D1504147

HISTORIC

DOCUMENTS

OF

1984

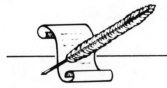

HISTORIC
DOCUMENTS
OF
1984

Cumulative Index 1980-84

Congressional Quarterly Inc.

The Library of Congress cataloged the first issue of this title as follows:

Historic documents.   1972—
    Washington. Congressional Quarterly Inc.

    1. United States—Politics and government—1945— —Yearbooks. 2. World politics—1945— —Yearbooks. I. Congressional Quarterly Inc.

E839.5H57   917.3′03′9205   72-97888
ISBN 0-87187-324-9

FOREWORD

Publication of *Historic Documents of 1984* carries through a 13th year the project Congressional Quarterly launched with *Historic Documents of 1972.* The purpose of this continuing series is to give students, scholars, librarians, journalists, and citizens convenient access to documents of basic importance in the broad range of public affairs.

To place the documents in perspective, each entry is preceded by a brief introduction containing background materials, in some cases a short summary of the document itself, and, where necessary, relevant subsequent developments. We believe these introductions will prove increasingly useful in future years when the events and questions now covered are less fresh in one's memory and the documents may be difficult to find.

Election-year politics held the national spotlight in 1984. Geraldine Ferraro became the first woman nominated for vice president by a major party, Jesse Jackson's presidential bid involved blacks in the political process in record numbers, and Ronald Reagan was re-elected president with an unprecedented electoral landslide of 525 votes.

It was also a year of Reagan administration successes on the Supreme Court. Affirming the administration's view, the Court ruled that inclusion of a Nativity scene as part of an official Christmas display did not violate First Amendment strictures on separation of church and state. In two other landmark decisions the Court limited the penalties against sex discrimination by federally aided schools and barred casting aside of seniority rules to protect the jobs of newly hired minority workers.

The year also marked renewed dialogue between the United States and the Soviet Union. In his first meeting with a ranking Soviet official, President Reagan discussed arms control talks with Foreign Minister Andrei Gromyko. The death of Soviet leader Yuri Andropov, after less than 15 months in office, and the questionable health of his successor, 73-year-old Konstantin Chernenko, necessarily raised questions about the future of U.S.-Soviet relations.

International attention focused on various trouble spots: the Persian Gulf, where fighting continued between Iran and Iraq; India, where street violence erupted following the assassination of prime minister Indira Gandhi and, in an unrelated tragedy, a gas leak at a Union Carbide plant poisoned more than 2,000 people; Nicaragua, where the Sandinista government protested the U.S. mining of its ports; and South Africa, where the government's apartheid policies roused widespread condemnation.

Historic Documents of 1984 contains statements, Court decisions, reports, special studies, and speeches related to these and other events of national and international significance. We have selected for inclusion as many as possible of the documents that in our judgment will be of more than transitory interest. Where space limitations prevented reproduction of the full texts, excerpts were used to set forth the essentials and, at the same time, to preserve the flavor of the materials.

The Editors

Washington, D.C., February 1985

Historic Documents of 1984

Editors: Margaret C. Thompson, Nancy A. Blanpied
Associate Editor: Barbara R. de Boinville
Contributors: Mary Ames Booker, Anne Chase, Carolyn Goldinger, James R. Ingram, Catherine P. Jaskowiak, Nancy Lammers, Carolyn Mc-Govern, Mary L. McNeil, John L. Moore, Molly Parrish, Patricia Pine, Elizabeth H. Summers
Cumulative Index: Jan Danis

How to Use This Book

The documents are arranged in chronological order. If you know the approximate date of the report, speech, statement, court decision, or other document you are looking for, glance through the titles for that month in the Table of Contents below.

If the Table of Contents does not lead you directly to the document you want, turn to the index at the end of the book. There you may find references not only to the particular document you seek but also to other entries on the same or a related subject. The index in this volume is a **five-year cumulative index** of Historic Documents covering the years 1980-1984.

The introduction to each document is printed in italic type. The document itself, printed in roman type, follows the spelling, capitalization, and punctuation of the original or official copy. In some cases, boldface headings in brackets have been added to highlight the organization of the text. Where the full text is not given, omissions of material are indicated by the customary ellipsis points.

TABLE OF CONTENTS

January

February

March

April

May

June

July

August

September

October

November

December

January

PRESIDENTIAL TASK FORCE ON FOOD ASSISTANCE

January 9, 1984

Ordered by President Ronald Reagan to make a "no-holds-barred"
study of reports that many needy Americans could not get enough to eat,
a 13-member commission made public a summary of its final report on
January 9. The task force concluded that, although "there is hunger in
America ... there is no evidence that widespread undernutrition is a
major health problem." But rather than calming the emotional issue of
hunger in the United States, the report served to reopen an acrimonious
debate.

A finding of the Task Force on Food Assistance that "allegations of
rampant hunger simply cannot be documented" drew vehement rebuttals
from advocates of the poor and charitable organizations and provoked a
mixed reaction from members of Congress. A major recommendation of
the task force, and the most controversial, was that states be allowed to
drop out of the federal food aid programs and instead receive a block
grant to distribute as they saw fit.

Background

Reports of increasing hunger, presented in the media and at congres-
sional hearings in 1983, placed the blame on the recession and on new re-
strictions in federal food program eligibility and benefits. The Reagan
administration insisted that food aid programs were more than adequate
and that isolated hardship cases had been blown out of proportion by the
media and by professional advocates for the poor. The amount the

3

federal government was spending on food aid, $18.6 billion in the current year, represented more money to help feed more people than ever before, administration officials said.

The significance of the issue in terms of domestic politics was pointed up in December 1983 when Edwin Meese III, Reagan's counsel, questioned reports of hunger, suggested there was cheating in free food programs, and defended the Reagan administration's policies toward the needy. Meese's remarks were met by a volley of criticism. (Historic Documents of 1983, p. 765)

A study of the question of hunger was ordered by Reagan in August 1983, and the task force was established with J. Clayborn La Force Jr., dean of the Graduate School of Management, University of California at Los Angeles, as chairman. It made public a summary of its report after three months of study and hearings.

Findings and Proposals

The task force found no overall monitoring of the nutritional status of Americans that could show whether the situation of the poor had worsened. It recommended that more timely data on nutrition be gathered. The summary said that the task force could "not doubt that there is hunger in America." Certain groups, it said, such as children whose parents could not provide a full diet, the homeless, and people whose resources were eaten up by rent, utility, and other bills, probably could not get enough to eat all the time. But the task force noted that the incidence of stunted growth and anemia had been going down for poor children and women, and it said that infant mortality rates had declined steadily for the previous 30 years.

Under the controversial block grant approach recommended by the task force, a state choosing to opt out of federal programs could instead receive a general food aid grant for some or all of the programs. Critics said that such an approach could mean the end of uniform eligibility and benefit standards in all states. Task force members said the grants would eliminate much of the red tape and inflexibility that bothered local officials. However, John Douglas Driggs, a task force member who opposed the change, said that the nation would lose the "leveling" effect of the national food programs that, to some extent, made up for differences among state welfare programs. The commission also recommended that heavier penalties be imposed on states for overpayment errors in the food stamp program.

Reaction

The issuance of the report summary set off a new round of criticism of Reagan policies. A 42-member coalition of religious, labor, civil rights, and elderly groups said that the summary "tells us little more than that hunger exists — and then proposes recommendations that would, on balance, make this tragic problem worse." Sen. Edward M. Kennedy, D-Mass., assailed the plan for block grants, saying, "In effect, this commission says to the hungry: Let them eat block grants." Robert Greenstein, the administrator of the federal Food and Nutrition Service in the Carter administration, warned that harsher penalties for error would drive states into the optional block grant program.

On the other hand, Sen. Jesse Helms, R-N.C., chairman of the Senate Agriculture Committee, found the study "well balanced" and predicted it would "disappoint those who wish to use the 'hunger issue' as a pretext for pouring more of the taxpayers' money into [federal food] programs."

Following are excerpts from the summary of the final draft report by the Presidential Task Force on Food Assistance, made public January 9, 1984. [Boldface headings in brackets have been added by Congressional Quarterly to highlight the organization of the text.]:

Introduction

Despite the very large expansion of federal programs that provide food assistance since the 1960's, many people claim today that hunger is widespread in America and that it is indeed growing. Two fundamental causes are commonly cited: the recent recession and efforts of the present Administration to limit federal spending on food assistance programs.

Because of the universally shared belief that the existence of real and widespread hunger is simply not acceptable in our society, President Reagan convened this Task Force and assigned us the task of examining the nation's food assistance programs and examining how, given the array of such programs, it has come about that claims of a resurgence of hunger can still be made in the United States. Furthermore, the President has asked the Task Force to examine the situation and, if appropriate to offer recommendations.

In carrying out these tasks, we have: (1) examined federal food assistance programs, (2) examined available statistical evidence concerning hunger and nutrition, (3) held hearings and listened to testimony from more than 100 witnesses in seven American cities, (4) conducted numerous site visits to food distribution facilities, and (5) gathered a great amount of information both through visitation and correspondence.

The issue before us is complex and requires careful and precise consideration. For example, we often hear the terms "hunger," "poverty," and "unemployment" being used interchangeably. While it is clear that there is some relation among these terms conceptually, they nonetheless are distinct in many respects. While it may be appropriate to assume that all hungry people are poor, for example, it is not appropriate to assume that all poor people are hungry. Also, the people who must rely on food assistance do not constitute a single general group whose problems can be understood or treated effectively in a single, general way. For example, groups having different distinguishing characteristics include the "traditional poor" (largely composed of the elderly poor and poor single-parent households), the "street people," and the "new poor" (recent victims of economic hard times).

The Social Safety Net

The social safety net consists of private, state, local, and federal programs to assist the poor and the hungry.

Private organizations tend to operate direct and immediate forms of assistance to the needy such as soup kitchens, shelters, food pantries and food banks. The extent of these activities has expanded in recent years as evidenced by data available from the food bank networks and surveys of soup kitchens and food pantries.

States and local communities contribute to the social safety net by: (1) sharing costs of some programs directed at the needy, (2) administering many of the federal programs, and (3) providing direct assistance to individuals in the form of programs designed to address needs that are not emphasized in federal program design. The latter contribution is principally in the form of general assistance programs that vary widely from state to state, and from county to county. Federal assistance and income transfer programs today represent a substantial portion of the total federal budget by historical standards. Federal food assistance, taking the form of cash, food stamps, or commodities, was authorized at $19 billion in fiscal year 1983, subsidizing more than 95 million meals per day during the year. As a rule, the Food Stamp Program is available to everyone in a household with incomes after deduction below the poverty line and limited assets. Other programs are specifically targeted at particular groups such as the elderly, infants, children, and pregnant women and mothers. Those participating in these other programs generally are, as intended, lower-income people. Federal food assistance programs have grown tremendously over the past two decades; in 1969 our nation spent approximately $2.8 billion (in 1983 dollars), in contrast to last year's $19 billion. . . .

Populations of Concern

The principal goal of this Task Force is to determine the extent to which needy individuals are not effectively served by the food assistance programs. To do this, it is essential that we understand the problems faced by the people these programs are intended to serve. People who need food assistance have diverse problems and needs. We focus on three main groups — the "traditional poor," the "new poor" and the homeless. The traditional poor are those groups which have for a long time experienced a relatively high incidence of poverty; notable among them are female-headed families and the elderly, although there are a wide range of other households that fall into this category as well. The new poor include individuals who have slipped into poverty as a result of extended spells of unemployment. The homeless, or "street people," are individuals with no apparent residence and an otherwise essentially undocumented existence, often bearing a personal history of mental disorders, or alcohol and/or drug abuse. We recognize that the problems of these groups are not all encompassing, or mutually exclusive, but we believe that their situations encompass many of the problems faced by low-income households. . . .

Public Sector Food Assistance Programs

The Task Force has examined the federal assistance programs to determine how they work, who they serve, and how they have changed in recent years. This section summarizes our findings. These findings are presented as neither criticism nor praise. Instead, we hope simply to clarify some misconceptions about these programs and point out what they do and do not accomplish.

The Food Stamp Program: The purpose of the Food Stamp Program is to provide low-income households with a more nutritious diet. Under the original rules of the program, households were required to pay a certain amount in cash for the bonus they received, and were allotted in food stamps an amount sufficient to cover the full cost of a basic, nutritious diet. Under current rules, participating households do not pay anything for the stamps, but receive only the food stamp bonus and are instead expected to contribute from their own income a certain portion of the cost of the same basic diet. . . .

It is frequently noted that many eligible individuals fail to participate (approximately 35-40 percent of eligibles) in the Food Stamp Program. This is often cited as evidence of failures in the Food Stamp Program itself. An analysis of available data indicates that while some deserving and eligible individuals are indeed not served by the program, a good deal of such non-participation occurs as a matter of a choice of less-needy families. Those not participating more often tend to be elderly or residents in rural areas. They tend to be households of smaller size and with relatively greater incomes, and therefore entitled to relatively small benefits. The reasons for nonparticipation vary. Some feel they do not need or want assistance; some feel there is a stigma from utilizing food stamps; others wish to avoid bureaucratic "hassles"; and others may not be aware of their eligibility.

However, there is concern that present program rules do not permit participation by certain low-income groups. First, low income families with assets exceeding the limits are not allowed to participate. In general this is good, because families that fail the asset test have been found to have fairly substantial resources, suggesting that the asset test is an effective means of screening out those who are not, in fact, needy. Yet, the recessions of the recent past have resulted in an increase in the number of "new poor" families, which are in fact needy even though they have assets that disqualify them from eligibility. Second, the Task Force has heard testimony that homeless people in some areas do not have access to the Food Stamp Program even though they are qualified under federal rules. The Department of Health and Human Services has reported to the Task Force that 19 states presently require recipients to possess a home street address.

The changes in the Food Stamp Program enacted in 1981 and 1982 are often the source of discussions that these changes have contributed fundamentally to a resurgence of hunger in America. Analysis of the effects of program changes is complicated by the fact that the recent recession has caused an increase in the number of families eligible for the program; hence the number of families receiving food stamps has increased, even though eligibility rules have been tightened. The primary change in eligibility has been the imposition of a cap on gross income at 130 percent of the poverty line which was imposed in the Omnibus Budget Reconciliation Act of 1981 (OBRA). The Congressional Budget Office estimated that the gross income cap eliminated about four percent of food stamp participants from the program.

Our own analysis of available data indicate that OBRA has not caused a decline in the percentage of people participating in the Food Stamp Program within the poverty population, the primary target population. Among families with incomes above the poverty line, the percentage of people participating did decline following OBRA, fairly substantially among individuals with family incomes well in excess of the poverty line. Households in poverty continue to have access to the Food Stamp Program.

Recent changes in the Food Stamp Program have also resulted in some small reductions in benefits....

The results of such complexity are predictable — long lines of frustrated people in food stamp offices, long interviews and high error rates. The Food and Nutrition Service of USDA [U.S. Department of Agriculture] estimates that more than $1 billion each year are distributed either in the form of excess entitlement payments or as payments to ineligible families. This represents more than 9 percent of all payments.

Another principal factor contributing to high error rates is the separation of administrative responsibility from liability for overpayments. The Food Stamp Program is funded completely by the federal government with the exception that half of the administrative costs are paid by the states. Historically, the costs of overpayments are borne solely by the federal government. A new plan was introduced in 1982, which is targeted to reduce error rates to five percent by FY 1985 (the target is nine percent in FY 1983 and seven percent in FY 1984). Under this plan, a state over the target error rate will lose five percent of federal administrative funds for each one percentage point difference between its actual error rate and the target. If the error rate is three percent or more above the target, the penalty rises to 10 percent for each one percentage point increase in the error rate.

Child Nutrition Programs: Each of the child nutrition programs — the National School Lunch Program, School Breakfast Program, Child Care Feeding Program, Summer Feeding Program, and the Special Milk Program — offers children, especially low-income children, the opportunity to partake of meals prepared away from their homes. Their stated purpose is to provide nutritional supplementation to a presumably vulnerable group....

NUTRITION SERVICES FOR THE ELDERLY

Price Support Programs and Commodities Distribution: Many witnesses before the Task Force have noted the irony that our government spends billions of dollars to provide food assistance to low-income families and at the same time spends billions of dollars to support and stabilize the prices of agricultural commodities. The agricultural price support programs in the U.S. are extremely complex and a full review and analysis of these programs is beyond the scope and mandate of the Task Force. It is impossible, however, to examine the problems of those who require food assistance without putting into perspective the government's impact on the price of food. In addition, the price control programs directly influence federal food assistance policies in that the "surplus" of food items is often distributed through the food assistance programs.

If the support prices are above free market prices for extended periods, USDA can and does accumulate huge stocks of surplus commodities. Because of this, USDA attempts to limit production by various mechanisms, most prominently acreage restrictions.

Most parties agree that by historical standards the costs of agricultural support programs have become excessive....

More than $1 billion in surplus food will be distributed under special food distribution programs in 1984. Another $300 million in commodities will be distributed through traditional USDA distribution programs. While special programs for commodity distribution help in the short run to reduce the accumulated surplus commodities, the very existence of such programs is mainly the consequence of commodity surpluses created by the price support programs. They are not the consequence of a clearly formulated food assistance policy. The programs generally offer only intermittent and unpredictable supplies and the commodities that are distributed do not constitute a nutritionally balanced diet. These programs also present important logistical problems in terms of transportation and storage.

The Task Force believes that the low-income population would be better served by a policy designed to permit agricultural prices to reach market levels than by the continued distribution of commodities under the existing price support system.

Given the existence of the large agricultural surpluses present today, however, the Task Force believes the federal government's efforts to distribute commodities are worthwhile. Efforts should be made to make distribution more efficient. The program's simplicity should also be maintained.

The Role of the Private Sector

Private charitable and philanthropic organizations constitute an integral part of the nation's food assistance safety net. It is our conviction that the existence of private sector institutions, including soup kitchens and food banks, does not imply the failure of federal food assistance policies, as some have argued. While the public sector effectively provides broad standardized coverage, the administering bureaucracies are by their nature relatively inefficient in meeting specialized and localized emergency needs. The private sector charities, however, are often models of compassion and efficiency that offer not only food, but a helping hand for a variety of problems. They provide a measure of social interaction for individuals, especially the homeless — individuals who often fear interacting with complex and impersonal public welfare programs but who trust and accept assistance from private local organizations. . . .

Government and the Private Sector: The USDA has for many years directly supported private sector feeding programs through its donations of commodities to charitable organizations. In 1983, USDA donated over $100 million in commodities under this program; this is more than double the amount donated in 1979 and 55 percent more than donated in 1980.

More generally, the federal and state governments have attempted to maintain a legal environment conducive to private sector activity by providing special tax incentives for charitable donations and limiting liability for individuals and organizations that make food donations.

Food assistance programs by private organizations are fueled by contributions. Tax law currently encourages these contributions through the deductibility of charitable donations. Corporations are entitled to enhanced deductions for charitable donations of goods from their inventories for the care of the needy, the ill and infants. Set forth in the Tax Reform Act of 1976, rules allowing "enhanced deductions" were an important economic incentive behind the recent rapid growth of the food bank industry. There is some current uncertainty, however as to how food donations are to be valued due to a recent ruling by the Internal Revenue Service. It has been argued that this uncertainty has discouraged firms from taking advantage of deductions to which they might be legally entitled. Enhanced charitable deductions also are available to corporate donors. Thus, non-corporate farmers have no supplemental tax incentive to donate food either directly from storage or through gleaning. . . .

As private efforts have expanded, there has also developed a partnership between public and private institutions in some food assistance efforts. The most prominent effort was the appropriation of $100 million in March 1983 for emergency food and shelter assistance as part of the "Jobs Bill." Half of this fund was distributed to states, the rest was allocated by a National Charities Board chaired by the Federal Emergency Management Agency (FEMA) to private charities. The United Way served as fiscal agent. These funds were expended, as required, by September 30th. An additional $40 million has been appropriated for expenditure before March 31st. The National Charity Board allocated funds to roughly 1000 of 4000 possible jurisdictions, primarily on the basis of local unemployment rates. Within these areas, local boards comprised of public officials and charitable organizations awarded grants to local charities. The emergency appropriation generated a spirit of cooperation and coordination among diverse charities. As an example, the United Way waived its managerial fees. It has been estimated that the program provided some 35 million meals and 2.5 million nights of lodging through 3500 private organizations.

While the emergency effort was effectively implemented, its potential as a permanent program is less certain. For the history of federal involvement strongly suggests that direct federal subsidization of private charities would almost certainly — in the end — come with strings attached; more specific rules about how funds are allocated and spent; what groups should be served; how records are to be kept, and so forth. These rules would restrict the private sector's flexibility and efficiency in meeting specialized needs. Other commentators argue against turning an *emergency* program into a permanent bureaucracy when the source of the emergency is a temporary phenomenon created by recession. . . .

How Much Hunger Is There in America?

Naturally, it is impossible to speak of food assistance without addressing the issue of hunger. Numerous witnesses have testified to us in the most forceful terms about the existence of widespread, and growing hunger in this country. Their statements served to underline what we all know: neither poverty nor the need for food assistance has been eradicated. Our site visits confirmed for us that there are a number of people who find it necessary at various times to avail themselves of food assistance programs in order to get enough to eat. There are people who must sometimes cut back on food expenditures to pay their rent and utility bills; toward the end of the month there are individuals and families who run out of money for food; there are homeless people who are unable to support themselves or even to avail themselves of existing public assistance programs.

Before we can discuss the extent of hunger in America, we must first make some effort to provide as precise a definition of the word as possible, for hunger is clearly a term that has come to mean rather different things to different people.

A definition of hunger: As we have already said, hunger cannot simply be equated with unemployment or poverty. Instead, we have found it useful to confine ourselves to two working definitions. The first is the scientific, clinical definition that would be used by a health professional. In this sense, hunger means the actual physiological effects of extended nutritional deprivation. The second is a necessarily looser interpretation relating more to a social phenomenon than to medical results. To many Americans hunger is also the inability, even occasionally, to obtain adequate food and nourishment. In this sense of the term, hunger can be said to be present even when there are no clinical symptoms of deprivation.

Hunger as medically defined: The medical textbook definition of hunger would be a weakened, disordered condition brought about by prolonged lack of food. In adults, the result of such hunger is a loss of weight leading eventually to reduced physical strength or impaired function. In children, the effect of prolonged lack of food is slower growth, or halted growth if the lack is severe enough, and loss of weight.

But physical disorders resulting from malnutrition may not be due only to insufficient caloric intake; a person's diet may be deficient in certain nutrients.

What evidence is there of clinical hunger in our country today? The United States does not have the kind of continuous national nutritional monitoring system that could give a complete answer to that question. Still, we do have some clear indicators. First, there is a continuous surveillance system in place, although not in all states, of two of the most vulnerable groups: children and pregnant women who use public health clinics. The most recent available data (which includes the first half of 1983) concerning these children indicate that the incidence of short stature has shown an overall tendency to decrease moderately over time, at least among children below two years of age, and that the incidence of anemia has probably decreased somewhat overall. Second, there are intermittent national health surveys of representative samples of the entire population. These surveys have not uncovered any major problems deriving from undernutrition.

Third, it can be noted that the infant mortality rate has been declining steadily in the U.S. over the last 30 years. This has been true for the nation as a whole, even during the last recession, although minor variations have been observed in some states. Infant mortality rates however, are influenced by many factors that have little or nothing to do with nutrition. Most of the decline in these rates is probably due to improved prenatal and neonatal medical care, along with better incomes, living standards, and nutrition.

We should not, however, take these clinical indicators to mean that no one suffers from clinical hunger. We know that there are people who find it impossible, for financial or other reasons, to get proper attention from physicians, and among these people there are those who suffer from the physiological symptoms associated with food shortages. Therefore, some undernutrition probably goes undetected. There are, for example, no studies of the nutritional status of the homeless, and among this very significant group there may well be important incidences of malnutrition and disease. With this possible exception, there is no evidence that widespread undernutrition is a major health problem in the United States.

Hunger as commonly defined: To many people hunger means *not* just symptoms that can be diagnosed by a physician; rather, it implies the existence of a social, not a medical problem. To most Americans, hunger means a situation where some people — even occasionally — cannot obtain an adequate amount of food, even if the shortage is not prolonged enough to cause health problems. This, of course, is the sense in which people ordinarily use the word. It is also the sense in which the witnesses before us and many of the reports and documents we have studied have spoken of hunger. This alternative definition of hunger relates directly to our communal commitment to ensure that everyone has adequate access to food, and to the nation's endeavors to provide food assistance.

And in this sense, we cannot doubt that there is hunger in America. This is the sad truth. It is easy to think of examples of this kind of hunger: children who sometimes are sent to bed hungry because their parents find it impossible to provide for them fully; the homeless who must depend on the largess of charity or who are forced to scavenge for food or beg; and people who do not eat properly in order that they have enough money to pay rent, utilities, and other bills.

Clinical hunger is relatively easy to quantify. People can be weighed and measured, and blood samples taken to indicate something about their nutritional status. But the ordinary, everyday sense in which the word hunger is used is much more difficult to identify and put a number to. How many people go hungry in the United States because their income is too low or because they are experiencing temporary financial setbacks? That is a question to which no one who has sincerely sought a true and responsible answer has been able to provide.

The extent of hunger in America: There is no official "hunger count" to estimate the number of hungry people. Those who argue that hunger is widespread and growing rely on indirect measures. The following are the main pieces of evidence used to support the claim that hunger is not only widespread but has grown worse in the last few years.

First, data have been presented to prove that there has been an increase in the number of people at or below the poverty line, and that their number is greater today than at any time in the last fifteen years. *Second,* there has been a significant increase in the number of people who seek food assistance. *Third,* there are many stories of poor families who run out of food stamps before the end of the month. *Fourth,* the fact that individuals eligible for food assistance programs frequently do not participate is often cited as proof that the programs are not reaching those in need.

Now, as important as each of these separate observations seems to be, together they nevertheless do not accurately indicate the extent of the hunger problem.

13

To begin with, while there has undoubtedly been an increase in the number of people officially defined as poor, there are also important reasons to believe that official poverty statistics do not adequately portray the economic circumstances of low-income people. These technical problems of measuring poverty do not mean that there is no hunger, or that there has been no increase in the amount of poverty or hunger in recent years; rather, they only mean that it is incorrect to simply point to changes in the poverty rate as an indication of the extent to which hunger has increased.

Furthermore, as incomes fall, people become eligible for food stamps and other food assistance benefits. These programs are designed to combat the hunger that is caused by unexpected reductions in income.

When incomes fall, and poverty increases, there is a concurrent humanitarian response from voluntary sources to complement the increase in public assistance programs. This is undoubtedly one of the reasons behind the growth of private sector food assistance efforts in recent years. . . .

All of these changes have contributed to the large increases in the amount of high-quality food available for distribution for free or at a minimal price. While it has become possible for private charitable organizations to offer far more services than several years ago, it should not necessarily be inferred that more private sector activity means that hunger has increased. . . .

The claim that people run out of food stamps before the end of the month, while undoubtedly true, also cannot be taken as incontrovertible evidence either of hunger or of failure of the Food Stamp Program. As explained earlier, food stamps are designed to *supplement* food purchasing power; they were never intended to provide income for all food expenditures. . . .

While it is true that the Food Stamp Program serves only about two-thirds of eligible families, this measure does not completely reflect an inadequacy of the program. . . . As a whole, eligible non-participants tend to be better off economically than participants. Needier families, including families with children, especially younger children, are more likely to participate.

This does not mean, however, that we cannot identify areas where improvements can be made so that food assistance is more available to those in need. . . .

While we have found evidence of hunger in the sense that some people have difficulties with access to food, we have also found that it is at present impossible to estimate the extent of that hunger. We cannot report on any indicator that will tell us where and by how much hunger has gone up in recent years. But we have also found that for the vast majority of low-income people, the private and public parts of the income maintenance and food assistance efforts are available, and sufficient for those who take advantage of them. We have not been able to substantiate allegations of rampant hunger. We regret our inability to document the degree of "non-clinical" hunger because such lack of definitive quantitative proof contributes to a climate in which policy discussions become unhelpfully heated and unsubstantiated assertions are then substituted for hard information.

Since general claims of widespread hunger can neither be positively refuted nor definitively proved, it is likely that hunger will remain as an issue on our national policy agenda for an indefinite future.

Recommendations

[ALLOW STATES TO ESTABLISH AUTONOMOUS PROGRAMS]

We have become convinced that people in need of food assistance would benefit if the programs or any subset of them were controlled at a more local level, such as the state or county. The gains from such a modification derive from allowing the states (1) more autonomy in allocating funds among the various food assistance programs, (2) greater discretion in administering programs, and (3) greater responsibility for assuring that funds are properly targeted toward those in need. The greater flexibility and improved administration that would be gained would help to increase the benefits available to the truly needy without at the same time increasing the cost to the taxpayer.

The tailoring of its food assistance program by a state would substantially improve its effectiveness since the circumstances of need often vary from state to state and even county to county. . . .

> Recommendation 1: The Task Force recommends that Congress make participation in existing federal food assistance programs optional for the states; states which choose to establish autonomous programs will instead receive one single appropriation to fund these programs. Allocations to states establishing autonomous programs shall be made according to a formula (based on changes in food costs and the state population in need) that would provide a predictable level of findings that meets the varying needs for food assistance in the state. States should have the option of continuing to participate in the federal Food Stamp Program while establishing autonomous control over the remaining programs. . . .

IMPROVE PROGRAM TARGETING AND ADMINISTRATION

Our major recommendations below relate to the potential for improvement in the Food Stamp Program. Many of the problems addressed in this section would be resolved for states that opt to undertake autonomous programs.

> Recommendation 2-a: Restore the food stamp allotment to 100 percent of the cost of the Thrifty Food Plan. . . .
> Recommendation 2-b: Raise asset limits for food stamp eligibility. We recommend that the asset limit be raised to $2,000 for non-elderly

15

households, $3,500 for elderly households. In addition, the exemption for an automobile should be raised to $5,000. . . .

Recommendation 2-c: Insure that individuals without fixed home addresses are eligible for participation in the Food Stamp Program. . . .

Recommendation 2-d: Cash out food stamp benefits for the disabled and the elderly; or allow states to permit SSI [Supplemental Security Income] recipients to use food stamps to purchase prepared meals. . . .

Recommendation 2-e: Simplify applications procedures in the Food Stamp Program. Specifically, we recommend the following:

    a. categorical eligibility for all AFDC and SSI households;

    b. a simpler definition of household, which includes all individuals at one address;

    c. adoption of standard decuctions to replace the present deductions for shelter costs and child care costs. We recommend that the standard deductions should be designed to reflect equitable variations in living costs across states. These deductions should be calculated to reflect actual deductions taken in each state such that average benefits remain unchanged. . . .

Recommendation 2-f: Require states to be fully responsible for overpayment errors in excess of 3 percent. . . .

Recommendation 2-g: Encourage states to keep food stamp offices open during some non-business hours, for example from 5 to 9 p.m. on some weekdays or during some hours on Saturday. This can be accomplished by closing offices an equivalent number of hours during regular working hours, thus keeping administrative costs approximately the same. . . .

Recommendation 2-h: Permit states to stagger the delivery of food stamps throughout the month and to adopt administrative procedures to promote staggered distribution by the states. . . .

Recommendation 2-i: Restrict eligibility for child-care home subsidies to homes in low incomes areas, for example, to areas where 50 percent or more of school lunches are served free or at a reduced rate. . . .

Recommendation 2-j: Reauthorize the WIC [Special Supplemental Food Program for Women, Infants and Children] program at current caseload levels for one year pending the reevaluation of the program under way in the USDA. . . .

ENCOURAGE PRIVATE SECTOR FOOD ASSISTANCE EFFORTS

Throughout our report, we have stressed the critical role played by private organizations in the nation's food assistance safety net. They are often models of compassion and efficiency, and are able to provide assistance to individuals that can not be reached through bureaucratic programs. We believe the government should continue to provide a climate which supports private organizations and allows them to accomplish their work without undue government interference. We have the following specific recommendations that will increase the government's support for these programs:

> Recommendation 3-a: The Task Force recommends that the U.S. Department of the Treasury clarify the rules under which corporations can take enhanced deductions for donations of food. . . .
>
> Recommendation 3-b: The Task Force recommends legislation that gives non-corporate taxpayers who are actively engaged in the production, wholesale, or retail marketing of food the same enhanced tax deductions for charitable donations of property that are now afforded to corporate taxpayers. . . .
>
> Recommendation 3-c: The Task Force recommends that the President encourage the military to participate actively and support cooperative programs with private-sector food assistance organizations. . . .

IMPROVE THE MEASUREMENT OF POVERTY AND NUTRITIONAL STATUS

In the course of its work, the Task Force was consistently troubled by the lack of appropriate information on the extent of hunger and poverty in the U.S. The absence of reliable data makes the evaluation of and solution to such problems considerably more difficult. The Task Force thus recommends that the federal government devote more effort to developing standards and means of measurement that more accurately portray the poverty status and the nutritional status of Americans.

> Recommendation 4-a: The Task Force recommends that the federal government explore new methods of measuring poverty and trends in poverty. . . .
>
> Recommendation 4-b: The Task Force recommends that the federal government take several steps designed to improve information on the nutritional status of Americans. . . .

U.S.-VATICAN
DIPLOMATIC RELATIONS
January 10, 1984

After 117 years of no formal contact, the United States and the Vatican January 10 announced agreement to establish full diplomatic relations. The step was described by a Reagan administration spokesman as recognition of Pope John Paul II's authority as a world leader in human rights. Congress had cleared the way for appointment of an ambassador in November 1983 when it repealed an 1867 law barring funds for a Vatican mission. President Ronald Reagan nominated William A. Wilson to the post. Wilson, a Southern California rancher and land developer, had been the president's personal envoy to the Vatican since 1981. The Senate confirmed the nomination by a vote of 81-13 March 7. But the wide margin of victory belied the controversial nature of the move, which was criticized as a violation of the constitutional separation of church and state.

A Checkered History

In a letter to the president of the Continental Congress, dated August 4, 1779, John Adams wrote, "Congress will probably never send a minister to his Holiness, who can do them no service, upon condition of receiving a Catholic legate or nuncio in return; or, in other words, an ecclesiastical tyrant, which, it is to be hoped, the United States will be too wise ever to admit into their territories." But only four months after Adams took office as president, in 1797, the first consul to represent the United States in the papal dominions was commissioned.

In defending diplomatic contacts with the Vatican, American presi-

dents traditionally offered the rationalization that it was possible to deal with the pope solely in his capacity as temporal sovereign and thus in a political and commercial, rather than religious, capacity. James K. Polk told Congress in 1847 that "a just regard to our commercial interests" warranted the appropriation of funds to support the opening of full diplomatic relations with the Papal States. The bill authorizing funds for the mission was approved by a wide margin. The appropriation provided only for a chargé d'affaires, a diplomatic representative inferior in rank to an ambassador or minister. Later, a minister-resident was assigned to the post. As Secretary of State James Buchanan instructed the American chargé in 1848, "Your efforts ... will be devoted exclusively to the cultivation of the most friendly civil relations with the papal government, and to the extension of commerce between the two countries. You will carefully avoid even the appearance of interfering in ecclesiastical questions, whether these relate to the United States or any other portion of the world."

Formal U.S. diplomatic ties to the Vatican were effectively severed in 1867, when Congress, responding to a move in Italy to reunite the independent Papal States with the rest of the country, refused to approve the Rome legation's budget. Rufus King, the minister-resident, was told that while the mission itself had not been closed, no more funds would be provided for its support. With the unification of Italy in 1870, the Papal States, having lost territory and seaports, declined in political and commercial importance. For the next 70 years official contacts between Washington and the Holy See were few and infrequent. Then, on December 23, 1939, President Franklin D. Roosevelt announced his intention to send Myron C. Taylor to Rome as his "personal represen-tative" to the pope. The purpose of the mission, Roosevelt stated in letters to Protestant and Jewish leaders, was to further the parallel peace efforts of the United States and the Vatican. Taylor, who was not a Catholic, remained in the post under President Harry S Truman. Presidents Richard Nixon, Gerald R. Ford, and Jimmy Carter also sent envoys to the Vatican, but Presidents Dwight D. Eisenhower, John F. Kennedy, and Lyndon B. Johnson did not.

Since 1870 the Vatican has consisted only of the 108 acres that serve as the headquarters of the Roman Catholic Church. As a city-state, Vatican City has fewer than 1,000 citizens. It issues its own license plates and postage stamps. The pope is the supreme executive, legislative, and judicial authority within the Vatican. Immediately beneath him is the secretary of state. It has been estimated that the Vatican has about $500 million of investments, in addition to innumerable art treasures.

Reaction

In support of its decision to resume official ties, administration spokesmen noted that 107 other countries had full diplomatic relations with the Vatican, which also maintained representation in all major United Nations organizations and retained permanent observers at the Common Market in Europe and the Organization of American States. Of the major powers, only the United States, the Soviet Union, and China had not sent ambassadors to Rome. Britain had established diplomatic ties with the Holy See in 1982, shortly before John Paul II's visit to that country, the first by a pope since King Henry II broke with the church in the 16th century. (Historic Documents of 1982, p. 409)

Administration officials also said the move did not violate the separation of church and state because the United States was recognizing the Holy See, rather than the Roman Catholic Church itself. "The United States holds Pope John Paul II in high esteem," said White House deputy press secretary Larry Speakes. "We respect the great moral and political influence which he and the Vatican exercise throughout the world. We admire the courageous stands he takes in defense of Western values." (Pope's travels to Central America and Poland, Historic Documents of 1983, pp. 241, 577)

Although Congress had cleared the way for the U.S.-Vatican ties with little debate and the administration announced the historic decision in what was described as a somewhat low-key manner, the action touched off a debate among religious groups. The strongest opposition came from fundamentalist Christians, many of whom had been firm supporters of Reagan in the 1980 election. "A bad precedent is being set" in appointing an ambassador, said the Rev. Jerry Falwell, leader of the Moral Majority. "I wonder when Mecca will want one. I told the White House if they give one to the pope, I may ask for one."

Other Protestant groups were critical of the move, as were Jewish groups and civil liberties organizations. A spokesman for the National Council of Churches, which encompassed 40 million Protestants and Eastern Orthodox Christians, reasserted the organization's longstanding policy that it was "improper for the United States government to send an ambassador to any church." Also opposed were the National Association of Evangelicals, representing 38,000 churches, the Baptist Joint Committee on Public Affairs, representing 26 million people, and Seventh-day Adventists. Opponents argued that the Vatican was primarily a church headquarters rather than a sovereign state and that the sending of an ambassador would therefore confer preferred status to a particular religion.

The reaction of Roman Catholics generally was guarded. Bishop James Malone, president of the National Conference of Catholic Bishops, issued a statement saying, "This matter has been discussed at length for many years. It is not a religious issue but a public policy question which, happily, has now been settled in this context." The Rev. Joseph O'Hara, editor of the Jesuit publication America, *said, "There will be divisions in Catholic opinion. The move will be applauded by many American*

Catholics, but others will be more restrained."

The establishment of formal ties elevated the Vatican's representative in Washington in 1984, Archbishop Pio Laghi, from apostolic delegate — the envoy of the pope in nations that had no diplomatic relations with the Holy See — to papal nuncio, the title of the permanent representative of the pope serving in foreign countries.

> *Following are the texts of the statements issued January 10, 1984, by the State Department and by the Vatican announcing establishment of full diplomatic relations between the Holy See and the United States:*

UNITED STATES ANNOUNCEMENT

The United States of America and the Holy See, in the desire to further promote the existing mutual friendly relations, have decided by common agreement to establish diplomatic relations between them at the level of embassy on the part of the United States of America and nunciature on the part of the Holy See, as of today, Jan. 10, 1984.

VATICAN ANNOUNCEMENT

The Holy See and the United States of America, in the desire to further promote the existing mutual friendly relations, have decided by common agreement to establish diplomatic relations between them on the level of embassy on the part of the United States of America and of nunciature on the part of the Holy See, as of today [Jan. 10, 1984].

VISIT OF CHINESE PREMIER ZHAO, U.S-CHINA TECHNOLOGY ACCORD

January 10, 12, 1982

Signaling an intention to improve relations, Premier Zhao Ziyang of the People's Republic of China (PRC) and President Ronald Reagan January 12 signed an industrial trade and technology agreement and renewed a science and technology accord. The pacts, initialed in Washington, D.C., were aimed at improving strained diplomatic and trade relations between the two countries. Zhao's U.S. trip, January 10-16, was the first by a Chinese premier and the first visit by a top-level official after Deng Xiaoping, then vice premier, visited the United States in 1979. The flamboyant vice premier's tour of the United States had resembled that of a U.S. politician on the hustings, with Deng campaigning on a theme of reassuring Americans that China's turn to the West was sincere.

In contrast, the businesslike atmosphere that surrounded the Zhao-Reagan exchange reflected the difficulties encountered in bilateral relations after Deng's visit. Differences over trade issues and Reagan's support for the Nationalist Chinese government on the island of Taiwan were among the major issues confronting the two leaders. As a leading conservative for more than 20 years, Reagan vowed repeatedly to stand by "free China" (Taiwan), where Nationalist Party leaders had fled after the 1949 takeover of the mainland by the Communist Party. U.S. policy toward Taiwan had been defined by Chinese leaders as the main obstacle to better relations between the United States and the PRC. A U.S.-China joint communiqué, signed Aug. 17, 1982, marked a step in defusing the Taiwan issue. In return for Peking's promise to seek reunification only by peaceful means, the Reagan administration promised a gradual reduction of arms sales to the island.

Premier Zhao made clear throughout his visit, however, that U.S. concessions on Taiwan were not satisfactory to Beijing and that the issue promised to remain a major stumbling block to true normalization of relations between the two nations. "Two possible futures lie ahead for Sino-U.S. ties," Zhao said. "One is sustained development of our friendly relations and cooperation. . . . [The other is] stagnation of our relations at the present level with frequent frictions and even setbacks."

Trade Relations

U.S.-China trade grew rapidly after Republican president Richard Nixon in 1972 journeyed to China and pledged to work for a "normalization of relations." Nixon's overture was followed in December 1978, when Democratic president Jimmy Carter announced agreement to establish full diplomatic ties. The economic impact of the thaw was dramatic: U.S.-Sino trade, which amounted to only $4.9 million in 1971, had climbed to $5.5 billion 10 years later. The most formidable obstacle to trade was lifted when the two countries signed an agreement in July 1979, giving China most-favored-nation status. The move had two major effects: it reduced tariffs on Chinese imports to the same level applied to Western trading partners, and it made China eligible for U.S. Export-Import Bank financing. The Ex-Im Bank, which promoted U.S. sales overseas by providing favorable financing terms, began lending to China in 1981. (U.S.-PRC diplomatic relations, Historic Documents of 1979, p. 135; previous U.S.-China agreements, Historic Documents of 1980, p. 829)

After tariffs were cut, trade between the two countries doubled in a year. As in any nascent relationship, however, there were rough spots. Because of U.S. controls on technology exports to China, sales stalled while the Chinese bought from other Western nations. The Reagan administration in June 1983 eased the controls, promoting China to the same rank as other friendly, non-aligned nations. The shift helped spur progress on trade-related issues. One source of friction, however was U.S. quotas on textile imports from China. In retaliation, the Chinese stopped buying U.S. wheat. Wheat growers lost 4.4 million tons in sales to China in 1983 as a result of the textiles dispute.

The two agreements signed by Zhao and Reagan in January 1984 were intended as a step in improving the two nations' troubled trade relations. A pact aimed at improving bilateral industrial cooperation called for the promotion of trade between the two countries, laying the groundwork for more specific joint development projects such as offshore oil drilling in the South China Sea.

Technology Exchanges

The second accord extended a joint commission that had been established in 1979 to encourage scientific and technological exchanges. A

24

major goal of the Chinese leadership was to develop the country's science and technology capabilities by adopting Western technological know-how to China's needs, rather than import potentially inappropriate technologies, an error made by many developing nations.

According to statistics, the Chinese had been somewhat successful in their endeavor. More than 130 contracts for technology transfer were concluded between 1973 and 1981, primarily for energy and power-generating equipment, electrical machinery, and precision instruments. China's main suppliers of this material were West Germany, followed by the United States, France, Britain, and Japan. Partly as result of the transfer, the Chinese State Statistical Bureau reported that industrial production rose by 10.2 percent in 1983, twice as fast as predicted.

But many problems still remained. According to State Economic Commission Minister Zhang Jinfu, "The technological level and the level of operation and management are on the whole comparatively backward in the 400,000 or so industrial enterprises existing in our country, the quality of products is low, the variety small in number, the consumption of energy resources and raw materials high, and the economic results poor."

Zhao's visit was followed by President Reagan's equally historic reciprocal trip to China April 26-May 1, during which he announced that an agreement between the two countries on the peaceful use of nuclear energy would be concluded. The agreement, reached after three years of negotiations, would clear the way for U.S. firms to sell to the Chinese nuclear reactors, components, and related engineering and design services. (Reagan trip. p. 287)

Following are excerpts from the remarks by President Ronald Reagan and Chinese Premier Zhao Ziyang of the People's Republic of China at Zhao's January 10, 1984, arrival in Washington, D.C., and the text of the January 12 accord on industrial and technological cooperation:

REAGAN, ZHAO REMARKS

The President. It gives me great pleasure to welcome you, Premier Zhao, to the United States.

Your visit recalls an old Chinese saying which asks: Is it not delightful to have friends come from afar? Well, yes, it is delightful to have you with us. Your presence symbolizes the growing trust and cooperation between our two countries.

For a decade, relations between the United States and the People's Republic of China have been building. Today, we know it is within our grasp to reap enormous rewards from the courage and foresight of those who opened the doors of Chinese-American friendship.

One of your predecessors, Premier Zhou Enlai, said in the early stages of our new relationship, "China places high hopes on the American people." Well, it is up to us, on both sides of the Pacific, to see to it that those high hopes become reality. For our part, we recognize the differences between our two countries, but we stand ready to nurture, develop, and build upon the many areas of accord to strengthen the ties between us.

China is now embarked on an exciting experiment designed to modernize the economy and quadruple the value of its national economic output by the year 2000. Premier Zhao, you eloquently described a key to achieving that end when you said that progress, and I quote, "lies in our efforts to emancipate our thinking in a bold way — to carry out reform with determination, to make new inventions with courage, and to break with the economic molds and conventions of all descriptions which fetter the development of productive force." These are words of vision. Our people understand and appreciate such vitality. We welcome the opportunity to walk at China's side in this endeavor.

Great strides of cooperation have already been made. In the last few years, each of our countries has tried to help the other build a better life. Our trade has flourished. The United States is now China's third largest trading partner. American investment in China exceeds that of all other countries. We're making available technology that will help open new horizons for your country.

Our citizens travel, study, and live in our respective countries in growing numbers. There are more than 10,000 Chinese students enrolled in American universities, and more than a hundred Chinese delegations arrive here each month. And more than a hundred thousand Americans now visit China each year. These exchanges between our countries, especially among our young people in the universities, are a source of joy for today and optimism for tomorrow. Only countries determined to be friends would be so open themselves. . . .

We have much to learn from each other. Your visit, Mr. Premier, provides a welcome opportunity to continue the open dialog that embodies the new spirit between our countries. We have much to discuss — matters of bilateral, regional, and global importance. We share many concerns, especially in the arena of international peace and stability. We stand on common ground in opposing expansionism and interference in the affairs of independent states. We are united by our commitment for international peace and our desire for economic progress.

I look forward to returning the honor of your visit when I travel to your country in the spring. . . .

The Premier. Mr. President and Mrs. Reagan, ladies and gentlemen, at the beginning of the new year, I have brought the American people the cordial greetings and good wishes of the 1 billion Chinese people. I would like to thank President Reagan for his kind invitation, which has offered me this opportunity to visit your great country.

As a friendly envoy of the Chinese people, I have come to visit your country for the purpose of seeking increased mutual understanding, stabilizing the relations between our two countries, enhancing Sino-U.S. friendship, and helping to preserve world peace. I believe this is not only the common aspiration of the Chinese and American peoples but also the expectation of the people of the world. . . .

This traditional friendship between our two peoples and the political foresight of the leaders of the two countries help to put an end to a long period of estrangement and confrontation between our two countries, and to bring about the normalization of our relations.

Since the establishment of diplomatic relations, the relations between China and the United States have, in the aggregate, made considerable progress. The friendly exchanges between our two peoples have greatly increased and their mutual understanding further deepened. Our exchanges and cooperation in the political, economic, cultural, scientific, technological, and other fields, have markedly expanded, but it should be considered that the growth of the Sino-U.S. relations is far below the level it should have attained. There have been ups and downs in the course of development, and there still exist difficulties and obstacles.

China has always attached importance to its relations with the United States and hopes to see their growth. U.S. Government leaders have also indicated on more than one occasion that they value Sino-U.S. relations and wish to see their development on a durable and stable basis.

I believe there is such a possibility. In order to turn the possibility into reality, it is necessary for both sides to show mutual respect for each other, to take into account the national interests of the other side as well as his own country in handling the problems before them.

So long as both China and the United States strictly abide by the principles as confirmed by both sides in the joint communiques, perform the obligations each undertook, it is possible for Sino-U.S. relations to leave behind doubts and uncertainties and embark on a smooth path.

Five years ago, Chinese leader Deng Xiaoping said at this podium that "great possibilities lie ahead for developing amicable cooperation between China and the United States." This remains our faith. Sino-U.S. relations are now at an important juncture. . . .

The world situation is at present more turbulent. The people of all countries are deeply worried about the future of the world. The United States and China, both being big countries, should be aware of their heavy responsibility for the maintenance of world peace.

In the next few days, I shall hold talks with President Reagan and other leaders of your government and exchange views with them on ways to develop Sino-U.S. relations and on international issues of common interest.

We never construe the significance of Sino-U.S. relations as being limited to ordinary bilateral relations, but regard them as an important affair affecting the overall world situation. We stand for peace, not only because China needs peace, friendship, and economic development but also because people of all countries want peace, friendship, and development.

The amicable coexistence of China and the United States is a major factor for maintaining world peace and stability. As long as the peoples of the world take their destiny into their own hands, it will be possible to maintain orld peace and prevent a new world war....

... This is an occasion for reviewing the past and looking ahead to the future. I believe that ... we will learn to live together better in amity....

INDUSTRIAL AND TECHNOLOGICAL ACCORD

The Government of the United States of America and the Government of the People's Republic of China (hereinafter referred to as the Parties):

Noting the development of economic and trade relations between the two countries;

Taking into account the characteristics and economic potential of the two countries and their respective levels of economic development;

Convinced of the desirability of promoting industrial and technological cooperation between the two countries on the basis of equality and mutual benefit;

Subject to and in implementation of the Agreement on Trade Relations between the United States of America and the People's Republic of China;

For the purpose of enhancing the friendship between the two peoples and further developing industrial and technological cooperation between the two countries;

Have agreed as follows:

Article I

1. The Parties shall take all appropriate steps to create favorable conditions for strengthening industrial and technological cooperation between the two countries in order to strive for a balance in their economic interests and the attainment of the harmonious development of such cooperation.

2. Such steps may include consultations to help identify and study proposals for industrial and technological cooperation projects, facilitation of contacts between potential participants in industrial and technological cooperation projects, assistance in arranging feasibility studies for industrial and technological cooperation projects and such other forms of cooperation as are mutually agreeable.

3. All activities under this Accord shall be subject to the respective applicable laws and regulations of the two countries.

Article II

1. Industrial and technological cooperation under this Accord shall be based on contracts or other arrangements between firms, companies and economic organizations of the two countries, in accordance with the respective applicable laws and regulations of the two countries.

2. The Parties recognize the importance of technology transfer and trade in technology products to the development of industrial and technological cooperation between the two countries. Accordingly, the Parties shall endeavor, in accordance with their respective laws and regulations, to promote and facilitate technology transfer and trade in technology products, so as to enhance the smooth conduct of industrial and technological cooperation between the two countries.

Article III

The Parties shall encourage industrial and technological cooperation according to the needs and capabilities of the two countries and on the basis of mutual benefit between firms, companies and economic organizations of the two countries. Such cooperation may include:

(1) construction of new industrial facilities and expansion and modernization of existing facilities in both countries;
(2) production, purchase, sale and leasing of machinery and equipment and high technology products;
(3) purchase and sale of industrial and agricultural materials and consumer goods;
(4) purchase, sale, license or commercial exchange of intellectual property rights, technical information or know-how, as well as provision of technical services, including training and exchange of specialists and technicians;
(5) co-production and co-marketing, including cooperation in using the technology and equipment of the other Party so as to foster the mutual expansion of the reciprocal trade between the two countries; and
(6) joint ventures, provision of services and construction works on a contractual basis, as well as other forms of industrial and technological cooperation which may be mutually agreed between firms, companies and economic organizations of the two countries.

Article IV

1. For the purpose of implementing this accord, the United States Government hereby nominates the Department of Commerce as its coordinating agency and the Chinese Government hereby nominates the Ministry of Foreign Economic Relations and Trade as its co-ordinating agency.

2.   The U.S.-China Joint Commission on Commerce and Trade shall place on the agenda of each session thereof industrial and technological cooperation between the two countries so as to review the implementation of this Accord, and make such recommendations as may be appropriate in pursuit of the objectives of this Accord.

3.   The U.S.-China Joint Commission on Commerce and Trade may, whenever the Parties deem it necessary, designate for a special purpose an ad hoc working group to assist it in its task. According to the needs of the specific task and by mutual agreement of the Parties, such ad hoc working group may include representatives of firms, companies and economic organizations of the two countries.

Article V

1.   Details of the activities undertaken by the Parties under this Accord, including financial facilitation and funding on as favorable terms and conditions as possible, shall be decided by mutual agreement, on the basis of the principles of the Agreement on Trade Relations between the United States of America and the People's Republic of China and in accordance with their respective applicable laws and regulations.

2.   The Trade and Development Program of the U.S. International Development Cooperation Agency shall consider the funding of feasibility studies of industrial and technological cooperation projects conducted under this Accord.

Article VI

This Accord shall be interpreted so as not to interfere with industrial and technological cooperation that might be conducted outside the Accord.

Article VII

This Accord shall enter into force upon signature and shall remain in force until January 31, 1986. This Accord shall be extended for successive terms of three years if neither party notifies the other of its intent to terminate this Accord at least thirty days before the end of a term.

Done at Washington this 12th day of January, 1984 in duplicate in the English and Chinese languages, both equally authentic.

KISSINGER COMMISSION REPORT ON CENTRAL AMERICA

January 11, 1984

The National Bipartisan Commission on Central America, appointed by President Ronald Reagan in July 1983 to make recommendations on U.S. policy in Central America, endorsed the thrust of Reagan's approach in a report released January 11. The president had appointed the panel in hopes of getting a broad consensus behind his program of supporting El Salvador against leftist guerrillas while pressuring Nicaragua to drop its pro-Soviet stance, but the panel's recommendations failed to quell political debate in Washington about U.S. policies. (Reagan policy, Historic Documents of 1983, p. 439)

Chaired by former secretary of state Henry A. Kissinger, the 12-member commission called for more than $8 billion in economic aid to the region through 1989 and for firm U.S. resistance to the expansion of Soviet and Cuban influence. It endorsed a "substantial" increase in military aid for El Salvador and backed indirectly Reagan's program of "covert" aid to anti-government rebels in Nicaragua. It also called on Reagan and Central American leaders to meet to decide on a plan for long-range economic development in the region. The panel said there was a "crisis" in Central America that was "real and acute" and the United States "must act to meet it, and act boldly."

The commission did not recommend using U.S. military forces to fight in Central America. But it did say the United States should consider military action against the Nicaraguan government as a "last resort" if it refused to stop supporting guerrilla movements in other countries. Reflecting congressional initiatives, the commission recommended one major departure from Reagan's policy. It would condition military aid to El Salvador and Guatemala on progress on human rights concerns such as curbing the activities of so-called "death squads." (State Department human rights report, Historic Documents of 1983, p. 189; 1984, p. 155)

Commission Report, Recommendations

In broad terms the 132-page report endorsed the Reagan view of why Central America was in turmoil, how that turmoil threatened the United States, and what should be done about it. Reciting the region's long history of poverty and injustice, and the more recent history of stymied economic growth, the commission said, "The roots of the crisis are both indigenous and foreign. Discontents are real, and for much of the population conditions of life are miserable," making the region "ripe for revolution." But, the commission said, "these conditions have been exploited by hostile outside forces — specifically Cuba, backed by the Soviet Union and now operating through Nicaragua — which will turn any revolution they capture into a totalitarian state, threatening the region and robbing the people of their hopes for liberty."

The United States was not threatened by "indigenous reform, even indigenous revolution" in Central America, the commission said. "But the intrusion of aggressive outside powers exploiting local grievances to expand their own political influence and military control is a serious threat to the United States, and to the entire hemisphere."

Saying the existing levels of U.S. military aid to El Salvador "are not sufficient to preserve even the existing military stalemate over a period of time," the commission called for "significantly increased levels of military aid as quickly as possible." The panel did not specify an amount but noted that the Pentagon had estimated a need for $400 million over fiscal years 1984-85 to "break the military stalemate."

The commission supported Reagan's policy of bolstering Central American economies with short-term aid. But it said the budget of $477 million in fiscal 1984 economic aid to Costa Rica, El Salvador, Guatemala, Honduras, Belize, and Panama was not adequate, and it recommended an additional $400 million.

Congressional Reaction

Members of Congress greeted the Kissinger commission report with the same partisan tone that for nearly three years had characterized the debate over U.S. policy toward Central America. Republicans embraced the report, predicting it would give President Reagan new leverage on Capitol Hill. Democrats, for the most part, attacked the recommendations that supported Reagan's actions and praised those elements that challenged his policies. One leading critic, Rep. Michael D. Barnes, D-Md., said the report would change few minds because "the issues are too important and the views in the country are too strongly held for the debate to end." One of eight non-voting, congressional "senior counselors" to the commission, Barnes complained that Reagan had "stacked" the panel with members receptive to his policies. But another counselor, Sen. Pete V. Domenici, R-N.M., said there was wide agreement "on about 99 percent of this report," adding, "I support it wholeheartedly."

Kissinger defended the report, saying it demonstrated "a remarkable consensus." Of the recommendations, he said, "We do not guarantee success, but without a program of this kind, success is surely not attainable." Nevertheless, the report contained several dissents that both sides were certain to use in attacking the commission's recommendations. Kissinger himself lodged a narrowly worded dissent against the recommended conditions on military aid to El Salvador.

Reagan Aid Package

Embracing most of the commission's recommendations on Central America, President Reagan February 4 proposed a five-year program of U.S. assistance to Central America. Unveiling the program at a White House ceremony attended by congressional leaders, Reagan said it included "a mix of developmental, political, diplomatic and security initiatives equitably and humanely pursued. We either do them all, or we jeopardize the chance for real progress in the region," he warned.

Reagan's proposal, formally sent to Congress February 17, included both short-term and long-term aid to the region. For the short term, Reagan asked Congress to add about $400 million in economic assistance and $259 million in military aid to funds already approved for fiscal 1984. For the longer term, Reagan accepted the commission's recommendation for a five-year program centering on $8.3 billion in economic aid. The president requested a nearly fivefold increase in aid to El Salvador in fiscal years 1984 and 1985. The request was $312 million, on top of the $64.8 million Congress already had approved for 1984.

The president accepted the panel's recommendation that military assistance to El Salvador be linked to improvements in human rights there. However, Reagan rejected conditions that would give Congress a role in deciding whether El Salvador merited the aid. "We believe that the administration is in the best position to control the spigot," a senior administration official told reporters.

Impact of El Salvador Elections

Congressional action on the aid package was in large part contingent on the outcome of the March 24 elections in El Salvador. The front-

runners in that contest were José Napoleón Duarte, the leader of the moderate Christian Democratic Party who headed an interim junta after the overthrow of the military dictatorship in 1979, and Roberto D'Aubuisson of the Nationalist Republican Alliance, a right-wing former Army major who was linked to the activity of the country's paramilitary death squads. Duarte won about 44 percent of the vote to D'Aubuisson's 30 percent, forcing a runoff May 6. In the runoff election, Duarte, who was supported by the Reagan administration, was declared the official winner with 55 percent of the vote.

The Salvadoran balloting weighed heavily on a House vote on El Salvador aid May 10. By a dramatic 212-208 vote, the House approved most of the president's request for military aid to the country, free of the stringent conditions sought by some Democrats.

Duarte visited the United States in late May and met with members of Congress, who generally had praise for the president-elect. Satisfied with his pledge to respect human rights and control the military, in 1984 Congress approved $196.55 million in military aid for El Salvador, more than twice the amount for fiscal 1982.

> *Following are excerpts from the report of the National Bipartisan Commission on Central America, released January 11, 1984.* (Boldface headings in brackets have been added by Congressional Quarterly to highlight the organization of the text.):

Toward Democracy and Economic Prosperity

The crisis in Central America has no single, simple cause, but the troubled performance of the region's economies has been a major factor. They were among the most dynamic in the world during the 1960s and early 1970s. But that growth was unevenly distributed and poverty continued to plague most of the region's people. As the Final Document of the Catholic Conference of Latin American Bishops at Puebla, Mexico recognized in 1979, there was a "growing gap between rich and poor," which the conference characterized as a "contradiction of Christian existence." This contributed to a growing political frustration in several countries, intensified by the fact that some sectors of these societies were enjoying economic success.

Then, in the late 1970s, production, export earnings, incomes, profits, and consumption all began to decline. The result was a sharp economic contraction in each country of the region. The effects have been particularly severe for those who were denied participation in the earlier era of rapid growth.

Yet our meetings with the leaders and people of Central America and our consideration of the facts put before us during the hearings have convinced us that the Central American economies can grow again, and that the fruits of that growth can be more equitably shared. This will require that:

- Economic growth goes forward in tandem with social and political modernization.
- Indigenous savings are encouraged and supplemented by substantial external aid.
- The nations of the region pursue appropriate economic policies.
- In particular, these policies recognize that success will ultimately depend on the re-invigoration of savings, growth, and employment.

The program the Commission envisions — aimed at promoting democratization, economic growth, human development and security — would break new ground. Most past U.S. development programs have been predominately economic. We argue here that the crisis in Central America cannot be considered in solely economic or social or security terms. The requirements for the development of Central America are a seamless web. The actions we recommend represent an attempt to address this complex interrelationship in its totality, not just in its parts. . . .

. . . We envision, in the short term, an emergency stabilization program and, in the medium and long term, a new multilateral regional organization to measure performance across the entire political, social, economic, and security spectrum, and to target external aid resources where they can provide the most significant impetus. In support of these efforts, we urge a five-year commitment by the United States to a substantially increased level of economic assistance. . . .

AN EMERGENCY STABILIZATION PROGRAM

We cannot wait to check the decline in economic activity and the deterioration in social conditions until a long-term program is in place. The Commission therefore urges the immediate adoption of an emergency stabilization program combining public and private efforts to halt the deterioration. Some of our recommendations are endorsements of existing initiatives. And, most important, it is critical that the Central American countries continue to implement economic stabilization programs and, especially, to pursue policies designed to foster increased investment and trade.

The program includes eight key elements:

We urge that the leaders of the United States and the Central American countries meet to initiate a comprehensive approach to the economic development of the region and the reinvigoration of the Central American Common Market. . . .

We encourage the greatest possible involvement of the private sector in the stabilization effort....

We recognize that the current climate of violence and uncertainty discourages private sector initiatives. Nevertheless, we believe it is imperative to increase the private sector's involvement as soon as possible. Thus, we recommend the establishment of an Emergency Action Committee of concerned private citizens and organizations with a mandate to provide advice on the development of new public-private initiatives to spur growth and employment in the region.

We recommend that the United States actively address the external debt problems of the region.

We urge new initiatives to deal with Central America's serious external debt problems. Although the United States and other creditor governments have agreed in principle to reschedule part of Costa Rica's external debt, none of the other countries of the region has formally asked for similar treatment. They should be encouraged to seek multilateral debt renegotiation; this would be a departure from existing practice which is essentially reactive....

We recommend that the United States provide an immediate increase in bilateral economic assistance.

Additional economic assistance should be made available in the current fiscal year. Total commitments of U.S. bilateral economic assistance to Belize, Costa Rica, El Salvador, Guatemala, Honduras, Nicaragua, and Panama in FY 1983 was [sic] $628 million; the request for appropriated funds for FY 1984 is $477 million. We recommend a supplemental appropriation of $400 million for the current fiscal year. Such an increase, if complemented by continued improvements in the economic policy programs of these countries and if quickly made available, would help stabilize current economic conditions. (Forecasts of the financial needs of the region are summarized in the appendix to this chapter.) We also recommend additional U.S. economic assistance in future years, which is discussed in the proposed medium-term program.

The bulk of this additional assistance should be channeled through the Agency for International Development (AID), with emphasis on creating productive jobs, providing general balance of payments support, and helping the recipient countries implement their economic stabilization programs. The purpose of this assistance would be to stop the continued decline in economic activity, and to signal a U.S. commitment to helping Central America address its deep-seated economic and political problems. Other donors, including Canada, Europe and Japan should be encouraged to provide similar additional help as soon as possible.

We recommend that a major thrust of expanded aid should be in labor intensive infrastructure and housing projects....

We recommend that new official trade credit guarantees be made available to the Central American countries.

The decline in the availability of trade finance has critically affected the flow of imports into Central America. A Trade Credit Insurance Program would provide U.S. government guarantees for short-term trade credit from U.S. commercial banks. Such a program could be administered by the Export-Import Bank, although the existing trade credit program is not available to Central American countries, in part because the risks of non-repayment are viewed as excessive. Therefore, every effort should be made to establish the program within existing legislation or to create new legislative authority for a program reflecting the need for special consideration in Central America. The novelty would be that the program would be available only for use in Central America.

We further recommend that participating U.S. commercial banks be required as a condition of their participation, to renegotiate their existing long-term credits in accordance with guidelines established by the debt task force described above. Thus, the program would contribute to easing debt service problems as well as to encouraging renewed commercial bank lending (albeit with a government guarantee) in Central America.

We also urge that a program be organized to provide seasonal credit to the agricultural sector which would meet a critical need in the region.

We recommend that the United States provide an emergency credit to the Central American Common Market Fund (CACMF).

The Central American countries have asked for a credit to refinance part of the accumulated trade deficits among themselves which have contributed to the contraction of intra-regional trade. The United States should use part of the increased economic aid for this purpose; the Central American countries that have been in surplus would be expected to transform the remainder of the deficits into long-term local currency credits. As the Central American countries have proposed, CACMF regulations should then be adjusted to avoid future build-ups of large unsettled balances. Since the debts that would be refinanced under this proposal are among central banks, there should be no adverse implications for other rescheduling efforts. . . .

We recommend that the United States join the Central American Bank for Economic Integration (CABEI).

The Central American countries are opening membership in CABEI to countries outside the region. We urge the U.S. to join this institution and to encourage other creditor countries to seek membership. The infusion of new resources would help reinvigorate the bank, which could channel much-needed funds to small-scale entrepreneurs and farmers, provide working capital to existing private sector companies, and encourage the development of new industries. Again, U.S. membership in CABEI would benefit all members of the Common Market.

[LONG-TERM PROGRAM]

The measures we have outlined above aim at short-term stabilization. Essentially, they are emergency economic measures made necessary by the severity of the economic downturn. They represent an effort to buy time to permit the Central American nations and their friends to build a broader structure of cooperation for the longer future. That longer-term future is our principal mandate, and we now turn to it. . . .

. . . Nevertheless, we are obliged to define medium-term objectives which are compatible with the interest of the United States:

Elimination of the climate of violence and civil strife.

Peace is an essential condition of economic and social progress. So too is elimination of the fear of brutality inflicted by arbitrary authority or terrorism. No need is more basic.

Development of democratic institutions and processes.

The United States should encourage the Central American nations to develop and nurture democratic cultures, institutions, and practices, including:

- Strong judicial systems to enhance the capacity to redress grievances concerning personal security, property rights, and free speech.
- Free elections, by seeking advice from technical experts and studying successful electoral systems, including Costa Rica's.
- Free and democratic trade unions. The importance of unions, which represent millions of rural and urban workers, has been firmly established in the region. They have been not only an economic force but a political one as well, opposing arbitrary rule and promoting democratic values. Labor unions will continue to have an important part to play in political development, as well as in improving the social and economic well-being of working men and women. Assuring an equitable distribution of economic benefits will require both job-oriented development strategies and trade unions to protect workers' rights.

Development of strong and free economies with diversified production for both external and domestic markets.

During the second half of this decade the Central American economies need to grow at per capita annual rates of at least 3 percent in real terms, which is close to the region's historical growth rate and is necessary to absorb new entrants to the labor force each year. This is an ambitious but realistic goal despite today's depressed conditions and the misfortunes of the recent past.

Sharp improvement in the social conditions of the poorest Central Americans. . . .

Substantially improved distribution of income and wealth. . . .

We urge a major increase in U.S. and other country financial and economic assistance for Central America.

Unless there is a substantial increase in aid, in our view, the prospects for recovery are bleak. The solution to the crisis of Central America does not lie along the path of austerity. We believe that the people of the region must at a minimum perceive a reasonable prospect that, with sustained effort on their part, they can reach 1980 levels of per capita economic activity by no later than 1990, and, with determination and luck, well before that. However, as we have repeatedly stressed, unless economic recovery is accompanied by social progress and political reform, additional financial support will ultimately be wasted. By the same token, without recovery, the political and security prospects will be grim.

Reaching that goal will require a significant effort. External financing needs between now and 1990 have been estimated at as much as $24 billion for the seven countries as a group. (Forecasts are summarized in the appendix.) The World Bank, the International Monetary Fund, the Inter-American Development Bank, other official creditors, private investors, and commercial banks are likely to provide at least half of these funds — especially if each Central American country follows prudent economic policies, if there is steady social and political progress, and if outside aggression is eliminated. The balance, as much as $12 billion, would have to be supplied by the United States. (As defined in the appendix, this total financing need includes the projected financing requirements of Nicaragua, which is not now a recipient of U.S. assistance.)

We have already proposed that U.S. economic assistance be increased in FY 1984 to cover part of this on an emergency basis.

We now propose that economic assistance over the five-year period beginning in 1985 total $8 billion. Although the macro-economic forecasts on which we base this proposal do not translate precisely into fiscal year federal budget requests, this global figure would include direct appropriations as well as contingent liabilities such as guarantees and insurance. In effect, this would represent a rough doubling of U.S. economic assistance from the 1983 level.

We recognize that such a proposal, at a time of serious concern in the United States about the level of governmental spending and the prospective size of the federal budget deficit, may be viewed with scepticism. However, we firmly believe that without such large-scale assistance, economic recovery, social progress, and the development of democratic institutions in Central America will be set back.

Because of the magnitude of the effort required and the importance of a long-term commitment, we further urge that Congress appropriate funds for Central America on a multiple-year basis. We strongly recommend a five year authorization of money, a portion of which would be channelled through the proposed Central American Development Organization, which is outlined later in this chapter. The balance would support economic assistance programs administered by existing U.S. government agencies.

Ultimately, the effectiveness of increased economic assistance will turn on the economic policies of the Central American countries themselves. As we have noted, most have begun to move away from some of the policies which contributed to the current crisis. However, we agree with what many experts have told us: that unless these reforms are extended economic performance will not significantly improve, regardless of the money foreign donors and creditors provide. In too many other countries, increased availability of financial resources has undermined reform by relieving the immediate pressure on policy makers. This must be avoided in Central America.

What is now required is a firm commitment by the Central American countries to economic policies, including reforms in tax systems, to encourage private enterprise and individual initiative, to create favorable investment climates, to curb corruption where it exists, and to spur balanced trade. These can lay the foundation for sustained growth.

The increased economic assistance we propose should be used to promote democracy, renew economic growth, improve living conditions, achieve better distribution of income and wealth, encourage more dynamic and open economies, and develop more productive agriculture. Specific programs are primarily the responsibilities of the recipient countries themselves. However, we strongly urge that the United States actively work to develop and nurture democratic institutions in the region.

We recommend that the United States expand economic assistance for democratic institutions and leadership training. . . .

[TRADE GROWTH]

Rapid Central American economic growth requires increased foreign exchange earnings. In the short run the region will continue to rely largely on the earnings which come from the export of commodities. The Commission considered, and rejected as ineffective or inappropriate, proposals to stabilize commodity prices or earnings. Thus, until demand recovers for the commodities which Central America produces, the prospects for significant increases in export earnings are limited.

The solution to this problem will necessarily be a slow one. Over the medium term, the Central American countries should try to broaden their export bases both in the agricultural and manufactured good sectors. More diversified exports would help to insulate the region from some of the swings in the international economy.

Central American export-promoting policies will come to naught, however, if the rest of the world fails to open its markets. The United States has taken the lead in this respect and the Caribbean Basin Initiative will provide additional encouragement for the development of new export industries.

The Central American countries should also try to free up foreign exchange resources by reducing energy imports. The United States and other donor nations possess relatively inexpensive technology that could be used in the region to identify and explore local energy resources.

We encourage the extension of duty-free trade to Central America by other major trading countries.

The CBI [Caribbean Basin Initiative] is a landmark piece of legislation and we hope that other countries will be willing to extend similar benefits to Central America. We urge the European Community to extend trade preferences to Central America under the Lome Agreement, since the U.S. is extending CBI benefits to Lome beneficiaries in the Caribbean. Other countries of Latin America should also be encouraged to offer special trade benefits to the Central American countries as their own economic recovery progresses.

We urge the United States to review non-tariff barriers to imports from Central America....

We recommend technical and financial support for export promotion efforts.

U.S. economic assistance should be used to provide technical and financial support for trading and export marketing companies and innovative export-oriented joint ventures between Central American and foreign entrepreneurs. This is already an important element of the current assistance program; in the future this should be a top priority....

We encourage the formation of a privately-owned venture capital company for Central America.

We recommend that a venture capital company — which might be called the Central American Development Corporation (CADC) — be established for Central America. This was suggested to us by several private business-men and organizations and represents an innovative way to promote investment in the region even under present difficult conditions. CADC, capitalized by private sector investors, would use its capital to raise funds which, in turn, would be lent to private companies active in Central America. It would be managed and directed by experienced entrepreneurs. Its loans would be made to commercially viable projects in high priority economic sectors for working capital or investment purposes. The U.S. government could support the CADC initiative through a long-term loan as it has for similar initiatives in other areas of the world....

We recommend that the financial underpinnings of the efforts to broaden land ownership be strengthened and reformed.

... In programs of land reform, ways should be found to ensure that the redistribution of land provides the new owners with a valid title, that governments promptly allocate resources as they become available to ensure that former owners are effectively compensated, and that in the end the system enhances incentives to expand the nation's total agricultural output....

... We have developed the outline of a structure which we have called the Central American Development Organization, or CADO. We put it forward not as the only design, but as a means of illustrating how the concept could be implemented.

Membership in CADO, as we envision it, would initially be open to the seven countries of Central America — Belize, Costa Rica, El Salvador, Guatemala, Honduras, Nicaragua and Panama — and to the United States. Associate member status would be available to any democracy willing to contribute significant resources to promote regional development. We would hope that the other Contadora countries would participate actively, as well as the nations of Europe, Canada and Japan. The organization's Chairman should be from the United States with an Executive Secretary from Central America.

The operating body of CADO, in which each full member would be represented, would assess the progress made by each Central American country toward economic, political and social objectives, as well as make recommendations on the allocation of economic resources. It would require of its members a high degree of integrity and judgment; they would be expected to bring to their task special competence and experience in the development process. We are convinced that the region has an impressive store of men and women, dedicated to the future progress of their people, who could fill these roles.

Representation should be drawn primarily from the private sector....

Central American participation in the program should turn on acceptance of and continued progress toward....

● Political pluralism, and a process of recurrent elections with competing political parties. Only nations prepared to base their governments on the free choice of their people should be eligible....

We recommend that an economic reconstruction fund be established within CADO and that the U.S. channel one-quarter of its economic assistance through such a fund. Loans to countries would be in support of development programs and policies including the implementation of growth-oriented economic policies, the establishment of genuine democratic institutions, and the adoption of programs to improve social conditions. They would be quick-disbursing, balance of payments support loans....

Human Development

... We recommend that the United States increase food aid on an emergency basis....

The United States and other countries can help Central Americans improve educational training opportunities. This should focus principally on building institutions, although in the short run direct training programs may be needed while institutions develop. The effort should start with a literacy program and continue with programs to help improve the quality and broaden the availability of formal education and vocational training programs.

We recommend that the Peace Corps expand its recruitment of front line teachers to serve in a new Literacy Corps. . . .

We recommend that Peace Corps activities be expanded at the primary, secondary, and technical levels in part by establishing a Central American Teacher Corps, recruited from the Spanish-speaking population of the United States. . . .

We recommend an expanded program of secondary level technical and vocational education. . . .

We recommend expansion of the International Executive Service Corps (IESC).

The IESC is a private, voluntary organization of retired American business executives. An expanded IESC effort in Central America, perhaps with some support from the U.S. Government, should give particular attention to training managers of small businesses. This would strengthen the economy, while also contributing to the development of the middle class. . . .

A major shortcoming of past U.S. educational assistance has been insufficient support for Central American universities. . . .

. . . [W]e recommend a program of 10,000 government-sponsored scholarships to bring Central American students to the United States. . . .

. . . [W]e recommend that existing technical assistance programs supported by AID should be expanded. . . .

We recommend a resumption of the AID-sponsored program to eradicate vector-borne diseases such as malaria and dengue fever. . . .

The recommendations we have made . . . constitute an ambitious program of human development in Central America. They cannot be accomplished by appropriations of money alone. Stability and security in the hemisphere depend on the existence of democratic and economically viable nations in Central America. In turn, this requires that their people be healthy, educated, properly housed and free.

To achieve this requires a consensus in the United States that the welfare of Central America is crucial to the well-being of the United States itself, and a commitment by thousands of corporations and individuals — as well as by the government — to help improve living conditions throughout Central America. We believe that if this development effort is to succeed, it must be supported by the educational and business institutions of this country. Such support is clearly in our own best interests, as well as in those of the Central American nations.

Central American Security Issues

... The conflicts that ravage the nations of Central America have both indigenous and foreign roots. Restoring peace and stability will require a combination of social and political reforms, economic advances, diplomatic pursuit and military effort. In earlier chapters we dealt with the social, economic and political aspects; in the next chapter, we will discuss possible diplomatic measures. We hope that negotiations will bear fruit so that the people of Central America can devote their energies to bettering their lives. That is our strong preference — a vigorous, concrete and comprehensive diplomatic effort is set forth in the next section. But even as military measures are needed to shield economic and social programs, so too are they essential as an adjunct to diplomacy....

We have stressed before, and we repeat here: indigenous reform movements, even indigenous revolutions, are not themselves a security concern of the United States. History holds examples of genuinely popular revolutions, springing wholly from native roots. In this hemisphere Mexico is a clear example. But during the past two decades we have faced a new phenomenon. The concerting of the power of the Soviet Union and Cuba to extend their presence and influence into vulnerable areas of the Western Hemisphere is a direct threat to U.S. security interests. This type of insurgency is present in Central America today.

The complexity of the political conflicts in Central America aggravates the situation in several countries and sometimes obscures the outlines of the different contests that are underway.

In Somoza's Nicaragua three broad groups were involved in the struggle for decisive control of that country: the Somoza machine, which dominated the country's government, army and economy; oppositionists who desired to establish democratic institutions including free elections and all the associated guarantees; and Marxist-Leninists who were tied to Cuba and the Soviet bloc.

After 1978 those in Nicaragua who opposed the Somoza regime joined together in a single "broad front" which eventually overthrew the Somozas. In the ensuing struggle, the Marxist-Leninist FSLN, with a monopoly of military power, took control of the machinery of government. They have since used that control effectively to exclude the democratic opposition from power. Some of the latter continue their struggle today as leaders of an armed insurgency against the Nicaraguan government.

In El Salvador two separate conflicts have raged since 1979. One conflict pits persons seeking democratic government and its associated rights and freedoms against those trying to maintain oligarchical rule and its associated privileges. A second conflict pits guerrillas seeking to establish a Marxist-Leninist state as part of a broader Central American revolution against those who oppose a Marxist-Leninist victory.

In each of these conflicts one of the parties has pursued its goals by violence. Both traditionalist death squads and murderous guerrillas have attacked political party, labor and peasant leaders working to establish and consolidate democratic institutions, killing them and dismantling their efforts to build democracy.

The co-existence of these conflicts greatly complicates the task of the democratic forces and their friends. Each violent group attempts to hide behind the other. Neither group has been willing to subordinate its desire for power to the civilized disciplines of the democratic process. The violence of the death squads weakens fragile democratic institutions at a time when they are already under attack by communist guerrillas. It wipes out democratic leaders, intimidates the less hardy, undermines freedom, and hampers the forces of democracy in their struggle against the armed guerrillas. Marxist-Leninist violence imposes the economic and social strains of war on El Salvador at the same time that it kills Salvadorans, progressively destroys the economy, disrupts and intimidates the democratic leaders and others, and weakens those struggling to consolidate democratic institutions. . . .

Cuba and Nicaragua did not invent the grievances that made insurrection possible in El Salvador and elsewhere. Those grievances are real and acute. In other chapters we have discussed ways of remedying them. But it is important to bear in mind three facts about the kind of insurgencies we confront:

- They depend on external support, which is substantially more effective when it includes the provision of privileged sanctuaries for the insurgents.

- They develop their own momentum, independent of the conditions on which they feed.

- The insurgents, if they win, will create a totalitarian regime in the image of their sponsors' ideology and their own. . . .

Propaganda support, money, sanctuary, arms, supplies, training, communications, intelligence, logistics, all are important in both morale and operational terms. Without such support from Cuba, Nicaragua and the Soviet Union, neither in El Salvador nor elsewhere in Central America would such an insurgency pose so severe a threat to the government. With such support, guerrilla forces could develop insurgencies in many other countries. The struggle in El Salvador is particularly severe because it is there that external support is at present most heavily concentrated.

Therefore, curbing the insurgents' violence in El Salvador requires, in part, cutting them off from their sources of foreign support.

. . . Unchecked, the insurgents can destroy faster than the reformers can build.

One reason for this is that an explicit purpose of guerrilla violence is to make matters worse: to paralyze the economy, to heighten social discords, to spread fear and despair, to weaken institutions and to undermine government authority — all so as to radicalize the people, and to persuade them that any alternative is better than what they have. . . .

None of this legitimizes the use of arbitrary violence by the right in El Salvador or elsewhere. Indeed, the grim reality is that many of the excesses we have condemned would be present even if there were no guerrilla war supported by outside forces. . . .

At the level of global strategy . . . the advance of Soviet and Cuban power on the American mainland affects the global balance. To the extent that a further Marxist-Leninist advance in Central America leading to progressive deterioration and a further projection of Soviet and Cuban power in the region required us to defend against security threats near our borders, we would face a difficult choice between unpalatable alternatives. We would either have to assume a permanently increased defense burden, or see our capacity to defend distant trouble-spots reduced, and as a result have to reduce important commitments elsewhere in the world. From the standpoint of the Soviet Union, it would be a major strategic coup to impose on the United States the burden of defending our southern approaches, thereby stripping us of the compensating advantage that offsets the burden of our transoceanic lines of communication. . . .

Beyond the issue of U.S. security interests in the Central American-Caribbean region, our credibility worldwide is engaged. The triumph of hostile forces in what the Soviets call the "strategic rear" of the United States would be read as a sign of U.S. impotence.

Thus, even in terms of the direct national security interests of the United States, this country has large stakes in the present conflict in Central America. . . .

The fundamental dilemma is as follows: both the national interests of the United States and a genuine concern for the long-term welfare of Central America create powerful incentives to provide all necessary assistance to defeat totalitarian guerrillas. At the same time one of the principal objectives of the guerrilla forces is to destroy the morale and efficiency of the government's administration and programs. . . .

. . . The United States obviously cannot accept, let alone support, the brutal methods practiced by certain reactionary forces in Central America. Some of these actions are related to counter-insurgency. Their common denominator is the systematic use of mass reprisals and selective killing and torture to dissuade the civil population from participating in the insurgency or from providing any help for the insurgents. . . .

Whatever their aims, these methods are totally repugnant to the values of the United States. . . .

The present level of U.S. military assistance to El Salvador is far too low to enable the armed forces of El Salvador to use these modern methods of counter-insurgency effectively. At the same time, the tendency in some quarters of the Salvadoran military towards brutality magnifies Congressional and Executive pressures for further cuts in aid. A vicious cycle results in which violence and denial of human rights spawn reductions in aid, and reductions in aid make more difficult the pursuit of an enlightened counter-insurgency effort. . . .

In the Commission's view it is imperative to settle on a level of aid related to the operational requirements of a humane anti-guerrilla strategy and to stick with it for the requisite period of time.

Another obstacle to the effective pursuit of anti-guerrilla strategy is a provision of current U.S. law under which no assistance can be provided to law enforcement agencies. This dates back to a previous period when it was believed that such aid was sometimes helping groups guilty of serious human rights abuses. The purpose of the legislation was to prevent the United States and its personnel from being associated with unacceptable practices. That concern is valid, but, however laudable its intentions, the blanket legal prohibition against the provision of training and aid to police organizations has the paradoxical effect, in certain cases, of inhibiting our efforts to improve human rights performance....

We therefore suggest that Congress examine this question thoroughly and consider whether Section 660 of the Foreign Assistance Act should be amended so as to permit — under carefully defined conditions — the allocation of funds to the training and support of law enforcement agencies in Central America....

[El Salvador Aid]

... The Salvadoran Government's National Campaign Plan combines military operations with follow-up civic actions to restore agriculture and commerce. The plan is designed to provide secure areas within which the Salvadoran *campesino* can grow, harvest and market his crops, and where industry can again operate. The plan assumes that sufficient security can be established countrywide to reduce the insurgency at least to a low level within two years. But the government's forces must be significantly and quickly strengthened if the plan is to succeed....

There might be an argument for doing nothing to help the government of El Salvador. There might be an argument for doing a great deal more. There is, however, no logical argument for giving some aid but not enough. The worst possible policy for El Salvador is to provide just enough aid to keep the war going, but too little to wage it successfully.

As we have already made clear in this report, the Commission has concluded that present levels of U.S. military assistance are inadequate.

We are not in a position to judge the precise amounts and types of increased aid needed. We note that the U.S. Department of Defense estimates that it would take approximately $400 million in U.S. military assistance in 1984 and 1985 to break the military stalemate and allow the National Campaign Plan to be carried out. The Department believes that thereafter assistance levels could be brought down to considerably more modest levels.

The Commission recommends that the United States provide to El Salvador — subject to the conditions we specify later in this chapter — significantly increased levels of military aid as quickly as possible, so that the Salvadoran authorities can act on the assurance that needed aid will be forthcoming....

The Commission believes that vigorous, concurrent policies on both the military and human rights fronts are needed to break out of the demoralizing cycle of deterioration on the one hand and abuses on the other. We believe policies of increased aid and increased pressure to safeguard human rights would improve both security and justice. A slackening on one front would undermine our objective on the other. El Salvador must succeed on both or it will not succeed on either.

The United States Government has a right to demand certain minimum standards of respect for human rights as a condition for providing military aid to any country.

With respect to El Salvador, military aid should, through legislation requiring periodic reports, be made contingent upon demonstrated progress toward free elections; freedom of association; the establishment of the rule of law and an effective judicial system; and the termination of the activities of the so-called death squads, as well as vigorous action against those guilty of crimes and the prosecution to the extent possible of past offenders. These conditions should be seriously enforced.

Implementation of this approach would be greatly facilitated through the device of an independent monitoring body, such as the Central American Development Organization spelled out in Chapter 4.

As an additional measure, the United States should impose sanctions, including the denial of visas, deportation, and the investigation of financial dealings, against foreign nationals in the United States who are connected with death-squad activities in El Salvador or anywhere else....

[The Search For Peace]

... [W]e believe that there is a chance for a political solution in Central America if the diplomacy of the United States is strategic in conception, purposeful in approach, and steadfast in execution. Our broad objectives should be:

- To stop the war and the killing in El Salvador.
- To create conditions under which Nicaragua can take its place as a peaceful and democratic member of the Central American community.
- To open the way to democratic development throughout the isthmus....

... [T]he Commission has concluded that power-sharing as proposed by the insurgents is not a sensible or fair political solution for El Salvador. There is no historical precedent suggesting that such a procedure would reconcile contending parties which entertain such deeply held beliefs and political goals, and which have been killing each other for years. Indeed, precedent argues that it would be only a prelude to a take-over by the insurgent forces....

Thus the El Salvador Government must take all appropriate measures to make the March 25 elections as safe and open as possible. This should include the introduction of outside observers to help insure the security and fairness of the process. . . .

1. The Salvadoran government would invite the FDR-FMLN [Democratic Revolutionary Front-Farabundo Marti National Liberation Front] to negotiate mutually acceptable procedures to establish a framework for future elections. . . .
2. As part of this framework a broadly representative Elections Commission would be established, including representatives of the FDR-FMLN. . . .
3. Violence should be ended by all parties so that mutually satisfactory arrangements can be developed among the government, pro-government parties, the different opposition groups and insurgent groups for the period of campaigning and elections. . . .
4. A system of international observation should be established to enhance the faith and confidence of all parties in the probity and equity of arrangements for elections. This might include senior advisers to the Elections Commission drawn from the OAS, Contadora nations or third countries agreed upon by all parties to the conflict. . . .

What happens in El Salvador will have important consequences in the other nations of Central America. If the shaky center collapses and the country eventually is dominated by undemocratic extremes, this will lead to increased pressures on El Salvador's neighbors. For Guatemala and Nicaragua, the experience of El Salvador could carry a clear message: the best means of earning the support of the United States, and of promoting political, social, and economic development, lies in adopting both the form and the substance of democracy.

In addition, events in El Salvador will have a major impact on developments in Nicaragua and on Nicaragua's relations with its neighbors. . . .

Therefore, though the Commission believes that the Sandinista regime will pose a continuing threat to stability in the region, we do not advocate a policy of static containment.

Instead, we recommend, first, an effort to arrange a comprehensive regional settlement. This would elaborate and build upon the 21 objectives of the Contadora Group. (For these see the annex to this chapter.) Within the framework of basic principles, it would:

- Recognize linkage between democratization and security in the region.
- Relate the incentives of increased development aid and trade concessions to acceptance of mutual security guarantees.
- Engage the United States and other developed nations in the regional peace system.
- Establish an institutional mechanism in the region to implement that system. . . .

The Commission believes . . . that whatever the prospects seem to be for productive negotiations, the United States must spare no effort to pursue the diplomatic route. Nicaragua's willingness to enter into a general agreement should be thoroughly tested through negotiations and actions. . . .

. . . As a broad generality, we do not believe that it would be wise to dismantle existing incentives and pressures on the Managua regime except in conjunction with demonstrable progress on the negotiating front. With specific reference to the highly controversial question of whether the United States should provide support for the Nicaraguan insurgent forces opposed to the Sandinistas now in authority in Managua, the Commission recognized that an adequate examination of this issue would require treatment of sensitive information not appropriate to a public report. However, the majority of the members of the Commission, in their respective individual judgments, believe that the efforts of the Nicaraguan insurgents represent one of the incentives working in favor of a negotiated settlement and that the future role of the United States in those efforts must therefore be considered in the context of the negotiating process. The Commission has not, however, attempted to come to a collective judgment on whether, and how, the United States should provide support for these insurgent forces. . . .

The four neighboring Contadora countries — Colombia, Mexico, Panama and Venezuela — have been active and creative in trying to develop a regional diplomacy that can meet the needs of Central America. Their role has been constructive in helping to define issues and to demonstrate the commitment of key Latin American nations to pursue stability and peaceful evolution within the region. . . .

Conclusion

We have concluded this exercise persuaded that Central America is both vital and vulnerable, and that whatever other crises may arise to claim the nation's attention the United States cannot afford to turn away from that threatened region. Central America's crisis is our crisis.

All too frequently, wars and threats of wars are what draw attention to one part of the world or another. So it has been in Central America. The military crisis there captured our attention, but in doing so it has also wakened us to many other needs of the region. However belatedly, it did "concentrate the mind."

In the case of this Commission, one effect of concentrating the mind has been to clarify the picture we had of the nations of Central America. It is a common failing to see other nations as caricatures rather than as portraits, exaggerating one or two characteristics and losing sight of the subtler nuances on which so much of human experience centers. As we have studied these nations, we have become sharply aware of how great a mistake it would be to view them in one-dimensional terms. An exceptionally complex interplay of forces has shaped their history and continues to define their identities and to affect their destinies.

We have developed a great sympathy for those in Central America who are struggling to control those forces, and to bring their countries successfully through this period of political and social transformation. As a regioa, Central America is in mid-passage from the predominantly authoritarian patterns of the past to what can, with determination, with help, with luck, and with peace, become the predominantly democratic pluralism of the future. That transformation has been troubled, seldom smooth, and sometimes violent. In Nicaragua, we have seen the tragedy of a revolution betrayed; the same forces that stamped out the beginnings of democracy in Nicaragua now threaten El Salvador. In El Salvador itself, those seeking to establish democratic institutions are beset by violence from the extremists on both sides. But the spirit of freedom is strong throughout the region, and the determination persists to strengthen it where it exists and to achieve it where it does not.

The use of Nicaragua as a base for Soviet and Cuban efforts to penetrate the rest of the Central American isthmus, with El Salvador the target of first opportunity, gives the conflict there a major strategic dimension. The direct involvement of aggressive external forces makes it a challenge to the system of hemispheric security, and, quite specifically, to the security interests of the United States. This is a challenge to which the United States must respond.

But beyond this, we are challenged to respond to the urgent human needs of the people of Central America. Central America is a region in crisis economically, socially and politically. Its nations are our neighbors, and they need our help. This is one of those instances in which the requirements of national interest and the commands of conscience coincide.

Through the years, there has been a sort of natural progression in this nation's ties with other parts of the world. At first they were almost exclusively with Europe. Then, without diminishing those ties with Europe, we expanded our trans-Pacific bonds. Now the crisis in Central America has served as a vivid reminder that we need to strengthen our ties to the south, as well as east and west.

Our response to the present crisis in Central America must not be a passing phenomenon. The United States was born of a vision, which has inspired the world for two centuries. That vision shines most brightly when it is shared. Just as we cherish our vision, we should encourage others to pursue their own. But in fact, what we want for ourselves is very largely what the people of Central America want for themselves. They do share the vision of the future that our ideals represent, and the time has come for us to help them not just to aspire to that vision, but to participate in it.

Our task now, as a nation, is to transform the crisis in Central America into an opportunity: to seize the impetus it provides, and to use this to help our neighbors not only to secure their freedom from aggression and violence, but also to set in place the policies, processes and institutions that will make them both prosperous and free. If, together, we succeed in this, then the sponsors of violence will have done the opposite of what they intended: they will have roused us not only to turn back the tide of totalitarianism but to bring a new birth of hope and of opportunity to the people of Central America.

Because this is our opportunity, in conscience it is also our responsibility.

COURT ON PRIVATE USE
OF HOME VIDEO RECORDERS
January 17, 1984

In a 5-4 decision January 17, the Supreme Court ruled that the non-commercial home taping of copyrighted television programs for personal use did not violate the federal Copyright Act of 1976. The decision, which came in the case of Sony Corp. *of America v.* Universal City Studios, *overturned a 1981 appeals court ruling that found Sony, some of its retailers, and its advertising agency liable for damages for contributing to copyright infringement by selling the company's popular Betamax video recorders.*

"One may search the Copyright Act in vain for any sign that the elected representatives of the millions of people who watch television every day have made it unlawful to copy a program for later viewing at home, or have enacted a flat prohibition against the sale of machines that make such copying possible," wrote Justice John Paul Stevens for the majority. Joining Stevens were Chief Justice Warren E. Burger and Justices William J. Brennan Jr., Byron R. White, and Sandra Day O'Connor.

The Court noted that most owners of video recorders used them principally to tape programs for viewing at a more convenient time, a practice known as "time-shifting." Under existing copyright law, any individual could reproduce a copyrighted work for a "fair use," which was defined by several criteria, including the purpose of the copying, the amount copied, and the effect on the market for the copyrighted work. The Court agreed with the findings of the U.S. district judge who first heard the case: time-shift recording was a "fair use."

Stevens noted that many copyright holders whose works were shown on television did not object to time-shift recording of their programs; in fact, they recognized it could enlarge the audience. And neither Universal nor Walt Disney productions proved that there would be anything other than minimal damage to the market for their works or the value of their works as a result of this sort of recording. "If the Betamax were used to make copies for a commercial or profit-making purpose, such use would presumptively be unfair," the Court said. But personal use did not fall in the prohibited area.

"When major technological innovations alter the market for copy-righted materials" it is up to Congress to adjust the law, Stevens wrote. "Congress has the constitutional authority and the institutional ability to accommodate fully the varied permutations of competing interests that are inevitably implicated by such new technology." Stevens said Congress might well "take a fresh look at this new technology, just as it so often has examined other innovations in the past. But it is not our job to apply laws that have not yet been written."

Background

Congress last overhauled the nation's copyright law in 1976, while the video recording industry was in its infancy. The 1976 law made no mention of video recording. Hollywood studios, however, saw the potential of the video recorder for taping their copyrighted programming and decided to test the scope of the law's protection.

The Sony case began in 1976, the year the new law was passed, when Universal and Disney sued the company. In 1979 a district court judge ruled for Sony, but that decision was reversed in 1981 by the 9th U.S. Circuit Court of Appeals, which held Sony liable as charged. The case was argued twice before the Supreme Court. The first time, January 18, 1983, only eight justices were present: Justice Brennan was absent that day. On July 6, the last day of the 1982-83 term, the justices set the case for reargument — presumably because they were deadlocked 4-4 on the issue. The case was reargued October 3, 1983.

Despite the legal uncertainty created by the 1981 ruling against Sony, sales of home video recorders had continued to grow at a rapid rate. Between late 1982 and early 1984, the number of American families owning such a device almost doubled, from five million to nine million. By 1990 the industry expected that nearly 40 million recorders would be in use.

Dissenting View

Justice Harry A. Blackmun wrote the dissent, joined by Justices Thurgood Marshall, Lewis F. Powell Jr., and William H. Rehnquist. They insisted that copyright law did not exempt the copying of protected materials for private use and that home taping of television programs did not meet the fair use test. There were no firm criteria for determining what was fair use, but most evidence indicated that it was intended to permit some copying of copyrighted works for productive or socially beneficial purposes, Blackmun wrote. "When a user reproduces an entire work and uses it for its original purpose, with no added benefit to the public, the doctrine of fair use usually does not apply," he said. "The making of a videotape recording for home viewing is an ordinary rather than a productive use of . . . copyrighted works."

Blackmun acknowleged that it might be "tempting" to "stretch the doctrine of fair use so as to permit unfettered use of this new technology in order to increase access to television programming. But such an extension risks eroding the very basis of copyright law, by depriving authors of control over their works and consequently of their incentive to create."

Home taping of TV programs could adversely affect the potential market for the programs, the dissent stated. Among other effects, such private taping reduces demand for showing these programs in movie theaters or for videotapes recorded by the producer for rental or sale. "Like so many other problems created by the interaction of copyright law with a new technology," Blackmun said, "there can be no really satisfactory solution to the problem presented here until Congress acts."

Reaction

Within hours of the decision, the entertainment industry announced it would seek relief from Congress. Jack Valenti, head of the Motion Picture Association of America and a principal spokesman for copyright holders, said that his group would press Congress aggressively for action. He said the decision was "just the opening shot" in a long fight to protect copyright holders. Valenti contended that if nothing were done the American public would be "the real loser" because the number of creative works would decline. Valenti noted that television ratings companies, such as the A. C. Nielsen Co., could determine if a television was attached to a home taping machine. Valenti said if advertising companies knew, for example, that 30 percent of the time programs were being taped — on machines that increasingly could excise commercials — they would request a 30 percent cut in the fees they paid the networks for advertising time. In turn, Valenti said, the networks would tell scriptwriters and other copyright holders that revenues were down, and they would pay less for creative works.

In early 1984 a number of bills were pending in House and Senate committees that would impose royalties on home taping machines and blank tape cassettes. The royalties would be paid to the Copyright

Royalty Tribunal, which would then disburse them to the holders of copyrights on TV movies and other programming material. But prospects for action on such legislation — which could raise the price to consumers of video recorders and blank tapes — appeared dim, especially in an election year.

> *Following are excerpts from the Supreme Court's January 17, 1984, decision in* Sony Corp. of America v. Universal City Studios *and from the dissenting opinion of Justice Harry A. Blackmun:*

<u>No. 81-1687</u>

Sony Corporation of America, et al., Petitioners *v.* Universal City Studios, Inc., etc., et al.	On writ of Certiorari to the United States Court of Appeals for the Ninth Circuit

[January 17, 1984]

JUSTICE STEVENS delivered the opinion of the Court.

Petitioners manufacture and sell home video tape recorders. Respondents own the copyrights on some of the television programs that are broadcast on the public airwaves. Some members of the general public use video tape recorders sold by petitioners to record some of these broadcasts, as well as a large number of other broadcasts. The question presented is whether the sale of petitioners' copying equipment to the general public violates any of the rights conferred upon respondents by the Copyright Act.

Respondents commenced this copyright infringment action against petitioners in the United States District Court for the Central District of California in 1976. Respondents alleged that some individuals had used Betamax video tape recorders (VTR's) to record some of respondents' copyrighted works which had been exhibited on commercially sponsored television and contended that these individuals had thereby infringed respondents' copyrights. Respondents further maintained that petitioners were liable for the copyright infringement allegedly committed by Betamax consumers because of petitioners' marketing of the Betamax VTR's. Respondents sought no relief against any Betamax consumer. Instead, they sought money damages and an equitable accounting of profits from petitioners, as well as an injunction against the manufacture and marketing of Betamax VTR's.

After a lengthy trial, the District Court denied respondents all the relief they sought and entered judgment for petitioners. The United States Court of Appeals for the Ninth Circuit reversed the District Court's judgment on respondent's copyright claim, holding petitioners liable for contributory infringement and ordering the District Court to fashion appropriate relief. We granted certiorari; since we had not completed our study of the case last Term we ordered reargument. We now reverse.

An explanation of our rejection of respondents' unprecedented attempt to impose copyright liability upon the distributors of copying equipment requires a quite detailed recitation of the findings of the District Court. In summary, those findings reveal that the average member of the public uses a VTR principally to record a program he cannot view as it is being televised and then to watch it once at a later time. This practice, known as "time-shifting," enlarges the television viewing audience. For that reason, a significant amount of television programming may be used in this manner without objection from the owners of the copyrights on the programs. For the same reason, even the two respondents in this case, who do assert objections to time-shifting in this litigation, were unable to prove that the practice has impaired the commercial value of their copyrights or has created any likelihood of future harm. Given these findings, there is no basis in the Copyright Act upon which respondents can hold petitioners liable for distributing VTR's to the general public. The Court of Appeals' holding that respondents are entitled to enjoin the distribution of VTR's, to collect royalties on the sale of such equipment or to obtain other relief, if affirmed, would enlarge the scope of respondents' statutory monopolies to encompass control over an article of commerce that is not the subject of copyright protection. Such an expansion of the copyright privilege is beyond the limits of the grants authorized by Congress.

I

The two respondents in this action, Universal Studios, Inc. and Walt Disney Productions, produce and hold the copyrights on a substantial number of motion pictures and other audiovisual works. In the current marketplace, they can exploit their rights in these works in a number of ways: by authorizing theatrical exhibitions, by licensing limited showings on cable and network television, by selling syndication rights for repeated airings on local television stations, and by marketing programs on prerecorded videotapes or videodiscs. Some works are suitable for exploitation through all of these avenues, while the market for other works is more limited.

Petitioner Sony manufactures millions of Betamax video tape recorders and markets these devices through numerous retail establishments, some of which are also petitioners in this action. Sony's Betamax VTR is a mechanism consisting of three basic components: (1) a tuner, which receives electromagnetic signals transmitted over the television band of the public airwaves and separates them into audio and visual signals; (2) a recorder, which records such signals on a magnetic tape; and (3) an adapter, which converts the audio and visual signals on the tape into a composite signal that can be received by a television set.

Several capabilities of the machine are noteworthy. The separate tuner in the Betamax enables it to record a broadcast off one station while the television set is tuned to another channel, permitting the viewer, for example, to watch two simultaneous news broadcasts by watching one "live" and recording the other for later viewing. Tapes may be reused, and programs that have been recorded may be erased either before or after viewing. A timer in the Betamax can be used to activate and deactivate the equipment at predetermined times, enabling an intended viewer to record programs that are transmitted when he or she is not at home. Thus a person may watch a program at home in the evening even though it was broadcast while the viewer was at work during the afternoon. The Betamax is also equipped with a pause button and a fast-forward control. The pause button, when depressed, deactivates the recorder until it is released, thus enabling a viewer to omit a commercial advertisement from the recording, provided, of course, that the viewer is present when the program is recorded. The fast forward control enables the viewer of a previously recorded program to run the tape rapidly when a segment he or she does not desire to see is being played back on the television screen.

The respondents and Sony both conducted surveys of the way the Betamax machine was used by several hundred owners during a sample period in 1978. Although there were some differences in the surveys, they both showed that the primary use of the machine for most owners was "time-shifting," — the practice of recording a program to view it once at a later time, and thereafter erasing it. Time-shifting enables viewers to see programs they otherwise would miss because they are not at home, are occupied with other tasks, or are viewing a program on another station at the time of the broadcast that they desire to watch.... Sony's survey indicated that over 80% of the interviewees watched at least as much regular television as they had before owning a Betamax. Respondents offered no evidence of decreased television viewing by Betamax owners.

Sony introduced considerable evidence describing television programs that could be copied without objection from any copyright holder, with special emphasis on sports, religious, and educational programming. For example, their survey indicated that 7.3% of all Betamax use is to record sports events, and representatives of professional baseball, football, basketball, and hockey testified that they had no objection to the recording of their televised events for home use.

Respondents offered opinion evidence concerning the future impact of the unrestricted sale of VTR's on the commercial value of their copyrights. The District Court found, however, that they had failed to prove any likelihood of future harm from the use of VTR's for time-shifting.

THE DISTRICT COURT'S DECISION

The lengthy trial of the case in the District Court concerned the private, home use of VTR's for recording programs broadcast on the public airwaves without charge to the viewer. No issue concerning the transfer of tapes to other persons, the use of home-recorded tapes for public performances, or the copying of programs transmitted on pay or cable television systems was raised. . . .

The District Court concluded that noncommercial home use recording of material broadcast over the public airwaves was a fair use of copyrighted works and did not constitute copyright infringement. It emphasized the fact that the material was broadcast free to the public at large, the noncommercial character of the use, and the private character of the activity conducted entirely within the home. Moreover, the court found that the purpose of this use served the public interest in increasing access to television programming, an interest that "is consistent with the First Amendment policy of providing the fullest possible access to information through the public airwaves." . . . Even when an entire copyrighted work was recorded, the District Court regarded the copying as fair use "because there is no . . . reduction in the market for 'plaintiff's original work.' "

As an independent ground of decision, the District Court also concluded that Sony could not be held liable as a contributory infringer even if the home use of a VTR was considered an infringing use. The District Court noted that Sony had no direct involvement with any Betamax purchasers who recorded copyrighted works off the air. Sony's advertising was silent on the subject of possible copyright infringement, but its instruction booklet contained the following statement:

> "Television programs, films, videotapes and other materials may be copyrighted. Unauthorized recording of such material may be contrary to the provisions of the United States copyright laws."

The District Court assumed that Sony had constructive knowledge of the probability that the Betamax machine would be used to record copyrighted programs, but found that Sony merely sold a "product capable of a variety of uses, some of them allegedly infringing." It reasoned:

> "Selling a staple article of commerce[,] *e.g.*, a typewriter, a recorder, a camera, a photocopying machine[,] technically contributes to any infringing use subsequently made thereof, but this kind of 'contribution,' if deemed sufficient as a basis for liability, would expand the theory beyond precedent and arguably beyond judicial management.
>
> "Commerce would indeed be hampered if manufacturers of staple items were held liable as contributory infringers whenever they 'constructively' knew that some purchasers on some occasions would use their product for a purpose which a court later deemed, as a matter of first impression, to be an infringement."

Finally, the District Court discussed the respondents' prayer for injunctive relief, noting that they had asked for an injunction either preventing the future sale of Betamax machines, or requiring that the machines be rendered incapable of recording copyrighted works off the air. The court stated that it had "found no case in which the manufacturers, distributors, retailers, and advertisers of the instrument enabling the infringement were sued by the copyright holders," and that the request for relief in this case "is unique."

It concluded that an injunction was wholly inappropriate because any possible harm to respondents was outweighed by the fact that "the Betamax could still legally be used to record noncopyrighted material or material whose owners consented to the copying. An injunction would deprive the public of the ability to use the Betamax for this noninfringing off-the-air recording."

THE COURT OF APPEALS' DECISION

The Court of Appeals reversed the District Court's judgment on respondents' copyright claim. It did not set aside any of the District Court's findings of fact. Rather, it concluded as a matter of law that the home use of a VTR was not a fair use because it was not a "productive use." It therefore held that it was unnecessary for plaintiffs to prove any harm to the potential market for the copyrighted works, but then observed that it seemed clear that the cumulative effect of mass reproduction made possible by VTR's would tend to diminish the potential market for respondents' works.

On the issue of contributory infringement, the Court of Appeals first rejected the analogy to staple articles of commerce such as tape recorders or photocopying machines. It noted that such machines "may have substantial benefit for some purposes" and do not "even remotely raise copyright problems." VTR's, however, are sold "for the primary purpose of reproducing television programming" and "virtually all" such programming is copyrighted material. The Court of Appeals concluded, therefore, that VTR's were not suitable for any substantial noninfringing use even if some copyright owners elect not to enforce their rights.

The Court of Appeals also rejected the District Court's reliance on Sony's lack of knowledge that home use constituted infringement. Assuming that the statutory provisions defining the remedies for infringement applied also to the nonstatutory tort of contributory infringement, the court stated that a defendant's good faith would merely reduce his damages liability but would not excuse the infringing conduct. It held that Sony was chargeable with knowledge of the homeowner's infringing activity because the reproduction of copyrighted materials was either "the most conspicuous use" or "the major use" of the Betamax product.

On the matter of relief, the Court of Appeals concluded that "statutory damages may be appropriate," that the District Court should reconsider its determination that an injunction would not be an appropriate remedy; and, referring to "the analogous photocopying area," suggested that a continuing royalty pursuant to a judicially created compulsory license may very well be an acceptable resolution of the relief issue.

II

Article I, Sec. 8 of the Constitution provides that:
"The Congress shall have power ... to Promote the Progress of Science and

useful Arts, by securing for limited Times to Authors and Inventors the exclusive Right to their respective Writings and Discoveries."

The monopoly privileges that Congress may authorize are neither unlimited nor primarily designed to provide a special private benefit. Rather, the limited grant is a means by which an important public purpose may be achieved. It is intended to motivate the creative activity of authors and inventors by the provision of a special reward, and to allow the public access to the products of their genius after the limited period of exclusive control has expired.

> "The copyright law, like the patent statute, makes reward to the owner a secondary consideration. In *Fox Film Corp.* v. *Doyal,* Chief Justice Hughes spoke as follows respecting the copyright monopoly granted by Congress. 'The sole interest of the United States and the primary object in conferring the monopoly lie in the general benefits derived by the public from the labors of authors.' It is said that reward to the author or artist serves to induce release to the public of the products of his creative genius." *United States* v. *Paramount Pictures.*

As the text of the Constitution makes plain, it is Congress that has been assigned the task of defining the scope of the limited monopoly that should be granted to authors or to inventors in order to give the public appropriate access to their work product. Because this task involves a difficult balance between the interests of authors and inventors in the control and exploitation of their writings and discoveries on the one hand, and society's competing interest in the free flow of ideas, information, and commerce on the other hand, our patent and copyright statutes have been amended repeatedly.

From its beginning, the law of copyright has developed in response to significant changes in technology. Indeed, it was the invention of a new form of copying equipment — the printing press — that gave rise to the original need for copyright protection. Repeatedly, as new developments have occurred in this country, it has been the Congress that has fashioned the new rules that new technology made necessary. Thus, long before the enactment of the Copyright Act of 1909, it was settled that the protection given to copyrights is wholly statutory. *Wheaton* v. *Peters* (1834). The remedies for infringement "are only those prescribed by Congress." *Thompson* v. *Hubbard* (1889).

The judiciary's reluctance to expand the protections afforded by the copyright without explicit legislative guidance is a recurring theme. . . . Sound policy, as well as history, supports our consistent deference to Congress when major technological innovations alter the market for copyrighted materials. Congress has the constitutional authority and the institutional ability to accommodate fully the varied permutations of competing interests that are inevitably implicated by such new technology.

In a case like this, in which Congress has not plainly marked our course, we must be circumspect in construing the scope of rights, created by a legislative enactment which never contemplated such a calculus of interests. In doing so, we are guided by Justice Stewart's exposition of the correct approach to ambiguities in the law of copyright:

"The limited scope of the copyright holder's statutory monopoly, like the limited copyright duration required by the Constitution, reflects a balance of competing claims upon the public interest: Creative work is to be encouraged and rewarded, but private motivation must ultimately serve the cause of promoting broad public availability of literature, music, and the other arts. The immediate effect of our copyright law is to secure a fair return for an 'author's' creative labor. But the ultimate aim is, by this incentive, to stimulate artistic creativity for the general public good. 'The sole interest of the United States and the primary object in conferring the monopoly,' this Court has said, 'lie in the general benefits derived by the public from the labors of authors.' *Fox Film Corp.* v. *Doyal....* When technological change has rendered its literal terms ambiguous, the Copyright Act must be construed in light of this basic purpose." *Twentieth Century Music Corp.* v. *Aiken.*

Copyright protection "subsists ... in original works of authorship fixed in any tangible medium of expression." This protection has never accorded the copyright owner complete control over all possible uses of his work. Rather, the Copyright Act grants the copyright holder "exclusive" rights to use and to authorize the use of his work in five qualified ways, including reproduction of the copyrighted work in copies. All reproductions of the work, however, are not within the exclusive domain of the copyright owner; some are in the public domain. Any individual may reproduce a copyrighted work for a "fair use," the copyright owner does not possess the exclusive right to such a use....

"Anyone who violates any of the exclusive rights of the copyright owner," that is, anyone who trespasses into his exclusive domain by using or authorizing the use of the copyrighted work in one of the five ways set forth in the statute, "is an infringer of the copyright." Conversely, anyone who is authorized by the copyright owner to use the copyrighted work in a way specified in the statute or who makes a fair use of the work is not an infringer of the copyright with respect to such use.

The Copyright Act provides the owner of a copyright with a potent arsenal of remedies against an infringer of his work, including an injunction to restrain the infringer from violating his rights, the impoundment and destruction of all reproductions of his work made in violation of his rights, a recovery of his actual damages and any additional profits realized by the infringer or a recovery of statutory damages, and attorneys fees.

The two respondents in this case do not seek relief against the Betamax users who have allegedly infringed their copyrights. Moreover, this is not a class action on behalf of all copyright owners who license their works for television broadcast, and respondents have no right to invoke whatever rights other copyright holders may have to bring infringement actions based on Betamax copying of their works. As was made clear by their own evidence, the copying of the respondents' programs represents a small portion of the total use of VTR's. It is, however, the taping of respondents own copyrighted programs that provides them with standing to charge Sony with contributory infringement. To prevail, they have the burden of proving that users of the Betamax have infringed their copyrights and that Sony should be held responsible for that infringement.

III

The Copyright Act does not expressly render anyone liable for infringement committed by another. In contrast, the Patent Act expressly brands anyone who "actively induces infringement of a patent" as an infringer, and further imposes liability on certain individuals labeled "contributory" infringers. The absence of such express language in the copyright statute does not preclude the imposition of liability for copyright infringements on certain parties who have not themselves engaged in the infringing activity." For vicarious liability is imposed in virtually all areas of the law, and the concept of contributory infringement is merely a species of the broader problem of identifying the circumstances in which it is just to hold one individual accountable for the actions of another.

Such circumstances were plainly present in *Kalem Co.* v. *Harper Brothers* (1911), the copyright decision of this Court on which respondents place their principal reliance. In *Kalem,* the Court held that the producer of an unauthorized film dramatization of the copyrighted book *Ben Hur* was liable for his sale of the motion picture to jobbers, who in turn arranged for the commercial exhibition of the film. Justice Holmes, writing for the Court, explained:

> "The defendant not only expected but invoked by advertisement the use of its films for dramatic reproduction of the story. That was the most conspicuous purpose for which they could be used, and the one for which especially they were made. If the defendant did not contribute to the infringement it is impossible to do so except by taking part in the final act. It is liable on principles recognized in every part of the law."

The use for which the item sold in *Kalem* had been "especially" made was, of course, to display the performance that had already been recorded upon it. The producer had personally appropriated the copyright owner's protected work and, as the owner of the tangible medium of expression upon which the protected work was recorded, authorized that use by his sale of the film to jobbers. But that use of the film was not his to authorize: the copyright owner possessed the exclusive right to authorize public performances of his work. Further, the producer personally advertised the unauthorized public performances, dispelling any possible doubt as to the use of the film which he had authorized.

Respondents argue that *Kalem* stands for the proposition that supplying the "means" to accomplish an infringing activity and encouraging that activity through advertisement are sufficient to establish liability for copyright infringement. This argument rests on a gross generalization that cannot withstand scrutiny. The producer in *Kalem* did not merely provide the "means" to accomplish an infringing activity; the producer supplied the work itself, albeit in a new medium of expression. Petitioners in the instant case do not supply Betamax consumers with respondents' works; respondents do. Petitioners supply a piece of equipment that is generally capable of copying the entire range of programs that may be televised: those that are uncopyrighted, those that are copyrighted but may be copied without objection from the copyright holder, and those that the copyright holder would prefer not to have copied. The Betamax can be used to make authorized or unauthorized uses of copyrighted works, but the range of its potential use is much broader than the particular infringing use of the film *Ben Hur* involved in *Kalem*. *Kalem* does not support respondents' novel theory of liability.

Justice Holmes stated that the producer had "contributed" to the infringement of the copyright, and the label "contributory infringement" has been applied in a number of lower court copyright cases involving an ongoing relationship between the direct infringer and the contributory infringer at the time the infringing conduct occurred. In such cases, as in other situations in which the imposition of vicarious liability is manifestly just, the "contributory" infringer was in a position to control the use of copyrighted works by others and had authorized the use without permission from the copyright owner. This case, however, plainly does not fall in that category. The only contact between Sony and the users of the Betamax that is disclosed by this record occurred at the moment of sale. The District Court expressly found that "no employee of Sony, Sonam or DDBI had either direct involvement with the allegedly infringing activity or direct contact with purchasers of Betamax who recorded copyrighted works off-the-air." And it further found that "there was no evidence that any of the copies made by Griffiths or the other individual witnesses in this suit were influenced or encouraged by [Sony's] advertisements."

If vicarious liability is to be imposed on petitioners in this case, it must rest on the fact that they have sold equipment with constructive knowledge of the fact that their customers may use that equipment to make unauthorized copies of copyrighted material. There is no precedent in the law of copyright for the imposition of vicarious liability on such a theory. The closest analogy is provided by the patent law cases to which it is appropriate to refer because of the historic kinship between patent law and copyright law.

In the Patent Code both the concept of infringement and the concept of contributory infringement are expressly defined by statute. The prohibition against contributory infringement is confined to the knowing sale of a component especially made for use in connection with a particular patent. There is no suggestion in the statute that one patentee may object to the sale of a product that might be used in connection with other patents. Moreover, the Act expressly provides that the sale of a "staple article or commodity of commerce suitable for substantial noninfringing use" is not contributory infringement.

When a charge of contributory infringement is predicated entirely on the sale of an article of commerce that is used by the purchaser to infringe a patent, the public interest in access to that article of commerce is necessarily implicated. A finding of contributory infringement does not, of course, remove the article from the market altogether; it does, however, give the patentee effective control over the sale of that item. Indeed, a finding of contributory infringement is normally the functional equivalent of holding that the disputed article is within the monopoly granted to the patentee.

For that reason, in contributory infringement cases arising under the patent laws the Court has always recognized the critical importance of not allowing the patentee to extend his monopoly beyond the limits of his specific grant. These cases deny the patentee any right to control the distribution of unpatented articles unless they are "unsuited for any commercial noninfringing use." *Dawson Chemical Co.* v. *Rohm & Haas Co.* (1980). Unless a commodity "has no use except through practice of the patented method," the patentee has no right to claim that its distribution constitutes contributory infringement. "To form the basis for contributory infringement the item must almost be uniquely suited as a component of the patented invention." P. Rosenberg, Patent Law Fundamentals (1982). "[A] sale of an article which though adapted to an infringing use is also adapted to other and lawful uses, is not enough to make the seller a contributory infringer. Such a rule would block the wheels of commerce." *Henry* v. *A. B. Dick Co.* (1912). . . .

We recognize there are substantial differences between the patent and copyright laws. But in both areas the contributory infringement doctrine is grounded on the recognition that adequate protection of a monopoly may require the courts to look beyond actual duplication of a device or publication to the products or activities that make such duplication possible. The staple article of commerce doctrine must strike a balance between a copyright holder's legitimate demand for effective — not merely symbolic — protection of the statutory monopoly, and the rights of others freely to engage in substantially unrelated areas of commerce. Accordingly, the sale of copying equipment, like the sale of other articles of commerce, does not constitute contributory infringement if the product is widely used for legitimate, unobjectionable purposes. Indeed, it need merely be capable of substantial noninfringing uses.

IV

The question is thus whether the Betamax is capable of commercially significant noninfringing uses. In order to resolve that question, we need not explore *all* the different potential uses of the machine and determine whether or not they would constitute infringement. Rather, we need only consider whether on the basis of the facts as found by the district court a significant number of them would be non-infringing. Moreover, in order to resolve this case we need not give precise content to the question of how much use is commercially significant. For one potential use of the Betamax plainly satisfies this standard, however it is understood: private, noncommercial time-shifting in the home. It does so both (A) because respondents have no right to prevent other copyright holders from authorizing it for their programs, and (B) because the District Court's factual findings reveal that even the unauthorized home time-shifting of respondents' programs is legitimate fair use.

A. AUTHORIZED TIME SHIFTING

Each of the respondents owns a large inventory of valuable copyrights, but in the total spectrum of television programming their combined market share is small. The exact percentage is not specified, but it is well below 10%. If they were to prevail, the outcome of this litigation would have a significant impact on both the producers and the viewers of the remaining 90% of the programming in the Nation. No doubt, many other producers share respondents' concern about the possible consequences of unrestricted copying. Nevertheless, the findings of the District Court make it clear that time-shifting may enlarge the total viewing audience and that many producers are willing to allow private time-shifting to continue, at least for an experimental time period. The District Court found:

"Even if it were deemed that home-use recording of copyrighted material constituted infringement, the Betamax could still legally be used to record noncopyrighted material or material whose owners consented to the copying. An injunction would deprive the public of the ability to use the Betamax for this noninfringing off-the-air recording.

"Defendants introduced considerable testimony at trial about the potential for such copying of sports, religious, educational and other programming. This included testimony from representatives of the Offices of the Commissioners of the National Football, Basketball, Baseball and Hockey Leagues and Associations, the Executive Director of National Religious Broadcasters and various educational communications agencies. Plaintiffs attack the weight of the testimony offered and also contend that an injunction is warranted because infringing uses outweigh noninfringing uses."

"Whatever the future percentage of legal versus illegal home-use recording might be, an injunction which seeks to deprive the public of the very tool or article of commerce capable of some noninfringing use would be an extremely harsh remedy, as well as one unprecedented in copyright law."

Although the District Court made these statements in the context of considering the propriety of injunctive relief, the statements constitute a finding that the evidence concerning "sports, religious, educational, and other programming" was sufficient to establish a significant quantity of broadcasting whose copying is now authorized, and a significant potential for future authorized copying....

If there are millions of owners of VTR's who make copies of televised sports events, religious broadcasts, and educational programs such as *Mister Rogers' Neighborhood,* and if the proprietors of those programs welcome the practice, the business of supplying the equipment that makes such copying feasible should not be stifled simply because the equipment is used by some individuals to make unauthorized reproductions of respondents' works. The respondents do not represent a class composed of all copyright holders. Yet a finding of contributory infringement would inevitably frustrate the interests of broadcasters in reaching the portion of their audience that is available only through time-shifting.

Of course, the fact that other copyright holders may welcome the practice of time-shifting does not mean that respondents should be deemed to have granted a license to copy their programs. Third party conduct would be wholly irrelevant in an action for direct infringement of respondents' copyrights. But in an action for *contributory* infringement against the seller of copying equipment, the copyright holder may not prevail unless the relief that he seeks affects only his programs, or unless he speaks for virtually all copyright holders with an interest in the outcome. In this case, the record makes it perfectly clear that there are many important producers of national and local television programs who find nothing objectionable about the enlargement in the size of the television audience that results from the practice of time-shifting for private home use. The seller of the equipment that expands those producers' audiences cannot be a contributory infringer if, as is true in this case, it has had no direct involvement with any infringing activity.

B. UNAUTHORIZED TIME SHIFTING

Even unauthorized uses of a copyrighted work are not necessarily infringing. An unlicensed use of the copyright is not an infringement unless it conflicts with one of the specific exclusive rights conferred by the copyright statute. *Twentieth Century Music Corp.* v. *Aiken* [1975]. Moreover, the definition of exclusive rights in § 106 of the present Act is prefaced by the words "subject to sections 107 through 118." Those sections describe a variety of uses of copyrighted material that "are not infringements of copyright notwithstanding the provisions of § 106." The most pertinent in this case is § 107, the legislative endorsement of the doctrine of "fair use."

That section identifies various factors that enable a Court to apply an "equitable rule of reason" analysis to particular claims of infringement. Although not conclusive, the first factor requires that "the commercial or nonprofit character of an activity" be weighed in any fair use decision. If the Betamax were used to make copies for a commercial or profit-making purpose, such use would presumptively be unfair. The contrary presumption is appropriate here, however, because the District Court's findings plainly establish that time-shifting for private home use must be characterized as a noncommercial, nonprofit activity. Moreover, when one considers the nature of a televised copyrighted audiovisual work, ... and that timeshifting merely enables a viewer to see such a work which he had been invited to witness in its entirety free of charge, the fact that the entire work is reproduced ... does not have its ordinary effect of militating against a finding of fair use.

This is not, however, the end of the inquiry because Congress has also directed us to consider "the effect of the use upon the potential market for or value of the copyrighted work." The purpose of copyright is to create incentives for creative effort. Even copying for noncommercial purposes may impair the copyright holder's ability to obtain the rewards that Congress intended him to have. But a use that has no demonstrable effect upon the potential market for, or the value of, the copyrighted work need not be prohibited in order to protect the author's incentive to create. The prohibition of such noncommercial uses would merely inhibit access to ideas without any countervailing benefit.

Thus, although every commercial use of copyrighted material is presumptively an unfair exploitation of the monopoly privilege that belongs to the owner of the copyright, noncommercial uses are a different matter. A challenge to a noncommercial use of a copyrighted work requires proof either that the particular use is harmful, or that if it should become widespread, it would adversely affect the potential market for the copyrighted work. Actual present harm need not be shown; such a requirement would leave the copyright holder with no defense against predictable damage. Nor is it necessary to show with certainty that future harm will result. What is necessary is a showing by a preponderance of the evidence that *some* meaningful likelihood of future harm exists. If the intended use is for commercial gain, that likelihood may be presumed. But if it is for a noncommercial purpose, the likelihood must be demonstrated. . . .

On the question of potential future harm from time-shifting, the District Court . . . rejected respondents' "fear that persons 'watching' the original telecast of a program will not be measured in the live audience and the ratings and revenues will decrease," by observing that current measurement technology allows the Betamax audience to be reflected. It rejected respondents' prediction "that live television or movie audiences will decrease as more people watch Betamax tapes as an alternative," with the observation that "[t]here is no factual basis for [the underlying] assumption." It rejected respondents' "fear that time-shifting will reduce audiences for telecast reruns," and concluded instead that "given current market practices, this should aid plaintiffs rather than harm them." And it declared that respondents' suggestion "that theater or film rental exhibition of a program will suffer because of time-shifting recording of that program" "lacks merit."

After completing that review, the District Court restated its overall conclusion several times, in several different ways. "Harm from time-shifting is speculative and, at best, minimal." "The audience benefits from the time-shifting capability have already been discussed. It is not implausible that benefits could also accrue to plaintiffs, broadcasters, and advertisers, as the Betamax makes it possible for more persons to view their broadcasts." "No likelihood of harm was shown at trial, and plaintiffs admitted that there had been no actual harm to date." "Testimony at trial suggested that Betamax may require adjustments in marketing strategy, but it did not establish even a likelihood of harm." "Television production by plaintiffs today is more profitable than it has ever been, and, in five weeks of trial, there was no concrete evidence to suggest that the Betamax will change the studios' financial picture."

The District Court's conclusions are buttressed by the fact that to the extent time-shifting expands public access to freely broadcast television programs it yields societal benefits. Earlier this year, in *Community Television of Southern California* v. *Gottfried* (1983), we acknowledged the public interest in making television broadcasting more available. Concededly, that interest is not unlimited. But it supports an interpretation of the concept of fair use that requires the copyright holder to demonstrate some likelihood of harm before he may condemn a private act of time-shifting as a violation of federal law.

When these factors are all weighed in the "equitable rule of reason" balance, we must conclude that this record amply supports the District Court's conclusion that home time-shifting is fair use. In light of the findings of the District Court regarding the state of the empirical data, it is clear that the Court of Appeals erred in holding that the statute as presently written bars such conduct.

In summary, the record and findings of the District Court lead us to two conclusions. First, Sony demonstrated a significant likelihood that substantial numbers of copyright holders who license their works for broadcast on free television would not object to having their broadcasts time-shifted by private viewers. And second, respondents failed to demonstrate that time-shifting would cause any likelihood of non-minimal harm to the potential market for, or the value of, their copyrighted works. The Betamax is, therefore, capable of substantial noninfringing uses. Sony's sale of such equipment to the general public does not constitute contributory infringement of respondent's copyrights.

V

"The direction of Art. I is that *Congress* shall have the power to promote the progress of science and the useful arts. When, as here, the Constitution is permissive, the sign of how far Congress has chosen to go can come only from Congress." *Deepsouth Packing Co.* v. *Laitram Corp.* (1972).

One may search the Copyright Act in vain for any sign that the elected representatives of the millions of people who watch television every day have made it unlawful to copy a program for later viewing at home, or have enacted a flat prohibition against the sale of machines that make such copying possible.

It may well be that Congress will take a fresh look at this new technology, just as it so often has examined other innovations in the past. But it is not our job to apply laws that have not yet been written. Applying the copyright statute, as it now reads, to the facts as they have been developed in this case, the judgment of the Court of Appeals must be reversed.

It is so ordered.

JUSTICE BLACKMUN, with whom JUSTICE MARSHALL, JUSTICE POWELL, and JUSTICE REHNQUIST join, dissenting.

A restatement of the facts and judicial history of this case is necessary, in my view, for a proper focus upon the issues. Respondents' position is hardly so "unprecedented" in the copyright law, nor does it really embody a "gross generalization," or a "novel theory of liability," and the like, as the Court, in belittling their claims, describes the efforts of respondents.

I

The introduction of the home videotape recorder (VTR) upon the market has enabled millions of Americans to make recordings of television programs in their homes, for future and repeated viewing at their own convenience. While this practice has proved highly popular with owners of television sets and VTRs, it understandably has been a matter of concern for the holders of copyrights in the recorded programs. A result is the present litigation, raising the issues whether the home recording of a copyrighted television program is an infringement of the copyright, and, if so, whether the manufacturers and distributors of VTRs are liable as contributory infringers. I would hope that these questions ultimately will be considered seriously and in depth by the Congress and be resolved there, despite the fact that the Court's decision today provides little incentive for congressional action. Our task in the meantime, however, is to resolve these issues as best we can in the light of ill-fitting existing copyright law.

It is no answer, of course, to say and stress, as the Court does, this Court's "consistent deference to Congress" whenever "major technological innovations" appear. Perhaps a better and more accurate description is that the Court has tended to evade the hard issues when they arise in the area of copyright law. I see no reason for the Court to be particularly pleased with this tradition or to continue it. Indeed, it is fairly clear from the legislative history of the 1976 Act that Congress meant to change the old pattern and enact a statute that would cover new technologies, as well as old. . . .

[Section II omitted]

III

The Copyright Clause of the Constitution, Art. I, § 8, cl. 8, empowers Congress "To promote the Progress of Science and useful Arts, by securing for limited Times to Authors and Inventors the exclusive Right to their respective Writings and Discoveries." This Nation's initial copyright statute was passed by the First Congress. Entitled "An Act for the encouragement of learning," it gave an author "the sole right and liberty of printing, reprinting, publishing and vending" his "map, chart, book or books" for a period of 14 years. Since then, as the technology available to authors for creating and preserving their writings has changed, the governing statute has changed with it. By many amendments, and by complete revisions in 1831, 1870, 1909, and 1976, authors' rights have been expanded to provide protection to any "original works of authorship fixed in any tangible medium of expression," including "motion pictures and other audiovisual works."

Section 106 of the 1976 Act grants the owner of a copyright a variety of exclusive rights in the copyrighted work, including the right "to reproduce the copyrighted work in copies or phonorecords." This grant expressly is made subject to §§ 107-118, which create a number of exemptions and limitations on the copyright owner's rights. The most important of these sections, for present purposes, is § 107; that section states that "the fair use of a copyrighted work . . . is not an infringement of copyright." '

The 1976 Act, like its predecessors, does *not* give the copyright owner full and complete control over all possible uses of his work. If the work is put to some use not enumerated in § 106, the use is not an infringement. See *Fortnightly Corp.* v. *United Artists* (1968). Thus, before considering whether home videotaping comes within the scope of the fair use exemption, one first must inquire whether the practice appears to violate the exclusive right, granted in the first instance by § 106(1), "to reproduce the copyrighted work in copies or phonorecords."

A

Although the word "copies" is in the plural in § 106(1), there can be no question that under the Act the making of even a single unauthorized copy is prohibited. The Senate and House Reports explain: "The references to 'copies or phonorecords,' although in the plural, are intended here and throughout the bill to include the singular." The Reports then describe the reproduction right established by § 106(1):

> "[T]he right 'to reproduce the copyrighted work in copies or phonorecords' means the right to produce a material object in which the work is duplicated, transcribed, imitated, or simulated in a fixed form from which it can be 'perceived, reproduced, or otherise communicated, either directly or with the aid of a machine or device.' As under the present law, a copyrighted work would be infringed by reproducing it in whole or in any substantial part, and by duplicating it exactly or by imitation or simulation."

The making of even a single videotape recording at home falls within this definition; the VTR user produces a material object from which the copyrighted work later can be perceived. Unless Congress intended a special exemption for the making of a single copy for personal use, I must conclude that VTR recording is contrary to the exclusive rights granted by § 106(1).

The 1976 Act and its accompanying reports specify in some detail the situations in which a single copy of a copyrighted work may be made without infringement concerns. Section 108(a), for example, permits a library or archives "to reproduce no more than one copy or phonorecord of a work" for a patron, but only under very limited conditions; an entire work, moreover, can be copied only if it cannot be obtained elsewhere at a fair price. . . . In other respects, the making of single copies is permissible only within the limited confines of the fair use doctrine. . . .

Indeed, it appears that Congress considered and rejected the very possibility of a special private use exemption. . . .

When Congress intended special and protective treatment for private use, moreover, it said so explicitly. One such explicit statement appears in

§ 106 itself. The copyright owner's exclusive right to *perform* a copyrighted work, in contrast to his right to reproduce the work in copies, is limited. Section 106(4) grants a copyright owner the exclusive right to perform the work "publicly," but does not afford the owner protection with respect to private performances by others. A motion picture is "performed" whenever its images are shown or its sounds are made audible. Like "sing[ing] a copyrighted lyric in the shower," *Twentieth Century Music Corp.* v. *Aiken* (1975), watching television at home with one's family and friends is now considered a performance. Home television viewing nevertheless does not infringe any copyright — but only because § 106(4) contains the word "publicly." . . . No such distinction between public and private uses appears in § 106(1)'s prohibition on the making of copies. . . .

B

The District Court in this case nevertheless concluded that the 1976 Act contained an implied exemption for "home-use recording." The court relied primarily on the legislative history of a 1971 amendment to the 1909 Act, a reliance that this Court today does not duplicate. That amendment, however, was addressed to the specific problem of commercial piracy of sound recordings. . . .

Unlike television broadcasts and other types of motion pictures, sound recordings were not protected by copyright prior to the passage of the 1971 Amendment. Although the underlying musical work could be copyrighted, the 1909 Act provided no protection for a particular performer's rendition of the work. Moreover, copyrighted musical works that had been recorded for public distribution were subject to a "compulsory license": any person was free to record such a work upon payment of a 2-cent royalty to the copyright owner. While reproduction without payment of the royalty was an infringement under the 1909 Act, damages were limited to three times the amount of the unpaid royalty. It was observed that the practical effect of these provisions was to legalize record piracy.

In order to suppress this piracy, the 1971 Amendment extended copyright protection beyond the underlying work and to the sound recordings themselves. Congress chose, however, to provide only limited protection: owners of copyright in sound recordings were given the exclusive right "[t]o reproduce [their works] and distribute [them] to the public." This right was merely the right of commercial distribution. . . .

Against this background the statements regarding home recording under the 1971 Amendment appear in a very different light. If home recording was "common and unrestrained" under the 1909 Act, . . . it was because sound recordings had no copyright protection and the owner of a copyright in the underlying musical work could collect no more than a 2-cent royalty plus 6 cents in damages for each unauthorized use. With so little at stake, it is not at all surprising that the Assistant Register "d[id] not see anybody going into anyone's home and preventing this sort of thing."

But the references to home sound recording in the 1971 Amendment's legislative history demonstrate no congressional intent to create a generalized home use exemption from copyright protection. Congress, having recognized that the 1909 Act had been unsuccessful in controlling home sound recording, addressed only the specific problem of commercial recording piracy. . . .

While the 1971 Amendment narrowed the sound recordings loophole in then existing copyright law, motion pictures and other audiovisual works have been accorded full copyright protection since at least 1912. . . . Congress continued this protection in the 1976 Act. Unlike the sound recording rights created by the 1971 Amendment, the reproduction rights associated with motion pictures under § 106(1) are not limited to reproduction for *public* distribution; the copyright owner's right to reproduce the work exists independently, and the "mere duplication of a copy may constitute an infringement even if it is never distributed." Moreover, the 1976 Act was intended as a comprehensive treatment of all aspects of copyright law. The reports accompanying the 1976 Act, unlike the 1971 House Report, contain no suggestion that home-use recording is somehow outside the scope of this all-inclusive statute. It was clearly the intent of Congress that no additional exemptions were to be implied.

I therefore find in the 1976 Act no implied exemption to cover the home taping of television programs, whether it be for a single copy, for private use, or for home use. Taping a copyrighted television program is infringement unless it is permitted by the fair use exemption contained in § 107 of the 1976 Act. I now turn to that issue.

IV

FAIR USE

The doctrine of fair use has been called, with some justification, "the most troublesome in the whole law of copyright." *Dellar* v. *Samuel Goldwyn, Inc.* (1939). . . . Although courts have constructed lists of factors to be considered in determining whether a particular use is fair, no fixed criteria have emerged by which that determination can be made. This Court thus far has provided no guidance; although fair use issues have come here twice, on each occasion the Court was equally divided and no opinion was forthcoming. *Williams & Wilkins Co.* v. *United States* (1973); *Benny* v. *Loew's, Inc.* (1956).

Nor did Congress provide definitive rules when it codified the fair use doctrine in the 1976 Act; it simply incorporated a list of factors "to be considered": the "purpose and character of the use," the "nature of the copyrighted work," the "amount and substantiality of the portion used," and, perhaps the most important, the "effect of the use upon the *potential* market for or value of the copyrighted work" (emphasis supplied). No particular weight, however, was assigned to any of these, and the list was not intended to be exclusive. The House and Senate Reports explain that § 107 does no more than give "statutory recognition" to the fair use doctrine; it was intended "to restate the present judicial doctrine of fair use, not to change, narrow, or enlarge it in any way." . . .

A

Despite this absence of clear standards, the fair use doctrine plays a crucial role in the law of copyright. The purpose of copyright protection, in the words of the Constitution, is to "promote the Progress of Science and useful Arts." Copyright is based on the belief that by granting authors the exclusive rights to reproduce their works, they are given an incentive to create, and that "encouragement of individual effort by personal gain is the best way to advance public welfare through the talents of authors and inventors in 'Science and the useful Arts.'" *Mazer* v. *Stein* (1954). The monopoly created by copyright thus rewards the individual author in order to benefit the public. *Twentieth Century Music Corp.* v. *Aiken* (1975); *Fox Film Corp.* v. *Doyal* (1932). . . .

There are situations, nevertheless, in which strict enforcement of this monopoly would inhibit the very "Progress of Science and useful Arts" that copyright is intended to promote. An obvious example is the researcher or scholar whose own work depends on the ability to refer to and to quote the work of prior scholars. . . . But there is a crucial difference between the scholar and the ordinary user. When the ordinary user decides that the owner's price is too high, and forgoes use of the work, only the individual is the loser. When the scholar forgoes the use of a prior work, not only does his own work suffer, but the public is deprived of his contribution to knowledge. . . .

A similar subsidy may be appropriate in a range of areas other than pure scholarship. The situations in which fair use is more commonly recognized are listed in § 107 itself; fair use may be found when a work is used "for purposes such as criticism, comment, news reporting, teaching, . . . scholarship, or research." The House and Senate Reports expand on this list somewhat, and other examples may be found in the case law. Each of these uses, however, reflects a common theme: each is a *productive* use, resulting in some added benefit to the public beyond that produced by the first author's work. The fair use doctrine, in other words, permits works to be used for "socially laudable purposes." . . .

I do not suggest, of course, that every productive use is a fair use. A finding of fair use still must depend on the facts of the individual case, and on whether, under the circumstances, it is reasonable to expect the user to bargain with the copyright owner for use of the work. The fair use doctrine must strike a balance between the dual risks created by the copyright system: on the one hand, that depriving authors of their monopoly will reduce their incentive to create, and, on the other, that granting authors a complete monopoly will reduce the creative ability of others. The inquiry is necessarily a flexible one, and the endless variety of situations that may arise precludes the formulation of exact rules. But when a user reproduces an entire work and uses it for its original purpose, with no added benefit to the public, the doctrine of fair use usually does not apply. There is then no need whatever to provide the ordinary user with a fair use subsidy at the author's expense.

The making of a videotape recording for home viewing is an ordinary rather than a productive use of the Studios' copyrighted works....

It may be tempting, as, in my view, the Court today is tempted, to stretch the doctrine of fair use so as to permit unfettered use of this new technology in order to increase access to television programming. But such an extension risks eroding the very basis of copyright law, by depriving authors of control over their works and consequently of their incentive to create. Even in the context of highly productive educational uses, Congress has avoided this temptation; in passing the 1976 Act, Congress made it clear that off-the-air videotaping was to be permitted only in very limited situations....

B

I recognize, nevertheless, that there are situations where permitting even an unproductive use would have no effect on the author's incentive to create, that is, where the use would not affect the value of, or the market for, the author's work. Photocopying an old newspaper clipping to send to a friend may be an example; pinning a quotation on one's bulletin board may be another. In each of these cases, the effect on the author is truly *de minimis*. Thus, even though these uses provide no benefit to the public at large, no purpose is served by preserving the author's monopoly, and the use may be regarded as fair.

Courts should move with caution, however, in depriving authors of protection from unproductive "ordinary" uses....

I therefore conclude that, at least when the proposed use is an unproductive one, a copyright owner need prove only a *potential* for harm to the market for or the value of the copyrighted work....

The Studios have identified a number of ways in which VTR recording could damage their copyrights. VTR recording could reduce their ability to market their works in movie theaters and through the rental or sale of pre-recorded videotapes or videodiscs; it also could reduce their rerun audience, and consequently the license fees available to them for repeated showings. Moreover, advertisers may be willing to pay for only "live" viewing audiences, if they believe VTR viewers will delete commercials or if rating services are unable to measure VTR use; if this is the case, VTR recording could reduce the license fees the Studios are able to charge even for first-run showings. Library-building may raise the potential for each of the types of harm identified by the Studios, and time-shifting may raise the potential for substantial harm as well....

In this case, the Studios and their *amici* demonstrate that the advent of the VTR technology created a potential market for their copyrighted programs. That market consists of those persons who find it impossible or inconvenient to watch the programs at the time they are broadcast, and who wish to watch them at other times. These persons are willing to pay for the privilege of watching copyrighted work at their convenience, as is evidenced by the fact that they are willing to pay for VTRs and tapes; undoubtedly, most also would be willing to pay some kind of royalty to copyright holders. The Studios correctly argue that they have been deprived of the ability to exploit this sizable market.

It is thus apparent from the record and from the findings of the District Court that time-shifting does have a substantial adverse effect upon the "potential market for" the Studios' copyrighted works. Accordingly, even under the formulation of the fair use doctrine advanced by Sony, time-shifting cannot be deemed a fair use.

V

CONTRIBUTORY INFRINGEMENT

From the Studios' perspective, the consequences of home VTR recording are the same as if a business had taped the Studios' works off the air, duplicated the tapes, and sold or rented them to members of the public for home viewing. The distinction is that home VTR users do not record for commercial advantage; the commercial benefit accrues to the manufacturer and distributors of the Betamax. I thus must proceed to discuss whether the manufacturer and distributors can be held contributorily liable if the product they sell is used to infringe.

It is well established that liability for copyright infringement can be imposed on persons other than those who actually carry out the infringing activity. *Kalem Co.* v. *Harper Brothers* (1911). . . . Although the liability provision of the 1976 Act provides simply that "[a]nyone who violates any of the exclusive rights of the copyright owner . . . is an infringer of the copyright," the House and Senate Reports demonstrate that Congress intended to retain judicial doctrines of contributory infringement.

The doctrine of contributory copyright infringement, however, is not well-defined. One of the few attempts at definition appears in *Gershwin Publishing Corp.* v. *Columbia Artists Management, Inc.* (CA2 1971). In that case the Second Circuit stated that "one who, with knowledge of the infringing activity, induces, causes or materially contributes to the infringing conduct of another, may be held liable as a 'contributory' infringer." While I have no quarrel with this general statement, it does not easily resolve the present case; the District Court and the Court of Appeals, both purporting to apply it, reached diametrically opposite results.

A

In absolving Sony from liability, the District Court reasoned that Sony had no direct involvement with individual Betamax users, did not participate in any off-the-air copying, and did not know that such copying was an infringement of the Studios' copyright. I agree with the *Gershwin* court that contributory liability may be imposed even when there has been no direct contact between the defendant and the infringer.... Moreover, a finding of contributory infringement has never depended on actual knowledge of particular instances of infringement; it is sufficient that the defendant have reason to know that infringement is taking place....

Nor is it necessary that the defendant be aware that the infringing activity violates the copying laws. Section 504(c)(2) of the 1976 Act provides for a reduction in statutory damages when an infringer proves he "was not aware and had no reason to believe that his or her acts constituted an infringement of copyright," but the statute establishes no general exemption for those who believe their infringing activities are legal. Moreover, such an exemption would be meaningless in a case such as this, in which prospective relief is sought; once a court has established that the copying at issue is infringement, the defendants are necessarily aware of that fact for the future. It is undisputed in this case that Sony had reason to know the Betamax would be used by some owners to tape copyrighted works off the air....

The District Court also concluded that Sony had not caused, induced, or contributed materially to any infringing activities of Betamax owners. In a case of this kind, however, causation can be shown indirectly; it does not depend on evidence that particular Betamax owners relied on particular advertisements....

The District Court found that Sony has advertised the Betamax as suitable for off-the-air recording of "favorite shows," "novels for television," and "classic movies," with no visible warning that such recording could constitute copyright infringement. It is only with the aid of the Betamax or some other VTR, that it is possible today for home television viewers to infringe copyright by recording off-the-air. Off-the-air recording is not only a foreseeable use for the Betamax, but indeed is its intended use. Under the circumstances, I agree with the Court of Appeals that if off-the-air recording is an infringement of copyright, Sony has induced and materially contributed to the infringing conduct of Betamax owners.

B

Sony argues that the manufacturer or seller of a product used to infringe is absolved from liability whenever the product can be put to any substantial noninfringing use. The District Court so held, borrowing the "staple article of commerce" doctrine governing liability for contributory infringement of patents.... This Court today is much less positive.... I do not agree that this technical judge-made doctrine of patent law, based in part on considerations irrelevant to the field of copyright ... should be imported wholesale into copyright law. Despite their common constitutional source ... patent and copyright protections have not developed in a parallel fashion, and this Court in copyright cases in the past has borrowed patent concepts only sparingly....

I therefore conclude that if a *significant* portion of the product's use is *noninfringing,* the manufacturers and sellers cannot be held contributorily liable for the product's infringing uses.... If virtually all of the product's use, however, is to infringe, contributory liability may be imposed; if no one would buy the product for noninfringing purposes alone, it is clear that the manufacturer is purposely profiting from the infringement, and that liability is appropriately imposed. In such a case, the copyright owner's monopoly would not be extended beyond its proper bounds; the manufacturer of such a product contributes to the infringing activities of others and profits directly thereby, while providing no benefit to the public sufficient to justify the infringement.

The Court of Appeals concluded that Sony should be held liable for contributory infringement, reasoning that "[v]ideotape recorders are manufactured, advertised, and sold for the primary purpose of reproducing television programming," and "[v]irtually all television programming is copyrighted material." While I agree with the first of these propositions, the second, for me, is problematic. The key question is not the amount of television programming that is copyrighted, but rather the amount of VTR usage that is infringing. Moreover, the parties and their *amici* have argued vigorously about both the amount of television programming that is covered by copyright and the amount for which permission to copy has been given. The proportion of VTR recording that is infringing is ultimately a question of fact, and the District Court specifically declined to make findings on the "percentage of legal versus illegal home-use recording." In light of my view of the law, resolution of this factual question is essential. I therefore would remand the case for further consideration of this by the District Court.

VI

The Court has adopted an approach very different from the one I have outlined. It is my view that the Court's approach alters dramatically the doctrines of fair use and contributory infringement as they have been developed by Congress and the courts. Should Congress choose to respond to the Court's decision, the old doctrines can be resurrected. As it stands, however, the decision today erodes much of the coherence that these doctrines have struggled to achieve.

The Court's disposition of the case turns on its conclusion that time-shifting is a fair use. Because both parties agree that time-shifting is the primary use of VTRs, that conclusion, if correct, would settle the issue of Sony's liability under almost any definition of contributory infringement. The Court concludes that time-shifting is fair use for two reasons. Each is seriously flawed.

The Court's first reason for concluding that time-shifting is fair use is its claim that many copyright holders have no objection to time-shifting, and that "respondents have no right to prevent other copyright holders from authorizing it for their programs." The Court explains that a finding of contributory infringement would "inevitably frustrate the interests of broadcasters in reaching the portion of their audience that is available only through time-shifting." Such reasoning, however, simply confuses the question of liability with the difficulty of fashioning an appropriate remedy. . . .

The Court's second stated reason for finding that Sony is not liable for contributory infringement is its conclusion that even unauthorized time-shifting is fair use. This conclusion is even more troubling. . . . There is no indication that the fair use doctrine has any application for purely personal consumption on the scale involved in this case, and the Court's application of it here deprives fair use of the major cohesive force that has guided evolution of the doctrine in the past. . . .

Because of the Court's conclusion concerning the legality of time-shifting, it never addresses the amount of noninfringing use that a manufacturer must show to absolve itself from liability as a contributory infringer. Thus, it is difficult to discuss how the Court's test for contributory infringement would operate in practice under a proper analysis of time-shifting. One aspect of the test as it is formulated by the Court, however, particularly deserves comment. The Court explains that a manufacturer of a product is not liable for contributory infringement as long as the product is "*capable* of substantial noninfringing uses." ([E]mphasis supplied). Such a definition essentially eviscerates the concept of contributory infringement. Only the most unimaginative manufacturer would be unable to demonstrate that a image-duplicating product is "capable" of substantial noninfringing uses. Surely Congress desired to prevent the sale of products that are used almost exclusively to infringe copyrights; the fact that noninfringing uses exist presumably would have little bearing on that desire.

More importantly, the rationale for the Court's narrow standard of contributory infringement reveals that, once again, the Court has confused the issue of liability with that of remedy. The Court finds that a narrow definition of contributory infringement is necessary in order to protect "the rights of others freely to engage in substantially unrelated areas of commerce." But application of the contributory infringement doctrine implicates such rights only if the remedy attendant upon a finding of liability were an injunction against the manufacture of the product in question. The issue of an appropriate remedy is not before the Court at this time, but it seems likely that a broad injunction is not the remedy that would be ordered. It is unfortunate that the Court has allowed its concern over a remedy to infect its analysis of liability.

VII

The Court of Appeals, having found Sony liable, remanded for the District Court to consider the propriety of injunctive or other relief. Because of my conclusion as to the issue of liability, I, too, would not decide here what remedy would be appropriate if liability were found. I concur, however, in the Court of Appeals' suggestion that an award of damages, or continuing royalties, or even some form of limited injunction, may well be an appropriate means of balancing the equities in this case. Although I express no view on the merits of any particular proposal, I am certain that, if Sony were found liable in this case, the District Court would be able to fashion appropriate relief. The District Court might conclude, of course, that a continuing royalty or other equitable relief is not feasible. The Studios then would be relegated to statutory damages for proved instances of infringement. But the difficulty of fashioning relief, and the possibility that complete relief may be unavailable, should not affect our interpretation of the statute.

Like so many other problems created by the interaction of copyright law with a new technology, "[t]here can be no really satisfactory solution to the problem presented here, until Congress acts." *Twentieth Century Music Corp.* v. *Aiken* (dissenting opinion). But in the absence of a congressional solution, courts cannot avoid difficult problems by refusing to apply the law. We must "take the Copyright Act . . . as we find it," *Fortnightly Corp.* v. *United Artists* (1968), and "do as little damage as possible to traditional copyright principles . . . until the Congress legislates." ([D]issenting opinion).

STATE OF THE UNION ADDRESS

January 25, 1984

President Ronald Reagan used the annual State of the Union address to remind Americans of the achievements of his administration during its first three years in office, while sharing credit with Congress for stemming the nation's "long decline." Delivered January 25 to a joint session of Congress, the nationally televised message was applauded by Republicans as an optimistic blueprint for the election year and derided by Democrats for ignoring the problems of minorities and women as well as troubles in Lebanon. Most of Reagan's ideas were aimed at his conservative constituency.

The president's journey to Capitol Hill was made amid unusual security measures, largely in reaction to a terrorist bombing blast in the Capitol in November 1983. Spectators were required to pass through checkpoints at the Capitol's outer rim, and police officers were stationed every few feet throughout the building.

In a last-minute addition to the speech, Reagan asked Congress to join him in a bipartisan effort to reduce the federal deficit by $100 billion between 1984 and 1987. His appeal came one week before the release of his fiscal 1985 budget, a document that projected huge deficits for years to come. (Budget message, p. 99) In a departure from his traditional anti-spending position, however, Reagan called for a new thrust into outer space, which he called "America's next frontier." He tried to blunt criticism of his administration's environmental policies by asking for more money to clean up hazardous wastes. The president also sought to modify his hawkish image by declaring that "a nuclear war cannot be won *and must never be fought," a phrase that drew an ovation from members of both parties. The comment continued a theme presented by Reagan in a major policy address on U.S.-Soviet relations delivered January 16 in which he emphasized the need to resume nuclear arms talks and to develop cooperation "built on deeds, not words."*

Major Economic, Space Proposals

In addition to his appeal to Congress, Reagan suggested the following economic steps:

● A constitutional amendment creating a line-item veto to allow presidents to eliminate funds for particular programs contained in appropriations bills passed by Congress. Reagan said he found this veto to be a "powerful tool" against wasteful spending when he was governor of California. But when other presidents had suggested it on a national level, Congress had refused to give up its spending control.

● A balanced budget constitutional amendment, which Reagan previously had endorsed. The Senate in 1982 approved the amendment requiring a balanced federal budget, but the House rejected the measure.

● An effort to simplify the federal tax code. Reagan directed Treasury Secretary Donald T. Regan to present specific recommendations that would make the tax system fairer, broaden the tax base, and bring the underground economy "into the sunlight."

One of Reagan's new initiatives was to ask the National Aeronautics and Space Administration (NASA) to build a permanently manned space station within a decade. The space station could be used for scientific experiments, communications, and possibly as a launching point for flights to other planets. It would be shared by government and industry and open to other friendly countries, Reagan said. NASA administrator James M. Beggs estimated it would cost $8 billion to put the laboratory into orbit by 1991 or 1992. More money would be needed to maintain and expand the facility, which initially could house six or eight people but eventually could handle 30 or more, Beggs said.

Environment, Family Values

During its first three years in office, the administration had been criticized by environmentalists for weak enforcement of pollution control laws and for disabling the Environmental Protection Agency (EPA) by cutting its budget. In his State of the Union message, Reagan tried to refute that image by proposing an extension of a program to fight toxic wastes and a larger budget for acid rain research, from a fiscal 1984 appropriation of $28.8 million to a fiscal 1985 level of $55.5 million, according to the EPA. Critics noted, however, that the funds would be used only for more research and not for implementing actual acid rain *controls.* (U.S.-Canadian acid rain report, Historic Documents of 1983, p. 197)

Reagan also called for renewal of the law creating the $1.6 billion "superfund" to clean up hazardous waste dumps, a switch from administration policies under former EPA administrator Anne M. Burford. The program was due to expire in 1985. The president's other environmental proposals called for the cleanup of the Chesapeake Bay and more money to acquire new park lands. He also said he would be more sensitive to state concerns about offshore oil drilling.

Under the theme of "strengthening traditional values," Reagan outlined a set of goals that reflected his conservative philosophy, among them a constitutional amendment permitting school prayer, a controversial measure pending in Congress. On education, Reagan said excellence must begin at home and in neighborhood schools, not with extra federal spending. He called for stricter school discipline, merit pay for teachers, and "putting parents back in charge." The president reaffirmed his support for tuition tax credits for parents who sent their children to private and parochial schools, a measure that the Senate had defeated in 1983. (Education report, Historic Documents of 1983, p. 413; tuition tax breaks, Historic Documents of 1983, p. 675)

On women's issues, Reagan said he favored equitable pension treatment and enforcement of delinquent child-support payments. Legislation on both issues was pending in Congress. (Supreme Court pension decision, Historic Documents of 1983, p. 691; Republicans and women's issues, Historic Documents of 1983, p. 755)

Foreign Policy Issues

Reagan offered the Soviet Union "an agenda for peace" he said was possible because of U.S. economic growth and restored military strength. "The United States is safer, stronger, and more secure in 1984 than before," the president said. "We can now move with confidence to seize the opportunities for peace — and we will." Reagan's peace agenda called for stronger allied relationships; "real and equitable reductions" in nuclear arms; reinforced peace efforts in the Middle East, Central America, and southern Africa; assistance for developing Western Hemisphere countries; and aid in the development of democratic institutions around the world.

The president asked Congress to accept the recommendations of the Kissinger commission on Central America, a bipartisan group that called for more than $8 billion in economic aid to the region through 1989 and a substantial increase in military aid for El Salvador. (Commission report, p. 31)

On Lebanon, Reagan commended Congress for agreeing in the fall of

1983 to keep U. S. Marines in Beirut through mid-1985 as "serving the cause of peace." However, following a rapid deterioration of conditions in the war-torn country, Reagan February 7 unexpectedly reversed his position and ordered the Marines participating in the multinational peacekeeping force to withdraw to ships offshore. The decision followed the resignation of Lebanese president Amin Gemayel's cabinet February 5 and a military collapse of the Lebanese army. Calls for withdrawing the forces had escalated after a terrorist bomb exploded October 23, 1983, killing more than 240 Marines. (Bombing of Marines in Beirut, Historic Documents of 1983, p. 933)

Reaction

Although Reagan drew bipartisan applause when he said, "we must bring federal deficits down," Democrats later were critical of the president's address. Senate Minority Leader Robert C. Byrd, D-W.Va., said the speech eloquently set forth the goals and hopes of Americans but lacked specific proposals about how to deal with the serious problems confronting the country. The Congressional Black Caucus issued a statement that said black unemployment remained at 18 percent and poverty was growing. "If you are poor, black, Hispanic, or a woman there was nothing for you in the president's State of the Union message," the caucus said. Rep. Patricia Schroeder, D-Colo., co-chair of the Congressional Caucus for Women's Issues, called Reagan's speech cosmetic and said he failed to address issues, such as economic inequities, that affected women. "Women weren't born Republicans. Women weren't born Democrats and women weren't born yesterday," she said.

Democrats followed Reagan's address with a 30-minute television show mixing live reaction with taped segments from around the country. The broadcast focused on broad themes of fairness and a vision of the future rather than on specific alternatives to administration proposals. "Are the policies of this administration fair to all Americans and what do these policies mean to our future?" asked Massachusetts governor Michael S. Dukakis, who moderated the Democratic response. "We'd like you to ask those questions with us, not just tonight but in the coming months."

On the Republican side, lawmakers praised Reagan's themes of spirit and unity and his focus on the economic recovery. Senate Majority Leader Howard H. Baker Jr., R-Tenn., said Reagan's words reminded him of President Dwight D. Eisenhower, "who made being president look easy but who gave us peace and prosperity and progress on every front. That's the kind of president Ronald Reagan has been."

Following is the text of President Ronald Reagan's nationally televised State of the Union address, delivered before a joint session of Congress January 25, 1983. (Boldface head-

ings in brackets have been added by Congressional Quarterly
to highlight the organization of the text.):

*Mr. Speaker, Mr. President, distinguished Members of the Congress,
honored guests and fellow citizens.*

Once again, in keeping with time-honored tradition, I have come to
report to you on the state of the Union, and I'm pleased to report that
America is much improved, and there's good reason to believe that
improvement will continue through the days to come.

You and I have had some honest and open differences in the year past.
But they didn't keep us from joining hands in bipartisan cooperation to
stop a long decline that has drained this nation's spirit and eroded its
health. There is renewed energy and optimism throughout the land.
America is back, standing tall, looking to the eighties with courage,
confidence, and hope.

The problems we're overcoming are not the heritage of one person,
party, or even one generation. It's just the tendency of government to grow,
for practices and programs to become the nearest thing to eternal life we
will ever see on this Earth. [*Laughter*] And there's always that well-
intentioned chorus of voices saying, "With a little more power and a little
more money, we could do so much for the people." For a time we forgot the
American dream is not one of making government bigger; it's keeping faith
with the mighty spirit of free people under God.

[The Decade of the 1980s]

As we came to the decade of the eighties we faced the worst crisis in our
postwar history. The seventies were years of rising problems and falling
confidence. There was a feeling government had grown beyond the consent
of the governed. Families felt helpless in the face of mounting inflation and
the indignity of taxes that reduced reward for hard work, thrift, and risk-
taking. All this was overlaid by an ever-growing web of rules and
regulations.

On the international scene, we had an uncomfortable feeling that we had
lost the respect of friend and foe. Some questioned whether we had the will
to defend peace and freedom. But America is too great for small dreams.
There was a hunger in the land for a spiritual revival; if you will, a crusade
for renewal. The American people said: Let us look to the future with
confidence, both at home and abroad. Let us give freedom a chance.

Americans were ready to make a new beginning, and together we have
done it. We are confronting our problems one by one. Hope is alive tonight
for millions of young families and senior citizens set free from unfair tax
increases and crushing inflation. Inflation has been beaten down from 12.4
to 3.2 percent, and that's a great victory for all the people. The prime rate
has been cut almost in half, and we must work together to bring it down
even more.

Together, we passed the first across-the-board tax reduction for everyone since the Kennedy tax cuts. Next year, tax rates will be indexed so inflation cannot push people into higher brackets when they get cost-of-living pay raises. Government must never again use inflation to profit at the people's expense.

Today, a working family earning $25,000, has $1,100 more in purchasing power than if tax and inflation rates were still at the 1980 levels. Real after-tax income increased 5 percent last year. And economic deregulation of key industries like transportation has offered more chances — or choices, I should say, to consumers and new changes — or chances for entrepreneurs, and protecting safety. Tonight, we can report and be proud of one of the best recoveries in decades. Send away the handwringers and the doubting Thomases. Hope is reborn for couples dreaming of owning homes and for risktakers with vision to create tomorrow's opportunities.

The spirit of enterprise is sparked by the sunrise industries of high-tech and by small businesspeople with big ideas — people like Barbara Proctor, who rose from a ghetto to build a multimillion-dollar advertising agency in Chicago; Carlos Perez, a Cuban refugee, who turned $27 and a dream into a successful importing business in Coral Gables, Florida.

People like these are heroes for the eighties. They helped 4 million Americans find jobs in 1983. More people are drawing paychecks tonight than ever before. And Congress helps — or progress helps everyone — well, Congress does, too — [laughter] — everyone. In 1983, women filled 73 percent of all the new jobs in managerial, professional, and technical fields.

[Restoring Values]

But we know that many of our fellow countrymen are still out of work, wondering what will come of their hopes and dreams. Can we love America and not reach out to tell them: You are not forgotten; we will not rest until each of you can reach as high as your God-given talents will take you.

The heart of America is strong; it's good and true. The cynics were wrong; America never was a sick society. We're seeing rededication to bedrock values of faith, family, work, neighborhood, peace and freedom — values that help bring us together as one people, from the youngest child to the most senior citizen.

The Congress deserves America's thanks for helping us restore pride and credibility to our military. And I hope that you're as proud as I am of the young men and women in uniform who have volunteered to man the ramparts in defense of freedom and whose dedication, valor, and skill increases so much our chance of living in a world at peace.

People everywhere hunger for peace and a better life. The tide of the future is a freedom tide, and our struggle for democracy cannot and will not be denied. This Nation champions peace that enshrines liberty, democratic rights, and dignity for every individual. America's new strength, confidence, and purpose are carrying hope and opportunity far from our shores. A world economic recovery is underway. It began here.

[Four Goals to Keep America Free]

We've journeyed far, but we have much farther to go. Franklin Roosevelt told us 50 years ago this month: "Civilization can not go back; civilization must not stand still. We have undertaken new methods. It is our task to perfect, to improve, to alter when necessary, but in all cases to go forward."

It's time to move forward again, time for America to take freedom's next step. Let us unite tonight behind four great goals to keep America free, secure, and at peace in the eighties together.

We can ensure steady economic growth. We can develop America's next frontier. We can strengthen our traditional values. And we can build a meaningful peace to protect our loved ones and this shining star of faith that has guided millions from tyranny to the safe harbor of freedom, progress, and hope.

Doing these things will open wider the gates of opportunity, provide greater security for all, with no barriers of bigotry or discrimination.

[ECONOMIC GROWTH]

The key to a dynamic decade is vigorous economic growth, our first great goal. We might well begin with common sense in Federal budgeting: government spending no more than government takes in.

We must bring Federal deficits down. But how we do that makes all the difference.

We can begin by limiting the size and scope of government. Under the leadership of Vice President Bush, we have reduced the growth of Federal regulations by more than 25 percent and cut well over 300 million hours of government-required paperwork each year. This will save the public more than $150 billion over the next 10 years.

The Grace commission — the Grace commission has given us some 2,500 recommendations for reducing wasteful spending, and they're being examined throughout the administration. Federal spending growth has been cut from 17.4 percent in 1980 to less than half of that today, and we've already achieved over $300 billion in budget savings for the period of 1982 to '86. But that's only a little more than half of what we sought. Government is still spending too large a percentage of the total economy.

Now, some insist that any further budget savings must be obtained by reducing the portion spent on defense. This ignores the fact that national defense is solely the responsibility of the Federal Government; indeed, it is its prime responsibility. And yet defense spending is less than a third of the total budget. During the years of President Kennedy and of the years before that, defense was almost half the total budget. And then came several years in which our military capability was allowed to deteriorate to a very dangerous degree. We are just now restoring, through the essential modernization of our conventional and strategic forces, our capability to meet our present and future security needs. We dare not shirk our responsibility to keep America free, secure, and at peace.

The last decade saw domestic spending surge literally out of control. But the basis for such spending had been laid in previous years. A pattern of overspending has been in place for half a century. As the national debt grew, we were told not to worry, that we owed it to ourselves.

Now we know that deficits are a cause for worry. But there's a difference of opinion as to whether taxes should be increased, spending cut, or some of both. Fear is expressed that government borrowing to fund the deficit could inhibit the economic recovery by taking capital needed for business and industrial expansion. Well, I think that debate is missing an important point. Whether government borrows or increases taxes, it will be taking the same amount of money from the private sector and, either way, that's too much. Simple fairness dictates that government must not raise taxes on families struggling to pay their bills. The root of the problem is that government's share is more than we can afford if we're to have a sound economy.

['Downpayment' on the Deficit]

We must bring down the deficits to ensure continued economic growth. In the budget that I will submit on February 1st, I will recommend measures that will reduce the deficit over the next 5 years. Many of these will be unfinished business from last year's budget.

Some could be enacted quickly if we could join in a serious effort to address this problem. I spoke today with Speaker of the House O'Neill, Senate Majority Leader Baker, Senate Minority Leader Byrd, and House Minority Leader Michel. I asked them if they would designate congressional representatives to meet with representatives of the administration to try to reach prompt agreement on a bipartisan deficit reduction plan. I know it will take a long hard struggle to agree on a full-scale plan. So what I have proposed is that we first see if we can agree on a downpayment.

Now, I believe there is basis for such an agreement, one that could reduce the deficits by about a hundred billion dollars over the next 3 years. We could focus on some of the less contentious spending cuts that are still pending before the Congress. These could be combined with measures to close certain tax loopholes, measures that the Treasury Department has previously said to be worthy of support. In addition, we could examine the possibility of achieving further outlay savings based on the work of the Grace commission.

If the congressional leadership is willing, my representatives will be prepared to meet with theirs at the earliest possible time. I would hope the leadership might agree on an expedited timetable in which to develop and enact that downpayment.

But a downpayment alone is not enough to break us out of the deficit problem. It could help us start on the right path. Yet, we must do more. So, I propose that we begin exploring how together we can make structural reforms to curb the built-in growth of spending.

[Budgeting Process]

I also propose improvements in the budgeting process. Some 43 of our 50 states grant their Governors the right to veto individual items in appropriation bills without having to veto the entire bill. California is one of those 43 states. As Governor, I found this line-item veto was a powerful tool against wasteful or extravagant spending. It works in 43 states. Let's put it to work in Washington for all the people.

It would be most effective if done by constitutional amendment. The majority of Americans approve of such an amendment, just as they and I approve of an amendment mandating a balanced Federal budget. Many States also have this protection in their constitutions.

To talk of meeting the present situation by increasing taxes is a Band-Aid solution which does nothing to cure an illness that has been coming on for half a century — to say nothing of the fact that it poses a real threat to economic recovery. Let's remember that a substantial amount of income tax is presently owed and not paid by people in the underground economy. It would be immoral to make those who are paying taxes pay more to compensate for those who aren't paying their share.

There is a better way. Let us go forward with an historic reform for fairness, simplicity and incentives, for growth. I am asking Secretary Don Regan for a plan for action to simplify the entire tax code so all taxpayers, big and small, are treated more fairly. And I believe such a plan could result in that underground economy being brought into the sunlight of honest tax compliance. And it could make the tax base broader, so personal tax rates could come down, not go up. I've asked that specific recommendations, consistent with those objectives, be presented to me by December 1984.

[EXPLORING SPACE AND PROTECTING THE ENVIRONMENT]

Our second great goal is to build on America's pioneer spirit — [laughter] — I said something funny? [Laughter] I said America's next frontier — and that's to develop that frontier. A sparkling economy spurs initiatives, sunrise industries, and makes older ones more competitive.

Nowhere is this more important than our next frontier: space. Nowhere do we so effectively demonstrate our technological leadership and ability to make life better on Earth. The Space Age is barely a quarter of a century old. But already we've pushed civilization forward with our advances in science and technology. Opportunities and jobs will multiply as we cross new thresholds of knowledge and reach deeper into the unknown.

Our progress in space — taking giant steps for all mankind — is a tribute to American teamwork and excellence. Our finest minds in government, industry, and academia have all pulled together. And we can be proud to say: We are first; we are the best; and we are so because we're free.

America has always been greatest when we dared to be great. We can reach for greatness again. We can follow our dreams to distant stars, living and working in space for peaceful, economic, and scientific gain. Tonight, I am directing NASA [National Aeronautics and Space Administration] to develop a permanently manned space station and to do it within a decade.

A space station will permit quantum leaps in our research in science, communications, in metals, and in lifesaving medicines which could be manufactured only in space. We want our friends to help us meet these challenges and share in their benefits. NASA will invite other countries to participate so we can strengthen peace, build prosperity, and expand freedom for all who share our goals.

Just as the oceans opened up a new world for clipper ships and Yankee traders, space holds enormous potential for commerce today. The market for space transportation could surpass our capacity to develop it. Companies interested in putting payloads into space must have ready access to private sector launch services. The Department of Transportation will help an expendable launch services industry to get off the ground. We'll soon implement a number of executive initiatives, develop proposals to ease regulatory constraints, and, with NASA's help, promote private sector investment in space.

As we develop the frontier of space, let us remember our responsibility to preserve our older resources here on Earth. Preservation of our environment is not a liberal or conservative challenge, it's common sense.

Though this is a time of budget constraints, I have requested for EPA one of the largest percentage budget increases of any agency. We will begin the long, necessary effort to clean up a productive, recreational area and a special national resource — the Chesapeake Bay.

To reduce the threat posed by abandoned hazardous waste dumps, EPA will spend $410 million, and I will request a supplemental increase of $50 million. And because the Superfund law expires in 1985, I have asked Bill Ruckelshaus to develop a proposal for its extension so there'll be additional time to complete this important task.

On the question of acid rain, which concerns people in many areas of the United States and Canada, I'm proposing a research program that doubles our current funding. And we'll take additional action to restore our lakes and develop new technology to reduce pollution that causes acid rain.

We have greatly improved the conditions of our national resources. We'll ask the Congress for $157 million beginning in 1985 to acquire new park and conservation lands. The Department of the Interior will encourage careful, selective exploration and production on [sic] our vital resources in an Exclusive Economic Zone within the 200-mile limit off our coasts — but with strict adherence to environmental laws and with fuller State and public participation.

[PRESERVING TRADITIONAL VALUES]

But our most precious resources, our greatest hope for the future, are the minds and hearts of our people, especially our children. We can help them build tomorrow by strengthening our community of shared values. This must be our third great goal. For us, faith, work, family, neighborhood, freedom, and peace are not just words; they're expressions of what America means, definitions of what makes us a good and loving people.

[Education and School Prayer]

Families stand at the center of our society. And every family has a personal stake in promoting excellence in education. Excellence does not begin in Washington. A 600-percent increase in Federal spending on education between 1960 and 1980 was accompanied by a steady decline in Scholastic Aptitude Test scores. Excellence must begin in our homes and neighborhood schools, where it's the responsibility of every parent and teacher and the right of every child.

Our children come first, and that's why I established a bipartisan National Commission on Excellence in Education, to help us chart a commonsense course for better education. And already, communities are implementing the Commission's recommendations. Schools are reporting progress in math and reading skills. But we must do more to restore discipline to schools; and we must encourage the teaching of new basics, reward teachers of merit, enforce tougher standards, and put our parents back in charge.

I will continue to press for tuition tax credits to expand opportunities for families and to soften the double payment for those paying public school taxes and private school tuition. Our proposal would target assistance to low- and middle-income families. Just as more incentives are needed within our schools, greater competition is needed among our schools. Without standards and competition there can be no champions, no records broken, no excellence in education or any other walk of life.

And while I'm on this subject, each day your Members observe a 200-year-old tradition meant to signify America is one nation under God. I must ask: If you can begin your day with a member of the clergy standing right here leading you in prayer, then why can't freedom to acknowledge God be enjoyed again by children in every schoolroom across this land?

America was founded by people who believed that God was their rock of safety. He is ours. I recognize we must be cautious in claiming that God is on our side, but I think it's all right to keep asking if we're on His side.

[Abortion]

During our first 3 years, we have joined bipartisan efforts to restore protection of the law to unborn children. Now, I know this issue is very controversial. But unless and until it can be proven that an unborn child is not a living human being, can we justify assuming without proof that it isn't? No one has yet offered such proof; indeed, all the evidence is to the contrary. We should rise above bitterness and reproach, and if Americans

91

could come together in a spirit of understanding and helping, then we could find positive solutions to the tragedy of abortion.

[Crime]

Economic recovery, better education, rededication to values, all show the spirit of renewal gaining the upper hand. And all will improve family life in the eighties. But families need more. They need assurance that they and their loved ones can walk the streets of America without being afraid. Parents need to know their children will not be victims of child pornography and abduction. This year we will intensify our drive against these and other horrible crimes like sexual abuse and family violence.

Already our efforts to crack down on career criminals, organized crime, drug pushers, and to enforce tougher sentences and paroles are having effect. In 1982 the crime rate dropped by 4.3 percent, the biggest decline since 1972. Protecting victims is just as important as safeguarding the rights of defendants.

[Creating Opportunities]

Opportunities for all Americans will increase if we move forward on fair housing and work to ensure women's rights, provide for equitable treatment in pension benefits and Individual Retirement Accounts, faciliate child care, and enforce delinquent parent support payments.

It's not just the home but the workplace and community that sustain our values and shape our future. So, I ask your help in assisting more communities to break the bondage of dependency. Help us to free enterprise by permitting debate and voting "yes" on our proposal for enterprise zones in America. This has been before you for 2 years. Its passage can help high-unemployment areas by creating jobs and restoring neighborhoods.

A society bursting with opportunities, reaching for its future with confidence, sustained by faith, fair play, and a conviction that good and courageous people will flourish when they're free — these are the secrets of a strong and prosperous America at peace with itself and the world.

[LASTING AND MEANINGFUL PEACE]

A lasting and meaningful peace is our fourth great goal. It is our highest aspiration. And our record is clear: Americans resort to force only when we must. We have never been aggressors. We have always struggled to defend freedom and democracy.

We have no territorial ambitions. We occupy no countries. We build no walls to lock people in. Americans build the future. And our vision of a better life for farmers, merchants, and working people, from the Americas to Asia, begins with a simple premise: The future is best decided by ballots, not bullets.

Governments which rest upon the consent of the governed do not wage war on their neighbors. Only when people are given a personal stake in deciding their own destiny, benefiting from their own risks, do they create societies that are prosperous, progressive, and free. Tonight, it is democracies that offer hope by feeding the hungry, prolonging life, and eliminating drudgery.

When it comes to keeping America strong, free, and at peace, there should be no Republicans or Democrats, just patriotic Americans. We can decide the tough issues not by who is right, but by what is right.

Together, we can continue to advance our agenda for peace. We can establish a more stable basis for peaceful relations with the Soviet Union; strengthen allied relationships across the board; achieve real and equitable reductions in the levels of nuclear arms; reinforce our peacemaking efforts in the Middle East, Central America, and southern Africa; insist — or assist developing countries, particularly our neighbors in the Western Hemisphere; and assist in the development of democratic institutions throughout the world.

The wisdom of our bipartisan cooperation was seen in the work of the Scowcroft commission, which strengthened our ability to deter war and protect peace. In that same spirit, I urge you to move forward with the Henry Jackson plan to implement the recommendations of the Bipartisan Commission on Central America.

Your joint resolution on the multinational peacekeeping force in Lebanon is also serving the cause of peace. We are making progress in Lebanon. For nearly 10 years, the Lebanese have lived from tragedy to tragedy, with no hope for their future. Now the multinational peacekeeping force and our marines are helping them break their cycle of despair. There is hope for a free, independent, and sovereign Lebanon. We must have the courage to give peace a chance. And we must not be driven from our objectives for peace in Lebanon by state-sponsored terrorism. We have seen this ugly spectre in Beirut, Kuwait, and Rangoon. It demands international attention. I will forward shortly legislative proposals to help combat terrorism. And I will be seeking support from our allies for concerted action.

Our NATO alliance is strong. 1983 was a banner year for political courage. And we have strengthened our partnerships and our friendships in the Far East. We're committed to dialog, deterrence, and promoting prosperity. We'll work with our trading partners for a new round of negotiations in support of freer world trade, greater competition, and more open markets.

A rebirth of bipartisan cooperation, of economic growth and military deterrence, and a growing spirit of unity among our people at home and our allies abroad underline a fundamental and far-reaching change. The United States is safer, stronger, and more secure in 1984 than before. We can now move with confidence to seize the opportunities for peace, and we will.

Tonight, I want to speak to the people of the Soviet Union, to tell them it's true that our governments have had serious differences, but our sons and daughters have never fought each other in war. And if we Americans have our way, they never will.

People of the Soviet Union, there is only one sane policy, for your country and mine, to preserve our civilization in this modern age: A nuclear war cannot be won and must never be fought. The only value in our two nations possessing nuclear weapons is to make sure they will never be used. But then would it not be better to do away with them entirely?

People of the Soviet: President Dwight Eisenhower, who fought by your side in World War II, said the essential struggle "is not merely man against man or nation against nation. It is man against war." Americans are people of peace. If your government wants peace, there will be peace. We can come together in faith and friendship to build a safer and far better world for our children and our children's children. And the whole world will rejoice. That is my message to you.

[American Heroes]

Some days when life seems hard and we reach out for values to sustain us or a friend to help us, we find a person who reminds us what it means to be Americans.

Sergeant Stephen Trujillo, a medic in the 2d Ranger Battalion, 75th Infantry, was in the first helicopter to land at the compound held by Cuban forces in Grenada. He saw three other helicopters crash. Despite the imminent explosion of the burning aircraft, he never hesitated. He ran across 25 yards of open terrain through enemy fire to rescue wounded soldiers. He directed two other medics, administered first aid, and returned again and again to the crash site to carry his wounded friends to safety.

Sergeant Trujillo, you and your fellow service men and women not only saved innocent lives; you set a nation free. You inspire us as a force for freedom, not for despotism; and yes, for peace, not conquest. God bless you.

And then there are unsung heroes: single parents, couples, church and civic volunteers. Their hearts carry without complaint the pains of family and community problems. They soothe our sorrow, heal our wounds, calm our fears, and share our joy.

A person like Father Ritter is always there. His Covenant House programs in New York and Houston provide shelter and help to thousands of frightened and abused children each year. The same is true of Dr. Charles Carson. Paralyzed in a plane crash, he still believed nothing is impossible. Today, in Minnesota, he works 80 hours a week without pay, helping pioneer the field of computer-controlled walking. He has given hope to 500,000 paralyzed Americans that someday they may walk again.

[The Greatness of America]

How can we not believe in the greatness of America? How can we not do what is right and needed to preserve this last best hope of man on Earth?

After all our struggles to restore America, to revive confidence in our country, hope for our future, after all our hard-won victories earned through the patience and courage of every citizen, we cannot, must not, and will not turn back. We will finish our job. How could we do less? We're Americans.

Carl Sandburg said, "I see America not in the setting sun of a black night of despair . . . I see America in the crimson light of a rising sun fresh from the burning, creative hand of God . . . I see great days ahead for men and women of will and vision."

I've never felt more strongly that America's best days and democracy's best days lie ahead. We're a powerful force for good. With faith and courage, we can perform great deeds and take freedom's next step. And we will. We will carry on the tradition of a good and worthy people who have brought light where there was darkness, warmth where there was cold, medicine where there was disease, food where there was hunger, and peace where there was only bloodshed.

Let us be sure that those who come after will say of us in our time, that in our time we did everything that could be done. We finished the race; we kept them free; we kept the faith.

Thank you very much. God bless you, and God bless America.

February

Features

PRESIDENT'S BUDGET MESSAGE

February 1, 1984

President Ronald Reagan sent Congress February 1 a budget marked by a huge projected deficit for the fiscal year beginning October 1, 1984. Urging deficit reductions, he nevertheless proposed a budget in which total outlays of $925.5 billion would greatly outweigh projected revenues of $745.1 billion. Large deficits were envisioned through 1987 but were expected to decline to $180 billion in that year. The deficit figures compared to a 1983 level of $195.4 billion, a record. In his budget message, however, Reagan credited his policies of the past three years with putting the United States "well on our way to sustained long-term prosperity."

Members of Congress reacted to the budget largely along party lines. Many Republicans called it "realistic" and most Democrats branded it "irresponsible." White House officials acknowledged that election-year pressures had played a role in framing a budget that avoided major tax-increase or spending-cut proposals. They portrayed the budget's proposed $180.4 billion deficit for fiscal 1985 as tentative, depending on the response to President Reagan's call January 25 for negotiations with congresssional leaders toward $100 billion in deficit reductions over three years. (State of the Union address, p. 81)

With a few exceptions, the basic outlines of Reagan's fiscal 1985 budget looked familiar: large increases in defense spending, a freeze on domestic spending programs, and minor tax increases with no retreat from the big tax cut he pushed through Congress in 1981. Reagan called for continued buildup of U.S. military forces, proposing $305 billion in budget authority, or a 13 percent rise in inflation-adjusted dollars. Budgets for the

Defense Department that the president previously had submitted called for inflation-adjusted increases of more than 10 percent. In the fiscal 1984 budget, Congress scaled that back to 5 percent. In addition to the sharply higher defense budget, more money was slated in 1985 for a number of select programs. In a concession to environmentalists, Reagan proposed a major effort to attack the problem of acid rain. There also would be more dollars for a crackdown on drug peddling by organized crime. The spending plan sought to achieve deficit reductions of $106 billion over the next three years by cutting Medicare and other programs and imposing modest tax hikes. And the president proposed adoption of two constitutional amendments intended to aid in limiting federal spending.

Among the changes from previous budgets, Reagan sought an 8.5 percent increase in operating funds for the Environmental Protection Agency after having proposed a $1.3 billion cut the previous year. The president also proposed increasing funds for low-income energy assistance and for block grants to states for primary and secondary education after having proposed to decrease or freeze funding for those programs in earlier budgets. Reagan shied away from an earlier idea to cut Medicare costs by about $2 billion in fiscal 1985, because Republican House members signaled that the effort would be rebuffed immediately. The budget called for Medicare savings of $1.05 billion or about half the amount originally discussed. The fiscal 1985 budget, however, contained some cuts in programs that benefited the elderly and poor. Included in this category were reductions in housing for the elderly, food and nutrition programs, Aid to Families with Dependent Children, Medicaid, and aid to low-income college students.

Deficit Reduction Plan

In his budget message Reagan said, "The long winter of transition from the misguided policies of the past, with their inflationary and growth-deadening side effects, is now yielding to a springtime of hope for America." But to continue the recovery, Reagan cautioned, "there must be substantial reductions in spending and strictly limited increases in receipts." The president proposed reductions and cost savings totaling $73 billion, and tax increases totaling $33.5 billion, over the next three years. A $32 billion portion of the spending reductions, however, was an accounting adjustment in defense spending. Another $14 billion was attributable to debt service savings. Actual proposed spending cuts amounted to only $5 billion in fiscal 1985, $10 billion in fiscal 1986, and $12 billion in fiscal 1987. The breakdown for revenue increases was: $7.8 billion in fiscal 1985, $11.6 billion in fiscal 1986, and $14.1 billion in fiscal 1987.

The president rebuffed the advice of several administration officials to resubmit the 1983 contingency tax plan, which would have kicked in if deficits were too high, and were contingent on spending cuts being achieved. Since the proposal was rejected out of hand in 1983, Reagan decided there was no point in resubmitting it in the fiscal 1985 budget. Instead, he directed the Treasury Department to complete a study and make recommendations by the end of 1984 on how to make the tax system simpler and fairer. Further, he urged Congress to enact in 1984 constitutional amendments requiring a balanced budget and permitting a president to veto line items in appropriations bills. He added, "Where Congress lacks the will to enforce upon itself the strict fiscal diet that is now necessary, it needs the help of the executive branch. We need a constitutional amendment granting the president the power to veto individual items in appropriations bills." But neither proposal was expected to fare well in Congress.

Economic Outlook

In assessing the economic results of the past year and looking ahead to the next year, the administration struck a note at times congratulatory, at others optimistic. According to the budget, 1983 was "one of the best years in the postwar period. . . ." The budget document added, "Although the magnitude of the recovery was somewhat surprising, the eventual reversal of the economic trends of the previous decade was expected. Indeed, it has been the goal of the administration's economic policies from its first days in office."

The administration singled out the "unwinding of inflation" as its most important economic accomplishment. But it acknowledged the role played by the Federal Reserve Board in this success. "A foundation for recovery" — built on low inflation, curtailed spending, an incentive-oriented tax system, and a reduction in regulatory interference — "is now in place," the budget document said. "If the new policies are maintained consistently," it continued, "the recent favorable economic trends are likely to strengthen and persist in the years ahead."

The administration's economic outlook reflected a cooling down of the economy, with all the major indexes continuing to improve, but at a slower pace. Specifically, the administration estimated that real output as measured by the gross national product (GNP) would grow 4.5 percent beginning with the fourth quarter of 1983 to the fourth quarter of 1984. The growth rate would be slightly higher than usual for the second year of a recovery. Output would grow 4 percent in 1985.

The administration expected the inflation rate to increase slightly to 5 percent from the fourth quarter of 1983 to the fourth quarter of 1984, and somewhat again in 1985 to 4.7 percent. The unemployment rate, which dropped sharply at the end of 1983, would continue to decline, but more slowly. It would average 7.8 percent in 1984 and 7.6 percent in 1985.

Interest costs, measured in relation to three-month Treasury bills, were projected to drop almost imperceptibly, averaging 8.5 percent in 1984 and, more significantly, 7.7 percent in 1985.

Council of Economic Advisers Chairman Martin Feldstein acknowledged February 1 that the budget's economic outlook assumed the adoption of $100 billion in deficit reductions plus unspecified "further significant actions in 1985." If those things happened, Feldstein said, "then I think we can have the preconditions for the kind of small real growth, favorable inflation, and interest rates that are the underlying assumptions in these calculations." If those things did not happen, Feldstein added, "it would not be the kind of healthy recovery with low inflation we would like to have." (Economic report, p. 119)

> *Following is the text of President Ronald Reagan's February 1, 1984, budget message to Congress. (Boldface headings in brackets have been added by Congressional Quarterly to highlight the organization of the text.):*

To the Congress of the United States:

In the past year, the Nation's prospects have brightened considerably. The economy has grown strongly — beyond expectation. Inflation has been reduced to its lowest rate in 16 years. Unemployment has declined faster than at any other time in 30 years. We are well on our way to sustained long-term prosperity without runaway inflation.

Our national security is being restored. Our domestic programs are being streamlined to reflect more accurately the proper scope of Government responsibility and intervention in our lives. Government operations are being made more effective and efficient, as steps are taken to reduce costs.

These developments are the result of the program I proposed 3 years ago to correct the severe economic and political problems caused by previous short-sighted and misguided policies and priorities. That program focused on long-range real growth. My tax proposals were designed to provide badly needed incentives for saving and productive investment. I supported the Federal Reserve in its pursuit of sound monetary policy. I worked with the Congress to reverse the growth of Government programs that had become too large or had outlived their usefulness, and as a result, domestic programs, which had been growing rapidly for 3 decades, have finally been contained. I worked to eliminate or simplify unnecessary or burdensome regulations.

To the Nation's great good fortune, the preceding Congress appreciated the fundamental soundness of this program and joined with my administration in helping to make it a reality. Frequently, because of entrenched constituency special interests, the political risks involved in doing so were great. I thanked Members then, and continue to be grateful, for the crucial support my program received. The Nation is now beginning to reap the solid fruits of our joint perseverance and foresight.

The economy's response has fully vindicated my economic program. During the past 2 years the percentage rise in consumer price index has been no more than it was during the first 6 months of 1980. Economic recovery has been vigorous during the past year, with real GNP rising over 6% and industrial production by 16%. Unemployment, though still unacceptably high, has declined by a record 2½ percentage points in a single year. Capacity utilization in American plants has risen dramatically. Business investment in new plant and equipment has risen 11½% in the past year, in real terms. American productivity, stagnant from 1977 to 1981, climbed 3.7% between the third quarter of 1982 and the third quarter of 1983. Interest rates declined substantially in mid-1982, followed by a major, sustained rally of the stock market that added half a trillion dollars to the net financial worth of American households. Real disposable personal income rose 5.1% in 1983. After a substantial decline, the U.S. dollar has rallied powerfully to its highest level in more than a decade.

We are not, however, out of the woods yet. Despite our success in reducing the rate of growth of nondefense spending in the last three budgets, spending in 1985 will exceed 1981 levels by 41%, reflecting continued increases in basic entitlement programs, essential increases in defense spending, and rapid growth of interest costs. Clearly, much remains to be done. The task of rebuilding our military forces to adequate levels must be carried to completion, and our commitment to provide economic and military support to small, poor nations that are struggling to preserve democracy must be honored. At the same time, further action is required to curb the size and growth of many programs and to achieve managerial efficiencies throughout Government, wherever the opportunity is present.

Three Years of Accomplishment

Last year, I reviewed the dramatic improvements during the preceding 2 years in Government operations, and in the way they affect the economy. I am happy to report that these improvements continued through a third year.

● Where the growth rate of spending was almost out of control at 17.4% a year in 1980, it will decline to 7.3% this year.

● Where spending grew 64% over the 4 years from 1977 to 1981, it will rise by only 41% over the 4-year period from 1981 to 1985, despite legislated cost-of-living adjustments and the needed defense buildup.

● The Federal tax system has been significantly restructured. Marginal income tax rates have been substantially reduced, greatly improving the climate for saving and investment. Depreciation reform has been enacted, restoring the value of depreciation allowances eroded by inflation. Tax loopholes have been closed, making the tax structure more equitable. Efforts have been made to shift to financing Government programs through user fees commensurate with benefits and services provided.

• Our military strength is being restored to more adequate levels.

• Domestic spending, which grew nearly 3-fold in real terms in a little more than 2 decades, will actually be lower this year than it was in 1981.

• The rapid growth of means-tested entitlement programs has been curbed. Eligibility criteria have been tightened to target benefits more to the truly needy, and significant steps have been taken to improve the efficiency and effectiveness of these programs. Unnecessarily frequent cost-of-living adjustments were pared back.

• The social security system has been rescued from the threat of insolvency raised by rampant inflation, excessive liberalizations, and lagging growth of its tax base.

• Unnecessary or excessive Federal credit activities have been eliminated or cut back. Improvements in the management and control of Federal credit activities are being pursued. The administration has supported the basic intent of proposed legislation that would move off-budget lending onto the unified budget, in order to provide better budgetary control over Federal lending.

• Proliferation of regulations and red tape has been stopped. The number of new Federal rules has fallen by over a quarter during the past three years, and hundreds of unnecessary old rules have been eliminated. For the first time, the *Federal Register* of new regulatory actions has grown shorter for three consecutive years; it is now one-third shorter than in 1980. Federal paperwork requirements have been cut by well over 300 million hours annually, and will be reduced even further in 1984. This has saved the American public over 150,000 work-years that had been spent every year filling out unnecessary Federal forms and reports. Our regulatory reform efforts to date will save individual citizens, businesses, and State and local governments over $150 billion over the next decade.

• Major management improvement initiatives are underway that will fundamentally change the way the Federal Government operates. The President's Council on Integrity and Efficiency has reported $31 billion in cost reductions or funds put to better use.

• The Federal nondefense work force has been reduced by 71,000 employees since I took office.

These are impressive accomplishments — accomplishments to be proud of and to build on. And together we can build on them. With this budget I call on all Members of the Congress once again for additional steps to ensure the firmness of our foundations and overcome the Nation's budget problem.

Maintaining Economic Recovery

Before us stands the prospect of an extended era of peace, prosperity, growth, and a rising standard of living for all Americans. What must we do to ensure that that promise shall be realized and enjoyed in the years to come? What must we do to ensure that the high price of adjustment to this new era paid by the Nation in recent years shall not have been paid in vain?

All signs point to continued strong economic growth, vigorous investment, and rising productivity, without renewed inflation — all but one. Only the threat of indefinitely prolonged high budget deficits threatens the continuation of sustained noninflationary growth and prosperity. It raises the specter of sharply higher interest rates, choked-off investment, renewed recession, and rising unemployment.

This specter must be laid to rest: just as fears of rampant inflation and its attendant evils are being laid to rest; just as fears of helplessness before growth in Soviet military might and all it threatens are being laid to rest; just as fears that the Nation's social security system would "go under" have been laid to rest. A number of actions will be required to lay it to rest. This budget requests these actions of Congress; it calls for measures to continue to curb the upward momentum of Federal spending and to increase Federal receipts. Other actions involve such fundamental reform of our fiscal procedures that they will require that the Constitution be amended.

Congress has each year enacted a portion of my budget proposals, while ignoring others for the time being. It is moving slowly, year by year, toward the full needed set of budget adjustments. I urge the Congress to enact this year not only the proposals contained in this budget, but also constitutional amendments providing for a line-item veto and for a balanced budget — rather than the fitful policy of enacting a half-hearted reform this year, another one next year, and so on.

Where Congress lacks the will to enforce upon itself the strict fiscal diet that is now necessary, it needs the help of the Executive Branch. We need a constitutional amendment granting the President power to veto individual items in appropriations bills. Forty-three of the fifty States give this authority to their governors. Congress has approved a line item veto for the District of Columbia, Puerto Rico, and the trust territories. It is now time for Congress to grant this same authority to the President. As Governor of California, I was able to use the line-item veto as a powerful tool against wasteful government spending. It works, and works well, in State government. Every number in this document bears testimony to the urgent need for the Federal Government to adopt this fundamental fiscal reform.

Let us also heed the people and finally support a constitutional amendment mandating balanced Federal budgets and spending limits. I encourage our citizens to keep working for this at the grassroots. If you want to make it happen, it will happen.

We must seek a bipartisan basis for fundamental reforms of Government spending programs. We need to reexamine just what, how, and how much the Federal Government should be doing — given our need for security and well-being and our desire to leave power and resources with the people. The President's Private Sector Survey on Cost Control (Grace Commission) has already come up with some interesting suggestions in this regard that, with the help of the Congress, will be adopted wherever possible.

To those who say we must raise taxes, I say wait. Tax increases pile unfair burdens on the people, hurt capital formation, and destroy incentives for growth. Tax cuts helped sustain the recovery, leading to faster growth and more jobs. Rather than risk sabotaging our future, let us go forward with an historic reform for fairness, simplicity, and growth. It is time to simplify the entire tax code so everyone is on equal footing.

The tax system must be made simpler and fairer; honest people should not pay for cheaters; the underground economy should come back into the sunlight; and everyone's tax rates should be reduced to spark more savings, investment, and incentives for work and economic growth. This is the blueprint for a brighter future and a fairer tax system. Therefore, I am directing the Department of the Treasury to complete a study with recommendations by the end of the year.

With these changes completed and the necessary fiscal tools in place, I am confident that we can devise a sweeping set of fiscal policy changes designed to reduce substantially the persistent Federal deficits that cloud our otherwise bright economic future. The plan must be based on these cardinal principles:

● It must be bipartisan. Overcoming the deficits and putting the Government's house in order will require everyone's best efforts.

● It must be fair. Just as all Americans will share in the benefits that are coming from recovery, all should share fairly in the burden of transition to a more limited role of Government in our society.

● It must be prudent. The strength of our national defense must be restored so that we can pursue prosperity in peace and freedom, while maintaining our commitment to the truly needy.

● Finally, it must be realistic. Government spending will not be curbed by wishful thinking.

In the meantime, the proposals in this budget provide important additional steps toward reducing the deficit.

Meeting Federal Responsibilities

My administration seeks to limit the size, intrusiveness, and cost of Federal activities as much as possible and to achieve the needed increase in our defense capabilities in the most cost-effective manner possible. This does not mean that appropriate Federal responsibilities are being abandoned, neglected, or inadequately supported. Instead, ways are being found to streamline Federal activity, to limit it to those areas and responsibilities that are truly Federal in nature; to ensure that these appropriate Federal responsibilities are performed in the most cost-effective and efficient manner; and to aid State and local governments in carrying out their appropriate public responsibilities in a similarly cost-effective manner. The Nation must ask for no more publicly-provided services and benefits than the taxpayers can reasonably be asked to finance.

EDUCATION

I have devoted considerable time this year to the problems of our schools. The record of the last two decades is not good, though relieved in places by the efforts of many dedicated teachers, administrators, parents, and students. It has been extremely gratifying to observe the response all across the country to my call for a renewed commitment to educational excellence. Excellence in education will only happen when the States and school districts, parents and teachers, and our children devote themselves to the hard work necessary to achieve it. Federal money cannot buy educational excellence. It has not in the past and will not in the future. What we will do in this budget is seek resources to help the States plan and carry out education reforms. My budget includes $729 million, about 50% more than Congress appropriated for 1984, for the education block grant and discretionary fund. States and localities will receive this increase in resources and be able to use the funds for education reform without Federal prescription and interference.

The budget also provides for stabilizing funding for almost all major education State grant programs at the 1984 level and in the future allows room for modest growth for most of these programs.

Finally, the budget reflects continued support of several more important initiatives that will strengthen American education:

● Enactment of tuition tax credits for parents who send their children to qualified private or religiously-affiliated schools.

● Establishment of education savings accounts to give middle- and lower-income families an incentive to save for their children's college education and, at the same time, to encourage a real increase in saving for economic growth.

● Reorientation of student aid programs to ensure that students and families meet their responsibilities for financing higher education.

● Permission for States or localities, if they so choose, to use their compensatory education funds to establish voucher programs to broaden family choice of effective schooling methods for educationally disadvantaged children.

● Assistance to States to train more mathematics and science teachers.

TRAINING AND EMPLOYMENT

While the economic forecast predicts continuing improvement in the economy and further steady declines in the unemployment rate, I recognize that there are those who lack the skills to find and hold steady jobs. This is particularly true for some of our youth. In the past, Federal training and employment programs have not always helped these people gain the skills needed for success in the job market. Instead the Government spent precious tax dollars funding temporary, dead-end, make-work jobs that did little, if anything, to prepare these people for holding real jobs in the private sector. My administration worked with the Congress to change that. The Job Training Partnership Act, which I signed into law in 1982, involves private industry in the design and delivery of job training programs. Each year it will train 1.5 million disadvantaged adults and youths, dislocated workers, and welfare recipients in skills needed for private sector jobs. Additional work experience for over 700,000 disadvantaged youths will be provided during the summer months. What is needed now is not more Government programs, but removal of Government-created barriers that make it difficult for youths who want to work to find jobs. It has long been acknowledged that the minimum wage is a barrier to job finding for youths, especially minority youths, who lack skills. Therefore, I am again asking the Congress to authorize a wage of 75% of the minimum wage for youths newly hired for jobs during the summer months. This will let employers lower their costs to levels more in line with the skills youths possess, and it will help many young people find jobs and gain valuable work experience. The legislation I have proposed includes protections for adult workers.

RESEARCH

Recognizing the Federal responsibility to maintain and strengthen U.S. leadership in science and technology, the budget proposes further increases of more than 10% in Government-wide funding for basic research. The $8 billion planned for support of such research represents a relatively small share of the budget, but it is a critical investment in the Nation's future. Basic research lays the foundation for a strong defense in the years to come and for new technologies and industries that will maintain U.S. industrial leadership, create new jobs, and improve our quality of life.

SPACE

Our civilian space program has made remarkable progress in the past year. The space shuttle, the world's most advanced space transportation system, has made eight pathbreaking trips into space and is progressing rapidly towards achieving routine operational status.

We can now look forward confidently to the next major challenge in space — a space station. The space station, to be placed in permanent Earth orbit in the early 1990's, is intended to enhance the Nation's science and application programs, to help develop advanced technologies potentially useful to the economy, and to encourage greater commercial use of space. The budget provides planning money to initiate this program.

NATIONAL DEFENSE

During the past 3 years, we have also taken decisive measures to increase our military strength to levels necessary to protect our Nation and our friends and allies around the world. At the same time, we have vigorously pursued diplomatic approaches, such as arms reduction talks, in an effort to ensure the principles of security and freedom for all.

The improvement in our defense posture has been across the board. Long-overdue modernization of our strategic forces is proceeding, while our conventional forces are also being modernized and strengthened. Successful recruiting and retention over the past 3 years have resulted in all of our armed services being more fully manned with capable, high-caliber men and women.

ENERGY

My administration has significantly reoriented the country's approach to energy matters toward reliance on market forces — instead of Government regulation and massive, indiscriminate Federal spending. This has resulted in greater energy production, more efficient use of energy, and more favorable energy prices. For example:

● The U.S. economy currently is using 30% less oil and gas per dollar's worth of output than it did 10 years ago when energy prices began to rise.

● Heating oil prices have been lower this past year than they were in January 1981, when I removed oil price controls. Gasoline prices have fallen to levels which, after adjustments for general inflation and sales taxes, are within 5% of those that prevailed in the U.S. in the 1950's.

Energy programs proposed in the budget are designed to complement market forces by focusing resources on limited but appropriate responsibilities of the Federal Government and by managing these programs well. Thus, for example, the budget proposes increased spending for basic and other long-term energy research. In addition, the administration continues its commitment to filling the strategic petroleum reserve. The reserve has more than tripled in size in the last three years.

HEALTH CARE

Progress has been made in slowing the explosive growth of health costs. As part of the Social Security Amendments of 1983, Congress enacted the Administration's proposed fixed price prospective payment system for hospital care. This replaced the previous Medicare hospital reimbursement system under which hospitals were reimbursed for their costs. The new prospective payment system has altered incentives and should lessen the rate of increase in hospital costs.

Under the proposals in this budget, physicians will be asked to maintain present fee levels for medicare through the next fiscal year. Tax incentives prompting overly-costly employee health insurance benefits would be revised to make users and providers more sensitive to costs. Finally, resources for biomedical research will increase.

TRANSPORTATION

My administration has sought to shift much of the costs of transportation from the general taxpayer to those who use transportation services and facilities. I signed into law several administration-backed proposals to increase excise taxes on aviation and highway users and thereby provide funding needed to revitalize and modernize these important segments of the Nation's transportation system. The proportion of the Department of Transportation's budget financed by user fees has risen from 49% in 1982 to 72% in 1985. The budget reflects the administration's continued commitment to the "users pay" principle by including receipts proposals for nautical and aviation aids, the inland waterway system, and construction and maintenance of deep-draft ports.

Recognizing the importance of safety in our transportation systems, the budget provides for significant improvements in this area. In addition, my administration secured passage of legislation designed to rebuild the Nation's highway and public transportation facilities. This legislation substantially increased funds available to the States and local communities to complete and repair the aging interstate highway system, to rehabilitate principal rural and urban highways and bridges, and to improve mass transit systems. The budget also provides for improvements in the safety of our transportation systems.

Improved ports and channels will help to make U.S. coal exports competitive in world markets. My administration will work with the Congress to provide for timely and efficient port construction. A system that recovers a significant portion of the cost of existing port maintenance and new port construction must be enacted prior to any new construction. In the last 3 years, my administration has sent several reasonable proposals to the Congress, and progress is being made. It is time for action on this important issue.

Reducing the Federal presence in commercial transportation, currently regulated by the Interstate Commerce Commission, the Civil Aeronautics Board, and the Federal Maritime Commission, will improve the efficiency of the industry. Authority for the Civil Aeronautics Board will expire next year, and its residual functions will be assumed by other agencies. The administration will continue to seek legislation to deregulate ocean shipping, and will propose legislation to deregulate oil pipelines and natural gas. Experience since the adoption of initial transportation deregulation legislation has shown clearly that both consumers and industry benefit from reduced Federal involvement in these activities.

CRIMINAL JUSTICE

My administration has continued to strengthen the Federal criminal justice system by seeking major legislative changes in immigration policy, sentencing, and bail procedures, and by seeking increased funding for law enforcement activities. An additional organized crime drug enforcement task force will be established in Florida, bringing the total number of task forces to 13. The budget proposes to bolster immigration control by strengthening border enforcement and improving the effectiveness of border inspection programs. Additional attorneys will be sought for the Internal Revenue Service and the Justice Department, underscoring my administration's determination to tackle the serious problem of tax protesters and evaders. The administration will enhance its efforts to identify, neutralize, and defeat foreign agents who pose a threat to the Nation.

INTERNATIONAL AFFAIRS

Our foreign policy is oriented toward maintaining peace through military strength and diplomatic negotiation; promoting market-oriented solutions to international economic problems; telling the story abroad of America's democratic, free-enterprise way of life; and reducing barriers to free trade both here and abroad.

• The security assistance portion of the international affairs program has been increased to assist friendly governments facing threats from the Soviet Union, its surrogates, and from other radical regimes.

• Development aid emphasizes encouraging the private sectors of developing nations and increasing U.S. private sector involvement in foreign assistance.

• The budget provides for continuing the major expansion of international broadcasting activities started last year. Television, exchanges of people, and other programs to improve communications with foreign countries are included.

• My administration will continue to work with the Congress to strengthen the management and coordination of the Government's international trade functions by consolidating them in a Department of International Trade and Industry.

The United States faces threats to its interests in many parts of the world. The Middle East, with its vital energy resources, is still in turmoil. In Central America, Marxist forces continue to threaten democratic governments, exploiting temporary economic dislocations and the continuing poverty of less developed countries. In Africa, the poorest nations of the world are facing the prospect of great privation, accentuated by drought. This budget addresses each of these concerns:

111

• It continues military and economic support for Israel and Egypt, with improved financial terms.

• It provides for a significant increase in assistance to Central America, the specific nature of which will be defined after our review of the recommendations of the National Bipartisan Commission on Central America.

• It provides special humanitarian aid to counter the immediate effects of African drought and proposes a longer-term program aimed at the root causes of Africa's economic problem.

Although now less than 2% of the budget, international programs are critical to American world leadership and to the success of our foreign policy.

CIVIL SERVICE RETIREMENT

There is growing recognition that civil service retirement has far more generous benefits and is much more costly than retirement programs in the private sector or in State and local governments. Accordingly, the administration continues its strong support of the civil service reform proposals advanced in last year's budget. In 1985, the administration will focus its legislative effort on three of those proposals, in modified form: cost-of-living adjustment (COLA) reform, a high 5-year salary average for the benefit formula, and increased employee and agency retirement contributions.

GI BILL RATE INCREASE

The budget proposes legislation to provide a 15% increase in the rates of educational assistance and special training allowances to GI bill trainees and disabled veterans receiving vocational rehabilitation assistance, effective January 1985. The increase will offset increased costs since GI bill benefits were last raised in 1981. It will provide an increase in monthly education benefit checks to 544,000 veterans and their dependents and survivors.

Continuing Reform of Our Federal System

The overall efficiency of Government in the United States can also be improved by a more rational sorting out of governmental responsibilities among the various levels of government in our Federal system — Federal, State, and local — and by eliminating or limiting overlap and duplication.

In 1981, the Congress responded to my proposals by consolidating 57 categorical programs into nine block grants. In 1982, a block grant was created for job training in the Jobs Training Partnership Act.

The administration is improving the management of intergovernmental assistance by providing State and local elected officials with greater opportunity to express their views on proposed Federal development and assistance actions before final decisions are made. Under Executive Order 12372, Intergovernmental Review of Federal Programs, which I signed in July 1982, Federal agencies must consult with State and local elected officials early in the assistance decision process and make every effort to accommodate their views. The Order also encourages the simplification of State planning requirements imposed by Federal law, and allows for the substitution of State-developed plans for federally required State plans where statutes and regulations allow.

Controlling Federal Credit Programs

Federal credit in all its forms imposes costs on the U.S. economy that must be weighed against its benefits. Federal intervention through guarantees and direct loans may misdirect investment and preempt capital that could be used more efficiently by unsubsidized, private borrowers. Because federally assisted borrowers are frequently less productive than private borrowers, large Federal credit demands, and the degree of subsidy involved in Federal credit activity, must be reduced if we are to improve prospects for economic growth.

The administration continues its strong commitment to control Federal direct loans and loan guarantees. It has supported the basic intent of proposed legislation to move off-budget Federal lending into the unified budget. It seeks other basic reforms in the way in which direct loans and loan guarantees are presented and controlled.

In the coming year, my administration will issue a directive establishing Government-wide policies on credit. This directive will be both an explicit statement of the administration's goal in providing credit assistance and a means of controlling the manner in which that assistance is provided.

Regulatory Reform

Federal regulation grew explosively throughout the 1970's. Whether well or poorly designed, whether aimed at worthy or dubious objectives, these rules have one thing in common: they "tax" and "spend" billions of dollars entirely within the private sector of the economy, unconstrained by public budget or appropriations controls.

My administration has taken steps to correct this problem. Under Executive Order 12291, all Federal regulations must be reviewed by the Office of Management and Budget before being issued to determine whether their social benefits will exceed their social costs. As a result of this review process, we have reversed the rate of growth of Federal regulations. Hundreds of ill-conceived proposals have been screened out, and hundreds of existing rules have been stricken from the books because they were unnecessary or ineffective. Equally important, numerous existing regulations have been improved, and new rules have been made as cost-effective as possible within statutory limits. We are steadily winding down economic controls that regulate prices, form barriers to entry for new firms, and other anti-competitive regulations. At the same time we are increasing the effectiveness of our programs promoting health, safety, and environmental quality.

Our regulatory reform program has been open and public. New rules and changes to existing rules now require public notice and comment. My Executive Order requires regulatory agencies to consider the interests of the general public as well as special interest groups in rulemaking proceedings. The Task Force on Regulatory Relief and the Office of Management and Budget have issued regular reports detailing the progress of regulatory reform efforts. *The Unified Agenda of Federal Regulations*, issued twice each year, describes all planned and pending regulatory changes in virtually all Federal agencies. The administration's *Regulatory Policy Guidelines*, published in August 1983, is the first comprehensive statement of regulatory policy ever to be issued.

I believe it is time the policies and procedures of Executive Order 12291 were enacted into law. Individual regulatory decisions will always be contentious and controversial, but surely we can all agree on the general need for regulatory reform. Making each Government rule as cost-effective as possible benefits everyone and strengthens the individual regulatory statutes. Regulation has become such an important role of the Federal Government that strong and balanced central oversight is becoming a necessity and a bi-partisan objective. The Laxalt-Leahy Regulatory Reform Act, which passed the Senate unanimously in 1982, would have accomplished this reform. I strongly urge the Congress to take up and pass similar legislation this year. In addition, my administration continues to support measures to deregulate financial institutions.

Improving the Efficiency of Government

It is important to continue to reduce the size of Government. It is equally important to use the remaining resources as efficiently and effectively as possible. My administration has begun to make great strides in doing exactly that.

During the past 3 years, we have initiated several Government-wide management improvement efforts under the guidance of the Cabinet Council on Management and Administration. They are:

—Reform 88;
—Personnel management reform;
—Federal field structure reform; and
—The President's Private Sector Survey on Cost Control.

These management improvement and cost reduction programs focus on 4 objectives:

—Reducing fraud, waste, and mismanagement;

—Improving agency operations;

—Developing streamlined Federal Government management systems; and

—Improving the delivery of services.

REDUCING FRAUD, WASTE, AND MISMANAGEMENT

This objective seeks better use of appropriated dollars. The President's Council on Integrity and Efficiency (PCIE) was formed in early 1981 and is made up of 18 department and agency Inspectors General. They recently reported $8.4 billion in cost reductions or funds put to better use in the last 6 months of 1983 and a total of $31 billion since they were appointed. The PCIE is beginning to direct its efforts toward preventing problems before they occur, through improved technology and better audit processes, as described in their latest report.

The PCIE also found that enormous waste was occurring because the Federal Government had never established an effective cash management system — despite the fact that it handles almost a trillion dollars in cash annually. This is currently being corrected by installing sophisticated, up-to-date systems that the Department of the Treasury estimates could save as much as $3½ billion a year.

When my administration came to office we found delinquent debt owed the Government rising at a rate of over 40% per year — with a total debt outstanding of over $240 billion. After only 2 years' efforts, this annual growth rate has been reduced to 2%. A credit pre-screening system is now being put in place, and automated collection centers are being installed.

Federal procurement involves annual expenditures of $170 billion. Procurement was an overly complex process with only 50% of our contract dollars awarded under competitive bid. My administration has replaced three sets of regulations with one, and we are now setting up a new pro-competitive policy to cut costs.

We have extended our fight to reduce waste and mismanagement to a direct attack on that nemesis that has always characterized the Federal Government: red tape and paperwork. We have already reduced the paperwork burden placed on the private sector by the Federal Government by well over 300 million hours. In this current fiscal year we intend to reduce the burden by another 130 million hours.

Further savings and improvements are possible. The President's Private Sector Survey on Cost Control (Grace Commission) developed numerous recommendations for savings and cost avoidance. These recommendations range from reducing costs of Federal employee retirement programs to upgrading the Government's seriously outdated and inefficient management and administrative systems. I have already included many of these ideas in this budget and will include more in future budgets. My administration will develop a tracking system to make sure they are carried out.

These are but a few of the efforts underway to make sure that appropriated funds go further and are used for the purposes for which they were intended.

IMPROVING AGENCY OPERATIONS

I am directing Federal agencies to coordinate their administrative activities so that they reduce their current operating costs immediately, rather than wait for future improvements in systems and technologies. Savings resulting from these efforts are reflected in this budget. These efforts include: (1) consolidating headquarters and regional administrative services; (2) requiring service centers to meet minimum productivity standards for processing documents; (3) using private sector contractors to provide support services where appropriate and economical; (4) reducing Federal civilian employment by 75,000 by the beginning of 1985, reducing higher graded staff, and improving personnel planning; (5) reducing office space by 10 %; (6) reducing printing plants by 25 % and publications by 25 %; and (7) eliminating the processing of documents altogether for most small agencies, by requiring them to obtain services from larger agencies that have efficient centers.

[STREAMLINING GOVERNMENT MANAGEMENT SYSTEMS]

As we are reducing the size of Government and reducing fraud, waste, and abuse, we also need to change fundamentally the way the Federal Government is managed. When I came into office, we found that the Federal Government lacked a well-planned compatible management process, so we set about developing one. This effort involves five major projects: (1) planning and budgeting, (2) financial management and accounting, (3) personnel management and payroll, (4) personal and real property, and (5) automatic data processing and telecommunications management. Responsibilities and resources for the development of each of these management systems have been assigned to those agencies that have or are capable of developing the most advanced management system in each category. Without this effort, the Federal Government would continue to operate in an inefficient manner that does not serve our citizens well.

IMPROVING THE DELIVERY OF SERVICES

My administration is looking seriously at the way the delivery of Federal services is handled across the country. The objective of this effort is to achieve improved service at lower cost, through improved technology and management techniques such as prescreening, computer matching, adjusted payment schedules, contractor and grantee performance incentives, and a streamlined field structure.

All of these efforts are being planned and coordinated centrally as part of the budget process. The results of these efforts will be reported to the Congress together with resulting savings and proposals to upgrade management of the Federal Government.

Conclusion

Vigorous, noninflationary economic recovery is well underway. The long winter of transition from the misguided policies of the past, with their inflationary and growth-deadening side-effects, is now yielding to a new springtime of hope for America. The hope of continued recovery to long-term noninflationary prosperity can be realized if we are able to work together on further deficit reduction measures. Bold, vigorous fiscal policy action to break the momentum of entrenched spending programs, together with responsible and restrained monetary policy, is essential to keep the recovery on track; essential to the Nation's future economic health and vitality. Limited measures to increase receipts will also be necessary to make our tax system fairer and more efficient. But it is important — more than important, *crucial* — to get the mix of spending restraint and receipts increases right. There must be substantial reductions in spending and strictly limited increases in receipts.

I call urgently upon the Congress, therefore, to take the actions proposed in this budget. Far too much is at stake to permit casual dismissal of these essential belt-tightening measures. The Nation has paid a high price for the prospect of a secure, prosperous, noninflationary future; that prospect must not be sacrificed to a sense of complacency, to an expedient ducking of the issues.

With confidence in the ultimate beneficial effects of our actions, let us seize the high ground and secure, for ourselves and our posterity, a bright and prosperous future — a future in which the glory that was America is again restored.

PRESIDENT'S ECONOMIC REPORT, ECONOMIC ADVISERS' REPORT

February 2, 1984

The Reagan administration February 2 released its annual economic report. The 343-page document included a seven-page report signed by President Ronald Reagan; the rest was the work of the president's Council of Economic Advisers (CEA), chaired by Martin Feldstein. The other members were William A. Niskanen and William Poole.

As with the budget message and State of the Union address, federal deficits were cited as the major economic worry. In his economic message accompanying the CEA report, Reagan termed the deficits "totally unacceptable" and said major plans to reduce them would be proposed in 1985. "The unwillingness of the Congress to accept the proposals that I offered has made it clear to me that we must wait until after this year's election to enact spending reductions coupled with tax simplifications that will eventually eliminate our budget deficit," he said. (Budget message, p. 99; State of the Union, p. 81)

The president's section of the report, however, generally was optimistic. Blaming the economic problems faced when he assumed office on "the inappropriate policies of the federal government," Reagan cited his accomplishments in reducing inflation, unemployment, and government regulation. Praising his administration's tax cut programs, the president said he had requested Treasury Secretary Donald Regan to develop a "fairer, simpler," and less burdensome tax system. Reagan referred again to proposals to increase the amount of tax-free contributions to Individual Retirement Accounts by married couples with only one wage earner.

The strong dollar was the principal cause of the huge U.S. trade deficit,

119

according to the president. But he said he was opposed to intervening in currency markets to alter the free value of the dollar. Reagan also said he remained "committed to the principle of free trade" and that it would be totally inappropriate to respond [to trade problems] by erecting trade barriers."

"As I look ahead, I am very optimistic about the prospects for the American economy," the president said. "If we continue to develop and pursue sound policies, our nation can achieve a long period of strong economic growth with low inflation."

Optimistic Scenario

The CEA report, required by law since 1946, projected that with sharp deficit reductions the economy would grow at a real — inflation adjusted — annual rate of approximately 4 percent for 1985 through 1988 and 3.75 percent in 1989. The president's economic advisers also envisioned a gradual decline in unemployment from an estimated 7.8 percent in 1984 to 5.7 percent in 1989. Using a measure of inflation based on the gross national product (GNP), the report said inflation would fall gradually from 5 percent in 1984 to 3.5 percent in 1989, in the CEA scenario. Interest rates on three-month Treasury bills also would drop from almost 8.5 percent in 1984 to about 5 percent in 1989.

The report cited recent growth in the economy and a decline in unemployment as evidence that Reagan's tax and spending cut policies, along with restrained monetary growth, had succeeded in turning around the "poor economic performance" of the 1970s. The report noted that the economy grew at an annual rate of 6.1 percent between the fourth quarter of 1982 and the fourth quarter of 1983 and that the unemployment rate had dropped from 10.7 percent in December 1982 to 8.2 percent one year later. In his testimony before the Joint Economic Committee, Feldstein said that "The near-term economic outlook is now far brighter and more certain than it was when I presented the administration's forecast to this committee a year ago."

Underlying Fears

But in sharp contrast to the administration's optimism about the state of the economy was the undercurrent of concern in the economic report about long-range deficit projections. The president's economic advisers warned that, without legislative remedies, the annual interest payment on the national debt could rise by $100 billion by 1989. In fiscal 1984 the interest payment was estimated to reach $149.5 billion. The report claimed a large federal interest burden would harm private investment as the government's borrowing needs restricted the amount of investment capital available to businesses and individuals. This could "reduce the *rate of capital formation and potential long-term growth of the economy," Feldstein testified. As the supply of funds available for investment diminished, interest rates would rise, he said. The Federal Reserve Board would then be pressured to increase the amount of money circulating in the economy, a move almost certain to reignite inflationary growth.*

In his economic message Reagan called for the continuation of restrained monetary growth in the face of such pressures and praised the Federal Reserve Board for its past efforts to curtail inflation. The report also noted that high interest rates and low inflation had made the dollar especially attractive on world markets, resulting in a record trade deficit of $65 billion in 1983 and a projected $110 billion in 1984 as U.S. goods became relatively more expensive.

During his appearance before the Joint Economic Committee, Feldstein said that proposals in the fiscal 1985 budget were insufficient to address the problem of mounting federal deficits. Without further action to lower deficits, Feldstein warned, the administration could not count on the high growth, low interest rates, and declining unemployment projected by the CEA. "I think the budget is inadequate to do the full job," the CEA chairman said. He added that the president's call for $100 billion in deficit reductions over the next three years was "clearly just a start."

Feldstein, who had come under fire late in 1983 for his public expressions of concern about the budget gap, said deficits would have to be cut to below 2 percent of GNP, or less than $100 billion in 1988, for the report's optimistic economic projections to materialize. The president's budget forecast a $152 billion shortfall in 1988. "If such deficit reductions are not enacted, the interest rates are not likely to fall over the next five years as we have projected and growth of real GNP is likely to be slower than we have assumed," Feldstein testified. "Moreover, larger deficits might induce a monetary policy that raises the rate of inflation in the years ahead."

The CEA's deficit forecasts were attacked by Regan during testimony before the Senate Budget Committee February 3. Regan disavowed the council's report and said of Feldstein, "I support this budget; apparently he doesn't."

In addition to warning about deficits, the economic advisers supported free-market solutions to the nation's agricultural problems, encouraged regulatory reform of the banking industry, and opposed "industrial policy" programs advocated by a number of Democrats.

Following is the text of President Ronald Reagan's Economic Report and excerpts from the Council of Economic Advisers' Economic Report, released February 2, 1983:

ECONOMIC REPORT OF THE PRESIDENT

To the Congress of the United States:

I have long believed that the vitality of the American economy and the prosperity of the American people have been diminished by inappropriate policies of the Federal Government: unnecessary government regulations that discouraged initiative and wasted scarce capital and labor; an inefficient and unfair tax system that penalized effort, saving, and investment; excessive government spending that wasted taxpayers' money, misused our Nation's resources, and created budget deficits that reduced capital formation and added to the burden of the national debt; and monetary policies that produced frequent business cycles and a path of increasing inflation.

I came to Washington to change these policies. The needed reforms are far from complete, but substantial progress can already be seen: the burden of regulation has been reduced, tax rates have been lowered and the tax structure improved, government spending on a wide range of domestic programs has been curtailed, and a sound monetary policy has been established.

Although the full favorable effect of those reforms on our Nation's rate of economic growth will take time to develop, some of the benefit of our economic policies is already visible in the current recovery. The economy's performance in 1983 was very gratifying to me. The 3.2 percent rise in consumer prices between 1982 and 1983 was the lowest rate of inflation since 1967. The recovery produced a sharp drop in unemployment and a substantial increase in the income of American families. The number of people at work increased by more than 4 million and the unemployment rate fell from a high of 10.7 percent in December 1982 to 8.2 percent in December 1983. The 6.1 percent rise in real gross national product (GNP) last year means that real annual income per person in the United States rose $700.

Reducing Unemployment

Despite the substantial reduction in unemployment, the number of unemployed workers remains unacceptably high. Continued economic recovery will mean millions of additional jobs in the years ahead and further declines in the rate of unemployment. In 1984 alone, the American economy is expected to add more than 3 million additional jobs. By the end of the decade, we will need 16 million new jobs to absorb a growing labor force. Only a strong and expanding economy can provide those jobs while achieving a progressively lower level of unemployment over the next 6 years.

Although economic growth is by far the most important way to reduce unemployment, special policies to help the structurally unemployed and particularly disadvantaged groups can also be helpful. To assist these individuals in developing job-related skills that will lead to productive careers in the private sector, I proposed the Job Training Partnership Act that I signed into law in 1982. Last year I proposed additional measures to increase opportunities for training and retraining. Although the Congress has enacted some of my employment proposals, I am still waiting for congressional action on others.

Of particular concern to me is the unemployment among teenagers. Such unemployment is not only a problem in itself, but is also indicative of lost opportunities to acquire on-the-job training and job-related skills. It is widely recognized that the minimum wage law is a substantial barrier to the employment of teenagers, especially minority teenagers. I have proposed that during the summer months the minimum wage for teenagers be reduced to 75 percent of the regular minimum wage. This reform would give many teenagers the opportunity to get a first job and acquire the skills needed to help them with subsequent employment and would not hurt adult employment. With an unemployment rate of nearly 50 percent among black teenagers and with only about 20 percent of black teenagers employed, we must act. The Federal Government must not be the source of barriers to employment.

Inflation and Monetary Policy

Reducing the rate of inflation was my most immediate economic goal when I arrived in Washington. In the preceding 24 months, the consumer price level had increased more than 27 percent. Many people feared the U.S. Government had lost its ability to control inflation. Until inflation was brought under control, a healthy recovery could not get under way.

The inflation rate has declined dramatically over the past 3 years. Between 1982 and 1983, the consumer price index rose only 3.2 percent. Americans can again have confidence in the value of the dollar, and they can save for the future without fearing that the purchasing power of these savings will be destroyed by inflation. I am firmly committed to keeping inflation on a downward path. We must never relax in our pursuit of price stability.

The basic requirement for a continued moderation of inflation is a sound monetary policy. I continue to support the Federal Reserve in its pursuit of price stability through sound monetary policy. Last year was a particularly difficult time for monetary policy because of the substantial changes in financial regulations. I am pleased that, in spite of these difficulties, the monetary aggregates at the end of the year were within their target ranges. I expect that in 1984 the Federal Reserve will expand the money stock at a moderate rate that is consistent with both a sustained recovery and continuing progress against inflation.

There are those who advocate a fast rate of money growth in an attempt to depress interest rates. Experience shows, however, that rapid money growth inevitably leads to an increased rate of inflation and higher interest rates. The only monetary policy that can bring interest rates down, and keep them down, is one that promotes confidence that inflation will continue to decline in the years ahead.

The Dollar and the Trade Deficit

The high interest rates in the United States and our low rate of inflation continue to make dollar securities an appealing investment for individuals and businesses around the world. In addition, the United States has been an attractive place for stock market investment and for direct business investment. The result has been a continued rise in the dollar's exchange value relative to other currencies of the world.

The sharp rise in the value of the dollar since 1980 has made it cheaper for Americans to purchase products from overseas, thereby helping us fight inflation. But the dollar's sharp rise has made it difficult for American businesses and farmers to compete in world markets. The decline in U.S. exports and the substantial rise in our imports has resulted in record trade deficits in 1982 and 1983. The trade deficit has been temporarily exacerbated by the international debt problems and by the more advanced stage of recovery in the United States than in the world at large.

Despite these problems, I remain committed to the principle of free trade as the best way to bring the benefits of competition to American consumers and businesses. It would be totally inappropriate to respond by erecting trade barriers or by using taxpayers' dollars to subsidize exports. Instead, we must work with the other nations of the world to reduce the export subsidies and import barriers that currently hurt U.S. farmers, businesses, and workers.

I am also firmly opposed to any attempt to depress the dollar's exchange value by intervention in international currency markets. Pure exchange market intervention cannot offset the fundamental factors that determine the dollar's value. Intervention in the foreign exchange market would be an exercise in futility that would probably enrich currency speculators at the expense of American taxpayers. A combination of exchange market intervention and expansionary monetary policy could reduce the dollar's exchange value, but only by causing an unacceptable increase in the rate of inflation. The dollar must therefore be allowed to seek its natural value without exchange market intervention.

Regulation

One of the four key elements of my program for economic recovery is a far-reaching program of regulatory relief. Substantial progress has been made during the last 3 years. The growth of new regulations has been reduced by more than a third. The demands on the private sector of government paperwork have been reduced by several hundred million hours a year. The Congress approved legislation that has led to substantial deregulation of financial markets and intercity bus transportation. The Federal Communications Commission, with our support, has reduced the regulation of broadcasting and of new communications technology, and the Interstate Commerce Commission and the Civil Aeronautics Board have gone far down the path of deregulation of competitive transportation markets. The benefits of these and other deregulation measures are now increasingly apparent to American consumers and businesses.

It is also apparent that substantial further deregulation and regulatory reform will require changes in the basic regulatory legislation. I urge the Congress to act on the several measures that I proposed last year on natural gas decontrol, financial deregulation, and reform of private pension regulation. I remain confident that there is a basis for agreement on measures that would reduce the burden of Federal regulations, while protecting our shared values and not jeopardizing safety.

Tax Reforms

The final installment of the 3-year personal tax cut took effect in July, giving a helpful boost to the economic recovery. The income tax rate at each income level has been reduced by about 25 percent since 1980. In 1984 a median income four-person family will pay about $1,100 less than it would have without these tax reductions. And, beginning in 1985, the tax brackets will be adjusted automatically so that inflation will no longer push taxpayers into higher brackets and increase the share of their income taken in taxes.

The Economic Recovery Tax Act of 1981 went beyond reducing tax rates to establish important reforms in the structure of the tax system. For businesses, the Accelerated Cost Recovery System increased the after-tax profitability of investments in plant and equipment. The sharp fall in inflation has also increased after-tax profitability. As a result, investment in business equipment has recently been quite strong despite the high real interest rates.

For individuals, the Economic Recovery Tax Act reduced the marriage tax penalty, the estate tax burden, and tax discrimination against saving. The response to the universal eligibility of Individual Retirement Accounts (IRAs) has been far greater than was originally expected. It is estimated that more than 15 million individuals now use IRAs to save for their retirement. Last year, I proposed to expand the opportunity for all married couples to use IRAs fully by allowing them to contribute up to $2,000 each per year to an IRA even if only one has wage income.

Further improvement and simplification of our tax system are sorely needed. The burden of taxation depends not only on the quantity of tax revenue that is collected but also on the quality of the tax system. I have asked the Secretary of the Treasury to develop a plan of action with specific recommendations to make our tax system fairer, simpler, and less of a burden on our Nation's economy. By broadening the tax base, personal tax rates could come down, not go up. Our tax system would stimulate greater economic growth and provide more revenue.

Government Spending

One of my principal goals when I came to Washington was to reverse the dramatic growth of Federal spending on domestic programs and to shift more resources to our Nation's defense. Although many doubted this could be done, both goals are being achieved. We must do everything that we can to avoid waste in defense as in other areas of government. But we must also be willing to pay the cost of providing the military capability to defend our country and to meet our responsibilities as the leading Nation of the free world. Outlays for defense had declined to only 5.2 percent of GNP in 1980, less than one-fourth of total government outlays. By the current fiscal year, defense outlays have increased to 6.7 percent of GNP and 28 percent of total outlays. Real defense outlays have grown 39 percent since 1980. Our spending on defense, however, remains a far smaller percentage of our national income than it was in 1960, when defense outlays took 9.7 percent of GNP.

Real spending has been cut on a wide range of domestic programs and activities. Many wasteful bureaucratic activities have been eliminated and the number of nondefense employees on the Federal payroll has been reduced by 71,000. We have examined every area of Federal Government spending, and sought to eliminate unnecessary and wasteful spending while protecting the benefits needed by the poor and the aged. As a result, total nondefense spending now takes a smaller share of our GNP than it did in 1980. Moreover, under present law, nondefense spending will continue to take a declining share of our GNP in the years ahead.

This reduction has been accomplished without any decrease in existing social security benefits or any change in the medicare benefits for the elderly. Spending on all other nondefense activities and programs has actually declined over 12 percent in real terms since 1980. Even with no further reductions in these activities and programs, their share of GNP in 1986 will be nearly back to the level of 1965.

I am committed to continuing the search for ways to reduce government spending. The budget that I am submitting to the Congress identifies significant savings in entitlement programs and reductions in outlays for other programs that are excessive or that are not the proper responsibility of the Federal Government. The Grace Commission has given us some 2500 ways to reduce wasteful spending that could save billions of dollars in the years ahead.

Budget Deficits

I have long believed that our Nation's budget must be balanced. A pattern of overspending by the Federal Government has produced a deficit in 22 of the last 23 years. My most serious economic disappointment in 1983 was therefore the failure of the Congress to enact the deficit reduction proposals that I submitted last January in my budget for fiscal 1984. We would be much closer to a balanced budget today if the Congress had enacted all of the spending cuts that I have requested since assuming office, and if the long recession and the sharp decline in inflation had not substantially reduced real tax revenue. In last year's budget I proposed changes in outlays and revenues that could put the deficit on a sharply declining path that, by 1988, would have been less than 2 percent of GNP and on its way to a balance of revenues and outlays.

The unwillingness of the Congress to accept the proposals that I offered has made it clear to me that we must wait until after this year's election to enact spending reductions coupled with tax simplification that will eventually eliminate our budget deficit. But we cannot delay until 1985 to start reducing the deficits that are threatening to prevent a sustained and healthy recovery. I have therefore called on the Democratic and Republican leaders in the Congress to designate representatives to work with the Administration on the development of a "downpayment" deficit reduction program.

I believe that this bipartisan group could develop a package that could be enacted this spring which would reduce the deficit by about $100 billion over the next 3 fiscal years. The package could include a number of the less contentious spending cuts that are pending before the Congress plus additional outlay savings based on the proposals of the Grace Commission. Additional revenue could be provided by measures to close certain tax loopholes — measures that the Department of the Treasury has previously said are worthy of support.

These deficit reductions can increase the public's confidence in our economic future and their faith in the ability of the political system to deal satisfactorily with the deficit. The downpayment package can be a first step toward full elimination of the remaining deficits. Even with a 3-year $100 billion package, the deficits projected for fiscal 1986 and beyond are totally unacceptable to me. They would be a serious threat to our Nation's economic health and a heavy burden to future generations. I am committed to finding ways to reduce further the growth of spending and to put the budget on a path that will lead to a balance between outlays and receipts. In 1985 I will submit a budget that can achieve this goal. But we must go further and make basic structural reforms in the budgetary process — including the line-item veto and the balanced budget amendment — that will keep spending under control and prevent deficits in the future.

Looking Ahead

As I look ahead, I am very optimistic about the prospects for the American economy. Substantial progress has been made in reforming the economic policies that will shape our economic future. If we continue to develop and pursue sound policies, our Nation can achieve a long period of strong economic growth with low inflation, and the American people can enjoy unprecedented prosperity and economic security.

ANNUAL REPORT OF THE COUNCIL OF ECONOMIC ADVISERS

The Strategy of Economic Policy

The economic recovery in 1983 was a very favorable combination of rising outputs, falling unemployment, and declining inflation. These economic improvements and the long-term economic strategy that the Reagan Administration has been pursuing since 1981 are a welcome change for the American economy.

The Administration's redirection of economic policy was a necessary antidote to the poor economic performance of the 1970s. The real earnings per week of the average employee were actually lower in 1980 than they had been a decade earlier. The unemployment rate doubled between the end of the 1960s and the start of the 1980s. The level of consumer prices more than doubled and the rate of inflation increased from 5.5 percent in 1970 to 12.4 percent in 1980. Net private capital investment declined from 7.1 percent of gross national product (GNP) in the 1960s to 6.4 percent of GNP in the 1970s and only 4.1 percent of GNP in 1980.

During these same years, the government expanded and tax burdens rose. Federal Government outlays for all nondefense programs rose from 10.3 percent of GNP in 1970 to 15.1 percent in 1980. Total Federal outlays rose from 20.2 percent of GNP to 22.4 percent of GNP despite the sharp fall in the GNP share devoted to defense.

Although Federal tax receipts took one-fifth of GNP in both 1970 and 1980, many taxpayers found themselves pushed by inflation into higher marginal tax brackets despite the absence of any rise in real income. A two-earner family earning twice the median income faced a marginal tax rate that was 26 percent in 1970 but 43 percent in 1980. The number of taxpayers facing marginal tax rates of 50 percent or higher rose more than five-fold during the decade. Inflation not only pushed people into higher tax brackets, but also distorted the measurement of interest income and capital gains, causing dramatic increases in the effective tax rates on real income from savings.

Nevertheless, the Federal budget moved from a position of near balance in 1970 (a deficit of only 0.3 percent of GNP) to a deficit of 2.3 percent of GNP in 1980.

By 1980 there was widespread agreement that the direction of economic policy had to be changed if economic performance was to improve. The accelerating growth of the money stock would have to be slowed in order to bring down inflation. The high marginal tax rates would have to be reduced and the tax structure reformed in order to take risks. The share of government domestic spending in GNP would have to be reduced in order to decrease the distorting effects of government programs, raise defense outlays, and reduce the budget deficit.

These aims guided the formation of the Administration's economic policy in 1981 and in the years since then. Now, 3 years later, monetary policy has been successful in reducing the rate of inflation. Government spending on domestic programs has been reduced to a smaller share of national income. Tax rates have been lowered and the tax system has been improved. . . .

ECONOMIC RECOVERY

The inherent vitality of the American economy was amply demonstrated in 1983. In this first full year of economic recovery, real GNP rose 6.1 percent and business output climbed 7.0 percent. Industrial production rose 16.3 percent in the 13 months following its November 1982 low, and the capacity utilization rate in manufacturing bounced back from 68.8 percent to 79.4 percent during this same period.

Civilian employment rose by 4.0 million in 1983 and the civilian unemployment rate declined from 10.7 percent in December 1982 to 8.2 percent a year later. Although unemployment remains unacceptably high, the progress in raising employment and reducing unemployment in virtually every demographic group has been gratifying. Civilian employment rose 4.0 percent between December 1982 and December 1983, while employment among blacks rose 5.0 percent and among teenagers rose 1.7 percent. The unemployment rate declined 2.5 percentage points, while the unemployment rate for blacks declined 3.1 percentage points and for teenagers declined 4.2 percentage points. Despite this progress, it is clear that more than cyclical recovery will be needed to reduce the very high unemployment rates among these problem groups. The Administration's employment and training policies and proposals . . . offer several ways of helping these individuals and others with temporary unemployment problems to find work.

The sharp increases in output and employment were accompanied by an inflation rate that was even lower than in the previous year. The GNP implicit price deflator rose only 4.1 percent in 1983 after rising 4.4 percent in 1982 and more than 8.7 percent in 1981. The consumer price index at the end of 1983 stood only 3.8 percent above the level of a year earlier, after rising 3.9 percent in 1982, 8.9 percent in 1981, and more than 12 percent in 1980. And the index of producer prices for finished goods rose only 0.6 percent in 1983, the smallest increase in nearly two decades and far below the 3.7 percent in 1982, 7.1 percent in 1981, and 11.8 percent in 1980.

The decline in price inflation accompanied smaller nominal wage increases and a slower rise in nominal compensation per hour. The 5.6 percent increase in compensation per hour was the slowest rise since 1967. In combination with the substantial cyclical improvement in productivity, the slow rise in compensation raised unit labor costs only 2.4 percent in 1983, far below the 7.9 percent rise in 1982 and the lowest since 1965.

Despite the slow rise in nominal compensation per hour, the low rate of inflation meant that real earnings and incomes increased significantly. Real average weekly earnings rose 2.5 percent in the 12 months to December 1983, after rising 0.5 percent in 1982 and declining in each of the 4 preceding years. Real personal income per capita rose 3.0 percent between the final quarter of 1982 and the final quarter of 1983 after rising a total of only 1.4 percent in the entire 3-year period between 1979 and 1982.

A significant problem in the otherwise outstanding recovery was the sharp decline in net exports. American imports rose while our exports of goods to the rest of the world declined. The U.S. merchandise trade deficit — the excess of imports of goods over our exports of goods — reached a record of about $65 billion in 1983, nearly twice 1982's record level of $36 billion. This trade deficit, and the even larger trade deficit projected for 1984, reflects several causes, including the decline of imports among less developed countries and the relatively advanced stage of the U.S. recovery, but of primary importance is the high real value of the dollar relative to other currencies. . . .

MONETARY POLICY

The fundamental guiding principle of the Administration's approach to monetary policy is that the rate of growth of the money stock should be reduced gradually until the rate is consistent with price stability. This principle is consistent with the general approach enunciated in recent years by the independent Federal Reserve.

Controlling the growth of the money stock may be viewed as a means of achieving a desirable path of nominal GNP. Because the growth of nominal GNP tends to follow the growth of the money stock, this strategy of monetary policy can be expected to be consistent with a gradual decline in the trend rate of growth of nominal GNP, although the mix of real growth and inflation is subject to other influences. In the remaining years of this decade, this decline in the rate of growth of nominal GNP should be compatible with both a continuing growth of real GNP and a continuing decline in the rate of inflation.

. . . An appropriate monetary policy must balance the principle of steady monetary deceleration with the need to take account of changes in asset preferences or institutional arrangements that cause sustained shifts in the velocity of money, i.e., sustained shifts in the ratio of nominal GNP to the money stock. There are, however, many uncertainties about the timing, magnitude, and direction of the effects of such financial changes on velocity.

The year 1983 was a time of significant change in financial regulations that substantially altered the nature of the monetary aggregates (M1, M2, and M3) and the pattern of portfolio demand for monetary assets. In December 1982 depository institutions were permitted to offer money market deposit accounts, a form of small-denomination time deposit with no limit on the permitted interest rate. These deposits are classified as a part of M2. Beginning in January 1983, Super-NOW accounts — checkable deposits with no ceiling on the interest rate — were permitted. These accounts are classified as part of M1.

The desirability of stable money growth rests on the stability of the demand for money relative to the stability of other relationships in the economy, and on the role of stable money growth in reducing inflationary expectations. A change in the available mix of financial assets or in the characteristics of the monetary aggregates may change the equilibrium ratios of nominal GNP to the monetary aggregates. The Federal Reserve can in principle adjust the supply of money to compensate for the shift in demand without altering the degree of liquidity in the economy or, equivalently, the likely growth of nominal GNP; however, because of the uncertainties mentioned above in practice it is often difficult to do so. As an example of these uncertainties, it is not clear at this time the extent to which the increases in the monetary aggregates in the early part of 1983 reflected demand shifts that will produce a sustained shift in the velocity of money. . . .

. . . The Federal Reserve appears to have followed a relatively passive strategy during the early months of the year. . . . This policy had the effect of not putting much pressure on interest rates. . . .

The Federal Reserve's approach to the very difficult task of adjusting the monetary policy to the new regulatory environment permitted major adjustments to occur in 1983 with minimal disruption in the financial markets. . . .

All too often at this stage of an economic recovery, as growth slows from the unsustainable pace of the recovery's first year, political pressures have built to try to reduce interest rates through raising money growth. The Administration rejects calls to abandon a sound monetary policy. Interest rates cannot prudently be lowered by creating more money. The Administration recognizes that if the Federal Reserve were to try to maintain a strong recovery through excessive expansion of money and credit the rate of inflation would inevitably rise and undercut the prospect for sustained growth of employment and output.

The Administration desires a steady growth of real GNP and a gradually declining inflation rate. The monetary policy consistent with this outcome is expected to be one of gradually declining rates of growth of the monetary aggregates. Although no regulatory changes comparable to those of 1982 and 1983 are expected, future shifts in institutional arrangements could cause changes in velocity that would require a recalibration of the money growth targets. It is important that any such recalibration be made only in response to a significant and persistent shift in velocity.

GOVERNMENT SPENDING

The second major aspect of the Administration's economic strategy is to reduce the burden of government domestic spending. For the first time in a half century, total appropriations for domestic programs began a sustained decline in real terms and total Federal spending on all nondefense programs began to take a declining share of the Nation's potential output.

... Even after adjusting for inflation, the Federal Government spent nearly four times as much on nondefense programs in 1980 as it had spent in 1960. Between 1930 and 1980 there was a dramatic increase in the role of the government and of government outlays in American economic life.

Of course, not all government outlays represent government purchases of goods or services. By 1980, 56 percent of Federal Government expenditures were transfers to individuals or to State and local governments. But transfers as well as direct purchases shift the use of the economy's resources and require a sacrifice by present or future taxpayers.

The speed at which many of the outlays grew was itself unintended and unanticipated, reflecting the so-called "entitlement" character of many of the programs introduced or modified in the 1960s or early 1970s. In such programs, the basic legislation does not appropriate a fixed amount of money for a particular purpose, but establishes rules that define who is eligible for benefits and the nature and amount of the benefits for which each person is eligible. Funds must then be made available for these benefits.

The medicare program is a good example of the unintended and unanticipated growth in outlays. Medicare was introduced in 1966 and immediately experienced costs that were far greater than had been generally anticipated. A decade ago, medicare outlays were less than $10 billion; in the current fiscal year, they will exceed $50 billion. Medicare actuaries now project that by 1989 the cost of the program will exceed $100 billion, or more than 2 percent of GNP. The dramatic growth of this program reflects greater utilization of health care services than had been anticipated and a very much faster rise in the cost of hospital care than had been forecast. For example, the cost of a day of hospital care, relative to all consumer prices, rose 67 percent in the decade before medicare was introduced, but jumped more than 100 percent in the decade after medicare began. ... The increase in utilization and the rapid rise in costs were not accidents of history but were in large part a direct response to the medicare program itself.

The medicare example is paralleled in a wide variety of other programs in such disparate areas as housing, nutrition, and disability insurance. Other new programs were enacted and old programs expanded without a proper understanding of the future burdens that they would impose on the economy. The members of the Congress who enacted these programs and the analysts who advised them frequently underestimated substantially the future costs of the programs that they were creating. They failed to anticipate that introducing new programs or liberalizing old program rules would markedly change economic behavior — that a higher level of retirement benefits would significantly reduce the average age of retirement, that the introduction of medicare and medicaid would contribute to an explosive growth of hospital costs, and that the more generous provision of disability benefits would be followed by a four-fold increase in the number of persons collecting disability checks.

In addition to underestimating future program costs, many analysts in the 1960s and early 1970s also overestimated the future growth of economic resources with which to pay for them. . . .

If the public had foreseen the future costs of the expanded social programs or the modest rate of economic growth during the past two decades, the Congress might not have enacted all of those programs and government would be smaller today. But once those programs were started, it became extremely difficult to stop them or even to reduce the level of benefits.

The Decline of Domestic Spending

Between 1960 and the end of the 1970s, government outlays on nondefense programs nearly doubled as a share of GNP. The government took a larger and larger share of the typical family's income and used it to finance programs that came to be widely regarded as neither generally useful nor directed at the truly needy. Many observers concluded that many well-intentioned programs were actually often exacerbating the very problems that they set out to solve. . . .

Since 1980 there has been a remarkable revolution in government spending. Social security benefits now take a decreasing share of GNP and all nondefense spending other than social security and medicare has already declined significantly as a share of GNP. . . .

Spending on social security benefits (including disability benefits as well as benefits for retirees and dependents) rose dramatically from 2.3 percent of GNP in 1960 to 5.3 percent in 1983. Although social security benefits will continue to grow in the future because of the increased number of retirees and rising benefit levels, the social security share of GNP has begun to decline and will shrink to 4.7 percent of GNP over the next 5 years.

The reduced share of GNP spent on all nondefense programs except social security and medicare has been even more dramatic. In 1980 government spending on these activities took 9.3 percent of GNP. In the 1984 fiscal year, that share is down to 7.5 percent of GNP. . . .

Between fiscal years 1980 and 1984 real government spending on all nondefense activities except social security and medicare will have fallen by 12.5 percent. This real 4-year decline, which includes outlays for everything from entitlement programs to the administrative costs of running government departments, is absolutely unprecedented. During each of the five 4-year periods between 1960 and 1980, this spending rose between 11 percent and 38 percent even after adjusting for inflation.

The changes that have been enacted since 1980 mean that the share of GNP spent on all nondefense activities except social security and medicare will continue to decline in the future even if the Congress adopts no further spending cuts. . . .

One implication of the very substantial reduction in nondefense spending is that it permits an increase in defense spending without an equal increase in tax revenue. The Administration's budget calls for a rise in defense spending from 5.2 percent of GNP in 1980 to 7.67 percent of GNP in 1989. For comparison, defense spending was 8.4 percent of GNP in 1970 and 9.7 percent of GNP in 1960.

Unfortunately, the rapid rise in interest on the national debt will absorb a substantial share of the budget savings achieved by reduced domestic spending. The net interest paid by the government will increase from 2.0 percent of GNP in 1980 to 2.6 percent in 1989, even if the rate of interest on Treasury bills declines from the current level of nearly 9 percent to less than 6 percent by the end of 1989. . . .

Despite the dramatic progress in reducing spending on domestic programs, government outlays are still projected to equal 23 percent of GNP in 1989, about 3 percentage points higher than in 1970 and 5 percentage points higher than in 1960. . . .

THE CHANGE IN TAX STRUCTURE

The third principal part of the Administration's economic strategy is to reduce the tax burden and restructure the tax system. The Economic Recovery Tax Act passed in 1981 substantially changed the quantity and quality of taxation. It reduced personal income tax rates by a cumulative 23 percent over 3 years. Special provisions reduced the tax on two-earner families, introduced the indexing of tax bracket and personal exemptions, and lowered the effective tax rates on income from saving and investment. The total Federal taxes paid by a median-income family, including both the personal income tax and the social security payroll taxes, will be $1,750 lower in 1984 than they would have been without the tax cuts. These changes represent a reduction of 36 percent in Federal income tax liabilities and of 26 percent in total tax liabilities.

The total share of GNP taken by taxes has come down significantly. . . . In fiscal 1980, all Federal taxes took 20.1 percent of GNP. In the current fiscal year, this tax share will be 18.7 percent of GNP. Continuing economic recovery and the rise in social security payroll taxes will raise the tax share of GNP to 19.4 percent by 1989, if there are no further legislative changes. Without the 1981 changes, the tax share would have risen substantially from the 20.1 percent share of 1980.

These tax reductions occurred despite the rise in the social security payroll tax. If the social security payroll tax is excluded, the reduction in all other taxes has been even greater, falling from 14.8 percent of GNP to

12.9 percent of GNP. This fall is equivalent to a $68 billion tax cut in 1984 alone.

The tax changes in the past 3 years have, however, gone far beyond reducing the amount of taxes and have achieved fundamental improvements in the nature of the tax system. The tax burden on the economy depends not only on the quantity of taxes but also on the quality. Although most taxes have adverse economic effects, some taxes are more harmful than others. Taxes are undesirable not only because they take away the fruits of labor, or risk-taking, and of savings, but also because they distort economic decisions and thereby lead to a wasteful misallocation of resources. Although there is no simple rule for improving the quality of taxes, there are a few useful principles. The most basic principle is to minimize the tax-induced distortions of economic choices — choices about which goods to buy, how much to work, how hard to save, and how to invest the capital that results from savings. A key implication of this principle is that the marginal tax rates paid on additional income or profits are more important than the average tax rates. A second implication is that taxes do more harm when levied on individuals or activities that are more responsive to tax rules. Taxes that reduce the incentive to save or that cause a misallocation of capital among different uses are particularly undesirable, because they unnecessarily increase the total economic burden of the tax system and reduce productivity and economic growth....

The favorable effect of these tax changes on saving can be expected to occur only gradually. At first, by transferring previously saved funds from existing accounts, many individuals can deposit the maximum $2,000 a year to an IRA without doing any additional saving. Some individuals may extend this period by borrowing. But, after a few years, most taxpayers will have exhausted all previously accumulated funds; they can then make additional IRA contributions only if they save more.

The new tax treatment of saving represents something far more basic than just an increased stimulus to saving. The universal availability of IRAs and the increase in IRA and Keogh limits will allow most American taxpayers to pay tax only on that part of their income that they do not save — that is, only on the part of their income that they consume. It is also true that two-thirds of taxpayers do not itemize deductions and therefore cannot deduct interest expenses. Thus, for most Americans, the income tax system has now been virtually transformed into a consumption tax. This is a very fundamental change in the character of our tax system.

An indirect but important source of reduction in the effective tax rate on the income from savings has been the fall in the rate of inflation....

The tax climate for business investment has also been substantially improved in the past 3 years. During the 1970s the rising rate of inflation combined with the old depreciation rules to raise very substantially the effective rate of tax on the income from investment in business plant and equipment. The 1981 changes in the tax rules governing depreciation, as modified in the Tax Equity and Fiscal Responsibility Act, and the sharp decline in inflation reduced this effective tax rate substantially. The result is higher after-tax rates of return on business investment, and therefore a renewed incentive to invest in plant and equipment.

The present strength of business investment in the face of very high real rates of interest can be attributed at least in part to the lower effective tax rates on business income and the higher real after-tax rates of return that result....

The recent reductions in high marginal tax rates and the improved tax treatment of saving and investment represent major improvements over earlier tax rules. Much more can and should be done, however, to reduce the adverse effects of the tax system on individual and business incentives and therefore on the potential income and growth of the economy. The President has emphasized his interest in further improvements of the tax law. The Administration will continue to examine possible directions for tax reform and will propose reforms aimed at making the tax system simpler, fairer, and more efficient.

REDUCING THE BUDGET DEFICIT

Despite the dramatic reduction in the share of national income taken by government domestic spending and the fundamental improvement in the character of our tax system, the Nation still faces the serious potential problem of a long string of huge budget deficits. Vigorous economic growth can eliminate the cyclical component of the deficit. But without legislative action, the structural component is likely to grow just as fast as the cyclical one shrinks. The Administration's economic projections imply that the budget deficit will remain roughly $200 billion a year — or about 5 percent of GNP — for the rest of the decade unless there is legislative action to reduce spending or raise revenue. Deficits of that size would represent a serious potential threat to the health of the American economy in the second half of this decade and in the more distant future.

Deficit Projection

The cyclical component of the budget deficit is the part of the deficit that occurs because the unemployment rate exceeds the inflation threshold level of unemployment, i.e., the minimum level of unemployment that can be sustained without raising the rate of inflation. This excess unemployment raises the deficit by depressing tax revenues and by increasing outlays on unemployment benefits and other cyclically sensitive programs.

The remaining part of the budget deficit, known as the structural component, is the amount of the deficit that would remain even if the unemployment rate were at the inflation threshold level. The Administration estimates that the inflation threshold level of unemployment is now 6.5 percent and will decline in the coming years as the relative number of inexperienced workers declines and as the Administration's employment policies are enacted and take effect.

... Because of the lower level of unemployment projected for 1984, a much larger share of the current year's deficit is structural. The projected deficit of $187 billion includes a cyclical component of $49 billion and a structural component of $138 billion. By 1989, the entire projected budget deficit is structural.

A rate of economic growth for the next 5 years that is sufficiently greater than the growth forecast by the Administration and by virtually all private forecasters could in principle eliminate the deficit without legislative action. However, a 1 percent increase in the current level of real GNP would reduce the budget deficit by only about $12 billion. It would require an increase of 40 percent in the projected growth rates over the next 6 years to eliminate the budget deficit by the end of the decade without a change in spending or tax rules. It would clearly be unwise to rely on such an unprecedented and improbably fast rate of growth. A prudent policy at this point must assume that economic growth alone will not eliminate these deficits.

The economic assumptions that are used to project the budget outlays and receipts are based on the premise that there will be a sound monetary policy and that future legislative changes will reduce budget deficits sharply in the years ahead. In the absence of legislative changes to reduce deficits substantially in future years, interest rates will be higher than projected and the real growth rate will probably be lower than projected. ...

Long-Term Consequences

The projected budget deficits would directly and substantially increase the future size of the national debt. If legislative action is not taken, the cumulative budget deficit would be more than $1,100 billion over the next 6 years. The annual interest on this extra debt alone would represent a permanent cost of about $60 billion in 1989, if interest rates fall as assumed, or at least $100 billion a year if the interest rates remain at their present level. These amounts are equivalent to between 10 percent and 17 percent of the personal and corporate income tax revenue now projected for 1989.

This growth of the national debt and the interest on the national debt shows that budget deficits do not eliminate the need for spending cuts or tax increases, but just postpone the time when extra spending cuts or larger tax increases must take effect to pay for current deficits.

The most important long-term economic effect of the prospective budget deficits would be to absorb a large fraction of domestic saving, and thereby reduce the rate of capital formation and slow the potential long-term growth of the economy. Federal borrowing to finance a budget deficit of 5 percent of GNP would absorb about two-thirds of all the net domestic saving that would otherwise be available to finance investment in plant and equipment and in housing. ...

If the current services budget deficits that are currently projected were actually to occur, the likely result would be to reduce net investment in plant and equipment to a substantially lower share of GNP than prevailed in the 1960s and 1970s. Net private investment has fallen from 6.7 percent of GNP in the three-decade period through 1979 to only 3.2 percent of GNP in the past 3 years. Much of this decline is attributable to the stage of the business cycle. The 1983 deficit strengthened the recovery and thereby boosted business fixed investment, although the government's competition for funds to finance the structural deficit also depressed the level of investment below what it would otherwise have been.

Deficits and the Recovery

The deficits will have effects on the economy recovery as well as on the capital stock and on long-term economic growth. To understand the effect of budget deficits on the economic recovery, it is important to distinguish the deficits in the early years of the recovery from the deficits that are projected for subsequent years. Although the projected future deficit would be likely to have serious adverse consequences on the character and possibly the duration of the recovery, the near-term deficits probably have a positive impact on the pace of recovery in 1983 and 1984. The tax cuts in 1982 and 1983 raised after-tax incomes and therefore contributed to the rise in consumer spending that has been responsible for so much of the recovery. Similarly, the direct fiscal stimulus of the large 1984 deficit will do more to raise demand in 1984 than the increased real interest rates that result from the 1984 deficit will do to depress demand.

It is the continuing string of large deficits projected out through the end of the decade and beyond that is the serious threat to the health of the near-term recovery. The prospect of such prolonged deficits inevitably raises the real long-term interest rate above what it otherwise would have been, reducing current activity in key interest-sensitive sectors and causing the recovery to be lopsided....

Budget Strategy

A major reduction in the structural budget deficit must therefore be achieved over the next several years. This must be done without causing a contraction of economic activity. Because the direct effect of reducing the budget deficit is to reduce government spending and private consumption, there must be an increase in investment and net exports if real incomes and economic activity are to remain at high levels.

A reduction in the level of the current or future budget deficits automatically stimulates investment and net exports by lowering the real rate of interest and the exchange value of the dollar. However, experience shows that the rise in investment and in exports follows the fall in interest rates and the exchange rate only with a substantial lag.

It would be unwise, therefore, to reduce the 1984 deficit by a very substantial amount. To reduce the deficit by a significant amount without jeopardizing the recovery, the financial markets should be given adequate advance notice of the intended deficit reduction. The result would be a stronger economy that could absorb the deficit reduction without a contraction of overall economic activity.

In the fiscal year 1984 budget that was presented to the Congress in January 1983, the Administration proposed a deficit reduction program that would begin with small reductions in the deficits of 1984 and 1985 but then would reduce the 1986 deficit by 41 percent and cut the 1988 deficit by 61 percent to only 1.6 percent of GNP. Unfortunately, the Congress failed to adopt those proposals.

The Administration is now taking a two-stage approach to dealing with the prospective budget deficits. The President has called upon the leaders of the Congress to establish a bipartisan group to work with the Administration to develop a "down payment" package that will reduce the deficit by about $100 billion over the next 3 fiscal years. The aim of these negotiations is to achieve a deficit reduction package in the next few months. This package would be comprised of some of the less contentious spending cuts still pending before the Congress, certain measures to close tax loopholes, and additional outlay savings achieved through improvements in management procedures and elimination of unnecessary or inefficient activities.

Such legislation to reduce the deficit by about $100 billion during the next 3 fiscal years would make a significant contribution to reducing deficits and the future national debt. It could also give increased confidence to the financial markets, business investors, and consumers that the projected deficits can be controlled and eventually eliminated. The result should be a stronger economy in 1984 and 1985.

Enacting a "down payment" package is just a first step in reducing budget deficits. The President has indicated that he will propose legislation in early 1985 that will further reduce deficits and point the way toward budget balance. If these proposals are enacted, the economy can enjoy continuing expansion and a reduced burden of national debt.

The United States in the World Economy: Challenges of Recovery

The international economy is in a much stronger position today than it was one year ago. In late 1982 the world was still in a severe recession, and prospects for recovery were uncertain; the third world debt crisis was a source of deep concern; and economic stagnation had given rise to strong protectionist pressures. In 1983 a vigorous recovery, originating in the United States, began to lead the world out of recession. Many of the high-debt countries made major strides toward successful adjustment. Despite increasing protectionist pressures, the open international trading system remained fundamentally intact.

But the outlook is not entirely sunny. The recovery is not a cure-all for the serious strains that remain in the world economy. From the U.S. point of view, the focus of these strains is the emergence of record trade deficits. Closely related to the problem of the trade deficits is the problem of the continued high value of the dollar in foreign exchange markets. There are also other economic troubles around the globe. Trade relations among the United States, Japan, and the European Community remain a source of friction. Much of Europe is lagging behind the recovery in North America. The high debt countries are finding the road back to financial health to be slow and painful. . . .

The most dramatic recent development in U.S. international economic relations is the rising trade deficit and associated capital inflow. The 1983 deficit in merchandise trade was about $65 billion, approaching twice the previous record, which was set in 1982. A deficit in the neighborhood of $110 billion is forecast for 1984, three times the 1982 level. The deficits signify loss of income and employment in those U.S. industries that depend on exports or compete with imports. A common reaction is one of concern. It is easy to draw the impression that there is a serious adverse long-run trend in the competitive standing of the United States in the world economy. The greatest danger is that such ideas will come to be believed, and that as a result, the Nation will opt for major departures from its traditional economic system. . . .

Although the 1983 and likely 1984 trade deficits are without precedent, they are not difficult to explain. To begin with, the United States has a normal or "structural" deficit in merchandise trade that is offset by a surplus in exports of services and therefore need not be a cause for special concern. But it is the recent increase in the trade deficit that has attracted attention. The increase can be broken down into three parts. First, the appreciation of the dollar has made it difficult for U.S. firms to compete in world markets. Second, there has been a substantial loss in net exports to debt-troubled countries. Third, the United States is experiencing more rapid growth in income, and therefore, in imports, than are Europe and Japan. These three factors concern economic perturbations that, though large, are believed to be temporary. The structural deficit is normal in that it would exist even in the absence of the temporary factors. . . .

The high value of the dollar in foreign exchange markets is the most important cause of the recent increases in the trade deficit. . . . [T]he dollar has appreciated sharply over the past 3 years. As of December 1983, the dollar had risen 52 percent against an average of 10 trading partners' currencies weighted by their shares in world trade, relative to the average for 1980. (Weighting countries by trade with the United States alone, which gives relatively less weight to Europe and relatively more to Canada and Japan, yields a smaller number.) Exchange rate trends sometimes match international differences in inflation rates, but that has not been the case in this episode. Very little of the appreciation of the dollar was offset by a more rapid increase in the foreign price level than in the U.S. price level. In other words the dollar appreciated not only in *nominal* terms, but in *real* terms as well. The real appreciation of the dollar between 1980 and December 1983 came to 45 percent. This means that U.S. firms are now offering their products on world markets at prices that on average have risen significantly relative to those of their competitors, when compared in a common currency....

... [T]he greatest danger, in the United States as elsewhere, is that the desire to boost exports and reduce imports will be reflected in protectionist measures. The only sound way to improve the U.S. trade balance is to adopt macroeconomic policies consistent with a recovery in which all sectors of the U.S. economy share. The only sound way to promote world trade is to adopt policies consistent with a recovery in which all members of the world economy share. In particular, it is essential to the favorable outcome of the debt problem that the debtor countries be allowed to increase exports to the industrialized countries. The liberal world trading system can only lose if its members resort to heightened barriers to the international flow of goods, services, capital, and labor. All parties can only gain if the debtor countries are restored to health.

Industrial Policy

Should the United States adopt an industrial policy? Proponents argue that such a strategy is necessary to revitalize our manufacturing sector. They claim that U.S. manufacturing has done poorly compared with the manufacturing sectors of other countries, and that we are losing our international competitiveness. These claims have led to the perception that manufacturing's share of our economy is eroding and that we are "deindustrializing." To reverse this alleged decline, some industrial policy advocates propose that the government encourage new high-technology industries and help older industries regain their former strength. They also recommend that the government assist declining industries to adjust more smoothly to lower levels of output and employment. Others propose government aid to prevent a decline in selected basic industries....

Some industrial policy advocates claim that the United States already has an industrial policy. They argue that such policies as trade protection and subsidies for exports and research and development are components of an industrial policy simply because they affect the composition of industrial output. The difference between our present policies and what they advocate, they say, is that the former is ad hoc industrial policy while the latter is coherent.

It is true that many Federal policies affect industrial output. But the argument about whether they constitute industrial policy, like all arguments about definitions, is pointless. What is relevant is whether the proposals of industrial policy advocates are a good idea. Should the U.S. Government have a larger role than it now has in deciding the composition of U.S. industry?

The answer is "no." An industrial policy would not solve the problems faced by U.S. industry and would instead create new problems. Industrial policy has a mixed record in Japan and has been unsuccessful in Europe. Most of the problems of U.S. industries can be solved with prudent monetary and fiscal policies. The best way to deal with the many changes in demand that occur in a dynamic economy is to allow investors and workers to respond to such changes. Because they reap the rewards of their successes and bear the costs of their failures, investors will seek out industries that pay the highest rates of return. Similarly, workers have incentives to work where they can earn the highest wages. The free movement of capital and labor in response to new profit opportunities and wage differentials increases growth. Government allocation of investment that ignores market signals usually stunts growth by diverting labor and capital from more productive uses. . . .

Food and Agriculture

American agriculture is one of the most successful examples of agricultural development in the world. The industry is very productive: only 3.1 percent of the civilian labor force produces enough to feed the entire domestic population at low cost and still export enough to earn almost 20 percent of the total export revenue of the United States. Although farmers in most countries earn much lower incomes than nonfarm workers, the average disposable income of the U.S. farm population over the past decade has averaged close to that of workers in the rest of the economy. Average wealth per farmer is much higher than of people employed in the rest of the economy, and half of American farmers have no debt.

Despite these successes, all is not well with American agriculture. Farm export earnings and asset values have declined for the past 2 years. Recent entrants and farmers who have recently expanded their businesses have experienced cash flow difficulties. Although the farm bankruptcy rate is well below that for nonfarm businesses, the number of farm bankruptcies has substantially increased. The fraction of the farm population with incomes below the poverty level is still almost double that for the nonfarm population.

In fiscal 1983, Federal Government outlays for farm price and income support programs totaled $18.9 billion, an increase of $12.3 billion in 2 years. To this must be added another $9.4 billion worth of payment-in-kind (PIK) commodities committed in 1983 to compensate farmers for reducing their crop acreage in order to reduce inventories. These programs cost taxpayers almost $12,000 per farm. While Federal expenditures have been curtailed in many domestic program areas, the cost of farm programs has exploded.

Farm programs affect not only the taxpayer but also the consumer. Some farm policies clearly benefit the consumer. In particular, federally sponsored research has lowered food costs by generating a steady increase in agricultural productivity. Other policies artificially raise food prices through price supports and restrictive marketing and trade practices. This reduces consumers' purchasing power.

The present Federal farm programs were designed to address the problems of farming as it existed in the 1930s, but American agriculture has changed dramatically since then. Farming has become a much more specialized, capital-intensive, and high-technology business. Many people justify farm income and price support programs on the basis of low farm incomes. But average farm family incomes of the commercial producers, to whom most benefits of the Federal programs go, are above income levels in the rest of the economy. Net farm incomes, however, vary substantially from year to year.

Exports now account for one-quarter of all farm sales. Yet present price support programs, along with the strong dollar, make U.S. agricultural products less competitive on world markets. If we value the foreign exchange earnings generated by farm exports and the market this provides for a quarter of the Nation's farm sales, our farm price and income support policies must become more market oriented than they are now....

Financial Market Deregulation

Over the past few years, financial markets have undergone sweeping changes of a magnitude not seen since the 1930s. Despite these changes, the process of market restructuring and regulatory reform remains incomplete. Additional regulatory changes of historic dimensions are being debated. The shape and scope of these reforms will be important to the American economy for decades to come.

The issues in financial regulation are many and complex. They include the safety and soundness of financial institutions, the problems of dealing constructively with changing technology, and the reduction of regulatory burdens to the maximum extent possible. Similar concerns are important in other industries where regulatory reform is being debated. But the financial regulatory reform issues are in many respects far larger.

Financial regulation is not simply a matter of protecting poorly informed investors — the usual focus of consumer protection regulation — but of protecting everyone. In the financial crises experienced in 1933 and earlier in U.S. history, well-informed, prudent investors and depositors found themselves ruined financially. From painful experience, we know that a failure of public policy with respect to financial markets can create damage that extends far beyond the financial services industry. Financial market failure can mean economy-wide failure — recession, widespread unemployment, and bankruptcies....

Of all the goals of financial regulation the goal of financial stability is paramount. In the 1930s, financial instability was widely attributed to the natural operation of competitive markets, and this view supported a very substantial extension of regulatory controls over financial markets. More recently, however, a renewed respect for the efficiency of competitive markets has developed, as well as increased recognition of the costs of regulation. Regulation tends to spread in unproductive directions and often causes industries to evolve less efficiently than they otherwise would. For these reasons, the promotion of efficiency by furthering competition is also an important regulatory goal. The purpose of regulation should not be to protect poorly managed individual firms from failure, but rather to prevent such failures from shaking the stability of the financial system as a whole. Regulations should be designed to achieve stability of the system, while individual firms are afforded the maximum possible freedom to compete and innovate....

The Outlook for 1984

... Administration policies are designed to achieve a long, sustainable economic expansion that takes the economy back to full employment with declining inflation. The assumption of 4.0 percent growth in real GNP for the 1985-88 period is a trend or average growth rate projection; the economy may grow somewhat more or less rapidly in any given year. In the Administration's view, any attempt to induce a substantially higher real growth rate by monetary stimulus might be temporarily successful, but growth accelerated in this way would not be sustainable. The result would soon be rising inflation and another recession....

... [T]he Administration has assumed a gradually declining rate of inflation over the 1985-89 period. This assumption reflects the view that the goal of stability in the general price level is appropriate because inflation not only is costly and inequitable in and of itself but also is disruptive of economic growth and employment stability. Also, eliminating inflation can be expected to reduce volatile changes in inflationary expectations, which are a major contributing factor to business cycle fluctuations.

The gradual reduction in inflation assumed by the Administration does not depend on a policy assumption that such a result will be "forced" by deliberate actions to choke off economic growth whenever there is any sign of a rise in inflation. Rather, the decline in inflation is the anticipated outcome of the assumed steady and predictable monetary and fiscal policies. As with real growth, it is expected that inflation may sometimes be higher and sometimes lower than the Administration's assumption, but that the trend will be downward as indicated.

Given the assumed decline in the inflation rate, it is reasonable to assume that the expected rate of inflation will also decline....

STATEMENTS ON DEATH
OF SOVIET LEADER ANDROPOV
February 10, 11, and 13, 1984

The Soviet leadership announced February 10 that Yuri V. Andropov died February 9 after a long kidney illness, less than 15 months after he succeeded Leonid I. Brezhnev as general secretary of the Communist Party of the Soviet Union (CPSU), the nation's top-ranking post. The Central Committee of the CPSU February 13 selected Konstantin U. Chernenko to succeed Andropov as general secretary and to lead the funeral commission. On April 11 Chernenko also was elected Soviet president. The assumption of the position of chief of state as well as party leader was viewed as a move to provide the new leader with additional prestige and flexibility, especially in foreign affairs. (Brezhnev death, Andropov background, Historic Documents of 1982, p. 871)

On learning of Andropov's death, President Ronald Reagan and Secretary of State George P. Shultz told Soviet leaders that the United States reaffirmed its desire "for constructive and realistic dialogue" with Moscow during the leadership transition period. The president February 11 devoted his weekly radio broadcast to the situation, saying, "There is no better time than now" for the United States and the Soviet Union to make an effort to negotiate their differences. "America is ready," Reagan said. "We would welcome negotiations."

Vice President George Bush, who headed the U.S. delegation to the funeral, met for 30 minutes with Chernenko February 14, the day of the funeral. In remarks to reporters February 15, Reagan said Chernenko had told the vice president that the United States and the Soviet Union should make certain "that regional conflicts did not get out of control"

145

and that there should be "safeguards against any inadvertent use of nuclear weapons." Reagan praised the "tone and words" of the new Soviet leader. But he added that Chernenko "did not retreat from . . . the basic Soviet position" of maintaining arms parity with the United States. Reagan said he thought "quiet diplomacy" was the best way to deal with the Soviets. "We seek whatever channels will be the most productive to us," he said.

Andropov's Legacy

Andropov had been selected to be general secretary after 15 years as the head of the KGB, the Soviet Union's internal security and intelligence agency. During his brief tenure, he attempted to improve the Soviet economy, which had long been plagued with waste and inefficiency. On assuming office, Andropov moved to shake up the bureaucracy, retiring ineffective ministers and promoting efficient managers to prominent positions. A disciplinarian, he was considered by many to be an independent thinker, good administrator, and astute politician. Under his leadership, there was some progress in combating corruption, but the heavy hand of government control of the arts and culture continued, as did harrassment of dissidents. After an initial impetus, some observers noted that Andropov's attempts at streamlining the government had been slowed by political infighting among old-line bureaucrats, as well as by his own poor health.

In foreign policy, Andropov's reign was less successful. The Soviet Union remained embroiled in the costly war in Afghanistan and burdened with expensive military commitments elsewhere. Negotiations with the People's Republic of China failed to bring about an improvement in the two nation's relations, which were noticeably cool. East-West relations deteriorated sharply with the breakdown of U.S.-Soviet arms control talks and the deployment by both nations of new kinds of medium-range nuclear missiles in Europe. The September 1, 1983, downing of a South Korean commercial airliner by the Soviet Union further complicated diplomacy. Two weeks before the plane incident, Andropov disappeared from view, and he did not reappear in public for nearly six months preceding his death. (Arms control talks, Historic Documents of 1983, p. 791; Korean airline tragedy, Historic Documents of 1983, p. 775).

These and other problems were among those confronting Andropov's successor.

Chernenko's Background

Born September 24, 1911, in the village of Bolshaya Tes, Chernenko joined the CPSU in 1931, graduating from a teachers' institute and the

Higher School of Party Organizers at the Central Committee. After completing army service, he worked his way up the party apparatus to the Kremlin, primarily in agitation and propaganda departments, as a protegé of Brezhnev. When Brezhnev became party secretary in 1956, Chernenko was assigned to the apparatus of the CPSU Central Committee, where he was named chief of Soviet propaganda. He became head of the Secretariat of the Presidium of the U.S.S.R. Supreme Soviet in 1960. Between 1966 and 1971 he was a candidate member of the CPSU Central Committee. In 1971 he was elected a member of the committee and in 1976 became its secretary. Chernenko became a member of the Politburo in 1978.

Although Chernenko assumed a more prominent position in the last year of Brezhnev's life — leading international delegations, speaking out on major issues, and appearing at public functions at the head of the Politburo just behind his patron — he was the losing candidate in November 1982, when Andropov was named to succeed Brezhnev. In an act of party loyalty, however, Chernenko himself nominated Andropov to become the new Soviet chief. Widely characterized as a "Bolshevik of the old mold," Chernenko was regarded as a conservative, unimaginative ideologue, loyal party member, and a firm believer in propaganda and party discipline. He was the oldest of the men named to lead the party since the Bolshevik revolution in 1917.

An announcement by Tass, the official Kremlin news agency, said the 12 members of the ruling Politburo unanimously recommended Chernenko's appointment and that the Central Committee, which had about 300 members, also was unanimous in approving the nomination.

Address to Central Committee, Appraisal

In a wide-ranging speech to the Central Committee immediately following his selection, Chernenko praised Andropov and endorsed many of his domestic policies, including the need for a "serious restructuring" of the economy. Concerning relations with Washington, he said Moscow remained committed to the policy of peaceful coexistence. "We need no military supriority. We do not intend to dictate our will to others. But we will not permit the military equilibrium that has been achieved to be upset," he said. "And let nobody have even the slightest doubt about that: We will further see to it that our country's defense capacity is strengthened, that we will have enough means to cool the hot heads of militant adventurists."

A number of diplomatic observers said they expected few dramatic changes in Soviet policy, particularly in light of the fact that Chernenko's appointment showed the aging "old guard" leadership remained in control. However, some viewed Chernenko as a transitional figure and a temporary extension of the Brezhnev era. "He clearly is not himself a major power," said Carl Jacobsen, director of Soviet and Strategic Studies at the Graduate School for International Studies at the University of Miami. "Chernenko is just a total mystery," said Peter Hauslohner, a political scientist at Yale University. "In terms of his personal qualifications, leadership or technical qualifications, his career betrays absolutely no talent, no particular leadership or problem-solving abilities." Dmitri K. Simes, a senior associate at the Carnegie Endowment for International Peace, cautioned against underestimating Chernenko. "He does not appear to be a formidable, dynamic leader, but I don't think you can reduce him to the simplistic image of an incompetent, colorless Soviet apparatchik [high-level bureaucrat]. He was sufficiently bright and forceful to understand what his colleagues wanted and to position himself sufficiently well during the Andropov rule," Simes said.

Following is the text of the February 10, 1983, Tass announcement on Soviet leader Andropov's death; excerpts from President Ronald Reagan's February 11 radio address; and excerpts from the February 13 speech by the new Communist Party general secretary Konstantin Chernenko. (Boldface headings in brackets have been added by Congressional Quarterly to highlight the organization of the text.):

TASS ANNOUNCEMENT

The Central Committee of the Communist Party of the Soviet Union, the Presidium of the USSR Supreme Soviet and the USSR Council of Ministers with deep sorrow inform the party and the entire Soviet people that Yuri Vladimirovich Andropov, General Secretary of the Central Committee of the Communist Party of the Soviet Union, President of the Presidium of the USSR Supreme Soviet, died after a long illness at 16 hours 50 minutes on February 9, 1984.

The name of Yuri Vladimirovich Andropov, an outstanding leader of the Communist Party and of the Soviet state, a staunch fighter for the ideals of communism and for peace, will always remain in the hearts of the Soviet people and all progressive people.

REAGAN RADIO ADDRESS

My fellow Americans:

I'd like to speak to you about a subject always on the minds of Americans, but of particular interest today in view of the death of Soviet leader Yuriy Andropov: our relations with the Soviet Union.

Changes of leadership have not happened often in the Soviet Union.

Yuriy Andropov was only the sixth Communist Party leader in the 66 years since the Russian Revolution. In recent months, he'd been totally absent from public view, so his death did not come as a shock to the world. Nevertheless, the importance of the U.S.-Soviet relationship makes his passing away a time for reflection on where that relationship is heading.

The changes in Moscow are an opportunity for both nations to examine closely the current state of our relations and to think about the future. We know that our relationship is not what we would like it to be. We've made no secret of our views as to the reasons why. What is needed now is for both sides to sit down and find ways of solving some of the problems that divide us.

In expressing my condolences to Mr. Andropov's family and to the Soviet Government, I emphasized once again America's desire for genuine cooperation between our two countries. Together we can help make the world a better, more peaceful place. This was also the message for the Soviet people in my address on Soviet-American relations last month. In that speech, as in my private communications with the late Chairman Andropov, I stressed our commitment to a serious and intensive dialog with the Soviet Union, one aimed at building a more constructive U.S.-Soviet relationship.

This commitment remains firm, and Vice President Bush will lead our delegation to Moscow for Mr. Andropov's funeral . . . .

As we engage in discussions with Soviet leaders, we recognize the fundamental differences in our values and in our perspectives on many international issues. We must be realistic and not expect that these differences can be wished away. But realism should also remind us that our two peoples share common bonds and interests. We are both relatively young nations with rich ethnic traditions and a pioneer philosophy. We have both experienced the terrible trauma of war. We have fought side by side in the victory over Nazi Germany. And while our governments have very different views, our sons and daughters have never fought each other. We must make sure they never do.

Avoiding war and reducing arms is a starting point in our relationship with the Soviet Union, but we seek to accomplish more. With a good-faith effort on both sides, I believe the United States and the Soviet Union could begin rising above the mistrust and ill will that cloud our relations. We could establish a basis for greater mutual understanding and constructive cooperation, and there's no better time to make that good-faith effort than now.

At this time of transition in the Soviet Union, our two nations should look to the future. We should find ways to work together to meet the challenge of preserving peace. Living in this nuclear age makes it imperative that we talk to each other, discuss our differences, and seek solutions to the many problems that divide us.

America is ready. We would welcome negotiations. And I repeat today what I've said before: We're prepared to meet the Soviets halfway in the search for mutually acceptable agreements. I hope the leaders of the Soviet

Union will work with us in that same spirit. I invite them to take advantage of the opportunities at hand to establish a more stable and constructive relationship. If the Soviet Government wants peace, then there will be peace....

CHERNENKO SPEECH

Dear Comrades,

I cordially thank the members of the Central Committee for the great honor bestowed on me — election as General Secretary of the Central Committee. I fully realize the enormous responsibility which is placed on me. I understand what important and exceptionally difficult work is to be done. I assure the Central Committee and the party that I will exert every effort, use all of my knowledge and experience to live up to this trust, to carry on together with you the principled policy of our party, which has been steadily and persistently implemented by Yuri Vladimirovich Andropov....

The convincing evidence of the correctness of the domestic and foreign policy of the CPSU [Communist Party of the Soviet Union], its conformity with the requirements and spirit of the times is the ardent countrywide support for this policy. The party firmly marches on the path upon which it embarked — the path of communist creativity and peace.

This is how it was in the past. This will always be so!

But we all realize, comrades, that the wish to advance on that path is not enough. We must be able not only to set correct goals, but also to work persistently for their attainment, overcoming any difficulties. It is necessary to evaluate realistically what has been achieved, without exaggerating and also without belittling them. Only this approach prevents mistakes in politics, the temptation to indulge in wishful thinking, makes it possible to see clearly, as Lenin said, "what we have done and what (we) have not ... yet done."

Yuri Vladimirovich Andropov was destined, comrades, to work at the head of our party and state for a short, painfully short time. We will all miss him. He passed away at the very height of great and intense work aimed at powerfully accelerating the development of the national economy, at overcoming the difficulties which our country encountered at the beginning of the eighties. But we all know what a large amount of work our party has succeeded in doing over that time, how many new and fruitful things have been introduced and reaffirmed in practice. Carrying on and further advancing by collective efforts the work started under the leadership of Yuri Vladimirovich is the best way of paying tribute to his memory and ensuring continuity in politics.

Continuity is not an abstract notion, but a real live cause. And its essence comes down primarily to moving forward, without stopping. This implies advancement relying on everything that has been accomplished earlier, creatively enriching it, concentrating the collective thought and the energy of the Communists, the working class and all people on the unresolved tasks, on the key problems of the present and future. All this imposes a deep obligation upon us.

The strength of our party is in its unity, adherence to Marxism-Leninism and ability to develop and guide the creative activity of the masses, to unite them ideologically and organizationally, under the guidance of the tested Leninist principles and methods. You know, comrades, what immense attention our Central Committee, Politburo of the Central Committee and Yuri Vladimirovich Andropov paid recently to the issues of perfecting the work of the state apparatus and improving the style of party leadership.

One of these issues is a clear distinction between the functions of party committees and the tasks of state and economic bodies, eliminating duplication in their performance. This is a major issue of political significance. Frankly speaking, not everything has been properly adjusted here. It happens that workers at Soviets, ministries and enterprises do not display the necessary independence, but leave to party bodies matters which they should handle themselves. The practice of substituting for economic managers disenchants the cadres. Moreover, this harbors the danger of weakening the role of the party committee as a body of political guidance. For party committees handling economic issues means, above all, being concerned with people engaged in the economy. This must always be borne in mind.

[Economic, Social Issues]

Comrades, a month and a half ago, at the December plenum of the Central Committee, we gave an all-round appraisal of the state of affairs in the country's social and economic development. The resolution it adopted emphasized the importance of maintaining the tempo achieved and general intent to get things going, steadily enhancing the level of party and state guidance over the economy, actively developing positive processes and imparting to them a stable character. It is our direct duty to implement the plenum's instructions in a consistent way.

All of our experience confirms: The most important source of the party's strength were, are and will be its contact with the masses, the civic activity of millions of working people and their practical attitude to production matters and to problems of public life. . . .

The broad response by the country's work collectives to the December plenum's call for raising by one per cent above plan labor productivity and additionally reducing production costs by 0.5 per cent gives rise to profound satisfaction. . . .

I think it is necessary to consider the question of directing all means and resources that will be obtained as a result, and they will not be insignificant, to improving the working and living conditions of Soviet people, medical services and housing construction. This would fully meet the supreme goal of party policy — all-round concern for the benefit of man.

In general, comrades, we must probably think of providing better material and moral incentive to working people for creative initiatives and innovation.

Social justice underlies the very foundation of the Soviet system. This constitutes its immense strength. That is why it is so important that it be strictly observed in everyday affairs, whether the matter concerns salaries or bonuses, distribution of apartments or passes (to a health resort), or awards, in brief, so that everything be fair, in accordance with each person's labor contribution to our common cause. . . .

The question of organization and order is a key, principled one for us. There can be no two views on this. Any slackness or irresponsibility brings to society not only material losses. They inflict serious social and moral damage. We, Communists, and millions of Soviet people understand this well. And it is quite natural that the measures adopted by the party with a view to enhancing labor, production, planning and state discipline and strengthening socialist law have evoked countrywide approval.

We have already succeeded in making some progress in this field, and everybody knows what salutary effect this has had on production, on our social life and simply on how people feel. Yet it would be wrong to believe that everything has already been done. No, comrades, life teaches that by no means should there be any relaxing here.

As far as the guidelines for the development of our economy are concerned, they have been clearly outlined by the party. Intensification, accelerated introduction of the achievements of science and technology into production and the implementation of large-scale comprehensive programs are all designed to raise, in the final analysis, the productive forces of our society to a qualitatively new level.

The system of economic management and our whole economic mechanism need a serious restructuring. Work in this direction has only been started. It includes a large-scale economic experiment for broadening the rights and increasing the responsibility of the enterprises. A search is under way for new forms and methods of management in the field of services. They will undoubtedly be very useful and will help us resolve the strategically important problem of increasing the effectiveness of the entire national economy. . . .

We expect from our economic executives more independence at all levels, a bold search and, if necessary, a well-justified risk in the name of increasing the effectiveness of the economy and ensuring a rise in the living standards of the people.

You know that in the past year the CPSU Central Committee and the government have drawn up and adopted a number of decisions on principled issues of economic development. These decisions have given the party and economic bodies certain levers for increasing the effectiveness of production and accelerating the country's economic development.

The planned measures, and these measures are not only of economic but also of great political significance, will be put into practice only if their implementation becomes the main component of every party organization's and every working person's everyday work. . . .

It is no less important now to ensure an increasingly closer interconnection between the economic, social and intellectual advancement of Soviet society. It is impossible to raise the economy to a qualitatively new level without creating the necessary social and ideological prerequisites for that. It is likewise impossible to resolve pressing problems of the development of socialist consciousness without resting upon a firm foundation of economic and social policy. . . .

[International Relations]

Comrades, in drawing up plans for the further development of our country, we cannot help but take into account the situation now developing in the world. And, as you know, it is now complicated and tense. The correct course of the party and the Soviet state in the sphere of foreign policy acquires still greater significance in these conditions. . . .

It is absolutely clear, comrades, that the success of the effort to preserve and strengthen peace depends in a considerable measure on how great the influence of the socialist countries in the world arena is and how vigorous, purposeful and coordinated their actions will be. Our countries have a vital stake in peace. In the name of this purpose we will strive to broaden cooperation with all the socialist countries. By developing and deepening comprehensively cohesion and cooperation with all countries of the socialist community in all fields, including certainly, such an important field as the economic one, we make a great contribution to the cause of peace, progress and the security of peoples.

Addressing the fraternal countries, we say: The Soviet Union will also be your reliable friend and true ally.

One of the fundamentals of our party's and the Soviet state's foreign policy has been and will remain solidarity with the peoples which have shattered the fetters of colonial dependence and embarked on the path of independent development. . . .

Now, about relations with the capitalist countries. The great Lenin bequeathed to us the principle of peaceful coexistence of states with different social systems. We are invariably loyal to this principle. Nowadays, in the age of nuclear weapons and superaccurate missiles, people need it as never before. Deplorably, some leaders of the capitalist countries, to all appearances, do not clearly realize, or do not wish to realize that.

We can very well see the threat created today to humankind by the reckless, adventurist actions of imperialism's aggressive forces — and we say it in full voice, drawing the attention of the peoples of the whole Earth to that danger. We need no military superiority. We do not intend to dictate our will to others. But we will not permit the military equilibrium that has been achieved to be upset. And let nobody have even the slightest doubt about that: We will further see to it that our country's defense capacity is strengthened, that we will have enough means to cool the hot heads of militant adventurists. This, comrades, is a very substantial prerequisite for preserving peace.

The Soviet Union as a great socialist power fully realizes its responsibility to the peoples for preserving and stregthening peace. We are open to peaceful, mutually beneficial cooperation with the states of all continents. We are for a peaceful settlement of all disputable international problems through serious, balanced and constructive talks. The USSR will cooperate in full measure with all states which are prepared to assist through practical deeds in lessening international tensions and creating an atmosphere of trust in the world. In other words, with those who will really lead things not to preparation for war but to a strengthening of the fundamentals of peace. We believe that with these aims full use shall be made of all the existing levers, including, certainly, the United Nations Organization, which has been created precisely for preserving and strengthening peace. . . .

STATE DEPARTMENT REPORT ON HUMAN RIGHTS PRACTICES
February 10, 1984

In its annual human rights report to Congress released February 10, the State Department said that serious human rights violations continued to be made throughout much of the world in 1983, with some significant progress observed in Central and South America.

The 1,485-page report covering 160 nations criticized deteriorating conditions in countries such as Iran and the Soviet Union, where the governments had intensified repression of citizens, often resorting to illegal detention, torture, and death. The Soviet Union was charged with an "escalation of efforts to eliminate free expression," notably among "Christians, Jews, free trade union organizers, and independent peace activists." The situation in Iran, with the increased persecution of religious minorities, was considered to be "one of the worst in the world," according to the report.

In contrast, however, the study found conditions improved throughout much of Latin America, where there was a "clear trend" toward genuine democracy. In releasing the report, Elliott Abrams, assistant secretary of state for human rights, made particular note of progress in Argentina, which in 1983 had made the successful transition from a military to civilian elected government. "The recent election in Argentina is only the latest of a series of victories for democracy in Central and South America," Abrams said. "The stereotype of a Latin America run entirely by dictators is being outdated." Other Latin American nations cited for improved human rights practices were Brazil, Panama, and Peru. (1983 human rights report, Historic Documents of 1983, p. 181)

Reagan Administration Policies

The introduction to Country Reports on Human Rights Practices *for 1983 outlined President Ronald Reagan's two-track policy of immediately speaking out against "gross affronts to human rights, such as the incarceration of Soviet dissidents in psychiatric wards," while at the same time pursuing the long-range goal of encouraging the development of democratic governments. "Too often our human rights policy has been simply reactive, responding to violations after they have occurred rather than working to prevent them," the report added.*

The introduction reflected the growing debate in Congress and among the American public over Reagan's policy of lending military and economic aid to Central America, notably to El Salvador, where human rights activists estimated that 35,000 civilians had been killed by death squads.

Human rights organizations that annually reviewed the State Department report, the Lawyers' Committee for International Human Rights, Americas Watch, and Helsinki Watch, applauded most of the evaluations as comprehensive but criticized the findings in several countries considered allies of the United States, including El Salvador. "There is political bias," concluded the groups in a joint statement.

Human Rights Defined

For its yearly analysis the State Department defined human rights within two broad categories. First was the "right to be free from governmental violations of integrity of the person — violations such as killings, torture, cruel, inhuman, or degrading treatment or punishment; arbitrary arrest or imprisonment; denial of fair public trial; and invasion of the home." Second, the report measured human rights as the "right to enjoy civil and political liberties, including freedom of speech, press, religion, and assembly; the right of citizens to participate in governing themselves; the right to travel freely within and outside one's own country; the right to be free from discrimination based on race or sex."

The study originally was mandated by the Foreign Assistance Act of 1961, which required an annual State Department review of human rights activities in nations receiving aid from the United States and, since 1979, in each country belonging to the United Nations. Used in part to determine the level of foreign aid to many countries, the government assessment was compiled for Congress with information furnished by U.S. missions abroad, international human rights organizations, press reports, and government data.

After providing in chilling detail the forms of repression practiced throughout much of the world, the 1983 report concluded that the Reagan administration policy of promoting democracy was vital to ensure the safeguarding of human rights. " 'Human rights' is not something added on to our foreign policy, but its ultimate purpose: the preservation and promotion of liberty in the world."

Following are excerpts from the State Department's Country Reports on Human Rights Practices for 1983, *released February 10, 1983:*

Argentina

In 1983 there was a dramatic improvement in human rights as Argentina successfully made the transition from a military Government to an elected civilian Government. There was also a continuous expansion of free and democratic political activity. Political debate was free and open, and all parties had full access to the media. There was a high level of public participation in the primaries, the campaign, and the October 30 elections. Dr. Raul Alfonsin of the Radical Civic Union was elected President on October 30 with 52 percent of the vote and was inaugurated on December 10. Over 14,000 national, provincial, and local officials were also chosen.

During 1983 there was also considerable progress toward respect for civil rights. Press restrictions were significantly relaxed and controls on the electronic media, largely government-owned, were less restrictive than at any time since the 1976 military coup. The judicial branch displayed increasing independence from the executive. For example, even prior to the transition to a civilian elected government the courts invalidated an executive decree and ordered arrests of a number of former military officers. Trade union freedom was greater than at any time in the recent past. Strikes occurred, including two national strikes, although they were technically illegal.

There were also major improvements in respect for individual rights during the year. The state of siege provision, which had permitted the curtailment of many civil and political freedoms since 1976, was lifted in October and the remaining prisoners held without trial under the state of siege were released during 1983 or remanded to civilian courts. In his inaugural address on December 10, President Alfonsin called for "the dismantling of the state's repressive machinery." . . .

For the third year in a row, there were no confirmed permanent disappearances in 1983. Human rights groups continued to demand a complete accounting for past disappearances and punishment for those responsible. The military Government published its "final report" on April 28, which said that all so-called "disappeared" persons were dead, in hiding, or living in exile. It subsequently promulgated a law granting an amnesty to those who had committed crimes in connection with the so-called "dirty war" against terrorism and a strict new anti-terrorism law. On December 27, President Alfonsin signed into law legislation approved earlier by both houses of congress repealing the amnesty law. In addition,

President Alfonsin decreed in December the creation of a 16-member National Commission on the Disappearance of Persons to help clarify the fate of people who disappeared. Alfonsin also ordered the Armed Forces Supreme Council to try all nine leaders of the military governments during the period 1976-1982 for "homicide, illegal imprisonment, and torture of prisoners" and ordered that legal action be taken against seven terrorist leaders for their crimes during that same period.

Argentina was beset by a number of severe economic problems in 1983. The military Government altered its earlier economic policies by reducing its reliance on the free market in an attempt to deal with an annual rate of inflation of approximately 400 percent and a large short-term foreign debt. Nevertheless, Argentina's population of 29.6 million had a per capita Gross National Product of over $4,000. Real wages increased by over 20 percent in 1983.

In summary, Argentina made dramatic progress in human rights in 1983. In little more than a year, the country went from a military government to a functioning democracy, complete with an independent judiciary, a free press, and a strong opposition....

Cuba

Cuba has been ruled for 25 years by one man, Fidel Castro, and a group which seized power in 1959. Working through the state bureaucracy, and a network of subordinate organizations, the Communist Party dominates all aspects of daily life, controlling the means of production and distribution of all goods, services and information, public communication, public welfare, and education, as well as national defense, foreign relations and public security. Internal security is under the direction of the Ministry of Interior, which operates the border guard (both sea and land) and several police forces, regulates migration, and maintains a system of neighborhood informers and block wardens known as the Committees for the Defense of the Revolution (CDR). Although extreme poverty is uncommon, scarcity is the hallmark of the Cuban economy, and many basic necessities are rationed. Long lines of Cubans wait for food and manufactured goods which are limited in quality and quantity.

New reports in 1983 confirmed information obtained in previous years that the Cuban Government continues to violate human rights on a large scale. For instance, in January 1983 death sentences were pronounced on several persons who tried to organize an independent trade union. Their defense attorneys were later detained without charges. There are credible reports that summary executions also have been carried out in various parts of the country. Some recently released political prisoners confirmed that Cuban authorities are still practicing torture and other forms of cruel and inhuman treatment or punishment. Other political prisoners have been kept in jail after the expiration of their sentences, and some former political prisoners have been re-arrested without explanation. A number of

HUMAN RIGHTS REPORT

lawyers and judges have been arrested on allegations of corrupt practices but who may actually have been resisting intensification of security restrictions on dissent in Cuba. There have been persistent reports that the suicide of Minister of Justice Dorticos, a former President of Cuba, was linked to his distress over this matter. Cuba continues to deny that it violates the most basic human rights of its citizens but has refused to allow representatives of outside human rights organizations to visit the country.

In the wake of economic distress in Cuba, it is probable that repression of human rights in Cuba will intensify. These conditions produced an explosion of popular discontent in 1980, leading to mass emigration when thousands eagerly responded to Cuban Government encouragement to enter the United States illegally by boat. With such a safety valve currently not available, Cuban authorities will be more watchful for signs of public restiveness or attempts to express dissatisfaction with the Cuban leadership or its policies. . . .

Cuban secret police commonly round up persons in nighttime arrests; friends, neighbors, and family members have no knowledge of their fate and frequently are too terrified to ask. . . .

Freedom of speech and press does not exist in Cuba. The media is used exclusively to disseminate officially approved news and opinion. The State owns and controls all means of communication. . . .

The Cuban Government routinely denies that any violations of human rights occur, but it refuses permission for any outside non-governmental organization to investigate charges that violations have occurred. . . .

El Salvador

El Salvador is a democratic republic governed by a multiparty Government of National Unity which was named by a Constituent Assembly elected freely in 1982. Democracy in El Salvador continues to be limited by the state of siege which suspends some constitutional rights in a response to the military emergency resulting from guerrilla attacks. The armed forces remain a significant political force in the country, and the extreme left does not participate in the political system. In October 1979 a right-wing military government was overthrown by a group of reformist military officers. This military junta was replaced in January 1980 by a joint Christian Democratic Party-Armed Forces government. After decades of social inequality and repression, this Government initiated major economic and political reforms. These reforms continue to progress although their benefits have been reduced by violent resistance from the extreme right and by relentless guerrilla warfare from the extreme left abetted by Cuba and Nicaragua. In 1983 El Salvador adopted a new constitution drafted by the Constituent Assembly in preparation for a presidential election in March 1984. With this election, the democratic structure envisaged by the coup of 1979 will be in place.

The Salvadoran Government's authority is currently being contested by

159

the Farabundo Marti National Liberation Front (FMLN) — a coalition of Marxist/Leninist-led guerrilla organizations. The political affiliate of this organization, the Revolutionary Democratic Front (FDR), includes elements of social democratic origin. One of the strategies of the FMLN involves the destruction of the Salvadoran economic infrastructure. Also targeted are municipal and national government installations, military personnel, and alleged government collaborators. The guerrillas and the FDR have published a general public program for a future government which includes a mixed economy and maintenance of certain individual liberties. In internal documents and speeches to their own organizations, FMLN leaders embrace the concepts of dictatorship of the proletariat, of the vanguard role of the revolutionary movement with regard to the rest of society, and of democratic centralism or disciplined adherence to decisions passed down by leaders. Political decisionmaking within the guerrilla movement takes place in some cases by bargaining among the leaders of its constituent factions, in other cases by intimidation and assassination. During 1983 one FMLN leader, Comandante Ana Maria (Melinda Amaya Montes) was murdered on the orders of another guerrilla leader Cayetano Carpio, who committed suicide when his involvement in the murder was discovered.

Abuse of human rights remains a central problem, despite efforts of the government to end violence from right-wing death squads, some of which have links to the security forces, and from its own security forces, as well as from the guerrilla left. The level of political violence remains high, but noncombatant deaths have declined steadily since a peak in 1980. The number of disappearances in 1983 remained at about the same level as in 1982. Elements within the Government security forces are still believed to use torture as arbitrary punishment or to extract information from suspected leftists. Individuals can be and are arrested without warrants, detained for investigation, sometimes for long periods before charges are brought, and, if charged with such crimes as sedition and treason, rarely brought to trial.

All human rights conditions in El Salvador are strongly affected by the ongoing civil strife. As is common during civil strife, the achievement of a public order that would protect each person's rights has been disrupted by military operations, partisan hatreds, acts of revenge, the satisfaction of personal grudges, pervasive fear, and a prevailing uncertainty dominated by violence. This situation contributed to, and is complicated by, the near-paralysis of the judicial system, which is caused in part by corruption and intimidation and which is most evident when crimes of a political nature are being considered. . . .

The most profound recent change has been the opening up of the political system and the restoration of government accountability through elections. This new political dynamic began with elections for a Constituent Assembly in March 1982. Some 1.5 million Salvadorans voted; only the extreme left refused to participate. The March 1982 elections produced an

Assembly in which no party held an absolute majority but which proved capable of drafting and approving a modern, liberal constitution. A multiparty Government of National Unity, named by the Constituent Assembly, has functioned slowly but successfully by consensus.

The new Constitution, which entered into force on December 20, 1983, establishes a republican, pluralistic form of government; strengthens the legislative branch and enhances judicial independence; improves safeguards for individual rights; establishes safeguards against excessive provisional detention and unreasonable searches; and protects the legal bases of land reform....

The Government of El Salvador is seeking a political solution to the armed conflict through a dialogue on democratic elections within El Salvador and participation in the regional Contadora process. El Salvador's Peace Commission remains prepared to meet with the armed left and its political associates to discuss their participation in free elections, including physical security for candidates and access to the media.

In 1980 the civilian-military junta enacted a wide-sweeping program of land reform to transfer land ownership from a small number of large holders to farmers who had previously worked the land as laborers, renters, or sharecroppers. Although plagued by problems including illegal evictions of beneficiaries, difficulties in compensating former owners, and violence, the land reform is making steady progress.

Major efforts are underway to ensure more effective functioning of the criminal justice system, including provision of greater judicial independence under the new Constitution and the creation of two legal reform commissions. The Government of El Salvador is developing programs to improve investigative capacities and protection for participants in the legal process and to modernize penal and evidentiary codes....

Far right death squads, some of which have had links with elements in the security forces, assumed a higher profile during the last half of 1983 by targeting prominent individuals and forcing the media to carry their communiques. The "Maximiliano Hernandez Martinez Anti-Communist Brigade," which had been relatively quiet since the March 1982 Constituent Assembly elections, resurfaced in September 1983 and claimed responsibility for a series of kidnappings and murders. Another group, the "Secret Anti-Communist Army," claimed responsibility for the murder of two civil servants in late June and for the torture and murder on September 10 of two Ministry of Education literacy campaign workers. More secretive squads operate in rural areas, kidnapping, torturing, and murdering their victims without claiming responsibility for these acts....

The Government has stepped up its campaign against death squad activity in response to the upsurge in killings claimed by death squads of the extreme right. On September 23, 1983, El Salvador's Ministry of Defense issued a statement repudiating "all terrorist actions from whatever source, because they constitute violations of human rights." On December 2, Minister of Defense Vides Casanova pledged "to bring before the law the members of these terrorist bands — whoever they may be and whatever reasons they might give to justify their illegal activity." On December 15, in an unusual act, the High Command of the Salvadoran Armed Forces and commanders of the military and the public security forces issued a statement endorsing the position of the Minister of Defense and pledging "to fight the death squads and the terrorist groups with all the means at our disposal until they are definitively eradicated from our country." President Magana, in his December 23 Christmas message to the nation, also spoke forcefully against the death squads, saying that to permit such activity is to promote a return to the law of the jungle. The President underscored his commitment and that of the Armed Forces' commanders to ensure the physical security of the citizenry. The Government's Political Commission and the Constituent Assembly have also spoken out forcefully against terrorists, including the death squads, as have political parties with a wide range of political philosophies. . . .

The guerrillas continue to be responsible for significant human rights violations, including murder. . . .

In addition to the civilian deaths which the press directly attributed to the guerrillas, the guerrillas are also responsible for the deaths of a significant, if indeterminate, number of civilians who are forcibly used as a shield against government forces in combat situations. The guerrillas have interfered with the Armed Forces battlefield communications to redirect military fire from the guerrillas themselves to civilian targets. . . .

Iran

Four years after the 1979 ouster of the Shah and the advent of the Islamic Revolution, Iran remains a revolutionary society. The regime is in the process of consolidating the revolution and building new political and social institutions. Iran is also a country at war. The fighting with Iraq began in September 1980 and continues with little hope for a negotiated settlement in the near future. An insurgency in Kurdish areas began about four years ago and continues.

Iran terms itself an Islamic Republic. It is theoretically "republican," in the sense that its Constitution, approved by popular referendum, follows a parliamentary pattern with a legislature, the Majlis, and a president elected by universal suffrage. Elections, however, are not free in that all candidates for office must be certified by the Ministry of Interior as meeting Islamic criteria. It is "Islamic" in its express belief that Iran should be governed by the "truth and justice" of the Koran under the leadership of Ayatollah Imam Khomeini and in the constitutional provision for a Council of Guardians, which reviews bills to assure that they comply with Islamic law.

The regime officially derives its legitimacy from the elected Majlis (Parliament) and from Islam. In practice, its hold on power is reinforced through intimidation, terror, and other harsh methods. Constitutional guarantees of human rights are ignored in practice.

Iran's political elite is composed of a group of Muslim clerics of the Shi'a sect, which predominates in Iran, and by laymen who have aligned themselves with these clerics. Opposition elements have not posed a serious threat to the regime since mid-1981 as a result of a government campaign to suppress political dissidents following a series of bombings that killed many of Iran's political leaders. Thousands of suspected Mujahedin (a major leftist opposition group) were arrested, and many were summarily executed. The regime eliminated one other potential opposition group in mid-1983 when it arrested an estimated 1,500 members of the Tudeh (Communist) Party, including much of the party leadership.

The regime, however, is not monolithic and there are major differences of opinion on economic issues such as private property ownership, government versus private control of foreign trade, labor versus management oriented industrial policy, and on a religious issue that centers on the question of divine sanction or authority for Khomeini's rule. . . .

The regime does not share Western concepts of individual freedom. Dissent from the political and religious views of the leadership is repressed. The ruling clerics' social views are imposed on everyone. The leadership's religiously justified codes of conduct are especially onerous as applied to women. Members of officially "recognized" religious minorities, Jews, Christians, and Zoroastrians, are permitted to practice their religions. The Baha'is, another religious minority in Iran, are not officially recognized by the regime. They are viewed as heretics and suffer from imprisonment, torture and execution at the hands of the Government. The regime remains strongly anti-Zionist and is distrustful of its religious minorities, but there have been no reports, at least since mid-1982, of arrests due solely to religious affiliation of members of the "recognized" religious minorities.

The war with Iraq that began in September, 1980 continues. . . .

The war has proved costly to both sides. Iran claims that roughly 100,000 of its soldiers have been killed since September, 1980. Economic resources have been diverted from development to the war effort. Both sides have attacked economic targets such as oil export terminals and factories. Iran claims that the war has created about one million refugees.

Iran holds an estimated 45,000 to 50,000 Iraqi prisoners of war. In general, treatment of the prisoners appears to meet international standards, although not all of these prisoners have been visited by international groups.

Iran's human rights record under the current regime remains one of the worst in the world, but, with the important exception of increased persecution of Baha'is, there was some improvement in 1983. . . . At least 1,500 prisoners . . . were amnestied in February and March of 1983. . . .

It is impossible to obtain even a rough estimate of the number of people killed for political reasons in Iran. It is equally impossible to estimate those executed for criminal offenses without benefit of a trial. . . .

Nicaragua

The National Directorate of the Sandinista National Liberation Front (FSLN), a group of nine Marxist revolutionary leaders who took control in July 1979, holds political power in Nicaragua. A three-man junta, composed of one member of the National Directorate and two civilians, serves as head of the Government of National Reconstruction. When it came to power with broad popular support, the Government promised to replace the discredited Somoza dictatorship with new social, political, and economic systems based on the principles of pluralism, free elections, a mixed economy, and observance of human rights. In the succeeding four years, the Government has not held elections but instead has consolidated its power and restricted civil liberties. Many original supporters of the Government have joined the armed opposition. Throughout 1983, armed anti-Government organizations conducted military operations on three fronts near the border areas and deep in the interior of the country. . . .

Respect for human rights, which deteriorated in 1982 with the imposition of the State of Emergency, continued to decline in 1983. The state of emergency declared in March 1982 remained in effect, continuing the suspension of many civil liberties guaranteed in the 1979 Statute of Rights and Guarantees. The Permanent Commission for Human Rights reported that the security forces, particularly the Directorate General of State Security, detained hundreds of suspected "counterrevolutionaries" (a term used loosely by the Government for anti-Government guerrillas, suspected guerrilla sympathizers, and subversives) and held many of them incommunicado indefinitely without formal charges. There are credible reports of torture and killing of detained persons by security forces.

The Government established Special Tribunals outside the judicial system to try the cases of suspected counterrevolutionaries, thus denying them such legal protection as the regular courts provide. Using both the powers of the Government and the capacity for intimidation of Sandinista organizations, the Government continued to harass opposition political parties, independent labor confederations, the private sector, the Catholic Church, and the independent media. The Government continued the prior censorship of print and electronic media. The various Sandinista organizations, particularly the ubiquitous Sandinista Defense Committees, sought out dissidents and coerced people into participating in Sandinista-sponsored activities. Through both legal and extra legal means, the Government seized the private property of several prominent citizens; it warned that neutrality in the struggle against armed opposition forces might be punishable by confiscation. The 10,000 Miskito Indians resettled from their Atlantic coast homelands in 1982 were prohibited from returning there. The Government forcibly evacuated additional inhabitants from the border areas of the country. About 1200 Miskito Indians fled to Honduras in December 1983. There are credible reports that Government security forces have killed and tortured Miskito Indians and have confiscated their food and property.

At the end of 1983 the Government declared an amnesty for most Miskitos, relaxed censorship of the only independent newspaper, and announced it would hold elections in 1985. Critics of the Government charged that these actions were only cosmetic changes that did not indicate genuine willingness to respect political pluralism. . . .

China

China is ruled by the Communist Party, which is headed by a small elite group dominated by Politburo Standing Committee member Deng Xiaoping. The party reserves to itself all power to decide political and economic policy and also sees itself as the final arbiter of social, cultural, and moral questions. When it achieved power in 1949, the party inherited a country with a long tradition of authoritarian rule. The party has built upon this tradition but has justified it with the Leninist doctrine of party control and considerably strengthened it through the use of all the instrumentalities available to the modern totalitarian state.

The experience of the 1966-76 Cultural Revolution — in which the populace (including most of the present leadership) was victimized by repeated, violent mass campaigns and the country was in a state of virtual anarchy — has apparently intensified the desire for order and stability. The leadership appeals to this desire in describing any potential threat to its own control as a threat to social order and in justifying a strong reaction to perceived challenges, whether from political dissidents or from the import of foreign attitudes and ideas. Since the death of Mao Zedong and the fall of his radical supporters, the "Gang of Four," in 1976, the Chinese system has entered a period of transition and experimentation. The party has reasserted central civilian authority — weakened during the Cultural Revolution — and the principle of collective leadership undermined by years of Mao's domination.

Today, power within the party is divided among a group of top leaders in several key organizations, including the Politburo and its Standing Committee, the Secretariat, and the Military Commission. Politburo Standing Committee member Deng Xiaoping, who is also chairman of the military commissions of both the party and the state and Chairman of the Party's Central Advisory Commission, holds a dominant position among these leaders. While arguing their policies in terms of Marxist-Leninist ideology and the writings of Mao Zedong, China's leaders state that these doctrines must be adapted to Chinese realities and that ideological tenets must be applied in the light of current conditions. This policy has resulted in a repudiation of some aspects of the Soviet economic model unsuited to Chinese conditions. The new policies, particularly in agriculture, are aimed at rewarding individual initiative, while preserving the framework of a centrally planned economy. . . .

. . . While not relinquishing its decisionmaking authority, the party has made a gesture towards broader participation in the political process through reinvigoration of such institutions as the National People's

Congress and the Chinese People's Political Consultative Conference and by conducting multicandidate local elections in 1980 and 1981. The party remains opposed to religion and officially atheist but has in recent years adopted a policy of limited religious toleration, under which religious activities have shown remarkable vitality and growth as places of worship have reopened for the first time since they were closed in the 1960s.

The overall trend towards a less tightly controlled society since the Cultural Revolution has been reflected in increased contacts with the outside, with tens of thousands of Chinese traveling abroad to study, conduct business, or visit relatives, while millions of overseas Chinese and hundreds of thousands of other foreigners have visited China annually. Emigration controls have also loosened considerably. . . .

On the other hand, there remain significant strictures on individual rights and freedoms. The regime does not tolerate criticism of the party's political role or of the fundamental structure of the Communist system, and it limits political debate. Critics who go beyond these limits to fault basic concepts are dealt with swiftly and sometimes harshly. . . .

Philippines

The Philippine Government is a mixed presidential-parliamentary system which reserves strong powers for the chief executive. Ferdinand Marcos, who has been President since 1965, dominates the political arena through his personal power, control of the ruling party, and a number of emergency executive powers carried over from the [1972] martial law period. . . .

Two insurgent groups are active. Both employ terrorist tactics, including murder, bombings, and extortion, to further their goals. Activities of the New People's Army have expanded over the past five years, and it now operates in more than two thirds of the provinces of the Philippines. In the south, the Moro National Liberation Front has waged a secessionist struggle since 1972. . . . The Government has mounted military, economic, and political efforts against both the insurgent groups. . . .

In 1983 there were human rights abuses by Government security forces, particularly members of the Philippine Constabulary and the Civilian Home Defense Forces, including harassment of civilians, arbitrary arrest, detention, disappearances, torture, and "salvaging," or summary execution of suspected insurgents or sympathizers. The majority of reports of abuses come from areas where Government forces are engaged in counterinsurgency operations. The Government periodically conducts investigations of abuses by the military, and senior officials have made public statements on the need for discipline and respect in military dealings with civilians. However, few individuals are seriously punished for abusive actions.

Former Senator Benigno S. Aquino, Jr., a leading opposition politician, was the victim of a political assassination at Manila Airport on August 21, upon his return from a three-year exile in the U.S., under conditions which generated widespread suspicion of the involvement of the military or government security forces. The murder is under investigation by an independent board.

In 1983, particularly following the Aquino assassination, there were increased public demonstrations and criticism of the Government, both in Manila and in key provincial cities, which the authorities tolerated to a greater extent than in the past. A Supreme Court ruling limited the Government's authority to prohibit public demonstrations.

Although the Government continued to exert significant control over the media and arrested a few journalists in the period following the Aquino assassination, it also tolerated more press criticism....

The number of persons detained on national security charges did not change appreciably from 1982, as some persons were released while others were arrested....

South Africa

South Africa is a multiracial country whose present constitution codifies the system of apartheid under which the white minority holds a monopoly of power in the country's national political institutions. Under apartheid, the rights of ethnic groups are regarded as more important than individual rights. The result has been a parliamentary democratic system run by the 16.2 percent of the South African population which is white. Persons of "colored" (mixed blood) and Asian descent have had no legal right to political participation at the national level, though a new constitution recently approved [in November 1983] by white voters would, if put into effect, permit a limited degree of power sharing at the national level, albeit with ultimate power in the hands of the whites. The overwhelming black majority has also been denied national political participation, except through the device of tribally-based "homelands" or "national states" created by the South African Government without regard to whether blacks live in or even wish to be associated with these areas. Black political rights are not addressed by the new Constitution. Within this narrow "whites only" context, national elections have been free and fair. The South African system combines Western-style human rights practices with limits on these practices. The press is outspoken, but circumscribed by government pressure. Free labor unions exist but, while the right of collective bargaining has been extended to a growing number of black unions, some of their leaders are subjected to official harassment and persecution. South Africa's judiciary is independent, but security legislation encroaches broadly on judicial power....

The conflict surrounding apartheid in South Africa has created an increasingly vicious cycle of violence involving African National Congress attacks against military and non-military targets in South Africa and South African raids against the African National Congress in neighboring states....

Although there were clear improvements, South Africa's fundamental human rights situation did not change in 1983. There remained no effective judicial remedy against the denationalization of blacks into "independent" tribal homelands or against forced resettlements. Indefinite detention without charge or access to attorney and other judicial acts without due process, such as banning, continue. The 83.3 percent of South Africa's population which is not part of the white minority suffers from pervasive discrimination which severely limits political, economic, and social life....

Union of Soviet Socialist Republics

... In September of [1983] ... the Soviet Union agreed to the Concluding Document of the Madrid meeting of representatives of the participating states of the Conference on Security and Cooperation in Europe. A follow-up to the Helsinki Accords of 1975, the Madrid Concluding Document is a reconfirmation of the participating nations' political commitment to respect "the universal significance of human rights and fundamental freedoms" and to "encourage the effective exercise of human rights and fundamental freedoms." Suppression of human rights continues in the Soviet Union despite this latest public commitment. In the short time since the Madrid meeting adjourned, at least six political prisoners are known to have been tried and sentenced to lengthy terms in labor camps: Iosif Begun, Sergey Grigoryants, Oleg Radzinskiy, Sergey Khodorovich, Vladimir Al'brekht, and Tat'yana Trusova.

Despite the Madrid Concluding Document's stipulation that all signatories "stress their determination to develop their laws and regulations in the field of civil, political, economic, social, cultural and other human rights and fundamental freedoms," new regulations went into effect in the Soviet Union on October 1 which allow the resentencing of prison camp inmates. At the same time, the authorities have further cut back emigration from the Soviet Union. Jewish emigration in 1983 was 51 percent below 1982 and 98 percent below the peak year of 1979....

Viewed as a whole, the past year has witnessed an escalation of efforts to eliminate free expression. Christians, Jews, free trade union organizers, and independent peace activists all have suffered intensified repression for having independently promoted cultural, political, or economic ideas, even those (e.g. peace and disarmament) which in principle are fully compatible with official Soviet policy....

CBO/GAO REPORT ON FINDINGS OF GRACE COMMISSION

February 18, 1984

Two research arms of Congress in a report issued February 18 challenged many of the findings of the President's Private Sector Survey on Cost Control (PPSSCC) in the federal government. The Congressional Budget Office (CBO) and the General Accounting Office (GAO) took aim at estimates of government cost savings by the PPSSCC, a panel of corporate executives known as the Grace Commission after its chairman, J. Peter Grace, chief executive of W. R. Grace & Co.

The Grace Commission, whose own final report was presented to President Ronald Reagan January 16, maintained that 2,478 managerial and structural reforms could "save" the government $424 billion in net cost reductions and revenue increases over a three-year period. But the CBO and GAO analyses claimed that the reforms proposed by the Grace Commission would save the government less than one-fourth the amount the panel estimated, or $98 billion over the same period. The commission also charged that Congress had interfered with attempts to cut costs by interfering in day-to-day executive agency decisions on pay scales, employee reorganizations, and contracting.

The two agencies also pointed out that the 36 task forces working on the Grace Commission study had in some instances been given overlapping work assignments and, as a consequence, some "savings" had been counted more than once in the overall estimate. Moreover, the GAO's Comptroller General Charles A. Bowsher noted that many of the major Grace Commission cost savings would require new legislation by Congress. While Grace himself indicated that all it would take was a good dose of sound business practice to root out government waste, many of his panel's reforms had been proposed by a number of presidents and proven politically treacherous over the previous two decades.

Grace Commission

Reagan established the PPSSCC by executive order on June 30, 1982, and named Grace as its chairman. An executive committee included 161 chief executive officers of major corporations and other experts from the private sector. The commission's mandate was to identify opportunities for increased efficiency and reduced costs achievable by executive or legislative action. The Grace Commission survey was privately financed at a cost of about $75 million, and its 650-page final summary report was in two volumes.

A key recommendation of the Grace Commission report was that the president be given "line item" veto power. That would permit him to knock out particular items he objected to in a bill without vetoing a large bill itself. Although Reagan himself had proposed such power in his State of the Union address, Congress was strongly opposed to the idea. (State of the Union address, p. 81)

Other major recommendations of the Grace panel were a means test to determine whether recipients of federal social welfare payments needed the benefits, for savings of $59 billion; lower civil service and military retirement benefits, for savings of $61 billion; repeal of the Davis-Bacon Act, which required federal contractors to pay higher wages than they otherwise would in some areas, for savings of $5 billion; and "privatizing" agencies that sold federally generated electricity, for savings of $20 billion.

CBO/GAO Analysis

In their joint report, the CBO and GAO noted that the Budget committees of both the Senate and the House wanted an analysis of the Grace Commission study "in time for use in developing the first budget resolution for 1985." With only a little more than a month to work in, the CBO and GAO said, their analysis was directed toward Grace reforms "that potentially could produce the largest budgetary savings." In contrast, the Grace Commission's report had taken 18 months to prepare.

In news conferences Grace maintained that his commission's report represented a study of federal management, not federal policy. However, the CBO and GAO reported that the "bulk of the cost savings" estimated by Grace's panel were "associated with proposals to change policies or to restructure programs." On the other hand, most of the recommendations in the Grace report, the CBO and GAO acknowledged, could be "characterized as management proposals to achieve greater efficiencies or to operate on a more business-like basis. . . ."

Following are excerpts from Analysis of the Grace Commission's Major Proposals for Cost Control, *a joint report released by the Congressional Budget Office and the General Accounting Office February 28, 1984.* (Boldface headings in brackets have been added by Congressional Quarterly to highlight the organization of the text.):

The outlook for the federal budget under current policies for the next five years is for large and growing deficits. The President's Private Sector Survey on Cost Control (PPSSCC) has submitted to the President nearly 2,500 recommendations, which it claims would save $424 billion over three years when fully implemented. The PPSSCC, better known as the Grace Commission, characterizes its recommendations as means for reducing program waste, correcting system failures, improving personnel management, and attacking structural deficiencies. The Congressional Budget Office (CBO) and the General Accounting Office (GAO) have reviewed nearly 400 of the PPSSCC recommendations that account for almost 90 percent of the potential three-year savings as estimated by the Grace Commission. To the extent possible, the impact of the PPSSCC proposals on the CBO baseline budget projections for fiscal years 1985-1989 was estimated, and an analysis of the likely program impact was made.

GAO analyzed whether the proposals could be implemented administratively or would require legislation, and focused its consideration on whether the proposals warrant support based on their individual merits. Many of the PPSSCC proposals were the subject of in-depth GAO reviews and evaluations. . . .

The CBO-GAO review found that the potential deficit reductions that might result in 1985-1987 from implementing most of these recommendations would be much smaller than the three-year savings projected by the Grace Commission. Without regard to the merits of the recommendations, the cumulative three-year deficit reduction for 1985-1987, including the off-budget deficit, is estimated to amount to $98 billion for those PPSSCC recommendations for which specific budget estimates could be prepared. This is 33 percent of the $298 billion of net three-year savings projected for these proposals by the Grace Commission and assumes that they are implemented by October 1, 1984. The CBO and PPSSCC estimates, however, are not fully comparable. The CBO estimates were calculated in federal budget accounting terms, whereas the PPSSCC estimates are characterized as planning figures and do not refer to specific years. Specific budget estimates could not be prepared for 122 of the commission recommendations reviewed because the proposals were too vague or necessary data were not available. The fact that their budget impact could not be evaluated does not imply, however, that they are not worthy of further study and possible implementation.

Most of these recommendations involve various management improvements that could be implemented administratively. The bulk of the potential savings, however, relate to recommendations that would require significant changes in current laws and policies. The federal spending generated by the policies and programs studied by the Grace Commission has been subject to close scrutiny before and should continue to be reviewed for possible savings. The magnitude of the savings projected by the Grace Commission for its proposals in these areas, however, is much too large to be attributed simply to eliminating waste and inefficiency. Rather, the PPSSCC proposals should be characterized for the most part as possible changes in public policy that could help reduce mounting federal deficits.

Although the majority of the Grace Commission recommendations can be characterized as management proposals to achieve greater efficiencies or to operate on a more business-like basis, the bulk of the cost savings estimated by the PPSSCC are associated with proposals to change policies or to restructure programs. All of these proposals would require Congressional action.

These proposals all represent tough decisions with difficult trade-offs. The CBO-GAO analysis reveals that the Grace Commission has not found an easy solution to the federal deficit problem, although it has helped to focus attention within the Administration and the Congress on ways to control the rising cost of government.

In GAO's opinion, about two-thirds of the revised PPSSCC recommendations have some degree of merit. Specifically, of the 396 recommendations assessed, GAO identified 242 as having some merit, 83 as not having merit, and 71 for which GAO had no basis for an opinion. Of the 242 recommendations GAO believed had merit, it had previously made similar or related recommendations in 150 cases. It is important to note, however, that many of the recommendations that do not have merit in GAO's opinion were among those with large savings estimates in the PPSSCC reports. It is also important to note that GAO does not agree that all of the proposals for which CBO estimated budgetary savings are feasible or desirable. Conversely, GAO believes that many proposals for which CBO was not able to estimate budgetary savings have merit and deserve further consideration. . . .

Focus of the CBO-GAO Analysis

Because the two Budget Committees were interested in having a CBO and GAO analysis of the PPSSCC recommendations in time for use in developing the first budget resolution for 1985, they requested that this joint report be issued in February 1984, little more than a month after the commission's final report was presented to the President. Given the short time available to review the many commission recommendations, we believed it essential to direct our analysis toward those PPSSCC proposals that potentially could produce the largest budgetary savings. As the final Grace Commission report to the President observes, and as presented in detail in CBO's recent baseline budget projections for 1985-1989, the prospect for the federal budget under current policies is large and growing deficits. Any serious proposals to reduce these deficits to less alarming levels deserve close attention.

Accordingly, we selected for review only those recommendations that the PPSSCC estimated could produce savings of $1 billion or more over a three-year period. Several other closely related recommendations were also selected for review. The result is that the joint CBO-GAO review covers 396 specific recommendations on 131 different issues as identified in PPSSCC reports. While this amounts to only 16 percent of the total number of recommendations made by the various task force and management office reports, the recommendations reviewed account for nearly 90 percent of the net three-year cost savings and revenue increases, and 95 percent of the cash accelerations, as estimated by the commission in its final report to the President.... Taken individually, most of the other PPSSCC recommendations were estimated by the commission to produce relatively small or no budgetary savings.

In examining the 396 PPSSCC recommendations selected for review, CBO and GAO staff examined the basis for the claimed savings potential, developed — where possible — estimates of the potential budgetary impact for fiscal years 1985-1989, identified the likely effect of the recommendations on the federal programs involved, and determined what actions would be necessary to implement them. In accordance with our respective roles and areas of expertise, CBO developed the budgetary estimates, while GAO focused on the merits of the recommendations, as well as program impact and implementation issues.

For purposes of analysis and discussion, the PPSSCC recommendations reviewed were grouped into 90 separate sets of proposals....

In assessing the merits of the PPSSCC's recommendations, GAO relied primarily on its prior and ongoing work, as well as its institutional knowledge developed through extensive and long-term review activities of virtually all major federal programs and activities. In fact, GAO's work, in a number of instances, formed the basis for the Grace Commission's recommendations.

Potential Budgetary Impact

The savings estimates for the Grace Commission proposals analyzed in this report for which CBO could determine the potential budgetary impact for 1985-1987 ... amount to $74.4 billion. Reductions in off-budget spending would add another $23.4 billion during 1985-1987, bringing the three-year total deficit reduction to $97.9 billion.

Savings ... for national defense programs are small — $9.2 billion over the first three years — because the budget impact for most of the proposals in this area could not be estimated. Budget savings in the national defense function would be larger in terms of budget authority because, under accrual accounting, the function would immediately reflect long-run retirement savings under the PPSSCC proposals.... Estimated savings for entitlements and other mandatory spending programs sum to

$15.0 billion for 1985-1987. Proposed reductions in nondefense discretionary spending and increased user charges are estimated to total $11.9 billion for this period. Another $13.0 billion in reduced outlays would result from proposals affecting federal civilian employment and compensation, with proposed revisions in the Civil Service Retirement program accounting for most of this amount. Potential revenue increases of $16.2 billion over the three-year period are also estimated, with the largest increase associated with the proposal to tax federal subsidies. Finally, the resulting reductions in the deficits over this period would lower net interest costs by another $9.1 billion using CBO's baseline interest rate assumptions. . . .

[COMPARISON WITH PPSSCC ESTIMATES]

It was possible to develop estimates of potential budgetary impact for 67 of the 90 sets of Grace Commission proposals analyzed in this report.

For the other 23 sets of proposals reviewed, budget estimates could not be prepared because either the proposals were too vague or the available information too scant. As noted earlier, the commission prepared what it characterized as planning figures for its proposals and did not attempt to make specific budget estimates. Furthermore, the commission noted in its reports that recommendations were not all based on the same level of research and analysis and that, as a result, their planning figures are not all of the same quality.

Where specific budget estimates could be made by CBO, 8 sets of PPSSCC proposals were found to have no budget impact for the next three years, 4 sets of proposals to entail added costs rather than savings, 9 sets to produce greater savings over three years than projected by the PPSSCC, and 46 sets to generate lower budget savings for 1985-1987 than implied by the Grace Commission three-year estimates. The total savings estimated by CBO for 1985-1987, including lower interest costs and off-budget savings, for the 67 sets of proposals for which budget impact estimates could be made is 33 percent of the $298.4 billion of net three-year savings projected for these proposals by the Grace Commission in its planning figures. . . .

The PPSSCC reports include several proposals that have already been acted upon by the Congress and are being implemented. As a result, the estimated budget effects of these proposals are included in CBO's baseline projections and no further savings are expected. Two examples are the proposals to raise Railroad Retirement payroll taxes and to increase debt collection through the use of private collection agencies. . . . Several other proposals would not have any near-term budget impact, such as the proposal to increase private participation in space programs and to improve the enforcement of the Social Security earning limit through an updated computer system.

Several Grace Commission proposals would add to federal budget costs rather than achieve savings. These include the proposals to reform the pay processes for federal employees to make them more comparable with the private sector. Because annual pay raises have been limited for a number of years to levels below those measured under the current comparability surveys, changes in these surveys would not produce savings but would raise costs. Also, the proposal to eliminate commodity donations to federal agencies would not affect the budget totals, and freezing the level of donations would add to storage costs.

In other instances, the CBO budget estimates for 1985-1987 are larger than the net three-year savings projected by the Grace Commission. The largest difference is for the effect of the PPSSCC proposal to replace the direct loan programs of the Farmers Home Administration (FmHA) and the Small Business Administration (SBA) with loan guarantees. The CBO savings estimate includes the effect of this proposal for off-budget financing of these loans by the Federal Financing Bank, which is not included in the Grace Commission estimate. CBO also has higher three-year savings estimates for the PPSSCC proposals to consolidate student loan programs in the Department of Education, to impose user fees for certain Coast Guard services, and to change the Civil Service Retirement system's accounting practices.

The CBO savings estimates ... were not constructed on the same basis as the Grace Commission estimates and, therefore, are not fully comparable. The CBO estimates show the potential budget impact for fiscal years 1985-1987, assuming implementation beginning October 1, 1984. As noted earlier, the PPSSCC estimates are said to represent potential savings during the first three years of implementation without regard to specific fiscal years. In some instances, the PPSSCC reports acknowledge that the recommendations could not be implemented in the next three years. In other instances, the reports make clear that the potential savings would come much later — in the 1990s or even later.

The CBO savings estimates also were calculated in federal budget accounting terms — that is, in terms of budget authority, outlays, and revenues. The CBO savings estimates for 1985-1987 ... are in terms of added revenues and/or lower outlays from the levels projected under a continuation of current laws and policies. Thus the CBO savings estimates indicate the potential effect of the PPSSCC proposals for reducing projected budget deficits. The Grace Commission savings estimates, on the other hand, were sometimes calculated in terms not used for the federal budget. As a result, many of the PPSSCC savings estimates are not true indicators of possible budget deficit reductions in the next three years. ...

Two other caveats should be considered in comparing the CBO and Grace Commission savings estimates. First, in order to develop many of the budget estimates, specific assumptions had to be made about the details of the proposals and how they would be implemented; in some instances, CBO analysts could not find the PPSSCC's assumptions in its published reports or background materials. Therefore, the CBO assumptions might not exactly reflect what the PPSSCC task forces assumed for their savings estimates. Second, a great amount of uncertainty should be attached to many of the PPSSCC and CBO savings estimates, particularly for proposals that call for substantial change in current laws, policies, and administrative practices. There usually is no way to determine exactly what happened in the past when laws, policies, or practices were similarly changed, so it is not possible to determine the extent to which projected effects for these changes were realized. As a result, a number of assumptions have to be made about how future changes will affect government spending and revenues, and these may not prove to be correct....

... On balance, ... it is CBO's judgment that the Grace Commission estimates of possible savings that could be derived from its recommendations during the next three years are overstated. This judgment apparently is shared by the Grace Commission.

PROPOSALS FOR THE NEXT THREE YEARS

In recent testimony before the Senate Finance Committee, Mr. Grace emphasized that the commission's three-year savings estimate of $424 billion did not refer to particular fiscal years and certainly not the next three. He identified a number of PPSSCC proposals, however, that he believed could be realized within the next three years with minimal political resistance. These proposals, which cover 44 issue areas in the PPSSCC reports, are in the area of inventory management, loan management, tax collections, cash management, reduced error rates, user charges for federal services, and general management. The PPSSCC three-year savings estimates for these proposals amount to $59 billion.

The CBO-GAO review of the Grace Commission reports covered 19 of these 44 issues identified by Mr. Grace. CBO was able to develop 1985-1987 budget estimates for 15 of these issues for which the commission estimated three-year savings of $33.3 billion. CBO estimates for these issues somewhat higher savings — amounting to $36.2 billion over the three-year period....

For three of the issues recommended by Mr. Grace, amounting to $7.7 billion in the PPSSCC three-year estimates, CBO found no budget impact relative to its baseline projections for two reasons. Either the savings would not be realized until after 1987, or the proposals already are being implemented. For three other issues, however, CBO estimates that there would be a greater budget impact during 1985-1987 than projected by the PPSSCC. As noted earlier, CBO projected greater savings for 1985-1987 for replacing FmHA and SBA direct loans with loan guarantees, for consolidating student loan programs, and for imposing user fees for certain Coast Guard services than estimated by the PPSSCC. For these three proposals, CBO estimates that the 1985-1987 budget impact would amount to $27.6 billion in deficit reductions compared to the PPSSCC three-year savings projection of only $4.6 billion. The remaining nine issues targeted by Mr. Grace that CBO was able to put into budget terms would produce deficit reductions of $8.5 billion. This CBO estimate is about 40 percent of the PPSSCC three-year savings projection.

The potential deficit reductions for 1985-1987 for the 44 issue areas selected by Mr. Grace presumably would be larger than the $36 billion that CBO was able to estimate. Congressional action would be needed to achieve most of these savings, and several would raise major policy issues.

Management Proposals

The majority of the Grace Commission recommendations selected for review are concerned with management issues, such as financial management, procurement practices, management of real property, and management of research and development programs. Approximately 40 percent of the three-year cost savings estimated by the Grace Commission for the 396 recommendations examined by CBO and GAO can be attributed to proposed management improvements. GAO has previously recommended many of these management improvements, and some are currently being implemented. About half of the PPSSCC estimated three-year savings could be achieved by administrative measures without further action by the Congress. The other half of the management savings would require Congressional action.

... It was possible to develop specific budget estimates for 32 sets of proposals involving 105 different recommendations. For these proposals, 20 sets of management proposals for which cost estimates could be prepared are projected to save $17.5 billion over three years, about 30 percent of the amount estimated by the Grace Commission. [O]f the remainder, 6 sets were found to have no effect on CBO's baseline projections for 1985-1987; 1 set would increase costs rather than produce savings; and 5 sets would result in slightly larger deficit reductions than estimated by the PPSSCC. The total amount of savings relative to CBO's baseline projections for 1985-1987 is estimated to be $21.5 billion, compared to $73.4 billion in three-year savings estimated by the PPSSCC.

The largest management saving would derive from augmenting the Internal Revenue Service's (IRS) staffing for collection of delinquent taxes and examination of tax returns, and from the disposition of tax cases brought before the U.S. Tax Court. CBO estimated savings amounting to $3.7 billion for 1985-1987 (and $13.0 billion over the five-year period 1985-1989) for this set of proposals, compared to $10.7 billion in three-year savings estimated by the PPSSCC. . . .

One of the largest three-year management savings projected by the Grace Commission was associated with a number of recommendations to improve federal work force productivity. The PPSSCC contends that the federal government, like any other employer, can improve productivity by changing its methods of operations, raising employees' skill levels, and investing more than it does now in work-facilitating equipment. CBO has tentatively estimated that the PPSSCC management proposals could lead to a federal productivity rise over four years of an extra 4.4 percent, which could yield net annual long-term compensation savings of some $1.8 billion. But because of the time required to accomplish changes, the near-term outlay savings would amount to only $0.5 billion for 1985-1987, compared to the PPSSCC three-year savings estimate of $17.1 billion.

Despite considerable federal activity and interest in improved productivity over the past 12 years, GAO has found agency efforts ill-prepared and poorly directed, disjointed, short-lived, and hence ineffective. Potential government-wide improvements in labor productivity, according to GAO calculations, would come mainly from five categories of federal work: compliance and enforcement of regulations, natural resource and environmental management, education and training, administration of loans and grants, and health-related services.

In four separate reports, the Grace Commission recommends more contracting out to private firms for certain support services, including maintenance, security, and data processing. . .

. . . CBO estimates that as many as 165,000 federal jobs, mostly blue-collar, could shift to private firms, with most of the job shifts occurring in defense agencies. In the near term, however, savings would be much smaller than the estimated long-term amounts because the proposals would have to be implemented gradually and there would be costs associated with transferring functions to the private sector, including payments to laid-off federal workers. CBO estimates that outlay savings for 1985-1989 would accumulate to about $0.7 billion. . . .

The Grace Commission made a number of other management proposals for which CBO was not able to estimate budget savings against its baseline projections. Either the proposals were so general in nature that estimating assumptions could not be made, or there were insufficient data available to use for preparing a savings estimate. . . .

Policy and Program Proposals

Of the 90 sets of PPSSCC proposals reviewed by the CBO and GAO, 36 sets involving 172 different recommendations are proposals to change policies or to restructure programs. As such they would require Congressional action. The Grace Commission's three-year savings estimates for these recommendations add to $225.8 billion, or 60 percent of the total three-year savings estimated by the commission for proposals analyzed in this report. CBO projects that these proposals could achieve deficit reductions amounting to over $75 billion during the next three years if implementation starts by October 1, 1984. . . .

In its analysis of PPSSCC'S policy and program proposals, GAO disagrees with several proposals, such as those to limit federal employees' compensation and benefits — proposals that represent some of the larger Grace commission savings estimates. On the other hand, GAO believes there is merit in several other policy proposals including those to repeal the Davis-Bacon and Service Contract Acts. . . .

CBO was able to develop budgetary impact estimates for all but one of the Grace Commission policy and program proposals. . . .

Three other PPSSCC proposals were estimated to result in added costs relative to the CBO baseline rather than savings. Two of these proposals involve reforming the process for determining pay comparability adjustments for federal white-collar and blue-collar employees. . . .

The other PPSSCC proposal that CBO estimates would increase costs rather than produce savings relative to its baseline projections involves the federal employees health benefit program (FEHBP). . . . GAO believes that there is no evidence to suggest that implementation of the PPSSCC recommendations would reduce costs by the commission's estimate of $1.4 billion. . . .

On the other hand, CBO estimates greater near-term savings relative to its baseline projections than implied by the PPSSCC three-year savings estimates for four other proposals. The largest difference is for the proposal to convert the direct loan programs of the Farmers Home Administration (FmHA) and the Small Business Administration (SBA) direct business loan program to partially guaranteed loan programs. The current FmHA and SBA loan guarantee maximum of 90 percent also would be reduced to 75 percent. . . . For 1985-1987, CBO estimates the savings of this proposal to be $23.2 billion in off-budget outlays. . . .

For 26 of the other Grace Commission proposals involving changes in policies and programs, CBO projects lower savings for 1985-1987 than implied by the PPSSCC three-year savings estimates. . . . CBO estimates 1985-1987 savings of $49.2 billion for these 26 proposals, or less than 25 percent of the PPSSCC three-year savings estimate. The bulk of the PPSSCC estimated three-year savings — almost 85 percent — is associated with proposals in just five areas. These proposals are to tax federal subsidies (estimated by PPSSCC at $58.9 billion); revise retirement benefits for federal employees ($58.1 billion); limit the growth in federal health care costs to GNP growth ($28.9 billion); sell the federal power marketing administrations and take other measures to reduce their costs ($19.1 billion); and repeal the Davis-Bacon, Walsh-Healey, and Service Contract Acts ($11.6 billion). If approved, CBO estimates that these proposals would yield savings of $30 billion for the next three fiscal years, and $79 billion for 1985-1989. . . .

COURT ON BANKRUPTCY

February 22, 1984

In a major setback for organized labor, the Supreme Court February 22 made it easier for financially ailing businesses to repudiate collective bargaining agreements. In a decision that subsequently was overturned by Congress, the Court voted 9-0 to permit a company attempting to reorganize its affairs under Chapter 11 of the federal Bankruptcy Code to abrogate its labor contract if a bankruptcy court found the contract was burdensome and that, on balance, the best interests of the company, its creditors, and its employees favored such a move. By a 5-4 vote, the Court also ruled that a company filing for bankruptcy could unilaterally disregard its collective bargaining agreement even before receiving court approval to do so. A company adopting that course could not be accused of an unfair labor practice by the National Labor Relations Board (NLRB), the Court said.

The decision came in the case of National Labor Relations Board v. Bildisco & Bildisco. *Bildisco, a building supplies distributor in New Jersey, filed for reorganization in 1980 and promptly ignored several aspects of its contract with a local of the International Brotherhood of Teamsters. The bankruptcy court permitted repudiation of that contract in 1981. The Teamsters union charged Bildisco with an unfair labor practice and challenged the bankruptcy court's decision. But the 3rd U.S. Circuit Court of Appeals upheld the court.*

Although the case involved a small company, a number of large firms, including Continental Airlines Corp. and Wilson Foods Corp., in 1983 abrogated union contracts after filing for Chapter 11 reorganization. At issue was how dire a company's financial state must be fore it could abrogate a collective bargaining agreement. While both sides in the dispute agreed that labor contracts involving a bankrupt company were different from other types of contracts, such as a rental agreement, they disagreed on the standard for allowing a company to get out of its contract. The NLRB argued that a company could reject a union contract only as a last resort and only if it was shown that the business was likely to fail unless the labor agreement was rejected. That position had been taken in 1975 by a federal appeals court in a case interpreting the then-existing bankruptcy laws. Union lawyers countered that a company, even if it had filed for bankruptcy, should be required to bargain with the union about changing the labor contract.

Bildisco contended it was not required to be on the brink of complete failure before changing a labor pact. The appeals court in 1982 agreed, rejecting the standard of the earlier case in favor of an approach that required "a balancing of the equities." The court required that the company must show some financial hardship and that the hardship must outweigh harm to the employees that might result from abrogating the labor contract.

The Court Ruling and Dissent

In affirming the appeals court ruling, the Supreme Court rejected the argument of the union and the NLRB that a company should be permitted to repudiate a labor contract only if it was on the brink of total collapse. Such a strict standard was at odds with the flexibility Congress built into the bankruptcy law, said Justice William H. Rehnquist, writing for the Court. He said, however, that a bankruptcy court should not permit repudiation unless it was persuaded that the company and the union had made "reasonable efforts" to negotiate "voluntary modification" of the agreement. As for a company's unilateral abrogation of a labor contract, Rehnquist said, "the filing of the petititon in bankruptcy means that the collective-bargaining agreement is no longer immediately enforceable, and may never be enforceable again." To permit the NLRB to move against unilateral repudiation of a labor contract would be at odds with the bankruptcy law's purpose "to give a debtor ... some flexibility and breathing space," he concluded. Rehnquist was joined in the ruling by Chief Justice Warren E. Burger and Justices Lewis F. Powell Jr., John Paul Stevens, and Sandra Day O'Connor.

Justices William J. Brennan Jr., Byron R. White, Thurgood Marshall, and Harry A. Blackmun dissented on the last point, finding such unilateral action a violation of federal labor law. Brennan predicted that the ruling would "spawn precisely the type of industrial strife" that labor laws were designed to prevent. He said he did not believe that a company could terminate a labor agreement without the permission of a bank-

ruptcy judge and be absolved of committing an unfair labor practice. Such a finding "seriously undermines the goals" of federal labor laws, Brennan said. "Plainly, the need to prevent economic warfare resulting from unilateral changes in terms and conditions of employment is as great after a bankruptcy petition has been filed as it is prior to that time."

A number of bankruptcy lawyers said that although the Court's decision might make it easier for companies to abrogate labor agreements, few companies would enter into bankruptcy proceedings for that reason. "I don't think any company in its right mind is going to file for bankruptcy unless it's in real financial trouble," said John Jerome, a New York City bankruptcy lawyer. "Sure, you might threaten the unions, but you're not going to file just because you think your wages are too high. Bankruptcy is supposed to be used as a shield and not as a sword."

The Court did not address the question of a company's liability if it annulled labor contracts but eventually was denied permission to do so by a bankruptcy court. Some labor law experts said it was probable a bankruptcy court would order the company to compensate its employees for back pay and benefits, without additional damages.

Labor, Congressional Reaction

The Court's decision was greeted with dismay at the annual meeting of the AFL-CIO executive council in Bal Harbour, Fla. Lane Kirkland, the labor federation's president, said unions would pursue "a legislative remedy." While the Bildisco decision was a major blow to union activists, it did not come as a complete surprise. "All along we knew our solution would have to come from Congress," said Howard Marlowe, a consultant to the AFL-CIO. Rep. Peter W. Rodino Jr., D-N.J., chairman of the House Judiciary Committee, called the decision "a puzzling misreading of congressional intent" and swiftly introduced legislation to overturn it. Rodino's bill would prohibit companies from unilaterally canceling labor contracts without bankruptcy court approval and would require proof that a company was likely to go out of business unless it repudiated its labor agreement. Rodino's bill, however, was entangled politically with two other controversial bankruptcy bills. One would restructure the nation's bankruptcy court system; the other would make it harder for consumers to declare bankruptcy, cancel their debts, and start their financial lives anew.

The situation was fluid because of an increasingly urgent need to act on the bankruptcy court legislation. In June 1982 the Supreme Court had invalidated the bankruptcy court structure set up in 1978 legislation. Since December 1982 the courts had been operating under an interim rule while Congress wrestled with legislation to correct the constitutional flaws cited by the justices.

Court Decision Overturned

The House March 21 passed legislation that would keep the bankruptcy courts in business. The bill also included the controversial labor contract provision. The strategy of linking the stronger protections for union contracts to the urgently needed courts bill angered Republicans, who charged that the labor proposal was being "railroaded" through the House without adequate consideration.

However, in adopting the conference report on the bankruptcy bill on June 29, Congress included a provision overturning the Court's decision. President Reagan signed the bill on July 10. The provision barred ailing companies from unilaterally throwing out their labor contracts. Instead, a company in financial straits would have to seek court approval to break its labor contract. Prior to filing such an application, the company would have to make a proposal to the union to alter the contract and seek to negotiate changes. A judge could allow rejection of the contract if he determined that the company made a good faith effort to accept the proposal "without good cause" and, on balance, all the factors "clearly favor" abrogation of the contract.

Following are excerpts from the majority opinion, written by Justice William H. Rehnquist, in National Labor Relations Board v. Bildisco & Bildisco, *holding that a bankruptcy court could free a company from its union contracts without requiring a company to prove that it would otherwise face immediate failure, and from the concurring and dissenting opinion of Justice William J. Brennan Jr., February 22, 1984:*

Nos. 82-818 and 82-852

National Labor Relations Board,
Petitioner
v.
Bildisco and Bildisco, Debtor-in-
Possession, et al.

Local 408, International
Brotherhood of Teamsters, etc.
Petitioner
v.
National Labor Relations Board
et al.

On writs of certiorari to the United States Court of Appeals for the Third Circuit

[January 25, 1982]

JUSTICE REHNQUIST delivered the opinion of the Court.

Two important and related questions are presented by these petitions for certiorari: (1) under what conditions can a Bankruptcy Court permit a debtor-in-possession to reject a collective-bargaining agreement; (2) may the National Labor Relations Board find a debtor-in-possession guilty of an unfair labor practice for unilaterally terminating or modifying a collective-bargaining agreement before rejection of that agreement has been approved by the Bankruptcy Court. We decide that the language "executory contract" in 11 U.S.C. § 365 of the Bankruptcy Code includes within it collective-bargaining agreements subject to the National Labor Relations Act, and that the Bankruptcy Court may approve rejection of such contracts by the debtor-in-possession upon an appropriate showing. We also decide that a debtor-in-possession does not commit an unfair labor practice when, after the filing of a bankruptcy petition but before court-approved rejection of the collective-bargaining agreement, it unilaterally modifies or terminates one or more provisions of the agreement. We therefore affirm the judgment of the Court of Appeals for the Third Circuit in these cases.

I

A

On April 14, 1980, respondent Bildisco and Bildisco ("Bildisco"), a New Jersey general partnership in the business of distributing building supplies, filed a voluntary petition in bankruptcy for reorganization under Chapter 11 of the Bankruptcy Code, 11 U.S.C. § 1101 *et seq.* Bildisco was subsequently authorized by the Bankruptcy Court to operate the business as debtor-in-possession under 11 U.S.C. § 1107.

At the time of the filing of the petition in bankruptcy, approximately 40 to 45 percent of Bildisco's labor force was represented by Local 408 of the International Brotherhood of Teamsters, Chauffeurs, Warehousemen and Helpers of America ("Union"). Bildisco had negotiated a three-year collective-bargaining agreement with the Union that was to expire on April 30, 1982, and which expressly provided that it was binding on the parties and their successors even though bankruptcy should supervene. Beginning in January 1980, Bildisco failed to meet some of its obligations under the collective-bargaining agreement, including the payment of health and pension benefits and the remittance to the Union of dues collected under the agreement. In May 1980, Bildisco refused to pay wage increases called for in the collective-bargaining agreement.

In December 1980, Bildisco requested permission from the Bankruptcy Court, pursuant to 11 U.S.C. § 365(a), to reject the collective-bargaining agreement. At the hearing on Bildisco's request the sole witness was one of Bildisco's general partners, who testified that rejection would save his company approximately $100,000 in 1981. The Union offered no witnesses of its own, but cross-examined the witness for Bildisco. On January 15,

1981, the Bankruptcy Court granted Bildisco permission to reject the collective-bargaining agreement and allowed the Union 30 days in which to file a claim for damages against Bildisco stemming from the rejection of the contract. The District Court upheld the order of the Bankruptcy Court, and the Union appealed to the Court of Appeals for the Third Circuit.

B

During mid-summer 1980, the Union filed unfair labor practice charges with the National Labor Relations Board ("Board"). The General Counsel of the Board issued a complaint alleging that Bildisco had violated § 8(a)(5) and § 8(a)(1) of the National Labor Relations Act ("NLRA"), 28 U.S.C. § 158(a)(5) and § 158(a)(1), by unilaterally changing the terms of the collective-bargaining agreement, in failing to pay certain contractually mandated fringe benefits and wage increases and to remit dues to the Union. Ultimately the Board found that Bildisco had violated § 8(a)(5) and § 8(a)(1) of the NLRA by unilaterally changing the terms of the collective-bargaining agreement and by refusing to negotiate with the Union. Bildisco was ordered to make the pension, health, and welfare contributions and to remit dues to the Union, all as required under the collective-bargaining agreement. The Board petitioned the Court of Appeals for the Third Circuit to enforce its order.

C

The Court of Appeals consolidated the Union's appeal and the Board's petition for enforcement of its order. That court held that a collective-bargaining agreement is an executory contract subject to rejection by a debtor-in-possession under § 365(a) of the Bankruptcy Code. The authority of the debtor-in-possession to seek rejection of the collective-bargaining agreement was not qualified by the restrictions of § 8(d) of the NLRA, which established detailed guidelines for midterm modification of collective-bargaining agreements, because in the court's view, the debtor-in-possession was a "new entity" not bound by the labor agreement. The Court of Appeals concluded, however, that given the favored status Congress has accorded collective-bargaining agreements, a debtor-in-possession had to meet a more stringent test than the usual business judgment rule to obtain rejection. The Court of Appeals ... required the debtor-in-possession to show not only that the collective-bargaining agreement is burdensome to the estate, but also that the equities balance in favor of rejection. The case was remanded to the Bankruptcy Court for reconsideration in light of the standards enunciated.

The Court of Appeals refused to enforce the Board's order, rejecting the Board's conclusion that Bildisco, as debtor-in-possession, was the alter-ego of the pre-petition employer. Under the Bankruptcy Code, a debtor-in-possession was deemed a "new entity" not bound by the debtor's prior collective-bargaining agreement. Because rejection relates back to the filing of a petition, the Court of Appeals held that if Bildisco were permitted to reject the contract, the Board was precluded from premising an unfair labor practice on Bildisco's rejection of the labor contract. The Court of Appeals implied that if the Bankruptcy Court determined that the collective-bargaining agreement should not be rejected, the Board could find a violation of § 8(d) of the NLRA.

We granted certiorari to review the decision of the Court of Appeals....

II

Section 365(a) of the Bankruptcy Code, 11 U.S.C. § 365, provides in full:

"(a) Except as provided in sections 765 and 766 of this title and in subsections (b), (c), and (d) of this section, the trustee, subject to the court's approval, may assume or reject any executory contract or unexpired lease of the debtor."

This language by its terms includes all executory contracts except those expressly exempted, and it is not disputed by the parties that an unexpired collective-bargaining agreement is an executory contract. Any inference that collective-bargaining agreements are not included within the general scope of § 365(a) because they differ for some purposes from ordinary contracts ... is rebutted by the statutory design of § 365(a) and by the language of § 1167 of the Bankruptcy Code. The text of § 365(a) indicates that Congress was concerned about the scope of the debtor-in-possession's power regarding certain types of executory contracts, and purposely drafted § 365(a) to limit the debtor-in-possession's power of rejection or assumption in those circumstances. Yet none of the express limitations on the debtor-in-possession's general power under § 365(a) apply to collective-bargaining agreements. Section 1167, in turn, expressly exempts collective-bargaining agreements subject to the Railway Labor Act, but grants no similar exemption to agreements subject to the NLRA. Obviously, Congress knew how to draft an exclusion for collective-bargaining agreements when it wanted to; its failure to do so in this instance indicates that Congress intended that § 365(a) apply to all collective-bargaining agreements covered by the NLRA.

None of the parties to this case dispute the foregoing proposition. But the Board contends that the standard by which the Bankruptcy Court must judge the request of a debtor-in-possession to reject a collective-bargaining contract must be stricter than the traditional "business judgment" standard applied by the courts to authorize rejection of the ordinary executory contract.... The Union also contends that the debtor-in-possession must comply with the procedural requirements of § 8(d) of the NLRA, or at a minimum, bargain to impasse before it may request the Bankruptcy Court either to assume or to reject the collective-bargaining agreement.

Although there is no indication in § 365 of the Bankruptcy Code that rejection of collective-bargaining agreements should be governed by a standard different from that governing other executory contracts, all of the Courts of Appeals which have considered the matter have concluded that the standard should be a stricter one. ... We agree with these Courts of Appeals that because of the special nature of a collective-bargaining contract, and the consequent "law of the shop" which it creates ..., a somewhat stricter standard should govern the decision of the Bankruptcy Court to allow rejection of a collective-bargaining agreement.

The Union and the Board argue that in light of the special nature of rights created by labor contracts, Bildisco should not be permitted to reject the collective-bargaining agreement unless it can demonstrate that its reorganization will fail unless rejection is permitted. This very strict standard was adopted by the Second Circuit in *Brotherhood of Railway and Airline Clerks* v. *REA Express, Inc.* (1975), decided under the former Bankruptcy Act three years before § 365(a) was passed by Congress. Under the canon of statutory construction that Congress is presumed to be aware of judicial interpretations of a statute, the Board argues that Congress should be presumed to have adopted the interpretation of the Second Circuit when it enacted § 365(a). ... The Board makes a related argument that Congress was fully aware of the strict standard for rejection established in *REA Express* and approved that standard when enacting § 365(a) of the Bankruptcy Code. In the legislative history accompanying § 82 of the Bankruptcy Act, a provision relating to municipal bankruptcies, the report of the House Committee on the Judiciary referred to *Kevin Steel Products*, and *REA Express*, as authority for the proposition that a stricter showing than the business judgment test was necessary to reject a collective-bargaining agreement. ... Since Congress made § 365(a) applicable to municipal bankruptcies, the Board argues that this reference to *REA Express* supports an inference that Congress adopted the *REA Express* standard for rejecting collective-bargaining agreements when it enacted § 365(a).

These arguments are wholly unconvincing. Quite simply, *Kevin Steel* and *REA Express* reflect two different formulations of a standard for rejecting collective-bargaining agreements. Congress cannot be presumed to have adopted one standard over the other without some affirmative indication of which it preferred. The reference in the House report to *Kevin Steel* and *REA Express* also cannot be considered a congressional endorsement of the stricter standard imposed on rejection of collective-bargaining agreements by the Second Circuit in *REA Express*, since the report indicates no preference for either formulation. At most, the House report supports only an inference that Congress approved the use of a somewhat higher standard than the business judgment rule when appraising a request to reject a collective-bargaining agreement.

The standard adopted by the Court of Appeals for the Second Circuit in *REA Express* is fundamentally at odds with the policies of flexibility and equity built into Chapter 11 of the Bankruptcy Code. The rights of workers under collective-bargaining agreements are important, but the *REA Express* standard subordinates the multiple, competing considerations underlying a Chapter 11 reorganization to one issue: whether rejection of the collective-bargaining agreement is necessary to prevent the debtor from going into liquidation. The evidentiary burden necessary to meet this stringent standard may not be insurmountable, but it will present difficulties to the debtor-in-possession that will interfere with the reorganization process.

We agree with the Court of Appeals below, and with the Court of Appeals for the Eleventh Circuit in a related case, *In re Brada-Miller Freight System, Inc.*, (1983), that the Bankruptcy Court should permit rejection of a collective-bargaining agreement under § 365(a) of the Bankruptcy Code if the debtor can show that the collective-bargaining agreement burdens the estate, and that after careful scrutiny, the equities balance in favor of rejecting the labor contract. The standard which we think Congress intended is a higher one than that of the "business judgment" rule, but a lesser one than that embodied in the *REA Express* opinion of the Court of Appeals for the Second Circuit.

Before acting on a petition to modify or reject a collective-bargaining agreement, however, the Bankruptcy Court should be persuaded that reasonable efforts to negotiate a voluntary modification have been made and are not likely to produce a prompt and satisfactory solution. The NLRA requires no less. Not only is the debtor-in-possession under a duty to bargain with the union under § 8(a)(5) of the NLRA, ... but the national labor policies of avoiding labor strife and encouraging collective bargaining generally require that employers and unions reach their own agreements on terms and conditions of employment free from governmental interference. ... The Bankruptcy Court need step into this process only if the parties' inability to reach an agreement threatens to impede the success of the debtor's reorganization. If the parties are unable to agree, a decision on the rejection of the collective-bargaining agreement may become necessary to the reorganization process. At such a point, action by the Bankruptcy Court is required, while the policies of the Labor Act have been adequately served since reasonable efforts to reach agreement have been made. That court need not determine that the parties have bargained to impasse or make any other determination outside the field of its expertise. ...

Since the policy of Chapter 11 is to permit successful rehabilitation of debtors, rejection should not be permitted without a finding that that policy would be served by such action. The Bankruptcy Court must make a reasoned finding on the record why it has determined that rejection should be permitted. Determining what would constitute a successful rehabilitation involves balancing the interests of the affected parties — the debtor, creditors, and employees. The Bankruptcy Court must consider the likelihood and consequences of liquidation for the debtor absent rejection, the reduced value of the creditors' claims that would follow from affirmance and the hardship that would impose on them, and the impact of rejection on the employees. In striking the balance, the Bankruptcy Court must consider not only the degree of hardship faced by each party, but also any qualitative differences between the types of hardship each may face.

The Bankruptcy Court is a court of equity, and in making this determination it is in a very real sense balancing the equities, as the Court of Appeals suggested. Nevertheless, the Bankruptcy Court must focus on the ultimate goal of Chapter 11 when considering these equities. The Bankruptcy Code does not authorize free-wheeling consideration of every conceivable equity, but rather only how the equities relate to the success of the reorganization. The Bankruptcy Court's inquiry is of necessity speculative and it must have great latitude to consider any type of evidence relevant to this issue.

III

The second issue raised by this case is whether the NLRB can find a debtor-in-possession guilty of an unfair labor practice for unilaterally rejecting or modifying a collective-bargaining agreement before formal rejection by the Bankruptcy Court. Much effort has been expended by the parties on the question of whether the debtor is more properly characterized as an "alter ego" or a "successor employer" of the pre-bankruptcy debtor, as those terms have been used in our labor decisions. . . . We see no profit in an exhaustive effort to identify which, if either, of these terms represents the closest analogy to the debtor-in-possession. Obviously if the latter were a wholly "new entity," it would be unnecessary for the Bankruptcy Code to allow it to reject executory contracts, since it would not be bound by such contracts in the first place. For our purposes, it is sensible to view the debtor-in-possession as the same "entity" which existed before the filing of the bankruptcy petition, but empowered by virtue of the Bankruptcy Code to deal with its contracts and property in a manner it could not have done absent the bankruptcy filing.

The fundamental purpose of reorganization is to prevent a debtor from going into liquidation, with an attendant loss of jobs and possible misuse of economic resources. . . . In some cases reorganization may succeed only if new creditors infuse the ailing firm with additional capital. We recognized the desirability of an analogous infusion of capital . . . ; a similarly beneficial recapitalization could be jeopardized if the debtor-in-possession were saddled automatically with the debtor's prior collective-bargaining agreement. Thus, the authority to reject an executory contract is vital to the basic purpose to a Chapter 11 reorganization, because rejection can release the debtor's estate from burdensome obligations that can impede a successful reorganization.

While all parties to this case ultimately concede that the Bankruptcy Court may authorize rejection of a collective-bargining agreement, the

Board and the Union nonetheless insist that a debtor-in-possession violates § 8(a)(5) and § 8(d) of the NLRA if it unilaterally changes the terms of the collective-bargaining agreement between the date of filing the bankruptcy petition and the date on which the Bankruptcy Court authorizes rejection of the agreement. But acceptance of such a contention would largely, if not completely, undermine whatever benefit the debtor-in-possession otherwise obtains by its authority to request rejection of the agreement. In a Chapter 11 reorganization, a debtor-in-possession has until a reorganization plan is confirmed to decide whether to accept or reject an executory contract, although a creditor may request the Bankruptcy Court to make such a determination within a particular time. In contrast, during a Chapter 7 liquidation the trustee has only 60 days from the order for relief in which to decide whether to accept or reject an executory contract. It seems to us that this difference between the two types of proceedings reflects the considered judgment of Congress that a debtor-in-possession seeking to reorganize should be granted more latitude in deciding whether to reject a contract than should a trustee in liquidation.

Under the Bankruptcy Code proof of claims must be presented to the Bankruptcy Court for administration, or be lost when a plan of reorganization is confirmed. . . . Action on claims that have been or could have been brought before the filing of a bankruptcy petition are, with limited exceptions not relevant here, stayed through the automatic stay provisions of the Bankruptcy Code. The Bankruptcy Code specifies that the rejection of an executory contract which had not been assumed constitutes a breach of the contract which relates back to the date immediately preceding the filing of a petition in bankruptcy. Consequently, claims arising after filing, such as result from the rejection of an executory contract, must also be presented through the normal administration process by which claims are estimated and classified. . . . Thus suit may not be brought against the debtor-in-possession under the collective-bargaining agreement; recovery may be had only through administration of the claim in bankruptcy.

While the Board insists that § 365(g)(1) deals only with priorities of payment, the implications from the decided cases are that the relation back of contract rejection to the filing of the petition in bankruptcy involves more than just priority of claims. Damages on the contract that result from the rejection of an executory contract, as noted, must be administered through bankruptcy and receive the priority provided general unsecured creditors. . . . If the debtor-in-possession elects to continue to receive benefits from the other party to an executory contract pending a decision to reject or assume the contract, the debtor-in-possession is obligated to pay for the reasonable value of those services, *Philadelphia Co.* v. *Dipple* (1941), which, depending on the circumstances of a particular contract, may be what is specified in the contract. . . . Should the debtor-in-possession elect to assume the executory contract, however, it assumes the contract *cum onere, In re Italian Cook Oil Corp.* (CA3 1951), and the expenses and liabilities incurred may be treated as administrative expenses, which are afforded the highest priority on the debtor's estate. . . .

The necessary result of the foregoing discussion is that the Board is precluded from, in effect, enforcing the contract terms of the collective-bargaining agreement by filing unfair labor practices against the debtor-in-possession for violating § 8(d) of the NLRA. Though the Board's action is nominally one to enforce § 8(d) of that Act, the practical effect of the enforcement action would be to require adherence to the terms of the collective-bargaining agreement. But the filing of the petition in bankruptcy means that the collective-bargaining agreement is no longer immediately enforceable, and may never be enforceable again. Consequently, Board enforcement of a claimed violation of § 8(d) under these circumstances would run directly counter to the express provisions of the Bankruptcy Code and to the Code's overall effort to give a debtor-in-possession some flexibility and breathing space. . . . We conclude that from the filing of a petition in bankruptcy until formal acceptance, the collective-bargaining agreement is not an enforceable contract within the meaning of NLRA § 8(d). . . .

The Union, but not the Board, also insists that the debtor-in-possession must comply with the mid-term contract modification procedures set forth in § 8(d) of the NLRA, 29 U.S.C. § 158(d). . . . Because the collective-bargaining agreement is not an enforceable contract within the meaning of § 8(d), it follows that the debtor-in-possession need not comply with the provisions of § 8(d) prior to seeking the Bankruptcy Court's permission to reject the agreement.

Section 8(d) applies when contractual obligations are repudiated by the unilateral actions of a party to the collective bargaining agreement. We have recognized that Congress's central purpose in enacting § 8(d) was to regulate the modification of collective-bargaining agreements and to facilitate agreement in place of economic warfare. *Allied Chemical & Alkali Workers of America, Local Union No. 1* v. *Pittsburgh Plate Glass Co.* (1971). . . . In a Chapter 11 case, however, the "modification" in the agreement has been accomplished not by the employer's unilateral action, but rather by operation of law. Since the filing of a petition in bankruptcy under Chapter 11 makes the contract unenforceable, § 8(d) procedures have no application to the employer's unilateral rejection of an already unenforceable contract. Indeed, even the Board concedes that the cumbersome and rigid procedures of § 8(d) need not be imported into bankruptcy proceedings.

The Union maintains, as a fall-back position, that even if § 8(d) procedures do not apply fully, the debtor-in-possession should be required to "bargain to impasse" prior to seeking rejection from the Bankruptcy Court. We interpret this contention to mean that the debtor-in-possession should not be permitted to seek rejection unless the duty to bargain has been excused because further negotiations would be fruitless, a standard little different from that imposed on all employers subject to the

NLRA. . . . Our rejection of the need for full compliance with § 8(d) procedures of necessity means that any corresponding duty to bargain to impasse under § 8(a)(5) and § 8(d) before seeking rejection must also be subordinated to the exigencies of bankruptcy. Whether impasse has been reached generally is a judgment call for the Board to make; imposing such a requirement as a condition precedent to rejection of the labor contract will simply divert the Bankruptcy Court from its customary area of expertise into a field in which it presumably has little or none.

Our determination that a debtor-in-possession does not commit an unfair labor practice by failing to comply with § 8(d) prior to formal rejection of the collective-bargaining agreement does undermine the policy of the NLRA, for that policy, as we have noted, is to protect the process of labor negotiations, not to impose particular results on the parties. See *H. K. Porter Co.* v. *NLRB* (1970); *NLRB* v. *Jones & Laughlin Steel Corp.* (1937). Nevertheless, it is important to note that the debtor-in-possession is not relieved of all obligations under the NLRA simply by filing a petition for bankruptcy. A debtor-in-possession is an "employer" within the terms of the NLRA, 11 U.S.C. § 152(1) and (2), and is obligated to bargain collectively with the employees' certified representative over the terms of a new contract pending rejection of the existing contract or following formal approval of rejection by the Bankruptcy Court. . . . But while a debtor-in-possession remains obligated to bargain in good faith under NLRA § 8(a)(5) over the terms and conditions of a possible new contract, it is not guilty of an unfair labor practice by unilaterally breaching a collective-bargaining agreement before formal Bankruptcy Court action.

Accordingly, the judgment of the Court of Appeals is

Affirmed.

JUSTICE BRENNAN, with whom JUSTICE WHITE, JUSTICE MARSHALL, and JUSTICE BLACKMUN join, concurring in part and dissenting in part.

The Court holds that under § 365 of the Bankruptcy Code, a Bankruptcy Court should permit a debtor in possession to reject a collective-bargaining agreement upon a showing that the agreement "burdens the estate, and that after careful scrutiny, the equities balance in favor of rejecting the labor contract." This test properly accommodates the policies of the National Labor Relations Act (NLRA) and the Bankruptcy Code, and I therefore join Parts I and II of the Court's opinion. But I cannot agree with the Court's holding in Part III that a debtor in possession does not commit an unfair labor practice if he unilaterally alters the terms of an existing collective-bargaining agreement after a bankruptcy petition has been filed, but before a Bankruptcy Court has authorized the rejection of that agreement. In so holding, the Court has completely ignored important policies that underlie the NLRA, as well as Parts I and II of its own opinion.

I

Two sections of the NLRA govern the alteration of existing collective-bargaining agreements. Section 8(a)(5) makes it an unfair labor practice for an employer "to refuse to bargain collectively with the representatives of his employees. . . ." Section 8(d) defines the § 8(a)(5) duty to "bargain collectively" as "the performance of the mutual obligation of the employer and the representative of the employees to meet at reasonable times and confer in good faith with respect to wages, hours, and other terms and conditions of employment." When a collective-bargaining agreement is "in effect," § 8(d) adds four additional requirements to the duty to bargain collectively: "no party to [a collective-bargaining contract] shall terminate or modify such contract unless" he (1) provides the other party to the contract with timely written notice of the proposed modification, (2) "offers to meet and confer with the other party," (3) provides timely notice to the Federal Mediation and Conciliation Service and any similar state agencies, and (4) "continues in full force and effect . . . all the terms and conditions of the existing contract for a period of sixty days after such notice is given or until the expiration date of such contract, whichever occurs later." Because § 8(d) defines the duty to bargain collectively that is imposed by § 8(a)(5), an employer who terminates or modifies a collective-bargaining agreement without complying with the requirements of § 8(d) violates § 8(a)(5). . . . A unilateral modification of an existing collective-bargaining agreement is, therefore, a violation of § 8(d) and § 8(a)(5). . . .

In this case, the National Labor Relations Board (Board) held that Bildisco had violated § 8(a)(5) of the NLRA by unilaterally altering the terms of its collective-bargaining agreement with Local 408 of the International Brotherhood of Teamsters, Chauffeurs, Warehousemen, and Helpers of America. Specifically, the Board found that Bildisco violated the terms of that agreement by its failure to (1) increase wages, (2) make pension, health, and welfare contributions, (3) remit dues to the union that were withheld from employees' wages, and (4) pay vacation benefits. Some of these activities occurred after Bildisco filed a voluntary petition in bankruptcy under Chapter 11 of the Bankruptcy Code, 11 U.S.C. § 1101 *et seq*, but before the Bankruptcy Court authorized Bildisco to reject its agreement with Local 408. During this period, Bildisco was operating its business as a debtor in possession. This aspect of the case, therefore, presents the question whether a debtor in possession violates § 8(d) and, as a result, § 8(a)(5) if he unilaterally modifies the terms of a collective-bargaining agreement in the interim between the filing of a bankruptcy petition and the rejection of that agreement.

II

The Court today rejects the Board's finding that Bildisco's unilateral modifications of its collective-bargaining agreement violated § 8(a)(5). The

Court supports this conclusion by asserting that enforcement of § 8(d) in the post-filing period "would run directly counter to the express provisions of the Bankruptcy Code." Yet, the Court points to no provision of that Code that purports to render § 8(d) inapplicable, and to no provision of the NLRA that would preclude the application of § 8(d). Indeed, the Court concedes that a debtor in possession generally must comply with the provisions of the NLRA.

Accordingly, in order to achieve its desired result, the Court is forced to infer from the Bankruptcy Code's general treatment of executory contracts, and from the policies that underlie that treatment, that Congress must have intended the filing of a bankruptcy petition to render § 8(d) inapplicable. The Court observes that during the post-petition period, the nondebtor party to an executory contract may not sue the debtor in possession to enforce the contract terms, but rather can only recover the reasonable value of any benefits conferred on the estate. By contrast, "though the Board's action is nominally one to enforce § 8(d) ... the practical effect of the enforcement action would be to require adherence to the terms of the collective-bargaining agreement." Because the Court finds that suspending the enforceability of executory contracts serves the goals of providing the debtor in possession with "flexibility and breathing space," the Court concludes that Congress could not have intended § 8(d) to remain applicable once a bankruptcy petition has been filed.

This argument is unpersuasive. However correct the Court may be in its description of the manner in which the Bankruptcy Code treats executory contracts generally and the policies that underlie that treatment, there is an unavoidable conflict between the Code and the NLRA with which the Court has simply failed to grapple. Permitting a debtor in possession unilaterally to alter a collective-bargaining agreement in order to further the goals of the Bankruptcy Code seriously undermines the goals of the NLRA....

The Court's concentration on the Bankruptcy Code and its refusal to accommodate that statute with the NLRA is particularly incongruous since the analysis in Part II of its opinion rests almost exclusively on the recognition that the two statutes must be accommodated. In that Part, the Court concludes that "because of the special nature of a collective-bargaining contract ... a somewhat stricter standard should govern the decision of the Bankruptcy Court to allow rejection of a collective-bargaining agreement." Surely, the "special nature of a collective-bargaining contract" must also be considered when determining whether Congress intended a debtor in possession to be able unilaterally to alter its terms. I can only conclude that the Court does not do so because an examination of the policies and provisions of both statutes inexorably leads to the conclusion that Congress did not intend the filing of a bankruptcy petition to affect the applicability of § 8(d), and that, as a result, a debtor in possession commits an unfair labor practice when he unilaterally alters the terms of an existing collective-bargaining agreement after a bankruptcy petition has been filed but prior to rejection of that agreement.

III

A

Because the issue in this case centers on the effect of filing a bankruptcy petition on the obligations of a debtor in possession under NLRA § 8(d), it is appropriate to begin by examining whether that provision would apply even in the absence of the countervailing provisions and policies of the Bankruptcy Code. In undertaking this threshold analysis, we must remember that we have previously recognized that § 8(d) must be construed flexibly to effectuate the purposes of the NLRA.... As we stated in *Lion Oil* [1956], a construction that does not serve the goals of the statute "is to be avoided unless the words chosen by Congress clearly compel it."

In addition, in resolving this threshold question we must be mindful of the deference to the Board's construction of the NLRA required by our decisions.... It is the Board's position that filing a bankruptcy petition does not affect the applicability of § 8(d).... Plainly, the Court's position that § 8(d) is inapplicable once a bankruptcy petition has been filed is contrary to the goals of the NLRA, and a careful examination of "the words Congress has chosen" reveals that they do not "clearly compel" this result.

By their terms, the notice and cooling-off requirements of § 8(d) apply when "there is in effect a collective-bargaining contract" and a "party to such contract" seeks to "terminate or modify" it. The Court of Appeals held that § 8(d) was inapplicable because the "debtor-in-possession is '[a] new entity ... created with its own rights and duties, subject to the supervision of the bankruptcy court.'" As a result, the Court of Appeals concluded that the debtor in possession is not a "party" to a collective-bargaining agreement within the meaning of § 8(d).

The Court today properly rejects the "new entity" theory, conceding that the debtor in possession is a party within the meaning of § 8(d). The Court nevertheless reaches an equally unsupportable result by concluding that once a bankruptcy petition has been filed, "the collective-bargaining agreement is not an enforceable contract within the meaning of NLRA § 8(d)." Of course, the phrase "enforceable contract" does not appear in § 8(d), so the Court's point must be that the collective-bargaining agreement is not "in effect" within the meaning of that section. Surely, the plain language of the statute does not compel this result....

Although enforcement of the contract is suspended during the interim period, the contract clearly has other characteristics that render it "in effect" during the interim period. For example, if the debtor in possession assumes the contract, that assumption relates back to the time that the bankruptcy petition was filed. As a result, "any compensation earned by and payable to the employee under the contract" after the petition is filed is a first priority administrative expense.... If the contract is eventually rejected, rejection constitutes a breach effective immediately before the date of the filing of the petition. The employees will have general unsecured claims for damages resulting from the breach. Some of these damages will stem from the employer's obligations under the contract in the post-filing period. Therefore, whether the contract is accepted or rejected, it will support a claim that arises out of the debtor's obligations in the post-petition period.

Additionally, even under the Court's approach, . . . during the interim between filing and rejection or assumption, the estate will be liable to the employees for the reasonable value of any services they perform. The contract rate frequently will be the measure of the reasonable value of those services. . . . For these reasons, it is inaccurate to say that the collective-bargaining agreement may not reasonably be considered "in effect" for purposes NLRA § 8(d). Other provisions of the NLRA, as well as the policies underlying that statute require that such a contract be considered "in effect."

The definitional sections of the NLRA plainly support the conclusion that Congress did not intend the filing of a bankruptcy petition to affect the applicability of § 8(d). As the Court notes, a debtor in possession is an "employer" within the meaning of the NLRA. Because § 8(a)(5) imposes the duty to bargain on employers, the Court properly concludes that § 8(a)(5) applies to debtors in possession. And because definition of the duty to bargain includes the notice and "cooling-off" requirements of § 8(d), the logical inference is that Congress intended these restrictions of unilateral alterations to apply to debtors in possession as well. It is most unlikely that Congress intended that the obligation to bargain apply to debtors in possession but not the definition of that duty.

B

The policies underlying the NLRA in general, and § 8(d) in particular, also strongly support the application of the notice and cooling-off requirements of § 8(d) in this context. As we explained in *First National Maintenance Corp.* v. *NLRB*, (1980), "[a] fundamental aim of the National Labor Relations Act is the establishment and maintenance of industrial peace to preserve the flow of interstate commerce. Central to achievement of this purpose is the promotion of collective bargaining as a method of defusing and chanelling conflict between labor and management. . . ." Because of the central role played by collective bargaining in achieving the goals of the NLRA, "[e]nforcement of the obligation to bargain collectively is crucial to the statutory scheme." *NLRB* v. *American National Insurance Co.*, 343 U.S. 395, 402 (1951). The notice and cooling-off requirements of § 8(d), which are components of the duty to bargain, are specifically designed to prevent labor strife resulting from unilateral modifications and terminations of collective-bargaining agreements. . . .

Plainly, the need to prevent "economic warfare" resulting from unilateral changes in terms and conditions of employment is as great after a bankruptcy petition has been filed as it is prior to that time. I do not think that there is any question that the threat to labor peace stemming from a unilateral modification of a collective-bargaining agreement is as great one day after a bankruptcy petition is filed as it was one day before the petition was filed. We cannot ignore these realities when construing the reach of the NLRA. . . .

The basis for § 8(d)'s prohibition against unilateral modifications is a congressional judgment that such modifications would be antithetical to labor peace. . . . In sum, were one to consider only the policies and provisions of the NLRA, there could be no question that Congress intended that § 8(d) remain applicable after a bankruptcy petition has been filed.

C

When we turn to the relevant provisions and policies of the Bankruptcy Code, we find nothing that alters this conclusion. As I have said, . . . the Court is unable to point to any provision of the Bankruptcy Code that by its terms renders § 8(d) inapplicable. Nor does the Court argue that there is anything in the Code that would forbid the debtor in possession from complying with the requirements of § 8(d). The question then is whether application of § 8(d) would so undermine the goals of the Bankruptcy Code that, despite the deleterious effect on the policies of the NLRA, Congress could not have intended that § 8(d) remain applicable once a bankruptcy petition has been filed.

As the Court correctly points out, the primary goal of Chapter 11 is to enable a debtor to restructure his business so as to be able to continue operating. Unquestionably, the option to reject an executory contract is essential to this goal. But the option to violate a collective-bargaining agreement before it is rejected is scarcely vital to insuring successful reorganization. For if a contract is so burdensome that even temporary adherence will seriously jeopardize the reorganization, the debtor in possession may seek the Bankruptcy Court's permission to reject that contract. Under the test announced by the Court today, his request should be granted. Indeed, because labor unrest is inimical to the prospects for a successful reorganization, and because unilateral modifications of a collective-bargaining agreement will often lead to labor strife, such unilateral modifications may more likely *decrease* the prospects for a successful reorganization.

The Court claims that requiring the debtor in possession to adhere to the terms of a collective-bargaining agreement conflicts with the "Code's overall effort to give the debtor in possession some flexibility and breathing space." Again the Court does not explain how enforcement of § 8(d) interferes with these policies; but I assume that the Court expects that the financial pressures created by requiring adherence to the collective-bargaining agreement would put pressure on the debtor in possession to reach a rapid and possibly premature judgment about whether to assume or reject a contract. It is apparent, however, that Congress did not believe that providing the debtor in possession with unlimited time to consider his options should outweigh all other considerations. . . . Congress . . . clearly concluded that, in certain circumstances, the rights of the nondebtor party would outweigh the need of the debtor in possession for unlimited flexibility and breathing space.

More importantly, I do not believe that the pressure to seek early rejection will frequently impede the reorganization process. As noted above, when a collective-bargaining agreement will seriously impede the reorganization, the debtor in possession should be able to obtain permission to reject the agreement. The major danger to the reorganization that stems from premature rejection of collective-bargaining agreements is that the debtor in possession will reject an agreement he would not have rejected upon further deliberation. If that agreement contains terms more favorable than any that he is later able to obtain through renegotiation the reorganization may be impaired. In the case of a collective-bargaining agreement, however, this danger is largely illusory. Because the union members will lose their jobs if the reorganization fails, it is highly likely that the debtor in possession will be able to negotiate a contract that is at least as favorable as the contract that he has rejected. . . .

<h2 style="text-align:center">IV</h2>

. . . The Court's holding that an employer, without committing an unfair labor practice, may disregard the terms of a collective-bargaining agreement after a bankruptcy petition has been filed, deprives the parties to the agreement of their "system of industrial government." Without this system, resolution of the parties' disputes will indeed be left to "the relative strength . . . of the contending forces." Of course, there is some tension between the policies underlying the Bankruptcy Code and a holding that § 8(d) remains applicable after a bankruptcy petition has been filed. Holding § 8(d) inapplicable in these circumstances, however, strikes at the very heart of the policies underlying that section and the NLRA, and will, I believe, spawn precisely the type of industrial strife that NLRA § 8(d) was designed to avoid. By contrast, I do not think that the prospects for a successful reorganization will be seriously impaired by holding that § 8(d) continues to apply. For this reason, I conclude that filing a bankruptcy petition does not affect the applicability of § 8(d), and that, as a result, a debtor in possession who unilaterally alters the terms of a collective-bargaining agreement commits an unfair labor practice.

COURT ON SEX BIAS
IN EDUCATION
February 28, 1984

The Supreme Court February 28 sharply curtailed the sweep of a ban on sex discrimination by federally aided schools and colleges. In a major victory for the Reagan administration, the Court ruled 6-3 that Title IX of the 1972 Education Amendments did not apply to all programs at a recipient institution but only to the particular program receiving government aid. With its decision in Grove City College v. Ball, *the Court placed its stamp of approval on the Reagan administration's reversal of earlier federal policy. Until 1983 the executive branch had consistently interpreted the law as covering an entire affected institution, not just particular programs at each school or college.*

In another part of the decision the justices were unanimous in rejecting Grove City's argument that it was not subject to Title IX because it received no federal aid directly. Federal dollars did find their way onto the campus as individual students received federal basic educational opportunity grants, also known as Pell grants. The Court held that such indirect aid was sufficient to bring Grove City College within the reach of Title IX. The administration had urged such a ruling on that point.

The effect of that ruling was to make every college and university in the country subject to Title IX; few, if any, remained as independent of federal aid as Grove City College. However, the Court's 6-3 ruling applying Title IX only to particular programs receiving federal aid sharply limited the law's effectiveness. On that point, the college and the administration successfully joined forces to urge the justices to reverse a

201

previous ruling by the 3rd U. S. Circuit Court of Appeals and a decade of administrative interpretation of the law.

The majority read the language of Title IX as confining its scope to particular programs. The critical provision prohibited sex discrimination in "any education program or activity receiving federal financial assistance." Only by ignoring that language could the justices conclude that federal student aid funds paid to the college as tuition represented federal aid to the entire institution, wrote Justice Byron R. White. "The fact that federal funds eventually reach the college's general operating budget cannot subject Grove City to institution-wide coverage." Under the broad view taken by the appeals court in the case, an entire school would become subject to Title IX if only one of its students received federal aid. "This result cannot be squared with Congress' intent," White declared.

In Grove City's case, the grants to students represented aid to the college's financial aid program, and only that program was subject to Title IX. Grove City College was required to sign federal forms assuring it was complying with Title IX in its student aid program, the Court held, and if it continued to refuse its students could lose their federal grants.

Criticism, Dissent

Although they concurred in the outcome, Justice Lewis F. Powell Jr., Chief Justice Warren E. Burger, and Justice Sandra Day O'Connor in a separate concurring opinion described the case as "an unedifying example of overzealousness on the part of the federal government." Pointing out that Grove City had never been charged with sex discrimination but simply with refusing to sign forms certifying its compliance with Title IX, the three justices criticized the government for choosing to litigate the case at all.

In a separate dissent, Justice John Paul Stevens criticized the majority for issuing an unnecessary advisory opinion on the breadth of Title IX coverage within an institution. All the Court was required to decide in this case was whether Grove City was a recipient of federal aid subject to Title IX, he contended. Justices William J. Brennan Jr. and Thurgood Marshall dissented from the majority's narrow view of Title IX's reach within a school or college. The majority "ignores the primary purposes for which Congress enacted Title IX," wrote Brennan.

"The absurdity of the Court's decision" was clear when one examined its practical effect, he continued. Grove City College's financial aid program could not discriminate on the basis of sex due to Title IX, but the admissions, athletic, or academic departments were under no such restriction. "The Court thus sanctions practices that Congress clearly could not have intended: For example, after today's decision, Grove City

College would be free to segregate male and female students in classes run by its mathematics department ... even though the affected students are attending the college with the financial assistance provided by federal funds," Brennan wrote.

Civil Rights, Congress Reaction

Civil rights lawyers warned that the Court's narrow reading of Title IX could lead to rulings that would similarly limit the scope of laws prohibiting racial bias and discrimination against the handicapped. Leaders of major civil rights groups met following the decision to discuss possible legislative responses.

The decision generated immediate protest on Capitol Hill. In November 1983 the House had voted 414-8 to oppose such a narrow interpretation of Title IX. Fifty members of the 98th Congress reiterated that view in a friend-of-the-court brief filed in the Grove City case. Rep. Patricia Schroeder, D-Colo., said the 1983 House vote had sent a clear message that Congress intended Title IX to be construed broadly, "but the Supreme Court must have had their earmuffs on."

Sen. Bob Packwood, R-Ore., introduced a bill designed to make it "crystal clear" that Title IX's ban on sex discrimination applied to an entire institution if any part of it received federal aid. "It is ... of little use to bar discrimination in any specific program in the institution if a woman cannot gain admittance to or participate in the institution because of its discriminatory policies," Packwood said.

A similar bill passed the House in 1984 but conservatives blocked its passage in the Senate and the legislation died with adjournment of the 98th Congress. Several new bills to offset the Grove City decision were introduced when the 99th Congress convened in January 1985. Both the Reagan administration and civil rights groups wanted the decision overturned, but they disagreed about how it should be done.

If Congress did not act, the Grove City ruling would reduce the burden of federal regulation for many educational institutions and lower the level of controversy provoked by the application of Title IX, particularly to athletic programs. Few athletic programs received federal aid directly, and the Court's ruling placed all such programs outside the reach of Title IX.

Following are excerpts from the Supreme Court's February 28, 1984, decision in Grove City College v. Bell, ruling that federally assisted educational institutions must comply with Title IX only in those programs receiving federal funds; from the concurring opinions of Justices Lewis F. Powell Jr. and John Paul Stevens; and from the dissent of Justice William J. Brennan Jr.:

No. 82-792

Grove City College, Individually and on Behalf of Its Students, et al., Petitioners v. Terrel H. Bell, Secretary of Education, et al.	On writ of certiorari to the United States Court of Appeals for the Third Circuit

[February 28, 1984]

JUSTICE WHITE delivered the opinion of the Court.

Section 901(a) of Title IX of the Education Amendments of 1972 prohibits sex discrimination in "any education program or activity receiving Federal financial assistance," and § 902 directs agencies awarding most types of assistance to promulgate regulations to ensure that recipients adhere to that prohibition. Compliance with departmental regulations may be secured by termination of assistance "to the particular program, or part thereof, in which ... noncompliance has been ... found" or by "any other means authorized by law."

This case presents several questions concerning the scope and operation of these provisions and the regulations established by the Department of Education. We must decide, first, whether Title IX applies at all to Grove City College, which accepts no direct assistance but enrolls students who receive federal grants that must be used for educational purposes. If so, we must identify the "education program or activity" at Grove City that is "receiving Federal financial assistance" and determine whether federal assistance to that program may be terminated solely because the College violates the Department's regulations by refusing to execute an Assurance of Compliance with Title IX. Finally, we must consider whether the application of Title IX to Grove City infringes the First Amendment rights of the College or its students.

I

Petitioner Grove City College is a private, coeducational, liberal arts college that has sought to preserve its institutional autonomy by consistently refusing state and federal financial assistance. Grove City's desire to avoid federal oversight has led it to decline to participate, not only in direct institutional aid programs, but also in federal student assistance programs under which the College would be required to assess students' eligibility and to determine the amounts of loans, work-study funds, or grants they should receive. Grove City has, however, enrolled a large number of students who receive Basic Educational Opportunity Grants

(BEOGs) under the Department of Education's Alternate Disbursement System (ADS).

The Department concluded that Grove City was a "recipient" of "Federal financial assistance" as those terms are defined in the regulations implementing Title IX, and, in July 1977, it requested that the College execute the Assurance of Compliance required by 34 CFR § 106.4 (1982). If Grove City had signed the Assurance, it would have agreed to

> "[c]omply, to the extent applicable to it, with Title IX . . . and all applicable requirements imposed by or pursuant to the Department's regulation . . . to the end that . . . no person shall, on the basis of sex, be . . . subjected to discrimination under any education program or activity for which [it] receives or benefits from Federal financial assistance from the Department."

When Grove City persisted in refusing to execute an Assurance, the Department initiated proceedings to declare the College and its students ineligible to receive BEOGs. The Administrative Law Judge held that the federal financial assistance received by Grove City obligated it to execute an Assurance of Compliance and entered an order terminating assistance until Grove City "corrects its noncompliance with Title IX and satisfies the Department that it is in compliance" with the applicable regulations.

Grove City and four of its students then commenced this action in the District Court for the Western District of Pennsylvania, which concluded that the students' BEOGs constituted "Federal financial assistance" to Grove City but held, on several grounds, that the Department could not terminate the students' aid because of the College's refusal to execute an Assurance of Compliance. *Grove City College* v. *Harris* (1980). The Court of Appeals reversed. (CA3 1982). It first examined the language and legislative history of Title IX and held that indirect, as well as direct, aid triggered coverage under § 901(a) and that institutions whose students financed their educations with BEOGs were recipients of federal financial assistance within the meaning of Title IX. Although it recognized that Title IX's provisions are program-specific, the court likened the assistance flowing to Grove City through its students to nonearmarked aid, and, with one judge dissenting, declared that "[w]here the federal government furnishes indirect or non-earmarked aid to an institution, it is apparent to us that the institution itself must be the 'program.' " Finally, the Court of Appeals concluded that the Department could condition financial aid upon the execution of an Assurance of Compliance and that the Department had acted properly in terminating federal financial assistance to the students and Grove City despite the lack of evidence of actual discrimination.

We granted certiorari, (1983), and we now affirm the Court of Appeals' judgment that the Department could terminate BEOGs received by Grove City's students to force the College to execute an Assurance of Compliance.

II

In defending its refusal to execute the Assurance of Compliance required by the Department's regulations, Grove City first contends that neither it nor any "education program or activity" of the College receives any federal financial assistance within the meaning of Title IX by virtue of the fact that some of its students receive BEOGs and use them to pay for their education. We disagree.

Grove City provides a well-rounded liberal arts education and a variety of educational programs and student services. The question is whether any of those programs or activities "receiv[es] Federal financial assistance" within the meaning of Title IX when students finance their education with BEOGs. The structure of the Education Amendments of 1972, in which Congress both created the BEOG program and imposed Title IX's nondiscrimination requirements, strongly suggests an affirmative conclusion. BEOGs were aptly characterized as a "centerpiece of the bill." ... In view of this connection and Congress' express recognition of discrimination in the administration of student financial aid programs, it would indeed be anomalous to discover that one of the primary components of Congress' comprehensive "package of federal aid" · was not intended to trigger coverage under Title IX.

It is not surprising to find, therefore, that the language of § 901(a) contains no hint that Congress perceived a substantive difference between direct institutional assistance and aid received by a school through its students. The linchpin of Grove City's argument that none of its programs receives any federal assistance is a perceived distinction between direct and indirect aid, a distinction that finds no support in the text of § 901(a). Nothing in § 901(a) suggests that Congress elevated form over substance by making the application of the nondiscrimination principle dependent on the manner in which a program or activity receives federal assistance. There is no basis in the statute for the view that only institutions that themselves apply for federal aid or receive checks directly from the federal government are subject to regulation.... As the Court of Appeals observed, "by its all inclusive terminology [§ 901(a)] appears to encompass all forms of federal aid to education, direct or indirect." We have recognized the need to " 'accord [Title IX] a sweep as broad as its language,' " *North Haven Board of Education* v. *Bell* (1982) (quoting *United States* v. *Price* (1966), and we are reluctant to read into § 901(a) a limitation not apparent on its face.

Our reluctance grows when we pause to consider the available evidence of Congress' intent. The economic effect of direct and indirect assistance often is indistinguishable, see *Mueller* v. *Allen* (1983) ... and the BEOG program was structured to ensure that it effectively supplements the College's own financial aid program. Congress undoubtedly comprehended this reality in enacting the Education Amendments of 1972. The legislative history of the amendments is replete with statements evincing Congress' awareness that the student assistance programs established by the amendments would significantly aid colleges and universities. In fact, one of the stated purposes of the student aid provisions was to "provid[e] assistance to institutions of higher education."

Congress' awareness of the purpose and effect of its student aid programs also is reflected in the sparse legislative history of Title IX itself. Title IX was patterned after Title VI of the Civil Rights Act of 1964. The drafters of Title VI envisioned that the receipt of student aid funds would trigger coverage, and, since they approved identical language, we discern no reason to believe that the Congressmen who voted for Title IX intended a different result. . . .

Persuasive evidence of Congress' intent concerning student financial aid may also be gleaned from its subsequent treatment of Title IX. We have twice recognized the probative value of Title IX's unique postenactment history, *North Haven Board of Education* v. *Bell, Cannon* v. *University of Chicago* [1979], and we do so once again. The Department's sex discrimination regulations made clear that "[s]cholarships, loans, [and] grants . . . extended directly to . . . students for payment to" an institution constitute federal financial assistance to that entity. Under the statutory "laying before" procedure of the General Education Provisions Act, Congress was afforded an opportunity to invalidate aspects of the regulations it deemed inconsistent with Title IX. The regulations were clear, and Secretary [of Health, Education and Welfare Caspar W.] Weinberger left no doubt concerning the Department's position that "the furnishing of student assistance to a student who uses it at a particular institution . . . [is] Federal aid which is covered by the statute." Yet, neither House passed a disapproval resolution. Congress' failure to disapprove the regulations is not dispositive, but, as we recognized in *North Haven Board of Education* v. *Bell*, it strongly implies that the regulations accurately reflect congressional intent. Congress has never disavowed this implication and in fact has acted consistently with it on a number of occasions.

With the benefit of clear statutory language, powerful evidence of Congress' intent, and a longstanding and coherent administrative construction of the phrase "receiving Federal financial assistance," we have little trouble concluding that Title IX coverage is not foreclosed because federal funds are granted to Grove City's students rather than directly to one of the College's educational programs. There remains the question, however, of identifying the "education program or activity" of the College that can properly be characterized as "receiving" federal assistance through grants to some of the students attending the College.

III

An analysis of Title IX's language and legislative history led us to conclude in *North Haven Board of Education* v. *Bell* that "an agency's authority under Title IX both to promulgate regulations and to terminate funds is subject to the program-specific limitations §§ 901 and 902." Although the legislative history contains isolated suggestions that entire institutions are subject to the nondiscrimination provision whenever one of their programs receives federal assistance, we cannot accept the Court of

Appeals' conclusion that in the circumstances present here Grove City itself is a "program or activity" that may be regulated in its entirety. Nevertheless, we find no merit in Grove City's contention that a decision treating BEOGs as "Federal financial assistance" cannot be reconciled with Title IXs program-specific language since BEOGs are not tied to any specific "education program or activity."

If Grove City participated in the BEOG program through the RDS [Regular Disbursement System], we would have no doubt that the "education program or activity receiving Federal financial assistance" would not be the entire College; rather, it would be its student financial aid program. RDS institutions receive federal funds directly, but can use them only to subsidize or expand their financial aid programs and to recruit students who might otherwise be unable to enroll. In short, the assistance is earmarked for the recipient's financial aid program. Only by ignoring Title IX's program-specific language could we conclude that funds received under the RDS, awarded to eligible students, and paid back to the school when tuition comes due represent federal aid to the entire institution.

We see no reason to reach a different conclusion merely because Grove City has elected to participate in the ADS. Although Grove City does not itself disburse students' awards, BEOGs clearly augment the resources that the College itself devotes to financial aid. As is true of the RDS, however, the fact that federal funds eventually reach the College's general operating budget cannot subject Grove City to institution-wide coverage. Grove City's choice of administrative mechanisms, we hold, neither expands nor contracts the breadth of the "program or activity" — the financial aid program — that receives federal assistance and that may be regulated under Title IX.

To the extent that the Court of Appeals' holding that BEOGs received by Grove City's students constitute aid to the entire institution rests on the possibility that federal funds received by one program or activity free up the College's own resources for use elsewhere, the Court of Appeals' reasoning is doubly flawed. First, there is no evidence that the federal aid received by Grove City's students results in the diversion of funds from the College's own financial aid program to other areas within the institution. Second, and more important, the Court of Appeals' assumption that Title IX applies to programs receiving a larger share of a school's own limited resources as a result of federal assistance earmarked for use elsewhere within the institution is inconsistent with the program-specific nature of the statute. Most federal educational assistance has economic ripple effects throughout the aided institution, and it would be difficult, if not impossible, to determine which programs or activities derive such indirect benefits. Under the Court of Appeals' theory, an entire school would be subject to Title IX merely because one of its students received a small BEOG or because one of its departments received an earmarked federal grant. This result cannot be squared with Congress' intent.

The Court of Appeals' analogy between student financial aid received by an educational institution and nonearmarked direct grants provides a more plausible justification for its holding, but it too is faulty. Student financial aid programs, we believe, are *sui generis*. In neither purpose nor effect can BEOGs be fairly characterized as unrestricted grants that institutions may use for whatever purpose they desire. The BEOG program was designed, not merely to increase the total resources available to educational institutions, but to enable them to offer their services to students who had previously been unable to afford higher education. It is true, of course, that substantial portions of the BEOGs received by Grove City's students ultimately find their way into the College's general operating budget and are used to provide a variety of services to the students through whom the funds pass. However, we have found no persuasive evidence suggesting that Congress intended that the Department's regulatory authority follow federally aided students from classroom to classroom, building to building, or activity to activity. In addition, as Congress recognized in considering the Education Amendments of 1972, the economic effect of student aid is far different from the effect of nonearmarked grants to institutions themselves since the former, unlike the latter, increases both an institution's resources and its obligations.... In that sense, student financial aid more closely resembles many earmarked grants.

We conclude that the receipt of BEOGs by some of Grove City's students does not trigger institution-wide coverage under Title IX. In purpose and effect, BEOGs represent federal financial assistance to the College's own financial aid program, and it is that program that may properly be regulated under Title IX.

IV

Since Grove City operates an "education program or activity receiving Federal financial assistance," the Department may properly demand that the College execute an Assurance of Compliance with Title IX. Grove City contends, however, that the Assurance it was requested to sign was invalid, both on its face and as interpreted by the Department, in that it failed to comport with Title IX's program-specific character. Whatever merit that objection might have had at the time, it is not now a valid basis for refusing to execute an Assurance of Compliance.

The Assurance of Compliance regulation itself does not, on its face, impose institution-wide obligations. Recipients must provide assurance only that "each education program or activity operated by ... [them] *and to which this part applies* will be operated in compliance with this part." ([E]mphasis added). The regulations apply, by their terms, "to every recipient and to *each education program or activity* operated by such recipient *which receives or benefits from Federal financial assistance.*" ([E]mphasis added). These regulations, like those at issue in *North Haven Board of Education* v. *Bell* (1982), "conform with the limitations Congress enacted in §§ 901 and 902." Nor does the Department now claim that its regulations reach beyond the College's student aid program. Furthermore, the Assurance of Compliance currently in use, like the one Grove City refused to execute, does not on its face purport to reach the entire College; it certifies compliance with respect to those "education programs and activities receiving Federal financial assistance." Under this opinion, consistent with the program-specific requirements of Title IX, the covered education program is the College's financial aid program.

A refusal to execute a proper program-specific Assurance of Compliance warrants termination of federal assistance to the student financial aid program. The College's contention that termination must be preceded by a finding of actual discrimination finds no support in the language of § 902, which plainly authorizes that sanction to effect "[c]ompliance with any requirement adopted pursuant to this section." Regulations authorizing termination of assistance for refusal to execute an Assurance of Compliance with Title VI had been promulgated and upheld long before Title IX was enacted, and Congress no doubt anticipated that similar regulations would be developed to implement Title IX. We conclude, therefore, that the Department may properly condition federal financial assistance on the recipient's assurance that it will conduct the aided program or activity in accordance with Title IX and the applicable regulations.

V

Grove City's final challenge to the Court of Appeals' decision — that conditioning federal assistance on compliance with Title IX infringes First Amendment rights of the College and its students — warrants only brief consideration. Congress is free to attach reasonable and unambiguous conditions to federal financial assistance that educational institutions are not obligated to accept. *E.g., Pennhurst State School & Hospital* v. *Halderman* (1981). Grove City may terminate its participation in the BEOG program and thus avoid the requirements of § 901(a). Students affected by the Department's action may either take their BEOGs elsewhere or attend Grove City without federal financial assistance. Requiring Grove City to comply with Title IX's prohibition of discrimination as a condition for its continued eligibility to participate in the BEOG program infringes no First Amendment rights of the College or its students.

Accordingly, the judgment of the Court of Appeals is

Affirmed.

JUSTICE POWELL, with whom CHIEF JUSTICE BURGER and JUSTICE O'CONNOR join, concurring.

As I agree that the holding in this case is dictated by the language and legislative history of Title IX, and the Regulations of the Department of Education, I join the Court's decision. I do so reluctantly and write briefly to record my view that the case is an unedifying example of overzealousness on the part of the Federal Government.

Grove City College (Grove City) may be unique among colleges in our country; certainly there are few others like it. Founded more than a century ago in 1876, Grove City is an independent, coeducational liberal arts college. It describes itself as having "both a Christian world view and a freedom philosophy," perceiving these as "interrelated." ... Some 140 of the College's students were receiving Basic Educational Opportunity Grants (BEOGs), and 342 had obtained Guaranteed Student Loans (GSLs). The grants were made directly to the students through the Department of Education, and the student loans were guaranteed by the federal government. Apart from this indirect assistance, Grove City has followed an unbending policy of refusing all forms of government assistance, whether federal, state or local. It was and is the policy of this small college to remain wholly independent of government assistance, recognizing — as this case well illustrates — that with acceptance of such assistance one surrenders a certain measure of the freedom that Americans always have cherished.

This case involves a Regulation adopted by the Department to implement § 901(a) of Title IX. It is well to bear in mind what § 901(a) provides:

> "No person in the United States shall, on the basis of sex, be excluded from participation in, be denied the benefits of, or be subjected to discrimination under any education program or activity receiving federal financial assistance...."

The sole purpose of the statute is to make unlawful *"discrimination"* by recipients of federal financial assistance on the "basis of sex." The undisputed fact is that Grove City does not discriminate — and so far as the record in this case shows — never has discriminated against anyone on account of sex, race, or national origin. This case has nothing whatever to do with discrimination past or present. The College therefore has complied to the letter with the sole purpose of § 901(a).

As the Court describes, the case arises pursuant to a Regulation adopted under Title IX that authorizes the Secretary to obtain from recipients of federal aid an "Assurance of Compliance" with Title IX and regulations issued thereunder. At the outset of this litigation, the Department insisted that by accepting students who received BEOG awards, Grove City's entire institution was subject to regulation under Title IX. The College, in view of its policies and principles of independence and its record of non-discrimination, objected to executing this Assurance. One would have thought that the Department, confronted as it is with cases of national importance that involve actual discrimination, would have respected the independence and admirable record of this college. But common sense and good judgment failed to prevail. The Department chose to litigate, and instituted an administrative proceeding to compel Grove City to execute an agreement to operate all of its programs and activities in full compliance with all of the regulations promulgated under Title IX — despite the College's record as an institution that had operated to date in full accordance with the letter and spirit of Title IX. . . .

The effect of the Department's termination of the student grants and loans would not have been limited to the College itself. Indeed, the most direct effect would have been upon the students themselves. Absent the availability of other scholarship funds, many of them would have had to abandon their college education or choose another school. It was to avoid these serious consequences, that this suit was instituted. The College prevailed in the District Court but lost in the Court of Appeals. Only after Grove City had brought its case before this Court, did the Department retreat to its present position that Title IX applies only to Grove City's financial aid office. On this narrow theory, the Department has prevailed, having taken this small independent college, which it acknowledges has engaged in no discrimination whatever, through six years of litigations with the full weight of the federal government opposing it. I cannot believe that the Department will rejoice in its "victory."

JUSTICE STEVENS, concurring in part and concurring in the result.

For two reasons. I am unable to join part III of the Court's opinion. First, it is an advisory opinion unnecessary to today's decision, and second, the advice is predicated on speculation rather than evidence.

The controverted issue in this litigation is whether Grove City College may be required to execute the "Assurance of Compliance with Title IX" tendered to it by the Secretary in order to continue receiving the benefits of the federal financial assistance provided by the BEOG program. The Court of Appeals affirmed the District Court's decision that Grove City is a "recipient" of federal financial assistance, and reversed its decision that the Secretary could not terminate federal financial assistance because Grove City refused to execute the Assurance. The Court today holds (in part II of its opinion) that Grove City is a recipient of federal financial assistance within the meaning of Title IX, and (in part IV) that Grove City must execute the Assurance of Compliance in order to continue receiving that assistance. These holdings are fully sufficient to sustain the judgment the Court reviews, as the Court acknowledges by affirming that judgment.

In part III of its opinion, the Court holds that Grove City is not required to refrain from discrimination on the basis of sex except in its financial aid program. In so stating, the Court decides an issue that is not in dispute. . . .

. . . The Court overlooks the fact that the regulation is in the disjunctive; Title IX coverage does not always depend on the actual receipt of federal financial assistance by a given program or activity. The record does not tell us how important the BEOG program is to Grove City, in either absolute or relative terms; nor does it tell us anything about how the benefits of the program are allocated within the institution. The Court decides that a small scholarship for just one student should not subject the entire school to coverage. But why should this case be judged on the basis of that hypothetical example instead of a different one? What if the record showed — and I do not suggest that it does — that all of the BEOG money was reserved for, or merely happened to be used by, talented athletes and that their tuition payments were sufficient to support an entire athletic program that would otherwise be abandoned? Would such a hypothetical program be covered by Title IX? And if this athletic program discriminated on the basis of sex, could it plausibly be contended that Congress intended that BEOG money could be used to enable such a program to survive? Until we know something about the character of the particular program, it is inappropriate to give advice about an issue that is not before us.

Accordingly, while I subscribe to the reasoning in parts I, II, and IV of the Court's opinion, I am unable to join part III.

JUSTICE BRENNAN, with whom JUSTICE MARSHALL joins, concurring in part and dissenting in part.

The Court today concludes that Grove City College is "receiving Federal financial assistance" within the meaning of Title IX of the Education Amendments of 1972 because a number of its students receive federal education grants. As the Court persuasively demonstrates in Part II of its opinion, that conclusion is dictated by "the need to accord [Title IX] a sweep as broad as its language," by reference to the analogous statutory language and legislative history of Title VI of the Civil Rights Act of 1964, by a reliance on the unique postenactment history of Title IX, and by recognition of the strong congressional intent that there is no "substantive difference between direct institutional assistance and aid received by a school through its students." For these same reasons, however, I cannot join Part III of the Court's opinion, in which the Court interprets the language in Title IX that limits application of the statute to "any education program or activity" receiving federal monies. By conveniently ignoring these controlling indicia of congressional intent, the Court also ignores the primary purposes for which Congress enacted Title IX. The result — allowing Title IX coverage for the College's financial aid program, but rejecting institution-wide coverage even though federal monies benefit the entire College — may be superficially pleasing to those who are uncomfortable with federal intrusion into private educational institutions, but it has no relationship to the statutory scheme enacted by Congress.

I

The Court has twice before had occasion to ascertain the precise scope of Title IX. See *North Haven Board of Education* v. *Bell* (1982); *Cannon* v. *University of Chicago* (1979). In both cases, the Court emphasized the broad congressional purposes underlying enactment of the statute....

... [A] careful examination of the statute's legislative history, the accepted meaning of similar statutory language in Title VI, and the postenactment history of Title IX will demonstrate that the Court's narrow definition of "program or activity" is directly contrary to congressional intent.

A

The statute that was eventually enacted as Title IX had its genesis in separate proposals considered by the House and the Senate, in 1970 and 1971, respectively. In the House, the Special Subcommittee on Education, under the leadership of Representative Edith Green, held extensive hearings during the summer of 1970 on "Discrimination Against Women." . . . Testimony offered during those hearings . . . focused on the evidence of pervasive sex discrimination in educational institutions. It therefore was not surprising that the version of the subcommittee's proposal that was eventually passed by the full House was limited in its application to federally assisted *education* programs or activities. . . . More important for present purposes, however, the House-passed bill retained the overall format of the subcommittee proposal, and therefore continued to incorporate the "program or activity" language and its enforcement provisions from Title VI.

In the Senate, action began on Title IX in 1971, when Senator [Birch] Bayh first introduced a floor amendment to the comprehensive education legislation then being considered. As then written, Senator Bayh's proposal was clearly intended to cover an entire institution whenever any education program or activity conducted by that institution was receiving federal monies. . . .

. . . There is nothing to suggest that the Senate had retreated from the underlying premise of the original amendment proposed by Senator Bayh in 1971 — that sex discrimination would be prohibited in any educational institution receiving Federal financial assistance. . . .

In sum, although the contemporaneous legislative history does not definitively explain the intended meaning of the program-specific language included in Title IX, it lends no support to the interpretation adopted by the Court. What is clear, moreover, is that Congress intended enforcement of Title IX to mirror the policies and procedures utilized for enforcement under Title VI. . . .

[Section II Omitted]

In sum, the program-specific language in Title IX was designed to ensure that the reach of the statute is dependent upon the scope of federal financial assistance provided to an institution. When that financial assistance is clearly intended to serve as federal aid for the entire institution, the institution as a whole should be covered by the statute's prohibition on sex discrimination. Any other interpretation clearly disregards the intent of Congress and severely weakens the antidiscrimination provisions included in Title IX. I therefore cannot join in Part III of the Court's opinion.

March

March

COURT ON PUBLIC DISPLAY
OF NATIVITY SCENE
March 5, 1984

In the most important ruling in recent years on the constitutional separation between church and state, the Supreme Court held March 5 that city officials of Pawtucket, R.I., did not violate the First Amendment when they included a Nativity scene, or crèche, as one of a number of traditional Christmas elements in the community's annual holiday display. The decision marked the first time the Court had permitted the official display of a symbol explicitly and exclusively Christian.

Writing for the majority in the 5-4 Lynch v. Donnelly decision, Chief Justice Warren E. Burger declared that the Constitution "affirmatively mandates accommodation, not merely tolerance, of all religions, and forbids hostility toward any." That declaration dovetailed with the Reagan administration's arguments for a change in the attitude of federal courts toward religion. Attorney General William French Smith, in a February 4 speech, spoke critically of lower federal courts' "increasing tendency to be hostile toward religion." The administration, which filed a brief supporting Pawtucket officials, supported the view that the First Amendment simply required the state to take an attitude of "benevolent neutrality" toward religion, according to Smith.

Although Roman Catholic bishops and fundamentalist Christians expressed approval of the decision, Jewish, Islamic, and some Christian groups decried it. Justice William J. Brennan, Jr., writing the minority opinion, held that it was a "plain fact that Pawtucket's action amounts to an impermissible governmental endorsement of a particular faith."

Pawtucket Case

For 40 years Pawtucket officials had erected a Christmas holiday display, which included a variety of Christmas decor — such as reindeer, Santa Claus's house and sleigh, a Christmas tree and colored lights — as well as the crèche at issue in Lynch v. Donnelly.

In 1980 several Pawtucket residents and the state affiliate of the American Civil Liberties Union challenged the inclusion of the crèche, arguing that it violated the First Amendment ban on government action establishing religion. (Dennis M. Lynch was the city's major at the time; Daniel Donnelly was one of the objectors.) A federal district court and the 1st U.S. Circuit Court of Appeals agreed. The city appealed to the Supreme Court to reverse the lower courts and permit it to continue using the Nativity scene in its Christmas display. Chief Justice Burger and Justices Byron R. White, Lewis F. Powell Jr., William H. Rehnquist, and Sandra Day O'Connor found the challenged practice permissible. Siding with the city, Burger wrote that it was useful, but not completely accurate, to speak of a "wall" of separation dividing church and state. "No significant segment of our society and no institutions within it can exist in a vacuum or in total or absolute isolation from all the other parts, much less from government," he said.

"There is an unbroken history of official acknowledgment by all three branches of government of the role of religion in American life from at least 1789," Burger continued. The chief justice also pointed to the long history of national observance of Thanksgiving and Christmas; the nation's motto, "In God We Trust"; the phrase "one nation under God" in the pledge of allegiance to the flag; and the inclusion of religious paintings in art galleries supported by public revenues. "This history may help explain why the Court consistently has declined to take a rigid, absolutist view of the Establishment Clause," he said.

When a law or official conduct was challenged as breaching the Establishment Clause, the Court examined it to see whether in fact it did establish any religion or tended to do so, Burger said. Applying that approach to Pawtucket's Christmas display, the majority found inclusion of the Nativity scene permissible. The crèche simply "depicts the historical origins" of Christmas, Burger wrote, and whatever benefit accrued "to one faith or religion or to all religions, is indirect, remote and incidental."

"We are satisfied that the city has a secular purpose for including the crèche, that the city has not impermissibly advanced religion, and that including the creche does not create excessive entanglement between religion and government," Burger concluded.

Dissenting Opinion

Justices Brennan, Thurgood Marshall, Harry A. Blackmun, and John Paul Stevens took issue with the majority. When public officials "appear to endorse the distinctively religious elements of this otherwise secular event [Christmas], they encroach upon First Amendment freedoms," Brennan argued. "For it is at that point that the government brings to the forefront the theological content of the holiday and places the prestige, power and financial support of a civil authority in the service of a particular faith."

A Nativity scene is "far more than a mere 'traditional' symbol of Christmas," Brennan said. "To suggest, as the Court does, that such a symbol is merely 'traditional' and therefore no different from Santa's house or reindeer is not only offensive to those for whom the crèche has profound significance, but insulting to those who insist for religious or personal reasons that the story of Christ is in no sense a part of 'history' nor an unavoidable element of our national 'heritage,' " Brennan wrote.

"Surely, this is a misuse of a sacred symbol," Blackmun said in a separate dissenting opinion. Joined by Stevens, he criticized the majority for ignoring the weight of precedent and for relegating the crèche to "the role of a neutral harbinger of the holiday season, useful for commercial, but devoid of any inherent meaning and incapable of enhancing the religious tenor of a display of which it is an integral part."

> *Following are excerpts from the Supreme Court's March 5, 1984, ruling in* Lynch v. Donnelly *that city officials of Pawtucket, R. I., did not violate the First Amendment when they included a Nativity scene as part of an official Christmas display; from the concurring opinion of Justice Sandra Day O'Connor; from the dissenting opinion of Justices William J. Brennan Jr., Thurgood Marshall, Harry A. Blackmun and John Paul Stevens; and from the dissenting opinion of Justices Blackmun and Stevens:*

<u>No. 82-1256</u>

Dennis Lynch, etc., et al., Petitioners *v.* Daniel Donnelly et al.	On writ of certiorari to the United States Court of Appeals for the First Circuit

[March 5, 1984]

THE CHIEF JUSTICE delivered the opinion of the Court.

We granted certiorari to decide whether the Establishment Clause of the

First Amendment prohibits a municipality from including a crèche, or Nativity scene, in its annual Christmas display.

I

Each year, in cooperation with the downtown retail merchants' association, the City of Pawtucket, Rhode Island, erects a Christmas display as part of its observance of the Christmas holiday season. The display is situated in a park owned by a nonprofit organization and located in the heart of the shopping district. The display is essentially like those to be found in hundreds of towns or cities across the Nation — often on public grounds — during the Christmas season. The Pawtucket display comprises many of the figures and decorations traditionally associated with Christmas, including, among other things, a Santa Claus house, reindeer pulling Santa's sleigh, candy-striped poles, a Christmas tree, carolers, cutout figures representing such characters as a clown, an elephant, and a teddy bear, hundreds of colored lights, a large banner that reads "SEASONS GREETINGS," and the crèche at issue here. All components of this display are owned by the City.

The crèche, which has been included in the display for 40 or more years, consists of the traditional figures, including the Infant Jesus, Mary and Joseph, angels, shepherds, kings, and animals, all ranging in height from 5″ to 5′. In 1973, when the present crèche was acquired, it cost the City $1365; it now is valued at $200. The erection and dismantling of the crèche costs the City about $20 per year; nominal expenses are incurred in lighting the crèche. No money has been expended on its maintenance for the past 10 years.

Respondents, Pawtucket residents and individual members of the Rhode Island affiliate of the American Civil Liberties Union, and the affiliate itself, brought this action in the United States District Court for Rhode Island, challenging the City's inclusion of the crèche in the annual display. The District Court held that the City's inclusion of the crèche in the display violates the Establishment Clause, *Donnelly* v. *Lynch* (D.R.I. 1981), which is binding on the states through the Fourteenth Amendment. The District Court found that, by including the crèche in the Christmas display, the City has "tried to endorse and promulgate religious beliefs" and that "erection of the crèche has the real and substantial effect of affiliating the City with the Christian beliefs that the crèche represents." This "appearance of official sponsorship," it believed, "confers more than a remote and incidental benefit on Christianity." Last, although the court acknowledged the absence of administrative entanglement, it found that excessive entanglement has been fostered as a result of the political divisiveness of including the crèche in the celebration. The City was permanently enjoined from including the crèche in the display.

A divided panel of the Court of Appeals for the First Circuit affirmed. *Donnelly* v. *Lynch* (1982). We granted certiorari (1983), and we reverse.

II

A

This Court has explained that the purpose of the Establishment and Free Exercise Clauses of the First Amendment is

> "to prevent, as far as possible, the intrusion of either [the church or the state] into the precincts of the other." *Lemon* v. *Kurtzman* (1971).

At the same time, however, the Court has recognized that

> "total separation is not possible in an absolute sense. Some relationship between government and religious organizations is inevitable."

In every Establishment Clause case, we must reconcile the inescapable tension between the objective of preventing unnecessary intrusion of either the church or the state upon the other, and the reality that, as the Court has so often noted, total separation of the two is not possible.

The Court has sometimes described the Religion Clauses as erecting a "wall" between church and state, see, *e.g., Everson* v. *Board of Education* (1947). The concept of a "wall" of separation is a useful figure of speech probably deriving from views of Thomas Jefferson. The metaphor has served as a reminder that the Establishment Clause forbids an established church or anything approaching it. But the metaphor itself is not a wholly accurate description of the practical aspects of the relationship that in fact exists between church and state.

No significant segment of our society and no institution within it can exist in a vacuum or in total or absolute isolation from all the other parts, much less from government. "It has never been thought either possible or desirable to enforce a regime of total separation. . . ." *Committee for Public Education & Religious Liberty* v. *Nyquist* (1973). Nor does the Constitution require complete separation of church and state; it affirmatively mandates accommodation, not merely tolerance, of all religions, and forbids hostility toward any. See, *e.g. Zorach* v. *Clauson* (1952); *McCollum* v. *Board of Education* (1948). Anything less would require the "callous indifference" we have said was never intended by the Establishment Clause. *Zorach.* Indeed, we have observed, such hostility would bring us into "war with our national tradition as embodied in the First Amendment's guaranty of the free exercise of religion." *McCollum.*

B

The Court's interpretation of the Establishment Clause has comported with what history reveals was the contemporaneous understanding of its guarantees. A significant example of the contemporaneous understanding of that Clause is found in the events of the first week of the First Session of the First Congress in 1789. In the very week that Congress approved the Establishment Clause as part of the Bill of Rights for submission to the states, it enacted legislation providing for paid chaplains for the House and Senate.

In *Marsh* v. *Chambers* (1983), we noted that seventeen Members of that First Congress had been Delegates to the Constitutional Convention where freedom of speech, press and religion and antagonism toward an established church were subjects of frequent discussion. We saw no conflict with the Establishment Clause when Nebraska employed members of the clergy as official Legislative Chaplains to give opening prayers at sessions of the state legislature.

The interpretation of the Establishment Clause by Congress in 1789 takes on special significance in light of the Court's emphasis that the First Congress:

> "was a Congress whose constitutional decisions have always been regarded, as they should be regarded, as of the greatest weight in the interpretation of that fundamental instrument," *Myers* v. *United States* (1926).

It is clear that neither the seventeen draftsmen of the Constitution who were Members of the First Congress, nor the Congress of 1789, saw any establishment problem in the employment of congressional Chaplains to offer daily prayers in the Congress, a practice that has continued for nearly two centuries. It would be difficult to identify a more striking example of the accommodation of religious belief intended by the Framers.

C

There is an unbroken history of official acknowledgement by all three branches of government of the role of religion in American life from at least 1789. Seldom in our opinions was this more affirmatively expressed that in Justice Douglas' opinion for the Court validating a program allowing release of public school students from classes to attend off-campus religious exercises. Rejecting a claim that the program violated the Establishment Clause, the Court asserted pointedly:

> "We are a religious people whose institutions presuppose a Supreme Being." *Zorach* v. *Schempp.*

See also *Abrington School District* v. *Schempp* (1963).

Our history is replete with official references to the value and invocation of Divine guidance in deliberations and pronouncements of the Founding Fathers and contemporary leaders. Beginning in the early colonial period long before Independence, a day of Thanksgiving was celebrated as a religious holiday to give thanks for the bounties of Nature as gifts from God. President Washington and his successors proclaimed Thanksgiving, with all its religious overtones, a day of national celebration and Congress made it a National Holiday more than a century ago. That holiday has not lost its theme of expressing thanks for Divine aid any more than has Christmas lost its religious significance.

Executive Orders and other official announcements of Presidents and of the Congress have proclaimed both Christmas and Thanksgiving National Holidays in religious terms. And, by Acts of Congress, it has long been the practice that federal employees are released from duties on these National Holidays, while being paid from the same public revenues that provide the compensation of the Chaplains of the Senate and the House and the military services. . . . Thus, it is clear that Government has long recognized — indeed it has subsidized — holidays with religious significance.

Other examples of reference to our religious heritage are found in the statutorily prescribed national motto "In God We Trust," which Congress and the President mandated for our currency and in the language "One nation under God," as part of the Pledge of Allegiance to the American flag. That pledge is recited by thousands of public school children — and adults — every year.

Art galleries supported by public revenues display religious paintings of the 15th and 16th centuries, predominantly inspired by one religious faith. The National Gallery in Washington, maintained with Government support, for example, has long exhibited masterpieces with religious messages, notably the Last Supper, and paintings depicting the Birth of Christ, the Crucifixion, and the Resurrection, among many others with explicit Christian themes and messages. The very chamber in which oral arguments on this case were heard is decorated with a notable and permanent — not seasonal — symbol of religion: Moses with Ten Commandments. Congress has long provided chapels in the Capitol for religious worship and meditation.

There are countless other illustrations of the Government's acknowledgement of our religious heritage and governmental sponsorship of graphic manifestations of that heritage. Congress has directed the President to proclaim a National Day of Prayer each year "on which [day] the people of the United States may turn to God in prayer and meditation at churches, in groups, and as individuals." Our Presidents have repeatedly issued such Proclamations. Presidential Proclamations and messages have also issued to commemorate Jewish Heritage Week (1981) and the Jewish High Holy Days (Sept. 29, 1981). One cannot look at even this brief resume without finding that our history is pervaded by expressions of religious beliefs such as are found in *Zorach*. Equally pervasive is the evidence of accommodation of all faiths and all forms of religious expression, and hostility toward none. Through this accommodation, as Justice Douglas observed, governmental action has "follow[ed] the best of our traditions" and "respect[ed] the religious nature of our people."

III

This history may help explain why the Court consistently has declined to take a rigid, absolutist view of the Establishment Clause. We have refused "to construe the Religion Clauses with a literalness that would undermine the ultimate constitutional objective *as illuminated by history.*" *Walz* v. *Tax Commission* (1970) (Emphasis added). In our modern complex society, whose traditions and constitutional underpinnings rest on and encourage diversity and pluralism in all areas, an absolutist approach in applying the Establishment Clause is simplistic and has been uniformly rejected by the Court.

Rather than mechanically invalidating all governmental conduct or statutes that confer benefits or give special recognition to religion in general or to one faith — as an absolutist approach would dictate — the Court has scrutinized challenged legislation or official conduct to determine whether, in reality, it establishes a religion or religious faith, or tends to do so.... Joseph Story wrote a century and a half ago:

> "The real object of the [First] Amendment was ... to prevent any national ecclesiastical establishment, which should give to an hierarchy the exclusive patronage of the national government."

In each case, the inquiry calls for line drawing; no fixed, *per se* rule can be framed. The Establishment Clause like the Due Process Clauses is not a precise, detailed provision in a legal code capable of ready application. The purpose of the Establishment Clause "was to state an objective, not to write a statute." *Walz.* The line between permissible relationships and those barred by the Clause can no more be straight and unwavering than due process can be defined in a single stroke or phrase or test. The Clause erects a "blurred, indistinct, and variable barrier depending on all the circumstances of a particular relationship." *Lemon.*

In the line-drawing process we have often found it useful to inquire whether the challenged law or conduct has a secular purpose, whether its principal or primary effect is to advance or inhibit religion, and whether it creates an excessive entanglement of government with religion. But, we have repeatedly emphasized our unwillingness to be confined to any single test or criterion in this sensitive area. See *e.g. Tilton* v. *Richardson* (1971); *Nyquist....*

In this case, the focus of our inquiry must be on the crèche in the context of the Christmas season. See, *e.g., Stone* v. *Graham* (1980) *(per curiam); Abington School District* v. *Schempp.* In *Stone,* for example, we invalidated a state statute requiring the posting of a copy of the Ten Commandments on public classroom walls. But the Court carefully pointed out that the Commandments were posted purely as a religious admonition, not "integrated into the school curriculum, where the Bible may constitutionally be used in an appropriate study of history, civilization, ethics, comparative religion, or the like." Similarly, in *Abington,* although the Court struck down the practices in two States requiring daily Bible readings in public schools, it specifically noted that nothing in the Court's holding was intended to "indicat[e] that such study of the Bible or of religion, when presented objectively as part of a secular program of education, may not be effected consistently with the First Amendment." Focus exclusively on the religious component of an activity would inevitably lead to its invalidation under the Establishment Clause.

The Court has invalidated legislation or governmental action on the ground that a secular purpose was lacking, but only when it has concluded there was no question that the statute or activity was motivated wholly by religious considerations.... Even where the benefits to religion were substantial ... we saw a secular purpose and no conflict with the Establishment Clause. Cf. *Larkin* v. *Grendel's Den* (1983).

The District Court inferred from the religious nature of the crèche that the City has no secular purpose for the display. In so doing, it rejected the City's claim that its reasons for including the crèche are essentially the same as its reasons for sponsoring the display as a whole. The District Court plainly erred by focusing almost exclusively on the crèche. When viewed in the proper context of the Christmas Holiday season, it is apparent that, on this record, there is insufficient evidence to establish that the inclusion of the crèche is a purposeful or surreptitious effort to express some kind of subtle governmental advocacy of a particular religious message. In a pluralistic society a variety of motives and purposes are implicated. The City, like the Congress and Presidents, however, has principally taken note of a significant historical religious event long celebrated in the Western World. The crèche in the display depicts the historical origins of this traditional event. . . .

The narrow question is whether there is a secular purpose for Pawtucket's display of the crèche. The display is sponsored by the City to celebrate the Holiday and to depict the origins of that Holiday. These are legitimate secular purposes. The District Court's inference, drawn from the religious nature of the crèche, that the City has no secular purpose was, on this record, clearly erroneous.

The District Court found that the primary effect of including the crèche is to confer a substantial and impermissible benefit on religion in general and on the Christian faith in particular. Comparisons of the relative benefits to religion of different forms of governmental support are elusive and difficult to make. But to conclude that the primary effect of incuding the crèche is to advance religion in violation of the Establishment Clause would require that we view it as more beneficial to and more an endorsement of religion, for example, than expenditure of large sums of public money for textbooks supplied throughout the country to students attending church-sponsored schools, *Board of Education* v. *Allen;* expenditure of public funds for transportation of students to church-sponsored schools, *Everson* v. *Board of Education;* federal grants for college buildings of church-sponsored institutions of higher education combining secular and religious education, *Tilton;* noncategorical grants to church-sponsored colleges and universities, *Roemer* v. *Board of Public Works* (1976); and the tax exemptions for church properties sanctioned in *Walz.* It would also require that we view it as more of an endorsement of religion than the Sunday Closing Laws upheld in *McGowan* v. *Maryland* (1961); the release time program for religious training in *Zorach;* and the legislative prayers upheld in *Marsh.*

We are unable to discern a greater aid to religion deriving from inclusion of the crèche than from these benefits and endorsements previously held not violative of the Establishment Clause. What was said about the legislative prayers in *Marsh* and implied about the Sunday Closing Laws in *McGowan* is true of the City's inclusion of the crèche: its "reason or effect merely happens to coincide or harmonize with the tenets of some . . . religions." See *McGowan.*

This case differs significantly from *Larkin* v. *Grendel's Den* and *McCollum* where religion was substantially aided. In *Grendel's Den,* important governmental power — a licensing veto authority — had been vested in churches. In *McCollum,* government had made religious instruction available in public school classrooms; the State had not only used the public school buildings for the teaching of religion, it had "afford[ed] sectarian groups an invaluable aid ... [by] provid[ing] pupils for their religious classes through use of the State's compulsory public school machinery." No comparable benefit to religion is discernible here.

The dissent asserts some observers may perceive that the City has aligned itself with the Christian faith by including a Christian symbol in its display and that this serves to advance religion. We can assume, *arguendo,* that the display advances religion in a sense; but our precedents plainly contemplate that on occasion some advancement of religion will result from governmental action. The Court has made it abundantly clear, however, that "not every law that confers an 'indirect,' 'remote,' or 'incidental' benefit upon [religion] is, for that reason alone, constitutionally invalid." *Nyquist.* ... Here, whatever benefit to one faith or religion or to all religions, is indirect, remote and incidental; display of the crèche is no more an advancement or endorsement of religion that the Congressional and Executive recognition of the origins of the Holiday itself as "Christ's Mass," or the exhibition of literally hundreds of religious paintings in governmentally supported museums.

The District Court found that there had been no administrative entanglement between religion and state resulting from the City's ownership and use of the crèche. But it went on to hold that some political divisiveness was engendered by this litigation. Coupled with its finding of an impermissible sectarian purpose and effect, this persuaded the court that there was "excessive entangelement." The Court of Appeals expressly declined to accept the District Court's finding that inclusion of the crèche has caused political divisiveness along religious lines, and noted that this Court has never held that political divisiveness alone was sufficient to invalidate government conduct.

Entanglement is a question of kind and degree. In this case, however, there is no reason to disturb the District Court's finding on the absence of administrative entanglement. There is no evidence of contact with church authorities concerning the content or design of the exhibit prior to or since Patucket's purchase of the crèche. No expenditures for maintenance of the crèche have been necessary; and since the City owns the crèche, now valued at $200, the tangible material it contributes is *de minimis*. In many respects the display requires far less ongoing, day-to-day interaction between church and state than religious paintings in public galleries. There is nothing here, of course, like the "comprehensive, discriminating, and continuing state surveillance" or the "enduring entanglement" present in *Lemon.*

The Court of Appeals correctly observed that this Court has not held that political divisiveness alone can serve to invalidate otherwise permissible conduct. And we decline to so hold today. This case does not involve a direct subsidy to church-sponsored schools or colleges, or other religious institutions, and hence no inquiry into potential political divisiveness is even called for, *Mueller* v. *Allen* (1983). In any event, apart from this litigation there is no evidence of political friction or divisiveness over the crèche in the 40-year history of Pawtucket's Christmas celebration. The District Court stated that the inclusion of the crèche for the 40 years has been "marked by no apparent dissension" and that the display has had a "calm history." Curiously, it went on to hold that the political divisiveness engendered by this lawsuit was evidence of excessive entanglement. A litigant cannot, by the very act of commencing a lawsuit, however, create the appearance of divisiveness and then exploit it as evidence of entanglement.

We are satisfied that the City has a secular purpose for including the crèche, that the City has not impermissibly advanced religion, and that including the crèche does not create excessive entanglement between religion and government.

IV

JUSTICE BRENNAN describes the crèche as a "re-creation of an event that lies at the heart of Christian faith." The crèche, like a painting, is passive; admittedly it is a reminder of the origins of Christmas. Even the traditional, purely secular displays extant at Christmas, with or without a crèche, would inevitably recall the religious nature of the Holiday. The display engenders a friendly community spirit of good will in keeping with the season. The crèche may well have special meaning to those whose faith includes the celebration of religious masses, but none who sense the origins of the Christmas celebration would fail to be aware of its religious implications. That the display brings people into the central city, and serves commercial interests and benefits merchants and their employees, does not, as the dissent points out, determine the character of the display. That a prayer invoking Divine guidance in Congress is preceded and followed by debate and partisan conflict over taxes, budgets, national defense, and myriad mundane subjects, for example, has never been thought to demean or taint the sacredness of the invocation.

Of course the crèche is identified with one religious faith but no more so than the examples we have set out from prior cases in which we found no conflict with the Establishment Clause. . . . It would be ironic, however, if the inclusion of a single symbol of a particular historic religious event, as part of a celebration acknowledged in the Western World for 20 centuries, and in this country by the people, by the Executive Branch, by the Congress, and the courts for two centuries, would so "taint" the City's exhibit as to render it violative of the Establishment Clause. To forbid the use of this one passive symbol — the crèche — at the very time people are taking note of the season with Christmas hymns and carols in public schools and other public places, and while the Congress and Legislatures

open sessions with prayers by paid chaplains would be a stilted over-
reaction contrary to our history and to our holdings. If the presence of the
crèche in this display violates the Establishment Clause, a host of other
forms of taking official note of Christmas, and of our religious heritage, are
equally offensive to the Constitution.

The Court has acknowledged that the "fears and political problems"
that gave rise to the Religion Clauses in the 18th Century are of far less
concern today. We are unable to perceive the Archbishop of Canterbury,
the Vicar of Rome, or other powerful religious leaders behind every public
acknowledgement of the religious heritage long officially recognized by the
three constitutional branches of government. Any notion that these
symbols pose a real danger of establishment of a state church is farfetched
indeed.

V

That this Court has been alert to the constitutionally expressed opposition to the establishment of religion is shown in numerous holdings
striking down statutes or programs as violative of the Establishment
Clause. . . . The most recent example of this careful scrutiny is found in the
case invalidating a municipal ordinance granting to a church a virtual veto
power over the licensing of liquor establishments near the church. *Grendel's Den.* Taken together these cases abundantly demonstrate the Court's
concern to protect the genuine objectives of the Establishment Clause. It is
far too late in the day to impose a crabbed reading of the Clause on the
country.

VI

We hold that, notwithstanding the religious significance of the crèche,
the City of Pawtucket has not violated the Establishment Clause of the
First Amendment. Accordingly, the judgment of the Court of Appeals is
reversed.

It is so ordered.

JUSTICE O'CONNOR, concurring.

I concur in the opinion of the Court. I write separately to suggest a
clarification of our Establishment Clause doctrine. The suggested approach leads to the same result in this case as that taken by the Court, and
the Court's opinion, as I read it, is consistent with my analysis. . . .

[Sections I and II omitted]

III

The central issue in this case is whether Pawtucket has endorsed Christianity by its display of the crèche. To answer that question, we must examine both what Pawtucket intended to communicate in displaying the crèche and what message the City's display actually conveyed. The purpose and effect prongs of the *Lemon* [1971] test represent these two aspects of the meaning of the City's action. . . .

The purpose prong of the *Lemon* test asks whether government's actual purpose is to endorse or disapprove of religion. The effect prong asks whether, irrespective of government's actual purpose, the practice under review in fact conveys a message of endorsement or disapproval. An affirmative answer to either question should render the challenged practice invalid.

A

The purpose prong of the *Lemon* test requires that a government activity have a secular purpose. That requirement is not satisfied, however, by the mere existence of some secular purpose, however dominated by religious purposes. In *Stone* v. *Graham* (1980), for example, the Court held that posting copies of the Ten Commandments in schools violated the purpose prong of the *Lemon* test, yet the State plainly had some secular objectives, such as instilling most of the values of the Ten Commandments and illustrating their connection to our legal system. . . . The proper inquiry under the purpose prong of *Lemon,* I submit, is whether the government intends to convey a message of endorsement or disapproval of religion.

Applying that formulation to this case, I would find that Pawtucket did not intend to convey any message of endorsement of Christianity or disapproval of nonChristian religions. The evident purpose of including the crèche in the larger display was not promotion of the religious content of the crèche but celebration of the public holiday through its traditional symbols. Celebration of public holidays, which have cultural significance even if they also have religious aspects, is a legitimate secular purpose.

The District Court's finding that the display of the crèche had no secular purpose was based on erroneous reasoning. The District Court believed that it should ascertain the City's purpose in displaying the crèche separate and apart from the general purpose in setting up the display. It also found that, because the tradition-celebrating purpose was suspect in the court's eyes, the City's use of an unarguably religious symbol "raises an inference" of intent to endorse. When viewed in light of correct legal principles, the District Court's finding of unlawful purpose was clearly erroneous.

B

Focusing on the evil of government endorsement or disapproval of religion makes clear that the effect prong of the *Lemon* test is properly interpreted not to require invalidation of a government practice merely because it in fact causes, even as a primary effect, advancement or inhibition of religion. The laws upheld in *Walz* v. *Tax Commission* (1970) (tax exemption for religious, educational, and charitable organizations), in *McGowan* v. *Maryland* (1960) (mandatory Sunday closing law), and in *Zorach* v. *Clauson*, (1952) (released time from school for off-campus religious instruction), had such effects, but they did not violate the Establishment Clause. What is crucial is that a government practice not have the effect of communicating a message of government endorsement or disapproval of religion. It is only practices having that effect, whether intentionally or unintentionally, that make religion relevant, in reality or public perception, to status in the political community.

Pawtucket's display of its crèche, I believe, does not communicate a message that the government intends to endorse the Christian beliefs represented by the crèche. Although the religious and indeed sectarian significance of the crèche, as the district court found, is not neutralized by the setting, the overall holiday setting changes what viewers may fairly understand to be the purpose of the display — as a typical museum setting, though not neutralizing the religious content of a religious painting, negates any message of endorsement of that content. The display celebrates a public holiday, and no one contends that declaration of that holiday is understood to be an endorsement of religion. The holiday itself has very strong secular components and traditions. Government celebration of the holiday, which is extremely common, generally is not understood to endorse the religious content of the holiday, just as government celebration of Thanksgiving is not so understood. The crèche is a traditional symbol of the holiday that is very commonly displayed along with purely secular symbols, as it was in Pawtucket.

These features combine to make the government's display of the crèche in this particular physical setting no more an endorsement of religion than such governmental "acknowledgments" of religion as legislative prayers of the type approved in *March* v. *Chambers* (1983), government declaration of Thanksgiving as a public holiday, printing of "In God We Trust" on coins, and opening court sessions with "God save the United States and this honorable court." Those government acknowledgments of religion serve, in the only ways reasonably possible in our culture, the legitimate secular purposes of solemnizing public occasions, expressing confidence in the future, and encouraging the recognition of what is worthy of appreciation in society. For that reason, and because of their history and ubiquity, those practices are not understood as conveying government approval of particular religious beliefs. The display of the crèche likewise serves a secular purpose — celebration of a public holiday with traditional symbols.

It cannot fairly be understood to convey a message of government endorsement of religion. . . .

JUSTICE BRENNAN, with whom JUSTICE MARSHALL, JUSTICE BLACKMUN and JUSTICE STEVENS join, dissenting.

The principles announced in the compact phrases of the Religion Clauses have, as the Court today reminds us, proven difficult to apply. Faced with that uncertainty, the Court properly looks for guidance to the settled test announced in *Lemon* v. *Kurtzman* (1971), for assessing whether a challenged governmental practice involves an impermissible step toward the establishment of religion. Applying that test to this case, the Court reaches an essentially narrow result which turns largely upon the particular holiday context in which the City of Pawtucket's nativity scene appeared. The Court's decision implicitly leaves open questions concerning the constitutionality of the public display on public property of a crèche standing alone, or the public display of other distinctively religious symbols such as a cross. Despite the narrow contours of the Court's opinion, our precedents in my view compel the holding that Pawtucket's inclusion of a life-sized display depicting the biblical description of the birth of Christ as part of its annual Christmas celebration is unconstitutional. Nothing in the history of such practices or the setting in which the City's crèche is presented obscures or diminishes the plain fact that Pawtucket's action amounts to an impermissible governmental endorsement of a particular faith.

I

Last Term, I expressed the hope that the Court's decision in *Marsh* v. *Chambers* (1983) would prove to be only a single, aberrant departure from our settled method of analyzing Establishment Clause cases. That the Court today returns to the settled analysis of our prior cases gratifies that hope. At the same time, the Court's less than vigorous application of the *Lemon* test suggests that its commitment to those standards may only be superficial. After reviewing the Court's opinion, I am convinced that this case appears hard not because the principles of decision are obscure, but because the Christmas holiday seems so familiar and agreeable. Although the Court's reluctance to disturb a community's chosen method of celebrating such an agreeable holiday is understandable, that cannot justify the Court's departure from controlling precedent. In my view, Pawtucket's maintenance and display at public expense of a symbol as distinctively sectarian as a crèche simply cannot be squared with our prior cases. And it is plainly contrary to the purposes and values of the Establishment Clause to pretend, as the Court does, that the otherwise secular setting of Pawtucket's nativity scene dilutes in some fashion the crèche's singular religiosity, or that the City's annual display reflects nothing more than an "acknowledgment" of our shared national heritage. Neither the character of the Christmas holiday itself, nor our heritage of religious expression supports this result. Indeed, our remarkable and precious religious diversity as a nation . . ., which the Establishment Clause seeks to protect, runs directly counter to today's decision.

A

As we have sought to meet new problems arising under the Establishment Clause, our decisions, with few exceptions, have demanded that a challenged governmental practice satisfy the following criteria:

> "First, the [practice] must have a secular legislative purpose; second, its principal or primary effect must be one that neither advances nor inhibits religion; finally, [it] must not foster 'an excessive government entanglement with religion.'"

This well-defined three-part test expresses the essential concerns animating the Establishment Clause. Thus, the test is designed to ensure that the organs of government remain strictly separate and apart from religious affairs, for "a union of government and religion tends to destroy government and degrade religion." *Engel* v. *Vitale* (1962). And it seeks to guarantee that government maintains a position of neutrality with respect to religion and neither advances nor inhibits the promulgation and practice of religious beliefs. *Everson* v. *Board of Education* (1947) ("Neither [a State nor the Federal Government] can pass laws which aid one religion, aid all religions, or prefer one religion over another"); *Epperson* v. *Arkansas* (1968); *Committee for Public Education* v. *Nyquist* (1973). In this regard, we must be alert in our examination of any challenged practice not only for an official establishment of religion, but also for those other evils at which the Clause was aimed — "sponsorship, financial support, and active involvement of the sovereign in religious activity." *Committee for Public Education* v. *Nyquist.*

Applying the three-part test to Pawtucket's crèche, I am persuaded that the City's inclusion of the crèche in its Christmas display simply does not reflect a "clearly secular purpose." *Nyquist.* Unlike the typical case in which the record reveals some contemporaneous expression of a clear purpose to advance religion, . . . or, conversely, a clear secular purpose, . . . here we have no explicit statement of purpose by Pawtucket's municipal government accompanying its decision to purchase, display and maintain the crèche. Governmental purpose may nevertheless be inferred. For instance, in *Stone* v. *Graham,* (1980), this Court found, despite the state's avowed purpose of reminding schoolchildren of the secular application of the commands of the decalogue, that the "pre-eminent purpose for posting the Ten Commandments on schoolroom walls is plainly religious in nature." In the present case, the City claims that its purposes were exclusively secular. Pawtucket sought, according to this view, only to participate in the celebration of a national holiday and to attract people to the downtown area in order to promote pre-Christmas retail sales and to help engender the spirit of goodwill and neighborliness commonly associated with the Christmas season.

Despite these assertions, two compelling aspects of this case indicate that our generally prudent "reluctance to attribute unconstitutional motives" to a governmental body, *Mueller* v. *Allen* (1983), should be overcome. First, as was true in *Larkin* v. *Grendel's Den, Inc.* (1982), all of Pawtucket's "valid secular objectives can be readily accomplished by other means." Plainly, the City's interest in celebrating the holiday and in promoting both retail sales and goodwill are fully served by the elaborate display of Santa Claus, reindeer, and wishing wells that are already a part of Pawtucket's annual Christmas display. More importantly, the nativity scene, unlike every other element of the Hodgson Park display, reflects a sectarian exclusivity that the avowed purposes of celebrating the holiday season and promoting retail commerce simply do not encompass. To be found constitutional, Pawtucket's seasonal celebration must at least be non-denominational and not serve to promote religion. The inclusion of a distinctively religious element like the crèche, however, demonstrates that a narrower sectarian purpose lay behind the decision to include a nativity scene. . . .

The "primary effect" of including a nativity scene in the City's display is, as the District Court found, to place the government's imprimatur of approval on the particular religious beliefs exemplified by the crèche. Those who believe in the message of the nativity receive the unique and exclusive benefit of public recognition and approval of their views. For many, the City's decision to include the crèche as part of its extensive and costly efforts to celebrate Christmas can only mean that the prestige of the government has been conferred on the beliefs associated with the crèche, thereby providing "a significant symbolic benefit to religion. . . ." *Larkin* v. *Grendel's Den, Inc.* . . . The effect on minority religious groups, as well as on those who may reject all religion, is to convey the message that their views are not similarly worthy of public recognition nor entitled to public support. It was precisely this sort of religious chauvinism that the Establishment Clause was intended forever to prohibit. . . .

Finally, it is evident that Pawtucket's inclusion of a crèche as part of its annual Christmas display does pose a significant threat of fostering "excessive entanglement." As the Court notes, the District Court found no administrative entanglement in this case, primarily because the City had been able to administer the annual display without extensive consultation with religious officials. . . . Of course, there is no reason to disturb that finding, but it is worth noting that after today's decision, administrative entanglements may well develop. Jews and other non-Christian groups, prompted perhaps by the Mayor's remark that he will include a Menorah in future displays, can be expected to press government for inclusion of their symbols, and faced with such requests, government will have to become involved in accommodating the various demands. . . . More importantly, although no political divisiveness was apparent in Pawtucket prior to the filing of respondents' lawsuit, that act, as the District Court found, unleashed powerful emotional reactions which divided the City along religious lines. The fact that calm had prevailed prior to this suit does not immediately suggest the absence of any division on the point for, as the District Court observed, the quiescence of those opposed to the crèche may have reflected nothing more than their sense of futility in opposing the majority. Of course, the Court is correct to note that we have never held that the potential for divisiveness alone is sufficient to invalidate a challenged governmental practice; we have, nevertheless, repeatedly emphasized that "too close a proximity" between religious and civil authorities, *Schempp* [1963] (BRENNAN, J., concurring), may represent a "warning signal" that the values embodied in the Establishment Clause are at risk. *Committee for Public Education* v. *Nyquist*. Furthermore, the Court should not blind itself to the fact that because communities differ in religious composition, the controversy over whether local governments may adopt religious symbols will continue to fester. In many communities, non-Christian groups can be expected to combat practices similar to Pawtucket's; this will be so especially in areas where there are substantial non-Christian minorities.

In sum, considering the District Court's careful findings of fact under the three-part analysis called for by our prior cases, I have no difficulty concluding that Pawtucket's display of the crèche is unconstitutional.

B

The Court advances two principal arguments to support its conclusion that the Pawtucket crèche satisfies the *Lemon* test. Neither is persuasive.

First. The Court, by focusing on the holiday "context" in which the nativity scene appeared, seeks to explain away the clear religious import of the crèche and the findings of the District Court that most observers understood the crèche as both a symbol of Christian beliefs and a symbol of the City's support for those beliefs.... Thus, although the Court concedes that the City's inclusion of the nativity scene plainly serves "to depict the origins" of Christmas as a "significant historical religious event," and that the crèche "is identified with one religious faith," we are nevertheless expected to believe that Pawtucket's use of the crèche does not signal the City's support for the sectarian symbolism that the nativity scene evokes....

The Court's struggle to ignore the clear religious effect of the crèche seems to me misguided for several reasons. In the first place, the City has positioned the crèche in a central and highly visible location within the Hodgson Park display....

Moreover, the City has done nothing to disclaim government approval of the religious significance of the crèche, to suggest that the crèche represents only one religious symbol among many others that might be included in a seasonal display truly aimed at providing a wide catalogue of ethnic and religious celebrations, or to disassociate itself from the religious content of the crèche. In *Abington School Dist.* v. *Schempp* [1963] we noted that reading aloud from the Bible would be a permissible schoolroom exercise only if it was "presented objectively as part of a secular program of education" that would remove any message of governmental endorsement of religion. Similarly, when the Court of Appeals for the District of Columbia approved the inclusion of a crèche as part of a national "Pageant of Peace" on federal parkland adjacent to the White House, it did so on the express condition that the government would erect "explanatory plaques" disclaiming any sponsorship of religious beliefs associated with the crèche. *Allen* v. *Morton* (CADC 1973). In this case, by contrast, Pawtucket has made no effort whatever to provide a similar cautionary message.

Third, we have consistently acknowledged that an otherwise secular setting alone does not suffice to justify a governmental practice that has the effect of aiding religion. In *Hunt* v. *McNair* (1973), for instance, we observed that "aid may normally be thought to have a primary effect of advancing religion ... when it [supports] a specifically religious activity in an otherwise secular setting." The demonstrably secular context of public education, therefore, did not save the challenged practice of school prayer in *Engel* or in *Schempp*. ...

Finally, and most importantly, even in the context of Pawtucket's seasonal celebration, the crèche retains a specifically Christian religious meaning. I refuse to accept the notion implicit in today's decision that non-Christians would find that the religious content of the crèche is eliminated by the fact that it appears as part of the city's otherwise secular celebration of the Christmas holiday. The nativity scene is clearly distinct in its purpose and effect from the rest of the Hodgson Park display for the simple reason that it is the only one rooted in a biblical account of Christ's birth. It is the chief symbol of the characteristically Christian belief that a divine Savior was brought into the world and that the purpose of this miraculous birth was to illuminate a path toward salvation and redemption. For Christians, that path is exclusive, precious and holy. But for those who do not share these beliefs, the symbolic re-enactment of the birth of a divine being who has been miraculously incarnated as a man stands as a dramatic reminder of their differences with Christian faith. When government appears to sponsor such religiously inspired views, we cannot say that the practice is " 'so separate and so indisputably marked off from the religious function,' that [it] may fairly be viewed as reflect-[ing] a neutral posture toward religious institutions." *Nyquist*. To be so excluded on religious grounds by one's elected government is an insult and an injury that, until today, could not by countenanced by the Establishment Clause.

Second. The Court also attempts to justify the crèche by entertaining a beguilingly simple, yet faulty syllogism. The Court begins by noting that government may recognize Christmas day as a public holiday; the Court then asserts that the crèche is nothing more than a traditional element of Christmas celebrations; and it concludes that the inclusion of a crèche as part of a government's annual Christmas celebration is constitutionally permissible. ... The Court apparently believes that once it finds that the designation of Christmas as a public holiday is constitutionally acceptable, it is then free to conclude that virtually every form of governmental association with the celebration of the holiday is also constitutional. The vice of this dangerously superficial argument is that it overlooks the fact that the Christmas holiday in our national culture contains both secular and sectarian elements. To say that government may recognize the holiday's traditional, secular elements of gift-giving, public festivities and community spirit, does not mean that government may indiscriminately embrace the distinctively sectarian aspects of the holiday....

When government decides to recognize Christmas day as a public holiday, it does no more than accommodate the calendar of public activities to the plain fact that many Americans will expect on that day to spend time visiting with their families, attending religious services, and perhaps enjoying some respite from pre-holiday activities.... If public officials go further and participate in the *secular* celebration of Christmas — by, for example, decorating public places with such secular images as wreaths, garlands or Santa Claus figures — they move closer to the limits of their constitutional power but nevertheless remain within the boundaries set by the Establishment Clause. But when those officials participate in or appear to endorse the distinctively religious elements of this otherwise secular event, they encroach upon First Amendment freedoms. For it is at that point that the government brings to the forefront the theological content of the holiday, and places the prestige, power and financial support of a civil authority in the service of a particular faith.

The inclusion of a crèche in Pawtucket's otherwise secular celebration of Christmas clearly violates these principles. Unlike such secular figures as Santa Claus, reindeer and carolers, a nativity scene represents far more than a mere "traditional" symbol of Christmas. The essence of the crèche's symbolic purpose and effect is to prompt the observer to experience a sense of simple awe and wonder appropriate to the contemplation of one of the central elements of Christian dogma — that God sent His son into the world to be a Messiah. Contrary to the Court's suggestion, the crèche is far from a mere representation of a "particular historic religious event." It is, instead, best understood as a mystical re-creation of an event that lies at the heart of Christian faith. To suggest, as the Court does, that such a symbol is merely "traditional" and therefore no different from Santa's house or reindeer is not only offensive to those for whom the crèche has profound significance, but insulting to those who insist for religious or personal reasons that the story of Christ is in no sense a part of "history" nor an unavoidable element of our national "heritage."

For these reasons, the crèche in this context simply cannot be viewed as playing the same role that an ordinary museum display does.... The Court seems to assume that forbidding Pawtucket from displaying a crèche would be tantamount to forbidding a state college from including the Bible or Milton's Paradise Lost in a course on English literature. But in those cases the religiously-inspired materials are being considered solely as literature. The purpose is plainly not to single out the particular religious beliefs that may have inspired the authors, but to see in these writings the outlines of a larger imaginative universe shared with other forms of literary expression. . . .

In this case, by contrast, the crèche plays no comparable secular role. . . . [T]he angels, shepherds, Magi and infant of Pawtucket's nativity scene can only be viewed as symbols of a particular set of religious beliefs. It would be another matter if the crèche were displayed in a museum setting, in the company of other religiously-inspired artifacts, as an example, among many, of the symbolic representation of religious myths. In that setting, we would have objective guarantees that the crèche could not suggest that a particular faith had been singled out for public favor and recognition. The effect of Pawtucket's crèche, however, is not confined by any of these limiting attributes. In the absence of any other religious symbols or of any neutral disclaimer, the inescapable effect of the crèche will be to remind the average observer of the religious roots of the celebration he is witnessing and to call to mind the scriptural message that the nativity symbolizes. . . .

II

Although the Court's relaxed application of the *Lemon* test to Pawtucket's crèche is regrettable, it is at least understandable and properly limited to the particular facts of this case. The Court's opinion, however, also sounds a broader and more troubling theme. Invoking the celebration of Thanksgiving as a public holiday, the legend "In God We Trust" on our coins, and the proclamation "God save the United States and this Honorable Court" at the opening of judicial sessions, the Court asserts, without explanation, that Pawtucket's inclusion of a crèche in its annual Christmas display poses no more of a threat to Establishment Clause values than these other official "acknowledgments" of religion. . . .

Intuition tells us that some official "acknowledgment" is inevitable in a religious society if government is not to adopt a stilted indifference to the religious life of the people. . . . It is equally true, however, that if government is to remain scrupulously neutral in matters of religious conscience, as our Constitution requires, then it must avoid those overly broad acknowledgments of religious practices that may imply governmental favoritism toward one set of religious beliefs. This does not mean, of course, that public officials may not take account, when necessary, of the separate existence and significance of the religious institutions and practices in the society they govern. Should government choose to incorporate some arguably religious element into its public ceremonies, that acknowledgment must be impartial; it must not tend to promote one faith or handicap another; and it should not sponsor religion generally over non-religion. Thus, in a series of decisions concerned with such acknowledgments, we have repeatedly held that any active form of public acknowledgment of religion indicating sponsorship or endorsement is forbidden. . . .

Despite this body of case law, the Court has never comprehensively addressed the extent to which government may acknowledge religion by, for example, incorporating religious references into public ceremonies and proclamations, and I do not presume to offer a comprehensive approach. Nevertheless, it appears from our prior decisions that at least three principles — tracing the narrow channels which government acknowledgments must follow to satisfy the Establishment Clause — may be identified. First, although the government may not be compelled to do so by the Free Exercise Clause, it may, consistently with the Establishment Clause, act to accommodate to some extent the opportunities of individuals to practice their religion.... And for me that principle would justify government's decision to declare December 25th a public holiday....

Second, our cases recognize that while a particular governmental practice may have derived from religious motivations and retain certain religious connotations, it is nonetheness permissible for the government to pursue the practice when it is continued today solely for secular reasons. As this Court noted with reference to Sunday Closing Laws in *McGowan* v. *Maryland,* the mere fact that a governmental practice coincides to some extent with certain religious beliefs does not render it unconstitutional. Thanksgiving Day, in my view, fits easily within this principle, for despite its religious antecedents, the current practice of celebrating Thanksgiving is unquestionably secular and patriotic....

Finally, we have noted that government cannot be completely prohibited from recognizing in its public actions the religious beliefs and practices of the American people as an aspect of our national history and culture.... While I remain uncertain about these questions, I would suggest that such practices as the designation of "In God We Trust" as our national motto, or the references to God contained in the Pledge of Allegiance can best be understood, in Dean Rostow's apt phrase, as a form a "ceremonial deism," protected from Establishment Clause scrutiny chiefly because they have lost through rote repetition any significant religious content....

The crèche fits none of these categories. Inclusion of the crèche is not necessary to accommodate individual religious expression.... Nor is the inclusion of the crèche necessary to serve wholly secular goals; it is clear that the City's secular purposes of celebrating the Christmas holiday and promoting retail commerce can be fully served without the crèche.... And the crèche, because of its unique association with Christianity, is clearly more sectarian than those references to God that we accept in ceremonial phrases or in other contexts that assure neutrality....

[Section III omitted]

IV

Under our constitutional scheme, the role of safeguarding our "religious heritage" and of promoting religious beliefs is reserved as the exclusive prerogative of our nation's churches, religious institutions and spiritual leaders. Because the Framers of the Establishment Clause understood that "religion is too personal, too sacred, too holy to permit its 'unhallowed perversion' by civil [authorities]," *Engel* v. *Vitale,* the clause demands that government play no role in this effort. The Court today brushes aside these concerns by insisting that Pawtucket has done nothing more than include a "traditional" symbol of Christmas in its celebration of this national holiday, thereby muting the religious content of the crèche. But the City's action should be recognized for what it is: a coercive, though perhaps small, step toward establishing the sectarian preferences of the majority at the expense of the minority, accomplished by placing public facilities and funds in support of the religious symbolism and theological tidings that the crèche conveys. As Justice Frankfurter, writing in *McGowan* v. *Maryland,* observed, the Establishment Clause "withdr[aws] from the sphere of legitimate legislative concern and competence a specific, but comprehensive area of human conduct: man's belief or disbelief in the verity of some transcendental idea and man's expression in action of that belief or disbelief." (separate opinion). That the Constitution sets this realm of thought and feeling apart from the pressures and antagonisms of government is one of its supreme achievements. Regrettably, the Court today tarnishes that achievement.

I dissent.

JUSTICE BLACKMUN, with whom JUSTICE STEVENS joins, dissenting.

As JUSTICE BRENNAN points out, the logic of the Court's decision in *Lemon* v. *Kurtzman* ... *compels* an affirmance here. If that case and its guidelines mean anything, the presence of Pawtucket's crèche in a municipally sponsored display must be held to be a violation of the First Amendment.

Not only does the Court's resolution of this controversy make light of our precedents, but also, ironically, the majority does an injustice to the crèche and the message it manifests.... The crèche has been relegated to the role of a neutral harbinger of the holiday season, useful for commercial purposes, but devoid of any inherent meaning and incapable of enhancing the religious tenor of a display of which it is an integral part. The city has its victory — but it is a Pyrrhic one indeed....

SENATE REJECTION OF
SCHOOL PRAYER AMENDMENT
March 20, 1984

The Senate dealt a sharp blow to President Ronald Reagan and his conservative religious supporters by rejecting March 20 a proposed constitutional amendment to permit organized, recited prayers in the nation's public schools. The 56-44 vote fell 11 short of the two-thirds majority needed to pass the prayer measure, S J Res 73. The vote came after more than two weeks of parliamentary maneuvering and intensive lobbying over the prayer issue.

With Vice President George Bush in the presiding officer's chair to demonstrate the administration's support for school prayer, 18 Senate Republicans joined 26 Democrats in voting against the amendment. Voting in favor were 37 Republicans and 19 Democrats. Opponents led by Sen. Lowell P. Weicker Jr., R-Conn., warned that children holding minority religious views — or none at all — would feel uncomfortable participating in a prayer alien to their beliefs and stigmatized if they refused to participate. "The issue really is not prayer in schools for our children," said Weicker. "They have that right today. No court case, no law, no Supreme Court ruling prevents any individual child or any adult in this nation from praying wherever or whenever they wish."

The prayer amendment was defeated in the Senate despite the fact that polls showed 80 percent of Americans supported the measure. Reagan, who made school prayer a key issue in his re-election campaign, undertook a strong personal lobbying effort in behalf of the measure. He called for an amendment in his January 25 State of the Union address, made it a central theme of a January 30 speech — his first official re-

election campaign appearance — and delivered a strong endorsement of prayer at a March 6 gathering of the National Association of Evangelicals. In an address on "religious values in public life," Reagan said, "America has begun a spiritual reawakening. Faith and hope are being restored. Americans are turning back to God." (State of the Union address, p. 81)

Prayer Debate History, Lobbying

The drive for a constitutional amendment on school prayer was an effort to overturn a series of Supreme Court decisions dating back to 1962 that effectively barred state-sponsored prayers and Bible readings from public schools. In the 1962 case, Engle v. Vitale, *the Court said the use of a non-denominational school prayer was "wholly inconsistent" with the First Amendment's bar to government establishment of religion. In two other cases a year later,* School District of Abington Township v. Schempp *and* Murray v. Curlett, *the Court declared that daily Bible readings in public school classrooms were likewise unconstitutional. In 1982 the Court, without comment, affirmed the ruling of a federal appeals court that struck down a Louisiana law permitting voluntary prayer sessions in public schools.*

In 1966 the Senate considered, but rejected, a school prayer amendment sponsored by Sen. Everett McKinley Dirksen, R-Ill., the late father-in-law of Majority Leader Howard H. Baker Jr., R-Tenn. In 1970 it added a school prayer measure to the Equal Rights Amendment, but the House rejected the school prayer portion.

The prayer issue divided members of the nation's clergy as well as the Senate. Fundamentalist leaders such as the Rev. Jerry Falwell of the Moral Majority were highly vocal and visible in their support of a prayer amendment, while leaders of mainline religious groups — Methodists, Lutherans, Jews, and Presbyterians among them — opposed any prayer amendment. The conservative religious media took up the prayer cause, airing programs on the issue daily and encouraging listeners to call their senators.

The grass-roots strategy worked well in the opening round of the debate. Early in the week of March 5, senators reported receiving dozens of calls daily advocating school prayer and only a smattering of calls, if any, opposing a constitutional amendment. But there was little consensus among supporters about the wording of the amendment and how it should work. Some advocates said the form of the prayers should be left entirely to volunteer students, while others said the amendment would give state and local officials full discretion over the form of the prayer.

On March 6 those opposing a prayer amendment counterattacked. Fourteen members of the clergy — including an Episcopal priest,

Protestant ministers and rabbis — held a news conference to explain their opposition to prayer. They were backed by such groups as Americans United for Separation of Church and State, People for the American Way, and the American Civil Liberties Union. "Whatever form it takes, proselytizing or evangelizing for a particular belief system in the realm of education is alien to the teachings of Christ," said the Rev. Charles Bergstrom of the Lutheran Council in the USA and a leader of the amendment opponents. "The United States of America cannot be viewed as a Protestant Sunday school.... The God I believe in cannot be expelled from school," he added.

Senate Debate, Reaction

The Senate began its long-promised debate amid an atmosphere of a revival meeting around much of the Capitol. A 12-hour vigil in support of school prayer was held in a congressional office building March 5, a human chain for prayer stretched for a few hours March 7 from the Capitol to the Supreme Court, and members of the clergy on both sides of the issue held informal meetings with the press and senators to present their views about the proposed amendment. Although the House had no prayer legislation before it, some representatives kept the chamber in session for an all-night talkathon on the subject March 5 to lend support to their Senate colleagues.

The administration-backed amendment, which the Senate rejected, would have allowed organized, recited prayer in public schools. Another proposal, sponsored by Sen. Orrin G. Hatch, R-Utah, would have allowed silent prayer or meditation in public schools. A third amendment, sponsored by Baker, was not specific about the type of prayer to be offered and simply stated that there was a right to pray voluntarily in public institutions.

Much of the Senate discussion on the issue was desultory, broken only infrequently by lively exchanges, particularly between Weicker and Hatch. Weicker contended that no amendment was needed to let children pray in school. "A child can pray during his lunch hour. A child can pray prior to an exam. A child can pray before he comes up to bat. A child can pray in school," Weicker said. Hatch countered that Weicker's argument was "a little bit like saying that a prisoner in the Gulag Archipelago can pray any time he wants to; in that sense anybody, of course, can pray if he is not caught."

Other senators also made spirited statements on the prayer issue. John C. Danforth, R-Mo., a prayer amendment opponent who was also an Episcopal priest, contended that the prayer debate "is not between the godly and the ungodly. For strongly held religious reasons, people have arrived at opposite conclusions...." Danforth added, "To many religious people, God is not dependent on the Supreme Court or Congress. Objects may be kept out of the classroom, chewing gum, for example. God is not chewing gum. He is the creator of heaven and earth."

The issue was "whether to restore the neutrality of the state in the free exercise of religion, or specifically reaffirm the antireligious bias of our schools," said Baker. "The government has no right either to force or forbid the voluntary exercise of religion in our schools and other places. Government cannot grant the right to pray; God grants that right. And government cannot prohibit the right to pray." Children would benefit from prayer and would look forward to it, said Jesse Helms, R-N.C., a longtime advocate of school prayer legislation. "Have you ever noticed how eagerly children take to prayer?" he asked. "They have no problem recognizing God, talking to Him, and thanking Him for the blessings He has given them." Helms said the Senate should "heed divine wisdom and the pleas of our children, and restore the right to pray in the schools once again. If we do, it is likely that not only will the children be closer to God, but that we — including . . . the Supreme Court — will be drawn closer as well."

Some senators were critical of Reagan's position, claiming that his support was more political than legislative and noting that the president had opposed a proposal for silent prayer they said had more support on Capitol Hill. On March 15, however, the Senate had voted 81-15 to table, and thus kill, a silent-prayer amendment offered by Sen. Alan J. Dixon, D-Ill. "I blame the failure of this amendment on President Reagn's unwillingness to reach a compromise," said Sen. Dennis DeConcini, D-Ariz., after the March 20 vote. "I believe there are political motives, to hammer the upcoming election. President Reagan was not willing to really get a prayer amendment."

After the Senate declined to adopt the amendment, the president said March 20. "The issue of free religious speech is not dead as a result of this vote. We suffered a setback, but we have not been defeated. Our struggle will go on." Other prayer supporters vowed to press their cause anew. "Round one is over, but so long as I am in the U.S. Senate, there will be many more rounds to come," said Helms. Gary Jarmin, a lobbyist for the pro-prayer group Christian Voice, said, "Politically, we've got something that we can take to the polls this November [1984], in 1986 and 1988." Pat Robertson, host of the 700 Club, a popular television ministry, said, "Like those of ancient Israel who cried out to their oppressors, 'Let my people go,' those of us who are oppressed by our political leadership today are also crying to them to let us go. Let us go — or we plan to let them go in November."

Groups that opposed the school prayer amendment were jubilant after the Senate vote. Barry Lynn, legislative counsel of the American Civil Liberties Union, called the vote a "resounding setback for those who wanted the schools of America doing the work of churches."

Related Actions

Less than two weeks after the Senate rejected the school prayer amendment, the Supreme Court agreed April 2 to review the constitutionality of an Alabama law permitting a moment of silence for prayer or meditation at the beginning of each school day. Even as it agreed to review the moment-of-silence law, however, the Court reaffirmed its opposition to formal spoken prayer in public schools. Without hearing arguments, the justices affirmed a lower court's decision that a second Alabama law, which permitted teachers to lead willing students in prayer at the beginning of class, was unconstitutional. The moment-of-silence case would be the first school prayer case to be argued before the Court since 1962-63, although in the intervening years, the Court had summarily — without hearing arguments — affirmed a number of lower court decisions that various forms of religious observances in public schools were unconstitutional.

On July 26, by an overwhelming majority, the House approved a measure to require schools to allow silent prayer in the classroom. Before agreeing to the proposal, the House rejected a stronger amendment that would have cut off federal funds to schools that prohibited silent or spoken prayer. The action came just one day after Congress cleared for the president's signature "equal access" legislation that would give student religious groups the same right to meet in school buildings before and after school on the same terms as other student groups. The bill would make it unlawful for a high school receiving federal funds to deny the use of its buildings to religious, political and other student groups for voluntary meetings if it allowed such access to other extracurricular groups.

Following is the text of S J Res 73, the proposed school prayer constitutional amendment rejected by the Senate March 20, 1984:

Nothing in this Constitution shall be construed to prohibit individual or group prayer in public schools or other public institutions. No person shall be required by the United States or any state to participate in prayer. Neither the United States nor any state shall compose the words of any prayer to be said in public schools.

COURT ON MEDIA LIBEL LAW
March 20, 1984

The Supreme Court March 20 expanded the vulnerability to libel suits of nationally circulated newspapers and magazines. Such publications could be sued in any state where they had substantial circulation, the justices ruled unanimously in two separate libel suits—one against Hustler *magazine, the other against* National Enquirer *and two of its employees.*

The Court's rulings effectively gave persons suing national publications for libel or defamation an almost unlimited choice of forum. It was expected to make defending such cases more costly and inconvenient for the media. Dealing only with jurisdictional questions, the decisions did not, however, change the substantive law of libel. The opinions, both written by Justice William H. Rehnquist, rejected arguments that the free press guarantee of the First Amendment gave the news media special protections against being sued for libel in distant forums.

Ruling in another case on April 30, however, the Court gave the press important reassurance of the First Amendment's protective scope, directing federal appeals judges to use special care and thoroughness in reviewing libel judgments in cases involving public figures. (Story, p. 299)

In Keeton v. Hustler Magazine, *the Court reversed two lower courts to hold that a libel suit against* Hustler, *an Ohio corporation, could be filed in New Hampshire because the magazine circulated in that state. Kathy Keeton, associate publisher of* Penthouse *magazine, a* Hustler *competitor, charged that* Hustler *in 1975 and 1976 published cartoons and stories libeling her. Keeton sued in federal courts in New Hampshire, which permitted an unusually long period for filing such suits, after a similar suit was dismissed in Ohio because it was filed too late.*

With some 10,000 to 15,000 copies of Hustler *magazine sold in New Hampshire each month,* Hustler *"must reasonably anticipate being haled into court there in a libel action based on the contents of its magazine," said Rehnquist. "There is no unfairness in calling it to answer for the contents of that publication wherever a substantial number of copies are regularly sold and distributed."*

In Calder v. Jones, *the Court affirmed that California courts had jurisdiction over a libel case brought by actress Shirley Jones against* National Enquirer *editor and president Iain Calder and John South, the writer of an allegedly libelous article concerning Jones' drinking habits. The two employees contested the jurisdiction; the weekly tabloid did not. Jones resided in California; the* National Enquirer *was published by a Florida corporation; the editor and writer lived in Florida. There was no dispute about whether the Enquirer, as a corporation, could be made to respond. The question — which had divided lower courts — was whether Calder and South could be made to travel across the country to California.*

Rehnquist noted that 600,000 copies of the paper were sold in California each week. "California is the focal point both of the story and of the harm suffered," he said. "Jurisdiction over petitioners is therefore proper in California based on the 'effects' of their Florida conduct in California." Unlike a factory worker, who had no control over product distribution, Rehnquist wrote, Calder and South "expressly aimed" their product (the article) at California. "They knew that the brunt of the injury would be felt by [Jones] in the state in which she lives and works and in which the National Enquirer *has its largest circulation."*

Rehnquist rejected the argument that the defendants, as individual employees, should not be subject to suit. He said they were "primary participants in an alleged wrongdoing." First Amendment concerns did not enter into the issue, Rehnquist concluded. Any "potential chill on protected First Amendment activity stemming from libel and defamation actions is already taken into account in the constitutional limitations on the substantive law governing such suits," he explained. "To reintroduce those concerns at the jurisdictional stage would be a form of double counting."

Following are excerpts from the Supreme Court's March 20 rulings in Keeton v. Hustler *and from the concurring opinion of Justice William J. Brennan Jr.; and in* Calder v. Jones, *holding that libel plaintiffs can make reporters and editors of national publications respond to suits in any state in which they had substantial circulation:*

No. 82-485

| Kathy Keeton, Petetitioner
v.
Hustler Magazine, Inc., et al. | On writ of certiorari to the United States Court of Appeals for the First Circuit |

[March 20, 1984]

JUSTICE REHNQUIST delivered the opinion of the Court.

Petitioner Kathy Keeton sued respondent Hustler Magazine, Inc., and other defendants in the United States District Court for the District of New Hampshire, alleging jurisdiction over her libel complaint by reason of diversity of citizenship. The district court dismissed her suit because it believed that the Due Process Clause of the Fourteenth Amendment to the United States Constitution forbade the application of New Hampshire's long-arm statute in order to acquire personal jurisdiction over respondent. The Court of Appeals for the First Circuit affirmed (CA 1 1982), summarizing its concerns with the statement that "the New Hampshire tail is too small to wag so large an out-of-state dog." We granted certiorari, and we now reverse.

Petitioner Keeton is a resident of New York. Her only connection with New Hampshire is the circulation there of copies of a magazine that she assists in producing. The magazine bears petitioner's name in several places crediting her with editorial and other work. Respondent Hustler Magazine, Inc., is an Ohio corporation, with its principal place of business in California. Respondent's contacts with New Hampshire consist of the sale of some 10 to 15,000 copies of *Hustler* magazine in that State each month. . . . Petitioner claims to have been libeled in five separate issues of respondent's magazine published between September 1975, and May 1976.

The Court of Appeals, in its opinion affirming the District Court's dismissal of petitioner's complaint, held that petitioner's lack of contacts with New Hampshire rendered the State's interest in redressing the tort of libel to petitioner too attenuated for an assertion of personal jurisdiction over respondent. The Court of Appeals observed that the "single publication rule" ordinarily applicable in multistate libel cases would require it to award petitioner "damages caused in *all* states" should she prevail in her suit, even though the bulk of petitioner's alleged injuries had been sustained outside New Hampshire. The court also stressed New Hampshire's unusually long (6-year) limitations period for libel actions. New Hampshire was the only State where petitioner's suit would not have been time-barred when it was filed. Under these circumstances, the Court of Appeals concluded that it would be "unfair" to assert jurisdiction over respondent. New Hampshire has a minimal interest in applying its unusual statute of limitations to, and awarding damages for, injuries to a nonresident occurring outside the State, particularly since petitioner suffered such a small proportion of her total claimed injury within the State.

We conclude that the Court of Appeals erred when it affirmed the dismissal of petitioner's suit for lack of personal jurisdiction. Respondent's regular circulation of magazines in the forum State is sufficient to support an assertion of jurisdiction in a libel action based on the contents of the magazine. This is so even if New Hampshire courts, and thus the District Court under *Klaxon Co.* v. *Stentor Co.* (1941), would apply the so-called "single publication rule" to enable petitioner to recover in the New Hampshire action her damages from "publications" of the alleged libel throughout the United States.

The district court found that "[t]he general course of conduct in circulating magazines throughout the state was purposefully directed at New Hampshire, and inevitably affected persons in the state." Such regular monthly sales of thousands of magazines cannot by any stretch of the imagination be characterized as random, isolated, or fortuitous. It is, therefore, unquestionable that New Hampshire jurisdiction over a complaint based on those contacts would ordinarily satisfy the requirement of the Due Process Clause that a State's assertion of personal jurisdiction over a nonresident defendant be predicated on "minimum contacts" between the defendant and the State. See *World-Wide Volkswagen Corp.* v. *Woodson* (1980); *International Shoe Corp.* v. *Washington* (1945). And, as the Court of Appeals acknowledged, New Hampshire has adopted a "long-arm" statute authorizing service of process on nonresident corporations whenever permitted by the Due Process Clause. Thus, all the requisites for personal jurisdiction over Hustler Magazine, Inc., in New Hampshire are present.

We think that the three concerns advanced by the Court of Appeals, whether considered singly or together, are not sufficiently weighty to merit a different result. The "single publication rule," New Hampshire's unusually long statute of limitations, and plaintiff's lack of contacts with the forum State do not defeat jurisdiction otherwise proper under both New Hampshire law and the Due Process Clause.

In judging minimum contacts, a court properly focuses on "the relationship among the defendant, the forum, and the litigation." *Shaffer* v. *Heitner* (1977). See also *Rush* v. *Savchuk* (1980). Thus, it is certainly relevant to the jurisdictional inquiry that petitioner is *seeking* to recover damages suffered in all States in this one suit. The contacts between respondent and the forum must be judged in the light of that claim, rather than a claim only for damages sustained in New Hampshire. That is, the contacts between respondent and New Hampshire must be such that it is "fair" to compel respondent to defend a multistate lawsuit in New Hampshire seeking nationwide damages for all copies of the five issues in question, even though only a small portion of those copies were distributed in New Hampshire.

The Court of Appeals expressed the view that New Hampshire's "interest" in asserting jurisdiction over plaintiff's multistate claim was minimal. We agree that the "fairness" of haling respondent into a New

Hampshire court depends to some extent on whether respondent's activities relating to New Hampshire are such as to give that State a legitimate interest in holding respondent answerable on a claim related to those activities. See *World-Wide Volkswagen Corp.* v. *Woodson* (1980); *McGee* v. *International Life Insurance Co.* (1957). But insofar as the State's "interest" in adjudicating the dispute is a part of the Fourteenth Amendment due process equation, as a surrogate for some of the factors already mentioned, see *Insurance Corp.* v. *Compagnie des Bauxites* (1982), we think the interest is sufficient.... This interest extends to libel actions brought by nonresidents. False statements of fact harm both the subject of the falsehood *and* the readers of the statement. New Hampshire may rightly employ its libel laws to discourage the deception of its citizens. There is "no constitutional value in false statements of fact." *Gertz* v. *Robert Welch, Inc.* (1974).

New Hampshire may also extend its concern to the injury that in-state libel causes within New Hampshire to a nonresident. The tort of libel is generally held to occur wherever the offending material is circulated. The reputation of the libel victim may suffer harm even in a state in which he has hiterto been anonymous. The communication of the libel may create a negative reputation among the residents of a jurisdiction where the plaintiff's previous reputation was, however small, at least unblemished....

... In sum, the combination of New Hampshire's interest in redressing injuries that occur within the State and its interest in cooperating with other States in the application of the "single publication rule" demonstrate the propriety of requiring respondent to answer to a multistate libel action in New Hampshire.

The Court of Appeals also thought that there was an element of due process "unfairness" arising from the fact that the statutes of limitations in every jurisdiction except New Hampshire had run on the plaintiff's claim in this case. Strictly speaking, however, any potential unfairness in applying New Hampshire's statute of limitations to all aspects of this nationwide suit has nothing to do with the jurisdiction of the Court to adjudicate the claims. "The issue is personal jurisdiction, not choice of law." *Hanson* v. *Denckla* (1958)....

The chance duration of statutes of limitations in nonforum jurisdictions has nothing to do with the contacts among respondent, New Hampshire, and this multistate libel action. Whether Ohio's limitations period is six months or six years does not alter the jurisdictional calculus in New Hampshire. Petitioner's successful search for a State with a lengthy statute of limitations is no different from the litigation strategy of countless plaintiffs who seek a forum with a favorable substantive or procedural rules or sympathetic local populations. Certainly Hustler Magazine, Inc., which chose to enter the New Hampshire market, can be charged with knowledge of its laws and no doubt would have claimed the benefit of them if it had a complaint against a subscriber, distributor, or other commercial partner.

Finally, implicit in the Court of Appeals' analysis of New Hampshire's interest is an emphasis on the extremely limited contacts of the *plaintiff* with New Hampshire. But we have not to date required a plaintiff to have "minimum contacts" with the forum State before permitting that State to assert personal jurisdiction over a nonresident defendant. On the contrary, we have upheld the assertion of jurisdiction where such contacts were entirely lacking. In *Perkins* v. *Benguet Mining Co.* (1952), none of the parties was a resident of the forum State; indeed, neither the plaintiff nor the subject-matter of his action had any relation to that State. Jurisdiction was based solely on the fact that the defendant corporation had been carrying on in the forum "a continuous and systematic, but limited, part of its general business." In the instant case, respondent's activities in the forum may not be so substantial as to support jurisdiction over a cause of action unrelated to those activities. But respondent is carrying on a "part of its general business" in New Hampshire, and that is sufficient to support jurisdiction when the cause of action arises out of the very activity being conducted, in part, in New Hampshire. . . .

It is undoubtedly true that the bulk of the harm done to petitioner occurred outside New Hampshire. But that will be true in almost every libel action brought somewhere other than the plaintiff's domicile. There is no justification for restricting libel actions to the plaintiff's home forum. The victim of a libel, like the victim of any other tort, may choose to bring suit in any forum with which the defendant has "certain minimum contacts ... such that the maintenance of the suit does not offend "traditional notions of fair play and substantial justice. *Milliken* v. *Meyer." International Shoe Co.* v. *Washington* (1945).

Where, as in this case, respondent Hustler Magazine, Inc., has continuously and deliberately exploited the New Hampshire market, it must reasonably anticipate being haled into court there in a libel action based on the contents of its magazine. *World-Wide Volkswagen Corp.* v. *Woodson* (1980). And, since respondent can be charged with knowledge of the "single publication rule," it must anticipate that such a suit will seek nationwide damages. Respondent produces a national publication aimed at a nationwide audience. There is no unfairness in calling it to answer for the contents of that publication wherever a substantial number of copies are regularly sold and distributed.

The judgment of the Court of Appeals is reversed and the cause is remanded for proceedings consistent with this opinion.

It is so ordered.

JUSTICE BRENNAN, concurring in the judgment.

I agree with the Court that "[r]espondent's regular circulation of magazines in the forum State is sufficient to support an assertion of jurisdiction in a libel action based on the contents of the magazine." These contacts between the respondent and the forum State are sufficiently important and sufficiently related to the underlying cause of action to foreclose any concern that the constitutional limits of the Due Process Clause are being violated. This is so, moreover, irrespective of the state's interest in enforcing its substantive libel laws or its unique statute of limitations. Indeed, as we recently explained in *Insurance Corp.* v. *Compagnie des Bauxites* (1982), these interests of the State should be relevant only to the extent that they bear upon the liberty interests of the respondent that are protected by the Fourteenth Amendment. "The restriction on state sovereign power described in *World-Wide Volkswagen Corp.* [v. *Woodson,* (1980)] must be seen as ultimately a function of the individual liberty interest preserved by the Due Process Clause. That Clause is the only source of the personal jurisdiction requirement and the Clause itself makes no mention of federalism concerns."

No. 82-1401

Iain Calder and John South, Appellants v. Shirley Jones	On appeal from the Court of Appeal of California, Second Appellate District

[March 20, 1984]

JUSTICE REHNQUIST delivered the opinion of the Court.

Respondent Shirley Jones brought suit in California Superior Court claiming that she had been libeled in an article written and edited by petitioners in Florida. The article was published in a national magazine with a large circulation in California. Petitioners were served with process by mail in Florida and caused special appearances to be entered on their behalf, moving to quash the service of process for lack of personal jurisdiction. The superior court granted the motion on the ground that First Amendment concerns weighed against an assertion of jurisdiction otherwise proper under the Due Process Clause. The California Court of Appeal reversed, rejecting the suggestion that First Amendment considerations enter into the jurisdictional analysis. We now affirm.

Respondent lives and works in California. She and her husband brought this suit against the National Enquirer, Inc., its local distributing company, and petitioners for libel, invasion of privacy, and intentional infliction of emotional harm. The Enquirer is a Florida corporation with its principal place of business in Florida. It publishes a national weekly newspaper with a total circulation of over 5 million. About 600,000 of those copies, almost twice the level of the next highest State, are sold in California. Respondent's and her husband's claims were based on an article that appeared in the Enquirer's October 9, 1979 issue. Both the Enquirer and the distributing company answered the complaint and made no objection to the jurisdiction of the California court.

Petitioner South is a reporter employed by the Enquirer. He is a resident of Florida, though he frequently travels to California on business. South wrote the first draft of the challenged article, and his byline appeared on it. He did most of his research in Florida, relying on phone calls to sources in California for the information contained in the article. Shortly before publication, South called respondent's home and read to her husband a draft of the article so as to elicit his comments upon it. Aside from his frequent trips and phone calls, South has no other relevant contacts with California.

Petitioner Calder is also a Florida resident. He has been to California only twice — once, on a pleasure trip, prior to the publication of the article and once after to testify in an unrelated trial. Calder is president and editor of the Enquirer. He "oversee[s] just about every function of the Enquirer." He reviewed and approved the initial evaluation of the subject of the article and edited it in its final form. He also declined to print a retraction requested by respondent. Calder has no other relevant contacts with California.

In considering petitioners' motion to quash service of process, the superior court surmised that the actions of petitioners in Florida, causing injury to respondent in California, would ordinarily be sufficient to support an assertion of jurisdiction over them in California. But the court felt that special solicitude was necessary because of the potential "chilling effect" on reporters and editors which would result from requiring them to appear in remote jurisdictions to answer for the content of articles upon which they worked....

The California Court of Appeal reversed.... But the court concluded that a valid basis for jurisdiction existed on the theory that petitioners intended to, and did, cause tortious injury to respondent in California. The fact that the actions causing the effects in California were performed outside the State did not prevent the State from asserting jurisdiction over a cause of action arising out of those effects. The court rejected the superior court's conclusion that First Amendment considerations must be weighed in the scale against jurisdiction.

A timely petition for hearing was denied by the Supreme Court of California. On petitioners' appeal to this Court, probable jurisdiction was postponed. We concluded that jurisdiction by appeal does not lie. *Kulko* v. *California* (1978). Treating the jurisdictional statement as a petition for writ of certiorari, as we are authorized to do, we hereby grant the petition.

The Due Process Clause of the Fourteenth Amendment to the United States Constitution permits personal jurisdiction over a defendant in any State with which the defendant has "certain minimum contacts ... such that the maintenance of the suit does not offend 'traditional notions of fair play and substantial justice.' *Milliken* v. *Meyer*." *International Shoe Co.* v. *Washington* (1945). In judging minimum contacts, a court properly focuses on "the relationship among the defendant, the forum, and the litigation." *Shaffer* v. *Heitner* (1980). The plaintiff's lack of "contacts" will not defeat otherwise proper jurisdiction, see *Keeton* v. *Hustler Magazine, Inc.,* but they may be so manifold as to permit jurisdiction when it would not exist in their absence. Here, the plaintiff is the focus of the activities of the defendants out of which the suit arises. See *McGee* v. *International Life Ins. Co.* (1957).

The allegedly libelous story concerned the California activities of a California resident. It impugned the professionalism of an entertainer whose television career was centered in California. The article was drawn from California sources, and the brunt of the harm, in terms both of respondent's emotional distress and the injury to her professional reputation, was suffered in California. In sum, California is the focal point both of the story and of the harm suffered. Jurisdiction over petitioners is therefore proper in California based on the "effects" of their Florida conduct in California. *World-Wide Volkswagen Corp.* v. *Woodson* (1980).

Petitioners argue that they are not responsible for the circulation of the article in California. A reporter and an editor, they claim, have no direct economic stake in their employer's sales in a distant State. Nor are ordinary employees able to control their employer's marketing activity. The mere fact that they can "foresee" that the article will be circulated and have an effect in California is not sufficient for an assertion of jurisdiction. *World-Wide Volkswagen Corp.* v. *Woodson; Rush* v. *Savchuk.* They do not "in effect appoint the [article their] agent for service of process." *World-Wide Volkswagen Corp.* v. *Woodson.* Petitioners liken themselves to a welder employed in Florida who works on a boiler which subsequently explodes in California. Cases which hold that jurisdiction will be proper over the manufacturer, *Buckeye Boiler Co.* v. *Superior Court* (1969); *Gray* v. *American Radiator & Standard Sanitary Corp.* (1961), should not be applied to the welder who has no control over and derives no direct benefit from his employer's sales in that distant State.

Petitioners' analogy does not wash. Whatever the status of their hypothetical welder, petitioners are not charged with mere untargeted negligence. Rather, their intentional, and allegedly tortious, actions were expressly aimed at California. Petitioner South wrote and petitioner Calder edited an article that they knew would have a potentially devastating impact upon respondent. And they knew that the brunt of that injury would be felt by respondent in the State in which she lives and works and in which the *National Enquirer* has its largest circulation. Under the circumstances, petitioners must "reasonably anticipate being haled into court there" to answer for the truth of the statements made in their article. *World-Wide Volkswagen Corp.* v. *Woodson; Kulko* v. *Superior Court* (1978); *Shaffer* v. *Heitner* (1977). An individual injured in California need not go to Florida to seek redress from persons who, though remaining in Florida, knowingly cause the injury in California.

Petitioners are correct that their contacts with California are not to be judged according to their employer's activities there. On the other hand, their status as employees does not somehow insulate them from jurisdic-

255

tion. Each defendant's contacts with the forum State must be assessed individually. See *Rush* v. *Savchuk* ("The requirements of *International Shoe* ... must be met as to each defendant over whom a state court exercises jurisdiction"). In this case, petitioners are primary participants in an alleged wrongdoing intentionally directed at a California resident, and jurisdiction over them is proper on that basis.

We also reject the suggestion that First Amendment concerns enter into the jurisdictional analysis. The infusion of such considerations would needlessly complicate an already imprecise inquiry. *Estin* v. *Estin* (1948). Moreover, the potential chill on protected First Amendment activity stemming from libel and defamation actions is already taken into account in the constitutional limitations on the substantive law governing such suits. See *New York Times, Inc.* v. *Sullivan* (1964); *Gertz* v. *Robert Welch, Inc.* (1974). To reintroduce those concerns at the jurisdictional stage would be a form of double counting. . . .

We hold that jurisdiction over petitioners in California is proper because of their intentional conduct in Florida calculated to cause injury to respondent in California. The judgment of the California Court of Appeal is

Affirmed.

SCIENTISTS', OTA REPORTS ON MISSILE DEFENSE IN SPACE
March 21, April 25, 1984

A year after President Ronald Reagan made his highly publicized "Star Wars" speech proposing a long-term effort to develop a sophisticated missile defense in space, two reports questioned the feasibility of that plan. In a paper issued March 21, a group of prominent scientists warned that the project would be technologically "unattainable" and prohibitively expensive. The study, issued by the Union of Concerned Scientists, was prepared by a nine-member panel that included Hans Bethe, a Nobel laureate in physics and one of the builders of the first atomic bomb, and Richard L. Garwin, a physicist who had participated in developing the first hydrogen bomb. ("Star Wars" speech, Historic Documents of 1983, p. 305)

Another study, released April 25, came to similar conclusions. The prospect of a workable anti-missile defense in space was "so remote that it should not serve as the basis of public expectation or national policy," according to the Office of Technology Assessment (OTA), a nonpartisan research arm of Congress. "This judgment appears to be the consensus among informed members of the defense technical community," the report said. The "technical prognosis for such a perfect or near-perfect defense is extremely pessimistic."

UCS, OTA Reports: Risks Cited

The UCS report warned that not only would a U.S. program to develop anti-satellite space weapons be doomed to failure, but it would stimulate a new offensive round of the arms race and lead to changes in U.S. and

257

Soviet nuclear strategy that would increase the risk of war. According to the scientists, orbiting space stations would be extremely vulnerable to known countermeasures. Major technical breakthroughs would be needed to develop laser or particle beam weapons powerful and accurate enough to intercept nuclear missiles across hundreds or even thousands of miles of space, and even if such weapons were developed, basing them would present intractable problems. A system of orbiting chemical laser stations would require more than 1,000 stations to ensure that sufficient numbers would be over Soviet missile bases at all times. Those lasers would cost about $70 billion simply to launch and would be highly vulnerable to Soviet attack, according to the UCS. The panel estimated that it would cost $40 billion to $300 billion to implement a ground-based laser defense shield. Such a system, it said, would require 20 percent to 60 percent of the entire electric generating capacity of the United States to be operable. Even a missile defense that was 95 percent effective — an impossible prospect — would leave the United States exposed to enough Soviet warheads to kill tens of millions of people in the event of a nuclear war, the UCS report concluded.

Like the UCS report, the OTA study cautioned against over-reliance on the feasibility of developing a "Star Wars" defense. The report, prepared by Ashton B. Carter of the Massachusetts Institute of Technology, warned that "All concepts identified as candidates for a future defense of population are known to be susceptible to countermeasures that would permit the Soviet Union to retain a degree of penetration with their future missile arsenal despite costly attempts to improve the U.S. defense."

Administration Program, Congressional Response

The reports were issued as the Reagan administration and Congress prepared to square off on the question of space weaponry. The administration requested $1.8 billion for its space weapons program, called the "Strategic Defense Initiative" (SDI), in fiscal 1985. Philosophical challenges to the SDI came from traditional proponents of arms control who argued that the plan could destabilize the U.S.-Soviet nuclear balance and was contrary to the 1972 U.S.-Soviet Antiballistic Missile Treaty (ABM), which prohibited both nations from deploying weapons in space. But administration officials and their congressional supporters argued that the Soviet Union already had disregarded the ABM treaty and was embarking on its own program of developing weapons in space.

Components of the administration's five-year $26 billion Strategic Defense Initiative included surveillance programs, which accounted for about 40 percent of the entire five-year budget. They were intended to identify Soviet missiles and distinguish warheads from the thousands of dummy targets they would eject. An additional 20 percent of the SDI budget was earmarked for "directed-energy" weapons — lasers and *atomic particle ray guns that would beam energy at Soviet missiles at the speed of light, across thousands of miles. "Kinetic energy" weapons — satellite-launched guided missiles designed to collide with Soviet missiles like bullets or to spray them with shrapnel like a shotgun — also accounted for about 20 percent of the budget.*

Defense Secretary Caspar W. Weinberger March 27 appointed Air Force Lieut. Gen. James A. Abrahamson program manager of the SDI. In his first appearance on Capitol Hill, Abrahamson April 24 said research for the system also would include protection against Soviet "tactical and theater-range" ballistic missiles aimed at Europe. "Our concept of an 'effective' defense is one which protects our allies as well as the United States," he said. Abrahamson acknowledged that deployment of the system would require some modifications of the ABM Treaty, "with Soviet agreement."

Several members of Congress questioned the feasibility of the SDI. Among them was Sen. John Glenn, D-Ohio, who said, "The President has misled the people of this country" into believing that the SDI would work. "If he wants to be Buck Rogers I understand that. But it is preposterous to carry on at this level" of spending. "The whole thing rests on specific technologies that haven't yet been invented," Glenn said.

Democratic presidential candidate Walter F. Mondale April 24 charged that Reagan was attempting to "open the heavens for warfare." Mondale proposed a "space freeze" to control anti-satellite weapons and curtail the administration's space defense effort.

Space Weapons and Arms Control Talks

Whether to inaugurate talks on controlling arms in space emerged as a major issue in U.S.-Soviet relations throughout 1984. Soviet President Konstantin U. Chernenko on June 11 called on the United States to negotiate a ban on the use of anti-satellite weapons before there were "drastic developments in the arms race in space," adding, "Tomorrow, it may be too late." President Reagan responded in a news conference three days later, saying, "We're ready, willing and able" to meet with the Soviets. ". . . The door is open."

On June 29 the official Soviet news agency Tass distributed a statement formally offering to begin "Soviet-American talks to prevent the militarization of space." Replying to the statement, National Security Affairs Adviser Robert C. McFarlane said the administration would be willing to join in the effort, but that it would also expect to discuss "mutually agreeable arrangements under which negotiations on the reduction of strategic and intermediate-range nuclear weapons can be resumed." Talks on both fronts had been at an impasse since November 1983, and relations between the two countries had become increasingly strained, as demonstrated pointedly by the Soviet boycott of the Summer Olympic games, held in Los Angeles in July and August 1984. (Arms talks, Historic Documents of 1983, p. 791)

Moscow immediately dismissed the U.S. position as "totally unsatisfactory," saying the Soviet Union "resolutely rejects the attempt to advance preconditions for talks." A July 1 Tass statement said the U.S. reply was "intended to turn outer space into an arena for the deployment of weapons of mass annihilation." The Reagan administration responded the next day that it had set no "preconditions" to a September meeting. During the next few days, President Reagan and Secretary of State George P. Shultz, in a series of meetings with Soviet Ambassador Anatoly F. Dobrynin, sought to reassure Moscow that Washington was willing to begin outer space negotiations. And on July 6 Moscow reaffirmed its offer to begin space weapons talks. "To these and no other talks, it invites the government of the U.S.A. and waits a positive response," a Tass statement said.

In late 1984 the two governments exchanged a number of proposals and counter proposals, but bitter rhetoric dimmed hopes for a dialogue. The impasse continued until January 7 and 8, 1985, when Shultz and Soviet Foreign Minister Andrei Gromyko met in Geneva and negotiated a resumption of talks on arms control, including space weaponry. The talks were to begin about three months later.

> *Following are excerpts from the March 21, 1984, report by the Union of Concerned Scientists on a "Space-Based Missile Defense," and from the Office of Technology Assessment background paper, "Directed Energy Missile Defense in Space," submitted to the Senate Foreign Relations Committee April 25, 1984:*

UCS REPORT

Overview

"I call upon the scientific community who gave us nuclear weapons to turn their great talents to the cause of mankind and world peace: to give us the means of rendering these nuclear weapons impotent and obsolete."

President Reagan, March 23, 1983

These words unveiled the President's Strategic Defense Initiative, a "comprehensive and intensive effort" with the "ultimate goal of eliminating the threat posed by strategic nuclear missiles." It proposes to rely on unborn generations of sophisticated space weapons that the Secretary of Defense told "Meet the Press" would provide a "thoroughly reliable and total" defense. We shall adopt Mr. [Caspar] Weinberger's words, and refer to the President's goal as *total ballistic missile defense*, or *total BMD* — what in the vernacular is now called "Star Wars."

Every sane person yearns to escape from the specter of nuclear annihilation. But that consensus still leaves a host of unanswered questions: will these BMD systems, which still are just conceptual designs, provide a total defense of our civilization against the Soviet missile force? That force now carries 9000 nuclear warheads, each far more powerful than the Hiroshima bomb, and able to arrive on US targets within 30 minutes. (The US arsenal is, of course, equally devastating.) If these defenses of the distant future could protect us totally against today's threat, could they cope with the Soviet strategic weapons of their own era?

What would the Soviets' response be? Would they devote themselves to a similar effort, and agree to reduce their offensive nuclear forces? Or would they perceive this new American program as an attempt to nullify Soviet nuclear forces — as a supplement to the emerging US capacity to destroy Soviet missiles in their silos? If so, would they not respond with a missile buildup and "countermeasures" to confound our defenses, so that they could still destroy the United States (just as the US can destroy the USSR)? Or would the Soviets not have this option, because our defense would be truly total — robust enough to foil any offensive countermove?

This report addresses these questions. It examines the proposed BMD systems in the light of the scientific facts and principles that will govern their performance.... There is general agreement that a defense of our population is impossible unless the vast majority of Soviet missiles can be intercepted in the first phase of their flight, while their booster engines emit a brilliant flame and before their multiple warheads are released. Otherwise, the subsequent layers of the BMD system will not be able to cope with the attack. We therefore devote the bulk of our attention to "boost phase" defense.

In assessing each BMD system, we first assume that it will perform as well as the constraints imposed by scientific law permit — that targets can be found instantly and aiming is perfect, that the battle management software is never in error, that all mirrors are optically perfect, that lasers with the required power output will become available, etc. Above all, we assume that the Soviets' forces remain static — that they do not build more missiles or install any countermeasures. Hence, our initial optimistic appraisal ignores the critical question of whether BMD will eventually work as well as it possibly could, and does not depend on classified information.

Even in this utopian regime, our findings concerning the proposed BMD schemes are that:

- Chemical laser "battle stations" in low orbits, or "space trucks" carrying "kill vehicles," will have to number in the thousands to give adequate coverage of the Soviet silo fields; simply lofting these stations into orbit would cost upwards of $70 billion.

- Excimer lasers on the ground, whose beams would be reflected towards boosters by over a thousand orbiting mirrors, would require power plants which alone would cost some $40 billion.
- The atmosphere and the earth's magnetic field combine to make particle beam weapons wholly implausible into the foreseeable future.

These cost estimates do not include research and development, or construction of space platforms, lasers, kill vehicles, mirrors, and command and control facilities. Just the R&D portion of this program has been described by Dr. Richard DeLauer, Under Secretary of Defense for Research and Engineering, as having at least eight components "every single one ... equivalent to or greater than the Manhattan Project." Furthermore, all costs will climb rapidly should the mirrors be imperfect, the time for aiming exceed several seconds, redundancy be desired. ... The full costs cannot even be estimated because the proposed technologies are still too immature, but it is clear that many hundreds of billions of dollars would be needed.

The proposal to launch x-ray lasers pumped by nuclear explosions at the time of an attack would require a new fleet of submarines, as there is no suitable base on land close enough to Soviet silos to allow interception in the time available. The laser's soft x-rays cannot penetrate the atmosphere, and they deliver a rather light blow from which the booster can readily be protected. These facts, when combined with the feasibility of shortening the boost so that it ends before the missile leaves the atmosphere, imply that the x-ray laser is not a viable BMD weapon.

These findings assume a minimal Soviet reaction to a US missile defense. But the Soviets have made it clear that they view the quest for total BMD as an unacceptable threat. They fear that such a BMD system would give us the option to strike first — an understandable fear since Mr. Weinberger has said that he would view a similar Soviet system as "one of the most frightening prospects" imaginable. And they have heard Administration officials speak of space-based BMD as a lever for stressing the USSR's technologically less sophisticated economy.

In the real world we must therefore expect a determined Soviet reaction, unconstrained by all existing agreements, because the very testing of our defensive weapons would violate our obligations under the ratified [1972] Anti-Ballistic Missile (ABM) Treaty. The Soviet reaction is likely to include:

- Offensive missiles designed to circumvent BMD, such as submarine-launched cruise missiles that cannot be intercepted from space.
- Fitting ICBMs with more powerful engines so that the boosters would burn out quickly and inside the atmosphere, which would stress any BMD system, and eliminate interception by kill vehicles and x-ray lasers.

- Cheap decoy ICBMs — boosters without warheads in fake silos — to overwhelm boost phase interceptors.
- Weapons that would exploit the fact that even a battleship's armor could not protect a space station from quite primitive types of attack.
- A Pandora's box of largely developed countermeasures that would vastly complicate the problem of targeting boosters and warheads.

All these countermeasures would exploit off-the-shelf weapons and techniques that exist today, in contrast to the unproven and improbable technologies on which our proposed defenses would rely. Hence, the Soviet response will be cheaper and far more reliable than our defenses, and available as those defenses emerge.

While this quest for a total defense against nuclear missiles would be endless, the decision to embark would have immediate political repercussions. Indeed, the first repercussion has already been heard: the US rebuff to Soviet overtures to negotiate constraints on anti-satellite (ASAT) weapons — a stance dictated by the plans for a space-based BMD system. The ABM Treaty could not survive the start of this endless journey, and with it all constraints on offensive forces would go overboard. The impact on NATO [the North Atlantic Treaty Organization] would be profound. Our allies in Europe would not be protected by an American BMD system, and this would inflame existing suspicion that the US intends to conduct nuclear operations in Europe without risk to itself. Alliance cohesion would erode because Europeans would hold the US responsible for exacerbating East-West tensions.

The risk to our survival would mount dramatically were we ever to begin erecting the BMD system. This budding system would be exceedingly vulnerable to attack. Nevertheless, its capabilities would be overvalued by our adversaries, and its installation could well be perceived as an attempt to disarm the Soviet Union. These circumstances could in themselves provoke open conflict.

If we get through this hazardous passage, will we have reached the promised land where nuclear weapons are "impotent and obsolete?" Obviously not. We would then have a defense of stupefying complexity, under the total control of a computer program whose proportions defy description, and whose performance will remain a deep mystery until the tragic moment when it would be called into action.

The President and his entourage occasionally argue that we must pursue this quest because the benefits of success outweigh the costs and risks. However, that is only an argument for a research program in strict conformity with the ABM Treaty. Such a program has always had our support. It is needed to protect us from Soviet surprises, and it might uncover concepts that could actually provide a viable defense. But there is an enormous gulf between such a program and a call from the ramparts for a national "experiment" to mount a defense based on untried technologies and provocative doctrines. We have delineated the costs and risks of such an "experiment." At best, the outcome would be a defense of precarious reliability, confronted by offensive nuclear forces designed to circumvent and overwhelm it, and a host of new "anti-BMD" weapons to attack our armada of space platforms which, in turn, would have to be defended by yet another fleet of anti-anti-BMD weapons.

It is difficult to imagine a more hazardous confrontation. And it is equally difficult to understand how anyone can believe that this is the path towards a less dangerous world. A direct and safe road is there for all to see — equitable and verifiable deep cuts in strategic offensive forces and immediate negotiations to ban all space weapons. If we are to take that road, we must abandon the misconception that nuclear explosives are military weapons, and the illusion that ever more sophisticated technology can, by itself, remove the perils that science and technology have created. We must, instead, recognize the overriding reality of the nuclear age — that we cannot regain safety by cleverly sawing off the thin, dry branch on which the Soviets are perched, for we cling to the same branch. . . .

SUMMARY

Our analysis makes clear that total ballistic missile defense — the protection of American society against the full weight of a Soviet nuclear attack — is unattainable if the Soviet Union exploits the many vulnerabilities intrinsic to all the schemes that have been proposed thus far. In none of the three phases of attack can one reasonably expect the success rates that would allow a layered BMD system to reduce the number of warheads arriving on US territory sufficiently to prevent unprecedented death and destruction. Instead, each phase presents intractable problems, and the resulting failure of the system compounds from one phase to the next.

A highly efficient boost phase intercept is a prerequisite of total BMD, but is doomed by the inherent limitations of the weapons, insoluble basing dilemmas, and an array of offensive countermeasures. As a result, the failure of midcourse systems is preordained. Midcourse BMD is plagued not so much by the laws of physics and geometry as by the sheer unmanageability of its task in the absence of a ruthless thinning out of the attack in boost phase.

Terminal phase BMD, finally, remains fundamentally unsuitable for area defense of population centers, as opposed to hard-point targets. There seems no way of defending soft targets on a continent-wide basis against the broad variety of attacks that could be tailored to circumvent and overwhelm terminal defenses. . . .

Political and Strategic Implications

The political and strategic dangers raised by the "Star Wars" initiative are at least as important as its technical flaws. Indeed, these dangers would weigh heavily against development of ballistic missile defenses even if the technical prospects for such systems were much brighter than they are. A US commitment to BMD would precipitate Soviet responses and a chain of actions and reactions that would radically change the strategic environment to the detriment of both countries' security. The offensive arms race would be greatly accelerated, arms control treaties undermined, and the nuclear peace made more precarious.

Of course, the technical and political issues are not completely unconnected. If it were possible to put in place overnight a fully effective, invulnerable defense against nuclear weapons, there could hardly be serious objections to doing so. But, as the preceding analysis has shown, such a system cannot be built now or, in all likelihood, ever. In the real world, BMD systems will be imperfect. Even under very optimistic assumptions about their ultimate performance, the process of improvement would be incremental and prolonged. During this extended and highly unstable transition period the strategic and political implications of BMD become critical.

While the alleged benefits of BMD are distant and hypothetical, the dangers are near-term and predictable. The adverse consequences of a commitment to BMD would be felt long before the actual deployment of mature technological systems, and quite likely even while the ABM Treaty was still technically being observed. These consequences would follow the familiar anticipated reactions syndrome, driven by the highly threatening nature of BMD and the worst-case assumptions that would dominate nuclear planning amid large uncertainties about the effectiveness of BMD systems and ambiguities about the intentions behind them. Accordingly, the dangers posed by a US policy of ballistic missile defense would be virtually independent of the level of performance that BMD systems might, decades in the future, finally achieve.

THE ABM TREATY

The ballistic missile defense envisaged by the Reagan administration is plainly inconsistent with the 1972 Anti-Ballistic Missile Treaty. As acknowledged in the President's Fiscal Year 1984 Arms Control Impact Statement, the treaty "bans the development, testing, and deployment of all ABM systems and components that are sea-based, air-based, space-based, or mobile land-based." The statement further notes explicitly that the ban on space systems applies to directed energy technologies. Under the interpretation of "development" offered by the US at the time the treaty was signed, the treaty's prohibitions take effect at the point that ABM systems or components enter the phase of field testing. . . .

The ABM Treaty is of great importance in both practical and symbolic terms. It embodies a joint recognition that effective territorial defense against nuclear weapons is technologically infeasible and that the pursuit of such a defense would be strategically destabilizing and would preclude the successful negotiation of restraints on offensive nuclear forces. These premises are still valid, and the treaty therefore remains firmly in the mutual interest of the two superpowers. Abandonment of the treaty by either country would be tantamount to a rejection of the arms control pr ɔcess per se, and would have highly damaging political as well as military consequences for the US-Soviet relationship. . . .

CONSEQUENCES FOR THE ARMS RACE AND ARMS CONTROL

A collapse of the ABM Treaty and the initiation of a BMD competition between the superpowers would have a devastating impact on the prospects for offensive arms control. Following an inevitable action-reaction pattern, the Soviets are certain to respond to an American BMD with new offensive measures. Both a quantitative and a qualitative escalation of the arms race would ensue. Adherence to the terms of the SALT II treaty — not ratified by the US but until now informally observed by both countries — would end, and hopes for new agreements would be undermined. . . .

In a world of BMD deployments, each superpower's first priority would be the maintenance of forces able to penetrate or circumvent the other's defenses. The resulting stimulus to the arms race would be aggravated by uncertainties about the effectiveness of defenses. . . .

CONSEQUENCES FOR DETERRENCE AND CRISIS STABILITY

In addition to the arms race consequences discussed above, the administration's BMD proposal would have a profoundly destabilizing effect on the nuclear balance, increasing the risk of nuclear war at times of US-Soviet confrontation and reducing the chances of bringing hostilities under control if war did occur.

These consequences run directly counter to the arguments often made by BMD advocates that US defenses would strengthen deterrence and, in the event deterrence fails, play an important damage-limitation role. Such arguments, it should be emphasized, are attempts to construct strategic rationales for only modestly capable BMD systems. . . .

Area defenses undermine deterrence because they magnify the advantage of striking first. Indeed, the modest BMD systems likely to be attainable in the foreseeable future would be useful only to the attacker. They would be easily defeated by a well-executed first strike, but might perform with some effectiveness against a poorly coordinated and weakened retaliatory strike.

As a result, these systems are likely to be perceived as components of a first strike strategy rather than as deterrent weapons, and to create strong incentives for preemptive attacks during periods of high tension. At such times, the fact that a first strike would be complicated by the adversary's BMD would be judged less relevant than the fear that, if one fails to attack first, effective retaliation may be impossible.

BMD, then, would aggravate the dangerous "use them or lose them" pressures that are already increasing due to the trend toward offensive weapons designed for counterforce. The result would be a serious weakening of mutual deterrence precisely at those times when it is most needed. . . .

OTA REPORT

[Sections 1-7 omitted]

8. Defensive Goals I: The Perfect Defense

No assessment of whether a defensive system "works" or not is meaningful without a clear and direct statement of the goal of the deployment. Though there has been much discussion of the feasibility of boost-phase BMD [ballistic missile defense] proponents and skeptics alike frequently leave unstated the standards against which they are judging the technical prospects. A "successful" BMD deployment could be defined as anything from a truly impenetrable shield, to a silo defense that merely costs less to build than it costs the Soviets to overcome, to a tangled deployment that just "creates uncertainty" for the attacker.

The most ambitious conceivable goal for BMD would be to take at literal face value the words of President Reagan in his so-called "Star Wars" speech of March 23, 1983, when he called for development of a defense capable of making nuclear weapons "impotent and obsolete." It is not clear that the President intended his words to be taken literally, nor that the Administration or anyone else is suggesting the United States seek a truly perfect or near-perfect defense. . . .

There is some confusion in the literature about the use of the term "mutual assured destruction" (MAD) in connection with the notion of perfect defense. In common strategic parlance, MAD refers to the *technological circumstance* of mutual vulnerability to catastrophic damage from nuclear weapons, not to a *chosen policy* to promote such vulnerability. There is a strategic school of thought that advocates a policy usually called "minimum deterrence," maintaining that the capability for assured destruction of Soviet society is the *only* requirement of U.S. strategic forces. However, many experts believe that effective deterrence and other national security objectives require nuclear forces capable of many other tasks than assured destruction. This section addresses itself to the question of whether MAD is an avoidable technological circumstance, *not* to whether minimum deterrence is a prudent strategic policy.

A sensible start at judging the prospect for near-perfect defense must involve two steps: first, an exact statement of what perfect defense means in the context of attack on society with nuclear weapons; second, some way of gauging the likelihood of success when the technological future cannot be accurately predicted. . . .

There is not and cannot be any "proof" that unknown future technologies will not provide near-perfect defensive protection of U.S. society against Soviet ICBMs. The question that needs to be answered is whether the prospects of near-perfect defense are so remote that such a notion has no place in reasonable public expectations or national policy. It is, after all, not provable that by the next century the United States and U.S.S.R. will not have patched up their political differences and have no need to target one another with nuclear weapons. The issue of the perfect defense is unavoidably one of technical judgment rather than of airtight proof.

Four misapprehensions seem common among non-technical people addressing the prospects for perfect defense.

The first misapprehension is to equate successful technology development of individual *devices* — lasers, power sources, mirrors, aiming and pointing mechanisms — with achievement of an efficient and robust defensive *system*. Millionfold increase in the brightness of some directed-energy device is a necessary, but is far from a sufficient, condition for successful defense. In the early 1960's, intercept of RVs [re-entry vehicles] with nuclear-tipped interceptor missiles was demonstrated — "a bullet could hit a bullet" — but 20 years later systems incorporating this "kill mechanism" are still considered relatively inefficient. In general, skeptics about the future of space-based directed-energy BMD do not confine their doubts to, or even emphasize, unforeseen problems in developing the individual components.

A second misapprehension arises in attempts to equate BMD development to past technological achievements, such as the Manhattan project's atomic bomb or the Apollo moon landings. The technically minded will recognize a vital difference between working around the constraints imposed by nature, which are predictable and unchanging, and competing with a hostile intelligence bent on sabotaging the enterprise. A dynamic opponent makes of BMD, first, a more difficult design problem, since the offense constructs the worst possible barriers to successful defense; and second, not one problem but many problems that need to be sidestepped simultaneously in the design, since the designer cannot be certain which tactics the offense will use.

A third misapprehension concerns the prospect for a "technological breakthrough" that would dispel all difficulties. Such breakthroughs are not impossible, but their mere possibility does not help in judging the prospects for the perfect defense. For one thing, an isolated technological breakthrough creating a new defensive component would not necessarily alleviate the system issues — vulnerability, dependability, susceptibility to countermeasures, cost — that determine overall effectiveness. Second, one can just as easily imagine offensive "breakthroughs," sometimes involving the same technologies. Thus the x-ray laser, if it matures, might turn out to have been better termed a breakthrough in strategic offense than a breakthrough in strategic defense.

A fourth misapprehension concerns the confidence with which predictions could be made about the performance of a complex system once in place. The "performance" of a system, as quoted in analyses, is the most likely outcome of an engagement of offense versus defense. Other outcomes, though less likely, might still be possible. Computing the relative likelihoods of *all* possible outcomes would be difficult even if one could quantify all technical uncertainties and statistical variances. Still, there would remain a residue of uncertainty about the performance of a system that had never been tested once in realistic wartime conditions, much less in a statistically significant ensemble of all-out nuclear wars. The defense would also have no chance to learn and adapt. In World War II, by contrast, air defense crews learned in raid after raid to inflict losses of several percent in attacking bombers. The only reason these modest losses assumed strategic significance was that they accumulated over many raids. Of course, the same uncertainties plague the offense as plague the defense. In general, the offense would tend to overestimate the defense's capability. This natural tendency toward "offense conservatism" is probably vitally important to the psychological and deterrent value of BMD as it is applied to less than-perfect goals. For the perfect defense goal (as defined above), however, it would seem that the uncertainty weighs heaviest on the defense. To the reckless, non-conservative defense, a wrong estimate of defense performance spells the difference between safety and socially mortal damage (or between deterrence and war). The reckless offense, on the other hand, is presumed desperate enough to try to inflict such damage on its enemy and willing to accept the consequences: it stands to lose little if its estimates are wrong and the defense *does* work perfectly after all.

With these misapprehensions out of the way, and recognizing clearly that there can be no question of "proof," it would seem that four major factors conspire to make extremely remote the prospect that directed-energy BMD (in concert with other layers if necessary) will succeed in reducing the vulnerability of U.S. population and society to the neighborhood of 100 megatons or less.

1. *Near-perfect defense of society is much harder and more expensive than partial defense of military targets. . . .*

2. *For every defense concept proposed or imagined, including all of the so-called "Star Wars" concepts, a countermeasure has already been identified. . . .*

3. *The Soviet Union does not configure its nuclear missile forces today to maximize damage to U.S. society and population, but it could do so if faced with near-perfect U.S. defenses. . . .*

4. *BMD by itself will not protect U.S. society from other methods of delivering nuclear weapons to U.S. soil or from other weapons of mass destruction. . . .*

9. Defensive Goals II: Less-Than-Perfect Defense

A host of less grandiose goals than perfect or near-perfect defense assume importance in certain theories about the workings of nuclear deterence and the requirements of U.S. security. Thoughtful observers debate not just the feasibility of achieving these goals but the validity and importance of the goals as well. The urgency one attaches to these goals determines the costs, risks, and harmful side effects one is willing to incur to fulfill them. Assessing the wisdom of less-than-perfect defense thus involves a complex and subjective balancing of goals and risks. . . .

Though various strategic goals for BMD can be distinguished in principle, in practice it might not be clear or agreed among all parties in the
United States what the purpose of a proposed deployment actually was.
Interpretations by the Soviet Union and other foreign nations of U.S. goals
might be quite different yet. . . .

1. *Strengthen deterrence by preventing preemptive destruction of
retaliatory forces.* It is widely recognized that the Soviet Union will soon
have, if it does not already, the combination of yields, numbers, and
accuracy in its ICBM forces to destroy most U.S. Minuteman ICBMs in
their silos. It is also widely agreed that vulnerable nuclear forces create
unwanted temptations for both sides to strike first if war seems likely. The
long and anguished search for survivable basing modes for the U.S. MX
(Peacekeeper) ICBM has to date turned up no clear favorites when
survivability is balanced against cost, technical risk, strategic effects, and
environmental impacts. BMD would substitute for or complement these
other basing modes. By shooting down a fraction of the opponent's
missiles, BMD would in effect "de-MIRV" ICBM forces.

Of course, turning to BMD to ease ICBM vulnerability is not without
problems. One problem is the prospect of a compensating Soviet BMD. . . .

2. *Strengthen deterrence by preventing the use of nuclear weapons as
decisive military tools for high-confidence "limited" strikes on conventional forces.* This goal is associated with so-called "warfighting" strategies
for nuclear weapons. According to analysts who hold this view, today's
"offense dominated" world creates dangerous temptations to resort to
nuclear weapons to accomplish militarily well-defined objectives. One can
imagine warheads simply being lobbed unopposed into another country in
any number or combination. Though surely the effects of these "limited"
attacks on nearby communities would not be so well-defined, the effect on
the opposing military machine might be truly dramatic, even decisive. This
use of nuclear weapons in wartime is possible with today's unopposed
offenses with considerable confidence and might therefore be tempting to
the combatants. Such temptations threaten nuclear deterrence and should
be eliminated. The goal of a comprehensive defense would be to make such
limited attacks infeasible, or at least to complicate the offense's estima-
tions of success to such a degree that it would not attempt an "experiment." Analysts who favor this approach usually maintain that Soviet
military doctrine inclines the Soviets towards a view of nuclear weapons as
military tools to a far greater degree than is common in U.S. thinking. . . .

Critics of this BMD goal object both to the warfighters' emphasis upon
the risk of this type of scenario and to the assumption that defense would
materially diminish that risk. In their view myriad detailed chinks in the
armor of deterrence can always be found, with or without defense and
worrying about them represents a loss of perspective on the basic difference between nuclear and conventional instruments of war. . . .

3. *Save Lives.* Another goal for BMD is purely humanitarian and seeks
no military or strategic advantage. If the defense did not interfere too
much with Soviet military targeting objectives (enough for the Soviets to

try to overcome it), and assuming the Soviets have no explicit aim to inflict human casualties, the United States could expect some reduction in fatalities in a nuclear war even from a modest defense. This reduction would necessarily be limited, since Soviet military objectives include destruction of many targets collocated with population. . . .

4. *Shape the course of the arms competition and arms control.* One version of this goal sees the Soviet tendency to upgrade and proliferate existing ICBM forces as the principal impediment to arms control. By introducing BMD (or even discussing it), according to this view, the United States makes the Soviets unsure about the next step in the arms competition and thus undercuts the momentum of Soviet strategic programs, especially ICBM modernization. . . .

Another line of argument holds that a major BMD initiative strengthens the U.S. negotiating position at START, [U.S.-Soviet Strategic Arms Reduction Talks]. An aggressive BMD program demonstrates U.S. technological prowess and hints at what the Soviets could face if this prowess were unleashed. . . .

5. *Respond to Soviet BMD efforts.* Many analysts view with alarm Soviet strategic defense activities, including upgrading of the Moscow ABM, development of a transportable terminal BMD system, construction of a radar in apparent violation of the ABM Treaty, development of defenses against the tactical ballistic missiles, incorporation of limited BMD capability in air defenses, and continued attention to other damage-limiting methods (civil defense, air defense, antisubmarine warfare, and countersilo ICBMs). A strong U.S. BMD research and development program might deter the Soviets from breaking out of the ABM Treaty and from continued encroachments on the Treaty's provisions. . . .

6. *Protect against accidental missile launches and attack from other nuclear powers.* These goals have been put forward several times in the past, most notably in the late 1960's when the Johnson Administration proposed the Sentinel ABM system to counter Chinese ICBMs, believed at that time to be fast-emerging. Neither goal figures prominently in today's discussion of BMD in the United States, though defense against Chinese, British, and French missiles could well loom larger in Soviet thinking. Emerging nuclear powers or terrorists would be unlikely to use ICBMs to deliver their small nuclear arsenals to the United States. BMD is therefore of little importance in staving off the threat to U.S. security posed by nuclear proliferation.

10. Principal Judgments and Observations

1. *The prospect that emerging "Star Wars" technologies, when further developed, will provide a perfect or near-perfect defense system, literally removing from the hands of the Soviet Union the ability to do socially mortal damage to the United States with nuclear weapons, is so remote that it should not serve as the basis of public expectation or national policy about ballistic missile defense (BMD). . . .*

2. *The wisdom of deploying less-than-perfect ballistic missile defenses remains controversial.* Less-than-perfect defenses would still allow the Soviet Union to destroy U.S. society in a massive attack but might call into question the effectiveness of smaller, specialized nuclear strikes. . . .

3. *The strategic goal of President Reagan's Strategic Defense Initiative calling for emphasized BMD research — perfect, near-perfect, or less-than-perfect defense against ballistic missiles — remains unclear.* . . .

4. *In all cases, directed-energy weapons and other devices with the specifications needed for boost-phase intercept of ICBMs have not yet been built in the laboratory, much less in a form suitable for incorporation in a complete defense system.* These devices include chemical lasers, excimer and free electron lasers, x-ray lasers, particle beams, lightweight high-velocity kinetic energy weapons, and microwave generators, together with tracking, aiming, and pointing mechanisms, power sources, and other essential accompaniments.

It is unknown whether or when devices with the required specifications can be built.

5. *Moreover, making the technological devices perform to the needed specifications in a controlled situation is not the crux of the technical challenge facing designers of an effective ballistic missile defense. A distinct challenge is to fashion from these devices a reliable defensive architecture, taking into account vulnerability of the defense components, susceptibility to future Soviet countermeasures, and cost relative to those countermeasures.* . . .

6. *It is clear that potent directed-energy weapons will be developed for other military purposes, even if such weapons are never incorporated into effective BMDs.* . . .

7. *For modest defensive goals requiring less-than-perfect performance, traditional reentry phase defenses and/or more advanced mid-course defenses might suffice.* Such defenses present less technical risk than systems that incorporate a boost-phase layer, and they could probably be deployed more quickly. . . .

8. *Deployment of missile defenses based on new technologies is forbidden by the Anti-Ballistic Missile (ABM) Treaty reached at SALT I.* The Treaty permits only restricted deployment of traditional BMDs using fixed, ground-based radars and interceptor missiles. Research into new technologies, and in selected cases development and testing of defense systems based on these technologies, are allowed within the Treaty.

9. *There is a close connection, not explored in detail in this Background Paper, between advanced BMD concepts and future anti-satellite (ASAT) systems.* . . .

April

April

PHYSICIANS' REPORTS ON TREATING THE HOPELESSLY ILL
April 12, 26, 1984

Doctors' treatment of terminally ill patients was the subject of two special reports appearing in the April 12 and 26 issues of The New England Journal of Medicine. *The first article, written by a team of 10 physicians, discussed the many factors affecting decisions about informing patients of the severity of their illness. "Although some physicians and families avoid frank discussions with patients, in our view, practically all patients, even disturbed ones, are better off knowing the truth," the authors concluded.*

The April 12 report was prepared by doctors who gathered for a conference at Harvard Medical School in October 1982. It was intended to provide guidelines for physicians who must make life-and-death decisions for seriously ill patients. The meeting, chaired by Dr. Daniel D. Federman, former president of the American College of Physicians, was attended by doctors from the Mayo Clinic and from the medical schools at Harvard, the University of Pittsburgh, Johns Hopkins, and the University of Texas, as well as the Hennepin County Medical Center in Minneapolis and the University of Virginia Medical Center. "The idea was that if a group of prominent physicians took the lead in suggesting what is possible that these principles might become accepted among the general physician population," said Dr. Sidney H. Wanzer of Emerson Hospital in Concord, Mass., who wrote the group's conclusions for publication.

In general, doctors should respect the patient's own wishes, but treatment that only prolonged a person's agony should in most cases not be undertaken, the authors concluded.

However, the second New England Journal of Medicine *article, based on a survey conducted at Boston's Beth Israel (one of Harvard Medical School's main teaching hospitals), found that doctors frequently did not talk with their patients about choices involved in cardiopulmonary resuscitation, among the most frequently practiced revival techniques. The study, undertaken by Drs. Susanna Bedell and Thomas Delbanco, reviewed 154 cases in which doctors tried to revive a patient's heart. The doctors had asked only 30 of the patients in advance whether they wanted such an attempt made. Of the 24 patients who survived in a mentally competent state, eight said they would have preferred to be allowed to die. Only one doctor in 10 had actually discussed resuscitation with his patients. One in five consulted family members, rather than the patient, even when the patient was fully competent. "The question of whether to perform or withhold cardiopulmonary resuscitation will always require attention to the balance between prolonging survival and decreasing suffering," the authors concluded. "Our study suggests that many patients may know what they want and welcome the chance to make their own contribution to this difficult debate."*

A Controversial Issue

The physician's responsibility to respect a terminally ill patient's wishes to forego life-sustaining treatment had been a topic of considerable debate in recent years, particularly as medical advances made prolongation of life through extraordinary measures increasingly possible. A March 1983 study by a presidential commission on medical ethics addressed the issue of deciding to forego life-sustaining measures, which it said involved "some of the most important and troubling ethical and legal questions in modern medicine." (Historic Documents of 1983, p. 279)

The debate was heightened in February 1984, when Colorado Gov. Richard D. Lamm remarked in a speech, "We've got a duty to die and get out of the way with all of our machines and artificial hearts ... and let the other society, our kids, build a reasonable effort." Responding to criticism of his comment, Lamm explained that he was trying to say that "we all have the duty to recognize and to leave instructions in our will" because machines "can keep us alive far beyond" the point where many people would want to live.

> *Following are excerpts from articles appearing in the April 12 and 26, 1984, issues of* The New England Journal of Medicine *on "The Physician's Responsibility Toward Hopelessly Ill Patients" and "Choices About Cardiopulmonary Resuscitation in the Hospital."* (Boldface headings in brackets have been added by Congressional Quarterly to highlight the organization of the text.):

THE PHYSICIAN'S RESPONSIBILITY TOWARD HOPELESSLY ILL PATIENTS

Sidney H. Wanzer, M.D., S. James Adelstein, M.D., Ronald E. Cranford, M.D., Daniel D. Federman, M.D., Edward D. Hook, M.D., Charles G. Moertel, M.D., Peter Safar, M.D., Alan Stone, M.D., Helen B. Taussig, M.D., and Jan van Eys, Ph.D., M.D.

. . . The patient's right to make decisions about his or her medical treatment is clear. That right, grounded in both common law and the constitutional right of privacy, includes the right to refuse life-sustaining treatment — a fact affirmed in the courts and recently supported by a presidential commission. Ideally, the right is exercised when the diagnosis and treatment are clear, the physician is skilled and sensitive, and the patient is competent and informed. Circumstances, however, are often less than ideal. . . . Disease, pain, drugs, and a variety of conditions altering mental states may severely reduce the patient's capacity for judgment. Since these circumstances can fluctuate, competency can be lost and regained, requiring reevaluation at intervals.

The principal obstacle to a patient's effective participation in decision making is lack of competence, and only when competence is lacking can others substitute their judgment for that of the patient. Therefore, the assessment of competence is a critical issue. Although legal determination of incompetence may at times be a matter for court review, this step can be safely bypassed when there is unanimity on the part of the physician and others consulted — family and close friends, and psychiatrists, if indicated. In arriving at the determination of incompetence, the physician must coordinate the various evaluations and opinions and document them clearly in the medical records. We believe that a hopelessly ill patient's refusal of life-sustaining treatment is not in itself a reason to question the patient's competency, no matter what the personal values of the physician or family may be.

If the terminally ill patient's ability to make decisions becomes progressively reduced, the physician must rely increasingly on the presumed or prestated wishes of the patient. It helps if there is a longstanding relationship between patient and physician, but in fact many adults have no personal physician. Terminally ill patients are often cared for by specialists or members of house staff who do not know what the patient would have wished or may not have the time or experience to handle difficult problems of this kind. Under these circumstances, it becomes important to have other means of determining the patient's desires. A written statement, prepared in advance of the patient's illness and diminished decision-making capacity, can be helpful in indicating to the physician the patient's preference with respect to terminal treatment. Such advance directions, or "living wills," are recognized by law in 15 states and the District of Columbia, and even in states where they have not been legally authorized, they provide important though not binding evidence of a patient's wishes.

Another aid to decision making in which the patient cannot participate effectively is a proxy, designated in advance by the patient to speak on his or her behalf. This option has only recently been provided by law in a few states — either as part of the state's "living will" legislation (Delaware's Death with Dignity Act of 1982 and Virginia's Natural Death Act of 1983) or (in California) as an amendment to the durable-power-of-attorney statute, extending the authorization to health-care decisions. Since the clinical circumstances of a future illness and available treatment options are unpredictable, a proxy chosen by the patient offers the advantage of decision making based on both an intimate knowledge of the patient's wishes and the physician's recommendations.

Neither the living will nor the proxy appointment is a perfect mechanism for projecting a patient's wishes into a period of future incompetency. The living will cannot predict all the various alternatives that become possible as acute illnesses arise, and in many cases, the document is not updated with any regularity. A proxy may not be available at the time of need, or he or she may have a conflict of interest, either emotionally or legally. Nevertheless, in spite of imperfections, the living will and the proxy can be of real assistance to the physician trying to decide the best course of treatment for the dying patient. In their absence, the physician must ascertain from family and friends the attitudes and wishes the patient would have expressed had competence been maintained.

The Physician's Role in Decision Making

The patient's right to accept or refuse treatment notwithstanding, the physician has a major role in the decision-making process. He or she has the knowledge, skills, and judgment to provide diagnosis and prognosis, to offer treatment choices and explain their implications, and to assume responsibility for recommending a decision with respect to treatment.

The physician's schooling, residency training, and professional oath emphasize positive actions to sustain and prolong life; the educational system has only recently given attention to ethical questions surrounding the intentional reduction of medical intervention. Physicians do not easily accept the concept that it may be best to do less, not more, for a patient. The decision to pull back is much more difficult to make than the decision to push ahead with aggressive support, and today's sophisticated and complex medical technology invites physicians to make use of all the means at their disposal — a temptation that must be recognized when evaluating how much or how little to do for the patient.

Coupled with the traditional pressures for aggressive treatment is the uncertainty of diagnosis and prognosis, making it difficult to predict the length and quality of the patient's life with or without treatment. If the attending physician is not expert in the particular area of the patient's illness, he or she should consult with those who are. If there is disagreement concerning the diagnosis or prognosis or both, the life-sustaining approach should be continued until reasonable agreement is reached. However, insistence on certainty beyond a reasonable point can handicap the physician dealing with treatment options in apparently hopeless cases. The rare report of a patient with a similar condition who survived is not an overriding reason to continue aggressive treatment. Such negligible statistical possibilities do not outweigh the reasonable expectations of outcome that will guide treatment decisions.

Physicians are strongly influenced by their personal values and unconscious motivations. Although they should not be forced to act against their moral codes, they should guard against being excessively influenced by unexamined inner conflicts, a tendency to equate a patient's death with professional failure, or unrealistic expectations.

Fear of legal liability often interferes with the physician's ability to make the best choice for the patient. Assessment of legal risks is sometimes made by lawyers whose primary objective is to minimize liability, whether real or imagined. Unfortunately, this may be done at the expense of humane treatment and may go against the expressed wishes of the patient or family. A recent case in California involving murder charges against two physicians who withdrew all life support from a comatose patient created a climate of heightened apprehension in the medical community. The action taken against the physicians was the first and only such criminal case in U.S. legal history. Fortunately, the charges were dismissed by the California Court of Appeal. Treatment of a dying patient always takes place in the context of changing law and changing social policy, but in spite of legal uncertainties, appropriate and compassionate care should have priority over undue fears of criminal or civil liability.

Another possible influence on the physician's thinking is consideration of monetary costs to society and the use of scarce treatment resources in the care of the hopelessly ill. In the past, cost was rarely an important factor in decision making, but today, as society tries to contain the soaring cost of health care, the physician is subject to insistent demands for restraint, which cannot be ignored. Financial ruin of the patient's family, as well as the drain on resources for treatment of other patients who are not hopelessly ill, should be weighed in the decision-making process, although the patient's welfare obviously remains paramount.

Communication with the Patient

When a physician discusses life-threatening illness with a patient, a number of questions arise. Is the patient capable of accepting the information? How much information should the patient be given? When should the physician inform the patient of a fatal illness? Can information be imparted without destroying all hope? There are no absolute answers to these questions, but the following principles seem reasonable.

Although some physicians and families avoid frank discussions with patients, in our view, practically all patients, even disturbed ones, are better off knowing the truth. A decision not to tell the patient the truth because of fear of his or her emotional or psychological inability to handle such information is rarely if ever justified, and in such a case the burden of proof rests on the person who believes that the patient cannot cope with frank discussion. The anxiety of dealing with the unknown can be far more upsetting than the grief of dealing with a known, albeit tragic, truth. A failure to transmit to the patient knowledge of terminal illness can create barriers in communication, and the patient is effectively placed in isolation at a time when emotional sharing is most needed.

The dying patient should be given only as much information as he or she wishes to handle. Some patients want to know every detail, whereas others, who have a limited ability to understand or a limited desire to know, want only the most general information.

The discussion of critical illness and the patient's right to accept or refuse life-prolonging treatment should occur as early as possible in the course of disease; ideally, it will already have taken place at a time when the patient was healthy. However, regardless of any discussions that may or may not have taken place, when fatal illness occurs, the physician — if possible, one with whom the patient has already developed rapport, not a stranger — should tell the patient of an unfavorable diagnosis or prognosis as soon as the information is firm. Such discussions may have to be repeated, since patients often find it difficult to assimilate all they need to know at any one time, and as illness progresses, continued communication will be required to meet changing needs.

When the prognosis is bad, the physician must help the terminally ill patient understand and deal with the prognosis and alternatives for treatment without destroying all hope. This can be done by reassuring the patient that he or she will not be abandoned and by emphasizing the positive measures that can be used for support. The emotional distress that accompanies such discussions is usually more than offset by the security of a consensus about terminal care.

Another important consideration with respect to doctor-patient communication is the matter of informed consent. There are three basic prerequisites for informed consent: the patient must have the capacity to reason and make judgments, the decision must be made voluntarily and without coercion, and the patient must have a clear understanding of the risks and benefits of the proposed treatment alternatives or nontreatment, along with a full understanding of the nature of the disease and the prognosis. Fulfillment of the third condition requires that the physician take the time to discuss the issues fully with the patient and outline the differences among alternatives, which are sometimes very difficult to estimate. Nevertheless, it is the physician's responsibility to ensure, as much as possible, that all the conditions for informed consents are met. In addition to being thoroughly informed, the patient must also understand clearly his or her right to make choices about the type of care to be received — a right many patients are not aware of. This is the cornerstone of all decision making and is the basis on which informed consent rests.

The preeminence of the patient's choice does not preclude the physician's responsibility to make and to share with the patient a personal judgment about what the patient should do. Patients often ask a trusted physician, "What would you do?" A direct answer is in order. Some patients want every possible day of life, regardless of how limited the quality, whereas others apparently prefer early death to prolongation of a very limited life on a day-to-day basis. Given what the physician knows about the individual patient, some order of preference for available treatment choices can be offered. In any case, it is unfair simply to provide a mass of medical facts and options and leave the patient adrift without any further guidance on the alternative courses of action and inaction.

The physician's traditional role as a source of comfort to patients and their families becomes especially important when the decision has been made to withhold treatment that prolongs dying. Competent patients who have chosen to be allowed to die may experience a resultant feeling of abandonment. The family may share this feeling on behalf of the dying patient and have difficulty grappling with the consequences of a decision in which they may or may not have played a part. Assiduous attention to the patient's physical and emotional comfort at this point is essential. The physician's availability at such times can be a source of great psychological comfort to both patient and family.

The physican has a special obligation to listen to the doubts and fears expressed by patients who are hopelessly or terminally ill. Although a rare patient may contemplate suicide, the physician cannot participate by assisting in the act, for this is contrary to law. On the other hand, the physician is not obligated to assume that every such wish is irrational and requires coercive intervention....

CHOICES ABOUT CARDIOPULMONARY RESUSCITATION IN THE HOSPITAL

Susanna E. Bedell, M.D., and Thomas L. Delbanco, M.D.

One of three patients who die at the Beth Israel Hospital undergoes cardiopulmonary resuscitation. The question of who should decide whether to perform or withhold resuscitation was once easily answered: the physician made the decisions about life and death. Today, the problem has become more complex as patients demand increasing responsibility for their own care and both administrators and doctors delineate appropriate guidelines for communication between the physician and patient. However, little is known about whether physicians actually discuss resuscitation with patients before the time of cardiac arrest.

We undertook a study that posed the following questions: How often and under what circumstances do physicians discuss the possibility of cardiopulmonary resuscitation with patients or their families? To what extent do physicians form attitudes about the appropriateness of resucitation for a given patient without direct communication with the patient? When are families, but not patients, consulted about resuscitation? How does the physician's perception compare with the patient's stated preference about resuscitation? How closely do the ideas of the private physician and the house officer parallel each other? Is there a discrepancy between what physicians say they ought to do and the reality of practice? . . .

Physicians expressed an opinion about their patients' attitudes toward cardiopulmonary resuscitation in 68 per cent of the cases. In 42 per cent of the cases the physician believed that the patient favored resuscitation, in 18 per cent the patient was considered ambivalent, and in 8 per cent the patient was thought to oppose resuscitation. For 32 per cent of the cases, the physician offered no opinion.

[Physicians' Communication]

Physicians did not often act according to their personal philosophy concerning the importance of consulting with patients about their desire for cardiopulmonary resuscitation. Seventy-six of the 82 private physicians (93 per cent) and all 75 of the house officers believed that patients should at least sometimes participate in decisions about resuscitation. . . . Only 15 of . . . 151 physicians (10 per cent) who believed in discussing resuscitation with patients actually talked with these patients before the arrest; 32 (21 per cent) discussed resuscitation with the family.

When considering that some physicians cared for more than one patient, we found that overall the private physicians discussed the possibility of resuscitation with 20 (13 per cent) of the 154 patients who had been resuscitated. There was no significant difference in the communication by private physicians and house officers. We were unable to identify any factor that was significantly associated with a greater or lesser likelihood that the physician discussed resuscitation with the patient before the arrest. Specifically, a physician's likelihood of communicating with a patient did not differ according to whether the patient was in the intensive-care unit or on a general ward, nor was there a significant difference according to whether the risk of arrest was estimated to be above or below 50 per cent. Similarly, physicians' expectations of survival after cardiopulmonary resuscitation did not influence the probability that resuscitation was discussed with the patient before the arrest, and no single disease category was significantly associated with the probability of such a discussion.

Similarly, the private physicians discussed cardiopulmonary resuscitation with 21 of the 134 families (16 per cent) of patients whom they had not consulted. Again, there was no significant difference between private physicians and house officers with respect to the frequency of discussions with such families. We found no circumstances under which physicians were significantly more likely to discuss resuscitation with the family; they did not talk more frequently with the families of the 21 patients who had a history of dementia.

To account for the possibility that the private physician and house officer were talking with different patients, we calculated the frequency with which either physician talked with a patient. Thirty of the 154 patients (19 per cent) had discussed cardiopulmonary resuscitation with either a private physician or a house officer (or both). Similarly, 51 of the 154 families (33 per cent) were consulted about resuscitation before the arrest. In 37 per cent of cases, one of the two physicians talked with the patient, the family, or both before the arrest. . . .

[Patients' Attitudes]

We compared the physicians' perceptions of their patients' attitudes with the stated preferences of the 25 survivors of cardiopulmonary resuscitation whom we interviewed. At the time of the initial hospital interview, 1 patient was too demented to respond, 1 was ambivalent, and 15 said that they desired resuscitation if it were necessary in the future. Eight stated unequivocally that they had not desired cardiopulmonary resuscitation and did not wish to be resuscitated in the future. Their reasons varied but were focused primarily on their discontent with a life style limited by chronic illness and their fear of further suffering at the time of arrest and resuscitation.

. . . [O]nly 1 of the 16 physicians caring for these eight patients believed that the patient had not desired resuscitation. Fourteen physicians stated that their patients were ambivalent or had desired resuscitation. At follow-up six months after discharage, six of the eight patients who had not desired cardiopulmonary resuscitation were still alive. By our scales, none was demented or depressed. Each repeated a desire not to be resuscitated.

Discussion

Our study suggests that physicians frequently form opinions about a patient's attitude toward cardiopulmonary resuscitation. Yet, they are unlikely to talk to their patients about resuscitation, even when they state that patients should always participate in decisions about resuscitation. The physician's perception may not correspond with the patient's stated preference, nor is there consistent agreement between two physicians about the patient's preference. Physicians also talk infrequently with patients' families. These attitudes and behaviors appear to be independent of the physician's estimate of the probability of arrest, the location of the patient in the hospital, or the patient's underlying disease.

There are several potential sources of bias in our study. First of all, the study was retrospective. However, since the questionnaires were administered shortly after cardiopulmonary resuscitation, we did not anticipate a problem with recall. Secondly, although it is possible that there was a discrepancy between stated and actual behavior, we expect that the direction of bias would have been toward overreporting communication with patients. In addition, in a situation where a single physician may treat more than one patient, bias from clustering may occur. Finally, the patients we interviewed were not a random sample. They were, by necessity, survivors of cardiopulmonary resuscitation.

There are myriad possible explanations for our observations about physicians' behavior, and some of our best clinical insights come from the comments of the study physicians. The private physicians in particular believed it is the doctor's responsibility to make decisions about resuscitation for patients. They said, moreover, that to involve the family would impose unnecessary guilt. These physicians believed that patients will initiate a discussion about resuscitation if they wish to and that they usually "tell you in other ways besides words that they do (or do not) want to be resuscitated." A discussion about cardiopulmonary resuscitation, initiated by the physician, would be "too threatening" a subject for most acutely ill patients and might in fact "bring on an arrest itself."

Among physicians who believed it appropriate for patients to participate in decisions about resuscitation, many were concerned by the complex logistical problem that cardiopulmonary resuscitation often presents. When should the physician consult a patient about his or her desire for resuscitation? Discussion must occur before the arrest itself; yet, the decision cannot be made so far in advance that it becomes irrelevant to a patient's immediate status. On the other hand, as one physician noted: "It is extremely difficult to discuss resuscitation with a patient or family when the arrest is totally unexpected."

We found inconsistencies between the perceptions and behavior of physicians. When patients are ambivalent about cardiopulmonary resuscitation, it is not surprising that the doctor's choice is for life. However, 8 per cent of resuscitations occurred in patients who were believed by the house officer or private physician to be opposed to cardiopulmonary resuscitation. Physicians offered several explanations. First of all, there was the concern that a "Do Not Resuscitate" order would mean that "fluid balance would not be maintained, that bloods would not be drawn, that the patient would simply be forgotten," although hospital policy explicitly forbids any diminution in the care of such patients. Secondly, some physicians complained that current policy is too cumbersome and a "Do Not Resuscitate" order is too difficult to obtain, even when a physician believes it is appropriate and in accordance with the patient's wishes. Finally, several physicians argued that no one would rationally refuse maximal medical technology and care. To quote one, "Who wouldn't want to be resuscitated?"

Today, there is increasing emphasis on the patient as an important participant in the decision-making process with respect to critical care. "Who is more likely to represent the patient's best interest than the patient himself?" Some suggest that an atmosphere in which terminal care and resuscitation are discussed openly helps patients explore their feelings on the subject. Yet, the concerns practicing physicians expressed in this study are realistic. Recommendations to increase direct communication and patient autonomy are perhaps easier said than done.

... [O]ur experience in talking directly with patients about resuscitation suggests that there are competent, emotionally stable patients who decide against cardiopulmonary resuscitation. All the survivors in our study readily discussed their arrest, its impact on their lives and family, and their attitudes toward resuscitation in the future. Most welcomed the opportunity to discuss their disease and functioning, as well as the complex familial and social factors that influenced their attitudes toward cardiopulmonary resuscitation. During our interviews, patients appeared able to set explicit limits on subjects they wished not to discuss. They also differentiated between the trauma of acute illness and the quality of life in general. Many seemed surprised at our questions and wondered how anyone could choose to forgo a life-saving intervention. On the other hand, those who said they would not be willing to undergo resuscitation again were equally straightforward and assured in their responses. We have shown, however, that physicians are more likely to recognize the preferences of patients who desire resuscitation than the preferences of those who do not. In addition, two physicians may disagree about a patient's willingness to undergo attempts at resuscitation. Such issues pose a serious liability for patients whose ideas about heroic or dignified death may differ greatly from those of their physicians.

Our findings raise other questions. In what circumstances do physicians speak with families rather than patients? We were unable to identify clear determinants; even when patients were demented, the physicans were unlikely to speak with the families. Are there situations in which it is clearly dangerous to discuss cardiopulmonary resuscitation with patients? Would it be worthwhile to address these issues routinely with all patients when they are admitted to the hospital? If this were to become standard practice, might it improve communication while minimizing the difficulty and possible danger of talking about resuscitation only in selected circumstances?

The question of whether to perform or withhold cardiopulmonary resuscitation will always require attention to the balance between prolonging survival and decreasing suffering. Our study suggests that many patients may know what they want and welcome the chance to make their own contribution to this difficult debate.

REAGAN'S TRIP TO CHINA

April 27, 30, 1984

Twelve years after President Richard Nixon made his historic journey to the communist People's Republic of China (PRC), opening the door to contact between the United States and the world's most populous nation, another conservative Republican president, Ronald Reagan, visited the PRC April 26-May 1. The president's journey to China came a little more than three months after the PRC's premier, Zhao Ziyang, visited the United States. (Story, p. 23)

Reagan's trip coincided with an upswing in the roller coaster cycle of relations between the United States and China that had occurred after formal diplomatic ties were established in 1979. The visit also illustrated that Reagan, previously a leading political foe of "Red China," had softened his views. There was a pragmatic element to the trip as well; it came at a time when friendly relations with Beijing (Peking) could help America's exporters and contribute to maintaining a strategic balance against the Soviet Union.

For Reagan, who like Nixon met with Chinese leaders in the Great Hall of the People and strolled along the Great Wall, the visit represented a boost to his stature as a world statesman. Perhaps because of his personal history, Reagan needed the full command of his diplomatic skills to keep relations between the two nations on an even keel. It was his first trip to a communist country, a visit that Reagan referred to as a "journey for peace."

Tangible results of the two countries' effort to improve ties on a broad spectrum of diplomatic and business issues were two accords signed by

287

Reagan and the Chinese leaders. The first renewed scientific and cultural exchanges that had been stalled after the United States granted asylum in April 1983 to the Chinese tennis player, Hu Na. The second agreement, designed to improve economic relations, was a treaty that reduced Chinese tax rates on U.S. business profits, investment income, capital gains, and pensions. American firms also would be allowed to take a U.S. tax credit for taxes paid in China. A controversial third agreement would allow U.S. companies to sell nuclear reactors and nuclear technology to the Chinese.

Nuclear Accord

The pact covering the sale of nuclear reactors and technology was a bone of contention between Reagan and some members of Congress. In the past, Congress allowed nuclear cooperation agreements to go forward without taking the legislative steps to reject them. But a number of lawmakers were nervous about selling nuclear plants to China. They pointed out that China, unlike other nuclear customers, was a communist nation with atomic weapons and uncertain alliances. There was concern that the Chinese might assist their close ally, Pakistan, in its effort to build a nuclear bomb to match that of its neighbor — and competitor — India. Moreover, China had not signed the 1968 Nuclear Non-proliferation Treaty, ratified by the United States, the Soviet Union, and 60 other nations. The treaty was aimed at halting the spread of nuclear weapons.

Addressing those misgivings, administration officials said Beijing had given private assurances that the PRC would not help other nations manufacture nuclear weapons. White House spokesmen pointed to a statement made by Permier Zhao when he visited the United States in January that "We do not engage in nuclear proliferation ourselves, nor do we help other countries develop nuclear weapons." Moreover, the State Department said that the PRC had agreed, for the first time, to require inspections by the Vienna-based International Atomic Energy Agency of any third country that bought nuclear equipment from China.

According to the State Department, the accord met the requirements of the Atomic Energy Act, guaranteeing that no nuclear materials and equipment provided by the United States would be used for military purposes; that nuclear material and equipment provided by the United States would not be transferred to a third country without permission from Washington; that the physical security of nuclear materials sold by the United States would be protected; and that nuclear fuels of U.S. origin would not be enriched, reprocessed or stored without consent from Washington because of the danger of the materials being diverted for weapons.

Despite these assurances, White House spokesman Larry Speakes June 21 said the accord probably would not be approved by Congress in

1984. Speakes said the administration remained "concerned about unsafeguarded nuclear activities in Pakistan." White House officials said that Reagan would not send the agreement to Congress until he received stronger pledges from China that U.S. technology would not be used to help other nations produce nuclear weapons.

The Chinese foreign ministry June 20 released a statement accusing the Reagan administration of deliberately holding up the agreement.

Soviet Union, Central America, Taiwan

Throughout his visit Reagan made note of the difference between the two major communist powers. While not mentioning the Soviet Union by name, he attacked the Russians in a speech delivered on April 27 at the Great Hall of the People. Reagan referred to the September 1983 Soviet destruction of a South Korean commercial jetliner as "wanton" act and spoke of the "brutal occupation" of Afghanistan by the Soviets. In contrast, he praised the PRC for liberalizing its socialist economy by increased reliance on private enterprise.

Some of the president's remarks were censored later by Chinese television, an action that was criticized by White House spokesman Speakes. "We regret the fact that statements by the president which would have given the Chinese people a better understanding of our country and its people were not included in Chinese media coverage of the speech," he said. According to The New York Times, *a Chinese official responded that it would have been inappropriate for Beijing to broadcast Reagan's attack on another nation over state television.* (Korean airline tragedy, Historic Documents of 1983, p. 775; invasion of Afghanistan, Historic Documents of 1979, p. 965)

As Reagan criticized Soviet actions, the president himself drew fire for his administration's policies toward Central America and the Middle East as well as U.S. support for the Nationalist Chinese government on Taiwan. During an April 27 meeting Premier Zhao told Reagan that U.S. policy in Central America was increasing the likelihood of war in the region. The Chinese premier also urged the president to negotiate with the Palestine Liberation Organization (PLO) in the Middle East. And he asked Reagan to halt deployment of U.S. intermediate-range missiles in Europe. At the same time, however, Zhao called on Moscow to resume arms control talks on those weapons. (The Soviet Union had walked out of the negotiations on November 23, 1983.) (Historic Documents of 1983, p. 791)

Zhao called on the president to cut back U.S. arms sales to Taiwan, describing the administration's policy as a major obstacle to improved relations between Washington and Beijing. In a subsequent interview on Chinese television, Reagan said the Taiwan issue was "a problem for the Chinese people on both sides of the strait to work out for themselves. We do not believe that we should involve ourselves in this internal affair."

In 1982 the Reagan administration had announced an agreement with Beijing that gradually would limit arms sales to Taiwan and phase them out at some point in the future. In return, the Chinese pledged to settle the issue of reunification in a peaceful manner. The PRC offered to open mail, sea, and air routes between the two nations, but Taiwan refused to discuss those matters. (Background on Taiwan, p. 23)

> *Following are excerpts from President Ronald Reagan's remarks to Chinese community leaders in Beijing on April 27, 1984; and the text of the U.S.-China accord on cultural exchanges, signed on April 30. (Boldface headings in brackets have been added by Congressional Quarterly to highlight the organization of the text.):*

REAGAN'S REMARKS

Thank you very much, Dr. Zhou Peiyuan, and all of you distinguished ladies and gentlemen. I'm honored to come before you today, the first American President ever to address your nation from the Great Hall of the People.

My wife, Nancy, and I have looked forward to visiting the people and treasures of your great and historic land, one of the world's oldest civilizations. We have marveled at Beijing's sweeping vistas, and we have felt the warmth of your hospitality touch our hearts. We only regret that our visit will be so brief. I'm afraid it will be as a Tang Dynasty poet once wrote, "looking at the flowers while riding horseback." But you have another saying from the book of Han which describes how Nancy and I feel: "To see a thing once is better than hearing about it a hundred times."

Twelve years ago former President Nixon arrived in Beijing, stepped down from Air Force One, and shook hands with former Premier Zhou Enlai. Premier Zhou would later tell him, "Your handshake came over the vastest ocean in the world — 25 years of no communication." With one handshake, America and China each turned a new page in their histories.

I believe that history beckons again. We have begun to write a new chapter for peace and progress in our histories with America and China going forward hand in hand — *xieshou bingjin.*

We must always be realistic about our relationship, frankly acknowledging the fundamental differences in ideology and institutions between our two societies. Yes, let us acknowledge those differences. Let us never minimize them. But let us not be dominated by them.

I have not come to China to hold forth on what divides us, but to build on what binds us. I have not come to dwell on a closed-door past, but to urge that Americans and Chinese look to the future, because together we can and will make tomorrow a better day.

When Premier Zhao was in the United States, he told us, "China has opened its door and will never close it again." Permit me to assure you today, America's door is open to you, and when you walk through, we'll welcome you as our neighbors and our friends.

We may live at nearly opposite ends of the world. We may be distinctly different in language, customs, and political beliefs. But on many vital questions of our time, there is little difference between the American and Chinese people. Indeed I believe if we were to ask citizens all over this world what they desire most for their children, and for their children's children, their answer, in English, Chinese, or any language, would likely be the same: We want peace. We want freedom. We want a better life. Their dreams, so simply stated, represent mankind's deepest aspirations for security and personal fulfillment. And helping them make their dreams come true is what our jobs are all about.

We can work together as equals in a spirt of mutual respect and mutual benefit. I believe in Chinese you say *Hu jing Hu hui.*

Well, America and China are both great nations. And we have a special responsibility to preserve world peace.

[Defense Policy, World Peace]

To help fulfill that responsibility, the United States is rebuilding its defenses, which had been neglected for more than a decade. Our people realize this effort is crucial if we're to deter aggression against America, our allies, and other friends. But we threaten no nation. America's troops are not massed on China's borders. And we occupy no lands. The only foreign land we occupy anywhere in the world is beneath gravesites where Americans shed their blood for peace and freedom. Nor do we commit wanton acts, such as shooting 269 innocent people out of the sky for the so-called cause of sacred airspace.

America and China both condemn military expansionism, the brutal occupation of Afghanistan, the crushing of Kampuchea; and we share a stake in preserving peace on the Korean peninsula.

I think our two peoples agree there can be only one sane policy to preserve our precious civilization in this modern nuclear age: A nuclear war cannot be won and must never be fought. And that's why we've proposed to the Soviet Union meaningful negotiations that go beyond rhetoric to actual arms reductions and why we must all work for the day when nuclear weapons will be banished from the face of the Earth. . . .

How did America, which began as an impoverished country and a melting pot, attracting immigrants from every corner of the globe, pull together and become the leading economic nation in the world? How did we go in so short a time from living by candlelight to exploring the frontiers of the universe by satellite, from each farmer laboring with horse and hoe for an entire year just to feed four people, to running his farm with the most modern machinery and producing enough to feed 75 people, making America the breadbasket of the world?

Well, we're people who've always believed the heritage of our past is the seed that brings forth the harvest of our future. And from our roots we have drawn tremendous power from two great forces — faith and freedom. America was founded by people who sought freedom to worship God and to trust in Him to guide them in their daily lives with wisdom, strength, goodness, and compassion. . . .

"Trust the people" — these three words are not only the heart and soul of American history but the most powerful force for human progress in the world today. Those who ignore this vital truth will condemn their countries to fall farther and farther behind in the world's competition for economic leadership in the 1980's and beyond, because look around us, the societies that have made the most spectacular progress in the shortest period of time are not the most rigidly organized nor even the richest in natural resources. No, it's where people have been allowed to create, compete, and build, where they've been permitted to think for themselves, make economic decisions, and benefit from their own risks, that societies have become the most prosperous, progressive, dynamic, and free. Nothing could be more basic to the spirit of progress for a farmer, laborer, or merchant than economic reward for legitimate risk and honest toil.

[China's Economic Role]

A little over a century ago, Ulysses S. Grant, who was then a former President, visited your country and saw China's great potential. "I see dawning . . ." Grant wrote, "the beginning of a change. When it does come, China will rapidly become a powerful and rich nation . . . The population is industrious, frugal, intelligent, and quick to learn."

Well, today, China's economy crackles with the dynamics of change: expansion of individual incentives for farmers in your new responsibility system; new bonuses for workers and more disciplined management in terms of profits and losses; improved methods of market distribution; opening your economy to the world through China's membership in the International Monetary Fund, the World Bank, and through your invitation to trade and invest, especially in your four Special Economic Zones; and your commitment to attract capital and scientific knowledge to create a high technology base for the future. All this reflects China's new role in the international economic community and your determination to modernize your economy and raise the standard of living of your people.

Unlike some governments which fear change and fear the future, China is beginning to reach out toward new horizons, and we salute your courage.

Progress, Premier Zhao has told us, "lies in our efforts to emancipate our thinking in a bold way — to carry out reform with determination, to make new inventions with courage, and to break with the economic molds and conventions of all descriptions which fetter the development of the productive force." Well, we Americans have always considered ourselves pioneers, so we appreciate such vitality and optimism.

Today, I bring you a message from my countrymen. As China moves forward in this new path, America welcomes the opportunity to walk by your side.

Incidentally, I know Premier Zhao has demonstrated mastery of his subject. When he was directing agricultural policies in Sichuan, the peasants went from food shortages and forced imports to bumper harvests and rising exports. In fact, I'm told that because of the work he did, it is said in Sichuan Province, "If you want rice, go see Zhao."

Well, China's growth is in China's hands. You will choose your own path to development. But we're not surprised to see the fresh breezes of incentives and innovation sweeping positive changes across China. And behind the statistics of economic growth are reports of personal success stories pointing to a new spirit of progress. Chairman Deng has a saying, "Seek truth from facts." Well, today in China, the reality of more small enterprises doing a thriving business, more families profiting from their own hard work and the bigger harvests they produce, and more investment in science and technology points to more opportunity for all....

[U.S.-China Cooperation]

The United States and China have an historic opportunity. We can expand our economic and scientific cooperation, strengthen the ties between our peoples, and take an important step toward peace and a better life. And there is much we can share.

We think progress in four areas is particularly promising: trade, technology, investment, and exchanges of scientific and managerial expertise.

In a few short years, two-way trade has risen sharply. The United States is now China's third largest trading partner. Our bilateral trade shows great promise for the future, particularly in areas such as machinery, technology, oil equipment, petroleum, agricultural and manufacturing products.

Last June, I instructed our government to liberalize controls over the export to China of high technology products, such as computers and laboratory instruments. Our policies on technology transfer will continue to evolve along with our overall relationship and the development of broader cooperation between us. May I emphasize to the members of the scientific community here today: The relaxing of export controls reflects my determination that China be treated as a friendly, non-allied nation and that the United States be fully prepared to cooperate in your modernization.

During Premier Zhao's visit to our country, we took another step forward, signing the United States-China Industrial and Technological Cooperation Accord. Our Joint Commission on Commerce and Trade will discuss implementation of the accord during their next meeting in Washington in May. We will focus our efforts on the sectors to which China has attached greatest priority. Our trade and development program will facilitate our progress.

Expanding cooperative ventures is another area of promising growth: American firms have invested almost $700 million in joint ventures and offshore oil exploration in China, making the United States your largest foreign investor. We welcome your determination to improve conditions for foreign business in China. Streamlining bureaucratic procedures, establishing a more predictable system for investment through domestic legislation and international agreements, reforming prices to make them internationally competitive, and providing foreign business people with the offices, housing, and schools they and their famiies need to work effectively, will stimulate more American investment.

For your part, some 50 Chinese firms have established offices or branches in the United States, and China has invested in several joint ventures in our country.

We intend to strengthen these trends. When Treasury Secretary Regan was here last month for the meeting of the Joint Economic Committee, he concluded a bilateral tax agreement. Monday, our two countries will sign this agreement, which, I'm pelased to report, will increase incentives for even closer cooperation between American and Chinese firms. And we're continuing to work toward conclusion of bilateral agreements on greater investment protection and many other areas of cooperation.

[Nuclear, Technology Agreements]

I am particularly proud that the United States and China have reached agreement on cooperation in the peaceful uses of atomic energy. As many of you know, the negotiations between our two countries go back almost to the beginning of my administration. We have held a total of six sessions in Washington and Beijing. We made great progress during Premier Zhao's visit, and our negotiations have just now concluded successfully. The result: an agreement for cooperation in peaceful uses of nuclear energy.

I understand that several of the people here made major contributions to this effort, which meets the requirements of both sides. Once approval is complete, it will open broad opportunities for joint work in development of the energy base which China needs for her modernization. Scientists, engineers, business leaders, and officials of both countries interested in peaceful nuclear energy will welcome this agreement. China has one of the world's most ambitious programs for expansion of electric power generation, and I believe that America's energy technology — not just in nuclear energy but across the board — is second to none, and perhaps most suitable for China's varied needs.

Our agreement is founded on important nonproliferation standards. We have noticed recent statements of China's nonproliferation policies, particularly those by Premier Zhao in Washington and Beijing over the past several months. Premier Zhao and I have discussed these matters directly. I can tell you that our countries share the same basic principles of preserving world peace and preventing the destabilizing spread of nuclear explosives. Neither of us will encourage proliferation nor assist any other country to acquire or develop any nuclear explosive device. Our cooperation in the peaceful uses of nuclear energy will be based on shared principles of nonproliferation.

There is also great potential in our joint efforts to increase managerial and scientific expertise. I know that many of you have heard through the Chinese press about the good work of the 9-month Dalian program of management training for industry, science, and technology. More than 750 graduates have received training in modern methods of industrial management. And I'm told some of you are graduates of that program. Well, I'm delighted to announce that we have agreed to establish a special new program there offering a full 3-year master's degree in business administration. The degree will be awarded by the State University of New York. We're to share with you the knowledge that is America's key technology — management and science skills to develop a nation.

Under our Joint Commission on Science and Technology, we have a very productive agreement with exchange programs in 21 specific areas. We're sharing the benefits of research in medicine, energy, and other technical fields. Our scientists are learning a great deal from each other in public health, agricultural sciences, and many other areas.

Cooperation in Space

Men and women of vision already see that working in the zero gravity environment of space offers dazzling opportunities to improve life on Earth. Experiments done on our space shuttle have shown that life-saving medicines can be manufactured in space with four times the purity of the same medicines on Earth. And they can be made over 400 times more rapidly, so 1 month's production of medicines in space yields as much as 30 years' production on the ground.

We also look forward to being able to manufacture large crystals of exceptional purity in space. These crystals are the basis of the semiconductor chips which run modern computers. By manufacturing them in zero gravity, we can make new strides toward producing larger, faster computers, the so-called supercomputers, and ultimately reduce the cost of computer manufacturing. We look forward to exploring with China the possibilities of cooperating in the development of space. . . .

In the humanities and social sciences, hundreds of American and Chinese scholars have visited each others' countries to teach and study subjects ranging from law and economics to poetry and history. For our part, we welcome this new Pacific tide. Let it roll peacefully on, carrying a two-way flow of people and ideas that can break down barriers of suspicion and mistrust, and build up bonds of cooperation and shared optimism.

The future is ours to build. Surmounting the risks and the fears of some may be difficult, but I'm convinced the challenge is worth it. The greatest victories come when people dare to be great, when they summon their spirits to brave the unknown and go forward together to reach a greater good. . . .

CULTURAL ACCORD

The Government of the United States of America and the Government of the People's Republic of China (hereafter referred to as "both sides"), desirous of enhancing friendly relations between the peoples of the two countries, and strengthening cultural cooperation between the two countries, based on the principles of mutual respect for sovereignty, of equality, reciprocity and mutual benefit, and in accordance with the Cultural Agreement signed on January 31, 1979, by the two governments, have agreed on the following program of cultural exchange between the two countries for the period 1984 and 1985.

I. Culture and the Arts

1. An official American Cultural Delegation, which might include but would not be limited to participants from the United States Information Agency, will visit China.

2. An official Chinese Cultural Delegation will visit the United States in the fall of 1985 to discuss and sign the 1986-1987 Implementing Accord to the U.S.-China Cultural Agreement.

3. Both sides will send one high quality small scale performing arts group to the other country for visits and performances during the life of the Accord. During such visits, artists may participate in workshops and give demonstrations and master classes. The specifics for sending performing arts groups will be decided through specific agreements signed by relevant organizations designated by each side respectively. Both sides agree to exchange views and propose suggestions on the types of performing arts groups to be exchanged during the life of the next implementing accord, so that preparations can begin early.

4. Both sides will hold one high quality art exhibit in the other country during the life of the Accord. This will be carried out by the U.S. side with the exhibit "Town and Country: Images of Urban and Rural Life in America, Paintings from the Brooklyn Museum" in China in 1984, and by the Chinese side with the exhibit "Chinese Traditional Painting: Five Modern Masters" in the United States in 1984 and 1985. The specifics for sending art exhibits will be decided through specific agreements signed by relevant organizations designated by each side respectively. Both sides agree to exchange views and propose suggestions on the types of art exhibits to be exchanged during the life of the next implementing accord, so that preparations can begin early.

5. Both sides will encourage the exchange of films, including the exchange of Film Weeks and film delegations to participate in Film Week activities. Both sides agree that exchange projects in this field will be decided through specific agreements signed by relevant organizations designated by each side respectively.

6. Both sides will encourage the sending of artists and experts in fields such as music, dance, drama, painting, sculpture, arts and crafts, photogra-

phy and film to the other country for visits, short-term lectures, professional exchanges and possible performances and exhibits.

II. Journalism, Broadcasting, and Television

1. Both sides will continue to encourage personnel and professional exchanges and facilitate the exchange of scripts and materials between the Voice of America and Radio Beijing.

2. The Director of the Voice of America and the Director of Radio Beijing will each lead a delegation for an exchange of visits and the Voice of America and Radio Beijing will exchange broadcasters for visits and professional exchange during the life of the Accord.

3. Both sides will encourage and facilitate the exchange of personnel and materials in the fields of print journalism, television, and radio. Both sides agree that exchange projects in these fields will be decided through separate discussion between relevant organizations from both countries.

III. Literature, Translation and Publication

Both sides will encourage the exchange of writers, translators and publishers in order to further mutual understanding of each other's culture, history and society.

IV. Libraries and Archives

1. Both sides will continue to facilitate the exchange of personnel, publications, and library materials between the Library of Congress and the National Library of China, as well as between other libraries in the two countries.

2. Both sides will continue to facilitate the exchange of personnel and archival materials between the National Archives and Records Service of the United States and other American archival organizations and the Chinese National Archives Bureau.

V. Education, Social Sciences, and Sports

Both sides agree that exchange projects in education, the social sciences and sports will be decided through separate discussions between relevant organizations from both countries.

VI. Parks and Related Matters

Both sides will encourage continued exchange of personnel and professional cooperation between the National Park Service of the United States and the Bureau of Landscape Architecture under the Ministry of Urban and Rural Construction and Environmental Protection of China. Both sides agree that specific exchange projects will be decided through separate discussions between the two above-mentioned organizations.

VII. Private Exchanges

Both sides will encourage and promote the expansion of non-governmental cultural exchanges to facilitate the future development of friendly relations between the peoples of the two countries.

VIII. Financial Provisions

1. Both sides agree that the necessary expenses for mutual visits by official delegations or individuals for official projects under this Accord will be borne as follows:

(A) The sending side will bear the two-way international travel expenses of the delegations or individuals.

(B) The receiving side will bear the expenses of board and lodging, transportation, and medical care or medical insurance, necessary to ensure the continuation of the program, when the delegation or individual is in its territory.

2. Both sides agree that payment of expenses for exchanges under this Accord involving exhibits, such as works of art, handicrafts, historical or archaeological objects, space objects, and other objects of special value or artistic interest, including expenses for accompanying staff, will be decided through specific agreements signed separately and based on the differing conditions in the two countries.

3. Both sides agree that the financial provisions for official projects under this Accord which involve mutual exchange of delegations of performing artists, including staff accompanying the delegations, will be as follows:

(A) The sending side will bear the delegations' two-way international travel expenses or the expenses from the receiving side to a third country, as well as the international transportation expenses of the properties, costumes, musical instruments, etc.

(B) The organization or organizations designated by the receiving side as host organization(s) will bear the expenses of the delegations' board and lodging, travel, and medical care or medical insurance necessary to ensure the continuation of the program within the receiving country, and transportation expenses of the properties, costumes, musical instruments, etc., while in the receiving country, and provide the necessary interpreters.

(C) Other financial matters will be negotiated separately.

4. If either side encounters financial difficulties in the course of carrying out an individual project a suitable adjustment or postponement of the project will be decided upon by consultation between the two sides.

IX. Entry Into Effect

The present Accord will enter into effect on the day of signature.

Done in duplicate at Beijing on this 30th day of April 1984, in the English and Chinese languages, both texts being equally authentic.

COURT ON FIRST AMENDMENT
PROTECTION FOR MEDIA
April 30, 1984

The Supreme Court April 30 gave the press important reassurance of the First Amendment's protective scope, ruling that appeals courts had special powers to scrutinize and reverse libel awards that trial judges and juries gave to public figures. A detailed review by appellate judges, going beyond the standard used in most cases, was necessary to ensure that libel awards did not curtail freedom of the press, the Court majority held.

'Actual Malice' Test

The Court's 6-3 ruling in the case of Bose Corp. v. Consumers Union of the United States *reinforced its landmark 1964 decision in* New York Times Co. v. Sullivan. *In that ruling, the Court held that a public figure could not successfully sue the press for libel without proof that the libelous material was published with "actual malice," that is, with knowledge that it was false or with reckless disregard for its truth or falsity.*

Coming 20 years after the Sullivan *ruling extended the First Amendment to libel suits, the* Bose *decision attested to the continuing vitality of the "actual malice" rule. Floyd Abrams, a New York attorney who had argued a number of major First Amendment cases before the Supreme Court, called it "the most significant libel ruling of the decade." Another libel defense attorney, Bruce W. Sanford, said the decision meant that "constitutional considerations are going to continue to pervade libel litigation."*

A study by the Libel Defense Resource Center found that libel plaintiffs won more than 80 percent of jury trials, but press defendants won more than 70 percent of appeals. Thus, the press had a major stake in the Supreme Court's approval for detailed appellate review.

The Court's decision gave news organizations an important weapon against a number of pending million-dollar judgments in cases brought by public figures. In cases decided March 20 the Court had ruled in favor of persons who sued two national magazines for libel. (Decisions, p. 247)

In the Bose *case, the Court overturned a $210,000 award to the company stemming from a 1970 article in* Consumer Reports, *a magazine that summarized product tests and evaluations conducted by Consumers Union. The article contained disparaging comments about a stereo speaker system produced by Bose, and the company sued for "product defamation." The libel award followed a trial jury's 1981 finding that some of the magazine's remarks about the Bose stereo speakers were false and were published with actual malice.*

In 1982 a Circuit Court of Appeals found the evidence upon which the award was based insufficient to prove malice. Bose challenged the appeals court's authority to re-examine the evidence, citing a federal rule that permitted an appeals court to overturn a trial court's finding of fact only if that finding was clearly erroneous.

Court Ruling and Dissent

The Supreme Court, however, affirmed the appeals court's ruling and its ability to judge the case, emphasizing the crucial role that courts played in guarding First Amendment freedoms. Independent review of libel awards by appellate judges was essential, Justice John Paul Stevens explained for the majority in the Bose *case. "The requirement of independent appellate review ... reflects a deeply held conviction that judges — and particularly members of this Court — must preserve the precious liberties established and ordained by the Constitution," Stevens wrote. "Judges, as expositors of the Constitution, must independently decide whether the evidence in the record is sufficient to cross the constitutional threshold that bars the entry of any judgment that is not supported by clear and convincing proof of 'actual malice.'"*

Chief Justice Warren E. Burger concurred in the Court's decision but did not join Stevens' opinion. Justices Byron R. White, William H. Rehnquist, and Sandra Day O'Connor dissented, finding the appeals court overstepped its authority. Rehnquist, writing for himself and O'Connor, criticized the majority for permitting appeals courts to "second guess" trial judges' findings on an author's state of mind — the key element in a finding of actual malice. "I am at a loss to see how appellate courts can even begin to make such determinations," he said.

*Following are excerpts from the Supreme Court's April 30,
1984, decision in* Bose Corp. v. Consumers Union of the
United States, *ruling that libel cases were entitled to special
scrutiny by appeals courts; the dissenting opinion of Justice
Byron R. White; and excerpts from the dissenting opinion of
Justice William H. Rehnquist, joined by Justice Sandra
Day O'Connor:*

<u>No. 82-1246</u>

Bose Corporation,
Petitioner
v.
Consumers Union of
the United States, Inc.

On writ of Certiorari to the United
States Court of Appeals for the
First Circuit

[April 30, 1984]

JUSTICE STEVENS delivered the opinion of the court.

An unusual metaphor in a critical review of an unusual loudspeaker
system gave rise to product disparagement litigation that presents us with
a procedural question of first impression: Does Rule 52(a) of the Federal
Rules of Civil Procedure prescribe the standard to be applied by the Court
of Appeals in its review of a District Court's determination that a false
statement was made with the kind of "actual malice" described in *New
York Times* v. *Sullivan* (1964)?

In the May 1970 issue of its magazine, "Consumer Reports," respondent
published a seven-page article evaluating the quality of numerous brands
of medium priced loudspeakers. In a boxed-off section occupying most of
two pages, respondent commented on "some loudspeakers of special
interest," one of which was the Bose 901 — an admittedly "unique and unconventional" system that had recently been placed on the market by
petitioner. After describing the system and some of its virtues, and after
noting that a listener "could pinpoint the location of various instruments
much more easily with a standard speaker than with the *Bose* system,"
respondent's article made the following statements:

> "Worse, individual instruments heard through the Bose system seemed to
> grow to gigantic proportions and tended to wander about the room. For
> instance, a violin appeared to be 10 feet wide and a piano stretched from wall
> to wall. With orchestral music, such effects seemed inconsequential. But we
> think they might become annoying when listening to soloists."

After stating opinions concerning the overall sound quality, the article
concluded: "We think the *Bose* system is so unusual that a prospective
buyer must listen to it and judge it for himself. We would suggest delaying

301

so big an investment until you were sure the system would please you after the novelty value had worn off."

Petitioner took exception to numerous statements made in the article, and when respondent refused to publish a retraction, petitioner commenced this product disparagement action in the United States District Court for the District of Massachusetts. After a protracted period of pretrial discovery, the District Court denied respondent's motion for summary judgment (1980), and conducted a 19-day bench trial on the issue of liability. In its lengthy, detailed opinion on the merits of the case (1981), the District Court ruled in respondent's favor on most issues. Most significantly, the District Court ruled that the petitioner is a "public figure" as that term is defined in *Gertz* v. *Robert Welsh, Inc.* (1974) for purposes of this case and therefore the First Amendment, as interpreted in *New York Times* v. *Sullivan, supra,* precludes recovery in this product disparagement action unless the petitioner proved by clear and convincing evidence that respondent made a false disparaging statement with "actual malice."

On three critical points, however, the District Court agreed with petitioner. First, it found that one sentence in the article contained a "false" statement of "fact" concerning the tendency of the instruments to wander. Based primarily on testimony by the author of the article, the District Court found that instruments heard through the speakers tended to wander "along the wall," rather than "about the room" as reported by respondent. Second, it found that the statement was disparaging. Third, it concluded "on the basis of proof which it considers clear and convincing, that the plaintiff has sustained its burden of proving that the defendant published a false statement of material fact with knowledge that it was false or with reckless disregard of its truth or falsity." Judgment was entered for petitioner on the product disparagement claim.

The United States Court of Appeals for the First Circuit reversed. (1982). The court accepted the finding that the comment about wandering instruments was disparaging. It assumed, without deciding, that the statement was one of fact, rather than opinion, and that it was false, observing that "stemming at least in part from the uncertain nature of the statement as one of fact or opinion, it is difficult to determine with confidence whether it is true or false." After noting that petitioner did not contest the conclusion that it was a public figure, or the applicability of the *New York Times* standard, the Court of Appeals held that its review of the "actual malice" determination was not "limited" to the clearly erroneous standard of Rule 52(a); instead, it stated that it "must perform a de novo review, independently examining the record to ensure that the district court has applied properly the governing constitutional law and that the plaintiff has indeed satisfied its burden of proof." It added, however, that it "was in no position to consider the credibility of witnesses and must leave such questions of demeanor to the trier of fact." Based on its own review of the record, the Court of Appeals concluded:

"[W]e are unable to find clear and convincing evidence that CU published the statement that individual instruments tended to wander about the room with knowledge that it was false or with reckless disregard of whether it was false or not. The evidence presented merely shows that the words in the article may not have described precisely what the two panelists heard during the listening test. CU was guilty of using imprecise language in the article — perhaps resulting from an attempt to produce a readable article for its mass audience. Certainly this does not support an inference of actual malice."

We granted certiorari to consider whether the Court of Appeals erred when it refused to apply the clearly erroneous standard of Rule 52(a) to the District Court's "finding" of actual malice.

I

To place the issue in focus, it is necessary to state in somewhat greater detail (a) the evidence on the "actual malice" issue; and (b) the basis for the District Court's determination.

Evidence of Actual Malice

At trial petitioners endeavored to prove that the key sentence embodied three distinct falsehoods about instruments heard through the Bose system: (1) that their size seemed grossly enlarged; (2) that they seemed to move; and (3) that their movement was "about the room."

Although a great deal of the evidence concerned the first two points, the District Court found that neither was false. It concluded that the average reader would understand that the reference to enlarged instruments was intended to describe the size of the area from which the sound seemed to emanate rather than to any perception about the actual size of the musical instruments being played, rejecting as "absurd" the notion that readers would interpret the figurative language literally. After referring to testimony explaining "that a certain degree of movement of the apparent sound source is to be expected with all stereo loudspeaker systems," the District Court recognized that the statement was accurate insofar as it reported that "instruments ... tended to wander...." Thus, neither the reference to the apparent size of the instruments, nor the reference to the fact that instruments appeared to move, was false.

The statement that instruments tended to wander "about the room" was found false because what the listeners in the test actually perceived was an apparent movement back and forth along the wall in front of them and between the two speakers. Because an apparent movement "about the room" — rather than back and forth — would be so different from what the average listener has learned to expect, the District Court concluded "that the location of the movement of the apparent sound source is just as critical to a reader as the fact that movement occurred."

The evidence concerning respondent's knowledge of this falsity focused on Arnold Seligson, an engineer employed by respondent. Seligson supervised the test of the Bose 901 and prepared the written report upon which the published article was based. His initial in-house report contained this sentence: "Instruments not only could not be placed with precision but appeared to suffer from giganticism and a tendency to wander around the room; a violin seemed about 10 ft. wide, a piano stretched from wall to wall, etc.' " Since the editorial revision from "around the room" to "about the room" did not change the meaning of the false statement, and since there was no evidence that the editors were aware of the inaccuracy in the original report, the actual malice determination rests entirely on an evaluation of Seligson's state of mind when he wrote his initial report, or when he checked the article against that report.

Seligson was deposed before trial and testified for almost six days at the trial itself. At one point in his direct examination, he responded at length to technical testimony by Dr. Bose, explaining the scientific explanation for the apparent movement of the source of sound back and forth across a wall. The trial judge then questioned Seligson, and that questioning revealed that the movement which Seligson had heard during the tests was confined to the wall. . . .

The District Court's Actual Malice Determination

The District Court's reasons for finding falsity in the description of the location of the movement of the wandering instruments provided the background for its ruling on actual malice. The court concluded that "no reasonable reader" would understand the sentence as describing lateral movement along the wall. Because the "average reader" would interpret the word "about" according to its "plain ordinary meaning," the District Court unequivocally rejected Seligson's testimony — and respondent's argument — that the sentence, when read in context, could be understood to refer to lateral movement.

On similar reasoning the District Court found Seligson's above-quoted explanation of the intended meaning of the sentence incredible. . . .

Notably, the District Court's ultimate determination of actual malice was framed as a conclusion and was stated in the disjunctive. Even though the District Court found it impossible to believe that Seligson — at the time of trial — was truthfully maintaining that the words "about the room" could fairly be read, in context, to describe lateral movement rather than irregular movement throughout the room, the District Court did not identify any independent evidence that Seligson realized the inaccuracy of the statement, or entertained serious doubts about its truthfulness, at the time of publication.

II

This is a case in which two well settled and respected rules of law point in opposite directions.

Petitioner correctly reminds us that Rule 52(a) provides:

"Findings of fact shall not be set aside unless clearly erroneous, and due regard shall be given to the opportunity of the trial court to judge of the credibility of the witnesses."

We have repeatedly held that the rule means what it says. *Inwood Laboratories, Inc.* v. *Ives Laboratories, Inc.* (1982); *Pullman-Standard* v. *Swint* (1982); *United States* v. *United States Gypsum Co.* (1948). It surely does not stretch the language of the rule to characterize an inquiry into what a person knew at a given point in time as a question of "fact." In this case, since the trial judge expressly commented on Seligson's credibility, petitioner argues that the Court of Appeals plainly erred when it refused to uphold the District Court's actual malice "finding" under the clearly erroneous standard of Rule 52(a).

On the other hand, respondent correctly reminds us that in cases raising First Amendment issues we have repeatedly held that an appellate court has an obligation to "make an independent examination of the whole record" in order to make sure "that the judgment does not constitute a for-bidden intrusion on the field of free expression." *New York Times* v. *Sullivan.* . . .

Our standard of review must be faithful to both Rule 52(a) and the rule of independent review applied in *New York Times* v. *Sullivan.* The conflict between the two rules is in some respects more apparent than real. The *New York Times* rule emphasizes the need for an appellate court to make an independent examination of the entire record; Rule 52(a) never forbids such an examination, and indeed our seminal decision on the rule expressly contemplated a review of the entire record, stating that a "finding is 'clearly erroneous' when although there is evidence to support it, the reviewing court *on the entire evidence* is left with the definite and firm conviction that a mistake has been committed." *United States* v. *Gypsum Co.* (emphasis supplied). Moreover, Rule 52(a) commands that "due regard" shall be given to the trial judge's opportunity to observe the demeanor of the witnesses; the constitutionally-based rule of independent review permits this opportunity to be given its due. Indeed, as we previously observed, the Court of Appeals in this case expressly declined to second-guess the district judge on the credibility of the witnesses.

The requirement that special deference be given to a trial judge's credibility determinations is itself a recognition of the broader proposition that the presumption of correctness that attaches to factual findings is stronger in some cases than in others. The same "clearly erroneous" standard applies to findings based on documentary evidence as to those based entirely on oral testimony, see *United States Gypsum Co.*, but the presumption has lesser force in the former situation than in the latter. Similarly, the standard does not change as the trial becomes longer and more complex, but the likelihood that the appellate court will rely on the presumption tends to increase when trial judges have lived with the controversy for weeks or months instead of just a few hours. One might therefore assume that the cases in which the appellate courts have a duty to exercise independent review are merely those in which the presumption that the trial court's ruling is correct is particularly weak. The difference between the two rules, however, is much more than a mere matter of degree. For the rule of independent review assigns to judges a constitutional responsibility that cannot be delegated to the trier of fact, whether the factfinding function be performed in the particular case by a jury or by a trial judge.

Rule 52(a) applies to findings of fact, including those described as "ultimate facts" because they may determine the outcome of litigation. See *Pullman-Standard* v. *Swint*. But Rule 52(a) does not inhibit an appellate court's power to correct errors of law, including those that may infect a so-called mixed finding of law and fact, or a finding of fact that is predicated on a misunderstanding of the governing rule of law. See *ibid.; Inwood Laboratories, Inc.* v. *Ives Laboratories, Inc.* Nor does Rule 52(a) "furnish particular guidance with respect to distinguishing law from fact." *Pullman-Standard* v. *Swint*. What we have characterized as "the vexing nature" of that distinction, *ibid.*, does not, however, diminish its importance, or the importance of the principles that require the distinction to be drawn in certain cases.

In a consideration of the possible application of the distinction to the issue of "actual malice," at least three characteristics of the rule enunciated in the *New York Times* case are relevant. First, the common law heritage of the rule itself assigns an especially broad role to the judge in applying it to specific factual situations. Second, the content of the rule is not revealed simply by its literal text, but rather is given meaning through the evolutionary process of common law adjudication; though the source of the rule is found in the Constitution, it is nevertheless largely a judge-made rule of law. Finally, the constitutional values protected by the rule make it imperative that judges — and in some cases judges of this Court — make sure that it is correctly applied....

The First Amendment presupposes that the freedom to speak one's mind is not only an aspect of individual liberty — and thus a good unto itself — but also is essential to the common quest for truth and the vitality of society as a whole. Under our Constitution "there is no such thing as a false idea. However pernicious an opinion may seem, we depend for its correction not on the conscience of judges and juries but on the competition of other ideas." *Gertz* v. *Robert Welch Inc.* Nevertheless, there are categories of communication and certain special utterances to which the majestic protection of the First Amendment does not extend because they "are no essential part of any exposition of ideas, and are of such slight social value as a step to truth that any benefit that may be derived from them is clearly outweighed by the social interest in order and morality." *Chaplinsky* v. *New Hampshire* (1942).

Libelous speech has been held to constitute one such category, see *Beauharnais* v. *Illinois* (1952); others that have been held to be outside the scope of the freedom of speech are fighting words, *Chaplinsky* v. *New Hampshire* (1942), incitement to riot, *Brandenburg* v. *Ohio* (1969), obscenity, *Roth* v. *United States* (1957), and child pornography, *New York* v. *Ferber* (1982). In each of these areas, the limits of the unprotected category, as well as the unprotected character of particular communications, have been determined by the judicial evaluation of special facts that have been deemed to have constitutional significance. In such cases, the Court has regularly conducted an independent review of the record both to be sure that the speech in question actually falls within the unprotected category and to confine the perimeters of any unprotected category within acceptably narrow limits in an effort to ensure that protected expression will not be inhibited. . . . The principle of viewpoint neutrality . . . also imposes a special responsibility on judges. . . .

. . . [I]n *New York Times* v. *Sullivan,* after announcing the constitutional requirement for a finding of "actual malice" in certain types of defamation actions, it was only natural that we should conduct an independent review of the evidence on the dispositive constitutional issue. . . .

In *Time, Inc.* v. *Pape* (1971), a case in which the federal District Court had entered a directed verdict, we again conducted an independent examination of the evidence on the question of actual malice, labeling our definition of "actual malice" as a "constitutional rule" and stating that the question before us was whether that rule had been correctly applied to the facts of the case. Again we stated that independent inquiries "of this kind are familiar under the settled principle that '[i]n cases in which there is a claim of denial of rights under the Federal Constitution, this Court is not bound by the conclusions of lower courts, but will re-examine the evidentiary basis on which those conclusions are founded," noting that "in cases involving the area of tension between the First and Fourteenth Amendments on the one hand and state defamation laws on the other, we have frequently had occasion to review 'the evidence in the . . . record to determine whether it could constitutionally support a judgment' for the plaintiff." *Ibid.* . . .

The requirement of independent appellate review reiterated in *New York Times* v. *Sullivan* is a rule of federal constitutional law. It emerged from the exigency of deciding concrete cases; it is law in its purest form under our common law heritage. It reflects a deeply held conviction that judges — and particularly members of this Court — must exercise such review in order to preserve the precious liberties established and ordained by the Constitution. The question whether the evidence in the record in a defamation case is of the convincing clarity required to strip the utterance of First Amendment protection is not merely a question for the trier of fact. Judges, as expositors of the Constitution, must independently decide whether the evidence in the record is sufficient to cross the constitutional threshold that bars the entry of any judgment that is not supported by clear and convincing proof of "actual malice."

III

The Court of Appeals was correct in its conclusions (1) that there is a significant difference between proof of actual malice and mere proof of falsity, and (2) that such additional proof is lacking in this case.

The factual portion of the District Court's opinion may fairly be read as including the following findings: (1) Seligson's actual perception of the apparent movement of the sound source at the time the Bose 901 was tested was "along the wall" rather than "about the room"; (2) even when the words in the disputed sentence are read in the context of the entire article, neither the "average reader," nor any other intelligent person, would interpret the word "about" to mean "across"; (3) Seligson is an intelligent, well educated person; (4) the words "about the room" have the same meaning for Seligson as they do for the populace in general; and (5) although he was otherwise a credible witness, Seligson's testimony that (a) he did not "know what made me pick that particular choice of words" and (b) that the word "about" meant what he had drawn on the board, is not credible. . . .

Aside from Seligson's vain attempt to defend his statement as a precise description of the nature of the sound movement, the only evidence of actual malice on which the District Court relied was the fact that the statement was an inaccurate description of what Seligson had actually perceived. Seligson of course had insisted "I know what I heard." The trial court took him at his word, and reasoned that since he did know what he had heard, and he knew that the meaning of the language employed did not accurately reflect what he heard, he must have realized the statement was inaccurate at the time he wrote it. "Analysis of this kind may be adequate when the alleged libel purports to be an eyewitness or other direct account of *events that speak for themselves." Time, Inc.* v. *Pape.*
. . . Here, however, adoption of the language chosen was "one of a number of possible rational interpretations" of an event "that bristled with ambiguities" and descriptive challenges for the writer. *Time, Inc.* v. *Pape.* The choice of such language, though reflecting a misconception, does not place the speech beyond the outer limits of the First Amendment's broad protective umbrella. Under the District Court's analysis, any individual using a malapropism might be liable, simply because an intelligent speaker would have to know that the term was inaccurate in context, even though he did not realize his folly at the time.

The statement in this case represents the sort of inaccuracy that is commonplace in the forum of robust debate to which the *New York Times* rule applies. "Realistically, . . . some error is inevitable; and the difficulties of separating fact from fiction convinced the court in *New York Times, Butts, Gertz,* and similiar cases to limit liability to instances where some degree of culpability is present in order to eliminate the risk of undue self-censorship and the suppression of truthful material." *Herbert* v. *Lando* (1979). "[E]rroneous statement is inevitable in free debate, and . . . must be protected if the freedoms of expression are to have the 'breathing space' that they 'need ... to survive.' " *New York Times* v. *Sullivan.*

The Court of Appeals entertained some doubt concerning the ruling that the *New York Times* rule should be applied to a claim of product disparagement based on a critical review of a loudspeaker system. We express no view on that ruling, but having accepted it for purposes of deciding this case, we agree with the Court of Appeals that the difference between hearing violin sounds move around the room and hearing them wander back and forth fits easily within the breathing space that gives life to the First Amendment. We may accept all of the purely factual findings of the District Court and nevertheless hold as a matter of law that the record does not contain clear and convincing evidence that Seligson or his employer prepared the loudspeaker article with knowledge that it contained a false statement, or with reckless disregard of the truth.

It may well be that in this case, the "finding" of the District Court on the actual malice question could have been set aside under the clearly erroneous standard of review, and we share the concern of the Court of Appeals that the statements at issue tread the line between fact and opinion. Moreover, the analysis of the central legal question before us may seem out of place in a case involving a dispute about the sound quality of a loudspeaker. But though the question presented reaches us on a somewhat peculiar wavelength, we reaffirm the principle of independent appellate review that we have applied uncounted times before. We hold that the clearly erroneous standard of Rule 52(a) of the Federal Rules of Civil Procedure does not prescribe the standard of review to be applied in reviewing a determination of actual malice in a case governed by *New York Times* v. *Sullivan.* Appellate judges in such a case must exercise independent judgment and determine whether the record establishes actual malice with convincing clarity.

The judgment of the Court of Appeals is affirmed.

It is so ordered.

THE CHIEF JUSTICE concurs in the judgment.

JUSTICE WHITE, dissenting.

Although I do not believe that the "reckless disregard" component of the *New York Times* malice standard is a question of historical fact, I agree with JUSTICE REHNQUIST that the actual knowledge component surely is. Here, the District Court found that the defamatory statement was written with actual knowledge of falsity. The Court of Appeals thus erred in basing its disagreement with the District Court on its *de novo* review of the record. The majority is today equally in error. I would remand to the Court of Appeals so that it may perform its task under the proper standard.

JUSTICE REHNQUIST, with whom JUSTICE O'CONNOR joins, dissenting.

There is more than one irony in this "Case of the Wandering Instruments," which subject matter makes it sound more like a candidate for inclusion in the "Adventures of Sherlock Holmes" than in a casebook on constitutional law. It is ironic in the first place that a constitutional principle which originated in *New York Times* v. *Sullivan* (1964) because of the need for freedom to criticize the conduct of public officials is applied here to a magazine's false statements about a commercial loudspeaker system.

It is also ironic that, in the interest of protecting the First Amendment, the Court rejects the "clearly erroneous" standard of review mandated by Fed. Rule of Civ. Proc. 52(a) in favor of a *"de novo"* standard of review for the "constitutional facts" surrounding the "actual malice" determination. But the facts dispositive of that determination — actual knowledge or subjective reckless disregard for truth — involve no more than findings about the mens rea of an author, findings which appellate courts are simply ill-prepared to make in any context, including the First Amendment context. Unless "actual malice" now means something different from the definition given to the term 20 years ago by this Court in *New York Times,* I do not think that the constitutional requirement of "actual malice" properly can bring into play any standard of factual review other than the "clearly erroneous" standard.

In this case the District Court concluded by what it found to be clear and convincing evidence that respondent's engineer Arnold Seligson had written the defamatory statement about Bose's product with actual knowledge that it was false. It reached that conclusion expressly relying on its determination about the credibility of Seligson's testimony. On appeal there was no issue as to whether the District Court had properly understood what findings were legally sufficient to establish "actual malice" nor was there any issue as to the necessary quantum of proof nor the proper allocation of the burden of proof of "actual malice." The issue on appeal thus was only the propriety of the District Court's factual conclusion that Bose had actually proven "actual malice" in this case. Yet the Court of Appeals never rebutted the District Court's conclusion that Seligson had actual knowledge that what he printed was false. Instead it concluded after de novo review that Seligson's language was merely "imprecise" and that as such, it would not "support an inference of actual malice."

It is unclear to me just what that determination by the Court of Appeals has to do with the mens rea conclusion necessary to the finding of "actual malice" and with the District Court's finding of actual knowledge here. In approving the Court of Appeals' de novo judgment on the "actual malice" question, for all the factual detail and rehearsal of testimony with which the majority's opinion is adorned, the Court never quite comes to grips with what factual finding it must focus on. At one point we are told that "the statement in this case represents the sort of inaccuracy that is commonplace in the forum of robust debate to which the New York Times rules applies," suggesting that the disparaging statement was perhaps not even false, or at any rate not false *enough*. One paragraph later, we are told that "as a matter of law ... the record does not contain clear and convincing evidence that Seligson or his employer prepared the loud-speaker article with knowledge that it contained a false statement, or with reckless disregard of the truth." The Court remarks that the question presented "reaches us on a somewhat peculiar wavelength," but that is scarcely a reason for transmitting the answer on an equally peculiar wavelength.

In my view the problem results from the Court's attempt to treat what is here, and in other contexts always has been, a pure question of fact, as something more than a fact — a so-called "constitutional fact." The Court correctly points out that independent appellate review of facts underlying constitutional claims has been sanctioned by previous decisions of this Court where "a conclusion of law as to a Federal right and a finding of fact are so intermingled as to make it necessary, in order to pass upon the Federal question, to analyze the facts." *Fiske* v. *Kansas*. But in other contexts we have always felt perfectly at ease leaving state of mind determinations, such as the actual knowledge and recklessness determinations involved here, to triers of fact with only deferential appellate review — for example, in criminal cases where the burden of proving those facts is even greater than the "clear and convincing" standard applicable under *New York Times*.

Presumably any doctrine of "independent review" of facts exists, not so that an appellate court may inexorably place its thumb on the scales in favor of the party claiming the constitutional right, but so that perceived shortcomings of the trier of fact by way of bias or some other factor may be compensated for. But to me, the only shortcoming here is an appellate court's inability to make the determination which the Court mandates today — the de novo determination about the state of mind of a particular author at a particular time. Although there well may be cases where the "actual malice" determination can be made on the basis of objectively reviewable facts in the record, it seems to me that just as often it is made, as here, on the basis of an evaluation of the credibility of the testimony of the author of the defamatory statement. I am at a loss to see how appellate courts can even begin to make such determinations. In any event, surely such determinations are best left to the trial judge.

It is of course true as the Court recognizes that "where particular speech falls close to the line separating the lawful and the unlawful, the possibility of mistaken fact-finding — inherent in all litigation — will create the danger that the legitimate utterance will be penalized." *Speiser* v. *Randall* (1958). But the *New York Times* rule adequately addresses the need to shield protected speech from the risk of erroneous fact-finding by placing the burden of proving "actual malice" on the party seeking to penalize expression. . . .

I think that the issues of "falsity" and "actual malice" in this case may be close questions, but I am convinced that the District Court, which heard the principal witness for the respondent testify for almost six days during the trial, fully understood both the applicable law and its role as a finder of fact. Because it is not clear to me that the de novo findings of appellate courts, with only bare records before them, are likely to be any more reliable than the findings reached by trial judges, I cannot join the majority's sanctioning of factual second guessing by appellate courts. I believe that the primary result of the Court's holding today will not be greater protection for First Amendment values, but rather only lessened confidence in the judgments of lower courts and more entirely factbound appeals.

I continue to adhere to the view expressed in *Pullman-Standard* v. *Swint* (1982), that Rule 52(a) "does not make exceptions or purport to exclude certain categories of factual findings from the obligation of a court of appeals to accept a district court's findings unless clearly erroneous." There is no reason to depart from that rule here, and I would therefore reverse and remand this case to the Court of Appeals so that it may apply the "clearly erroneous" standard of review to the factual findings of the District Court.

May

New Ireland Forum

May 2, 1984

The New Ireland Forum, a coalition of four political parties from both parts of Ireland, issued a report May 2 that outlined the major political, religious, and economic problems of the island and proposed three ways to reunite Northern Ireland and the Republic of Ireland.

Irish Prime Minister Garret FitzGerald established the Forum in May 1983 to search for a solution to the continuing crisis in Northern Ireland. All democratic parties that had rejected violence as a way of achieving Irish unity and had elected parliamentary members in the North or South were invited to participate in the Forum. Four nationalist parties opted to take part: the Fine Gael and the Labour Party, which made up Ireland's coalition government, the opposition Irish Fianna Fail Party, and Northern Ireland's Social Democratic and Labor Party. These parties represented about 75 percent of the island's five million people, North and South, and 90 percent of the nationalist, primarily Catholic, vote. Sinn Fein, the political arm of the Irish Republican Army, was deliberately excluded because of its support for the IRA terrorist campaign. The Protestant unionist parties of the North rejected the invitation to take part in the Forum. While the nationalist point of view was the only one formally represented, the Forum did solicit and receive views from all segments of Irish society.

At the opening of the Forum in May 1983 at Dublin Castle, the speakers agreed that the only way to end the conflict in Northern Ireland was to find a way to reunite the island. John Hume, leader of the North's Social Democratic and Labour Party, expressed the challenge of this undertaking: "I suggest that we begin by humbly admitting that no more difficult task ever confronted the Irish people. I suggest that we also understand clearly why we are attempting it — not because it would be gratifying to succeed, not because it would be interesting to attempt, not because it would be to our political advantage. Only because it would be dangerously irresponsible not to do this now."

Background

Tensions between the Protestant majority and the Catholic minority in Northern Ireland date back to the Elizabethan period of English history and the Protestant Reformation. The Reformation firmly established the Church of England, with the British monarch as its supreme head, as the official religion of Britain. But the Protestant religious movement never took root in Ireland, mostly due to poor lines of communication and a language barrier.

By the time Elizabeth I came to the throne in 1558, England in theory had ruled Ireland for hundreds of years. But in practice, British rule there had been ineffectual. Irish kings fought each other and their English-appointed authorities for control of territory and, by the late 16th century, anarchy reigned. Elizabeth decided the time had come to secure effective British control of Ireland. She sent British troops to impose order and began a policy of settling English colonists there. The most extensive and successful area of English colonization was in the province of Ulster (Northern Ireland).

In Ulster, the British confiscated the holdings of Catholic landowners and redistributed the land to Scottish and English settlers. In addition, many Scottish Presbyterians, fleeing religious persecution in their own country, settled in Belfast and the surrounding area. Thus, a large Protestant population grew in Northern Ireland.

Sectarian antagonism between the two religious groups thrived from that point. The Irish Catholics resented having their lands taken from them by the English settlers, and the Protestants, fearful of Catholic reprisals, made security their paramount concern. Through the years a vicious cycle of Catholic repression and rebellion repeated itself. The Protestants, who maintained close ties to Britain, controlled the North. Catholics in Ulster were often victims of political, economic, and cultural discrimination. Both groups, as the Forum report noted, "lived under the shadow of sectarian politics and the fear of domination of one tradition by the other."

The Government of Ireland Act of 1920 resulted in partition of the country, retaining Northern Ireland under British control. Protestant Unionists, who made up approximately two-thirds of the North's population, took pride in their association with Britain. Irish nationalism, the minority sentiment in Ulster, "found sovereign and international expression.... through the establishment of an independent, democratic state in the South," the Forum report pointed out.

The situation in Northern Ireland had grown increasingly critical since 1969 when violence erupted in Ulster. The dormant IRA was revived and renewed its terrorist campaign to end Northern Ireland's separation from the Republic. In an attempt to protect its citizens, the British Army was deployed on the streets of Ulster. A cold war atmosphere punctuated by repeated terrorist activities and reprisals continued, at great human cost. Since the renewal of violence in 1969, the Forum has estimated that more than 2,300 people have died, and thousands have been wounded. The financial costs also have been high. The report estimated that Britain has spent over $6,500 million, Ireland over $1,300 million. High unemployment, projected to reach 32 percent by the 1990s if no solution to the crisis could be reached, was an additional social and economic cost to the politically unstable area.

As the situation in the North continued to deteriorate, the violence threatened to spill into the Republic. The New Ireland Forum met "to deliberate on the shape of a new Ireland in which people of differing identities would live together in peace...."

Unitary State

The Forum urged creation of a "unitary state," governed from Dublin, that would embrace the whole island and provide "irrevocable guarantees for the protection and preservation of both the unionist and nationalist identities." A new non-denominational constitution would be necessary, Forum members noted.

The report outlined two other possible solutions for ending the country's civil strife: a federal/confederal system with separate parliaments in Dublin and Belfast sharing a common president and body to oversee foreign policy and security; and a "joint authority" system, with London and Dublin sharing equal responsibility for the government of Northern Ireland, and dual citizenship for the North's residents.

The report marked the first time since the island's partition that nationalists had recognized the right of unionists to retain their British identity. The proposal of a new constitution guaranteeing full civil and religious liberties also indicated a conciliatory shift in approach.

However, Northern Ireland's unionist parties immediately rejected the Forum report, labeling it a "waste of time" and a republican scheme to "destroy Northern Ireland."

Following are excerpts from the New Ireland Forum report released May 2, 1984:

317

Preface

The New Ireland Forum was established for consultations on the manner in which lasting peace and stability could be achieved in a new Ireland through the democratic process and to report on possible new structures and processes through which this objective might be achieved.

Participation in the Forum was open to all democratic parties which reject violence and which have members elected or appointed to either House of the Oireachtas or the Northern Ireland Assembly. Four political parties took part in the Forum: the Fianna Fail Party, the Fine Gael Party, the Labour Party and the Social Democratic and Labour Party (SDLP). These four parties together represent over ninety per cent of the nationalist population and over three-quarters of the entire population of Ireland. The parties which participated in the Forum would have greatly preferred that discussions on a new Ireland should have embraced the elected representatives of both the unionist and nationalist population. However, the Forum sought the views of people of all traditions who agreed with its objectives and who reject violence. The establishment and work of the Forum have been of historic importance in bringing together, for the first time since the division of Ireland in 1920, elected nationalist representatives from North and South to deliberate on the shape of a new Ireland in which people of differing identities would live together in peace and harmony and in which all traditions would find an honoured place and have equal validity. . . .

Introduction

The Forum has been inbued with an overriding sense of the importance and urgency of its task. It was established against a background of deep division, insecurity and violence that threatens society, primarily in Northern Ireland but also in the Republic and to a certain extent in Britain. The continuing crisis in Northern Ireland has reached critical proportions, involving intense human suffering and misery for many thousands of people. The persistence of division and of conflict on such a scale poses a fundamental challenge to those who support and practice democratic principles as a means to resolve political problems; in particular, since Britain exercises direct responsibility, it is a serious reflection on successive British Governments. More than thirty years after European statesmen successfully resolved to set aside their ancient quarrels and to work together in the European Community, the continuation of the conflict in Northern Ireland represents a dangerous source of instability in Western Europe and a challenge to the democratic values which Europe shares in common with North America and the rest of the Western World. . . .

The analysis by the Forum of the crisis in Northern Ireland . . . illustrates the inherent instability of the 1920 constitutional arrangements which resulted in the arbitrary division of Ireland. Each generation since has suffered from the discrimination, repression and violence which has stemmed from those constitutional arrangements.

The study by DKM Economic Consultants shows that the economic outlook for the North is very bleak as long as the present political paralysis and violence continue. This study indicates that on the basis of foreseeable economic trends, and in the absence of a political settlement leading to an end to violence, there would be virtual stagnation in the economy and a further substantial increase in unemployment. Unemployment in the North would increase from an estimated 122,000 in 1984 to as much as 166,000 (about 32 per cent of civil employment) by the 1990's. Without political progress the scale of economic and social problems will increase greatly, exacerbating a highly dangerous situation. This will make increasingly intolerable the social and economic burden for both sections of the community in the North. It will also lead to a major increase in the financial burden on Britain because of the mounting cost of security and the increased expenditure necessary to shore up the economy and living standards of the area. For the South, there will be a further diversion of resources to security where expenditure is already disproportionately greater than that of Britain, while the adverse effects on the economy, particularly of the border areas, will be prolonged.

The immediate outlook for the North is extremely dangerous unless an acceptable political solution is achieved. The long-term damage to society worsens each day that passes without political progress. In political, moral and human terms there is no acceptable level of violence. There are at present no political institutions to which a majority of people of the nationalist and unionist traditions can give their common allegiance or even acquiesce in. The fundamental society bonds which hold people together in a normal community, already tenuous in the abnormal conditions of Northern Ireland, have been very largely sundered by the events and experiences of the past fifteen terrible years. However, despite the drawing apart of the two traditions since 1969, respect for basic human values was for a time maintained within each tradition. But as sensibilities have become dulled and despair has deepened, there has been a progressive erosion of basic values which is in danger of becoming irreversible. The immense challenge facing political leaders in Britain and Ireland is not merely to arrest the cancer but to create the conditions for a new Ireland and a new society acceptable to all its people.

The need for progress towards this objective is now so urgent that there can be no justification for postponing action. A major reassessment by Britain which at present exercises direct responsibility for Northern Ireland is required. There is an overwhelming need to give urgent and sustained priority to the initiation of a political process leading to a durable solution.

The conflict inherent in the Northern situation has surfaced dramatically in the last 15 years and the situation is progressively deteriorating within the present structures. The alienation of nationalists in Northern Ireland from political and civil institutions, from the security forces and from the manner of application of the law has increased to major proportions. There is fear, insecurity, confusion and uncertainty about the future in the unionist section of the community. Northern Ireland today is characterized by the fact that neither section of the community is happy with the status quo or has confidence in or a sense of direction about the future. It is essential that any proposals for political progress should remove nationalist alienation and assure the identity and security of both unionists and nationalists. Accordingly, in the search for the basis of a political solution the British and Irish Governments must together initiate a process which will permit the establishment and development of common ground between both sections of the community in Northern Ireland and among all the people of this island. . . .

Framework for a New Ireland: Present Realities and Future Requirements

The major realities identified in the Forum's analysis of the problem, as set out in earlier chapters, may be summarized as follows:

(1) Existing structures and practices in Northern Ireland have failed to provide either peace, stability or reconciliation. The failure to recognize and accommodate the identity of Northern nationalists has resulted in deep and growing alienation on their part from the system of political authority.

(2) The conflict of nationalist and unionist identities has been concentrated within the narrow ground of Northern Ireland. This has prevented constructive interaction between the two traditions and fostered fears, suspicions and misunderstandings.

(3) One effect of the division of Ireland is that civil law and administration in the South are seen, particularly by unionists, as being unduly influenced by the majority ethos on issues which Protestants consider to be a matter for private conscience and there is a widespread perception that the South in its laws, attitudes, and values does not reflect a regard for the ethos of Protestants. On the other hand, Protestant values are seen to be reflected in the laws and practices in the North.

(4) The present formal position of the British Government, namely the guarantee, contained in Section 1 of the Northern Ireland Constitution Act, 1973, has in its practical application had the effect of inhibiting the dialogue necessary for political progress. It has had the additional effect of removing the incentive which would otherwise exist on all sides to seek a political solution.

(5) The above factors have contributed to conflict and instability

with disastrous consequences involving violence and loss of life on a large scale in Northern Ireland.

(6) The absence of political consensus, together with the erosion of the North's economy and social fabric, threatens to make irreversible the drift into more widespread civil conflict with catastrophic consequences.

(7) The resulting situation has inhibited and placed under strain the development of normal relations between Britain and Ireland.

(8) The nationalist identity and ethos comprise a sense of national Irish identity and a democratically founded wish to have that identity institutionalized in a sovereign Ireland united by consent.

(9) The unionist identity and ethos comprise a sense of Britishness, allied to their particular sense of Irishness and a set of values comprising a Protestant ethos which they believe to be under threat from a Catholic ethos, perceived as reflecting different and often opposing values.

(10) Irish nationalist attitudes have hitherto in their public expression tended to underestimate the full dimension of the unionist identity and ethos. On the other hand, unionist attitudes and practices have denied the right of nationalists to meaningful political expression of their identity and ethos.

(11) The basic approach of British policy has created negative consequences. It has shown a disregard of the identity and ethos of nationalists. In effect, it has underwritten the supremacy in Northern Ireland of the unionist identity. Before there can be fundamental progress Britain must re-assess its position and responsibility.

Having considered these realities, the Forum proposes the following as necessary elements of a framework within which a new Ireland could emerge:

(1) A fundamental criterion of any new structures and processes must be that they will provide lasting peace and stability.

(2) Attempts from any quarter to impose a particular solution through violence must be rejected along with the proponents of such methods. It must be recognized that the new Ireland which the Forum seeks can come about only through agreement and must have a democratic basis.

(3) Agreement means that the political arrangements for a new and sovereign Ireland would have to be freely negotiated and agreed to by the people of the North and by the people of the South.

(4) The validity of both the nationalist and unionist identities in

Ireland and the Democratic rights of every citizen on this island must be accepted; both of these identities must have equally satisfactory, secure and durable, political, administrative and symbolic expression and protection.

(5) Lasting stability can be found only in the context of new structures in which no tradition will be allowed to dominate the other, in which there will be equal rights and opportunities for all, and in which there will be provision for formal and effective guarantees for the protection of individual human rights and of the communal and cultural rights of both nationalists and unionists.

(6) Civil and religious liberties and rights must be guaranteed and there can be no discrimination or preference in laws or administrative practices, on grounds of religious belief or affiliation; government and administration must be sensitive to minority beliefs and attitudes and seek consensus.

(7) New arrangements must provide structures and institutions including security structures with which both nationalists and unionists can identify on the basis of political consensus; such arrangements must overcome alienation in Northern Ireland and strengthen stability and security for all the people of Ireland.

(8) New arrangements must ensure the maintenance of economic and social standards and facilitate, where appropriate, integrated economic development, North and South. . . .

(9) The cultural and linguistic diversity of the people of all traditions, North and South, must be preserved and fostered as a source of enrichment and vitality.

(10) Political action is urgently required to halt disillusionment with democratic politics and the slide towards further violence. Britain has a duty to respond *now* in order to ensure that the people of Northern Ireland are not condemned to yet another generation of violence and sterility. The parties in the Forum by their participation in its work have already committed themselves to join in a process directed towards that end. . . .

The particular structure of political unity which the Forum would wish to see established is a unitary state, achieved by agreement and consent, embracing the whole island of Ireland and providing irrevocable guarantees for the protection and preservation of both the unionist and nationalist identities. A unitary state on which agreement had been reached would also provide the ideal framework for the constructive interaction of the diverse cultures and values of the people of Ireland. . . .

The Forum in the course of its work, in both public and private sessions, received proposals as to how unionist and nationalist identities and interests could be accommodated in different ways and in varying degrees in a new Ireland.... In addition to the unitary state, two structural arrangements were examined in some detail — a federal/confederal state and joint authority....

Unitary State

A unitary state would embrace the island of Ireland governed as a single unit under one government and one parliament elected by all the people of the island. It would seek to unite in agreement the two major identities and traditions in Ireland. The democratic basis of a unitary state in Ireland has always existed in modern times. Historically up to 1922 Ireland was governed as a single unit and prior to the Act of Union in 1801 was constitutionally a separate and theoretically equal kingdom. Such a state would represent a constitutional change of such magnitude as to require a new constitution that would be non-denominational. This constitution could only be formulated at an all-round constitutional conference convened by the British and Irish Governments. Such a constitution would contain clauses which would guarantee civil and religious liberties to all the citizens of the state on a basis that would entail no alteration nor diminution of the provisions in respect of civil and religious liberties which apply at present to the citizens of Northern Ireland. These guarantees could not subsequently be changed, except in accordance with special procedures....

In a unitary state, there would be a single legal and judicial system throughout the island....

Political and administrative arrangements in a unitary state would be devised to ensure that unionists would not be denied power or influence in a state where nationalists would be in a majority....

A unitary state would have a single police service recruited from the whole island so designed that both nationalists and unionists could identify with it on the basis of political consensus.

A redefined relationship between Britain and Ireland would take account of the unionist sense of Britishness. In a unitary state persons in Ireland, North and South, who at present hold British citizenship would continue to have such citizenship and could pass it on to their children without prejudice to the status of Irish citizenship which they would automatically acquire. The state could develop structures, relationships and associations with Britain which could include an Irish-British Council with intergovernmental and interparliamentary structures which would acknowledge the unique relationship between Ireland and Britain and which would provide expression of the long-established connections which unionists have with Britain.

All the cultural traditions in Ireland, North and South, would be guaranteed full expression and encouragement. The educational system would reflect the two main traditions on the island. The Irish language and culture would continue to be fostered by the state, and would be made more accessible to everyone in Ireland without any compulsion or imposition on any section.

A unitary state achieved by agreement between the nationalist and unionist traditions would for the first time allow full participation by all traditions in the affairs of the island. This would require a general and more explicit acknowledgement of a broader and more comprehensive Irish identity. A unitary state would promote administrative and economic efficiency in the island by ending duplication and separate planning and investment programmes and by facilitating integrated promotion of investment, exports and tourism. Natural resources, oil, gas and minerals will be developed for the benefit of all the people of Ireland and could make a significant contribution to securing the economic basis of the state. With no scope for conflicts of jurisdiction and with single taxation and currency systems, the implementation of an integrated economic policy suitable to the largely similar needs of the economies, North and South, would be facilitated, with consequent benefit. Integrated economic policies would ensure a united voice in advancing vital interests of both parts of Ireland, especially in the European Community, within which both North and South have common interests in areas such as agriculture and regional policy which diverge from the interests of Britain.

Federal/Confederal State

A two state federal/confederal Ireland based on the existing identities, North and South, would reflect the political and administrative realities of the past 60 years and would entrench a measure of autonomy for both parts or Ireland within an all-Ireland framework. While protecting and fostering the identities and ethos of the two traditions, it would enable them to work together in the common interest.

In a federal/confederal constitution would be non-denominational and capable of alteration only by special procedures. There would be safeguards within each state and in the country as a whole for the protection of individual and minority rights. There would be a federal/confederal Supreme Court to interpret the constitution and to adjudicate on any conflicts of jurisdiction between federal/confederal and state governments. . . . There would either be a special Bill of Rights or, alternatively, all the rights already defined and accepted in international conventions to which Ireland and the U.K. are signatories would be incorporated in the new federal or confederal constitution. This constitution could only be formulated at an all-round constitutional conference convened by the British and Irish governments.

In a federation, residual power would rest with the central government. Certain powers would be vested in the two individual states. A confederation would comprise the two states which would delegate certain specified powers to a confederal government.

In a federal/confederal arrangement, each state would have its own parliament and executive. Authority for security would be vested in the federal/confederal government in order to gain widespread acceptability and to ensure that the law and order functions were administered in the most effective and impartial manner.

In a federation, the federal parliament could have one or two Chambers, a House of Representatives, and/or a Senate.... The federal government would be approved by and be responsible to the federal parliament. The powers held at the federal level would be a matter for negotiation but in an Irish context matters such as agriculture, industry, energy, transport, industrial promotion and marketing might be more efficiently administered on an island basis at federal level, while other services such as education, health, housing and social welfare might best be administered by the individual states. The functions of Head of State could be carried out by a President, the office alternating between persons representative of the Northern and Southern states.

In a confederal arrangement, the powers held at the center could be relatively limited, (for example, foreign policy, external and internal security policy and perhaps currency and monetary policy), requiring a less elaborate parliamentary structure at the confederal level....

A federal/confederal arrangement would, in particular, provide institutions giving unionists effective power and influence in a new Ireland. The Northern parliament would have powers which could not be removed by an Act of another parliament. Exising civil and religious rights in the North would be unaffected. With a federal/confederal framework unionists would have parallel British citizenship and could maintain special links with Britain. Mechanisms for ensuring full Northern participation in the federal/confederal civil service would have to be devised. Provision would be made for the full recognition and symbolic expression of both traditions.

A federal/confederal arrangement would allow the retention within the North and South of many laws and practices reflecting the development of both areas over the past 60 years. All the cultural traditions in Ireland, North and South, would be guaranteed full expression and encouragement.

A federal/confederal arrangement would allow all those living on the island to share and give expression to the common aspects of their identity while at the same time maintaining and protecting their separate beliefs and way of life. The central authority would promote their common interests while the state authorities protected individual interests.

Joint Authority

Under joint authority, the London and Dublin governments would have equal responsibility for all aspects of the government of Northern Ireland. This arrangement would accord equal validity to the two traditions in Northern Ireland and would reflect the current reality that the people of the North are divided in their allegiances. The two governments, building on existing links and in consultation with nationalist and unionist opinion, would establish joint authority designed to ensure a stable and secure system of government.

Joint authority would give political, symbolic and administrative expression of their identity to Northern nationalists without infringing the parallel wish of unionists to maintain and to have full operational expression of their identity. It would be an unprecedented approach to the unique realities that have evolved within Ireland and between Britain and Ireland. . . .

. . . Joint citizenship rights would be conferred automatically on all persons living in Northern Ireland, resulting in no diminution of the existing rights of Irish or British citizenship of persons living in Northern Ireland. . . .

Under joint authority the two traditions in Northern Ireland would find themselves on a basis of equality and both would be able to find an expression of their identity in the new institutions. . . .

POPE'S TRIP TO THE FAR EAST

May 3, 6, 8, 10, and 11, 1984

Pope John Paul II arrived in Seoul, South Korea, May 3, beginning a 10-day odyssey in Asia and the Pacific. While South Korea was the primary stop on the trip, visits to Papua New Guinea, the Solomon Islands, and Thailand demonstrated the reach of the Roman Catholic Church.

En route from Rome to Seoul, the pontiff stopped briefly in Alaska May 2, meeting with President Ronald Reagan, who was returning from a six-day visit to the People's Republic of China. The two men exchanged public remarks at Fairbanks International Airport and met privately for about 20 minutes while the papal plane was refueled. (Reagan China trip, p. 287)

South Korea Visit

The pope's four-day tour of South Korea marked the bicentennial of Roman Catholicism in that country. In recent years the number of Catholics, as well as those of other Christian religions, had grown at a rapid rate. Upon his arrival at the Seoul-Kimbo International Airport May 3, the pope praised this "marvelous flowering of the Christian faith" among the predominantly Buddhist and Confucian population. Approximately one-fourth of Korea's 41 million people were Christians; of that number 1.7 million were Roman Catholics.

Security at the airport welcoming ceremony was tight, as it was throughout John Paul II's Korean visit. Approximately 1,600 carefully selected people welcomed the pontiff in an atmosphere of stiff formality. In his airport remarks, the pope touched on the themes of peace and human rights, two subjects to which he returned throughout his trip. He called upon South Korea to build "a more human society of true justice and peace," and he ended his remarks with a prayer for the reunification of North and South Korea through "dialogue, mutual trust and brotherly love."

During his Korean visit, John Paul II spoke to a variety of groups, including industrial workers, Korean youth, bishops, representatives of culture and the arts, members of the international diplomatic corps, and leaders of non-Christian religions. In a slightly controversial move, he celebrated mass in the southern city of Kwangju, which became a symbol of political repression after the killing of hundreds of students during a 1980 uprising.

The central event of the pope's Korean tour, however, was the canonization ceremony of 103 Korean martyrs who died during persecutions in the mid-1800s. The canonization was the first to take place outside the Vatican since the 13th century. Approximately 800,000 people attended the May 6 ceremony in Seoul. In his homily the pontiff dwelt on the unique beginnings of the Catholic Church in Korea, a community "founded entirely by lay people."

Relaxed Island Welcome

In contrast to the formality and preoccupation with security that marked his Korean stops, a relaxed and informal atmosphere prevailed during the pontiff's two days in Papua New Guinea and the Solomon Islands. Tribal warrior and grass-skirted dancers welcomed the pope at a spontaneous airport reception upon his arrival in Papua May 7. The pontiff delighted crowds by speaking in pidgin English and Motu, the country's principal vernacular languages.

Approximately one-third of New Guinea's three million people were Roman Catholics. According to island missionaries, however, elements of the native culture often mingled with Catholic observances. Polygamy and animal sacrifices to calm evil spirits, for example, continued among some of the islanders.

The pope celebrated mass in pidgin English in the highland town of Mount Hagen on May 8, and later that day addressed local bishops in Port Moresby, the capital of Papua New Guinea. The following day he visited Guadalcanal on the Solomons.

The pope traveled to Thailand on May 10 for the last leg of his Far Eastern tour. At a mass in Bangkok the pontiff addressed the position of the church in a Buddhist land; only 200,000 of Thailand's 48 million people were Catholics. In his homily the pope told a crowd of 45,000 that "as people of Thailand you are heirs of the ancient and venerable wisdom" of Buddhism, and he noted that the Buddhist tradition "provides a fertile terrain for the seed of God's word."

In perhaps one of the most moving events of his trip, the pontiff visited on May 11 the refugee camp at Phanat Nikhom, 60 miles south of Bangkok. The camp served as a processing center for more than 17,000 exiles from Vietnam, Laos, and Cambodia. "Never forget your identity as free people who have a rightful place in the world," the pope told the refugees.

After his visit to the camp, the pontiff addressed top Thai officials regarding the refugees' plight. He praised Thailand's role in accepting so many exiles and thanked the many groups and individuals working to help the homeless. However, the pope continued, "Resettlement alone can never be the final answer to these people's plight. They have a right to go back to their native land with its national sovereignty and its right to independence and self determination."

Following are excerpts from Pope John Paul II's address in Seoul, South Korea, May 3, 1984; the pope's homily during canonization ceremonies in Seoul May 6; an address delivered May 8 in Port Moresby, Papua New Guinea, to bishops of Papua New Guinea and the Solomon Islands; a homily delivered during mass in Bangkok, Thailand, on May 10; and a speech delivered May 11 to Thai officials in Bangkok:

REMARKS ON ARRIVAL IN SEOUL

... 1. "Is it not a joy indeed to have a friend come from afar?" We hear these words in the opening lines of Confucius' analects. May I echo them by saying: Is it not a great joy indeed to go to visit a far-off friend? ...

... For, ever since assuming the office of Peter's successor in Rome some five years ago, I have always prayed that one day I might be granted the grace and joy of coming to visit the wonderful land and the dear people of Korea. And I have always felt particularly close to you in my heart. And now here I am, come as your friend and as an apostle of peace — of God's own peace — to your entire land.

2. Yours is a beautiful land that through trials and tempests of a venerable history has known how to emerge ever new, full of life and youth. Yours is a proud and sturdy people which, in meeting great cultures and neighboring powers, has remained true to its personal identity, bearing splendid fruits in art, religion and human living. Your ancestors embraced such overwhelming spiritual worlds as Confucianism and Buddhism, yet made them truly their own, enhanced them, lived them and even transmitted them to others. Wonhyo and Sosan, T'oege and Yulgok eloquently express this feat.

So also today the marvelous flowering of the Christian faith in Korea promises to bring spiritual enrichment both to yourselves and to others. The bicentennial of the Catholic Church in your country gives me the occasion to proclaim that faith in Jesus Christ can indeed bring that enrichment to the culture, wisdom and dignity of the Korean people. . . .

Today Korea is known and admired by all for its courage, its industry and its will to build up a model nation from the ashes. The tragic division of a once peaceful people imposed from without, the deep wounds from the Korean conflict and further tragedies of more recent years — all this cannot, however, dampen or break your will to overcome obstacles and to be reunited again as one happy family.

The untold sacrifices made to achieve this end through rapid industrialization and economic growth will, I sincerely hope, bring about first of all a more human society of true justice and peace, where all life is upheld as sacrosanct, where to live is to work for the good of others, where to govern is to serve, where no one is used as a tool, no one left out and no one downtrodden, where all can life in real brotherhood. . . .

We know that in order to be fully human man must transcend himself and seek the ultimate reality and meaning of life. This was the witness of a Yyi Ch'adon in your own heritage. So it is, in another way, the witness of the 103 martyrs of Korea, outstanding among 10,000 others who followed the footsteps of Jesus of Nazareth in dying for the truth of eternal life.

Permit me at this time to extend my heartfelt good wishes to the venerable Buddhist community about to celebrate May 8 the coming of Buddha. I also desire to extend fraternal greetings to the Protestant community on their centenary of generous service and witness in this land.

4. I pray that your beloved fatherland, now tragically divided into two for over a generation, will be reunited as one family, not through confrontation and hostility, but through dialogue, mutual trust and brotherly love, giving the lie to a world more and more given to mistrust, hatred and the violence of arms. And all the sufferings of the past and present will not have been in vain, along the road of purification that leads to resurrection and new life. . . .

HOMILY IN SEOUL

"Was it not necessary that the Christ should suffer these things and enter into his glory" (Lk. 24:26)?

1. These words taken from today's Gospel were spoken by Jesus as he was going from Jerusalem to Emmaus in the company of two of his disciples. They did not recognize him, and as to the unknown person they described to him all that had happened in Jerusalem in these last days. They spoke of the passion and death of Jesus on the cross. They spoke of their own shattered hopes: "We had hoped that he was the one to redeem Israel" (Lk. 24:21). These hopes were buried with the death of Jesus.

The two disciples were downhearted. Even though they had heard that the women and the apostles, on the third day after his death, had failed to find the body of Jesus in the tomb, nevertheless they were completely unaware that he had been seen alive. The disciples did not know that at that precise moment they were actually looking at him, that they were walking in his company. . . .

2. Then Jesus began to explain to them from sacred scripture that it was precisely through suffering that the Messiah had to reach the glory of the resurrection. The words alone, however, did not have the full effect. Even though their hearts were burning within them while they listened to this unknown person, nevertheless he still remained for them an unknown person. It was only during the evening meal, when he took bread, said the blessing, broke it and gave it to them that "their eyes were opened and they recognized him" (Lk. 24:31), but he then disappeared from their sight. Having recognized the risen Lord, they became witnesses for all time of the resurrection of Jesus Christ.

Through them, through all the apostles, through the men and women who were witnesses of the life and death of Jesus Christ, of his Gospel and resurrection, the truth about him spread first to Jerusalem, next to all Judea, and then to other countries and peoples. It entered into the history of humanity.

3. The truth about Jesus Christ also reached Korean soil. It came by means of books brought from China. And in a most marvelous way, divine grace soon moved your scholarly ancestors first to an intellectual quest for the truth of God's word and then to a living faith in the risen Savior.

Yearning for an ever greater share in the Christian faith, your ancestors sent one of their own in 1784 to Peking, where he was baptized. From this good seed was born the first Christian community in Korea, a community unique in the history of the church by reason of the fact that it was founded entirely by lay people. This fledgling church, so young and yet so strong in faith, withstood wave after wave of fierce persecution. Thus, in less than a century it could already boast of some 10,000 martyrs. The years 1791, 1801, 1827, 1839, 1846 and 1866 are forever signed with the holy blood of your martyrs and engraved in your hearts.

Even though the Christians in the first half-century had only two priests from China to assist them, and these only for a time, they deepened their unity in Christ through prayer and fraternal love; they disregarded social classes and encouraged religious vocations. And they sought ever closer union with their bishop in Peking and the pope in faraway Rome.

After years of pleading for more priests to be sent, your Christian ancestors welcomed the first French missionaries in 1836. Some of these too are numbered among the martyrs who gave their lives for the sake of the Gospel and who are being canonized today in this historic celebration.

The splendid flowering of the church in Korea today is indeed the fruit of the heroic witness of the martyrs. Even today their undying spirit sustains the Christians in the church of silence in the north of this tragically divided island.

4. Today then it is given to me, as the bishop of Rome and successor of St. Peter in that apostolic See, to participate in the jubilee of the church on Korean soil. I have already spent several days in your midst as a pilgrim, fulfilling as bishop and pope my service to the sons and daughters of the beloved Korean nation. Today's litergy constitutes the culminating point of this pastoral service.

For behold: Through this liturgy of canonization the blessed Korean martyrs are inscribed in the list of the saints of the Catholic Church. These are true sons and daughters of your nation, and they are joined by a number of missionaries from other lands. They are your ancestors, according to the flesh, language and culture. At the same time they are your fathers and mothers in the faith, a faith to which they bore witness by the shedding of their blood.

From the 13-year-old Peter Yu to the 72-year-old Mark Chong, men and women, clergy and laity, rich and poor, ordinary people and nobles, many of them descendants of earlier unsung martyrs — they all gladly died for the sake of Christ....

Today the church on Korean soil desires in a solemn way to give thanks to the Most Holy Trinity for the gift of the redemption. It is of this gift that St. Peter writes: "You were ransomed ... not with perishable things such as silver or gold, but with the precious blood of Christ" (1 Pt. 1:18-19). To this lofty price, to this price of the redemption, your church desires, on the basis of the witness of the Korean martyrs, to add an enduring witness of faith, hope and charity.

Through this witness may Jesus Christ be ever more widely known in your land: the crucified and risen Christ, Christ, the way and the truth and the life. Christ, true God: the son of the living God. Christ, true man: the son of the Virgin Mary....

ADDRESS TO BISHOPS IN NEW GUINEA

... 2. As we meet here today, I rejoice in the way that God has brought to rich fruition the missionary work of the past century. There has indeed been a great flowering of the Christian faith on these islands, despite the many obstacles which must often have seemed insurmountable. I am thinking of various difficulties, including those of travel, lack of roads and communications, and the problems of trying to proclaim Christ to people of hundreds of different languages and dialects....

I rejoice too in the way that the young missionary churches are making great strides toward maturity. Examples of this, to mention only a few, are the institution of the ordinary ecclesiastical hierarchy by Paul VI in 1966 and, more recently, the establishment of the metropolitan Sees of Honiara and Mount Hagen.

3. The church in your countries has been endowed by the Holy Spirit with unity in diversity. The faithful belong to a great variety of cultures and backgrounds, as is reflected in their many languages and traditions.

The missionaries too come from all over the world and different religious institutes. Your dioceses differ widely from one another in both their historical development and their present pastoral situations. And in the midst of all this diversity you are one in faith, hope and charity, one in the doctrine and disciple of the Catholic Church, one in the unity of the Father, the Son and the Holy Spirit.

4. One of the many ways in which this unity is made visible is collaboration and joint action by the Bishops' Conference of Papua New Guinea and Solomon Islands. I wish to encourage you in this important collegial endeavor, which is linked to your fraternal charity and your pastoral zeal for the universal mission entrusted to you as successors of the apostles. Today, more than ever before in the church's history, there is a need for a forum in which bishops can share their insights and experiences, pool their resources and draw up programs for meeting the urgent challenges and problems of the church and society....

6. Allow me now to direct your attention to the topic of the laity. For many years I have heard of the outstanding contribution to evangelization which has been made by your catechists and lay church leaders. They have made and continue to make a truly indispensable contribution to the life and mission of the church in your countries. Their roles as translators and assistants to the priests and religious are extremely important, as are their proper tasks of catechesis, Christian service and the permeating of society with the leaven of the Gospel. I commend you in your encouragement and support of these lay leaders in your churches, especially through your training centers, which perform an extremely valuable service for catechesis and evangelization.

I am also pleased to know of the many lay movements which are thriving here. When such movements act in union with the local church, they are indeed a sign of the Holy Spirit at work among your people and they can help the laity to integrate the faith more fully into their daily lives. At the same time, these movements require the pastoral guidance and care of the clergy. I know that you are fully aware of this need and have in recent years made provision for the appointment of ecclesiastical representatives to such groups, who help them to avoid possible errors and to serve the cause of truth and charity among the faithful.

In speaking of the laity, I cannot fail to mention that vital part of every community: the family. In every society today marriage and family life are threatened by moral and social evils. And yet at no time in history has the stability and vitality of a Christian home been more necessary. As bishops, we have a great responsibility to assist families and married couples. Our special service is to proclaim the truth of the Gospel, to hand on in its purity and entirety the church's teaching on marriage and family life. We owe it to Jesus Christ never to doubt the power of his grace to triumph in the lives of his people.

7. As I visit your churches, which are so full of promise for the future, I wish to encourage you in your efforts to foster vocations to the priesthood and religious life. Your young churches are moving quickly toward greater

responsibility for themselve and less reliance on missionaries and the help of other Christians around the world, and so the need for religious and priestly vocations is becoming particularly acute. For the most crucial factor in this time of transition is a steady increase of indigenous vocations, accompanied by careful provision for the spiritual, educational and cultural formation of these young men and women. . . .

HOMILY IN BANGKOK

. . . There can be no more appropriate gathering at the beginning of my visit to your country, dear Catholics of Thailand, than for us to join together in the name of Christ and to celebrate together this memorial of our redemption. It is important for you to gather every Sunday in this way, for at Mass you discover over and over again your source of unity as brothers and sisters in Christ, closely bound one to another. You may form a small part of the population of your country and be a small flock of Christ's followers, but Christ the Good Shepherd cares for you and watches over you with a special love. And as you join your hearts and minds to Christ in this sacrifice, you are at the same time spiritually united with the whole church of Christ, the universal assembly of believers, both living and dead, that constitutes the one body of Christ.

2. As a church you are constantly presented with the unique opportunity of reflecting on the mysterious nature of divine providence, which chooses you to hear Christ's message and to bear witness to God's love made manifest in the person of Jesus our savior. What kind of world is it in which God calls you to witness to Christ? One aspect of it was indicated to us by your cardinal at the beginning of this liturgy. You have the privilege of living in a kingdom whose citizens enjoy religious freedom, where men and women are free to worship God according to the dictates of an upright conscience. For this situation — which corresponds to a universal right of all people — I join you in thanking God.

Added to this, you find yourselves in a world where the majority of your fellow citizens embrace Buddhism, that complex of religious beliefs and philosophical ideas which is rooted in Thai history, culture and psychology and which profoundly influences your identity as a nation. To a certain extent one can say then that as people of Thailand you are heirs of the ancient and venerable wisdom contained therein.

3. How can you as Christians, members of the Catholic Church, who recognize Christ as the savior of the world, respond to Christ's call of discipleship, living as you do immersed in a religious environment different from your own?

Sacred scripture gives insights for an answer to this question. The second reading from the Letter of St. James speaks of an earthly wisdom which is opposed to "the wisdom from above," which is pure, peaceable, gentle, open to reason, full of mercy and good fruits, without uncertainty or insincerity. Your cultural heritage as Thai people is intimately linked to the indigenous Buddhist tradition, which provides a fertile terrain for the seed of God's word, proclaimed by Jesus Christ, to take root and grow. In the practice of Buddhism can be discerned a noble tendency to strive to separate oneself from an "earthly wisdom," in order to discover and achieve an interior purification and liberation. This aim is pursued through prayer and meditation, coupled with the practice of moral virtue. As the Second Vatican Council so clearly pointed out, the church looks with sincere respect upon the religious wisdom contained in non-Christian traditions and rejects nothing that is true and holy in them (cf. *Nostra Aetate,* 2). The fruits of a "peaceable" and "gentle" wisdom are manifestly evident in the Thai character and are esteemed and respected by those who have the good fortune to meet you and come to know this spiritual quality within you. . . .

5. The Christian life is lived through faith in the redeeming power of the cross and resurrection of Christ; it is the response of those who sincerely desire to follow the way of the Gospel outlined by the Beatitudes. How does this wisdom revealed by Christ manifest itself in the lives of those who experience the redeeming power of his cross and resurrection? Again our scriptural readings offer us light for meditation. Pre-eminent among the fruits which come from above is the gift of peace, the theme of today's liturgy and the intention for which we offer this Mass. In our first reading from prophet Isaiah we learn that peace will be the effect of righteousness. But it will come about only if the Spirit is "poured upon us from on high.". . .

Our responsibility to pray for the gift of peace does not exempt us from the duty of taking positive, concrete action in working for peace. I speak here of the peace that comes from justice and love of neighbor and which is linked to the peace of Christ that comes from God. Our commitment to peace means resisting temptations to violence; it involves the constant mastery of the passions, respect for the dignity of others, compassion, meekness and all those qualities which flow from a heart that is configured to the image of the heart of Christ, the Prince of Peace.

Here too, as people who are enriched by the Buddhist tradition of your country, you are endowed with a special sensitivity to the renunciation of violence in the vindication of personal rights, and so the Lord's injunction to be peacemakers strikes a resonant chord in your minds and hearts, helping you not to fall victim to the many temptations to violence that haunt the world.

6. From this perspective we can better understand the meaning of St. James' words: "The harvest of righteousness is sown in peace by those who make peace" (Jas. 3:18). How can this happen? It takes place in the Christian by his or her acceptance of the way of life outlined by Christ in the Sermon on the Mount. This program is the new wisdom that comes from above and remains in sharp contrast to the wisdom of this world. It is opposed by materialism and hedonism.

The beatitude "Blessed are the peacemakers, for they shall be called children of God" takes on particular relevance in this context. The true peacemaker is one who not only renounces the use of violence as the normal course of action, but who also has the courage to combat the enemies of peace. The peacemaker struggles, not with physical weapons or against another individual or nation, but against that selfishness, in all its forms, which impedes us from seeing others as brothers and sisters in the one human family. He fights against indifference or apathy in the face of poverty, pain or suffering, for in the Christian vision of human life these conditions neither justify fatalism nor are they signs of being accursed. Rather, they lead us to our redemption when they are joined to the cross and resurrection of Jesus Christ, our saving Lord, whose innocent suffering remains forever a sign of hope for all humanity. . . .

ADDRESS TO THAI OFFICIALS

. . . 2. The Catholic Church is a universal community whose members belong to almost all countries and continents, nations, races, languages and cultures. She sees as an important part of her mission the task of seeking out ways for understanding and peaceful collaboration among peoples, and she promotes initiatives which safeguard and defend the God-given dignity of the human person.

For this reason, I wish to take the opportunity tonight to call to your attention, as representatives of government and nations, a problem of immense magnitude. To keep silent about it would be a kind of denial of what the Catholic Church teaches about human dignity and about how individuals and nations can and should respond in defense of that dignity. I speak of the plight of the thousands and thousands of refugees currently living in this country. My deep concern for their welfare and future impels me to mention the subject in this assembly and to speak out on their behalf.

Through the courtesy of the Thai government, I had the opportunity this morning to visit the refugee camp at Phanat Nikhom, a processing and transit center for over 17,000 men, women and children who have been exiled from their own countries and have sought asylum here in Thailand. It was a particularly moving experience for me because, as I looked into the faces of so many suffering human beings, at the same time I realized that there were thousands more in a similar situation, living in the various other camps in this country.

The sad lot of these courageous and unfortunate people cannot be ignored by the international community. Indeed the conscience of humanity must be made ever more aware of the evils of the situation, so that prompt and decisive action may be taken toward an adequate solution.

3. The poverty of these victims of political unrest and civil strife is so extreme at virtually all levels of human existence that it is difficult for the outsider to fathom it. Not only have they lost their material possessions

and the work which once enabled them to earn a living for their families and prepare a secure future for their children, but their families themselves have been uprooted and scattered: husbands and wives separated, children separated from their parents. In their native lands they have left behind the tombs of their ancestors, and thus in a very real way they have left behind a part of themselves, thereby becoming still poorer.

Many of the refugees have endured dangers in their flight by sea or land. All too many were given up for lost or died en route, often the victims of shameless exploitation. Arriving here completely destitute, they have found themselves in a state of total dependence on others to feed them, clothe them, shelter them and make every decision for their future.

And how much greater is the poverty of the aged, the infirmed and the handicapped, who experience particular difficulty in finding a country willing to give them stable asylum. These countless victims are indeed enduring a cruel misfortune: Unable to return to their own countries, they cannot remain indefinitely in their present state. What are they to do? Does the path which they have been forced to follow offer them real hope for the future?

4. The desperate appeals of these suffering men, women and children have been heard by many compassionate people, both in Thailand and round the world, who offer a ray of hope. At this time I would like to express my admiration and appreciation to the various groups who have assisted the refugees during their stay in this country.

In the first place, I wish to express my gratitude to the government and people of Thailand. They are to be thanked especially for having agreed to be, for many years now, the country of first asylum for thousands and thousands of refugees from other parts of Southeast Asia. The international community knows the difficulties which they have encountered. These difficulties are not only of a material nature. The internal and external political order of the nation has been affected by the steady influx of refugees. The departures of these same people to resettlement countries has not proceeded at nearly the same rate....

I also acknowledge with profound esteem the work of the U.N. High Commission for Refugees. This organization's great solicitude for the protection and assistance of refugees throughout the world has moved it not only to assume, with the constant help of the governments, the financial burdens of first asylum, but also responsibility for encouraging nations to accept refugees and to offer them a real chance of settling down and making a new life. The generous response of these many host nations is well-known and has certainly earned the enduring gratitude of the refugees.

Similar human solidarity is being manifested in a very clear way by numerous non-governmental organizations, both of a confessional and non-confessional nature. I would like to single out the work of the Catholic Office for Emergency Relief and Refugees, and I am also glad to mention the many other national and international organizations which are cooperating in this urgent mission of mercy. These bodies have assisted the refugees by providing educational facilities, by helping to safeguard their cultural identity and by offering them moral and psychological support.

In addition, the contribution of many Catholic organizations is an expression of the generosity and solidarity of numerous local churches in other parts of the world....

5. However, the many efforts being made toward relieving the suffering of the refugees should not be a convenient excuse for the international community to stop being concerned for the ultimate future of these people. The fact remains that it is something repugnant and abnormal for hundreds of thousands of human beings to have to leave their own countries because of their race, ethnic origin, political convictions or religion, or because they are in danger of violence or even death from civil strife or political turmoil. Exile seriously violates the human conscience and the norms of life in society; it is clearly contrary to the Universal Declaration on Human Rights and to international law itself.

Consequently, the governments of the world and the international community at large must focus their attention on long-range political solutions to the complex problem.

Resettlement alone can never be the final answer to these people's plight. They have a right to go back to their roots, to return to their native land with its national sovereignty and its right to independence and self-determination; they have a right to all the cultural and spiritual relationships which nourish and sustain them as human beings.

6. In the final analysis, the problem cannot be solved unless the conditions are created whereby genuine reconciliation may take place: reconciliation between nations, between various sectors of a given national community, within each ethnic group and between ethnic groups themselves. In a word, there is an urgent need to forgive and forget the past and to work together to build a better future....

7. Ladies and gentlemen, from this place tonight I wish to renew the appeals I have made on other occasions to representatives of governments and international organizations to increase and intensify all efforts so that the refugees both here in Thailand and elsewhere may be received back into their homeland, in which they have a natural human right to live in freedom, dignity and peace.

The Catholic Church, for her part, offers the assurance of her unflagging support for any measures which pursue this goal. She likewise pledges her constant availability to assist, as much as she can and solely out of her love and respect for the human person, in any efforts aimed at re-establishing the just conditions and circumstances to which every refugee has a human right and without which true and lasting peace cannot be possible....

WORLD COURT ON MINING OF NICARAGUAN HARBORS

May 10, 1984

The disclosure early in April that the CIA had played a direct role in laying underwater mines in three Nicaraguan ports created an uproar in Congress and was met by strong opposition from a number of foreign governments. Acting on charges brought by Nicaragua, the World Court, headquartered in The Hague, Netherlands, unanimously ruled on May 10 that the United States should "cease and refrain" from any attempts to blockade or mine Nicaraguan harbors.

Details of the mining were disclosed by members of Congress and administration officials opposed to the secret operation. At least seven vessels, including a Soviet tanker, a Dutch dredger, and the Japanese ship Terushio, *were damaged by exploding mines.*

After the World Court's ruling, the State Department said that "nothing contained in the measures indicated by the court is inconsistent with current United States policy or activities with respect to Nicaragua." U.S. officials earlier had said that the mining ended in late March and that it would not be resumed.

Mining of Ports

It appeared doubtful that Reagan administration officials had anticipated the extent of criticism that followed the disclosure of the mining operation, planned and supervised by the CIA in support of the administration policy of providing help for guerrillas fighting Nicaragua's leftist Sandinista government. The basis for U.S. policy toward Nicaragua was presented by President Ronald Reagan April 4. The president told a news conference that "the present government of Nicaragua is exporting revolution to El Salvador ... and is helping, supporting and arming and training the guerrillas that are trying to overthrow a duly elected government. And as long as they do that, we're going to try and inconvenience that government of Nicaragua until they quit that kind of action." (Kissinger Commission Report on Central America, p. 31)

The mining of the three ports — Puerto Corinto and Puerto Sandino on the Pacific coast and El Bluff on the Atlantic — began about March 1. According to press reports, the mines were assembled in Honduras and El Salvador and dropped from CIA-owned speedboats operated by Nicaraguan rebels and by Latin American employees of the CIA. A larger vessel that served as the nerve center for the operation was manned by both Americans and an elite unit of Latin Americans.

U.S. officials said that the mines, triggered by the sound of ships passing over them, could cause extensive damage but were unlikely to sink large ships. When its tanker was damaged at Puerto Sandino, the Soviet Union made a formal protest to the United States, and Britain also condemned the mining. France offered to help Nicaragua remove the mines.

Congressional Reaction

As the role of the CIA became public knowledge, the covert operation came under heavy attack by leading members of both parties in Congress. Both chambers adopted resolutions condemning the mining. In the Senate, the furor was intensified by a dispute over whether members of the Senate Intelligence Committee had been "fully and currently informed" about major covert operations, as required by a 1980 law. In a blistering letter to CIA Director William J. Casey, Committee Chairman Barry Goldwater, R-Ariz., April 9 complained that he had not been apprised of the situation and called the mining "an act of war."

Later, reporters wrote that the House Select Committee on Intelligence had been briefed about the mining on January 31. While the subject was mentioned by intelligence officials to the Senate committee on March 13, it was not discussed in detail until committee staff members were briefed on April 2.

U.S. support for covert operations in Nicaragua had been a source of controversy in Congress since 1982, when Reagan sought emergency funds for CIA aid in supplies and support services to the more than 10,000 guerrillas, called contras, who were battling the Sandinista government. The Democratic House voted twice in 1982 and once in May 1984 to suspend aid to the contras. Under a compromise with the Republican-controlled Senate enacted in late 1984, President Reagan was required to return to Congress in March 1985 if he wished to continue that aid.

World Court Ruling

The Reagan administration tried to blunt the propaganda impact of an adverse ruling by the World Court by announcing, before Nicaragua had formally brought its charge to the court, that it would not accept the court's jurisdiction in cases involving Central America for two years. Nicaragua, the administration said, was misusing the court and trying to divert world attention from its support of subversion in neighboring El Salvador. However, State Department lawyers represented the United States before the tribunal, explaining that they were appearing because of the United States' "deep and longstanding commitment to the . . . court as an important institution for resolving differences of a juridical character between states." Officials said the United States would abide by the court's decision.

Formally called the International Court of Justice, the court was established in 1945 under a statute that was part of the United Nations Charter. Depending entirely on world opinion and moral suasion, the 15-member court had no machinery to enforce its decisions. The U.S. move to deny the court jurisdiction was the first time this country had taken such an action to block resolution of a specific dispute. Administration lawyers argued that because Nicaragua never had filed an official statement of ratification accepting the court's jurisdiction, it could not sue or be sued by it. Nicaraguan lawyers contested that argument, and the court rejected the U.S. challenge April 24.

In its complaint Nicaragua asserted that the United States was "training, supplying and directing military and paramilitary actions against the people and Government of Nicaragua, resulting in extensive loss of lives and property." In its interim ruling, the court voted unanimously against the U.S. request to reject Nicaragua's application for a restraining order. In a second decision, the court also ruled 14-1 that Nicaragua's sovereignty "should be fully respected and should not in any way be jeopardized by any military and paramilitary activities which are prohibited by the principles of international law." The dissenting vote was by the American judge on the court, Stephen Schwebel. He said that U.S. allegations against Nicaragua were "of a gravity no less profound" than the charges Nicaragua had brought against the United States.

> *Following are excerpts from the charges brought by Nicaragua against the United States, the text of the interim restraining order by the International Court of Justice, and excerpts from the dissent filed by Judge Stephen Schwebel, May 10, 1984:*

1. Whereas in the . . . Application the Republic of Nicaragua, invoking the declarations of acceptance of the jurisdiction of the Court deposited by both States under Article 36 of the Statute of the Court, recounts a series

of events over the period from March 1981 up to the present day, as a result of which Nicaragua claims to have suffered grievous consequences, and claims that "the United States of America is using military force against Nicaragua and intervening in Nicaragua's internal affairs, in violation of Nicaragua's sovereignty, territorial integrity and political independence and of the most fundamental and universally-accepted principles of international law"; and whereas, on the basis of the facts alleged in the Application, it requests the Court to adjudge and declare:

"(a) That the United States, in recruiting, training, arming, equipping, financing, supplying and otherwise encouraging, supporting, aiding, and directing military and paramilitary actions in and against Nicaragua, has violated and is violating its express charter and treaty obligations to Nicaragua and, in particular, its charter and treaty obligations under [United Nations and other charters and conventions]. . . .

(b) That the United States, in breach of its obligation under general and customary international law, has violated and is violating the sovereignty of Nicaragua by:

— armed attacks against Nicaragua by air, land and sea;
— incursions into Nicaraguan territorial waters;
— aerial trespass into Nicaraguan airspace;
— efforts by direct and indirect means to coerce and intimidate the Government of Nicaragua.

(c) That the United States, in breach of its obligations under general and customary international law, has used and is using force and the threat of force against Nicaragua.

(d) That the United States, in breach of its obligation under general and customary international law, has intervened and is intervening in the affairs of Nicaragua.

(e) That the United States, in breach of its obligation under general and customary international law, has infringed and is infringing the freedom of the high seas and interrupting peaceful maritime commerce.

(f) That the United States, in breach of its obligation under general and customary international law, has killed, wounded and kidnapped and is killing, wounding and kidnapping citizens of Nicaragua.

(g) That, in view of its breaches of the foregoing legal obligations, the United States is under a particular duty to cease and desist immediately:

from all use of force — whether direct or indirect, overt or covert — against Nicaragua, and from all threats of force against Nicaragua;

from all violations of the sovereignty, territorial integrity or political independence of Nicaragua, including all intervention, direct or indirect, in the internal affairs of Nicaragua;

from all support of any kind — including the provision of

training, arms, ammunition, finances, supplies, assistance, direction or any other form of support — to any nation, group, organization, movement or individual engaged or planning to engage in military or paramilitary actions in or against Nicaragua;

from all efforts to restrict, block or endanger access to or from Nicaraguan ports;

and from all killings, woundings and kidnappings of Nicaraguan citizens.

(h) That the United States has an obligation to pay Nicaragua, in its own right and as *parens patriae* for the citizens of Nicaragua, reparations for damages to person, property and the Nicaraguan economy caused by the foregoing violations of international law in a sum to be determined by the Court. Nicaragua reserves the right to introduce to the Court a precise evaluation of the damages caused by the United States";

2. Having regard to the request dated 9 April 1984 and filed in the Registry the same day, whereby the Republic of Nicaragua, relying on Article 41 of the Statute of the Court and Articles 73, 74, 75 and 78 of the Rules of Court, urgently requests the Court to indicate the following provisional measures to be in effect while the Court is seised of the case introduced by the above-mentioned Application:

"— That the United States should immediately cease and desist from providing, directly or indirectly, any support — including training, arms, ammunition, supplies, assistance, finances, direction or any other form of support — to any nation, group, organization, movement or individual engaged or planning to engage in military or paramilitary activities in or against Nicaragua;

— That the United States should immediately cease and desist from any military or paramilitary activity by its own officials, agents or forces in or against Nicaragua and from any other use or threat of force in its relations with Nicaragua".…

The COURT,

A. Unanimously,

Rejects the request made by the United States of America that the proceedings on the Application filed by the Republic of Nicaragua on 9 April 1984, and on the request filed the same day by the Republic of Nicaragua for the indication of provisional measures, be terminated by the removal of the case from the list;

B. *Indicates,* pending its final decision in the proceedings instituted on 9 April 1984 by the Republic of Nicaragua against the United States of America, the following provisional measures:

1. Unanimously,

The United States of America should immediately cease and refrain from any action restricting, blocking or endangering access to or from Nicaraguan ports, and, in particular, the laying of mines;

2. By fourteen votes to one,

The right to sovereignty and to political independence possessed by
the Republic of Nicaragua, like any other State of the region or of
the world, should be fully respected and should not in any way be
jeopardized by any military and paramilitary activities which are
prohibited by the principles of international law, in particular the
principle that States should refrain in their international relations
from the threat or use of force against the territorial integrity or the
political independence of any State, and the principle concerning
the duty not to intervene in matters within the domestic jurisdiction of a State, principles embodied in the United Nations Charter
and the Charter of the Organization of American States. . . .

3. Unanimously,

The Governments of the United States of America and the Republic of Nicaragua should each of them ensure that no action of any
kind is taken which might aggravate or extend the dispute submitted to the Court.

4. Unanimously,

The Governments of the United States of America and the Republic of Nicaragua should each of them ensure that no action is taken
which might prejudice the rights of the other Party in respect of the
carrying out of whatever decision the Court may render in the case.

C. Unanimously,

Decides further that, until the Court delivers its final judgment in
the present case, it will keep the matters covered by this Order
continuously under review.

D. Unanimously,

Decides that the written proceedings shall first be addressed to the
questions of the jurisdiction of the Court to entertain the dispute and
of the admissibility of the Application;

And reserves the fixing of the time-limits for the said written
proceedings, and the subsequent procedure, for further decision.

Done in English and in French, the English text being authoritative,
at the Peace Palace, The Hague, this tenth day of May, one thousand
nine hundred and eighty-four, in four copies, one of which will be
placed in the archives of the Court, and the other transmitted
respectively to the Government of the United States of America, to
the Government of the Republic of Nicaragua, and to the Secretary-
General of the United Nations for transmission to the Security
Council.

   (Signed) T. O. ELIAS, President.
   (Signed) Santiago TORRES BERNARDEZ, Registrar.

Dissenting Opinion of Judge Schwebel

I have voted in favour of the Court's rejection of the United States
request to dismiss Nicaragua's case on jurisdictional grounds. I have

supported the Court's indication of three provisional measures, namely:
- the United States should not restrict access to and from Nicaraguan ports, particularly by mine-laying;
- the United States and Nicaragua should each ensure that no action is taken which might aggravate or extend the dispute before the Court;
- the United States and Nicaragua should each ensure that no action is taken which might prejudice the rights of the other in implementing whatever decision the Court may render.

I emphatically dissent, however, from a fourth provisional measure which appears as operative paragraph 2 of the Court's Order. That paragraph provides that:

> "The right to sovereignty and to political independence possessed by the Republic of Nicaragua, like any other State of the region or of the world, should be fully respected and should not in any way be jeopardized by any military or paramilitary activities which are prohibited by the principles of international law. . . ."

In my view, that paragraph's emphasis upon the rights of Nicaragua — in a case in which Nicaragua itself is charged with violating the territorial integrity and political independence of its neighbours — is unwarranted. Worse than that, it is incompatible with the principles of equality of States and of collective security which are paramount in contemporary international law and which the Court, as the principal judicial organ of the United Nations, is bound to uphold. . . .

▼▼▼

INTERMENT OF VIETNAM UNKNOWN SERVICEMAN
May 28, 1984

The remains of the only unidentified American serviceman killed in Vietnam were laid to rest on Memorial Day, May 28, in the Tomb of the Unknowns in Arlington National Cemetery outside Washington, D.C., during a state funeral led by President Ronald Reagan. The Vietnam unknown joined three other unknown servicemen from World Wars I and II and Korea (the latter an undeclared war) as a representative of the 58,012 military personnel who died in the nation's longest foreign war. The tradition of commemorating an unknown soldier began in 1921, when Congress appropriated funds to build a monument to the fallen soldiers who could not be identified.

In his speech Reagan spoke of the reconciliation that he saw occurring between supporters and opponents of the divisive war. "We Americans have learned to listen to each other and to trust each other again," he said. "We've learned that government owes the people an explanation and needs their support for its actions at home and abroad. And we have learned, and I pray this time for good, the most valuable lesson of all: The preciousness of human freedom. It has been a lesson relearned not just by Americans but by all the people of the world."

Reagan's voice broke with emotion as he wondered about the kind of man the unknown might have been. "As a child, did he play on some street in a great American city? Did he work beside his father on a farm in America's heartland? Did he marry? Did he have children? Did he look expectantly to return to a bride?

"We'll never know the answers to those questions about his life. We do

347

know, though, why he died. He saw the horrors of war but bravely faced them, certain his own cause and his country's cause was a noble one; that he was fighting for human dignity, for free men everywhere."

Interment Ceremony

The flag-draped coffin lay in state in the rotunda of the Capitol for three days while tens of thousands came to pay their respects. At noon on Memorial Day, the coffin was placed on a horse-drawn caisson and was carried along the three mile route to Arlington National Cemetery, preceded by military bands and color guards from the service academies.

The presence of 300 Vietnam veterans dressed in battle fatigues and blue jeans following the columns of bands lent a somber note to the already subdued event. Military officials refused to allow them to participate in the official parade but made no effort to stop them from marching. Walking in step behind a single bagpiper, the group carried black flags in memory of the 2,489 servicemen and civilians still reported missing. Many veterans watching from the sidelines left their families to join the column, and others saluted. Watchers along the parade route responded to the veterans with applause and cheers.

Problems in Designating an Unknown

The process of designating an unknown serviceman from Vietnam took more than 10 years after the last American soldier left the jungles of Southeast Asia. Because of advances in forensic science, it was easier for pathologists to identify human remains than had previously been the case. Moreover, because casualties were evacuated swiftly by helicopter, those who died often were identified immediately. Only four bodies at the military's Central Identification Laboratory in Honolulu remained unidentified at the end of 1982. Subsequently, two of the four were identified, and researchers believed that the remains of the third might be those of a Vietnamese. To avoid any possibility that the unknown might be traced or identified, the Pentagon destroyed all records that may have indicated where the body was found.

Some veterans groups resisted designating an unknown serviceman from the Vietnam War so long as 2,000 military personnel and civilians still were listed either as prisoners of war or as missing in action. The president sought to reassure the families and friends of those persons in his speech. "One way to honor those who served or may still be serving in Vietnam is to gather here and rededicate ourselves to securing the answers for the families of those missing in action," Reagan said. "I ask the members of Congress, the leaders of veterans' groups and the citizens of an entire nation, present or listening, to give these families your help and your support, for they still sacrifice and suffer. Vietnam is not over for them; they cannot rest until they know the fate of those they loved and watched march off to serve their country. Our dedication to their cause must be strengthened with these events today. We write no last chapters, we close no books, we put away no final memories."

A Divisive Memory

From the time in 1955 when President Dwight D. Eisenhower first sent 900 military advisers to South Vietnam after the French left in 1954 to help the South Vietnamese defeat communist North Vietnam and the guerrilla fighters in the south known as the National Liberation Front (NLF), U.S. involvement in the war was highly controversial. Supporters argued that if South Vietnam was allowed to fall to the communist National Liberation Front, other nations in Southeast Asia would suffer a similar fate. But opponents charged that the United States was propping up an unpopular regime in South Vietnam.

The war divided the United States along class as well as political lines. The military draft system allowed college students to postpone their term of service. Until 1971, when President Richard Nixon instituted a national draft lottery, young men from middle- and upper-middle class families often escaped the military service, while those from poor and working class backgrounds did not. The percentage of blacks and Hispanics who served in Vietnam was greater than their percentage in the general population.

On returning to the United States, veterans often felt betrayed when they found that there was little popular support at home for the war. Few civilians were involved in any kind of war effort; men and women went about their daily lives with little recognition of the sacrifices made by those who served in Vietnam. The ambivalence became more pronounced after 1969, when it was revealed that American soldiers in 1968 had murdered more than 100 unarmed Vietnamese peasants, including small children, in the village of My Lai. The event severely tarnished the image of U.S. servicemen and made many Americans distrustful of returning veterans.

In spite of the remote nature of the war, it still caused deep political and social divisions in the country. Thousands of young men who were unable to achieve conscientious objector status fled to Canada and Scandinavia, becoming exiles until 1974, when President Gerald Ford issued a conditional clemency program for Vietnam-era military deserters and draft evaders.

Opposition to the war was only one element of the culture of the late 1960s and early 1970s that separated young men and women from their parents, but it probably was the strongest force. Many middle-aged Americans who had served their country in World War II found the vocal opposition to the war inexplicable and unpatriotic. The comments of Vice President Spiro T. Agnew about peace demonstrators, describing them as an "effete corps of impudent snobs," were echoed in many parts of the country. In New York City a crowd of construction workers on their lunch break attacked an antiwar demonstration, sending many of the protestors to the hospital. Even the American flag became a symbol of divisiveness rather than a universal emblem. Conservatives often wore tiny flag pins on their lapels, while antiwar demonstrators mocked the flag by wearing it on the backs of their coats and the seats of their pants.

As Nixon wound down U.S. involvement in the war, antiwar protests subsided as well. By 1972 the last U.S. ground troops were withdrawn from Vietnam, and all American personnel had left by 1975, when the country fell to the communists. However, many observers believed the scars left by the war would linger for many years to come.

Following is the text of the speech delivered May 28, 1984, by President Ronald Reagan, at the memorial service and entombment of the Vietnam Unknown Serviceman:

Memorial Day is a day of ceremonies and speeches. Throughout America today, we honor the dead of our wars. We recall their valor and their sacrifices. We remember they gave their lives so that others might live.

We're also gathered here for a special event — the national funeral for an unknown soldier who will today join the heroes of three other wars.

When he spoke at a ceremony at Gettysburg in 1863, President Lincoln reminded us that through their deeds, the dead had spoken more eloquently for themselves than any of the living ever could and that we living could only honor them by rededicating ourselves to the cause for which they so willingly gave a last full measure of devotion.

Well, this is especially so today, for in our minds and hearts is the memory of Vietnam and all that that conflict meant for those who sacrificed on the field of battle and for their loved ones who suffered here at home.

Not long ago, when a memorial was dedicated here in Washington to our Vietnam veterans, the events surrounding that dedication were a stirring reminder of America's resilience, of how our nation could learn and grow and transcend the tragedies of the past.

During the dedication ceremonies, the rolls of those who died and are still missing were read for three days in a candlelight ceremony at the National Cathedral. And the veterans of Vietnam who were never welcomed home with speeches and bands, but who were never defeated in battle and were heroes as surely as any who have ever fought in a noble cause, staged their own parade on Constitution Avenue. As America watched them — some in wheelchairs, all of them proud — there was a feeling that as a nation we were coming together again and that we had, at long last, welcomed the boys home.

"A lot of healing . . . went on," said one combat veteran who helped organize support for the memorial. And then there was this newspaper account that appeared after the ceremonies. I'd like to read it to you.

"Yesterday, crowds returned to the memorial. Among them was Herbie Petit, a machinist and former Marine from New Orleans. 'Last night,' he said, standing near the wall, 'I went out to dinner with some other ex-Marines. There was also a group of college students in the restaurant. We started talking to each other and before we left they stood up and cheered us.

'The whole week,' Petit said, his eyes red, 'it was worth it just for that.' "

It has been worth it. We Americans have learned to listen to each other and to trust each other again. We have learned that government owes the people an explanation and needs their support for its actions at home and abroad. And we have learned, and I pray this time for good, the most valuable lesson of all — the preciousness of human freedom. It has been a lesson relearned not just by Americans but by all the people of the world. Yet, while the experience of Vietnam has given us a stark lesson that ultimately must move the conscience of the world, we must remember that we cannot today, as much as some might want to, close this chapter in our history, for the war in Southeast Asia still haunts a small but brave group of Americans — the families of those still missing in the Vietnam conflict.

They live day and night with uncertainty, with an emptiness, with a void that we cannot fathom. Today, some sit among you. Their feelings are a mixture of pride and fear. They're proud of their sons or husbands, fathers or brothers, who bravely and nobly answered the call of their country, but some of them fear that this ceremony writes a final chapter, leaving those they love forgotten.

Well, today, then, one way to honor those who served or may still be serving in Vietnam is to gather here and rededicate ourselves to securing the answers for the families of those missing in action. I ask the members of Congress, the leaders of veterans' groups and the citizens of an entire nation, present or listening, to give these families your help and your support, for they still sacrifice and suffer.

Vietnam is not over for them; they cannot rest until they know the fate of those they loved and watched march off to serve their country. Our dedication to their cause must be strengthened with these events today. We write no last chapters. We close no books. We put away no final memories. An end to America's involvement in Vietnam cannot come before we have achieved the fullest possible accounting of those missing in action.

This can only happen when their families know with certainty that this nation discharged her duty to those who served nobly and well. Today, a united people call upon Hanoi with one voice: Heal the sorest wound of this conflict, return our sons to America, end the grief of those who are innocent and undeserving of any retribution.

The unknown soldier who has returned to us today and whom we lay to rest is symbolic of all our missing sons, and we will present him with the Congressional Medal of Honor, the highest military decoration we can bestow.

About him, we may well wonder as others have: As a child, did he play on some street in a great American city? Did he work beside his father on a farm in America's heartland? Did he marry? Did he have children? Did he look expectantly to return to a bride?

We'll never know the answers to those questions about his life. We do know, though, why he died. He saw the horrors of war but bravely faced them, certain his own cause and his country's cause was a noble one; that he was fighting for human dignity, for free men everywhere. Today we pause to embrace him and all who served us so well in a war whose end offered no parades, no flags, and so little thanks. We can be worthy of the values and ideals for which our sons sacrificed, worthy of their courage in the face of a fear that few of us will ever experience — by honoring their commitment and devotion to duty and country.

Many veterans of Vietnam still serve in the armed forces, work in our offices, on our farms, in our factories. Most have kept their experiences private, but most have been strengthened by their call to duty. A grateful nation opens her heart today in gratitude for their sacrifice, for their courage and their noble service. Let us, if we must, debate the lessons learned at some other time; today we simply say with pride: Thank you, dear son, and may God cradle you in his loving arms.

We present to you our nation's highest award, the Congressional Medal of Honor, for service above and beyond the call of duty in action with the enemy during the Vietnam era.

Thank you.

June

LONDON ECONOMIC SUMMIT

June 8, 9, 1984

The leaders of seven industrialized democracies met amid pomp and pageantry in London, England, June 7-9, 1984, to discuss economic issues affecting their countries and the world. Responding to pleas from developing nations struggling with debt burdens, the leaders agreed to encourage lower interest rates and to stretch out the Third World debt repayment.

For President Ronald Reagan, the London conference came on the third and final leg of a trip that also included a visit to Ballyporeen in County Tipperary, Ireland, the home of his Irish forebears, and participation in somber ceremonies in Normandy, France, commemorating the 40th anniversary of the Allied landings in World War II (D-Day).

In the concluding hours of the leaders' discussions, an estimated 150,000 demonstrators marched through central London protesting American nuclear policy. British authorities kept the marchers well away from all of the leaders' meeting sites.

The economic summit meeting was the 10th in a series begun in 1975 at the suggestion of Valery Giscard D'Estaing, then president of France. Participating in the 1984 meeting besides Reagan were the heads of government of Britain, Canada, France, Italy, Japan, and West Germany.

U.S. Budget Deficit

Observers said that Reagan's most significant achievement at the meeting was heading off specific criticism in the final communiqué of the

355

large U.S. budget deficits and high interest rates. Reagan came under fire from the other six leaders who contended that the deficits, expected to stay near $200 billion throughout the 1980s, were pushing up interest rates and vastly exacerbating the debt problems of Third World nations.

Other leaders told reporters that Reagan had assured them privately that further steps would be taken to reduce the deficit. A working draft of the communiqué pointed specifically to the American deficit, but the final statement contained only a general reference to the interrelated problems of inflation, high interest rates, and deficits.

Jacques Delors, the French finance minister, was quoted in The New York Times *as saying, "It was not our intention to embarrass a government in the midst of an election." President Reagan's campaign for reelection was only weeks away.*

Third World Debt

Leaders of eight Latin American nations appealed to the seven summit powers to focus at the meeting on the problems of Third World nations, which owed more than $800 billion in foreign loans. Repayment problems had been aggravated by a one-and-one-half percentage-point rise in U.S. interest rates since January 1984.

The seven western leaders reiterated a decision made at the 1983 summit in Williamsburg, Va., to deal with problems of debtor nations on a case-by-case basis. They also agreed to encourage commercial banks to stretch out repayments by countries that had adopted the stringent economic austerity plans proposed by the International Monetary Fund. Finally, the leaders authorized the World Bank to make longer-term loans, and they promised to channel more foreign direct investment to developing nations. (Williamsburg summit, Historic Documents of 1983, p. 507)

Other Issues

President Reagan joined Japanese prime minister Yashuhiro Nakasone in seeking the approval of the other leaders on a specific year, 1985, to begin planning a new round of international trade negotiations and another year, 1986, to begin the talks. But the final communiqué, while supporting the principle of antiprotectionist talks, carefully sidestepped the recommended schedule.

The summit leaders agreed to a conference, probably in 1986 — similar to the Bretton Woods Conference that laid the foundations of the postwar monetary system — to consider alternatives to the existing system. Critics believed that the floating exchange rate system in effect since 1972 was too volatile and had severely disrupted world trade.

Reagan was rebuffed by the other leaders in seeking a specific agreement on sharing oil supplies in the event of a Persian Gulf crisis, spurred by the ongoing bitter war between Iraq and Iran. Finally, the leaders approved a weaker declaration on combating terrorism than British prime minister Margaret Thatcher had proposed.

Security and defense issues played a relatively small role in the economic summit conference. In a statement on East-West relations, the leaders declared the need for "solidarity and resolve" in dealing with the Soviet Union.

Following are the texts of the declaration on economic values, issued June 8, 1984; and the economic declaration, the declaration on East-West relations, the declaration on international terrorism, and the statement on the Iran/Iraq conflict, issued June 9, 1984, at the conclusion of the economic summit meeting in London of the heads of government of Britain, Canada, France, Japan, Italy, the United States, and West Germany:

DECLARATION ON DEMOCRATIC VALUES

We, the Heads of State or Government of seven major industrial democracies with the President of the Commission of the European Communities, assembled in London for the Tenth Economic Summit meeting, affirm our commitment to the values which sustain and bring together our societies.

2. We believe in a rule of law which respects and protects without fear or favour the rights and liberties of every citizen, and provides the setting in which the human spirit can develop in freedom and diversity.

3. We believe in a system of democracy which ensures genuine choice in elections freely held, free expression of opinion and the capacity to respond and adapt to change in all its aspects.

4. We believe that, in the political and economic systems of our democracies, it is for Governments to set conditions in which there can be the greatest possible range and freedom of choice and personal initiative; in which the ideals of social justice, obligations and rights can be pursued; in which enterprise can flourish and employment opportunities can be available for all; in which all have equal opportunities of sharing in the benefits of growth and there is support for those who suffer or are in need; in which the lives of all can be enriched by the fruits of innovation, imagination and scientific discovery; and in which there can be confidence in the soundness of the currency. Our countries have the resources and will jointly work to master the tasks of the new industrial revolution.

5. We believe in close partnership among our countries in the conviction that this will reinforce political stability and economic growth in the world as a whole. We look for cooperation with all countries on the basis of

respect for their independence and territorial integrity, regardless of differences between political, economic and social systems. We respect genuine non-alignment. We are aware that economic strength places special moral responsibilities upon us. We reaffirm our determination to fight hunger and poverty throughout the world.

6. We believe in the need for peace with freedom and justice. Each of us rejects the use of force as a means of settling disputes. Each of us will maintain only the military strength necessary to deter aggression and to meet our responsibilities for effective defence. We believe that in today's world the independence of each of our countries is of concern to us all. We are convinced that international problems and conflicts can and must be resolved through reasoned dialogue and negotiation and we shall support all efforts to this end.

7. Strong in these beliefs, and endowed with great diversity and creative vigour, we look forward to the future with confidence.

ECONOMIC DECLARATION

We, the Heads of State or Government of seven major industrialised countries and the President of the Commission of the European Communities, have gathered in London from 7 to 9 June 1984 at the invitation of the Rt Hon Margaret Thatcher FRS MP, the Prime Minister of the United Kingdom, for the tenth annual Economic Summit.

2. The primary purpose of these meetings is to enable Heads of State or Government to come together to discuss economic problems, prospects and opportunities for our countries and for the world. We have been able to achieve not only closer understanding of each other's positions and views but also a large measure of agreement on the basic objectives of our respective policies.

3. At our last meeting, in Williamsburg in 1983, we were already able to detect clear signs of recovery from world recession. That recovery can now be seen to be established in our countries. It is more soundly based than previous recoveries in that it results from the firm efforts made in the Summit countries and elsewhere over recent years to reduce inflation.

4. But its continuation requires unremitting efforts. We have to make the most of the opportunities with which we are now presented to reinforce the basis for enduring growth and the creation of new jobs. We need to spread the benefits of recovery widely, both within the industrialised countries and also to the developing countries, especially the poorer countries who stand to gain more than any from a sustainable growth of the world economy. High interest rates, and failure to reduce inflation further and damp down inflationary expectations, could put recovery at risk. Prudent monetary and budgetary policies of the kind that have brought us so far will have to be sustained and where necessary strengthened. We reaffirm the commitment of our Governments to those objectives and policies.

5. Not the least of our concerns is the growing strain of public expenditure in all our countries. Public expenditure has to be kept within the limits of what our national economies can afford. We welcome the increasing attention being given to these problems by national governments and in such international bodies as the Organisation for Economic Cooperation and Development (OECD).

6. As unemployment in our countries remains high, we emphasise the need for sustained growth and creation of new jobs. We must make sure that the industrial economies adapt and develop in response to demand and to technological change. We must encourage active job training policies and removal of rigidities in the labour market, and bring about the conditions in which more new jobs will be created on a lasting basis, especially for the young. We need to foster and expand the international trading system and liberalise capital markets.

7. We are mindful of the concerns expressed by the developing countries, and of the political and economic difficulties which many of them face. In our discussion of each of the issues before us we have recognised the economic interdependence of the industrialised and developing countries. We reaffirm our willingness to conduct our relations with them in a spirit of goodwill and cooperation. To this end we have asked Ministers of Finance to consider the scope for intensified discussion of international financial issues of particular concern to developing countries in the IBRD [International Bank for Reconstruction and Development] Development Committee, an appropriate and broadly representative forum for this purpose.

8. In our strategy for dealing with the debt burdens of many developing countries, a key role has been played by the International Monetary Fund (IMF), whose resources have been strengthened for the purpose. Debtor countries have been increasingly ready to accept the need to adjust their economic policies, despite the painful and courageous efforts it requires. In a climate of world recovery and growing world trade, this strategy should continue to enable the international financial system to manage the problems that may still arise. But continuously high or even further growing levels of international interest rates could both exacerbate the problems of the debtor countries and make it more difficult to sustain the strategy. This underlines the importance of policies which will be conducive to lower interest rates and which take account of the impact of our policies upon other countries.

9. We have therefore agreed:—

(1) to continue with and where necessary strengthen policies to reduce inflation and interest rates, to control monetary growth and where necessary reduce budgetary deficits;

(2) to seek to reduce obstacles to the creation of new jobs:
— by encouraging the development of industries and services in response to demand and technological change, including in innovative small and medium-size businesses;
— by encouraging the efficient working of the labour market;

— by encouraging the improvement and extension of job training;

— by encouraging flexibility in the patterns of working time;

— and by discouraging measures to preserve obsolescent production and technology;

(3) to support and strengthen work in the appropriate international organizations, notably the OECD, on increasing understanding of the sources and patterns of economic change, and on improving economic efficiency and promoting growth, in particular by encouraging innovation and working for a more widespread acceptance of technological change, harmonising standards and facilitating the mobility of labour and capital;

(4) to maintain and wherever possible increase flows of resources, including official development assistance and assistance through the international financial and development institutions, to the developing countries and particularly to the poorest countries; to work with the developing countries to encourage more openness towards private investment flows; and to encourage practical measures in those countries to conserve resources and enhance indigenous food and energy production. Some of us also wish to activate the Common Fund for Commodities;

(5) in a spirit of co-operation with the countries concerned, to confirm the strategy on debt and continue to implement and develop it flexibly case by case; we have reviewed progress and attach particular importance to:

— helping debtor countries to make necessary economic and financial policy changes, taking due account of political and social difficulties;

— encouraging the IMF in its central role in this process, which it has been carrying out skillfully;

— encouraging closer cooperation between the IMF and the International Bank for Reconstruction and Development over the medium and long term;

— in cases where debtor countries are themselves making successful efforts to improve their position, encouraging more extended multi-year rescheduling of commercial debts and standing ready where appropriate to negotiate similarly in respect of debts to governments and government agencies;

— encouraging the flow of long-term direct investment; just as there is need for industrial countries to make their markets more open for the exports of developing countries, so these countries can help themselves by encouraging investment from the industrial countries;

— encouraging the substitution of more stable long-term finance, both direct and portfolio; for short-term bank lending;

(6) to invite Finance Ministers to carry forward, in an urgent and thorough manner, their current work on ways to improve the operation of the international monetary system, including exchange rates, surveillance, the creation, control and distribution of international liquidity and the role of the IMF; and to complete the present phase of their work in the first half of 1985 with a view to discussion at an early meeting of the IMF Interim Committee. The question of a further allocation of Special

Drawing Rights is to be reconsidered by the IMF Interim Committee in September 1984;

(7) to carry forward the procedures agreed at Versailles and at Williamsburg for multilateral monitoring and surveillance of convergence of economic performance toward lower inflation and higher growth;

(8) to seek to improve the operation and stability of the international financial system, by means of prudent policies among the major countries, by providing an adequate flow of funding to the international financial institutions, and by improving international access to capital markets in industrialised countries;

(9) to urge all trading countries, industrialised and developing alike, to resist continuing protectionist pressures, to reduce barriers to trade and to make renewed efforts to liberalise and expand international trade in manufactures, commodities and services;

(10) to accelerate the completion of current trade liberalisation programmes, particularly the 1982 GATT work programme, in cooperation with other trading partners; to press forward with the work on trade in services in the international organisations; to reaffirm the agreement reached at the OECD Ministerial Meeting in May 1984 on the important contribution which a new round of multilateral trade negotiations would make to strengthening the open multilateral trading system for the mutual benefit of all economies, industrial and developing; and, building on the 1982 GATT work programme, to consult partners in the GATT with a view to decisions at an early date on the possible objectives, arrangements and timing for a new negotiating round.

10. We are greatly concerned about the acute problems of poverty and drought in parts of Africa. We attach major importance to the special action programme for Africa, which is being prepared by the World Bank and should provide renewed impetus to the joint efforts of the international community to help.

11. We have considered the possible implications of a further deterioration of the situation in the Gulf for the supply of oil. We are satisfied that, given the stocks of oil presently available in the world, the availability of other sources of energy, and the scope for conservation in the use of energy, adequate supplies could be maintained for a substantial period of time by international cooperation and mutually supportive action. We will continue to act together to that end.

12. We note with approval the continuing consensus on the security and other implications of economic relations with Eastern countries, and on the need to continue work on this subject in the appropriate organisations.

13. We welcome the further report of the Working Group on Technology, Growth and Employment created by the Versailles Economic Summit, and the progress made in the eighteen areas of cooperation, and invite the Group to pursue further work and to report to Personal Representatives in time for the next Economic Summit. We also welcome the invitation of the Italian Government to an international conference to be

held in Italy in 1985 on the theme of technological innovation and the creation of new jobs.

14. We recognise the international dimension of environmental problems and the role of environmental factors in economic development. We have invited Ministers responsible for environmental policies to identify areas for continuing cooperation in this field. In addition we have decided to invite the Working Group on Technology, Growth and Employment to consider what has been done so far and to identify specific areas for research on the causes, effects and means of limiting environmental pollution of air, water and ground where existing knowledge is inadequate, and to identify possible projects for industrial cooperation to develop cost-effective techniques to reduce environmental damage. The Group is invited to report on these matters by 31 December 1984. In the meantime we welcome the invitation from the Government of the Federal Republic of Germany to certain Summit countries to an international conference on the environment in Munich on 24-27 June 1984.

15. We thank the Prime Minister of Japan for his report on the Hakone Conference of Life Sciences and Mankind, organised by the Japan Foundation in March 1984, and welcome the intention of the French Government to sponsor a second Conference in 1985.

16. We believe that manned space stations are the kind of programme that provides a stimulus for technological development leading to strengthened economies and improved quality of life. Such stations are being studied in some of our countries with a view to their being launched in the framework of national or international programmes. In that context each of our countries will consider carefully the generous and thoughtful invitation received from the President of the United States to other Summit countries to participate in the development of such a station by the United States. We welcome the intention of the United States to report at the next Summit on international participation in their programme.

17. We have agreed to meet again next year and have accepted the Federal Chancellor's invitation to meet in the Federal Republic of Germany.

DECLARATION ON EAST-WEST RELATIONS

1. We had a substantial discussion of East-West relations. We stressed that the first need is for solidarity and resolve among us all.

2. At the same time, we are determined to pursue the search for extended political dialogue and long-term cooperation with the Soviet Union and her allies. Contacts exist and are being developed in a number of fields. Each of us will pursue all useful opportunities for dialogue.

3. Our aim is security and the lowest possible level of forces. We wish to see early and positive results in the various arms control negotiations and

the speedy resumption of those now suspended. The United States has offered to re-start nuclear arms control talks anywhere, at any time, without preconditions. We hope that the Soviet Union will act in a constructive and positive way. We are convinced that this would be in the common interest of both East and West. We are in favour of agreements which would build confidence and give concrete expression, through precise commitments, to the principle of the non-use of force.

4. We believe that East and West have important common interests: in preserving peace; in enhancing confidence and security; in reducing the risks of surprise attack or war by accident; by improving crisis management techniques; and in preventing the spread of nuclear weapons.

DECLARATION ON TERRORISM

1. The Heads of State and Government discussed the problem of international terrorism.

2. They noted that hijacking and kidnapping had declined since the Declaration of Bonn (1978), Venice (1980) and Ottawa (1981) as a result of improved security measures, but that terrorism had developed other techniques, sometimes in association with traffic in drugs.

3. They expressed their resolve to combat this threat by every possible means, strengthening existing measures and developing effective new ones.

4. They were disturbed to note the ease with which terrorists move across international boundaries, and gain access to weapons, explosives, training and finance.

5. They viewed with serious concern the increasing involvement of states and governments in acts of terrorism, including the abuse of diplomatic immunity. They acknowledged the inviolability of diplomatic missions and other requirements of international law: but they emphasised the obligations which that law also entails.

6. Proposals which found support in the discussion included the following:

— closer co-operation and co-ordination between police and security organisations and other relevant authorities, especially in the exchange of information, intelligence and technical knowledge;

— scrutiny by each country of gaps in its national legislation which might be exploited by terrorists;

— use of the powers of the receiving state under the Vienna Convention in such matters as the size of diplomatic missions, and the number of buildings enjoying diplomatic immunity;

— action by each country to review the sale of weapons to states supporting terrorism;

— consultation and as far as possible cooperation over the expulsion or exclusion from their countries of known terrorists, including persons of diplomatic status involved in terrorism.

7. The Heads of State and Government recognised that this is a problem which affects all civilised states. They resolved to promote action through competent international organisations and among the international community as a whole to prevent and punish terrorist acts.

STATEMENT ON THE IRAN/IRAQ CONFLICT

1. We discussed the Iraq/Iran conflict in all its various aspects.

2. We expressed our deep concern at the mounting toll in human suffering, physical damage and bitterness that this conflict has brought; and at the breaches of international humanitarian law that have occurred.

3. The hope and desire of us all is that both sides will cease their attacks on each other and on the shipping of other states. The principle of freedom of navigation must be respected. We are concerned that the conflict should not spread further and we shall do what we can to encourage stability in the region.

4. We encourage the parties to seek a peaceful and honourable settlement. We shall support any efforts designed to bring this about, particularly those of the United Nations Secretary-General.

5. We also considered the implications for world oil supplies on the lines set out in the Economic Declaration. We noted that the world oil market has remained relatively stable. We believe that the international system has both the will and the capacity to cope with any foreseeable problems through the continuation of the prudent and realistic approach that is already being applied.

COURT ON SENIORITY/
AFFIRMATIVE ACTION
June 12, 1984

The Supreme Court ruled June 12 in a 6-3 decision that federal courts may not override the "last hired, first fired" rules of valid seniority systems to protect the jobs of newly hired minority workers. The case, Firefighters Local Union No. 1784 v. Stotts, was one of the most highly charged affirmative action cases to reach the Court in several years.

Background

The case stemmed from a 1980 consent decree between Memphis, Tennessee, and the Justice Department, which committed the city to increase the number of blacks hired and promoted by the Memphis fire department. The city had entered into the consent agreement after black firefighters filed suit, charging discrimination.

During a 1981 fiscal crisis Memphis announced the need to lay off a substantial number of municipal employees. The 1980 consent decree said nothing about what would happen in the event of layoffs. Under the established fire department seniority plan, at least 40 junior firefighters were to be laid off; 25 were white, 15 black. Several blacks, including fire captain Carl Stotts, petitioned the district court to protect the jobs of newly hired black firefighters so that minority job gains resulting from the consent decree would be preserved. The court directed the fire department to ignore its seniority system to save the jobs of the black officers. As a result of the court order, three white firefighters were laid off for a month and several others were "bumped" into lower positions. The

*firefighters union and the city unsuccessfully challenged the order in the
6th U.S. Circuit Court of Appeals.*

Majority Decision

*The majority decision, written by Justice Byron R. White, reversed the
appellate court ruling. Chief Justice Warren E. Burger and Justices
Lewis F. Powell Jr., William H. Rehnquist Jr., and Sandra Day O'Connor
joined in the majority decisions. O'Connor filed an additional concurring
opinion. Justice John Paul Stevens voted with the majority to reverse the
appeals court, but filed a separate opinion to reflect a different line of
reasoning.*

*The decision was based on Title VII of the Civil Rights Act of 1964,
which prohibited employment discrimination based on race or sex but
explicitly protected "bona fide" seniority systems, so long as they were
not established with the purpose of discriminating. White wrote that
Title VII's exemption for seniority systems limited the authority of the
lower court judge to modify the 1980 consent decree.*

*White rejected the appeals court's view that federal judges had the
power to issue orders to carry out the purposes of agreements like the
consent decree. In enacting Title VII, he wrote, Congress intended "to
provide make-whole relief only to those who have been actual victims of
illegal discrimination." White said that the appellate court's order, in
effect, granted retroactive seniority to the newly hired blacks, in violation
of a 1977 Supreme Court decision, Teamsters v. United States. That
ruling, the leading decision on the seniority protections contained in
Title VII, established that retroactive seniority was available only to
individuals who could show not only that they were members of a group
that had been discriminated against, but also that they personally were
victims of discrimination. In the Memphis case, White wrote, "There was
no finding that any of the blacks protected from layoff had been a victim
of discrimination."*

Dissenting View

*Justice Harry A. Blackmun, joined by Justices William J. Brennan Jr.,
and Thurgood Marshall, filed a dissenting opinion. Blackmun contended
that the Court should have dismissed the case as moot because all of the
white firefighters laid off as a result of the 1981 court order were back at
work. White argued, however, that the order had a continuing effect and
would govern the city's actions in any future layoff. The matter of back
pay for the whites still was open as well, he noted.*

*Blackmun argued that the majority had taken too narrow a view of the
federal judge's power to implement the original consent decree. "[P]ar-
ties to a consent decree typically agree to confer upon supervising courts*

the authority to ensure that the purposes of a decree are not frustrated by unforeseen circumstances."

The dissenters also disagreed with the majority's contention that only individual members of a disadvantaged group who could prove discrimination were entitled to compensatory seniority. The purpose of affirmative action remedies under Title VII, Blackmun wrote, "is not to make whole any particular individual, but rather to remedy the present class-wide effects of past discrimination or to prevent similar discrimination in the future."

Reactions

The decision was a clear victory for the city, the union, and the Reagan administration, which had filed a friend-of-the-court brief in the case. The administration had long been opposed to the use of employment quotas based on race or sex. Solicitor General Rex E. Lee, who had argued the administration's position before the Court, hailed the decision as "one of the greatest victories of all time." Union leaders praised the ruling as well. In light of the decision, the Justice Department announced it would begin a review of all affirmative action decrees and agreements involving the federal government.

Union leaders applauded the decision. Albert Shanker, president of the American Federation of Teachers, called it "a very important decision, adding, "We believe seniority rules are good in the long run for minorities because they're objective." But most representatives of women's and minority groups viewed the decision as a setback to affirmative action. Benjamin L. Hooks, executive director of the National Association for the Advancement of Colored People, said the ruling provided "a backdoor method" for communities to continue discrimination. However, Charles S. Sims, national staff counsel for the American Civil Liberties Union, said he was disappointed but that the decision was "by no means a disaster."

The Court's decision was closely tied to the particular facts of the Memphis case, leaving open the question of its impact on cases where valid seniority systems were not at issue. While opponents of affirmative action, including administration officials, put the broadest possible interpretation on the decision, some civil rights lawyers maintained that the impact of the ruling would be limited.

Following are excerpts from the Supreme Court's June 12, 1984, decision in Firefighters Local Union No. 1784 v. Stotts, *ruling that a court may not order an employer to protect the jobs of recently hired black employees at the expense of whites who have more seniority; and from the dissent by Justice Harry A. Blackmun.*

Nos. 82-206 and 82-229

Firefighters Local Union No. 1784,
     Petitioner
          v.
   Carl W. Stotts Et Al.   On writs of Certiorari to the United
                                States Court of Appeals for the
Memphis Fire Department Et Al.,   Sixth Circuit
     Petitioners
          v.
  Carl W. Stotts, Etc., Et Al.

[June 12, 1984]

JUSTICE WHITE delivered the opinion of the Court.

Petitioners challenge the Court of Appeals' approval of an order enjoining the City of Memphis from following its seniority system in determining who must be laid off as a result of a budgetary shortfall. Respondents contend that the injunction was necessary to effectuate the terms of a Title VII consent decree in which the City agreed to undertake certain obligations in order to remedy past hiring and promotional practices. Because we conclude that the order cannot be justified, either as an effort to enforce the consent decree or as a valid modification, we reverse.

I

In 1977 respondent Carl Stotts, a black holding the position of fire-fighting captain in the Memphis, Tennessee, Fire Department, filed a class action complaint in the United States District Court for the Western District of Tennessee. The complaint charged that the Memphis Fire Department and other city officials were engaged in a pattern or practice of making hiring and promotion decisions on the basis of race in violation of Title VII of the Civil Rights Act of 1964, 42 U. S. C. §2000e *et seq.,* as well as 42 U. S. C. §§1981 and 1983. The District Court certified the case as a class action and consolidated it with an individual action subsequently filed by respondent Fred Jones, a black fire-fighting private in the Department, who claimed that he had been denied a promotion because of his race. Discovery proceeded, settlement negotiations ensued, and in due course, a consent decree was approved and entered by the District Court on April 25, 1980.

The stated purpose of the decree was to remedy the hiring and promotion practices "of the Department with respect to blacks." Accordingly, the City agreed to promote 13 named individuals and to provide backpay to 81 employees of the Fire Department. It also adopted the long-term goal of increasing the proportion of minority representation in each job classification in the Fire Department to approximately the proportion of blacks in the labor force in Shelby County, Tennessee. However, the city did not, by agreeing to the decree, admit "any violations of law, rule or regulation with respect to the allegations" in the complaint. The plaintiffs waived any further relief save to enforce the decree, and the District Court retained jurisdiction "for such further orders as may be necessary or appropriate to effectuate the purposes of this decree."

The long-term hiring goal outlined in the decree paralleled the provisions of a 1974 consent decree, which settled a case brought against the City by the United States and which applied citywide. Like the 1974 decree, the 1980 decree also established an interim hiring goal of filling on an annual basis 50 percent of the job vacancies in the Department with qualified black applicants. The 1980 decree contained an additional goal with respect to promotions: the Department was to attempt to ensure that 20 percent of the promotions in each job classification be given to blacks. Neither decree contained provisions for layoffs or reductions in rank, and neither awarded any competitive seniority. The 1974 decree did require that for purposes of promotion, transfer, and assignment, seniority was to be computed "as the total seniority of that person with the city."

In early May, 1981, the City announced that projected budget deficits required a reduction of non-essential personnel throughout the City Government. Layoffs were to be based on the "last hired, first fired" rule under which citywide seniority, determined by each employee's length of continuous service from the latest date of permanent employment, was the basis for deciding who would be laid off. If a senior employee's position were abolished or eliminated, the employee could "bump down" to a lower ranking position rather than be laid off. As the Court of Appeals later noted, this layoff policy was adopted pursuant to the seniority system "mentioned in the 1974 decree and .... incorporated in the City's memorandum with the Union."

On May 4, at respondents' request, the District Court entered a temporary restraining order forbidding the layoff of any black employee. The Union, which previously had not been a party to either of these cases, was permitted to intervene. At the preliminary injunction hearing, it appeared that 55 then-filled positions in the Department were to be eliminated and that 39 of these positions were filled with employees having "bumping" rights. It was estimated that 40 least-senior employees in the fire-fighting bureau of the department would be laid off and that of these 25 were white and 15 black. It also appeared that 56 percent of the employees hired in the department since 1974 had been black and that the percentage of black employees had increased from approximately 3 or 4 percent in 1974 to 11½ percent in 1980.

On May 18, the District Court entered an order granting an injunction. The Court found that the consent decree "did not contemplate the method to be used for reduction in rank or lay-off," and that the layoff policy was in accordance with the City's seniority system and was not adopted with any intent to discriminate. Nonetheless, concluding that the proposed layoffs would have a racially discriminatory effect and that the seniority system was not a bona fide one, the District Court ordered that the City "not apply the seniority policy insofar as it will decrease the percentage of black lieutenants, drivers, inspectors and privates that are presently employed . . . ." On June 23, the District Court broadened its order to include three additional classifications. A modified layoff plan, aimed at protecting black employees in the seven classifications so as to comply with the court's order, was presented and approved. Layoffs pursuant to the modified plan were then carried out. In certain instances, to comply with the injunction, non-minority employees with more seniority than minority employees were laid off or demoted in rank.

On appeal, the Court of Appeals for the Sixth Circuit affirmed despite its conclusion that the District Court was wrong in holding that the City's seniority system was not bona fide. Characterizing the principal issue as "whether the district court erred in modifying the 1980 Decree to prevent minority employment from being affected disproportionately by unanticipated layoffs," the Court of Appeals concluded that the District Court had acted properly. After determining that the decree was properly approved in the first instance, the court held that the modification was permissible under general contract principles because the City "contracted" to provide "a substantial increase in the number of minorities in supervisory positions" and the layoffs would breach that contract. Alternatively, the court held that the District Court was authorized to modify the decree because new and unforeseen circumstances had created a hardship for one of the parties to the decree. Finally, articulating three alternative rationales, the court rejected petitioners' argument that the modification was improper because it conflicted with the City's seniority system, which was immunized from Title VII attack under § 703(h) of that Act, 42 U. S. C. § 2000e-2(h).

The City and the Union filed separate petitions for certiorari. The two petitions were granted, and the cases were consolidated for oral argument.

II

We deal first with the claim that these cases are moot. Respondents submit that the injunction entered in this case was a preliminary injunction dealing only with the 1981 layoffs, that all white employees laid off as a result of the injunction were restored to duty only one month after their layoff, and that those who were demoted have now been offered back their old positions. Assertedly, the injunction no longer has force or effect, and the cases are therefore moot. For several reasons, we find the submission untenable.

First, the injunction on its face ordered "that the defendants not apply the seniority policy proposed insofar as it will decrease the percentage of black" employees in specified classifications in the Department. The seniority policy was the policy adopted by the City and contained in the collective bargaining contract with the Union. The injunction was affirmed by the Court of Appeals and has never been vacated. It would appear from its terms that the injunction is still in force and that unless set aside must be complied with in connection with any future layoffs.

Second, even if the injunction itself applied only to the 1981 layoffs, the predicate for the so-called preliminary injunction was the ruling that the consent decree must be construed to mean and, in any event, must be modified to provide that layoffs were not to reduce the percentage of blacks employed in the fire department. Furthermore, both the District Court and the Court of Appeals, for different reasons, held that the seniority provisions of the City's collective bargaining contract must be disregarded for the purpose of achieving the mandated result. These rulings remain undisturbed, and we see no indication that respondents concede in urging mootness that these rulings were in error and should be reversed. To the contrary, they continue to defend them. Unless overturned, these rulings would require the City to obey the modified consent decree and to disregard its seniority agreement in making future layoffs.

Accordingly, the inquiry is not merely whether the injunction is still in effect, but whether the mandated modification of the consent decree continues to have an impact on the parties such that the case remains alive. We are quite unconvinced — and it is the respondents' burden to convince us, *County of Los Angeles* v. *Davis* (1979) — that the modification of the decree and the *pro tanto* invalidation of the seniority system is of no real concern to the city because it will never again contemplate layoffs that if carried out in accordance with the seniority system would violate the modified decree. For this reason alone, the case is not moot.

Third, the judgment below will have a continuing effect on the City's management of the Department in still another way. Although the City has restored or offered to restore to their former positions all white employees who were laid off or demoted, those employees have not been made whole: those who were laid off have lost a month's pay, as well as seniority that has not been restored; and those employees who "bumped down" and accepted lesser positions will also have back-pay claims if their demotions were unjustified. Unless the judgment of the Court of Appeals is reversed, however, the layoffs and demotions were in accordance with the law, and it would be quite unreasonable to expect the City to pay out money to which the employees had no legal right. Nor would it feel free to respond to the seniority claims of the three white employees who, as the City points out, lost competitive seniority in relation to all other individuals who were not laid off, including those minority employees who would have been laid off but for the injunction. On the other hand, if the Court of Appeals' judgment is reversed, the City would be free to take a wholly different position with respect to backpay and seniority.

Undoubtedly, not much money and seniority are involved, but the amount of money and seniority at stake does not determine mootness. As long as the parties have a concrete interest in the outcome of the litigation, the case is not moot notwithstanding the size of the dispute. *Powell* v. *McCormack* (1969). Moreover, a month's pay is not a negligible item for those affected by the injunction, and the loss of a month's competitive seniority may later determine who gets a promotion, who is entitled to bid for transfers or who is first laid off if there is another reduction in force. These are matters of substance, it seems to us, and enough so to foreclose any claim of mootness. Cf. *Franks* v. *Bowman Transportaton Co.* (1976); *Powell* v. *McCormack; Bond* v. *Floyd* (1966).

In short, respondents successfully attacked the City's initial layoff plan and secured a judgment modifying the consent decree, ordering the City to disregard its seniority policy, and enjoining any layoffs that would reduce the percentage of blacks in the Department. Respondents continue to defend those rulings, which, as we have said, may determine the City's disposition of back pay claims and claims for restoration of competitive seniority that will affect respondents themselves. It is thus unrealistic to claim that there is no longer a dispute between the City and respondents with respect to the scope of the consent decree. Respondents cannot invoke the jurisdiction of a federal court to obtain a favorable modification of a consent decree and then insulate that ruling from appellate review by claiming that they are no longer interested in the matter, particularly when the modification continues to have adverse effects on the other parties to the action.

III

The issue at the heart of this case is whether the District Court exceeded its powers in entering an injunction requiring white employees to be laid off, when the otherwise applicable seniority system would have called for the layoff of black employees with less seniority. We are convinced that the Court of Appeals erred in resolving this issue and in affirming the District Court.

A

The Court of Appeals first held that the injunction did no more than enforce the terms of the agreed-upon consent decree. This specific-performance approach rests on the notion that because the City was under a general obligation to use its best efforts to increase the proportion of blacks on the force, it breached the decree by attempting to effectuate a layoff policy reducing the percentage of black employees in the Department even though such a policy was mandated by the seniority system adopted by the City and the Union. A variation of this argument is that since the decree permitted the District Court to enter any later orders that "may be necessary or appropriate to effectuate the purposes of this decree," the City had agreed in advance to an injunction against layoffs that would reduce the proportion of black employees. We are convinced, however, that both of these are improvident constructions of the consent decree.

It is to be recalled that the "scope of a consent decree must be discerned within its four corners, and not by reference to what might satisfy the purposes of one of the parties to it" or by what "might have been written had the plaintiff established his factual claims and legal theories in litigation." *United States* v. *Armour & Co.* (1971). Here, as the District Court recognized, there is no mention of layoffs or demotions within the four corners of the decree; nor is there any suggestion of an intention to depart from the existing seniority system or from the City's arrangements with the Union. We cannot believe that the parties to the decree thought that the City would simply disregard its arrangements with the Union and the seniority system it was then following. Had there been any intention to depart from the seniority plan in the event of layoffs or demotions, it is much more reasonable to believe that there would have been an express provision to that effect. This is particularly true since the decree stated that it was not "intended to conflict with any provisions" of the 1974 decree, and since the latter decree expressly anticipated that the City would recognize seniority. It is thus not surprising that when the City anticipated layoffs and demotions, it in the first instance faithfully followed its preexisting seniority system, plainly having no thought that it had already agreed to depart from it. It therefore cannot be said that the express terms of the decree contemplated that such an injunction would be entered.

The argument that the injunction was proper because it carried out the purposes of the decree is equally unconvincing. The decree announced that its purpose was "to remedy past hiring and promotion practices" of the Department, and to settle the dispute as to the "appropriate and valid procedures for hiring and promotion. The decree went on to provide the agreed-upon remedy, but as we have indicated, that remedy did not include the displacement of white employees with seniority over blacks. Furthermore, it is reasonable to believe that the "remedy" which it was the purpose of the decree to provide, would not exceed the bounds of the remedies that are appropriate under Title VII, at least absent some express provision to that effect. As our cases have made clear, however, and as will be reemphasized below, Title VII protects bona fide seniority systems, and it is inappropriate to deny an innocent employee the benefits of his seniority in order to provide a remedy in a pattern or practice suit such as this. We thus have no doubt that the City considered its system to be valid and that it had no intention of departing from it when it agreed to the 1980 decree.

Finally, it must be remembered that neither the Union nor the non-minority employees were parties to the suit when the 1980 decree was entered. Hence the entry of that decree cannot be said to indicate any agreement by them to any of its terms. Absent the presence of the Union or the non-minority employees and an opportunity for them to agree or disagree with any provisions of the decree that might encroach on their rights, it seems highly unlikely that the City would purport to bargain away non-minority rights under the then-existing seniority system. We therefore conclude that the injunction does not merely enforce the agreement of the parties as reflected in the consent decree. If the injunction is to stand, it must be justified on some other basis.

B

The Court of Appeals held that even if the injunction is not viewed as compelling compliance with the terms of the decree, it was still properly entered because the District Court had inherent authority to modify the decree when an economic crisis unexpectedly required layoffs which, if carried out as the City proposed, would undermine the affirmative action outlined in the decree and impose an undue hardship on respondents. This was true, the court held, even though the modification conflicted with a bona fide seniority system adopted by the City. The Court of Appeals erred in reaching this conclusion.

Section 703(h) of Title VII provides that it is not an unlawful employment practice to apply different standards of compensation, or different terms, conditions, or privileges of employment pursuant to a bona fide seniority system, provided that such differences are not the result of an intention to discriminate because of race. It is clear that the City had a seniority system, that its proposed layoff plan conformed to that system, and that in making the settlement the City had not agreed to award competitive seniority to any minority employee whom the City proposed to lay off. The District Court held that the City could not follow its seniority system in making its proposed layoffs because its proposal was discriminatory in effect and hence not a bona fide plan. Section 703(h), however, permits the routine application of a seniority system absent proof of an intention to discriminate. *Teamsters* v. *United States* (1977). Here, the District Court itself found that the layoff proposal was not adopted with the purpose or intent to discriminate on the basis of race. Nor had the City in agreeing to the decree admitted in any way that it had engaged in intentional discrimination. The Court of Appeals was therefore correct in disagreeing with the District Court's holding that the layoff plan was not a bona fide application of the seniority system, and it would appear that the City could not be faulted for following the seniority plan expressed in its agreement with the Union. The Court of Appeals nevertheless held that the injunction was proper even though it conflicted with the seniority system. This was error.

To support its position, the Court of Appeals first proposed a "settlement" theory, *i.e.*, that the strong policy favoring voluntary settlement of Title VII actions permitted consent decrees that encroached on seniority systems. But at this stage in its opinion, the Court of Appeals was supporting the proposition that even if the injunction was not merely enforcing the agreed-upon terms of the decree, the District Court had the authority to modify the decree over the objection of one of the parties. The settlement theory, whatever its merits might otherwise be, has no application when there is no "settlement" with respect to the disputed issue.

Here, the agreed-upon decree neither awarded competitive seniority to the minority employees nor purported in any way to depart from the seniority system.

A second ground advanced by the Court of Appeals in support of the conclusion that the injunction could be entered notwithstanding its conflict with the seniority system was the assertion that "[i]t would be incongruous to hold that the use of the preferred means of resolving an employment discrimination action decreases the power of a court to order relief which vindicates the policies embodied within Title VII, and 42 U.S.C. §§ 1981 and 1983." The court concluded that if the allegations in the complaint had been proved, the District Court could have entered an order overriding the seniority provisions. Therefore, the court reasoned, "[t]he trial court had the authority to override the Firefighter's Union seniority provisions to effectuate the purpose of the 1980 Decree."

The difficulty with this approach is that it overstates the authority of the trial court to disregard a seniority system in fashioning a remedy after a plaintiff has successfully proved that an employer has followed a pattern or practice having a discriminatory effect on black applicants or employees. If individual members of a plaintiff class demonstrate that they have been actual victims of the discriminatory practice, they may be awarded competitive seniority and given their rightful place on the seniority roster. This much is clear from *Franks* v. *Bowman Transportation Co.* (1976) and *Teamsters* v. *United States* (1977). *Teamsters*, however, also made clear that mere membership in the disadvantaged class is insufficient to warrant a seniority award; each individual must prove that the discriminatory practice had an impact on him. Even when an individual shows that the discriminatory practice has had an impact on him, he is not automatically entitled to have a non-minority employee laid off to make room for him. He may have to wait until a vacancy occurs, and if there are non-minority employees on layoff, the Court must balance the equities in determining who is entitled to the job. See also *Ford Motor Co.* v. *EEOC* (1982). Here, there was no finding that any of the blacks protected from layoff had been a victim of discrimination and no award of competitive seniority to any of them. Nor had the parties in formulating the consent decree purported to identify any specific employee entitled to particular relief other than those listed in the exhibits attached to the decree. It therefore seems to us that in light of *Teamsters,* the Court of Appeals imposed on the parties as an adjunct of settlement something that could not have been ordered had the case gone to trial and the plaintiffs proved that a pattern or practice of discrimination existed.

Our ruling in *Teamsters* that a court can award competitive seniority only when the beneficiary of the award has actually been a victim of illegal discrimination is consistent with the policy behind § 706(gg) of Title VII, which affects the remedies available in Title VII litigation. That policy, which is to provide make-whole relief only to those who have been actual victims of illegal discrimination, was repeatedly expressed by the sponsors of the Act during the congressional debates. Opponents of the legislation that became Title VII charged that if the bill were enacted, employers could be ordered to hire and promote persons in order to achieve a racially balanced work force even though those persons had not been victims of illegal discrimination. Responding to these charges, Senator Humphrey explained the limits on a court's remedial powers as follows:

> "No court order can require hiring, reinstatement, admission to membership, or payment of back pay for anyone who was not fired, refused employment or advancement or admission to a union by an act of discrimination forbidden by this title. This is stated expressly in the last sentence of Section 707(e) [enacted without relevant change as §706(g)]. . . . Contrary to the allegations of some opponents of this title, there is nothing in it that will give any power to the Commission or to any court to require . . . firing . . . of employees in order to meet a racial 'quota' or to achieve a certain racial balance. That bugaboo has been brought up a dozen times; but is nonexistent.". . .

Similar assurances concerning the limits on a court's authority to award make-whole relief were provided by supporters of the bill throughout the legislative process. For example, following passage of the bill in the House, its Republican House sponsors published a memorandum describing the bill. Referring to the remedial powers given the courts by the bill, the memorandum stated: "Upon conclusion of the trial, the federal court may enjoin an employer or labor organization from practicing further discrimination and may order the hiring or reinstatement of an employee or the acceptance or reinstatement of a union member. *But Title VII does not permit the ordering of racial quotas in business or unions. . . .*"

The Court of Appeals holding that the District Court's order was permissible as a valid Title VII remedial order ignores not only our ruling in *Teamsters* but the policy behind § 706(g) as well. Accordingly, that holding cannot serve as a basis for sustaining the District Court's order.

Finally, the Court of Appeals was of the view that the District Court ordered no more than that which the City unilaterally could have done by way of adopting an affirmative action program. Whether the City, a public employer, could have taken this course without violating the law is an issue we need not decide. The fact is that in this case the city took no such action and that the modification of the decree was imposed over its objection.

We thus are unable to agree either that the order entered by the District Court was a justifiable effort to enforce the terms of the decree to which the City had agreed or that it was a legitimate modification of the decree that could be imposed on the City without its consent. Accordingly, the judgment of the Court of Appeals is reversed.

It is so ordered.

JUSTICE BLACKMUN, with whom JUSTICE BRENNAN and JUSTICE MARSHALL join, dissenting.

Today's opinion is troubling less for the law it creates that for the law it ignores. The issues in these cases arose out of a preliminary injunction that prevented the city of Memphis from conducting a particular layoff in a particular manner. Because that layoff has ended, the preliminary injunction no longer restrains any action that the city wishes to take. The Court nevertheless rejects respondents' claim that these cases are moot because the Court concludes that there are continuing effects from the preliminary injunction and that these create a continuing controversy. The Court appears oblivious, however, to the fact that any continuing legal consequences of the preliminary injunction would be erased by simply vacating the Court of Appeals' judgment, which is this Court's longstanding practice with cases that become moot.

Having improperly asserted jurisdiction, the Court then ignores the proper standard of review. The District Court's action was a preliminary injunction reviewable only on an abuse of discretion standard; the Court treats the action as a permanent injunction and decides the merits, even though the District Court has not yet had an opportunity to do so. On the merits, the Court ignores the specific facts of these cases that make inapplicable the decisions on which it relies. Because, in my view, the Court's decision is demonstrably in error, I respectfully dissent.

I

Mootness

"The usual rule in federal cases is that an actual controversy must exist at stages of appellate or certiorari review and not simply at the date the action is initiated." *Roe* v. *Wade* (1973). In the absence of a live controversy, the constitutional requirement of a "case" or "controversy," see U.S. Const., Art. III, deprives a federal court of jurisdiction. Accordingly, a case, although live at the start, becomes moot when intervening acts destroy the interest of a party to the adjudication. *DeFunis* v. *Odegaard* (1974). In such a situation, the federal practice is to vacate the judgment and remand the case with a direction to dismiss. *United States* v. *Munsingwear, Inc.* (1950).

Application of these principles to the present cases is straightforward. The controversy underlying the suits is whether the city of Memphis' proposed layoff plan violated the 1980 consent decreee. The District Court granted a preliminary injunction limiting the proportion of Negroes that the city could lay off as part of its efforts to solve its fiscal problems. Because of the injunction, the city chose instead to reduce its workforce according to a modified layoff plan under which some whites were laid off despite their greater seniority over the blacks protected by the preliminary injunction. Since the preliminary injunction was entered, however, the layoffs all have terminated and the city has taken back every one of the workers laid off pursuant to the modified plan. Accordingly, the preliminary injunction no longer restraints the city's conduct, and the adverse relationship between the opposing parties concerning its propriety is gone. A ruling in this situation thus becomes wholly advisory, and ignores the basic duty of this Court "to decide actual controversies by a judgment which can be carried into effect, and not to give opinions upon moot questions or abstract propositions, or to declare principles or rules of law which cannot affect the matter in issue in the case before it.' " *Oil Workers* v. *Missouri* (1960), quoting *Mills* v. *Green* (1895). The proper disposition, therefore, is to vacate the judgment and remand the cases with directions to dismiss them as moot.

The purpose of vacating a judgment when it becomes moot while awaiting review is to return the legal relationships of the parties to their status prior to initiation of the suit. The Court explained in *Munsingwear* that vacating a judgment

> "clears the path for future relitigation of the issues between the parties and eliminates a judgment, review of which was prevented through happenstance. When that procedure is followed, the rights of all parties are preserved; none is prejudiced by a decision which in the statutory scheme was only preliminary."

Were the Court to follow this procedure in these cases, as clearly it should, the legal rights of the parties would return to their status prior to entry of the preliminary injunction. In the event that future layoffs became necessary, respondents would have to seek a new injunction based on the facts presented by the new layoffs, and petitioners could oppose the new injunction on any and all grounds, including arguments similar to those made in these cases.

Struggling to find a controversy on which to base its jurisdiction, the Court offers a variety of theories as to why these cases remain live. First, it briefly suggests that the cases are not moot because the preliminary injunction continues in effect and would apply in the event of a future layoff. My fundamental disagreement with this contention is that it incorrectly interprets the preliminary injunction. Even if the Court's interpretation of the preliminary injunction is correct, however, it is nonetheless true that if the judgment in these cases were vacated, the preliminary injunction would not apply to a future layoff.

The Court's second argument against mootness is remarkable. The Court states that even if the preliminary injunction applies only to the 1981 layoffs, the "rulings" that formed the "predicate" for the preliminary injunction "remain undistrubed." The Court then states:

> "[W]e see no indication that respondents concede in urging mootness that these rulings were in error and should be reversed. To the contrary, they continue to defend them. Unless overturned, these rulings would require the City to obey the modified consent decree and to disregard its seniority agreement in making future layoffs."

Two aspects of this argument provoke comment. It is readily apparent that vacating the judgment in these cases would also vacate whatever "rulings" formed the "predicate" for that judgment. There simply is no such thing as a "ruling" that has a life independent of the judgment in these cases and that would bind the city in a future layoff if the judgment in these cases were vacated. The Court's argument, therefore, is nothing more than an oxymoronic suggestion that the judgment would somehow have a res judicata effect even if it was vacated — a complete contradiction in terms.

Moreover, and equally remarkable, is the notion that respondents must concede that the rulings below were in error before they can argue that the case is moot. To my knowledge, there is nothing in this Court's mootness doctrine that requires a party urging mootness to concede the lack of merit in this case. Indeed, a central purpose of mootness doctrine is to avoid an unnecessary ruling on the merits.

The Court's third argument against mootness focuses on the wages and seniority lost by white employees during the period of their layoffs — and it is undisputed that some such pay and seniority were lost. The Court does not suggest, however, that its decision today will provide the affected workers with any backpay or seniority. It is clear that any such backpay or retroactive seniority for laidoff workers would have to come from the city, not from respondents. But the city and the union are both *petitioners* here, not adversaries, and respondents have no interest in defending the city from liability to the union in a separate proceeding. For that reason, these suits involve the wrong adverse parties for resolution of any issues of backpay and seniority.

The Court, nevertheless, suggests that the backpay and seniority issues somehow keep these cases alive despite the absence of an adversarial party. The Court states:

> "Unless the judgment of the Court of Appeals is reversed, however, the layoffs and demotions were in accordance with the law, and it would be quite unreasonable to expect the City to pay out money to which the employees had no legal right. Nor would it feel free to respond to the seniority claims of the three white employees who . . . lost competitive seniority in relation to all other individuals who were not laid off, including these minority employees who would have been laid off but for the injunction. On the other hand, if the Court of Appeals' judgment is reversed, the City would be free to take a wholly different position with respect to back pay and seniority."

Although the artful ambiguity of this passage renders it capable of several interpretations, none of them provides a basis on which to conclude that these cases are not moot. The Court may mean to suggest that the city has no legal obligation to provide backpay and retroactive seniority, but that it might voluntarily do so if this Court opines that the preliminary injunction was improper. A decision in that situation, however, would be an advisory opinion in the full sense — it would neither require nor permit the city to do any thing that it cannot do already.

It is more likely that the Court means one of two other things. The Court may mean that if the Court of Appeals' decision is left standing, it would have some kind of preclusive effect in a suit for back pay and retroactive seniority brought by the union against the city. Alternatively, the Court may mean that if the city sought voluntarily to give union members the back pay and retroactive seniority that they lost, the respondents could invoke the preliminary injunction to prohibit the city from doing so.

Even if both of these notions were correct — which they clearly are not, they are irrelevant to the question of mootness. The union has not filed a suit for backpay or seniority, nor has the preliminary injunction prevented the city from awarding retroactive seniority to the laidoff workers. . . . By vacating this judgment as moot, the Court would ensure that in the event that a controversy over backpay and retroactive seniority should arise, the parties in these cases could relitigate any issues concerning the propriety of the preliminary injunction as it relates to that controversy. Thus, the Court today simply has its reasoning backwards. It pretends that these cases present a live controversy because the judgment in them might affect future litigation; yet the Court's longstanding practice of vacating moot judgments is designed precisely to prevent that result.

By going beyond the reach of the Court's Article III powers, today's decision improperly provides an advisory opinion for the city and the union. With regard to the city's ability to give retroactive seniority and backpay to laidoff workers, respondents concede that neither the preliminary injunction nor the Court of Appeals' judgment prohibits the city from taking such action. The city has not claimed any confusion over its ability to make such an award; it simply has chosen not to do so. Thus, the opinion today provides the city with a decision to ensure that it can do something that it has not claimed any interest in doing and has not been prevented from doing, and that respondents concede they have no way of stopping.

With regard to the union, the Court's imagined controversy is even more hypothetical. The Court concedes that there is doubt whether, in fact, the union possesses any enforceable contractual rights that could form the basis of a contract claim by the union against the city. It is also unclear how the propriety of the preliminary injunction would affect the city's defenses in such a suit. In any event, no such claims have been filed. Thus, today's decision is provided on the theory that it might affect a defense that the city has not asserted, in a suit that the union has not brought, to enforce contractual rights that may not exist.

II

Because there is now no justiciable controversy in these cases, today's decision by the Court is an improper exercise of judicial power. It is not my purpose in dissent to parallel the Court's error and speculate on the appropriate disposition of these nonjusticiable cases. In arriving at its result, however, the Court's analysis is misleading in many ways, and in other ways it is simply in error. Accordingly, it is important to note the Court's unexplained departures from precedent and from the record.

A

Assuming *arguendo* that these cases are justiciable, then the only question before the Court is the validity of a *preliminary* injunction that prevented the city from conducting layoffs that would have reduced the number of Negroes in certain job categories within the Memphis Fire Department. In granting such relief, the District Court was required to consider respondents' likelihood of success on the merits, the balance of irreparable harm to the parties, and whether the injunction would be in the public interest. *University of Texas* v. *Camenisch; Doran* v. *Salem Inn, Inc.* The question before a reviewing court "is simply whether the issuance of the injunction, in light of the applicable standard, constituted an abuse of direction."

The Court has chosen to answer a different question. The Court's opinion does not mention the standard of review for a preliminary injunction, and does not apply that standard to these cases. Instead, the Court treats the cases as if they involved a *permanent* injunction, and addresses the question whether the city's proposed layoffs violated the consent decree. That issue was never resolved in the District Court because the city did not press for a final decision on the merits. The issue, therefore, is not properly before this Court. After taking jurisdiction over a controversy that no longer exists, the Court reviews a decision that was never made. . . .

B

After ignoring the appropriate standard of review, the Court then focuses on an issue that is not in these cases. It begins its analysis by stating that the "issue at the heart of this case" is the District Court's power to "ente[r] an injunction requiring white employees to be laid off." That statement, with all respect, is simply incorrect. On its face, the preliminary injunction prohibited the city from conducting layoffs in accordance with its seniority system "insofar as it will decrease the percentage of black[s] . . . presently employed" in certain job categories. The preliminary injunction did not require the city to lay off any white employees at all. In fact, several parties interested in the suit, including the union, attempted to persuade the city to avoid layoffs entirely by reducing the working hours of all fire department employees. Thus, although the District Court order reduced the city's options in meeting its fiscal crisis, it did not require the dismissal of white employees. The choice of a modified layoff plan remained that of the city.

This factual detail is important because it makes clear that the preliminary injunction did not abrogate the contractual rights of white employees. If the modified layoff plan proposed by the city to comply with the District Court's order abrogated contractual rights of the union, those rights remained enforceable. . . .

III

Assuming, as the Court erroneously does, that the District Court entered a permanent injunction, the question on review then would be whether the District Court had authority to enter it. In affirming the District Court, the Court of Appeals suggested at least two grounds on which respondents might have prevailed on the merits.

The first of these derives from the contractual characteristics of a consent decree. Because a consent decree "is to be construed for enforcement purposes essentially as a contract," *United States* v. *ITT Continental Baking Co.* (1975), respondents had the right to specific performance of the terms of the decree. If the proposed layoffs violated those terms, the District Court could issue an injunction requiring compliance with them. Alternatively, the Court of Appeals noted that a court of equity has inherent power to modify a consent decree in light of changed circumstances. Thus, if respondents could show that changed circumstances justified modification of the decree, the District Court would have authority to make such a change.

A

Respondents based their request for injunctive relief primarily on the first of these grounds, and the Court's analysis of this issue is unpersuasive. The District Court's authority to enforce the terms and purposes of the consent decree was expressly reserved in [paragraph] 17 of the decree itself: "The Court retains jurisdiction of this action for such further orders as may be necessary or appropriate to effectuate the purposes of this decree." Respondents relied on that provision in seeking the preliminary injunction. The decree obligated the city to provide certain specific relief to particular individuals, and to pursue a long-term goal to "raise the black representation in each job classification on the fire department to levels approximating the black proportion of the civilian labor force in Shelby County." The decree set more specific goals for hiring and promotion opportunities as well. To meet these goals, the decree "require[d] reasonable, good faith efforts on the part of the City."

In support of their request for a preliminary injunction, respondents claimed that the proposed layoffs would adversely affect blacks significantly out of proportion to their representation. They argued that the proposed layoffs were "designed to thwart gains made by blacks" under the decree. Their argument emphasized that the Mayor had "absolute discretion to choose which job classifications" were to be affected by the layoffs, and that the "ranks chosen by the Mayor for demotion are those where blacks are represented in the greatest number." Respondents claimed that such a layoff plan "violates the spirit of the 1980 Consent Decree." Had respondents been able to prove these charges at trial, they may well have constituted a violation of the city's obligation of good faith under the decree. On the basis of these claims, the limited evidence presented at the hearing prior to the issuance of the preliminary injunction, and the District Court's familiarity with the city's past behavior, the District Court enjoined the city from laying off blacks where the effect would have been to reduce the percentage of black representation in certain job categories. By treating the District Court's injunction as a permanent one, however, the Court first deprives respondents of the opportunity to substantiate these claims, and then faults them for having failed to do so. But without determining whether these allegations have any substance, there is simply no way to determine whether the proposed layoff plan violated the terms of the consent decree.

Even if respondents could not have shown that the proposed layoff plan conflicted with the city's obligation of good faith, [paragraph] 17 of the Decree also empowered the District Court to enter orders to "effectuate the purposes" of the decree. Thus, if the District Court concluded that the layoffs would frustrate those purposes, then the decree empowered the District Court to enter an appropriate order. . . .

The Court rejects the argument that the injunctive relief was a proper exercise of the power to enforce the purposes of the decree principally on the ground that the remedy agreed upon in the consent decree did not specifically mention layoffs. This treatment of the issue is inadequate. The power of the District Court to enter further orders to effectuate the purposes of the decree was a part of the agreed remedy. The parties negotiated for this, and it is the obligation of the courts to give it meaning. In an ideal world, a well-drafted consent decree requiring structural change might succeed in providing explicit directions for all future contingencies. But particularly in civil rights litigation in which implementation of a consent decree often takes year, such foresight is unattainable. Accordingly, parties to a consent decree typically agree to confer upon supervising courts the authority to ensure that the purposes of a decree are not frustrated by unforeseen circumstances. . . . The District Judge in these cases, who presided over the negotiation of the consent decree, is in a unique position to determine the nature of the parties' original intent, and he has a distinctive familiarity with the circumstances that shaped the decree and defined its purposes. Accordingly, he should be given special deference to interpret the general and any ambiguous terms in the decree. It simply is not a sufficient response to conclude, as the Court does, that the District Court could not enjoin the proposed layoff plan merely because layoffs were not specifically mentioned in the consent decree. . . .

B

The Court of Appeals also suggested that respondents could have prevailed on the merits because the 1981 layoffs may have justified a modification of the consent decree. . . .

The Court rejects this ground for affirming the preliminary injunction, not by examining the purposes of the *consent decree* and whether the proposed layoffs justified a modification of the decree, but rather by reference to Title VII. The Court concludes that the preliminary injunction was improper because it "imposed on the parties as an adjunct of settlement something that could not have been ordered had the case gone to trial and the plaintiffs proved that a pattern or practice of discrimination existed." Thus, the Court has chosen to evaluate the propriety of the preliminary injunction by asking what type of relief the District Court could have awarded had respondents litigated their Title VII claim and prevailed on the merits. Although it is far from clear whether that is the right question, it is clear that the Court has given the wrong answer.

Had respondents prevailed on their Title VII claims at trial, the remedies available would have been those provided by § 706(g), 42 U.S.C. § 2000e-5(g). Under that section, a court that determines that an employer has violated Title VII may "enjoin the respondent from engaging in such unlawful employment practice, and order such affirmative action as may be appropriate, which may include, *but is not limited to,* reinstatement or hiring of employees, with or without back pay . . ., *or any other equitable relief as the court deems appropriate"* (emphasis added). The scope of the relief that could have been entered on behalf of respondents had they prevailed at trial therefore depends on the nature of relief that is "appropriate" in remedying Title VII violations.

In determining the nature of "appropriate" relief under § 706(g), courts have distinguished between individual relief and race-conscious class relief. Although overlooked by the Court, this distinction is highly relevant here. In a Title VII class-action suit of the type brought by respondents, an individual plaintiff is entitled to an award of individual relief only if he can establish that he was the victim of discrimination. That requirement grows out of the general equitable principles of "make whole" relief; an individual who has suffered no injury is not entitled to an individual award. See *Teamsters* v. *United States* (1977). If victimization is shown, however, an individual is entitled to whatever retroactive seniority, backpay, and promotions are consistent with the statute's goal of making the victim whole. *Franks* v. *Bowman Transportation Co.* . . .

In Title VII class-action suits, the Courts of Appeals are unanimously of the view that race-conscious affirmative relief can also be "appropriate" under § 706(g). . . . The purpose of such relief is not to make whole any particular individual, but rather to remedy the present class-wide effects of past discrimination or to prevent similar discrimination in the future. Because the discrimination sought to be alleviated by race-conscious relief is the classwide effects of past discrimination, rather than discrimination against identified members of the class, such relief is provided to the class as a whole rather than to its individual members. . . .

In the instant case, respondents' request for a preliminary injunction did not include a request for individual awards of retroactive seniority — and, contrary to the implication of the Court's opinion, the District Court did not make any such awards. Rather, the District Court order required the city to conduct its layoffs in a race-conscious manner; specifically, the preliminary injunction prohibited the city from conducting layoffs that would "decrease the percentage of black[s]" in certain job categories. The city remained free to lay off any individual black so long as the percentage of black representation was maintained.

Because these cases arise out of a consent decree, and a trial on the merits has never taken place, it is of course impossible for the Court to know the extent and nature of any past discrimination by the city. . . .

For reasons never explained, the Court's opinion has focused entirely on what respondents have actually shown, instead of what they might have shown had trial ensued. It is improper and unfair to fault respondents for failing to show "that any of the blacks protected from layoff had been a victim of discrimination," for the simple reason that the claims on which such a showing would have been made never went to trial. The whole point of the consent decree in these cases — and indeed the point of most Title VII consent decrees — is for both parties to avoid the time and expense of litigating the question of liability and identifying the victims of discrimination. . . .

In discussing § 706(g), the Court relies on several passages from the legislative history of the Civil Rights Act of 1964 in which individual legislators stated their views that Title VII would not authorize the imposition of remedies based upon race. And while there are indications that many in Congress at the time opposed the use of race-conscious remedies, there is authority that supports a narrower interpretation of § 706(g). . . .

. . . As has been observed, moreover, the Courts of Appeals are unanimously of the view that race-conscious remedies are not prohibited by Title VII. Because the Court's opinion does not even acknowledge this consensus, it seems clear that the Court's conclusion that the District Court "ignored the policy" of § 706(g) is a statement that the race-conscious relief ordered in these cases was broader than necessary, not that race-conscious relief is never appropriate under Title VII.

IV

By dissenting, I do not mean glibly to suggest that the District Court's preliminary injunction necessarily was correct. Because it seems that the affected whites have no contractual rights that were breached by the city's modified layoff plan, the effect of the preliminary injunction was to shift the pain of the city's fiscal crisis onto innocent employees. This Court has recognized before the difficulty of reconciling competing claims of innocent employees who themselves are neither the perpetrators of discrimination nor the victims of it. . . . If the District Court's preliminary injunction was proper, it was because it correctly interpreted the original intent of the parties to the consent decree, and equitably enforced that intent in what admittedly was a zero-sum situation. If it was wrong, it was because it improperly interpreted the consent decree, or because a less painful way of reconciling the competing equities was within the court's power. In either case, the District Court's preliminary injunction terminated many months ago, and I regret the Court's insistence upon necessarily reviving a past controversy.

COURT ON SUSPECTS' RIGHTS

June 12, 1984

The Supreme Court June 12 ruled, 5-4, that police did not have to advise a criminal suspect of his constitutional rights if by doing so it would compromise public safety. In the ruling on the case, New York v. Quarles, the Court for the first time carved out an exception to the Miranda rule barring use of statements or evidence obtained from a suspect who had not been warned of his constitutional rights. The statement of rights had evolved from the Court's 1966 landmark ruling in Miranda v. Arizona. After that decision, arrested suspects were entitled to be advised of their right to remain silent, to have a lawyer present during questioning, and to have a court-appointed lawyer if they could not afford counsel. However, in some situations, the Court held in Quarles, "concern for public safety must be paramount to adherence to the literal language of the prophylactic rules enunciated in Miranda. . . . We think police officers can and will distinguish almost instinctively between questions necessary to secure the . . . safety of the public and questions designed solely to elicit testimonial evidence from a suspect."

The case involved Benjamin Quarles, a rape suspect, who was appre-hended by police in a supermarket after a chase. He had been armed; he was no longer armed when apprehended. Asked by the arresting officer where his gun was, Quarles responded, "The gun is over there." The weapon was located by the police, who only then advised Quarles of his rights. Three New York State courts subsequently ruled that neither Quarles' responses nor the gun itself could be used as evidence in prosecution for possession of an illegal firearm. The state appealed, backed by the Reagan administration.

Majority, Dissenting Opinions

By a 6-3 vote, the Court held that the gun could be used as evidence. By a 5-4 vote, the Court permitted the use of Quarles' statement locating the gun. "We do not believe that the doctrinal underpinnings of Miranda require that it be applied in all its rigor to a situation in which police officers ask questions reasonably prompted by a concern for the public safety," wrote Justice William H. Rehnquist, joined by Chief Justice Warren E. Burger and Justices Byron R. White, Harry A. Blackmun, and Lewis F. Powell Jr. In this case, Rehnquist said, the police were justified in asking their question by the "immediate necessity" of locating a loaded gun that was probably somewhere in the supermarket. The suspect had an empty gun holster when the police seized him.

Justice Sandra Day O'Connor agreed that the gun could be used as evidence but would not permit use of the statement indicating its whereabouts. "Were the Court writing from a clean slate, I could agree," she said. "But Miranda is now the law and ... the Court has not provided sufficient justification for departing from it or for blurring its now clear strictures."

Justices Thurgood Marshall, William J. Brennan Jr., and John Paul Stevens joined in disagreeing on both points. "In a chimerical quest for public safety, the majority has abandoned the rule that brought 18 years of doctrinal tranquility to the field of custodial interrogations," Marshall wrote for the three. "A public safety exception destroys forever the clarity of Miranda both for law enforcement officers and members of the judiciary...." Marshall accused the majority of ignoring the Fifth Amendment by endorsing "the introduction of coerced self-incriminating statements in criminal prosecutions." The ruling, he said, "condemns the American judiciary to a new era of post hoc inquiry into the propriety of custodial interrogations." The dissenters suggested that the gun might be admissible under the "inevitable discovery" exception recognized the day before in the case of Nix v. Williams, permitting the use of evidence collected through police misconduct when it would inevitably have been discovered.

Following are excerpts from the Supreme Court's June 12, 1984, decision in New York v. Quarles, recognizing a public-safety exception to the rule that police may not question a suspect until they have warned him of his rights; from the dissenting and concurring opinion of Justice Sandra Day O'Connor; and from the dissenting opinion of Justices Thurgood Marshall, William J. Brennan Jr., and John Paul Stevens:

No. 82-1213

New York

v.

Benjamin Quarles

On Writ of Certiorari to the Court of Appeals of New York

[June 12, 1984]

JUSTICE REHNQUIST delivered the opinion of the Court.

Respondent Benjamin Quarles was charged in the New York trial court with criminal possession of a weapon. The trial court suppressed the gun in question, and a statement made by respondent, because the statement was obtained by police before they read respondent his "*Miranda* rights." That ruling was affirmed on appeal through the New York Court of Appeals. We granted certiorari, and we now reverse. We conclude that under the circumstances involved in this case, overriding considerations of public safety justify the officer's failure to provide *Miranda* warnings before he asked questions devoted to locating the abandoned weapon.

On September 11, 1980, at approximately 12:30 a.m., Officer Frank Kraft and Officer Sal Scarring were on road patrol in Queens, New York, when a young woman approached their car. She told them that she had just been raped by a black male, approximately six feet tall, who was wearing a black jacket with the name "Big Ben" printed in yellow letters on the back. She told the officers that the man had just entered an A & P supermarket located nearby and that the man was carrying a gun.

The officers drove the woman to the supermarket, and Officer Kraft entered the stores while Officer Scarring radioed for assistance. Officer Kraft quickly spotted respondent, who matched the description given by the woman, approaching a check-out counter. Apparently upon seeing the officer, respondent turned and ran toward the rear of the store, and Officer Kraft pursued him with a drawn gun. When respondent turned the corner at the end of an aisle, Officer Kraft lost sight of him for several seconds, and upon regaining sight of respondent, ordered him to stop and put his hands over his head.

Although more than three other officers had arrived on the scene by that time, Officer Kraft was the first to reach respondent. He frisked him and discovered that he was wearing a shoulder holster which was then empty. After handcuffing him, Officer Kraft asked him where the gun was. Respondent nodded in the direction of some empty cartons and responded, "the gun is over there." Officer Kraft thereafter retrieved a loaded .38 caliber revolver from one of the cartons, formally placed respondent under arrest, and read him his *Miranda* rights from a printed card. Respondent indicated that he would be willing to answer questions without an attorney present. Officer Kraft then asked respondent if he owned the gun and where he had purchased it. Respondent answered that he did own it and that he had purchased it in Miami, Florida.

In the subsequent prosecution of respondent for criminal possession of a weapon, the judge excluded the statement, "the gun is over there," and the gun because the officer had not given respondent the warnings required by our decision in *Miranda* v. *Arizona* (1966), before asking him where the gun was located. The judge excluded the other statements about respondent's ownership of the gun and the place of purchase, as evidence tainted by the prior *Miranda* violation. The Appellate Division of the Supreme Court of New York affirmed without opinion.

The Court of Appeals granted leave to appeal and affirmed by a 4-3 vote. It concluded that respondent was in "custody" within the meaning of *Miranda* during all questioning and rejected the state's argument that the exigencies of the situation justified Officer Kraft's failure to read respondent his *Miranda* rights until after he had located the gun. The court declined to recognize an exigency exception to the usual requirements of *Miranda* because it found no indication from Officer Kraft's testimony at the suppression hearing that his subjective motivation in asking the question was to protect his own safety or the safety of the public. For the reasons which follow, we believe that this case presents a situation where concern for public safety must be paramount to adherence to the literal language of the prophylactic rules enunciated in *Miranda*.

The Fifth Amendment guarantees that "[n]o person ... shall be compelled in any criminal case to be a witness against himself." In *Miranda* this Court for the first time extended the Fifth Amendment privilege against compulsory self-incrimination to individuals subjected to custodial interrogation by the police. The Fifth Amendment itself does not prohibit all incriminating admission; "[a]bsent some officially *coerced* self-accusation, the Fifth Amendment privilege is not violated by even the most damning admissions." *United States* v. *Washington* (1977) (emphasis added). The *Miranda* Court, however, presumed that interrogation in certain custodial circumstances is inherently coercive and held that statements made under those circumstances are inadmissible unless the suspect is specifically informed of his *Miranda* rights and freely decides to forgo these rights....

In this case we have before us no claim that respondent's statements were actually compelled by police conduct which overcame his will to resist.... Thus the only issue before us is whether Officer Kraft was justified in failing to make available to respondent the procedural safeguards associated with the privilege against compulsory self-incrimination since *Miranda*.

The New York Court of Appeals was undoubtedly correct in deciding that the facts of this case come within the ambit of the *Miranda* decision as we have subsequently interpreted it. We agree that respondent was in police custody because we have noted that "the ultimate inquiry is simply whether there is a 'formal arrest or restraint on freedom of movement' of the degree associated with a formal arrest," *California* v. *Beheler* (1983) *(per curiam)*, quoting *Oregon* v. *Mathiason* (1977) *(per curiam)*. Here Quarles was surrounded by at least four police officers and was handcuffed when the questioning at issue took place. As the New York Court of

Appeals observed, there was nothing to suggest that any of the officers were any longer concerned for their own physical safety. The New York Court of Appeals' majority declined to express an opinion as to whether there might be an exception to the *Miranda* rule if the police had been acting to protect the public, because the lower courts in New York had made no factual determination that the police had acted with that motive.

We hold that on these facts there is a "public safety" exception to the requirement that *Miranda* warnings be given before a suspect's answers may be admitted into evidence, and that the availability of that exception does not depend upon the motivation of the individual officers involved. In a kaleidoscopic situation such as the one confronting these officers, where spontaneity rather than adherence to a police manual is necessarily the order of the day, the application of the exception which we recognize today should not be made to depend on *post hoc* findings at a suppression hearing concerning the subjective motivation of the arresting officer. Undoubtedly most police officers, if placed in Officer Kraft's position, would act out of a host of different, instinctive, and largely unverifiable motives — their own safety, the safety of others, and perhaps as well the desire to obtain incriminating evidence from the suspect.

Whatever the motivation of individual officers in such a situation, we do not believe that the doctrinal underpinnings of *Miranda* require that it be applied in all its rigor to a situation in which police officers ask questions reasonably prompted by a concern for the public safety. The *Miranda* decision was based in large part on this Court's view that the warning which it required police to give to suspects in custody would reduce the likelihood that the suspects would fall victim to constitutionally impermissible practices of police interrogation in the presumptively coercive environment of the station house. The dissenters warned that the requirement of *Miranda* warnings would have the effect of decreasing the number of suspects who respond to police questioning. The *Miranda* majority, however, apparently felt that whatever the cost to society in terms of fewer convictions of guilty suspects, that cost would simply have to be borne in the interest of enlarged protection for the Fifth Amendment privilege.

The police in this case, in the very act of apprehending a suspect, were confronted with the immediate necessity of ascertaining the whereabouts of a gun which they had every reason to believe the suspect had just removed from his empty holster and discarded in the supermarket. So long as the gun was concealed somewhere in the supermarket, with its actual whereabouts unknown, it obviously posed more than one danger to the public safety: an accomplice might make use of it, a customer or employee might later come upon it.

In such a situation, if the police are required to recite the familiar *Miranda* warnings before asking the whereabouts of the gun, suspects in Quarles' position might well be deterred from responding. Procedural safeguards which deter a suspect from responding were deemed acceptable in *Miranda* in order to protect the Fifth Amendment privilege; when the primary social cost of those added protections is the possibility of fewer convictions, the *Miranda* majority was willing to bear that cost. Here, had *Miranda* warnings deterred Quarles from responding to Officer Kraft's question about the whereabouts of the gun, the cost would have been something more than merely the failure to obtain evidence useful in convicting Quarles. Officer Kraft needed an answer to his question not simply to make his case against Quarles but to insure that further danger to the public did not result from the concealment of the gun in a public area.

We conclude that the need for answers to questions in a situation posing a threat to the public safety outweighs the need for the prophylactic rule protecting the Fifth Amendment's privilege against self-incrimination. We decline to place officers such as Officer Kraft in the untenable position of having to consider, often in a matter of seconds, whether it best serves society for them to ask the necessary questions without the *Miranda* warnings and render whatever probative evidence they uncover inadmissible, or for them to give the warnings in order to preserve the admissibility of evidence they might uncover but possibly damage or destroy their ability to obtain that evidence and neutralize the volatile situation confronting them.

In recognizing a narrow exception to the *Miranda* rule in this case, we acknowledge that to some degree we lessen the desirable clarity of that rule. At least in part in order to preserve its clarity, we have over the years refused to sanction attempts to expand our *Miranda* holding.... As we have in other contexts, we recognize here the importance of a workable rule "to guide police officers, who have only limited time and expertise to reflect on and balance the social and individual interests involved in the specific circumstances they confront." *Dunaway* v. *New York* (1979). But as we have pointed out, we believe that the exception which we recognize today lessens the necessity of that on-the-scene balancing process. The exception will not be difficult for police officers to apply because in each case it will be circumscribed by the exigency which justifies it. We think police officers can and will distinguish almost instinctively between questions necessary to secure their own safety or the safety of the public and questions designed solely to elicit testimonial evidence from a suspect.

The facts of this case clearly demonstrate that distinction and an officer's ability to recognize it. Officer Kraft asked only the question necessary to locate the missing gun before advising respondent of his rights. It was only after securing the loaded revolver and giving the warnings that he continued with investigatory questions about the ownership and place of purchase of the gun. The exception which we recognize today, far from complicating the thought processes and on-the-scene judgments of police officers, will simply free them to follow their legitimate instincts when confronting situations presenting a danger to the public safety.

We hold that the Court of Appeals in this case erred in excluding the statement, "the gun is over there," and the gun because of the officer's failure to read respondent his *Miranda* rights before attempting to locate the weapon. Accordingly we hold that it also erred in excluding the subsequent statements as illegal fruits of a *Miranda* violation. We therefore reverse and remand for further proceedings not inconsistent with this opinion.

It is so ordered.

JUSTICE O'CONNOR, concurring in part in the judgment and dissenting in part.

In *Miranda* v. *Arizona* (1966), the Court held unconstitutional, because inherently compelled, the admission of statements derived from in-custody questioning not preceded by an explanation of the privilege against self-incrimination and the consequences of foregoing it. Today, the Court concludes that overriding considerations of public safety justify the admission of evidence — oral statements and a gun — secured without the benefit of such warnings. In so holding, the Court acknowledges that it is departing from prior precedent and that it is "lessen[ing] the desirable clarity of [the *Miranda*] rule. Were the Court writing from a clean slate, I could agree with its holding. But *Miranda* is now the law and, in my view, the Court has not provided sufficient justification for departing from it or for blurring its now clear strictures. Accordingly, I would require suppression of the initial statement taken from the respondent in this case. On the other hand, nothing in *Miranda* or the privilege itself requires exclusion of nontestimonial evidence derived from informal custodial interrogation, and I therefore agree with the Court that admission of the gun in evidence is proper....

The *Miranda* Court itself considered objections akin to those raised by the Court today. In dissent, JUSTICE WHITE protested that the *Miranda* rules would "operate indiscriminately in all criminal cases, regardless of the severity of the crime or the circumstances involved." But the *Miranda* Court would not accept any suggestion "that society's need for interrogation [could] outweig[h] the privilege." To that Court, the privilege against self-incrimination was absolute and therefore could not be "abridged."

Since the time *Miranda* was decided, the Court has repeatedly refused to bend the literal terms of that decision. To be sure, the Court has been sensitive to the substantial burden the *Miranda* rules place on local law enforcement efforts, and consequently has refused to extend the decision or to increase its strictures on law enforcement agencies in almost any way.... But wherever an accused has been taken into "custody" and subjected to "interrogation" without warnings, the Court has consistently prohibited the use of his responses for prosecutorial purposes at trial.... As a consequence, the "meaning of *Miranda* has become reasonably clear and law enforcement practices have adjusted to its strictures." *Rhode Island* v. *Innis* (1980) (BURGER, C. J., concurring)....

In my view, a "public safety" exception unnecessarily blurs the edges of the clear line heretofore established and makes *Miranda's* requirements more difficult to understand. In some cases, police will benefit because a reviewing court will find that an exigency excused their failure to administer the required warnings. But in other cases, police will suffer because, though they thought an exigency excused their noncompliance, a reviewing court will view the "objective" circumstances differently and require exclusion of admissions thereby obtained. The end result will be a finespun new doctrine on public safety exigencies incident to custodial interrogation, complete with the hair-splitting distinctions that currently plague our Fourth Amendment jurisprudence. . . .

The justification the Court provides for upsetting the equilibrium that has finally been achieved — that police cannot and should not balance considerations of public safety against the individual's interest in avoiding compulsory testimonial self-incrimination — really misses the critical question to be decided. . . . *Miranda* has never been read to prohibit the police from asking questions to secure the public safety. Rather, the critical question *Miranda* addresses is who shall bear the cost of securing the public safety when such questions are asked and answered: the defendant or the State. *Miranda,* for better or worse, found the resolution of that question implicit in the prohibition against compulsory self-incrimination and placed the burden on the State. When police ask custodial questions without administering the required warnings, *Miranda* quite clearly requires that the answers received be presumed compelled and that they be excluded from evidence at trial. . . .

The Court concedes, as it must, both that respondent was in "custody" and subject to "interrogation" and that his statement "the gun is over there" was compelled within the meaning of our precedent. . . . In my view, since there is nothing about an exigency that makes custodial interrogation any less compelling, a principled application of *Miranda* requires that respondent's statement be suppressed. . . .

Citizens in our society have a deeply rooted social obligation "to give whatever information they may have to aid in law enforcement." *Miranda* v. *Arizona*. Except where a recognized exception applies, "the criminal defendant no less than any other citizen is obliged to assist the authorities." *Roberts* v. *United States* (1980). The privilege against compulsory self-incrimination is one recognized exception, but it is an exception nonetheless. Only the introduction of a defendant's own *testimony* is proscribed by the Fifth Amendment's mandate that no person "shall be compelled in any criminal case to be a witness against himself." That mandate does not protect an accused from being compelled to surrender *nontestimonial* evidence against himself. See *Fisher* v. *United States* (1976).

The distinction between testimonial and nontestimonial evidence was explored in some detail in *Schmerber* v. *California* [1966], a decision this Court handed down within a week of deciding *Miranda*. The defendant in *Schmerber* had argued that the privilege against self-incrimination barred the state from compelling him to submit to a blood test, the results of which would be used to prove his guilt at trial. The State, on the other hand, had urged that the privilege prohibited it only from compelling the accused to make a formal testimonial statement against himself in an official legal proceeding. This Court rejected both positions. It favored an approach that protected the "accused only from being compelled to testify against himself, or otherwise provide the State with evidence of a testimonial or communicative nature." The blood tests were admissible because they were neither testimonial nor communicative in nature.

. . . Thus, *Schmerber* resolved the dilemma by allowing admission of the nontestimonial, but not the testimonial, products of the State's compulsion.

The Court has applied this bifurcated approach in its subsequent cases as well. . . . Thus, based on the distinction first articulated in *Schmerber,* "a strong analytical argument can be made for an intermediate rule whereby[,] although [the police] cannot require the suspect to speak by punishment or force, the nontestimonial [evidence derived from] speech that is [itself] excludable for failure to comply with the *Miranda* code could still be used." H. Friendly, Benchmarks, 280 (1967).

To be sure, admission of nontestimonial evidence secured through informal custodial interrogation will reduce the incentives to enforce the *Miranda* code. But that fact simply begs the question of *how much* enforcement is appropriate. There are some situations, as the Court's struggle to accommodate a "public safety" exception demonstrates, in which the societal cost of administering the *Miranda* warnings is very high indeed. The *Miranda* decision quite practically does not express any societal interest in having those warnings administered for their own sake. Rather, the warnings and waiver are only required to ensure that "testimony" used against the accused at trial is voluntarily given. Therefore, if the testimonial aspects of the accused's custodial communications are suppressed, the failure to administer the *Miranda* warnings should cease to be of concern (where interference with assistance of counsel has no affect on trial, no Sixth Amendment violation lies). The harm caused by failure to administer *Miranda* warnings relates only to admission of testimonial self-incriminations, and the suppression of such incriminations should by itself produce the optimal enforcement of the *Miranda* rule. . . .

JUSTICE MARSHALL, with whom JUSTICE BRENNAN and JUSTICE STEVENS join, dissenting.

The police in this case arrested a man suspected of possessing a firearm in violation of New York law. Once the suspect was in custody and found to be unarmed, the arresting officer initiated an interrogation. Without being advised of his right not to respond, the suspect incriminated himself by locating the gun. The majority concludes that the State may rely on this incriminating statement to convict the suspect of possessing a weapon. I disagree. The arresting officers had no legitimate reason to interrogate the suspect without advising him of his rights to remain silent and to obtain assistance of counsel. By finding on these facts justification for unconsented interrogation, the majority abandons the clear guidelines enunciated in *Miranda* v. *Arizona* (1966), and condemns the American judiciary to a new era of *post hoc* inquiry into the propriety of custodial interrogations. More significantly and in direct conflict with this Court's long-standing interpretation of the Fifth Amendment, the majority has endorsed the introduction of coerced self-incriminating statements in criminal prosecutions. I dissent....

The majority's entire analysis rests on the factual assumption that the public was at risk during Quarles' interrogation. This assumption is completely in conflict with the facts as found by New York's highest court. Before the interrogation began, Quarles had been "reduced to a condition of physical powerlessness."...

The majority's treatment of the legal issues presented in this case is no less troubling than its abuse of the facts. Before today's opinion, the Court had twice concluded that, under *Miranda* v. *Arizona,* police officers conducting custodial interrogations must advise suspects of their rights before any questions concerning the whereabouts of incriminating weapons can be asked. *Rhode Island* v. *Innis* (1980); *Orozo* v. *Texas* (holding). Now the majority departs from these cases and rules that police may withhold *Miranda* warnings whenever custodial interrogations concern matters of public safety.

... In a chimerical quest for public safety, the majority has abandoned the rule that brought eighteen years of doctrinal tranquility to the field of custodial interrogations. As the majority candidly concedes, a public-safety exception destroys forever the clarity of *Miranda* for both law enforcement officers and members of the judiciary. The Court's candor cannot mask what a serious loss the administration of justice has incurred.

This case is illustrative of the chaos the "public-safety" exception will unleash....

Though unfortunate, the difficulty of administering the "public-safety" exception is not the most profound flaw in the majority's decision. The majority has lost sight of the fact that *Miranda* v. *Arizona* and our earlier custodial-interrogation cases all implemented a constitutional privilege against self-incrimination. The rules established in these cases were designed to protect criminal defendants against prosecutions based on coerced self-incriminating statements. The majority today turns its back on these constitutional considerations, and invites the government to prosecute through the use of what necessarily are coerced statements....

In fashioning its "public-safety" exception to *Miranda*, the majority makes no attempt to deal with the constitutional presumption established by that case. The majority does not argue that police questioning about issues of public safety is any less coercive than custodial interrogations into other matters. The majority's only contention is that police officers could more easily protect the public if *Miranda* did not apply to custodial interrogations concerning the public's safety. But *Miranda* was not a decision about public safety; it was a decision about coerced confessions. Without establishing that interrogations concerning the public's safety are less likely to be coercive than other interrogations, the majority cannot endorse the "public-safety" exception and remain faithful to the logic of *Miranda* v. *Arizona*....

Indeed, in the efficacy of the "public-safety" exception lies a fundamental and constitutional defect. Until today, this Court could truthfully state that the Fifth Amendment is given "broad scope" "where there has been genuine compulsion of testimony." *Michigan* v. *Tucker* [1974]. Coerced confessions were simply inadmissible in criminal prosecutions. The "Public-safety" exception departs from this principle by expressly inviting police officers to coerce defendants into making incriminating statements, and then permitting prosecutors to introduce those statements at trial. Though the majority's opinion is cloaked in the beguiling language of utilitarianism, the Court has sanctioned *sub silentio* criminal prosecutions based on compelled self-incriminating statements. I find this result in direct conflict with the Fifth Amendment's dictate that "No person . . . shall be compelled in any criminal case to be a witness against himself." . . .

POPE'S TRIP TO SWITZERLAND

June 12, 15, 17, 1984

Pope John Paul II landed in Zurich on June 12, beginning a six-day tour of Switzerland. More than 47 percent of the country's 6.3 million inhabitants are Catholic; 44.5 percent are Protestant.

The pope's itinerary for this, his twenty-second foreign trip, was characteristically rigorous. From Zurich he traveled June 12 to Lugano, the center of Italian-Swiss Roman Catholicism, and then to Geneva. The pontiff met with a number of groups June 13 in Fribourg, the site of Switzerland's major Roman Catholic university. The following day his schedule included stops near Bern, the country's capital. There he met with members of the Swiss government, a group of ambassadors, and representatives of Switzerland's 18,300 Jews. The pontiff spent the fourth day of his visit in Einsiedeln at that city's famous Benedictine abbey. Other major stops before his return to Rome June 17 included Lucerne and Sion, the capital of the Alpine canton of Valais.

Unity, Obedience Themes

In Geneva the pontiff met with representatives from the World Council of Churches June 12 and spoke at a worship service in the council's Ecumenical Center. While noting that "separations and ... frequent differences in methods of operation" existed between Catholics and Protestants, the pope stated that he regarded Catholic participation in the ecumenical movement as a priority. He cited his visit to the Protestant council as a sign of his "will for unity."

The pontiff also visited in Geneva the European center of the Orthodox church. There he spoke of the Roman Catholic will to mend the age-old split between the Eastern and Western churches.

Unity within the Catholic church and the duty of clerical obedience were themes John Paul II stressed in his addresses to Swiss clergy. At several points during his tour, the pope encountered criticism from a group of theologians of the Vatican's stand on a variety of issues. In Einsiedeln June 15 he received a list of grievances from Rev. Markus Fischer, representative of the German-speaking priests of Switzerland. The complaints generally concerned issues on which some of the clergy believed the pope took too conservative a stand, including celibacy of priests, the role of women in the church, and laicization of priests who had married. The pope questioned whether the concerns were shared by most of the Swiss clergy, but he did address some of the issues. In particular, the pontiff remained firm in his rejection of laicization, the process of allowing married priests to return to the lay state, and of any weakening of the priestly vow of chastity.

On June 17 the pope celebrated mass at the airport at Sion. A crowd of 80,000, the largest of the tour, gave the pope his warmest reception. During the mass, the pope ordained nine priests and reminded all priests of their duty to obey their bishops and the pope, Bishop of Rome.

The pontiff's message was meant, in part, for Archbishop Marcel Lefebvre, who headed the most troublesome dissident movement of the Catholic church. Ten miles from Sion, in the village of Econe, Lefebvre founded a seminary from which he directed his traditionalist, or integrist, movement. Lefebvre and his followers rejected many of the teachings of the Second Vatican Council, such as celebration of the mass in the vernacular and active involvement in the ecumenical movement. Lefebvre's dissident movement worried the Vatican, and church officials had predicted that the pope would not ignore Lefebvre in his speeches.

> *Following are excerpts from Pope John Paul II's address to the World Council of Churches at Geneva June 12, 1984; from an address to representatives of the priests of Switzerland delivered at Einsiedeln June 15; and from a homily delivered June 17 during a mass in Sion, Switzerland:*

ADDRESS IN GENEVA

... 1. Thank you for having invited me to visit you here in the Ecumenical Center during my visit to the Catholics of Switzerland. How fitting it is that we should meet to pray together and to talk as brothers and sisters at this season of the year when Christians throughout the world celebrate the event of Pentecost. ...

Pentecost, the gift of the Spirit, is for the church the ever-living source of its unity and the beginning of its mission. Our meeting coincides with the spirit of these days.

The simple fact of my presence here among you, as bishop of Rome paying a fraternal visit to the World Council of Churches, is a sign of this will for unity. From the beginning of my ministry as bishop of Rome, I have insisted that the engagement of the Catholic Church in the ecumenical movement is irreversible and that the search for unity was one of its pastoral priorities. . . .

2. To be sure, the Catholic Church entered on the hard ecumenical task bringing with it a conviction. Despite the moral afflictions which have marked the life of its members and even of its leaders in the course of history, it is convinced that in the ministry of the bishop of Rome it has preserved the visible pole and guarantee of unity in full fidelity to the apostolic tradition and to the faith of the fathers. . . .

To be in communion with the bishop of Rome is to give visible evidence that one is in communion with all who confess that same faith, with those who have confessed it since Pentecost and with those who will confess it until the day of the Lord shall come. That is our Catholic conviction, and our fidelity to Christ forbids us to give it up. We also know that it is a difficulty for most of you, whose memories are perhaps marked by certain sorrowful recollections for which my predecessor Pope Paul VI asked your forgiveness. But we have to discuss this in all frankness and friendship, with the seriousness full of promise shown in the work done to prepare the Faith and Order study on baptism, eucharist and ministry. If the ecumenical movement is really led by the Holy Spirit, the time for that will come. . . .

The defense of human beings and their dignity, their liberty, their rights, the fuller meaning of their existence are a major concern of the Catholic Church. Wherever it can, it strives to make its contribution to promoting the conditions required for human development in the full truth of human existence created and redeemed by God, convinced that "man is the primary route that the church must travel in fulfilling her mission" (*Redemptor Hominis,* 14).

By intervening in favor of human beings, whatever the political regime of the country, it insists on making the distinction and relative autonomy of church from state. It is respectful of the noble and difficult function of those who have charge of the common good. It undertakes a dialogue with them and enters into the stable relation of a common agreement to enable peace and justice to progress. At the same time it judges that it is not its role to intervene in the forms of government which people choose for their temporal affairs or to preach violence in order to change them. But it invites its lay members to take an active part in their administration and orientation according to evangelical principles, and it keeps its freedom in order to judge from an ethical point of view the conditions which favor the progress of people and of communities or which, on the contrary, are gravely harmful to the rights of people or to civil and religious liberty (cf.

Pastoral Constitution on the Church in the Modern World, 42, 75).

On the latter point the Catholic Church desires that other Christian churches and communities raise their voices along with hers so that the citizens' authentic freedom of conscience and of worship is guaranteed as well as the liberty of the churches to train their ministers and to provide them with the means they need to develop the faith of their peoples. Many persons of good will and from international organizations understand today the importance of this fundamental right. But faced with the gravity of the facts, it seems to me necessary that, together, all Christians and Christian communities — when they have the possibility of expressing themselves — should give their common witness on what is vital to them.

10. Further we should meet together more and more in all fields where human beings, because of the burden of their environment, experience great difficulties on the social, ethical or religious levels in living according to the dignity of their vocation. So many human values — equity in relationships, authenticity of love, fraternal and generous openness to others — are obscured in the lives of individuals and of families. Despite our separations and the frequent differences in methods of operation, we often meet on the level of social thought and action, and we witness to one and the same vision, based on the same reading of the Gospel. Certainly it happens that we differ about the means. Our positions on ethical questions are not always the same. But what unites us already allows us to hope that a day will come when we shall arrive at a convergence on this fundamental ground.

Yes, the will "to follow Christ" in his love for those who are in need leads us to common action. And temporary though it be, this communion in evangelical service lets us glimpse what our whole and perfect communion in faith, charity and the eucharist could be, will be. It is not then a purely chance encounter inspired only by pity in the face of misery or a reaction in the face of injustice. It belongs to our march together toward unity. . . .

ADDRESS AT EINSIEDELN

1. It is a great joy for me to meet you, and I attribute capital importance to this meeting. You priests of the 26 cantons of Switzerland have gathered at Einsiedeln. You have been delegated by your fellow priests or have come of your own accord. Through you I address all the clergy of your country. It is given to you every day to accomplish an irreplaceable work, basically, that the whole church in Switzerland may grow in truth, in charity, in holiness. . . .

I have read and have carefully listened to the body of questions and the preoccupations which have been frankly expounded. I have received them seriously. I do not know whether they correspond to the thoughts and concerns of the clergy of Switzerland as a whole, whom I wish to address. It seems to me that the crucial problem is that of announcing the Gospel of

Jesus Christ to the world which is yours, an often indifferent world, tempted by materialism, sometimes atheist. That is what I want to talk to you about.

But beforehand I will try to clarify certain problems which are worrying you and which concern relations between the local church and the universal church, whose charge the Lord has entrusted to me in a particular way. And on this point my duty as pope is to confirm my brothers, to point out the way, to teach the will of Jesus Christ and his church.

2. The Second Vatican Council was certainly a providential moment for various reasons. Among other things it was a providential event for the unity and universality of the church. It is in this sense that it is necessary to view its ecumenical content as well as the problem of the church's relationship with "non-Christian religions" and again, the church's situation in the world of our time. The council there laid down new bases for comprehending the church's mission and enabling her to carry it out. It is the same with the mission of priests.

3. The teaching on the collegiality of the episcopate, which I have just been discussing with your bishops, has a very close link with the question of the unity and universality of the church. Without taking up the whole of that theme again, I would remind you that the bishops' mission always has a "universal" character. . . .

Against that background, the identity of the priest which comes to him from the sacrament of orders is not only confirmed, it is also reinforced and renewed. As I have just said to the bishops, it in no way means "clericalization"of the laity, even less "laicization" of the clergy. It is along the line of deepening their own identity that priests can truly realize the council, individually and in common. It was in this framework that the resolutions of the 1971 synod took their place, particularly those concerning the basis of motivations and obligation to preserve celibacy in the Latin church (Part 2, no. 4).

I myself addressed this problem in a first letter to priests on the occasion of Holy Thursday 1979. I said, "The importance of this problem is so grave, its link with the language of the Gospel itself is so close, that we cannot . . . in this summary think in categories different from those which were used by the council, the Synod of Bishops and the great Pope Paul VI. . . . In order to be disposed to such service (of the people of God), to such solicitude, to such love, the priest's heart must be free. Celibacy is a sign of a liberty in view of service" (8).

According to the tradition of the Catholic Church, celibacy is not only a juridical adjunct to the sacrament of orders, but it is also a personal commitment, a commitment assumed in all maturity, toward Christ and the church. Dispensations, even if they are possible, cannot do away with, diminish or cause the character of that commitment to be disregarded. Fidelity to a state in life that has been taken on is required for the dignity of the person itself. What exigency the Gospel and the church demonstrate in the case of spouses!

6. Having clarified these questions in response to your preoccupations, I now come to the pastoral situation, which may appear discouraging to a certain number of you.

What you actually feel deeply is the progressive pressure of a world which does without God or thinks it can do without God. This is manifested statistically at the level of the number of baptisms requested or of religious practice. But it is a widespread phenomenon, broader and deeper, and affects the faith itself: Some doubt, others alter the faith or refuse it. Such a situation is characteristic of the affluent societies of the Western world. Priests might be tempted to become discouraged in it. It is a grave matter to see assemblies diminish and observe that the world seems to be sinking into religious indifference or is attaching itself to "false gods.". . .

The priest acts in *persona Christi* — in the name of the head of the body, notably through the sacraments, but also in announcing the Gospel. We must rejoice to see the laity and women religious making their valuable contribution in manifold forms of catechesis and preparation for the sacraments, but the priest keeps his specific responsibility there. It is from his mouth that God's word is quite especially awaited (cf. PO, 4), and he retains the ordinary ministry of the sacraments, together with the deacon in certain cases.

It is in this sense, finally, that the priest has to enjoy the autonomy necessary for his ministry. He is not the community's delegate: He is sent to it. Obedience to his bishop, the witness given by a simple and poor life, his celibacy, go to emphasize his particular relationship with Christ and the community.

Dear friends, fidelity to our marvelous vocation establishes us in a fullness of joy that nothing can tarnish, no one can take from us. I wish you that perfect joy promised those who follow the Lord. And I hope that it shall radiate through you upon the face of the ecclesial community. May Our Lady, *causa nostrae laetitiae,* keep you in joy!

11. To end, I have one more question for you. It concerns the essentially universal character of your sacerdotal mission. With the bishop and under his leadership, the priest has a direct responsibility in the particular church and an indirect responsibility for the church as a whole. This is true in any case for every Christian.

The church is living a period of struggle for justice and for peace in the world of today. By reason of what she is, she tries to take part in that struggle. As at her beginning and then in various periods of her history, the church of our time is yet again the church of martyrs. Among these are the laity, there are also bishops and priests, who in various ways "bear with ill treatment for the sake of the name of Jesus" (cf. Acts 5:41). They suffer because of their pastoral service in truth and love.

Dear friends, be united with our brothers. Be in solidarity with them. Their testimony helps you, among other things, to appreciate the requirements of the priesthood at their right value for each of us, for us who live here in countries where religious liberty fundamentally exists.

The testimony of those brothers of whom I have been speaking shows how far love for Christ, love for the church and for immortal souls can go!

Let us learn this love! Let us learn it with humility, every day! It is from that love that the church grows.

In the shrine of Einsiedeln, I pray the mother of Christ that the church in Switzerland may grow. That it may progress thanks to such love!

HOMILY AT SION

... In the context of today's eucharistic liturgy, some sons of your Switzerland — from Sion or other Swiss dioceses or institutes — are going to become priests "according to the order of Melchizedek" (cf. Ps. 109 (110): 4; Heb. 5:6, 7:17), by receiving the sacrament of orders....

Those who receive sacerdotal ordination today become ministers of the sacrifice accomplished for the salvation of the world. They make it present. They are ministers of the eucharist: Their sacerdotal life develops from that center. All the rest will be a preparation for or an echo of this sacramental act. Day after day they will be present to human existence and will have to lead their brothers to the redemption achieved by Christ and celebrated in the eucharist....

Priests are at the same time guides to their neighbor on the way to salvation.

They remain in the midst of the people of God and say like Moses, "Lord, deign to go in the midst of us" (Ex. 34:9)....

They are teachers of truth, through announcing the Gospel, through arousing and strengthening faith, by pointing out the way to follow in order to remain on the path of salvation. They are the guardians of the uprightness of consciences. And so they are servants of that God who proclaimed to Moses: "The Lord, the Lord, a merciful and gracious God, slow to anger and rich in kindness and fidelity" (Ex. 34:7). They are servants of Jesus Christ through whom God forgives our faults and our sins, and makes us into a people belonging to him....

... The other aspects of their sacerdotal life, which I will only indicate, develop around those central functions. The priest participates in the task of the unique mediator who is Christ. But he knows his weakness. He does nothing of himself. He is strong with the strength of God, through a permanent disposition which consecrates his very being. But he has to try to respond. He must seek the holiness which befits the minister of Christ, with the Holy Spirit who has been given to him through the laying on of hands. He has to offer himself entirely together with him, he has "to live what he accomplishes" (cf. Ordination Prayer, on handing over the bread and the wine). He has to transmit what he has contemplated. He has to be a man of prayer, now in solitude like Moses on the mountain, now as the leader or president of the prayer of his brothers.

On the plain, he must live near people, simply, poorly, at their service, like Christ, who came to serve. He will take account of their worries and their speech when announcing the Gospel of Jesus Christ — the whole Gospel — in a way capable of being understood. But he must also initiate them into the mystery at the same time. Through his way of living, the priest must be seen as the man linked with Jesus Christ, notably through celibacy. He becomes "the living sign of the world to come, which is already present through faith and charity" (cf. *Presbyterorum Ordinis,* 16). He is "the man for others." He must be a witness, a prophet. He will courageously also accept becoming a sign of contradiction in his turn, sometimes being the suffering servant, but he will always be the man of the peace which Christ came to bring on earth. . . .

He will do all this as a collaborator with his bishop, who for his part acts in union with the successor of St. Peter. When the priest is obedient to both of these, he lives in communion with the whole church. Indeed his priesthood has that of the local bishop's as its foundation, and the local bishop is the father of the presbyterium as a whole. In this way the priest can contribute to the building up of the church in unity. He does not dispose of God's gifts according to his own will. According to St. Paul, he is "an administrator of the mysteries of God. The first requirement of an administrator is that he prove trustworthy" (1 Cor. 4:1-2).

Everything that the priest is has its reason for being ultimately in the church, through the church and for the church. So he must love the church, feel and think with the church (*sentire cum ecclesia*): not the church of the past or the church which is not yet present, but the concrete church present now, whose wrinkles and stains also must be wiped away through his humble help. This love makes the priest ready for the oblation which the church expects from him for the salvation of all. . . .

The ministerial priesthood is such an important, such a necessary, office that we should all be concerned for vocations. The Diocese of Sitten decided in 1978 to sharpen all Christians' awareness of this theme. I hope that even more fruit will grow from that, among you here as in the other Swiss dioceses to which these new priests will return.

Of course, the whole people of the baptized is called upon to be active in the life of the Christian community and to take part in bearing witness to the Gospel in the world. The priest's mission is precisely in service to such participation. But his mission has its particular nature and has no substitute. There is no dualism or competition here, but only a necessary, reciprocal fulfillment, in respect to each other's own calling, and there the bishops must give guidance toward a harmonious working together. The church community corresponds fully to its mission and readiness for commitment only when vocations to the priesthood can bud and ripen in it, and without them the community itself cannot develop. Vocation and mission — to office or apostolate — always come from God, from the most holy Trinity. . . .

TRUDEAU'S FAREWELL ADDRESS

June 14, 1982

Prime Minister Pierre Elliot Trudeau on June 16 stepped down as leader of Canada's Liberal Party, a position he had held for 16 years. John Turner, a former Trudeau Cabinet officer, succeeded Trudeau as Liberal leader and was sworn in as prime minister on June 30. On September 4, however, Conservative Brian Mulroney won a landslide victory over Turner in the national election, to become Canada's 18th prime minister. Mulroney's Progressive Conservative Party won the biggest political majority in Canada's history, effectively ending the Trudeau era.

Trudeau's Tenure

Trudeau announced February 29 his plans to resign from public office. He had served as prime minister for 16 years — longer than any other Canadian prime minister except William Lyon MacKenzie King, who held the position for a total of 22 years. Trudeau was swept into office in 1968, setting off a frenzy that the press termed "Trudeaumania." From that time on, his political agenda and accomplishments and his flamboyant personal style dominated Canadian life. His period in office was interrupted only once when Joe Clark, the former Conservative leader, headed a minority government from June 1979 to March 1980.

Under Trudeau's leadership, Canada became officially bilingual and multicultural. His handling of the French-English conflict was, in the estimation of many political analysts, his greatest achievement. He

407

worked to integrate French Canadians, who made up roughly one-quarter of the country's population, into the English-dominated culture and economy. He also successfully battled attempts by Quebec, a predominantly French-speaking province, to separate from the nation.

Trudeau worked to repatriate and amend the British North America Act of 1867, Canada's founding document. In November 1981, after a decade of infighting, a majority of Canada's provincial premiers approved a new constitution and charter of rights; in April 1982 Queen Elizabeth II transferred full authority over the Canadian constitution from Britain to Canada. (Historic Documents of 1982, p. 317)

A third major undertaking of the Trudeau administration was the attempt to "canadianize" the country's economy and lessen its dependence on the United States. To this end, Trudeau limited foreign investment in energy fields and established a Foreign Investment Review Agency to determine whether foreign investments were in Canada's best interests.

Trudeau spent his last months in office promoting a personal peace and disarmament plan. He visited Moscow, Washington, Peking, and a number of European capitals in an attempt to bridge the widening gap between the United States and the Soviet Union regarding arms limitations. Some observers pointed out that his crusade provided Trudeau and his Liberal Party with positive press coverage and visibility and with an opportunity for a much-needed boost in the popularity polls. Others remarked that the international focus of Trudeau's disarmament project provided him with a graceful way to exit from domestic politics and helped to establish a role as an elder statesman.

The Liberal leadership convention in Ottawa June 14 opened with an emotional tribute to Trudeau. He then gave a farewell address, praising Liberal Party values and touching on some of the major accomplishments of his career. Trudeau, who had withheld his backing from any candidate, ended his speech with a pledge to support whomever was elected. "[Y]ou will find me there following him because we have much more building to do!" he asserted.

General Election Campaign

The Liberals elected Turner, a corporate lawyer, as the new party leader on June 16. He was sworn in as prime minister two weeks later. Hoping to capitalize on the Liberals' improved standings in the popularity polls following the convention, Turner called for an early election. September 4 was set as election day.

Montreal attorney Brian Mulroney, leader of the Progressive Conservative Party, was Turner's primary opponent. In early July, when Turner scheduled the September election, he led Mulroney in popular support.

However, a series of gaffes and a wooden campaign style hurt Turner. By early August Mulroney, an attractive and articulate campaigner, led in the polls.

The two candidates held remarkably similar views on campaign issues. Both were fiscal conservatives; both stressed the need to cut the federal deficit. Both men, however, supported costly Liberal social welfare programs. The two agreed on the need to improve Canadian-U.S. relations, and both pledged support for the program of official bilingualism begun by Trudeau.

The candidates' views on a variety of issues may have been close, but the outcome of the race was not. On September 4, Canadian voters handed Mulroney and his Conservative Party the biggest political majority in the country's history. The Conservatives won 211 of 282 seats in the House of Commons. Mulroney was sworn in as prime minister on September 17.

> *Following are excerpts of Pierre Elliott Trudeau's farewell address, delivered in English and French, as prime minister to the Liberal Party of Canada leadership convention in Ottawa, June 14:*

... I thought that these fifteen or twenty past years were, in a certain sense, a period of adolescence for our country, a coming of age. Norman Jewison talked about seeing our identity from abroad. Really, those years were years of turmoil and revolt and search for identity and the slow learning of maturity for our country. I will not fall into the trap of talking about those fifteen, sixteen years together. I hope historians will do it gently. And I will not talk either about the future that lies ahead.

You delegates, you Liberals, are here in this city at this time to choose the person who will lead our party into the future; and I will leave it to the candidates, those from whom you will choose your leader, to talk to you about that future. But it seemed to me, as I saw these various events rushing before our eyes and listened to the reminiscences and tributes, it seemed to me that I discovered something more of the Liberal Party. I discovered again something we always knew: that liberalism is not so much a program, it is not so much a series of policies, it is an approach to politics, it is a belief in people.

The answers of today to the problems of yesterday become, in their turn, the problems of tomorrow which the people of the day after tomorrow will have to answer.

A country is not something you build like the pharaohs built the pyramids, and leave standing there to defy eternity. A country is something that is built every day out of certain basic values, those that many of you were good enough to mention in your speeches and in your songs[,] those values, for instance, that we see in the Canadian Charter of Rights, which for the first time gives all of us an identity rooted in a Constitution that no government can destroy.

Liberalism is dealing with change. It is meeting challenge. Liberalism is reform. We have the inheritance of Locke and Jefferson and Montesquieu and Acton and Mill. They taught us that problems that men create can be solved by men of good will, if they apply their reason to those problems. That is what Liberals do. They see the difficulties. They look for rational solutions. They make sure that reason prevails over prejudice. They tear down the barriers that separate what a country is from what it can become. They remove obstacles to freedom and liberty so that each human being can fulfill himself or herself according to his potential. They do not seek to equalize everybody. They do ensure that equality of opportunity is there for all, so that each can fulfill himself. They confront the powerful. They confound the secure. They challenge the conventional. They are asking questions all the time. They are looking for answers to those problems which prevent a country from fulfilling its destiny; and they see examples throughout the history of our party.

Our party was defined in 1877 by Wilfrid Laurier, when in Quebec City at the Canadian Club he stated: "I am a Liberal. I am one of those who think that everywhere in human affairs, there are abuses to be corrected. There are strengths to be developed. There are new horizons to see." Wilfrid Laurier did in fact see those new horizons. He opened Canada to other countries of the world. He brought Canada into the 20th century.

Mackenzie King, after him, saw that the weak in our society needed protection. He saw that true liberalism is not giving freedom to everybody — freedom to the strong to oppress the weak. He ushered in that great series of Liberal reforms, from old age pensions to family allowances, unemployment insurance and all those great measures that made Canada the foremost democracy in giving services to its people.

Louis St. Laurent, while building a strong nation in this country, and a solid economy, saw during the postwar period the major problems which only now we are starting to tackle: the East-West problem which caused him to create the Atlantic Alliance with our allies. He saw the North-South problem, and it was in the time of St. Laurent that the Colombo Plan, the first of the great undertakings to share with the Third World, was begun.

Then it was Lester Pearson, with all his love and knowledge, who sought further improvement and gave us Medicare and the Canada Assistance Plan. But he also taught the world and taught the United Nations the way of peacekeeping.

These are leaders. They were looking at the problems of the day and bringing solutions for the times. I said earlier I am not going to talk about the solutions we tried to bring in the last fifteen years. But just remember, just look back. Let us not talk of things we did. Let us just think of people.

Fifteen years ago, a woman had never sat in the Speaker's chair of the House of Commons or of the Senate. A woman had never occupied the post of lieutenant-governor or of governor-general. A woman had never sat on the Supreme Court of Canada, or even been a member of a superior Court in Canada. No one voted until they were twenty-one. There was no Jew in the Canadian cabinet and there never had been. There were none on the benches of the Supreme court. There was no French-Canadian who had ever been Minister of Finance, or Minister of Trade, for that matter. There was no Negro Canadian sitting in the Senate, nor a Greek, nor an Italian. There was no Indian who had been a member of the Canadian cabinet nor lieutenant-governor of a province. There was no provision in the Constitution stating that aboriginal rights were entrenched and did exist.

The people of Canada have reached a certain maturity. And when abroad, as I think Norman Jewison was saying, they look at Canada, they see a country with compassion, with an ideal of sharing.

They see a country which is a meeting of cultures. They see a country where the rich provinces help the poor provinces, where the French-speaking people and the English-speaking people live together, and where we have replaced the language of biculturalism by multiculturalism, because we recognize that Canada is more than two founding races when in reality the Indians and the Eskimos, two of them in the Senate, were there before us.

Liberalism is setting people free, but it is setting people free not only through the heritage of those philosophers. Liberalism is not only a party of purpose, it is a party of the people.

Our roots as Liberals in this country (I am not talking about Jefferson here. I am not talking about the former democracies or the old democracies. I am talking about our country and our roots.) Go back to Mackenzie and to Papineau, those people who dared to challenge the establishment, the family compact. Our roots go back to the "rouges" of Quebec and the Clear Grits of Ontario.

They were the radicals of those days. They believed in universal franchise and they ushered in mass democracy of which we are the inheritors today. They were our ancestors, these Liberals.

I have found that in any of the reforms — the difficult reforms that we have tried to bring in throughout my years — whenever the going was tough and we were opposed by the multinationals or by the provincial premiers, or by the superpowers, I found that if our case was right all we had to do to win was to talk over the heads of the premiers, over the heads of the multinationals, over the heads of the superpowers to the people of this land, to the people of Canada.

That is how we won the referendum, by going over the heads of all those pretentious intellectuals from the Parti Québécois and talking to the people of Quebec, and saying to them: "This country belongs to you!"

That is how we brought the Constitution home, after fifty-four years of politicians, federal and provincial, trying to come to grips with this problem. Fifty-four years of frustration, where we were dealing not with what the people wanted, but with more power for the federal government or more power for the provinces. What did the Liberal Party finally do? We brought in the "people's package." We said to the people: Forget the powers that the premiers want and forget the powers that the federal government wants to keep. Do you want a constitution of your own, do you want us to patriate it, do you want a charter of rights? And the people said yes! And that is how we got it!

I remember my caucus, and I remember those days in 1980 after the election when we were saying: "Okay, we are going to the people." And as in that clip that you showed, I said: "If we cannot get it from the premiers, we will get it through a referendum. We will ask the people." And I was discussing what we should do. Should we get just patriation, or should we maybe add some linguistic rights? They said: "Hell, no. Let us go first class."

They said to me: "We'll go in a Cadillac!"

And that is how we got the Charter, because these men in the caucus and these women said the people want nothing less than first-class, and they got it.

So it was with every reform, whether it be Petro-Canada or canadianizing our economy, FIRA [Foreign Investment Review Agency], whether it be extending . . . remembering fifteen years ago, our territorial sea was a piddling three miles. Even the Northwest Passage was not in Canadian waters. And now, a 200-mile territorial zone in which we control the resources of the sea and under the sea. This is part of our identity, as our Bill of Rights is.

So remember this, because tonight I am stepping down as your leader. In two days, we will be choosing a new leader and you will find me there with you following him, because we have much more building to do!

Such splendid loves I dreamed of . . . and we will dream some more. Our hopes are high. Our faith in the people is great. Our courage is strong and our dreams for this beautiful country will never die.

COURT ON ANTITRUST LAW

June 19, 1984

Reversing a 37-year-old doctrine of federal antitrust law, the Supreme Court on June 19 ruled that a corporation and its wholly owned subsidiary could not be charged with conspiracy to restrain trade in violation of antitrust statutes. The 5-3 ruling was a victory for the Reagan administration, which had mounted a major assault on key elements of federal antitrust policy.

The Court's decision in the case, Copperweld Corp. v. Independence Tube Corp., *did not answer the question of whether a corporation and its partially owned subsidiary could be found liable under section one of the Sherman Antitrust Act. Nor did it immunize companies and their subsidiaries from liability for violating other sections of antitrust laws.*

Known as the "intra-enterprise conspiracy doctrine," the legal doctrine the Court reversed had grown out of a 1947 decision in United States v. Yellow Cab Co. *That decision held that a parent company and its subsidiary could be held liable for conspiring to curtail trade or competition. While the Reagan administration and many businesses asked the Court to reverse the 1947 doctrine, the attorneys general of 47 states urged the Court to keep it.*

Background

Congress moved into federal regulation of commercial enterprise in 1890 with the passage of the Sherman Antitrust Act "to protect commerce against unlawful restraints and monopolies." Federal regulation of commerce was further strengthened in 1914 by passage of the Clayton Act and the Federal Trade Commission Act.

The "intra-enterprise conspiracy doctrine" was based on section one of the Sherman Act, which prohibited "every contract, combination in the form of trust or otherwise, or conspiracy in restraint of trade or commerce." Section two of the Sherman Act prohibited monopolies. The Reagan administration's attack on antitrust policy was directed at the existing ban on resale price maintenance; the general presumption that it was illegal for suppliers to "tie" two products together, forcing a consumer who bought one to buy the other; and the view that a company and its subsidiary could conspire in violation of the antitrust laws.

Copperweld Case

In the Copperweld case, the Court overturned a $7.5 million damage award to Independence Tube Corp. that had been based on a finding that Copperweld and its wholly owned subsidary, Regal Tube Co., violated antitrust laws when they urged suppliers and customers not to deal with Independence. A new competitor to Regal in the structural steel tubing market, Independence had been formed by a former Regal official. The damage award was upheld in 1982 by the 7th U.S. Circuit Court of Appeals. Copperweld asked the Supreme Court to overturn the damage award and to repudiate the "intra-enterprise conspiracy doctrine" as inconsistent with economic reality. Ruling in Copperweld's favor were Chief Justice Warren E. Burger and Justices Harry A. Blackmun, Lewis F. Powell Jr., William H. Rehnquist, and Sandra Day O'Connor. Justices William J. Brennan Jr., Thurgood Marshall, and John Paul Stevens dissented, while Justice Byron R. White did not participate.

Writing for the majority, Chief Justice Burger said that "While this Court has previously seemed to acquiesce in the intra-enterprise conspiracy doctrine, it has never explored or analyzed in detail the justifications for such a rule." A parent company and a wholly owned subsidiary, Burger wrote, "have a complete unity of interest. They are not unlike a multiple team of horses drawing a vehicle under the control of a single driver." He continued, "Indeed, the very notion of an 'agreement' in Sherman Act terms between a parent and a wholly owned subsidiary lacks meaning."

The dissenting justices criticized the Court majority for making a sweeping declaration that a wholly owned subsidiary was incapable of conspiring with its parent to restrain trade. In the Copperweld case, Justice Stevens wrote, the challenged activities had "precious little to do with effective integration between parent and subsidiary corporations." Rather, he said, their purpose was to "exclude a potential competitor of the subsidiary from the market."

Other Antitrust Cases

In another case, the Court on March 27 ruled that it was not invariably an antitrust violation for the provider of a service to require a customer to buy a second service along with the first. In Jefferson Parish Hospital District No. 2 v. Hyde, *it held unanimously that a hospital in the New Orleans, Louisiana, area did not engage in illegal anti-competitive conduct when it granted a single firm the right to provide anesthesia services for all surgery at the hospital.*

Finally, the Court ruled 7-2 on June 27 that the National Collegiate Athletic Association (NCAA) had violated antitrust law by preventing individual schools from negotiating the rights to football telecasts. The ruling, in NCAA v. University of Oklahoma, *came on a suit against the NCAA by the University of Georgia and the University of Oklahoma and appeared to represent strict enforcement of the antitrust laws.*

> *Following are excerpts from the Supreme Court's June 19 decision in* Copperweld Corp. v. Independence Tube Corp., *declaring that a corporation and its wholly owned subsidiary could not be charged with conspiring to restrain trade in violation of antitrust laws; and from the dissenting opinion of Justice John Paul Stevens:*

No. 82-1260

Copperweld Corporation, et al., Petitioners *v.* Independence Tube Corporation	On writ of Certiorari to the United States Court of Appeals for the Seventh Circuit

[June 19, 1984]

CHIEF JUSTICE BURGER delivered the opinion of the Court.

We granted certiorari to determine whether a parent corporation and its wholly owned subsidiary are legally capable of conspiring with each other under §1 of the Sherman Act.

I

A

The predecessor to petitioner Regal Tube Co. was established in Chicago in 1955 to manufacture structural steel tubing used in heavy equipment, cargo vehicles, and construction. From 1955 to 1968 it remained a wholly owned subsidiary of C. E. Robinson Co. In 1968 Lear Siegler, Inc., purchased Regal Tube Co. and operated it as an unincorporated division. David Grohne, who had previously served as vice president and general manager of Regal, became president of the division after the acquisition.

In 1972 petitioner Copperweld Corp. purchased the Regal division from Lear Siegler; the sale agreement bound Lear Siegler and its subsidiaries not to compete with Regal in the United States for five years. Copperweld then transferred Regal's assets to a newly formed, wholly owned Pennsylvania corporation, petitioner Regal Tube Co. The new subsidiary continued to conduct its manufacturing operations in Chicago but shared Copperweld's corporate headquarters in Pittsburgh.

Shortly before Copperweld acquired Regal, David Grohne accepted a job as a corporate officer of Lear Siegler. After the acquisition, while continuing to work for Lear Siegler, Grohne set out to establish his own steel tubing business to compete in the same market as Regal. In May 1972 he formed respondent Independence Tube Corp., which soon secured an offer from the Yoder Co. to supply a tubing mill. In December 1972 respondent gave Yoder a purchase order to have a mill ready by the end of December 1973.

When executives at Regal and Copperweld learned of Grohne's plans, they initially hoped that Lear Siegler's noncompetition agreement would thwart the new competitor. Although their lawyer advised them that Grohne was not bound by the agreement, he did suggest that petitioners might obtain an injunction against Grohne's activities if he made use of any technical information or trade secrets belonging to Regal. The legal opinion was given to Regal and Copperweld along with a letter to be sent to anyone with whom Grohne attempted to deal. The letter warned that Copperweld would be "greatly concerned if [Grohne] contemplates entering the structural tube market ... in competition with Regal Tube" and promised to take "any and all steps which are necessary to protect our rights under the terms of our purchase agreement and to protect the know-how, trade secrets, etc. which we have purchased from Lear Siegler." Petitioners later asserted that the letter was intended only to prevent third parties from developing reliance interests that might later make a court reluctant to enjoin Grohne's operations. When Yoder accepted respondent's order for a tubing mill on February 19, 1973, Copperweld sent Yoder one of these letters; two days later Yoder voided its acceptance. After respondent's efforts to resurrect the deal failed, respondent arranged to have a mill supplied by another company, which performed its agreement even though it too received a warning letter from Copperweld. Respondent began operations on September 13, 1974, nine months later than it could have if Yoder had supplied the mill when originally agreed.

Although the letter to Yoder was petitioners' most successful effort to discourage those contemplating doing business with respondent, it was not their only one. Copperweld repeatedly contacted banks that were considering financing respondent's operations. One or both petitioners also approached real estate firms that were considering providing plant space to respondent and contacted prospective suppliers and customers of the new company.

B

In 1976 respondent filed this action in the District Court against petitioners and Yoder. The jury found that Copperweld and Regal had conspired to violate § 1 of the Sherman Act, 26 Stat. 209, as amended, 15 U.S.C. § 1, but that Yoder was not part of the conspiracy. It also found that Copperweld, but not Regal, had interfered with respondent's contractual relationship with a potential customer of respondent, Deere Plow & Planter Works, and had slandered respondent to Deere; and that Yoder had breached its contract to supply a tubing mill. . . .

C

The United States Court of Appeals for the Seventh Circuit affirmed. It noted that the exoneration of Yoder from antitrust liability left a parent corporation and its wholly owned subsidiary as the only parties to the § 1 conspiracy. The court questioned the wisdom of subjecting an "intra-enterprise" conspiracy to antitrust liability, when the same conduct by a corporation and an unincorporated division would escape liability for lack of the requisite two legal persons. However, relying on its decision in *Photovest Corp.* v. *Fotomat Corp.* (1979), the Court of Appeals held that liability was appropriate "when there is enough separation between the two entities to make treating them as two independent actors sensible." It held that the jury instructions took account of the proper factors for determining how much separation Copperweld and Regal in fact maintained in the conduct of their businesses. It also held that there was sufficient evidence for the jury to conclude that Regal was more like a separate corporate entity than a mere service arm of the parent.

We granted certiorari to reexamine the intra-enterprise conspiracy doctrine, and we reverse.

II

Review of this case calls directly into question whether the coordinated acts of a parent and its wholly owned subsidiary can, in the legal sense contemplated by § 1 of the Sherman Act, constitute a combination or conspiracy. The so-called "intra-enterprise conspiracy" doctrine provides that § 1 liability is not foreclosed merely because a parent and its subsidiary are subject to common ownership. The doctrine derives from declarations in several of this Court's opinions.

In no case has the Court considered the merits of the intra-enterprise conspiracy doctrine in depth. Indeed, the concept arose from a far narrower rule. Although the Court has expressed approval of the doctrine on a number of occasions, a finding of intra-enterprise conspiracy was in all but perhaps one instance unnecessary to the result.

The problem began with *United States* v. *Yellow Cab Co.* (1947). The Court stated that even restraints in a vertically integrated enterprise were not "necessarily" outside the Sherman Act. . . .

. . . In *Yellow Cab,* the affiliation of the defendants was irrelevant because the original acquisitions were *themselves* illegal. An affiliation "flowing from an illegal conspiracy" would not avert sanctions. Common ownership and control were irrelevant because restraint of trade was "the primary object of the combination," which was created in a " 'deliberate, calculated' " manner. Other language in the opinion is to the same effect. . . .

The ambiguity of the *Yellow Cab* holding yielded the one case giving support to the intra-enterprise conspiracy doctrine. In *Kiefer-Stewart Co.* v. *Joseph E. Seagram & Sons, Inc.* (1951), the Court held that two wholly owned subsidiaries of a liquor distiller were guilty under § 1 of the Sherman Act for jointly refusing to supply a wholesaler who declined to abide by a maximum resale pricing scheme. The Court off-handedly dismissed the defendants' argument that "their status as 'mere instrumentalities of a single manufacturing-merchandising unit' makes it impossible for them to have conspired in a manner forbidden by the Sherman Act." With only a citation to *Yellow Cab* and no further analysis, the Court stated that the

> "suggestion runs counter to our past decisions that common ownership and control does not liberate corporations from the impact of the antitrust laws"

and stated that this rule was "especially applicable" when defendants "hold themselves out as competitors."

Unlike the *Yellow Cab* passage, this language does not pertain to corporations whose initial affiliation was itself unlawful. In straying beyond *Yellow Cab,* the *Kiefer-Stewart* Court failed to confront the anomalies an intra-enterprise doctrine entails. It is relevant nonetheless that, were the case decided today, the same result probably could be justified on the ground that the subsidiaries conspired with wholesalers other than the plaintiff. An intra-enterprise conspiracy doctrine thus would no longer be necessary to a finding of liability on the facts of *Kiefer-Stewart.* . . .

In short, while this Court has previously seemed to acquiesce in the intra-enterprise conspiracy doctrine, it has never explored or analyzed in detail the justifications for such a rule; the doctrine has played only a relatively minor role in the Court's Sherman Act holdings.

III

Petitioners, joined by the United States as *amicus curiae,* urge us to repudiate the intra-enterprise conspiracy doctrine. The central criticism is that the doctrine gives undue significance to the fact that a subsidiary is separately incorporated and thereby treats as the converted activity of two entities what is really unilateral behavior flowing from decisions of a single enterprise.

We limit our inquiry to the narrow issue squarely presented: whether a parent and its wholly owned subsidiary are capable of conspiring in violation of § 1 of the Sherman Act. We do not consider under what circumstances, if any, a parent may be liable for conspiring with an affiliated corporation it does not completely own.

A

The Sherman Act contains a "basic distinction between concerted and independent action." *Monsanto Co.* v. *Spray-Rite Service Corp.* (1984). The conduct of a single firm is governed by § 2 alone and is unlawful only when it threatens actual monopolization. It is not enough that a single firm appears to "restrain trade" unreasonably, for even a vigorous competitor may leave that impression. For instance, an efficient firm may capture unsatisfied customers from an inefficient rival, whose own ability to compete may suffer as a result. This is the rule of the marketplace and is precisely the sort of competition that promotes the consumer interests that the Sherman Act aims to foster. In part because it is sometimes difficult to distinguish robust competition from conduct with long-run anti-competitive effects, Congress authorized Sherman Act scrutiny of single firms only when they pose a danger of monopolization. Judging unilateral conduct in this manner reduces the risk that the antitrust laws will dampen the competitive zeal of a single aggressive entrepreneur.

Section 1 of the Sherman Act, in contrast, reaches unreasonable restraints of trade effected by a "contract, combination . . . or conspiracy" between *separate* entities. It does not reach conduct that is "wholly unilateral." *Albrecht* v. *Herald Co.* (1968); accord *Monsanto Co.* v. *Spray-Rite Corp.* . . . .

The reason Congress treated concerted behavior more strictly than unilateral behavior is readily appreciated. Concerted activity inherently is fraught with anticompetitive risk. It deprives the marketplace of the independent centers of decisionmaking that competiton assumes and demands. In any conspiracy, two or more entities that previously pursued their own interests separately are combining to act as one for their common benefit. This not only reduces the diverse directions in which economic power is aimed but suddenly increases the economic power moving in one particular direction. Of course, such mergings of resources may well lead to efficiencies that benefit consumers, but their anticompetitive potential is sufficient to warrant scrutiny. . . .

B

The distinction between unilateral and concerted conduct is necessary for a proper understanding of the terms "contract, combination . . . or conspiracy" in § 1. Nothing in the literal meaning of those terms excludes coordinated conduct among officers or employees of the *same* company. But it is perfectly plain that an internal "agreement" to implement a single, unitary firm's policies does not raise the antitrust dangers that § 1 was designed to police. The officers of a single firm are not separate economic actors pursuing separate economic interests, so agreements among them do not suddenly bring together economic power that was previously pursuing divergent goals. Coordination within a firm is as likely to result from an effort to compete as from an effort to stifle competition. In the marketplace, such coordination may be necessary if a business enterprise is to compete effectively. For these reasons, officers or employees of the same firm do not provide the plurality of actors imperative for a § 1 conspiracy.

There is also general agreement that § 1 is not violated by the internally coordinated conduct of a corporation and one of its unincorporated divisions. Although this court has not previously addressed the question, there can be little doubt that the operations of a corporate enterprise organized into divisions must be judged as the conduct of a single actor. The existence of an unincorporated division reflects no more than a firm's decision to adopt an organizational division of labor. A division within a corporate structure pursues the common interests of the whole rather than interests separate from those of the corporation itself; a business enterprise establishes divisions to further its own interests in the most efficient manner. Because coordination between a corporation and its division does not represent a sudden joining of two independent sources of economic power previously pursuing separate interests, it is not an activity that warrants § 1 scrutiny.

Indeed, a rule that punished coordinated conduct simply because a corporation delegated certain responsibilities to autonomous units might well discourage corporations from creating divisions with their presumed benefits. This would serve no useful antitrust purpose but could well deprive consumers of the efficiencies that decentralized management may bring.

C

For similar reasons, the coordinated activity of a parent and its wholly owned subsidiary must be viewed as that of a single enterprise for purposes of § 1 of the Sherman Act. A parent and its wholly owned subsidiary have a complete unity of interest. Their objectives are common, not disparate; their general corporate actions are guided or determined not by two separate corporate consciousnesses, but one. They are not unlike a multiple team of horses drawing a vehicle under the control of a single driver. With or without a formal "agreement," the subsidiary acts for the benefit of the parent, its sole shareholder. If a parent and a wholly owned subsidiary do "agree" to a course of action, there is no sudden joining of economic resources that had previously served different interests, and there is no justification for § 1 scrutiny.

Indeed, the very notion of an "agreement" in Sherman Act terms between a parent and a wholly owned subsidiary lacks meaning. . . .

The intra-enterprise conspiracy doctrine looks to the form of an enterprise's structure and ignores the reality. Antitrust liability should not depend on whether a corporate subunit is organized as an unincorporated division or a wholly owned subsidiary. A corporation has complete power to maintain a wholly owned subsidiary in either form. The economic, legal, or other considerations that lead corporate management to choose one structure over the other are not relevant to whether the enterprise's conduct seriously threatens competition. . . .

If antitrust liability turned on the garb in which a corporate subunit was clothed, parent corporations would be encouraged to convert subsidiaries into unincorporated divisions. . . .

The error of treating a corporate division differently from a wholly owned subsidiary is readily seen from the facts of this case. Regal was operated as an unincorporated division of Lear Siegler for four years before it became a wholly owned subsidiary of Copperweld. Nothing in this record indicates any meaningful difference between Regal's operations as a division and its later operations as a separate corporation. Certainly nothing suggests that Regal was a greater threat to competiton as a subsidiary of Copperweld than as a division of Lear Siegler. Under either arrangement, Regal might have acted to bar a new competitor from entering the market. In one case it could have relied on economic power from other quarters of the Lear Siegler corporation; instead it drew on the strength of its separately incorporated parent, Copperweld. From the standpoint of the antitrust laws, there is no reason to treat one more harshly than the other. As Chief Justice Hughes cautioned, "[r]ealities must dominate the judgment." *Appalachian Coals, Inc. v. United States.*

D

Any reading of the Sherman Act that remains true to the Act's distinction between unilateral and concerted conduct will necessarily disappoint those who find that distinction arbitrary. . . .

The appropriate inquiry in this case, therefore, is not whether the coordinated conduct of a parent and its wholly owned subsidiary may ever have anticompetitive effects, as the dissent suggests. Nor is it whether the term "conspiracy" will bear a literal construction that includes parent corporations and their wholly owned subsidiaries. For if these were the proper inquiries, a single firm's conduct wuld be subject to § 1 scrutiny whenever the coordination of two employes was involved. Such a rule would obliterate the Act's distinction between unilateral and concerted conduct, contrary to the clear intent of Congress as interpreted by the weight of judicial authority. See *supra*, n. 15. Rather, the appropriate inquiry requires us to explain the logic underlying Congress' decision to exempt unilateral conduct from § 1 scrutiny, and to assess whether that logic similarly excludes the conduct of a parent and its wholly owned subsidiary. Unless we second-guess the judgment of Congress to limit § 1 to concerted conduct, we can only conclude that the coordinated behavior of a parent and its wholly owned subsidiary falls outside the reach of that provision.

Although we recognize that any "gap" the Sherman Act leaves is the sensible result of a purposeful policy decision by Congress, we also note that the size of any such gap is open to serious question. Any anticompetitive activities of corporations and their wholly owned subsidiaries meriting antitrust remedies may be policed adequately without resort to an intra-enterprise conspiracy doctrine. A corporation's initial acquisition of control will always be subject to scrutiny under § 1 of the Sherman Act and § 7 of the Clayton Act, 38 Stat. 731, 15 U.S.C. § 18. Thereafter, the enterprise is fully subject to § 2 of the Sherman Act and § 5 of the Federal Trade Commission Act, 38 Stat. 719, 15 U.S.C. § 45. That these statutes are adequate to control dangerous anticompetitive conduct is suggested by the fact that not a single holding of antitrust liability by this Court would today be different in the absence of an intra-enterprise conspiracy doctrine. It is further suggested by the fact that the Federal Government, in its administration of the antitrust laws, no longer accepts the concept that a corporation and its wholly owned subsidiaries can "combine" or "conspire" under § 1. Elimination of the intra-enterprise conspiracy doctrine with respect to corporations and their wholly owned subsidiaries will therefore not cripple antitrust enforcement. It will simply eliminate treble damages from private state tort suits masquerading as antitrust actions.

IV

We hold that Copperweld and its wholly owned subsidiary Regal are incapable of conspiring with each other for purposes of § 1 of the Sherman Act. To the extent that prior decisions of this Court are to the contrary, they are disapproved and overruled. Accordingly, the judgment of the Court of Appeals is reversed.

It is so ordered.

JUSTICE STEVENS, with whom JUSTICE BRENNAN and JUSTICE MARSHALL join, dissenting.

It is safe to assume that corporate affiliates do not vigorously compete with one another. A price fixing or market allocation agreement between two or more such corporate entities does not, therefore, eliminate any competition that would otherwise exist. It makes no difference whether such an agreement is labeled a "contract," a "conspiracy" or merely a policy decision, because it surely does not unreasonably restrain competition within the meaning of the Sherman Act. The Rule of Reason has always given the courts adequate latitude to examine the substance rather than the form of an arrangement when answering the question whether collective action has restrained competition within the meaning of § 1.

Today the Court announces a new per se rule: a wholly-owned subsidiary is incapable of conspiring with its parent under § 1 of the Sherman Act. Instead of redefining the word "conspiracy," the Court would be better advised to continue to rely on the Rule of Reason. Precisely because they do not eliminate competition that would otherwise exist but rather enhance the ability to compete, restraints which enable effective integration between a corporate parent and its subsidiary — the type of arrangement the Court is properly concerned with protecting — are not prohibited by § 1. Thus, the Court's desire to shield such arrangements from antitrust liability provides no justification for the Court's new rule.

In contrast, the case before us today presents the type of restraint that has precious little to do with effective integration between parent and subsidiary corporations. Rather, the purpose of the challenged conduct was to exclude a potential competitor of the subsidiary from the market. The jury apparently concluded that the two defendant corporations — Copperweld and its subsidiary Regal — had successfully delayed Independence's entry into the steel tubing business by applying a form of economic coercion to potential suppliers of financing and capital equipment, as well as to potential customers. Everyone seems to agree that this conduct was tortious as a matter of state law. This type of exclusionary conduct is plainly distinguishable from vertical integration designed to achieve competitive efficiencies. If, as seems to be the case, the challenged conduct was manifestly anticompetitive, it should not be immunized from scrutiny under § 1 of the Sherman Act.

[Section I omitted]

II

The language of § 1 of the Sherman Act is sweeping in its breadth: "Every contract, combination in the form of trust or otherwise, or conspiracy, in restraint of trade or commerce among the several States, is declared to be illegal."... This broad construction is illustrated by the Court's refusal to limit the statute to actual agreements. Even mere acquiescence in an anticompetitive scheme has been held sufficient to satisfy the statutory language.

Since the statute was written against the background of the common law, reference to the common law is particularly enlightening in construing the statutory requirement of a "contract, combination in the form of trust or otherwise, or conspiracy." Under the common law, the question whether affiliated corporations constitute a plurality of actors within the meaning of the statute is easily answered. The well-settled rule is that a corporation is a separate legal entity; the separate corporate form cannot be disregarded. The Congress that passed the Sherman Act was well-acquainted with this rule. . . . Thus it has long been the law of criminal conspiracy that the officers of even a single corporation are capable of conspiring with each other or the corporation. This Court has held that a corporation can conspire with its employee, and that a labor union can "combine" with its business agent within the meaning of § 1. This concept explains the *Timken* Court's statement that the affiliated corporations in that case made "agreements between legally separate persons," 341 U.S., at 598. Thus, today's holding that agreements between parent and subsidiary corporations involve merely unilateral conduct is at odds with the way that this Court has traditionally understood the concept of a combination or conspiracy, and also at odds with the way in which the Congress that enacted the Sherman Act surely understood it.

Holding that affiliated corporations cannot constitute a plurality of actors is also inconsistent with the objectives of the Sherman Act. Congress was particularly concerned with "trusts," hence it named them in § 1 as a specific form of "combination" at which the statute was directed. Yet "trusts" consisted of affiliated corporations. As Senator Sherman explained:

> "Because these combinations are always in many States and, as the Senator from Missouri says, it will be very easy for them to make a corporation within a State. So they can; but that is only one corporation of the combination. The combination is always of two or more, and in one case of forty-odd corporations, all bound together by a link that holds them under the name of trustees, who are themselves incorporated under the laws of one of the States.". . .

Thus, the corporate subsidiary, when used as a device to eliminate competition, was one of the chief evils to which the Sherman Act was addressed. The anomaly in today's holding is that the corporate devices most similar to the original "trusts" are now those which free an enterprise from antitrust scrutiny.

III

The Court's reason for rejecting the concept of a combination or conspiracy among a parent corporation and its wholly-owned subsidiary is that it elevates form over substance — while in form the two corporations are separate legal entities, in substance they are a single integrated enterprise and hence cannot comprise the plurality of actors necessary to satisfy § 1. In many situations the Court's reasoning is perfectly sensible, for the affiliation of corporate entities often is procompetitive precisely because, as the Court explains, it enhances efficiency. A challenge to conduct that is merely an incident of the desirable integration that accompanies such affiliation should fail. However, the protection of such conduct provides no justification for the Court's new rule, precisely because such conduct cannot be characterized as an unreasonable restraint of trade violative of § 1. Conversely, the problem with the Court's new rule is that it leaves a significant gap in the enforcement of § 1 with respect to anticompetitive conduct that is entirely unrelated to the efficiencies associated with integration.

Since at least *United States* v. *Colgate & Co.* (1919) § 1 has been construed to require a plurality of actors. This requirement, however, is a consequence of the plain statutory language, not of any economic principle. As an economic matter, what is critical is the presence of market power, rather than a plurality of actors. From a competitive standpoint, a decision of a single firm possessing power to reduce output and raise prices above competitive levels has the same consequence as a decision by two firms acting together who have acquired an equivalent amount of market power through an agreement not to compete. Unilateral conduct by a firm with market power has no less anticompetitive potential than conduct by a plurality of actors which generates or exploits the same power, and probably more, since the unilateral actor avoids the policing problems faced by cartels. . . .

. . . When conduct restrains trade not merely by integrating affiliated corporations but rather by restraining the ability of others to compete, that conduct has competitive significance drastically different from procompetitive integration. In these cases, the affiliation assisted exclusionary conduct; it was not the competitive equivalent of unilateral integration but instead generated power to restrain marketwide competition. . . .

In this case, it may be that notices to potential suppliers of respondent emanating from Copperweld carried more weight than would notices coming only from Regal. There was evidence suggesting that Regal and Copperweld were not integrated, and that the challenged agreement had little to do with achieving precompetitive efficiencies and much to do with protecting Regal's market position. The Court does not even try to explain why their common ownership meant that Copperweld and Regal were merely obtaining benefits associated with the efficiencies of integration. Both the District Court and the Court of Appeals thought that their agreement had a very different result — that it raised barriers to entry and imposed an appreciable marketwide restraint. The Court's discussion of the justifications for corporate affiliation is therefore entirely abstract — while it dutifully lists the procompetitive justifications for corporate affiliation, it fails to explain how any of them relate to the conduct at issue in this case. What is challenged here is not the fact of integration between Regal and Copperweld, but their specific agreement with respect to Independence. That agreement concerned the exclusion of Independence from the market, and not any efficiency resulting from integration. The facts of this very case belie the conclusion that affiliated corporations are incapable of engaging in the kind of conduct that threatens marketwide competition. The Court does not even attempt to assess the competitive significance of the conduct under challenge here — it never tests its economic assumptions against the concrete facts before it. Use of economic theory without reference to the competitive impact of the particular economic arrangement at issue is properly criticized when it produces overly broad per se rules of antitrust liability; criticism is no less warranted when a per se rule of antitrust immunity is adopted in the same way.

In sum, the question that the Court should ask is not why a wholly owned subsidiary should be treated differently from a corporate division, since the immunity accorded that type of arrangement is a necessary consequence of *Colgate*. Rather the question should be why two corporations that engage in a predatory course of conduct which produces a marketwide restraint on competition and which, as separate legal entities, can be easily fit within the language of § 1, should be immunized from liability because they are controlled by the same godfather. That is a question the Court simply fails to confront. I respectfully dissent.

COURT ON CLEAN AIR
ENFORCEMENT BY EPA
June 25, 1984

President Ronald Reagan's campaign to lighten the regulatory burden on business and industry took a giant step forward June 25 when the Supreme Court reinstated controversial clean air regulations that environmentalists had challenged as too permissive. The Court's decision in the three cases, Environmental Protection Agency v. Natural Resources Defense Council (NRDC), Chevron USA Inc. v. NRDC, American Iron and Steel Institute v. NRDC, *came by a vote of 6-0. Supporting the administration were Chief Justice Warren E. Burger and associate justices Harry A. Blackmun, William J. Brennan Jr., Lewis F. Powell Jr., John Paul Stevens, and Byron R. White. Justices Sandra Day O'Connor, William H. Rehnquist, and Thurgood Marshall took no part in the decision.*

The Court held that the 1981 decision of the Environmental Protection Agency (EPA) to permit states to use the "bubble concept" for enforcing the Clean Air Act in areas that had not yet met clean air standards was "a reasonable accommodation of manifestly competing interests." Use of this concept permitted existing plants to make major changes in their facilities without complying with all of the law's standards governing new sources of pollution. As long as pollution from a new source in one part of a plant was offset by reductions in emissions from another part, the plant as a whole could be treated as though it were a single unit enclosed in a "bubble." Jimmy Carter's administration had rejected use of the bubble concept, but the Reagan EPA adopted it.

In 1982 the U.S. Court of Appeals for the District of Columbia, acting in a suit brought by the Natural Resources Defense Council, blocked

*EPA's clean air regulations, finding them inconsistent with the purpose
of the Clean Air Act — to improve the quality of the nation's air. The administration and industry representatives appealed, asking the justices
to find that the appeals court had overstepped its proper role in blocking
the regulations.*

*Underlying the clean air issue in the case were a number of larger
questions closely related to the administration's efforts to ease the
burden of federal regulation on business. The clean air case, focusing on
the power of an agency to redefine key terms as it implemented
regulatory legislation, was seen as the administration's second line of
attack on federal regulation. Its first, frontal assault — directly rescinding certain regulations — resulted in a major defeat in June 1983, when
the Court rejected as arbitrary and capricious the administration's
attempt to rescind a requirement that all cars be equipped with passive
safety restraints — automatic seat belts or air bags. In that case, the
Court told the administration it had to provide reasoned justification for
rescinding regulations. With rescission made considerably more difficult,
the use of redefinition as an alternative route to deregulation became
more important.*

Administration, Environmentalist Views

*The legal arguments in the clean air case concerned the proper
definition of a "major stationary source" of pollution. The 1977 Clean Air
Act Amendments (PL 95-95) required new sources of pollution in "nonattainment" areas where national clean air standards had not been met
to undergo strict review before they were constructed. Under PL 95-95 a
company wishing to build a new pollution-emitting source in an area with
unhealthy air could do so only after showing that the state had a
complete air pollution control program, that emissions from the new unit
would be offset by a reduction in pollution elsewhere, that the new source
emitted pollution at the lowest achievable rate, that all the company's
units in the state were in compliance with clean air requirements and —
in areas where clean air deadlines had been extended from 1982 to 1987
— that the benefits of the new source outweighed its costs.*

*Administration and industry arguments for the bubble concept focused
primarily on the balance of power between courts and executive agencies,
the proper federal-state relationship in clean air enforcement, and the
need to avoid stifling economic growth. "The decision of the court of
appeals ... constitutes an unwarranted usurpation of the authority
reserved to the administrative agency," according to the administration
brief. "Nobody in Congress focused sharply or pointedly" on the definition of "major stationary source" of pollution when the Clean Air Act
Amendments were passed in 1977, the government argued, and so the
task of defining the term was left to the EPA. The EPA definition was*

reasonable, consistent with the law, and should be upheld by federal judges, who had limited power to review such executive decisions, the administration said.

Furthermore, the government argued, the bubble concept was in line with the intent of Congress to give states flexibility in deciding how to enforce the Clean Air Act and improve air quality while permitting economic growth. By exempting many in-plant changes from the costly and often slow process of clean air review, the concept actually encouraged replacement of older polluting equipment with cleaner new units, the administration said.

Chevron's brief underscored the last point, pointing to the company's nearly completed modernization of a refinery in the San Francisco Bay area, an improvement exempted from the review process under the bubble concept. The modernization reduced total emissions from the refinery, but was the sort of change that might not have taken place, the brief said, if Chevron had known that it would have had to undergo the clean air review and compliance process the appeals court ruling required for each such change.

The environmentalists, on the other hand, contended that EPA's definition of "stationary source" as an entire plant "conflict[ed] with the terms, legislative history and purpose of the Clean Air Act." The NRDC said the administation played "the unseemly role of a willing amnesiac" in assuming that because Congress did not include a definition of "source" in 1977, it left that key word undefined. The Clean Air Act of 1970 defined the term as "any building, structure, facility or installation" emitting air pollutants, and Congress in 1977 clearly intended EPA to continue using that definition, the NRDC said. EPA's 1981 redefinition of "source" sharply reversed the rule in effect since passage of the 1970 act, the brief continued. The redefinition was both contrary to the law and arbitrary, unsupported by any emperical evidence that it would encourage improvement in the nation's air quality, the NRDC concluded.

There was no disagreement on the stringent review requirements for an entirely new plant built in a non-attainment area, according to the NRDC. The question simply was over the application of those requirements to new units within existing plants — a category that accounted for more than 90 percent of the new air-polluting projects built in areas with unhealthy air. Nearly all of these were required to undergo pre-construction review before adoption of the bubble concept; henceforth they would all be exempt, warned the council.

Court Decision

Finding the "bubble concept" a reasonable policy choice for EPA to make, Justice Stevens emphasized the agency's broad power to make *such decisions and the courts' limited role in reviewing them. "A court may not substitute its own construction of a statutory provision for a reasonable interpretation made by the administrator of an agency," he wrote. Because Congress did not define "major stationary source," the key term at issue in the case, the Court looked to the purposes of the permit program used to enforce the Clean Air Act. In that program, Stevens wrote, "Congress sought to accommodate the conflict between the economic interest in permitting capital improvements to continue and the environmental interest in improving air quality." EPA, he said, was well within its authority when it decided that in areas where air quality standards had not yet been met, an entire plant could be considered a single source.*

In amending the Clean Air Act in 1977, Congress did not expressly address that definitional issue, Stevens noted. For the Court's purposes, he said, the reason for congressional inaction was irrelevant. "Judges are not experts in the field, and are not part of either political branch of the government. Courts must, in some cases, reconcile competing political interests, but not on the basis of the judges' personal policy preferences.

"In contrast, an agency to which Congress has delegated policy-making responsibilities may, within the limits of that delegation, properly rely upon the incumbent administration's views of wise policy to inform its judgments.

"While agencies are not directly accountable to the people," Stevens continued, "the Chief Executive is, and it is entirely appropriate for this political branch of the Government to make such policy choices — resolving the competing interests which Congress itself either inadvertently did not resolve, or intentionally left to be resolved by the agency charged with the administration of the statute in light of everyday realities." When an agency's interpretation of a law was challenged by those who argued primarily that it reflected an unwise policy, the challenge must fail, Stevens said. "In such a case, federal judges — who have no constituency — have a duty to respect legitimate policy choices made by those who do."

Following are excerpts from the Supreme Court's June 25, 1984, decision in Environmental Protection Agency v. Natural Resources Defense Council (NRDC), Chevron USA Inc. v. NRDC, *and* American Iron and Steel Institute v. NRDC, *ruling that the Environmental Protection Agency was acting within its power when it adopted the so-called "bubble concept" for enforcing key provisions of the Clean Air Act in areas that had not yet attained national clean air standards:*

Chevron, U.S.A., Inc.,
Petitioner
v.
82-1005 Natural Resources
Defense Council, Inc., et al.

American Iron and Steel Institute,
et al.,
Petitioners
v.
82-1247 Natural Resources
Defense Council Inc., et al.

On writs of certiorari to the United
States Court of Appeals for the
District of Columbia Circuit

William D. Ruckelshaus,
Administrator,
Environmental Protection Agency
Petitioner
v.
82-1591 Natural Resources
Defense Council, Inc., et al.

[June 25, 1984]

JUSTICE STEVENS delivered the opinion of the Court.

In the Clean Air Act Amendments of 1977, Pub. L. 95-95, Congress enacted certain requirements applicable to States that had not achieved the national air quality standards established by the Environmental Protection Agency (EPA) pursuant to earlier legislation. The amended Clean Air Act required these "nonattainment" States to establish a permit program regulating "new or modified major stationary sources" of air pollution. Generally, a permit may not be issued for a new or modified major stationary source unless several stringent conditions are met. The EPA regulation promulgated to implement this permit requirement allows a State to adopt a plantwide definition of the term "stationary source." Under this definition, an existing plant that contains several pollution-emitting devices may install or modify one piece of equipment without meeting the permit conditions if the alteration will not increase the total emissions from the plant. The question presented by this case is whether EPA's decision to allow States to treat all of the pollution-emitting devices within the same industrial group as though they were encased within a single "bubble" is based on a reasonable construction of the statutory term "stationary source."

I

The EPA regulations containing the plantwide definition of the term stationary source were promulgated on October 14, 1981. Respondents filed a timely petition for review in the United States Court of Appeals for the District of Columbia Circuit.... The Court of Appeals set aside the regulations. *National Resources Defense Council, Inc.* v. *Gorsuch* (1982).

The court observed that the relevant part of the amended Clean Air Act "does not explicitly define what Congress envisioned as a 'stationary source, to which the permit program ... should apply," and further stated that the precise issue was not "squarely addressed in the legislative history." In light of its conclusion that the legislative history bearing on the question was "at best contradictory," it reasoned that "the purposes of the nonattainment program should guide our decision here." Based on two of its precedents concerning the applicability of the bubble concept to certain Clean Air Act programs, the court stated that the bubble concept was "mandatory" in programs designed merely to maintain existing air quality, but held that it was "inappropriate" in programs enacted to improve air quality. Since the purpose of the permit program — its *"raison d'etre,"* in the court's view — was to improve air quality, the court held that the bubble concept was inapplicable in this case under its prior precedents. It therefore set aside the regulations embodying the bubble concept as contrary to law. We granted certiorari to review the judgment, and we now reverse.

The basic legal error of the Court of Appeals was to adopt a static judicial definition of the term stationary source when it had decided that Congress itself had not commanded that definition. Respondents do not defend the legal reasoning of the Court of Appeals. Nevertheless, since this Court reviews judgments, not opinions, we must determine whether the Court of Appeals' legal error resulted in an erroneous judgment on the validity of the regulations.

II

When a court reviews an agency's construction of the statute which it administers, it is confronted with two questions. First, always, is the question whether Congress has directly spoken to the precise question at issue. If the intent of Congress is clear, that is the end of the matter; for the court, as well as the agency, must give effect to the unambiguously expressed intent of Congress. If, however, the court determines Congress has not directly addressed the precise question at issue, the court does not simply impose its own construction on the statute, as would be necessary in the absence of an administrative interpretation. Rather, if the statute is silent or ambiguous with respect to the specific issue, the question for the court is whether the agency's answer is based on a permissible construction of the statute.

"The power of an administrative agency to administer a congressionally created ... program necessarily requires the formulation of policy and the making of rules to fill any gap left, implicitly or explicitly, by Congress." *Morton* v. *Ruiz* (1974). If Congress has explicitly left a gap for the agency to fill, there is an express delegation of authority to the agency to elucidate a specific provision of the statute by regulation. Such legislative regulations are given controlling weight unless they are arbitrary, capricious, or manifestly contrary to the statute. Sometimes the legislative delegation to an agency on a particular question is implicit rather than explicit. In such a case, a court may not substitute its own construction of a statutory provision for a reasonable interpretation made by the administrator of an agency.

We have long recognized that considerable weight should be accorded to an executive department's construction of a statutory scheme it is entrusted to administer. . . .

In light of these well-settled principles it is clear that the Court of Appeals misconceived the nature of its role in reviewing the regulations at issue. Once it determined, after its own examination of the legislation, that Congress did not actually have an intent regarding the applicability of the bubble concept to the permit program, the question before it was not whether in its view the concept is "inappropriate" in the general context of a program designed to improve air quality, but whether the Administrator's view that it is appropriate in the context of this particular program is a reasonable one. Based on the examination of the legislation and its history which follows, we agree with the Court of Appeals that Congress did not have a specific intention on the applicability of the bubble concept in these cases, and conclude that the EPA's use of that concept here is a reasonable policy choice for the agency to make. . . .

[Sections III and IV omitted]

V

The legislative history of the portion of the 1977 Amendments dealing with nonattainment areas does not contain any specific comment on the "bubble concept" or the question whether a plantwide definition of a stationary source is permissible under the permit program. It does, however, plainly disclose that in the permit program Congress sought to accommodate the conflict between the economic interest in permitting capital improvements to continue and the environmental interest in improving air quality. . . .

VI

As previously noted, prior to the 1977 Amendments, the EPA had adhered to a plantwide definition of the term, "source" under a NSPS [new source performance standards] program. After adoption of the 1977

Amendments, proposals for a plantwide definition were considered in at least three formal proceedings.

In January 1979, the EPA considered the question whether the same restriction on new construction in nonattainment areas that had been included in its December 1976 ruling should be required in the revised SIP's [State Implementation Plans] that were scheduled to go into effect in July 1979. After noting that the 1976 ruling was ambiguous on the question "whether a plant with a number of different processes and emission points would be considered a single source," the EPA, in effect, provided a bifurcated answer to that question. In those areas that did not have a revised SIP in effect by July 1979, the EPA rejected the plantwide definition; on the other hand, it expressly concluded that the plantwide approach would be permissible in certain circumstances if authorized by an approved SIP....

In April, and again in September 1979, the EPA published additional comments in which it indicated that revised SIP's could adopt the plant-wide definition of source in nonattainment areas in certain circumstances.... On the latter occasion, the EPA made a formal rulemaking proposal that would have permitted the use of the "bubble concept" for new installations within a plant as well as for modifications of existing units.... Significantly, the EPA expressly noted that the word "source" might be given a plantwide definition for some purposes and a narrower definition for other purposes.... The EPA's summary of its proposed ruling discloses a flexible rather than rigid definition of the term "source" to implement various policies and programs....

In August 1980, however, the EPA adopted a regulation that, in essence, applied the basic reasoning of the Court of Appeals in this case. The EPA took particular note of the two then-recent Court of Appeals decisions, which had created the bright-line rule that the bubble concept should be employed in a program designed to maintain air quality but not in one designed to enhance air quality. Relying heavily on those cases, EPA adopted a dual definition of "source" for nonattainment areas that required a permit whenever a change in either the entire plant, or one of its components, would result in a significant increase in emissions even if the increase was completely offset by reductions elsewhere in the plant. The EPA expressed the opinion that this interpretation was "more consistent with congressional intent" than the plantwide definition because it "would bring in more sources or modifications for review," but its primary legal analysis was predicated on the two Court of Appeals decisions.

In 1981 a new administration took office and initiated a "Government-wide reexamination of regulatory burdens and complexities." In the context of that review, the EPA reevaluated the various arguments that had been advanced in connection with the proper definition of the term "source" and concluded that the term should be given the same definition in both nonattainment areas and PSD [preventing significant deterioration] areas.

In explaining its conclusion, the EPA first noted that the definitional issue was not squarely addressed in either the statute or its legislative history and therefore that the issue involved an agency "judgment as how to best carry out the Act." It then set forth several reasons for concluding that the plantwide definition was more appropriate. It pointed out that the dual definition "can act as a disincentive to new investment and modernization by discouraging modifications to existing facilities" and "can actually retard progress in air pollution control by discouraging replacement of older, dirtier processes or pieces of equipment with new, cleaner ones." Moreover, the new definition "would simplify EPA's rules by using the same definition of 'source' for PSD, nonattainment new source review and the construction moratorium. This reduces confusion and inconsistency." Finally, the agency explained that additional requirements that remained in place would accomplish the fundamental purposes of achieving attainment with NAAQ's [National Ambient Air Quality Standards] as expeditiously as possible. These conclusions were expressed in a proposed rulemaking in August 1981 that was formally promulgated in October....

VII

In this Court respondents expressly rejected the basic rationale of the Court of Appeals' decision. That court viewed the statutory definition of the term "source" as sufficiently flexible to cover either a plantwide definition, a narrower definition covering each unit within a plant, or a dual definition that could apply to both the entire "bubble" and its components. It interpreted the policies of the statute, however, to mandate the plantwide definition in programs designed to maintain clean air and to forbid it in programs designed to improve air quality. Respondents place a fundamentally different construction on the statute. They contend that the text of the Act requires the EPA to use a dual definition — if either a component of a plant, or the plant as a whole, emits over 100 tons of pollutant, it is a major stationary source. They thus contend that the EPA rules adopted in 1980, insofar as they apply to the maintenance of the quality of clean air, as well as the 1981 rules which apply to nonattainment areas, violate the statute....

... We find that the legislative history [of the act] as a whole is silent on the precise issue before us. It is, however, consistent with the view that the EPA should have broad discretion in implementing the policies of the 1977 Amendments.

More importantly, that history plainly identifies the policy concerns that motivated the enactment; the plantwide definition is fully consistent with one of those concerns — the allowance of reasonable economic growth — and, whether or not we believe it most effectively implements the other, we must recognize that the EPA has advanced a reasonable explanation for its conclusion that the regulations serve the environmental objectives as well.... Indeed, its reasoning is supported by the public record developed in the rulemaking process, as well as by certain private studies.

Our review of the EPA's varying interpretations of the word "source" — both before and after the 1977 Amendments — convinces us that the agency primarily responsible for administering this important legislation has consistently interpreted it flexibly — not in a sterile textual vacuum, but in the context of implementing policy decisions in a technical and complex arena. The fact that the agency has from time to time changed its interpretation of the term source does not, as respondents argue, lead us to conclude that no deference should be accorded the agency's interpretation of the statute. An initial agency interpretation is not instantly carved in stone. On the contrary, the agency, to engage in informed rulemaking, must consider varying interpretations and the wisdom of its policy on a continuing basis. Moreover, the fact that the agency has adopted different definitions in different contexts adds force to the argument that the definition itself is flexible, particularly since Congress has never indicated any disapproval of a flexible reading of the statute.

Significantly, it was not the agency in 1980, but rather the Court of Appeals that read the statute inflexibly to command a plantwide definition for programs designed to maintain clean air and to forbid such a definition for programs designed to improve air quality. The distinction the court drew may well be a sensible one, but our labored review of the problem has surely disclosed that it is not a distinction that Congress ever articulated itself, or one that the EPA found in the statute before the courts began to review the legislative work product. We conclude that it was the Court of Appeals, rather than Congress or any of the decisionmakers who are authorized by Congress to administer this legislation, that was primarily responsible for the 1980 position taken by the agency....

The arguments over policy that are advanced in the parties' briefs create the impression that respondents are now waging in a judicial forum a specific policy battle which they ultimately lost in the agency and in the 32 jurisdictions opting for the bubble concept, but one which was never waged in the Congress. Such policy arguments are more properly addressed to legislators or administrators, not to judges.

In this case, the Administrator's interpretation represents a reasonable accommodation of manifestly competing interests and is entitled to deference: the regulatory scheme is technical and complex, the agency considered the matter in a detailed and reasoned fashion, and the decision involves reconciling conflicting policies. Congress intended to accommodate both interests, but did not do so itself on the level of specificity presented by this case. Perhaps that body consciously desired the Administrator to strike the balance at this level, thinking that those with great expertise and charged with responsibility for administering the provision would be in a better position to do so; perhaps it simply did not consider the question at this level; and perhaps Congress was unable to forge a coalition on either side of the question, and those on each side decided to take their chances with the scheme devised by the agency. For judicial purposes, it matters not which of these things occurred.

Judges are not experts in the field, and are not part of either political branch of the Government. Courts must, in some cases, reconcile competing political interests, but not on the basis of the judges' personal policy preferences. In contrast, an agency to which Congress has delegated policymaking responsibilities may, within the limits of that delegation, properly rely upon the incumbent administration's views of wise policy to inform its judgments. While agencies are not directly accountable to the people, the Chief Executive is, and it is entirely appropriate for this political branch of the Government to make such policy choices — resolving the competing interests which Congress itself either inadvertently did not resolve, or intentionally left to be resolved by the agency charged with the administration of the statute in light of everyday realities.

When a challenge to an agency construction of a statutory provision, fairly conceptualized, really centers on the wisdom of the agency's policy, rather than whether it is a reasonable choice within a gap left open by Congress, the challenge must fail. In such a case, federal judges — who have no constituency —have a duty to respect legitimate policy choices made by those who do. The responsibilities for assessing the wisdom of such policy choices and resolving the struggle between competing views of the public interest are not judicial ones: "Our Constitution vests such responsibilities in the political branches." *TVA* v. *Hill* (1978).

We hold that the EPA's definition of the term "source" is a permissible construction of the statute which seeks to accommodate progress in reducing air pollution with economic growth. . . .

The judgment of the Court of Appeals is reversed.

It is so ordered.

COMMON MARKET SUMMIT

June 26, 1984

A long-festering budget controversy that threatened the financial and political future of the European Community (EC) was resolved — at least temporarily — June 25-26 at a summit meeting of the heads of government of the 10 member nations. Convening in Fontainebleau, France, the leaders worked out an agreement on the size of Britain's annual contribution to the EC that was satisfactory to that country's prime minister, Margaret Thatcher.

Had the dilemma not been resolved, many observers believed, the budget deadlock might have led to the breaking up of the EC, or Common Market as it was known, reversing the trend toward the economic integration of Western Europe that went back to the years immediately after World War II. At the end of an earlier EC summit, held in Brussels, Belgium, March 19-20, 1984, President François Mitterrand of France had said that if the disagreement continued, it could turn Europe into "an abandoned construction site."

The dispute revolved around the fact that Britain's contribution to the EC exceeded the amount it received in subsidies. To reduce the gap, Prime Minister Thatcher had requested a rebate, and she refused to permit any action on the Common Market's budget until her demands were met. Thatcher told reporters at the end of the Fontainebleau meeting, "We've got a settlement we've been trying to get for five years."

Participants at the meeting also decided to establish a standing committee to study such joint projects as common history textbooks, a

European anthem, a united European radio and television network, and a European passport (available January 1, 1985, from Denmark, France, Italy, Luxembourg, and Ireland and due shortly from the other five EC countries), projects long sought for European unification.

But while there was some euphoria over settling the issue of Britain's contribution to the community and agreeing to study social and political cooperation, major problems remained. Foremost among them was an expected $1.8 billion shortfall in the community's revenues for 1984.

Background

The European Community (formerly called the European Economic Community) had its roots in a commencement address by Secretary of State George C. Marshall at Harvard University in June 1947. Presenting his "European Recovery Plan" — later to be known as the Marshall Plan — he offered U.S. economic aid to support a cooperative effort by the European nations to overcome the devastating effects of World War II.

The objectives of the EC, which was established in 1957 by the Treaties of Rome, were to remove all quotas and trade barriers among member countries and to set common policies for agriculture and trade with non-member nations. The unification process represented by the EC was broadly supported as Europe prospered in the 1950s and 1960s. But a decade of economic decline, triggered by a quadrupling of Mideast oil prices in 1973-74, had more recently dampened European enthusiasm for further moves toward economic and political integration.

The 10 member nations of the EC in 1984 were Belgium, Denmark, France, Greece, Ireland, Italy, Luxembourg, the Netherlands, the United Kingdom, and West Germany. Spain and Portugal were expected to enter the community in 1986.

Budget Problems

The EC increased its own financial resources in 1970 by allocating all customs duties and agricultural levies on imports from non-member states to the community. The member nations also agreed to contribute to the EC 1 percent of all the value added taxes (VAT) imposed within their nations. (Resembling a sales tax in terms of its impact on consumers, the value added tax was an incremental excise levied on the value added, for example, at each stage of the production and distribution of a commodity.)

However, the EC required a large amount of income. Beginning in 1962, it had subsidized farm production throughout the community by paying farmers for all commodities without regard to demand. Aimed at reducing the Common Market's dependence on agricultural imports, the policy had become a drain on EC funds, accounting for two-thirds of its total budget.

Britain's long argument with the EC stemmed directly from the Common Market's expensive farm subsidy policy. Because agriculture was relatively unimportant to its economy, Britain received proportionally less than the other Common Market countries from the EC's farm price supports. Indeed, in recent years Britain's contributions had amounted to about $2 billion a year more than the country received in subsidies and other assistance.

Agreement Reached, Dispute Reopened

To bring about what it considered to be a fairer net contribution, Britain had demanded a $900 million rebate from the EC and assurances that its payments would be reduced in the future. Prime Minister Thatcher's government also advocated strong steps to stop agricultural spending by the community from soaring even higher.

Under the terms of the Fontainebleau agreement, Britain would receive cash rebates of about $800 million in its 1984 contribution and $600 million for 1983. After 1984 Britain would receive 66 percent of all the value added taxes it contributed to the EC, less all EC expenditures in that country. After the settlement was announced, Gaston Thorn, president of the EC's commission, said, "We've got Europe going again." A spokesman for Mitterrand was quoted in The New York Times *as saying, "We're finally freed of this paralyzing obsession."*

Nonetheless, problems lay ahead for the community. During a meeting of EC foreign ministers July 18-25, Britain refused to approve a supplementary budget for 1984 to cover the expected huge shortfall, caused primarily by the common agricultural policy (CAP). After Britain rejected a proposal to make interest-free advance payments to cover the budget deficit, the EC executive commission announced a number of alternative measures, including selling surplus butter and meat to the Soviet Union and Iran at heavily subsidized prices, expected to add another $150 million to the 1984 deficit.

A further blow was dealt to the Fontainebleau agreement when the European Parliament in Strasbourg voted 212-70 on July 27 to block payment of the 1983 $600 million rebate to Britain. Leaders of the parliament said they could not vote to give a country a rebate when the community as a whole faced a budget crisis. The reaction of British leaders was harsh. Thatcher called the decision "absolutely despicable." But she added that Britain's criticism was aimed at parliament and not the leaders of the other EC nations. After the Thatcher government had made concessions, the parliament October 20, 1984, agreed on a vote of 218-34 to release the $600 million rebate.

Following is the text adopted by the leaders of the 10-nation
European Community at the conclusion of a summit meet-
ing in Fontainebleau, France, June 26, 1984:

The European Council, meeting at Fontainebleau on June 25 and 26, 1984, adopted the decisions on questions left in abeyance at its meeting in Brussels on March 19 and 20, 1984.

The European Council also confirmed the points of agreement which it had reached in Brussels. It took note of the progress made in regard to new policies and discussed environment and health issues. It adopted new guidelines for the reactivation of European cooperation.

Budgetary Imbalances

1. Expenditure policy is ultimately the essential means of resolving the question of budgetary imbalances.

However, it has been decided that any Member State sustaining a budgetary burden which is excessive in relation to its relative prosperity may benefit from a correction at the appropriate time.

The basis for the correction is the gap between the share of Value Added Tax (VAT) payments and the share of expenditure allocated in accordance with the present criteria.

2. As far as the United Kingdom is concerned, the following arrangement is adopted:
   - for 1984, a lump sum of 1 billion ECUs* is fixed;
   - from 1985 the gap (base of the correction) as defined in paragraph 1 is, for the period referred to in paragraph 4, corrected annually at 66 percent.

3. The corrections foreseen in paragraph 2 will be deducted from the United Kingdom's normal VAT share in the budget year following the one in respect of which the correction is granted. The resulting cost for the other Member States will be shared among them according to their normal VAT share, adjusted to allow the Federal Republic of Germany's share to move to 2/3 of its VAT share.

4. The correction formula foreseen in paragraph 2 (second indent) will be a part of the decision to increase the VAT ceiling to 1.4 percent, their durations being linked.

One year before the new ceiling is reached, the Commission will present to the Council of Ministers a report setting out the state of play on:
   - the result of the budgetary discipline;
   - the Community's financial needs;
   - the breakdown of the budgetary costs among Member States, having regard to their relative prosperity, and the consequences to be drawn from this for the application of the budgetary corrections.

The Council of Ministers will reexamine the question as a whole and will take the appropriate decisions ex novo.

Own Resources and Enlargement

The maximum rate of mobilization of VAT will be 1.4 percent on January 1, 1986; this maximum rate applies to every Member State and will enter into force as soon as the ratification procedures are completed, and by January 1, 1986 at the latest.

The maximum rate may be increased to 1.6 percent on January 1, 1988 by unanimous decision of the Council of Ministers and after agreement has been given in accordance with national procedures.

The European Council confirms that the negotiations for the accession of Spain and Portugal should be completed by September 30, 1984 at the latest. Between now and then the Community will have to make every effort to create the right conditions for the success of this enlargement, both in the negotiations with Spain on fisheries to ensure the conservation of fish stocks and also by reforming the common organization of the wine market to ensure that the quantities of wine produced in the Community are controlled, and by means of a fair balance between agricultural and industrial agreements.

Financing of the 1984 Budget

The European Council agreed that, pending national parliaments' ratification of the increase in own [sic] resources, steps will be taken at the next (Budget) Council of Ministers meeting to cover the needs of the 1984 budget to ensure that the Community operates normally.

Dismantling of Positive Monetary Compensatory Amounts in the Federal Republic of Germany

The European Council asks the Commission to propose, and the Council of Ministers to decide on, measures which will enable VAT relief for German agriculture under the German national budget to be increased from 3 percent to 5 percent with effect from July 1, 1984 until December 31, 1988 in compensation for dismantling the monetary compensatory amounts; the compensation shall not exceed the amounts dismantled.

Social Policy

The European Council asks the Commission to carry out the work program set out in the Community's medium-term social action plan and to forge ahead with the work stemming from the Council of Ministers' conclusions on technological change and social adjustment and with that on production organization.

A People's Europe

The European Council considers it essential that the Community respond to the expectations of the people of Europe by adopting measures to strengthen and promote its identity and its image both for its citizens and for the rest of the world. An ad hoc Committee will be set up to prepare and coordinate this action. It will be composed of representatives of the Heads of State or of Government of the Member States.

The European Council approves the agreement reached on the principle of creating a European passport and asks the Council of Ministers to take the necessary decisions to ensure that this passport is actually available to Member States' nationals by January 1, 1985 at the latest.

It asks the Council of Ministers and the Member States to put in hand without delay a study of the measures which could be taken to bring about in the near future, and in any case *before the middle of 1985:*

● a single document for the movement of goods;

● the abolition of all police and customs formalities for people crossing intra-Community frontiers;

● a general system for ensuring the equivalence of university diplomas, in order to bring about the effective freedom of establishment within the Community.

The Committee will examine inter alia the following suggestions;

● symbols of the Community's existence, such as a flag and an anthem;

● formation of European sports teams;

● streamlining procedures at frontier posts;

● minting of a European coinage, namely the ECU.

It would also like the Member States to take steps to encourage young people to participate in projects organized by the Community beyond its frontiers, and in particular to support the creation of national committees of European volunteers for development, bringing together young Europeans who wish to work on development projects in the third world.

The ad hoc Committee will also examine the following suggestions:

● measures to combat drug abuse;

● the twinning of children's classes.

The Commission will contribute to the proceedings of the Committee within the limits of its powers.

Ad Hoc Committee on Institutional Affairs

The European Council decided to set up an ad hoc Committee consisting of personal representatives of the Heads of State and of Government, on the lines of the "Spaak Committee." **

The Committee's function will be to make suggestions for the improvement of the operation of European cooperation in both the Community field and that of political, or any other, cooperation.

The President of the European Council will take the necessary steps to implement that decision.

---

* European Currency Unit = \$.80 on June 22, 1984.
** The Speak Committee laid the groundwork for the Community's founding Treaties of Rome.

July

COURT ON PUBLIC
BROADCASTING EDITORIALS
July 2, 1984

The Supreme Court July 2 held that Congress violated the First Amendment when it prohibited editorials on public radio and television stations that accepted grants from the Corporation for Public Broadcasting. By a 5-4 vote in Federal Communications Commission v. League of Women Voters of California, *the Court struck down the ban, a provision of the Public Broadcasting Act of 1967. The law was challenged in 1979 by the Pacifica Foundation, which owned several non-commercial radio stations. The foundation was backed by the League of Women Voters of California and Rep. Henry A. Waxman, D-Calif. After Jimmy Carter's administration refused to defend the ban, the case was dismissed. It was revived, however, when Ronald Reagan's administration announced it would defend the law.*

"Were a similar ban on editorializing applied to newspapers and magazines, we would not hesitate to strike it down as violative of the First Amendment," wrote Justice William J. Brennan Jr. for the majority. He conceded that the government had more leeway to regulate broadcasters, primarily because there were only a limited number of frequencies available and because the government, in issuing licenses for use of those frequencies, wished to ensure that they were used in the public interest. Even in that context, the Court said, the editorializing ban must fall. First, it was aimed at "precisely that form of speech which the framers of the Bill of Rights were most anxious to protect — speech that is 'indispensable to the discovery and spread of political truth'...."

Second, Brennan continued, the ban reached only one particular kind of speech, and that affected speech was defined by its content. When

449

government acted to curtail expression of a point of view on matters of public interest, it provided "the purest example" of the kind of law the First Amendment was enacted to prevent.

Administration, Court Arguments

The Reagan administration defended the ban as necessary to protect public broadcasting stations from becoming vehicles of government propaganda or easy targets for capture by private interest groups. Neither argument was sufficient to justify such a sweeping ban, the majority ruled, pointing to a variety of other means for safeguarding the independence of public broadcasters. The government argued that controversial editorials by public broadcasters could anger members of Congress to the point that funding for public broadcasting would be terminated or drastically reduced. That was too speculative a basis upon which to ground such a drastic limitation of speech, the majority concluded.

Chief Justice Warren E. Burger and Associate Justices William H. Rehnquist and Byron R. White dissented, finding the editorial ban a permissible condition on the spending of government funds. "Congress simply has decided not to subsidize stations" that engaged in editorializing, a decision quite within its power to make, wrote Rehnquist. According to Rehnquist, the majority decision made the government appear as the "Big Bad Wolf," while Pacifica was portrayed as "Little Red Riding Hood."

In a separate dissent, Justice John Paul Stevens said he felt that the government's interest in maintaining its neutrality in the marketplace of ideas, avoiding either censorship or propaganda, outweighed the ban's impact on protected speech. "Members of Congress, not members of the judiciary, live in the world of politics," Stevens continued. "When they conclude that there is a real danger of political considerations influencing the dispensing of this money and that this provision is necessary to insulate grantees from political pressures ... that judgment is entitled to our respect."

In two footnotes, the Court hinted that it — like the Reagan administration — was ready to reconsider the need for any government regulation of broadcast stations. With cable and satellite television systems providing viewers access to a wide variety of broadcast stations, there was growing criticism of the scarcity rationale for broadcast regulation, the Court observed. The justices made clear, however, that the first move had to come from Congress or the Federal Communications Commission (FCC). "We are not prepared," Brennan wrote, "to reconsider our longstanding approach without some signal from Congress or the FCC that technological developments have advanced so far that some revision of the system of broadcast regulation may be required."

In a second footnote, the Court noted that the FCC was considering repeal of the "fairness doctrine," which required adequate and fair coverage of both sides of political issues. Modification or repeal of that doctrine on the basis that it effectively curtailed, rather than enhanced, speech would force the Court to reconsider the constitutional basis for its decisions upholding that doctrine, Brennan wrote.

Broadcasters' Reactions

As quoted in the July 3 edition of The New York Times, *a number of broadcasters approved the Court's decision but questioned its immediate impact. "It means an important affirmation of our having parity in the fourth estate," said John Jay Iselin, president of WNET/Channel 13, "and that all people work equally under the First Amendment. This rule was unconstitutional. But, in fact, there will not be much immediate change over how we perform our duties and exercise our responsibilities."*

Iselin said the decision would have more of an impact on editorializing of local issues but that it probably would not be useful to the station for national issues. "I think it would be good for us at some point in the future if we had the resources to develop an editorial posture," Iselin said. "But it would be vis à vis the metropolitan community. I think we have more city or regional license to express an opinion than editorializing nationally. There's a philosophical question here, over who would develop such a policy, and the answer is the board of trustees. We have a public trust. We are a not-for-profit organization. I can't see getting into the editorial business immediately."

According to Philip Tymon, the station manager at WBAI-FM, an affiliate of the Pacifica Foundation, the decision "could mean as many problems as benefits for us." He said, "there's no real movement within Pacifica to start editorializing. I would not want to be creating editorials around here. But we've been told, at least, whatever it means, that the federal government believes that noncommercial stations have the same rights as commercial ones. This is important to know, because it has to do with whether or not you take government money. . . . Even though it's a fairly recent development that we do take government money, it's important to us to know that our First Amendment rights not be limited just because we do."

> *Following are excerpts from the Supreme Court's July 2, 1984, decision in* Federal Communications Commission v. League of Women Voters of California, *striking down a 1967 law banning editorials on public broadcast stations that accepted federal funds; from the dissenting opinion by Justice John Paul Stevens; and from the dissenting opinion by Justice William H. Rehnquist:*

No. 82-912

Federal Communications   On appeal from the United States
        Commission   District Court for the Central Dis-
              v.   trict of California
League of Women Voters of
        California et al.

[July 2, 1984]

JUSTICE BRENNAN delivered the opinion of the Court.

Moved to action by a widely felt need to sponsor independent sources of broadcast programming as an alternative to commercial broadcasting, Congress set out in 1967 to support and promote the development of noncommercial, educational broadcasting stations. A keystone of Congress' program was the Public Broadcasting Act of 1967, Pub. L. No. 90-129, which established the Corporation for Public Broadcasting, a nonprofit corporation authorized to disburse federal funds to noncommercial television and radio stations in support of station operations and educational programming. Section 399 of that Act, as amended by the Public Broadcasting Amendments Act of 1981, Pub. L. No. 97-35, forbids any "noncommercial educational broadcasting station which receives a grant from the Corporation" to "engage in editorializing." In this case, we are called upon to decide whether Congress, by imposing that restriction, has passed a "law . . . abridging the freedom of speech, or of the press" in violation of the First Amendment of the Constitution.

I

A

The history of noncommercial, educational broadcasting in the United States is as old as broadcasting itself. In its first efforts to regulate broadcasting, Congress made no special provision for noncommercial, educational broadcasting stations. Under the Radio Act of 1927 and the Communications Act of 1934, such stations were subject to the same licensing requirements as their commercial counterparts. As commercial broadcasting rapidly expanded during the 1930s, however, the percentage of broadcast licenses held by noncommercial stations began to shrink. In 1939, recognizing the potential effect of these commercial pressures on educational stations, the Federal Communications Commission (FCC or Commission) decided to reserve certain frequencies for educational radio, and in 1945, the Commission allocated 20 frequencies on the new FM spectrum exclusively for educational use. . . . Similarly, in 1952, with the advent of television, the FCC reserved certain television channels solely for educational stations. Helped in part by these allocations, a wide variety of noncommercial stations, some funded by state and local governments and others by private donations and foundation grants, developed during this period.

It was not until 1962, however, that Congress provided any direct financial assistance to noncommercial, educational broadcasting. This first step was taken with the passage of the Educational Television Facilities Act of 1962, Pub. L. No. 87-447, which authorized the former Department of Health, Education & Welfare (HEW) to distribute $32 million in matching grants over a five-year period for the construction of noncommercial television facilities.

Impetus for expanded federal involvement came in 1967 when the Carnegie Corporation sponsored a special commission to review the state of educational broadcasting. Finding that the prospects for an expanded public broadcasting system rested on "the vigor of its local stations," but that these stations were hobbled by chronic underfinancing, the Carnegie Commission called upon the Federal Government to supplement existing state, local, and private financing so that educational broadcasting could realize its full potential as a true alternative to commercial broadcasting. . . . In fashioning a legislative proposal to carry out this vision, the Commission recommended the creation of a nonprofit, nongovernmental "Corporation for Public Television" to provide support for noncommercial broadcasting, including funding for new program production, local station operations, and the establishment of satellite interconnection facilities to permit nationwide distribution of educational programs to all local stations that wished to receive and use them.

The Commission's report met with widespread approval and its proposals became the blueprint for the Public Broadcasting Act of 1967, which established the basic framework of the public broadcasting system of today. Titles I and III of the Act authorized over $38 million for continued HEW construction grants and for the study of instructional television. Title II created the Corporation for Public Broadcasting (CPB or Corporation), a nonprofit, private corporation governed by a 15-person, bipartisan board of directors appointed by the President with the advice and consent of the Senate. The Corporation was given power to fund "the production of educational television and radio programs for national or regional distribution," to make grants to local broadcasting stations that would "aid in financing local educational . . . programming costs of such stations," and to assist in the establishment and development of national interconnection facilities. Aside from conferring these powers on the Corporation, Congress also adopted other measures designed both to ensure the autonomy of the Corporation and to protect the local stations from governmental interference and control. For example, all federal agencies, officers, and employees were prohibited from "exercis[ing] any direction, supervision or control" over the Corporation or local stations, and the Corporation itself was forbidden to "own or operate any television or radio broadcast station," and was further required to "carry out its purposes and functions . . . from interference with or control of program content" of the local stations.

B

Appellee Pacifica Foundation is a nonprofit corporation that owns and operates several noncommercial educational broadcasting stations in five major metropolitan areas. Its licensees have received and are presently receiving grants from the Corporation and are therefore prohibited from editorializing by the terms of § 399, as originally enacted and as recently amended. In April 1979, appellees brought this suit in the United States District Court for the Central District of California challenging the constitutionality of former § 399. In October 1979, the Department of Justice informed both Houses of Congress and the District Court that it had decided not to defend the constitutionality of the statute. The Senate then adopted a resolution directing its counsel to intervene as *amicus curiae* in support of § 399. Counsel appeared and subsequently obtained dismissal of the lawsuit for want of a justiciable controversy because the Government had decided not to enforce the statute. While appellees' appeal from this disposition was pending before the Court of Appeals for the Ninth Circuit, however, the Department of Justice under a new Administration announced that it would defend the statute. The Court of Appeals then remanded the case to the District Court; the District Court permitted the Senate counsel to withdraw from the litigation, and, finding that a concrete controversy was now presented, vacated its earlier order of dismissal. While the suit was pending before the District Court, Congress, as already mentioned, . . . amended § 399 by confining the ban on editorializing to noncommercial stations that receive Corporation grants and by separately prohibiting all noncommercial stations from making political endorsements, irrespective of whether they receive federal funds. Subsequently, appellees amended their complaint to reflect this change, challenging only the ban on editorializing.

The District Court granted summary judgment in favor of appellees, holding that § 399's ban on editorializing violated the First Amendment. The court rejected the Government's contention that "§ 399 serves a compelling government interest in ensuring that funded noncommercial broadcasters do not become propaganda organs for the government." Noting the diverse sources of funding for noncommercial stations, the protections built into the Public Broadcasting Act to ensure that noncommercial broadcasters remain free of governmental influence, and the requirements of the FCC's fairness doctrine which are designed to guard against one-sided presentation of controversial issues, the District Court concluded that the asserted fear of government control was not sufficiently compelling to warrant § 399's restriction on speech. The court also rejected the contention that the restriction on editorializing as necessary to ensure that government funding of noncommercial broadcast stations does not interfere with the balanced presentation of opinion on those stations. The Government appealed from the District Court judgment directly to this Court. . . . We postponed consideration of the question of our jurisdiction to the merits, and we now affirm.

II

We begin by considering the appropriate standard of review. The District Court acknowledged that our decisions have generally applied a different First Amendment standard for broadcast regulation than in other areas, but after finding that no special characteristic of the broadcast media justified application of a less stringent standard in this case, it held that § 399 could survive constitutional scrutiny only if it served a "compelling" governmental interest. Claiming that the court drew the wrong lessons from our prior decisions concerning broadcast regulation, the Government contends that a less demanding standard is required. It argues that Congress may, consistently with the First Amendment, exercise broad power to regulate broadcast speech because the medium of broadcasting is subject to the "special Characteristic" of spectrum scarcity — a characteristic not shared by other media — which calls for more exacting regulation. This power, in the Government's view, includes authority to restrict the ability of all broadcasters, both commercial and noncommercial, to editorialize. Moreover, given the unique role of noncommercial broadcasting as a source of "programming excellence and diversity that the commercial sector could not or would not produce," Congress was entitled to impose special restrictions such as § 399 upon these stations. The Government concludes by urging that § 399 is an appropriate and essential means of furthering "important" governmental interests, which leaves open the possibility that a wide variety of views on matters of public importance can be expressed through the medium of noncommercial educational broadcasting.

At first glance, of course, it would appear that the District Court applied the correct standard. Section 399 plainly operates to restrict the expression of editorial opinion on matters of public importance, and, as we have repeatedly explained, communication of this kind is entitled to the most exacting degree of First Amendment protection. *E.g., Minneapolis Star & Tribune Co.* v. *Minnesota Commissioner of Revenue* (1983); *First National Bank of Boston* v. *Bellotti* (1978); *Buckley* v. *Valeo* (1976); *Thornhill* v. *Alabama* (1940). Were a similar ban on editorializing applied to newspapers and magazines, we would not hesitate to strike it down as violative of the First Amendment. *E. g., Mills* v. *Alabama* (1966). But, as the Government correctly notes, because broadcast regulation involves unique considerations, our cases have not followed precisely the same approach that we have applied to other media and have never gone so far as to demand that such regulations serve "compelling" governmental interests. At the same time, we think the Government's argument loses sight of concerns that are important in this area and thus misapprehends the essential meaning of our prior decisions concerning the reach of Congress' authority to regulate broadcast communication.

The fundamental principles that guide our evaluation of broadcast regulation are by now well established. First, we have long recognized that Congress, acting pursuant to the Commerce Clause, has power to regulate the use of this scarce and valuable national resource. The distinctive feature of Congress' efforts in this area has been to ensure through the regulatory oversight of the FCC that only those who satisfy the "public interest, convenience and necessity" are granted a license to use radio and television broadcast frequencies.

Second, Congress may, in the exercise of this power, seek to assure that the public receives through this medium a balanced presentation of information on issues of public importance that otherwise might not be addressed if control of the medium were left entirely in the hands of those who own and operate broadcasting stations. Although such governmental regulation has never been allowed with respect to the print media, *Miami Herald Publishing Co.* v. *Tornillo* (1974), we have recognized that "differences in the characteristics of new media justify differences in the First Amendment standards applied to them." *Red Lion Broadcasting Co.* v. *FCC* (1969). The fundamental distinguishing characteristic of the new medium of broadcasting that, in our view, has required some adjustment in First Amendment analysis is that "[b]roadcasting frequencies are a scarce resource [that] must be portioned out among applicants." *Columbia Broadcasting System, Inc.* v. *Democratic National Committee* (1973). Thus our cases have taught that, given spectrum scarcity, those who are granted a license to broadcast must serve in a sense as fiduciaries for the public by presenting "those views and voices which are representative of his community and which would otherwise by necessity, be barred from the airwaves." *Red Lion.* As we observed in that case, because "[i]t is the purpose of the First Amendment to preserve an uninhibited marketplace of ideas in which truth will ultimately prevail, . . . the right of the public to receive suitable access to social, political, esthetic, moral and other ideas and experiences [through the medium of broadcasting] is crucial here [and it] may not constitutionally be abridged either by the Congress or the FCC."

Finally, although the government's interest in ensuring balanced coverage of public issues is plainly both important and substantial, we have, at the same time, made clear that broadcasters are engaged in a vital and independent form of communicative activity. As a result, the First Amendment must inform and give shape to the manner in which Congress exercises its regulatory power in this area. Unlike common carriers, broadcasters are "entitled under the First Amendment to exercise 'the widest journalistic freedom consistent with their public [duties].' " *Columbia Broadcasting System, Inc.* v. *FCC*, (1981). See also *FCC* v. *Midwest Video Corp.* (1979). Indeed, if the public's interest in receiving a balanced presentation of views is to be fully served, we must necessarily rely in large part upon the editorial initiative and judgment of the broadcasters who bear the public trust. . . .

Thus, although the broadcasting industry plainly operates under restraints not imposed upon other media, the thrust of these restrictions has generally been to secure the public's First Amendment interest in receiving a balanced presentation of views on diverse matters of public concern. As a result of these restrictions, of course, the absolute freedom to advocate one's own positions without also presenting opposing viewpoints — a freedom enjoyed, for example, by newspaper publishers and soapbox orators — is denied to broadcasters. But, as our cases attest, these restrictions have been upheld only when we were satisfied that the restriction is narrowly tailored to further a substantial governmental interest, such as ensuring adequate and balanced coverage of public issues. . . .

III

We turn now to consider whether the restraint imposed by § 399 satisfies the requirements established by our prior cases for permissible broadcast regulation. Before assessing the government's proffered justifications for the statute, however, two central features of the ban against editorializing must be examined, since they help to illuminate the importance of the First Amendment interests at stake in this case.

A

First, the restriction imposed by § 399 is specifically directed at a form of speech — namely, the expression of editorial opinion — that lies at the heart of First Amendment protection. In construing the reach of the statute, the FCC has explained that "although the use of noncommercial educational broadcast facilities by licensees, their management or those speaking on their behalf for the propagation of the licensee's own views on public issues is not permitted, such prohibition should not be construed to inhibit any *other* presentations on controversial issues of public importance." *In re Complaint of Accuracy in Media, Inc.* (1973) (emphasis added). The Commission's interpretation of § 399 simply highlights the fact that what the statute forecloses is the expression of editorial opinion on "controversial issues of public importance." As we recently reiterated in *NAACP* v. *Claiborne Hardware Co.* (1982), "expression on public issues 'has always rested on the highest rung of the hierarchy of First Amendment values.' " . . .

. . . Preserving the free expression of editorial opinion, therefore, is part and parcel of "our profound national commitment . . . that debate on public issues should be uninhibited, robust, and wide-open." *New York Times* v. *Sullivan* (1964). . . . Indeed, the pivotal importance of editorializing as a means of satisfying the public's interest in receiving a wide variety of ideas and views through the medium of broadcasting has long been recognized by the FCC; the Commission has for the past 35 years actively encouraged commercial broadcast licensees to include editorials on public affairs in their programming. Because § 399 appears to restrict precisely that form of speech which the Framers of the Bill of Rights were most anxious to protect — speech that is "indispensable to the discovery and spread of political truth" — we must be especially careful in weighing the in*erests that are asserted in support of this restriction and in assessing the precision with which the ban is crafted. *Whitney* v. *California* (1927) (Brandeis, J., concurring).

Second, the scope of § 399's ban is defined solely on the basis of the content of the suppressed speech. A wide variety of non-editorial speech "by licensees, their management or those speaking on their behalf," *In re Complaint of Accuracy in Media, Inc., supra,* is plainly not prohibited by § 399. Examples of such permissible forms of speech include daily announcements of the station's program schedule or over-the-air appeals for contributions from listeners. Consequently, in order to determine whether a particular statement by station management constitutes an "editorial" proscribed by § 399, enforcement authorities must necessarily examine the content of the message that is conveyed to determine whether the views expressed concern "controversial issues of public importance." *Ibid.*

As JUSTICE STEVENS observed in *Consolidated Edison Co.* v. *Public Service Commission* (1980), however, "[a] regulation of speech that is motivated by nothing more than a desire to curtail expression of a particular point of view on controversial issues of general interest is the purest example of a 'law ... abridging the freedom of speech, or of the press.' A regulation that denies one group of persons the right to address a select audience on 'controversial issues of public policy' is plainly such a regulation." Section 399 is just such a regulation, for it singles out noncommercial broadcasters and denies them the right to address their chosen audience on matters of public importance....

B

In seeking to defend the prohibition on editorializing imposed by § 399, the Government urges that the statute was aimed at preventing two principal threats to the overall success of the Public Broadcasting Act of 1967. According to this argument, the ban was necessary, first, to protect noncommercial educational broadcasting stations from being coerced, as a result of federal financing, into becoming vehicles for government propagandizing or the objects of governmental influence; and, second, to keep these stations from becoming convenient targets for capture by private interest groups wishing to express their own partisan viewpoints. By seeking to safeguard the public's right to a balanced presentation of public issues through the prevention of either governmental or private bias, these objectives are, of course, broadly consistent with the goals identified in our earlier broadcast regulation cases. But, in sharp contrast to the restrictions upheld in *Red Lion* or in *Columbia Broadcasting System, Inc.* v. *FCC,* which left room for editorial discretion and simply required broadcast editors to grant others access to the microphone, § 399 directly prohibits the broadcaster from speaking out on public issues even in a balanced and fair manner. The Government insists, however, that the hazards posed in the "special" circumstances of noncommercial educational broadcasting are so great that § 399 is an indispensable means of preserving the public's First Amendment interests. We disagree. . . .

. . . [A]n examination of both the overall legislative scheme established by the 1967 Act and the character of public broadcasting demonstrates that the interest asserted by the Government is not substantially advanced by § 399. First, to the extent that federal financial support creates a risk that stations will lose their independence through the bewitching power of governmental largesse, the elaborate structure established by the Public Broadcasting Act already operates to insulate local stations from governmental interference. . . .

Even if these statutory protections were thought insufficient to the task, however, suppressing the particular category of speech restricted by § 399 is simply not likely, given the character of the public broadcasting system, to reduce substantially the risk that the Federal Government will seek to influence or put pressure on local stations. An underlying supposition of the Government's argument in this regard is that individual noncommercial stations are likely to speak so forecefully on particular issues that Congress, the ultimate source of the station's Federal funding, will be tempted to retaliate against these individual stations by restricting appropriations for all of public broadcasting suggests that such a risk is speculative at best. There are literally hundreds of public radio and television stations in communities scattered throughout the United States and its territories. . . . Given that central fact, it seems reasonable to infer that the editorial voices of these stations will prove to be as distinctive, varied, and idiosyncratic as the various communities they represent. More importantly, the editorial focus of any particular station can fairly be expected to focus largely on issues affecting only its community. Accordingly, absent some showing by the Government to the contrary, the risk that local editorializing will place all of public broadcasting in jeopardy is not sufficiently pressing to warrant § 399's broad suppression of speech. . . .

Furthermore, the manifest imprecision of the ban imposed by § 399 reveals that its proscription is not sufficiently tailored to the harms it seeks to prevent to justify its substantial interference with broadcasters' speech. Section 399 includes within its grip a potentially infinite variety of speech, most of which would not be related in any way to governmental affairs, political candidacies or elections. Indeed, the breadth of editorial commentary is as wide as human imagination permits. But the Government never explains how, say, an editorial by local station management urging improvements in a town's parks or museums will so infuriate Congress or other Federal officials that the future of public broadcasting will be imperiled unless such editorials are suppressed. Nor is it explained how the suppression of editorials alone serves to reduce the risk of governmental retaliation and interference when it is clear that station management is fully able to broadcast controversial views so long as such views are not labelled as its own. . . .

Finally, although the Government certainly has a substantial interest in ensuring that the audiences of noncommercial stations will not be led to think that the broadcaster's editorials reflect the official view of the government, this interest can be fully satisfied by less restrictive means that are readily available. To address this important concern, Congress could simply require public broadcasting stations to broadcast a disclaimer every time they editorialize which would state that the editorial represents only the view of the station's management and does not in any way represent the views of the Federal Government or any of the station's other sources of funding. . . .

In sum, § 399's broad ban on all editorializing by every station that receives CPB funds far exceeds what is necessary to protect against the risk of governmental interference or to prevent the public from assuming that editorials by public broadcasting stations represent the official view of government. The regulation impermissibly sweeps within its prohibition a wide range of speech by wholly private stations on topics that do not take a directly partisan stand or that have nothing whatever to do with federal, state or local government. . . .

Finally, the public's interest in preventing public broadcasting stations from becoming forums for lopsided presentations of narrow partisan positions is already secured by a variety of other regulatory means that intrude far less drastically upon the "journalistic freedom" of noncommercial broadcasters. *Columbia Broadcasting System, Inc.* v. *Democratic National Committee, supra.* The requirements of the FCC's fairness doctrine, for instance, which apply to commercial and noncommercial stations alike, ensure that such editorializing would maintain a reasonably balanced and fair presentation of controversial issues. Thus, even if the management of a noncommercial educational station were inclined to seek to further only its own partisan views when editorializing, it simply could not do so. . . .

We therefore hold that even if some of the hazards at which § 399 was aimed are sufficiently substantial, the restriction is not crafted with sufficient precision to remedy those dangers that may exist to justify the significant abridgement of speech worked by the provision's broad ban on editorializing. The statute is not narrowly tailored to address any of the government's suggested goals. Moreover, the public's "paramount right" to be fully and broadly informed on matters of public importance through the medium of noncommercial educational broadcasting is not well served by the restriction, for its effect is plainly to diminish rather than augment "the volume and quality of coverage" of controversial issues. *Red Lion, supra.* Nor do we see any reason to deny noncommercial broadcasters the right to address matters of public concern on the basis of merely speculative fears of adverse public or governmental reactions to such speech. . . .

[Section IV omitted]

460

V

In conclusion, we emphasize that our disposition of this case rests upon a narrow proposition. We do not hold that the Congress or the FCC are without power to regulate the content, timing, or character of speech by noncommercial educational broadcasting stations. Rather, we hold only that the specific interests sought to be advanced by § 399's ban on editorializing are either not sufficiently substantial or are not served in a sufficiently limited manner to justify the substantial abridgement of important journalistic freedoms which the First Amendment jealously protects. Accordingly, the judgment of the District Court is

Affirmed.

JUSTICE STEVENS, dissenting.

. . . The quality of the interest in maintaining government neutrality in the free market of ideas — of avoiding subtle forms of censorship and propaganda — outweigh the impact on expression that results from this statute. Indeed, by simply terminating or reducing funding, Congress could curtail much more expression with no risk whatever of a constitutional transgression. . . .

The statute does not violate the fundamental principle that the citizen's right to speak may not be conditioned upon the sovereign's agreement with what the speaker intends to say. On the contrary, the statute was enacted in order to protect that very principle — to avoid the risk that some speakers will be rewarded or penalized for saying things that appeal to — or are offensive to — the sovereign. The interests the statute is designed to protect are interests that underlie the First Amendment itself.

In my judgment the interest in keeping the Federal Government out of the propaganda arena is of overriding importance. That interest is of special importance in the field of electronic communication, not only because that medium is so powerful and persuasive, but also because it is the one form of communication that is licensed by the Federal Government. When the Government already has great potential power over the electronic media, it is surely legitimate to enact statutory safeguards to make sure that it does not cross the threshold that separates neutral regulation from the subsidy of partisan opinion. . . .

Members of Congress, not members of the Judiciary, live in the world of politics. When they conclude that there is a real danger of political considerations influencing the dispensing of this money and that this provision is necessary to insulate grantees from political pressures in addition to the other safeguards, that judgment is entitled to our respect. . . .

JUSTICE REHNQUIST, with whom THE CHIEF JUSTICE and JUSTICE WHITE join, dissenting.

All but three paragraphs of the Court's lengthy opinion in this case are devoted to the development of a scenario in which the government appears as the "Big Bad Wolf," and appellee Pacifica as "Little Red Riding Hood." In the Court's scenario the Big Bad Wolf cruelly forbids Little Red Riding Hood from taking to her grandmother some of the food that she is carrying in her basket. Only three paragraphs are used to delineate a truer picture of the litigants, wherein it appears that some of the food in the basket was given to Little Red Riding Hood by the Big Bad Wolf himself, and that the Big Bad Wolf had told Little Red Riding Hood in advance that if she accepted his food she would have to abide by his conditions. Congress in enacting § 399 of the Public Broadcasting Act has simply determined that public funds shall not be used to subsidize noncommercial, educational broadcasting stations which engage in "editorializing" or which support or oppose any political candidate. I do not believe that anything in the First Amendment to the United States Constitution prevents Congress from choosing to spend public monies in that manner. . . .

The Court's three-paragraph discussion of why § 399, repeatedly re-examined and retained by Congress, violates the First Amendment is to me utterly unpersuasive. Congress has rationally determined that the bulk of the taxpayers whose monies provide the funds for grants by the CPB would prefer not to see the management of local educational stations promulgate its own private views on the air at taxpayer expense. Accordingly Congress simply has decided not to subsidize stations which engage in that activity. . . .

The Court seems to believe that Congress actually subsidizes editorializing only if a station uses federal money specifically to cover the expenses that the Court believes can be isolated as editorializing expenses. But to me the Court's approach ignores economic reality. CPB's unrestricted grants are used for salaries, training, equipment, promotion, etc. — financial expenditures which benefit all aspects of a station's programming, including management's editorials. Given the impossibility of compartmentalizing programming expenses in any meaningful way, it seems clear to me that the only effective means for preventing the use of public monies to subsidize the airing of management's views is for Congress to ban a subsidized station from all on-the-air editorializing. . . .

This is not to say that the government may attach *any* condition to its largess; it is only to say that when the government is simply exercising its power to allocate its own public funds, we need only find that the condition imposed has a rational relationship to Congress' purpose in providing the subsidy and that it is not primarily "aimed at the suppression of dangerous ideas." *Cammarano* v. *United States* (1959), quoting *Speiser* v. *Randall* (1958). In this case Congress' prohibition is directly related to its purpose in providing subsidies for public broadcasting, and it is plainly rational for Congress to have determined that taxpayer monies should not be used to subsidize management's views or to pay for management's exercise of partisan politics. Indeed, it is entirely rational for Congress to have wished to avoid the appearance of government sponsorship of a particular view or a particular political candidate.

Furthermore, Congress' prohibition is strictly neutral. In no sense can it be said that Congress has prohibited only editorial views of one particular ideological bent. Nor has it prevented public stations from airing programs, documentaries, interviews, etc. dealing with controversial subjects, so long as management itself does not expressly endorse a particular viewpoint. And Congress has not prevented station management from communicating its own views on those subjects through any medium other than subsidized public broadcasting. . . .

. . . Because Congress' decision to enact § 399 is a rational exercise of its spending powers and strictly neutral, I would hold that nothing in the First Amendment makes it unconstitutional. Accordingly, I would reverse the judgment of the District Court.

COURT ON SEX DISCRIMINATION IN COMMERCIAL ORGANIZATIONS

July 3, 1984

Do civic and other membership groups such as the U.S. Jaycees have a right to restrict their membership to one sex? That question was argued before the Supreme Court April 18 in the case of Roberts v. United States Jaycees. *By a 7-0 decision the Court held July 3 that states could require the organization to admit women as full members. A state's interest in ensuring equal treatment for its women citizens outweighed any First Amendment rights of the Jaycees involving freedom of speech or of association, the justices said.*

In handing down its decision, upholding the Minnesota Supreme Court, the U.S. Supreme Court overturned a ruling by the 8th U.S. Circuit Court of Appeals that a Minnesota law barring discrimination in public accommodations could not be used to challenge the Jaycees' refusal to admit women as full members. At least 38 states and many cities had anti-discrimination laws similar to Minnesota's. Some of them already had been invoked against restrictive practices of such organizations as the Rotary Club and the Boy Scouts.

Background and Arguments

The Jaycees, until 1965 the U.S. Junior Chamber of Commerce, was a civic organization for young men between the ages of 18 and 35 that actively sought members from the general public. It had about 295,000 members in 7,500 locals in 1981. Women could become associates but could not be full members with the right to vote and hold office in the organization. In 1974 and 1975 the Minneapolis and St. Paul chapters of the Jaycees disregarded the organization's bylaws and began admitting women to full membership. The national organization moved to revoke the local chapters' charters.

In admitting women, the two maverick chapters invoked Minnesota's Human Rights Act, which banned sex discrimination in public accommodations — defined as facilities "whose goods, services, facilities, privileges, advantages or accommodations are extended, offered, sold or otherwise made available to the public." In 1982 a U.S. district judge held that the Jaycees was subject to the state ban. A year later, however, the appeals court overturned that ruling, declaring that the Jaycees' First Amendment freedom of association was violated by the application of the state law.

At stake in the case, said the Jaycees' brief, was "the right of the people to decide for themselves who shall be their friends and associational companions." The question was "whether a membership organization composed of private persons may, without government interference, confine its purpose to providing beneficial service to something less than the whole of society...." Minnesota's law, the Jaycees argued, could be used to force the Junior League to accept male members, to compel the National Association for the Advancement of Colored People to begin serving the special interests of white people, and to prevent ethnic groups from limiting their membership to the people who shared their cultural heritage. Minnesota had demonstrated no compelling interest weighty enough to justify that burden on the Jaycees' First Amendment freedom to associate, the organization contended. Furthermore, the Jaycees' brief attacked the state law as unconstitutionally vague, providing no standards for other groups to use to determine whether they too were a "public accommodation" within its reach.

Defending the applicability of its law to the Jaycees, Minnesota asserted that there was no constitutional right of association apart from the specific First Amendment rights of expression. The freedom of association "is a derivative right whose existence the court has sometimes deemed necessary in order to protect the collective exercise by individuals of enumerated First Amendment rights such as free speech or assembly," the state argued. Furthermore, Minnesota's brief pointed out, the Court had explicitly rejected the argument that the First Amendment protected the right of those who believed in racial segregation to practice that belief by excluding blacks from certain institutions.

The justices should "reject as constitutionally groundless the idea that the First Amendment protects not only the right to espouse sex discrimination, but in the context of the Jaycees, the right to practice it," declared the state. "The Jaycees can point to no organization goal to which women cannot and do not aspire, no organization function which women cannot perform, and no organization position regarding which sex mandates a point of view," the state argued. "Allowing women to vote, hold office and receive awards will therefore change nothing about the organization except its sexually restrictive nature."

The application of the sex discrimination ban to the Jaycees was justified by the state's compelling interest in ensuring equality of access to the marketplace for women, argued the state, pointing out that the Jaycees marketed and sold membership in their organization, just as other businesses sold goods and services.

Impact of Court's Decision

It was unclear what impact the Court's ruling might have on other all-male organizations such as the Kiwanis and Elks clubs. Minnesota attorney general Hubert H. Humphrey III said, "I think it's a significant case and it probably will provide states further basis to make sure there is no discrimination in the public marketplace." However, Justice William J. Brennan Jr., writing for the majority, indirectly referred to the limited implications of the decision, stressing that "the local chapters of the Jaycees are large and basically unselective groups.... Apart from age and sex, neither the national organization nor the local chapters employs any criteria for judging applicants for membership, and new members are routinely recruited and admitted with no inquiry into their backgrounds." As a result, he concluded, "the Jaycees chapters lack the distinctive characteristics that might afford constitutional protection to the decision of its members to exclude women." Such discrimination "deprives persons of their individual dignity and denies society the benefits of wide participation in political, economic and cultural life...."

Two types of freedom of association were protected by the First Amendment, explained Brennan for the Court. The freedom of intimate association protected highly personal relationships, primarily those among family members. The Jaycees could not invoke that freedom because it was too large and unselective a group, he wrote. On the other hand, Brennan continued, the Jaycees could argue that their freedom of expressive association — the joining together of like-minded persons to work together toward shared goals — was violated when it was compelled to admit women as full members. Nonetheless, "The right to associate for expressive purposes is not, however, absolute," Brennan wrote. "We are persuaded that Minnesota's compelling interest in eradicating discrimination against its female citizens justifies the impact that application of the statute to the Jaycees may have on the male members' associational freedoms."

Brennan rejected the Jaycees' argument that the organization had uniquely male views on public controversies that might be undermined by admission of women. That argument, he said, reflected "unsupported generalizations about the relative interests and perspectives of men and women.... In the absence of a showing far more substantial than that

467

attempted by the Jaycees, we decline to indulge in the sexual stereotyp-
ing that underlies [the organization's] contention."

Justice Sandra Day O'Connor agreed with the Court's decision, but she
wrote separately to set out her view that commercial associations such as
the Jaycees enjoyed only minimum constitutional protection for their
freedom of association, while groups formed primarily for expressive
purposes had much broader protection under the First Amendment.

Justices Byron R. White, Thurgood Marshall, Lewis F. Powell Jr., and
John Paul Stevens fully agreed with the opinion. Justice William H.
Rehnquist agreed with the result but did not join the opinion. Chief
Justice Warren E. Burger, once president of a local Jaycees chapter in
Minnesota, and Justice Harry A. Blackmun, also a Minnesotan, did not
take part in the Court's consideration of the case.

> *Following are excerpts from the Supreme Court's July 3,*
> *1984, decision in* Roberts v. *United States Jaycees, ruling*
> *that states could open all-male commercial groups to*
> *women, and from the concurring opinion of Justice Sandra*
> *Day O'Connor:*

<u>No. 83-724</u>

Kathryn R. Roberts, Acting Commissioner, Minnesota Department of Human Rights, et al. *v.* United States Jaycees	On appeal from the United States Court of Appeals for the Eighth Circuit

[July 3, 1984]

JUSTICE BRENNAN delivered the opinion of the Court. [The CHIEF
JUSTICE and JUSTICE BLACKMUN took no part in the decision of this
case.]

This case requires us to address a conflict between a State's efforts to
eliminate gender-based discrimination against its citizens and the constitutional freedom of association asserted by members of a private
organization. In the decision under review, the Court of Appeals for the
Eighth Circuit concluded that, by requiring the United States Jaycees to
admit women as full voting members, the Minnesota Human Rights Act
violates the First and Fourteenth Amendment rights of the organization's
members. We noted probable jurisdiction, and now reverse.

I

A

The United States Jaycees (Jaycees), founded in 1920 as the Junior Chamber of Commerce, is a nonprofit membership corporation, incorporated in Missouri with national headquarters in Tulsa, Oklahoma. The objective of the Jaycees, as set out in its bylaws, is to pursue

"such educational and charitable purposes as will promote and foster the growth and development of young men's civic organizations in the United States, designed to inculcate in the individual membership of such organization a spirit of genuine Americanism and civic interest, and as a supplementary education institution to provide them with opportunity for personal development and achievement and an avenue for intelligent participation by young men in the affairs of their community, state and nation, and to develop true friendship and understanding among young men of all nations."

The organization's bylaws establish seven classes of membership, including individual or regular members, associate individual members, and local chapters. Regular membership is limited to young men between the ages of 18 and 35, while associate membership is available to individuals or groups ineligible for regular membership, principally women and older men. An associate member, whose dues are somewhat lower than those charged regular members, may not vote, hold local or national office, or participate in certain leadership training and awards programs. The bylaws define a local chapter as "any young men's organization of good repute existing in any community within the United States, organized for purposes similar to and consistent with those" of the national organization. The ultimate policymaking authority of the Jaycees rests with an annual national convention, consisting of delegates from each local chapter, with a national president and board of directors. At the time of trial in August 1981, the Jaycees had approximately 295,000 members in 7,400 local chapters affiliated with 51 state organizations. There were at that time about 11,915 associate members. The national organization's Executive Vice President estimated at trial that women associate members make up about two percent of the Jaycees' total membership.

New members are recruited to the Jaycees through the local chapters, although the state and national organizations are also actively involved in recruitment through a variety of promotional activities. A new regular member pays an initial fee followed by annual dues; in exchange, he is entitled to participate in all of the activities of the local, state, and national organizations. The national headquarters employs a staff to develop "program kits" for use by local chapters that are designed to enhance individual development, community development, and members' management skills. These materials include courses in public speaking and personal finances as well as community programs related to charity, sports, and public health. The national office also makes available to members a range of personal products, including travel accessories, casual wear, pins, awards, and other gifts. The programs, products, and other activities of the organization are all regularly featured in publications made available to the membership, including a magazine entitled "Future."

B

In 1974 and 1975, respectively, the Minneapolis and St. Paul chapters of the Jaycees began admitting women as regular members. Currently, the memberships and boards of directors of both chapters include a substantial portion of women. As a result, the two chapters have been in violation of the national organization's bylaws for about 10 years. The national organization has imposed a number of sanctions on the Minneapolis and St. Paul chapters for violating the bylaws, including denying their members eligibility for state or national office or awards programs, and refusing to count their membership in computing votes at national conventions.

In December 1978, the president of the national organizations advised both chapters that a motion to revoke their charters would be considered at a forthcoming meeting of the national board of directors in Tulsa. Shortly after receiving this notification, members of both chapters filed charges of discrimination with the Minnesota Department of Human Rights. The complaints alleged that the exclusion of women from full membership required by the national organization's bylaws violated the Minnesota Human Rights Act (Act), which provides in part:

"It is an unfair discriminatory practice:

"To deny any person the full and equal enjoyment of the goods, services, facilities, privileges, advantages, and accommodations of a place of public accommodation because of race, color, creed, religion, disability, national origin or sex." Minn. Stat. § 363.03, subd. 3 (1982).

The term "place of public accommodation" is defined in the Act as "a business, accommodation, refreshment, entertainment, recreation, or transportation facility of any kind, whether licensed or not, whose goods, services, facilities, privileges, advantages or accommodations are extended, offered, sold, or otherwise made available to the public."

After an investigation, the Commissioner of the Minnesota Department of Human Rights found probable cause to believe that the sanctions imposed on the local chapters by the national organization violated the statute and ordered that an evidentiary hearing be held before a state hearing examiner. Before that hearing took place, however, the national organization brought suit against various state officials, appellants here, in the United States District Court for the District of Minnesota, seeking declaratory and injunctive relief to prevent enforcement of the Act. The complaint alleged that, by requiring the organization to accept women as regular members, application of the Act would violate the male members' constitutional rights of free speech and association. With the agreement of the parties, the District Court dismissed the suit without prejudice, stating that it could be renewed in the event the state administrative proceeding resulted in a ruling adverse to the Jaycees....

Subsequently, the Jaycees amended their complaint in the District

Court to add a claim that the Minnesota Supreme Court's interpretation of the Act rendered it unconstitutionally vague and overbroad. The federal suit then proceeded to trial, after which the District Court entered judgment in favor of the state officials. *United States Jaycees* v. *McClure* (Minn. 1982). On appeal, a divided Court of Appeals for the Eighth Circuit reversed (1983). The Court of Appeals determined that, because "the advocacy of political and public causes, selected by the membership, is a not insubstantial part of what [the Jaycees] does," the organization's right to select its members is protected by the freedom of association guaranteed by the First Amendment. It further decided that application of the Minnesota statute to the Jaycees' membership policies would produce a "direct and substantial" interference with that freedom, because it would necessarily result in "some change in the Jaycees' philosophical cast," and would attach penal sanctions to those responsible for maintaining the policy. The court concluded that the State's interest in eradicating discrimination is not sufficiently compelling to outweigh this interference with the Jaycees' constitutional rights, because the organization is not wholly "public," the state interest had been asserted selectively, and the anti-discrimination policy could be served in a number of ways less intrusive of First Amendment freedoms.

Finally, the court held, in the alternative, that the Minnesota statute is vague as construed and applied and therefore unconstitutional under the Due Process Clause of the Fourteenth Amendment. In support of this conclusion, the court relied on a statement in the opinion of the Minnesota Supreme Court suggesting that, unlike the Jaycees, the Kiwanis Club is "private" and therefore not subject to the Act. By failing to provide any criteria that distinguish such "private" organizations from the "public accommodations" covered by the statute, the Court of Appeals reasoned, the Minnesota Supreme Court's interpretation rendered the Act unconstitutionally vague.

II

Our decisions have referred to constitutionally protected "freedom of association" in two distinct senses. In one line of decisions, the Court has concluded that choices to enter into and maintain certain intimate human relationships must be secured against undue intrusion by the State because of the role of such relationships in safeguarding the individual freedom that is central to our constitutional scheme. In this respect, freedom of association receives protection as a fundamental element of personal liberty. In another set of decisions, the Court has recognized a right to associate for the purpose of engaging in those activities protected by the First Amendment — speech, assembly, petition for the redress of grievances, and the exercise of religion. The Constitution guarantees freedom of association of this kind as an indispensable means of preserving other individual liberties.

The intrinsic and instrumental features of constitutionally protected association may, of course, coincide. In particular, when the State interferes with individuals' selection of those with whom they wish to join in a common endeavor, freedom of association in both of its forms may be implicated. The Jaycees contend that this is such a case. . . .

A

The Court has long recognized that, because the Bill of Rights is designed to secure individual liberty, it must afford the formation and preservation of certain kinds of highly personal relationships a substantial measure of sanctuary from unjustified interference by the State. *E.g., Pierce* v. *Society of Sisters* (1925); *Meyer* v. *Nebraska* (1923). Without precisely identifying every consideration that may underlie this type of constitutional protection, we have noted that certain kinds of personal bonds have played a critical role in the culture and traditions of the Nation by cultivating and transmitting shared ideals and beliefs; they thereby foster diversity and act as critical buffers between the individual and the power of the State. . . . Moreover, the constitutional shelter afforded such relationships reflects the realization that individuals draw much of their emotional enrichment from close ties with others. Protecting these relationships from unwarranted state interference therefore safeguards the ability independently to define one's identity that is central to any concept of liberty. . . .

 . . . Family relationships, by their nature, involve deep attachments and commitments to the necessarily few other individuals with whom one shares not only a special community of thoughts, experiences, and beliefs but also distinctively personal aspects of one's life. Among other things, therefore, they are distinguished by such attributes as relative smallness, a high degree of selectivity in decisions to begin and maintain the affiliation, the seclusion from others in critical aspects of the relationship. As a general matter, only relationships with these sorts of qualities are likely to reflect the considerations that have led to an understanding of freedom of association as an intrinsic element of personal liberty. Conversely, an association lacking these qualities — such as a large business enterprise — seems remote from the concerns giving rise to this constitutional protection. Accordingly, the Constitution undoubtedly imposes constraints on the State's power to control the selection of one's spouse that would not apply to regulations affecting the choice of one's fellow employees. . . .

Between these poles, of course, lies a broad range of human relationships that may make greater or leser claims to constitutional protection from particular incursions by the State. Determining the limits of state authority over an individual's freedom to enter into a particular association therefore unavoidably entails a careful assessment of where that relationship's objective characteristics locate it on a spectrum from the most intimate to the most attenuated of personal attachments. See generally

Runyon v. *McCrary* (1976) (POWELL, J., concurring). We need not mark the potentially significant points on this terrain with any precision. We note only that factors that may be relevant include size, purpose, policies, selectivity, congeniality, and other characteristics that in a particular case may be pertinent. In this case, however, several features of the Jaycees clearly place the organization outside of the category of relationships worthy of this kind of constitutional protection.

The undisputed facts reveal that the local chapters of the Jaycees are large and basically unselective groups. . . . Apart from age and sex, neither the national organization nor the local chapters employs any criteria for judging applicants for membership, and new members are routinely recruited and admitted with no inquiry into their backgrounds. . . . Furthermore, despite their inability to vote, hold office, or receive certain awards, women affiliated with the Jaycees attend various meetings, participate in selected projects, and engage in many of the organization's social functions. . . .

In short, the local chapters of the Jaycees are neither small nor selective. Moreover, much of the activity central to the formation and maintenance of the association involves the participation of strangers to that relationship. Accordingly, we conclude that the Jaycees chapters lack the distinctive charactacteristics that might afford constitutional protection to the decision of its members to exclude women. We turn therefore to consider the extent to which application of the Minnesota statute to compel the Jaycees to accept women infringes the group's freedom of expressive association.

B

An individual's freedom to speak, to worship, and to petition the Government for the redress of grievances could not be vigorously protected from interference by the State unless a correlative freedom to engage in group effort toward those ends were not also guaranteed. . . .

The right to associate for expressive purposes is not, however, absolute. Infringements on that right may be justified by regulations adopted to serve compelling state interests, unrelated to the suppression of ideas, that cannot be achieved through means significantly less restrictive of associational freedoms. . . . We are persuaded that Minnesota's compelling interest in eradicating discrimination against its female citizens justifies the impact that application of the statute to the Jaycees may have on the male members' associational freedoms.

On its face, the Minnesota Act does not aim at the suppression of speech, does not distinguish between prohibited and permitted activity on the basis of viewpoint, and does not license enforcement authorities to administer the statute on the basis of such constitutionally impermissible criteria. . . . Nor do the Jaycees contend that the Act has been applied in this case for the purpose of hampering the organization's ability to express its views. Instead, as the Minnesota Supreme Court explained, the Act reflects the State's strong historical commitment to eliminating discrimination and assuring its citizens equal access to publicly available goods and services.... That goal, which is unrelated to the suppression of expression, plainly serves compelling state interests of the highest order....

...[I]n explaining its conclusion that the Jaycees local chapters are "place[s] of public accommodations" within the meaning of the Act, the Minnesota court noted the various commercial programs and benefits offered to members and stated that, "[l]eadership skills are 'goods,' [and] business contacts and employment promotions are 'privileges' and 'advantages'...." Assuring women equal access to such goods, privileges, and advantages clearly furthers compelling state interests.

In applying the Act to the Jaycees, the State has advanced those interests through the least restrictive means of achieving its ends. Indeed, the Jaycees have failed to demonstrate that the Act imposes any serious burdens on the male members' freedom of expressive association. See *Hishon* v. *King & Spalding* (1984) (law firm "has not shown how its ability to fulfill [protected] function[s] would be inhibited by a requirement that it consider [a woman lawyer] for partnership on her merits"); (POWELL, J., concurring).... To be sure, as the Court of Appeals noted, a "not insubstantial part" of the Jaycees' activities constitutes protected expression on political, economic, cultural, and social affairs.... There is, however, no basis in the record for concluding that admission of women as full voting members will impede the organization's ability to engage in these protected activities or to disseminate its preferred views....

In any event, even if enforcement of the Act causes some incidental abridgement of the Jaycees' protected speech, that effect is no greater than is necessary to accomplish the State's legitimate purposes....

III

We turn finally to appellee's contentions that the Minnesota Act, as interpreted by the State's highest court, is unconstitutionally vague and overbroad. The void-for-vagueness doctrine reflects the principle that "a statute which either forbids or requires the doing of an act in terms so vague that [persons] of common intelligence must necessarily guess at its meaning and differ as to its application, violates the first essential of due process of law." *Connally* v. *General Construction Co.* (1925). The requirement that government articulate its aims with a reasonable degree of clarity ensures that state power will be exercised only on behalf of policies reflecting an authoritative choice among competing social values, reduces the danger of caprice and discrimination in the administration of the laws, enables individuals to conform their conduct to the requirements of law, and permits meaningful judicial review....

We have little trouble concluding that these concerns are not seriously implicated by the Minnesota Act, either on its face or as construed in this case. In deciding that the Act reaches the Jaycees, the Minnesota Supreme

Court used a number of specific and objective criteria — regarding the organization's size, selectivity, commercial nature, and use of public facilities — typically employed in determining the applicability of state and federal anti-discrimination statutes to the membership policies of assertedly private clubs. . . . The Court of Appeals seemingly acknowledged that the Minnesota court's construction of the Act by use of these familiar standards ensures that the reach of the statute is readily ascertainable. It nevertheless concluded that the Minnesota court introduced a constitutionally fatal element of uncertainty into the statute by suggesting that the Kiwanis Club might be sufficiently "private" to be outside the scope of the Act. . . . Like the dissenting judge in the Court of Appeals, however, we read the illustrative reference to the Kiwanis Club, which the record indicates has a formal procedure for choosing members on the basis of specific and selective criteria, as simply providing a further refinement of the standards used to determine whether an organization is "public" or "private." . . . By offering this counter-example, the Minnesota Supreme Court's opinion provided the statute with more, rather than less, definite content. . . .

IV

The judgment of the Court of Appeals is

Reversed.

JUSTICE O'CONNOR, concurring in part and concurring in the judgment.

I join Parts I and III of the Court's opinion, which set out the facts and reject the vagueness and overbreadth challenges to the Minnesota statute. With respect to Part II-A of the Court's opinion, I agree with the Court that the Jaycees cannot claim a right of association deriving from this Court's cases concerning "marriage, procreation, contraception, family relationships, and child rearing and education." *Paul* v. *Davis* (1976). Those cases, "while defying categorical description," identify certain zones of privacy in which certain personal relationships or decisions are protected from government interference. Whatever the precise scope of the rights recognized in such cases, they do not encompass associational rights of a 295,000-member organization whose activities are not "private" in any meaningful sense of that term.

I part company with the Court over its First Amendment analysis in Part II-B of its opinion. I agree with the Court that application of the Minnesota law to the Jaycees does not contravene the First Amendment, but I reach that conclusion for reasons distinct from those offered by the Court. I believe the Court has adopted a test that unadvisedly casts doubt on the power of States to pursue the profoundly important goal of ensuring nondiscriminatory access to commercial opportunities in our society. At the same time, the Court has adopted an approach to the general problem presented by this case that accords insufficient protection to expressive associations and places inappropriate burdens on groups claiming the protection of the First Amendment.

I

The Court analyzes Minnesota's attempt to regulate the Jaycees' membership using a test that I find both over-protective of activities undeserving of constitutional shelter and under-protective of important First Amendment concerns. The Court declares that the Jaycees' right of association depends on the organization's making a "substantial" showing that the admission of unwelcome members "will change the message communicated by the group's speech." . . . I am not sure what showing the Court thinks would satisfy its requirement of proof of a membership-message connection, but whatever it means, the focus on such a connection is objectionable.

Imposing such a requirement, especially in the context of the balancing-of-interests test articulated by the Court, raises the possibility that certain commercial associations, by engaging occasionally in certain kinds of expressive activities, might improperly gain protection for discrimination. The Court's focus raises other problems as well. How are we to analyze the First Amendment associational claims of an organization that invokes its right, settled by the Court in *NAACP* v. *Alabama* (1958), to protect the privacy of its membership? And would the Court's analysis of this case be different if, for example, the Jaycees membership had a steady history of opposing public issues thought (by the Court) to be favored by women? It might seem easy to conclude, in the latter case, that the admission of women to the Jaycees' ranks would affect the content of the organization's message, but I do not believe that should change the outcome of this case. Whether an association is or is not constitutionally protected in the selection of its membership should not depend on what the association says or why its members say it.

The Court's readiness to inquire into the connection between membership and message reveals a more fundamental flaw in its analysis. The Court pursues this inquiry as part of its mechanical application of a "compelling interest" test, under which the Court weighs the interests of the State of Minnesota in ending gender discrimination against the Jaycees' First Amendment right of association. The Court entirely neglects to establish at the threshold that the Jaycees is an association whose activities or purposes should engage the strong protections that the First Amendment extends to expressive associations.

On the one hand, an association engaged exclusively in protected expression enjoys First Amendment protection of both the content of its message and the choice of its members. . . .

On the other hand, there is only minimal constitutional protection of the freedom of *commercial* association. There are, of course, some constitutional protections of commercial speech — speech intended and used to promote a commercial transaction with the speaker. But the State is free to impose any rational regulation on the commercial transaction itself. The Constitution does not guarantee a right to choose employees, customers, suppliers, or those with whom one engages in simple commercial transactions, without restraint from the State. A shopkeeper has no constitutional right to deal only with persons of one sex. . . .

Many associations cannot readily be described as purely expressive or purely commercial. No association is likely ever to be exclusively engaged in expressive activities, if only because it will collect dues from its members or puchase printed materials or rent lecture halls or serve coffee and cakes at its meetings. And innumerable commercial associations also engage in some incidental protected speech or advocacy. . . .

In my view, an association should be characterized as commercial, and therefore subject to rationally related state regulation of its membership and other associational activities when, and only when, the association's activities are not predominantly of the type protected by the First Amendment. It is only when the association is predominantly engaged in protected expression that state regulation of its membership will necessarily affect, change, dilute, or silence one collective voice that would otherwise be heard. An association must choose its market. Once it enters the marketplace of commerce in any substantial degree it loses the complete control over its membership that it would otherwise enjoy if it confined its affairs to the marketplace of ideas. . . .

In summary, this Court's case law recognizes radically different constitutional protections for expressive and non-expressive associations. . . .

II

Minnesota's attempt to regulate the membership of the Jaycees chapters operating in that State presents a relatively easy case for application of the expressive-commercial dichotomy. Both the Minnesota Supreme Court and the United States District Court, which expressly adopted the state court's findings, made findings of fact concerning the commercial nature of the Jaycees activities. The Court of Appeals, which disagreed with the District Court over the legal conclusions to be drawn from the facts, did not dispute any of those findings. *United States Jaycees* v. *McClure* (CA8 1983). "The Jaycees is not a political party, or even primarily a political pressure group, but the advocacy of political and public causes, selected by the membership, is a not insubstantial part of what it does. . . . [A] good deal of what the [Jaycees] does indisputably comes within the right of association . . . in pursuance of the specific ends of speech, writing, belief, and assembly for redress of grievances."

There is no reason to question the accuracy of this characterization. Notwithstanding its protected expressive activities, the Jaycees — otherwise known as the Junior Chamber of Commerce — is, first and foremost, an organization that, at both the national and local levels, promotes and practices the art of solicitation and management. The organization claims that the training it offers its members gives them an advantage in business, and business firms do indeed sometimes pay the dues of individual memberships for their employees. Jaycees members hone their solicitation and management skills, under the direction and supervision of the organization, primarily through their active recruitment of new members. . . .

Recruitment and selling are commercial activities, even when conducted for training rather than for profit. The "not insubstantial" volume of protected Jaycees activity found by the Court of Appeals is simply not enough to preclude state regulation of the Jaycees' commercial activities. The State of Minnesota has a legitimate interest in ensuring nondiscriminatory access to the commercial opportunity presented by membership in the Jaycees. The members of the Jaycees may not claim constitutional immunity from Minnesota's antidiscrimination law by seeking to exercise their First Amendment rights through this commercial organization.

For these reasons, I agree with the Court that the Jaycees' First Amendment challenge to the application of Minnesota's public accommodations law is meritless. I therefore concur in Parts I and III of the Court's opinion and in the judgment.

COURT ON PRISONERS' RIGHTS

July 3, 1984

In decisions handed down July 3, a sharply divided Supreme Court severely limited constitutional protection for the rights of prison inmates and pretrial detainees. The Court made plain that the Constitution provided far less protection for the privacy, property, and privileges of persons in penal institutions than it did for the general population. Deferring to prison officials and citing the need to preserve institutional security as the overriding objective of prison administrators, Chief Justice Warren E. Burger announced the justices' decisions that:

• The Fourth Amendment guarantees against unreasonable search and seizure did not apply in prison cells; prisoners were subject to random searches of their cells at any time.

• The Constitution's promise that the government would not deprive someone of his property without due process of law was not violated by a prison guard's intentional destruction of an inmate's personal property, such as letters, photographs and books, items legally in the inmate's possession, if the state provided the inmate with a way to obtain a remedy for this deprivation.

• Neither prison inmates nor pretrial detainees had any constitutional right to "contact visits" at which they were permitted to embrace or touch their spouses, families, or friends.

• Inmates had no constitutional right to observe searches of their cells.

Alvin Bronstein, director of the National Prison Project of the American Civil Liberties Union, predicted that the major impact of the rulings was "that they will send a message to already weary federal trial and appeals court judges to stop paying attention to these cases." Bronstein said the decisions would make it "more difficult to convince judges they must step in and do something in a particular situation."

Hudson v. Palmer

The first two issues arose in Hudson v. Palmer, *begun by Russell Thomas Palmer Jr., a Virginia prisoner, after his personal books and papers were destroyed by a prison guard searching Palmer's cell. Palmer won a ruling from the 4th U.S. Circuit Court of Appeals that he had a constitutionally protected privacy interest in his cell that was violated by the search. However, the appeals court held that because the state provided a mechanism for him to obtain a remedy for the destruction of his property, its destruction did not violate his constitutional rights.*

The justices unanimously agreed that the state remedy for Palmer's property loss was sufficient, but the question of privacy divided them 5-4. "...[S]ociety is not prepared to recognize as legitimate any subjective expectation of privacy that a prisoner might have in his prison cell," wrote Chief Justice Burger for the majority, which included associate justices William H. Rehnquist, Sandra Day O'Connor (who wrote a separate concurring opinion), Byron R. White, and Lewis F. Powell Jr. "[A]ccordingly, the Fourth Amendment proscription against unreasonable searches does not apply within the confines of the prison cell," he continued. "The recognition of privacy rights for prisoners in their individual cells simply cannot be reconciled with the concept of incarceration and the needs and objectives of penal institutions."

"Virtually the only place inmates can conceal weapons, drugs and other contraband is in their cells. Unfettered access to these cells by prison officials, thus, is imperative if drugs and contraband are to be ferreted out and sanitary surroundings are to be maintained," Burger explained.

In a vigorous dissent, which Justice John Paul Stevens read from the bench in an unusual divergence from normal practice, Stevens, William J. Brennan Jr., Thurgood Marshall, and Harry A. Blackmun challenged the majority's ruling as regressive. "Measured by the conditions that prevail in a free society, neither the possessions nor the slight residuum of privacy that a prison inmate can retain in his cell can have more than the most minimal value. From the standpoint of the prisoner, however, that trivial residuum may mark the difference between slavery and humanity," Stevens wrote.

The Fourth Amendment declared that unjustified searches and seizures were such a threat to liberty that they must be forever condemned, he continued. The courts "have a special obligation to protect the rights

COURT ON PRISONERS' RIGHTS

of prisoners," Stevens said, labeling inmates "truly the outcasts of society." In the decision, he said, the Court had adopted a "hands off" approach to prison administration "that I thought it had abandoned forever. . . ."

Block v. Rutherford

The issue of contact visits and observation of cell searches came to the Court in Block v. Rutherford, *involving the Los Angeles County jail, which housed more than 5,000 male pretrial detainees and convicts. A suit begun in 1975 led to rulings by a federal district court and the 9th Circuit Court of Appeals granting some detainees the right to contact visits and requiring that inmates be permitted to watch when their cells were searched.*

Jail officials appealed, and by a 6-3 vote the Supreme Court overturned the lower courts' rulings. Burger wrote the majority opinion, accepting the argument of prison officials that, in the interest of security, they must have the discretion to ban all contact visits. Marshall, Brennan, and Stevens dissented, charging that the majority seemed "willing to sanction any prison condition for which they can imagine a colorable rationale, no matter how oppressive or ill justified that condition is in fact." Under previous precedents, the Court ruled that inmates awaiting trial could not be subject to "punishment," but could be subjected to constraints necessary for security.

Marshall said the Court had "turned a deaf ear to inmates' claims that the conditions of their confinement violate the federal Constitution." He added that "permitting low-risk pretrial detainees who have been incarcerated for more than a month ... to have contact visits with their [families]" would not undermine security.

Blackmun concurred with the majority in denying contact visitations and said he recognized the "danger of excessive judicial intervention" into the prison administration. "At the same time, however," he said, "careless invocations of 'deference' run the risk of returning us to the passivity of several decades ago, when the then-prevailing barbarism and squalor of many prisons were met with a judicial blind eye and a 'hands off' approach."

> *Following are excerpts from the Supreme Court's July 3, 1984, decisions in* Hudson v. Palmer *and* Block v. Rutherford, *ruling that prison inmates had no constitutional protection against destruction of personal papers by prison guards and that prison administrators had broad discretion to restrict inmates' rights in order to ensure security; and from the dissenting opinions by Justices John Paul Stevens and Thurgood Marshall:*

481

Nos. 82-1630 and 82-6695

Ted S. Hudson, Petitioner,
v.
Russell Thomas Palmer, Jr.

Russell Thomas Palmer, Jr.,
Petitioner
v.
Ted S. Hudson

On writs of Certiorari to the United States Court of Appeals for the Fourth Circuit

[July 3, 1984]

CHIEF JUSTICE BURGER delivered the opinion of the Court.

We granted certiorari in No. 82-1630 to decide whether a prison inmate has a reasonable expectation of privacy in his prison cell entitling him to the protection of the Fourth Amendment against unreasonable searches and seizures. We also granted certiorari in No. 82-6695, the cross-petition, to determine whether our decision in *Parratt* v. *Taylor* (1981), which held that a negligent deprivation of property by state officials does not violate the Fourteenth Amendment if an adequate postdeprivation state remedy exists, should extend to intentional deprivations of property.

I

The facts underlying this dispute are relatively simple. Respondent Palmer is an inmate at the Bland Correctional Center in Bland, Va., serving sentences for forgery, uttering, grand larceny, and bank robbery convictions. On September 16, 1981, petitioner Hudson, an officer at the Correctional Center, with a fellow officer, conducted a "shakedown" search of respondent's prison locker and cell for contraband. During the "shakedown," the officers discovered a ripped pillowcase in a trashcan near respondent's cell bunk. Charges against Palmer were instituted under the prison disciplinary procedures for destroying state property. After a hearing, Palmer was found guilty on the charge and was ordered to reimburse the State for the cost of the material destroyed; in addition, a reprimand was entered on his prison record.

Palmer subsequently brought this *pro se* action in United States District Court under 42 U.S.C. § 1983. Respondent claimed that Hudson had conducted the shakedown search of his cell and had brought a false charge against him solely to harass him, and that, in violation of his Fourteenth Amendment right not to be deprived of property without due process of law, Hudson had intentionally destroyed certain of his noncontraband personal property during the September 16 search. Hudson denied each allegation; he moved for and was granted summary judgment. The District

Court accepted respondent's allegations as true but held nonetheless, relying on *Parratt* v. *Taylor* that the alleged destruction of respondent's property, even if intentional, did not violate the Fourteenth Amendment because there were state tort remedies available to redress the deprivation, and that the alleged harassment did not "rise to the level of a constitutional deprivation."

The Court of Appeals affirmed in part, reversed in part, and remanded for further proceedings. (CA4 1983). The court affirmed the District Court's holding that respondent was not deprived of his property without due process. The court acknowledged that we considered only a claim of negligent property deprivation in *Paratt* v. *Taylor*. It agreed with the District Court, however, that the logic of *Paratt* applies equally to unauthorized intentional deprivations of property by state officials: "[O]nce it is assumed that a postdeprivation remedy can cure an unintentional but negligent act causing injury, inflicted by a state agent which is unamenable to prior review, then that principle applies as well to random and unauthorized intentional acts." The Court of Appeals did not discuss the availability and adequacy of existing state law remedies; it presumably accepted as correct the District Court's statement of the remedies available under Virginia law.

The Court of Appeals reversed the summary judgment on respondent's claim that the shakedown search was unreasonable. The court recognized that *Bell* v. *Wolfish* (1979) authorized irregular unannounced shakedown searches of prison cells. But the court held that an individual prisoner has a "limited privacy right" in his cell entitling him to protection against searches conducted solely to harass or to humiliate. The shakedown of a single prisoner's property, said the court, is permissible only if "done pursuant to an established program of conducting random searches of single cells or groups of cells reasonably designed to deter or discover the possession of contraband" or upon reasonable belief that the particular prisoner possessed contraband. Because the Court of Appeals concluded that the record reflected a factual dispute over whether the search of respondent's cell was routine or conducted to harass respondent, it held that summary judgment was inappropriate, and that a remand was necessary to determine the purpose of the cell search.

We granted certiorari. We affirm in part and reverse in part.

II

A

The first question we address is whether respondent has a right of privacy in his prison cell entitling him to the protection of the Fourth Amendment against unreasonable searches. As we have noted, the Court of Appeals held that the District Court's summary judgment in petitioner's favor was premature because respondent had a "limited privacy right" in his cell that might have been breached. The court concluded that, to protect this privacy right, shakedown searches of an individual's cell should be performed only "pursuant to an established program of conducting random searches ... reasonably designed to deter or discover the possession of contraband" or upon reasonable belief that the prisoner possesses contraband. Petitioner contends that the Court of Appeals erred in holding that respondent had even a limited privacy right in his cell, and urges that we adopt the "bright line" rule that prisoners have no legitimate expectation of privacy in their individual cells that would entitle them to Fourth Amendment protection.

We have repeatedly held that prisons are not beyond the reach of the Constitution. No "iron curtain" separates one from the other. *Wolff* v. *McDonnell* (1974). Indeed, we have insisted that prisoners be accorded those rights not fundamentally inconsistent with imprisonment itself or incompatible with the objectives of incarceration....

However, while persons imprisoned for crime enjoy many protections of the Constitution, it is also clear that imprisonment carries with it the circumscription or loss of many significant rights. See *Bell* v. *Wolfish.* These constraints on inmates, and in some cases the complete withdrawal of certain rights, are "justified by the considerations underlying our penal system." *Price* v. *Johnston* (1948); see also *Bell* v. *Wolfish,* and cases cited; *Wolff* v. *McDonnell.* The curtailment of certain rights is necessary, as a practical matter, to accommodate a myriad of "institutional needs and objectives" of prison facilities, *Wolff* v. *McDonnell,* chief among which is internal security, see *Pell* v. *Procunier* (1974). Of course, these restrictions or retractions also serve, incidentally, as reminders that, under our system of justice, deterrence and retribution are factors in addition to correction.

We have not before been called upon to decide the specific question whether the Fourth Amendment applies within a prison cell, but the nature of our inquiry is well defined. We must determine here, as in other Fourth Amendment contexts, if a "justifiable" expectation of privacy is at stake. *Katz* v. *United States* (1967). The applicability of the Fourth Amendment turns on whether "the person invoking its protection can claim a 'justifiable,' a 'reasonable,' or a 'legitimate expectation of privacy' that has been invaded by government action." *Smith* v. *Maryland* (1979), and cases cited....

Notwithstanding our caution in approaching claims that the Fourth Amendment is inapplicable in a given context, we hold that society is not prepared to recognize as legitimate any subjective expectation of privacy that a prisoner might have in his prison cell and that, accordingly, the Fourth Amendment proscription against unreasonable searches does not apply within the confines of the prison cell. The recognition of privacy rights for prisoners in their individual cells simply cannot be reconciled with the concept of incarceration and the needs and objectives of penal institutions.

Prisons, by definition, are places of involuntary confinement of persons who have a demonstrated proclivity for antisocial criminal, and often violent, conduct....

The administration of a prison, we have said, is "at best an extraordinarily difficult undertaking." *Wolff* v. *McDonnell; Hewitt* v. *Helms* (1983). But it would be literally impossible to accomplish the prison objectives identified above if inmates retained a right of privacy in their cells. Virtually the only place inmates can conceal weapons, drugs, and other contraband is in their cells. Unfettered access to these cells by prison officials, thus, is imperative if drugs and contraband are to be ferretted out and sanitary surroundings are to be maintained.

Determining whether an expectation of privacy is "legitimate" or "reasonable" necessarily entails a balancing of interests. The two interests here are the interest of society in the security of its penal institutions and the interest of the prisoner in privacy within his cell.... We strike the balance in favor of institutional security, which we have noted is "central to all other correction goals," *Pell* v. *Procunier*. A right of privacy in traditional Fourth Amendment terms is fundamentally incompatible with the close and continual surveillance of inmates and their cells required to ensure institutional security and internal order. We are satisfied that society would insist that the prisoner's expectation of privacy always yield to what must be considered the paramount interest in institutional security. We believe that it is accepted by our society that "[l]oss of freedom of choice and privacy are inherent incidents of confinement." *Bell* v. *Wolfish*....

[Section B omitted]

III

We hold that the Fourth Amendment has no applicability to a prison cell. We hold also that, even if petitioner intentionally destroyed respondent's personal property during the challenged shakedown search, the destruction did not violate the Fourteenth Amendment since the Commonwealth of Virginia has provided respondent an adequate postdeprivation remedy.

Accordingly, the judgment of the Court of Appeals reversing and remanding the District Court's judgment on respondent's Fourth and Fourteenth Amendments claim is reversed. The judgment affirming the District Court's decision that respondent has not been denied due process under the Fourteenth Amendment is affirmed.

It is so ordered.

JUSTICE STEVENS, with whom JUSTICE BRENNAN, JUSTICE MARSHALL and JUSTICE BLACKMUN join, concurring in part and dissenting in part.

This case comes to us on the pleadings. We must take the allegations in Palmer's complaint as true. Liberally construing this pro se complaint as we must, it alleges that after examining it, prison guard Hudson maliciously took and destroyed a quantity of Palmer's property, including legal materials and letters, for no reason other than harassment.

For the reasons stated in ... the opinion of the Court, I agree that Palmer's complaint does not allege a violation of his constitutional right to procedural due process. The reasoning in ... the Court's opinion, however, is seriously flawed — indeed, internally inconsistent. The Court correctly concludes that the imperatives of prison administration require random searches of prison cells, and also correctly states that in the prison context "[o]f course, there is a risk of maliciously motivated searches, and of course, intentional harassment of even the most hardened criminal cannot be tolerated by a civilized society." But the Court then holds that no matter how malicious, destructive or arbitrary a cell search and seizure may be, it cannot constitute an unreasonable invasion of privacy or possessory interest that society is prepared to recognize as reasonable.

Measured by the conditions that prevail in a free society, neither the possessions nor the slight residuum of privacy that a prison inmate can retain in his cell, can have more than the most minimal value. From the standpoint of the prisoner, however, that trivial residuum may mark the difference between slavery and humanity....

Personal letters, snapshots of family members, a souvenir, a deck of cards, a hobby kit, perhaps a diary or a training manual for an apprentice in a new trade, or even a Bible — a variety of inexpensive items may enable a prisoner to maintain contact with some part of his past and an eye to the possibility of a better future. Are all of these items subject to unrestrained perusal, confiscation or mutilation at the hands of a possibly hostile guard? Is the Court correct in its perception that "society" is not prepared to recognize *any* privacy or possessory interest of the prison inmate — no matter how remote the threat to prison security may be?

I

Even if it is assumed that Hudson had no reasonable expectation of privacy in most of the property at issue in this case because it could be inspected at any time, that does not mean he was without Fourth Amendment protection. For the Fourth Amendment protects Palmer's possessory interests in this property entirely apart from whatever privacy interests he may have in it....

There can be no doubt that the complaint adequately alleges a "seizure" within the meaning of the Fourth Amendment. Palmer was completely deprived of his possessory interests in his property; by taking and destroying it, Hudson was asserting "dominion and control" over it; hence his conduct "did constitute a seizure." The fact that the property was destroyed hardly alters the analysis — the possessory interests the Fourth Amendment protects are those of the citizen. From the citizen's standpoint, it makes no difference what the government does with his property once it takes it from him; he is just as much deprived of his possessory interests when it is destroyed as when it is merely taken....

... To hold that a prisoner's possession of a letter from his wife, or a picture of his baby, has no protection against arbitrary or malicious perusal, seizure or destruction would not, in my judgment, comport with any civilized standard of decency....

II

Once it is concluded that Palmer had adequately alleged a "seizure,' the question becomes whether the seizure was "unreasonable." Questions of Fourth Amendment reasonableness can be resolved only by balancing the intrusion on constitutionally protected interests against the law enforcement interests justifying the challenged conduct.

It is well-settled that the discretion accorded prison officials is not absolute. A prisoner retains those constitutional rights not inconsistent with legitimate penological objectives. There can be no penological justification for the seizure alleged here....

Depriving inmates of any residuum of privacy or possessory rights is in fact plainly *contrary* to institutional goals. Sociologists recognize that prisoners deprived of any sense of individuality devalue themselves and others and therefore are more prone to violence toward themselves or others. At the same time, such an approach undermines the rehabilitative function of the institution....

In the final analysis, however, any deference to institutional needs is totally undermined by the fact that Palmer's property was not contraband. If Palmer were allowed to possess the property, then there can be no contention that any institutional need or policy justified the seizure and destruction of the property. Once it is agreed that random searches of a prisoner's cell are reasonable to ensure that the cell contains no contraband, there can be no need for seizure and destruction of noncontraband items found during such searches. To accord prisoners any less protection is to declare that the prisoners are entitled to no measure of human dignity or individuality — not a photo, a letter, or anything except standard-issue prison clothing would be free from arbitrary seizure and destruction. Yet that is the view the Court takes today. It declares prisoners to be little more than chattels, a view I thought society had outgrown long ago.

III

By adopting its "bright line" rule, the Court takes the "hands off" approach to prison administration that I thought it had abandoned forever when it wrote in *Wolff* v. *McDonnell* (1974), that

> "though his rights may be diminished by the needs and exigencies of the institutional environment, a prisoner is not wholly stripped of constitutional protections when he is imprisoned for crime. There is no iron curtain drawn between the Constitution and the prisons of this country."

... Today's holding cannot be squared with the text of the Constitution, nor with common sense....

... The Fourth Amendment is part of that fundamental law; it represents a value judgment that unjustified search and seizure so greatly threatens individual liberty that it must be forever condemned as a matter of constitutional principle. The courts, of course, have a special obligation to protect the rights of prisoners. Prisoners are truly the outcasts of society. Disenfranchised, scorned and feared, often deservedly so, shut away from public view, prisoners are surely a "discrete and insular minority.". . .

By telling prisoners that no aspect of their individuality, from a photo of a child to a letter from a wife, is entitled to constitutional protection, the Court breaks with the ethical tradition that I had thought was enshrined forever in our jurisprudence.

Accordingly, I respectfully dissent from the Court's judgment in No. 82-1630 and from Part II-A of its opinion.

No. 83-317

Sherman Block, Sheriff of the County of Los Angeles, et al., Petitioners, *v.* Dennis Rutherford et al.	On writ of Certiorari to the United States Court of Appeals for the Ninth Circuit

[July 3, 1984]

CHIEF JUSTICE BURGER delivered the opinion of the Court.

We granted certiorari to decide whether pretrial detainees have a right guaranteed by the United States Constitution to contact visits and to observe shakedown searches of their cells by prison officials.

I

Los Angeles County Central Jail is one of seven principal facilities operated by the Sheriff of Los Angeles County. The three-story jail complex, located in downtown Los Angeles, is the largest jail in the country, with a capacity of over 5,000 inmates. It is the primary facility in Los Angeles County for male pretrial detainees, the vast majority of whom remain at the facility at most a few days or weeks while they await trial.

In 1975, respondents, pretrial detainees at Central Jail, brought a class action under 42 U.S.C. §§ 1983, 1985 against the County Sheriff, certain administrators of Central Jail, and the County Board of Supervisors, challenging various policies and practices of the Jail and conditions of their confinement. Only respondents' challenges to the policy of the Jail denying pretrial detainees contact visits with their spouses, relatives, children, and friends, and to the Jail's practice of permitting irregularly scheduled shakedown searches of individual cells in the absence of the cell occupants are before this Court. The District Court sustained both of these challenges. *Rutherford* v. *Pitchess* (CD Cal. 1978).

The District Court agreed with respondents that "the ability of a man to embrace his wife and his children from time to time during the weeks or months while he is awaiting trial is a matter of great importance to him," yet it recognized that "unrestricted contact visitation would add greatly" to security problems at the Jail. The court ultimately concluded, however, that the danger of permitting *low security risk* inmates to have "physical contact with their loved ones" was not sufficiently great to warrant deprivation of such contact. Striking what it believed was a "reasonable balance" between the twin considerations of prison security and the constitutional rights of the inmates, the court tentatively proposed to order contact visitation for those inmates who "have received other than high risk classification," and who have been incarcerated for more than two weeks.

With respect to the cell searches, the District Court concluded that allowing inmates to watch from a distance while their cells are searched would allay inmate concerns that their personal property will be unnecessarily confiscated or destroyed. The court concluded that "[f]uture shakedowns should be made while the respective inmates remain outside their cells but near enough to observe the process and raise or answer any relevant inquiry." The District Court viewed both of its proposed orders as "the least restrictive alternatives consistent with the purpose of [respondents'] incarceration.". . .

On appeal the Court of Appeals for the Ninth Circuit remanded the case to the District Court for consideration in light of our intervening decision in *Bell* v. *Wolfish* (1979), noting, among other things, that we rejected in *Wolfish* the suggestion that existence of less restrictive means for achievement of security objectives is proof of an exaggerated response to security concerns.

The District Court on remand reaffirmed its prior orders, "[finding] nothing in *Bell* v. *Wolfish* that render[ed] inappropriate any of the . . . challenged orders.". . .

On petitioner's second appeal, the Court of Appeals affirmed the District Court's orders requiring that certain of the detainees be allowed contact visits and that inmates be allowed to watch searches of their cells. *Rutherford* v. *Pitchess* (1983). . . .

We granted certiorari because of both the importance of the issue to the administration of detention facilities and the conflict among the Federal Courts of Appeals. We reverse.

[Section II omitted]

III

A

Petitioner's first contention is that it was error to conclude that even low risk detainees incarcerated for more than a month are constitutionally entitled to contact visits from friends and relatives. Petitioners maintain, as they have throughout these proceedings that, in the interest of institutional and public security, it is within their discretion as officials of a detention facility to impose an absolute prohibition on contact visits. The District Court did not find, nor did the Court of Appeals suggest, that the purpose of petitioners' policy of denying contact visitation is to punish the inmates. To the contrary, the District Court found that petitioners are fully cognizant of the possible value of contact visitation, and it commended petitioners for their conscientious efforts to accommodate the large numbers of inmates at Central.

The question before us, therefore, is narrow: whether the prohibition of contact visits is reasonably related to legitimate governmental objectives. More particularly, because there is no dispute that internal security of detention facilities is a legitimate governmental interest, our inquiry is simply whether petitioners' blanket prohibition on contact visits at Central Jail is reasonably related to the security of that facility.

That there is a valid, rational connection between a ban on contact visits and internal security of a detention facility is too obvious to warrant extended discussion. The District Court acknowledged as much. Contact visits invite a host of security problems. They open the institution to the introduction of drugs, weapons, and other contraband. Visitors can easily conceal guns, knives, drugs, or other contraband in countless ways and pass them to an inmate unnoticed by even the most vigilant observers. And these items can readily be slipped from the clothing of an innocent child, or transferred by other visitors permitted close contact with inmates. . . .

. . . Petitioners' flat prohibition on contact visits cannot be considered a more excessive response to the same security objectives. . . . In any event, we have emphasized that we are unwilling to substitute our judgment on these difficult and sensitive matters of institutional administration and security for that of "the persons who are actually charged with and trained in the running," of such facilities. In sum, we conclude that petitioners' blanket prohibition is an entirely reasonable, nonpunitive response to the legitimate security concerns identified, consistent with the Fourteenth Amendment. . . .

B

It has been the petitioners' practice, as it is of all such facilities, to conduct irregular or random "shakedown" searches of the cells of detainees while the detainees are away at meals, recreation, or other activities. Respondents do not dispute the need for these searches; they challenge the searches only to the extent that detainees are not permitted to observe them.

Petitioners respond that their method of conducting cell searches is a security measure virtually identical to that challenged in *Wolfish.* . . .

. . . The security concerns that we held justified the same restriction in *Wolfish* are no less compelling here. Moreover, we could not have been clearer in our holding in *Wolfish* that this is a matter lodged in the sound discretion of the institutional officials. We reaffirm that, "proper deference to the informed discretion of prison authorities demands that they, and not the courts, make the difficult judgments which reconcile conflicting claims affecting the security of the institution, the welfare of the prison staff, and the property rights of the detainees."

Accordingly, the judgment of the Court of Appeals is reversed.

It is so ordered.

JUSTICE MARSHALL, with whom JUSTICE BRENNAN and JUSTICE STEVENS join, dissenting.

This case marks the third time in recent years that the Court has turned a deaf ear to inmates' claims that the conditions of their confinement violate the Federal Constitution. See *Rhodes* v. *Chapman* (1981); *Bell* v. *Wolfish* (1979). Guided by an unwarranted confidence in the good faith and "expertise" of prison administrators and by a pinched conception of the meaning of the Due Process Clauses and the Eighth Amendment, a majority of the Court increasingly appears willing to sanction any prison condition for which they can imagine a colorable rationale, no matter how oppressive or ill justified that condition is in fact. So, here, the Court upholds two policies in force at the Los Angeles County Central Jail. Under one, a pretrial detainee is not permitted any physical contact with members of his family, regardless of how long he is incarcerated pending his trial or how slight is the risk that he will abuse a visitation privilege. Under the other, detainees are not allowed to observe searches of their cells, despite the fact that such searches frequently result in arbitrary destruction or confiscation of the detainees' property. In my view, neither of these policies comports with the Constitution.

... [N]either petitioners nor the majority have shown that permitting low-risk pretrial detainees who have been incarcerated for more than a month occasionally to have contact visits with their spouses and children would frustrate the achievement of any substantial state interest. Because such visitation would significantly alleviate the adverse impact of the Jail's current policies upon respondents' familial rights, its deprivation violates the Due Process Clause. . . .

COURT ON STUDENT AID/
DRAFT REGISTRATION
July 5, 1984

By a vote of 6-2, the Supreme Court July 5 overturned a 1983 decision by a U.S. district court judge who had ruled that a law linking federal student aid to draft registration was a bill of attainder, imposing punishment on individuals for their past behavior. The Constitution flatly bans such acts.

The Supreme Court held in the case of Selective Service System v. Minnesota Public Interest Research Group *that Congress acted to encourage draft registration, not to punish non-registrants, when it denied financial aid to college students who failed to register.*

The student aid provision had been enacted as part of the fiscal 1983 defense authorization bill (PL 97-252). Implementation of the ban was delayed by the challenge to the law brought by the Minnesota Public Interest Research Group on behalf of several young men who had not registered with the Selective Service System.

The law, which had been fully enforced since October 1, 1983, required students applying for federal aid to sign a form certifying that they had registered for the draft or were not required to do so — because, for example, they were female. More than 300,000 students who had not registered for the draft registered after the law took effect.

Background

Although implementation of the law was suspended during the lower court's consideration of the case, the Supreme Court in June 1983 allowed the government to start enforcing it. The law applied to all college students who received loans and grants from the federal government after July 1, 1983. But many colleges could not implement it that fast, so the Education Department did not require strict enforcement until October. After that time, colleges were barred from releasing federal aid checks to students until they had signed the required form.

The Education Department and the Selective Service System had no estimates of how many students had been denied federal grants and loans — or chose not to apply for aid — as a result of the law. But officials believed few had been affected, in light of the high rate of compliance. Joan Lamb, a spokesman for the Selective Service, said that about 97 percent of those required to register had done so by early 1984, with a total of 12 million men on the draft rolls.

It was not clear how effective the law was as an inducement for nonregistrants to sign up with the Selective Service, but Lamb attributed a jump in registration in the summer of 1983 to the widely publicized inauguration of the new requirement. In August and September 1983, Lamb said, about 75,000 more people registered than normally would have been expected.

After widespread protests from students and some colleges, bills to repeal the law were introduced in Congress, but none of them advanced beyond the hearing stage. During Senate debate in July 1983 on the fiscal 1984 defense authorization bill, an amendment to repeal the student aid language was tabled, and thus killed, 71-23.

The Challengers' Case

Students challenging the law with the help of the Minnesota Public Interest Research Group claimed it "was intended to and clearly does punish an identifiable group without the protections of a trial." The challengers contended the law was similar to an 1865 law that was the first of three to be invalidated as a bill of attainder by the Supreme Court. In 1867 the Court ruled 5-4 that the law was unconstitutional because it punished individuals for past conduct, without a trial, by excluding them from practicing their profession.

The 1982 law operated in similar fashion, the student challengers claimed. It punished certain young men for failing to register for the draft by denying them the federal aid they needed to finance a college education, thereby foreclosing that education and certain career opportunities. "There can be no doubt that the loss of such opportunities constitutes an onerous punishment in our society," argued the challengers' attorneys. "Post-secondary vocational training and college degrees have become the sine qua non of advancement in today's society. To disable a citizen from pursuing such training is to inflict a severe penalty."

The students also contended the law violated the Fifth Amendment's guarantee that individuals would not be compelled to incriminate themselves. By requiring all applicants for federal student aid to certify their draft registration, the law presented non-registrants with a cruel and impermissible "trilemma," the challengers said. Such students must either incriminate themselves by admitting their failure to register, commit perjury by certifying their registration falsely, or forgo financial aid, higher education, and their chosen careers.

The Government's Case

The government insisted the law was not intended to punish those who failed to register for the draft, but rather to encourage registration by those who failed to do so out of "inadvertence, neglect or willful refusal." The law, the government asserted, "promotes a fair allocation of increasingly scarce federal monies, since it rewards students who have performed the legal duty imposed on them by the Military Selective Service Act."

Like the challengers, the government dusted off an old bill-of-attainder case for comparison. In 1950, the Justice Department noted, the Supreme Court held that it was permissible for Congress to deny certain benefits to labor unions whose officers failed to file statements disclaiming membership in the Communist Party. That law was not a bill of attainder, the Court ruled, because any union officer who had been or was a member of the party could disaffiliate himself and sign the affidavit.

Although under the law young men had to register for the draft within 30 days of turning 18, federal regulations permitted late registrants to receive student aid. The Court should use those regulations as a basis for rejecting the bill-of-attainder challenge, the government argued. In a footnote, the government acknowledged that failure to register within 30 days of the 18th birthday was a criminal offense. However, the note continued, no registrant had ever been prosecuted for late registration.

The government dismissed the Fifth Amendment argument as well, saying nothing in the law compelled self-incrimination. Young men who did not register for the draft "have the option of simply not applying for federal aid, and so furnishing no information whatever to the government."

Court Decision

Writing for the Court, Chief Justice Warren E. Burger said the denial of a government benefit did not constitute punishment. Congress intended, he said, "not to punish anyone, but to promote compliance with the draft registration requirement and fairness in the allocation of scarce resources." Furthermore, Burger said, the denial of aid was not perma-

nent. A young man ineligible for aid because he had not registered for the draft had a 30-day grace period within which he could register and become eligible for aid.

The Court found evidence in the language and legislative history of the law that Congress intended to give non-registrants a 30-day grace period, during which they might sign up, after they were notified that they were ineligible for federal aid.

The Court majority did not resolve the question of whether such late registration compelled self-incrimination in violation of the Fifth Amendment. Justices William J. Brennan Jr. and Thurgood Marshall felt that it did, and that the law for that reason was unconstitutional. Justice Harry A. Blackmun did not participate in the decision.

> *Following are excerpts from the Supreme Court's July 5, 1984, decision in* Selective Service System v. Minnesota Public Interest Research Group, *upholding the constitutionality of the draft registration law, and from the dissenting opinion of Justice Thurgood Marshall:*

No. 83-276

Selective Service System et al. *v.* Minnesota Public Interest Research Group et al.	On appeal from the United States District Court for the District of Minnesota

[July 5, 1984]

CHIEF JUSTICE BURGER delivered the opinion of the Court. [JUSTICE BLACKMUN took no part in the decision of this case.]

We noted probable jurisdiction to decide (a) whether § 1113 of the Department of Defense Authorization Act of 1983, which denies federal financial assistance under Title IV of the Higher Education Act of 1965 to male students who fail to register for the draft under the Military Selective Service Act, is a Bill of Attainder; and (b) whether § 1113 compels those students who elect to request federal aid to incriminate themselves in violation of the Fifth Amendment.

I

Section 3 of the Military Selective Service Act, 50 U.S.C. App. § 453, empowers the President to require every male citizen and male resident alien between the ages of 18 and 26 to register for the draft. Section 12 of that Act imposes criminal penalties for failure to register. On July 2, 1980,

President Carter issued a Proclamation requiring young men to register within 30 days of their 18th birthday. Presidential Proclamation No. 4771 (1981).

Appellees are anonymous individuals who were required to register before September 1, 1982. On September 8, Congress enacted the Department of Defense Authorization Act of 1983, Pub. L. 97-252, 96 Stat. 718. Section 113(f)(1) provides that any person who is required to register and fails to do so "in accordance with any proclamation" issued under the Military Selective Service Act "shall be ineligible for any form of assistance or benefit provided under title IV of the Higher Education Act of 1965." Section 1113(f)(2) requires applicants for Title IV assistance to file with their institutions of higher education a statement attesting to their compliance with the draft registration law and regulations issued under it. Sections 1113(f)(3) and (4) require the Secretary of Education, in agreement with the Director of Selective Service, to prescribe methods for verifying such statements of compliance and to issue implementing regulations.

Regulations issued in final form on April 11, 1983, ... provide that no applicant may receive Title IV aid unless he files a statement of compliance certifying that he is registered with the Selective Service or that, for a specified reason, he is not required to register. The regulations allow a student who has not previously registered, although required to do so, to establish eligibility for Title IV aid by registering, filing a statement of registration compliance, and, if required, verifying that he is registered. The statement of compliance does not require the applicant to state the date that he registered.

In November 1982 the Minnesota Public Interest Research Group filed a complaint in the United States District Court for the District of Minnesota seeking to enjoin the operation of § 1113. The District Court dismissed the Minnesota Group for lack of standing but allowed three anonymous students to intervene as plaintiffs. The intervenors alleged that they reside in Minnesota, that they need financial aid to pursue their educations, that they intend to apply for Title IV assistance, and that they are legally required to register with the Selective Service but have failed to do so. This suit was informally consolidated with a separate action brought by three other anonymous students making essentially the same allegations as the intervenors.

In March 1983 the District Court granted a preliminary injunction restraining the Selective Service System from enforcing § 1113. After finding that appellees had demonstrated a threat of irreparable injury, the court held that appellees were likely to succeed on the merits. . . .

On June 16, 1983, the District Court entered a permanent, nationwide injunction against the enforcement of § 1113. The court held that the regulations making late registrants eligible for aid were inconsistent with the statute and concluded that the statute was an unconstitutional attainder. It also held the statute to violate appellees' constitutional privilege against compelled self-incrimination.

On June 29, we stayed the District Court's June 16 order pending the timely docketing and final disposition of this appeal. *Selective Service System* v. *Doe*. We noted probable jurisdiction on December 5, 1983, and we reverse.

II

The District Court held that § 1113 falls within the category of congressional actions that Art. I, § 9, cl. 3 of the Constitution bars by providing that "[n]o Bill of Attainder . . . shall be passed." A Bill of Attainder was most recently described by this Court as "a law that legislatively determines guilt and inflicts punishment upon an identifiable individual without provision of the protections of a judicial trial." *Nixon* v. *Administrator of General Services* (1977); see *United States* v. *O'Brien* (1968); *United States* v. *Lovett* (1946). The Government argues that § 1113 does not satisfy any of these three requirements, *i.e.,* specification of the affected persons, punishment, and lack of a judicial trial.

A

In forbidding Bills of Attainder, the draftsmen of the Constitution sought to prohibit the ancient practice of the Parliament in England of punishing without trial "specifically designated persons or groups." *United States* v. *Brown* (1965). Historically, Bills of Attainder generally named the persons to be punished. However, "[t]he singling out of an individual for legislatively precribed punishment constitutes an attainder whether the individual is called by name or described in terms of conduct which, because it is past conduct, operates only as a designation of particular persons." *Communist Party of the United States* v. *Subversive Activities Control Board* (1961). When past activity serves as "a point of reference for the ascertainment of particular persons ineluctably designated by the legislature" for punishment, the Act may be an attainder. See *Cummings* v. *Missouri* (1867).

In *Cummings* the Court struck down a provision of the Missouri post-Civil War Reconstruction Constitution that barred persons from various professions unless they stated under oath that they had not given aid or comfort to persons engaged in armed hostility to the United States and had never " 'been a member of, or connected with, any order, society, or organization, inimical to the government of the United States.' " The Court recognized that the oath was required, not "as a means of ascertaining whether parties were qualified" for their professions, but rather to effect a punishment for having associated with the Confederacy....

The District Court in this case viewed § 1113 as comparable to the provisions of the Reconstruction laws declared unconstitutional ... because it thought the statute singled out nonregistrants and made them ineligible for aid based on their past conduct, *i.e.,* failure to register.... Having construed § 1113 as precluding late registration, the District Court read the statute to be retrospective, in that it denies financial assistance to an identifiable group — nonregistrants — based on their past conduct....

We reject the District Court's view that § 1113 requires registration within the time fixed by Proclamation No. 4771. That view is plainly inconsistent with the structure of § 1113 and with the legislative history....

... § 1113's requirements, far from irreversible, can be met readily by either timely or late filing. "Far from attaching to ... past and ineradicable actions," ineligibility for Title IV benefits "is made to turn upon continuingly contemporaneous fact" which a student who wants public assistance can correct. *Communist Party of the United States* v. *Subversive Activities Control Board.*

B

... In deciding whether a statute inflicts forbidden punishment, we have recognized three necessary inquiries: (1) whether the challenged statute falls within the historical meaning of legislative punishment; (2) whether the statute, "viewed in terms of the type and severity of burdens imposed, reasonably can be said to further nonpunitive legislative purposes"; and (3) whether the legislative record "evinces a congressional intent to punish." We conclude that under these criteria § 1113 is not a punitive Bill of Attainder....

[Sections 1, 2 and C omitted]

III

Appellees assert that § 1113 violates the Fifth Amendment by compelling nonregistrants to acknowledge that they have failed to register timely when confronted with certifying to their schools that they have complied with the registration law. Pointing to the fact that the willful failure to register within the time fixed by Proclamation No. 4771 is a criminal offense punishable under 50 U.S.C. § 462, they contend that § 1113 requires them — since in fact they have not registered — to confess to a criminal act and that this is "compulsion" in violation of their Fifth Amendment rights.

However, a person who has not registered clearly is under no compulsion to seek financial aid; if he has not registered, he is simply ineligibile for aid. Since a nonregistrant is bound to know that his application for federal aid would be denied, he is in no sense under any "compulsion" to seek that aid. He has no reason to make any statement to anyone as to whether or not he has registered.

If appellees decide to register late, they could, of course, obtain Title IV aid without providing any information to their school that would incriminate them, since the statement to the school by the applicant is simply that he is in compliance with the registration law; it does not require him to disclose whether he was a timely or a late registrant.... A late registrant is therefore not required to disclose any incriminating information in order to become eligible for aid....

IV

We conclude that § 1113 does not violate the proscription against Bills of Attainder. Nor have appellees raised a cognizable claim under the Fifth Amendment.

The judgment of the District Court is

Reversed.

JUSTICE MARSHALL, dissenting.

In 1980, after a 5-year suspension, the United States Government reinstituted registration for military service. By Presidential Proclamation, all men born after January 1, 1960, were required to register with the Selective Service System within 30 days of their 18th birthday. The issue in this case is not whether Congress has authority to implement the law, but whether the method it has chosen to do so offends constitutional guarantees of individual rights. I conclude that § 1113 fails to pass constitutional muster on two grounds. First, it compels self-incrimination, in violation of the Fifth Amendment. Second, it violates the right to equal protection of the laws guaranteed under the Due Process Clause of the Constitution.

I

At the time of the enactment of the statute before the Court today, Congress understood that, of the draft-eligible population of 9,039,000 men, some 674,000 had failed to register, and many more registrants had failed to provide current mailing addresses. Explanations for this widespread dereliction of legal duty have been as varied as the proposals to obtain full compliance....

Both the agency and Congress have crafted strategies to increase compliance with the law, such as increasing publicity programs, declaring a grace period when nonregistrants could comply without fear of prosecution, and posting lists of registrants in their local post offices. To identify and locate nonregistrants, Selective Service has collected Social Security numbers on draft registration forms, and located nonregistrants through computer data bank sharing with the Department of Health and Human Services and through mail forwarding by the Internal Revenue Service. Several persons have been prosecuted for their failure to register, and the names of others have been forwarded to the Department of Justice for investigation and possible prosecution; the attendant publicity is seen by the agency as an effective method of communicating the duty to register and the seriousness of the failure to do so.

It is in this context that Congress considered and adopted the statute before the Court.... As the Court holds today, the purpose of this statute was not to penalize nonregistrants, but to encourage compliance with the legal duty to provide information to the Selective Service System.

It is tempting to succumb to the comfortable conclusions the majority draws after its glancing review of this legislation. After all, the Government has an explicit constitutional duty to provide for the common defense.... The statute at issue has something to do with promoting full compliance with the registration law, which in turn promotes fairness in allocating burdens in the event of reinstitution of involuntary induction. Much of the legislative rhetoric promoting § 1113 seems unexceptional: youth should accept the obligations as well as the privileges of a democracy. Nevertheless, mindful that "[i]t is the duty of courts to be watchful for the constitutional rights of the citizen, and against any stealthy encroachments thereon," *Boyd* v. *United States* (1886), I must dissent.

II

I do not have to disagree with the majority that § 1113 does not violate the constitutional prohibition against bills of attainder.... The majority emphasizes the "nonpunitive spirit" of the legislation implicit in the fact that Congress "allowed *all* nonregistrants to qualify for Title IV aid simply by registering late." Congress did not, however, grant immunity from criminal prosecution for that act of late registration. Absent such a grant, § 1113 must be struck because it compels self-incrimination.

The Fifth Amendment privilege against coerced self-incrimination extends to every means of government information gathering....

I do not take issue with the majority's conclusion that the Title IV application process itself does not require a student to divulge incriminating information to the educational institution. The neutrality of this compliance verification system is central to the majority's acceptance of the permissible, regulatory purpose of the statute. However, our inquiry cannot stop there. Although § 1113 does not coerce an admission of nonregistration, it does coerce registration with the Selective Service System, and hence individual reporting of self-incriminating information directly to the Federal Government.

If appellees were to register with Selective Service now so that they could submit statements of compliance to obtain financial aid for their schooling, they would still be in violation of federal law ... by registering late.... Failure to comply with Selective Service registration requirements within 30 days of one's eighteenth birthday is a felony, punishable by imprisonment for up to five years and/or a fine of up to $10,000....

There can be little doubt that a late registration creates a "real and appreciable" hazard of incrimination and prosecution, and that the risk is not "so improbable that no reasonable man would suffer it to influence his conduct." *Brown* v. *Walker* (1896)....

Having established that late registration is an incriminating act, the question to be asked is whether the Government has exercised its powers in a way that deprives appellees the freedom to refrain from self-incrimination through late registration. *Garrity* v. *New Jersey* (1967); *Malloy* v. *Hogan* (1964). When the Government extracts incriminating information by the leverage of the threat of penalties, including the "threat of substantial economic sanction," *Lefkowitz* v. *Turley* [1973], the information is not volunteered. . . .

The threat of the denial of student aid is substantial economic coercion, and falls within the ambit of these cases. For students who had received federal education aid before enactment of § 1113, termination of aid is coercive because it could force these students to curtail their studies, thereby forfeiting their investment in prior education and abandoning their hopes for obtaining a degree. Five of the six appellees in these cases fall into this category. Students who have not previously received federal aid may also be coerced by § 1113. All students understand that entry into most professions and technical trades requires postsecondary education. For students who cannot otherwise afford this education, compliance with § 1113 is coerced by the threat of foreclosing future employment opportunities. . . .

. . . I therefore completely agree with appellees that this enforcement mechanism violates the Fifth Amendment's proscription against self-incrimination as interpreted in our previous cases, and would strike the provision down on this ground alone.

Moreover, I do not understand the Court today to dispute that § 1113 raises serious Fifth Amendment problems. The Court concedes that it would be incriminating for appellees to register with the Selective Service now. . . . The majority incorrectly assumes, however, that appellees must claim their privilege against self-incrimination before they can raise a Fifth Amendment claim in this lawsuit. What the majority fails to recognize is that it would be just as incriminating for appellees to exercise their privilege against self-incrimination when they registered as it would be to fill out the form without exercising the privilege. . . .

. . . The defect in § 1113 is that it denies students seeking federal aid the freedom to withhold their identities from the Federal Government. If appellees assert their Fifth Amendment privilege by their silence, they are penalized for exercising a constitutional right by the withholding of education aid. If they succumb to the economic coercion either by registering, or by registering but claiming the privilege as to particular disclosures, they have incriminated themselves.

Thus, I cannot accept the majority's view that appellee's Fifth Amendment claims are not ripe for review. . . .

In sum, appellees correctly state that this law coerces them into self-incrimination in the face of a substantial risk of prosecution. . . .

III

The aspect of the law that compels self-incrimination is doubly troubling because a discrete subgroup of nonregistrants bears the brunt of the statute. The Federal Government has a duty under the Due Process Clause of the Fifth Amendment to guarantee to all its citizens the equal protection of the laws. *Rostker* v. *Goldberg* (1981); *Bolling* v. *Sharpe* (1954). Section § 1113, in my view, violates that constitutional duty. . . .

The majority is factually incorrect when it states that the statute at issue in this case treats all nonregistrants alike. "Only low-income and middle-income students will be caught in this trap," as was pointed out in floor debate on § 1113. Title IV education aid is awarded on the basis of need. . . . Although federal education aid is significant for a large segment of post-secondary students, more than three out of four post-secondary students dependent on family incomes under $6,000 are receiving Title IV aid. . . . In contrast, only 8% of students dependent on families with incomes over $30,000 receive any Department of Education-funded financial aid. . . .

As appellees argued in the District Court and in their briefs to this Court, by linking draft compliance with education aid, Congress has created a de facto classification based on wealth, and has laid an unequal hand on those who have committed precisely the same offense of failing to register with the Selective Service within 30 days of their eighteenth birthday. *Cf. Yick Wo* v. *Hopkins* (1886). Further, § 1113 clearly burdens these individuals' interest in access to education, which "provides the basic tools by which individuals might lead economically productive lives to the benefit of us all." *Plyler* v. *Doe* (1982). . . .

IV

As the District Court noted, the issue before us "turns not on whether the registration law should be enforced, but in what manner." *Doe* v. *Selective Service System* (1983). For the reasons stated above, I find § 1113 of the Military Appropriations Act of 1982 violative of the Fifth Amendment, both because it compels self-incrimination, and because it violates due process by denying persons the equal protection of the laws. I respectfully dissent.

COURT ON EXCLUSIONARY RULE

July 5, 1984

Seventy years after a unanimous Supreme Court excluded illegally obtained evidence from use at federal trials, the Court agreed to permit use of such evidence if the police who seized it thought they were acting legally. The justices July 5 by 6-3 approved this "good faith" exception to the exclusionary rule in deciding the case of United States v. Leon. *In so doing, the Court reversed a 9th U.S. Circuit Court of Appeals decision excluding evidence in a federal narcotics case because the search warrant used to seize it later was found to be based on insufficient information.*

It was the second time within a month that the Court had carved out an exception to the rule. In the case of Nix v. Williams, *the Court June 11 approved an "inevitable discovery" exception permitting the use of evidence collected through police misconduct when it would inevitably have been discovered.*

The Reagan administration had urged the Court to endorse a good faith exception, and the Senate on Feb. 7 had passed a bill to create one by statute. That bill, however, remained bottled up in the House Judiciary Committee. Attorney General William French Smith said of the July 5 Court decision that it "gives the American people a result we have sought for some time, by better striking the balance between the rights of the accused and the rights of society to protect itself.... The Court's decision will help restore respect for the criminal justice system by allowing the use of some of the most reliable and relevant evidence in the fact-finding process. It gives recognition to the principle that the ascertainment of truth is a priority in our criminal justice system."

Nix Case

The Nix case began on Christmas Eve 1968, when a 10-year-old girl was murdered in Des Moines, Iowa. A suspect, Robert Anthony Williams, was quickly apprehended. During a long car ride, police — without formally questioning Williams — elicited from him the whereabouts of the girl's body, which was the subject of an intensive search. Williams was subsequently convicted of murder.

In 1977 the Supreme Court reversed Williams' conviction, holding that police had violated his right to legal counsel by using the long car ride as a time to persuade him to lead them to the body. Williams was retried and convicted again. At the second trial, evidence about the location and condition of the body was used by the prosecution. Williams again challenged his conviction, arguing that the body was found because of police misconduct and the evidence should not be admitted. Prosecutors insisted that the body would inevitably have been found by the searchers, without Williams' cooperation, and so his statement should be admitted as evidence.

In 1983 the 8th U.S. Circuit Court of Appeals reversed Williams' second conviction. The appeals court held that the state could not invoke an "inevitable discovery" exception unless it proved that the police misconduct was inadvertent, that the police acted in good faith. The state appealed, backed by the Reagan administration, arguing that the Supreme Court should recognize the inevitable discovery exception without any requirement of a showing of good faith.

By a 7-2 vote the Court agreed that "logic, experience, and common sense" dictated recognition of this exception. It could be invoked, Chief Justice Warren E. Burger wrote, "if the prosecution can establish by a preponderance of the evidence that the information ultimately or inevitably would have been discovered by lawful means. . . ." Denying prosecutors the use of this evidence "would do nothing whatever to promote the integrity of the trial process, but would inflict a wholly unacceptable burden on the administration of criminal justice," Burger continued.

The dissenting justices — William J. Brennan Jr. and Thurgood Marshall — agreed that the "inevitable discovery" exception was proper but argued that prosecutors should be required to meet a higher standard of proof before invoking it. They would require proof by clear and convincing evidence — rather than by a preponderance of the evidence — that the item in question would inevitably have been discovered.

Leon Case

Writing for the Court in the Leon case, Justice Byron R. White justified a good faith exception by a simple cost-benefit analysis and limited it — for the time being — to situations in which police obtained a warrant and executed a search in accord with it, only to have the warrant later found to be defective. The exclusionary rule had no deterrent effect on police in that situation, White explained, and simply "cannot pay its way."

Brennan, Marshall, and John Paul Stevens dissented. "The Court's victory over the Fourth Amendment is complete," Brennan declared for himself and Marshall. He called the ruling the climax of the "Court's gradual but determined strangulation of the rule" over the last decade and predicted that the majority would soon relax the exclusionary rule even in cases where police acted without a warrant. Stevens, in a separate dissent, said the Court was on the verge of converting "the Bill of Rights into an unenforced honor code that police may follow in their discretion."

Although he concurred with the majority, Justice Harry A. Blackmun sounded a cautionary note. "If it should emerge from experience that, contrary to our expectations, the good faith exception ... results in a material change in police compliance with the Fourth Amendment, we shall have to reconsider what we have undertaken here," he said.

The majority described the exclusionary rule as a judicial remedy intended to deter police from violating the Fourth Amendment guarantee against unreasonable search and seizure by denying them the use of evidence obtained in violation of that guarantee. White explained that "when an officer acting with objective good faith has obtained a search warrant ... and has acted within its scope ... there is no police illegality and thus nothing to deter."

Nor did the rule deter judges and magistrates from issuing invalid warrants, the majority said. "Judges and magistrates are not adjuncts to the law-enforcement team; as neutral judicial officers, they have no stake in the outcome of particular criminal prosecutions. The threat of exclusion thus cannot be expected significantly to deter them."

White said it cost society too much — in terms of weakened prosecutions — to apply the rule rigidly. "Particularly when law enforcement officers have acted in objective good faith or their transgressions have been minor, the magnitude of the benefit conferred on such guilty defendants offends basic concepts of the criminal justice system," he wrote. "We conclude that the marginal or nonexistent benefits produced by suppressing evidence obtained in objectively reasonable reliance on a subsequently invalidated search warrant cannot justify the substantial costs of exclusion."

The dissenters took a far broader view of the exclusionary rule's purpose. For them, the use of illegally obtained evidence in court inflicted a second constitutional injury upon a defendant and destroyed the integrity of the judicial system that permitted its use. "The major-

ity," wrote Brennan, "ignores the fundamental constitutional importance of what is at stake here. . . . [T]he task of combating crime and convincing the guilty will in every era seem of such critical and pressing concern that we may be lured by the temptations of expediency into forsaking our commitment to protecting individual liberty and privacy. It was for that very reason that the framers of the Bill of Rights insisted that law enforcement efforts be permanently and unambiguously restricted in order to preserve personal freedoms."

Other Cases

In a companion case, Massachusetts v. Sheppard, the Court by 7-2 applied the new exception to admit once-suppressed evidence in a murder case. White again wrote the opinion; Brennan and Marshall dissented. In that case, the home of a murder suspect was searched and a number of incriminating pieces of evidence were found. The warrant, however, was a makeshift form used because no proper forms were available and was found to be technically defective, even though the supporting affidavit prepared by the police was correct and would have justified the issuance of a warrant. As in the Leon case, the police had acted in good faith, assistant district attorneys had approved the warrant applications, and they had been signed and issued by judicial officers.

In a third case decided July 5, the Court held 5-4 that the exclusionary rule could not be invoked at all in civil deportation proceedings. Sandra Day O'Connor wrote the Court's opinion in Immigration and Naturalization Service v. Lopez-Mendoza; Brennan, White, Marshall, and Stevens dissented.

> *Following are excerpts from the Supreme Court's July 5, 1984, decision in United States v. Leon permitting the use of illegally obtained evidence in federal trials if the police who seized it thought they were acting legally, and in "good faith"; from the concurring opinion of Justice Blackmun; and from the dissenting opinions of justices Stevens and Brennan:*

No. 82-1771

United States, Petitioner v. Alberto Antonio Leon Et Al.	}	On writ of Certiorari to the United States Court of Appeals for the Ninth Circuit

[July 5, 1984]

JUSTICE WHITE delivered the opinion of the Court.

This case presents the question whether the Fourth Amendment exclusionary rule should be modified so as not to bar the use in the prosecution's case-in-chief of evidence obtained by officers acting in reasonable reliance on a search warrant issued by a detached and neutral magistrate but ultimately found to be unsupported by probable cause. To resolve this question, we must consider once again the tension between the sometimes competing goals of, on the one hand, deterring official misconduct and removing inducements to unreasonable invasions of privacy and, on the other, establishing procedures under which criminal defendants are "acquitted or convicted on the basis of all the evidence which exposes the truth." *Alderman* v. *United States* (1969).

I

In August 1981, a confidential informant of unproven reliability informed an officer of the Burbank Police Department that two persons known to him as "Armando" and "Patsy" were selling large quantities of cocaine and methaqualone from their residence at 620 Price Drive in Burbank, Cal. The informant also indicated that he had witnessed a sale of methaqualone by "Patsy" at the residence approximately five months earlier and had observed at that time a shoebox containing a large amount of cash that belonged to "Patsy." He further declared that "Armando" and "Patsy" generally kept only small quantities of drugs at their residence and stored the remainder at another location in Burbank.

On the basis of this information, the Burbank police initiated an extensive investigation focusing first on the Price Drive residence and later on two other residences as well. Cars parked at the Price Drive residence were determined to belong to respondents Armando Sanchez, and Patsy Stewart, who had no criminal record. During the course of the investigation, officers observed an automobile belonging to respondent Ricardo Del Castillo, who had previously been arrested for possession of 50 pounds of marihuana, arrive at the Price Drive residence. The driver of that car entered the house, exited shortly thereafter carrying a small paper sack, and drove away. A check of Del Castillo's probation records led the officers to respondent Alberto Leon, whose telephone number Del Castillo had listed as his employer's. Leon had been arrested in 1980 on drug charges, and a companion had informed the police at that time that Leon was heavily involved in the importation of drugs into this country. Before the current investigation began, the Burbank officers had learned that an informant had told a Glendale police officer that Leon stored a large quantity of methaqualone at his residence in Glendale. During the course of this investigation, the Burbank officers learned that Leon was living at 716 South Sunset Canyon in Burbank.

Subsequently, the officers observed several persons, at least one of whom had prior drug involvement, arriving at the Price Drive residence and leaving with small packages; observed a variety of other material activity at the two residences as well as at a condominium at 7902 Via Magdalena; and witnessed a variety of relevant activity involving respondents' automobiles. The officers also observed respondents Sanchez and Stewart board separate flights for Miami. The pair later returned to Los Angeles together, consented to a search of their luggage that revealed only a small amount of marihuana, and left the airport. Based on these and other observations summarized in the affidavit, Officer Cyril Rombach of the Burbank Police Department, an experienced and well-trained narcotics investigator, prepared an application for a warrant to search 620 Price Drive, 716 South Sunset Canyon, 7902 Via Magdalena, and automobiles registered to each of the respondents for an extensive list of items believed to be related to respondents' drug-trafficking activities. Officer Rombach's extensive application was reviewed by several Deputy District Attorneys.

A facially valid search warrant was issued in September 1981 by a state superior court judge. The ensuing searches produced large quantities of drugs at the Via Magdalena and Sunset Canyon addressses and a small quantity at the Price Drive residence. Other evidence was discovered at each of the residences and in Stewart's and del Castillo's automobiles. Respondents were indicted by a grand jury in the District Court for the Central District of California and charged with conspiracy to possess and distribute cocaine and a variety of substantive counts.

The respondents then filed motions to suppress the evidence seized pursuant to the warrant. The District Court held an evidentiary hearing and, while recognizing that the case was a close one, granted the motions to suppress in part. It concluded that the affidavit was insufficient to establish probable cause, but did not suppress all of the evidence as to all of the respondents because none of the respondents had standing to challenge all of the searches. In response to a request from the Government, the court made clear that Officer Rombach had acted in good faith, but it rejected the Government's suggestion that the Fourth Amendment exclusionary rule should not apply where evidence is seized in reasonable, good-faith reliance on a search warrant.

The District Court denied the Government's motion for reconsideration and a divided panel of the Court of Appeals for the Ninth Circuit affirmed. . . .

The Government's petition for certiorari expressly declined to seek review of the lower courts' determinations that the search warrant was unsupported by probable cause and presented only the question "[w]hether the Fourth Amendment exclusionary rule should be modified so as not to bar the admission of evidence seized in reasonable, good-faith reliance on a search warrant that it subsequently held to be defective." We granted certiorari to consider the propriety of such a modification. . . .

We have concluded that, in the Fourth Amendment context, the exclusionary rule can be modified somewhat without jeopardizing its ability to perform its intended functions. Accordingly, we reverse the judgment of the Court of Appeals.

II

Language in opinions of this Court and of individual Justices has sometimes implied that the exclusionary rule is a necessary corollary of the Fourth Amendment, *Mapp* v. *Ohio* (1961); *Olmstead* v. *United States* (1928), or that the rule is required by the conjunction of the Fourth and Fifth Amendments. *Mapp* v. *Ohio* (Black, J., concurring); *Agnello* v. *United States* (1925). These implications need not detain us long. The Fifth Amendment theory has not withstood critical analysis or the test of time, see *Andresen* v. *Maryland* (1976), and the fourth Amendment "has never been interpreted to proscribe the introduction of illegally seized evidence in all proceedings or aainst all persons." *Stone* v. *Powell* (1976).

A

... Whether the exclusionary sanction is appropriately imposed in a particular case, our decisions make clear, is "an issue separate from the question whether the Fourth Amendment rights of the party seeking to invoke the rule were violated by police conduct." *Illinois* v. *Gates* [1983]. Only the former question is currently before us, and it must be resolved by weighing the costs and benefits of preventing the use in the prosecution's case-in-chief of inherently trustworthy tangible evidence obtained in reliance on a search warrant issued by a detached and neutral magistrate that ultimately is found to be defective.

The substantial social costs exacted by the exclusionary rule for the vindication of Fourth Amendment rights have long been a source of concern. "Our cases have consistently recognized that unbending application of the exclusionary sanction to enforce ideals of governmental rectitude would impede unacceptably the truth-finding functions of judge and jury." *United States* v. *Payner* (1980). An objectionable collateral consequence of this interference with the criminal justice system's truth-finding function is that some guilty defendants may go free or receive reduced sentences as a result of favorable plea bargains. Particularly when law enforcement officers have acted in objective good faith or their transgressions have been minor, the magnitude of the benefit conferred on such guilty defendants offends basic concepts of the criminal justice system. *Stone* v. *Powell*. Indiscriminate application of the exclusinary rule, therefore, may well "generat[e] disrespect for the law and the administration of justice." Accordingly, "[a]s with any remedial device, the application of the rule has been restricted to those areas where its remedial objectives are thought most efficaciously served." *United States* v. *Calandra* [1974]; see *Stone* v. *Powell; United States* v. *Janis* (1976).

B

Close attention to those remedial objectives has characterized our recent decisions concerning the scope of the Fourth Amendment exclusionary rule. The Court has, to be sure, not seriously questioned, "in the absence of a more efficacious sanction, the continued application of the rule to suppress evidence from the [prosecution's] case where a Fourth Amendment violation has been substantial and deliberate...." *Franks* v. *Delaware* (1978); *Stone* v. *Powell.* Nevertheless, the balancing approach that has evolved in various contexts — including criminal trials — "forcefully suggest[s] that the exclusionary rule be more generally modified to permit the introduction of evidence obtained in the reasonable good-faith belief that a search or seizure was in accord with the Fourth Amendment." *Illinois* v. *Gates* (WHITE, J., concurring in the judgment).

In *Stone* v. *Powell,* the Court emphasized the costs of the exclusionary rule, expressed its view that limiting the circumstances under which Fourth Amendment claims could be raised in federal habeas corpus proceedings would not reduce the rule's deterrent effect, and held that a state prisoner who has been afforded a full and fair opportunity to litigate a Fourth Amendment claim may not obtain federal habeas relief on the ground that unlawfully obtained evidence had been introduced at his trial. Cf. *Rose* v. *Mitchell* (1979). Proposed extensions of the exclusionary rule to proceedings other than the criminal trial itself have been evaluated and rejected under the same analytic approach....

As yet, we have not recognized any form of good-faith exception to the Fourth Amendment exclusionary rule. But the balancing approach that has evolved during the years of experience with the rule provides strong support for the modification currently urged upon us. As we discuss below, our evaluation of the costs and benefits of suppressing reliable physical evidence seized by officers reasonably relying on a warrant issued by a detached and neutral magistrate leads to the conclusion that such evidence should be admissible in the prosecution's case-in-chief.

III

A

Because a search warrant "provides the detached scrutiny of a neutral magistrate, which is a more reliable safeguard against improper searches than the hurried judgment of a law enforcement officer 'engaged in the often competitive enterprise of ferreting out crime,'" *United States* v. *Chadwick* (1971) (quoting *Johnson* v. *United States* (1948)), we have expressed a strong preference for warrants and declared that "in a doubtful or marginal case a search under a warrant may be sustainable where without one it would fail."...

... To the extent that proponents of exclusion rely on its behavioral effects on judges and magistrates in these areas, their reliance is misplaced. First, the exclusionary rule is designed to deter police misconduct rather than to punish the errors of judges and magistrates. Second, there exists no evidence suggesting that judges and magistrates are inclined to ignore or subvert the Fourth Amendment or that lawlessness among these actors requires application of the extreme sanction of exclusion.

Third, and most important, we discern no basis, and are offered none, for believing that exclusion of evidence seized pursuant to a warrant will have a significant deterrent effect on the issuing judge or magistrate. Many of the factors that indicate that the exclusionary rule cannot provide an effective "special" or "general" deterrent for individual offending law enforcement officers apply as well to judges or magistrates. And, to the extent that the rule is thought to operate as a "systemic" deterrent on a wider audience, it clearly can have no such effect on individuals empowered to issue search warrants. Judges and magistrates are not adjuncts to the law enforcement team; as neutral judicial officers, they have no stake in the outcome of particular criminal prosecutions. The threat of exclusion thus cannot be expected significantly to deter them. Imposition of the exclusionary sanction is not necessary meaningfully to inform judicial officers of their errors, and we cannot conclude that admitting evidence obtained pursuant to a warrant while at the same time declaring that the warrant was somehow defective will in any way reduce judicial officers' professional incentives to comply with the Fourth Amendment, encourage them to repeat their mistakes, or lead to the granting of all colorable warrant requests.

B

If exclusion of evidence obtained pursuant to a subsequently invalidated warrant is to have any deterrent effect, therefore, it must alter the behavior of individual law enforcement officers or the policies of their departments. . . .

. . . But even assuming that the rule effectively deters some police misconduct and provides incentives for the law enforcement profession as a whole to conduct itself in accord with the Fourth Amendment, it cannot be expected, and should not be applied, to deter objectively reasonable law enforcement activity. . . .

This is particularly true, we believe, when an officer acting with objective good faith has obtained a search warrant from a judge or magistrate and acted within its scope. In most such cases, there is no police illegality and thus nothing to deter. It is the magistrate's responsibility to determine whether the officer's allegations establish probable cause and, if so, to issue a warrant comporting in form with the requirements of the Fourth Amendment. In the ordinary case, an officer cannot be expected to question the magistrate's probable-cause determination or his judgment that the form of the warrant is technically sufficient. "[O]nce the warrant issues, there is literally nothing more the policeman can do in seeking to comply with the law." Penalizing the officer for the magistrate's error, rather than his own, cannot logically contribute to the deterrence of Fourth Amendment violations.

C

We conclude that the marginal or nonexistent benefits produced by suppressing evidence obtained in objectively reasonable reliance on a subsequently invalidated search warrant cannot justify the substantial costs of exclusion....

... The good-faith exception for searches conducted pursuant to warrants is not intended to signal our unwillingness strictly to enforce the requirements of the Fourth Amendment, and we do not believe that it will have this effect. As we have already suggested, the good-faith exception, turning as it does on objective reasonableness, should not be difficult to apply in practice. When officers have acted pursuant to a warrant, the prosecution should ordinarily be able to establish objective good faith without a substantial expenditure of judicial time....

If the resolution of a particular Fourth Amendment question is necessary to guide future action by law enforcement officers and magistrates, nothing will prevent reviewing courts from deciding that question before turning to the good-faith issue.... We have no reason to believe that our Fourth Amendment jurisprudence would suffer by allowing reviewing courts to exercise an informed discretion in making this choice.

IV

When the principles we have enunciated today are applied to the facts of this case, it is apparent that the judgment of the Court of Appeals cannot stand. The Court of Appeals applied the prevailing legal standards to Officer Rombach's warrant application and concluded that the application could not support the magistrate's probable-cause determination. In so doing, the court clearly informed the magistrate that he had erred in issuing the challenged warrant. This aspect of the court's judgment is not under attack in this proceeding.

Having determined that the warrant should not have issued, the Court of Appeals understandably declined to adopt a modification of the Fourth Amendment exclusionary rule that this Court had not previously sanctioned. Although the modification finds strong support in our previous cases, the Court of Appeals' commendable self-restraint is not to be criticized. We have now re-examined the purposes of the exclusionary rule and the propriety of its application in cases where officers have relied on a subsequently invalidated search warrant. Our conclusion is that the rule's purposes will only rarely be served by applying it in such circumstances....

Accordingly, the judgment of the Court of Appeals is

Reversed.

JUSTICE BLACKMUN, concurring.

... I join the Court's opinion in this case and the one in *Massachusetts* v. *Sheppard, post,* because I believe that the rule announced today advances the legitimate interests of the criminal justice system without sacrificing the individual rights protected by the Fourth Amendment. I write separately, however, to underscore what I regard as the unavoidably provisional nature of today's decisions....

What must be stressed, however, is that any empirical judgment about the effect of the exclusionary rule in a particular class of cases necessarily is a provisional one. By their very nature, the assumptions on which we proceed today cannot be cast in stone. To the contrary, they now will be tested in the real world of state and federal law enforcement, and this Court will attend to the results. If it should emerge from experience that, contrary to our expectations, the good faith exception to the exclusionary rule results in a material change in police compliance with the Fourth Amendment, we shall have to reconsider what we have undertaken here. The logic of a decision that rests on untested predictions about police conduct demands no less....

JUSTICE STEVENS, dissenting.

... The exclusionary rule is designed to prevent violations of the Fourth Amendment. "Its purpose is to deter — to compel respect for the constitutional guaranty in the only effectively available way, by removing the incentive to disregard it." *Elkins* v. *United States* (1960). If the police cannot use evidence obtained through warrants issued on less than probable cause, they have less incentive to seek those warrants, and magistrates have less incentive to issue them.

Today's decisions do grave damage to that deterrent function. Under the majority's new rule, even when the police know their warrant application is probably insufficient, they retain an incentive to submit it to a magistrate, on the chance that he may take the bait. No longer must they hesitate and seek additional evidence in doubtful cases....

... The Court's approach — which, in effect, encourages the police to seek a warrant even if they know the existence of probable cause is doubtful — can only lead to an increased number of constitutional violations.

Thus, the Court's creation of a double standard of reasonableness inevitably must erode the deterrence rationale that still supports the exclusionary rule. But we should not ignore the way it tarnishes the role of the judiciary in enforcing the Constitution....

... Courts simply cannot escape their responsibility for redressing constitutional violations if they admit evidence obtained through unreasonable searches and seizures, since the entire point of police conduct that violates the Fourth Amendment is to obtain evidence for use at trial. If such evidence is admitted, then the courts become not merely the final and necessary link in an unconstitutional chain of events, but its actual motivating force. "If the existing code does not permit district attorneys to have a hand in such dirty business it does not permit the judge to allow such iniquities to succeed." *Olmstead* v. *United States* (1928) (Holmes, J., dissenting). Nor should we so easily concede the existence of a constitutional violation for which there is no remedy. To do so is to convert a Bill of *Rights* into an unenforced honor code that the police may follow in their discretion. The Constitution requires more; it requires a *remedy*. If the Court's new rule is to be followed, the Bill of Rights should be renamed....

JUSTICE BRENNAN, with whom JUSTICE MARSHALL joins, dissenting.

Ten years ago in *United States* v. *Calandra* (1974), I expressed the fear that the Court's decision "may signal that a majority of my colleagues have positioned themselves to reopen the door [to evidence secured by official lawlessness] still further and abandon altogether the exclusionary rule in search-and-seizure cases." Since then, in case after case, I have witnessed the Court's gradual but determined strangulation of the rule. It now appears that the Court's victory over the Fourth Amendment is complete. That today's decision represents the *piece de resistance* of the Court's past efforts cannot be doubted, for today the Court sanctions the use in the prosecution's case-in-chief of illegally obtained evidence against the individual whose rights have been violated — a result that had previously been thought to be foreclosed.

The court seeks to justify this result on the ground that the "costs" of adhering to the exclusionary rule in cases like those before us exceed the "benefits." But the language of deterrence and of cost/benefit analysis, if used indiscriminately, can have a narcotic effect. It creates an illusion of technical precision and ineluctability. It suggests that not only constitutional principle but also empirical data supports the majority's result. When the Court's analysis is examined carefully, however, it is clear that we have not been treated to an honest assessment of the merits of the exclusionary rule, but have instead been drawn into a curious world where the "costs" of excluding illegally obtained evidence loom to exaggerated heights and where the "benefits" of such exclusion are made to disappear with a mere wave of the hand.

The majority ignores the fundamental constitutional importance of what is at stake here. While the machinery of law enforcement and indeed the nature of crime itself have changed dramatically since the Fourth Amendment became part of the Nation's fundamental law in 1791, what the Framers understood then remains true today — that the task of combatting crime and convicting the guilty will in every era seem of such critical and pressing concern that we may be lured by the temptations of expediency into forsaking our commitment to protecting individual liberty and privacy. It was for that very reason that the Framers of the Bill of Rights insisted that law enforcement efforts be permanently and unambiguously restricted in order to preserve personal freedoms. In the constitutional scheme they ordained, the sometimes unpopular task of ensuring that the government's enforcement efforts remain within the strict boundaries fixed by the Fourth Amendment was entrusted to the courts. As James Madison predicted in his address to the First Congress on June 8, 1789:

> "If [these rights] are incorporated into the Constitution, independent tribunals of justice will consider themselves in a peculiar manner the guardians of those rights; they will be an impenetrable bulwark against every assumption of power in the Legislative or Executive; they will naturally be led to resist every encroachment upon rights expressly stipulated for in the Constitution by the declaration of rights." 1 Annals of Cong. 439 (1789).

If those independent tribunals lose their resolve, however, as the Court has done today, and give way to the seductive call of expediency, the vital guarantees of the Fourth Amendment are reduced to nothing more than a "form of words." *Silverthorne Lumber Co.* v. *United States* (1920).

A proper understanding of the broad purposes sought to be served by the Fourth Amendment demonstrates that the principles embodied in the exclusionary rule rest upon a far firmer constitutional foundation than the shifting sands of the Court's deterrence rationale. But even if I were to accept the Court's chosen method of analyzing the question posed by these cases, I would still conclude that the Court's decision cannot be justified. . . .

. . . [A]s troubling and important as today's new doctrine may be for the administration of criminal justice in this country, the mode of analysis used to generate that doctrine also requires critical examination, for it may prove in the long run to pose the greater threat to our civil liberties. . . .

. . . [A]s critics of the exclusionary rule never tire of repeating, the Fourth Amendment makes no express provision for the exclusion of evidence secured in violation of its commands. A short answer to this claim, of course, is that many of the Constitution's most vital imperatives are stated in general terms and the task of giving meaning to these precepts is therefore left to subsequent judicial decision-making in the context of concrete cases. . . .

A more direct answer may be supplied by recognizing that the Amendment, like other provisions of the Bill of Rights, restrains the power of the government as a whole; it does not specify only a particular agency and exempt all others. The judiciary is responsible, no less than the executive, for ensuring that constitutional rights are respected.

When that fact is kept in mind, the role of the courts and their possible involvement in the concerns of the Fourth Amendment comes into sharper focus. Because seizures are executed principally to secure evidence, and because such evidence generally has utility in our legal system only in the context of a trial supervised by a judge, it is apparent that the admission of illegally obtained evidence implicates the same constitutional concerns as the initial seizure of that evidence. Indeed, by admitting unlawfully seized evidence, the judiciary becomes a part of what is in fact a single governmental action prohibited by the terms of the Amendment....

... [T]he Court has frequently bewailed the "cost" of excluding reliable evidence. In large part, this criticism rests upon a refusal to acknowledge the function of the Fourth Amendment itself. If nothing else, the Amendment plainly operates to disable the government from gathering information and securing evidence in certain ways. In practical terms, of course, this restriction of official power means that some incriminating evidence inevitably will go undetected if the government obeys these constitutional restraints. It is the loss of that evidence that is the "price" our society pays for enjoying the freedom and privacy safeguarded by the Fourth Amendment.... Understood in this way, the Amendment directly contemplates that some reliable and incriminating evidence will be lost to the government; therefore, it is not the exclusionary rule, but the Amendment itself that has imposed this cost.

In addition, the Court's decisions over the past decade have made plain that the entire enterprise of attempting to assess the benefits and costs of the exclusionary rule in various contexts is a virtually impossible task for the judiciary to perform honestly or accurately.... To the extent empirical data is available regarding the general costs and benefits of the exclusionary rule, it has shown, on the one hand, as the Court acknowledges today, that the costs are not as substantial as critics have asserted in the past....

... Rather than seeking to give effect to the liberties secured by the Fourth Amendment through guesswork about deterrence, the Court should restore to its proper place the principle framed 70 years ago ... that an individual whose privacy has been invaded in violation of the Fourth Amendment has a right grounded in that Amendment to prevent the government from subsequently making use of any evidence so obtained....

At the outset, the Court suggests that society has been asked to pay a high price — in terms either of setting guilty persons free or of impeding the proper functioning of trials — as a result of excluding relevant physical evidence in cases where the police, in conducting searches and seizing evidence, have made only an "objectively reasonable" mistake concerning the constitutionality of their actions. But what evidence is there to support such a claim?

Significantly, the Court points to none, and, indeed, as the court acknowledges, recent studies have demonstrated that the "costs" of the exclusionary rule — calculated in terms of dropped prosecutions and lost convictions — are quite low....

... [T]he Court's "reasonable mistake" exception to the exclusionary rule will tend to put a premium on police ignorance of the law. Armed with the assurance provided by today's decision that evidence will always be admissible whenever an officer has "reasonably" relied upon a warrant, police departments will be encouraged to train officers that if a warrant has simply been signed, it is reasonable, without more, to rely on it. Since in close cases there will no longer be any incentive to err on the side of constitutional behavior, police would have every reason to adopt a "let's-wait-until-its-decided" approach in situations in which there is a question about a warrant's validity or the basis for its issuance. . . .

Although the Court brushes these concerns aside, a host of grave consequences can be expected to result from its decision to carve this new exception out of the exclusionary rule. A chief consequence of today's decision will be to convey a clear and unambiguous message to magistrates that their decisions to issue warrants are now insulated from subsequent judicial review. Creation of this new exception for good faith reliance upon a warrant implicitly tells magistrates that they need not take much care in reviewing warrant applications, since their mistakes will from now on have virtually no consequence: If their decision to issue a warrant was correct, the evidence will be admitted; if their decision was incorrect but the police relied in good faith on the warrant, the evidence will also be admitted. Inevitably, the care and attention devoted to such an inconsequential chore will dwindle. Although the court is correct to note that magistrates do not share the same stake in the outcome of a criminal case as the police, they nevertheless need to appreciate that their role is of some moment in order to continue performing the important task of carefully reviewing warrant applicatons. Today's decision effectively removes that incentive.

Moreover, the good faith exception will encourage police to provide only the bare minimum of information in future warrant applications. The police will now know that if they can secure a warrant, so long as the circumstances of its issuance are not "entirely unreasonable," all police conduct pursuant to that warrant will be protected from further judicial review. . . . The long-run effect unquestionably will be to undermine the integrity of the warrant process. . . .

When the public, as it quite properly has done in the past as well as in the present, demands that those in government increase their efforts to combat crime, it is all too easy for those government officials to seek expedient solutions. In contrast to such costly and difficult measures as building more prisons, improving law enforcement methods, or hiring more prosecutors and judges to relieve the overburdened court systems in the country's metropolitan areas, the relaxation of Fourth Amendment standards seems a tempting, costless means of meeting the public's demand for better law enforcement. In the long run, however, we as a society pay a heavy price for such expediency, because as Justice Jackson observed, the rights guaranteed in the Fourth Amendment "are not mere second-class rights but belong in the catalog of indispensable freedoms." *Brinegar* v. *United States* (1949) (dissenting opinion). Once lost, such rights are difficult to recover. There is hope, however, that in time this or some later Court will restore these precious freedoms to their rightful place as a primary protection for our citizens against overeaching officialdom.

I dissent.

WORLD POPULATION PROBLEMS

July 11 and August 14, 1984

Meeting in Mexico City August 6-14, the United Nations International Conference on Population reviewed a "world population plan of action" that had been adopted at a meeting a decade earlier. A four-page Mexico City Declaration of Population and Development, issued the last day of the conference, said that although "considerable progress" had been made following the earlier U.N. meeting held in Bucharest, Romania, "millions of people still lack access to safe and effective family planning methods."

The Mexico City declaration came five weeks after a much longer and more pessimistic report on world population growth had been published by the World Bank. That report, issued July 11, projected a doubling of the earth's population by the year 2050 and urged stronger policies to slow the rapid rate of increase. The World Bank report went so far as to raise the question of whether, for some countries, it might not already be "too late" to curb the rapid population growth.

Both the Mexico City declaration and the World Bank report emphasized the need for governments of developing countries to initiate family planning activities. However, that broadly held position was challenged by the U.S. delegation at the conference. Indeed, the delegation, whose members were named by the Reagan administration, blamed the governments themselves for interfering in national economies and thus holding back economic development. The United States also contended that the development of free market economies was "the natural mechanism for slowing population growth."

Mexico City Conference

The Mexico City declaration stated that the experience with population policies in recent years had been "encouraging." But it stressed the "interrelated" problems of accelerating Third World birth rates, joblessness, and urbanization and said that "[m]ajor efforts" must be made to ensure that couples and individuals could exercise their "basic human rights" to decide "freely, responsibly, and without coercion" how many children they would have.

Some observers at the conference saw the Reagan administration position at Mexico City as growing out of a decade-old policy that barred the use of U.S. funds for abortions. The chairman of the U.S. delegation, former senator James L. Buckley, R-N.Y., struck a somewhat optimistic note. He said that the United States recognized "that a number of countries face critical problems" but that it rejected "the notion that we are caught up in a global population crisis."

Reporting on the conference for The New York Times, *Richard J. Meislin wrote that other delegates had "shown, for the most part, an uncommon consensus that voluntary family planning is the key element in the economic growth of developing countries."*

World Bank Report

The lengthy World Bank report, entitled World Development Report 1984, *marshaled facts and arguments against the idea that economic development would lead to lower birth rates. In some countries, it said, development might not be possible at all unless slower population growth could be achieved soon. The population analysis on which the report was based was the most comprehensive that the World Bank had ever undertaken. The report said that world population growth accelerated dramatically in the 20th century, from 0.5 percent to an unprecedented 2 percent. Between 1950 and 1984 it grew from 2.5 billion to almost 4.8 billion.*

Looking ahead to 2050, the report said that India might replace China as the most populous country with 1.7 billion people. It said that the population of all the developing nations would have burgeoned from 3.6 billion to 8.4 billion. The report projected the population of Bangladesh at 450 million in 2150. The population of the countries in sub-Sahara Africa might double from 440 million to 880 million in the next 20 years. Moreover, by the time world population stabilized in 2150, the report said, sub-Sahara Africa and South Asia would have about 50 percent of the world's population, as compared with 30 percent in 1984.

While birth rates (at about 2 percent in 1984) peaked at 2.4 percent in 1965, the report cautioned that most of the decline was accounted for by the success of population control measures in one country, China. To make matters worse, the bank, officially called the International Bank for Reconstruction and Development, said that some of its assumptions of future growth rates were "based more on hope than on present trends."

Emphasis on Population Control

The report said that fertility declines in the late 1960s and into the 1970s had been "much more closely associated with adult literacy and life expectancy than with gross national product per capita." Indeed, the bank said, between 1965 and 1975 birth rates dropped less in Brazil and Venezuela, where urbanization and industrialization were taking place, than in Sri Lanka, Thailand, and Turkey.

The report reiterated that the two most important policies leading to a lower birth rate in developing nations were promotion of family planning and female education. "The effect of the two together. . .," the bank said, "has been powerful."

The bank stressed the crucial importance of population control activities by the governments of the developing nations. For example, it said that government policy could affect decisions on family size by taxing and spending in ways that would provide parents with incentives and disincentives to limit their fertility. Governments also could offer "rewards" for women who deferred pregnancy, and they could provide insurance and old-age security for parents restricting the size of their families.

McNamara Article

Writing in the Summer 1984 issue of Foreign Affairs, *Robert S. McNamara, president of the World Bank from 1968 to 1981, warned that a slight decline in population growth rates in the 1970s must not be taken as a sign that the world no longer faced grave population problems. Editorial writers and commentators, he said, had been quick to call the population explosion "another non-crisis." "But this assessment is simply wrong," McNamara wrote.*

In his article, entitled "Time Bomb or Myth: The Population Problem," McNamara blamed the "fuzziness of policy instruments" and the "delay in obtaining results" for dulling the sense of urgency that surrounded the population problem 10 or 20 years earlier. He recommended that each nation with a rapid rate of population growth set quantitative population goals. If such goals had been established 10 years earlier, McNamara said, "no major developing country" with the possible exception of China would be satisfied with its demographic progress.

McNamara said that the World Bank's population study task force and the Population Council were the sources for the material he used in his article.

Following are excerpts from the report, World Development ment Report 1984, *on rapid world population growth, published July 11, 1984, by the International Bank for Reconstruction and Development; and the text of the Mexico City Declaration on Population and Development, issued August 14, 1984, by the United Nations International Conference on Population:*

WORLD DEVELOPMENT REPORT

Population and Demographic Change

While the causes of poor economic performance can be traced back twenty years, the links between demography and development can be understood only by going back even farther into the past. In the long run of history, the second half of the twentieth century stands out for its remarkable population growth. Consider that in the year 1 the world had about 300 million people. Its population then took more than 1,500 years to double. Though the general trend was rising, population growth was not steady; the balance of births over deaths was tenuous, and crises such as war or plague periodically reduced populations in parts of the world. Only in the eighteenth century did the number of people start to rise steadily. From 1750 until well into the twentieth century, the world's population grew at the then unprecedented rate of about 0.5 percent a year, faster in today's developed countries, slower elsewhere. World population size doubled again, this time in about 150 years; it had reached about 1.7 billion by 1900. In the twentieth century, growth continued to accelerate, from 0.5 to 1 percent until about 1950 and then to a remarkable 2 percent. In just over thirty years, between 1950 and today, world population nearly doubled again — growing from 2.5 billion to almost 4.8 billion. . . .

Since 1950 population growth has been concentrated largely in the developing countries. Though a postwar baby boom combined with falling mortality in the industrial countries, the population growth rate never exceeded 1 percent in Europe and seldom exceeded 1.5 percent in North America. At its peak, fertility in the United States meant that families had on average little more than three children; in Europe and Japan postwar families were even smaller. By the 1970s, in most developed countries fertility had fallen to a level near or even below "replacement" — about two children per couple being the level which, over the long run, holds population constant (demographic terms are defined in the glossary).

The postwar experience of developing countries was not only different but historically unprecedented. Driven by falling mortality and continued high fertility, their population growth rate rose above 2 percent a year. It peaked at 2.4 percent in the 1960s. It is now around 2.0 percent a year, because of a slightly greater decline in birth rates than in death rates.... Further decline in population growth will not come automatically. Much of the slowdown so far can be attributed to China, where fertility is already low, close to an average of two children per family. Most families in other developing countries now have at least four children, in rural areas five and more. In a few countries in which fertility fell in the 1970s, there is evidence that it has leveled off recently. For parts of South Asia and the Middle East, forecasts of a lower rate of population growth are based more on hope than on present trends. For much of Africa and Central America, population growth rates are rising and could rise still further. In Africa couples say they want more children than in fact they are having, while mortality — though high — can be expected to decline.

Furthermore, population "momentum" means that growth rates in developing countries will remain high for several decades even if couples have fewer children ... absolute annual increases will be close to or more than 80 million people a year in developing countries well into the next century. The baby "bulge" that resulted from the trends of high fertility and falling mortality that started twenty years ago is now entering childbearing age. In China, for example, the number of women aged twenty to thirty-four almost doubled between 1950 and 1980; throughout the 1980s, as the children born in the 1960s enter their twenties, the number of women marrying and bearing children will continue to increase. To reduce population growth to 1 percent a year by the early 1990s, couples in China would need to have fewer than two children on average.

These considerations should not obscure the central fact that the world's population growth rate is falling. The latter part of the twentieth century has been a demographic watershed, the high point of several centuries of accelerating growth and the beginning of what demographers project to be a continuous decline, until world population stabilizes sometime in the twenty-second century. Though absolute numbers will continue to increase for several decades, the issue now is how quickly the rate of increase can be slowed down — and how individual countries (and the international community) are to cope with continued growth in the meantime....

THE DEMOGRAPHIC FUTURE

... [If] World Bank population projections ... are correct, world population would stabilize around the year 2150, having risen from almost 4.8 billion to more than 11 billion.... It would reach 9.8 billion by the year 2050. The population of today's developed countries would grow from about 1.2 billion today to 1.4 billion in 2050, while that of those countries now classified as developing would grow from over 3.6 billion to 8.4 billion. By the time world population stabilized, the population of India would be 1.7 billion, making it the most populous nation on earth. Bangladesh, a country about the size of the state of Wisconsin in the United States, would have a population of 450 million. Nigeria, Ethiopia, Zaire, and Kenya, among the most populous countries in Africa, would have populations of 620 million, 230 million, 170 million, and 150 million, respectively. As a group, sub-Saharan Africa and South Asia — today's poorest countries, with the fastest population growth — would account for 50 percent of the world's people, compared with 30 percent today.

Even allowing for some error in such projections, it is clear that future population increases will be concentrated in what are now the poorer areas of the globe; the average level of human welfare will depend largely on the degree to which economic and social transformation occurs in these areas.

Are the assumptions that produce these projections realistic, and what do they imply for future human welfare? The critical assumptions are that the decline in mortality will continue until life expectancy of about eighty years is reached, and that fertility will decline to replacement level — in developing countries between the years 2005 and 2045, depending on recent mortality levels, fertility trends, and family planning efforts; and in most developed countries in the year 2010. (In the several developed countries in which fertility is now below replacement level, it is assumed to rise and then stabilize at replacement.)

In some respects these assumptions are optimistic. Consider the poor countries of Africa and South Asia. Even with rapid income growth and advances in literacy in the next two decades, they are not likely to reach the income and literacy levels that triggered fertility declines in such countries as Brazil, Korea, and Malaysia in the 1960s. . . . Yet their fertility is projected to decline significantly — and even with those declines their populations will more than double in the next fifty years. A pessimist might wonder whether for some countries it is not already too late — whether rising unemployment and increasing landlessness will overwhelm social and political institutions; whether fragile administrative systems will be unable to maintain health programs; whether, in countries that are already crowded and still heavily reliant on agriculture, mortality will rise to check further population growth.

Such speculative pessimism needs to be set against the concrete reasons for optimism. The experience of the past two decades shows that economic growth and social development are possible, even starting at low initial income levels, and that developing countries can take conscious steps to influence their demographic futures. Both mortality and fertility — the latter matters much more for population growth — can be brought down more quickly than projected. Declines need not rely, solely or even primarily, on per capita income growth. Educational change can occur rapidly; policy effort can make a difference. Moreover, the actions that would speed the demographic transition are also those which would increase economic growth. . . .

. . .The experience of the past two decades of population policy is encouraging. Many countries have shown that effective measures can be taken to slow population growth. . . .

The Setting for High Fertility

Why do the poor have many children? ... There are several good reasons why, for poor parents, the economic costs of children are low, the economic (and other) benefits of children are high, and having many children makes economic sense.

First, where wages are low, the difference between children's and mother's earnings will be small; income lost by the mother during a child's infancy may be easily recouped by the child later on. In poor rural areas, especially, children can help a lot. Nepalese village boys and girls of six to eight years work three to four hours a day caring for farm animals and helping with younger siblings. Javanese teenagers work eight to ten hours a day. Many Bangladeshi children work even longer hours; children in the Philippines and in Sri Lanka, where fertility is lower, work somewhat less. Sometimes children may also earn cash incomes. In the Philippines those in their late teens contribute as much to household cash income as do adults. And much of women's traditional work — in farming, crafts, and petty retailing — can be combined with looking after children. Other family members, including older siblings, are readily available to help.

In developed countries, by contrast, a major cost of children to parents is time lost from work — usually by the mother — or the cost, inconvenience, and uncertainty of finding child care. Nor do children contribute much to household chores and income as they grow up....

A second reason that having many children can make economic sense is the lack of schooling opportunities, particularly from the age of twelve or so. For young children of primary-school age, school can often be combined with work in the house or on the farm, especially if there is a school in the village. But the choice between school and work becomes harder as children grow up. If they do not go to secondary school, they can work more themselves and, by caring for younger siblings, allow their mothers to work more. The apparent disadvantages of secondary schooling are compounded if children must live away from home or travel long distances to get to school.

As parents' income rises, as schooling opportunities improve, and as education becomes more clearly the key to future success for children, parents everywhere send their children to school and keep them there longer. In turn they often have fewer children — because schooling itself and the loss of children's help are costly, and because having two or three educated children becomes a better "investment" (for the parents and for the children too) than having many who cannot be educated.

High infant and child mortality are a third reason for having many children. Although mortality has fallen, in many parts of the developing world it is still high. One out of five children dies before reaching the age of one in some parts of Africa; one out of seven in much of Bangladesh, India, and Pakistan. Parents may feel the need to have many babies to be sure that a few survive....

Fourth, poor parents are worried about who will take care of them when they are old or ill. In Indonesia, Korea, the Philippines, Thailand, and Turkey 80 to 90 percent of parents surveyed said they expect to rely on their children to support them in their old age. In Egypt, especially in rural areas, poor and uneducated parents are much more likely to expect to live with (and be supported by) their children when they are old than are rich and educated parents. For many adults, the need for support in their old age outweighs the immediate cost of children.

One reason parents look to children for help in disability and old age is the lack of safe alternatives. In developed countries there are trusted institutions (banks, pensions, government bonds, insurance, and mutual aid societies) that help individuals to earn today and to save and spend tomorrow. In poor countries, capital markets are not nearly so well developed. In parts of South Asia, there is no tradition of community support; elsewhere, community support is weakening as mobility increases. For the rural poor, children are the best possible annuity, a way to transform today's production into consumption many years hence. . . .

The Need for Public Policy

There are two broad justifications for government action to encourage people to have fewer children. The first is the gap between the private and social gains from having many children. Suppose that, even as each couple hopes to benefit from many children, it wishes its neighbors would have fewer, so that its children would face less competition for land and jobs. In other words, the couple's wish for society as a whole is different from its wish for itself. One reason private and social gains differ is the existence of "externalities": parents do not internalize the costs of their children to society as a whole. For example, one family's children will have little effect on the availability of land; but the children born of many families will. The same is true of the effects on forests or pasture. To narrow this gap between private and social perceptions, governments can act as custodians of society. They are meant to have longer time horizons than their individual constituents, and to weigh the interests of future generations against those of the present. . . .

The second justification for government action to reduce fertility is that people may have more children than they want, or would want had they more information about, and better access to, easier fertility control. For example, couples may lack (or disbelieve) information about falling child mortality — or about their chance to reduce the risks to their existing children by keeping numbers down — and thus have more children than needed to reach desired family size. They may not be fully aware of the health risks, to mothers and children, of many and closely spaced births. The very idea of planning pregnancies may be unknown, especially if social norms dictate early marriage for young women and if couples do not discuss sexual matters.

Even if they know about family planning, couples may not know how to practice it. They may be reluctant to ask questions, especially if their parents pressure them to have many children. Or they may lack ready access to modern contraceptives and be forced to rely on traditional methods such as rhythm and withdrawal, which are less effective in preventing conception, or on abortion, which, if primitively performed, puts the mother's life at risk.

In this situation, the role of the government is critical. . . .

Current Demographic Change in Developing Countries

Only in a few developing countries have population growth rates fallen below 2 percent a year in the past two decades. In many, population is still growing by more than 3 percent a year. In general, growth is fastest in the poorest countries. This delinking of population growth and prosperity in what is now the developing world began after World War I, when mortality began to decline. . . .

The current demographic conditions of developing countries can be summed up in seven statements.

1. The postwar rate of population growth in developing countries is without precedent. Though in the past two decades rates of population growth in some countries have been falling because of birth rate declines, rates of growth are still unusually high, and birth rates are not declining everywhere.

In 1984 the world's population will increase by about 80 million. Most of the increase, abut 73 million, will occur in developing countries, now comprising about three-quarters of world population. The combination of continued high fertility and much-reduced mortality has led to population growth of between 2 and 4 percent in most low- and middle-income countries, compared with 1 percent and less in most developed countries. Growth at 3 percent a year means that in seventy years population grows eightfold; at 1 percent a year it merely doubles. Current population growth in the developing economies is a phenomenon for which economic and demographic history offers no real precedent.

For developing countries as a group, population growth rates rose from 2.0 percent in 1950 to 2.4 percent in 1965, largely because of falling death rates. . . . Since then, death rates have continued to fall but birth rates have declined even more, so that growth has slowed somewhat. The rate of natural increase (and of population growth) in developing countries is now about 2 percent a year.

The fall in the average growth rate is due almost entirely to the birth rate decline in China, which alone accounts for a third of all the people in developing countries and where the birth rate has fallen by over 50 percent since 1965. . . . Birth rates have also fallen in other countries of East Asia — in Hong Kong, Korea, Thailand, and Singapore by more than 30 percent, in Indonesia and elsewhere by 20 to 30 percent. In these generally

529

middle-income economies, a demographic transition to low fertility is clearly underway. . . .

2. The high fertility and falling infant mortality of the mid-1960s mean that in developing countries today about 40 percent of populations are aged fifteen or younger.

In countries such as Kenya, where fertility has declined little or not at all, more than 50 percent of the population is younger than fifteen, compared with only 20 to 25 percent in developing countries. . . . Although the proportion of old people is smaller in developing countries, the dependency ratio — the proportion of the population under fifteen and over sixty-four — is on average higher. In Japan, for example, there are roughly two people of working age to support one who is either too old or too young to work; in Kenya, the ratio is less than one-to-one. Other things being equal, if income per worker were identical in Japan and Kenya, income per person in Japan would nevertheless be at least 30 percent higher. Even within the same country there are comparable differences in age structure — and hence in dependency burdens — among families. In urban Maharashtra state (India), about half the people in the poorest 10 percent of households are younger than fifteen; in richest 20 percent, only one in five is younger than fifteen.

3. Neither internal nor international migration offers real solutions to population growth. High rates of natural population increase account more for the rapid growth of cities in developing countries than does rural-urban migration. Despite extensive rural-urban migration, population growth in rural areas of low-income Asia and Africa still averages 2 percent or more a year. The present scale of international migration, both permanent and temporary, constitutes a small proportion of the populations of developing countries.

Cities in developing countries are growing at almost twice the rate of overall populations. . . . More than half the increase is due to the balance of births over deaths; the rest is due to migration from rural areas and the re-classification of rural areas to urban status. Historically, the urban populations of some of today's developed countries have grown even faster — for example, the urban population of the United States increased about 6 percent a year between 1830 and 1860. But today's developing countries have started from a much larger base, so the absolute increases are much greater. From 1950 to 1980 the urban population of all developing countries (excluding China) increased by 585 million — compared with total urban population in the developed countries in 1950 of just over 300 million.

Latin America is the most urbanized of developing-country regions. In 1980 about two-thirds of its people were urban dwellers, a level reached in today's developed countries only in 1950. Low-income Asia and Africa are still overwhelmingly rural; their current urbanization level of about 25 percent was reached in the developed countries before 1900. . . .

Despite the rapid growth of cities, the urban share of today's developing-country populations is not increasing especially fast. This is because not only urban but also rural populations are growing rapidly, and in low-income countries from a large base, so that a considerable growth of numbers will continue in the countryside for the rest of this decade and beyond. In India, for example, though urban rates of population growth are likely to be about four times higher than rural rates in the next two decades, and the urban population could increase by 170 million, the rural population will still increase by 130 million. . . .

Compared with rates of intercontinental migration from Europe in the eighteenth and nineteenth centuries, present-day permanent emigration rates are small: between 1970 and 1980 emigration absorbed about 3 percent of population growth in Europe and Latin America, less than 1 percent in Asia and Africa. . . . For India, a large low-income country, the emigration rate was only 0.2 percent. Only for a few countries are permanent emigration rates high, and these tend to be the relatively better-off, middle-income countries: Greece, Hong Kong, and Portugal. . . .

4. More often than not, current fertility and mortality rates are inversely related to income — but this rule has many significant exceptions. . . .

In general, the higher a country's average income, the lower its fertility and the higher its life expectancy. Some of the 100 countries used in the analysis are identified in the figures.

Sub-Saharan Africa and the Indian subcontinent (Bangladesh, India, and Pakistan) have the highest levels of fertility and mortality and the lowest incomes; fertility averages five to eight children per woman, and life expectancy is as low as fifty years. Countries of East Asia and Latin America have lower fertility (three to five children), higher life expectancy (about sixty years), and higher incomes. Some countries have moved faster than others: Brazil, Indonesia, Mexico, and Thailand are some of the countries that achieved relatively large reductions in fertility between 1972 and 1982. At the other extreme, fertility rose slightly in a few African countries. . . .

It is wrong to conclude, however, that countries must get richer before they can lower fertility and raise life expectancy. Average income is only one of the factors involved. . . . [S]ome countries have significantly lower fertility than the norm for those with their income level. Examples include China, Colombia, India, Indonesia, Korea, Thailand, and Sri Lanka. By contrast, countries with relatively high fertility (given their income) include Algeria, Jordan, and Morocco, most countries of sub-Saharan Africa, Venezuela, and even with its recent decline in fertility, Mexico. China, Costa Rica, and Sri Lanka have relatively high life expectancy. These exceptions demonstrate the importance of the availability and distribution of health and educational services, the extent to which adult women enjoy a status independent of childrearing, and the access of the poor to family planning services. . . .

5. The relation between income and life expectancy, and between income and fertility, has shifted over time....

[T]he same average income is associated with lower fertility and higher life expectancy in 1982 than in 1972. Since the 1920s, and especially since the end of World War II, the main reasons for rising life expectancy in developing countries have been better public health systems, educational advances, and the greater political stability that permitted these. For example, a quarter of Sri Lanka's decline in mortality after 1945 is attributable solely to the control of malaria. Rising incomes and associated improvement in nutrition and sanitation have in general played a lesser role. As a result, life expectancy is higher in developing countries than it was in today's developed countries at the turn of the century, despite income and education levels that in many countries are still lower....

6. Mortality has declined everywhere, and fertility has started to decline in many countries. But there is considerable variation, and in some regions and countries the declines now seem to be stalled at relatively high levels.

Almost all countries outside Africa have experienced some fertility decline in the past two decades. But since 1975 the decline seems to have slowed and even stopped in countries such as Costa Rica, India, Korea, and Sri Lanka, where fertility levels are still relatively high (though low given income levels in these countries). In contrast, once fertility started falling in today's developed countries, it went on falling more or less continuously. Though fertility rose in Europe and the United States for two decades after World War II, total fertility rates rose only a little above 3 even during this baby boom and have declined to less than 2 since....

7. Further declines in mortality rates will boost population growth much less from now on than they did in the 1950s and 1960s.

For most of the developing world, the time when declining mortality produced surges in population is passing rapidly. In part this is because mortality, though still high compared with developed countries, has already fallen considerably. But there are other reasons. Mortality declines affect population growth less when fertility is falling, and is and will be the case in most countries. Long-range population growth is less dependent on the addition of people whose lives are saved than on the number of children they subsequently bear. When fertility is high, saving a baby's life adds a great deal of reproductive potential. To save the lives of an infant girl and boy who will go on to have 6 children is to add those people plus (perhaps) their 36 grandchildren, 216 great grandchildren, and so on. But as fertility declines, so does the amount of extra reproductive capacity.... Furthermore, as mortality declines, more and more deaths are shifted from younger to older ages. To extend the life of someone sixty years old is to keep the population just one person larger than it would otherwise be, not to boost it by that person plus descendants....

Three points are clear from these projections.

• Even with rapid fertility (and mortality) decline, the developing world's population would more than double by the year 2050, rising to 6.9

billion. The population of Indonesia would still increase from 153 million to about 300 million, that of Bangladesh from 93 million to about 230 million, and that of India from 717 million to 1.4 billion.... For countries of Africa, Central America, and the Middle East, where the proportion of young people is higher and where fertility is still high and would take longer to decline to replacement level, the increases would be much greater. Even with rapid fertility decline, Kenya would not reach replacement-level fertility until 2015, and today's population of 18 million would increase to almost 70 million by 2050. Under the standard declines, replacement-level fertility would not be attained until 2030, and Kenya's population would grow to 120 million by 2050. With rapid fertility decline, El Salvador's population would still grow from 5 million to 12 million.

• Population growth beyond the year 2000 depends critically on falling fertility in the next decade or two.... [T]he difference in population size between the standard and rapid declines is not great in 2000 — less than 20 percent in most countries. Under any assumption, the populations of most developing countries are likely to increase by 50 percent or more by 2000; a few, including Kenya and Nigeria, will almost double. By the year 2050, however, the differences will be huge. If fertility falls sooner rather than later in Kenya, population there in 2050 will be reduced by about 50 million compared with what it would otherwise be, against today's total population of 18 million.

• In determining the ultimate size of world population, fertility matters more than mortality. Rapid mortality decline combined with standard fertility decline would produce population in developing countries 7 percent larger in the year 2050 than that resulting from the standard mortality decline. In contrast, rapid fertility decline would produce a population 25 percent smaller in the year 2050 than that resulting from the standard fertility decline. Combined with rapid mortality decline, the population would still be 20 percent smaller.... Insofar as mortality and fertility declines are linked, the combined rapid path for both is more realistic; it illustrates the relatively small effect that rapid mortality decline would have on population size, especially if fertility is falling. However, the implications of a faster mortality decline are not the same for all regions. In Latin America and in East Asia, where mortality is already low and fertility has fallen, the population in 2050 would be only 2 to 3 percent greater if rapid mortality decline were added to rapid fertility decline. But where mortality and fertility remain high — as in sub-Saharan Africa and South Asia — rapid mortality decline combined with standard fertility decline would produce a population in 2050 about 10 percent greater. But even that difference is much smaller than the difference between rapid and standard fertility decline: South Asia's population would be more than 20 percent smaller and Africa's about 50 percent smaller with a rapid rather than a standard decline in fertility....

These differences between rapid and standard declines in fertility have far-reaching consequences. To take the example of Bangladesh ... [the table on page 535 shows] what would happen to its population density and the size of its school-age and working-age population under the standard and rapid assumptions about declining fertility. Under both, population and average density will increase for the next seventy years. But the pressure on land (reflected in the projections of agricultural densities), already high, would more than double by the year 2050 under the standard assumption; under the rapid assumption, it would be higher than now in the year 2000 but would then begin to fall. The number of school-age children would almost double under the standard fertility decline by the year 2000; were fertility rates to decline rapidly, the number would still increase by 50 percent by the year 2000 but would then stop increasing....

Some countries have chosen to set quantitative targets based on feasible target declines in mortality and fertility.... Bangladesh has already adopted a goal of a total fertility rate of 2.0 in the year 2000, lower than the rate assumed for it under a rapid path of fertility decline. Thailand is aiming for a total fertility rate of 2.6 by 1986, and Indonesia for a rate of 2.7 by 1990. India is aiming for a crude birth rate of 21 per thousand by 1996. The rapid declines in mortality and fertility provide only one possible set of goals. They take no real account of national differences in the seriousness of the population problem, or of the social, political, and administrative possibilities in dealing with it....

Slowing Population Growth

Experience has shown that as development progresses fertility falls. Yet, because current rates of population growth are so much greater in the developing world than they were at comparable income levels in today's developed countries, many developing countries cannot afford to wait for fertility to decline spontaneously....

It was once assumed that reducing fertility in developing countries would require a typical sequence of economic advance: urbanization, industrialization, a shift from production in the household to factory production, and incomes rising to levels enjoyed by today's developed countries. This view seemed to be confirmed by the fertility declines of the 1960s, which were largely confined to the industrializing economies of Korea, Singapore, and Hong Kong. But fertility declines beginning in other developing countries in the late 1960s, and spreading to more in the 1970s, have been related to a different kind of development: education, health, and the alleviation of poverty. Birth rate declines have been much more closely associated with adult literacy and life expectancy than with GNP per capita. Despite high average incomes, rapid industrialization, and fast economic growth, birth rates fell less in Brazil and Venezuela between 1965 and 1975 than in Sri Lanka, Thailand, and Turkey, where income gains and social services have been more evenly distributed....

But such changes come only gradually. Education, for example, cannot be transformed overnight. Nationally, literacy rates today are strongly

Projections of population size in selected countries, 2000 and 2050
(millions)

Country	1982 Population	Population in 2000			Population in 2050		
		Standard fertility and mortality decline	Rapid fertility decline and standard mortality decline	Rapid fertility and mortality decline	Standard fertility and mortality decline	Rapid fertility decline and standard mortality decline	Rapid fertility and mortality decline
Bangladesh	93	157	136	139	357	212	230
Brazil	127	181	168	169	279	239	247
Egypt	44	63	58	58	102	84	88
El Salvador	5	8	8	8	15	12	13
India	717	994	927	938	1,513	1,313	1,406
Indonesia	153	212	197	198	330	285	298
Kenya	18	40	34	35	120	69	73
Korea, Rep. of	39	51	49	50	67	63	65
Mexico	73	109	101	101	182	155	160
Nigeria	91	169	143	147	471	243	265

influenced by their level in the past; in households, children are more likely to attend school if their mothers did, regardless of family income level. Expanding opportunities for women relies in part on educating women — but this occurs more slowly where parents see only limited opportunities for their daughters. In rural areas, credit and labor markets cannot be transformed overnight. All the more reason, therefore, to act now — especially because some of these changes also take time to lower fertility.

Other complementary policies can have more immediate effects. Promotion of later marriage and longer breastfeeding can reduce the birth rate at the same time it raises welfare. And the experience of many developing countries shows that public support for family planning programs, by narrowing the gap between actual family size and what couples would want if they could more easily choose, can lower fertility quickly. Where family planning services are widespread and affordable, fertility has declined more rapidly than social and economic progress alone would predict. Some examples are Colombia, Costa Rica, India, Thailand, Tunisia, and, more recently, Indonesia and Mexico.

By taxing and spending in ways that provide couples with specific incentives and disincentives to limit their fertility, government policy can also affect fertility in the short run. Government can offer "rewards" for women who defer pregnancy; it can compensate people who undergo sterilization for loss of work and travel costs; and it can provide insurance and old-age security schemes for parents who restrict the size of their families.

Each of these public policies works through signals which influence individual and family decisions — when to marry, whether to use contraception, how long to send children to school, and whether and how much family members work. The level and pattern of government expenditure — for example, for health and education — has great potential for affecting such decisions. Education and primary health care account for between a fifth (Malawi) and a third (Tunisia) of public budgets in low-income and middle-income countries. Taxes similarly affect behavior through, for example, tax-free allowances for children and fees or subsidies on services that children use. The effects of taxes and subsidies can differ depending on the situation. Tuition and book charges might discourage parents from sending children to school and so indirectly contribute to higher fertility. But once it is clear that education is valuable, such charges are likely to encourage people to have fewer children in order to give them a better education. . . .

Socioeconomic Factors and Fertility

One possible remedy for population growth can be ruled out at the start: accepting a rise in death rates, or even a slower decline than is possible. High death rates do slow population growth. But the main reason for wanting slower growth is to improve people's well-being — to move quickly toward a balance of low death and birth rates, thus completing the demographic transition.

REDUCING INFANT AND CHILD MORTALITY

High infant mortality is part of the setting that promotes high fertility. . . . Parents who expect some children to die may insure themselves by giving birth to more babies than they want or expect to survive. High infant mortality can cause high fertility for biological reasons as well: breastfeeding delays the return of regular ovulation, so the interval between a birth and the next conception may be shortened if a baby dies.

In the short term, the prevention of ten infant deaths yields one to five fewer births, depending on the setting. Thus lower infant and child mortality leads to somewhat larger families and faster rates of population growth than otherwise. But effects in the long term are more important. With improved chances of survival, children receive more attention from their parents, and parents are willing to spend more on their children's health and education. Lower mortality not only helps parents to achieve their desired family size with fewer births, it leads them to want a smaller family as well. . . .

RAISING INCOME

Since the children are a source of satisfaction, one might expect richer parents to have more of them. Within the same socioeconomic group, this is often so: among small farmers, for example, those with more land often have higher fertility (although their fertility is lower than the fertility of the landless. . . . Rising incomes are also associated with decreased breastfeeding, which raises fertility unless contraceptives are used. Where marriages are delayed by the need for a dowry, or by the costs of setting up a household, rising incomes permit earlier marriage and earlier childbearing — and thus higher fertility. But these effects are transitory and may be avoided altogether. They can be offset by the social changes that accompany economic growth — such as education and family planning programs — and that work to lower fertility.

This relation adds up to a well-established fact: in the long run, people with more income want fewer children. Alternative uses of time — earning money, developing and using skills, enjoying leisure — become more attractive, particularly to women who are primarily responsible for bringing up children. Parents start to want healthier and better-educated but fewer children. Education of children becomes more attractive as job opportunities depend less on traditional factors — class origin or family background — and more on education and associated skills. And children's work becomes less important to family welfare. Higher income means an increased surplus to invest in land or other assets. . . .

EDUCATING PARENTS

More education for women is one of the strongest factors in reducing fertility. It is true that, in poorer countries, women with a few years of primary schooling have slightly higher fertility than do women with no education at all, especially in rural areas. Some education may be associated with a lower rate of sterility, and it often leads to a decline in breastfeeding not offset by greater use of contraceptives.

In time, however, the effect of education in reducing fertility becomes increasingly clear. In all countries, women who have completed primary school have fewer children than women with no education, and everywhere the number of children declines regularly (and usually substantially) as the education of mothers increases above the primary-school level. The differences can be large — about four children between the highest and lowest educational groups in Colombia, for example....

Studies also show that educating women makes a greater difference than does educating men in reducing family size. There are several plausible reasons for this. Children cost women more than they do men, in time and energy....

MAKING CONTRACEPTION EASIER

... [F]ertility declines everywhere have been eventually tied to increasing use of contraception. Use of contraception is partly a function of a couple's wish to avoid (or to postpone) additional children; the number of children desired is related to the social and economic factors discussed above. But use of contraception is also related to its costs, that is, to the costs of limiting or postponing births. People have regulated family size for centuries — through abortion, withdrawal, sexual abstinence, and even infanticide. But these methods are all costly in terms of reduced emotional, psychological, and, in the case of traditional abortion, physical well-being. Moreover, except for complete abstinence and infanticide, they do not always work. Under these circumstances, risking an additional child may seem less costly than preventing a birth, and even the stated "desired family size" may be higher than it would be if birth control were easier.

It follows that programs to provide publicly subsidized information and access to modern methods of contraception can reduce fertility. They do so in several ways: by making it easier for couples to have only the children they want; by spreading the idea of birth control as something individuals can do; and by providing information about the private and social benefits of smaller families, which may itself alter desired family size....

Incentives and Disincentives

To complement family planning services and social programs that help to reduce fertility, governments may want to consider financial and other incentives and disincentives as additional ways of encouraging parents to have fewer children. Incentives may be defined as payments given to an individual, couple, or group to delay or limit childbearing or to use contraceptives. They extend further the subsidy governments provide when they use public resources to deliver family planning services. Disincentives are the withholding of social benefits from those whose family size exceeds a desired norm.

Incentives and disincentives serve three main purposes.

● They encourage birth control by calling attention to family planning, spreading information about its availability, motivating individuals to consider it more seriously, and compensating for costs and inconvenience that might discourage potential users.

● They alter the costs and benefits of children and may therefore affect desired family size.... Incentives offer alternative ways to ensure the benefits children might otherwise provide; disincentives raise the costs of children. Where large families are not in the interests of society as a whole, society may benefit more by providing incentives that lower fertility than by bearing the social costs of high fertility.

● They help inform people about society's population goals and the damaging effects of rapid population growth and large families.

Payments to people who volunteer for sterilization are usually meant to compensate for travel and work time lost; like incentives and free family planning services, they provide a subsidy that encourages smaller family size (though they are usually offered to all clients regardless of family size). Some population programs also provide bonus payments as incentives to family planning workers; they are meant not to increase demand for services but to improve supply, and are discussed in the next chapter.

Incentives and disincentives give individuals a choice. They provide direct and voluntary tradeoffs between the number of children and possible rewards or penalties. But choice will be preserved only if programs are well designed and carefully implemented....

EXAMPLES AND EXPERIENCE

Although various forms of incentives and disincentives now exist in over thirty countries in the developing world, it is still not possible to estimate exactly how much influence they have had on fertility. In countries in which they have been tried, they have been accompanied by social change, family planning services, and (in the case of China) various social pressures that make it impossible to distinguish their separate effects.

Disincentives built into benefit or tax systems are the most common. Ghana, Malaysia, Pakistan, and the Philippines limit income tax deductions, child allowances, and maternity benefits beyond a few births; to encourage spacing, Tanzania allows working women paid maternity leave only once every three years. But these policies affect only the small minority who are public employees or who pay taxes. Singapore has disincentives which affect more people because of the country's higher income, comprehensive health services, urbanized setting, and extensive public housing. Singapore's disincentives include limitation of income tax relief to the first three children, restriction of paid maternity leave to the first two pregnancies and an increase in childbirth costs after the first two deliveries. Singapore also gives children from smaller families priority in school admission and ignores family size in the allocation of state housing, so smaller families enjoy more space per person. Attitudinal studies suggest that these disincentives, particularly the school admission policy, are much more influential in Singapore than are the more common tax disincentives. Disincentives were introduced gradually in Singapore beginning in 1969, more than a decade after fertility had started to fall. The timing and pattern of the fertility decline thereafter suggests that they have had some impact. . . .

China has the most comprehensive set of incentives and disincentives, designed (most recently) to promote the one-child family. Since the early 1970s women undergoing various types of fertility-related operations have been entitled to paid leave: in urban areas fourteen days for induced abortion; ten days for tubal ligation; two to three days for insertion or removal of an IUD; and in the case of postnatal sterilization, seven extra days over the normal fifty-six days of paid maternity leave. Since 1979 the central government has been encouraging, even requiring, each area and province to draw up its own rewards and penalties. Sichuan, for example, provides for a monthly subsidy to one-child families of five yuan (8 percent of the average worker's wage) until the child is fourteen years old. The child will have priority in admission to schools and in obtaining a factory job. In rural areas in Hunan, parents of only one child receive annual bonuses until their child is fourteen years old and private plots and housing lots big enough for a two-child family. In some urban areas, a single child is allotted adult food rations. Most factories and other work units give preference in the allocation of scarce housing to single-child families. In some cases, medical and educational entitlements are granted preferentially to parents whose only child is a girl — one way, the government hopes, of overcoming the preference for sons.

Penalties for excessive fertility also vary by area in China. In some places, couples who have a second child must return any bonuses obtained for the first child. A couple having a second child may be required to pay for the privilege. (In one brigade in Beijing studied by foreign researchers, several couples have been willing to pay more than twice the annual collective income distributed to each brigade member in order to have a second child.) Parents may have to pay a higher price for grain that they buy for a second child whose birth has not been authorized under the planned-birth program. Some areas and provinces impose taxes, which can be as high as 10 percent of family income, only on third and later-born children. Similarly, mothers may not be entitled to paid maternity leave for a third child, and parents may have to pay all its medical expenses. In

1983 the State Family Planning Commission proposed a tax of 10 percent of family wages on urban dwellers with two or more children, unless one or the other partner is sterilized. . . .

Supplying Family Planning Services

Family planning programs have evolved in various ways, but a typical pattern begins with services being provided only by private family planning associations and a few concerned doctors and nurses. These groups gradually show that family planning is feasible and acceptable and start pressing for government support. Once persuaded, governments typically provide family planning through the public health system. But because health care is often underfinanced and concentrated in urban areas, and because family planning competes with other medical priorities, the quality of services is uneven and available to only a small proportion of people. . . .

Public family planning programs are now at different stages of development in different regions.

● *East Asia*. Governments have a longstanding commitment to reduce population growth. They have been extremely successful in improving access to family planning services and in widening the range of contraceptive methods available. Large numbers of field workers have been recruited to provide family planning, and sometimes basic health care, in villages in China, Indonesia, and Thailand. Contraceptive use has increased dramatically during the past decade.

● *South Asia*. Official commitment to reduce fertility is strong, but results have been mixed. Contraceptive use is highest in Sri Lanka and several states in southern India, and is lowest in Nepal and Pakistan. The demand for contraception is still constrained by high infant mortality and by a preference for large families. At the same time, recent surveys have revealed substantial unmet need for both limiting and spacing births. Most programs have yet to achieve the rural spread found in East Asia and have tended to emphasize sterilization. Other methods have been largely supplied through subsidized commercial outlets.

● *Latin America and the Caribbean*. At first, widespread demand for family planning was met largely by private doctors, pharmacies, and nonprofit organizations, primarily in urban areas. Government support was weak, in part because of opposition from some religious authorities. The 1970s saw a growing interest on the part of governments and a greater tolerance by religious authorities. Most governments now support family planning services for health and humanitarian purposes; Barbados, Colombia, the Dominican Republic, El Salvador, Guatemala, Haiti, Jamaica, Mexico, and Trinidad and Tobago do so to reduce fertility as well. In rural areas, access to services is still inadequate in most countries.

● *Middle East and North Africa*. Some countries in North Africa — Egypt, Morocco, and Tunisia, for example — have long-established programs to reduce fertility. About half the countries in the Middle East provide family planning to improve child spacing and to promote health; only Turkey's program seeks to reduce fertility. In a few Middle Eastern countries, contraception is illegal. In others, cultural practices often confine women to their households, which makes it difficult for them to seek out family planning services. Programs that include home visits by family planning workers are not well developed.

● *Sub-Saharan Africa.* Of forty-one governments for which data are available, only nine have demographic objectives. Most governments that support family planning do so for health reasons, and twelve countries still provide no official backing for family planning. Where services exist, they are provided through health care systems that have only limited coverage, particularly in rural areas. Throughout Africa couples want large families, and infant mortality is high. There is some demand for family planning but it is poorly met by existing programs. As traditional ways of child spacing (prolonged breastfeeding and sexual abstinence) erode, the demand for modern contraception increases. Private organizations have helped to demonstrate that demand and to press for government support. . . .

The Policy Agenda

"Population policy" is the province of government. By choosing how many resources and how much political authority to invest in a policy, a government determines the policy's effectiveness. In its broadest sense, population policy is concerned with population distribution as well as with population growth. . . . In the area of fertility reduction, inaction is itself a choice which has implications for both future policy and the room for maneuver that a government will later have. Religious and cultural conditions cannot be ignored in designing an effective policy to reduce fertility; actions culturally and politically acceptable in one country might be rejected in others. But religious and cultural characteristics do not rule out effective action. In every part of the developing world during the past decade some governments have made significant progress in developing a policy to reduce population growth.

Choosing from policy options is a matter for local decision. But foreign aid for population programs can help developing countries meet their population policy objectives and can increase the impact of aid in other parts of the economy. . . .

A population policy to lower fertility needs to be distinguished from public support for family planning services. Family planning support has wider social goals than fertility reduction but more limited population goals than overall population policy. Family planning programs provide information and services to help people achieve their own fertility objectives. By contrast, population policy involves explicit demographic goals. It employs a wide range of policies, direct and indirect, to change the signals that otherwise induce high fertility. Effective policy requires action by many ministries, and thus an interministerial approach to setting policy and monitoring its results. And it requires clear direction and support from the most senior levels of government.

Family planning programs and other socioeconomic policies that can reduce fertility are often pursued by governments to achieve overall development objectives, irrespective of their effect on fertility. What distinguishes countries with a population policy from those without one is an explicit demographic objective and the institutional mechanisms to translate that objective into effective policy....

Population Change: Success and New Challenge

The accumulating evidence on population change in developing countries underscores the strong link between fertility decline and the general level of socioeconomic development, and the contribution that family planning programs can make to slowing population growth. Differences in fertility among and within countries are related less to income per person than to life expectancy, female literacy, and the income of poorer groups. They are also related to availability of family planning services. Thus Sri Lanka has lower fertility than India, and India has lower fertility than Pakistan. Colombia has lower fertility than Brazil, and Brazil has lower fertility than Peru. Egypt has lower fertility than Morocco. Countries which have made a substantial and sustained effort in family planning have achieved remarkable success; where education is widespread, the success is even more striking....

But there is also evidence that further fertility decline, and the initiation of decline where it has not begun, will not come automatically. There are two points to bear in mind. One is that in most developing countries desired family size is about four. It is higher in rural areas and among the less educated. Without sustained improvements in living conditions, desired family size could remain around four — implying population growth rates at or above 2 percent. The second is that family planning programs, successful as they have been, have by no means reached their full potential. In virtually every country surveyed, many couples who say they want no more children do not use contraception — usually because they have poor access to modern services. In many areas where services are available, discontinuation rates are high — often because few effective methods are offered, and because follow-up services are limited.

It has been almost two decades since the peak of population growth in developing countries was passed. But the turnaround to slower growth has been slow and has not occurred everywhere. Increases in population size are projected to mount for another two decades, and in many countries of the developing world, populations will triple in size by the year 2050, even assuming substantial declines in fertility. Two decades after the turnaround, the slow pace of change and its uneven incidence point more than ever to rapid population growth as a central development concern....

MEXICO CITY DECLARATION ON POPULATION AND DEVELOPMENT

1. The International Conference on Population met in Mexico City from 6 to 14 August 1984, to appraise the implementation of the World Population Plan of Action, adopted by consensus at Bucharest, ten year [sic] ago. The Conference reaffirmed the full validity of the principles and objectives of the World Population Plan of Action and adopted a set of recommendations for the further implementation of the Plan in the years ahead.

2. The world has undergone far-reaching changes in the past decade. Significant progress in many fields important for human welfare has been made through national and international efforts. However, for a large number of countries it has been a period of instability, increased unemployment, mounting external indebtedness, stagnation and even decline in economic growth. The number of people living in absolute poverty has increased.

3. Economic difficulties and problems of resource mobilization have been particularly serious in the developing countries. Growing international disparities have further exacerbated already serious problems in social and economic terms. Firm and widespread hope was expressed that increasing international co-operation will lead to a growth in welfare and wealth, their just and equitable distribution and minimal waste in use of resources, thereby promoting development and peace for the benefit of the world's population.

4. Population growth, high mortality and morbidity, and migration problems continue to be causes of great concern requiring immediate action.

5. The Conference confirms that the principal aim of social, economic and human development, of which population goals and policies are integral parts, is to improve the standards of living and quality of life of the people. This Declaration constitutes a solemn undertaking by the nations and international organizations gathered in Mexico City to respect national sovereignty to combat all forms of racial discrimination including *apartheid,* and to promote social and economic development, human rights and individual freedom.

* * * *

6. Since Bucharest the global population growth rate has declined from 2.03 to 1.67 percent per year. In the next decade the growth rate will decline more slowly. Moreover, the annual increase in numbers is expected to continue and may reach 90 million by the year 2000. Ninety percent of that increase will occur in developing countries and at that time 6.1 billion people are expected to inhabit the Earth.

7. Demographic differences between developed and developing coun-

tries remain striking. The average life expectancy at birth, which has increased almost everywhere, is 73 years in developed countries, while in developing countries it is only 57 years and families in developing countries tend to be much larger than elsewhere. This gives cause for concern since social and population pressures may contribute to the continuation of the wide disparity in welfare and the quality of life between developing and developed countries.

8. In the past decade, population issues have been increasingly recognized as a fundamental element in development planning. To be realistic, development policies, plans and programmes must reflect the inextricable links between population, resources, environment and development. Priority should be given to action programmes integrating all essential population and development factors, taking fully into account the need for rational utilization of natural resources and protection of the physical environment and preventing its further deterioration.

9. The experience with population policies in recent years is encouraging. Mortality and morbidity rates have been lowered, although not to the desired extent. Family planning programmes have been successful in reducing fertility at relatively low cost. Countries which consider that their population growth rate hinders their national development plans should adopt appropriate population policies and programmes. Timely action could avoid the accentuation of problems such as overpopulation, unemployment, food shortages, and environmental degradation.

10. Population and development policies reinforce each other when they are responsive to individual, family and community needs. Experience from the past decade demonstrates the necessity of the full participation by the entire community and grass-roots organizations in the design and implementation of policies and programmes. This will ensure that programmes are relevant to local needs and in keeping with personal and social values. It will also promote social awareness of demographic problems.

11. Improving the status of women and enhancing their role is an important goal in itself and will also influence family life and size in a positive way. Community support is essential to bring about the full integration and participation of women into all phases and functions of the development process. Institutional, economic and cultural barriers must be removed and broad and swift action taken to assist women in attaining full equality with men in the social, political and economic life of their communities. To achieve this goal, it is necessary for men and women to share jointly responsibilities in areas such as family life, child-caring and family planning. Governments should formulate and implement concrete policies which would enhance the status and role of women.

12. Unwanted high fertility adversely affects the health and welfare of individuals and families, especially among the poor, and seriously impedes social and economic progress in many countries. Women and children are the main victims of unregulated fertility. Too many, too close, too early

and too late pregnancies are a major cause of maternal, infant and childhood mortality and morbidity.

13. Although considerable progress has been made since Bucharest, millions of people still lack access to safe and effective family planning methods. By the year 2000 some 1.6 billion women will be of childbearing age, 1.3 billion of them in developing countries. Major efforts must be made now to ensure that all couples and individuals can exercise their basic human rights to decide freely, responsibly and without coercion, the number and spacing of their children and to have the information, education and means to do so. In exercising this right, the best interests of their living and future children as well as the responsibility towards the community should be taken into account.

14. Although modern contraceptive technology has brought considerable progress into family planning programmes, increased funding is required in order to develop new methods and to improve the safety, efficacy and acceptability of existing methods. Expanded research should also be undertaken in human reproduction to solve problems of infertility and subfecundity.

15. As part of the overall goal to improve the health standards for all people, special attention should be given to maternal and child health services within a primary health care system. Through breast-feeding, adequate nutrition, clean water, immunization programmes, oral rehydration therapy and birth spacing, a virtual revolution in child survival could be achieved. The impact would be dramatic in humanitarian and fertility terms.

16. The coming decades will see rapid changes in population structures with marked regional variations. The absolute numbers of children and youth in developing countries will continue to rise so rapidly that special programmes will be necessary to respond to their needs and aspirations, including productive employment. Aging of populations is a phenomenon which many countries will experience. This issue requires attention particularly in developed countries in view of its social implications and the active contribution the aged can make to the social, cultural and economic life in their countries.

17. Rapid urbanization will continue to be a salient feature. By the end of the century, 3 billion people, 48 per cent of the world's population, might live in cities, frequently very large cities. Integrated urban and rural development strategies should therefore be an essential part of population policies. They should be based on a full evaluation of the costs and benefits to individuals, groups and regions involved, should respect basic human rights and use incentives rather than restrictive measures.

18. The volume and nature of international migratory movements continue to undergo rapid changes. Illegal or undocumented migration and refugee movements have gained particular importance; labor migration of considerable magnitude occurs in all regions. The outflow of skills remains a serious human resource problem in many developing countries. It is

indispensable to safeguard the individual and social rights of the persons involved and to protect them from exploitation and treatment not in conformity with basic human rights; it is also necessary to guide these different migration streams. To achieve this, the co-operation of countries of origin and destination and the assistance of international organizations are required.

19. As the years since 1974 have shown, the political commitment of Heads of State and other leaders and the willingness of Governments to take the lead in formulating population programmes and allocating the necessary resources are crucial for the further implementation of the World Population Plan of Action. Governments should attach high priority to the attainment of self-reliance in the management of such programmes, strengthen their administrative and managerial capabilities, and ensure co-ordination of international assistance at the national level.

20. The years since Bucharest have also shown that international cooperation in the field of population is essential for the implementation of recommendations agreed upon by the international community and can be notably successful. The need for increased resources for population activities is emphasized. Adequate and substantial international support and assistance will greatly facilitate the efforts of Governments. It should be provided wholeheartedly and in a spirit of universal solidarity and enlightened self-interest. The United Nations family should continue to perform its vital responsibilities.

21. Non-governmental organizations have a continuing important role in the implementation of the World Population Plan of Action and deserve encouragement and support from Governments and international organizations. Members of Parliament, community leaders, scientists, the media and others in influential positions are called upon to assist in all aspects of population and development work.

* * * *

22. At Bucharest, the world was made aware of the gravity and magnitude of the population problems and their close interrelationship with economic and social development. The message of Mexico City is to forge ahead with effective implementation of the World Population Plan of Action aimed at improving standards of living and quality of life for all peoples of this planet in promotion of their common destiny in peace and security.

23. IN ISSUING THIS DECLARATION, ALL PARTICIPANTS AT THE INTERNATIONAL CONFERENCE ON POPULATION REITERATE THEIR COMMITMENT AND REDEDICATE THEMSELVES TO THE FURTHER IMPLEMENTATION OF THE PLAN.

DEMOCRATIC PARTY PLATFORM

July 17, 1984

Democrats left their convention in San Francisco July 19 with a platform that created few divisions in the party, but one few candidates were enthusiastic about using in their fall campaigns. The platform, adopted in an emphatic but seldom angry four-hour debate July 17, drew heavily from the campaign themes of former vice president Walter F. Mondale, the Democratic nominee. It also contained significant contributions from his rivals for the nomination, Colorado Sen. Gary Hart and the Rev. Jesse Jackson.

The platform theoretically was the Democrats' basic issues document for the 1984 elections. But although party leaders promised a document that all Democrats could "run on, win on and govern on," most congressional candidates were reluctant to embrace the platform as a whole. Among incumbents in Congress, there were few plans to tout the Democratic party, the 1984 platform also was a vehicle designed to unite platform selectively.

Fashioning the Platform

The process of assembling the platform was an important exercise for the party. In four months of hearings and drafting sessions, the Democrats invited dozens of interest groups to weave their goals and ideals into the platform. The variegated document became a symbol of the party's all-inclusive philosophy, as it grew to roughly 45,000 words after countless pressure groups had their say.

The 1984 Democratic platform was loyal to traditional Democratic ideology, with commitments to unions, blacks, feminists, the poor, environmentalists, and other liberal constituencies. But it also included new ideas from the party's younger generation, especially on economic policy. The platform did not call for major new social spending, making it economically more conservative than Democratic documents of the past 50 years. But in its support for homosexual rights, the availability of abortions, and other "lifestyle" issues, it was socially more liberal than earlier platforms.

The platform's central theme was an attack on President Ronald Reagan's administration. The document indicted the president's record on topics ranging from budget deficits to civil rights to arms control, and it laid out what Democrats proposed as an alternative.

Besides giving a voice to the various interest groups that composed the Democratic Party, the 1984 platform also was a vehicle designed to unite the three presidential contenders. Negotiations continued up to the last minute on the five minority planks presented to the convention delegates July 17 by Jackson and Hart. But Mondale's forces demonstrated a firm grip on the delegates, soundly defeating Jackson planks on defense spending, "no first use" of nuclear weapons, and runoff primaries. Mondale accepted Hart's plank restricting the use of U.S. troops overseas. Mondale also compromised on a Jackson plank outlining the party's affirmative action policy.

The debate on the five minority planks was lackluster compared with the heated platform struggles between President Jimmy Carter and Massachusetts Sen. Edward M. Kennedy at the 1980 convention. (Historic Documents of 1980, p. 711)

One person conspicuously absent from the convention platform debate was Geraldine A. Ferraro, who chaired the committee that produced the document. Ferraro was to run the program July 17 — until Mondale asked her to be his running mate. When asked why Ferraro was not handling the platform, Mondale quipped, "There's been a somewhat altered change in Mrs. Ferraro's professional plans over the next eight years."

Nuclear Issue, Peace Plank

The first sign that Mondale would surmount the Jackson challenges came on the "no first use" plank. After a brief debate, it was defeated, with 1,405.7 delegates voting for it and 2,216.3 against. As adopted by the platform committee June 23, the document said a Democratic president would "move toward" a policy in which the United States would not initiate a nuclear attack. But Jackson wanted an immediate commitment to "no first use." Jackson supporters said it was "morally and militarily insane" even to consider using nuclear weapons. But Mondale backers said the platform's arms control language was strong enough. Also, Mondale argued that NATO's conventional forces needed to be strengthened before the United States could adopt a "no first use" stance.

In contrast to the opposition to Jackson's national security planks, Hart's "peace plank" was readily accepted by Mondale. Delegates adopted it by a 3,271.8 to 351.2 vote. The plank delineated conditions under which a Democratic president would not "hazard American lives or engage in unilateral military involvement" abroad. It was dubbed the Persian Gulf—Central America plank, because the underlying message was that U.S. troops should not be sent to those regions unless American objectives were clear and diplomatic efforts had been exhausted.

Mondale's supporters opposed the plank when the platform committee considered it in June. At that time they said the plank would put a Democratic president "in a political or diplomatic straitjacket." But Mondale softened his stand in San Francisco. By accepting the plank, Mondale also hoped to distinguish Democratic foreign policy from Reagan's "saber-rattling" international agenda, as one Mondale supporter put it.

Runoffs, Affirmative Action

Jackson's two other minority reports dealt with issues of special interest to his black constituency: runoff primaries in the South and affirmative action. His call to abolish runoff primaries was defeated, but a compromise version of the affirmative action plank was accepted.

Ten Southern states used runoff primaries when no candidate received a majority in the first primary. Jackson claimed these second elections diluted minority voting strength because white voters often reverted to racial loyalty when a runoff choice was between a white and a black candidate. Supporters of second primaries argued that they prevented the nomination of fringe candidates who could receive a plurality in first-round primaries when more credible candidates split the vote. There also was strong sentiment against Jackson's plank from conservative Southerners who did not want the national party dictating their state election procedures.

The other dispute was whether the platform should reject the use of quotas to overturn discrimination in employment and education. As adopted in June, the platform specifically rejected quotas, but called for affirmative action goals and timetables to end discrimination in hiring, promotions, and education.

Following is the text of the platform adopted at the 1984 Democratic National Convention in San Francisco, July 17, 1984:

Preamble

A fundamental choice awaits America — a choice between two futures.

It is a choice between solving our problems, and pretending they don't exist; between the spirit of community, and the corrosion of selfishness; between justice for all, and advantage for some; between social decency and social Darwinism; between expanding opportunity and contracting horizons; between diplomacy and conflict; between arms control and an arms race; between leadership and alibis.

America stands at a crossroads.

Move in one direction, and the President who appointed James Watt will appoint the Supreme Court majority for the rest of the century. The President who proposed deep cuts in Social Security will be charged with rescuing Medicare. The President who destroyed the Environmental Protection Agency will decide whether toxic dumps get cleaned up. The President who fought the Equal Rights Amendment will decide whether women get fair pay for their work. The President who launched a covert war in Central America will determine our human rights policy. The President who abandoned the Camp David process will oversee Middle East policy. The President who opposed every nuclear arms control agreement since the bomb went off will be entrusted with the fate of the earth.

We offer a different direction.

For the economy, the Democratic Party is committed to economic growth, prosperity, and jobs. For the individual, we are committed to justice, decency, and opportunity. For the nation, we are committed to peace, strength, and freedom.

In the future we propose, young families will be able to buy and keep new homes — instead of fearing the explosion of their adjustable-rate mortgages. Workers will feel secure in their jobs — instead of fearing layoffs and lower wages. Seniors will look forward to retirement — instead of fearing it. Farmers will get a decent return on their investment — instead of fearing bankruptcy and foreclosure.

Small businesses will have the capital they need — instead of credit they can't afford. People will master technology — instead of being mastered or displaced by it. Industries will be revitalized — not abandoned. Students will attend the best colleges and vocational schools for which they qualify — instead of trimming their expectations. Minorities will rise in the mainstream of economic life — instead of waiting on the sidelines. Children will dream of better days ahead — and not of nuclear holocaust.

Our Party is built on a profound belief in America and Americans.

We believe in the inspiration of American dreams, and the power of progressive ideals. We believe in the dignity of the individual, and the enormous potential of collective action. We believe in building, not wrecking. We believe in bridging our differences, not deepening them. We believe in a fair society for working Americans of average income; an opportunity society for enterprising Americans; a caring society for Americans in need through no fault of their own — the sick, the disabled, the hungry, the elderly, the unemployed; and a safe, decent and prosperous society for all Americans.

We are the Party of American values — the worth of every human being; the striving toward excellence; the freedom to innovate; the inviolability of law; the sharing of sacrifice; the struggle toward justice; the pursuit of happiness.

We are the Party of American progress — the calling to explore; the challenge to invent; the imperative to improve; the importance of courage; the perennial need for fresh thinking, sharp minds, and ambitious goals.

We are the Party of American strength — the security of our defenses; the power of our moral values; the necessity of diplomacy; the pursuit of peace; the imperative of survival.

We are the Party of American vision — the trustees of a better future. This platform is our road map toward that future.

Chapter I: Economic Growth, Prosperity, and Jobs

INTRODUCTION

Building a prosperous America in a changing world: that is the Democratic agenda for the future. To build that America, we must meet the challenge of long-term, sustainable, noninflationary economic growth. Our future depends on it.

To a child, economic growth means the promise of quality education. To a new graduate, it means landing a good first job. To a young family, growth means the opportunity to own a home or a car. To an unemployed worker, it means the chance to live in dignity again. To a farmer, growth means expanding markets, fair prices, and new customers. To an entrepreneur, it means a shot at a new business. To our nation, it means the ability to compete in a dramatically changing world economy. And to all in our society, growth — and the prosperity it brings — means security, opportunity, and hope. Democrats want an economy that works for everyone — not just the favored few.

For our party and our country, it is vital that 1984 be a year of new departures.

We have a proud legacy to build upon: the Democratic tradition of caring, and the Democratic commitment to an activist government that understands and accepts its responsibilities.

Our history has been proudest when we have taken up the challenges of our times, the challenges we accept once again in 1984 — to find new ways, in times of accelerating change, to fulfill our historic commitments. We will continue to be the party of justice. And we will foster the productivity and growth on which justice depends.

For the 1980s, the Democratic Party will emphasize two fundamental economic goals. We will restore rising living standards in our country. And we will offer every American the opportunity for secure and productive employment.

Our program will be bold and comprehensive. It will ask restraint and cooperation from all sectors of the economy. It will rely heavily on the private sector as the prime source of expanding employment. And it will treat every individual with decency and respect.

A Democratic Administration will take four key steps to secure a bright future of long-term economic growth and opportunity for every American:

• Instead of runaway deficits, a Democratic Administration will pursue overall economic policies that sharply reduce deficits, bring down interest rates, free savings for private investment, prevent another explosion of inflation and put the dollar on a competitive footing.

• Instead of government by neglect, a Democratic Administration will establish a framework that will support growth and productivity and assure opportunity.

• In place of conflict, a Democratic Administration will pursue cooperation, backed by trade, tax and financial regulations that will serve the long-term growth of the American economy and the broad national interest.

• Instead of ignoring America's future, a Democratic Administration will make a series of long-term investments in research, infrastructure, and above all in people. Education, training and retraining will become a central focus in an economy built on change.

THE FUTURE IF REAGAN IS REELECTED

"Since the Reagan Administration took office, my wife and I have lost half our net worth. Took us 20 years to build that up, and about three to lose it. That is hard to deal with...."

> David Sprague, Farmer, Colorado (Democratic Platform Committee Hearing, Springfield, Illinois, April 27, 1984)

"There's got to be something wrong with our government's policy when it's cheaper to shut a plant down than it is to operate it.... The Houston Works plant sits right in the middle of the energy capital of the world and 85 percent of our steel went directly into the energy-related market, yet Japan could sit their products on our docks cheaper than we can make it and roll it there."

> Early Clowers, President, Steel Workers Local 2708 (Democratic Platform Committee Hearing, Houston, Texas, May 29, 1984).

A Democratic future of growth and opportunity, of mastering change rather than hiding from it, of promoting fairness instead of widening inequality, stands in stark contrast to another four years of Ronald Reagan. Staying the course with Ronald Reagan raises a series of hard questions about a bleak future.

What would be the impact of the Republican deficit if Mr. Reagan is reelected?

A second Reagan term would bring federal budget deficits larger than any in American history — indeed, any in world history. Under the Republican's policies, the deficit will continue to mount. Interest rates, already rising sharply, will start to soar. Investments in the future will be slowed, then stopped. The Reagan deficits mortgage the future and threaten the present.

Mr. Reagan has already conceded that these problems exist. But as he said in his 1984 Economic Report to the Congress, he prefers to wait until after the election to deal with them. And then, he plans "to enact spending reductions coupled with tax simplification that will eventually eliminate our budget deficit."

What will Mr. Reagan's plan for "tax simplification" mean to average Americans if he is reelected?

Ronald Reagan's tax "reforms" were a bonanza for the very wealthy, and a disaster for poor and middle-class Americans. If reelected, Mr. Reagan will have more of the same in store. For him, tax simplification will mean a further freeing of the wealthy from their obligation to pay their fair share of taxes and an increasing burden on the average American.

How will Mr. Reagan's "spending reductions" affect average Americans if he is reelected?

If he gets a second term, Mr. Reagan will use the deficit to justify his policy of government by subtraction. The deficits he created will become his excuse for destroying programs he never supported. Medicare, Social Security, federal pensions, farm price supports and dozens of other people-oriented programs will be in danger.

If Mr. Reagan is reelected, will our students have the skills to work in a changing economy?

If we are to compete and grow, the next generation of Americans must be the best-trained, best-educated in history. While our competitors invest in educating their children, Mr. Reagan cuts the national commitment to our schools. While our competitors spend greater and greater percentages of their GNP on civilian research and development, this President has diverted increasing portions of ours into military weaponry. These policies are short-sighted and destructive.

If Mr. Reagan is reelected, will basic industries and the workers they employ be brought into the future?

The Republican Administration has turned its back on basic industries and their communities. Instead of putting forward policies to help revitalize and adjust, Mr. Reagan tells blameless, anxious, displaced workers to abandon their neighborhoods and homes and "vote with their feet."

America's economic strength was built on basic industries. Today, in a changing economy, they are no less important. Strong basic industries are vital to our economic health and essential to our national security. And as major consumers of high technology, they are catalysts for growth in newly emerging fields. We need new approaches to ensure strong American basic industries for the remainder of this century and beyond.

Can the road to the future be paved with potholes?

Adequate roads and bridges, mass transit, water supply and sewage treatment facilities, and ports and harbors are essential to economic growth. For four years, the Reagan Administration has refused to confront adequately the growing problems in our infrastructure. Another term will bring four more years of negligence and neglect.

If Mr. Reagan is reelected, how many children will join the millions already growing up at risk?

Between 1980 and 1982, more than two million younger Americans joined the ranks of the poor: the sharpest increase on record.

With the Reagan Administration's cutbacks in prenatal care and supplemental food programs have come infant mortality rates in parts of our cities rivaling those of the poorest Latin American nations. Black infants are now twice as likely as white infants to die during the first year of life.

Cuts in school lunch and child nutrition programs have left far too many children hungry and unable to focus on their lessons.

Teenage prostitution, alcohol and drug abuse, depression, and suicide have all been linked to child abuse. The Administration has abandoned most avenues to breaking the cycle of abuse. Funding to prevent and treat child physical abuse has been cut in half. And funds to help private groups set up shelters for runaway youth are being diverted elsewhere.

If Mr. Reagan is reelected, will we ensure that our children are able to enjoy a clean, healthy environment?

Protecting our natural heritage — its beauty and its richness — is not a partisan issue. For eighty years, every American President has understood the importance of protecting our air, our water, and our health. Today, a growing population puts more demands on our environment. Chemicals which are unsafe or disposed of improperly threaten neighborhoods and families. And as our knowledge expands, we learn again and again how fragile life and health — human and animal — truly are.

Ensuring the environmental heritage of future generations demands action now. But the Reagan Administration continues to develop, lease, and sell irreplaceable wilderness lands. While thousands of toxic waste sites already exist, and more and more are being created constantly, the Reagan Administration is cleaning them up at a rate of only 1.5 per year. The environmental legacy of Ronald Reagan will be long-lasting damage that can *never* truly be undone.

If Mr. Reagan is reelected, will we be able to heat our homes and run our factories?

Twice in the past, our country has endured the high costs of dependence on foreign oil. Yet the Reagan Administration is leaving us vulnerable to another embargo or an interruption in oil supply. By failing adequately to fill the Strategic Petroleum Reserve, and trusting blindly to the market to "muddle through" in a crisis this Administration has wagered our national security on its economic ideology. One rude shock from abroad or just one "market failure," and our country could find itself plunged into another energy crisis.

The New Economic Reality:
Five Reagan Myths

Underlying the Reagan approach to the economy are five key myths; myths that determine and distort the Reagan economic policy, and ensure that it is not the basis for long-term growth.

The world has changed, but Ronald Reagan does not understand.

First, and most fundamental, the Reagan Administration continues to act as if the United States were an economic island unto itself. But we have changed from a relatively isolated economy to an economy of international interdependence. In fact, the importance of international trade to the U.S. economy has roughly doubled in a decade. Exports now account for almost 10 percent of GNP — and roughly 20 percent of U.S. manufactured goods. One in six manufacturing jobs now depends on exports, and one in three acres is now planted for the overseas market. Imports have also doubled in importance.

Financial markets are also closely linked. U.S. direct investments and commercial loans overseas now amount to hundreds of billions of dollars. A debt crisis in Mexico will affect balance sheets in San Francisco. A recession in Europe will limit the profits of U.S. subsidiaries operating in the European market. Lower overseas profits will limit the flow of earnings back to the United States — one important way the U.S. has found to help pay for the rising tide of imports. Hundreds of billions of dollars in foreign short-term capital invested here are sensitive to small shifts in interest rates or the appearance of added risk. It is only partly bad loans that brought Continental Illinois to the brink of bankruptcy. Heavily dependent on short-term foreign deposits, Continental Illinois was particularly vulnerable. Rumors that were false at the time were enough to set off a run on the bank.

The strength of American steel, the competitiveness of the U.S. machine tool industry, and the long-term potential of U.S. agriculture are no longer matters decided exclusively in Washington or by the American market. America must look to Tokyo, Paris, and the money markets in Singapore and Switzerland. Policy based on the myth that America is independent of the world around us is bound to fail.

Second, this Administration has ignored the enormous changes sweeping through the American work force.

The maturing of the baby boom generation, the sharp increase in the percentage of women seeking work, and the aging of the work force all have to be taken into account.

Decade by decade, more and more women have moved into the work force. This large-scale movement is already changing the nature of professions, altering the patterns of child care and breaking down sex-based distinctions that have existed in many types of employment.

In Ronald Reagan's vision of America, there are no single parent families; women only stay at home and care for children. Reagan's families do not worry about the effects of unemployment on family stability; they do not worry about decent housing and health care; they do not need child care. But in the real world, most Americans do. Providing adequate child care for the millions of American children who need it, and for their parents, is surely not a responsibility which belongs solely to the federal government. But, like the responsibility for decent housing and health care, it is one where federal leadership and support are essential.

The work force is also aging. For the first time in this century, the average American is 31 years of age. Coupled with greater longevity and the gradual elimination of mandatory retirement rules, older workers can be expected to increase steadily their share of the total work force.

Moreover, the kinds of jobs available in our economy are changing rapidly. The combined pressures of new products, new process technology, and foreign competition are changing the face of American industry.

New technologies, shifting economics and deregulation have opened up dozens of new careers both in traditional industrial concerns and in new businesses. Many of them did not exist at all only a few years ago.

And the change is far from over. In setting national policy, a government that ignores that change is bound to fail. In setting national policy, a government that ignores the future is short-changing the American people.

Third, the Reagan program has ignored the fundamental changes that are sweeping through the structure of American industry, the diversity of the economy and the challenges various sectors face. New products and new ways of manufacturing are part of the change. High technology is creating new competitive industries, and holding out the promise of making older industries competitive once again. Foreign competition has also had a major impact. But the tide runs much deeper than that.

In the past decade, small business and new entrepreneurs have become more and more of a driving force in the American economy. Small businesses are a growing force in innovation, employment, and the long-term strength of the American economy.

Technology itself appears to be changing the optimal size of American businesses. And unlike the conglomerate mergers of the 1960s, renewed emphasis on quality and efficient production has shifted the focus back to industry-specific experience.

An Administration that sets tax policy, spending priorities, and an overall growth program without understanding the new dynamics and the diversity of American industry is weakening, rather than strengthening the American economy.

Reaganomics is based on the theory that blanket tax cuts for business and the rich would turn directly into higher productivity, that private investors and industry would use the money saved to restore our edge in innovation and competitiveness.

In practice, the theory failed because it did not take into account the diversity within our economy. The economy is composed of a set of complex public and private institutions which are intricately interrelated and increasingly influenced by the pressures of international competition. In the international economy, multinational companies and governments cooperate to win trade advantage, often at American expense.

We are coming to understand that in an expanding number of markets, industrial strategies, rather than just the energies of individual firms, influence competitive success. Indeed, success in marketing a product may depend more on the quality and productivity of the relationship between government and business than on the quality of the product. While several foreign industrial strategies have failed, foreign governments are becoming more sophisticated in the design and conduct of their industrial strategies. The Reagan Administration is not.

Fourth, the Reagan Administration has acted as if deficits do not count. The deficits are huge and are expected to get larger — and they are a major negative factor in everything from high interest rates to the third world debt crisis.

— Because of the huge tax cuts to benefit the wealthy, and an enormous military buildup bought on credit, the federal deficit in 1983 was equivalent to 6% of our GNP. In dollars it amounted to almost 200 billion — more than three times larger than the deficit Ronald Reagan campaigned against in 1980.

— Under the budget Reagan proposed to Congress earlier this year, the annual deficit would grow to $248 billion by 1989, and unless he makes major changes in current policy, it will exceed $300 billion. Reagan doubled the national debt during his first term. Given eight years, he will have tripled it. According to the proposed budget, at the end of his second term Reagan *by himself* will have put this country *three times deeper* into debt than *all our other Presidents combined*.

— As the Reagan debt hangs over us, more and more of our tax dollars are going nowhere. By 1989, the percentage of federal revenues to be spent on deficit interest payments alone will have doubled. *These unproductive payments will claim a staggering 42¢ on every personal income tax dollar we pay.* This huge allocation will do nothing to reduce the principal of the debt; it will only finance the interest payments.

— The interest payments on Reagan's debt are grossly out of line with historical spending patterns. Since 1981, more money has been squandered on *interest payments* on the Reagan-created debt alone than has been saved by all of Reagan's cuts in domestic spending. Non-defense discretionary spending, to be productively invested in programs to benefit the poor and middle class, and to build our social capital, is being overwhelmed by the enormous sums of money wasted on interest payments. By 1989, the annual payment will account for twice the percentage of federal revenue that we have ever set aside for such discretionary programs.

— Interest payments on the debt are rising at an alarming rate. Today the annual payment has already reached $110 billion — twice what it was four years ago. During a second Reagan term, it will double *again*, reaching $207 billion by 1989.

— The consequences for the individual taxpayer are enormous. Deficit increases under Reagan so far are equivalent to $2,387 levied from every woman, man and child alive in the United States today.

— The consequences for the nation as a whole are also enormous. The massive government borrowing necessary to service the debt will amount to about three-quarters of the entire nation's net savings between 1983 and 1986.

The pressure of the deficits on interest rates has sucked in a wave of overseas investment. Some of those investments have been made in manufacturing plants or other commercial enterprises. Much of the foreign money, however, is in the form of portfolio holdings or even more liquid short-term bank deposits. It is an uncertain source of savings for a long-term investment program. To a limited degree, it puts the country in the same risky position as Continental Illinois Bank which relied heavily on short-term foreign deposits to make long-term domestic loans.

High interest rates will eventually take their toll on domestic investment, make their own contribution to inflationary pressure (while eventually slowing growth and inflation), and increase the tensions in the domestic banking system. They will also have a potentially devastating impact on the international economy. Each percentage point rise in U.S. interest rates adds $3-5 billion to the annual debt payments of the developing world. High American interest rates have also put added pressure on interest rates in the industrial democracies, dampening their own prospects for growth, and their ability to buy our goods.

Fifth, and finally, the Reagan Administration has virtually wished away the role of government. When it comes to the economy, *its view is that the government that governs best is one that governs not at all.*

A Democratic Administration must answer this challenge by reaffirming the principle that government must both "provide for the common defense" *and* "promote the general welfare" as coequal responsibilities under the Constitution. If the Democratic Party can succeed in correcting the present imbalance, it will reverse the cycle of pain and despair, and recapture the initiative in the area of social and economic progress.

The Reagan Administration succeeded in shifting massive resources from human needs functions of the Federal budget to military-related functions and created unprecedented deficits, based on the assumption that government should have a diminished responsibility for social progress, and thus, for the welfare of the needy and disadvantaged in society. The resulting Reagan-induced recession caused tremendous suffering, threw millions of people out of work, terminated or reduced benefits, and raised the national misery index.

Mr. Reagan denies government's critical role in our economy. Government cannot, and should not, dominate our free enterprise economy. But American prosperity has been most pronounced when the government played a supportive or catalytic role in the nation's economic fortunes. There are a wide variety of examples stretching back through our entire history: government investments in roads and research, in education and training; government initiatives in opening up new economic possibilities, initiatives that started with the decision to protect domestic markets shortly after the Revolution to the ongoing commercial development of space.

Agriculture is a clear example of government cooperation with a highly competitive private sector that has yielded a harvest of economic results that is the envy of the world. The government helps fund the research, helps spread it through the economy, educates the modern farmer, influences production levels, and helps develop new markets overseas. It is America's most conspicuous example of a successful industrial strategy — combining the cooperative efforts of business, government and our universities.

Reagan's Recession and A Recovery Built on Debt

The Economic Roller Coaster — Following the first oil shock in 1973, the United States embarked on a ten year economic roller coaster. The up and down performance of the economy was paralleled by erratic macroeconomic policy. There were wide swings from stimulative fiscal and monetary policies causing raging inflation, to government-engineered recessions.

The frequency of the cycles created a climate of uncertainty that was tailor-made to discourage and distort investment. Each cycle left the economy weaker than the one before. At the end of each recession the level of inflation was higher, and at the end of each recovery the level of unemployment had risen.

Even more disturbing was the decline in the rate of growth of productivity. By the end of the 1970s, productivity growth first stopped and then fell. Productivity growth has finally resumed — but the rate of growth remains disappointing compared both to our own economic past and the performance of other industrial economies.

Reaganomics and an Election Year Recovery — Ronald Reagan swept into office on the promise of a smaller government and a bigger private sector, of higher GNP and lower inflation, and of the elimination of federal deficits.

First, he proposed huge tax cuts. Mr. Reagan went so far as to suggest that the growth caused by his tax cuts would be so rapid that total tax revenues would actually rise even while tax rates were cut.

Second, he promised a huge defense build-up.

Third, he promised stable prices. How was he going to contain prices while stimulating rapid growth? His answer was tight money.

Fourth, the supply-siders promised growth and stable prices without the intervening pain of a recession. In effect, Reagan promised tight money without tears.

Cut taxes but raise more revenues. Arm to the teeth. Growth with stable prices. Tight money and no hard times. It just did not work out that way.

561

Worse, there was never any reason to expect that it would. Reagan's kind of tax cuts were based neither on rational economic theory nor on any empirical evidence. And wishing simply did not make it so. George Bush was right when he called Reaganomics "voodoo economics."

Instead of growth, the country had plunging production and record unemployment. Instead of increased savings and investment, the country had bankruptcy and economic decline. The Reagan policies, which were supposed to break the cycle of inflation and recession, only made it worse.

Reagan cut domestic programs, but more than offset those cuts with vastly increased defense spending. The Government significantly reduced the growth of the money supply and kept real interest rates high. For a recession, real interest rates reached record highs. These interest rates brought an added problem. They attracted foreign funds and helped drive up the international value of the dollar. American business was faced with a double whammy — empty order books and high interest rates. For the increasingly large part of American business that either sells overseas or competes with imports at home, the over-valued dollar abroad meant their products cost far more compared to the foreign competition.

Reagan effectively created a tax on exports and a subsidy for imports. It was a climate that forced record bankruptcies, enormous unemployment, plant closings, and major corporate reorganizations. It was the largest and most severe economic collapse since the Great Depression.

The Reagan Administration then prepared for the election year by "staying the course" in fiscal policy (pumping up demand with huge deficits) and sharply reversing the course in monetary policy.

The Federal Reserve Board rapidly expanded the supply of money and the economy ceased to decline and began to recover.

The Millions Left Behind — But millions of Americans were left behind. Over the last two years, 1.8 million men and women became discouraged workers and more than 5.4 million have fallen into poverty. Nearly half of all minority youth are unemployed, and Black males have effectively lost 13 percent of their labor force participation in the last two decades. Unemployment on Indian reservations continues to be among the highest in the nation. The U.S.-Mexico border has been devastated by the currency devaluations and economic crisis in Mexico. Small businesses have closed; American families are suffering hunger and poor health, as unemployment exceeds depression rates. Women continue to receive less than 60 percent of the wages that men receive, with minority women receiving far less. Millions of other Americans, including the growing number of women heading poor households or those who have been hard-hit by plant closings or obsolescent skills, avidly seek training or retraining in occupations that hold real promise for sustained employment opportunities in the future.

Millions of Americans, including those in the industrial and agricultural heartland, have been severely affected by the recent recession and the transformation in American industry that accompanied it. Furthermore, the changes seem to have come very quickly, and they do not seem to be over. Many Americans worked in auto, steel, machine tool, textile, agriculture and small business and related industries. Today for many of them, the recovery is a fiction, or seems very fragile. Plant closings have hit hard and job security and loss of health and pension benefits evoke memories from the past.

Investment in jobs for all Americans constitutes the key investment for the future of the nation. For every one million workers who go back to work, our country produces an additional $60-70 billion in goods and adds $25 billion to the Federal treasury. The Democratic Party will work aggressively to stimulate employment, rebuild trade and encourage labor-intensive industrialization.

Seven Threats to the Recovery

The current election year recovery is in serious jeopardy, threatened by a series of major economic problems:
• Unless corrective action is taken soon, the current $180 billion deficit will balloon even larger by the end of the decade.
• Interest rates are high and rising. The prime rate has jumped one and one half percentage points. A credit crunch is rapidly approaching in which federal borrowing for the deficit will overwhelm private demand for funds to fuel the recovery. Mortgage rates have risen to a point where home sales and housing starts are beginning to fall. The variable rate mortgage that buffers the thrift industry against high interest rates may, in the near future, put the entire industry under pressure as steadily rising rates put mortgage payments beyond the reach of the average homeowner.
• The Federal Reserve Board faces a deficit dilemma. By expanding the money supply to help finance the deficit, the Federal Reserve runs the risk of runaway inflation. But if it limits growth by restricting the money supply, high interest rates will distort growth or tip the economy back into recession.
• The Reagan Administration has done nothing to solve America's repeated problem of reconciling steady growth with stable prices, except by causing a deep recession. Continuing high levels of unemployment still exist in various communities across the country. Many jobs have disappeared. The Reagan Administration is not interested in new forms of fighting inflation — its anti-inflation program amounts to little more than unemployment, tight money and union busting. It is a highly cynical economic selective service that drafts only the poor and the middle class to fight the war against inflation. Unrestrained by the demands of another election, a second Reagan Administration will be even less concerned about the impact of deep recession on the average working American.
• Our trade deficit is a looming disaster for the national economy. An overvalued dollar, itself the product of high interest rates, helped create a nearly $70 billion trade deficit in 1983. It will be almost twice as large in 1984. Borrowing to support the deficits and buying abroad to maintain a

recovery tilted toward consumption are eroding America's position as a creditor nation.

● America is very much a part of the international economy. And the recovery overseas has been slow to catch hold. European economies are strained by the impact of high American interest rates on their own economies. For many developing countries, growth has been slowed or even reversed by the overhang of an enormous burden of commercial and official debt. If they cannot buy our products, our economy must slow.

● The sheer size of the international debt burden is itself a threat to the recovery. It is not only a question of falling exports to Latin America. The American and international financial system has been put in peril by the weakening of debtor nations' ability to repay their debt to U.S. banks as interest rates rise.

Howard Baker called Mr. Reagan's policies a "riverboat gamble." We now know the outcome. The very wealthiest in our society have been big winners — but future generations of Americans will be the losers.

The Americans coming of age today face a future less secure and less prosperous than their parents did — unless we change course. We have an obligation to our children and to their children. We Democrats have a different vision of our future.

THE DEMOCRATIC ALTERNATIVE:
A PROSPEROUS AMERICA IN A CHANGING WORLD

"There's a lot of people out there only making $3.35 an hour, and that's been since '81. That's a long time to be making $3.35 an hour. . . . Costs of living have gone up considerably. The insurance has gone up, gas, lights, water. It's a whole lot different now, it's not the same as '81. I know times have changed, but why can't the $3.35 change with them? I would like to know if anybody can answer. I urge the Democratic Party to develop policies and protect working people."

> Doris Smith, Steward, SEIU Local 706 (Democratic Platform Committee Hearing, Houston, Texas, May 29, 1984)

"We do not have a surplus as long as one member of my family is hungry. He may live next door or on the other side of the world. However, it should not be the producer's responsibility to provide cheap food at the expense of his own children."

> Roberta Archer, Farmer, Springfield, Illinois (Democratic Platform Committee Hearing, Springfield, Illinois, April 27, 1984)

"In the four years prior to Mr. Reagan taking over, I was fortunate to have four good years of employment, and I was able to put money aside in savings accounts which since have been exhausted. My unemployment benefits are exhausted too. . . . I may not qualify for any type of public assistance and the standard of living I was accustomed to for my wife and myself and my family has drastically changed. . . . But we as Democrats can join together in harmony and unison and we decide what is the future or the fate of our people and what is good for all of us. So I am very proud to be a Democrat."

> James Price, unemployed mine worker (Democratic Platform Committee Hearing, Birmingham, Alabama, April 24, 1984)

Democratic growth is not just a matter of good numbers, but of opportunities for people. Jobs and employment are at the center of Democratic thinking. It is not only a question of legislation or appropriations. Rather, it is a philosophy that views employment as the ongoing concern of the country. Work in America is not an idle concept — but a definition of self, a door to future opportunity, and the key step in securing the economic necessities of the present.

An America at work is a moral obligation as well as the most effective way to return our economy to a high growth path. Employed people stimulate the economy, their taxes pay for the expenses of government and their production adds to our national wealth. Moreover, the social and economic fabric of the nation will be strengthened as millions of Americans who presently are frozen out of productive and dignified employment become contributing citizens.

The potential for America is unlimited. It is within our means to put America back on a long-term path that will assure both growth and broad-based economic opportunity. That is what the next Democratic Administration will do. First, we will adopt overall economic policies that will bring interest rates down, free savings for private investment, prevent another explosion of inflation, and put the dollar on a competitive basis. Second, we will invest for our future — in our people, and in our infrastructure. Third, we will promote new partnerships and participation by all levels of government, by business and labor, to support growth and productivity. Finally, government will work with the private sector to assure that American businesses and American workers can compete fully and fairly in a changing world economy.

Overall Economic Policies:
A Firm Ground for Growth

A Democratic Administration will pursue economic policies which provide the basis for long-term economic growth and will allow us to fulfill our commitment to jobs for all Americans who want to work. A key part of the effort will be reducing and eventually eliminating the deficits that currently form a dark cloud over the nation's future. In addition, monetary policy must be set with an eye to stability and to the strengths or weaknesses of the economy. Finally, we will pursue policies that will promote price stability and prevent inflation from breaking out again.

Reducing the Reagan Budget Deficits

After plunging the nation into a deficit crisis, President Reagan refuses to take part in efforts to solve it. He postpones hard decisions until after the Presidential election, refusing to compromise, refusing to address revenues and defense spending seriously, refusing all but a "down payment" on the deficit. The President continues to stand apart from serious, comprehensive efforts to cut the deficit. There must be statesmanship and compromise here, not ideological rigidity or election year politics.

The Democratic Party is pledged to reducing these intolerable deficits. We will reassess defense expenditures; create a tax system that is both adequate and fair; control skyrocketing health costs without sacrificing quality of care; and eliminate other unnecessary expenditures. Through efficiency and toughness, we will restore sanity to our fiscal house.

We oppose the artificial and rigid Constitutional restraint of a balanced budget amendment. Further we oppose efforts to call a federal constitutional convention for this purpose.

Rational Defense Spending — In the last three years, the Defense Department was told by this Administration that it could have anything it wanted, and at any price. As Democrats, we believe in devoting the needed resources to ensure our national security. But military might cannot be measured solely by dollars spent. American military strength must be secured at an affordable cost. We will reduce the rate of increase in defense spending. Through careful reevaluation of proposed and existing weapons, we will stop throwing away money on unworkable or unnecessary systems; through military reform we will focus defense expenditure on the most cost-effective military policies. We will insist that our allies contribute fairly to our collective security, and that the Department of Defense reduces its scandalous procurement waste.

And above all else, we will seek sensible arms control agreements as a means of assuring that there will be a future for our children and that we as a nation will have the resources we need to invest for the future.

Tax Reform — America needs a tax system that encourages growth and produces adequate revenues in a fair, progressive fashion. The Democratic Party is committed to a tax policy that embodies these basic values.

The present system is unfair, complex, and encourages people to use a wide range of loopholes to avoid paying their fair share of taxes. The combination of loopholes for the few and high rates for the many is both unfair and anti-growth. It distorts investment, diverting creative energies into tax avoidance. And it makes the tax code even less comprehensible to the average American.

Our tax code must produce sufficient revenue to finance our defense and allow for investment in our future, and we will ask every American to pay his or her fair share. But by broadening the tax base, simplifying the tax code, lowering rates, and eliminating unnecessary, unfair and unproductive deductions and tax expenditures, we can raise the revenues we need and promote growth without increasing the burden on average taxpayers.

Ronald Reagan's tax program gave huge breaks to wealthy individuals and to large corporations while shifting the burden to low and moderate income families. The Democratic Party is pledged to reverse these unsound policies. We will cap the effect of the Reagan tax cuts for wealthy

Americans and enhance the progressivity of our personal income tax code, limiting the benefits of the third year of the Reagan tax cuts to the level of those with incomes of less than $60,000. We will partially defer indexation while protecting average Americans. We will close loopholes, eliminate the preferences and write-offs, exemptions, and deductions which skew the code toward the rich and toward unproductive tax shelters. Given the fact that there has been a veritable hemorrhage of capital out of the federal budget, reflected in part by the huge budget deficit, there must be a return to a fair tax on corporate income. Under the Reagan Administration, the rate of taxation on corporations has been so substantially reduced that they are not contributing their fair share to federal revenues. We believe there should be a 15% minimum corporate tax. In addition, our tax code has facilitated the transfer of capital from the United States to investments abroad, contributing to plant closing without notice in many communities and loss of millions of jobs. We will toughen compliance procedures to reduce the $100 billion annual tax evasion.

Our country must move to a simpler, more equitable, and more progressive tax system. Our tax code can let the market put our country's savings to the best use. There must be a fair balance between corporate and personal tax increases. Wealthier taxpayers will have to shoulder a greater share of the new tax burdens. Economic distortions must be eliminated.

Controlling Domestic Spending — A balanced program for reducing Republican megadeficits must also deal with the growing costs of domestic programs. But this must be done in a way that is fair to average Americans.

Social Security is one of the most important and successful initiatives in the history of our country, and it is an essential element of the social compact that binds us together as a community. There is no excuse — as the Reagan Administration has repeatedly suggested — for slashing Social Security to pay for excesses in other areas of the budget. We will steadfastly oppose such efforts, now and in the future.

It is rather in the area of health care costs that reform is urgently needed. By 1988, Medicare costs will rise to $106 billion; by the turn of the century, the debt of the trust fund may be as great as $1 trillion. In the Republican view, the problem is the level of benefits which senior citizens and the needy receive. As Democrats, we will protect the interests of health care beneficiaries. The real problem is the growing cost of health care services.

We propose to control these costs, and to demand that the health care industry become more efficient in providing care to all Americans, both young and old. We will limit what health care providers can receive as reimbursement, and spur innovation and competition in health care delivery. The growth of alternative health care delivery systems such as HMOs, PPOs and alternatives to long-term care such as home care and social HMOs should be fostered so that high quality care will be available at a lower cost. We must learn the difference between health care and sick care.

Unlike the Republicans, we recognize that investing in preventive health care saves dollars as well as lives, and we will make the needed investment. The states must be the cornerstone of our health care policies, but a Democratic Administration will provide the leadership at the federal level to assure that health care is available to all who need help at a cost we can afford. In addition, we pledge to scour the budget for other areas of wasteful or unnecessary spending.

Monetary Policy for Growth

Reducing the deficit is the first step toward lowering interest rates and establishing the basis for fair tax and budget policies. But even with a Democratic fiscal policy reining in the deficit, the task of the Federal Reserve Board will be critical. Monetary policy must work to achieve stable real interest rates, the availability of capital for long-term investments, predictable long-term policy and stable prices. We reject the rigid adherence to monetary targets that has frequently characterized the Reagan monetary policy. Whatever targeting approach the Federal Reserve Board adopts, it must be leavened with a pragmatic appraisal of what is happening in the harsh world of the real economy, particularly the impact on unemployment, interest rates, and the international value of the dollar.

An Anti-Inflation Program

We have learned that sustained economic growth is impossible in a climate of high inflation or of inflationary expectations. The Reagan Administration's only prescription for inflation is recession — deliberate high unemployment — coupled with a relentless assault on the collective bargaining power and rights of working men and women. The Democratic Party believes that these tactics are both unacceptable and ineffective.

We will develop the following five-step program to stabilize prices:
- — Growth — full order books encourage investments in new plants and equipment and research and development. The productivity growth that comes in tandem with new investment will help offset — point for point — any increase in cost.
- — Increased flexibility in the marketplace — will also help keep inflationary pressures under control. There is no single policy that will make the U.S. economy more adaptable. Rather, there is a series of smaller steps which will help keep prices stable. In general, competitive markets are more likely to restrain sudden surges of prices than are markets dominated by a few large firms. No Democratic Administration will forget the use of old fashioned antitrust policy to keep markets competitive and prices down.
- — Trade policy — is also an important component of any effective anti-inflation program. Expanding world markets for American goods increase the gains from large scale production and stimulate research

and development on new products and processes.

— The price-wage spiral — as part of any effective anti-inflation program, serious policies to address the price-wage spirals and other inflationary pressures we have experienced in the past must be developed.

— We believe that an attack on sectoral sources of inflation — in food, fuel, utilities, health care, and elsewhere — is essential without economic distortions. Our agriculture, energy, and health programs will all promote sectoral price stability while assuring fair treatment for average Americans, including working men and women and family farmers. For example, the Strategic Petroleum Reserve is one clear response to reducing the chance of another oil shock. The very presence of reserves in the U.S., Japan, and elsewhere reduces the likelihood of panic buying to replace suddenly threatened oil supplies. In this context, a far-reaching energy policy that emphasizes conservation and the development of alternative energy supplies will also help stabilize energy prices. And lower interest rates from reduced budget deficits will reduce upward pressure on housing costs and bring housing back within the reach of millions of Americans now excluded from the market.

Investing in People

America's greatest resource is our people. As Democrats, we affirm the need for both public and private investment — in our children; in our educational institutions and our students; in jobs, training, and transitional assistance for our workers — to build America's future. If we choose wisely, these investments will be returned to our country many times over. They are essential if we are to create an America with high-quality jobs and rising opportunities for all. And they are vital if we are to safeguard our competitive position in the world economy.

Investing in Children

Simple decency demands that we make children one of our highest national priorities. But the argument for so acting goes well beyond that. Programs for children represent the most critical investment we can make in our ability to compete in future world markets and maintain a strong national defense in the decades ahead.

Above all else, the Democratic Party stands for making the proper investment in coming generations of Americans.

Preventive efforts must be at the heart of the broad range of health, child care, and support programs for children. Helping these children makes good moral sense — and sound economic sense. Measles vaccine alone has saved $1.3 billion in medical costs in just ten years. Supplemental food programs for low-income pregnant women and infants save $3 for every dollar spent.

By improving access to medical care before and after birth, we can promote a generation of healthy mothers and healthy babies. Seeing that supplemental food programs for low-income pregnant women and infants reach all those eligible will do more than save the $40,000 now spent to treat one low birth weight infant in a neo-natal ward. It will also reduce the risk of birth defects for such infants.

We recognize that a hungry child is a child who cannot learn. Restoring school breakfast and school lunches for millions of children will improve their alertness and concentration in school.

Child care must also be a top priority. Helping communities establish afterschool care programs will remove millions of American children from the serious risks they now face of injury, abuse and alienation by staying at home alone. Encouraging employers, churches, public centers, and private groups to provide quality, affordable child care will give millions of children whose parents must work the kind of adult supervision necessary to thrive. And setting up centers for child care information and referral will assist parents wherever they reside to locate quality care for their children.

Preventing child abuse must be at the forefront of Democratic Party concern. Local, community-based child abuse prevention programs must be strengthened and expanded. A child who learns first about the risks of sexual abuse in school will be less likely to become the target of repeated victimization. Federal challenge grants could encourage states to make local prevention efforts a real priority.

Prompt intervention efforts must also be provided for children in crisis. If we are to make any headway in breaking the cycle of child abuse, both victims and offenders must have access to treatment programs.

Juvenile offenders must not be left in adult jails where the only skills they acquire are those of the career criminal. Safe shelter and assistance must be available for the hundreds of thousands of runaway children at risk of exploitation in our cities. Local, state, and federal law enforcement agencies must refine ways to locate children who have been abducted. And children in foster care must not be allowed to graduate to the streets at age 18 without ever having known a permanent home.

We must ensure that essential surveys on children's health and welfare status are reinstated. We know more about the number of matches sold than about the number of children across the country who die in fires while alone at home. Likewise, we know less about hunger and malnutrition among children than we do about the health of the nation's poultry stock.

The Democratic Party affirms its commitment to protecting the health and safety of children in the United States. Existing laws mandating the use of automobile child restraints must be enforced, and child safety seat loaner or rental programs and public education programs must be encouraged, in order to reduce significantly the leading cause of death and serious injury among children between the ages of six months and five years — motor vehicle crashes.

The crises devastating many of our nation's youth is nowhere more dramatically evidenced than in the alarming rate of increase in teenage suicide. Over 6,000 young people took their lives in 1983, and for each actual suicide 50 to 100 other youths attempted suicide. The underlying causes of teenage suicide, as well as its full scope, are not adequately researched or understood. We must commit ourselves to seek out the causes, formulate a national policy of prevention, and provide guidance to our state and local governments in developing means to stem this devastating tide of self-destruction. We support the creation of a national panel on teenage suicide to respond to this challenge.

A Democratic Administration which establishes these priorities can reduce the risks for our young people and improve the odds. By so doing, it will serve their future ... and ours.

Investing in Education

No public investment is more important than the one we make in the minds, skills and discipline of our people. Whether we are talking about a strong economy, a strong defense or a strong system of justice, we cannot achieve it without a strong educational system. Our very future in international economic competition depends on skilled workers and on first-rate scientists, engineers, and managers.

We Democrats are committed to equity in education. We will insist on excellence, discipline, and high standards. Quality education depends on students, teachers and parents performing at the highest levels of achievement.

Today, education in America needs help. But, the Reagan Administration offers misleading homilies about the importance of education while aggressively slashing education programs.

This is intolerable. We know that every dollar we invest in education is ultimately returned to us six-fold. We know that the education of our citizens is critical to our democracy.

There are four key goals that a Democratic program for educational excellence must address: strengthening local capacity to innovate and progress in public education and encourage parental involvement; renewing our efforts to ensure that all children, whatever their race, income, or sex have a fair and equal chance to learn; attracting the most talented young people into teaching and enabling them to remain and develop in their profession; and ensuring that all American families can send their children on to college or advanced training.

Primary and Secondary Education — While education is the responsibility of local government, local governments already strapped for funds by this Administration cannot be expected to bear alone the burden of undertaking the efforts we need for quality education — from teacher training, to the salaries needed to attract and retain able teachers, to new labs, to new programs to motivate talented and gifted students, to new ties between businesses and schools — without leadership at the federal level.

Democrats will provide that leadership. We call for the immediate restoration of the cuts in funding of education programs by the Reagan Administration, and for a major new commitment to education. We will create a partnership for excellence among federal, state and local governments. We will provide incentives to local school districts to concentrate on science, math, communications and computer literacy; to provide access to advanced technology. In all of these fields, but particularly in computers, there is a growing danger of a two-tier education system. The more affluent districts have adequate hardware and teachers prepared to use it. Many districts are left completely behind or saddled with a modern machine but no provision for faculty training. Every American child should have the basic education that makes computer literacy possible and useful. Major attention must be given to recruiting the finest young people into teaching careers, and to providing adequate staff development programs that enable educators to increase their effectiveness in meeting the needs of all students.

Vocational education should be overhauled to bring instructional materials, equipment, and staff up to date with the technology and practices for the workplace and target assistance to areas with large numbers of disadvantaged youth. We will insist that every child be afforded an equal opportunity to fulfill his or her potential. We will pay special attention to the needs of the handicapped.

Education is an important key to the upward mobility of all citizens and especially the disadvantaged, despite the fact that racial discrimination and other prejudices have set limits to such achievement.

The Reagan Administration has singled out for extinction the proven most successful education program — compensatory education for disadvantaged children. The Democratic Party will reverse this malicious onslaught and dramatically strengthen support in order to provide educational equity for all children.

Bilingual education enables children to achieve full competence in the English language and the academic success necessary to their full participation in the life of our nation. We reject the Reagan double-talk on bilingual education and commit ourselves to expanding and increasing its effectiveness.

We will emphasize the importance of preventing one-third of our student body nationwide from dropping out of school in the first place. And, we will supplement community-based programs encouraging students who have left school due to teenage parenthood, alcohol and drug abuse, or economic difficulties at home to complete their educations.

Recognizing that young people who are never given an opportunity for a job will be less likely to hold one in adulthood, we will also emphasize training and employment opportunities for youth. In so doing, we need to establish a genuine working partnership with the private sector.

Private schools, particularly parochial schools, are also an important part of our diverse educational system. Consistent with our tradition, the Democratic Party accepts its commitment to constitutionally acceptable methods of supporting the education of all pupils in schools which do not racially discriminate, and excluding so-called segregation academies. The Party will continue to support federal education legislation which provides for the equitable participation in federal programs of all low and moderate income pupils.

For its part, when added to the traditional educational institutions of family, school and church, television has enormous promise as a teacher. When children spend more time in front of the television set than they do in the classroom, we must ask how television can help children, and why commercial broadcasters do so little programming for children today despite their legal responsibility as "public trustees" of the airwaves granted to them. The National Science Board, for instance, has recommended that commercial television stations be required to air a certain amount of information/educational programming for children each week. Properly developed, television can be an enormously efficient and effective supplemental teaching tool.

Higher Education — We will make certain that higher education does not become a luxury affordable only by the children of the rich. That is Ronald Reagan's America. In our America, no qualified student should be deprived of the ability to go on to college because of financial circumstance.

The Democratic Party reaffirms the importance of historically Black colleges. Today the survival of many of these colleges is threatened. The programs that assist them, which have been severely weakened in recent years, must be greatly strengthened with funding targeted toward Black and Hispanic institutions.

An explosion in demand for certain types of engineers, scientists and other technical specialists is creating a shortage of faculty and PhD candidates. We must encourage colleges and universities to train more scientists and engineers. More than one hundred years ago the Morrill Land Grant Act provided for agricultural colleges and programs that today still help keep American agriculture the world leader. We need a similar program today to encourage the training of scientists and engineers. At the same time, we must not neglect the arts and humanities, which enrich our spirit. The private sector must also recognize its responsibility to join partnerships which strengthen our diverse public and private higher education system.

Finally, all our educational institutions must adapt to growing numbers of adults returning to school to upgrade their skills, acquire new skills, prepare themselves for entirely new occupations, and enrich their lives.

Investing in the Arts

America is truly growing and prosperous when its spirit flourishes. The arts and humanities are at the core of our national experience. Creativity and the life of the mind have defined us at our best throughout our history. As scholars or artists, the museum-goers or students, craftsmen and craftswomen or the millions who use our libraries, countless Americans have a stake in a nation that honors and rejoices in intelligence and imagination.

The Democratic Party will set a new national tone of respect for learning and artistic achievement. Not only will the federal agencies that support them be strengthened and freed from political intimidation, but the White House itself will once again be a place where American cultural and intellectual life — in all its rich diversity — is honored. Excellence must start at the top.

Finally, the Democratic Party is also committed to the survival of public television and radio stations, which allow all Americans, regardless of ability to pay, to appreciate high quality, alternative programming. We oppose the efforts of the Reagan Administration to enact draconian cuts which would totally undermine the viability of this nation's excellent public broadcasting system, a broadcasting system which has given the country Sesame Street, 3-2-1 Contact, and other superb children's as well as cultural and public affairs programming.

Jobs, Training and Transitional Assistance

We must have a growing economy if we are to have jobs for all Americans who seek work. But even in a growing economy, the pressures of competition and the pace of change ensure that while jobs are being created, others are being destroyed. Prosperity will not be evenly distributed among regions and communities. We must make special efforts to help families in economic transition who are faced with loss of homes, health benefits, and pensions. And far too many of our young people, especially minorities, do not have the training and skills they need to get their first job. Democrats believe that it is a national responsibility to ensure that the burdens of change are fairly shared and that every young American can take the first step up the ladder of economic opportunity.

Of the 8.5 million Americans still out of work, 40 percent are under 25. Unemployment among teenagers stands at almost 20 percent. Less than three percent of the jobs created in the last three and a half years have gone to young people. Black and Hispanic youth have a double burden. Unemployment for black teenagers stands at 44 percent — a 20 percent increase in the last three years. Hispanic teens face a 26 percent unemployment rate.

As disturbing as these figures are, they do not tell the whole story. The unemployment rate measures only those teenagers who were actively looking for work, not those who have given up, completely discouraged by the lack of opportunity. Again the burden falls disproportionately on minority youth.

The Reagan Administration has dismantled virtually all of the successful programs to train and employ young people. Today, we are spending less to put young people to work than we were even under the last *Republican* Administration — 70 percent less, when inflation is taken into account. Youth unemployment has skyrocketed, while government efforts to combat it have dwindled to a trickle.

Unless we address this problem now, half of an entire generation may never know what it means to work. America cannot successfully compete in the world economy if a significant portion of our future work force is illiterate, unskilled, and unemployable.

The Democratic Party must give our young people new skills and new hope; we must work hand in hand with the private sector if job training is to lead to jobs. Specifically, targeted efforts are needed to address the urgent problem of unemployment among minority teenagers. We must provide job training for those who have dropped out of school, and take every step to expand educational opportunity for those still in school. We must recognize the special needs of the over-age 50 worker and the displaced homemaker. Through education, training and retraining we must reduce these dangerously high levels of unemployment.

We must provide an opportunity for workers, including those dislocated by changing technologies, to adapt to new opportunities; we must provide workers with choices as to which skills they wish to acquire. We know that Americans want to work. We are committed to ensuring that meaningful job training is available — for our students, for housewives returning to the workplace, and for those displaced by changing patterns of technology or trade.

— The federal government will develop a major comprehensive national job skills development policy that is targeted on the chronically unemployed and underemployed. We must train and place these Americans in high-demand labor shortage occupations, working with the private sector so that maximum employment and job creation can be achieved.
— We will overhaul the currently antiquated unemployment compensation system, and adequately fund job search listings of local employment agencies.
— We will also launch meaningful training programs that lead to job placement for women who receive public assistance, in order to break the cycle of dependence and to raise their standard of living. Instead of punitive reductions in AFDC and other benefits for women who seek training and employment while receiving such assistance, beneficiaries should be given a transition period during which they are permitted to earn income in a formal training program while receiving full benefits.
— We will seriously examine new approaches to training and retraining programs that could be financed directly by government, by labor and management, or by tax free contributions.
— If cancellations of specific weapons systems result in significant economic dislocations and job loss, it is a national responsibility to address the human consequences of national policy.

Investing in Infrastructure

Economic growth requires that America invest in our infrastructure as well as in our people. Investing in infrastructure means rebuilding our bridges and roads and sewers, and we are committed to doing that. But it also means investing in our cities, in decent housing and public transportation, and in regulatory systems for finance and telecommunication that will provide a sound basis for future economic growth.

Investing in our Cities

The Democratic Party recognizes the value of prosperous local government, and within that context we recognize that a healthy city is essential to the well-being of the nation, state, county and surrounding local governments.

Our nation's economic life depends on the economic growth of our cities. Our cities are not only the treasuries from which the nation draws its wealth; they are the centers of industry, the centers of art and culture, the breeding ground for economic innovation, and home to the majority of the American people. Our cities are among this country's greatest achievements, and they can be our country's greatest engine of economic growth.

Cities can be active partners with the federal government and private enterprises for creating new growth. They can be a dynamic entrepreneurial force — by encouraging education and research, by incubating promising new industries, by steering resources toward those most in need, and by fostering new cooperative arrangements among public agencies and private business. Cities can be a leading force for rebuilding the nation's economy.

But to do this, cities need state and national leadership which values the role of city and county government. Cities need a President willing to work and consult with mayors and county executives. They need an Administration which puts the needs of urban America on the top of the national agenda — because no plan for economic strength will survive when our cities are left behind.

Today, the Reagan Administration has turned its back on the cities. By sapping our cities' strength, this Administration is sapping our country's strength. Only the intervention of the Congress has prevented further and more devastating cuts in city-oriented programs. The Democratic Party believes in making our cities' needs a federal priority once again. We want to see again cities where people have jobs and adequate housing, cities whose bridges and mass transit are being maintained, and whose neighborhoods are safe to live in. And that will take a commitment by our federal government to help our cities again.

Toward that end, the Democratic Party pledges:
— a commitment to full employment. We believe the federal government must develop a major, comprehensive national job skills devel-

opment policy targeted on the chronically unemployed and underemployed. We must launch special training programs for women who receive public assistance. We need to increase government procurement opportunities for small and minority firms and to encourage deposits of federal funds in minority-owned financial institutions. And to build for the future, the Democratic Party calls for a new national commitment to education, which must include raising standards, insisting on excellence, and giving all children a chance to learn, regardless of race, income or sex.

— a commitment to rebuilding the infrastructure of America. We need to inventory facility needs, set priorities and establish policies for the repair, maintenance, and replacement of public works by all levels of government. We need to create a federal capital budget to separate operating and capital outlays. We will consult local governments in decisions affecting the design and performance standards of facilities constructed under federal programs. And we need to create a national reconstruction fund to provide affordable loans to states and localities for infrastructure projects. This will not only rebuild the infrastructure of our cities but provide badly needed employment for people who live there.

— a commitment to housing. We must restore government's positive role in helping all Americans find adequate and affordable housing. We reaffirm our commitment to public housing for the most disadvantaged members of our society. We must strengthen our commitment to the operation and rehabilitation of current government-assisted housing. We must maintain and expand the flow of mortgage capital, and bring interest rates down with sensible economic policies. We must pull together the patchwork of housing programs and cut through the red tape to make it easier for cities to receive the assistance to meet their own unique needs. We must upgrade and replenish housing in minority communities and create more units for poor and low-income people. And we must enforce fair housing standards to prohibit discrimination in the housing market.

Our Party must be a vehicle for realizing the hopes, the aspirations, and the dreams of the people of this country. And that includes the people who live in cities.

Physical Infrastructure

This nation's physical infrastructure — our bridges and roads, our ports, our railroads, our sewers, our public transit and water supply systems — is deteriorating faster than we can repair it. The gap between the necessary improvements and available resources grows every year. State and local governments, strapped by Reaganomics, have been forced repeatedly to defer maintenance, and to abandon plans for construction.

As Democrats, we recognize that infrastructure is the basis for efficient commerce and industry. If our older industrial cities are to grow, if our expanding regions are to continue to expand, then we must work with state and local governments to target our investment to our most important infrastructure. There is work to be done in rebuilding and maintaining our infrastructure, and there are millions of American men and women in need of work. The federal government must take the lead in putting them back to work, and in doing so, providing the basis for private sector investment and economic growth. We need to inventory facility needs, set priorities, and establish policies for the repair, maintenance and replacement of the public works by all levels of government. We need a capital budget to separate paying for these long-term investments from regular expenditures. Futhermore, we need a national reconstruction fund to provide affordable loans to states and localities for infrastructure projects.

Finance Infrastructure

At the heart of our economy is the financial infrastructure: a set of diverse interdependent institutions and markets which are the envy of the world. We must preserve their strengths. Until very recently, the United States operated with a domestic financial system that was built in response to the stock market crash of 1929, the massive series of bank failures that accompanied the Great Depression, and the speculative excesses of the stock market. There was an emphasis on placing different types of financial activities in different institutions. Commercial banks were not to float stock market issues. Investment bankers could. Neither took equity positions in individual companies. Separate savings and credit institutions were established to support housing and consumer durables. Soundness of the system, liquidity, investor and depositor protection, neutrality of credit and capital decisions, and a wide variety of financial institutions to serve the varying needs of business and consumers have been the fundamental goals.

Bit by bit, the American financial system began to change. The domestic financial market became closely tied to the international market, which in turn had become larger, more competitive, and more volatile. Inflation, technology, the growth of foreign competition, and institutional innovation all combined to create strong pressures for change. The 1980s brought a deregulation of interest rates and a wave of deregulatory decisions by financial regulators.

These changes raise serious threats to our traditional financial goals. Before leaping into a highly uncertain financial future, the country should take a careful look at the direction deregulation is taking, and what it means to our financial system and the economy.

Telecommunications

Telecommunications is the infrastructure of the information age. The last decade has seen an explosion in new technologies, expanded competition, and growing dependence on high quality telecommunications.

Nationwide access to those networks is becoming crucial to full participation in a society and economy that are increasingly dependent upon the rapid exchange of information. Electronically-delivered messages, and not the written word, are becoming the dominant form of communication. A citizen without access to telecommunications is in danger of fading into isolation. Therefore, the proper regulation of telecommunications is critical. We must encourage competition while preventing regulatory decisions which substantially increase basic telephone rates and which threaten to throw large numbers of low-income, elderly, or rural people off the telecommunications networks. We must also insure that workers in the telecommunications industry do not find their retirement or other earned benefits jeopardized by the consequences of divestiture.

This electronic marketplace is so fundamental to our future as a democracy (as well as to our economy) that social and cultural principles must be as much a part of communications policy as a commitment to efficiency, innovation, and competition. Those principles are diversity, the availability of a wide choice of information services and sources; access, the ability of all Americans, not just a privileged few, to take advantage of this growing array of information services and sources; and opportunity, a commitment to education and diverse ownership, particularly by minorities and women, that will give every American the ability to take advantage of the computer and the telecommunications revolution. We support the Fairness Doctrine and Equal Time requirements, along with other laws and regulations to the electronic media which encourage or require responsiveness to community needs and a diversity of viewpoints.

Housing

Decent, affordable housing has been a goal of national public policy for almost half a century, since the United States Housing Act of 1937. The Democratic Party has repeatedly reaffirmed the belief that American citizens should be able to find adequate shelter at reasonable cost. And we have been unwavering in our support of the premise that government has a positive role to play in ensuring housing opportunities for less fortunate Americans, including the elderly and the handicapped, not served by the private market.

In the last four years this long-standing commitment to decent shelter has been crippled by the underfunding, insensitivity, high interest rates, and distorted priorities of the Reagan Administration.

The Democratic Party has always accorded housing the high priority it deserves. One essential quality will characterize this commitment in the future. It must and will be comprehensive.

By advocating a comprehensive policy which addresses the totality of our housing needs, we do not mean to suggest that all concerns have an equal claim on resources or require the same level of governmental intervention. The bulk of our resources will be concentrated on those most in need, and government must take a leadership role where others cannot or will not participate.

Within a comprehensive framework for policy development and constituency building, we will establish priorities according to principles of compassion and equity. We would like to see a special effort in two areas in the first years of a new Democratic Administration.

First, we must intensify our commitment to the adequate operation, management, and rehabilitation of the current inventory of government-assisted housing. This housing stock is not one, but the only option for the least fortunate among our lower income families and senior citizens. It is the right thing to do and it makes economic sense to preserve our own economic investment.

Second, we must maintain and expand the flow of mortgage capital. The American dream of home ownership will fall beyond the reach of this generation and future ones if government fails to help attract new sources of capital for housing.

We will draw on our historic commitment to housing, and the best insights and energies of today's Democratic Party, to address the future housing needs of all the American people. The Democratic Party will develop short-range emergency responses to the problem of homelessness as well as long-range solutions to its causes. The Democratic Party will support upgrading and replenishment of the housing stock in minority communities, with more affordable units available so that poor and low income people can buy units with low interest loans. Also, fair housing standards need to be vigorously enforced by the federal, state and local governments in order to deal with persistent discrimination in the housing market for buyers and renters. Finally, the expansion of public housing and other publicly-assisted housing programs is a necessity due to the growth in the homeless population and in the high cost of commercially available units.

Transportation

Democrats vigorously support the concept of promoting competition in transportation and the elimination of unnecessary and inefficient regulation of the railroad industry. Democrats also insist on insuring a fair rate for captive shippers. It was the Democratic Party which was primarily responsible for the passage of the Staggers Rail Act of 1980, which was designed to accomplish these objectives.

The Democratic Party is committed to a policy of administering the transportation laws in a manner which will encourage competition and provide protection for captive shippers.

A comprehensive maritime policy that is tailored to the realities of today's international shipping world and to the economic, political, and military needs of the United States is a necessity. Such a policy should address all facets of our maritime industry — from shipping to shipbuilding and related activities — in an integrated manner.

A Framework for Growth

The American economy is a complex mix, incorporating any number of different actors and entities — private businesses, professional societies, charitable institutions, labor unions, regional development councils, and local school boards. The economy is driven by millions of individual decisions on spending and saving, on investing and wages. Government is only one force among many woven into the fabric of American economic life. Just as the wrong overall economic policy can disrupt the best private decisions, the best government economic policies will not put us on a path to long-term growth unless business, labor, and other private institutions meet their responsibilities and rise to the competitive challenge of a new era.

Private Sector Responsibilities

In many cases, the private sector is already playing a major role in laying the basis for future growth and meeting broad community responsibilities. In other cases, however, short-term considerations have been allowed to predominate at the expense of the long-term needs of the national economy.

A recent wave of mergers has been particularly troubling. Any number of large corporations have focused their energies arranging the next merger or defending against the latest takeover bid.

Many of our major competitors have targeted their efforts on investments in new methods of producing cheaper, high-quality products. To respond to the growing pressure of foreign competition, America's private sector must meet several challenges:
- Investing strategically — the more U.S. companies focus on long-term strategies to improve their competitive positions, the better off the entire economy will be.
- Managing cost and quality — U.S. companies will have to place similar emphasis on controlling costs and quality to effectively meet the best of the foreign competition.
- Competing internationally — U.S. business like other institutions in the country need to pay greater attention to the international market place.

Partnership, Cooperation and Participation

Partnership, cooperation and participation are central to economic growth. We need new cooperative institutions, and a steady redefinition of how labor and management, universities, the private sector, and state and local governments can work together.
- National cooperation — In developing a long-term growth strategy, there are several particularly important functions that today are poorly performed or poorly coordinated by the government: coordina-

tion and policy coherence; developing and disseminating useful economic information; anticipating economic problems; and developing long-term consensus between public and private sectors. To better accomplish these tasks, it is time that a national Economic Cooperation Council was created. Its charter would be simple and basic: (1) to collect, analyze, and disseminate economic data; (2) to create a forum where the gap between business, labor, and government is bridged, where all three develop the trust, understanding, and cooperation necessary to improve productivity; and, (3) to identify national priorities, make recommendations on how best to reach those goals, and help build consensus for action.

— State involvement — Under the guise of increasing the power of state government, the Reagan Administration has actually given the states only the power to decide what programs to cut or eliminate, because of the substantially decreased funding it has made available to the states. Should it be baby clinics, child immunization against disease, day care, maternal health, or youth services? The Democratic Party believes a strong partnership of federal, state and local governments is basic to effective and efficient decision-making, problem-solving, and provision of adequate services. We must also encourage cooperation between states and the private sector. State development agencies are already seeking closer ties to both business and universities. And universities are increasingly looking to the private sector in setting their research agendas.

— Local and community involvement — Citizen involvement in governance should be as great as possible. The responsibility for general governance, the delivery of programs and services, and the resolution of problems should be with the level of government that is closest to the citizenry and that can still discharge those responsibilities effectively and efficiently. These levels of government must assure basic civil liberties and justice for all citizens. They must not be abrogated by any local jurisdiction. The federal government should focus on the importance of local initiatives. For example, vocational education is an area where local schools and local business will increasingly be brought together. Financial stability and adequate authority are essential prerequisites to developing successful public-private partnerships and maximizing citizen involvement in governance.

Government financial and technical assistance programs should give preference to viable worker and/or community-owned or -run businesses, especially as a response to plant shutdowns.

Broadening Labor-Management Cooperation

We support greater employee participation in the workplace. Employees should have an opportunity to make a greater contribution to workplace productivity and quality through actual ownership of the company, employee representation on corporate boards, quality work circles, and greater worker participation in management decisions. The government should encourage employee participation and ownership, particularly as an alternative to plant shutdowns. It is destructive of labor-management relations when concessions extracted from labor to preserve jobs are converted, after the restoration of profitability, into management bonuses, rather than restoring the concessions that the workers made. Such practices offend our sense of fairness, as does the Reagan Administration-inspired union-busting. Essential to fairness in the workplace is the basic right of workers to organize collectively.

Consumer Protection

The Democratic Party strongly reaffirms its commitment to federal programs which are designed to enhance and protect the health and safety of all Americans. Under the Reagan Administration, the critical missions of agencies such as the Consumer Product Safety Commission (CPSC), the National Highway Traffic Safety Administration (NHTSA), the Food and Drug Administration (FDA), the Occupational Safety and Health Administration (OSHA), the Mine Safety and Health Administration (MSHA), and the Federal Trade Commission (FTC) have been ignored and subverted.

The Reagan Administration proposed abolishing the CPSC, which has recalled over 300 million dangerous and defective products in its 10 year history. When it failed to accomplish this, the Administration attempted to submerge CPSC in the Department of Commerce. Also failing in this attempt, the Reagan Administration inflicted massive budget and personnel cuts on the Commission. The impact has been far reaching: recalls declined 66%, inspections were cut in half and over half of CPSC's regional offices have been closed. The result has been a paralysis of mission and an America more susceptible to dangerous products.

The record at the NHTSA, the agency mandated to reduce the appalling annual highway deaths of more than 50,000 Americans, is just as shameful. The President has appointed administrators with no safety background and even less commitment to the public health mission of the agency. Critical lifesaving safety standards, such as one requiring automatic crash protection in cars, have been revoked. The enforcement of defect and recall programs, designed to remove dangerous vehicles from our roads, has been cut back. Recalls are at an all-time low and only one safety standard has been proposed in four years.

At OSHA and MSHA, we have witnessed a retreat from agency mandates to provide safe and healthful working conditions for this nation's working men and women. Existing standards have been weakened or revoked and not one single new standard has been implemented. Similarly, at the FDA there has been an important shift away from removing dangerous and ineffective drugs in favor of weakening standards for products. The FTC has run roughshod over the nation's antitrust laws, allowing 9 of the 10 largest mergers in history to occur.

The dangerous trends in all these areas must be immediately reversed to allow these vital health and safety agencies to pursue their missions aggressively, to protect and enhance the health and safety of all Americans.

Individual Empowerment

The Democratic Party's commitment to full equality is as much a part of providing individual opportunity as it is part of a program of social justice. At the heart of our values as a nation is our belief in independence. Anyone who has brought home a paycheck, bought a car, or paid off a mortgage knows the pride that economic self-sufficiency brings. And anyone who has lost a job, watched one's children go hungry, or been denied a chance at success knows the terrible indignity that comes with dependence.

As Democrats, we share that belief in independence. Our goal is to allow the greatest number of people the greatest opportunity for self-sufficiency.

As a Party, we are committed to preparing people to stand on their own; that is why we insist on adequate nutrition for our children and good educations for our young people. We are committed to permitting independence; that's why we believe discrimination on any basis must come to an end. We believe that independence should be prolonged for as long as possible; to ensure it continues even after retirement, we support Social Security and Medicare. And we believe we must preserve the self-respect of those who are unable to be completely self-sufficient — the very young, the unskilled, the disabled, the very old — and to help them toward as much independence as possible. As much as it is a strategy for long run economic growth, individual empowerment must itself be an operating philosophy. In the welfare system, in education, and in the laws affecting everyone from shareholders to the average voter, the Democratic Party will ask if the individual is being made stronger and more independent.

America in a World Economy

The reality of international competition in the 1980s requires government policies which will assure the competitiveness of American industry and American workers. Democrats will support and encourage innovation and research and development in both the private and public sector. We will seek to strengthen America's small businesses. And we will pursue trade policies and industrial strategies to ensure that our workers and our businesses can compete fully and fairly in the international arena.

Innovation

Innovation — in process and product technology — is at the heart of our ability to compete in a world economy and produce sustained economic growth at home. And research and development, critical as it is for our growing high technology industries, is no less important for our basic industries. In the past generation, our world leadership in innovation has been increasingly jeopardized. We have not invested enough — or widely enough — to match our major competitors.

Research and Development — Since the mid-1960s, all the other major industrial nations have increased their expenditures for research and development more rapidly than we have. Over the past decade, manufacturing productivity rose more than four times faster in Japan, more than three times faster in France, and more than twice as fast in both West Germany and the United Kingdom than in the United States. And the number of patents granted to Americans each year has plunged by 40 percent.

The United States should revise its downward trend and increase the percentage of GNP devoted to commercially-rated R&D as a long-term spending goal. We must be at the cutting edge, and we will not get there without cooperation between the government and the private sector. As Democrats, our goal is to increase civilian research and development in this country, to expand its commercial application, and to provide more industries with the opportunity to take advantage of it.

At the national level, this means enhanced support for undergraduate and graduate training in science, mathematics, and engineering; increased support to refurbish and modernize university research laboratories; increased support for the National Science Foundation and similar efforts; and a commitment to civilian research and development.

Centers of Excellence — In the past generation, scientists and engineers, together with educators and business leaders throughout the United States, have begun countless new, high technology businesses such as those in Boston, Massachusetts, California's Silicon Valley, North Carolina's Research Triangle, greater Denver, Colorado, and Austin, Texas to establish this country as a leader in the next generation of high technology industries — biotechnology, polymer sciences, robotics, photovoltaics, marine sciences, microelectronics. The Democratic Party will encourage and support centers that provide for cooperation of academic and entrepreneurial excellence, thereby strengthening our scientific and technological resources and creating tomorrow's jobs.

Small and Minority Business

The Democratic Party recognizes that small businesses create many, if not most of the new jobs in our country, and are responsible for much of the innovation. They are thus our greatest hope for the future. Our capacity as a nation to create an environment that encourages and nurtures innovative new businesses will determine our success in providing jobs for our people. In the private sector, spurring innovation means paying special attention to the needs of small, including minority and women-owned, and rapidly growing businesses on the cutting edge of our economy.

This will require incentives for research and development and for employee education and training, including relaxing certain restrictions on pension fund investment; targeted reform that stimulates the flow of capital into new and smaller businesses; a tax code that is no longer biased against small and rapidly growing firms; vigorous enforcement of our antitrust laws, coupled with antitrust policies that permit clearly legitimate joint research and development ventures; expanded small business access to the Export-Import Bank and other agencies involved in export promotion; and targeted reform that provides for the delivery of community-based, community-supported management assistance, and innovative means of making seed capital available for companies in our large cities, as well as our rural communities.

Rules and regulations should not weigh more heavily on new firms or small businesses than they do on the large, well-established enterprise. Risk taking is a key to economic growth in a modern industrial society. If anything, rules and regulations should encourage it.

The Small Business Administration must once again be responsive to the needs of entrepreneurs, including minorities and women. In addition, the heads of the Small Business Administration, the Minority Business Development Administration and other government agencies must ensure that the needs of smaller minority businesses are met at the regional and local levels. To further meet the needs of smaller minority businesses, we favor increasing government procurement, opportunities for smaller minority firms, encouraging deposits of federal funds in minority-owned financial institutions, and vigorously implementing all set-aside provisions for minority businesses.

The Democratic Party pledges to bring about these reforms and create a new era of opportunity for the entrepreneurs who have always led the way in our economy.

Meeting the Challenge of Economic Competition

Thirty years ago, half of all goods produced in the world were made in the United States. While we have greatly expanded our output of services, our share of manufactured products is now just one-fifth of the world's total. Once dominant U.S.-industries are now hard-pressed. In April, our trade deficit reached a stunning $12.2 billion for one month. At that rate, we would lose two million or more jobs this year alone. We will not allow our workers and our industries to be displaced by either unfair import competition, or irrational fiscal and monetary policies.

Some of these difficulties we have brought on ourselves, with short-sighted strategies, inadequate investment in plant, equipment, and innovation, and fiscal and monetary policies that have impaired our international competitiveness by distorting the value of the dollar against foreign currencies. But other difficulties have been thrust upon us by foreign nations.

The reality of the 1980s is that the international economy is the arena in which we must compete. The world economy is an integrated economy; the challenge for our political leadership is to assure that the new arena is in fact a fair playing field for American businesses and consumers. We are committed to pursuing industrial strategies that effectively and imaginatively blend the genius of the free market with vital government partnership and leadership. As Democrats, we will be guided by the following principles and policies.

— We need a vigorous, open and fair trade policy that builds America's competitive strength and that allows our nation to remain an advanced, diversified economy while promoting full employment and raising living standards in the United States and other countries of the world; opens overseas markets for American products; strengthens the international economic system; assists adjustment to foreign competition; and recognizes the legitimate interests of American workers, farmers and businesses.

— We will pursue international negotiations to open markets and eliminate trade restrictions, recognizing that the growth and stability of the Third World depends on its ability to sell its products in international markets. High technology, agriculture and other industries should be brought under the General Agreement on Trade and Tariffs. Moreover, the developing world is a major market for U.S. exports, particularly capital goods. As a result, the U.S. has a major stake in international economic institutions that support growth in the developing world.

— We recognize that the growth and development of the Third World is vital both to global stability and to the continuing expansion of world trade. The U.S. presently sells more to the Third World than to the European Community and Japan combined. If we do not buy their goods, they cannot buy ours, nor can they service their debt. Consequently, it is important to be responsive to the issues of the North/South dialogue such as volatile commodity prices, inequities in the functioning of the international financial and monetary markets, and removal of barriers to the export of Third World goods.

— If trade has become big business for the country, exports have become critical to the economic health of a growing list of American industries. In the future, national economic policy will have to be set with an eye to its impact on U.S. exports. The strength of the dollar, the nature of the U.S. tax system, and the adequacy of export finance all play a role in making U.S. exports internationally competitive.

— The United States continues to struggle with trade barriers that affect its areas of international strength. Subsidized export financing on the part of Europe and Japan has also created problems for the United States, as has the use of industrial policies in Europe and Japan. In some cases, foreign governments target areas of America's competitive strength. In other cases, industrial targeting has been used to maintain industries that cannot meet international competition — often diverting exports to the American market and increasing the burden of adjustment for America's import-competing industries. We will ensure that timely and effective financing can be obtained by American businesses through the Export-Import Bank, so that they can compete effectively against subsidized competitors from abroad.

— A healthy U.S. auto industry is essential to a strong trade balance and economy. That industry generates a large number of American jobs and both develops and consumes new technology needed for economic vitality. We believe it is a sound principle of international trade for foreign automakers which enjoy substantial sales in the United States to invest here and create jobs where their markets are. This can promote improved trade relations and a stronger American and world economy. We also believe U.S. automakers need to maintain high volume small car production in the U.S. With the U.S. auto companies' return to profitability (despite continued unemployment in the auto sector), we urge expanded domestic investment to supply consumers with a full range of competitive vehicles. We support efforts by management and labor to improve auto quality and productivity, and to restrain prices.

— Where foreign competition is fair, American industry should compete without government assistance. Where competition is unfair, we must respond powerfully. We will use trade law and international negotiations to aid U.S. workers, farmers, and business injured by unfair trade practices.

— We need industrial strategies to create a cooperative partnership of labor, capital, and management to increase productivity and to make America competitive once more. Our keystone industries must be modernized and rebuilt, through industry-wide agreements. Where necessary, through Presidential leadership, we must negotiate industrial modernization and growth agreements that commit management to new domestic investment, higher levels of employment and worker training, as well as commit labor to ease the introduction of new technologies.

— There must be a broad consensus and commitment among labor, business and financial institutions that industry should and can be assisted, and in a particular way. We believe that all parties to modernization agreements must contribute to their success and that the government must be prepared to use a range of tools — including tax, import, and regulatory relief, and appropriate financing mechanisms — to assist this revitalization. There should be a primary emphasis on private capital in any such agreements.

— The problems of individual industries, rather than industry as a whole, is another area in which an Economic Cooperation Council will be effective. In the case of a particular industry, the Council would select sub-councils to solve specific problems. Key members of the interested businesses and unions, financial institutions, academic specialists and other concerned and knowledgeable parties would meet to hammer out proposed strategies and agreements. It is not a question of picking winners and losers. Nor is it even always a question of some industries being more important than others.

Rather, it is an opportunity for government and the private sector to forge a consensus to capture new markets, to restore an industry to competitive health, or to smooth the transition of workers and firms to new opportunities.

— We want industries to modernize so as to restore competitiveness where it is flagging. If temporary trade relief is granted, the *quid pro quo* for relief will be a realistic, hardheaded modernization plan which will restore competitiveness involving commitments by all affected parties. The public is entitled to receive a fair return on its investment. Where government initiatives are necessary to save an industry like steel, auto or textiles, we must see that those initiatives meet the needs of the whole community — workers as well as executives, taxpayers and consumers as well as stockholders.

— To facilitate the efforts of workers and communities to keep plants open and operating and, in cases which closings are unavoidable, to help workers and communities to adapt, we support a requirement that companies give advance notification of plant closings or large-scale layoffs to their employees, surrounding communities and local governments. Where plants are nonetheless closed, we will help workers and communities to adapt.

— Finally, we need a vigorous effort to redress the currency distortions that are undermining our international competitiveness. In addition to reducing our budget deficit, we will press for improved economic coordination with the major industrialized nations; work with Japan and other countries to further liberalize currency and investment regulations; and negotiate toward agreements that will blunt speculative currency swings and restore stability and predictability to the international monetary system.

Agriculture

Agriculture — America's largest, most fundamental industry — has been plunged into its worst depression since Herbert Hoover presided over the farm economy's collapse half a century ago. During President Reagan's stewardship of our nation's agriculture economy: real prices paid to farmers for their commodities have plummeted by twenty-one percent; real interest rates paid by farmers have increased by as much as 1,200 percent; real farm income has fallen to its lowest level since 1933; debt owed by U.S. farmers and ranchers has swelled to $215 billion; and farm foreclosures and forced sales have tripled.

Ronald Reagan has hung a "for sale" sign on America's independent, family-based system of agricultural production. While these farmers have raised their production efficiency to record highs, Reagan's policies have forced down their prices, income, and financial worth.

The Reagan Administration has been unwilling to take sensible, fiscally responsible action needed to halt this accelerating downward cycle in agriculture. Because of this failure of leadership, nearly 200,000 good farmers and ranchers, including minority farmers, have gone out of business since he took office in 1981. This is a rate of more than 1,000 families pushed off their land every week, the equivalent of all the farms and ranches in California and Iowa, our two largest agricultural states. Hundreds of thousands of the remaining enterprises teeter on the brink of bankruptcy and cannot survive another four years of this Administration's agricultural mismanagement.

This collapse is happening despite the fact that Ronald Reagan has squandered taxpayers' money on his farm policies, spending $31 billion on his programs last year alone. That is *six times more* than any other President in history has spent on farm programs, and it is *$9 billion more* than was spent on farm programs *in all eight years* of President Kennedy's and President Johnson's Administrations combined.

Like 1932 and 1960, this election year represents a watershed for American agriculture. At stake is the survival of the family farm. Under President Reagan's policies of high costs and low prices, these family farmers cannot survive. They will continue to go out of business at a historic pace, to be replaced by an industrialized structure of agriculture that is dominated by conglomerates, giant farm combinations, and tax loss ventures. Already, under Reagan, 65 percent of net farm income has been concentrated in the hands of the largest 1 percent of farms, up from 42 percent just three years ago.

The Democratic Party renews its commitment to the family farm structure of American agriculture. We believe that the public need for a reliable supply of high-quality, reasonably priced food and fiber is best met by family farm enterprises whose primary business is farming or ranching. It is from hundreds of thousands of those competitive, diverse, decentralized, entrepreneurial families that the public gains superior agricultural efficiency and productivity. Accordingly, it is in these farming families that the public finds its most sensible investment. In addition, these farmers are the ones who show greatest concern for good conservation practices, quality of food, and rural values. We need more of these farmers, not fewer.

The Democratic Party pledges action. We must solve the immediate farm crisis through a combination of humanitarian aid programs abroad, aggressive promotion of farm exports, and a fair moratorium on farm debt and foreclosure by federal credit agencies to family farm borrowers being forced out of business through no fault of their own, until a long-term program addressing the farm credit crisis can be put into place. Beginning next January with the writing of a new long-term farm bill, the Democratic Party pledges to rebuild a prosperous system of family farms and ranches. We will forge a new agreement on a farm and food policy that assures a fair deal for family farmers, consumers, taxpayers, conservationists, and others with a direct stake in the organizational structure of the food economy.

Our goal is to restore the faith of family farmers that their hard work, ingenuity, efficiency, and good stewardship will be rewarded with profit, rather than debt. We seek a program that is focused specifically on the true family farm, that encourages long-term financial planning, that is tied to locally-approved soil conservation programs, and that reduces federal budget costs for farm programs.

We will target federal assistance toward true family-sized and beginning farmers' operations. We will stop good, efficient farmers from being thrown off their farms, while structuring incentives so as to achieve maximum participation in farm commodity programs. We will bring farm credit interest rates down and set supports at levels that at least enable farmers to recover actual production costs. We will use the full range of programs to reduce excess production when necessary to assure fair prices to farmers. As the overall economy improves, we will gradually adjust price supports toward a firm goal of parity of income. We will give new emphasis to producer-controlled marketing arrangements. We will revitalize the farmer-owned commodity reserve system. We will put in place tax policies that are fair to farmers, while removing unproductive incentives for investors seeking to avoid taxes. We must protect family farmers from land speculators and we must protect both farmers and consumers from income losses resulting from exorbitant pricing of middlemen. We will renew our country's historic commitment to agricultural science and education, to rural services such as cooperative electrification and telephones. We oppose Reagan Administration proposals that would more than double interest rates to rural cooperatives, and sharply reduce rural electric loan levels.

The Democratic Party reaffirms its commitment to soil and water conservation. We will actively promote the production of ethanol and other biomass sources of renewable energy and encourage conversion to energy self-sufficient farming operations.

Finally, we must reverse the annual decrease in the value and volume of U.S. farm exports which has occurred in each year of Ronald Reagan's term. Our farm exports are vital to the nation's prosperity and provide a major part of total farm income. We must restore the ability of U.S. farm products to compete in world markets, and increase world-wide demand for American agricultural products. To do this, we must make major changes in Ronald Reagan's economic policies, and correct his grossly distorted currency exchange rates, which have caused American competitiveness in international trade to decline. We must also resist efforts to lower commodity price supports; such action would only lower farm income without addressing the economic policies which are the root cause of declining competitiveness of U.S. farm products in world markets.

Critical to the recovery of farm income and exports will be the pursuit of economic policies that contribute to worldwide economic recovery. Flexible export credit programs and assurances of long-term availability of U.S. farm products will also be necessary to restore America's preeminence as an agricultural exporter and end the destruction of the family farm brought on by Ronald Reagan.

Managing Our Natural Resources

Our economy, the quality of our lives, and the kind of opportunities that we leave to our children all depend on how well we manage our wealth of natural resources. We must harvest enough timber and food, produce enough minerals, coal, oil and gas, and provide enough electric power to keep our economy growing. We must be prepared to avoid severe dislocations when conflicts in other parts of the world force energy prices to climb. At the same time that we encourage enhanced energy production, we must recognize that conserving irreplaceable resources, using energy efficiently instead of wasting it, and protecting our environment help guarantee a better life for twenty-first century America.

Protecting Our National Security

President Reagan has reduced our ability to defend our economy from the disruptions that would come if conflicts in other countries interrupt the world's oil supply. While the percentage of our oil imports from the Middle East has dropped, U.S. oil imports from other countries have increased. If war in the Middle East cuts back oil supplies from that region, Europe and Japan will pay higher prices to get replacement oil; a bidding war among oil-importing nations means that the price of oil all over the world, including the United States, will rise dangerously.

Ronald Reagan has refused to prepare us for that day. He has refused to fill the Strategic Petroleum Reserve as quickly as authorized by law, and in case of emergency, he has made clear that his policy will be simply to allow those who can pay the most to buy whatever supplies are available.

Our Party must spell out a comprehensive program for energy security. We should accelerate the filling of the Strategic Petroleum Reserve, so that it can play its intended role as a temporary national oil supply during future energy emergencies. And in an oil crisis, a Democratic President will make every effort to ensure that essential users — schools, farmers, hospitals, local bus and rail systems — have the supplies they need at reasonable prices. The Democratic Party will ensure that the especially vulnerable — the unemployed, the elderly, the poor — will not be unfairly forced to share the burden of rising oil prices.

Developing U.S. Energy Supplies

In today's complex world, no industrial nation can be fully self-sufficient. The United States and all countries in the free world depend on each other for resources, as markets, or as economic and political allies. But the strength of our own economy and the influence we exercise in the rest of the world are sure to be increased if we are capable of supplying more, not less, of our own energy.

America is blessed with abundant coal and natural gas, substantial supplies of oil, and plentiful reserves of uranium. Although very costly to process, vast supplies of oil shales and tar sands represent future energy sources. Significant contributions to our energy supply can be made by utilizing renewable resources and indigenous energy, such as active and passive solar systems, windpower, geothermal and ocean thermal power, and the recovery of gas from agricultural waste, coal mines, and garbage dumps. These proven energy sources, as well as more experimental energy systems, should be encouraged for the positive environmental and economic contribution they can make to our energy security.

The Democratic Party supports the aggressive promotion of coal exports, research and development into better technologies for using coal, and assurances that rates for transporting coal are fair and reasonable. To ensure that the environment and worker safety are fully protected as coal production increases to meet our national energy needs, we will vigorously implement and strictly enforce laws governing worker safety, land reclamation, air and water quality, and the protection of agriculture, fish, and wildlife.

The Democratic Party will support research and development for solar energy and other renewable energy systems, and will provide incentives for use of solar and other emerging energy systems. We will vigorously pursue our solar energy efforts and dramatically increase funding for the Solar Energy and Energy Conservation Bank and low-income weatherization, which could put hundreds of thousands of unemployed people to work weatherizing and installing solar energy systems in millions of American homes, especially the homes of low-income Americans. We oppose the Reagan Administration's efforts to fund these programs through petroleum price overcharge refunds from the oil companies.

We will support the federal research and development efforts slashed by the Reagan Administration, to promote the discovery of new energy supplies and energy use technologies.

The Democratic Party strongly opposes the Reagan Administration's policy of aggressively promoting and further subsidizing nuclear power. Today, millions of Americans are concerned about the safety of nuclear power plants and their radioactive waste. We recognize the safety and economic factors which bring into question the viability of this energy source.

We will insist on the highest possible standards of safety and protection of public health with respect to nuclear power, including siting, design, operation, evacuation plans, and waste disposal procedures. We will require nuclear power to compete fairly in the marketplace. We will reexamine and review all federal subsidies to the nuclear industry, including the Price-Anderson Act's limits on the liability of the industry which will be considered for re-authorization in the next Congress. A Democratic Administration will give the Nuclear Regulatory Commission the integrity, competence, and credibility it needs to carry out its mandate to protect the public health and safety. We will expand the role of the public in NRC procedures.

The Democratic Party believes high-level radioactive waste and other hazardous materials should be transported only when absolutely necessary. We will guarantee states full participatory rights in all decisions affecting the movement of high-level radioactive waste within their borders. We will require radioactive waste and hazardous materials emergency response plans along transportation routes, similar to those required for nuclear power plants. The Democratic Party will act swiftly to ensure states' authority to regulate routes and schedules for radioactive and other hazardous shipments.

We will ensure that no offshore oil and gas exploration will be taken up that is inconsistent with the protection of our fisheries and coastal resources. The leasing of public lands, both onshore and offshore, will be based on present demand and land use planning processes, and will be undertaken in ways that assure fair economic return to the public, protection of the environment and full participation by state and local governments. The Coastal Zone Management Act should be amended to require initial leasing decisions to be consistent with federally approved state and territorial coastal zone management plans. Interior states should be given consultation and concurrence rights with respect to onshore leases comparable to the rights afforded coastal states with respect to offshore leases.

We believe that synthetic fuels research and development support should emphasize environmental protection technologies and standards and hold out reasonable hope of long-term economic viability. The Democratic Party proposes to reevaluate the Synthetic Fuels Corporation.

Energy Conservation

The high cost of producing and using energy now constitutes a substantial share of U.S. capital spending. Energy conservation has become essential to our economy as well as our national security.

Strict standards of energy efficiency for home appliances, for example, could save enough money in the next 15 years to avoid the need for 40 new power plants. Better insulated houses and apartments can sharply reduce power and heating bills for families throughout America, and help utilities avoid the high cost of building more expensive powerplants.

Ronald Reagan sees no role for government in conserving energy, and he has gutted promising conservation efforts. The Democratic Party supports extension of the existing tax credits for business and residential energy conservation and renewable energy use, and expansion of those tax credits to include the incorporation of passive solar designs in new housing. The Democratic Party also supports faithful implementation of existing programs for energy efficiency standards for new appliances; upgrading of fuel efficiency standards for new automobiles; establishment of comparable fuel efficiency standards for new light trucks and vans; and development of an energy efficiency rating system to be used to advise homebuyers at the time of sale of the likely future energy costs of houses.

Lifeline Utility Rates — Recognizing that the elderly and the poor suffer most from high energy costs, the Democratic Party supports special, lower electricity and natural gas rates for senior citizens and low-income Americans.

Recycling — The Democratic Party recognizes that recovering and recycling new materials can conserve energy and natural resources, create additional jobs, reduce the costs of material goods, eliminate solid waste and litter, and avoid pollution. We will increase efforts to recover and recycle useful materials from municipal waste.

Protecting Our Environment

Americans know that industrial production and economic development do not have to mean ruined land or polluted air and water. Sound resource management, careful planning, and strict pollution control enforcement will allow us to have a prosperous economy and a healthy environment. For the last four years the Reagan Administration has assumed a radical position, working to eliminate the environmental protections forged through years of bipartisan cooperation.

Ronald Reagan's first appointees to key environmental positions have already been forced to resign. But the American people are entitled to more than the absence of scandal — they demand real action to protect the health and safety of our families and communities. The Democratic Party supports revitalizing the Environmental Protection Agency by providing it with a budget increase adequate to allow it to carry out its substantially increased responsibility to protect the people and enforce the law.

Hazardous Wastes — Thousands of dump sites across America contain highly dangerous poisons that can threaten the health and safety of families who live nearby or who depend on water supplies that could be contaminated by the poisons. Although Congress has established the Superfund for emergency cleanup of these dangerous sites, President Reagan refuses to use it vigorously. The Democratic Party is committed to enforcing existing laws, to dramatically increasing Superfund resources to clean up all sites that threaten public health, and to assuring that everyone whose health or property is damaged has a fair opportunity to force the polluters to pay for the damage. This increased support should be financed at least in part through new taxes on the generation of hazardous wastes, so companies have an economic incentive to reduce the volume and toxicity of their dangerous wastes.

The Resource Conservation and Recovery Act should be expanded to include major new requirements for safer management of newly generated toxic waste. High priority must be given to establishing and implementing a program to phase out the land disposal of untreated hazardous waste, requiring instead that it be treated by chemical, biological, or thermal processes that render it harmless and safe for disposal. The Environmental Protection Agency also should adopt standards to ensure that the safest possible methods of managing particular wastes are used, and that available methods are used to reduce the volume and toxicity of waste produced by industry.

Clean Air and Water — The Democratic Party supports a reauthorized and strengthened Clean Air Act. Statutory requirements for the control of toxic air pollutants should be strengthened, with the environmental agency required to identify and regulate within three years priority air pollutants known or anticipated to cause cancer and other serious diseases. The Democratic Party calls for an immediate program to reduce sulfur dioxide emissions by 50% from 1980 levels within the next decade; this program shall include interim reductions within five years of its enactment. Our effort should be designed to reduce environmental and economic damage from acid rain while assuring such efforts do not cause regional economic dislocations. Every effort should be made to mitigate any job losses associated with any national acid rain program.

The Democratic Party is committed to strengthening the Clean Water Act to curb both direct and indirect discharge of toxic pollutants into our nation's waters, and supports a strengthened Environmental Protection Agency to assure help to American cities in providing adequate supplies of drinking water free of toxic chemicals and other contaminants.

Workplace Safety — The Democratic Party believes all Americans, in their workplaces and communities, have the right to know what hazardous materials and chemicals they may have been exposed to and how they may protect their health from such exposure. The Democratic Party supports appropriate funding levels for the Occupational Safety and Health Administration, reversing the Reagan budget cuts in that agency; vigorous enforcement of occupational safety and health standards; and worker right-to-know requirements.

Pesticides and Herbicides — The Democratic Party is committed to establishing standards and deadlines requiring all pesticides and herbicides to be thoroughly tested to ensure they do not cause cancer, birth defects, or other adverse health effects. We support rigorous research and information programs to develop and assist farmers with the use of integrated pest management and non-chemical pest control methods to reduce the health risk of controlling agricultural pests, and the establishment of strict deadlines to ensure that pesticides are fully tested and in compliance with health and safety standards. The Democratic Party is committed to ensuring that our nation's food supply is free of pesticides whose danger to health has been demonstrated, and believes it is irresponsible to allow the export to other nations of herbicides and pesticides banned for use in the U.S. and will act swiftly to halt such exports.

EPA Budget — The Democratic Party opposes the Reagan Administration's budget cuts, which have severely hampered the effectiveness of our environmental programs. The Environmental Protection Agency should receive a budget that exceeds in real dollars the agency's purchasing power when President Reagan took office, since the agency's workload has almost doubled in recent years.

Managing our Public Lands — The Democratic Party believes in retaining ownership and control of our public lands, and in managing those lands according to the principles of multiple use and sustained yield, with appropriate environmental standards and mitigation requirements to protect the public interest. The Democratic Party supports the substantial expansion of the National Wilderness Preservation System, with designations of all types of ecosystems, including coastal areas, deserts, and prairies as well as forest and alpine areas. Congressional decisions to designate wilderness should include evaluations of mineral resources and other potential land values.

The Democratic Party supports adequate funding of and restoration of federal programs to protect fully national parks, wildlife refuges, and wilderness areas from external and internal threats. Development activities within national wildlife refuges which are not compatible with the purposes for which the refuges were designated should not be allowed. The letter and the spirit of the Alaska National Interest Lands Conservation Act of 1980 should be followed, with an end to unsound land exchanges and other efforts to circumvent the law.

A new Democratic Party will provide adequate appropriations for the Land and Water Conservation Fund.

Wetlands — The Democratic Party supports coherent and coordinated federal policies to protect our nation's valuable and disappearing wetlands, which are critical nurseries for commercial fisheries and vital ecological, scenic, and recreational sources. These policies will include more active efforts to acquire threatened wetland areas, consideration of new tax incentives to encourage private efforts to preserve instead of develop wetlands, and elimination of current incentives that encourage wetlands destruction.

Wildlife — Fishing, hunting, and enjoyment of America's wildlife can continue to be an important part of our natural heritage only through active programs to maintain the diversity and abundance of plants, animals, and natural habitats. The Democratic Party supports protection of endangered species, land management to maintain healthy populations of wildlife, and full United States participation to implement international wildlife treaties.

Water Policy — The Democratic Party recognizes that finite and diminishing quantities of water, and often antiquated, inadequate, or inefficient water supply systems, threaten economic growth and the quality of life in all regions of the country. New water project starts, in the West by the Bureau of Reclamation, and in the rest of the country by the Corps of Engineers, are critical. We recognize that strong federal leadership is necessary to meet these needs, and to do so in environmentally sound ways.

The Democratic Party supports the creation of a national water resources planning board and a comprehensive review of the nation's water needs. We support major new water policy efforts addressing several national needs:

— We will help meet our nation's infrastructure needs, including the construction of new projects which are economically and environmentally sound. In the West, new reclamation water project starts are critical. In all cases, we will consider innovative and nonstructural alternatives on an equal basis.

— We will examine the water quantity and water quality issues associated with providing adequate water supply.

— We will help meet navigation, flood control, and municipal water supply system needs, with new assistance.

Federal water policy efforts must be carefully coordinated with affected state governments, making possible not only cooperative financing of water investments but a commensurate sharing of decision-making authority and responsibility.

Chapter II: Justice, Dignity and Opportunity

INTRODUCTION

Fulfilling America's highest promise, equal justice for all: that is the Democratic agenda for a just future.

For many of our citizens, it is only in the last two decades that the efforts of a broad, bipartisan coalition have begun to give real meaning to the dream of freedom and equality. During that time Democrats, spurred by the Civil Rights Movement, have enacted landmark legislation in areas including voting, education, housing and employment.

A nation is only as strong as its commitment to justice and equality. Today, a corrosive unfairness eats at the underpinnings of our society. Civil rights laws and guarantees — only recently achieved after hardfought battles, personal sacrifice and loss of life — are imperiled by an Administration that consciously seeks to turn the clock back to an era when second-class citizenship for women and minorities, disenfranchisement, and *de jure* and *de facto* segregation were very much the facts of life for well over half of America's population. Moreover, justice encompasses more than our nation's laws. The poor, the female, the minority — many of them just like boats stuck on the bottom — have come to experience an implacable and intractable foe in the Reagan Administration.

A new Democratic Administration will understand that the age-old scourge of discrimination and prejudice against many groups in American society is still rampant and very much a part of the reason for the debilitating circumstances in which disadvantaged peoples are forced to live. Although strides have been made in combatting discrimination and defamation against Americans of various ethnic groups, much remains to be done. Therefore, we pledge an end to the Reagan Administration's punitive policy toward women, minorities, and the poor and support the reaffirmation of the principle that the government is still responsible for protecting the civil rights of all citizens. Government has a special responsibility to those whom society has historically prevented from enjoying the benefits of full citizenship for reasons of race, religion, sex, age, national origin and ethnic heritage, sexual orientation, or disability.

The goal for the coming decades is not only full justice under the law, but *economic* justice as well. In the recent past, we have put our nation on the road toward achieving equal protection of all our citizens' human rights. The challenge now is to continue to press that cause, while joining a new battle — to assure justice and opportunity in the workplace, and in the economy.

Justice for all in today's America and the America of tomorrow demands not one, but two broad guarantees. First, we must guarantee that our nation will reinforce and extend its commitment to human rights and equal opportunity. And second, we must guarantee progress on the new frontier for the future: economic and social justice.

We are determined to enforce the laws guaranteeing equal opportunity, and to complete the civil rights agenda cast aside by the Reagan Administration. No President has the right to do what this Administration has done: to read selectively from the United States Code and simply ignore the laws ensuring basic rights and opportunities because they conflict with this Administration's ideology. As Democrats, we pledge to reverse the trend towards lawlessness which has characterized this Administration, and to keep our commitments to all in our community who look to the government for defense of their rights.

But we recognize that while a first step toward a just society is to guarantee the right of all workers to compete equally for a job, the next step is assuring that enough new jobs are created to give meaningful employment to all our workers for the future.

If in past decades we won the right for minorities to ride at the front of the bus, in coming years we must assure that minorities have the opportunity to own the bus company.

It will not be enough to say that our nation must offer equal access to health care — we must put comprehensive health care within the reach of all of our citizens, at a price all can afford.

It will not do simply to guarantee women a place in the work force — women deserve an equal chance at a career leading to the board of directors.

As Democrats, we believe that human rights and an economy of opportunity are two sides of the same coin of justice. No economic program can be considered just unless it advances the opportunity of all to live a better, more dignified life. No American is afforded economic justice when he or she is denied an opportunity to reap the rewards of economic growth.

Economic justice is also economic common sense. Any who doubt that should consider the toll of welfare, crime, prisons, public housing and urban squalor on our national wealth. We will pay a high price for all the disadvantaged or disenfranchised if we fail to include them in the new economic revolution.

As Democrats, therefore, we pledge to pursue a new definition of justice that meets the new demands of our time. Under a Democratic Administration, equality and fairness under the law will be matched by justice in the economy and in the workplace.

THE FUTURE IF REAGAN IS REELECTED

"Twenty years after the Equal Pay Act should have eradicated the last vestige of economic discrimination against women, employers have made little progress in integrating their work force.... It is the Republican governor of Washington State, and the Republican County Executive of Nassau County, New York, who are committing public resources to mount a legal defense for their jurisdictions' blatant sex discrimination practices.... The Reagan Administration from the outset has made it abundantly clear that civil rights and economic justice are to be sacrificed on the altar of corporate greed...."

> Diana Rock, Director of Women's Rights, American Federation of State, County, and Municipal Employees (Democratic Platform Committee Hearing, Cleveland, Ohio, May 21, 1984)

"The Reagan Administration, upon taking office in 1981, set upon a concerted effort to roll back civil rights protections. This attack is underway in agency enforcement, court litigation, legislative initiative, and nominations of federal appointees."

> Virna M. Canson, Regional Director, West Coast Region, NAACP (Democratic Platform Committee Hearing, Los Angeles, California, May 14, 1984)

The neglect of our historic human rights commitment will already be recorded as the first legacy of Ronald Reagan's years in the White House. But suppose Mr. Reagan is reelected.

What would become of America's commitment to equal justice and opportunity if Mr. Reagan is reelected?

The hard truth is that if Mr. Reagan is reelected our most vigorous defender of the rule of law — the United States Supreme Court — could be lost to the cause of equal justice for another generation. Today, five of the nine members of the Court are over 75. Our next President will likely have the opportunity to shape that Court, not just for his own term — or even for his own lifetime — but for the rest of ours, and for our children's too.

There can be little doubt that a Supreme Court chosen by Ronald Reagan would radically restrict constitutional rights and drastically reinterpret existing laws. Today, the fundamental right of a woman to reproduction freedom rests on the votes of six members of the Supreme Court — five of whom are over 75. That right could easily disappear during a second Reagan term. Already, the protections against employment discrimination have been restricted by the Court; a Reagan Court surely would reduce them further. The same is true for the right of workers to have a healthy and safe workplace, and to organize collectively in unions. Although the statute protecting voting rights has been extended through a massive bipartisan effort, opposed by the Reagan Administration, a Reagan Supreme Court could still effectively nullify it simply by erecting impossible standards of proof. Not long ago, the Court decided it should hire independent counsel to argue that tax exemptions for racially discriminatory schools were unlawful because the Justice Department refused to do so. Can anyone imagine a Reagan Court doing that? How much easier it would be for a Reagan Court simply to agree with a Reagan Department of Justice.

If Mr. Reagan is reelected, who would protect women and minorities against discrimination?

In the first year after the Reagan Administration assumed office, the number of cases involving charges of employment discrimination filed in court by the EEOC dropped by more than 70 percent. During this Administration, the EEOC has refused to process a single comparable worth case filed by a woman. Meanwhile, the Reagan Justice Department has sought to destroy effective affirmative action remedies, and even to undermine *private* plans to reduce discrimination in employment. The actions of the Reagan Administration serve only to delay the day when fairness is achieved and such remedial measures are, therefore, no longer needed.

It is now clear that if Mr. Reagan is reelected, women and minorities seeking protection of their rights would be forced to contend not only with their employers, but with a hostile government. Equal employment opportunity and equity would remain elusive dreams.

If Mr. Reagan is reelected, who would assure access to justice?

Since the day of its inauguration, the Reagan Administration has conducted a continuous, full-scale war against the federal Legal Services Corporation, whose only job is to ensure that the poor are fairly heard in court, and that they get equal access to our system of justice. Thirty percent of the Corporation's lawyers have been laid off, and the Administration has used every means it could find to stack its Board with people hostile to the very concept of equal justice for the poor.

In the America of Ronald Reagan, you will only get as much justice as you pay for.

If Mr. Reagan is reelected, who would protect the rights of workers?

The Republican Administration has consistently viewed the dollar costs to businesses of providing a safe workplace as more important than the impact of injury and disease on working men and women. It has appointed officials to the National Labor Relations Board who openly oppose the rights of workers to organize and bargain collectively. The Department of Labor has ignored its mandate to enforce fair labor standards and has sought to reverse hard-won gains in protections for worker health and safety.

What would happen if Mr. Reagan is reelected? Will the right to bargain collectively be eviscerated through Republican-approved abuses of the bankruptcy laws? Will the National Labor Relations Act be converted into a tool that limits working men and women and empowers only their employers? Who will ensure that our next generation does not suffer the effects of toxic substances in the workplace — substances whose existence is not even revealed to the worker?

If Mr. Reagan is reelected, who would protect the rights of senior citizens?

Speaking at Philadelphia in 1980 during his campaign, Ronald Reagan vowed to a large audience of senior citizens his strong support for Social Security. He assured thousands of senior citizens on that occasion that as President he would see to it that every commitment made by the federal government to the senior citizens was faithfully kept.

Ronald Reagan violated that promise shortly after he became President. In 1981, speaking to a joint session of Congress, President Reagan said, "We will not cut Medicare." In a matter of weeks thereafter President Reagan asked the Congress of the United States to cut $88 billion in 1981 and the following four years from Social Security programs. He proposed to reduce by a third the number of people protected by the disability insurance program. He proposed to reduce by a third the benefits a senior citizen would receive if he or she retired at 62. He proposed to cut out the burial program for recipients of Social Security.

He proposed to cut millions from programs that Democratic Administrations had provided for the education of the children of the elderly covered by Social Security, slashing the list of beneficiaries of these programs by hundreds of thousands of sons and daughters of men and women covered by Social Security. And he called for the abolition of the $122-a-month minimum benefit program, which would have dropped over three million people from Social Security altogether.

The American people then revolted, and so did the Congress. The Democratic Party put a stop to the decimation of the Social Security program, but not before President Reagan had cut $19 billion from Social Security benefits in 1981 and the ensuing four years. Democrats in Congress forced the restoration of the $122-a-month minimum benefit program to those who were covered before the Reagan cuts, but never succeeded in extending coverage to the additional 7,000 people a month who would have become eligible after the Reagan cuts.

Instead of keeping his word that he would not cut Medicare, Reagan forced Congress every year beginning in 1981 to cut billions from the Medicare program. When Social Security developed financial problems due to massive unemployment in 1982, the Reagan Administration moved to "solve" them by cutting benefits further. Only the Democrats on the Social Security Commission prevented him from doing that.

If Mr. Reagan is reelected, how would we teach our children to respect the law?

We cannot teach our children to respect the law when they see the highest officials of government flaunting it at their will. Lawlessness has been a pattern in this Administration — and it is a pattern that is unlikely to be altered if Reagan and the Republicans stay in the White House.

More than forty top Republican officials have already been implicated in all kinds of wrongdoing. Murky transactions on the fringe of organized crime, accepting gifts from foreign journalists and governments, misusing government funds, lying under oath, stock manipulations, taking interest-free loans from wealthy businessmen who later receive federal jobs — all of these are part of business as usual with Ronald Reagan's appointees.

The Republicans profess to stand for "law and order." But this is the same Administration that vetoed the bipartisan anti-crime bill in 1982. And when it comes to laws they do not like — whether they concern toxic wastes, pure food and drugs, or worker health and safety — this Administration simply makes believe they do not exist. The same is true overseas: this Administration is just as willing to ignore international law as domestic law. When we finally learned of its illegal mining of Nicaragua's harbors, the Reagan Administration hastily attempted, the night before Nicaragua sued us, to withdraw jurisdiction over the question from the World Court. But even this maneuver was carried out in an illegal fashion that the World Court later set aside.

This Republican Administration has been unprecedentedly eager to limit public debate by instituting "security agreements" that censor ex-officials, "revising" the Freedom of Information Act, refusing visas to foreign visitors who might provide another perspective on American policies overseas, and denying our war correspondents their historic position alongside our troops. This comes as no surprise: in the first term the Reagan Administration had a lot to hide. What would happen in a second?

If Mr. Reagan is reelected, what would happen to our unfinished civil rights agenda?

The answer is clear: an Administration which refuses to enforce the laws that are on the books can hardly be expected to respect — or even recognize — the rights of those who are not already specifically protected by existing law.

Nowhere is this Administration's hostility to equal rights and equal justice more apparent than in its attitude to the Equal Rights Amendment. As soon as the Reagan faction took control of the Republican Party at its convention in 1980, it ended that Party's forty-year commitment to passage of the Equal Rights Amendment. So long as this Administration remains in office, the proponents of unamended ERA have nothing less than an enemy in the White House. And if this is true for the women of America, it is equally true for disadvantaged minorities who must depend on this government's sense of justice to secure their rights and lead independent lives.

Since assuming office, the Reagan Administration has shown more hostility — indeed, more outright and implacable aggression — toward the American ideal of equal justice for all than even its harshest critics would have predicted in 1980. Given its first-term record, even our most pessimistic forecasts for four more Republican years may well fall short of the mark. No one knows the full extent of the damage Reagan could wreak on this country in another term. But we do know one thing: we cannot afford to find out.

THE DEMOCRATIC ALTERNATIVE:
EQUAL JUSTICE FOR ALL

"The Democratic Party is challenged as never before to redirect the present dangerous course of our nation and our world, and to provide meaningful work at adequate pay for all our citizens and justice for all Americans.

"The dream of a nation fully committed to peace, jobs, and justice has fast become a nightmare under this Administration....

"Our choice today is to become just a new party in power in November with new faces and new pledges — or a truly great party with the courage to develop a new vision and a new direction for the sake of our nation and our world."

    Coretta Scott King (Democratic Platform Committee Hearing, Washington, D.C., June 11, 1984)

"The Equal Rights Amendment is the only guarantee of full equality the women of this nation can trust and count on. We have seen in the past three and one-half years an administration that has gone out of its way to prove that laws, court decisions, executive orders, and regulations are not enough — they can be changed by a new majority, overturned, swept aside, underfunded, or rescinded. Only when the legislative protections against such discrimination are grounded in the bedrock of the Constitution can we feel that the vagaries of changing political climates or a hostile administration will not wipe out those protections."

    Judy Goldsmith, President, National Organization for Women (Democratic Platform Committee Hearing, Washington, D.C., June 12, 1984)

Equal justice for all, in a Democratic future, means that every individual must have a fair and equal opportunity to fulfill his or her potential, and to be an independent, working member of our society — and it is the commitment of our Party to secure that opportunity.

We are determined to build an America of self-sufficient, independent people. We will enforce the laws guaranteeing equal opportunity and human rights, and complete the unfinished civil rights agenda. We will keep our commitments to all of the members of our community who rely upon our word to stay, or to become, independent — our senior citizens, those who served in the Armed Forces, the handicapped and disabled, the members of our American family who are trapped in poverty, and all Americans who look to government to protect them from the pain, expense, and dislocation caused by crime. And in fulfilling these and all the duties of government, a Democratic Administration will stand as an example to all of integrity and justice.

Equal Justice Under Law

Many have suffered from historical patterns of discrimination and others, because of their recent immigration in sizeable numbers, are subject to new forms of discrimination. Over the years, the Democratic Party has voiced a commitment to eradicating these injustices. In 1948, the Democratic Platform for the first time contained a plank committing this Party to the cause of civil rights. For almost forty years, we have fought proudly for that cause. In 1964, a Democratic President and a Democratic Congress enacted the landmark legislation prohibiting discrimination in employment and public accommodations. And for nearly two decades, a bipartisan commitment has existed in Congress and in the White House to expand and enforce those laws. Until Ronald Reagan.

This Administration has sought to erode the force and meaning of constitutionally-mandated and court-sanctioned remedies for long-standing patterns of discriminatory conduct. It has attempted to create new standards under each of our nation's civil rights laws by requiring a showing of intent to discriminate, and case-by-case litigation of class-wide violations. Its interpretation of two recent Supreme Court decisions attempts to sound the death knell for equal opportunity and affirmative action. In one case, the Administration interpreted the Court's decision as requiring that equal opportunity mandates associated with the receipt of *all* federal monies apply only to the specific program receiving federal funds. In the other, the Administration is using a ruling in favor of a *bona fide* seniority system to assault all affirmative action plans. As Democrats, we disagree. Instead, we reaffirm our long-standing commitment to civil rights for all and we pledge to enforce the laws guaranteeing equal opportunity for all Americans. The next Democratic Administration will offer unwavering support for the following:

A Strong, Independent Civil Rights Commission — A Democratic Administration will return the Commission on Civil Rights to an independent status and increase its funding. The Commission must be restored to its original mission of ensuring the enforcement of civil rights by those federal agencies charged with the task.

Strengthened Civil Rights Enforcement — We will restore a strong Equal Employment Opportunity Commission and renew the commitment of the Department of Justice and the Department of Labor to enforce civil rights laws and executive orders. A Democratic Administration will, by vigorously enforcing laws and strengthening education and training opportunities, increase minority participation in the workplace and eliminate wage inequities which leave minorities at the bottom of the pay scale.

Equal Educational Opportunity — The Democratic Party pledges to do all it can, beginning this year, to reverse the decision of the United States Supreme Court in the Grove City College case, and to restore as the law of the land the prohibition of any use of federal financial assistance to subsidize discrimination because of race, national origin, sex, age, or disability. Fulfilling this commitment means that every institution which receives government funds must guarantee equality and equal opportunity in all of its programs.

Religious Liberty and Church/State Separation — The current Administration has consistently sought to reverse in the courts or overrule by constitutional amendment a long line of Supreme Court decisions that preserve our historic commitment to religious tolerance and church/state separation. The Democratic Platform affirms its support of the principles of religious liberty, religious tolerance and church/state separation and of the Supreme Court decisions forbidding violation of those principles. We pledge to resist all efforts to weaken those decisions.

Ensure Fair Housing — We will enhance the authority of the Department of Housing and Urban Development to enforce our fair housing laws. A Democratic Administration will work to provide the Department with the resources and the power to seek cease and desist orders to prevent housing discrimination against minorities, women and families with children.

Affirmative Action — The Democratic Party firmly commits itself to protect the civil rights of every citizen and to pursue justice and equal treatment under the law for all citizens. The Party reaffirms its longstanding commitment to the eradication of discrimination in all aspects of American life through the use of affirmative action, goals, timetables, and other verifiable measurements to overturn historic patterns and historic burdens of discrimination in hiring, training, promotions, contract procurement, education, and the administration of all Federal programs. A Democratic Administration will resist any efforts to undermine the progress made under previous Democratic administrations and shall strongly enforce Federal civil rights standards such as equal opportunity, affirmative action in employment, contract procurement, education, and training. The Federal Government must set an example and be a model for private employers, making special efforts in both recruitment, training, and promotion to aid minority Americans in overcoming both the historic patterns and the historic burdens of discrimination. We will reverse the regressive trend of the Reagan Administration by making a commitment to increase recruitment, hiring, training, retraining, procurement, and promotional opportunity at the Federal level to aid minority Americans and women. We call on the public and private sectors to live up to and enforce all civil rights laws and regulations, i.e., Equal Employment Opportunity Programs, Title VI and Title VII of the Civil Rights Act, the Fair Housing Laws, and affirmative action requirements.

Eliminate Ethnic-Stereotyping and Recognize Ethnic Diversity — While strides have been made in combatting discrimination and defamation against Americans of various ethnic groups, ethnic stereotyping continues. We support cooperation and understanding between racial, ethnic, and cultural groups and reject those who promote division based on fear or stereotyping which have their basis in social and economic inequity. We encourage respect for America's ethnic diversity.

Equal Access to Justice — Democrats believe that all our government processes should be open to all Americans, and that no essential right should be denied based on wealth or status. We therefore strongly support a well-funded, unrestricted Legal Services Corporation to ensure that none of our citizens is denied the full benefits of our judicial system. No American should suffer illegality or abuse simply because he or she is poor. And lawyers for the poor must not be prevented from acting in accordance with the same ethical canons as apply to lawyers for the rich: to represent their clients with all the zeal, devotion, energy, and creativity that the law allows.

Equal Rights for Women — A top priority of a Democratic Administration will be ratification of the unamended Equal Rights Amendment. In a Democratic America, the Constitution will be amended to provide:

Section 1. Equality of rights under the law shall not be denied or abridged by the United States or by any State on account of sex.

Section 2. The Congress shall have the power to enforce, by appropriate legislation, the provisions of this article.

Section 3. This article shall take effect two years after the date of ratification.

We will insist on pay equity for women. Today, white women who can find work earn, on average, only 62 cents for every dollar earned by white men. Black women earn only 58 cents for every dollar earned by white men, and Hispanic women only 56 cents. The earnings gap — and the occupational segregation of women which it reflects — extends to all women at every educational level, but is most pronounced among black and other women of color who are confronted by historical and contemporary racial barriers which transcend sex. The Democratic Party defines nondiscrimination to encompass both equal pay for equal work *and* equal pay for work of comparable worth, and we pledge to take every step, including enforcement of current law and amending the Constitution to include the unamended ERA, to close the wage gap. We also support efforts to reform private and civil service pension rules to ensure equal treatment for women, prohibit discrimination in insurance practices, and improve enforcement of child-support obligations. Our Party also recognizes that women cannot compete equally with men so long as they are expected to choose between having a job and having a family. The Democratic Party calls for universally available day-care with federal or business funding, for meaningful part-time work, and for flex-time on the job so that women — and men — can shape even full-time jobs around their family schedules.

Political Empowerment for Minorities and Women — The Democratic Party is committed to placing women as well as minorities in positions of power in government. We establish the goal of doubling the number of minorities and women in Congress by 1988. We will create and fund a talent bank of minorities and women to fill policy positions in the next Administration. We will recruit women and minorities to run for Governorships and all state and local offices. The Democratic Party (through all of its campaign committees) will commit to spending maximum resources to elect women and minority candidates and offer these candidates in-kind services, including political organizing and strategic advice. And the bulk of all voter registration funds will be spent on targeted efforts to register minorities and women.

Reproductive Freedom — The Democratic Party recognizes reproductive freedom as a fundamental human right. We therefore oppose government interference in the reproductive decisions of Americans, especially government interference which denies poor Americans their right to privacy by funding or advocating one or a limited number of reproductive choices only. We fully recognize the religious and ethical concerns which many Americans have about abortion. But we also recognize the belief of many Americans that a woman has a right to choose whether and when to have a child. The Democratic Party supports the 1973 Supreme Court decision on abortion rights as the law of the land and opposes any constitutional amendment to restrict or overturn that decision. We deplore violence and harassment against health providers and women seeking services, and will work to end such acts. We support a continuing federal interest in developing strong local family planning and family life education programs and medical research aimed at reducing the need for abortion.

The Rights of Workers — This nation established a labor policy more than a generation ago whose purpose is to encourage collective bargaining and the right of workers to organize to obtain this goal. The Democratic Party is committed to extending the benefit of this policy to all workers and to removing the barriers to its administration. To accomplish this, the Democratic Party supports: the repeal of Section 14B of the National Labor Relations Act; labor law reform legislation; a prohibition on the misuse of federal bankruptcy law to prevent the circumvention of the collective bargaining process and the destruction of labor-management contracts; and legislation to allow building trades workers the same peaceful picketing rights currently afforded industrial workers. We support the right of public employees and agricultural workers to organize and bargain collectively, and we will act to assure that right. Inasmuch as farm workers are excluded from coverage under the National Labor Relations Act, the Democratic Party recognizes the heroic efforts of farm workers to gain contracts and their right under the law to use boycotts as an effective tool to achieve such ends. We must restore to federal workers their First Amendment rights by reforming the Hatch Act. We must also protect federal and private sector workers from invasions of their privacy by prohibiting the use of polygraphs and other "Truth Test" devices. In addition, the Mine Health Safety Act and the Occupational Health and Safety Act must be properly administered, with the concern of the worker being the highest priority. All efforts to weaken or undermine OSHA's basic worker protection provisions, or to shirk the duty to enforce them, are unacceptable and intolerable. For the victims of occupational disease, we insist on legislation to assure just compensation and adequate health care for these workers as well as vigorous enforcement action by OSHA to eradicate the causes of occupational disease. All fair labor standards acts, such as the minimum wage and Davis-Bacon protections, must be effectively enforced. We reject the so-called "sub-minimum wage" as an appropriate tool of social or economic policy. We strongly oppose workfare which penalizes welfare recipients and undercuts the basic principle of equal pay for equal work. Workfare is not a substitute for a jobs program.

The Responsibility of Economic Institutions — The Democratic Party continues to support the struggle of all citizens to secure economic equality. Therefore, we support policies calling for increased involvement of minorities and women in job training and apprenticeship programs. The Democratic Party encourages all economic institutions, including business and labor, to work actively to ensure that leadership at all levels of decision-making reflects the ethnic and gender diversity of the relevant work force by expanding opportunities for training and advancement.

Enforcing the Voting Rights Act — The right to vote — and to have one's vote counted fully and fairly — is the most important civil right of every American citizen. For without it, no other social, economic, or political rights can be fully realized.

Nothing is more shameful in the record of the Reagan Administration than its willful refusal to fulfill its responsibility to guarantee the voting rights of every American. Instead of moving America forward by expanding voting rights and by eliminating barriers to voting by minority citizens, the Reagan Administration fought a year-long, rear-guard action against efforts to strengthen the Voting Rights Act.

The Democratic Party commits itself to a wholly different course than that of the Reagan Administration. For while we are proud of our record of commitment to civil rights in the past, we recognize that the test of our commitment is what a Democratic Administration will do in the future. Despite the great progress in securing voting rights for minority Americans in the past, there remain throughout our nation voting rules, practices, and procedures that have been and are used to discriminate against many citizens to discourage or deny their right to register and to vote, or dilute their vote when they do. A Democratic President and Administration pledge to eliminate any and all discriminatory barriers to full voting rights, whether they be at-large requirements, second-primaries, gerrymandering, annexation, dual registration, dual voting or other practices. Whatever law, practice, or regulation discriminates against the voting rights of minority citizens, a Democratic President and Administration will move to strike it down.

This is more than a verbal pledge. For minority citizens have waited far too long already to realize their full voting rights.

To prevent any further delay, the Democratic Party pledges to fund a serious, in-depth study of the use of second primaries and other practices throughout the nation that may discriminate against voting rights. This study shall be completed in ample time prior to the 1986 elections for the Party to act. The Democratic Party commits to use its full resources to eliminate any second primary, gerrymandering, at-large requirements, annexation, dual registration, dual voting or other voting practices that discriminate or act to dilute votes of minority citizens.

Wherever a runoff primary or other voting practice is found to be discriminatory, the State Party shall take provable, positive steps to achieve the necessary legislative or party rules changes.

Provable positive steps shall be taken in a timely fashion and shall include the drafting of corrective legislation, public endorsement by the state Party of such legislation, efforts to educate the public on the need for such legislation, active support for the legislation by the state Party lobbying state legislators, other public officials, Party officials and Party members, and encouraging consideration of the legislation by the appropriate legislative committees and bodies.

A Democratic Administration pledges also that the Justice Department shall initiate a similar study, and use the full resources of the law to eliminate any voting practice, such as second primaries, gerrymandering, annexation, dual registration, dual voting, or any other practice that discriminates or acts to dilute votes of minority citizens.

A Democratic President and Administration will use the full resources of the Voting Rights Act of 1982, with its strengthened enforcement powers, to investigate and root out any and all discriminatory voting barriers. A Democratic President will appoint as Attorney General, as Assistant Attorney General for Civil Rights, and throughout the Justice Department individuals with a proven record of commitment to enforcing civil rights and voting rights for all our citizens. The full resources of the Justice Department shall be used to investigate fully and speedily all alleged instances of discriminatory barriers. And a Democratic Administration shall use the full resources of the law, the power of government, and shall seek new legislation, if needed, to end discrimination in voting wherever it exists.

We are committed to a massive, nationwide campaign to increase registration and voting participation by women and minorities, including blacks, Asian Americans, native Americans, and Hispanics. Moreover, our Party must call for the creation of a new program to strengthen our democracy and remove existing obstacles to full participation in the electoral process. We should allow registration and voting on the same day (same day plans have worked well in several states) and we should provide mail-in registration forms throughout our communities. We should consider holding our elections on weekends or holidays, instituting 24-hour voting days, staggering voting times, and closing all polling places across the country at the same time.

We call on the television networks and all other media in the case of presidential elections to refrain from projecting winners of national races, either implicitly or explicitly, while any polls are still open in the continental United States; in the case of state elections, to refrain from projecting winners within a state, either implicitly or explicitly, while any polls in that state are still open.

Voting Rights for the District of Columbia — The Democratic Party supports self-determination for the District of Columbia that guarantees local control over local affairs and full voting representation in Congress. Towards this end, the Democratic Party supports the attainment of statehood for New Columbia; ratification of the District of Columbia Voting Rights Amendment; legislative, judicial, and fiscal autonomy; and a formula-based federal payment.

Puerto Rico — We continue to support Puerto Rico's right to enjoy full self-determination and a relationship that can evolve in ways that will most benefit U.S. citizens in Puerto Rico. The Democratic Party respects and supports the desire of the people of Puerto Rico, by their own will freely-expressed in a peaceful and democratic process, to associate in permanent union with the United States either as a commonwealth or as a state or to become an independent nation. We are also committed to respecting the cultural heritage of the people of Puerto Rico and to the elimination of the discriminatory or unfair treatment of Puerto Ricans as U.S. citizens under federal programs.

A Fair and Humane Immigration Policy — Our nation's outdated immigration laws require comprehensive reform that reflects our national interests and our immigrant heritage. Our first priority must be to protect the fundamental human rights of American citizens and aliens. We will oppose any "reforms" that violate these rights or that will create new incentives for discrimination against Hispanic Americans and other minorities arising from the discriminatory use of employer sanctions. Specifically, we oppose employer sanctions designed to penalize employers who hire undocumented workers. Such sanctions inevitably will increase discrimination against minority Americans. We oppose identification procedures that threaten civil liberties, as well as any changes that subvert the basic principle of family unification. And we will put an end to this Administration's policies of barring foreign visitors from our country for political or ideological reasons. We strongly oppose "bracero" or guest-worker programs as a form of legalized exploitation. We firmly support a one-tiered legalization program with a 1982 cut-off date.

The Democratic Party will implement a balanced, fair, and non-discriminatory immigration and refugee policy consistent with the principle of affording all applications for admission equal protection under the law. It will work for improved performance by the Immigration and Naturalization Service in adjudicating petitions for permanent residence and naturalization. The Party will also advocate reform within the INS to improve the enforcement operations of the Service consistent with civil liberties protection. The correction of past and present bias in the allocation of slots for refugee admissions will be a top priority. Additionally, it will work to ensure that the Refugee Act of 1980, which prohibits discrimination on the basis of ideology and race in adjudicating asylum claims, is complied with. The Party will provide the necessary oversight of the Department of State and the Immigration and Naturalization Service so as to ensure that the unjustifiable treatment visited upon the Haitian refugees will never again be repeated.

The Democratic Party will formulate foreign policies which alleviate, not aggravate, the root causes of poverty, war, and human rights violations and instability which compel people to flee their homelands.

We support the creation of an international body on immigration to address the economic development problems affecting Mexico and Latin American countries which contribute to unauthorized immigration to the U.S. and to respond to the backlog of approved immigrant visas.

To pursue these and other goals, the Democratic Party nominee upon election shall establish the following national advisory committees to the President and the national Democratic Party: civil rights and justice; fair housing; affirmative action; equal rights for women; rights for workers; immigration policy; and voting rights. These committees shall be representative on the basis of geography, race, sex, and ethnicity.

Dignity for All — As Democrats, we take pride in our accomplishments of the past decades in enacting legislation to assure quality and in fighting the current efforts of this Administration to turn its back on equal opportunity. But we also recognize that so long as any Americans are subject to unfair discrimination, our agenda remains unfinished. We pledge to complete the agenda, and to afford dignity for all.

— We reaffirm the dignity of all people and the right of each individual to have equal access to and participation in the institutions and services of our society. To ensure that government is accessible to those Americans for whom English is a second language, we call for federal hiring and training initiatives to increase the number of government employees skilled in more than one language. All groups must be protected from discrimination based on race, color, sex, religion, national origin, language, age, or sexual orientation. We will support legislation to prohibit discrimination in the workplace based on sexual orientation. We will assure that sexual orientation *per se* does not serve as a bar to participation in the military. We will support an enhanced effort to learn the cause and cure of AIDS, and to provide treatment for people with AIDS. And we will ensure that foreign citizens are not excluded from this country on the basis of their sexual orientation.

— We have long failed to treat the original inhabitants of this land with the dignity they deserve. A Democratic Administration will work in partnership with Indian nations to target assistance to address the twin problems of unemployment and poverty, recognizing appropriate Native American rights to self-determination and the federal government's fiduciary responsibility to the Native American nations. We will take the lead in efforts to resolve water and other natural resource claims of Native Americans. We must also reevaluate the mission of the Bureau of Indian Affairs in light of its troubled record.

— We owe history and ourselves a formal apology and a promise of redress to Japanese Americans who suffered unjust internment during World War II. No commitment to civil liberties could be complete without a formal apology, restitution of position, status or entitlements and reparations to those who suffered deprivation of rights and property without due process forty years ago.

— The Democratic Party strongly condemns the Ku Klux Klan, the American Nazi Party, and other hate groups. We pledge vigorous federal prosecution of actions by the Klan and American Nazi Party that violate federal law, including the enactment of such laws in jurisdictions where they do not exist. We further condemn those acts, symbols, and rituals, including cross-burnings, associated with anti-civil rights activities. We urge every state and local government to pursue vigorous protection of actions by the Klan and Nazi Party and other such groups that violate state or local law.

Americans Abroad — Americans abroad play a vital role in promoting the ideals, culture, and economic well-being of the United States. They are entitled to equitable treatment by their government and greater participation in decisions which directly affect them.

The Democratic Party will work to remedy the unique problems that U.S. citizens encounter abroad. In particular, we will consider ways to: protect their rights; eliminate citizenship inequities; make it easier for them to vote; have their interests actively represented in the federal government; provide them with fair coverage in federal social programs; honor the principles of residency in taxation; and ensure the adequate education of federal dependents abroad.

Insular Areas — The territories are in spirit full partners in the American political family; they should always be so treated. Their unique circumstances require the sensitive application of federal policy and special assistance. Their self-determination, along with that of the Trust Territory of the Pacific Islands, is an American commitment.

Democrats will work with the territories to improve their relationship with the rest of the United States and obtain equal rights for their citizens, including the right to vote for President. A Democratic President and Congress will coordinate their interests as foreign and domestic policy is made. We are committed to providing territorial America with essential assistance and equitable participation in federal programs. We will promote the growth and ensure the competitive position of territorial private sectors. It is Democratic policy that, together with the territories, the United States should strive to assist and develop closer relations with the territories' neighbors in the Caribbean and Pacific regions.

Economic Justice: Keeping Our Commitments

For some, the goal of independence requires greater support and assistance from government. We pledge to provide that support. Justice demands that we keep our commitments and display our compassion to those who most need our help — to veterans and seniors, to disadvantaged minorities, to the disabled and the poor — and we will.

A Healthy America — As Democrats we believe that quality health care is a necessity for everyone. We reaffirm our commitment to the long-term goal of comprehensive national health insurance and view effective health care cost containment as an essential step toward that goal. Health cost containment must be based on a strong commitment to quality of service delivery and care. We also pledge to return to a proper emphasis on basic scientific research and meeting the need for health professionals — areas devastated by the Reagan Administration.

Sickle Cell Anemia — Sickle Cell disease is a catastrophic illness that affects thousands of persons annually. Its victims include, but are not limited to, blacks, Hispanics, and persons of Mediterranean ancestry including Turks, Greeks, and Italians. Its morbidity rate is particularly high among infants, women and children.

Despite the compelling need for a national policy of sickle cell disease prevention and control, the present Administration has dramatically reduced the federal commitment to research and funding. The Democratic Party, on the other hand, pledges to make sickle cell a national health priority because we believe that only the federal government can adequately focus the necessary resources to combat such a major public health problem. Specifically, we pledge that a Democratic Administration will restore the National Sickle Cell Anemia Control Act to provide health parity to those individuals and families whose lives are threatened by this chronic and debilitating disorder.

Opportunities for the Elderly — There are more than 26 million Americans over the age of 65, and their numbers are growing rapidly. Most have spent a lifetime building America and raising the next generation, and when they choose to retire — and it should be their choice — they deserve to retire with dignity and security. Yet for millions of Americans, particularly women, minorities, and ethnic Americans, old age means poverty, insecurity, and desperation.

Beginning with President Franklin D. Roosevelt, the Democratic Party has been dedicated to the well-being of the senior citizens of America. President Roosevelt gave to the elderly Social Security. The following Democratic Administrations provided the elderly with Medicare, the Older Americans Act, the nutrition program, low-cost housing, elderly employment programs and many others to make lives longer, healthier and happier for senior citizens, those who have done so much to make America the great nation it is today. This Reagan Republican Administration is the first administration to stop the progress of aid to the elderly and to cut back on every helpful program which Democratic Administrations had enacted for our elders.

Now we have a crisis facing the country with respect to Medicare. Funds will be short in four years. Again, the Reagan Republican Administration, speaking recently through the Social Security Advisory Council, proposed that the way to meet this financial crisis was to make the people already paying into Medicare pay more and to cut benefits by raising the age of eligibility from 65 to 67.

Too many elderly people covered by Medicare are not able to pay the deductible now required by Medicare. We Democrats will never add more to the burdens of the people now covered by Medicare. Nor will we Democrats allow benefits to be cut under Medicare by raising the age of eligibility, for we know that Medicare, which Democratic leadership established in 1964, is the only chance that millions of senior citizens have to get the health care they need.

To date, the needs of America's ethnic elderly have not been met. Ethnic American elderly number over seven million persons, or approximately one quarter of the total population of people over 65. A close examination of data from the U.S. Census reveals that nearly one-half of this ethnic population who are 65 years of age or older do not speak English. To assure the well-being of ethnic seniors who comprise a large segment of our elderly population, we should promote programs to strengthen family life, care for the elderly, and spur neighborhood revitalization and development of "language barrier-free" social and health services.

We also know that the number of senior citizens as a percentage of the population is rapidly growing. The Democratic Party is committed to the principle of forbidding any discrimination on account of age against the elderly, either in holding a job or obtaining one. We offer to the elderly an opportunity for additional training or retraining that will enable them to do better at the jobs they have or to turn to other jobs which they would like better.

In short, the Democratic Party, which for so long has been the champion of the elderly, assures the senior citizens of America that it will maintain its longstanding good faith with them. Whatever is right and good for the senior citizen shall always be close to the heart of the Democratic Party and ever a primary dedication of our Party.

It is the cherished aim and high purpose of the Democratic Party to make the last part of the long journey of life for our senior citizens as long, as healthy and as happy as may be.

As Democrats, we are proud of the programs we have created — Social Security and Medicare — to allow our senior citizens to live their lives independently and with dignity, and we will fight to preserve and protect those programs. We will work for decent housing and adequate nutrition for our senior citizens, and we will enforce the laws prohibiting age discrimination. We will not break faith with those who built America.

The Social Security Administration long had a reputation for administrative efficiency and high quality public service. Problems which have emerged under the current Administration — the financing crises, a deteriorating computer system, and arbitrary terminations of benefits to hundreds of thousands of disabled Americans — threaten the agency's ability to carry out its mission. The current Administration's policies have shaken people's confidence in the entire Social Security system.

The policies and operations of the Social Security Administration must be carefully and fully investigated to reform its operations so that the elderly and disabled receive the services and treatment to which they are entitled. In particular, we should explore the recommendation that the

Social Security Administration become an independent agency.

Opportunities for Disabled Americans — There are nearly 36 million people with disabilities in the United States, who look to our government for justice. As Democrats, we have long recognized that a disability need not be an obstacle to a productive, independent life and we have fought to guarantee access to facilities, and adequate training and support to meet the special needs of the disabled. This Administration has closed its eyes to those needs, and in so doing, violated a fundamental trust by seeking to condemn millions of disabled Americans to dependency. We will honor our commitments. We will insist that those who receive federal funds accommodate disabled employees — a requirement this Administration sought to eliminate. We will insist that benefits be available for those who cannot work, and that training is available for those who need help to find work.

The Democratic Party will safeguard the rights of the elderly and disabled to remain free from institutionalization except where medically indicated. The rights of the disabled within institutions should be protected from violations of the integrity of their person. Also, we will promote accessible public transportation, buildings, make voting booths accessible, and strictly enforce laws such as the entire Rehabilitation Act of 1973.

Opportunities for Veterans — This country has a proud tradition of honoring and supporting those who have defended us. Millions of Americans in the years after World War II went to college and bought their homes thanks to GI benefits. But for the latest generation of American veterans, needed support and assistance have been missing.

The nation has begun to welcome home with pride its Vietnam veterans, as reflected in the extraordinary Vietnam Veterans Memorial which was built through public contributions. The Democratic Party shares the nation's commitment to Vietnam veterans.

No President since the beginning of the Vietnam War has been so persistently hostile to Vietnam veterans programs as Ronald Reagan. He has sought to dismantle the Readjustment Counseling Centers, opposed employment and Agent Orange benefits, as well as basic due process at the Veterans Administration, including judicial review.

The Vietnam War divided our nation. Many of the rifts remain, but all agree on the respect due Vietnam veterans for their distinguished service during a troubled time. The Democratic Party pledges to reverse Ronald Reagan's Vietnam veteran policies, helping our nation come together as one people. And we believe it is especially important that we end discrimination against women and minority veterans, particularly in health and education programs.

We believe that the government has a special obligation to all of this nation's veterans, and we are committed to fulfilling it — to providing the highest quality health care, improving education and training, providing the assistance they need to live independent and productive lives.

Opportunities for the Poor — For the past four years, this Administration has callously pursued policies which have further impoverished those at the bottom of the economic ladder and pushed millions of Americans, particularly women and children, below the poverty line. Thanks to the Reagan budget cuts, many of the programs upon which the poor rely have been gutted — from education to housing to child nutrition. Far from encouraging independence, the Administration has penalized those seeking to escape poverty through work, by conditioning assistance on nonparticipation in the workplace. The figures tell part of the story:

— Today, 15 percent of all Americans live below the poverty line;
— Over three million more children are in poverty today than there were in 1979;
— Over half of all black children under age three live in poverty;
— More than one-third of all female-headed households are below the poverty line, and for non-white families headed by women with more than one child, the figure is 70 percent.

But the numbers tell only part of the story; numbers do not convey the frustration and suffering of women seeking a future for themselves and their children, with no support from anyone; numbers do not recount the pain of growing numbers of homeless men and women with no place to sleep, or of increasing infant mortality rates among children born to poor mothers. Numbers do not convey the human effects of unemployment on a once stable and strong family.

As Democrats, we call upon the American people to join with us in a renewed commitment to combat the feminization of poverty in our nation so that every American can be a productive, contributing member of our society. In that effort, our goal is to strengthen families and to reverse the existing incentives for their destruction. We therefore oppose laws requiring an unemployed parent to leave the family or drop out of the work force in order to qualify for assistance and health care. We recognize the special need to increase the labor force participation of minority males, and we are committed to expanding their opportunities through education and training and to enforcing the laws which guarantee them equal opportunities. The plight of young mothers must be separately addressed as well: they too need education and training, and quality child care must be available if they are to participate in such programs. Only through a nation that cares and a government that acts can those Americans trapped in poverty move toward meaningful independence.

The Hungry and the Homeless — In the late 1960s, the nation discovered widespread hunger and malnutrition in America, especially among poor children and the elderly. The country responded with a national effort, of which Americans should be justly proud. By the late 1970s, medical researchers found that hunger had nearly been eliminated.

Since 1980, however, hunger has returned. High unemployment, coupled with deep cutbacks in food assistance and other basic support programs for poor families have led to conditions not seen in this country for years. Studies in hospitals and health departments document increases in numbers of malnourished children. Increasing numbers of homeless wander our cities' streets in search of food and shelter. Religious organizations, charities and other agencies report record numbers of persons standing in line for food at soup kitchens and emergency food pantries.

Strong action is needed to address this issue and to end the resurgence of hunger in America. The Democratic Party is committed to reversing regressive Reagan policies and to providing more adequate food aid for poor families, infants, children, elderly and handicapped persons. It is time to resume the national effort, jettisoned in 1980, to ensure that less fortunate Americans do not go without adequate food because they are too poor to secure a decent diet. As Democrats, we call upon the American people to join with us in a renewed commitment to fight hunger and homelessness so that every American can be a productive, contributing member of our society.

Hunger is an international problem as well. In many countries it threatens peace and stability. The United States should take the lead in working with our allies and other countries to help wipe hunger from the face of the earth.

A Democratic President will ensure that the needs of the world's children are given priority in all U.S. foreign assistance programs and that international assistance programs are geared toward increasing self-reliance of local populations and self-sufficiency in food production.

Integrity in Government

As Democrats, we believe that the American people are entitled to a government that is honest, that is open, and that is fully representative of this nation and its people, and we are committed to providing it.

After four years in which the roll of dishonor in the Administration has grown weekly and monthly — from Richard Allen to Rita Lavelle, from Thomas Reed to James Watt — it is time for an end to the embarrassment of Republican cronyism and malfeasance. Our appointments will be ones of which Americans can be proud. Our selection process in staffing the government will be severe. We will not tolerate impropriety in a Democratic Administration.

We must work to end political action committee funding of federal political campaigns. To achieve that, we must enact a system of public financing of federal campaigns. At the same time, our Party should assure that a system of public financing be responsive to the problem of underrepresentation of women and minorities in elective offices.

We Democrats are not afraid to govern in public and to let the American people know and understand the basis for our decisions. We will reverse current Administration policies that permit the widespread overclassification of documents lacking a relationship to our national security. We will rescind Reagan Administration directives imposing undue burdens on citizens seeking information about their government through the Freedom of Information Act.

We will insist that the government, in its relations with its own employees, set a standard of fairness which is a model for the private sector. We believe, moreover, that an Administration that cannot run its own house fairly cannot serve the American people fairly. We will ensure that government's number one priority is the performance of its mission under the law, and not the implementation of the narrow political agenda of a single Party. Sound management and fair government cannot be administered by a politicized work force. Neither can it be accomplished by a demoralized work force. A Democratic Administration will not devalue the pay, benefits, and retirement rights of federal workers guaranteed under the law. We will work to reverse personnel policies, including the contracting out of work traditionally performed by public employees, that have made it impossible for current federal employees to recommend a career in federal service to our nation's young people.

Our judicial system must be one in which excellence and access are the foundations. It is essential to recruit people of high integrity, outstanding competence, and high quality of judgment to serve in our nation's judiciary. And we oppose efforts to strip the federal courts of their historic jurisdiction to adjudicate cases involving questions of federal law and constitutional right.

Crime

No problem has worried Americans more persistently over the past 20 years than the problem of crime. Crime and the fear of crime affect us all, but the impact is greatest on poor Americans who live in our cities. Neither a permissive liberalism nor a static conservatism is the answer to reducing crime. While we must eliminate those elements — like unemployment and poverty — that foster the criminal atmosphere, we must never let them be used as an excuse.

Although the primary responsibility for law enforcement rests at the local level, Democrats believe the federal government can play an important role by encouraging local innovation and the implementation of new crime control methods as their effectiveness is shown. And when crime spills across state borders, the federal government must take the lead, and assume responsibility for enforcing the law. This Administration has done neither. It has talked "law and order" while cutting law enforcement budgets. It has decried the influence of drugs, while cutting back on customs enforcement.

As a result, drug trafficking and abuse have risen to crisis proportions in the United States. In 1983, an estimated 60 tons of cocaine, 15,000 tons of marijuana, and 10 tons of heroin entered the United States, clear evidence that we are losing the effort overseas to control the production and transshipment of these and other dangerous drugs. Domestically, the illicit trafficking in drugs is a $100 billion per year business; the economic and social costs to our society are far higher.

Today, in our country, there are 25 million regular abusers of marijuana, close to 12 million abusers of cocaine, and half a million heroin addicts. Since 1979, hospital emergency room incidents — including deaths —

related to cocaine have soared 300 percent; incidents related to heroin have climbed 80 percent. According to the 1983 National High School Survey on Drug Abuse, 63 percent of high school seniors have tried an illicit drug, and 40 percent have tried a drug other than marijuana. Alcohol abuse is also a serious problem which must be faced.

— For this reason, the Democratic Party believes it is essential to make narcotics control a high priority on the national agenda, and a major consideration in our dealings with producer and transshipment countries, particularly if they are recipients of U.S. assistance.

— At the national level, the effort must begin by introducing a comprehensive management plan to eliminate overlap and friction between the 113 different federal agencies with responsibilities for fighting crime, particularly with respect to the control of drug traffic. We must provide the necessary resources to federal agencies and departments with responsibility for the fight against drugs.

— To spur local law enforcement efforts, establishment of an independent criminal justice corporation should be considered. This corporation could serve as a means of encouraging community-based efforts, such as neighborhood citizen watches, alternative deployment patterns for police, and community service sentencing programs, which have proven effectiveness.

— Violent acts of bigotry, hatred and extremism aimed at women, racial, ethnic and religious minorities, and gay men and lesbians have become an alarmingly common phenomenon. A Democratic Administration will work vigorously to address, document, and end all such violence.

— We believe that victims of crime deserve a workable program of compensation. We call for sentencing reforms that routinely include monetary or other forms of restitution to victims. The federal government should ensure that victims of violent federal crime receive compensation. We need to establish a federal victim compensation fund, to be financed, in part, by fines and the proceeds from the sale of goods forfeited to the government.

— We support tough restraints on the manufacture, transportation, and sale of snubnosed handguns, which have no legitimate sporting use and are used in a high proportion of violent crimes.

— We will establish a strong federal-state partnership to push for further progress in the nationwide expansion of comprehensive, community-based anti-drunk driving programs. With the support of citizens, private-sector business and government at all levels; we will institutionalize fatality and injury reduction on the nation's highways.

— We support fundamental reform of the sentencing process so that offenders who commit similar crimes receive similar penalties. Reform should begin with the establishment of appropriately drafted sentencing guidelines, and judges deviating from such guidelines should be required to provide written reasons for doing so.

— Finally, we believe that the credibility of our criminal courts must be restored. Our courts should not be attacked for failing to eliminate the major social problem of crime — courts of justice were not designed, and were never intended, to do that. A Democratic Administration will encourage experimentation with alternative dispute-resolution mechanisms, diversion programs for first and nonviolent offenders, and other devices to eliminate the congestion in our courts and restore to them an atmosphere in which they can perform their intended job: doing real individualized justice, in an orderly way.

Chapter III: Peace, Security, and Freedom

INTRODUCTION

Building a safer future for our nation and the world: that is the Democratic agenda for our national security. Every responsibility before our nation, every task that we set, pales beside the most important challenge we face — providing new leadership that enhances our security, promotes our values, and works for peace.

The next American President will preside over a period of historic change in the international system. The relatively stable world order that has prevailed since World War II is bursting at the seams from the powerful forces of change — the proliferation of nuclear and conventional weapons, the relentless Soviet military buildup, the achievement of rough nuclear parity between the Soviet Union and the United States, the increasingly interdependent nature of the international economic order, the recovery and rise of European and Asian powers since the devastation of the Second World War, and the search for a new American political consensus in the wake of Vietnam and Lebanon and in the shadow of a regional crisis in Central America.

The greatest foreign policy imperative of the Democratic Party and of the next President is to learn from past mistakes and adapt to these changes, rather than to resist or ignore them. While not underestimating the Soviet threat, we can no longer afford simplistically to blame all of our troubles on a single "focus of evil," for the sources of international change run even deeper than the sources of superpower competition. We must see change as an opportunity as well as a challenge. In the 1980s and beyond, America must not only make the world safe for diversity; we must learn to thrive on diversity.

The Democratic Party believes that it is time to harness the full range of America's capacity to meet the challenges of a changing world. We reject the notion that America is beset by forces beyond its control. Our commitment to freedom and democracy, our willingness to listen to contrasting viewpoints, and our ingenuity at devising new ideas and arrangements have given us advantages in an increasingly diverse world that no totalitarian system can match.

The Democratic Party has a constructive and confident vision of America's ability to use all of our economic, political, and military resources to pursue our wide-ranging security and economic interests in a diverse and changing world. We believe in a responsible defense policy that will increase our national security. We believe in a foreign policy that respects our allies, builds democracy, and advances the cause of human rights. We believe that our economic future lies in our ability to rise to the challenge of international economic competition by making our own industries more competitive. Above all, we believe that our security requires the direct, personal involvement of the President of the United States to limit the Soviet military threat and to reduce the danger of nuclear war.

We have no illusions about the forces arrayed against the democratic cause in our time. In the year made famous by George Orwell, we can see the realization of many of his grimmest prophecies in the totalitarian Soviet state, which has amassed an arsenal of weapons far beyond its defensive needs. In the communist and non-communist world, we find tyrannical regimes that trample on human rights and repress their people's cry for economic justice.

The Reagan Administration points to Soviet repression — but has no answer other than to escalate the arms race. It downgrades repression in the noncommunist world, by drawing useless distinctions between "totalitarian" and "authoritarian" regimes.

The Democratic Party understands the challenge posed by the enemies of democracy. Unlike the Reagan Administration, however, we are prepared to work constructively to reduce tensions and make genuine progress toward a safe world.

The Democratic Party is confident that American ideals and American interests reinforce each other in our foreign policy: the promotion of democracy and human rights not only distinguishes us from our adversaries, but it also builds the long-term stability that comes when governments respect their people. We look forward to the 21st Century as a century of democratic solidarity where security, freedom, and peace will flourish.

Peace, freedom and security are the essence of America's dream. They are the future of our children and their children.

This is the test where failure could provide no opportunity to try once more. As President Kennedy once warned: "We have the power to make this the best generation of mankind in the history of the world — or to make it the last."

THE FUTURE IF REAGAN IS REELECTED

"Star Wars is not the path toward a less dangerous world. A direct and safe road exists: equitable and verifiable deep cuts in strategic offensive forces. We must abandon the illusion that ever more sophisticated technology can remove the perils that science and technology have created."

> Statement by Dr. Jerome B. Wiesner, Dr. Carl Sagan, Dr. Henry Kendall, and Admiral Noel Gayler (Democratic Platform Committee Hearing, Washington, D.C., June 12, 1984)

"The minister of the apartheid government recently boasted of the fruitful relationship between Pretoria and Washington since the advent of the Reagan regime. Now apartheid South Africa has acquired the military muscle to bomb, to maim, to kill men, women, and children, and to bully these states into negotiating with apartheid through the threat of increased military action. This may be hailed as a victory for apartheid and for the Reagan Administration, but in truth it can only create anger and contempt in the African people."

> Professor Dennis Brutus, Northwestern University (former political prisoner in South Africa) (Democratic Platform Committee Hearing, New York, New York, April 9, 1984)

Suppose Mr. Reagan is reelected. How would he deal with the serious threats that face us and our children?

Under Mr. Reagan, the nuclear arms race would continue to spiral out of control. A new generation of destabilizing missiles will imperil all humanity. We will live in a world where the nuclear arms race has spread from earth into space.

Under Mr. Reagan, we would continue to overemphasize destabilizing and redundant nuclear weapons programs at the expense of our conventional forces. We will spend billions for weapons that do not work. We will continue to ignore proposals to improve defense management, to get a dollar's worth for each dollar spent, and to make our military more combat-effective and our weapons more cost-effective.

Under Mr. Reagan, regional conflicts would continue to be dangerously mismanaged. Young Americans may be sent to fight and die needlessly. The spread of nuclear materials to new nations and the spread of sophisticated conventional weapons to virtually every nation on earth will continue unabated.

Can America afford a President so out of touch with reality that he tells us, "I think the world is safer and further removed from a possible war than it was several years ago"?

Can America afford the recklessness of a President who exposed American Marines to mortal danger and sacrificed 262 of them in a bungled mission in Lebanon against the advice of the Joint Chiefs of Staff, and brought upon us the worst U.S. military disaster since the Vietnam War?

Can America afford the irresponsibility of a President who undermines confidence in our deterrent with misleading allegations of Soviet nuclear "superiority" and whose Administration beguiles the American public with false claims that nuclear war can be survived with enough shovels?

Can America afford the unresponsiveness of a President who thwarts the will of the majority of Americans by waging a secret war against Nicaragua?

In a second Reagan term, will our heavens become a nuclear battleground?

In 1980, candidate Ronald Reagan promised the American people a more secure world. Yet, as President:

- He has raced to deploy new weapons that will be destabilizing and difficult to verify. He has pressed for a multi-billion dollar chemical weapons program. He has launched his trillion dollar "Star Wars" arms race in space.
- He has relaxed controls on nuclear proliferation, thus enhancing the risk that nuclear weapons will be acquired and used by unstable governments and international terrorists.
- He has become the first President since the Cold War to preside over the complete collapse of all nuclear arms negotiations with the Soviets.
- He has rejected SALT II, threatened the ABM Treaty, and abandoned the goal of a complete ban on nuclear weapons tests that has been pursued by every President since Eisenhower. He has refused to seek negotiations to limit anti-satellite weapons that could threaten our vital early-warning and military satellites. Over 250 strategic missiles and bombers that would have been eliminated under SALT II are still in Soviet hands.

Can we afford four more years of a Pentagon spending binge?

In 1980, candidate Ronald Reagan and the Republican Party promised the American people a defense spending increase "to be applied judiciously to critically needed programs." Yet, as President:

- He has initiated the largest peacetime defense build-up in our history with no coherent plan for integrating the increased programs into an effective military posture.
- He has slighted training and readiness of our conventional forces in favor of big ticket nuclear items, "preparing," in the words of General Maxwell Taylor, "for the least possible threats to the neglect of the most probable."
- He has brought us the worst-managed and most wasteful Defense Department in history. Under the Pentagon's wasteful purchasing system, the American taxpayer has paid $435 for a $17 claw hammer, $1100 for a 22-cent plastic steel cap, over $2000 for a 13-cent plain round nut, and $9600 for a $9 Allen wrench.

Can we afford four more years of dangerous foreign policy failures?

In 1980, candidate Ronald Reagan and the Republican Party promised "to put America on a sound, secure footing in the international arena." Yet, as President:

- He has contributed to the decline of U.S.-Soviet relations to a perilous point. Instead of challenges, he has used easy and abusive anti-Soviet rhetoric as a substitute for strength, progress, and careful use of power.

— He has strained vital U.S. alliances through his bungled efforts to stop the Soviet natural gas pipeline, his inflammatory nuclear rhetoric and policies, and his failure to support the efforts of our democratic allies to achieve a negotiated political solution in Central America.

— He has had as many Middle East policies as he has had staff turnovers. First, he offered strategic cooperation to Israel as if it were a gift. Then he took it away to punish Israel as if it were not our ally. Then he pressured Israel to make one-sided concessions to Jordan. Then he demanded that Israel withdraw from Lebanon. Then he pleaded with them to stay. Then he did not accept their offer of medical help for our wounded Marines. He undercut American credibility throughout the Middle East by declaring Lebanon a vital interest of the United States and then withdrawing.

— He has failed to understand the importance for the United States of a solid relationship with the African continent — not only from the perspective of human decency, but also from enlightened concern for our own self-interest. By his lack of sensitivity and foresight, he has ignored the fate of millions of people who need our help in developing their economies and in dealing with the ravages of drought, and he has jeopardized our relations with countries that are important to U.S. security and well-being.

— He has brought us a strategy in Central America and the Caribbean that has failed. Since he took office, the region has become much more unstable; the hemisphere is much more hostile to us; and the poverty is much deeper. Today in El Salvador, after more than a billion dollars in American aid, the guerrillas are stronger than they were three years ago, and the people are much poorer. In Nicaragua, our support for the *contras* and for the covert war has strengthened the totalitarians at the expense of the moderates. In Honduras, an emerging democracy has been transformed into a staging ground for possible regional war. And in Costa Rica our backing for rebels based there is in danger of dragging that peaceful democracy into a military confrontation with Nicaragua. In Grenada, Mr. Reagan renounced diplomacy for over two years, encouraging extremism, instability, and crisis. By his failure to avoid military intervention, he divided us from our European allies and alienated our friends throughout the Western hemisphere. And by excluding the press, he set a chilling precedent, greatly hampering public scrutiny of his policies. After three and one-half years of Mr. Reagan's tunnel vision, extremism is stronger, our democratic friends are weaker, and we are further than ever from achieving peace and security in the region.

— He is the first President to fail to support publicly the ratification of the Genocide Convention. His Vice President has praised the Philippine dictator for his "love of democracy," his first Secretary of State announced that human rights would be replaced as a foreign policy priority, and his first nominee for Assistant Secretary of State for

Human Rights was rejected by the U.S. Senate as unfit for that post. He has closely identified the United States with the apartheid regime in South Africa, and he has time and again failed to confront dictators around the globe.

This is an unprecedented record of failure. But President Reagan is content to make excuses for failure.

President Reagan blames Congress and the Democratic Party. He rebukes Americans deeply and genuinely concerned about the threat of nuclear war. He rails at the Soviet Union — as if words alone, without strategy or effective policy, will make that nation change its course.

It is time for Democrats and Americans to apply a tough standard to Ronald Reagan. Let us paraphrase the question he asked in 1980: Are we safer today than we were three and a half years ago? Are we further from nuclear war? After more than a thousand days of Mr. Reagan, is the world anywhere less tense, anywhere closer to peace?

Americans throughout this land are answering with a resounding no.

President Reagan himself is responsible — responsible for four years of a failed foreign policy. America elects its President to lead. It does not elect its President to make excuses.

The Democratic Party believes that it is time to harness the full power of America's spirit and capacity to meet the challenges of a changing world.

The Democratic Party has a different and positive vision of America's future. What is at stake may be freedom and survival itself.

THE DEMOCRATIC ALTERNATIVE: A SAFER FUTURE FOR OUR NATION AND THE WORLD

"I do not see why we think of Democracy as so weak and so vulnerable. Let us for heaven's sake have some confidence in America and not tremble, fearing that our society will fall apart at the least rattle of the door. If I were constructing this platform, I would ask that its planks be carved out of self-confidence, and planted in belief in our own system."

Historian Barbara Tuchman (Democratic Platform Committee Hearing, New York, New York, April 9, 1984)

"The Democratic Party requires a foreign policy which approaches the problems that confront us primarily in their national and regional contexts, rather than viewing them, as the Reagan Administration does, almost exclusively as a manifestation of the 'evil empire's' efforts to extend its sway over the entire globe. What we need is a foreign policy which promotes the cause of human rights by opposing tyranny on the part of left as well as right wing governments, rather than a foreign policy, like the one we have now, which supports virtually every reactionary and repressive regime that professes to be anti-communist."

Honorable Stephen J. Solarz, U.S. Representative, New York (Democratic Platform Committee Hearing, New York, New York, April 9, 1984)

There is no higher goal for the Democratic Party than assuring the national security of the United States. This means a strong national defense, vigorous pursuit of nuclear arms control, and a foreign policy dedicated to advancing the interests of America and the forces of freedom and democracy in a period of global transformation. This will require new leadership, strong alliances, skillful diplomacy, effective economic cooperation, and a foreign policy sustained by American strength and ideals. And to hold the support of the American people, our leaders must also be careful and measured in the use of force.

The Democratic Party is committed to a strong national defense. Democrats know that a relentless Soviet military build-up — well beyond its defensive needs — directly challenges world security, our democratic values, and our free institutions. On the nature of the Soviet threat and on the essential issue of our nation's security, Americans do not divide. On the common interest in human survival, the American and Soviet peoples do not divide.

Maintaining strong and effective military forces is essential to keeping the peace and safeguarding freedom. Our allies and adversaries must never doubt our military power or our will to defend our vital interests. To that end, we pledge a strong defense built in concert with our allies, based on a coherent strategy, and supported by a sound economy.

In an age of about 50,000 nuclear weapons, however, nuclear arms control and reductions are also essential to our security. The most solemn responsibility of a President is to do all that he or she can to prevent a single nuclear weapon from ever being used. Democrats believe that mutual and verifiable controls on nuclear arms can, and must be, a serious integral part of national defense. True national security requires urgent measures to freeze and reverse the arms race, not the pursuit of the phantom of nuclear superiority or futile Star Wars schemes.

The Democratic Party believes that the purpose of nuclear weapons is to deter war, not to fight it. Democrats believe that America has the strength and tenacity to negotiate nuclear arms agreements that will reduce the risk of nuclear war and preserve our military security.

Today we stand at one of the most critical junctures in the arms race since the explosion of the first atomic bomb. Mr. Reagan wants to open the heavens for warfare.

His Star Wars proposal would create a vulnerable and provocative "shield" that would lull our nation into a false sense of security. It would lead our allies to believe that we are retreating from their defense. It would lead to the death of the ABM Treaty — the most successful arms control treaty in history — and this trillion-dollar program would provoke a dangerous offensive and defensive arms race.

If we and our allies could defend our populations effectively against a nuclear war, the Democratic Party would be the first to endorse such a scheme. Unfortunately, our best scientists agree that an effective population defense is probably impossible. Therefore, we must oppose an arms race where the sky is no longer the limit.

Arms Control and Disarmament

Ronald Reagan is the first American President in over twenty years who has not reached any significant arms control agreements with the Soviet Union, and he is the first in over fifty years who has not met face to face with Soviet leaders. The unjustified Soviet walkout from key nuclear talks does not excuse the arms control failures of the Administration.

To reopen the dialogue, a Democratic President will propose an early summit with regular, annual summits to follow, with the Soviet leaders, and meetings between senior civilian and military officials, in order to reduce tensions and explore possible formal agreements. In a Democratic Administration, the superpowers will not communicate through megaphones.

A new Democratic Administration will implement a strategy for peace which makes arms control an integral part of our national security policy. We must move the world back from the brink of nuclear holocaust and set a new direction toward an enduring peace, in which lower levels of military spending will be possible. Our ultimate aim must be to abolish all nuclear weapons in a world safe for peace and freedom.

This strategy calls for immediate steps to stop the nuclear arms race, medium-term measures to reduce the dangers for war, and long-term goals to put the world on a new and peaceful course.

The first practical step is to take the initiative, on January 20, 1985, to challenge the Soviets to halt the arms race quickly. As President Kennedy successfully did in stopping nuclear explosions above ground in 1963, a Democratic President will initiate temporary, verifiable, and mutual moratoria, to be maintained for a fixed period during negotiations so long as the Soviets do the same, on the testing of underground nuclear weapons and anti-satellite weapons; on the testing and deployment of all weapons in space; on the testing and deployment of new strategic ballistic missiles now under development; and on the deployment of nuclear-armed, sea-launched cruise missiles.

These steps should lead promptly to the negotiation of a comprehensive, mutual and verifiable freeze on the testing, production, and deployment of all nuclear weapons.

Building on this initiative, the Democratic President will:

— update and resubmit the SALT II Treaty to the Senate for its advice and consent.

— pursue deep, stabilizing reductions in nuclear arsenals within the framework of SALT II, in the meantime observing the SALT II limits ourselves and insisting that the Soviets do likewise.

— propose the merging of the intermediate-range and strategic arms limitations negotiations, if the President judges that this could advance a comprehensive arms limitation agreement with the Soviet Union.

— immediately resubmit to the Senate for its advice and consent the

1974 Threshold Test Ban Treaty and the 1976 Peaceful Nuclear Explosions Treaty.

— conclude a verifiable and Comprehensive Test Ban Treaty.

— reaffirm our commitment to the ABM Treaty, ensure U.S. compliance, and vigorously demand answers to questions about Soviet compliance through the Standing Consultative Commission and other appropriate channels.

— actively pursue a verifiable, anti-satellite weapons treaty and ban on weapons in space.

— seek a verifiable international ban on the production of nuclear weapons-grade fissile material, such as plutonium and highly enriched uranium.

— undertake all-out efforts to halt nuclear proliferation.

— terminate production of the MX missile and the B-1 bomber.

— prohibit the production of nerve gas and work for a verifiable treaty banning chemical weapons.

— establish U.S.-Soviet nuclear risk reduction centers and other improved communications for a crisis.

— invite the most eminent members of the scientific community to study and report on the worldwide human suffering and the long-term environmental damage which would follow in the days after a nuclear war, and take into account as fully as possible the results of such study in the formulation of our nuclear weapons and arms control policies.

— strengthen broad-based, long-term public support for arms control by working closely with leaders of grass-roots, civic, women's, labor, business, religious and professional groups, including physicians, scientists, lawyers, and educators.

— provide national leadership for economic adjustment for affected communities and industries, and retraining for any defense workers affected by the termination or cutbacks in weapons programs.

— initiate, in close consultation with our NATO allies, a strategy for peace in Europe including:

— achieving a balance of conventional forces in order to reduce reliance on nuclear weapons and to permit the Atlantic Alliance to move toward the adoption of a "no first use" policy;

— mutually pulling back battlefield nuclear weapons from the frontlines of Europe, in order to avoid the necessity of having to make a "use them or lose them" choice should hostilities erupt in Europe.

— negotiating new approaches to intermediate nuclear force limits along the lines of the "walk in the woods" proposal, and then seeking to move closer to zero INF deployments by the U.S. and U.S.S.R.;

— negotiating significant mutual and balanced reductions in conventional forces of both NATO and the Warsaw Pact, and confidence-building measures to reduce the dangers of a surprise attack.

We are under no illusion that these arms control proposals will be easy to achieve. Most will involve patience and dedication, and above all leadership in the pursuit of peace, freedom, and security. The Soviets are tough negotiators and too often seek to use arms control talks for their propaganda purposes. On this issue — preventing nuclear war — America must lead, and the Democratic Party intends to lead. Without our leadership the nations of the world will be tempted to abandon themselves, perhaps slowly at first, but then relentlessly to the quest for nuclear weapons, and our children will look back with envy upon today's already dangerous nuclear world as a time of relative safety.

Defense Policy

The Reagan Administration measures military might by dollars spent. The Democratic Party seeks prudent defense based on sound planning and a realistic assessment of threats. In the field of defense policy, the Democratic Administration will:

— Work with our NATO and other allies to ensure our collective security, especially by strengthening our conventional defenses so as to reduce our need to rely on nuclear weapons, and to achieve this at increased spending levels, with funding to continue at levels appropriate to our collective security, with the firm hope that successful steps to reduce tensions and to obtain comprehensive and verifiable arms control agreements will guarantee our nation both military security and budgetary relief.

— Cancel destabilizing or duplicative weapons systems, while proceeding in the absence of appropriate arms control agreements with necessary modernization of our strategic forces.

— Scale back the construction of large, expensive and vulnerable nuclear carriers.

— Modernize our conventional forces by balancing new equipment purchases with adequate resources spent on training, fuel, ammunition, maintenance, spare parts, and airlift and sealift to assure combat readiness and mobility, and by providing better equipment for our Reserves and National Guard.

— Reorganize Pentagon management and strengthen the JCS system to reduce interservice rivalries, promote military leadership over bureaucratic skills, assure effective execution of policies and decisions, undertake better multi-year planning based upon realistic projections of available resources, and reduce conflicts of interest.

— Ensure open and fair competitive bidding for procurement of necessary equipment and parts, and establish a system of effective, independent testing of weapons for combat conditions.

— Implement a program of military reform. Our forces must be combat ready; our doctrines should emphasize out-thinking and out-maneuvering our adversaries; and our policies should improve military organization and unit cohesion.

— Press our European allies to increase their contributions to NATO defense to levels of effort comparable to our own — an approach that the Administration undercut by abandoning the NATO-wide agreement concluded by its Democratic predecessor — and pursue improved trans-Atlantic economic cooperation and coordination of arms procurement.

— Recognize that the heart of our military strength is people, Americans in uniform who will have the skills and the will to maintain the peace. The men and women of our armed services deserve not only proper pay and benefits, but the nation's recognition, respect and gratitude as well.

— Recognize the importance of the intelligence community and emphasize its mission as being dedicated to the timely collection and analysis of information and data. A Democratic Administration will also recognize the urgent need to de-politicize the intelligence community and to restore professional leadership to it.

— Oppose a peacetime military draft or draft registration.

— Oppose efforts to restrict the opportunities of women in the military based solely on gender. The Reagan Administration has used the combat designation as an arbitrary and inappropriate way to exclude women from work they can legitimately perform. Women nurses and technicians, for example, have long served with distinction on the front lines; women must not be excluded from jobs that they are trained and able to perform.

— Seek ways to expand programs such as VISTA, the Young Adult Conservation Corps, and the Peace Corps.

These and other qualitative improvements will ensure effective American strength at affordable cost. With this strength, we will restore the confidence of our fellow citizens and our allies; we will be able to mount an effective conventional defense; and we will present our adversaries with a credible capability to deter war.

The Democratic Party is committed to reversing the policies of the Reagan Administration in the area of military and defense procurement. Public accounts reveal a four-year record of waste, fraud, conflicts of interest, and indications of wrongdoing. Administration officials have engaged in practices that have cost the taxpayers billions of dollars. Further, the Reagan Administration has ignored legal remedies to stop the abuses, recover the funds, and punish those responsible.

A Democratic President will demand full disclosure of all information, launch a thorough investigation, and seek recovery of any tax funds illegally spent. This will be a major step towards restoring integrity to defense procurements and reducing unnecessary expenditures in the defense budget.

Foreign Policy

The purpose of foreign policy is to attain a strong and secure United States and a world of peace, freedom and justice. On a planet threatened by dictatorships on the left and right, what is at stake may be freedom itself. On a planet shadowed by the threat of a nuclear holocaust, what is at stake may be nothing less than human survival.

A Democratic Administration will comprehend that the gravest political and security dangers in the developing world flow from conditions that open opportunities for the Soviet Union and its surrogates: poverty, repression and despair. Against adversaries such as these, military force is of limited value. Such weapons as economic assistance, economic and political reform, and support for democratic values by, among other steps, funding scholarships to study at U.S. colleges and universities, must be the leading elements of our presence and the primary instruments of American influence in the developing countries.

To this end, a Democratic President will strengthen our Foreign Service, end the present practice of appointing unqualified persons as Ambassadors, strengthen our programs of educational and cultural exchange, and draw upon the best minds in our country in the quest for peace.

A Democratic Administration will initiate and establish a Peace Academy. In the interests of balancing this nation's investment in the study of making war, the Peace Academy will study the disciplines and train experts in the arts of waging peace.

The Democratic Party is committed to ensuring strong representation of women and minorities in military and foreign policy decisionmaking positions in our government.

In addition, a Democratic President will understand that as Commander-in-Chief, he or she directs the forces of peace as well as those of war, and will restore an emphasis on skilled, sensitive, bilateral and multilateral diplomacy as a means to avert and resolve international conflict.

A Democratic President will recognize that the United States, with broad economic, political, and security interests in the world, has an unparalleled stake in the rule of international law. Under a Democratic Administration, there will be no call for clumsy attempts to escape the jurisdiction of the International Court of Justice, such as those put forth by the Reagan Administration in connection with its mining of the harbors of Nicaragua.

A Democratic President will reverse the automatic militarization of foreign policy and look to the causes of conflict to find out whether they are internal or external, whether they are political or primarily social and economic.

In the face of the Reagan Administrations's cavalier approach to the use of the military force around the world, the Democratic Party affirms its commitment to the selective, judicious use of American military power in consonance with Constitutional principles and reinforced by the War Powers Act.

A Democratic President will be prepared to apply military force when vital American interests are threatened, particularly in the event of an attack upon the United States or its immediate allies. But he or she will not hazard American lives or engage in unilateral military involvement:

- Where our objectives are not clear;
- Until all instruments of diplomacy and non-military leverage, as appropriate, have been exhausted;
- Where our objectives threaten unacceptable costs or unreasonable levels of military force;
- Where the local forces supported are not working to resolve the causes of conflict;
- Where multilateral or allied options for the resolution of conflict are available.

Further, a Democratic Administration will take all reasonable domestic action to minimize U.S. vulnerability to international instability, such as reducing Western alliance on Persian Gulf oil and other strategic resources. To this end, a Democratic Administration will implement, with our allies, a multilateral strategy for reduction of allied dependence on critical resources from volatile regions of the world.

U.S. covert operations under a Democratic President will be strictly limited to cases where secrecy is essential to the success of an operation and where there is an unmistakable foreign policy rationale. Secrecy will not be used simply to hide from the American people policies they might be expected to oppose.

Finally, a Democratic President will recognize our democratic process as a source of strength and stability, rather than an unwelcome restraint on the control of foreign policy. He or she will respect the War Powers Resolution as a reflection of wise judgment that the sustained commitment of America's fighting forces must be made with the understanding and support of Congress and the American people. A Democratic President will understand that United States leadership among nations requires a proper respect for law and treaty obligations, and the rights of men and women everywhere.

Europe and the Atlantic Alliance — American leadership is not about standing up to your friends. It is about standing up with them, and for them. In order to have allies, we must act like one.

Maintaining a strong alliance is critically important. We remain absolutely committed to the defense of Europe, and we will work to ensure that our allies carry their fair share of the burden of the common defense. A Democratic Administration in turn will commit itself to increased consultation on security affairs. We must work to sustain and enhance Western unity.

We must persuade the next generation of Europeans that America will use its power responsibly in partnership with them. We Democrats affirm that Western security is indivisible. We have a vital interest in the security of our allies in Europe. And it must always remain clear that an attack upon them is the same as an attack upon us — by treaty and in reality.

A strong Western alliance requires frank discussions among friends about the issues that from time to time divide us. For example, we must enter into meaningful negotiations with the European Community to reduce their agricultural export subsidies which unfairly impair the competitiveness of American agricultural products in third-country markets.

A Democratic President will encourage our European friends to resolve their long-standing differences over Ireland and Cyprus.

The Democratic Party supports an active role by the United States in safeguarding human rights in Northern Ireland and achieving an enduring peaceful settlement of that conflict. We oppose the use of plastic bullets in Northern Ireland, and we urge all sides to reject the use of violence. The Democratic Party supports a ban on all commercial transactions by the U.S. government with firms in England and Ireland that practice, on an on-going basis, discrimination in Northern Ireland on the basis of race, religion, or sex. We affirm our strong commitment to Irish unity — achieved by consent and based on reconciliation of all the people of Ireland. The Democratic Party is greatly encouraged by the historic and hopeful Report of the New Ireland Forum which holds the promise of a real breakthrough. A Democratic President will promptly appoint a special envoy and urge the British as well as the political leaders in Northern Ireland to review the findings and proposals of the Forum with open hearts and open minds, and will appeal to them to join a new initiative for peace. The Congress and a Democratic President will stand ready to assist this process, and will help promote jobs and investments, on a non-discriminatory basis, that will represent a significant contribution to the cause of peace in Ireland.

In strong contrast to President Reagan's failure to apply effective diplomacy in Cyprus and the Eastern Mediterranean, a Democratic President will act with urgency and determination to make a balanced policy in the area and a peaceful resolution of the Cyprus dispute a key foreign policy priority. A Democratic President will utilize all available U.S. foreign policy instruments and will play an active, instead of a passive, role in the efforts to secure implementation of U.N. Resolutions so as to achieve removal of Turkish troops, the return of refugees, reestablishment of the integrity of the Republic of Cyprus, and respect for all citizens' human rights on Cyprus.

United States — Soviet Relations — U.S. relations with the Soviet Union are a critical element of our security policy. All Americans recognize the threat to world peace posed by the Soviet Union. The U.S.S.R. is the only adversary with the capability of destroying the United States. Moreover, Americans are more generally concerned about the Soviet leadership's dangerous behavior internationally and the totalitarian nature of their regime. The Brezhnev Doctrine proclaims Soviet willingness to maintain communist regimes against the opposition of their own people. Thus, Soviet troops have invaded and today continue to wage war on the proud people of Afghanistan. In Poland, a military government, acting under Soviet pressure, has sought to crush the indomitable spirit of the Polish people and to destroy Solidarity, a free trade Union movement of ten million members and the first such movement in a communist country. In recent years, the Soviet Union and its allies have played a more aggressive role in countries around the world. At the same time, the Soviet military arsenal, nuclear and conventional, far exceeds that needed for its defense.

Yet we also recognize that the Soviets share a mutual interest in survival. They, too, have no defense against a nuclear war. Our security and their security can only be strengthened by negotiation and cooperation.

To shape a policy that is both firm and wise, we must first stand confident and never fear the outcome of any competition between our systems. We must see the Soviet Union as it is — neither minimizing the threats that Soviet power and policies pose to U.S. interests, nor exaggerating the strength of a Soviet regime beset by economic stagnation and saddled with a bankrupt and sterile ideology. We must join with our allies and friends to maintain an effective deterrent to Soviet power. We must pursue a clear, consistent and firm policy of peaceful competition toward the Soviet Union, a steady and pragmatic approach that neither tolerates Soviet aggression and repression nor fuels Soviet paranoia.

The job of an American President is both to check Soviet challenges to our vital interests, and to meet them on the common ground of survival. The risk of nuclear war cannot be eliminated overnight. But every day it can be either increased or decreased. And one of the surest ways to increase it is to cut off communications.

The Democratic Party condemns continued Soviet persecution of dissidents and refuseniks, which may well have brought Nobel laureate Andrei Sakharov and his wife to the verge of death in internal exile in Gorki. We will not be silent when Soviet actions, such as the imprisonment of Anatoly Shcharansky and Ida Nudel and thousands of others, demonstrate the fundamentally repressive and anti-Semitic nature of the Soviet regime. A Democratic Administration will give priority to securing the freedom to emigrate for these brave men and women of conscience including Jews and other minorities, and to assuring their fair treatment while awaiting permission to leave. These freedoms are guaranteed by the Universal Declaration of Human Rights and by the Helsinki Final Act which the Soviets have signed and with whose provisions they must be required to comply. Jewish emigration, which reached the level of fifty thousand per year during the last Democratic Administration and which has virtually ended under its Republican successor, must be renewed through firm, effective diplomacy. We also recognize that Jewish emigration reached its height at the same time there was an American Administration dedicated to pursuing arms control, expanding mutually beneficial trade, and reducing tensions with the Soviet Union — fully consistent with the interests of the United States and its allies. It is no contradiction to say that while pursuing an end to the arms race and reducing East-West tensions, we can also advance the cause of Soviet Jewish emigration.

Eastern Europe — We must respond to the aspirations and hopes of the peoples of Eastern Europe and encourage, wherever possible, the forces of change and pluralism that will increase these people's freedom from Soviet tyranny and communist dictatorship. We should encourage Western European countries to pursue independent foreign policies and to permit greater liberalization in domestic affairs, and we should seek independent relationships to further these objectives with them.

The Democratic Party condemns the Soviet repression by proxy in Poland and the other countries of Eastern Europe. The emergence of the free trade union Solidarity is one of the most formidable developments in post-war Europe and inspires all who love freedom. The struggle of the Polish people for a democratic society and religious freedom is eloquent testimony to their national spirit and bravery that even a brutal martial law regime cannot stamp out.

Today the Jaruzelski regime claims to have ended the harshest repressive measures. Yet it continues to hold political prisoners, it continues to mistreat them, and it continues to hunt down members of Solidarity.

The Democratic Party agrees with Lech Walesa that the underground Solidarity movement must not be deprived of union freedoms. We call for the release of all political prisoners in Poland and an end to their harassment, the recognition of the free trade union Solidarity, and the resumption of progress toward liberty and human rights in that nation. A Democratic President will continue to press for effective international sanctions against the Polish regime until it makes satisfactory progress toward these objectives.

The Middle East — The Democratic Party believes that the security of Israel and the pursuit of peace in the Middle East are fundamental priorities for American foreign policy. Israel remains more than a trusted friend, a steady ally, and a sister democracy. Israel is strategically important to the United States, and we must enter into meaningful strategic cooperation.

The Democratic Party opposes this Administration's sales of highly advanced weaponry to avowed enemies of Israel, such as AWACS aircraft and Stinger missiles to Saudi Arabia. While helping to meet the legitimate defensive needs of states aligned with our nation, we must ensure Israel's military edge over any combination of Middle East confrontation states. The Democratic Party opposes any consideration of negotiations with the PLO, unless the PLO abandons terrorism, recognizes the state of Israel, and adheres to U.N. Resolutions 242 and 338.

Jerusalem should remain forever undivided with free access to the holy places for people of all faiths. As stated in the 1976 and 1980 platforms, the Democratic Party recognizes and supports the established status of Jerusalem as the capital of Israel. As a symbol of this stand, the U.S.

Embassy should be moved from Tel Aviv to Jerusalem.

The Democratic Party condemns this Administration's failure to maintain a high-level Special Negotiator for the Middle East, and believes that the Camp David peace process must be taken up again with urgency. No nation in the Middle East can afford to wait until a new war brings even worse destruction. Once again we applaud and support the example of both Israel and Egypt in taking bold steps for peace. We believe that the United States should press for negotiations among Israel, Jordan, Saudi Arabia, and other Arab states. We re-emphasize the fundamental principle that the prerequisite for a lasting peace in the Middle East remains an Israel with secure and defensible borders, strong beyond a shadow of a doubt; that the basis for peace is the unequivocal recognition of Israel's right to exist by all other states; and that there should be a resolution of the Palestinian issue.

The United States and our allies have vital interests in the Persian Gulf. We must be prepared to work with our allies in defense of those interests. We should stand by our historic support for the principle of freedom of the high seas. At the same time, we and our allies should employ active diplomacy to encourage the earliest possible end to the Iran/Iraq conflict.

The Western Hemisphere — The Western Hemisphere is in trouble. Central America is a region at war. Latin America is experiencing the most serious economic crisis in 50 years. The Inter-American system is on the verge of collapse. Concern about U.S. policies has risen sharply.

It is time to make this Hemisphere a top priority. We need to develop relations based on mutual respect and mutual benefit. Beyond essential security concerns, these relations must emphasize diplomacy, development and respect for human rights. Above all, support for democracy must be pursued. The Reagan Administration is committing the old error of supporting authoritarian military regimes against the wishes of the people they rule, but the United States was not founded, and defended for 200 years with American blood, in order to perpetuate tyranny among our neighbors.

The Hemisphere's nations must strive jointly to find acceptable solutions with judgments and actions based on equally-applied criteria. We must condemn violations of human rights, aggression, and deprivation of basic freedoms wherever they occur. The United States must recognize that the economic and debt crisis of Latin America also directly affects us.

The Reagan Administration has badly misread and mishandled the conflict in Central America. The President has chosen to dwell on the strategic importance of Central America and to cast the struggle in almost exclusively East-West terms. The strategic importance of Central America is not in doubt, nor is the fact that the Soviet Union, Cuba and Nicaragua have all encouraged instability and supported revolution in the region. What the President ignores, however, are the indigenous causes of unrest. Historically, Central America has been burdened by widespread hunger and disease. And the historic pattern of concentrated wealth has done little to produce stable democratic societies.

Sadly, Mr. Reagan has opted for the all too frequent American response to the unrest that has characterized Central America — military assistance. Over the past 100 years, Panama, Nicaragua, and Honduras have all been occupied by U.S. forces in an effort to suppress indigenous revolutionary movements. In 1954, CIA-backed forces successfully toppled the Government of Guatemala.

President Reagan's massive transfusions of military aid to El Salvador are no substitute for the social and economic reforms that are necessary to undermine the appeal the guerrillas hold for many Salvadorans. The changes and upheavals in El Salvador and Nicaragua are home-grown, but they are exacerbated by forces from outside of Central America. The undoubted communist influence on these revolutions cannot be nullified by the dispatch of naval and air armadas to the waters off Nicaragua and thousands of troops to the jungles of Honduras. The solution lies with a new policy that fosters social, economic and political reforms that are compatible with our legitimate vital interests while accommodating the equally legitimate forces of change.

America must find a different approach. All too often, the United States thinks in terms of what it can do *for* the nations of Latin America and the Caribbean region. Rarely does it think in terms of what it can do *with* them. Even with the best of intentions, the difference is more than rhetorical, for paternalism can never be disguised and it is always resented — whether we choose to label it a "special relationship" or to call it a "defensive shield." Acting *for* the nations of the Hemisphere rather than acting in concert *with* them is the surest way of repeating the mistakes of the past and casting a dark shadow over the future.

It need not be. There is an alternative, a good alternative. The great Mexican patriot Benito Juarez pointed the way and said it best: "Between men as between nations, respect for the rights of others is peace." Working *with* our hemispheric neighbors produces understanding and cooperation. Doing someting *for* them produces resentment and conflict.

Democrats know there is a real difference between the two and a Democratic President will seek the advice and counsel of the authentic democratic voices within the region — voices that may be heard north and south, east and west; the voices of President Miguel de la Madrid of Mexico, President Belisario Betancur of Colombia, and President Raul Alfonsin of Argentina; the voices of President Jorge Blanco of the Dominican Republic, Prime Minister Tom Adams of Barbados, and President Alberto Monge of Costa Rica. By consulting with and listening carefully to these leaders and their democratic colleagues elsewhere in the region, the next Democratic President of the United States will fashion a policy toward the region which recognizes that:

— the security and well-being of the Hemisphere are more a function of economic growth and development than of military agreements and arms transfers;

— the mounting debt crisis throughout the region poses a broader threat to democratic institutions and political stability than does any insurgency or armed revolutionary movement;

— there is an urgent and genuine need for far-reaching economic, social and political reforms in much of the region and that such reforms are absolutely essential to the protection of basic human rights;

— the future belongs as much to the people of the region — the politically forgotten and the economically deprived — as it does to the rich and powerful elite;

— preservation and protection of U.S. interests in the Hemisphere requires mutual respect for national sovereignty and demilitarization of the region, prior consultation in accordance with the Rio Treaty and the OAS Charter regarding the application of the Monroe Doctrine, the use of military force, and a multilateral commitment to oppose the establishment of Soviet and Cuban military bases, strategic facilities, or combat presence in Central America or elsewhere in Latin America;

— efforts to isolate Cuba only serve to make it more dependent on the Soviet Union; U.S. diplomatic skills must be employed to reduce that level of dependence and to explore the differences that divide us with a view to stabilizing our relations with Cuba. At the same time we must continue to oppose firmly Cuban intervention in the internal affairs of other nations. Progress in our relationship will depend on Cuba's willingness to end its support for violent revolution, to recognize the sovereignty and independence of other nations by respecting the principle of non-intervention, to demonstrate respect for human rights both inside and outside of Cuba, and to abide by international norms of behavior.

Mindful of these realities and determined to stop widening, militarizing, and Americanizing the conflict, a Democratic President's immediate objective will be to stop the violence and pursue a negotiated political solution in concert with our democratic allies in the Contadora group. He or she will approach Central American policy in the following terms:

— First, there must be unequivocal support for the Contadora process and for the efforts by those countries to achieve political solutions to the conflicts that plague the Central American region.

— Second, there must be a commitment on the part of the United States to reduce tensions in the region. We must terminate our support for the *contras* and other paramilitary groups fighting in Nicaragua. We must halt those U.S. military exercises in the region which are being conducted for no other real purpose than to intimidate or provoke the Nicaraguan government or which may be used as a pretext for deeper U.S. military involvement in the area. And, we must evidence our firm willingness to work for a demilitarized Central America, including the mutual withdrawal of all foreign forces and military advisers from the region. A Democratic President will seek a multilateral framework to protect the security and independence of the region which will include regional agreements to bar new military bases, to restrict the numbers and sophistication of weapons being introduced into Central America, and to permit international inspection of borders. This diplomatic effort can succeed, however, only if all countries in Central America, including Nicaragua, will agree to respect the sovereignty and integrity of their neighbors, to limit their military forces, to reject foreign military bases (other than those provided for in the Panama Canal Treaties), and to deny any external force or power the use of their territories for purposes of subversion in the region. The viability of any security agreement for Central America would be enhanced by the progressive development of pluralism in Nicaragua. To this end, the elections proposed for November are important; how they are conducted will be an indication of Nicaragua's willingness to move in the direction of genuine democracy.

— Third, there must be a clear, concise signal to indicate that we are ready, willing and able to provide substantial economic resources, through the appropriate multilateral channels, to the nations of Central America, as soon as the Contadora process achieves a measure of success in restoring peace and stability in the region. In the meantime, of course, we will continue to provide humanitarian aid and refugee relief assistance. The Democratic Administration will work to help churches and universities which are providing sanctuary and assistance to Guatemalan, Haitian, and Salvadoran refugees, and will give all assistance to such refugees as is consistent with U.S. law.

— Fourth, a Democratic President will support the newly elected President of El Salvador in his efforts to establish civilian democratic control, by channeling U.S. aid through him and by conditioning it on the elimination of government-supported death squads and on progress toward his objectives of land reform, human rights, and serious negotiations with contending forces in El Salvador, in order to achieve a peaceful democratic political settlement of the Salvadoran conflict.

— Fifth, a Democratic President will not use U.S. armed forces in or over El Salvador or Nicaragua for the purpose of engaging in combat unless:

1) Congress has delcared war or otherwise authorized the use of U.S. combat forces, or

2) the use of U.S. combat forces is necessary to meet a clear and present danger of attack upon the U.S., its territories or possessions or upon U.S. embassies or citizens, consistent with the War Powers Act.

These are the key elements that evidence very real differences between the Democrats' approach to Central America and that of the Reagan Administration. And these are the key elements that will offer the American public a choice — a very significant choice — between war and peace in the Central American region.

A Democratic President would seek to work with the countries of the Caribbean to strengthen democratic institutions. He or she would not overlook human rights, by refusing to condemn repression by the regimes of the right or the left in the region. A Democratic President would give high priority to democracy, freedom, and to multilateral development. A Democratic President would encourage regional cooperation and make of that important area a showplace rather than a footstool for economic development. Finally, support for democracy must be pursued in its own right, and not just as a tactic against communism.

Human rights principles were a cornerstone of President Carter's foreign policy and have always been a central concern in the Inter-American system. Regional multilateral action to protect and advance human rights is an international obligation.

A Democratic President must not overlook human rights, refusing to condemn repression by the regimes of the right or the left in the region. Insistence that government respect their obligations to their people is a criterion that must apply equally to all. It is as important in Cuba as in El Salvador, Guatemala as in Nicaragua, in Haiti as in Paraguay and Uruguay.

A Democratic Administration would place protection of human rights in a core position in our relations with Latin America and the Caribbean. It would particularly seek multilateral support for such principles by strengthening and backing the Inter-American Commission on Human Rights, and by encouraging the various private organizations in the hemisphere dedicated to monitoring and protecting human rights.

Africa — The Democratic Party will advocate a set of bold new initiatives for Third World nations in general and Africa in particular. Hunger, drought, and famine have brought untold suffering to millions in Africa. This human misery — and the armies of nationless — requires a policy of substantial increases in humanitarian assistance, a major thrust in agricultural technology transfer, and cessation of the unfortunate tendency to hold such aid hostage to East-West confrontation or other geopolitical aims. The United States also must offer substantially greater economic assistance to these nations, while engaging in a North-South multilateral dialogue that addresses mutual economic development strategies, commodities pricing, and other treaties relevant to international trade. A Democratic President will join with our friends within and outside the continent in support of full respect for the sovereignty and territorial integrity of all African states. Africa is the home of one-eighth of the world's population and a continent of vast resources. Our national interest demands that we give this rich and diverse continent a much higher priority.

A Democratic President will reverse the Reagan Administration's failed policy of "constructive engagement" and strongly and unequivocally oppose the apartheid regime in South Africa. A Democratic Administration will:

— exert maximum pressure on South Africa to hasten the establishment

of a democratic, unitary political system within South Africa.
— pursue scrupulous enforcement of the 1977 U.N. arms embargo against South Africa, including enforcement of restrictions on the sale of "dual use" equipment.
— impose a ban on all new loans by U.S. business interests to the South African government and on all new investments and loans to the South African private sector, until there is substantial progress toward the full participation of all the people of South Africa in the social, political, and economic life in that country and toward an end to discrimination based on race or ethnic origin.
— ban the sale or transfer of sophisticated computers and nuclear technology to South Africa and the importation of South African gold coins.
— reimpose export controls in effect during the Carter Administration which were relaxed by the Reagan Administration.
— withdraw landing rights to South African aircraft.

The Democratic Party condemns South Africa for unjustly holding political prisoners. Soviet harassment of the Sakharovs is identical to South African house arrests of political opponents of the South African regime. Specifically, the detention of Nelson Mandela, leader of the African National Congress, and Winnie Mandela must be brought to the world's attention, and we demand their immediate release. In addition, we demand the immediate release of all other political prisoners in South Africa.

A Democratic Administration will work as well toward legitimate rights of self-determination of the peoples of Namibia by:
— demanding compliance with U.N. Security Council Resolution 435 — the six-year-old blueprint for Namibian independence;
— imposing severe fines on U.S. companies that violate the United Nations Decree prohibiting foreign exploitation of Namibian mineral wealth until Namibia attains independence;
— progressively increasing effective sanctions against South Africa unless and until it grants independence to Namibia and abolishes its own abhorrent apartheid system.

Asia — Our relationship with the countries of Asia and the Pacific Basin will continue to be of increasing importance. The political, cultural, economic, and strategic ties which link the United States to this region cannot be ignored.

With our Asian friends and allies, we have a common cause in preserving the security and enhancing democracy in the area.

With our Asian trading partners, we share a common interest in expanding commerce and fair trade between us, as evidenced by the 33 percent of total American trade now conducted with those countries.

And with the growing number of Asian/Pacific-Americans, we welcome the strength and vitality which increased cultural ties bring to this country.

Our relationship with Japan is a key to the maintenance of peace, security, and development in Asia and the Pacific region. Mutual respect, enhanced cooperation, and steady diplomacy must guide our dealings with Japan. At the same time, as allies and friends, we must work to resolve areas of disagreement. A Democratic President, therefore, will press for increased access to Japanese as well as other Asian markets for American firms and their products. Finally, a Democratic President will expect Japan to continue moving toward assuming its fair share of the burden of collective security — in self-defense as well as in foreign assistance and democratic development.

Our security in the Pacific region is also closely tied to the well-being of our long-time allies, Australia and New Zealand. A Democratic President will honor and strengthen our security commitment to ANZUS as well as to other Southest Asian friends.

Our relationship with the People's Republic of China must also be nurtured and strengthened. The Democratic Party believes that our developing relations with the PRC offer a historic opportunity to bring one quarter of the world's population into the community of nations, to strengthen a counterweight to Soviet expansionism, and to enhance economic relations that offer great potential for mutual advantage. At the same time, we recognize our historic ties to the people on Taiwan and we will continue to honor our commitments to them, consistent with the Taiwan Relations Act.

Our own principles and interests demand that we work with those in Asia, as well as elsewhere, who can encourage democratic institutions and support greater respect for human rights. A Democratic President will work closely with the world's largest democracy, India, and maintain mutually beneficial ties. A Democratic President will press for the restoration of full democracy in the Philippines, further democratization and the elimination of martial law in Taiwan, the return to freedom of speech and press in South Korea, and restoration of human rights for the people of East Timor. Recognizing the strategic importance of Pakistan and the close relationship which has existed between our two countries, a Democratic President would press to restore democracy and terminate its nuclear weapons program. Finally, a Democratic President would press for the fullest possible accounting of Americans still missing in Indochina.

For the past four years, the Soviet Union has been engaged in a brutal effort to crush the resistance of the people of Afghanistan. It denies their right to independence. It is trying to stamp out their culture and to deny them the right to practice their religion, Islam. But despite appalling costs, the people of Afghanistan continue to resist — demonstrating the same qualities of human aspiration and fortitude that made our own nation great. We must continue to oppose Soviet aggression in Afghanistan. We should support the efforts of the Afghanistan freedom fighters with material assistance.

If the Soviet Union is prepared to abide by the principles of international law and human dignity, it should find the U.S. prepared to help produce a peaceful settlement.

Global Debt and Development

The Democratic Party will pursue policies for economic development, for aid and trade that meet the needs of the people of the developing world and that further our own national interest. The next Democratic President will support development policies that meet the basic needs of the poor for food, water, energy, medical care, and shelter rather than "trickle down" policies that never reach those on the bottom. The next Democratic Administration will give preference in its foreign assistance to countries with democratic institutions and respect for human rights.

A Democratic President will seek to cut back record U.S. budget deficits and interest rates not only for our own economic well-being, but to reduce the economic crisis confronting so many industrialized and developing states alike.

Mr. Reagan has perceived national security in very limited and parochial terms, and thus has failed completely to grasp the significance of the international debt which now has sky-rocketed to some $800 billion. In 1983, some thirty nations accounting for half of this total were forced to seek restructuring of their debts with public and private creditors because they were unable to meet their debt payments.

The U.S. economy is directly linked to the costs of these loans through their variable interest rates (tied to the U.S. prime rate). A rise in the U.S. prime rate by one percent added more than $4 billion to the annual interest costs associated with these external debts. The struggle to meet their external debts has slashed the purchasing power of these developing countries and forced them to curtail imports from the U.S. This accounts for one-third to one-half of the adverse turn in the U.S. trade deficit, which is projected to reach $130 billion this year. The social and political stability of these developing countries is seriously challenged by the debt crisis. In light of the interdependence of the international economy, the crisis also threatens the very foundation of the international financial system. To answer these dangers, the Democratic Administration will:

— Call immediately for discussions on improving the functioning of the international monetary systems and on developing a comprehensive long-term approach to the international debt problem.

— Instruct the Treasury Department to work with the Federal Reserve Board, U.S. bank regulators, key private banks, and the finance ministers and central bankers of Europe and Japan, to develop a short-term program for reducing the debt service obligations of less developed countries, while 1) preserving the safety and soundness of the international banking system and 2) ensuring that the costs of the program are shared equitably among all parties to existing and rescheduled debts.

— Recommend an increase in the lending capacity of the World Bank, as well as an increase in the lending capacity of the Export-Import Bank of the U.S., to ensure that debtor nations obtain adequate capital for investment in export industries.

— Review international trade barriers which limit the ability of these countries to earn foreign exchange.

Security assistance can, in appropriate circumstances, help our friends meet legitimate defense needs. But shifting the balance from economic development toward military sales, as has occurred over the past three and one-half years, sets back the cause of peace and justice, fuels regional arms races, and places sophisticated weapons in the hands of those who could one day turn them back upon us and upon our friends and allies. The Democratic Party seeks now, as in the past, effective international agreements to limit and reduce the transfer of conventional arms.

A Democratic President will seize new opportunities to make major advances at limited cost in the health and survival of the world's poorest people — thus enabling more people to contribute to and share in the world's resources, and promoting stability and popular participation in their societies. Recognizing that unrestrained population growth constitutes a danger for economic progress and political stability, a Democratic President will restore full U.S. support for national and international population programs that are now threatened by the policies of the Reagan Administration.

A Democratic President will work to see the power and prestige of the U.S. fully committed to the reform and strengthening of the United Nations and other international agencies in the pursuit of their original purposes — peace, economic and social welfare, education, and human rights.

Because of the economic instability caused by global debts and by other problems, unprecedented migration into the United States and other parts of the world is occurring in the form of economic refugees. The Democratic Party will support economic development programs so as to aid nations in reducing migration from their countries, and thereby reduce the flow of economic refugees to the U.S. and other parts of the world.

Rather than scuttling the international Law of the Sea negotiations after over a decade of bipartisan U.S. involvement, a Democratic President will actively pursue efforts to achieve an acceptable Treaty and related agreements that protect U.S. interests in all uses of ocean space.

Human Rights and Democratic Solidarity

The Democratic Party believes that we need new approaches to replace the failed Republican policies. We need sustained, personal, presidential leadership in foreign policy and arms control. We need a President who will meet with the Soviets to challenge them to reduce the danger of nuclear war, who will become personally involved in reviving the Camp David peace process, who will give his or her full support to the Contadora negotiations, and who will press the South Africans to repeal their policies of apartheid and destabilization. We need a President who will understand that human rights and national security interests are mutually supportive. We need a President to restore our influence, enhance our security, pursue democracy and freedom, and work unremittingly for peace. With firm purpose, skill, sensitivity, and a recovery of our own pride in what we are — a Democratic President will build an international alliance of free people to promote these great causes.

A Democratic President will pursue a foreign policy that advances basic civil and political rights — freedom of speech, association, thought and religion, the right to leave, freedom of the integrity of the person, and the prohibition of torture, arbitrary detention and cruel, inhuman and degrading treatment — and that seeks as well to attain basic, economic, social, and cultural rights. A Democratic President's concern must extend from the terror of the Russian Gulag to the jails of Latin generals. The banning of South African blacks is no more acceptable than the silencing of Cuban poets. A Democratic President will end U.S. support for dictators throughout the world from Haiti to the Philippines. He or she will support and defend the observance of basic human rights called for in the Universal Declaration of Human Rights and the Helsinki Final Act. He or she will seek, through both quiet diplomacy and public measures, the release of political prisoners and the free immigration of prosecuted individuals and peoples around the world. He or she will seek U.S. ratification of the Genocide Convention, the International Covenants on Human Rights, and the American Convention on Human Rights, as well as the establishment of a U.N. High Commissioner for Human Rights. He or she will fulfill the spirit as well as the letter of our legislation calling for the denial of military and economic assistance to governments and systematically violate human rights.

The Democratic Party believes that whether it is in response to totalitarianism in the Soviet Union or repression in Latin America and East Asia, to apartheid in South Africa or martial law in Poland, to terrorism in Libya or the reign of terror in Iran, or to barbaric aggression in Southeast Asia and Afghanistan, the foreign policy of the United States must be unmistakably on the side of those who love freedom.

As Democrats and as Americans, we will make support for democracy, human rights, and economic and social justice the cornerstone of our policy. These are the most revolutionary ideas on our planet. They are not to be feared. They are the hallmarks of the democratic century that lies before us.

MONDALE, FERRARO
ACCEPTANCE SPEECHES
July 19, 1984

Ending a long and difficult nomination campaign with a display of party unity and a historic vice presidential choice, Walter F. Mondale July 19 sounded the opening themes of his challenge to President Ronald Reagan: family, fairness, the flag, and the future.

Accepting their nominations July 19 before cheering, flag-waving delegates at the Democratic National Convention in San Francisco, the presidential candidate and his running mate, Rep. Geraldine A. Ferraro of New York, served notice that they would hold Reagan to account for his policies in their uphill battle to capture the White House. "Here is the truth about the [nation's] future," Mondale told the Democrats as they wrapped up their four-day convention. "We are living on borrowed money and borrowed time."

Emphasis on Unity

The spectacle of Mondale and Ferraro, with their families, celebrating with delegates in the jammed Moscone Center, capped a week in which the Democrats came together to choose their ticket and shore up party unity. Toward that end, the convention succeeded to a greater degree than had seemed possible when the former vice president was battling Sen. Gary Hart of Colorado and the Rev. Jesse Jackson in the primaries and caucuses. There was little acrimony over consideration of the party platform. And, once Mondale was nominated, the three rivals seemed to put aside their most visible differences. (Platform, p. 549)

The 56-year-old Minnesotan had been the apparent winner since the final round of primaries on June 5, when he took New Jersey, which gave him the 1,967 pledged delegates needed to take the nomination. Mondale finished the convention balloting with nearly 1,000 votes more than Hart, his closest competitor, yet he was by no means the overwhelming choice. He polled 2,191 votes — about 55 percent of a possible 3,933.

Despite fears that radical and homosexual elements in San Francisco would stage confrontations in the streets outside the convention center — evoking memories of the party's 1968 catastrophe in Chicago — there were no violent incidents, although there were several minor confrontations between demonstrators and police. Several hundred thousand homosexuals and labor union members marched peacefully in separate demonstrations July 15, and protestors representing a variety of causes gathered throughout convention week in the giant parking lot across the street from the convention center.

Cuomo Keynote Address

The Democratic unity displayed in San Francisco — so different from the 1980 convention, when the struggle between Carter and Sen. Edward M. Kennedy of Massachusetts left the party torn and battered — was due largely to delegates' deeply felt antipathy to the policies of the Reagan administration. The unusual harmony was also due, at least in part, to Gov. Mario M. Cuomo of New York, who electrified delegates with his keynote address on the opening night, July 16. In an eloquent appeal for family values and compassion for the poor, he set the tone for the rest of the convention. His speech was rivaled in intensity only by Ferraro's nomination by acclamation July 19 and an impassioned speech given by Jackson on July 17.

Speaking forcefully but without dramatic oratorical flourishes, and repeatedly interrupted by emotional applause, Cuomo combined an appeal to Democratic traditions with specific attacks on the domestic and foreign policies of the Reagan administration. Noting Reagan's reference to America as "a shining city on a hill," Cuomo said that "the hard truth is that not everyone is sharing in this city's splendor and glory."

"There is despair, Mr. President," Cuomo continued, "in the faces that you don't see, in the places that you don't visit in your shining city."

The theme of family unity was a major thread running throughout Cuomo's speech. Democrats, he said, were united by "a single fundamental idea that describes better than most text books and any speech that I could write what a proper government should be. The idea of family. Mutuality. The sharing of benefits and burdens for the good of all." In one of the speech's most emotional moments, Cuomo referred to his own father, who had arrived from Italy more than 50 years before. "I learned about our kind of democracy from my father. And, I learned about our obligation to each other from him and from my mother."

Mondale, Ferraro Speeches

The product of weeks of intensive work by the candidate and a team of advisers, Mondale's acceptance speech July 19 was a carefully drawn outline for his campaign against Reagan. Although the former vice president had been criticized for lacking speech-making flair during the nomination campaign, he repeatedly brought delegates to their feet during his address.

To introduce Mondale, the party turned to Kennedy, one of its most effective practitioners of rousing oratory. Kennedy's booming voice filled the hall with denunciations of Reagan and the Republican Party, which he called a "cold citadel of privilege."

"By his choice of Geraldine Ferraro, Walter Mondale has already done more for this country in one short day than Ronald Reagan has done in four long years in office," he said, as delegates cheered and stomped their feet.

Shortly before Mondale's address, aides had passed out thousands of small American flags to delegates, so the crowd was a sea of red, white, and blue when the former vice president arrived on the podium.

Pledging a government of "new realism" that would combine strong but conciliatory foreign policies with tough economic initiatives, Mondale vowed in his address to squeeze the budget and raise taxes to reduce soaring deficits. He spoke of "values," of "paying your dues" and "rising on merit."

That theme ran through Ferraro's acceptance speech, delivered earlier the evening of July 19, as delegates interrupted her repeatedly with applause and chants of "Gerry, Gerry." To Ferraro, the first woman put on the national ticket by a major party, her nomination by acclamation was a special honor. Quoting the late Rev. Martin Luther King Jr., she said that " 'Occasionally in life there are moments which cannot be completely explained in words. Their meaning can only be articulated by the inaudible language of the heart.'

"Tonight is such a moment for me. My heart is filled with pride."

Following are the texts of former vice president Walter F. Mondale's speech accepting the Democratic presidential nomination and New York Rep. Geraldine A. Ferraro's speech accepting the vice presidential nomination, both delivered July 19, 1984. (Boldface headings in brackets have been added by Congressional Quarterly to highlight the organization of the texts.):

MONDALE ACCEPTANCE SPEECH

My fellow Democrats, my fellow Americans:

I accept your nomination. Behind us now is the most wide open race in political history.

It was noisy — but our voices were heard. It was long — but our stamina was tested. It was hot — but the heat was passion, and not anger. It was a roller coaster — but it made me a better candidate, and it will make me a stronger president of the United States.

I do not envy the drowsy harmony of the Republican Party. They squelch debate; we welcome it. They deny differences; we bridge them. The are uniform; we are united. They are a portrait of privilege; we are a mirror of America.

Just look at us at here tonight: Black and white, Asian and Hispanic, Native and immigrant, young and old, urban and rural, male and female — from yuppie to lunchpail, from sea to shining sea. We're all here tonight in this convention speaking for America. And when we in this hall speak for America, it is America speaking.

> When we speak of family, the voice is Mario Cuomo's.
> When we speak of change, the words are Gary Hart's.
> When we speak of hope, the fire is Jesse Jackson's.
> When we speak of caring, the spirit is Ted Kennedy's.
> When we speak of patriotism, the strength is John Glenn's.
> When we speak of the future, the message is Geraldine Ferraro.
> And now we leave San Francisco — together.

[Future of America]

And over the next hundred days, in every word we say, and every life we touch, we will be fighting for the future of America.

Joan and I are parents of three wonderful children who will live much of their lives in the twenty-first century. This election is a referendum on their future — and on ours. So tonight I'd like to speak to the young people of America — and to their parents and to their grandparents.

I'm Walter Mondale. You may have heard of me — but you may not really know me. I grew up in the farm towns of southern Minnesota. My dad was a preacher, and my mom was a music teacher. We never had a dime. But we were rich in the values that were important; and I've carried those values with me ever since.

They taught me to work hard; to stand on my own; to play by the rules; to tell the truth; to obey the law; to care for others; to love our country; to cherish our faith.

My story isn't unique.

In the last few weeks, I've deepened my admiration for someone who shares those same values. Her immigrant father loved our country. Her widowed mother sacrificed for her family. And her own career is an American classic: Doing your work. Earning your way. Paying your dues. Rising on merit.

My presidency will be about those values. My vice president will be Geraldine Ferraro.

Tonight, we open a new door to the future. Mr. Reagan calls it "tokenism." We call it America.

Ever since I graduated from Elmore High, I've been a Democrat. I was attorney general of my state; then a U.S. senator. Then, an honest, caring man — Jimmy Carter — picked me as his running mate and in 1976 I was elected vice president. And in 1980, Ronald Reagan beat the pants off us.

So tonight, I want to say something to those of you across our country who voted for Mr. Reagan — Republicans, Independents, and yes, some Democrats: I heard you. And our party heard you.

After we lost we didn't tell the American people that they were wrong. Instead, we began asking you what our mistakes had been. And for four years, I listened to all of the people of our country. I traveled everywhere. It seemed like I had visited every acre of America.

It wasn't easy. I remember late one night, as I headed from a speech in one city to a hotel a thousand miles away, someone said to me, "Fritz, I saw you on TV. Are those bags under your eyes natural?" And I said, "No, I got them the old-fashioned way. I earned them."

To the thousands of Americans who welcomed me into your homes and into your businesses, your churches and synagogues: I thank you.

You confirmed my belief in our country's values. And you helped me learn and grow.

[New Realism]

So, tonight we come to you with a new realism: Ready for the future, and recapturing the best in our tradition.

We know that America must have a strong defense, and a sober view of the Soviets.

We know that government must be as well-managed as it is well-meaning.

We know that a healthy, growing private economy is the key to the future.

We know that Harry Truman spoke the truth when he said: "A President ... has to be able to say *yes* and *no*, but mostly no."

Look at our platform. There are no defense cuts that weaken our security; no business taxes that weaken our economy; no laundry lists that raid our Treasury.

We are wiser, stronger, and focused on the future. If Mr. Reagan wants to re-run the 1980 campaign: Fine. Let them fight over the past. We're fighting for the American future — and that's why we're going to win this campaign.

One last word to those who voted for Mr. Reagan.

I know what you were saying. But I also know what you were not saying.

You did not vote for a $200 billion deficit.

You did not vote for an arms race.

You did not vote to turn the heavens into a battleground.

You did not vote to savage Social Security and Medicare.

You did not vote to destroy family farming.

You did not vote to trash the civil rights laws.

You did not vote to poison the environment.

You did not vote to assault the poor, the sick, and the disabled.

And you did not vote to pay fifty bucks for a fifty-cent light bulb.

Four years ago, many of you voted for Mr. Reagan because he promised you'd be better off. And today, the rich are better off. But working Americans are worse off, and the middle class is standing on a trap door.

Lincoln once said that ours is to be a government of the people, by the people, and for the people. What we have today is a government of the rich, by the rich, and for the rich. And we're going to make a change in November. Look at the record.

[Reagan Record]

First, there was Mr. Reagan's tax program. What happened was, he gave each of his rich friends enough tax relief to buy a Rolls Royce — and then he asked your family to pay for the hub caps.

Then they looked the other way at the rip-offs, soaring utility bills, phone bills, medical bills.

Then they crimped our future. They let us be routed in international competition, and now the help-wanted ads are full of listings for executives, and for dishwashers — but not much in between.

Then they socked it to workers. They encouraged executives to vote themselves huge bonuses — while using King Kong tactics to make workers take Hong Kong wages.

Mr. Reagan believes that the genius of America is in the boardrooms and exclusive country clubs. I believe that the greatness can be found in the men and women who built our nation; do its work; and defend our freedom.

[Truth About the Future]

If this administration has a plan for a better future, they're keeping it a secret.

Here is the truth about the future: We are living on borrowed money and borrowed time. These deficits hike interest rates, clobber exports, stunt investment, kill jobs, undermine growth, cheat our kids, and shrink our future.

Whoever is inaugurated in January, the American people will have to pay Mr. Reagan's bills. The budget will be squeezed. Taxes will go up. And anyone who says they won't is not telling the truth to the American people.

I mean business. By the end of my first term, I will reduce the Reagan budget deficit by two-thirds.

Let's tell the truth. It must be done, it must be done. Mr. Reagan will raise taxes, and so will I. He won't tell you. I just did.

There's another difference. When he raises taxes, it won't be done fairly. He will sock it to average-income families again, and leave his rich friends alone. And I won't stand for it. And neither will you and neither will the American people.

To the corporations and freeloaders who play the loopholes or pay no taxes, my message is: Your free ride is over.

To the Congress, my message is: We must cut spending and pay as we go. If you don't hold the line, I will: That's what the veto is for.

Now that's my plan to cut the deficit. Mr. Reagan is keeping his plan secret until after the election. That's not leadership; that's salesmanship. And I think the American people know the difference.

I challenge tonight, I challenge Mr. Reagan to put his plan on the table next to mine — and then let's debate it on national television before the American people. Americans want the truth about the future — not after the election.

When the American economy leads the world, the jobs are here, the prosperity is here for our children. But that's not what's happening today. This is the worst trade year in American history. Three million of our best jobs have gone overseas.

Mr. Reagan has done nothing about it. They have no plan to get our competitive edge back. But we do. We will cut the deficits, reduce interest rates, make our exports affordable, and make America number one again in the world economy.

We will launch a renaissance in education, in science, and learning. A mind is a terrible thing to waste. And this must be the best-educated, best-trained generation in American history. And I will lead our nation forward to the best system that this nation has ever seen. We must do it, we must do it.

It is time for America to have a season of excellence. Parents must turn off that television; students must do their homework; teachers must teach; and America compete. We'll be number one if we follow those rules; let's get with it in America again.

To big companies that send our jobs overseas, my message is: We need those jobs here at home. And our country won't help your business — unless your business helps our country.

To countries that close their markets to us, my message is: We will not be pushed around any more. We will have a president who stands up for American workers and American businesses and American farmers in international trade.

When I grew up, and people asked us to imagine the future we were full of dreams. But a few months ago, when I visited a grade school class in Texas and asked the children to imagine the future, they talked to me about nuclear war.

As we've neared the election, this administration has begun to talk about a safer world. But there's a big difference: As president, I will work for peace from my first day in office — and not from my first day campaigning for re-election.

As president, I will reassert American values. I'll press for human rights in Central America, and for the removal of all foreign forces from the region. And in my first hundred days, I will stop the illegal war in Nicaragua.

We know the deep differences with the Soviets. And America condemns their repression of dissidents and Jews; their suppression of Solidarity; their invasion of Afghanistan; their meddling around the world.

But the truth is that between us, we have the capacity to destroy the planet. Every president since the bomb went off understood that and talked with the Soviets and negotiated arms control. Why has this administration failed? Why haven't they tried? Why can't they understand the cry of Americans and human beings for sense and sanity in control of these God awful weapons? Why, why?

Why can't we meet in summit conferences with the Soviet Union at least once a year? Why can't we reach agreements to save this earth? The truth is, we can.

President Kennedy was right when he said: We must never negotiate out of fear. But we must never fear to negotiate. For the sake of civilization we must negotiate a mutual, verifiable nuclear freeze before those weapons destroy us all.

[A Second Mondale Term]

The second term of the Mondale-Ferraro Administration will begin in 1989.

By the start of the next decade, I want to ask our children their dreams, and hear not one word about nuclear nightmares.

By the start of the next decade, I want to walk into any classroom in America and hear some of the brightest students say, "I want to be a teacher."

By the start of the next decade, I want to walk into any public health clinic in America and hear the doctor say, "We haven't seen a hungry child this year."

By the start of the next decade, I want to walk into any store in America and pick up the best product, of the best quality, at the best price; and turn it over; and read, "Made in the U.S.A."

By the start of the next decade, I want to meet with the most successful business leaders anywhere in America, and see as many minorities and women in that room as I see here in this room tonight.

By the start of the next decade, I want to point to the Supreme Court and say, "Justice is in good hands."

Before the start of the next decade, I want to go to my second Inaugural, and raise my right hand, and swear to "preserve, protect, and defend" a Constitution that includes the Equal Rights Amendment.

My friends, America is a future each generation must enlarge; a door each generation must open; a promise each generation must keep.

For the rest of my life, I want to talk to young people about their future.

And whatever their race, whatever their religion, whatever their sex, I want to hear some of them say what I say — with joy and reverence — tonight: "I want to be president of the United States."

Thank you very much.

FERRARO ACCEPTANCE SPEECH

Ladies and gentlemen of the convention: My name is Geraldine Ferraro. I stand before you to proclaim tonight: America is the land where dreams can come true for all of us.

As I stand before the American people and think of the honor this great convention has bestowed upon me, I recall the words of Dr. Martin Luther King Jr., who made America stronger by making America more free.

He said: "Occasionally in life there are moments which cannot be completely explained by words. Their meaning can only be articulated by the inaudible language of the heart."

Tonight is such a moment for me.

My heart is filled with pride.

My fellow citizens, I proudly accept your nomination for vice president of the United States.

And I am proud to run with a man who will be one of the great presidents of this century, Walter F. Mondale.

[The Future]

Tonight, the daughter of a woman whose highest goal was a future for her children talks to our nation's oldest party about a future for us all.

Tonight, the daughter of working Americans tells all Americans that the future is within our reach — if we're willing to reach for it.

Tonight, the daughter of an immigrant from Italy has been chosen to run for [vice] president in the new land my father came to love.

Our faith that we can shape a better future is what the American dream is all about. The promise of our country is that the rules are fair. If you work hard and play by the rules, you can earn your share of America's blessings.

Those are the beliefs I learned from my parents. And those are the values I taught my students as a teacher in the public schools of New York City.

At night, I went to law school. I became an assistant district attorney, and I put my share of criminals behind bars. I believe: If you obey the law, you should be protected. But if you break the law, you should pay for your crime.

When I first ran for Congress, all the political experts said a Democrat could not win in my home district of Queens. But I put my faith in the people and the values that we shared. And together, we proved the political experts wrong.

In this campaign, Fritz Mondale and I have put our faith in the people. And we are going to prove the experts wrong again.

We are going to win, because Americans across this country believe in the same basic dream.

[Elmore, Minn., and Queens]

Last week, I visited Elmore, Minn., the small town where Fritz Mondale was raised. And soon Fritz and Joan will visit our family in Queens.

Nine hundred people live in Elmore. In Queens, there are 2,000 people on one block. You would think we would be different, but we're not.

Children walk to school in Elmore past grain elevators; in Queens, they pass by subway stops. But, no matter where they live, their future depends on education — and their parents are willing to do their part to make those schools as good as they can be.

In Elmore, there are family farms; in Queens, small businesses. But the men and women who run them all take pride in supporting their families through hard work and initiative.

On the Fourth of July in Elmore, they hang flags out on Main Street; in Queens, they fly them over Grand Avenue. But all of us love our country, and stand ready to defend the freedom that it represents.

[Playing by the Rules]

Americans want to live by the same set of rules. But under this administration, the rules are rigged against too many of our people.

It isn't right that every year, the share of taxes paid by individual citizens is going up, while the share paid by large corporations is getting smaller and smaller. The rules say: Everyone in our society should contribute their fair share.

It isn't right that this year Ronald Reagan will hand the American people a bill for interest on the national debt larger than the entire cost of the federal government under John F. Kennedy.

Our parents left us a growing economy. The rules say: We must not leave our kids a mountain of debt.

It isn't right that a woman should get paid 59 cents on the dollar for the same work as a man. If you play by the rules, you deserve a fair day's pay for a fair day's work.

It isn't right that — that if trends continue — by the year 2000 nearly all of the poor people in America will be women and children. The rules of a decent society say, when you distribute sacrifice in times of austerity, you don't put women and children first.

It isn't right that young people today fear they won't get the Social Security they paid for, and that older Americans fear that they will lose what they have already earned. Social Security is a contract between the last generation and the next, and the rules say: You don't break contracts. We're going to keep faith with older Americans.

We hammered out a fair compromise in the Congress to save Social Security. Every group sacrificed to keep the system sound. It is time Ronald Reagan stopped scaring our senior citizens.

It isn't right that young couples question whether to bring children into a world of 50,000 nuclear warheads.

That isn't the vision for which Americans have struggled for more than two centuries. And our future doesn't have to be that way.

Change is in the air, just as surely as when John Kennedy beckoned America to a new frontier; when Sally Ride rocketed into space and when Rev. Jesse Jackson ran for the office of president of the United States.

By choosing a woman to run for our nation's second highest office, you sent a powerful signal to all Americans. There are no doors we cannot unlock. We will place no limits on achievement.

If we can do this, we can do anything.

Tonight, we reclaim our dream. We're going to make the rules of American life work fairly for all Americans again.

To an Administration that would have us debate all over again whether the Voting Rights Act should be renewed and whether segregated schools should be tax exempt, we say, Mr. President: Those debates are over.

On the issue of civil, voting rights and affirmative action for minorities, we must not go backwards. We must — and we will — move forward to open the doors of opportunity.

To those who understand that our country cannot prosper unless we draw on the talents of all Americans, we say: We will pass the Equal Rights Amendment. The issue is not what America can do for women, but what women can do for America.

To the Americans who will lead our country into the 21st century, we say: We will not have a Supreme Court that turns the clock back to the 19th century.

To those concerned about the strength of American family values, as I am, I say: We are going to restore those values — love, caring, partnership — by including, and not excluding, those whose beliefs differ from our own. Because our own faith is strong, we will fight to preserve the freedom of faith for others.

To those working Americans who fear that banks, utilities, and large special interests have a lock on the White House, we say: Join us; let's elect a people's president; and let's have government by and for the American people again.

To an Administration that would savage student loans and education at the dawn of a new technological age, we say: You fit the classic definition of a cynic; you know the price of everything, but the value of nothing.

To our students and their parents, we say: We will insist on the highest standards of excellence because the jobs of the future require skilled minds.

To young Americans who may be called to our country's service, we say: We know your generation of Americans will proudly answer our country's call, as each generation before you.

This past year, we remembered the bravery and sacrifice of Americans at Normandy. And we finally paid tribute — as we should have done years ago — to that unknown soldier who represents all the brave young Americans who died in Vietnam.

Let no one doubt, we will defend America's security and the cause of freedom around the world. But we want a president who tells us what America is fighting for, not just what we are fighting against. We want a president who will defend human rights — not just where it is convenient — but wherever freedom is at risk — from Chile to Afghanistan, from Poland to South Africa.

To those who have watched this administration's confusion in the Middle East, as it has tilted first toward one and then another of Israel's long-time enemies and wondered. "Will America stand by her friends and sister democracy?" We say: America knows who her friends are in the Middle East and around the world.

America will stand with Israel always.

Finally, we want a President who will keep America strong, but use that strength to keep America and the world at peace. A nuclear freeze is not a slogan: It is a tool for survival in the nuclear age. If we leave our children nothing else, let us leave them this Earth as we found it — whole and green and full of life.

I know in my heart that Walter Mondale will be that president.

A wise man once said, "Every one of us is given the gift of life, and what a strange gift it is. If it is preserved jealously and selfishly, it impoverishes and saddens. But if it is spent for others, it enriches and beautifies."

My fellow Americans: We can debate policies and programs. But in the end what separates the two parties in this election campaign is whether we use the gift of life — for others or only ourselves.

Tonight, my husband, John, and our three children are in this hall with me. To my daughters, Donna and Laura, and my son, John Jr., I say: My mother did not break faith with me . . . and I will not break faith with you. To all the children of America, I say: The generation before ours kept faith with us, and like them, we will pass on to you a stronger, more just America.

Thank you.

August

August

REPUBLICAN PARTY PLATFORM

August 21, 1984

After four days of spirited debate, the 106-member Republican Platform Committee August 17 adopted a 1984 campaign document that conformed in virtually all respects to the themes President Ronald Reagan had sounded during his first term in office. The platform was ratified with no debate by delegates to the Republican National Convention in Dallas August 21. On almost every aspect of public policy, the document stood in stark contrast to the platform adopted by the Democrats at their July 16-19 convention in San Francisco. (Democratic platform, p. 549)

However, in its strong stand against tax increases and its criticism of the independent Federal Reserve Board, the Republican platform went further than the White House wanted. Administration operatives led by former transportation secretary Drew Lewis sought to soften the tax plank, but while they succeeded in modifying some of the language, they were unable to alter it substantially. The tax section of the Republican platform pledged that the party would continue efforts to lower tax rates and would support tax reform that "will lead to a fair and simple tax system." The platform said the party believed that a "modified flat tax — with specific exemptions for such items as mortgage interest — is a most promising approach."

Taxes had mushroomed as an election issue when Democratic presidential nominee Walter F. Mondale said in his acceptance speech at the Democratic National Convention July 19 that regardless of who won in November, tax increases would be necessary in 1985 to combat record federal budget deficits. Mondale also accused Reagan of having a secret plan to raise taxes. (Mondale speech, p. 547)

Despite a vigorous hour-long debate August 16, the GOP platform committee refused to endorse either the proposed Equal Rights Amendment (ERA) — which Reagan opposed — or compromise language stating that the Republican Party respected those who supported the amendment. The committee also turned aside challenges by party moderates to language endorsing voluntary prayer in public schools and opposing federal financing for abortions under any circumstances. Some moderate delegates had considered trying to offer a minority plank on the ERA stating respect for differing Republican views on the issue. But moderates determined that they lacked support to bring a floor challenge.

Major Planks

The platform included the following major points:

● Unqualified opposition to tax increases, which were dismissed as a "misguided effort to balance the budget."

● A call for passage by Congress of a constitutional amendment to require a balanced federal budget.

● Support for a constitutional convention to write a balanced budget amendment if Congress failed to act on the issue.

● Criticism of Federal Reserve Board policies as "destabilizing," and a suggestion that the gold standard "may be a useful mechanism" for achieving the goal of stable prices.

● Support for the administration's policy in Central America, specifically its support of the government in El Salvador.

● A pledge of party support for putting the United States in a superior military position in the world, although the term "military superiority" that appeared in the 1980 platform was not used in 1984. (1980 platform, Historic Documents of 1980, p. 567)

● A call for repealing the windfall profits tax on oil.

● Support for abolition of the Department of Energy.

● Opposition to quotas to remedy discrimination because they "are the most insidious form of discrimination against the innocent."

● Support for a constitutional amendment to ban abortion and reaffirmation of a statement in the 1980 platform that Reagan should appoint federal judges who opposed abortion.

● Support for the right of students to engage in voluntary school prayer.

Domestic Issues

A multi-section chapter entitled "Security for the Individual" covered the environment, education, individual rights, and "our constitutional system." On the environment, the platform said the party "endorses a strong effort to control and clean up toxic wastes." It asserted further that the GOP "supports the continued commitment to clean air and clean water. This support includes the implementation of meaningful clean air and clean water acts."

The 1980 platform had called for abolition of the Department of Education, which was created in 1979 at the urging of President Jimmy Carter. The 1984 GOP platform stated that education was a "local function, a state responsibility and a federal concern. The federal role should be limited." However, it stopped short of urging that the federal department be disbanded.

In the section on individual rights, the platform devoted several paragraphs to GOP support for women's rights. In one section, the document stated, "President Reagan believes, as do we, that all members of our party are free to work individually for women's progress." At another point, the platform called for "assuring that women have equal opportunity, security and real choices for the promising future." But while it called for "equal pay for equal work," the document said that "with equal emphasis, we oppose the concept of 'comparable worth.' We believe that the free-market system can determine the value of jobs better than any government authority."

On the issue of abortion, the platform picked up language from the 1980 document supporting a constitutional amendment to ban abortion and supporting a ban on federal funding for abortion. An amendment that called for support of federal funding for abortions in the case of rape or incest was rejected.

Foreign Affairs, Defense Issues

In the foreign affairs area, the Republicans took dead aim at the Democrats. The platform declared that the Soviet Union's "globalist ideology and its leadership obsessed with military power make it a threat to freedom and peace on every continent. The Carter-Mondale Administration ignored that threat, and the Democratic candidates underestimate it today. The Carter-Mondale illusion that the Soviet leaders share our ideals and aspirations is not only false but a profound danger to world peace." The platform added that Republicans "reaffirm our belief that Soviet behavior at the negotiating table cannot be divorced from Soviet behavior elsewhere."

This section was similar in tone to the 1980 platform, which declared "the premier challenge facing the United States, its allies and the entire globe is to check the Soviet Union's global ambitions." Although the 1984 campaign document did not contain the call for outright U.S. "military superiority" that appeared in the 1980 platform, the notion that the United States should be the superior power in the world ran through the *chapter. The platform also stated that the Republicans "enthusiasti-cally" supported the development of "non-nuclear, space-based defensive systems" designed to protect the United States from incoming missiles.*

> *Following is the text of the platform adopted on August 21 by delegates to the Republican National Convention in Dallas, Texas. (Boldface headings in brackets have been added by Congressional Quarterly to highlight the organiza-tion of the text):*

Preamble

This year, the American people will choose between two diametrically opposed visions of what America should be.

The Republican Party looks at our people and sees a new dawn of the American spirit.

The Democratic Party looks at our nation and sees the twilight of the American soul.

Republicans affirm that now, as throughout history, the spiritual and intellectual genius of the American people will create a better nation and maintain a just peace. To Republicans, creativity and growth are impera-tives for a new era of opportunity for all.

The Republican Party's vision of America's future, the heart of our 1984 Platform, begins with a basic premise:

> From freedom comes opportunity; from opportunity comes growth; from growth comes progress.

This is not some abstract formula. It is the vibrant, beating heart of the American experience. No matter how complex our problems, no matter how difficult our tasks, it is *freedom* that inspires and guides the American Dream.

If everything depends on freedom — and it does — then securing freedom, at home and around the world, is one of the most important endeavors a free people can undertake.

Thus, the title of our Platform, "America's Future: Free and Secure," is more than a summary of our Platform's message. It is the essence.

The Democratic Party understands none of this. It thinks our country has passed its peak. It offers Americans redistribution instead of expan-sion, contraction instead of growth, and despair instead of hope. In foreign policy it asserts the rhetoric of freedom, but in practice it follows a policy of withdrawal and isolation.

The Democratic Party, in its 1984 Platform, has tried to expropriate the optimism and vision that marked the 1980 Republican Platform.

Rhetorical pilfering of Republican ideals cannot disguise one of history's major ironies: the party whose 1932 standard-bearer told the American people, as president, that all we have to fear is fear itself has itself become the party of fear.

Today we declare ourselves the Party of Hope — not for some but for all.

It has been said that mercy must have a human heart and pity a human face. We agree. Democrats measure social programs in terms of government activity alone. But the divine command to help our neighbor is directed to each individual and not to a bureaucratic machine. Not every problem cries out for a federal solution.

We must help the poor *escape* poverty by building an economy which creates more jobs, the greatest poverty fighter of them all. Not to help the poor is to abandon them and demean our society; but to help the poor without offering them a chance to escape poverty is ultimately to degrade us all.

The great tasks of compassion must be accomplished both by people who care and by policies which foster economic growth to enhance all human development.

In all these areas, at home and abroad, Ronald Reagan has demonstrated the boldness of vision, the optimism for our future, and the confidence in the American people that can transform human lives and the life of a nation. That is what we expect from a President who, wounded by an assassin, walked his way into a hospital and cheerfully assured the world that he and his country would not be deterred from their destiny.

His example has shaped the 1984 Republican Platform, given it meaning and inspired its vision. We stand with President Reagan and with Vice President Bush to make it a reality.

Economic Freedom and Prosperity

FREE ENTERPRISE, DEMOCRACY, AND THE ROLE OF GOVERNMENT

Free enterprise is fundamental to the American way of life. It is inseparable from the social, religious, political, and judicial institutions which form the bedrock of a nation dedicated to individual freedom and human rights.

Economic growth enables all citizens to share in the nation's great physical and spiritual wealth, and it is maximized by giving them the fullest opportunity to engage in economic activities and to retain the rewards of their labor.

Our society provides both a ladder of opportunity on which all can climb to success and a safety net of assistance for those who need it. To safeguard both, government must protect property rights, provide a sound currency, and minimize its intrusions into individual decisions to work, save, invest, and take risks.

The role of the federal government should be limited. We reaffirm our conviction that State and local governments closest to the people are the best and most efficient. While President Reagan has done much to alleviate federal regulatory and bureaucratic burdens on individuals and businesses, Congress has failed to act. The size and scope of the federal government remains much too large and must be reduced.

During the Carter-Mondale Administration, no group of Americans was spared from the impact of a failing economy. Family budgets were stretched to the limit to keep pace with increases in taxes and costs of food, energy, and housing. For the first time, owning a home slipped out of reach for millions. Working people saw their wage increases outpaced by inflation. Older Americans saw their savings and retirement incomes consumed by basic living costs. Young people found job opportunities narrowing. Disadvantaged Americans faced an inefficient and wasteful bureaucracy which perpetuated programs of dependency. American business and industry faced recession, unemployment, and upheaval, as high interest rates, inflation, government regulation, and foreign competition combined to smother all enterprise and strike at our basic industries.

When President Reagan took office in 1981, our economy was in a disastrous state. Inflation raged at 12.4 percent. The cost of living had jumped 45 percent in the Carter-Mondale years. The prime rate was 21.5 percent. Federal spending increases of 17 percent per year, massive tax rate increases due to inflation, and a monetary policy debasing the dollar had destroyed our economic stability.

We brought about a new beginning. Americans are better off than they were four years ago, and they're still improving. Almost six and one-half million have found jobs since the recovery began, the largest increase in our history. One and one-half million have come in manufacturing — a part of our economy designated for stagnation and government control by Democrats. More than 107 million Americans, more than ever before, are working. Their industry proves that policies which increase incentives for work, saving, and investment do lead to economic growth, while the redistributionist policies of the past did cause unemployment, declining incomes, and idle industries.

We will therefore continue to return control over the economy to the people. Our policies will maximize the role of the individual and build on the success of the past four years: (a) the most rapid decline in unemployment of any post-World War II recovery; (b) inflation dramatically reduced; (c) interest rates significantly cut; (d) a 25 percent cut in federal tax rates; (e) automatic tax increases eliminated by indexing tax rates; (f) the financial holdings of American families increased by over $1.8 trillion; (g) oil prices down 35 percent in real terms; and (h) 300 million hours once devoted to government paperwork returned to individuals and business.

Our most important economic goal is to expand and continue the economic recovery and move the nation to full employment without inflation. We therefore oppose any attempts to increase taxes, which would harm the recovery and reverse the trend to restoring control of the economy to individual Americans. We favor reducing deficits by continuing and expanding the strong economic recovery brought about by the policies of this Administration and by eliminating wasteful and unnecessary government spending. Mondale-Ferraro, by contrast, boast that they will raise taxes, with ruinous effects on the economy.

To assure workers and entrepreneurs the capital required to provide jobs and growth, we will further expand incentives for personal saving. We will expand coverage of the Individual Retirement Account, especially to homemakers, and increase and index the annual limits on IRA contributions. We will increase the incentives for savings by moving toward the reduction of taxation of interest income. We will work for indexation of capital assets and elimination of the double taxation of dividends to increase the attractiveness of equity investments for small investors.

We oppose withholding on dividend and interest income. It would discourage saving and investment, create needless paperwork, and rob savers of their due benefits. A higher personal savings rate is key to deficit control. We therefore oppose any disincentives to thrift.

History has proven again and again that wage and price controls will not stop inflation. Such controls only cause shortages, inequities, and ultimately high prices. We remain firmly opposed to the imposition of wage and price controls.

We are committed to bringing the benefits of economic growth to all Americans. Therefore, we support policies which will increases opportunities for the poorest in our society to climb the economic ladder. We will work to establish enterprise zones in urban and rural America; we will work to enable those living in government-owned or subsidized housing to purchase their homes.

As part of our effort to reform the tax system, we will reduce disincentives to employment which too often result in a poverty trap for poor American families.

FISCAL AND MONETARY POLICY

Taxation

A major goal of all Republicans in 1980 was to reduce the oppressive tax rates strangling Americans. The tax burden, which had increased steadily during the Carter-Mondale Administration, was at a record high and scheduled to go even higher. Taxes as a percentage of GNP rose from 18.2 percent in 1976 to 21 percent in 1981 and would have reached 24 percent by 1984. The tax bill for the median-income family of four had risen from $1,713 in 1976 to $2,778 in 1980 and would have reached $3,943 in 1984.

Double-digit inflation had pushed individuals into ever higher marginal tax brackets. High marginal tax rates reduced the incentive for work, saving, and investment, and retarded economic growth, productivity, and job creation.

With the Economic Recovery Tax Act of 1981, we carried out the first phase of tax reduction and reform by cutting marginal tax rates by 25 percent. Tax brackets were indexed to prevent tax hikes through bracket creep. In addition, families received further relief by reducing the marriage penalty and lowering estate and gift taxes.

Businesses and workers benefitted when we replaced outdated depreciation systems with the accelerated cost recovery system, reduced capital gains tax rates, and lowered the pressures which high tax rates place on wage demands. Investment in plants and equipment has increased 16.5 percent since 1982, resulting in 6.3 million new jobs.

In 1980, we promised the American people a tax cut which would be progressive and fair, reducing tax rates across-the-board. Despite Democrat opposition we succeeded in reducing the tax rates of all taxpayers by about 25 percent with low-income taxpayers receiving a slightly larger percentage tax reduction than high-income taxpayers. These sound economic policies have succeeded. We will continue our efforts to further reduce tax rates and now foresee no economic circumstances which would call for increased taxation.

The bulk of the tax cut goes to those who pay most of the taxes: middle-income taxpayers. Nearly three-fourths of its benefits go to taxpayers earning less than $50,000. In fact, these taxpayers now pay a smaller percentage of total income taxes than they did in 1980; and those earning more than $50,000 pay a larger percentage of total income taxes than they did in 1980.

As a result, the income tax system is fairer now than it was under Carter-Mondale. To keep it fair, Republicans indexed the tax code: starting in 1985, individual tax brackets, the zero bracket amount, and the personal exemption will be adjusted annually for inflation. As a result, cost of living raises will no longer push taxpayers into higher brackets.

For years, congressional big spenders used inflation as a silent partner to raise taxes without taking the heat for passing tax increases. With indexing, taxpayers will be protected against that theft. Low- and moderate-income taxpayers benefit the most from indexing and would bear the brunt of the hidden tax increases if it were repealed.

Nearly 80 percent of the tax increase from the repeal of indexing would fall on taxpayers earning less than $50,000. For a family of four earning $10,000, repeal of indexing would result in a staggering 40 percent tax increase over the next five years. We pledge to preserve tax indexing. We will fight any attempt to repeal, modify, or defer it.

The Republican Party pledges to continue our efforts to lower tax rates, change and modernize the tax system, and eliminate the incentive-destroying effects of graduated tax rates. We therefore support tax reform that will lead to a fair and simple tax system and believe a modified flat tax — with specific exemptions for such items as mortgage interest — is a most promising approach.

For families, we will restore the value of personal exemptions, raising it to a minimum of $2,000 and indexing to prevent further erosion. We will preserve the deduction for mortgage interest payments. We will propose an employment income exclusion to assure that tax burdens are not shifted to the poor. Tax reform must not be a guise for tax increases. We believe such an approach will enhance the income and opportunities of families and low- and middle-income Americans.

We oppose taxation of churches, religious schools, or any other religious institutions. However, we do believe that any business income unrelated to the religious function of the institution should be subject to the same taxes paid by competing businesses.

We oppose the setting of artificially high interest rates which would drastically curtail the ability of sellers to finance sales of their own property. Rather, we encourage marketplace transfer of homes, farms, and smaller commercial properties.

Spending and Budget

The Republican Party believes the federal budget must be balanced. We are committed to eliminating deficits and the excessive spending that causes them. In 1980, federal spending was out of control, increasing at a rate of over 17 percent. We have cut that growth rate by almost two-thirds.

But Congress ignored many of the President's budget reforms. It scaled back and delayed the tax cuts. As a result, we began to pay the price for the irresponsible spending and tax policies of the Carter-Mondale Administration. The resulting recession dramatically increased the deficit, and government spending continues at an unacceptable level.

Democrats claim deficits are caused by Americans' paying too little in taxes. Nonsense. We categorically reject proposals to increase taxes in a misguided effort to balance the budget. Tax and spending increases would reduce incentives for economic activity and threaten the recovery.

Even when we achieve full employment and with robust economic growth, federal spending — including credit programs and other off-budget items — will remain too high. As a percentage of GNP, it must be reduced.

The congressional budget process is bankrupt. Its implementation has not brought spending under control, and it must be thoroughly reformed. We will work for the constitutional amendment requiring a balanced federal budget passed by the Republican Senate but blocked by the Democrat-controlled House and denounced by the Democrat Platform. If Congress fails to act on this issue, a constitutional convention should be convened to address only this issue in order to bring deficit spending under control.

The President is denied proper control over the federal budget. To remedy this, we support enhanced authority to prevent wasteful spending, including a line-item veto.

Monetary Policy

Our 1980 Platform promised to bring inflation under control. We did it. This cruelest tax — hitting hardest at the poor, the aged, and those on fixed incomes — raged up to 13.3 percent under Carter-Mondale. We have brought it down to about 4 percent and we strive for lower levels.

The effects of our program have been dramatic. Real, after-tax incomes are rising. Food prices are stable. Interest rates have fallen dramatically, leading to a resurgence in home building, auto purchases, and capital investment.

Just as our tax policy has only laid the groundwork for a new era of prosperity, reducing inflation is only the first step in restoring a stable currency. A dollar now should be worth a dollar in the future. This allows real economic growth without inflation and is the primary goal of our monetary policy.

The Federal Reserve Board's destabilizing actions must therefore stop. We need coordination between fiscal and monetary policy, timely information about Fed decisions, and an end to the uncertainties people face in obtaining money and credit. The Gold Standard may be a useful mechanism for realizing the Federal Reserve's determination to adopt monetary policies needed to sustain price stability.

Domestically, a stable dollar will mean lower interest rates, rising real wages, guaranteed value for retirement and education savings, growth of assets through productive investment, affordable housing, and greater job security.

Internationally, a stable dollar will mean stable exchange rates, protection for contract prices, commodity prices which change only when real production changes, greater resources devoted to job-creating investment, less protectionist pressure, and increased trade and income for all nations.

REGULATORY REFORM

Our 1980 Platform declared that "excessive regulation remains a major component of our nations's spiraling inflation and continues to stifle private initiatives, individual freedom, and State and local government autonomy." President Reagan's regulatory reform program contributed significantly to economic recovery by removing bureaucratic roadblocks and encouraging efficiency. In many fields, government regulation either did not achieve its goals or made limited improvements at exorbitant cost. We have worked with industry and labor to get better results through cooperation rather than coercion.

The flood of regulation has stopped. The number of new regulations has been halved. Unrestrained growth in the size and spending of the regulatory workforce has stopped. Some $150 billion will thereby be saved over the next decade by consumers and businesses. In the past four years alone, 300 million hours of government-mandated paperwork were eliminated. We have reduced the regulatory burden on Americans by making government rules as cost-effective as possible. We must maintain this progress through comprehensive regulatory reform legislation and a constitutional procedure which will enable Congress to properly oversee executive branch rules by reviewing and, if necessary, overturning them.

So consumers can have the widest choice of services at the lowest possible prices, Republicans commit themselves to breaking down artificial barriers to entry created by antiquated regulations. With the explosion of computer technologies just beginning to enhance our way of life, we will encourage rather than hinder innovative competition in telecommunications and financial services.

There are still federal statutes that keep Americans out of the workforce. Arbitrary minimum wage rates, for example, have eliminated hundreds of thousands of jobs and, with them, the opportunity for young people to get productive skills, good work habits, and a weekly paycheck. We encourage the adoption of a youth opportunity wage to encourage employers to hire and train inexperienced workers.

We demand repeal of prohibitions against household manufacturing. Restrictions on work in the home are intolerable intrusions into our private lives and limit economic opportunity, especially for women and the homebound.

SUPPORT FOR SMALL BUSINESS

America's small business entrepreneurs have led the way in fueling economic recovery. Almost all the 11 million non-farm businesses in the United States are small, but they provide over 50 million jobs. We must keep them strong to ensure lasting prosperity. Republicans reaffirm our historic ties with independent business people and pledge continued efforts to help this energetic segment of our economy.

We have created a climate conducive to small business growth. Our tax rate reductions increased incentives for entrepreneurial activity and provided investment capital through incentives to save. Reduced capital gains taxes further stimulated capital formation and increased the return on small business investment. Greater depreciation allowances encouraged modernization. Estate tax changes will allow families to keep the rewards of their labors.

We have insisted on less federal interference with small business. As a result, burdensome regulations were reduced, and runaway agencies like OSHA were reined in. We have ensured that the federal government pays its bills on time or pays interest penalties.

Presidential action has focused needed attention on increased government procurement from small and minority businesses. In FY 1983 the Small Business Administration directed $2.3 billion in federal sole-source contracts to minority firms through its 8(a) program — a 45 percent increase over 1980. This record amount was achieved along with management improvements that eliminated past abuses in that program.

Three million women business owners are generating $40 billion in annual receipts and creating many new jobs. Yet, their enterprises face barriers in credit, access to capital, and technical assistance. They lag far behind in federal procurement contracts. We are dedicated to helping them become full partners in the economic mainstream of small business.

To them and to all who make America grow, we reaffirm our commitment to reduce marginal tax rates further. We oppose any scheme to roll back the estate tax cuts and will seek further reductions for family businesses. Moreover, we support lower capital gains tax rates and indexation of asset values to protect investors from inflation.

We will create enterprise zones to revitalize economically depressed areas by offering simplified regulation and lower taxes for small businesses that relocate there.

We will make it easier for small businesses to compete for government contracts, not only to assist the private sector but also to provide competition and greater cost control in federal purchases.

In a continuing effort to offset our balance of trade, we reaffirm our strong support for this nation's tourism industry.

SCIENCE AND TECHNOLOGY

We pledge to continue the Reagan Administration's science and technology policies, which have enhanced economic recovery and our nation's research capability.

We have refocused federal research and development spending on basic research, and it has increased more than 50 percent.

We propose to extend the incremental research and development tax credit to stimulate greater activity in the private sector.

To allow U.S. firms to compete on an equal footing with foreign companies, we will permit U.S. firms to cooperate in joint research and development projects.

ENERGY

In 1980, energy prices were at all-time highs and rising rapidly. The OPEC cartel had an iron grip on free world economies. Oil imports rose, and domestic production fell under Carter-Mondale price controls and allocations. Competition in energy markets declined.

We have all but eliminated those disastrous policies. President Reagan's immediate decontrol of oil prices precipitated a decline in real oil prices and increased competition in all energy markets. Oil price decontrol crippled the OPEC cartel.

The results have been dramatic. Imported oil prices are down 35 percent in real terms. The real price of gasoline is at a five-year low. Energy consumption has declined relative to economic growth. Energy efficiency increased by 12 percent since 1980, with lower costs to businesses and families. The Strategic Petroleum Reserve is now four times larger than in 1980, providing significant protection against any disruption in imports.

We will complete America's energy agenda. Natural gas should be responsibly decontrolled as rapidly as possible so that families and businesses can enjoy the full benefits of lower prices and greater production, as with decontrolled oil. We are committed to the repeal of the confiscatory windfall profits tax, which has forced the American consumer to pay more for less and left us vulnerable to the energy and economic stranglehold of foreign producers.

While protecting the environment, we should permit abundant American coal to be mined and consumed. Environmentally sound development of oil and natural gas on federal properties (which has brought the taxpayers $20 billion in revenue in the last four years) should continue. We believe that as controls have been lifted from the energy marketplace, conservation and alternative sources of energy, such as solar, wind, and geothermal, have become increasingly cost-effective. We further take pride in the fact that Reagan Administration economic policies have created an environment most favorable to the small businesses that pioneer these alternative technologies.

We now have a sound, long-term program for disposal of nuclear waste. We will work to eliminate unnecessary regulatory procedures so that nuclear plants can be brought on line quickly, efficiently, and safely. We call for an energy policy, the stability and continuity of which will restore and encourage public confidence in the fiscal stability of the nuclear industry.

We are committed to the termination of the Department of Energy. President Reagan has succeeded in abolishing that part which was telling Americans what to buy, where to buy it, and at what price — the regulatory part of DOE. Then he reduced the number of bureaucrats by 25 percent. Now is the time to complete the job.

AGRICULTURE

Securing a Prosperous Rural America

The Republican Party is thankful for, and proud of, the ability of American farmers and ranchers to provide abundant, high quality, and nutritious food and fiber for all our citizens and millions more throughout the world. This unmatched ability to produce is basic to this country's high standard of living. We recognize that a prosperous agriculture is essential to the future of America and to the health and welfare of its people. We have set the stage for securing prosperity in rural America. In 1979, farm and ranch production costs increased 19 percent, in 1983 they actually declined by almost 3 percent. The prime interest rate has been brought down from 21.5 percent to 13 percent. Our reputation as a reliable world food and fiber supplier has been restored. Despite that remarkable beginning, much remains to be done.

We believe well managed, efficient American farm and ranch operations are the most cost-effective and productive food and fiber suppliers in the world, and therefore have the inherent economic capability and right to make a profit from their labor, management, and investments. The primary responsibility of government with respect to agriculture is to create the opportunity for a free and competitive economic and policy environment supportive of the American farmers' and ranchers' industrious and independent spirit and innovative talent. We further believe that, to the extent some well-managed and efficient farms and ranches are temporarily unable to make a profit in the marketplace, it is in the public interest to provide reasonable and targeted assistance.

The Carter-Mondale Administration, and 28 years of a Congress rigidly controlled by the Democrats and out of touch with the people, brought farmers and ranchers to the hardest times since the Great Depression. Farm and ranch incomes fell to disastrous levels. Uncontrolled inflation and the highest interest rates in over a century prevented farmers from operating at a profit, and 300,000 of them went out of business under Carter-Mondale.

In the span of but four devastating years, the Carter-Mondale Administration managed to jeopardize this country's agricultural heritage by putting America's farmers $78 billion further in debt (a 75 percent increase) and inflating farmers' annual food and fiber production costs by $46 billion (55 percent increase). These irresponsible inflationary policies led to spiraling land values and to the illusion of enhanced debt-bearing wealth. This paper wealth was converted into very real and unavoidable debt. Debt payments, combined with record cost of production levels, have presented many farmers and ranchers with severe cash flow problems. On top of all that came the Carter-Mondale grain embargo of 1980. Thus, one begins to understand the origins of the financial stress farmers and ranchers are experiencing today. Adding insult to injury, farmers and ranchers found themselves blamed as Carter-Mondale inflation ballooned consumer food costs by $115 billion, a 50 percent increase in four years.

Republicans support a sound agricultural credit policy, including the Farm Credit System, to meet agriculture's expanding credit needs. We support an extensive examination of agricultural and rural credit and crop insurance programs to assure they are adequately serving our farmers and rural residents.

Interest Rates and Farm and Ranch Indebtedness

The magnitude of indebtedness and the level of interest rates significantly influence farm and ranch profitability. The interrelationship between high interest rates and the high value of the dollar has caused an erosion in our competitive position in export markets. Republicans recognize that lower interest rates are vital to a healthy farm and ranch economy and pledge that an economic priority of the first order will be the further lowering of interest rates by intensifying our efforts to cut federal spending to achieve a balanced budget and reform Federal Reserve policy.

Republicans are very much aware of the devastating impact which high interest rates have had, and continue to have, on the viability of America's farmers and ranchers. We also realize that, unless interest rates decline significantly in the near future, the character of American agriculture and rural life will be tragically changed. For these reasons, we pledge to pursue every possible course of action, including the consideration of temporary interest rate reductions, to ensure the American farmer or rancher is not a patient that dies in the course of a successful economic operation.

Republicans are cognizant that there are many well-managed, efficient, farm and ranch operations which face bankruptcy and foreclosure. The foreclosures and resulting land sales will jeopardize the equity positions of neighboring farms and ranches, compounding financial problems in agriculture. Republicans pledge to implement comprehensive Farmers Home Administration and commercial farm and ranch debt restructuring procedures, including the establishment of local community farm and ranch finance committees, which shall advise borrowers, lenders, and government officials regarding debt restructuring alternatives and farmer and rancher eligibility.

Setting the Stage for
Farm and Ranch Recovery

Sensitive to the needs of farmers and ranchers, we have made the best of the tools available to deal with the Carter-Mondale failure. Among the many specific accomplishments of the Reagan Administration in agriculture, Republicans are proud to have:

• Lifted the Carter-Mondale grain embargo and demonstrated by word and deed that farm and ranch product embargoes will not be used as a tool of foreign policy, negotiated a long term agreement with the Soviet Union, and strengthened our credibility as a reliable supplier by enacting contract sanctity legislation.

• Increased food assistance and agricultural export financing programs to over $7 billion, a record level.

• Challenged unfair export subsidy practices and aggressively countered them with "blended credit" and other export expansion programs.

• Achieved major breakthroughs in Japan's beef and citrus quotas, allowing our exports to double over four years.

• Resisted protectionist efforts by other industries, such as domestic content legislation, that would cause a backlash against U.S. farm and ranch exports.

• Developed and implemented the PIK program to draw down burdensome reserve stocks of major commodities created by the Carter-Mondale embargo.

• Reformed bankruptcy law to provide for accelerated distribution of farm products in bankrupt elevators, acceptance of warehouse receipts and scale tickets as proof of ownership, and allowing a lien against elevator assets for unpaid farmers.

• Eliminated the marriage penalty for a surviving spouse and protected family farms and ranches by exempting, by 1987, up to $600,000 from estate taxes.

• Accelerated depreciation of farm and ranch equipment and buildings and increased the exemption for agricultural vehicles from the heavy vehicle use tax.

• Increased the gasoline tax exemption by 50 percent for alcohol fuels, stimulating demand for domestic grain production and reducing dependency on foreign oil.

• Worked with rural credit and farm and ranch lending institutions to assure adequate capital at the lowest possible interest rates.

• Responded to the emergency financial needs of farmers and ranchers stricken by drought and flood.

We want real profits for farmers and ranchers. We have begun the turnaround on farm and ranch incomes. Sound fiscal, monetary, and growth-oriented tax policies are essential if farmers are to realize sufficient and enduring profits. We support legislation to permit farmers, ranchers, and other self-employed individuals to deduct from their gross income up to one-half of the cost of their personal hospitalization insurance premiums.

Government policies should strengthen the ability of farmers and ranchers to provide quality products at reasonable rates of return in an expanding economy. We believe that federal farm programs should be tailored to meet economic needs and requirements of today's structurally diverse and internationally oriented agriculture. These programs must be sensitive to potential impacts on all agriculture, especially non-program commodities, livestock, agribusiness and rural communities.

Republicans believe that the future of American agriculture lies in the utilization of our rich farmland, advanced technology, and hard working farm and ranch people, to supply food and fiber to the world. Traditional farm programs have threatened the confidence of America's farmers and ranchers and exhausted the patience of American taxpayers. We reject the policy of more of the same, and we further reject the Democrats' public utility vision of agriculture which views it as a problem to be minimized by further political and bureaucratic management. Our new programs will bring the flexibility to adjust to rapidly changing export market conditions and opportunities, and, in a timely and effective manner, respond to the inherent, uncontrollable risks of farming and ranching.

Rural Americans impart a special strength to our national character, important to us all. Whether farmers or not, all rural citizens should have the same consideration as those who live in towns and cities in economic development, energy, credit, transportation availability, and employment. Opportunities for non-farm jobs have become increasingly important to farm and ranch families, enhancing life and work in rural America.

Toward Fair and Expanded Markets and Responding to Hunger

Agriculture is an international advantage for the United States. But a successful farm and ranch policy demands earnest attention to building on the strength of our domestic production capacity and to developing world markets, for American agriculture cannot be prosperous without exports.

Our farmers and ranchers must have full access to world markets and should not have to face unfair export subsidies and predatory dumping by other producing nations without redress. Republicans believe that unfair trade practices and non-tariff barriers are so serious that a comprehensive renegotiation of multilateral trade arrangements must be undertaken to revitalize the free, fair, and open trade critical to worldwide economic growth.

The Republican Party is unalterably opposed to the use of embargoes of grain or other agricultural products as a tool of foreign policy. The Carter-Mondale grain embargo is still — more than any other factor — the cause of the present difficulties in American agriculture and possibly the irretrievable loss of foreign markets. Republicans say "Never again." The Democratic Platform says nothing.

America has a long history of helping those in need, and the responsibility for food assistance has been shared by federal and State governments and neighborhood volunteers. Federal expenditures in this area exceeded $19 billion in 1983, the highest amount ever. Numerous private and public efforts assure that adequate food is available. This expresses faith in our future and reflects our people's goodness.

We will provide adequate resources in programs ranging from food stamps to school lunches for the truly needy. We also recognize that fraud and abuse must be eliminated from those programs. We stress maximum local control consistent with national objectives.

Reducing Excessive Regulation in Agriculture

Excessive federal regulations, many imposed by the Carter-Mondale Administration, have been a crushing burden.

In 1980, we pledged to make sensible reductions in regulations that drained the profitability from farming, ranching, and commercial fishing. We did just that. We restored balance to the Interior Department's ineffective predator-control policies, and we moderated the EPA's and the FDA's excessive adherence to "zero risk" standards concerning the use of pesticides, antibiotics, food additives, and preservatives.

Republicans favor modernizing our food-safety laws, providing guidelines for risk-benefit assessment, peer review, and regulatory flexibility consistent with other health and safety policies.

Soil and Water Conservation

Agriculture must be both economically and environmentally sustainable. The soil and water stewardship of our farmers, ranchers, watermen, and rural people is commendable. Republicans believe that long-term soil, water, and other conservation policies, emphasizing environmentally sound agricultural productivity, rangeland protection, fish and wildlife habitat, and balanced forestry management, must be a top priority. Conservation practices must be intensified and integrated with farm programs to safeguard our most valuable resources. Volunteer participation, emphasizing State and local control and adequate incentives, is essential to effective conservation.

Water Policy

In 1980, we pledged a water policy which addressed our national diversity in climate, geography, reclamation needs, and patterns of land ownership. We promised a partnership between the States and federal government which would not destroy traditional State supremacy in water law, and which would avert a water crisis in the coming decades. That partnership is now working to meet these challenges.

The Future of Farming

American agriculture is the world's most successful because of the hard work and creativity of family farmers and ranchers. They have benefitted immensely from agricultural research, extension, and teaching, unequalled in the world. Cooperative extension, operating in every county, brings the results of USDA and Land Grant University research to rural America. We support these programs, with special attention to marketing efficiencies, reduced production costs, and new uses for farm and ranch commodities. We also encourage the establishment of regional international research and export trade centers.

Our agricultural people have developed the ideals of free enterprise and have based their enterprise on our culture's basic element, the family. The family farm and ranch is defined as a unit of agriculture production managed as an enterprise where labor and management have an equity interest in the business and a direct gain or loss from its operation. Family farms and ranches are the heart, soul, and backbone of American agriculture; it is the family farm that makes our system work better than any other.

Our rural and coastal people developed a great diversity of support organizations. They organized farm and ranch cooperatives, and rural electric and telephone cooperatives to provide essential services. They established farm and ranch organizations to work for better farm policies and to improve the quality of rural life. Republicans note with particular pride and enthusiasm the vital impact women have always had in American farming and ranching, and we support efforts to increase their role.

American agriculture has always relied upon the hardworking people who harvest seasonal and perishable crops. Republicans support comprehensive farm-labor legislation, fair to workers *and* employers, to protect consumers from work stoppages which disrupt the flow of food.

Republicans also recognize the tremendous efforts of commercial fishers to bring nutritious seafood products to market, thus strengthening America's food base.

Our agriculture is both a global resource and a tremendous opportunity. Only America possesses the natural, technological, management, and labor resources to commercially develop agriculture's next frontier.

We are encouraged by innovation in agriculture, and applaud its diversity, creativity, and enterprise. Commercial applications of new technology and marketing and management innovations are creating additional opportunities for farming and ranching. Republicans have set the stage for building a new prosperity into our fundamentally strong agricultural system. We renew our national commitment to American farmers and ranchers.

INTERNATIONAL ECONOMIC POLICY

The recent tremendous expansion of international trade has increased the standard of living worldwide. Our strong economy is attracting investment in the United States, which is providing capital needed for new jobs, technology, higher wages, and more competitive products.

We are committed to a free and open international trading system. All Americans benefit from the free flow of goods, services and capital, and the efficiencies of a vigorous international market. We will work with all of our international trading partners to eliminate barriers to trade, both tariff and non-tariff. As a first step, we call on our trading partners to join in a new round of trade negotiations to revise the General Agreement on Tariffs and Trade in order to strengthen it. And we further call on our trading partners to join us in reviewing trade with totalitarian regimes.

But free trade must be fair trade. It works only when all trading partners accept open markets for goods, services, and investments. We will review existing trade agreements and vigorously enforce trade laws including assurance of access to all markets for our service industries. We will pursue domestic and international policies that will allow our American manufacturing and agricultural industries to compete in international markets. We will not tolerate the loss of American jobs to nationalized, subsidized, protected foreign industries, particularly in steel, automobiles, mining, footwear, textiles, and other basic industries. This production is sometimes financed with our own tax dollars through international institutions. We will work to stop funding of such projects that are detrimental to our own economy.

The greatest danger today to our international trade is a growing protectionist sentiment. Tremendous fluctuations in exchange rates have rendered long-term international contracts virtually useless. We therefore urge our trading partners to join us in evaluating and correcting the structural problems of the international monetary system, to base it on more stable exchange rates and free capital markets.

Further, we support reorganization of trade responsibilities in order to reduce overlap, duplication, and waste in the conduct of international trade and industry.

Revisions in that system will stabilize trade relations so that debtor nations can repay their debts. These debts are the direct result of their domestic policies, often mandated by multilateral institutions, combined with the breakdown of the international monetary system. Slower economic growth, reduced imports, and higher taxes will not relieve debt burdens, but worsen them. The only way to repay the debts is to create productive capacity to generate new wealth through economic expansion, as America has done.

Austerity should be imposed not on people, but on governments. Debtor nations seeking our assistance must increase incentives for growth by encouraging private investment, reducing taxes, and eliminating subsidies, price controls, and politically motivated development projects.

Security for the Individual

America was built on the institutions of home, family, religion, and neighborhood. From these basic building blocks came self-reliant individuals, prepared to exercise both rights and responsibilities.

In the community of individuals and families, every generation has relearned the art of self-government. In our neighborhoods, Americans have traditionally taken care of their needs and aided the less fortunate. In the process we developed, independent of government, the remarkable network of "mediating institutions" — religious groups, unions, community, and professional associations. Prominent among them have been innumerable volunteer groups, from fire departments and neighborhood-watch patrols to meals-on-wheels and the little leagues.

Public policy long ignored these foundations of American life. Especially during the two decades preceding Ronald Reagan's election, the federal government eroded their authority, ignored their rights, and attempted to supplant their functions with programs at once intrusive and ineffectual. It thereby disrupted our traditional patterns of caring, sharing, and helping. It elbowed out the voluntary providers of services and aid instead of working through them.

By centralizing responsibility for social programs in Washington, liberal experimenters destroyed the sense of community that sustains local institutions. In many cases, they literally broke up neighborhoods and devastated rural communities.

Washington's governing elite thought they knew better than the people how to spend the people's money. They played fast and loose with our schools, with law enforcement, with welfare, with housing. The results were declining literacy and learning, an epidemic of crime, a massive increase in dependency, and the slumming of our cities.

Worst of all, they tried to build their brave new world by assaulting our basic values. They mocked the work ethic. They scorned frugality. They attacked the integrity of the family and parental rights. They ignored traditional morality. And they still do.

Our 1980 Republican Platform offered a renewed vision. We based it upon home, family, and community as the surest guarantees of both individual rights and national greatness. We asserted, as we do now, the ethical dimension of public policy: the need to return to enduring principles of conduct and firm standards of judgment.

The American people responded with enthusiasm. They knew that our roots, in family, home, and neighborhood, do not tie us down. They give us strength. Once more we call upon our people to assert their supervision over government, to affirm their rights against government, to uphold their interests within government.

HOUSING AND HOMEOWNERSHIP

Homeownership is part of the American Dream. For the last two decades, that dream has been endangered by bad public policy. Government unleashed a dreadful inflation upon homebuyers, driving mortgage rates beyond the reach of average families, as the prime rate rose more than 300 percent (from 6.5 percent to 21.5 percent). The American worker's purchasing power fell every year from 1977 through 1980.

No wonder the housing industry was crippled. Its workers faced recurrent recessions. The boom-and-bust cycle made saving foolish, investment risky, and housing scarce.

Federal housing blighted stable low-income neighborhoods, disrupting communities which people had held together for generations. Only government could have wasted billions of dollars to create the instant slums which disgrace our cities.

In our 1980 Platform, we pledged to reverse this situation. We have begun to do so, despite obstructionism from those who believe that the taxpayer's home is government's castle.

We attacked the basic problem, not the symptoms. We cut tax rates and reduced inflation to a fraction of the Carter-Mondale years. The median price house that would cost $94,800 if Carter-Mondale inflation had continued now costs $74,200. The average monthly mortgage payment, which rose by $342 during the Carter-Mondale years, has increased just $24 since January 1981. The American Dream has made a comeback.

To sustain it, we must finish the people's agenda.

We reaffirm our commitment to the federal-tax deductibility of mortgage interest payments. In the States, we stand with those working to lower property taxes that strike hardest at the poor, the elderly, and large families. We stand, as well, with Americans earning possession of their homes through "sweat-equity" programs.

We will, over time, replace subsidies and welfare projects with a voucher system, returning public housing to the free market.

Despite billions of dollars poured into public housing developments, conditions remain deplorable for many low-income Americans who live in them. These projects have become breeding grounds for the very problems they were meant to eliminate. Their dilapidated and crumbling structures testify to decades of corrupt or incompetent management by poverty bureaucrats.

Some residents of public housing developments have reversed these conditions by successfully managing their own housing units through creative self-help efforts. It is abundantly clear that their pride of ownership has been the most important factor contributing to the efficiency of operation, enhancing the quality of housing, improving community morale, and providing incentives for their self-improvement. The Republican Party therefore supports the development of programs which will lead to homeownership of public housing developments by current residents.

We strongly believe in open housing. We will vigorously enforce all fair housing laws and will not tolerate their distortion into quotas and controls.

Rent controls promise housing below its market cost but inevitably result in a shortage of decent homes. Our people should not have to underwrite any community which erodes its own housing supply by rent control.

Sound economic policy is good housing policy. In our expanding economy, where people are free to work and save, they will shelter their families without government intrusion.

WELFARE

Helping the less fortunate is one of America's noblest endeavors, made possible by the abundance of our free and competitive economy. Aid should be swift and adequate to ensure the necessities of a decent life.

Over the past two decades, welfare became a nightmare for the taxpayer and the poor alike. Fraud and abuse were rampant. The costs of public assistance are astronomical, in large part because resources often benefit the welfare industry rather than the poor.

During the 1970s, the number of people receiving federal assistance increased by almost 300 percent, from 9 million to 35 million, while our population increased by only 11.4 percent. This was a fantastic and unsustainable universalization of welfare.

Welfare's indirect effects were equally bad. It became a substitute for urgently needed economic reforms to create more entry-level jobs. Government created a hellish cycle of dependency. Family cohesion was shattered, both by providing economic incentives to set up maternal households and by usurping the breadwinner's economic role in intact families.

The cruelest result was the maternalization of poverty, worsened by the breakdown of the family and accelerated by destructive patterns of conduct too long tolerated by permissive liberals. We endorse programs to assist female-headed households to build self-sufficiency, such as efforts by localities to enable participants to achieve permanent employment.

We have begun to clean up the welfare mess. We have dramatically reduced the poor's worst enemy — inflation — thereby protecting their purchasing power. Our resurgent economy has created over six million new jobs and reduced unemployment by 30 percent.

We have launched real welfare reforms. We have targeted benefits to the needy through tighter eligibility standards, enforced child-support laws, and encouraged "workfare" in the States. We gave States more leeway in managing welfare programs, more assistance with fraud control, and more incentives to hold down costs.

Only sustained economic growth, continuing our vigorous recovery, can give credible hope to those at the bottom of the opportunity ladder.

The working poor deserve special consideration, as do low-income families struggling to provide for their children. As part of comprehensive simplification of the federal tax code, we will restore the real value of their personal tax exemptions so that families, particularly young families, can establish their economic independence.

Federal administration of welfare is the worst possible, detached from community needs and careless with the public's money. Our long tradition of State and local administration of aid programs must be restored. Programs and resources must be returned to State and local governments and not merely exchanged with them. We will support block grants to combine duplicative programs under State administration.

We must also recognize and stimulate the talents and energy of low-income neighborhoods. We must provide new incentives for self-help activities that flow naturally when people realize they *can* make a difference. This is especially critical in foster care and adoption.

Because there are different reasons for poverty, our programs address different needs and must never be replaced with a unitary income guarantee. That would betray the interest of the poor and the taxpayers alike.

We will employ the latest technology to combat welfare fraud in order to protect the needy from the greedy.

Whenever possible, public assistance must be a transition to the world of work, except in cases, particularly with the aged and disabled, where that is not appropriate. In other cases, it is long overdue.

Remedying poverty requires that we sustain and broaden economic recovery, hold families together, get government's hand out of their pocketbooks, and restore the work ethic.

HEALTH

Our tremendous investment in health care has brought us almost miraculous advances. Although costs are still too high, we have dramatically enhanced the length and quality of life for all.

Faced with Medicare and Medicaid mismanagement, government tried to ration health care through arbitrary cuts in eligibility and benefits.

Meanwhile, inflation drove up medical bills for us all. Economic incentives were backwards, with little awareness of costs by individual patients. Reimbursement mechanisms were based on expenses incurred, rather than set prospectively. Conspicuously absent were free-market incentives to respond to consumer wishes. Instead, government's heavy hand was everywhere.

We narrowly averted disaster. We moved creatively and carefully to restructure incentives, to free competition, to encourage flexible new approaches in the States, and to identify better means of health-care delivery. Applying these principles, we will preserve Medicare and Medicaid. We will eliminate the excesses and inefficiencies which drove costs unacceptably high in those programs. In order to assure their solvency and to avoid placing undue burdens on beneficiaries, reform must be a priority. The Republican Party reaffirms its commitment to assure a basic level of high quality health care for all Americans. We reaffirm as well our opposition to any proposals for compulsory national health insurance.

While Republicans held the line against government takeover of health care, the American people found private ways to meet new challenges. There has been a laudable surge in preventive health care and an emphasis upon personal responsibility for maintaining one's health. Compassionate innovation has developed insurance against catastrophic illness, and capitated "at risk" plans are encouraging innovation and creativity.

We will maintain our commitment to health excellence by fostering research into yet-unconquered diseases. There is no better investment we as a nation can make than in programs which hold the promise of sounder health and longer life. For every dollar we spend on health research, we save many more in health care costs. Thus, what we invest in medical research today will yield billions of dollars in individual productivity as well as savings in Medicare and Medicaid. The federal government has been the major source of support for biomedical research since 1945. That research effort holds great promise for combatting cancer, heart disease, brain disorders, mental illness, diabetes, Alzheimer's disease, sickle cell anemia and numerous other illnesses which threaten our nation's welfare. We commit to its continuance.

Many health problems arise within the family and should be dealt with there. We affirm the right and responsibility of parents to participate in decisions about the treatment of children. We will not tolerate the use of federal funds, taxed away from parents, to abrogate their role in family health care.

Republicans have secured for the hospice movement an important role in federal health programs. We must do more to enable persons to remain within the unbroken family circle. For those elderly confined to nursing homes or hospitals, we insist that they be treated with dignity and full medical assistance.

Discrimination in health care is unacceptable; we guarantee, especially for the handicapped, non-discrimination in the compassionate healing that marks American medicine.

Government must not impose cumbersome health planning that causes major delays, increases construction costs, and stifles competition. It should not unduly delay the approval of new medicines, nor adhere to outdated safety standards hindering rapidly advancing technology.

We must address ailments, not symptoms, in health-care policy. Drug and alcohol abuse costs thousands of lives and billions of dollars every year. We reaffirm our vigorous commitment to alcohol and drug abuse prevention and education efforts. We salute the citizens' campaign, launched from America's grassroots, against drunk driving. We applaud those States which raised the legal drinking age.

Much illness, especially among the elderly, is related to poor nutrition. The reasons are more often social than economic: isolation, separation from family, and often a mismatch between nutritional needs and available assistance. This reinforces our efforts to protect federal nutrition programs from fraud and abuse, so that their benefits can be concentrated upon the truly needy.

A supportive environment linking family, home, neighborhood, and workplace is essential to sound health policy. The other essential step is to encourage the individual responsibility and group assistance that are uniquely American.

ENVIRONMENT

It is part of the Republican philosophy to preserve the best of our heritage, including our natural resources. The environment is not just a scientific or technological issue; it is a human one. Republicans put the needs of people at the center of environmental concerns. We assert the people's stewardship of our God-given natural resources. We pledge to meet the challenges of environmental protection, economic growth, regulatory reform, enhancement of our scenic and recreational areas, conservation of our non-renewable resources, and preservation of our irreplaceable natural heritage.

Americans were environmentalists long before it became fashionable. Our farmers cared for the earth and made it the world's most bountiful. Our families cared for their neighborhoods as an investment in our children's future. We pioneered the conservation that replenished our forests, preserved our wildlife, and created our national park system.

The American people have joined together in a great national effort to protect the promise of our future by conserving the rich beauty and bounty of our heritage. As a result, by almost any measure, the air is cleaner than it was 10 years ago, and fish are returning to rivers where they had not been seen for generations.

Within the last four years, dramatic progress has been made in protecting coastal barrier islands, and we began the Park Preservation and Restoration Program to restore the most celebrated symbols of our heritage. We support programs to restore and protect the nation's estuaries, wetland resources, and beaches.

The Republican Party endorses a strong effort to control and clean up toxic wastes. We have already tripled funding to clean up hazardous waste dumps, quadrupled funding for acid rain research, and launched the rebirth of the Chesapeake Bay.

The environmental policy of our nation originated with the Republican Party under the inspiration of Theodore Roosevelt. We hold it a privilege to build upon the foundation which we have laid. The Republican Party supports the continued commitment to clean air and clean water. This support includes the implementation of meaningful clean air and clean water acts. We will continue to offer leadership to reduce the threat to our environment and our economy from acid rain, while at the same time preventing economic dislocation.

Even as many environmental problems have been brought under control, new ones have been detected. And all the while, the growth and shifts of population and economic expansion, as well as the development of new industries, will further intensify the competing demands on our national resources.

Continued progress will be much more difficult. The environmental challenges of the 1980s are much more complex than the ones we tried to address in the 1970s, and they will not yield quickly to our efforts. As the science and administration of environmental protection have become more sophisticated, we have learned of many subtle and potentially more dangerous threats to public health and the environment.

In setting out to find solutions to the environmental issues of the 1980s and 1990s, we start with a healthy appreciation of difficulties involved. Detecting contamination, assessing the threat, correcting the damage, setting up preventive measures, all raise questions of science, technology, and public policy that are as difficult as they are important. However, the health and well being of our citizens must be a high priority.

The number of people served by waste water treatment systems has nearly doubled just since 1970. The federal government should offer assistance to State and local governments in planning for the disposal of solid and liquid wastes. A top priority nationwide should be to eliminate the dumping of raw sewage.

We encourage recycling of materials and support programs which will allow our economic system to reward resource conservation.

We also commit ourselves to the development of renewable and efficient energy sources and to the protection of endangered or threatened species of plants and wildlife.

We will be responsible to future generations, but at the same time, we must remember that quality of life means more than protection and preservation. As Teddy Roosevelt put it, "Conservation means development as much as it does protection." Quality of life also means a good job, a decent place to live, accommodation for a growing population, and the continued economic and technological development essential to our standard of living, which is the envy of the whole world.

TRANSPORTATION

America's overall transportation system is unequalled. Generating over 20 percent of our GNP and employing one of every nine people in the work force, it promotes the unity amid diversity that uniquely characterizes our country. We travel widely, and we move the products of field and factory more efficiently and economically than any other people on earth.

And yet, four years ago, the future of American transportation was threatened. Over several decades, its vigor and creativity had been stunted by the intrusion of government regulation. The results were terribly expensive, and consumers paid the price. Our skies and highways were becoming dangerous and congested. With the same vision that marked President Eisenhower's beginning of the Interstate Highway System, the Reagan Administration launched a massive modernization of America's transport systems.

An expanded highway program is rebuilding the nation's roads and bridges and creating several hundred thousand jobs in construction and related fields. Driving mileage has increased by 8 percent, but greater attention to safety has led to a 17 percent reduction in fatalities, saving more than 8,000 lives yearly.

In public transit, we have redefined the federal role to emphasize support for capital investment, while restoring day-to-day responsibility to local authorities.

Our National Airspace Plan is revolutionizing air traffic control. It will improve flight safety and double the nation's flight capacity, providing better air service and stimulating economic growth.

Regulatory reform is revitalizing American transportation. Federal agencies had protected monopolies by erecting regulatory barriers that hindered the entry of new competitors. Small businesses and minority enterprises were virtually excluded. Prices were set, not by the public through free exchange, but by Washington clerks through green eyeshades.

Republicans led the successful fight to break government's stranglehold. The deregulation of airline economics (not their safety!) will be completed on December 30, 1984, when the Civil Aeronautics Board closes its doors forever. Through our regulatory reform efforts, the rail and trucking industries are now allowed to compete in both price and service. We also led the fight to deregulate interstate bus operations by enacting the Bus Regulatory Reform Act of 1982. While returning to a more free and competitive marketplace, we have ensured that small communities in rural America will retain necessary services through transitional assistance like the Essential Air Service Program, which will continue for four more years.

The Shipping Act of 1984 secured the first major reform of maritime law, as it applies to the U.S. liner trade, since 1916. This major step introduces genuine competition to the maritime industry, while enhancing our ability to compete against international cartels. Important in peacetime, critical in times of conflict, one of our proudest industries had long been neglected. We have expanded employment and brought hope of a future worthy of its past. The Reagan defense program now provides more work for our shipyards than at any time since World War II. We seek to halt the decline of our commercial fleet and restore it to economic strength and strategic capacity to fulfill its national obligations. We also seek to maximize the use of our nation's existing port facilities and shipbuilding and repair capability as a vital transportation resource that should be preserved in the best long-term interest of this country.

The American people benefit from regulatory reform. Air travelers now have a remarkable range of options, and flight is within reach of the average family budget. In the trucking business, increased competition has lowered prices and improved service.

The future of America's freight rail system is again bright. As a result of our reforms, the major private railroads have climbed back to profitability. Government red tape caused their red ink; by cutting the former, we are wiping out the latter. In addition, we transformed Conrail from a multi-billion dollar drain on the taxpayers into an efficient, competitive freight railroad. Returning Conrail as a financially sound single entity to private ownership, with service and jobs secure, will provide the nation with an improved rail freight system to promote economic growth. It will also return to the Treasury a significant portion of the taxpayers' investment, virtually unheard of for a federal project. We support improved passenger rail service where economically justified. We have made substantial progress in reducing the taxpayers' subsidy to Amtrak while maintaining services for which there is genuine demand. The Reagan Administration is selling the Alaska Railroad to the State of Alaska and transferring Conrail's commuter lines to the jurisdictions they serve.

The Republican Party believes that the nation's long-term economic growth will depend heavily on the adequacy of its public works infrastructure. We will continue to work to reverse the long-term decline that has occurred. We should foster development of better information on the magnitude and effectiveness of current federal, State and local government capital expenditures and innovative financing mechanisms which would improve our capacity to leverage limited federal funds more effectively.

America's leadership in space depends upon the vitality of free enterprise. That is why we encourage a commercial space-transportation industry. We share President Reagan's vision of a permanent manned space station within a decade, viewing it as the first stepping stone toward creating a multi-billion dollar private economy in space. The permanent presence of man in space is crucial both to developing a visionary program of space commercialization and to creating an opportunity society on Earth of benefit to all mankind. We are, after all, the people who hewed roads out of the wilderness. Our families crossed ocean, prairie, and desert no less dangerous than today's space frontier to reach a new world of opportunity. And every route they took became a highway of liberty. Like them, we know where we are going: forward, toward a future in our hands. Because of them, and because of us, our children's children will use space transportation to build both prosperity and peace on earth.

EDUCATION AND YOUTH

Our children are our hope and our future. For their sake, President Reagan has led a national renewal to get back to the "basics" and excellence in education. Young people have turned away from the rebellion of the 1960s and the pessimism of the 1970s. Their hopeful enthusiasm speaks better for a bright future than any government program.

During the Reagan Administration, we restored education to prominence in public policy. This change will clearly benefit our youth and our country. By using the spotlight of the Oval office, the Reagan Administration turned the nation's attention to the quality of education and gave its support to local and State improvement efforts. Parents and all segments of American society responded overwhelmingly to the findings of the National Commission on Excellence in Education, appointed by President Reagan. Its report, along with others from prominent experts and foundations, provided the impetus for educational reform.

Ronald Reagan's significant and innovative leadership has encouraged and sustained the reform movement. He catapulted education to the forefront of the national agenda and will be remembered as a president who improved education.

Unlike the Carter-Mondale Democrats, Republicans have levelled with parents and students about the problems we face together. We find remedies to these problems in the common sense of those most concerned: parents and local leaders. We support the decentralization necessary to put education back on the right track. We urge local school communities, including parents, teachers, students, administrators, and business and civic leaders, to evaluate school curricula — including extra-curricular activities and the time spent in them — and their ultimate effect upon students and the learning process. We recognize the need to get "back to basics" and applaud the dramatic improvements that this approach has already made in some jurisdictions.

In schools, school districts, and States throughout our land, the past year andone-half has been marked by unprecedented response to identified education deficiencies. *The Nation Responds*, a recent report by the Reagan Administration, referred to a "tidalwave of school reform which promises to renew American education." According to that report:

- Forty-eight States are considering new high school graduation requirements and 35 have approved changes.
- Twenty-one States report initiatives to improve textbooks and instructional material.
- Eight States have approved lengthening the school day, seven are lengthening the school year, and 18 have mandates affecting the amount of time for instruction.
- Twenty-four States are examining master teacher or career ladder programs, and six have begun statewide or pilot programs.
- Thirteen States are considering changes in academic requirements for

extra-curricular and athletic programs, and five have already adopted more rigorous standards.

Education is a matter of choice, and choice in education is inevitably political. All of education is a passing on of ideas from one generation to another. Since the storehouse of knowledge is vast, a selection must be made of what to pass on. Those doing the selecting bring with them their own politics. Therefore, the more centralized the selection process, the greater the threat of tyranny. The more diversified the selection process, the greater the chance for a thriving free marketplace of ideas as the best insurance for excellence in education.

We believe that education is a local function, a State responsibility, and a federal concern. The federal role in education should be limited. It includes helping parents and local authorities ensure high standards, protecting civil rights, and ensuring family rights. Ignoring that principle, from 1965 to 1980, the United States indulged in a disastrous experiment with centralized direction of our schools. During the Carter-Mondale Administration, spending continued to increase, but test scores steadily declined.

This decline was not limited to academic matters. Many schools lost sight of their traditional task of developing good character and moral discernment. The result for many was a decline in personal responsibility.

The key to the success of educational reform lies in accountability: for students, parents, educators, school boards, and all governmental units. All must be held accountable in order to achieve excellence in education. Restoring local control of education will allow parents to resume the exercise of their responsibility for the basic education, discipline, and moral guidance of their children.

Parents have the primary right and responsibility for the education of their children; and States, localities, and private institutions have the primary responsibility for supporting that parental role. America has been a land of opportunity because America has been a land of learning. It has given us the most prosperous and dynamic society in the world.

The Republican Party recognizes the importance of good teachers, and we acknowledge the great effort many put forth to achieve excellence in the classroom. We applaud their numerous contributions and achievements in education. Unfortunately, many teachers are exhausted by their efforts to support excellence and elect to leave the classroom setting. Our best teachers have been frustrated by lowered standards, widespread indifference, and compensation below the true value of their contribution to society. In 1980-81 alone, 4 percent of the nation's math and science teachers quit the classroom. To keep the best possible teachers for our children, we support those education reforms which will result in increased student learning, including appropriate class sizes, appropriate and adequate learning and teaching materials, appropriate and consistent grading practices, and proper teacher compensation, including rewarding exceptional efforts and results in the classroom.

Classroom materials should be developed and produced by the private sector in the public marketplace, and then selections should be made at the State, local, and school levels.

We commend those States and local governments that have initiated challenging and rigorous high school programs, and we encourage all States to take initiatives that address the special educational needs of the gifted and talented.

We have enacted legislation to guarantee equal access to school facilities by student religious groups. Mindful of our religious diversity, we reaffirm our commitment to the freedoms of religion and speech guaranteed by the Constitution of the United States and firmly support the rights of students to openly practice the same, including the right to engage in voluntary prayer in schools.

While much has been accomplished, the agenda is only begun. We must complete the block-grant process begun in 1981. We will return revenue sources to State and local governments to make them independent of federal funds and of the control that inevitably follows.

The Republican Party believes that developing the individual dignity and potential of disabled Americans is an urgent responsibility. To this end, the Republican Party commits itself to prompt and vigorous enforcement of the rights of disabled citizens, particularly those rights established under the Education for All Handicapped Children Act, Section 504 of the Rehabilitation Act of 1973, and the Civil Rights of Institutionalized Persons Act. We insist on the highest standards of quality for services supported with federal funds.

In addition, government should seek out disabled persons and their parents to make them knowledgeable of their rights.

We will work toward providing federal funds to State and local governments sufficient to meet the degree of fiscal participation already promised in law.

We are committed to excellence in education for all our children within their own communities and neighborhoods. No child should be assigned to, or barred from, a school because of race.

In education, as in other activities, competition fosters excellence. We therefore support the President's proposal for tuition tax credits. We will convert the Chapter One grants to vouchers, thereby giving poor parents the ability to choose the best schooling available. Discrimination cannot be condoned, nor may public policies encourage its practice. Civil rights enforcement must not be twisted into excessive interference in the education process.

Teachers cannot teach and students cannot learn in an undisciplined environment. We applaud the President's promise to provide protection to teachers and administrators against suits from the unruly few who seek to disrupt the education of the overwhelming majority of students.

We urge the aggressive enforcement of the Protection of Pupil Rights amendment (also known as the Hatch Amendment, 20 U.S.C. 1232h) in order to protect pupils' and parents' rights. The amendment prohibits requiring any pupil to reveal personal or family information as part of any federally supported program, test, treatment, or psychological examination unless the school first obtains written consent of the pupil's parents.

The recent Grove City and Hillsdale College cases have raised questions about the extension of federal interference with private colleges, universities, and schools. Since federal aid, no matter how indirect, is now being linked to nearly every aspect of American life, great care must be taken in defining such terms as "federal financial assistance," "indirect" assistance, and "recipient" of assistance. We are deeply concerned that this kind of federal involvement in the affairs of some of the nation's fine private universities, colleges, and schools, many of which have remained stubbornly free of federal entanglements, can only bring with it unintended results. As the historical party of Lincoln and individual rights, we support enactment of legislation which would ensure protection of those covered under Title IX.

We urge States to establish partnerships with the scientific and business worlds to increase the number of teachers in these critical areas of learning. We also recognize a vast reservoir of talent and experience among retirees and other Americans competent to teach in these areas and ready to be tapped.

We endorse experiments with education such as enterprise zones and Cities-in-Schools. We reaffirm our commitment to wipe out illiteracy in our society. Further, we encourage the Congress and the States to reassess the process for aiding education, awarding funds on the basis of academic improvement rather than on daily attendance.

We are aware that good intentions do not always produce the desired results. We therefore urge our schools to evaluate their sex education programs to determine their impact on escalating teenage pregnancy rates. We urge that school officials take appropriate action to ensure parent involvement and responsibility in finding solutions to this national dilemma.

We support and encourage volunteerism in the schools. President Reagan's Adopt-a-School program is an example of how private initiative can revitalize our schools, particularly inner-city schools, and we commend him for his example.

Our emphasis on excellence includes the nation's colleges and universities. Although their achievements are unequalled in the world — in research, in proportion of citizens enrolled, in their contribution to our democratic society — we call upon them for accountability in good teaching and quality curricula that will ensure competent graduates in the world of work.

We pledge to keep our colleges and universities strong. They have been far too dependent on federal assistance and thus have been tied up in federal ted tape. Their independence is an essential part of our liberty. Through regulatory reform, we are holding down the costs of higher education and reestablishing academic freedom from government. This is especially important for small schools, religious institutions, and the historically black colleges, for which President Reagan's Executive Order 12320 has meant new hope and vigor. We further reaffirm and support a regular Black College Day which honors a vital part of our educational community.

Republicans applaud the information explosion. This literacy-based knowledge revolution, made possible by computers, tapes, television, satellites, and other high technology innovations, buttressed by training programs through the business sector and foundations, is a tribute to American ingenuity. We urge our schools to educate for the ever-changing demands of our society and to resist using these innovations as substitutes for reasoning, logic, and mastery of basic skills.

We encourage excellence in the vocational and technical education that has contributed to the self-esteem and productivity of millions. We believe the best vocational and technical education programs are rooted in strong academic fundamentals. Business and industry stand ready to establish training partnerships with our schools. Their leadership is essential to keep America competitive in the future.

In an age when individuals may have four or five different jobs in their working career, vocational education and opportunities for adult learning will be more important than ever. The challenge of learning for citizenship and for work in an age of change will require new adaptations and innovations in the process of education. We urge the teaching profession and educational institutions at all levels to develop the maximum use of new learning opportunities available through learning-focused high technology. This technology in education and in the workplace is making possible, and necessary, the continuing education of our adult population. The participation by adults in educational offerings within their communities will strengthen the linkages among the places where Americans live, work, and study.

Important as technology is, by itself it is inadequate for a free society. The arts and humanities flourish in the private sector, where a free market in ideas is the best guarantee of vigorous creativity. Private support for the arts and humanities has increased over the last four years, and we encourage its growth.

We support the National Endowments for the Arts and Humanities in their efforts to correct past abuses and focus on developing the cultural values that are the foundation of our free society. We must ensure that these programs bring the arts and humanities to people in rural areas, the inner city poor, and other underserved populations.

CRIME

One of the major responsibilities of government is to ensure the safety of its citizens. Their security is vital to their health and to the well-being of their neighborhoods and communities. The Reagan Administration is committed to making America safe for families and individuals. And Republican programs are paying dividends.

For the first time in the history of recorded federal crime statistics, rates of serious crime have dropped for two consecutive years. In 1983, the overall crime rate dropped 7 percent; and in 1982, the overall crime rate dropped 3 percent. In 1982 (the latest year for which figures are available), the murder rate dropped 5 percent, the robbery rate was down 6 percent, and forcible rape dropped 5 percent. Property crimes also declined: burglary decreased 9 percent, auto theft declined 2 percent, and theft dropped 1 percent.

Republicans believe that individuals are responsible for their actions. Those who commit crimes should be held strictly accountable by our system of justice. The primary objective of the criminal law is public safety; and those convicted of serious offenses must be jailed swiftly, surely, and long enough to assure public safety.

Republicans respect the authority of State and local law enforcement officials. The proper federal role is to provide strong support and coordination for their efforts and to vigorously enforce federal criminal laws. By concentrating on repeat offenders, we are determined to take career criminals off the street.

Additionally, the federal law enforcement budget has been increased by nearly 50 percent. We added 1,900 new investigators and prosecutors to the federal fight against crime. We arrested more offenders and sent more of them to prison. Convictions in organized crime cases have tripled under the Reagan Administration. We set up task forces to strike at organized crime and narcotics. In the year since, 3,000 major drug traffickers have been indicted, and nearly 1,000 have already been convicted. We are helping local authorities search for missing children. We have a tough new law against child pornography. Republicans initiated a system for pooling information from local, State and federal law enforcement agencies: the Violent Criminal Apprehension Program (VI-CAP). Under this program, State and local agencies have the primary law enforcement responsibility, but cross-jurisdictional information is shared rapidly so that serial murderers and other violent criminals can be identified quickly and then apprehended.

Under the outstanding leadership of President Reagan and Vice President Bush's Task Force on Organized Crime, the Administration established the National Narcotics Border Interdiction System. We set up an aggressive Marijuana Eradication and Suppression Program, gave the FBI authority to investigate drugs, and coordinated FBI and DEA efforts. We reaffirm that the eradication of illegal drug traffic is a top national priority.

We have levelled with the American people about the involvement of foreign governments, especially Communist dictators, in narcotics traffic: Cuba, the Soviet Union, Bulgaria — and now the Sandinistas in Nicaragua — are international "pushers," selling slow death to young Americans in an effort to undermine our free society.

The Republican Party has deep concern about gratuitous sex and violence in the entertainment media, both of which contribute to the problem of crime against children and women. To the victims of such crimes who need protection, we gladly offer it.

We have begun to restore confidence in the criminal justice system. The Carter-Mondale legal policy had more concern for abstract criminal rights than for the victims of crime. It hurt those least able to defend themselves: the poor, the elderly, school children, and minorities. Republican leadership has redressed that imbalance. We have advanced such reforms as restitution by convicted criminals to their victims; providing victims with full explanations of what will occur before, during, and after trial; and assuring that they may testify at both trial and sentencing.

The Republican Senate has twice passed, with one dissenting vote, a comprehensive federal anti-crime package which would:

- Establish uniform, predictable and fair sentencing procedures, while abolishing the inconsistencies and anomalies of the current parole system;
- Strengthen the current bail procedures to allow the detention of dangerous criminals, who under current law are allowed to roam the streets pending trial;
- Increase dramatically the penalties for narcotic traffickers and enhance the ability of society to recoup ill-gotten gains from drug trafficking;
- Narrow the overly broad insanity defense; and
- Provide limited assistance to states and localities for the implementation of anti-crime programs of proven effectiveness.

In addition, the Republican Senate has overwhelmingly passed Administration-backed legislation which would:

- Restore a federal constitutionally valid federal death penalty;
- Modify the exclusionary rule in a way recently approved by the Supreme Court; and
- Curtail abuses by prisoners of federal *habeas corpus* procedures.

The Democrat bosses of the House of Representatives have refused to allow a vote on our initiatives by the House Judiciary Committee, perennial graveyard for effective anti-crime legislation, or by the full House despite our pressure and the public's demand.

The best way to deter crime is to increase the probability of detection and to make punishment certain and swift. As a matter of basic philosophy, we advocate preventive rather than merely corrective measures. Republicans advocate sentencing reform and secure, adequate prison construction. We concur with the American people's approval of capital punishment where appropriate and will ensure that it is carried out humanely.

Republicans will continue to defend the constitutional right to keep and bear arms. When this right is abused and armed felonies are committed, we believe in stiff, mandatory sentencing. Law-abiding citizens exercising their constitutional rights must not be blamed for crime. Republicans will continue to seek repeal of legislation that restrains innocent citizens more than violent criminals.

OLDER AMERICANS

We reaffirm our commitment to the financial security, physical well-being, and quality of life of older Americans. Valuing them as a treasure of wisdom and experience, we pledge to utilize their unique talents to the fullest.

During the Carter-Mondale years, the silent thief of inflation ruthlessly preyed on the elderly's savings and benefits, robbing them of their retirement dollars and making many dependent on government handouts.

No more. Due to the success of Reaganomics, a retiree's private pension benefits are worth almost $1,000 more than if the 1980 inflation rate had continued. Average monthly Social Security benefits have increased by about $180 for a couple and by $100 a month for an individual. Because President Reagan forged a hard-won solution to the Social Security crisis, our elderly will not be repeatedly threatened with the program's impending bankruptcy as they were under the irresponsible policies of the Carter-Mondale Administration. We will work to repeal the Democrats' Social Security earnings-limitation, which penalizes the elderly by taking one dollar of their income for every two dollars earned.

Older Americans are vital contributors to society. We will continue to remove artificial barriers which discourage their participation in community life. We reaffirm our traditional opposition to mandatory retirement.

For those who are unable to care for themselves, we favor incentives to encourage home-based care.

We are combatting insidious crime against the elderly, many of whom are virtual prisoners in their own homes for fear of violence. We demand passage of the President's Comprehensive Crime Control package, stalled by the Democrat-controlled House Judiciary Committee. We support local initiatives to fight crime against the elderly.

Older Americans want to contribute, to live with the dignity and respect they have earned, and to have their special needs recognized. The Republican Party must never turn its back on our elderly, and we ensure that we will adequately provide for them during their golden years so they can continue to enjoy our country's high standard of living, which their labors have helped provide.

ADVANCING OPPORTUNITY

Throughout this Platform are initiatives to provide an opportunity ladder for the poor, particularly among minorities, in both urban and rural areas. Unlike the Carter-Mondale Administration that locked them into the welfare trap, Republicans believe compassion dictates our offering real opportunities to minorities and the urban poor to achieve the American Dream.

We have begun that effort; and as a pledge of its continuance, this Platform commits us, not to a war of class against class, but to a crusade for prosperity for all.

For far too long, the poor have been trapped by the policies of the Democratic Party which treat those in the ghetto as if their interests were somehow different from our own. That is unfair to us all and an insult to the needy. Their goals are ours; their aspirations we share.

To emphasize our common bond, we have addressed their needs in virtually every section of this Platform, rather than segregating them in a token plank. To those who would see the Republican future for urban America, and for those who deserve a better break, we offer the commitments that make up the sinew of this Platform.

Congress must pass enterprise zones, to draw a green line of prosperity around the red-lined areas of our cities and to help create jobs and entrepreneurial opportunities.

We offer the boldest breakthrough in housing policy since VA mortgages: we offer opportunities for private ownership of housing projects by the poor themselves.

We pledge comprehensive tax reform that will give America back what was its post-war glory: a pro-family tax code with a dramatic work incentive for low-income and welfare families.

We offer hope, not despair; more opportunities for education through vouchers and tuition tax relief; and increased participation in the private enterprise system through the reform of counterproductive taxes and regulations.

Together with our emphatic commitment to civil rights, Republican programs will achieve, for those who feel left out of our society's progress, what President Reagan has already secured for our country: a new beginning to move America to full employment and honest money for all.

A Free and Just Society

In 1980, the Republican Party offered a vision of America's future that applied our traditions to today's problems. It is the vision of a society more free and more just than any in history. It required a break with the worn-out past, to redefine the role of government and its relationship with individuals and their institutions. Under President Reagan's leadership, the American people are making that vision a reality.

The American people want an opportunity society, not a welfare state. They want government to foster an environment in which individuals can develop their potential without hindrance.

The Constitution is the ultimate safeguard of individual rights. As we approach the Constitutional Bicentennial in 1987, Republicans are restoring its vitality, which had been transgressed by Democrats in Congress, the executive, and in the courts.

We are renewing the federal system, strengthening the States, and returning power to the people. That is the surest course to our common goal: a free and just society.

697

INDIVIDUAL RIGHTS

The Republican Party is the party of equal rights. From its founding in 1854, we have promoted equality of opportunity.

The Republican Party reaffirms its support of the pluralism and freedom that have been part and parcel of this great country. In so doing, it repudiates and completely disassociates itself from people, organizations, publications, and entities which promulgate the practice of any form of bigotry, racism, anti-semitism, or religious intolerance.

Americans demand a civil rights policy premised on the letter of the Civil Rights Act of 1964. That law requires equal rights; and it is our policy to end discrimination on account of sex, race, color, creed, or national origin. We have vigorously enforced civil rights statutes. The Equal Employment Opportunity Commission has recovered record amounts of back pay and other compensation for victims of employment discrimination.

Just as we must guarantee opportunity, we oppose attempts to dictate results. We will resist efforts to replace equal rights with discriminatory quota systems and preferential treatment. Quotas are the most insidious form of discrimination: reverse discrimination against the innocent. We must always remember that, in a free society, different individual goals will yield different results.

The Republican Party has an historic commitment to equal rights for women. Republicans pioneered the right of women to vote, and our party was the first major party to advocate equal pay for equal work, regardless of sex.

President Reagan believes, as do we, that all members of our party are free to work individually for women's progress. As a party, we demand that there be no detriment to that progress or inhibition of women's rights to full opportunity and advancement within this society.

Participation by women in policy-making is a strong commitment by the Republican Party and by President Reagan. He pledged to appoint a woman to the United States Supreme Court. His promise was not made lightly; and when a vacancy occurred, he quickly filled it with the eminently qualified Sandra Day O'Connor of Arizona.

His Administration has also sought the largest number of women in history to serve in appointive positions within the executive branch of government. Three women serve at Cabinet level, the most ever in history. Jeane Kirkpatrick, the U.S. Representative to the United Nations, Elizabeth Dole, Secretary of Transportation, and Margaret Heckler, Secretary of Health and Human Services, head a list of over 1,600 women who direct policy and operations of the federal government.

The Republican Party continues to search for interested and qualified women for all government positions. We will continue to increase the number of first-time appointments for women serving in government at all levels.

Our record of economic recovery and growth is an additional important accomplishment for women. It provides a stark contrast to the Carter-Mondale legacy to women: a shrinking economy, limited job opportunities, and a declining standard of living.

Whether working in or outside the home, women have benefitted enormously from the economic progress of the past four years. The Republican economic expansion added over six million new jobs to the economy. It increased labor force participation by women to historic highs. Women's employment has risen by almost four and one-half million since the last Carter-Mondale year. They obtained almost one million more new jobs than men did. Economic growth due to Republican economic policies has produced a record number of jobs so that women who want to work outside the home now have unmatched opportunity. In fact, more than 50 percent of all women now have jobs outside the home.

The spectacular decline in inflation has immeasurably benefitted women working both in and outside the home. Under President Reagan, the cost increase in everyday essentials — food, clothing, housing, utilities — has been cut from the Carter-Mondale highs of over 10 percent a year to just over 4 percent today. We have ushered in an era of price stability that is stretching take-home pay hundreds of dollars farther. In 1982, for the first time in 10 years, women experienced a real increase in wages over inflation.

Lower interest rates have made it possible for more women, single and married, to own their homes and to buy their own automobiles and other consumer goods.

Our 25 percent reduction in marginal tax rates provided important benefits to women, as did the virtual elimination of the "widow's tax" which had jeopardized retirement savings of senior women. At the same time, we raised the maximum child care tax credit from $400 to $720 per family. We will continue to actively seek the elimination of discrimination against homemakers with regard to Individual Retirement Accounts so that single-income couples can invest the same amount in IRAs as two-income couples.

In addition, President Reagan has won enactment of the Retirement Equity Act of 1984. That legislation, strongly supported by congressional Republicans, makes a comprehensive reform of private pension plans to recognize the special needs of women.

Our record of accomplishment during the last four years is clear, but we intend to do even better over the next four.

We will further reduce the "marriage penalty," a burden upon two-income, working families. We will work to remove artificial impediments in business and industry, such as occupational licensing laws, that limit job opportunities for women, minorities, and youth or prevent them from entering the labor force in the first place.

For low-income women, the Reagan Administration has already given States and localities the authority, through the Job Training Partnership Act, to train more recipients of Aid to Families with Dependent Children for permanent, not make-work, jobs. We have increased child support collections from $1.5 billion to $2.4 billion and enacted a strong child support enforcement law. We will continue to stress welfare reforms which promote individual initiative, the real solution to breaking the cycle of welfare dependency.

With women comprising an increasing share of the work force, it is essential that the employment opportunities created by our free market system be open to individuals without regard to their sex, race, religion, or ethnic origin. We firmly support an equal opportunity approach which gives women and minorities equal access to all jobs — including the traditionally higher-paying technical, managerial, and professional positions — and which guarantees that workers in those jobs will be compensated in accord with the laws requiring equal pay for equal work under Title VII of the Civil Rights Act. We are creating an environment in which individual talents and creativity can be tapped to the fullest, while assuring that women have equal opportunity, security, and real choices for the promising future. For all Americans, we demand equal pay for equal work. With equal emphasis, we oppose the concept of "comparable worth." We believe that the free market system can determine the value of jobs better than any government authority.

The Department of Justice has identified 140 federal statutes with gender-based distinctions. Proposed legislation will correct all but 18; six are still under study; the rest, which actually favor women, will remain as is. President Reagan's Fifty States Project, designed to identify State laws discriminating against women, has encouraged 42 States to start searches, and 26 have begun amending their laws. The Department has filed more cases dealing with sex discrimination in employment than were filed during a comparable period in the Carter-Mondale Administration.

Working with Republicans in Congress, President Reagan has declared 1983-1992 the Decade of Disabled Persons. All Americans stand to gain when disabled citizens are assured equal opportunity.

The Reagan Administration has an outstanding record in achieving accessibility for the handicapped. During the past two years, minimum guidelines have at last been adopted, and the Uniform Federal Accessibility Standard has become fact.

The Republican Party realizes the great potential of members of the disabled community in this country. We support all efforts being made at the federal level to remove artificial barriers from our society so that disabled individuals may reach their potential and participate at the maximum level of their abilities in education, employment, and recreation. This includes the removal, in so far as practicable, of architectural, transportation, communication and attitudinal barriers. We also support efforts to provide disabled Americans full access to voting facilities.

We deplore discrimination because of handicap. The Reagan Administration was the first to combat the insidious practice of denying medical care or even food and water to disabled infants. This issue has vast implications for medical ethics, family autonomy, and civil rights. But we find no basis, whether in law or medicine or ethics, for denying necessities to an infant because of the child's handicap.

We are committed to enforcing statutory prohibitions barring discrimination against any otherwise qualified handicapped individuals, in any program receiving federal financial assistance, solely by reason of their handicap.

We recognize the need for watchful care regarding the procedural due process rights of persons with handicaps both to prevent their placement into inappropriate programs or settings and to ensure that their rights are represented by guardians or other advocates, if necessary.

For handicapped persons who need care, we favor family-based care where possible, supported by appropriate and adequate incentives. We increased the tax credit for caring for dependents or spouses physically or mentally unable to care for themselves. We also provided a deduction of up to $1,500 per year for adopting a child with special needs that may otherwise make adoption difficult.

We are committed to seeking out gifted children and their parents to make them knowledgeable of their educational rights.

We reaffirm the right of all individuals freely to form, join, or assist labor organizations to bargain collectively, consistent with State laws and free from unnecessary government involvement. We support the fundamental principle of fairness in labor relations. We will continue the Reagan Administration's "open door" policy toward organized labor and its leaders. We reaffirm our long-standing support for the right of States to enact "Right-to-Work" laws under section 14(b) of the Taft-Hartley Act.

The political freedom of every worker must be protected. Therefore, we strongly oppose the practice of using compulsory dues and fees for partisan political purposes. Also, the protection of all workers must be secured. Therefore, no worker should be coerced by violence or intimidation by any party to a labor dispute.

The healthy mix of America's ethnic, cultural, and social heritage has always been the backbone of our nation and its progress throughout our history. Without the contributions of innumerable ethnic and cultural groups, our country would not be where it is today.

For millions of black Americans, Hispanic Americans, Asian Americans, and members of other minority groups, the past four years have seen a dramatic improvement in their ability to secure for themselves and for their children a better tomorrow.

That is the American Dream. The policies of the Reagan Administration have opened literally millions of doors of opportunity for these Americans, doors which either did not exist or were rapidly being slammed shut by the no-growth policies of the Carter-Mondale Administration.

We Republicans are proud of our efforts on behalf of all minority groups, and we pledge to do even more during the next four years.

We will continue to press for enactment of economic and social policies that promote growth and stress individual initiative of minority Americans. Our tax system will continue to be overhauled and reformed by making it fairer and simpler, enabling the families of minorities to work and save for their future. We will continue to push for passage of enterprise zone legislation, now bottled up in the Democrat-controlled House of Representatives. That bill, discussed elsewhere in this platform, will help minority Americans living in cities and urban areas to get jobs, to start their own businesses, and to reap the fruits of entrepreneurship by tapping their individual initiative, energy, and creativity.

We honor and respect the contributions of minority Americans and will do all we can to see that our diversity is enhanced during the next four years. Active contributions by minorities are the threads that weave the fabric that is America and make us stronger as a nation. We recognize these individuals and their contributions and will continue to promote the kinds of policies that will make their dreams for a better America a reality. The party of Lincoln will remain the party of equal rights for all.

We continue to favor whatever legislation may be necessary to permit American citizens residing in the Virgin Islands, Guam, and Puerto Rico to vote for president and vice president in national elections.

We support the right of Indian Tribes to manage their own affairs and resources. Recognizing the government-to-government trust responsibility, we are equally committed to working towards the elimination of the conditions of dependency produced by federal control. The social and economic advancement of Native Americans depends upon changes they will chart for themselves. Recognizing their diversity, we support the President's policy of responsibly removing impediments to their self-sufficiency. We urge the nations of the Americas to learn from our past mistakes and to protect native populations from exploitation and abuse.

Native Hawaiians are the only indigenous people of our country who are not officially designated as Native Americans. They should share that honored title. We endorse efforts to preserve their culture as a unique element in the human tapestry that is America.

FAMILY PROTECTION

Republicans affirm the family as the natural and indispensable institution for human development. A society is only as strong as its families, for they nurture those qualities necessary to maintain and advance civilization.

Healthy families inculcate values — integrity, responsibility, concern for others — in our youth and build social cohesion. We give high priority to their well-being. During the 1970s, America's families were ravaged by worsening economic conditions and a Washington elite unconcerned with them.

We support the concept of creating Family Education Accounts which would allow tax-deferred savings for investment in America's most crucial asset, our children, to assist low- and middle-income families in becoming self-reliant in meeting the costs of higher education.

In addition, to further assist the young families of America in securing the dream of homeownership, we would like to review the concept of

Family Housing Accounts which would allow tax-exempt savings for a family's first home.

Preventing family dissolution, a leading cause of poverty, is vital. It has had a particularly tragic impact on the elderly, women, and minorities. Welfare programs have devastated low-income families and induced single parenthood among teens. We will review legislation and regulations to examine their impact on families and on parental rights and responsibilities. We seek to eliminate incentives for family break-up and to reverse the alarming rate of pregnancy outside marriage. Meanwhile, the Republican Party believes that society must do all that is possible to guarantee those young parents the opportunity to achieve their full educational and parental potential.

Because of Republican tax cuts, single people and married people without dependents will have in 1984 basically the same average tax rates they had in 1960. The marriage penalty has been reduced. However, a couple with dependents still pays a greater portion of their income in taxes than in 1960. We reaffirm that the personal exemption for children be no less than for adults, and we will at least double its current level. The President's tax program also increased tax credits for child care expenses. We will encourage private sector initiatives to expand on-site child care facilities and options for working parents.

The problem of physical and sexual abuse of children and spouses requires careful consideration of its causes. In particular, gratuitous sex and violence in entertainment media contribute to this sad development.

We and the vast majority of Americans are repulsed by pornography. We will vigorously enforce constitutional laws to control obscene materials which degrade everyone, particularly women, and depict the exploitation of children. We commend the Reagan Administration for creating a commission on pornography and the President for signing the new law to eliminate child pornography. We stand with our President in his determination to solve the problem.

We call upon the Federal Communications Commission, and all other federal, State, and local agencies with proper authority, to strictly enforce the law regarding cable pornography and to implement rules and regulations to clean up cable pornography and the abuse of telephone service for obscene purposes.

IMMIGRATION

Our history is a story about immigrants. We are proud that America still symbolizes hope and promise to the world. We have shown unparalleled generosity to the persecuted and to those seeking a better life. In return, they have helped to make a great land greater still.

We affirm our country's absolute right to control its borders. Those desiring to enter must comply with our immigration laws. Failure to do so not only is an offense to the American people but it is fundamentally unjust to those in foreign lands patiently waiting for legal entry. We will preserve the principle of family reunification.

With the estimates of the number of illegal aliens in the United States ranging as high as 12 million and better than one million more entering each year, we believe it is critical that responsible reforms of our immigration laws be made to enable us to regain control of our borders.

The flight of oppressed people in search of freedom has created pressures beyond the capacity of any one nation. The refugee problem is global and requires the cooperation of all democratic nations. We commend the President for encouraging other countries to assume greater refugee responsibilities.

OUR CONSTITUTIONAL SYSTEM

Our Constitution, now almost 200 years old, provides for a federal system, with a separation of powers among the three branches of the national government. In that system, judicial power must be exercised with deference towards State and local officials; it must not expand at the expense of our representative institutions. It is not a judicial function to reorder the economic, political, and social priorities of our nation. The intrusion of the courts into such areas undermines the stature of the judiciary and erodes respect for the rule of law. Where appropriate, we support congressional efforts to restrict the jurisdiction of federal courts.

We commend the President for appointing federal judges committed to the rights of law-abiding citizens and traditional family values. We share the public's dissatisfaction with an elitist and unresponsive federal judiciary. If our legal institutions are to regain respect, they must respect the people's legitimate interests in a stable, orderly society. In his second term, President Reagan will continue to appoint Supreme Court and other federal judges who share our commitment to judicial restraint.

The Republican Party firmly believes that the best governments are those most accountable to the people. We heed Thomas Jefferson's warning: "When all government, in little as in great things, shall be drawn to Washington as the center of all power, it will render powerless the checks provided of one government on another."

For more responsible government, non-essential federal functions should be returned to the States and localities wherever prudent. They have the capability, knowledge, and sensitivity to local needs required to better administer and deliver public services. Their diverse problems require local understanding. The transfer of rights, responsibilities, and revenues to the "home front" will recognize the abilities of local government and the limitations of a distant federal government.

We commend the President for the bold initiatives of his "New Federalism." The enacted block grants discussed elsewhere in this Platform are a positive step. But the job of making government more accountable to the people has just begun. We strongly favor the expansion of block-grant funding and other means to restore our nation's federal foundation.

More than 40 years ago, a grave injustice was done to many Americans of Japanese ancestry. Uprooted from their homes in a time of crisis, loyal citizens and residents were treated in a way which contravened the fundamental principles of our people. We join them and their descendants in assuring that the deprivation of rights they suffered shall never again be permitted in this land of liberty.

[Government Services]

To benefit all Americans, we support the privatization of government services whenever possible. This maximizes consumer freedom and choice. It reduces the size and cost of government, thus lessening the burden on taxpayers. It stimulates the private sector, increases prosperity, and creates jobs. It demonstrates the primacy of individual action which, within a free market economy, can address human needs most effectively.

Within the executive branch, the Reagan Administration has made government work more efficiently. Under the direction of the Office of Personnel Management, non-defense government employment was reduced by over 100,000. The overwhelming majority of federal employees are dedicated and hard-working. Indeed, we have proposed to base their pay and retention upon performance so that outstanding federal employees may be properly rewarded.

The federal government owns almost a third of our nation's land. With due recognition of the needs of the federal government and mindful of environmental, recreational, and national defense needs, we believe the sale of some surplus land will increase productivity and increase State and local tax bases. It will also unleash the creative talents of free enterprise in defense of resource and environmental protection.

The expression of individual political views is guaranteed by the First Amendment; government should protect, not impinge upon First Amendment rights. Free individuals must have unrestricted access to the process of self-government. We deplore the growing labyrinth of bewildering regulations and obstacles which have increased the power of political professionals and discouraged the participation of average Americans. Even well-intentioned restrictions on campaign activity stifle free speech and have a chilling effect on spontaneous political involvement by our citizens.

The holding of public office in our country demands the highest degree of commitment to integrity, openness, and honesty by candidates running for all elective offices. Without such a commitment, public confidence rapidly erodes. Republicans, therefore, reaffirm our commitment to the fair and consistent application of financial disclosure laws. We will continue our support for full disclosure by all high officials of the government and candidates in positions of public trust. This extends to the financial holdings of spouses or dependents, of which the official has knowledge, financial interest, or benefit. We will continue to hold all public officials to the highest ethical standards and will oppose the inconsistent application of those standards on the basis of gender.

Republicans want to encourage, not restrict, free discourse and association. The interplay of concerned individuals, sometimes acting collectively to pursue their goals, has led to healthy and vigorous debate and better understanding of complex issues. We will remove obstacles to grassroots participation in federal elections and will reduce, not increase, the federal role.

Republicans believe that strong, competitive political parties contribute mightily to coherent national policies, effective representation, and responsive government. Forced taxpayer financing of campaign activities is political tyranny. We oppose it.

In light of the inhibiting role federal election laws and regulations have had, Congress should consider abolishing the Federal Election Commission.

We are the party of limited government. We are deeply suspicious of the amount of information which governments collect. Governments limited in size and scope best ensure our people's privacy. Particularly in the computer age, we must ensure that no unnecessary information is demanded and that no disclosure is made which is not approved. We oppose national identification cards.

We support reasonable methods to fight those who undermine national security, prevent crosschecks of government benefit records to conceal welfare fraud, or misuse financial secrecy laws to hide their narcotics profits under the guise of a right to privacy.

Private property is the cornerstone of our liberty and the free enterprise system. The right of property safeguards for citizens all things of value: their land, merchandise and money, their religious convictions, their safety and liberty, and their right of contract to produce and sell goods and services. Republicans reaffirm this God-given and inalienable right.

[Abortion]

The unborn child has a fundamental individual right to life which cannot be infringed. We therefore reaffirm our support for a human life amendment to the Constitution, and we endorse legislation to make clear that the Fourteenth Amendment's protections apply to unborn children. We oppose the use of public revenues for abortion and will eliminate funding for organizations which advocate or support abortions. We commend the efforts of those individuals and religious and private organizations that are providing positive alternatives to abortion by meeting the physical, emotional, and financial needs of pregnant women and offering adoption services where needed.

We applaud President Reagan's fine record of judicial appointments, and we reaffirm our support for the appointment of judges at all levels of the judiciary who respect traditional family values and the sanctity of innocent human life.

America Secure and the World at Peace

THE FUTURE OF OUR FOREIGN POLICY

President Reagan has restored the American people's faith in the principles of liberal democracy. Today, we have more confidence in the self-evident truths of democracy than at any time since World War II.

The first principle of that faith is that all human beings are created equal in the natural human right to govern themselves.

Just as we assert the right of self-government, it follows that all people throughout the world should enjoy that same human right. This moral principle must be the ideal by which our policy toward other nations is directed.

We Republicans emphasize that there is a profound moral difference between the actions and ideals of Marxist-Leninist regimes and those of democratic governments, and we reject the notions of guilt and apology which animate so much of the foreign policy of the Democratic Party. We believe American foreign policy can only succeed when it is based on unquestioned faith in a single idea: the idea that all human beings are created equal, the founding idea of democracy.

The supreme purpose of our foreign policy must be to maintain our freedom in a peaceful international environment in which the United States and our allies and friends are secure against military threats, and democratic governments are flourishing in a world of increasing prosperity.

This we pledge to our people and to future generations: we shall keep the peace by keeping our country stronger than any potential adversary.

The Americas

Our future is intimately tied to the future of the Americas. Family, language, culture, and trade link us closely with both Canada, our largest trading partner, and our southern neighbors.

The people of both Mexico and Canada are of fundamental importance to the people of the United States of America, not just because we share a common border, but because we are neighbors who share both history and a common interest for the present and future. Under President Reagan, our relations with both countries are being carried out in a serious, straight-forward manner in a climate of mutual respect. As our countries seek solutions to common problems on the basis of our mutual interests, we recognize that each country has a unique contribution to make in working together to resolve mutual problems.

The security and freedom of Central America are indispensable to our own. In addition to our concern for the freedom and overall welfare of our neighbors to the south, two-thirds of our foreign trade passes through the Caribbean and the Panama Canal. The entire region, however, is gravely threatened by Communist expansion, inspired and supported by the Soviet Union and Cuba. We endorse the principles of the Monroe Doctrine

707

as the strongest foundation for United States policy throughout the hemisphere.

We encourage even closer ties with the countries of South America and consider the strengthening of representative governments there as a contribution to the peace and security of us all. We applaud the Organization of American States for its efforts to bring peace and freedom to the entire hemisphere.

Republicans have no illusions about Castro's brutal dictatorship in Cuba. Only our firmness will thwart his attempts to export terrorism and subversion, to destroy democracy, and to smuggle narcotics into the United States. But we also extend a constructive, hopeful policy toward the Cuban people. Castro resents and resists their desire for freedom. He fears Radio Marti, President Reagan's initiative to bring truth to our Cuban neighbors. He is humiliated by the example of Cuban-born Americans, whose spiritual and material accomplishments contrast starkly with Communist failures in their birthplace. We believe in friendship between the Cuban and the American peoples, and we envision a genuine democracy in Cuba's future.

We support the President in following the unanimous findings of the Bipartisan Commission on Central America, first proposed by the late Senator Henry "Scoop" Jackson of Washington.

Today, democracy is under assault throughout the hemisphere. Marxist Nicaragua threatens not only Costa Rica and Honduras, but also El Salvador and Guatemala. The Sandinista regime is building the largest military force in Central America, importing Soviet equipment, Eastern bloc and PLO advisers, and thousands of Cuban mercenaries. The Sandinista government has been increasingly brazen in its embrace of Marxism-Leninism. The Sandinistas have systematically persecuted free institutions, including synagogue and church, schools, the private sector, the free press, minorities, and families and tribes throughout Nicaragua. We support continued assistance to the democratic freedom fighters in Nicaragua. Nicaragua cannot be allowed to remain a Communist sanctuary, exporting terror and arms throughout the region. We condemn the Sandinista government's smuggling of illegal drugs into the United States as a crime against American society and international law.

The heroic effort to build democracy in El Salvador has been brutally attacked by Communist guerrillas supported by Cuba and the Sandinistas. Their violence jeopardizes improvements in human rights, delays economic growth, and impedes the consolidation of democracy. El Salvador is nearer to Texas than Texas is to New England, and we cannot be indifferent to its fate. In the tradition of President Truman's postwar aid to Europe, President Reagan has helped the people of El Salvador defend themselves. Our opponents object to that assistance, citing concern for human rights. We share that concern, and more than that, we have taken steps to help curb abuses. We have firmly and actively encouraged human rights reform, and results have been achieved. In judicial reform, the murderers of the American nuns in 1980 have been convicted and sentenced; and in political reform, the right to vote has been exercised by 80 percent of the voters in the fair, open elections of 1982 and 1984. Most important, if the Communists seize power there, human rights will be extinguished, and tens of thousands will be driven from their homes. We, therefore, support the President in his determination that the Salvadoran people will shape their own future.

We affirm President Reagan's declaration at Normandy: there is a profound moral difference between the use of force for liberation and the use of force for conquest and territorial expansion. We applaud the liberation of man and mind from oppression everywhere.

We applaud the liberation of Grenada, and we honor those who took part in it. Grenada is small, and its people few; but we believe the principle established there, that freedom is worth defending, is of monumental importance. It challenges the Brezhnev doctrine. It is an example to the world.

The Caribbean Basin Initiative is a sound program for the strengthening of democratic institutions through economic development based on free people and free market principles. The Republican Party strongly supports this program of integrated, mutually reinforcing measures in the fields of trade, investment, and financial assistance.

We recognize our special-valued relationship with Puerto Rico and the Virgin Islands; and we will support special measures to ensure that they will benefit and prosper from the Caribbean Basin Initiative, thereby reinforcing a stronghold of democracy and free enterprise in the Caribbean. The Republican Party reaffirms its support of the right of Puerto Rico to be admitted into the Union after it freely so determines, through the passage of an admission bill which will provide for a smooth fiscal transition, recognize the concept of a multicultural society for its citizens, and secure the opportunity to retain their Spanish language and traditions.

The Soviet Union

Stable and peaceful relations with the Soviet Union are possible and desirable, but they depend upon the credibility of American strength and determination. As our power waned in the 1970s, our very weakness was provocative. The Soviets exploited it in Afghanistan, the Middle East, Africa, Southeast Asia, and the Western Hemisphere. Our policy of peace through strength encourages freedom-loving people everywhere and provides hope for those who look forward one day to enjoying the fruits of self-government.

We hold a sober view of the Soviet Union. Its globalist ideology and its leadership obsessed with military power make it a threat to freedom and peace on every continent. The Carter-Mondale Administration ignored that threat, and the Democratic candidates underestimate it today. The Carter-Mondale illusion that the Soviet leaders share our ideals and aspirations is not only false but a profound danger to world peace.

Republicans reaffirm our belief that Soviet behavior at the negotiating table cannot be divorced from Soviet behavior elsewhere. Over-eagerness to sign agreements with the Soviets at any price, fashionable in the Carter-Mondale Administration, should never blind us to this reality. Any future agreement with the Soviets must require full compliance, be fully verifiable, and contain suitable sanctions for non-compliance. Carter-Mondale efforts to cover up Soviet violations of the 1972 Strategic Arms Limitations agreement and Anti-ballistic Missile Treaty emboldened the Soviets to strengthen their military posture. We condemn these violations, as well as recent violations of chemical and toxic weapons treaties in Afghanistan, Southeast Asia, and the Iran-Iraq war. We insist on full Soviet compliance with all treaties and executive agreements.

We seek to deflect Soviet policy away from aggression and toward peaceful international conduct. To that end, we will seek substantial reductions in nuclear weapons, rather than merely freezing nuclear weapons at their present dangerous level. We will continue multilateral efforts to deny advanced Western technology to the Soviet war machine.

We will press for Soviet compliance with all international agreements, including the 1975 Helsinki Final Act and the U.N. Declaration on Human Rights. We will continue to protest Soviet anti-semitism and human rights violations. We admire the courage of such people as Andrei Sakharov, his wife Yelena Bonner, Anatole Shcharansky, Ida Nudel and Josef Begun, whose defiance of Soviet repression stands as a testament to the greatness of the human spirit. We will press the Soviet Union to permit free emigration of Jews, Christians, and oppressed national minorities. Finally, because the peoples of the Soviet empire share our hope for the future, we will strengthen our information channels to encourage them in their struggle for individual freedom, national self-determination, and peace.

Europe

Forty years after D-Day, our troops remain in Europe. It has been a long watch, but a successful one. For four decades, we have kept the peace where, twice before, our valiant fought and died. We learned from their sacrifice.

We would be in mortal danger were Western Europe to come under Soviet domination. Fragmenting NATO is the immediate objective of the Soviet military buildup and Soviet subversion. During the Carter-Mondale years, the Soviets gained a substantial military and diplomatic advantage in Europe. They now have three times as many tanks as we do and almost a monopoly on long-range theater nuclear forces. To keep the peace, the Reagan-Bush Administration is offsetting the Soviet military threat with the defensive power of the Alliance. We are deploying Pershing II and Cruise missiles. Remembering the Nazi Reich, informed voters on both sides of the Atlantic know they cannot accept Soviet military superiority in Europe. That is why the British, Italian, and West German parliaments have approved Euromissile deployments, and why new NATO base agreements were concluded successfully in Portugal, Spain, Turkey, and Greece. This is a victory for the Reagan-Bush Administration and our European friends.

The United States again leads the Alliance by offering hope of a safer future. As America's strength is restored, so is our allies' confidence in the future of freedom. We will encourage them to increase their contributions to our common defense.

To strengthen NATO's Southern Flank, we place the highest priority on resolving the Cyprus dispute and maintaining our support for both Greece and Turkey, with non-recognition of regimes imposed in occupied territory. We share a deep concern for peace and justice in Northern Ireland and condemn all violence and terrorism in that strife-torn land.

We stand in solidarity with the peoples of Eastern Europe: the Poles, Hungarians, East Germans, Czechs, Rumanians, Yugoslavs, Bulgarians, Ukrainians, Baltic peoples, Armenians, and all captive nations who struggle daily against their Soviet masters. The heroic efforts of Lech Walesa and the Solidarity movement in Poland are an inspiration to all people yearning to be free. We are not neutral in their struggle, wherever the flame of liberty brightens the black night of Soviet oppression.

The tragic repression of the Polish people by the Soviet-inspired military dictatorship in Poland has touched the American people. We support policies to provide relief for Polish nationals seeking asylum and refuge in the United States.

The Middle East

President Reagan's Middle East policy has been flexible enough to adapt to rapidly changing circumstances, yet consistent and credible so that all nations recognize our determination to protect our vital interests. The President's skillful crisis management throughout the Iran-Iraq war has kept that conflict from damaging our vital interests. His peace efforts have won strong bipartisan support and international applause. And his willingness to stand up to Libya has made peace-loving states in the region feel more secure.

The 1979 Soviet invasion of Afghanistan, which surprised the Carter-Mondale Administration, brought Soviet forces less than 400 miles from the strategic Straits of Hormuz. The seizure of American hostages in Iran that year caught the United States unprepared and unable to respond. Lebanon is still in turmoil, despite our best efforts to foster stability in that unhappy country. With the Syrian leadership increasingly subject to Soviet influence, and the Palestine Liberation Organization and its homicidal subsidiaries taking up residence in Syria, U.S. policy toward the region must remain vigilant and strong. Republicans reaffirm that the United States should not recognize or negotiate with the PLO so long as that organization continues to promote terrorism, rejects Israel's right to exist, and refuses to accept U.N. Resolutions 242 and 338.

The bedrock of that protection remains, as it has for over three decades, our moral and strategic relationship with Israel. We are allies in the defense of freedom. Israel's strength, coupled with United States assistance, is the main obstacle to Soviet domination of the region. The sovereignty, security, and integrity of the state of Israel are moral imperatives. We pledge to help maintain Israel's qualitative military edge over its adversaries.

Today, relations between the United States and Israel are closer than ever before. Under President Reagan, we have moved beyond mere words to extensive political, military, and diplomatic cooperation. U.S.-Israeli strategic planning groups are coordinating our joint defense efforts, and we are directly supporting projects to augment Israel's defense industrial base. We support the legislation pending for an Israel-U.S. free trade area.

We recognize that attacks in the U.N. against Israel are but thinly disguised attacks against the United States, for it is our shared ideals and democratic way of life that are their true target. Thus, when a U.N. agency denied Israel's right to participate, we withheld our financial support until that action was corrected. And we have worked behind the scenes and in public in other international organizations to defeat discriminatory attacks against our ally.

Our determination to participate actively in the peace process begun at Camp David has won us support over the past four years from moderate Arab states. Israel's partner in the Camp David accords, Egypt, with American support, has been a constructive force for stability. We pledge continued support to Egypt and other moderate regimes against Soviet and Libyan subversion, and we look to them to contribute to our efforts for a long-term settlement of the region's destructive disputes.

We believe that Jerusalem should remain an undivided city with free and unimpeded access to all holy places by people of all faiths.

Asia and the Pacific

Free Asia is a tremendous success. Emulating the United States economically and politically, our friends in East Asia have had the world's highest economic growth rates. Their economies represent the dynamism of free markets and free people, in stark contrast to the dreary rigidity and economic failures of centrally planned socialism. U.S. investments in Asia now exceed $30 billion, and our annual trade surpasses that with any other region.

Unable to match this progress, the Soviet Union, North Korea, and Vietnam threaten the region with military aggression and political intimidation. The Soviet rape of Afghanistan, the criminal destruction of the KAL airliner, the genocide in Vietnam, Cambodia and Laos, the steady growth of Soviet SS-20 forces in East Asia, the rapid increase of the Soviet Pacific Fleet, the continuing build-up of North Korean forces and the brutal bombing of South Korean leaders in Rangoon, the recent deployment of Soviet forces at Cam Ranh Bay, the continued occupation of

Cambodia by the Vietnamese, and chemical and biological weapons attacks against defenseless civilian populations in Afghanistan and Southeast Asia are some of the more obvious threats to the peace of Asia and to America's friends there.

Republicans salute the brave people of Afghanistan, struggling to regain their freedom and independence. We will continue to support the freedom fighters and pledge our continuing humanitarian aid to the thousands of Afghan refugees who have sought sanctuary in Pakistan and elsewhere.

To preserve free Asia's economic gains and enhance our security, we will continue economic and security assistance programs with the frontline states of Korea, Thailand, and Pakistan. We will maintain defense facilities in Korea, Japan, the Philippines, and the Indian Ocean to protect vital sea lanes.

We will promote economic growth while we strengthen human rights and the commitment to both democracy and free markets. We will help friendly nations deal with refugees and secure their help against drug cultivation and trafficking.

Our relations with Japan are central to America's role in the Far East, and they have never been better. The world's second-largest industrial power can make an increasingly important contribution to peace and economic development over much of Asia. We applaud Japan's commitment to defend its territory, air space, and sea lanes. We are heartened by its increases in defense spending and urge Japan to further expand its contribution to the region's defense. We have made progress in our trade relations and affirm that, with good will on both sides, broader agreement is likely.

In keeping with the pledge of the 1980 Platform, President Reagan has continued the process of developing our relationship with the People's Republic of China. We commend the President's initiatives to build a solid foundation for the long-term relations between the United States and the People's Republic, emphasizing peaceful trade and other policies to promote regional peace. Despite fundamental differences in many areas, both nations share an important common objective: opposition to Soviet expansionism.

At the same time, we specifically reaffirm our concern for, and our moral commitment to, the safety and security of the 18 million people on Taiwan. We pledge that this concern will be constant, and we will continue to regard any attempt to alter Taiwan's status by force as a threat to regional peace. We endorse, with enthusiasm, President Reagan's affirmation that it is the policy of the United States to support and fully implement the provisions of the Taiwan Relations Act. In addition, we fully support self determination for the people of Hong Kong.

The Republic of Korea is a stalwart ally. To deter aggression, we will maintain our forces there which contribute to our common defense. Our growing economic relations are good for both countries and enhance our influence to foster a democratic evolution there.

We prize our special relationship with the Philippines. We will make every effort to promote the economic development and democratic principles they seek. Because the Clark and Subic Bay bases are vital to American interests in the Western Pacific, we are committed to their continued security.

We recognize the close and special ties we have maintained with Thailand since the days of Abraham Lincoln. Thailand stands tall against the imperialist aggression of Vietnam and the Soviet Union in Southeast Asia.

We hail the economic achievements of the Association of Southeast Asian Nations. We will strengthen economic and political ties to them and support their opposition to the Vietnamese occupation of Cambodia.

Almost a decade after our withdrawal from Vietnam, thousands of Americans still do not know the fate of their fathers, brothers, and sons missing in action. Our united people call upon Vietnam and Laos with one voice: return our men, end the grief of the innocent, and give a full accounting of our POW-MIAs. We will press for access to investigate crash sites throughout Indochina. We support the efforts of our private citizens who have worked tirelessly for many years on this issue.

Africa

Africa faces a new colonialism. The tripartite axis of the Soviet Union, Cuba, and Libya has unleased war and privation upon the continent. We are committed to democracy in Africa and to the economic development that will help it flourish. That is why we will foster free-market, growth-oriented, and liberalized trading policies.

As part of reforming the policies of the International Development Association, we have assisted in directing a larger proportion of its resources to sub-Saharan Africa. To nurture the spirit of individual initiative in Africa, our newly created African Development Foundation will work with African entrepreneurs at the village level. In addition, through our rejection of the austerity programs of international organizations, we are bringing new hope to the people of Africa that they will join in the benefits of the growing, dynamic world economy.

We will continue to provide necessary security and economic assistance to African nations with which we maintain good relations to help them develop the infrastructure of democratic capitalism so essential to economic growth and individual accomplishment. We will encourage our allies in Europe and east Asia to coordinate their assistance efforts so that the industrialized countries will be able to contribute effectively to the economic development of the continent. We believe that, if given the choice, the nations of Africa will reject the model of Marxist state-controlled economies in favor of the prosperity and quality of life that free economies and free people can achieve.

We will continue to assist threatened African governments to protect themselves and will work with them to protect their continent from subversion and to safeguard their strategic minerals. The Reagan-Bush

Administration will continue its vigorous efforts to achieve Namibian independence and the expulsion of Cubans from occupied Angola.

We reaffirm our commitment to the rights of all South Africans. Apartheid is repugnant. In South Africa, as elsewhere on the continent, we support well-conceived efforts to foster peace, prosperity, and stability.

Foreign Assistance and Regional Security

Developing nations look to the United States for counsel and guidance in achieving economic opportunity, prosperity, and political freedom. Democratic capitalism has demonstrated, in the United States and elsewhere, an unparalleled ability to achieve political and civil rights and long-term prosperity for ever-growing numbers of people. We are confident that democracy and free enterprise can succeed everywhere. A central element in our programs of economic assistance should be to share with others the beneficial ideas of democratic capitalism, which have led the United States to economic prosperity and political freedom.

Our bilateral economic assistance program should be directed at promoting economic growth and prosperity in developing nations. Therefore, we support recently enacted legislation untying our programs from the policies of austerity of international organizations such as the International Monetary Fund.

We have changed the Carter-Mondale policy of channeling increasing proportions of U.S. assistance through multinational institutions beyond our control. We strongly support President Reagan's decision not to increase funding for the International Development Association because of its predilection for nations with state-dominated economic systems. Our contribution to the International Fund for Agricultural Development will be eliminated due to its consistent bias toward non-market economies. And the anti-American bureaucracy of the U.N.'s Educational, Scientific and Cultural Organization (UNESCO) will no longer be supported by U.S. taxpayers. We will not support international organizations inconsistent with our interests. In particular, we will work to eliminate their funding of Communist states.

Prominent among American ideals is the sanctity of the family. Decisions on family size should be made freely by each family. We support efforts to enhance the freedom of such family decisions. We will endeavor to assure that those who are responsible for our programs are more sensitive to the cultural needs of the countries to which we give assistance.

As part of our commitment to the family and our opposition to abortion, we will eliminate all U.S. funding for organizations which in any way support abortion or research on abortion methods.

To strengthen bilateral foreign assistance, we will reduce or eliminate assistance to nations with foreign policies contrary to our interests and strengthen the Secretary of State's hand by ensuring his direct control over assistance programs.

Foreign military assistance strengthens our security by enabling friendly

715

nations to provide for their own defense, including defense against terrorism.

Terrorism is a new form of warfare against the democracies. Supported by the Soviet Union and others, it ranges from PLO murder to the attempted assassination of the Pope. Combatting it requires an integrated effort of our diplomacy, armed forces, intelligence services, and law-enforcement organizations. Legislative obstacles to international cooperation against terrorism must be repealed, followed by a vigorous program to enhance friendly nations' counter-terrorist forces. In particular, we seek the cooperation of our hemispheric neighbors to deal comprehensively with the Soviet and Cuban terrorism now afflicting us.

International Organizations

Americans cannot count on the international organizations to guarantee our security or adequately protect our interests. The United States hosts the headquarters of the United Nations, pays a fourth of its budget, and is proportionally the largest contributor to most international organizations; but many members consistently vote against us. As Soviet influence in these organizations has grown, cynicism and the double standard have become their way of life.

This is why President Reagan announced that we will leave the worst of these organizations, UNESCO. He has put the U.N. on notice that the U.S. will strongly oppose the use of the U.N. to foster anti-semitism, Soviet espionage, and hostility to the United States. The President decisively rejected the U.N. Convention on the Law of the Sea and embarked instead on a dynamic national oceans policy, animated by our traditional commitment to freedom of the seas. That pattern will be followed with regard to U.N. meddling in Antarctica and outer space. Enthusiastically endorsing those steps, we will apply the same standards to all international organizations. We will monitor their votes and activities, and particularly the votes of member states which receive U.S. aid. Americans will no longer silently suffer the hypocrisy of many of these organizations.

Human Rights

The American people believe that United States foreign policy should be animated by the cause of human rights for all the world's peoples.

A well-rounded human rights policy is concerned with specific individuals whose rights are denied by governments of the right or left, and with entire peoples whose Communist governments deny their claim to human rights as individuals and acknowledge only the "rights" derived from membership in an economic class. Republicans support a human rights policy which includes both these concerns.

Republican concern for human rights also extends to the institutions of free societies — political parties, the free press, business and labor organizations — which embody and protect the exercise of individual rights. The National Endowment for Democracy and other instruments of U.S. diplomacy foster the growth of these vital institutions.

By focusing solely on the shortcomings of non-Communist governments, Democrats have missed the forest for the trees, failing to recognize that the greatest threat to human rights is the Communist system itself.

Republicans understand that the East-West struggle has profound human rights implications. We know that Communist nations, which profess dedication to human rights, actually use their totalitarian systems to violate human rights in an organized, systematic fashion.

The Reagan-Bush Administration has worked for positive human rights changes worldwide. Our efforts have ranged from support for the Helsinki Accords to our support of judicial and political reform in El Salvador.

The Republican Party commends President Reagan for accepting the Honorary Chairmanship of the campaign to erect a U.S. Holocaust Memorial in Washington, D.C. and supports the efforts of the U.S. Holocaust Council in erecting such a museum and educational center. The museum will bear witness to the victims and survivors of the Holocaust.

For Republicans, the struggle for human freedom is more than an end in itself. It is part of a policy that builds a foundation for peace. When people are free to express themselves and choose democratic governments, their free private institutions and electoral power constitute a constraint against the excesses of autocratic rulers. We agree with President Truman, who said: "In the long run our security and the world's hopes for peace lie not in measures of defense or in the control of weapons, but in the growth and expansion of freedom and self-government."

To this end, we pledge our continued effort to secure for all people the inherent, God-given rights that Americans have been privileged to enjoy for two centuries.

Advocacy for Democracy

To promote and sustain the cause of democracy, America must be an active participant in the political competition between the principles of Communism and of democracy.

To do this, America needs a strong voice and active instruments of public diplomacy to counter the Communist bloc's massive effort to disinform and deceive world public opinion. Republicans believe that truth is America's most powerful weapon.

The Reagan-Bush Administration has elevated the stature of public diplomacy in the councils of government and increased the United States Information Agency budget by 44 percent in four years. New programs have been launched in television, citizen exchanges, and dissemination of written information. The National Endowment for Democracy has enlisted the talent of private American institutions, including the AFL-CIO and the U.S. Chamber of Commerce, to educate our friends overseas in the ways of democratic institutions. A sustained billion-dollar effort is modernizing and expanding the Voice of America, strengthening the Voice's signal, lengthening its broadcasts, improving its content, adding new language services and replacing antiquated equipment. Radio Marti, the new broadcast service to Cuba, will begin to broadcast the truth about Cuba to the Cuban people.

Initial steps have been taken to improve the capabilities of Radio Free Europe and Radio Liberty, which serve the captive nations of the Soviet bloc. We pledge to carry out a thorough improvement program for these radios, including new transmitters and other means of penetrating the jamming which denies the RFE/RL signal to millions of captive people, including the increasingly discontented Soviet minorities, behind the Iron Curtain.

Because of the importance we place on people-to-people exchange programs, Republicans support the dedicated work of Peace Corps volunteers. America must nurture good relations not only with foreign governments but with other peoples as well. By encouraging the free flow of ideas and information, America is helping to build the infrastructure of democracy and demonstrating the strength of our belief in the democratic example. The United States Peace Corps, reflecting traditional American values, will follow the White House initiative promoting free enterprise development overseas in third world countries.

The tradition of addressing the world's peoples, advocating the principles and goals of democracy and freedom, is as old as our Republic. Thomas Jefferson wrote the Declaration of Independence "with a decent respect to the opinions of mankind." This popular advocacy is even more important today in the global struggle between totalitarianism and freedom.

THE FUTURE OF OUR NATIONAL SECURITY

Republicans look to the future with confidence that we have the will, the weapons, and the technology to preserve America as the land of the free and the home of the brave. We stand united with President Reagan in his hope that American scientists and engineers can produce the technology and the hardware to make nuclear war obsolete.

The prospect for peace is excellent because America is strong again. America's defenses have only one purpose: to assure that our people and free institutions survive and flourish.

Our security requires both the capability to defend against aggression and the will to do so. Together, will and capability deter aggression. That is why the danger of war has grown more remote under President Reagan.

When he took office, defense policy was in disarray. The Carter-Mondale Administration had diminished our military capability and had confused the pursuit of peace with accommodating totalitarianism. It could not respond to the determined growth of Soviet military power and a more aggressive Soviet foreign policy.

We are proud of a strong America. Our military strength exists for the high moral purpose of deterring conflict, not initiating war. The deterrence of aggression is ethically imperative. That is why we have restored America's defense capability and renewed our country's will. Americans are again proud to serve in the Armed Forces and proud of those who serve.

We reaffirm the principle that the national security policy of the United States should be based upon a strategy of peace through strength, a goal of the 1980 Republican Platform.

Maintaining a technological superiority, the historical foundation of our policy of deterrence, remains essential. In other areas, such as our maritime forces, we should continue to strive for qualitative superiority.

President Reagan committed our nation to a modernized strategic and theater nuclear force sufficient to deter attack against the United States and our allies, while pursuing negotiations for balanced, verifiable reductions of nuclear weapons under arms control agreements.

In order to deter, we must be sufficiently strong to convince a potential adversary that under no circumstances would it be to its advantage to initiate conflict at any level.

We pledge to do everything necessary so that, in case of conflict, the United States would clearly prevail.

We will continue to modernize our deterrent capability while negotiating for verifiable arms control. We will continue the policies that have given fresh confidence and new hope to freedom-loving people everywhere.

Arms Control for the Future

Americans, while caring deeply about arms control, realize that it is not an end in itself, but can be a major component of a foreign and defense policy which keeps America free, strong, and independent.

Sharing the American people's realistic view of the Soviet Union, the Reagan Administration has pursued arms control agreements that would reduce the level of nuclear weaponry possessed by the superpowers. President Reagan has negotiated with flexibility, and always from a position of strength.

In the European theater, President Reagan proposed the complete elimination of intermediate-range nuclear missiles. In the START talks with the Soviet Union, he proposed the "build-down" which would eliminate from the U.S. and Soviet arsenals two existing nuclear warheads for each new warhead.

The Soviet Union has rejected every invitation by President Reagan to resume talks, refusing to return unless we remove the Pershing II and Cruise missiles which we have placed in Europe at the request of our NATO allies. Soviet intransigence is designed to force concessions from the United States even before negotiations begin. We will not succumb to this strategy. The Soviet Union will return to the bargaining table only when it recognizes that the United States will not make unilateral concessions or allow the Soviet Union to achieve nuclear superiority.

The Soviet Union, by engaging in a sustained pattern of violations of arms control agreements, has cast severe doubt on its own willingness to negotiate and comply with new agreements in a spirit of good faith. Agreements violated by the Soviet Union include SALT, the Anti-Ballistic Missile Treaty of 1972, the Helsinki Accords, and the Biological and Toxin Weapons Convention of 1972. This pattern of Soviet behavior is clearly designed to obtain a Soviet strategic advantage.

To deter Soviet violations of arms control agreements, the United States must maintain the capability to verify, display a willingness to respond to Soviet violations which have military significance, and adopt a policy whereby the defense of the United States is not constrained by arms control agreements violated by the Soviet Union.

We support the President's efforts to curb the spread of nuclear weapons and to improve international controls and safeguards over sensitive nuclear technologies. The President's non-proliferation policy has emphasized results, rather than rhetoric, as symbolized by the successful meeting of nuclear supplier states in Luxembourg in July of this year. We endorse the President's initiative on comprehensive safeguards and his efforts to encourage other supplier states to support such measures.

Defense Resources

The first duty of government is to provide for the common defense. That solemn responsibility was neglected during the Carter-Mondale years. At the end of the Eisenhower era, nearly 48 percent of the federal budget was devoted to defense programs, representing 9.1 percent of our gross national product. By 1980, under Carter-Mondale, defense spending had fallen to only 5 percent of gross national product and represented only 24 percent of the federal budget. The Reagan Administration has begun to correct the weaknesses caused by that situation by prudently increasing defense resources. We must continue to devote the resources essential to deter a Soviet threat — a threat which has grown and should be met by an improved and modernized U.S. defense capability. Even so, the percentage of the Reagan Administration budget spent on defense is only about half that of the Eisenhower-Kennedy era.

Readiness

In 1980, our military forces were not ready to perform their missions in the event of emergency. Many planes could not fly for lack of spare parts; ships could not sail for lack of skilled personnel; supplies were insufficient for essential training or sustained combat. Today, readiness and sustainability have improved dramatically. We not only have more equipment, but it is in operating condition. Our military personnel have better training, pride, and confidence. We have improved their pay and benefits. Recruiting and retaining competent personnel is no longer a problem.

Under the Democrats, the All-Volunteer Force was headed for disastrous failure. Because of the Carter-Mondale intransigence on military pay and benefits, we saw the shameful spectacle of patriotic service families being forced below the poverty level, relying on food stamps and other welfare programs. The quality of life for our military has been substantially improved under the Reagan Administration. We wholeheartedly support the all-volunteer armed force and are proud of our historic initiative to bring it to pass.

From the worst levels of retention and recruiting in post-war history in 1979, we have moved to the highest ever recorded. We are meeting 100 percent of our recruiting needs, and 92 percent of our recruits are high school graduates capable of mastering the skills needed in the modern armed services. In 1980, 13 percent of our ships and 25 percent of our aircraft squadrons reported themselves not combat ready because of personnel shortages. Today, those figures have dropped to less than 1 percent and 4 percent respectively.

Today, the United States leads the world in integrating women into the military. They serve in a variety of non-combat assignments. We have made significant strides in numbers of women and their level of responsibility. Female officer strength has grown by 24 percent under the Reagan Administration and is projected to increase, with even greater increases for non-commissioned officers.

Conventional and Strategic Modernization

In 1980, we had a "hollow Army," a Navy half its numbers of a decade earlier, and an Air Force badly in need of upgrading. The Army is now receiving the most modern tanks, fighting vehicles, and artillery. The Navy has grown to 513 ships with 79 more under construction this year, well on its way toward the 600-ship, 15-carrier force necessary for our maritime strategy. The Air Force has procured advanced tactical aircraft. By decade's end, our intertheater lift capacity will have increased by 75 percent. We pledge to rescue a shipbuilding industry consigned to extinction by the Carter-Mondale team.

Since the end of World War II, America's nuclear arsenal has caused the Soviet Union to exercise caution to avoid direct military confrontation with us and our close allies.

Our nuclear arms are a vital element of the Free World's security system.

Throughout the 1970s and up to the present, the Soviet Union has engaged in a vast buildup of nuclear arms. In the naive hope that unilateral restraint by the United States would cause the Soviet Union to reverse course, the Carter-Mondale Administration delayed significant major features of the strategic modernization our country needed. There was no arms race because only the Soviet Union was racing, determined to achieve an intimidating advantage over the Free World. As a result, in 1980, America was moving toward a position of clear nuclear inferiority to the Soviets.

President Reagan moved swiftly to reverse this alarming situation and to reestablish an effective margin of safety before 1990. Despite obstruction from many congressional Democrats, we have restored the credibility of our deterrent.

Reserve and Guard Forces

We salute the men and women of the National Guard and the Reserves. The Carter-Mondale team completely neglected our vital Reserve and Guard forces, leaving them with obsolete equipment, frozen pay, and thousands of vacancies.

The Reagan Administration has transformed our Reserve and National Guard. The Naval Reserve will ultimately operate 40 of the fleet's 600 ships. Navy and Marine Air Reserve units now receive the most modern aircraft, as do the Air Force Reserve and Guard. Army Reserve and Guard units now receive the latest tanks, infantry fighting vehicles, and artillery. Reserve pay has increased 30 percent, and reserve components are having record success in filling their positions. Our country counts on the Reserves and the Guard, and they can count on us.

Management Reform

The Republican Party advocates a strong defense and fiscal responsibility at the same time. This Administration has already made major advances in eliminating the deep-rooted procurement problems we inherited. Republicans have changed the way the Pentagon does business, encouraging greater economy and efficiency, stretching the taxpayer's dollar.

Learning nothing from past mistakes, the Carter-Mondale Administration returned to centralized defense management. The predictable result: competition fell to only 15 percent of Pentagon procurement; programs were mired in disastrous cost overruns and disputes; outrageous and exorbitant prices were paid for spare parts; and the taxpayers' money was wasted on a grand scale.

We have tackled this problem head-on. We returned management to the Services and began far-reaching reforms. To hold down costs, we more than doubled competition in Pentagon procurement. We appointed Competition Advocate Generals in each Service and an overall Inspector General for the Pentagon. We increased incentives for excellent performance by contractors, and we have applied immediate penalty for poor performance. Our innovative approaches have already saved the taxpayers billions of dollars.

Spare parts acquisition has undergone thorough reform. Improving spare parts management, involving a Department of Defense inventory of almost four million items, is a complex and massive management challenge. The Pentagon's new 10-point program is already working. Old contracts are being revamped to allow competition, high prices are being challenged, and rigorous audits are continuing. As an example, a stool cap for a navigator's chair, once priced at $1,100, was challenged by an alert Air Force Sergeant. It now costs us 31 cents. The Pentagon obtained a full refund and gave the Sergeant a cash reward.

Our men and women in uniform deserve the best and most reliable weapons that this country can offer. We must improve the reliability and performance of our weapons systems, and warranties can be a very positive contribution to defense procurement practices, as can be the independent office of operational testing and evaluation, which was another positive Republican initiative.

The acquisition improvement program now includes program stability, multi-year procurement, economic production rates, realistic budgeting, and increased competition. The B-1B bomber, replacing our aging B-52 force, is ahead of schedule and under cost. We support our anti-submarine warfare effort and urge its funding at its current level. For the last two years, the Navy has received nearly 50 ships more than three years ahead of schedule and nearly $1 billion under budget. The *U.S.S. Theodore Roosevelt*, our newest aircraft carrier, is 17 months ahead of schedule and almost $74 million under cost.

We have reformed inefficient procurement practices established decades ago, and we will continue to ensure the most gain from each defense dollar.

The Tasks Ahead

The damage to our defenses through unilateral disarmament cannot be repaired quickly. The hollow Army of the Carter-Mondale Administration is hollow no more, and our Navy is moving toward a 600-ship force.

We share President Reagan's determination to restore credible security for our country. Our choice is not between a strong defense or a strong economy; we must succeed in both, or we will succeed in neither.

Our forces must be second to none, and we condemn the notion that one-sided military reduction will induce the Soviets to seek peace. Our military strength not only provides the deterrent necessary for a more peaceful world, but it is also the best incentive for the Soviets to agree to arms reduction.

Veterans

America is free because of its veterans. We owe them more than thanks. After answering the call to arms, they brought leadership and patriotism back to their communities. They are a continuing resource for America. Through their membership in veterans' service activities, they have strongly supported President Reagan's defense policy. Knowing firsthand the sacrifices of war, they have spoken out frequently for a strong national defense.

Veterans have earned their benefits; these must not be taken away. The help we give them is an investment which pays our nation unlimited dividends.

We have accomplished a great deal. We are meeting the needs of women veterans and ensuring them equal treatment. We must prepare to meet the needs of aging veterans.

We are addressing the unique readjustment problems of Vietnam veterans by expanding the store-front readjustment counseling program, extending vocational training and job placement assistance, and targeting research toward understanding delayed stress reaction in combat veterans. We have moved to alleviate the uncertainty of veterans exposed to Agent Orange by providing nearly 129,000 medical exams and by launching an all-out, government-wide research effort.

We are making major strides in improving health care for veterans. VA hospital construction has expanded to meet community needs, and benefits for disabled veterans have been improved.

We will maintain the veterans' preferences for federal hiring and will improve health, education, and other benefits. We support the Reagan Administration's actions to make home ownership attainable by more veterans, as well as our program to help veterans in small business compete for government contracts. We will extend to all veterans of recent conflicts, such as Lebanon and Grenada, the same assistance.

In recognition of the unique commitment and personal sacrifices of military spouses, President Reagan has called upon the nation to honor them and proclaimed a day of tribute. We will remember them and advance their interests.

National Intelligence

Knowing our adversaries' capabilities and intentions is our first line of defense. A strong intelligence community focuses our diplomacy and saves billions of defense dollars. This critical asset was gravely weakened during the Carter-Mondale years.

We will continue to strengthen our intelligence services. We will remove statutory obstacles to the effective management, performance, and security of intelligence sources and methods. We will further improve our ability to influence international events in support of our foreign policy objectives, and we will strengthen our counterintelligence facilities.

Strategic Trade

By encouraging commerce in militarily significant technology, the Carter-Mondale Administration actually improved Soviet military power. Because of that terrible error, we are now exposed to significant risk and must spend billions of defense dollars that would otherwise have been unnecessary.

The Reagan Administration halted the Carter-Mondale folly. We have strengthened cooperative efforts with our allies to restrict diversion of militarily critical technologies. We will increase law-enforcement and counterintelligence efforts to halt Soviet commercial espionage and illegal exploitation of our technology.

Terrorism

International terrorism is not a random phenomenon but a new form of warfare waged by the forces of totalitarianism against the democracies.

In recent years, certain states have sponsored terrorist actions in pursuit of their strategic goals. The international links among terrorist groups are now clearly understood; and the Soviet link, direct and indirect, is also clearly understood. The Soviets use terrorist groups to weaken democracy and undermine world stability.

Purely passive measures do not deter terrorists. It is time to think about appropriate preventive or pre-emptive actions against terrorist groups before they strike.

Terrorism is an international problem. No one country can successfully combat it. We must lead the free nations in a concerted effort to pressure members of the League of Terror to cease their sponsorship and support of terrorism.

A Secure Future

During the Carter-Mondale Administration, the Soviets built more weapons, and more modern ones, than the United States. President Reagan has begun to reverse this dangerous trend. More important, he has begun a process that, over time, will gradually but dramatically reduce the Soviet Union's ability to threaten our lives with nuclear arms.

His leadership came none too soon. The combined damage of a decade of neglect and of relentless Soviet buildup, despite treaties and our restraint, will not be undone easily.

Today, the Soviet Union possesses over 5,000 intercontinental nuclear warheads powerful and accurate enough to destroy hard military targets, and it is flight-testing a whole new generation of missiles. The Carter-Mondale Administration left this country at a decided disadvantage, without a credible deterrent. That is why President Reagan embarked on a modernization program covering all three legs of the strategic triad.

Republicans understood that our nuclear deterrent forces are the ultimate military guarantor of America's security and that of our allies. That is why we will continue to support the programs necessary to modernize our strategic forces and reduce the vulnerabilities. This includes the earliest possible deployment of a new small mobile ICBM.

While the Carter-Mondale team hid beneath an umbrella of wishful thinking, the Soviet Union made every effort to protect itself in case of conflict. It has an operational anti-satellite system; the United States does not. A network of huge ultra-modern radars, new anti-missile interceptors, new surface-to-air missiles, all evidence the Soviet commitment to self-protection.

President Reagan has launched a bold new Strategic Defense Initiative to defend against nuclear attack. We enthusiastically support President Reagan's Strategic Defense Initiative. We enthusiastically support the development of non-nuclear, space-based defensive systems to protect the United States by destroying incoming missiles.

Recognizing the need for close consultation with our allies, we support a comprehensive and intensive effort to render obsolete the doctrine of Mutual Assured Destruction (MAD). The Democratic Party embraces Mutual Assured Destruction. The Republican Party rejects the strategy of despair and supports instead the strategy of hope and survival.

We will begin to eliminate the threat posed by strategic nuclear missiles as soon as possible. Our only purpose (one all people share) is to reduce the danger of nuclear war. To that end, we will use superior American technology to achieve space-based and ground-based defensive systems as soon as possible to protect the lives of the American people and our allies.

President Reagan has asked, "Would it not be better to save lives than to avenge them?" The Republican Party answers, "Yes!"

REAGAN, BUSH
ACCEPTANCE SPEECHES
August 23, 1984

A jubilant Republican Party wound up its August 20-23 convention in Dallas, Texas, confident that President Ronald Reagan and Vice President George Bush would be "the winning team" in November. With the ticket's renomination certain beforehand, the 33rd Republican National Convention was more a celebration than a business meeting of GOP activists. Behind the cheering and display of party unity, however, there was a current of dissent: Moderates, who were greatly outnumbered, voiced unhappiness with the party's direction and its platform. (Platform, p. 661)

During convention week, speaker after speaker criticized the Democrats, saying they represented a legacy of "malaise" from Jimmy Carter's administration and promised only a future of fear. Reagan, too, emphasized that theme in his 55-minute acceptance speech August 23. To repeated interruptions of applause and cheers, he drew sharp differences between Republicans and Democrats, and between himself and the Democratic presidential nominee, Walter F. Mondale. "The choices this year are not just between two different personalities or between two political parties," Reagan said. "They are between two different visions of the future, two fundamentally different ways of governing — their government of pessimism, fear and limits ... or ours of hope, confidence and growth."

In his acceptance speech earlier in the evening, Bush vigorously touted the Reagan administration's record. "Under this president, more lands have been acquired for parks, more for wilderness," he said. "The quality

*of life is better — and that's a fact." In foreign affairs, Bush said,
"... there is new confidence in the U.S. leadership around the world. ...
Because our president stood firm in defense of freedom, America has
regained respect throughout the world. ..."*

*Speakers in previous sessions had sought to make the same points.
They tried to link former Vice President Mondale to the policies and
problems of the administration in which he had served. "Carter-Mondale" became their shorthand for a list of evils: inflation, high interest
rates, foreign policy failures, and sagging national spirit.*

*GOP leaders also were anxious to portray the Democratic ticket and
the party's leadership as out of step with most Democrats. They gave the
spotlight to Democrats-turned-Republicans, giving one of their warmest
welcomes to Jeane J. Kirkpatrick, the U.S. representative to the United
Nations, whom one party leader referred to as "an enlightened Democrat." Kirkpatrick delivered a foreign policy speech during the opening
session August 20. The party's leaders also made clear they were making
a pitch for women voters, in response to the candidacy of Rep. Geraldine
A. Ferraro, D-N.Y., Mondale's running mate.*

Opening Ceremonies, Ford Speech

*The administration was firmly in control of events inside the Dallas
Convention Center. Conditions outside the hall were almost as controlled
as events inside. Police were ever present, but demonstrations were, by
and large, tepid. One major reason was the record-breaking heat: It
prompted some protesters to leave town and delegates and the press to
stay in the air-conditioned indoors.*

*The official August 20 opening ceremonies were a mix of the patriotic
and the political. About 50 young people carrying flags and wearing
smocks decorated with red, white, and blue elephants lined the interior of
the hall; delegates then sang "The Star-Spangled Banner" and recited
the pledge of allegiance.*

*The evening session was the GOP's "ladies' night." Four of the six
speakers were women, including Katherine D. Ortega, the U.S. treasurer,
and Kirkpatrick. Although Ortega was billed as the keynote speaker, it
was Democrat Kirkpatrick who received the most sustained and vigorous
applause from the delegates. Kirkpatrick had harsh words for her fellow
Democrats, charging that they "treat foreign affairs as an afterthought."
She asserted that the Carter administration "did not seem to notice
much, care much, or do much" about a host of international problems.*

*Following adoption of the platform the next day, the highlight of the
August 21 evening session was a speech by former president Gerald R.
Ford. Delegates gave Ford and his wife, Betty, a rousing welcome. Ford
wasted no time attacking the Democratic nominee, telling delegates:*

"Mondale wants this election to be a 'referendum on the future.' I can't blame him for wanting to forget the past, the four years of Carter-Mondale from 1977 through 1980. Who wants to remember four years of roaring inflation, skyrocketing interest rates and so-called 'malaise?' "

Goldwater Address, Renominations

Before Reagan and Bush were renominated on the evening of August 22, Sen. Barry Goldwater, Ariz., addressed the convention. Goldwater, the party's presidential nominee in 1964, said he wanted to talk to the delegates about "freedom." He opened his speech with a slogan from his campaign 20 years earlier: "Let me remind you," he said, "extremism in the defense of liberty is no vice." Goldwater charged that the Democrats at their convention "turned their backs on our own heritage. Indeed, they would have us ashamed of our freedom and our ability to defend it. To me, the worst part was that they said nicer things about the Soviet Union than about our own military services."

The delegates then proceeded to renominate Reagan and Bush. Although the outcome came as no surprise, there was a state-by-state roll call on the nominations, with Reagan receiving 2,233 votes and Bush receiving 2,231 votes. U.N. Representative Kirkpatrick received one vice presidential vote from a delegate in Alabama, and Rep. Jack F. Kemp, N.Y., got one vote from Nebraska.

It was a festive night for Republicans, and one that was days in the making. Dozens of Dallas teenagers had painted "Reagan-Bush" posters for the scheduled 15-minute demonstration to celebrate the nominations. Hundreds of red, white, and blue balloons dropped from the ceiling at the appropriate moment.

Nevadan Paul Laxalt, the president's closest friend in the Senate, put Reagan's name in nomination. He delivered a rousing speech, emphasizing the problems of the "Carter-Mondale" administration and highlighting successes under Reagan. Gov. George Deukmejian of California placed Bush's name in nomination. Deukmejian, too, took aim at the Democrats. Their message, he asserted, is "a message of fear. Fear that the prosperity they couldn't produce will end if we re-elect the team that produced it, Ronald Reagan and George Bush.... We're not afraid. We're not scared. We're confident."

Acceptance Speeches

On the final night of the convention, Reagan and Bush came to the hall to claim their nominations. With standing room only in the 17,000-seat arena, guests were lined up three deep in some places for an evening of balloons, speeches, and patriotic music. Delegates were shown a short film about Bush. At its conclusion, the vice president came to the podium and received a long ovation. Bush launched an attack on the Democrats, charging that "for over half a century, the liberal Democrats have pursued a philosophy of tax and spend, tax and spend."

Shortly thereafter, the hall was darkened, and for 18 minutes a film on Reagan's accomplishments was shown. With testimonials, footage of foreign trips, and voice-over narrative by Reagan, it sought to portray the president as a concerned leader and statesman. When the film was over, Reagan came to the podium amid a thunderous ovation. After about 10 minutes the crowd quieted, allowing him to speak. But the audience interrupted him repeatedly with applause and chants of "Four more years!" and "U.S.A!"

> *Following are the texts of President Ronald Reagan's and Vice President George Bush's speeches to the Republican National Convention in Dallas August 23, accepting the party's renomination to a second term. (Boldface headings in brackets have been added by Congressional Quarterly to highlight the organization of the text.):*

REAGAN ACCEPTANCE SPEECH

Thank you very much. Mr. Chairman, Mr. Vice President, delegates to this convention, and fellow citizens:

In 75 days, I hope we enjoy a victory that is the size of the heart of Texas.

Nancy and I extend our deep thanks to the Lone Star State and the "Big D" — the city of Dallas — for all their warmth and hospitality.

Four years ago, I didn't know precisely every duty of this office, and not too long ago, I learned about some new ones from the first-graders of Corpus Christi School in Chambersburg, Pa.

Little Leah Kline was asked by her teacher to describe my duties.

She said: "The president goes to meetings. He helps the animals. The president gets frustrated. He talks to other presidents."

How does wisdom begin at such an early age?

[Clear Political Choice]

Tonight, with a full heart and deep gratitude for your trust, I accept your nomination for the presidency of the United States.

I will campaign on behalf of the principles of our party which lift America confidently into the future.

America is presented with the clearest political choice of half a century.

The distinction between our two parties and the different philosophy of our political opponents are at the heart of this campaign and America's future.

I've been campaigning long enough to know that a political party and its leadership can't change their colors in four days.

We won't, and no matter how hard they tried, our opponents didn't in San Francisco.

We didn't discover our values in a poll taken a week before the convention.

And we didn't set a weathervane on top of the Golden Gate Bridge before we started talking about the American family.

The choices this year are not just between two different personalities, or between two political parties.

They are between two different visions of the future, two fundamentally different ways of governing — their government of pessimism, fear and limits — or ours of hope, confidence, and growth.

Their government sees people only as members of groups; ours serves all the people of America as individuals.

Theirs lives in the past, seeking to apply the old and failed policies to an era that has passed them by; ours learns from the past and strives to change by boldly charting a new course for the future.

Theirs lives by promises, the bigger, the better. We offer proven, workable answers.

[Inflation and Interest Rates]

Our opponents began this campaign hoping that America has a poor memory.

Well, let's take them on a little stroll down memory lane.

Let's remind them of how a 4.8 percent inflation rate in 1976 became back-to-back years of double-digit inflation — the worst since World War I — punishing the poor and the elderly, young couples striving to start their new lives, and working people struggling to make ends meet.

Inflation was not some plague borne on the wind.

It was a deliberate part of their official economic policy needed, they said, to maintain prosperity.

They didn't tell us that with it would come the highest interest rates since the Civil War.

As average monthly mortgage payments more than doubled, home building nearly ground to a halt, tens of thousands of carpenters and others were thrown out of work.

And who controlled both houses of the Congress and the executive branch at the time?

Not us. Not us.

Campaigning across America in 1980, we saw evidence everywhere of industrial decline.

And in rural America, farmers' costs were driven up by inflation; they were devastated by a wrongheaded grain embargo, and were forced to borrow money at exorbitant interest rates just to get by, and many of them didn't get by.

Farmers have to fight insects, weather, and the marketplace — they shouldn't have to fight their own government.

The high interest rates of 1980 were not talked about in San Francisco.

[Taxes]

But how about taxes?

They were talked about in San Francisco.

Will Rogers once said he never met a man he didn't like.

But if I could paraphrase Will, our friends in the other party have never met a tax they didn't like — they didn't like, or hike.

Under their policies, tax rates have gone up three times as much for families with children as they have for everyone else over these past three decades.

In just the five years before we came into office, taxes roughly doubled.

Some who spoke so loudly in San Francisco of fairness were among those who brought about the biggest, single, individual tax increase in our history in 1977, calling for a series of increases in the Social Security payroll tax and in the amount of pay subject to the tax.

The bill they passed called for two additional increases between now and 1990, increases that bear down hardest on those at the lower income levels.

The Census Bureau confirms that, because of the tax laws we inherited, the number of households at or below the poverty level paying federal income tax more than doubled between 1980 and 1982.

Well, they received some relief in 1983 when our across-the-board tax cut was fully in place, and they'll get more help when indexing goes into effect this January.

Our opponents have repeatedly advocated eliminating indexing.

Would that really hurt the rich?

No, because the rich are already in the top brackets.

But those working men and women who depend on a cost-of-living adjustment just to keep abreast of inflation would find themselves pushed into a higher tax bracket and wouldn't even be able to keep even with inflation because they'd be paying a higher income tax.

That's "bracket creep" and our opponents are for it; and we're against it.

It's up to us to see that all our fellow citizens understand that confiscatory taxes, costly social experiments and economic tinkering were not just the policies of a single administration.

For the 26 years prior to January of 1981, the opposition party controlled both houses of Congress.

Every spending bill and every tax for more than a quarter of a century has been of their doing.

About a decade ago, they said federal spending was out of control, so they passed a budget control act, and, in the next five years, ran up deficits of $260 billion. Some control.

In 1981, we gained control of the Senate and executive branch. With the help of some concerned Democrats in the House we started a policy of tightening the federal budget instead of the family budget.

A task force chaired by Vice President George Bush — the finest vice president this country has ever had — it eliminated unnecessary regulations that had been strangling business and industry.

[Poor Americans]

And while we have our friends down memory lane, maybe they'd like to recall a gimmick they designed for their 1976 campaign.

As President Ford told us the night before last, adding the unemployment and inflation rates, they got what they called a Misery Index — in '76 it came to 12½ percent.

And they declared the incumbent had no right to seek re-election with that kind of Misery Index.

Four years ago in the 1980 election, they didn't mention the Misery Index.

Possibly because it was then over 20 percent.

And do you know something?

They won't mention it in this election either; it's down to 11.6, and dropping.

By nearly every measure, the position of poor Americans worsened under the leadership of our opponents.

Teenage drug use, out-of-wedlock births, and crime increased dramatically.

Urban neighborhoods and schools deteriorated.

Those whom government intended to help discovered a cycle of dependency that could not be broken.

Government became a drug — providing temporary relief, but addiction as well.

And let's get some facts on the table that our opponents don't want to hear.

The biggest annual increase in poverty took place between 1978 and 1981 — over 9 percent each year in the first two years of our administration. Well, I should — pardon me, I didn't put a period in there.

In the first two years of our administration, that annual increase fell to 5.3 percent.

And 1983 was the first year since 1978 that there was no appreciable increase in poverty at all.

Pouring hundreds of billions of dollars into programs in order to make people worse off was irrational and unfair.

[Faith in the Human Process]

It was time we ended this reliance on the government process and renewed our faith in the human process.

In 1980, the people decided with us that the economic crisis was not caused by the fact that they lived too well. Government lived too well.

It was time for tax increases to be an act of last resort, not of first resort.

The people told the liberal leadership in Washington, "Try shrinking the size of government before you shrink the size of our paychecks."

Our government was also in serious trouble abroad.

We had aircraft that couldn't fly and ships that couldn't leave port.

Many of our military were on food stamps because of meager earnings, and re-enlistments were down.

Ammunition was low, and spare parts were in short supply.

Many of our allies mistrusted us.

In the four years before we took office, country after country fell under the Soviet yoke.

Since Jan. 20, 1981, not one inch of soil has fallen to the communists.

But worst of all, worst of all, Americans were losing the confidence and optimism about the future that has made us unique in the world.

Parents were beginning to doubt that their children would have the better life that has been the dream of every American generation.

We can all be proud that pessimism is ended.

America is coming back and is more confident than ever about the future.

Tonight, we thank the citizens of the United States — whose faith, and unwillingness to give up on themselves or this country saved us all.

Together, we began the task of controlling the size and activities of the government by reducing the growth of its spending while passing a tax program to provide incentives to increase productivity for both workers and industry.

Today, a working family earning $25,000 has about $2,900 more in purchasing power than if tax and inflation rates were still at the 1980 level.

Today, of all the major industrial nations of the world, America has the strongest economic growth; one of the lowest inflation rates; the fastest rate of job creation — 6½ million jobs in the last year and a half; a record 600,000 business incorporations in 1983; and the largest increase in real, after-tax personal income since World War II.

We're enjoying the highest level of business investment in history, and America has renewed its leadership in developing the vast new opportunities in science and high technology.

America is on the move again, and expanding toward new areas of opportunity for everyone.

Now, we're accused of having a secret.

Well, if we have, it is that we're going to keep the mighty engine of this nation revved up.

And that means a future of sustained economic growth without inflation that's going to create for our children and grandchildren a prosperity that finally will last.

[Defense and Foreign Policy]

Today, our troops have newer and better equipment, their morale is higher.

The better armed they are, the less likely it is they will have to use that equipment.

But if, heaven forbid, they are ever called upon to defend this nation, nothing would be more immoral than asking them to do so with weapons inferior to those of any possible opponent.

We have also begun to repair our valuable alliances, especially our historic NATO alliance.

Extensive discussions in Asia have enabled us to start a new round of diplomatic progress there.

In the Middle East, it remains difficult to bring an end to historic conflicts — but we're not discouraged.

And we shall always maintain our pledge never to sell out one of our closest friends — the state of Israel.

Closer to home, there remains a struggle for survival for free Latin American states — allies of ours, they valiantly struggle to prevent communist takeovers fueled massively by the Soviet Union and Cuba.

Our policy is simple: We are not going to betray our friends, reward the enemies of freedom or permit fear and retreat to become American policies — especially in this hemisphere.

None of the four wars in my lifetime came about because we were too strong.

It is weakness that invites adventurous adversaries to make mistaken judgments.

America is the most peaceful, least warlike nation in modern history.

We are not the cause of all the ills of the world.

We are a patient and generous people.

But for the sake of our freedom and that of others, we cannot permit our reserve to be confused with a lack of resolve.

['New Realism']

When we talk of the plight of our cities, what would help more than our enterprise zones bill which provides tax incentives for private industry to help rebuild and restore decayed areas in 75 sites all across America?

If they really wanted a future of boundless new opportunities for our citizens, why have they buried enterprise zones, over the years, in committee?

Our opponents are openly committed to increasing your tax burden.

We are committed to stopping them, and we will.

They call their policy the "new realism."

But their "new realism" is just the "old liberalism."

They will place higher and higher taxes on small businesses, on family farms and every working family so that government may once again grow at the people's expense.

You know, we could say they spend money like drunken sailors but that would be unfair to drunken sailors.

(Cheers from crowd, chants of "four more years.")

All right, I agree. All right. I was going to say it would be unfair because the sailors are spending their own money.

Our tax policies are and will remain pro-work, pro-growth, and pro-family.

We intend to simplify the entire tax system; to make taxes more fair, easier to understand, and, most important, to bring the tax rates of every American further down, not up.

Now, if we bring them down far enough, growth will continue strong; the underground economy will shrink; the world will beat a path to our door; and no one will be able to hold America back; and the future will be ours.

[Reduce Risk of Nuclear War]

Another part of our future, the greatest challenge of all, is to reduce the risk of nuclear war by reducing the levels of nuclear arms.

I have addressed parliaments, have spoken to parliaments in Europe and Asia during these last 3½ years declaring that a nuclear war cannot be won and must never be fought.

And those words in those assemblies were greeted with spontaneous applause.

There are only two nations who by their agreement can rid the world of those doomsday weapons, the United States of America and the Soviet Union.

For the sake of our children and the safety of this earth, we ask the Soviets — who have walked out of our negotiations — to join us in reducing and, yes, ridding the earth of this awful threat.

[If Democrats Win in November]

When we leave this hall tonight, we begin to place those clear choices before our fellow citizens.

We must not let them be confused by those who still think that G.N.P. stands for Gross National Promises.

But after the debates, the position papers, the speeches, the conventions, the television commercials, primaries, caucuses, and slogans — after all this, is there really any doubt at all about what will happen if we let them win this November?

Is there any doubt that they will raise our taxes?

That they will send inflation into orbit again?

That they will make government bigger than ever, and deficits even worse?

Raise unemployment?

Cut back our defense preparedness?

Raise interest rates?

Make unilateral and unwise concessions to the Soviet Union?

And they'll do all that in the name of compassion.

It's what they've done to America in the past, but if we do our job right, they won't be able to do it again.

[Renew the Mandate of 1980]

In 1980 —

It's getting late.

In 1980, we asked the people of America: Are you better off than you were four years ago?

Well, the people answered by choosing us to bring about a change.

We have every reason now, four years later, to ask that same question again, for we have made a change, the American people joined and helped us.

Let us ask for their help again to renew the mandate of 1980, to move us further forward on the road we presently travel.

The road of common sense, of people in control of their own destiny; the road leading to prosperity and economic expansion in a world at peace.

As we ask for their help, we should also answer the central question of public service: Why are we here? What do we believe in?

Well, for one thing, we're here to see that government continues to serve the people and not the other way around.

Yes, government should do all that is necessary, but only that which is necessary.

We don't lump people by groups or special interests, and let me add, in the party of Lincoln, there is no room for intolerance, and, not even a small corner for anti-Semitism or bigotry of any kind.

Many people are welcome in our house, but not the bigots.

We believe in the uniqueness of each individual.

We believe in the sacredness of human life.

For some time now we've all fallen into a pattern of describing our choice as left or right.

It has become standard rhetoric in discussions of political philosophy.

But is that really an accurate description of the choice before us?

Go back a few years to the origin of the terms and see where left or right would take us if we continued far enough in either direction.

Stalin. Hitler. One would take us to communist totalitarianism and the other to the totalitarianism of Hitler.

Isn't our choice really not one of left or right, but of up or down: down through the welfare state to statism, to more and more government largesse, accompanied always by more government authority, less individual liberty and ultimately totalitarianism, always advanced as for our own good.

The alternative is the dream conceived by our founding fathers, up to the ultimate in individual freedom consistent with an orderly society.

We don't celebrate Dependence Day on the Fourth of July.

We celebrate Independence Day.

We celebrate the right of each individual to be recognized as unique, possessed of dignity and the sacred right to life, liberty and the pursuit of happiness.

At the same time, with our independence goes a generosity of spirit more evident here than in almost any other part of the world.

Recognizing the equality of all men and women, we're willing and able to lift the weak, cradle those who hurt, and nurture the bonds that tie us together as one nation under God.

Finally, we are here to shield our liberties, not just for now or for a few years, but forever.

[Leaving the Democratic Party]

Could I share a personal thought with you tonight?

Because tonight is kind of special for me.

It is the last time, of course, that I will address you under these circumstances.

I hope you'll invite me back to future conventions.

Nancy and I will be forever grateful for the honor you've done us, for the opportunity to serve, and for your friendship and trust.

I began political life as a Democrat, casting my first vote in 1932 for Franklin Delano Roosevelt.

That year, the Democrats called for a 25 percent reduction in the cost of government by abolishing useless commissions and offices and consolidating departments and bureaus, and giving more authority to state governments.

As the years went by and those promises were forgotten, did I leave the Democratic Party, or did the leadership of that party leave not just me but millions of patriotic Democrats who believed in the principles and philosophy of that platform?

One of the first to declare this was a former Democratic nominee for president — Al Smith, the happy warrior — who went before the nation in 1936 to say on television — on radio — that he could no longer follow his party's leadership, and that he was "taking a walk."

As Democrat leaders have taken their party further and further away from its first principles, it's no surprise that so many responsible Democrats feel that our platform is closer to their views, and we welcome them to our side.

Four years ago we raised a banner of bold colors — no pale pastels.

['A Shining City on a Hill']

We proclaimed a dream of an America that would be "a shining city on a hill."

We promised that we'd reduce the growth of the federal government, and we have.

We said we intended to reduce interest rates and inflation, and we have.

We said we would reduce taxes to provide incentives for individuals and business to get our economy moving again. We said — and we have.

We said there must be jobs with a future for our people, not government make-work programs, and, in the last 19 months, as I've said, 6½ million new jobs in the private sector have been created.

We said we would once again be respected throughout the world, and we are.

We said we would restore our ability to protect our freedom on land, sea, and in the air, and we have.

We bring to the American citizens in this election year a record of accomplishment and the promise of continuation.

We came together in a "national crusade to make America great again," and to make "a new beginning."

Well, now, it's all coming together.

[Springtime of Hope]

With our beloved nation at peace, we are in the midst of a springtime of hope for America.

Greatness lies ahead of us.

Holding the Olympic Games here in the United States began defining the promise of this season.

All through the spring and summer, we marveled at the journey of the Olympic Torch as it made its passage, east to west.

Over 9,000 miles, by some 4,000 runners, that flame crossed a portrait of our nation.

From our Gotham City, New York, to the cradle of liberty, Boston, across the Appalachian springtime, to the city of the big shoulders, Chicago.

Moving south toward Atlanta, over to St. Louis past its Gateway Arch, across wheat fields into the stark beauty of the Southwest and then up into the still snow-capped Rockies.

And after circling the greening Northwest, it came down to California, across the Golden Gate, and finally into Los Angeles.

And all along the way, that torch became a celebration of America. And, we all became participants in the celebration.

Each new story was typical of this land of ours.

There was Ansel Stubbs, a youngster of 99, who passed the torch in Kansas to a 4-year-old, Katie Johnson.

In Pineville, Ky., it came at 1 a.m., so hundreds of people lined the streets with candles.

At Tupelo, Miss., at 7 a.m. on a Sunday morning, a robed church choir sang "God Bless America" as the torch went by.

The torch went through the Cumberland Gap, past the Martin Luther King Jr. Memorial, down the Santa Fe Trail and alongside Billy the Kid's grave.

In Richardson, Texas, it was carried by a 14-year-old boy in a special wheelchair.

In West Virginia, the runner came across a line of deaf children and let each one pass the torch for a few feet, and at the end those youngsters' hands talked excitedly in their sign language.

Crowds spontaneously began singing "America the Beautiful" or "The Battle Hymn of the Republic."

And then, in San Francisco, a Vietnamese immigrant, his little son held on his shoulders, dodged photographers and policemen to cheer a 19-year-old black man pushing an 88-year-old white woman in a wheelchair as she carried the torch.

My friends, that's America.

We cheered in Los Angeles as the flame was carried in and the giant Olympic torch burst into a billowing fire in front of the teams.

The youth of 140 nations assembled on the floor of the coliseum.

And in that moment, maybe you were struck as I was with the uniqueness of what was taking place before 100,000 people in the stadium, most of them citizens of our country, and over a billion worldwide watching on television.

There were athletes representing 140 countries here to compete in the one country in all the world whose people carry the bloodlines of all those 140 countries and more.

Only in the United States is there such a rich mixture of races, creeds, and nationalities — only in our melting pot.

[Liberty]

And that brings to mind another torch, the one that greeted so many of our parents and grandparents.

Just this past Fourth of July, the torch atop the Statue of Liberty was hoisted down for replacement.

We can be forgiven for thinking maybe it was just worn out from lighting the way to freedom for 17 million new Americans.

So now we'll put up a new one.

The poet called Miss Liberty's torch the "lamp beside the golden door."

Well, that was the entrance to America and it still is.

And now you really know why we are here tonight.

The glistening hope of that lamp is still ours.

Every promise, every opportunity is still golden in this land.

And through that golden door our children can walk into tomorrow with the knowledge that no one can be denied the promise that is America.

Her heart is full; her door is still golden, her future bright.

She has arms big enough to comfort and strong enough to support.

For the strength in her arms is the strength of her people.

She will carry on in the eighties unafraid, unashamed, and unsurpassed.

In this springtime of hope, some lights seem eternal.

America's is.

Thank you, God bless you, and God bless America.

BUSH ACCEPTANCE SPEECH

Thank you very much.

Mr. Chairman, madam chairman, and my fellow Republicans, and my fellow Americans.

I accept your nomination and the honor and challenge it represents.

Four years ago in Detroit, I pledged my total dedication and energies to support our president. And that has been a very easy pledge to keep. Tonight, I pledge again my every effort to support President Reagan as he leads this nation into four more years of prosperity, opportunity and peace.

In 1980, America needed Governor Reagan in the White House to restore power to the grassroots and to give the American people fresh hope and a new beginning.

In 1984, America needs President Reagan in the White House for a second term to finish the job — to keep this country moving forward.

But we can't move forward, we can't move forward, if we have a majority in Congress that wants to go back.

With your all-out effort, we will maintain control of the Senate — and we'll get a House of Representatives that will move forward with President Reagan and the party of the future — not backward with Tip O'Neill and the party of the past.

[Taxes]

For over half a century, the liberal Democrats have pursued this philosophy of tax and spend, tax and spend.

And, sure enough, out of that Moscone Center in San Francisco, that temple of doom, came Mr. Mondales's first promise — a solemn promise to raise everyone's taxes.

Well, Mr. Mondale calls this promise to raise taxes a lot of courage, an act of courage. But it wasn't courage — it was just habit, because he is a gold medal winner when it comes to increasing the tax burden of the American people.

Well, President Reagan, with strong support in Congress, cut tax rates across the board for every single American — and he'll keep those rates cut.

And the message the American people got from San Francisco was, "We'll raise your taxes."

But our message from Dallas is: The American people want less spending, less regulation, and not more taxes.

They want to keep America's dynamic economy strong.

They want to reduce the deficits by making government more efficient, holding the line on spending, and through economic growth.

And as for a balanced budget, our message is this: Let the big spenders in Congress step aside. Give us the balanced budget amendment.

Give us the line-item veto and watch what this president can do.

I heard that speaker in San Francisco last month exhorting his fellow Democrats with the cry, "Our time has come; our time has come."

The American people have a message for the tax raisers, the free spenders, the excess regulators — the government-knows-best handwringers, those who would promise every special interest group everything — and that message is this: "Your time has passed; your time has passed."

No matter how your rhetoric tries to move away from your voting records, no matter how hard you try to turn your back on Jimmy Carter, no matter how much you now talk about family values, this country will not retreat. You've had your chance. Your time has passed.

[President's Accomplishments]

This president has turned this country's economy around. Since we came into office, productivity is up; personal savings are up; consumer spending is up; housing starts are up; take-home pay is up; inflation — the cruelest tax of all — is down, and more Americans are at work than at any time in the history of the United States.

More Americans are enjoying our country because our parks are cleaner and our air is purer. Under this president, more lands have been acquired for parks, more for wilderness. The quality of life is better. And that's a fact.

You know more Americans are giving to help others. Private contributions in the great tradition of neighbor helping neighbor are up. And that's a fact.

And at the same time, government help for the truly needy is up. The Social Security system has been strengthened and saved by our president's leadership and a truly bipartisan effort in Congress.

More Americans now have a chance for quality education. Test scores are up in our schools. In striving for excellence, we have re-emphasized fundamentals. We believe in teaching kids to read, and to write, to add and to subtract. We believe in classroom discipline and in merit pay for teachers. We believe in local control of schools. And we believe kids should not be prohibited from prayer. And that's a fact.

We're waging all-out war against narcotics in our schools, in our neighborhoods, and across the land. We will not rest until American society is free from the threat of drug pushers and that's a fact.

More Americans are safe. Crime is down, and that's a fact.

President Reagan and I think it's time that we worried less about the criminals and more about the victims of crime.

As for our judicial system, it's always been my view that the Supreme Court should not be all caught up and involved in the political arena. But, since the Democrats made this an issue in San Francisco, let me say that the American people want a Supreme Court that will interpret the Constitution, and not legislate.

We heard that liberal convention in San Francisco attack the president regarding the Supreme Court. But the record shows that President Reagan's sole appointment to the court, Sandra Day O'Connor, is an outstanding justice. And that's a fact.

And, one more fact, and let this be heard loud and clear: Ronald Reagan has protected and will continue to protect the rights of all Americans. Discrimination based on race, religion, sex or age will never be tolerated by this president nor this vice president. And, furthermore, we condemn the vicious anti-Semitism of Louis Farrakhan and the ugly bigotry of the Ku Klux Klan.

Of course, problems remain. Of course, problems remain. And, yes, there's still much to be done to provide opportunity for those Americans that truly need help. But the answer doesn't lie in going back to the "malaise" days of Carter and Mondale.

The answer doesn't lie in Mr. Mondale's new spending programs — programs that John Glenn estimated would cost up to $170 billion more; or in Mondale deficits that Fritz Holling estimated at $400 billion. It doesn't lie in the programs of a man that Gary Hart called "mush."

Instead, the answer lies in a dynamic private sector that provides jobs, jobs with dignity. The answer lies in limited government and unlimited confidence in the American people.

[New Confidence in U.S. Leadership]

Just as there's a new confidence — a new optimism — there is new confidence in U.S. leadership around the world. Since becoming vice president, I've gone to 59 countries. Talked to the leaders of those countries and to many other foreign leaders who have come here.

Forgotten is the Carter-Mondale era of vacillation — of weakness — of lecturing to our friends and then letting them down. In this hemisphere, when 1,000 American lives were threatened and when four small Caribbean countries called out for U.S. support to give democracy a chance, President Reagan acted.

And I don't care what Walter Mondale says about it or what Tip O'Neill says about it. Grenada was a proud moment in the history of the United States of America.

Because our president stood firm in defense of freedom, America has regained respect throughout the world. And, because President Reagan has made America stronger, chances for world peace — true, lasting peace — are stronger.

Our European alliance has never been more solid. More countries in Central and South America have turned to democracy since Ronald Reagan became president. Thirteen Latin American countries have held democratic elections since 1980.

We have strengthened our friendships with countries in the Pacific. We are doing more to foster democratic change and to help the hungry in Africa. We are reaching out to more countries in the Middle East and our strategic relations with Israel have never been stronger.

And, one last point on foreign affairs.

I am proud to serve with a president who is working for peace and I am proud to serve with a president who doesn't go around apologizing for the United States of America.

[Message of Optimism, Hope]

As vice president, I've had the opportunity to watch this president in action. I've seen a real leader make tough decisions. No longer do we read and hear stories about the job of president being too big for any one person. Gone are the days of blaming the American people for what was really a failure not of the people, but of our national leadership.

Four years ago, we came into office to restore our economy, expand opportunity for all Americans and secure a lasting peace.

Much has been done. Much remains to be done. But this we know: more Americans today believe we have strong, principled, firm leadership in the White House.

This is the message we will take from this convention — a message of optimism, a message of hope.

Three decades ago, a great American president stood on the Capitol steps and made his second inaugural address.

"May we pursue the right without self-righteousness," said Dwight Eisenhower.

"May we know unity without conformity."

"May we grow in strength without pride in self."

"May we, in our dealings with all the people of the Earth, ever speak truth and serve justice."

And, finally, said President Eisenhower, "May the light of freedom . . . flame brightly, until at last the darkness is no more."

Now, as in President Eisenhower's day, these words reflect the true spirit and aspirations of the American people.

May we continue to keep the light of freedom burning. And may we continue to move forward in the next four years — on the high road to peace, prosperity and opportunity — united behind a great president, Ronald Reagan.

Thank you all, very, very much.

SENATE COMMITTEE REPORT ON THE PERSIAN GULF WAR
August 27, 1984

The Senate Foreign Relations Committee issued a staff report August 27 assessing the volatile political situation in the Persian Gulf and the status of the four-year-old war between Iraq and Iran. The report covered historical background of the conflict, military conditions, U.S. policy in the region, the political perspectives of Iraq, Iran, and neighboring states, and the impact of the war on the world's energy needs. Begun in September 1980, the Iraq-Iran war was regarded as a highly dangerous conflict, given its potential for escalation and the impact it could have on the global oil supply. The struggle was one of the bloodiest in recent history.

Ancient Enmity

The Iraq-Iran struggle had its roots in a centuries-old conflict between Arabs and Persians. Iraq is an Arab country; Iran is Persian. According to some historians, the rivalry stretches back almost 5,000 years. In 2700 B.C. the Sumerians, who lived in part of modern-day Iraq, battled the people of Elam, who lived on the Iranian plateau. Iraqis compared the contemporary struggle with the battle of Qadisiyah in 637 A.D. In that contest the Arabs routed the Indo-European Persians and took control of Mesopotamia.

Religious, as well as cultural, differences played a part in the most recent feud. The Arabs established Islam as the religion of the region. Ironically, most Arab states, including Iraq, practiced a more secular

747

form of Islam than the fundamentalist version practiced under Ayatollah Khomeini in Iran. In 1979 Khomeini deposed the shah of Iran and led an Islamic revolution, establishing a government based on Shiite beliefs. (Historic Documents of 1979, p. 867)

Most of Iraq's population were made up of Shiite Moslems, but the country was ruled by the Sunni Baathists under President Saddam Hussein. Khomeini had made it clear, as the Senate Foreign Relations Committee report noted, that he "would not be satisfied until an Islamic Republic was established in Iraq under the rule of the Shia majority." He called on Iraq's Shiites to overthrow the Hussein government. In addition to politically divergent views, a personal antagonism existed between the two leaders. In 1978, at the request of the shah, Hussein expelled Khomeini from Iraq, where the Shiite cleric had lived in exile for 15 years. This ill will between Khomeini and Hussein added to the long-standing tension between the two countries.

For years the two countries had argued over their border, the sovereignty of three islands at the mouth of the Persian Gulf, and the Shatt-al-Arab waterway at the mouth of the Gulf. The waterway provided Iraq with its primary access to the sea and linked the major oil ports of both countries to the Gulf. Iraq and Iran supposedly settled the dispute over these points at a meeting in Algiers in March 1975. Under the Algiers pact, both countries agreed to stop interfering in the internal affairs of the other. The land frontier was redefined and the southern boundary was set in the middle of the Shatt-al-Arab. Following this agreement, relations between the countries improved. However, Khomeini's rise to power in 1979 brought a quick deterioration of Iraq-Iran ties.

Iraqi Attack

On September 17, 1980, Iraq abrogated the Algiers pact, charging Iran with noncompliance. Four days later Iraq launched an air attack on 11 Iranian bases in the Khuzestan Province. The attack backed up Hussein's demands for Iraqi sovereignty over the Shatt-al-Arab, for a realignment of the border to the north, and a return to "Arab" sovereignty of the three islands.

The blitzkrieg nature of the assault was intended to provide Iraq with a quick victory. Hussein hoped to capitalize on the disorganized state of Iran's military, which was regrouping after the revolution. He also hoped to gain the support of Iran's Arab population in the Khuzestan area. Iraqi forces planned to seize quick control of the Shatt-al-Arab, the Iranian port of Khorramshahr, and the oil refinery complex of Abadan. A quick victory might have increased Iraq's influence in the Middle East and Hussein's prestige as a prominent leader of the Arab world.

But the plan did not work. Iraqi forces battled for almost a month to take Khorramshahr and after a year still did not have control of Abadan, although the refinery was badly damaged. Contrary to Iraq's calculations, Iranian Arabs did not join forces with the Iraqis, the Iranian military did not crack, and the Khomeini regime did not collapse. The two armies battled for months. News reports termed the war "static" and a "no-win conflict." After a year of fighting, Iraq had captured some 8,000 square miles of Iranian territory but had been unable to attain Iranian recognition of Iraqi sovereignty over the Shatt-al-Arab.

Costly Stalemate

Late in 1981 and early in 1982 Hussein made several overtures to end the war. He offered to pull out Iraqi forces from Iran if the latter would recognize Iraqi sovereignty over the waterway. Iran refused. The Iranian army was better organized and the country more united than at the start of the war. From the Iranian perspective, the war was a battle to rid Iran of Arab invaders. Bolstered by events, Iran launched a major offensive in Khuzestan and forced Iraqi soldiers to retreat in March of 1982.

On June 10, 1982, Iraq declared a truce and ceasefire, but Iran rejected the offer. Iraq withdrew its forces from Iran June 20-29, hoping to negotiate a settlement. Iran, however, was not interested in negotiations. On July 13 Iranian forces, numbering almost 80,000, attacked Iraq. Furious fighting cost both sides many lives. Khomeini in a radio broadcast called upon the Iraqi people to "rise up" against the "blasphemous regime" of Hussein. But the war dragged on through 1982 — a costly stalemate. Estimates in August 1982 gave totals of 80,000 killed, 200,000 wounded, and 45,000 captured.

In February 1983 Iran launched a new offensive in Iraq. News accounts described the "human waves" of young Iranian volunteers and revolutionary guards who marched with suicidal determination toward the Iraqi lines. More than anything else, some analysts stated, it was the attitude of these Iranian fighters, motivated by thoughts of martyrdom and revenge, that was the turning tide of the war in Iran's favor. With a population almost three times that of Iraq, Iran was able to enlist a far greater number of recruits, many reportedly boys in their early teens.

One step that Iraq took to counter the superior number of Iranian soldiers was to use internationally outlawed chemical weapons. In March 1984 the U.S. State Department accused Iraq of having used mustard gas; later in 1984, reports that Iraq also was using nerve gas remained unconfirmed.

Unable to persuade Iran to negotiate an end to the war, Iraq in the spring of 1983 threatened to use its superior air power to attack Iranian ports and tankers carrying Iranian oil through the Gulf. In response, Iran threatened to close the Gulf to prevent other countries from exporting oil.

Attacks on oil tankers escalated in 1984, doubling insurance rates for maritime traffic in the Gulf. Kharg Island at the head of the Gulf, where almost 90 percent of Iranian oil exports were handled, became a prime target of Iraqi attacks.

Ground fighting continued along the Iraqi border in 1984. In late February an Iranian offensive in Iraq resulted in tremendous losses for both sides. On February 23 an estimated 7,300 soldiers were reported killed in 24 hours. In early March Iran began to move hundreds of thousands of soldiers to the Iraqi front for what could be the largest offensive in the war. The offensive attempt remained on hold, however, at the time the Senate report was released.

Mediation Attempts

A number of mediation attempts had been made since the onset of the war. The United Nations Security Council adopted resolutions in 1980, 1982, and 1983 calling for a ceasefire, and a United Nations representative traveled to the area in search of a settlement. The Gulf Cooperation Council (comprised of Kuwait, Saudi Arabia, Bahrain, Qatar, the United Arab Emirates, and Oman) and the 42-nation Organization of the Islamic Conference made repeated attempts to mediate. Representatives from individual countries, including Turkey, India, Algeria, and Japan, also made efforts to de-escalate the conflict. All attempts at settlement foundered, however, on Iran's demands that Iraq pay substantial war reparations and that Hussein and his government be identified as the aggressors and be punished.

Iraq held the edge in the conflict by mid-1984. Iraq's Arab neighbors, fearful of the implications of an Iranian victory, provided Iraq with billions of dollars to finance its war effort. The Soviet Union, abandoning its early support of Iran, had become Iraq's largest weapon supplier. France was Iraq's other major arms source, having provided $5 billion worth of equipment, including Super Etendard fighter jets and Exocet missiles.

Since 1982, when Iraq offered to negotiate an end to the war, U.S. policy had tilted toward Iraq. The United States had taken a number of steps to shore up Iraq's position by providing $1 billion in commodity credits, an Export-Import Bank guarantee for 85 percent of construction costs of an Aqaba pipeline, and strong support for a fairly effective arms embargo against Iran.

Committee Report Findings

In July 1984 five staff members from the Senate Foreign Relations Committee made two visits to the Persian Gulf area to assess the situation. They visited Iraq and other Gulf states, but not Iran. On August 27 the committee issued a report based on the staff's findings.

The study reported that the military balance had tilted toward Iraq, primarily due to its superior air weapons and the effectiveness of the arms embargo against Iran. The report stated that launching of the long-awaited Iranian offensive would probably lead to an Iranian defeat. However, the study noted, Iraqi morale was low and the country was weary of the prolonged war effort.

The report also touched on the issue of prisoners of war. An estimated 50,000 to 60,000 Iraqi soldiers were being held as POWs in Iran, and 10,000 to 15,000 Iranians were being held in Iraq. Both sides, according to the International Committee of the Red Cross, had violated requirements of the Geneva Convention for the treatment of prisoners. The Senate committee report claimed that the Iranian-held POWs, however, were being treated worse than those those held in Iraq. Reportedly, those Iraqi prisoners who refused to be converted to Iran's revolutionary cause were either executed or used as human minesweepers.

The committee staff members also visited U.S. military facilities in the region, reporting that 11,500 U.S. military personnel were on duty in the Persian Gulf and Arabian Sea areas. The Soviets also maintained a military presence in the region. The report maintained that because the United States and Soviet Union were both helping Iraq in an attempt to end the conflict, "there is no serious concern that the Iran-Iraq war could engage the superpowers in hostilities." Assessing the energy situation, the report stated that the tanker war "is having remarkably little effect on Persian Gulf exports." Should exports be shut off because of the war, increased Saudi production could avert a crisis. A shut-off of Saudi oil, however, "would have a severe impact on the price and availability of oil."

Following is the Executive Summary of the "War In The Gulf" *prepared for the United States Senate Committee on Foreign Relations, released August 27, 1984:*

U.S. Policy in the Region

The stakes in the Persian Gulf are high for the United States and its Western allies. It remains vital for the West as a source of imported petroleum despite the current oil "glut."

There is greater calm in most Gulf countries and in the international oil market than most observers had predicted.

Earlier this year there was considerable concern in the Gulf region that the United States would use military force prematurely to keep the Gulf open and then be forced by U.S. public opinion to pull out. In the last several months, the Administration has allayed these concerns by placing emphasis on military involvement only through invitation rather than by unilateral decision. This policy is also supported by the British and the French.

The United States supports an immediate peace between Iraq and Iran without victor and without vanquished. Since 1982, when the Iraqis agreed to negotiate without conditions, United States policy has tilted toward Iraq. The United States has undertaken a number of steps to shore up Iraq and to forestall an Iranian victory.

The Soviets seek new opportunities in the Gulf and the Middle East generally by attempting to expand their influence among parties on both sides of the Iraq-Iran conflict. They have tilted toward Iraq, as has the United States, while at the same time increasing military support for Iran's ally Syria and maintaining lines of communication with Iran. They would like to be in a position to mediate an end to the war in order to regain credibility in the area. While fundamental United States and Soviet interests remain at odds in the Gulf, both have some immediate goals in common. As a result, there is no serious concern that the current Iran-Iraq war could engage the superpowers in hostilities.

The Military Situation

The Iran-Iraq military balance has shifted in Iraq's favor during the past year as a result of the worldwide arms embargo on Iran and massive arms sales to Iraq by the Soviets and French. Iraq does have two potentially serious military liabilities: its lack of strategic depth and the morale of Iraqi troops. It is our assessment that an Iranian assault on Iraq would probably lead to a defeat for Iran unless Iraqi morale collapses. Having publicly heightened expectations for a major assault that it is unlikely to win, Iran faces a dilemma. The debate continues in Iran and is complicated by Ayatollah Khomeini's poor health.

If Iran decides not to attack Iraq directly, it might increase military and diplomatic pressure on the Gulf Cooperation Council (GCC) states [Kuwait, Saudi Arabia, Bahrain, Qatar, the United Arab Emirates, Oman.] Iraq has incentives to escalate the tanker war to bring further economic pressure to bear on Iran. A massive Iraqi attack on Iran's oil exporting facilities at Kharg Island remains a distinct possibility.

Closing the Gulf would be an act of desperation for Iran. Iran has the capability to close the Gulf in the absence of assistance to the Gulf states from countries outside the region. Western powers could reopen the Gulf, and this might lead to devastating air strikes on Iranian ports and airbases. While the United States might find it necessary to take such action, it could provide political and military opportunities for the Soviets in Iran. Therefore, a high priority of U.S. diplomacy should be to promote a settlement of the war.

Sources in the area say that without the capabilities provided to the Saudis by U.S. arms sales, the Saudis might well now be seeking direct support of U.S. Air Force fighter aircraft to defend their oil fields. Instead, Saudi Arabia's combat aircraft in the Dhahran region combined with early warning from the U.S.-operated AWACs and KC-10 refueling tankers give the Saudis the capability to defend against both a small surprise attack and a sustained attack by the Iranian Air Force. A surprise attack in force would be difficult to stop entirely. Saudi Arabia has the capability to retaliate against attacks on its territory, although its will to do so is questioned by some.

The Saudis are vulnerable to sabotage. They rely on harsh punishment to deter saboteurs and redundancy in their export capacity to continue the flow of oil to the West.

The United States currently has 11,500 sailors and soldiers in the Persian Gulf and Arabian Sea area. Despite its size, the U.S. presence is unobtrusive. U.S. military personnel in the war zone are generally not unduly vulnerable, although there is some risk. Our destroyers in the Gulf itself are primarily symbolic, but the Carrier Battle Group in the Arabian Sea has a deterrent capability. The United States does not now have the capability in the region to stop the tanker war, but there are significant U.S. military assets earmarked for the U.S. Central Command (CENTCOM) that could. Senior U.S. military commanders in the region do not envision realistic contingencies that would require U.S. ground troops, except for security guard duty.

U.S. access to the military facilities of Gulf Cooperation Council countries is crucial if the United States should agree to protect shipping in the Gulf. The change in possible adversaries from the Soviet Union to Iran clouds the political picture somewhat and raises the question whether the facilities necessary for a substantial U.S. military effort would be forthcoming.

Coordination with the NATO allies on Persian Gulf issues has improved.

Virtually all the Gulf Cooperation Council states have asked the United States for additional arms sales to cope with the current military tension in the area. Some of these requests appear to be in excess of regional needs.

Senior U.S. military officials in Saudi Arabia estimate that the 200 Stinger launchers with 400 missiles already in Saudi hands are adequate to provide gap-filler defense for the oil-rich Eastern Province. The Stingers are stored in concrete ammunition storage bunkers with a two-key security system. Additional protective measures are being taken.

Political Perspectives

There are few signs of war in Baghdad, but below the surface there is war weariness. Iraqi officials now speak with a greater degree of confidence about the war than they did a year ago.

The regime's reliance on repressive measures and Saddam Hussein's personality cult may limit the quality of advice that he gets.

Iraq's economy remains in serious but manageable shape.

The United States' position on the war has led to an Iraqi desire to strengthen relations with the United States. Iraqi officials are trying to allay U.S. concerns about their support for terrorism and their use of chemical weapons. Iraq does not, however, want to resume full diplomatic relations with the United States at this time.

Several key Iranian leaders appear to be reaching the conclusion that the costs of continuing military efforts are becoming too great. There is no indication, however, that Ayatollah Khomeini has changed his basic position in support of the war. With limited options, an Iranian diplomatic effort seems to be under way to separate Iraq from the GCC states and to gain some influence in Moscow.

A wide diversity of views exists among the Gulf Cooperation Council states. All share a common perception that an escalation in the war poses severe risks for them. In general, the further north one goes in the Gulf, the more support one finds for Iraq's position in the war.

United States-Saudi relations suffered briefly after the failure in Lebanon, but U.S. support during the tanker war has renewed good relations. United States and Saudi interests in the Persian Gulf are generally consistent, but the extent of potential cooperation should not be exaggerated. Significant bilateral problems could develop over arms sales and policy questions related to Israel.

Kuwait is particularly vulnerable to Iranian sabotage efforts, air raids, and terrorist acts. Their industrial facilities and societal structure are both very vulnerable and Iran has significant incentives to undermine Kuwaiti support for Iraq. The Kuwaitis are searching in many quarters for ways to defend themselves.

The UAE [United Arab Emirates] and Oman both stress the need to avoid a direct Arab-Iranian confrontation. Neither would be eager to allow the United States to use its military facilities for operations against Iran.

The $300 million U.S. military construction program in Oman is 75 percent completed, but some problems remain including the question of U.S. access to Omani facilities.

Energy Assessment

Non-Communist world petroleum demand declined in 1983 for the fourth consecutive year. One result is an excess oil production capacity worldwide estimated at from 10 to 12 million barrels per day (mbd), of which only 3 mbd is located outside the Persian Gulf.

Downward pressure on oil prices continues. The outlook for global petroleum demand is for a gradual pick-up. The pressure among Gulf producers is for more production not less. If they are able to produce, prices are likely to remain stable or decline.

At present, the tanker war is having remarkably little effect on Persian Gulf exports through the Strait of Hormuz.

If oil exports from Iraq, Kuwait, Iran and the Neutral Zone were shut off, this reduction could be accommodated by expanded Saudi production. A shut-off of Saudi oil would have a severe impact on the price and availability of oil. . . .

September

THE VATICAN ON THE 'THEOLOGY OF LIBERATION'

September 3, 1984

The Vatican released a formal critique September 3 on "liberation theology," a controversial blend of Christian doctrine and Marxist social theory that had developed in many Third World nations, particularly in Latin America, advocating radical means to achieve social change. The statement's purpose was to "draw the attention of pastors, theologians and all the faithful to the deviations" of certain liberation theologies "which use, in an insufficiently critical manner, concepts borrowed from various currents of Marxist thought."

Entitled "Instruction on Certain Aspects of the 'Theology of Liberation,'" the 36-page statement represented the most comprehensive attempt that church officials in Rome had made to deal with the doctrinal problems created by leftist theologies. The document was certain to intensify the growing controversy between radical and conservative Roman Catholic clergy in Latin America. Since 1980 the Vatican had been increasing pressure on church officials to bring activist priests in line with the more conservative outlook of Pope John Paul II, whose views were shaped, in part, by his long service as a prelate in communist-controlled Poland and his exposure to a European brand of Marxism, allegedly different from the socio-religious philosophy of espoused "liberation" theologians.

Liberation Theology

The controversial theology was first defined by Rev. Gustavo Gutiérrez of Peru in his seminal book A Theology of Liberation, *published in 1971.*

His work was followed by similar analyses by concerned theologians of Latin America. The philosophy developed as priests and nuns, appalled by social injustices they observed, began drawing on Marxist concepts to analyze the economic inequities and to justify their own political activism. But liberation theology extends far beyond attacking the social inequality that exists between the landowners and the military of Latin America on the one hand, and the peasantry on the other. The control of the major industrial nations over the resources of developing economies is seen as the true enemy. ". . . [T]here can be authentic development for Latin America only if there is liberation from the domination exercised by the great capitalist countries, especially by the most powerful, the United States of America," wrote Father Gutiérrez in his critical work. It is a theology not primarily devoted to social action but rather to the broader concept of the politics of underdevelopment.

The core of Marxist theory is that there is a historical inevitability about the ultimate triumph of socialism. Marx's concept of dialectical materialism stated that capitalism contained within itself the seeds of its own destruction. As wealth becomes increasingly concentrated, the working class — upon whom the capitalists depend to produce — becomes increasingly impoverished. Ultimately, to survive, the working class must seize control of the means of production or starve. According to Marx, this process is inevitable, a product of historical economic forces. There is no place for any otherworldly forces, making Marxist theory anathema to the Vatican from its inception.

Encouraged by the Second Vatican Council's appeal that the church express a "preferential option for the poor" and by the Conference of Latin American Bishops' endorsement, held in Medellín, Colombia, in 1968, of liberation theology, some Roman Catholic clerics began to interpret the Bible as a call for social change, buttressing their arguments with Marxist social analysis. The Vatican statement, however, gave little encouragement to these clerics. "It is difficult, and perhaps impossible, to purify these borrowed concepts of an ideological inspiration which is incompatible with Christian faith and the ethical requirements which flow from it," the authors warned.

The Role of the Clergy

The Vatican statement also shed light on the hierarchy's view of the proper role of the clergy in countries where glaring social inequality existed. The church should not condone this situation, according to the document, but neither should the clergy take part in political parties or movements: "The acute need for radical reforms . . . should not let us lose sight of the fact that the source of injustice is in the hearts of men. Therefore it is only by making an appeal to the moral potential of the person and to the constant need for interior conversion that social change will . . . truly be in the service of man."

Church officials in Rome leveled their severest criticism at the use of the concept of inevitable class struggle — with its overtones of violence — by the liberation theologians, calling this notion "contrary to any ethic which is respectful of persons." In addition, their critique continued, these religious philosophies had accepted the viewpoint of the revolutionary class as the "single true point of view," a stance that threatened to divide the church itself. "There is a denunciation of the members of the hierarchy and the magisterium as objective representatives of the ruling class which has to be opposed."

Political Involvement

The effects of the Vatican statement were likely to be felt in several countries. In Nicaragua, for example, the clergy actively supported the Sandinista revolution in 1976 and four priests holding office in the Marxist-inspired Sandinista government were ordered to resign by their bishop. Political involvement by activist clergy also was evident in nearby El Salvador, where 18 priests and lay workers, including the nation's archbishop and a group of nuns from the United States, had been killed, presumably by rightist "death squads."

Salvadoran clerics feared a fatal division within the church in response to the Vatican's statement. A Salvadoran priest was quoted in the New York Times *as saying, "The right will use this to say we are leftists who have been condemned by the pope ... And the leftists will tell the rightists that they don't understand reality. I don't think it will force priests out of the church, but it will polarize us."*

The pope had made clear earlier his opposition to political involvement on the part of Roman Catholic clergy. In 1980 the pontiff forced an activist priest, Rep. Robert F. Drinan, D-Mass., to resign from the U.S. Congress. (Historic Documents of 1980, p. 411)

Church spokesmen in the United States greeted the Vatican statement with general approval. But critical responses were heard from other quarters. The Rev. Peter-Hans Kolvenbach, superior general of the Jesuit order, expressed his strong support of Latin American liberation theologians and church workers. Father Kolvenbach said there existed a range of philosophy within liberation theology, and that the terminology of Marxism would be fitting under certain conditions. The Jesuits, having defined a joint mission of faith and justice in their 32nd general congregation in 1975, assumed a leading role in promoting the debated theology. The Jesuit leader also expressed the opinion that a further, more positive statement would be forthcoming from the Vatican. His expectation was supported by the pope's September 17 homily in Edmonton, Alberta, that lashed out at the nations of the North and their responsibility to aid the poor countries of the South. (Pope's Canadian pilgrimage, p. 777)

Following are excerpts from "Instruction on Certain Aspects of the 'Theology of Liberation'" prepared by the Vatican Congregation for the Doctrine of the Faith in response to the growing political involvement of clerics, released September 3, 1984:

The Gospel of Jesus Christ is a message of freedom and a force for liberation. In recent years this essential truth has become the object of reflection for theologians, with a new kind of attention which is itself full of promise.

Liberation is first and foremost liberation from the radical slavery of sin. Its end and its goal is the freedom of the children of God, which is the gift of grace. As a logical consequence, it calls for freedom from many different kinds of slavery in the cultural, economic, social and political spheres, all of which derive ultimately from sin and so often prevent people from living in a manner befitting their dignity. To discern clearly what is fundamental to this issue and what is a byproduct of it is an indispensable condition for any theological reflection on liberation.

Faced with the urgency of certain problems, some are tempted to emphasize, unilaterally, the liberation from servitude of an earthly and temporal kind. They do so in such a way that they seem to put liberation from sin in second place and so fail to give it the primary importance it is due. Thus, their very presentation of the problems is confused and ambiguous. Others, in an effort to learn more precisely what are the causes of the slavery which they want to end, make use of different concepts without sufficient critical caution. It is difficult, and perhaps impossible, to purify these borrowed concepts of an ideological inspiration which is incompatible with Christian faith and the ethical requirements which flow from it.

The Sacred Congregation for the Doctrine of the Faith does not intend to deal here with the vast theme of Christian freedom and liberation in its own right. . . .

The present instruction has a much more limited and precise purpose: to draw the attention of pastors, theologians and all the faithful to the deviations and risks of deviation, damaging to the faith and to Christian living, that are brought about by certain forms of liberation theology which use, in an insufficiently critical manner, concepts borrowed from various currents of Marxist thought.

This warning should in no way be interpreted as a disavowal of all those who want to respond generously and with an authentic evangelical spirit to the "preferential option for the poor." It should not at all serve as an excuse for those who maintain an attitude of neutrality and indifference in the face of the tragic and pressing problems of human misery and injustice. It is, on the contrary, dictated by the certitude that the serious ideological deviations which it points out tend inevitably to betray the cause of the poor. More than ever, it is important that numerous Christians, whose faith is clear and who are committed to live the Christian life in its fullness, become involved in the struggle for justice, freedom and human dignity because of their love for their disinherited, oppressed and persecuted brothers and sisters. More than ever, the church intends to condemn abuses, injustices and attacks against freedom, wherever they occur and whoever commits them. She intends to struggle, by her own means, for the defense and advancement of the rights of mankind, especially of the poor.

I. An Aspiration

1. The powerful and almost irresistible aspiration that people have for liberation constitutes one of the principal signs of the times which the church has to examine and interpret in the light of the Gospel. This major phenomenon of our time is universally widespread, though it takes on different forms and exists in different degrees according to the particular people involved. It is, above all, among those people who bear the burdens of misery and in the heart of the disinherited classes that this aspiration expresses itself with the greatest force. . . .

4. Consequently mankind will no longer passively submit to crushing poverty with its effects of death, disease and decline. He resents this misery as an intolerable violation of his native dignity. Many factors, and among them certainly the leaven of the Gospel, have contributed to an awakening of the consciousness of the oppressed.

5. It is widely known even in still illiterate sections of the world that, thanks to the amazing advances in science and technology, mankind, still growing in numbers, is capable of assuring each human being the minimum of goods required by his dignity as a person.

6. The scandal of the shocking inequality between the rich and the poor — whether between rich and poor countries, or between social classes in a single nation — is no longer tolerated. On one hand, people have attained an unheard-of abundance which is given to waste, while on the other hand so many live in such poverty, deprived of the basic necessities, that one is hardly able even to count the victims of malnutrition.

7. The lack of equity and of a sense of solidarity in international transactions works to the advantage of the industrialized nations so that the gulf between the rich and the poor is ever widening. Hence derives the feeling of frustration among Third World countries and the accusations of exploitation and economic colonialism brought against the industrialized nations.

8. The memory of crimes of a certain type of colonialism and of its effects often aggravates these injuries and wounds.

9. The Apostolic See, in accord with the Second Vatican Council and together with the episcopal conferences, has not ceased to denounce the scandal involved in the gigantic arms race which, in addition to the threat which it poses to peace, squanders amounts of money so large that even a fraction of it would be sufficient to respond to the needs of those people who want for the basic essentials of life.

II. Expressions of This Aspiration

1. The yearning for justice and for the effective recognition of the dignity of every human being needs, like every deep aspiration, to be clarified and guided.

2. In effect, a discernment process is necessary which takes into account both the theoretical and the practical manifestations of this aspiration. For there are many political and social movements which present themselves as authentic spokesmen for the aspirations of the poor and claim to be able, though by recourse to violent means, to bring about the racial changes which will put an end to the oppression and misery of people.

3. So the aspiration for justice often finds itself the captive of ideologies which hide or pervert its meaning and which propose to people struggling for their liberation goals which are contrary to the true purpose of human life. They propose ways of action which imply the systematic recourse to violence, contrary to any ethic which is respectful of persons.

4. The interpretation of the signs of the times in the light of the Gospel requires, then, that we examine the meaning of this deep yearning of people for justice, but also that we study with critical discernment the theoretical and practical expressions which this aspiration has taken on.

III. Liberation, a Christian Theme

1. Taken by itself, the desire for liberation finds a strong and fraternal echo in the heart and spirit of Christians.

2. Thus, in accord with this aspiration, the theological and pastoral movement known as "liberation theology" was born, first in the countries of Latin America, which are marked by the religious and cultural heritage of Christianity, and then in other countries of the Third World, as well as in certain circles in the industrialized countries.

3. The expression "theology of liberation" refers first of all to a special concern for the poor and the victims of oppression, which in turn begets a commitment to justice. Starting with this approach, we can distinguish several often contradictory ways of understanding the Christian meaning of poverty and the type of commitment to justice which it requires. As with all movements of ideas, the "theologies of liberation" present diverse theological positions. Their doctrinal frontiers are badly defined.

4. The aspiration for liberation, as the term itself suggests, repeats a theme which is fundamental to the Old and New Testaments. In itself, the expression "theology of liberation" is a thoroughly valid term: It designates a theological reflection centered on the biblical theme of liberation and freedom, and on the urgency of its practical realization.

The meeting, then, of the aspiration for liberation and the theologies of liberation is not one of mere chance. The significance of this encounter between the two can be understood only in light of the specific message of revelation, authentically interpreted by the magisterium of the church.

IV. Biblical Foundations

1. Thus a theology of liberation correctly understood constitutes an invitation to theologians to deepen certain essential biblical themes with a concern for the grave and urgent questions which the contemporary yearning for liberation and those movements which more or less faithfully echo it pose for the church. We dare not forget for a single instant the situations of acute distress which issue such a dramatic call to theologians.

2. The radical experience of Christian liberty is our first point of reference. Christ, our liberator, has freed us from sin and from slavery to the law and to the flesh, which is the mark of the condition of sinful mankind. Thus it is the new life of grace, fruit of justification, which makes us free. This means that the most radical form of slavery is slavery to sin. Other forms of slavery find their deepest root in slavery to sin. That is why freedom in the full Christian sense, characterized by the life in the Spirit, cannot be confused with a license to give in to the desires of the flesh. Freedom is a new life in love.

3. The "theologies of liberation" make wide use of readings from the Book of Exodus. The exodus, in fact, is the fundamental event in the formation of the chosen people. It represents freedom from foreign domination and from slavery. One will note that the specific significance of the event comes from its purpose, for this liberation is ordered to the foundation of the people of God and the covenant cult celebrated on Mt. Sinai. That is why the liberation of the exodus cannot be reduced to a liberation which is principally or exclusively political in nature. Moreover, it is significant that the term freedom is often replaced in scripture by the very closely related term *redemption*....

10. At the same time, the requirements of justice and mercy, already proclaimed in the Old Testament, are deepened to assume a new significance in the New Testament. Those who suffer or who are persecuted are identified with Christ. The perfection that Jesus demands of his disciples (Mt. 5:18) consists in the obligation to be merciful "as your heavenly Father is merciful" (Lk. 6:36).

11. It is in light of the Christian vocation to fraternal love and mercy that the rich are severely reminded of their duty. St. Paul, faced with the disorders of the church of Corinth, forcefully emphasizes the bond which exists between participation in the sacrament of love and sharing with the brother in need.

12. New Testament revelation teaches us that sin is the greatest evil, since it strikes man in the heart of his personality. The first liberation, to which all others must make reference, is that from sin....

14. Consequently, the full ambit of sin, whose first effect is to introduce disorder into the relationship between God and man, cannot be restricted to "social sin." The truth is that only a correct doctrine of sin will permit us to insist on the gravity of its social effects.

15. Nor can one localize evil principally or uniquely in bad social, political or economic "structures" as though all other evils came from them

so that the creation of the "new man" would depend on the establishment of different economic and socio-political structures. To be sure, there are structures which are evil and which cause evil and which we must have the courage to change. Structures, whether they are good or bad, are the result of man's actions and so are consequences more than causes. The root of evil, then, lies in free and responsible persons who have to be converted by the grace of Jesus Christ in order to live and act as new creatures in the love of neighbor and in the effective search for justice, self-control and the exercise of virtue.

To demand first of all a radical revolution in social relations and then to criticize the search for personal perfection is to set out on a road which leads to the denial of the meaning of the person and his transcendence, and to destroy ethics and its foundation, which is the absolute character of the distinction between good and evil. Moreover, since charity is the principle of authentic perfection, that perfection cannot be conceived without an openness to others and a spirit of service....

VI. A New Interpretation of Christianity

1. It is impossible to overlook the immense amount of selfless work done by Christians, pastors, priests, religious or laypersons, who, driven by a love for their brothers and sisters living in inhuman conditions, have endeavored to bring help and comfort to countless people in the distress brought about by poverty. Among these, some have tried to find the most effective means to put a quick end to the intolerable situation.

2. The zeal and the compassion which should dwell in the hearts of all pastors nevertheless run the risk of being led astray and diverted to works which are just as damaging to man and his dignity as is the poverty which is being fought, if one is not sufficiently attentive to certain temptations....

4. To some it even seems that the necessary struggle for human justice and freedom in the economic and political sense constitutes the whole essence of salvation. For them, the Gospel is reduced to a purely earthly gospel.

5. The different theologies of liberation are situated between the preferential option for the poor forcefully reaffirmed without ambiguity after Medellin at the conference of Puebla on the one hand, and the temptation to reduce the Gospel to an earthly gospel on the other....

9. In this present document, we will only be discussing developments of that current of thought which, under the name "theology of liberation," proposes a novel interpretation of both the content of faith and of Christian existence which seriously departs from the faith of the church and, in fact, actually constitutes a practical negation.

10. Concepts uncritically borrowed from Marxist ideology and recourse to theses of a biblical hermeneutic marked by rationalism are at the basis of the new interpretation which is corrupting whatever was authentic in the generous initial commitment on behalf of the poor.

VII. Marxist Analysis

1. Impatience and a desire for results has led certain Christians, despairing of every other method, to turn to what they call "Marxist analysis."

2. Their reasoning is this: An intolerable and explosive situation requires effective action which cannot be put off. Effective action presupposes a scientific analysis of the structural causes of poverty. Marxism now provides us with the means to make such an analysis, they say. Then one simply has to apply the analysis to the Third-World situation, especially in Latin America. . . .

6. In the case of Marxism, in the particular sense given to it in this context, a preliminary critique is all the more necessary since the thought of Marx is such a global vision of reality that all data received from observation and analysis are brought together in a philosophical and ideological structure, which predetermines the significance and importance to be attached to them. The ideological principles come prior to the study of the social reality and are presupposed in it. Thus no separation of the parts of this epistemologically unique complex is possible. If one tries to take only one part, say, the analysis, one ends up having to accept the entire ideology. That is why it is not uncommon for the ideological aspect to be predominant among the things which the "theologians of liberation" borrow from Marxist authors.

7. The warning of Paul VI remains fully valid today: Marxism as it is actually lived out poses many distinct aspects and questions for Christians to reflect upon and act on. However, it would be "illusory and dangerous to ignore the intimate bond which radically unites them, and to accept elements to the Marxist analysis without recognizing its connections with the ideology, or to enter into the practice of class struggle and of its Marxist interpretation while failing to see the kind of totalitarian society to which this process slowly leads."

8. It is true that Marxist thought ever since its origins, and even more so lately, has become divided and has given birth to various currents which diverge significantly from one another. To the extent that they remain fully Marxist, these currents continue to be based on certain fundamental tenets which are not compatible with the Christian conception of humanity and society. In this context certain formulas are not neutral, but keep the meaning they had in the original Marxist doctrine. This is the case with the "class struggle." This expression remains pregnant with the interpretation that Marx gave it, so it cannot be taken as the equivalent of "severe social conflict," in an empirical sense. Those who use similar formulas, while claiming to keep only certain elements of the Marxist analysis and yet to reject this analysis taken as a whole, maintain at the very least a serious confusion in the minds of their readers.

9. Let us recall the fact that atheism and the denial of the human person, his liberty and his rights, are at the core of Marxist theory. This theory, then, contains errors which directly threaten the truths of the faith

regarding the eternal destiny of individual persons. Moreover, to attempt to integrate into theology an analysis whose criterion of interpretation depends on this atheistic conception is to involve oneself in terrible contradictions. What is more, this misunderstanding of the spiritual nature of the person leads to a total subordination of the person to the collectivity and thus to the denial of the principles of a social and political life which is in keeping with human dignity.

10. A critical examination of the analytical methods borrowed from other disciplines must be carried out in a special way by theologians. It is the light of faith which provides theology with its principles. That is why the use of philosophical positions or of human sciences by the theologian has a value which might be called instrumental, but yet must undergo a critical study from a theological perspective. In other words, the ultimate and decisive criterion for truth can only be a criterion which is itself theological. It is only in the light of faith and what faith teaches us about the truth of man and the ultimate meaning of his destiny, that one can judge the validity or degree of validity of what other disciplines propose, often rather conjecturally, as being the truth about man, his history and his destiny.

11. When modes of interpretation are applied to the economic, social and political reality of today, which are themselves borrowed from Marxist thought, they can give the initial impression of a certain plausibility to the degree that the present-day situation in certain countries is similar to what Marx described and interpreted in the middle of the last century. On the basis of these similarities, certain simplifications are made which, abstracting from specific essential factors, prevent any really rigorous examination of the causes of poverty and prolong the confusion.

12. In certain parts of Latin America the seizure of the vast majority of the wealth by an oligarchy of owners bereft of social consciousness, the practical absence or the shortcomings of a rule of law, military dictators making a mockery of elementary human rights, the corruption of certain powerful officials, the savage practices of some foreign capital interests constitute factors which nourish a passion for revolt among those who thus consider themselves the powerless victims of a new colonialism in the technological, financial, monetary or economic order. The recognition of injustice is accompanied by a pathos which borrows its language from Marxism, wrongly presented as though it were scientific language.

13. The first condition for any analysis is total openness to the reality to be described. That is why a critical consciousness has to accompany the use of any working hypotheses that are being adopted. One has to realize that these hypotheses correspond to a particular viewpoint which will inevitably highlight certain aspects of the reality while leaving others in the shade. This limitation, which derives from the nature of human science, is ignored by those who, under the guise of hypotheses recognized as such, have recourse to such an all-embracing conception of reality as the thought of Karl Marx.

VIII. Subversion of the Meaning of Truth and Violence

1. This all-embracing conception thus imposes its logic and leads the "theologies of liberation" to accept a series of positions which are incompatible with the Christian vision of humanity. In fact, the ideological core borrowed from Marxism which we are referring to exercises the function of a determining principle. It has this role in virtue of its being described as "scientific," that is to say, true of necessity.

In this core we can distinguish several components.

2. According to the logic of Marxist thought, the "analysis" is inseparable from the praxis and from the conception of history to which this praxis is linked. The analysis is for the Marxist an instrument of criticism, and criticism is only one stage in the revolutionary struggle. This struggle is that of the proletarian class, invested with its mission in history.

3. Consequently, for the Marxist, only those who engage in the struggle can work out the analysis correctly.

4. The only true consciousness, then, is the partisan consciousness.

It is clear that the concept of truth itself is in question here, and it is totally subverted: There is no truth, they pretend, except in and through the partisan praxis.

5. For the Marxist, the praxis and the truth that comes from it are partisan praxis and truth because the fundamental structure of history is characterized by class struggle. There follows, then, the objective necessity to enter into the class struggle, which is the dialectical opposite of the relationship of exploitation, which is being condemned. For the Marxist, the truth is a truth of class: There is no truth but the truth in the struggle of the revolutionary class.

6. The fundamental law of history, which is the law of the class struggle, implies that society is founded on violence. To the violence which constitutes the relationship of the domination of the rich over the poor, there corresponds the counterviolence of the revolution, by means of which this domination will be reversed.

7. The class struggle is presented as an objective, necessary law. Upon entering this process on behalf of the oppressed, one "makes" truth, one acts "scientifically." Consequently, the conception of the truth goes hand in hand with the affirmation of necessary violence, and so, of a political amorality. Within this perspective, any reference to ethical requirements calling for courageous and radical institutional and structural reforms makes no sense.

8. The fundamental law of class struggle has a global and universal character. It is reflected in all the spheres of existence: religious, ethical, cultural and institutional. As far as this law is concerned, one of these spheres is autonomous. In each of them this law constitutes the determining element.

9. In particular, the very nature of ethics is radically called into question because of the borrowing of these theses from Marxism. In fact, it is the

transcendent character of the distinction between good and evil, the principle of morality, which is implicitly denied in the perspective of the class struggle.

IX. The Theological Application of This Core

....2. It is not the fact of social stratification with all its inequity and injustice, but the theory of class struggle as the fundamental law of history which has been accepted by these "theologies of liberation" as a principle. The conclusion is drawn that the class struggle thus understood divides the church herself, and that in light of this struggle even ecclesial realities must be judged.

The claim is even made that it would maintain an illusion with bad faith to propose that love in its universality can conquer what is the primary structural law of capitalism.

3. According to this conception, the class struggle is the driving force of history. History thus becomes a central notion. It will be affirmed that God himself makes history. It will be added that there is only one history, one in which the distinction between the history of salvation and profane history is no longer necessary. To maintain the distinction would be to fall into "dualism." Affirmations such as these reflect historicist immanentism. Thus there is a tendency to identify the kingdom of God and its growth with the human liberation movement and to make history itself the subject of its own development, as a process of the self-redemption of man by means of the class struggle.

This identification is in opposition to the faith of the church as it has been reaffirmed by the Second Vatican Council....

If one holds that a person should not be the object of hate, it is claimed nevertheless that if he belongs to the objective class of the rich he is primarily a class enemy to be fought. Thus the universality of love of neighbor and brotherhood become an eschatological principle, which will only have meaning for the "new man" who arises out of the victorious revolution.

8. As far as the church is concerned, this system would see her only as a reality interior to history, herself subject to those laws which are supposed to govern the development of history in its immanence. The church, the gift of God and mystery of faith, is emptied of any specific reality by this reductionism. At the same time it is disputed that the participation of Christians who belong to opposing classes at the same eucharistic table still makes any sense.

9. In its positive meaning the "church of the poor" signifies the preference given to the poor, without exclusion, whatever the form of their poverty, because they are preferred by God. The expression also refers to the church of our time, as communion and institution and on the part of her members, becoming more fully conscious of the requirement of evangelical poverty.

10. But the "theologies of liberation," which reserve credit for restoring

to a place of honor the great texts of the prophets and of the Gospel in defense of the poor, go on to a disastrous confusion between the poor of the scripture and the proletariat of Marx. In this way they pervert the Christian meaning of the poor, and they transform the fight for the rights of the poor into a class fight within the ideological perspective of the class struggle. For them, the "church of the poor" signifies the church of the class which has become aware of the requirements of the revolutionary struggle as a step toward liberation and which celebrates this liberation in its liturgy.

11. A further remark regarding the expression "church of the people" will not be out of place here. From the pastoral point of view, this expression might mean the favored recipients of evangelization to whom, because of their condition, the church extends her pastoral love first of all. One might also refer to the church as people of God, that is, people of the new covenant established in Christ.

12. But the "theologies of liberation" of which we are speaking mean by church of the people a church of the class, a church of the oppressed people whom it is necessary to "conscientize" in the light of the organized struggle for freedom. For some, the people, thus understood, even become the object of faith.

13. Building on such a conception of the church of the people, a critique of the very structures of the church is developed. It is not simply the case of fraternal correction of pastors of the church whose behavior does not reflect the evangelical spirit of service and is linked to old-fashioned signs of authority which scandalize the poor. It has to do with a challenge to the sacramental and hierarchical structure of the church, which was willed by the Lord himself. There is a denunciation of members of the hierarchy and the magisterium as objective representatives of the ruling class which has to be opposed. Theologically, this position means that ministers take their origin from the people, who therefore designate ministers of their own choice in accord with the needs of their historic revolutionary mission. . . .

XI. Orientations

1. The warning against the serious deviations of some "theologies of liberation" must not at all be taken as some kind of approval, even indirect, of those who keep the poor in misery, who profit from that misery, who notice it while doing nothing about it or who remain indifferent to it. The church, guided by the Gospel of mercy and by the love for mankind, hears the cry for justice and intends to respond to it with all her might.

2. Thus a great call goes out to all the church: With boldness and courage, with farsightedness and prudence, with zeal and strength of spirit, with a love for the poor which demands sacrifice, pastors will consider the response to this call a matter of the highest priority, as many already do.

3. All priests, religious and lay people who hear this call for justice and who want to work for evangelization and the advancement of mankind will

do so in communion with their bishop and with the church, each in accord with his or her own specific ecclesial vocation.

4. Aware of the ecclesial character of their vocation, theologians will collaborate loyally and with a spirit of dialogue with the magisterium of the church. They will be able to recognize in the magisterium a gift of Christ to his church and will welcome its word and its directives with filial respect.

5. It is only when one begins with the task of evangelization understood in its entirety that the authentic requirements of human progress and liberation are appreciated. This liberation has as its indispensable pillars: the truth about Jesus the savior, the truth about the church and the truth about man and his dignity.

It is in light of the Beatitudes, and especially the Beatitude of the poor of heart, that the church, which wants to be the church of the poor throughout the world, intends to come to the aid of the noble struggle for truth and justice. She addresses each person, and for that reason, every person. She is the "universal church. The church of the incarnation. She is not the church of one class or another. And she speaks in the name of truth itself. This truth is realistic." It leads to a recognition "of every human reality, every injustice, every tension and every struggle."

6. An effective defense of justice needs to be based on the truth of mankind, created in the image of God and called to the grace of divine sonship. The recognition of the true relationship of human beings to God constitutes the foundation of justice to the extent that it rules the relationships between people. That is why the fight for the rights of man, which the church does not cease to reaffirm, constitutes the authentic fight for justice.

7. The truth of mankind requires that this battle be fought in ways consistent with human dignity. That is why the systematic and deliberate recourse to blind violence, no matter from which side it comes, must be condemned. To put one's trust in violent means in the hope of restoring more justice is to become the victim of a fatal illusion: Violence begets violence and degrades man. It mocks the dignity of man in the person of the victims, and it debases that same dignity among those who practice it.

8. The acute need for radical reforms of the structures which conceal poverty and which are themselves forms of violence should not let us lose sight of the fact that the source of injustice is in the hearts of men. Therefore it is only by making an appeal to the moral potential of the person and to the constant need for interior conversion that social change will be brought about which will truly be in the service of man. For it will only be in the measure that they collaborate freely in these necessary changes through their own initiative and in solidarity, that people, awakened to a sense of their responsibility, will grow in humanity.

The inversion of morality and structures is steeped in a materialist anthropology which is incompatible with the dignity of mankind.

9. It is therefore an equally fatal illusion to believe that these new structures will of themselves give birth to a "new man" in the sense of the

truth of man. The Christian cannot forget that it is only the Holy Spirit, who has been given to us, who is the source of every true renewal and that God is the Lord of history.

10. By the same token, the overthrow by means of revolutionary violence of structures which generate violence is not *ipso facto* the beginning of a just regime. A major fact of our time ought to evoke the reflection of all those who would sincerely work for the true liberation of their brothers: Millions of our own contemporaries legitimately yearn to recover those basic freedoms of which they were deprived by totalitarian and atheistic regimes which came to power by violent and revolutionary means, precisely in the name of the liberation of the people. This shame of our time cannot be ignored: While claiming to bring them freedom, these regimes keep whole nations in conditions of servitude which are unworthy of mankind. Those who, perhaps inadvertently, make themselves accomplices of similar enslavements betray the very poor they mean to help.

11. The class struggle as a road toward a classless society is a myth which slows reform and aggravates poverty and injustice. Those who allow themselves to be caught up in fascination with this myth should reflect on the bitter examples history has to offer about where it leads. They would then understand that we are not talking here about abandoning an effective means of struggle on behalf of the poor for an ideal which has no practical effects. On the contrary, we are talking about freeing oneself from a delusion in order to base oneself squarely on the Gospel and its power of realization.

12. One of the conditions for necessary theological correction is giving proper value to the social teaching of the church. This teaching is by no means closed. It is, on the contrary, open to all the new questions which are so numerous today. In this perspective, the contribution of theologians and other thinkers in all parts of the world to the reflection of the church is indispensable today.

13. Likewise the experience of those who work directly for evangelization and for the advancement of the poor and the oppressed is necessary for the doctrinal and pastoral reflection of the church. In this sense it is necessary to affirm that one becomes more aware of certain aspects of truth by starting with praxis, if by that one means pastoral praxis and social work which keeps its evangelical inspiration.

14. The teaching of the church on social issues indicates the main lines of ethical orientation. But in order that it be able to guide action directly, the church needs competent people from a scientific and technological viewpoint, as well as in the human and political sciences. Pastors should be attentive to the formation of persons of such capability who live the Gospel deeply. Lay persons, whose proper mission is to build society, are involved here to the highest degree.

15. The theses of "theologies of liberation" are widely popularized under a simplified form in formation sessions or in what are called "base groups" which lack the necessary catechetical and theological preparation as well as the capacity for discernment. Thus these theses are accepted by

generous men and women without any critical judgment being made.

16. That is why pastors must look after the quality and the content of catechesis and formation, which should always present the whole message of salvation and the imperatives of true liberation within the framework of this whole message.

17. In this full presentation of Christianity, it is proper to emphasize those essential aspects which the "theologies of liberation" especially tend to misunderstand or to eliminate, namely: the transcendence and gratuity of liberation in Jesus Christ, true God and true man; the sovereigny of grace; and the true nature of the means of salvation, especially of the church and the sacraments. One should also keep in mind the true meaning of ethics, in which the distinction between good and evil is not relativized, the real meaning of sin, the necessity for conversion and the universality of the law of fraternal love.

One needs to be on guard against the politicization of existence, which, misunderstanding the entire meaning of the kingdom of God and the transcendence of the person, begins to sacralize politics and betray the religion of the people in favor of the projects of the revolution.

18. The defenders of orthodoxy are sometimes accused of passivity, indulgence or culpable complicity regarding the intolerable situations of injustice and the political regimes which prolong them. Spiritual conversion, the intensity of the love of God and neighbor, zeal for justice and peace, the gospel meaning of the poor and of poverty, are required of everyone and especially of pastors and those in positions of responsibility. The concern for the purity of the faith demands giving the answer of effective witness in the service of one's neighbor, the poor and the oppressed in particular, in an integral theological fashion. By the witness of their dynamic and constructive power to love, Christians will thus lay the foundations of this "civilization of love" of which the conference of Puebla spoke, following Paul VI. Moreover there are already many priests, religious and lay people who are consecrated in a truly evangelical way for the creation of a just society.

Conclusion

The words of Paul VI in his "Profession of Faith," express with full clarity the faith of the church, from which one cannot deviate without provoking, besides spiritual disaster, new miseries and new types of slavery.

"We profess our faith that the kingdom of God, begun here below in the church of Christ, is not of this world, whose form is passing away, and that its own growth cannot be confused with the progress of civilization, of science, of human technology, but that it consists in knowing ever more deeply the unfathomable riches of Christ, to hope ever more strongly in things eternal, to respond ever more ardently to the love of God, to spread ever more widely grace and holiness among men. But it is this very same love which makes the church constantly concerned for the true temporal good of mankind as well. Never ceasing to recall to her children that they have no lasting dwelling here on earth, she urges them also to contribute, each according to his own vocation and means, to the welfare of their earthly city, to promote justice, peace and brotherhood among men, to lavish their assistance on their brothers, especially on the poor and the most dispirited. The intense concern of the church, the bride of Christ, for the needs of mankind, their joys and their hopes, their pains and their struggles, is nothing other than the great desire to be present to them in order to enlighten them with the light of Christ and join them all to him, their only savior. It can never mean that the church is conforming to the things of this world nor that she is lessening the earnestness with which she awaits her Lord and the eternal kingdom."

This instruction was adopted at an ordinary meeting of the Sacred Congregation for the Doctrine of the Faith and was approved at an audience granted to the undersigned cardinal prefect by His Holiness Pope John Paul II, who ordered its publication.

Given at Rome, at the Sacred Congregation for the doctrine of the Faith, Aug. 6, 1984, the feast of the Transfiguration of Our Lord.

Cardinal Joseph Ratzinger
Prefect

Archbishop Alberto Bovone
Secretary

CANADIAN PILGRIMAGE OF POPE JOHN PAUL II
September 10, 12, 14, and 17

On September 9 Pope John Paul II arrived in Quebec City, becoming the first pontiff to visit Canada. The 12-day tour was the longest trip yet taken by John Paul outside Italy since his elevation to the papacy in 1978.

A rugged itinerary took the pope coast to coast, with stops in almost every major Canadian city. He spent the first four days of the tour in Quebec Province, whose residents made up almost half of Canada's 11.4 million Roman Catholics. Even in this Catholic stronghold, however, the importance of the church had decreased considerably since the 1960s, making it an important stay for the pope.

Forty-six percent of Canada's population were Catholic, and there were large turnouts throughout the land for the pontiff's appearances. In Montreal September 11, the pope beatified Sister Marie-Leonie, a nun who founded a religious order dedicated to serving priests. From Montreal the pope headed to St. John's, Newfoundland, to Moncton, New Brunswick, and Halifax, Nova Scotia. He then made stops in Toronto, Winnipeg, Edmonton, Vancouver, and Fort Simpson. The pontiff completed his tour with two days in Ottawa September 19 and 20. Throughout the trip, crowds greeted John Paul warmly.

Social Themes

Although the pope addressed a range of issues during his Canadian journey, he repeatedly returned to the themes of peace, justice, and

777

human rights. The rights of the handicapped, of American Indians and Eskimos, of refugees and migrants, and of the French-speaking minority in Canada received particular attention. John Paul placed a special emphasis on peace and justice, dedicating a mass to those themes in Ottawa on the last day of his visit.

The pope spoke out against global injustice and inequality in a September 17 homily in Edmonton, Alberta. At an outdoor mass, he spoke out in unusually harsh terms against the disparity between rich and poor countries. "[T]his poor South will judge the rich North. And the poor people and poor nations — poor in different ways, not only lacking food, but also deprived of freedom and other human rights — will judge those people who take these goods away from them, amassing to themselves the imperialistic monopoly of economic and political supremacy at the expense of others."

The pontiff's remarks echoed the theme of a Vatican statement released two weeks earlier on the growing "theology of liberation" movement advocating drastic social change in underdeveloped countries, notably in Latin America. ("Theology of Liberation," p. 759) The Vatican's statement, prepared by the Sacred Congregation for the Doctrine of Faith, condemned the Marxist analysis used by liberation theologians. The pope's Edmonton message, however, was a counterpoint to this critique, stressing the need for action to aid the poorer nations.

From fishing village to urban center, the pope did not hesitate to tackle controversial topics or to speak out strongly on any number of social issues. At the Basilica of St. John the Baptist in St. John's, Newfoundland, for example, he called for government financing of religious schools. The message, he later stated, was directed to all governments where there was a lack of fluidity between church and state. Although the strength of the Church had declined in Canada, its importance remained evident as there was no constitutional distinction between church and state in the country, and religious universities were publicly financed.

Although the pope said his remarks were not specifically directed toward the United States, the relationship between religion and politics was receiving a great deal of attention during the 1984 U.S. presidential campaign. The pope's statement that "[W]e cannot leave God at the schoolhouse door" was relevant to U.S. debates over tuition tax credits for religious school education and the U.S. Supreme Court's rulings against state aid for such schools and banning organized prayer in public schools.

Technology and Christian Unity

In Toronto, the center of Canada's technological and industrial development, the pontiff addressed the social implications of technology and *urged that it be used to serve mankind in keeping with Christian values. A "technological mentality" exists, he stated, that challenges "gospel values" and moral priorities. "[T]he needs of the poor must take priority over the desires of the rich; the rights of workers over the maximization of profits; the preservation of the environment over uncontrolled industrial expansion; production to meet social needs over production for military purposes," he stressed in an address to leaders of other Christian faiths September 14 in Toronto.*

Following are excerpts from Pope John Paul II's speech to a group of handicapped persons in Quebec City September 10; from an address September 12 to Canadian Catholic educators in St. John's, Newfoundland; from an address to Christian leaders September 14 in Toronto; and from a homily delivered in Edmonton, Alberta, September 17, 1984:

THE HANDICAPPED IN MODERN SOCIETY

1. I have very much wanted to meet personally with you, you who suffer in your bodies from illness or accident. I would like to greet each and every one of you, as well as all those who surround you with affection and assistance and who help you to love life and to make it blossom in you like a gift from God. I mean, of course, your parents, your friends and all the people who work in this center. I would also like to extend my greetings to the other handicapped men and women in Quebec and throughout Canada. Like Jesus of Nazareth, I want to come near you and to explore with you the spiritual meaning of your suffering and your hope for a full life. . . .

Our societies, thank God, appear to be becoming progressively more aware of the situation of the handicapped. They have rights which have often been neglected. On Dec. 9, 1975, the United Nations issued a statement on these rights which deserves our praise. In addition, the United Nations decreed 1981 the International Year of the Handicapped. However, all these good intentions must take form in every region. For this to happen there are psychological and material obstacles to overcome and progress to be made.

The church has always taken a vivid interest in this question. Over the centuries it fostered many undertakings involving great generosity in order, like Christ, to come to the aid of the handicapped. It did this because it was convinced of the unique value of every person. . . . I would like now to say once again clearly and forcefully: The handicapped person is a human subject in the full sense with all the innate, sacred and inviolable rights that that entails. This is true whether the person be handicapped by physical disability, whether due to birth defect, chronic disease or accident, or by mental or sensory deficiency. It is true too no matter how great the person's affliction might be. We must facilitate his or her participation in all facets of social life and at all possible levels: in the family, at school, at work, in the community, in politics and religion. In practice this presupposes the absolute respect of the human life of the handicapped person from his or her conception through every stage of development.

We must attempt to overcome not only handicaps, but also their causes. Often they are natural. A deformation of the organism or a disease; sometimes they are related to war or pollution, alcohol or drug abuse or careless driving. There may be psychological and moral causes; a spiritual "ecology" is as important as an ecology of nature. We must help families who are in distress and deserve our help. To this end, we must build centers like this one where there is sensitivity to family bonds. We must provide training, suitable employment with a just wage, promotion opportunities and security to spare the handicapped traumatic experiences. All this requires imagination and boldness in order to develop various kinds of ideal initiatives. It also requires the aid of public authorities. . . . It is important, finally, that the handicapped person not only be loved and helped but that he or she be as aware as possible of his or her dignity and resources, of his or her ability to will, to communicate, to cooperate, to love and give while continuing daily the battle to maintain and develop his or her potential.

Unquestionably, the quality of a society or civilization is measured by the respect it has for its weakest members. A technically perfect society where only fully productive members are accepted must be considered totally unworthy of human beings, perverted as it is by a type of discrimination that is no less reprehensible than racial discrimination. The handicapped person is one of us and shares in our humanity. To recognize and promote his or her dignity and rights is to recognize our own dignity and rights. . . .

SUPPORT ASKED FOR CATHOLIC SCHOOLS

. . . It is indeed a joy and privilege to join this gathering of educators, to speak to those who carry out one of the most important tasks of the church and of society. The task of the teacher and the school is indeed a sacred trust conveyed to them by parents and families. . . .

To you it is given to create the future and give it direction by offering to your students a set of values with which to assess their newly discovered knowledge. . . .

2. As you pursue your professional and spiritual goals as teachers or as educational administrators you experience the ambiguities and conflicts which characterize our contemporary society. In the span of a single lifetime we have seen enormous changes in social values, in economic circumstances and in technological innovations. As educators you must cope with these changes since they are the daily experience and fare of your students.

At the same time as a teacher and a school system seek to adapt continually to the new, they must affirm and preserve the meaning and importance of perennial truths and values. Educators must be ready to grasp firmly the challenge of providing a kind of education whose curriculum will be inspired more by reflection than by technique, more by the search for wisdom than the accumulation of information.

In the same way the radically different cultural expressions and activities of our time, especially those which catch the popular attention of young people, demand that educators be open to new cultural influences and be capable of interpreting them for young people in the light of the Christian faith and of Christ's universal command of love....

3. An extremely important aspect of your role is that you are called to lead the young to Christ, to inspire them to follow him, to show them his boundless love and concern for them through the example of your own life. Through you, as through a clear window on a sunny day, students must come to see and know the richness and the joy of a life lived in accordance with his teaching, in response to his challenging demands. To teach means not only to impart what we know, but also to reveal who we are by living what we believe. It is this latter lesson which tends to last the longest. En masse, the students of the world are today repeating to their Catholic teachers those words recorded in the Gospel of St. John and originally addressed to the apostle Philip: "We wish to see Jesus" (Jn. 12:21). This is indeed a vital task of the Catholic teacher: to show Jesus to the young....

5. Young people today are buffeted in every direction by loud and competing claims upon their attention and allegiance. From around the world they hear daily messages of conflict and hostility, of greed and injustice, of poverty and despair. Amid this social turmoil, young people are eager to find solid and enduring values which can give meaning and purpose to their lives....

6. Young people are hungry today for truth and justice because they are hungry for God. To respond to that hunger is the highest calling of the Christian educator. In partnership with the parents, who bear the primary responsibility for the education of their children, the teacher is called upon to reflect in faithful and discerning fashion God's presence in the world.

Teachers and parents must strive for a mature spirituality in their own lives, a strength and relevance of faith which can withstand the assault of conflicting values upon the home and the school. If the teaching of the Gospel is visible in your daily lives, it will have visible influence upon the young whom you teach....

8. ... Catholic schools can provide young people with insights and spiritual incentives badly needed in a materialistic and fragmented world. Catholic schools speak of the meaning of life, of values and of faith that make for a meaningful life. Similarly, since individualism is often alienating, Catholic schools must hand on and reinforce a sense of community, of social concern and the acceptance of difference and diversity in pluralistic societies....

While striving for excellence in the areas of professional and technical training, Catholic schools must never forget that their ultimate purpose is to prepare young people to take up, in Christian freedom, their personal and social responsibility for the pilgrimage of all humanity to eternal life.

For these same reasons Catholic schools, while always committed to intellectual development, will also heed the gospel imperative of serving all students and not only those who are the brightest and most promising. Indeed, in accord with the spirit of the Gospel and its option for the poor, they will turn their attention particularly to those most in need.

9. All men and women — and all children — have a right to education. Closely linked to this right to education is the right of parents, of families, to choose according to their convictions the kind of education and the model of school which they wish for their children (Universal Declaration of Human Rights, Art. 26). Related as well is the no less sacred right of religious freedom.

In a society such as Canada's, freedom to associate and enter into certain group or institutional endeavors with the aim of fulfilling their expectations according to their own values is a fundamental democratic right. This right implies that parents have a real possibility to choose, without undue financial burden placed upon them, appropriate schools and educational systems for their children. . . .

Society is called to provide for and support with public funding those types of schools that correspond to the deepest aspirations of its citizens. The role of the modern state is to respond to these expectations within the limits of the common good. A state thereby promotes harmony and, in a pluralistic situation such as Canada, this effectively fosters respect for the wide diversity of this land. To ignore this diversity and the legitimate claims of the people within various groups would be to deny a fundamental right to parents.

Governments have the responsibility, therefore, to ensure the freedom of ecclesial communions to have appropriate educational services with all that such a freedom implies: teacher training, buildings, research funding, adequate financing and so forth.

In a pluralistic society it is surely a challenge to provide all citizens with satisfactory educational services. In dealing with this complex challenge one must not ignore the centrality of God in the believer's outlook on life. A totally secular school system would not be a way of meeting this challenge. We cannot leave God at the schoolhouse door. Dear teachers and parents, the Catholic school is in your hands. It is a reflection of your convictions. Its very existence depends on you. It is one of those privileged places, together with the family and the parish community, where our faith is handed on. . . .

Our world searches for a new sense of meaning and coherence. A Catholic school through the ministry of Catholic teachers is a privileged place for the development and communication of a world view rooted in the meaning of creation and redemption. You are called, dear educators and parents, to create those schools which will transmit the values which you would hand on to those who will come after you. And always remember that it is Christ who says: Go and teach!

CHRISTIAN UNITY
IN A TECHNOLOGICAL AGE

1. I am deeply pleased to join in the prayer of praise and petition with all of you who represent the different churches and Christian communions throughout Canada. With deep respect and love I greet you all in the words of the apostle Paul: "Grace to you and peace from God the Father and the Lord Jesus Christ" (2 Thes. 1:2). I also wish to greet with deep respect the leaders of the other faiths who have come here today. I thank you for your presence at this ecumenical service. . . .

4. In my first encyclical letter, *Redemptor Hominis*, written shortly after my election to the See of Peter, I state:

"In the present historical situation of Christianity and the world, the only possibility we see of fulfilling the church's universal mission with regard to ecumenical questions is that of seeking sincerely, perseveringly, humbly and also courageously the ways of drawing closer and of union. Pope Paul VI gave us his personal example for this. We must therefore seek unity without being discouraged at the difficulties that can appear or accumulate along that road; otherwise we would be unfaithful to the word of Christ, we would fail to accomplish his testament" (No. 6).

The experience of the past six years since my election has confirmed even more in my heart the evangelical obligation "of seeking sincerely, perseveringly, humbly and also courageously the ways of drawing closer and of union."

5. We cannot turn back on this difficult but vital task, for it is essentially linked with our mission of proclaiming to all humanity the message of salvation. The restoration of the complete unity of Christians, for which we so greatly yearn and pray, is of crucial importance for the evangelization of the world. Millions of our contemporaries still do not know Christ, and millions more who have heard of Christ are hindered from accepting the Christian faith because of our tragic divisions. Indeed, the reason Jesus prayed that we might be one was precisely "so that the world might believe" (Jn. 17:21). The proclamation of the good news of our Lord Jesus Christ is greatly obstructed by doctrinal division among the followers of the savior. On the other hand, the work of evangelization bears fruit when Christians of different communions, though not yet fully one, collaborate as brothers and sisters in Christ to the degree possible and with respect for their particular traditions.

As the third millennium of Christianity approaches, we are faced with a rapidly expanding technology which raises numerous opportunities as well as obstacles to evangelization. While it engenders a number of beneficial effects for humanity, it has also ushered in a technological mentality which challenges gospel values. The temptation exists of pursuing technological development for its own sake, as if it were an autonomous force with built-in imperatives for expansion, instead of seeing it as a resource to be placed at the service of the human family. A second temptation exists which would tie technological development to the logic of profit and constant economic expansion without due regard for the rights of workers or the needs of the poor and helpless. A third temptation is to link technological development to the pursuit or maintenance of power instead of using it as an instrument for freedom.

To avoid these dangers, all such developments need to be examined in terms of the objective demands of the moral order and in the light of the gospel message. United in the name of Christ, we need to ask critical questions and assert basic moral principles which have a bearing on technological development. For instance, the needs of the poor must take priority over the desires of the rich; the rights of workers over the maximization of profits; the preservation of the environment over uncontrolled industrial expansion; production to meet social needs over production for military purposes. These challenges present us with important areas of ecumenical collaboration and form a vital part of our mission of proclaiming the Gospel of Christ. And before all of this we lift up our hearts to God, the Father of our Lord Jesus Christ....

6. Ecumenical collaboration, as we have discovered, can take many forms: working together in projects of fraternal service, engaging in theological dialogue and joint ventures to understand our troubled past, cooperative actions for justice and for the humanizing of the technological society, and many others. All of these are of great value and need to be continued in earnest, especially those which promote the truth and help us grow in fraternal charity. At the same time, we all need to remember the primacy of the spiritual activities which the Second Vatican Council considered as the very soul of the ecumenical movement (Cf. *Unitatis Redintegratio,* 8). I am referring to the faithful practice of public and private prayer for reconciliation and unity, and the pursuit of personal conversion and holiness of life. Without these, all other efforts will lack depth and the vitality of faith. We would too quickly forget what St. Paul teaches, namely, that "all this is from God, who through Christ reconciled us to himself and gave us the ministry of reconciliation" (2 Cor. 5:18).

There can be no progress toward unity among us where there is no growth in holiness of life. In the Beatitudes Jesus indicates the way to holiness: "Blessed are the poor in spirit.... Blessed are those who mourn.... Blessed are the meek.... Blessed are those who hunger and thirst for righteousness...." (Mt. 5:3ff). In seeking to be counted among these "blessed ones," we shall grow in holiness ourselves; but at the same time we shall also be making a contribution to the unity of all followers of Christ and thus to the reconciliation of the world. True holiness of life, which draws us closer to the heart of the Savior, will strengthen our bonds of charity with all people and especially with other Christians.

Let us, then, strive to be counted among those "blessed ones" of the Beatitudes, "hungering and thirsting for righteousness" in a technological age, praying for unity with one another and with all who believe in Christ, yearning in hope for the day when "there will be only one flock and one shepherd" (Jn. 10:16).

DEVELOPMENT: THE PROGRESS OF ALL THE DISADVANTAGED

"I will hear what the Lord God has to say, a voice that speaks of peace. Mercy and faithfulness have met; justice and peace have embraced" (Ps. 84 (85):8, 10).

Dear brothers and sisters in Christ,

1. These are words of today's liturgy, taken from the responsorial psalm. The God of the covenant is a God of peace. Peace on earth is a good that belongs to his kingdom and to his salvation. This good is obtained in justice and faithfulness to the divine commandments. This good, which is peace, is promised to us in different spheres: as the interior good of our conscience, as the good of our human living together and finally as a social and international good.

This last meaning was above all what Paul VI had in mind when he wrote these memorable words: "The new name for peace is development." And he wrote these words in the encyclical *Populorum Progessio* (87).

2. Today we come together here in Edmonton to make this theme of the development or progress of peoples the principal object of our meditations and prayers in the eucharistic sacrifice....

Our faith in Jesus Christ finds here a kind of final expression: "The Father judges no one, but has given all judgment to the Son." (Jn. 5:22). In today's Gospel Christ stands before us as our judge. He has a special right to make this judgment. Indeed he became one of us, our brother. This brotherhood with the human race — and at the same time his brotherhood with every single person — has led him to the cross and the resurrection. Thus he judges in the name of his solidarity with each person and likewise in the name of our solidarity with him, who is our brother and redeemer and whom we discover in every human being: "I was hungry ... I was thirsty ... I was a stranger ... naked ... sick ... in prison. . ." (Mt. 25:35-36).

And those called to judgment — on his right hand and on his left — will ask: When and where? When and where have we seen you like this? When and where have we done what you said? Or: When and where have we not done it?

The answer: "Truly, I say to you, as you did it to one of the least of these my brethren, you did it to me" (Mt. 25:40). And, on the contrary: "As you did it not to one of the least of these, you did it not to me" (Mt. 25:45).

4. "To one of the least of these my brethren." Thus: to man, to an individual human being in need.

Yet, the Second Vatican Council, following the whole of tradition, warns us not to stop at an "individualistic" interpretation of Christian ethics, since Christian ethics also has its social dimension. The human person lives in a community, in society. And with the community he shares hunger and thirst and sickness and malnutrition and misery and all the deficiencies that result therefrom. In his or her own person the human being is meant to experience the needs of others.

So it is that Christ the judge speaks of "one of the least of the brethren," and at the same time he is speaking of each and of all.

Yes. He is speaking of the whole universal dimension of injustice and evil. He is speaking of what today we are accustomed to call the North-South contrast. Hence not only East-West, but also North-South: the increasingly wealthier North and the increasingly poorer South.

Yes, the South — becoming always poorer. And the North — becoming always richer. Richer too in the resources of weapons with which the superpowers and blocs can mutually threaten each other. And they threaten each other — such an argument also exists — in order not to destroy each other.

This is a separate dimension — and according to the opinion of many it is the dimension in the forefront — of the deadly threat which hangs over the modern world, which deserves separate attention.

Nevertheless, in the light of Christ's words, this poor South will judge the rich North. And the poor people and poor nations — poor in different ways, not only lacking food, but also deprived of freedom and other human rights — will judge those people who take these goods away from them, amassing to themselves the imperialistic monopoly of economic and political supremacy at the expense of others.

5. The Gospel of today's liturgy is very rich in content. It is relevant to the different spheres of injustice and human evil. In the midst of each of these situations stands Christ himself, and as redeemer and judge he says: "You did it to me," "You did it not to me."

Nevertheless he wishes, in this final judgment — which is constantly in preparation and which in a certain sense is constantly present — to bear witness first of all to the good that has been done.

And here also that significant expression of the teaching of the church takes a start, whose principal formulation becomes the encyclical *Populorum Progessio.* What was the inner concern of Paul VI and the universal church became a dynamic action and a loud appeal that echoes to this day:

"It is not just a matter of eliminating hunger or even of reducing poverty. The struggle against destitution, though urgent and necessary, is not enough. It is a question, rather, of building a world where every man, no matter what his race, religion or nationality, can live a fully human life, freed from servitude imposed on him by other men or by natural forces. A world where freedom is not an empty word and where the poor man Lazarus can sit down at the same table with the rich man" (no. 47).

Yes, "development" is the new name for peace. Peace is necessary. It is an imperative of our time. And so is this development or progress: the progress of all the disadvantaged. . . .

7. Today we are praying in Canada, in the city of Edmonton, for the progress of peoples. Hence, according to the words of Pope Paul VI we are praying for peace because we are praying for what constitutes its contemporary meaning. . . .

May the God of Peace be with us! This cry brings with it the whole drama of our age, the whole threat. The nuclear threat? Certainly!

But even more: the whole threat of injustice, the threat coming from the rigid structures of those systems which man is not able to pass through — those systems which do not permit themselves to go out toward man, to go out toward the development of peoples, to go out toward justice, with all its requirements, and toward peace.

Is the global account not perhaps ever increasing — the global account of what we "have not done for one of the least of the brethren"? For millions of the least of the brethren? For billions?

This must also be said here in Canada, which is as vast as a continent. And at the same time here, from this very place, it must likewise be said to all people of good will and to all groups, communities, organizations, institutions, nations and governments, that everything we "have done" and what we will still do, what we will plan and will do with greater energy and determination — all of this really matters.

And the account is increasing and must increase of what we "have done" for one person, for millions, for billions: the account of good in human history. . . .

May justice and peace embrace (cf. Ps. 84 (85):10) once again at the end of the second millennium which prepares us for the coming of Christ, in glory. Amen.

ARGENTINE REPORT ON THE DISAPPEARANCE OF PERSONS
September 20, 1984

After nine months and thousands of hours of testimony, Argentina's National Commission on the Disappearance of Persons delivered its 50,000-page report to President Raúl Alfonsín on September 20, 1984, blaming the armed forces for the "dirty war" that swept up an estimated 9,000 victims in the late 1970s.

The investigators dismissed the suggestion that the anti-terrorist campaign waged by squads of armed men in civilian dress was the work of right-wing vigilante groups. Ernesto Sábato, head of the commission, said in the introduction to the report, "How can one talk of 'individual excesses'... From our information, it appears that this technology of hell was carried out by sadistic but controlled agents."

The 11-member commission was appointed shortly after Alfonsín, the first elected leader of Argentina after eight years of military rule, took office in December 1983. Attempting to resolve the serious human rights issue that had racked the country, the new president ordered the courts-martial of nine members of the first three military juntas that had ruled the country between 1976 and 1981.

To further aid the criminal proceedings, the president repealed an amnesty law passed by the military government in the last days in office to protect its leaders against prosecution. But as Alfonsín wrestled with a shaky economy and fear of alienating the armed forces with a vigorous campaign against the rank and file, attempts to bring those persons responsible for the mass abductions to justice began to slow down by the end of 1984.

Death Squads

The wave of government-sponsored kidnappings, torture, and death that paralyzed Argentina in the late 1970s came as a response to the anti-government activities of the Montoneros, a leftist guerrilla movement, and other leftist groups. The Montoneros carried out numerous assassinations, bombings, and kidnappings between 1970 and 1979, when it was dismantled by security forces. The group was responsible for the kidnappings of several prominent businessmen who paid huge ransoms for their release.

A few military leaders of that era defended their policies after Alfonsín took office, claiming that the assault on the Montoneros and leftist sympathizers was necessary to fight the unconventional tactics of the guerrillas. However, many people with few or no political affiliations were pulled from the streets and locked in secret prisons along with suspected terrorists.

In the early months of Alfonsín's leadership, friends and relatives of the victims hoped that the missing would be restored to them. However, as stories of mass graves and secret prisons were revealed, the possibility that the victims were still alive grew increasingly slim. In March 1984, a hillside cemetery in the city of Cordoba yielded hundreds of bodies that witnesses said had been killed by firing squads. Grave diggers and a few of the actual managers of the torture chambers came forward to testify about the deaths of other captives. According to their statement, some prisoners were burned alive and others were tied together and dropped out of airplanes flying over the Atlantic Ocean.

Although the commission documented the disappearance of 8,900 persons and the existence of 340 secret prisons, it did not help the families of victims who wanted specific information on each of the missing individuals. The day the report was issued, the Mothers of the Plaza de Mayo, Argentina's best-known human rights group, held a demonstration before the Argentine Congress to protest the lack of action against the military. After the promotion of 18 Army and Navy officers accused of participating in the wave of terror was approved by the Argentine Senate in September 1984, human rights activists questioned the elected government's commitment to seeing that those responsible for the kidnappings and torture would be punished.

Fragile Democracy

Taking office, Alfonsín promised to punish the lower-level officers who carried out the atrocities, as well as the leaders who ordered them. He pushed a bill through Congress giving the military courts jurisdiction over human rights cases. The strategy behind this act was twofold. First, by giving the military control over such prosecutions, the government gave the armed forces the opportunity to clean its own house and break with the policies of its former leaders. Second, this approach was expected to make convictions easier to obtain because military courts were not bound by the same strict rules of evidence as the civilian courts.

But the nine-member Armed Forces Supreme Council, the country's highest military tribunal, demonstrated its reluctance to condemn the abductions when the cases of nine junta members charged with massive human rights violations were referred to civilian courts in October 1984 after the tribunal ruled that the orders issued by the junta to fight the leftists were "unobjectionable." As a final blow to the president's plan to resolve the cases through a military process, the tribunal resigned en masse November 14, leaving hundreds of human rights cases unsettled.

The fate of Argentina's prosecution against the official terror of the late 1970s hung in the balance in late 1984 as Alfonsín wrestled with the political challenge from the military and the nation's massive foreign debt, contributed, in part, by Argentina's war against Great Britain over the Falkland Islands. (Historic Documents of 1982, p. 283) *But as quoted in* Newsweek *magazine, the president pledged to continue legal proceedings saying, "We are convinced that in order to build our country we cannot look back with a sense of revenge. But neither can we build a democracy without ethical standards. And that would have been the case if we had acted as if nothing had happened in Argentina. We will be working [under] due process of law to find the truth."*

Following are excerpts from the introduction of the report prepared by the National Commission on the Disappearance of Persons and presented to Argentine president Raúl Alfonsín September 20, 1984:

During the decade of the 1970's Argentina was convulsed by a terror that came as much from the extreme right as from the extreme left, a phenomenon that has occurred in many other countries. It happened in Italy, which for many years suffered under the merciless actions of fascists, the Red Brigades and similar groups. But not at any moment did that nation abandon the principles of law to combat these groups. They worked with absolute effectiveness through the courts, offering the accused all the guarantees of defense in a trial. When a member of a security force suggested to General Della Chiesa on the occasion of Aldo Moro's kidnapping that they torture a prisoner to get information, the general responded with these memorable words: "Italy can permit itself to lose an Aldo Moro, but not to institute torture."

It did not happen like this in our country. The armed forces responded with a terrorism infinitely worse than that of the combatant. From March 24, 1976, they relied on the power and the immunity of an absolute state to kidnap, torture and assassinate thousands of human beings.

Our commission was not instituted to pass judgment, because for this we have the courts, but to investigate the fate of the disappeared during those fateful years. But having received thousands of declarations and depositions, verified or determined the existence of hundreds of clandestine detention sites and accumulated more than 50,000 documented pages, we are certain that the military dictatorship produced the greatest and most savage tragedy of our history. And even if we must wait for justice to give the last word, we cannot silence what we have heard, read and recorded, all of which goes beyond what can be considered simply delinquent to reach the dark category of inhuman crimes. . . .

From the voluminous documentation we have gathered, we deduce that human rights were violated by the organs of the state through the repression of the armed forces. And they were not violated sporadically but systematically, always in a similar way. How could it not be attributed to a methodology of terror planned by the high command? How, under a vigorously military regime, could such crimes have been committed by perverse individuals acting on their own, with all the power and access to information this implies? How can one talk of "individual excesses?" From our information, it appears that this technology of hell was carried out by sadistic but controlled agents. . . .

The kidnapping operations demonstrated precise organization, at times in the work places of those who had been denounced. Others were carried out in the street in daylight. When the victim was looked for at night in his home, armed squads surrounded the district and entered by force, terrorizing parents and children, often gagging them and forcing them to watch the events. They took hold of the person they had been looking for, beat him brutally, hooded him and finally dragged the person to a car or truck, while the rest of the squad often destroyed what was left behind or stole what could be carried away. From there they headed toward a den with a door that could have been inscribed with the words that Dante read on the gates of hell: "All hope abandon, ye who enter here."

In this way, in the name of national security, thousands and thousands of human beings, generally young and even teen-agers, became part of a dark and ghostly category, that of the "disappeared." A word — sad Argentine privilege — now written in Spanish in the world press.

During the course of our investigations we were insulted and threatened by those who committed the crimes, who, far from repenting, again repeat the well-known reasons for the "dirty war." They talk of the country's salvation and of their Western and Christian values — the precise values that they dragged between the bloody walls of the repression dens. And they accuse us of not propitiating national reconciliation, of inciting hatred and resentment, of preventing forgetting. But this is not so. . . . We believe that reconciliation will not be possible until after the guilty repent and justice, based on truth, is done. . . .

Great calamities are always instructive. Without a doubt the most terrible drama that this nation has suffered in all of its history during the period of the military dictatorship initiated in March 1976 will be useful to make us understand that only democracy is capable of preserving a people from such horror, that only it can maintain and save those sacred and essential rights of the human creature. Only with this, will we be sure that never again in our country will events be repeated that have made us tragically famous in the civilized world. . . .

IMF — WORLD BANK CONFERENCE

September 24, 1984

Finance ministers and central bankers from 148 countries met in Washington, D.C., September 24-26, 1984, for the 39th annual meeting of the International Monetary Fund (IMF) and the World Bank. Against a backdrop of an improving world economy, the tone of the meeting was generally optimistic. But speakers, led by Jacques de Larosière, managing director of the IMF, warned that the economic recovery in Third World countries was endangered by the adoption of protectionist measures among the industrial nations.

The industrial countries turned aside a call for a rich nation—poor nation conference that had been suggested by the so-called Cartagena group of 11 Latin American debtor nations. Financial leaders of those countries had met in Cartagena, Colombia, in June 1984 to discuss reforms in the system of paying and restructuring the region's massive foreign debt.

As an alternative to the comprehensive conference the Latin American countries wanted, representatives of the industrial nations, led by U.S. Secretary of the Treasury Donald Regan, agreed that the April 1985 meeting of the IMF and World Bank would take up a range of issues affecting the poor countries, including trade, interest rates, and the role of the IMF.

The IMF and the World Bank, formally known as the International Bank for Reconstruction and Development, were set up at an international monetary conference at Bretton Woods, New Hampshire, in 1944.

Intended to complement each other, the IMF makes loans to cash-short nations while the World Bank makes longer-term loans for such projects as the construction of ports and roads.

Economic Growth

The Washington, D.C., meeting was told by de Larosière that "1984 is shaping up as the best year for economic growth in the industrial countries in at least eight years." He said that "International trade has rebounded strongly. Inflation has been substantially reduced. And the balance of payments situation of heavily indebted developing countries has improved dramatically."

According to new IMF forecasts, the volume of world trade in 1984 would expand by 8.5 percent and the gross national products (GNPs) of the industrial nations would grow an average of 5 percent. Growth in the United States, seen by the IMF in April 1984 as 5 percent, instead would be 7.3 percent, according to the new forecasts.

Addressing the meeting, President Ronald Reagan said, "Our own economy is dramatically changed from only three years. . . . Born in the safe harbor of freedom, economic growth gathered force and rolled out in a rising tide that has reached distant shores."

Protectionist Fears

A number of the principal speakers saw a threat to the more fragile recovery in the Third World in what they described as a growing protectionist trend in the industrial nations. Trouble for the developing nations' trade was seen in the IMF's forecasts. While the IMF slightly raised its forecast of the volume of exports of the developing nations in 1984, it lowered its forecast of the volume of their imports.

De Larosière told his audience that temporary protectionist measures tended to "become entrenched and spread. They do not just poison the trading climate in certain industries, but weaken the fabric of international economic and political cooperation as a whole."

A. W. Clausen, president of the World Bank, said it was of "crucial importance" that industrial nations "stop simply making general declarations of interest and start taking concrete steps to liberalize trade. . . ."

Argentine Agreement

For most of the finance ministers and bankers attending the meeting, the best news was the successful conclusion on September 25, 1984, of long negotiations between Argentina and the IMF on terms that likely would make available to that country billions of dollars in loans from both the monetary fund and commercial banks. The announcement of the agreement on a program of austerity for Argentina that would clear the way for the fresh credits was made at the meeting in a speech by Bernardo Grinspun, Argentina's economy minister.

The IMF had demanded stringent reductions in public spending as a condition for new loans. President Raúl Alfonsín, however, had been afraid that excessive austerity would result in civil unrest. Alfonsín had been installed in December 1983 as head of a democratic government in Argentina after eight years of military rule. (Historic Documents of 1983, p. 455)

> *Following are excerpts from the statement of Jacques de Larosière to the Board of Governors of the International Monetary Fund, and excerpts from the address of A. W. Clausen to the Board of Governors of the World Bank and the International Finance Corporation, September 24, 1984. (Boldface headings in brackets have been added by Congressional Quarterly to highlight the organization of the text.):*

STATEMENT BY JACQUES de LAROSIÈRE

Mr. Chairman, two years ago, our annual meetings took place in an atmosphere of gathering crisis in the world economy. The worldwide recession had brought economic activity to a low ebb, and the debt problems of several major developing countries threatened an unraveling of the international financial system.

Recalling this underlines how far we have come since Toronto. Since early 1983, economic expansion has proceeded at a rapid pace in the United States, and there is increasing evidence that growth is reviving in the rest of the industrial world. International trade has rebounded strongly. Inflation has been substantially reduced. And the balance of payments situation of heavily indebted developing countries has improved dramatically.

There are, however, important problems that continue to present difficult challenges to policymakers. Interest rates are still very high in real terms. Although they do not appear to have impeded recovery so far, high interest rates undermine its longer-term sustainability and compound the problems of heavily indebted developing countries. Many developing countries still have a long way to go before being able to combine balance of payments viability with their needs of domestic economic development. This is particularly true for many smaller developing countries and low-income countries. In the industrial world, unemployment remains at very high levels, especially in Western Europe.

In my remarks today, I will address these problems and how they must be tackled so as to consolidate the improvements that have recently taken place in the world environment. . . .

1. Sustaining expansion in industrial countries

1984 is shaping up as the best year for economic growth in the industrial countries in at least eight years. The IMF staff expects output to be 5 percent higher than in 1983, with the majority of industrial countries recording an acceleration in their growth rate. Encouragingly, this strengthening in the economic situation has not been accompanied by any acceleration of inflation. Price increases in 1984 are expected to average about 4½ percent, a little less than in 1983, and the best performance in almost 15 years. Also encouraging has been the strength of fixed investment. . . .

There are, however, difficult challenges to be met in broadening the basis of the present expansion and making it more durable. A particular problem lies in the geographically unbalanced nature of the upswing. In Europe, growth has not yet made much of a dent in the unemployment problem. In the United States, on the other hand, policies have to ensure that the growth of nominal demand is made consistent with the avoidance of a resurgence of inflation. In particular, continued and determined action to reduce the budget deficit is essential. This would also assist in bringing down reliance on foreign savings to a more sustainable level and relieve pressures on interest rates. . . .

The way to achieve lower interest rates is not through accommodative monetary policy — this would simply rekindle inflationary fears — but through a fiscal policy that reduces the share of savings absorbed by the public sector. This involves action both to bring down fiscal deficits and to curb the growth of public expenditures. If government deficits remain high, markets will remain fearful that the temptation to monetize debt will become difficult to resist. Even if this temptation is resisted, the pre-emption of savings to finance fiscal deficits will eventually squeeze out interest-sensitive expenditure, particularly business investment. Of course, private spending can also be crowded out by tax-financed government outlays; it is therefore of the utmost importance that adequate restraint be exercised over government expenditures.

Financial policies, however, are only part of the story. We need also to make sure that markets are flexible enough to adapt to the demands of rapidly changing technology, and to absorb the available labor force. This is an area in which the different institutional settings of countries will require different policy responses. . . .

2. Growth and adjustment in developing countries

The improving situation in the industrial countries is having a beneficial effect in the third world. A number of developing countries have taken advantage of these conditions by implementing courageous and deter-mined adjustment programs. With better conditions and improved poli-cies, exports of developing countries to the industrial world have grown rapidly over the past year (by 18 percent in dollar terms), imparting a badly needed stimulus to growth and contributing to a further improve-ment in balance of payments positions. . . .

The fact that the adjustment process in developing countries is now moving from the import-compression phase to the export-expansion phase is also making for faster output growth. For the first time in four years, output in these countries, as a group, is expected to grow appreciably faster than population, and a further acceleration to 4½ percent is in prospect for 1985.

These positive developments should not be allowed to obscure the many aspects of the present picture that give cause for concern. The present trends in growth follow several years in which living standards in many developing countries have been stagnant or declining. It must also be borne in mind that economic performance has been highly uneven across countries, with African and Latin American countries having been severely affected. . . . Though Asian countries have generally experienced satisfac-tory growth rates, we must not forget that this is still the region with the largest number of people in economic distress. Lastly, the debt situation of many developing countries the world over remains precarious and vulner-able to adverse developments, whether of a domestic or external character.

The key issue is how developing countries burdened with heavy indebt-edness can regain the momentum of their economic advance. This is a question that concerns us greatly in the Fund. We have studied it closely, both in the context of our support for member countries' programs of adjustment and of the Fund's surveillance of world economic developments. . . .

3. International collaboration

Grasping the opportunities and meeting the challenges of the present situation will require not only domestic political commitment, but also a high degree of international collaboration. The world economy has become increasingly interdependent, and all countries need to recognize the ways in which their policies interact with those of their trading and financial partners. . . .

Collaboration on the part of international lenders, both public and private, has over the past year been crucial in underpinning adjustment efforts and in bringing about an orderly evolution of the debt situation. There are no miracle solutions, no global panaceas in this field. It is only by maintaining and improving collaboration between all the parties concerned on a case-by-case basis that continued progress can be realized. . . .

ADDRESS BY A. W. CLAUSEN

Mr. Chairman, Governors, Ladies and Gentlemen:

Welcome to these Annual Meetings....

Since last we gathered here a year ago, much progress has been made toward securing global economic recovery. The recovery is well under way in most industrial countries, and inflation has declined. Developing country economic performance in 1984 is likely to be better than in 1983, and improve even further in 1985.

Economic growth in the member countries of the Organization for Economic Cooperation and Development (OECD) is expected to top 4 percent this year. In the developing countries as a group, economic growth is now projected to rise from 1 percent in 1983 to 3.5 percent in 1984.

Industrial country growth in 1984 can be expected to stimulate an increase in developing country export volumes of about 7.5 percent this year. And that, together with a limited amount of net borrowing, will allow imports to grow by about 6.0 percent this year, so providing for some restoration of depleted reserves. This is heartening. But let us not forget that the strength and durability of this trend depends heavily on continued recovery in the industrial nations....

[Trends]

As we have consistently emphasized, there are, of course, no quick and easy solutions to the major problems confronting the developing countries. In the fields of trade, debt, economic management, and population, there is a long haul ahead of them. And that means a long haul ahead of the international community as a whole....

In looking ahead to see how the Bank can best respond to the needs of our borrowing members in the next decade, we have tried to analyze the economic prospects that developing countries might face under various assumptions. That analysis is set out at length in our 1984 World Development Report, and the main message is clear: whatever the domestic efforts of our borrowing members, the nature of the prospects facing them still depends heavily on the courses of action which the industrialized world decides to pursue.

We cannot predict which road the industrialized world will take — the road of reform, which we believe is essential, or the road of "business as usual," which we believe exposes the world to considerable risk. But one thing is certain: whichever road is taken, the economic environment in which the developing countries will be struggling to grow in the late Eighties and early Nineties will be significantly different from that of the Seventies. And in some repects it is almost certain to be worse....

The dangers of a continuation of the protectionist trend are abundantly evident. An era of sustained real growth for the industrialized countries, as well as recovery for the developing countries, is going to be a mere pipedream unless trade liberalization is revived. . . .

It is now of crucial importance that governments stop simply making general declarations of interest and start taking concrete stops to liberalize trade before what was achieved in the Sixties and Seventies is more than offset by what is being perpetrated in the Eighties. The launching of a new round of multilateral trade negotiations, under the auspices of the GATT, and focused in particular on non-tariff barriers and issues of concern to the developing countries, cannot come too soon. In the absence of such negotiations, and with continuing protectionist pressures, the medium-term environment will be fraught with uncertainties. . . .

[Proposals]

How the institutions of The World Bank can best contribute to the effort to secure a more vibrant world economy in coming years is the subject of detailed discussions now underway with your Executive Board. We are reviewing every element in the future evolution of your institutions to determine their most effective roles for the remainder of this century in the light of the broad economic trends that we perceive.

This is a challenging and exciting undertaking. We are not deviating in this effort from our most basic objectives: to assist in the attainment of economic and social progress in our developing member countries and to work to alleviate poverty in those countries. Since the Bank went into business almost 40 years ago, there has been a continuing evolution of the institution, enabling it to become ever more effective in assisting developing nations in rapidly changing global economic conditions. That evolutionary process has quickened in most recent times. The moment is therefore ripe for a comprehensive review of our strategies. In particular, we have to recognize three new facts of life about the Bank's relationship with the international community.

First, as our assessment of the medium-term environment confirms, the Bank's borrowers are becoming increasingly differentiated in their economic performance and prospects, creditworthiness, and demand for Bank assistance;

Second, the Bank's ability to respond effectively is increasingly affected by its relations with other lenders; and

Third, there are increasing uncertainties over the volume of resources we can mobilize and how much we can lend. . . .

We need your encouragement and support. . . . Increased strength and increased innovation will be the keys to the Bank's effectiveness as a major participant in the action program for Sub-Sarahan Africa. Strength and innovation will be the keys to success in our efforts to assist institutional change and the resumption of growth and investment in the heavily indebted countries. In short, a strong, innovative Bank can really make a substantial difference to the international cooperative effort to accelerate Third World development. And that cooperative effort must not be allowed to falter for lack of faith in our collective ability to succeed. . . .

For there is no acceptable reason why we should fail. Here in this hall today is an assembly of men and women with the greatest experience and understanding of the problems, and the clearest recognition of the solutions, as has ever been convened. And I venture to suggest that all of us here are of one mind on this: that the economic situation, though serious in much of the developing world, is categorically not hopeless. To think otherwise is to declare a vote of no confidence in ourselves; to reject all belief in the power of ingenuity and determination to meet the challenge; and worst of all, to dash the hopes of a better life for millions upon millions of our fellow human beings....

DONOVAN INDICTMENT

September 24, October 2, 1984

Secretary of Labor Raymond J. Donovan, New York state senator Joseph L. Galiber, Schiavone Construction Co., and Jopel Contracting and Trucking Corp., along with eight business associates, were indicted by a Bronx County, N. Y., grand jury on September 24, 1984. The 137-count indictment charged the two companies and their officials with grand larceny, falsifying business records, and filing false documents in connection with construction of the 63rd Street East River subway tunnel.

Donovan's involvement marked the first time a sitting Cabinet member was formally indicted. Donovan was executive vice president of Schiavone Construction until 1981, when he resigned to join the Reagan Cabinet.

Fraudulent Business Practices

Jopel Contracting and Trucking Corp., owned by William P. Masselli, a reputed organized crime figure, and Galiber, a black, were hired by Schiavone Construction Co., one of the main contractors in the $186 million federally financed project. Ten percent of all payments for work on the project were required by federal and state law to go to minority business enterprises. The investigation leading to the indictment centered around the questionable status of Jopel Contracting and Trucking as a legitimate minority business. Evidence was uncovereed that Galiber had made no actual investment in the firm and that the alleged *minority business enterprise had been formed for the purpose of meeting the federal and state requirements.*

The indictment charged that Schiavone Construction's quarterly reports to the New York City Transit Authority overstated the amounts paid to Jopel Contracting and Trucking. According to District Attorney Mario Merola, Schiavone Construction purchased $1 million in equipment that it claimed to rent to Jopel, although the equipment was operated by Schiavone employees. The rental charges for this equipment were then deducted from payments from the NYC Transit Authority to Jopel as a minority contractor. By this method, Schiavone Construction was able to increase the amount attributable to a minority business.

The Murder Indictment

A second indictment charged Masselli and Joseph Bugliarelli with the 1978 murder of Salvatore Frascone. Frascone, a Mafia "soldier," had been a friend of Louis Nargi, a competitor of Jopel for subcontracting work from Schiavone Construction. Frascone had protested Masselli's takeover of Nargi's trucking business. Information about the killing was offered to authorities by Michael Orlando, a driver for Masselli (reputed to be a member of the Genovese family) at the time of the murder. Orlando was serving a prison term in 1984 for truck hijacking. In exchange for immunity, Orlando told how he and Masselli had killed Frascone.

Orlando's confession led investigators to the suspicious relationship between the Jopel and Schiavone businesses. Orlando had cooperated with authorities before. As a Federal Bureau of Investigation informer in 1979, Orlando had facilitated the electronic surveillance of the South Bronx warehouse from which Masselli operated Jopel Contracting. This FBI surveillance produced 892 tapes suggesting the fraudulent operations of the two companies.

The 1982 Investigation

The 1982 investigation of the relationship between Schiavone Construction and Jopel Contracting, conducted by Special Prosecutor Leon Silverman under the Federal Ethics in Government Act, found "insufficient credible evidence" that Secretary Donovan had violated federal law. (Historic Documents of 1982, p. 587) District Attorney Merola, whose jurisdiction was broader, stated that he benefited from evidence uncovered by Silverman, as well as that developed by Justice Department prosecutors in Manhattan and Brooklyn, and by Bronx County detectives and prosecutors over a period of two years.

Two related murders that occurred during the period of the Silverman investigation were unsolved at the time of the indictment. A scheduled witness, Frederick S. Furino, and Nathan Masselli, the son of scheduled witness William Masselli, were killed in 1982.

Reaction

At the October 2 arraignment, Donovan pleaded not guilty to the charges. He stated after the arraignment, "I commented yesterday, without having seen the indictment, that it was not worth the paper it was written on. Now that I've seen it, I realize that I overstated its value." He attacked the "actions and the obviously partisan timing of the Bronx district attorney." Donovan asked President Ronald Reagan to grant him a leave of absence without pay "to assure that this matter does not become part of the current election campaign" and to allow Donovan to devote his attention to fighting the charges.

Rep. Tony Coelho, D-Calif., chairman of the Democratic Congressional Campaign Committee, criticized Reagan for agreeing to Donovan's leave of absence. Walter F. Mondale, the Democratic presidential nominee, said the administration should "immediately determine whether there is a substantial or reasonable basis" for the charges, "and, if so, [Donovan] should be removed." Sen. Orrin G. Hatch, R-Utah, chairman of the Labor and Human Resources Committee, agreed with Donovan that "there's a lot of politics involved" in the timing of the indictment, which came five days before the statute of limitations would have expired on a crucial count.

Following are the text of the press release from the Office of the Bronx District Attorney dated October 2, 1984 announcing the two indictments; and excerpts of the indictment of the Schiavone Construction Co., Raymond J. Donovan, Ronald A. Schiavone, Jopel Contracting and Trucking Corp., Joseph L. Galiber, William P. Masselli, and others filed September 24, 1984:

PRESS RELEASE

Bronx District Attorney Mario Merola today announced the handing up of two indictments by a Bronx grand jury, one naming U.S. Secretary of Labor Raymond J. Donovan, State Sen. Joseph L. Galiber and eight other corporate executives on charges of grand larceny and the other naming two men on charges of murder in connection with dealings of two corporations also named in the first indictment.

The first indictment also names the Schiavone Construction Co. and the Jopel Contracting and Trucking Corp., along with the 10 men, in addition to the single count of grand larceny in the 2nd degree, with 125 counts of falsifying business records in the 1st degree and eleven counts of offering a false instrument for filing in the 1st degree.

The grand larceny charge carries a maximum of seven years in prison, if convicted, and each of the other counts carries up to four years in prison. The corporations face fines in the millions of dollars.

The murder indictment, which carries a maximum penalty of life in prison, names William P. Masselli and Joseph Bugliarelli.

The indictment charges that "the said defendants, acting in concert with each other and another, in the county of the Bronx, on or about Sept. 22, 1978, with intent to cause the death of Salvatore Frascone, caused the death of Salvatore Frascone by shooting him with a deadly weapon, to wit: a loaded revolver."

Named along with Donovan, who was executive vice president of the Schiavone Co. at the time of the alleged crimes, and Galiber, who was associated with Masselli, who then headed up the Jopel Corp., were:

—Ronald A. Schiavone, Chairman of the Board and Chief Executive Officer.

—Richard C. Callaghan, Senior Vice President.

—Joseph A. DiCarolis, President and Chief Operating Officer.

—Morris J. Levin, Secretary and Counsel to the Corporation.

—Albert J. Magrini, Vice President for Construction.

—Gennaro Liguori, Second Vice President.

—William P. Masselli.

—Robert Genuario, Treasurer of a joint venture of companies involved with the construction of a subway tunnel.

The grand larceny count in the 137 count indictment charges that:

"The said defendants, acting in concert with each other and others, in the County of the Bronx, on or about and between October 1, 1979 and September 24, 1984, did steal property with a value exceeding one thousand five hundred dollars, to wit: payments of money by the New York City Transit Authority on Contract number C-20198 for construction of Section 5B of a rapid transit railroad, such contract awarded in 1978 at a bid of approximately 186 million dollars."

One of the charges of Falsifying Business Records, states that:

"The said defendants, acting in concert with each other and others, in the County of the Bronx, on or about October 1, 1979, with intent to defraud, made and caused a false entry in the business records of an enterprise, to wit: Schiavone Equipment Backcharge to Period ending 9/29/79 by Jopel Contracting and Trucking Corporation, with false entry reported in an amount greater than the true amount, with the intent to commit another crime and to aid and conceal the commission thereof."

One of the charges of the crime of Offering a False Instrument for Filing in the First Degree, specifies that:

"The said defendants, acting in concert with each other and others, in the County of the Bronx, on or about June 30, 1980, with intent to defraud the state and any political subdivision thereof and knowing that a written instrument, namely, a quarterly report to the New York City Transit Authority on Contract number C-20198 regarding payments made to minority business enterprises, contained a false statement and false information, to wit: payments to June 1, 1980 to Jopel Constr. & Trucking, an alleged minority firm, reported in an amount greater than the true amount, did offer and present it to a public office and public servant, namely the New York City Transit Authority, with the knowledge and belief that it would be filed with registered, recorded in and otherwise become a part of the records of such public office and public servant."

Merola said the cases against those named in the indictments were the result of nearly two years of work by a team comprised of Assistant District Attorney Stephen Bookin and Det. Sgt. Michael Geary and Det. Lawrence Doherty.

Merola singled out for particular praise Edward McDonald, Chief of the Organized Crime Strike Force of the U.S. Government in the Eastern District of New York, noting that McDonald had turned over to him the evidence to get the probe into focus and rolling.

INDICTMENT
SUPREME COURT OF THE STATE OF NEW YORK

Indictment No. 45482/84

The People of the State of New York

against

Schiavone Construction Company, Raymond J. Donovan, Ronald A. Schiavone, Richard C. Callaghan, Joseph A. DiCarolis, Morris J. Levin, Albert J. Magrini, Gennaro Liguori, Robert Genuario, Jopel Contracting and Trucking Corporation, Joseph L. Galiber, and William P. Masselli,

Defendants.

Counts
  Grand larceny in the second degree (1 count)
  Falsifying business records in the first degree (125 counts)
  Offering a false instrument for filing in the first degree (11 counts)

September 24, 1984
A true bill

Mario Merola
District Attorney

The GRAND JURY of the COUNTY OF BRONX, by this indictment accuse defendants, Schiavone Construction Company, Raymond J. Donovan, Ronald A. Schiavone, Richard C. Callaghan, Joseph A. DiCarolis, Morris J. Levin, Albert J. Magrini, Gennaro Liguori, Robert Genuario, Jopel Contracting and Trucking Corporation, Joseph L. Galiber, and William P. Masselli, of the Crime of Grand Larceny in the Second Degree committed as follows:

The said defendants, acting in concert with each other and others, in the County of Bronx, on or about and between October 1, 1979 and September 24, 1984, did steal property with a value exceeding one thousand five hundred dollars, to wit: payments of money by the New York City Transit Authority on Contract number C-20198 for construction of Section 5B of a rapid transit railroad, such contract awarded in 1978 at a bid of approximately 186 million dollars.

SECOND COUNT:

And the GRAND JURY Aforesaid, by this indictment, further accuse said defendants, of the crime of Falsifying Business Records in the First Degree committed as follows:

The said defendants, acting in concert with each other and others, in the County of Bronx, on or about October 1, 1979, with intent to defraud, made and caused a false entry in the business records of an enterprise, to wit: Schiavone Equipment Backcharge to Period Ending 9/29/79 by Jopel Contracting and Trucking Corporation, such false entry reported in an amount greater than the true amount, with the intent to commit another crime and to aid and conceal the commission thereof. . . .

THIRTY-SEVENTH COUNT:

And the GRAND JURY Aforesaid, by this indictment, further accuse said defendants, of the crime of Falsifying Business Records in the First Degree committed as follows:

The said defendants, acting in concert with each other and others, in the County of Bronx, on or about June 30, 1980, with intent to defraud, made and caused a false entry in the business records of an enterprise, to wit: quarterly report to the New York City Transit Authority on Contract number C-20198 regarding payments to June 1, 1980 to Jopel Constr. & Trucking, an alleged minority firm, such false entry reported in an amount greater than the true amount, with the intent to commit another crime and to aid and conceal the commission thereof.

THIRTY-EIGHTH COUNT:

And the GRAND JURY Aforesaid, by this indictment, further accuse said defendants of the crime of Offering a False Instrument For Filing in the First Degree committed as follows:

The said defendants, acting in concert with each other and others, in the County of Bronx, on or about June 30, 1980, with intent to defraud the state and any political subdivision thereof and knowing that a written instrument, namely, a quarterly report to the New York City Transit Authority on Contract number C-20198 regarding payments made to minority business enterprises, contained a false statement and false information, to wit: payments to June 1, 1980 to Jopel Constr. & Trucking, an alleged minority firm, reported in an amount greater than the true amount, did offer and present it to a public office and public servant, namely the New York City Transit Authority, with the knowledge and belief that it would be filed with, registered, recorded in and otherwise become a part of the records of such public office and public servant.

THIRTY-NINTH COUNT:

And the GRAND JURY Aforesaid, by this indictment, further accuse said defendants, of the crime of Falsifying Business Records in the First Degree committed as follows:

The said defendants, acting in concert with each other and others, in the County of Bronx, on or about February 26, 1982, with intent to defraud, made and caused a false entry in the business records of an enterprise, to wit: quarterly report to the Urban Mass Transit Administration regarding MBE construction statistics for the period April 1-June 30, 1980, such false entry reported in an amount greater than the true amount, with the intent to commit another crime and to aid and conceal the commission thereof. . . .

REAGAN AND GROMYKO ADDRESS THE UNITED NATIONS
September 24, 27, 1984

In a move that surprised many observers, President Ronald Reagan took a major step to reopen a dialogue with the Soviet Union in the fall of 1984 by inviting Soviet foreign minister Andrei A. Gromyko to confer at the White House. The president's action was an attempt to get nuclear arms talks in motion that had been stalled since 1983. The Soviet delegation had broken off those negotiations, protesting the deployment of new intermediate-range nuclear missiles in Western Europe.

Gromyko had come to the United States to address an opening session of the 39th United Nations General Assembly in New York City. Reagan, also speaking to the General Assembly, gave a speech that signaled a new, conciliatory approach toward the Russians.

In the past, it had not been unusual for an American president to confer with Gromyko during the veteran diplomat's annual visits to the United Nations. Such meetings between Gromyko and the president had been routine since the administration of Franklin Roosevelt, but they were abruptly halted when President Jimmy Carter refused to see the foreign minister after the Soviet invasion of Afghanistan in 1979. (Historic Documents of 1979, p. 965) For Reagan, however, the invitation represented a marked departure from his past policy; it was, in fact, his first meeting with a ranking Soviet official since he became president in 1981.

The Reagan-Gromyko meeting took place at a crucial point in U.S.-Soviet relations. The Soviet government's verbal attacks on the United

States had grown increasingly abrasive during the Reagan administration in the face of the president's harsh anti-Soviet stance and the military buildup he had launched. In addition, negotiations on limiting medium- and long-range nuclear armaments had come to a complete halt after the Soviet delegation made good its threat to walk away from the table if the United States insisted on deploying the Pershing II and cruise missiles, aimed at Russia, in North Atlantic Treaty Organization countries. The Soviet delegation had refused to resume the talks unless the missiles were removed.

During the summer of 1984, the Soviets had shown some interest in resuming negotiations that were limited to the topic of preventing development of anti-satellite weapons for use in outer space. However, a Reagan administration proposal to discuss this topic in conjunction with other arms control issues was rejected, and preliminary discussions broke down.

Reagan's initiative also coincided with the presidential election less than six weeks away. Walter F. Mondale, Reagan's Democratic opponent, had made a major campaign issue out of the president's failure to meet with the Soviets, pointing out repeatedly that Reagan was the first president since Herbert Hoover not to have done so — a circumstance, Mondale said, that heightened the risk of nuclear war. The Democratic candidate questioned whether Reagan's overture was a real quest for dialogue or a political maneuver calculated to portray Reagan to voters as a peacemaker.

Gromyko also sought a meeting with Mondale during his New York visit, perhaps in an effort to avoid leaving the impression that Moscow was trying to influence the election. The two conferred on September 27. Some observers speculated that Gromyko agreed to see Reagan in September because the Kremlin no longer believed that its refusal to talk would hurt Reagan politically and bring someone else into the White House who might prove easier to deal with than Reagan.

Reagan's Speech to the United Nations

Reagan's U.N. address on September 24 stood in sharp contrast to the speech he made one year earlier to the General Assembly after a Korean airliner that strayed over Soviet territory had been shot down. (Historic Documents of 1983, p. 775) The anti-Soviet rhetoric that had punctuated his 20-year political career was absent from the 1984 address. "We're ready to be the friend of any country that is a friend to us and a friend of peace," he told the assembly, while Gromyko watched impassively. Reagan quoted Mahatma Gandhi and Saint Ignatius Loyola, founder of the Society of Jesus, in the speech. "America has repaired its strength," he declared. "We are ready for constructive negotiations with the Soviet Union."

Although Reagan did not make specific arms control proposals, he did suggest several possible formats that might be used for future talks: regular Cabinet-level meetings between American and Soviet officials; observations of one another's nuclear test sites; exchanges of information about plans for military growth, such as projected weapons development; regular consultations between American and Soviet experts on "regional" disputes, such as those in Afghanistan, the Middle East, and Central America; and formation of an "umbrella" group to deal with a variety of arms control issues.

The Russian Response

A dispatch from the New York office of Tass, the official Soviet news agency, declared that Reagan's speech contained "no indications of any change in the essence of the present U.S. policy," and Gromyko's September 27 speech to the United Nations seemed to confirm that view. Gromyko launched into a strongly worded criticism of U.S. foreign policy during the previous 40 years that seemed to throw cold water on Reagan's overture. "The Soviet Union believes that it is precisely concrete deeds and not verbal assurances that can lead to the normalization of the situation in our relations with the U.S.," he proclaimed. Gromyko called on the United States to "remove the obstacles it has erected to the holding of talks" and expressed the Soviet Union's interest in four other points: prevention of the militarization of space, a freeze on the nuclear arsenals of both superpowers, complete prohibition of nuclear testing, and a mutual pledge not to be the first to use nuclear weapons.

Many observers were cautious about taking Gromyko's speech as an indicator of Moscow's reaction, however, pointing out that the Soviets would need time to digest Reagan's speech and that the foreign minister was a wily professional diplomat whose skill in dealing with Washington had earned him the respect of many American officials and a reputation of inscrutability.

The Washington Talks

After Gromyko met with Reagan on September 28, administration spokesmen indicated that, although no substantive agreements emerged from the meeting, both sides did plan to continue their contacts, a point that was confirmed in a Tass report covering Gromyko's visit. A spokesman for Secretary of State George P. Shultz, who also conferred with Gromyko twice while the foreign minister was in the United States, told newspaper correspondents that the meetings had resulted in a good give-and-take about the problems of nuclear weapons.

Another indication from Moscow came on October 16 when Soviet President Konstantin Chernenko, in an unusual interview with a foreign reporter, told a Washington Post *correspondent that "Soviet-American relations could be improved if the United States would demonstrate a genuine interest" in one of the four issues Gromyko listed in his U.N. address. Chernenko's comments gave hope that the stalled nuclear missile talks would be resumed in the near future if progress in one of the areas was made.* (Chernenko interview, p. 917)

Following are excerpts from President Ronald Reagan's September 24 address to an opening session of the 39th United Nations General Assembly, and Soviet foreign minister Andrei A. Gromyko's address to that body September 27. (Boldface headings in brackets have been added by Congressional Quarterly to highlight organization of the text.):

REAGAN ADDRESS

Mr. President, Mr. Secretary General, distinguished Heads of State, Ministers, Representatives, and guests — first of all, I wish to congratulate President Lusaka on his election as President of the General Assembly. I wish you every success, Mr. President, in carrying out the responsibilities of this high international office....

It's an honor to be here, and I thank you for your gracious invitation. I would speak in support of the two great goals that led to the formation of this organization, the cause of peace and the cause of human dignity.

The responsibility of this Assembly, the peaceful resolution of disputes between peoples and nations, can be discharged successfully only if we recognize the great common ground upon which we all stand — our fellowship as members of the human race, our oneness as inhabitants of this planet, our place as representatives of billions of our countrymen whose fondest hope remains the end to war and to the repression of the human spirit. These are the important central realities that bind us, that permit us to dream of a future without the antagonisms of the past. Just as shadows can be seen only where there is light, so too can we overcome what is wrong only if we remember how much is right. And we will resolve what divides us only if we remember how much more unites us.

This chamber has heard enough about the problems and dangers ahead. Today, let us dare to speak of a future that is bright and hopeful and can be ours only if we seek it. I believe that future is far nearer than most of us would dare to hope....

Let me ... briefly outlin[e] the major goals of American foreign policy, and then explor[e] with you the practical ways we're attempting to further freedom and prevent war. By that I mean, first, how we have moved to strengthen ties with old allies and new friends; second, what we're doing to help avoid the regional conflicts that could contain the seeds of world conflagration; and third, the status of our efforts with the Soviet Union to reduce the level of arms.

[Policy Objectives]

Let me begin with a word about the objectives of American foreign policy, which have been consistent since the post-war era, and which fueled the formation of the United Nations and were incorporated into the UN Charter itself.

The UN Charter states two overriding goals: "to save succeeding generations from the scourge of war, which twice in our lifetime has brought untold sorrow to mankind," and "to reaffirm faith in fundamental human rights, in the dignity and worth of the human person, in the equal rights of men and women of nations large and small.". . .

But I would like also to emphasize that our concern for protecting human rights is part of our concern for protecting the peace.

The answer is for all nations to fulfill the obligations they freely assumed under the Universal Declaration of Human Rights. It states: "The will of the people shall be the basis of the authority of government; this will shall be expressed in periodic and genuine elections." The Declaration also includes these rights: "to form and to join trade unions," "to own property alone as well as in association with others," "to leave any country including his own and to return to his country," and to enjoy "freedom of opinion and expression." Perhaps the most graphic example of the relationship between human rights and peace is the right of peace groups to exist and to promote their views. In fact, the treatment of peace groups may be a litmus test of government's true desire for peace.

In addition to emphasizing this tie between the advocacy of human rights and the prevention of war, the United States has taken important steps, as I mentioned earlier, to prevent world conflict. The starting point and cornerstone of our foreign policy is our alliance and partnership with our fellow democracies. For 35 years, the North Atlantic Alliance has guaranteed the peace in Europe. In both Europe and Asia, our alliances have been the vehicle for a great reconciliation among nations that had fought bitter wars in decades and centuries past. And here in the Western Hemisphere, north and south are being lifted on the tide of freedom and are joined in a common effort to foster peaceful economic development. . . .

The people of the United States will remain faithful to their commitments. But the United States is also faithful to its alliances and friendships with scores of nations in the developed and developing worlds with differing political systems, cultures and traditions. The development of ties between the United States and China, a significant global event of the last dozen years, shows our willingness to improve relations with countries ideologically very different from ours.

We're ready to be the friend of any country that is a friend to us and a friend of peace. And we respect genuine nonalignment. . . .

The United States welcomes diversity and peaceful competition. We do not fear the trends of history. We are not ideologically rigid. We do have principles, and we will stand by them. . . .

[International Conflicts]

But any economic progress as well as any movement in the direction of greater understanding between the nations of the world are, of course, endangered by the prospect of conflict at both the global and regional level. . . .

We're engaged, for example, in diplomacy to resolve conflicts in Southern Africa, working with the Front Line States and our partners in the Contact Group. Mozambique and South Africa have reached an historic accord on non-aggression and cooperation. South Africa and Angola have agreed on a disengagement of forces from Angola, and the groundwork has been laid for the independence of Namibia, with virtually all aspects of Security Council Resolution 435 agreed upon. Let me add that the United States considers it a moral imperative that South Africa's racial policies evolve peacefully but decisively toward a system compatible with basic norms of justice, liberty, and human dignity. . . .

In Central America, the United States has lent support to a diplomatic process to restore regional peace and security. We have committed substantial resources to promote economic development and social progress.

The growing success of democracy in El Salvador is the best proof that the key to peace lies in a political solution. Free elections brought into office a government dedicated to democracy, reform, economic progress and regional peace. Regrettably, there are forces in the region eager to thwart democratic change — but these forces are now on the defensive. The tide is turning in the direction of freedom. We call upon Nicaragua, in particular, to abandon its policies of subversion and militarism, and to carry out the promises it made to the Organization of American States to establish democracy at home.

The Middle East has known more than its share of tragedy and conflict for decades, and the United States has been actively involved in peace diplomacy for just as long. We consider ourselves a full partner in the quest for peace. The record of the 11 years since the October War shows that much can be achieved through negotiations; it also shows that the road is long and hard:

— Two years ago, I proposed a fresh start toward a negotiated solution to the Arab-Israeli conflict. My initiative of September 1st, 1982, contains a set of positions that can serve as a basis for a just and lasting peace. That initiative remains a realistic and workable approach, and I am committed to it as firmly as on the day I announced it. And the foundation stone of this effort remains Security Council Resolution 242, which in turn was incorporated in all its parts in the Camp David Accords.

— The tragedy of Lebanon has not ended. Only last week, a despicable act of barbarism by some who are unfit to associate with humankind reminded us once again that Lebanon continues to suffer. In 1983, we helped Israel and Lebanon reach an agreement that, if implemented, could have led to the full withdrawal of Israeli forces in the context of the withdrawal of all foreign forces. This agreement was blocked, and the long agony of the Lebanese continues. . . .

— In the Gulf, the United States has supported a series of Security Council resolutions that call for an end to the war between Iran and Iraq that has meant so much death and destruction and put the world's economic well-being at risk. Our hope is that hostilities will soon end, leaving each side with its political and territorial integrity intact, so that both may devote their energies to addressing the needs of their people and a return to relationships with other states.

— The lesson of experience is that negotiations work. The peace treaty between Israel and Egypt brought about the peaceful return of the Sinai, clearly showing that the negotiating process brings results when the parties commit themselves to it. The time is bound to come when the same wisdom and courage will be applied with success to reach peace between Israel and all of its Arab neighbors in a manner that assures security for all in the region, the recognition of Israel and a solution to the Palestinian problem.

In every part of the world, the United States is similarly engaged in peace diplomacy as an active player or a strong supporter.

— In Southeast Asia, we have backed the efforts of ASEAN to mobilize international support for a peaceful resolution of the Cambodian problem, which must include the withdrawal of Vietnamese forces and the election of a representative government. . . .

— In Afghanistan, the dedicated efforts of the Secretary General and his representatives to find a diplomatic settlement have our strong support. I assure you that the United States will continue to do everything possible to find a negotiated outcome which provides the Afghan people with the right to determine their own destiny, allows the Afghan refugees to return to their own country in dignity and protects the legitimate security interests of all neighboring countries. . . .

[U.S. — Soviet Relations]

The United States has been and will always be a friend of peaceful solutions. This is no less true with respect to my country's relations with the Soviet Union.

When I appeared before you last year, I noted that we cannot count on the instinct for survival alone to protect us against war. Deterrence is necessary but not sufficient. America has repaired its strength; we have invigorated our alliances and friendships. We are ready for constructive negotiations with the Soviet Union.

We recognize that there is no sane alternative to negotiations on arms control and other issues between our two nations, which have the capacity to destroy civilization as we know it. I believe this is a view shared by virtually every country in the world and by the Soviet Union itself.

And I want to speak to you today on what the United States and the Soviet Union can accomplish together in the coming years, and the concrete
steps that we need to take.

You know, as I stand here and look out from this podium, there in front
of me, I can see the seat of the representative from the Soviet Union. And
not far from that seat, just over to the side, is the seat of the representative
from the United States. In this historic assembly hall, it's clear there's not
a great distance between us. Outside this room, while there still will be
clear differences, there's every reason why we should do all that is possible
to shorten that distance. And that's why we're here. Isn't that what this
organization is all about?

[DIPLOMATIC OBJECTIVES]

Last January 16th, I set out three objectives for U.S.-Soviet relations
that can provide an agenda for our work over the months ahead. First, I
said, we need to find ways to reduce, and eventually, to eliminate the
threat and use of force in solving international disputes. Our concern over
the potential for nuclear war cannot deflect us from the terrible human
tragedies occurring every day in the regional conflicts I just discussed.
Together, we have a particular responsibility to contribute to political
solutions to these problems, rather than to exacerbate them through the
provision of even more weapons.

I propose that our two countries agree to embark on periodic consultations at policy level about regional problems. We will be prepared, if the
Soviets agree, to make senior experts available at regular intervals for
in-depth exchanges of views. I've asked Secretary Shultz to explore this
with Foreign Minister Gromyko. Spheres of influence are a thing of the
past. Differences between American and Soviet interests are not. The
objectives of this political dialogue will be to help avoid miscalculation,
reduce the potential risk of U.S.-Soviet confrontation, and help the people
in areas of conflict to find peaceful solutions. . . .

Our second task must be to find ways to reduce the vast stockpiles of armaments in the world. I am committed to redoubling our negotiating
efforts to achieve real results. In Geneva, a complete ban on chemical
weapons; in Vienna, real reductions to lower and equal levels in Soviet and
American, Warsaw Pact and NATO conventional forces; in Stockholm,
concrete practical measures to enhance mutual confidence, to reduce the
risk of war, and to reaffirm commitments concerning non-use of force.

In the field of nuclear testing, improvements in verification essential to
ensure compliance with the Threshold Test Ban and Peaceful Nuclear
Explosions agreements; and in the field of non-proliferation, close cooperation to strengthen the international institutions and practices aimed at
halting the spread of nuclear weapons, together with redoubled efforts to
meet the legitimate expectations of all nations that the Soviet Union and
the United States will substantially reduce their own nuclear arsenals. We

and the Soviets have agreed to upgrade our hotline communications facility, and our discussions of nuclear non-proliferation in recent years have been useful to both sides. We think there are other possibilities for improving communications in this area that deserve serious exploration.

I believe the proposal of the Soviet Union for opening U.S.-Soviet talks in Vienna provided an important opportunity to advance these objectives. We've been prepared to discuss a wide range of issues of concern to both sides, such as the relationship between defensive and offensive forces and what has been called the militarization of space. During the talks we would consider what measures of restraint both sides might take while negotiations proceed. However, any agreement must logically depend on our ability to get the competition in offensive arms under control and to achieve genuine stability at substantially lower levels of nuclear arms.

Our approach in all these areas will be designed to take into account concerns the Soviet Union has voiced. It will attempt to provide a basis for an historic breakthrough in arms control. I'm disappointed we were not able to open our meeting in Vienna earlier this month, on the date originally proposed by the Soviet Union. I hope we can begin these talks by the end of the year, or shortly thereafter.

The third task I set in January was to establish a better working relationship between the Soviet Union and the United States, one marked by greater cooperation and understanding. We've made some modest progress. We have reached agreements to improve our hotline, extend our 10-year economic agreement, enhance consular cooperation and explore coordination of search and rescue efforts at sea.

We've also offered to increase significantly the amount of U.S. grain for purchase by the Soviet[s], and to provide the Soviets a direct fishing allocation off U.S. coasts. But there's much more we could do together. I feel particularly strongly about breaking down the barriers between the peoples of the United States and the Soviet Union, and between our political, military and other leaders.

Now, all of these steps that I've mentioned, and especially the arms control negotiations, are extremely important to a step-by-step process toward peace. But let me also say that we need to extend the arms control process to build a bigger umbrella under which it can operate — a road map, if you will, showing where, during the next 20 years or so, these individual efforts can lead. This can greatly assist step-by-step negotiations and enable us to avoid having all our hopes or expectations — or expectations ride on any single set of series of negotiations. If progress is temporarily halted at one set of talks, this newly-established framework for arms control could help us take up the slack at other negotiations.

[BINATIONAL COOPERATION]

Today, to the great end of lifting the dread of nuclear war from the peoples of the Earth, I invite the leaders of the world to join in a new beginning. We need a fresh approach to reducing international tensions. History demonstrates beyond controversy that just as the arms competition has its root in political suspicions and anxieties, so it can be channeled in more stabilizing directions and eventually be eliminated, if those political suspicions and anxieties are addressed as well.

Toward this end, I will suggest to the Soviet Union that we institutionalize regular ministerial or cabinet-level meetings between our two countries on the whole agenda of issues before us, including the problem of needless obstacles to understanding. To take but one idea for discussion: In such talks, we could consider the exchange of outlines of five-year military plans for weapons development and our schedules of intended procurement.

We would also welcome the exchange of observers at military exercises and locations. And I propose that we find a way for Soviet experts to come to the United States nuclear test site and for ours to go to theirs to measure directly the yields of tests of nuclear weapons. We should work toward having such arrangements in place by next spring. I hope that the Soviet Union will cooperate in this undertaking and reciprocate in a manner that will enable the two countries to establish the basis for verification for effective limits on underground nuclear testing.

I believe such talks could work rapidly toward developing a new climate of policy understanding, one that is essential if crises are to be avoided and real arms control is to be negotiated.... How much progress we will make and at what pace, I cannot say. But we have a moral obligation to try....

Now some may dismiss such proposals and my own optimism as simplistic American idealism. And they will point to the burdens of the modern world and to history. Well, yes, if we sit down and catalog year by year, generation by generation, the famines, the plagues, the wars, the invasions mankind has endured, the list will grow so long, and the assault on humanity so terrific that it seems too much for the human spirit to bear.

But isn't this narrow and shortsighted, and not at all how we think of history? Yes, the deeds of infamy or injustice are all recorded, but what shines out from the pages of history is the daring of the dreamers and the deeds of the builders and the doers. These things make up the stories we tell and pass on to our children. They comprise the most enduring and striking fact about human history: that through the heartbreak and tragedy man has always dared to perceive the outline of human progress, the steady growth in not just the material well-being, but the spiritual insight of mankind.

There have been tyrants and murderers, and for a time they can seem invincible. But in the end, they always [fall.] Think on it ... always. All through history, the way of truth and love has always won. That was the belief and the vision of Mahatma Gandhi. He described that, and it remains today a vision that is good and true.

"All is gift," is said to have been the favorite expression of another great spiritualist, a Spanish soldier who gave up the ways of war for that of love and peace. And if we're to make realities of the two great goals of the United Nations Charter — the dreams of peace and human dignity — we must take to heart these words of Ignatius Loyola; we must pause long enough to contemplate the gifts received from Him who made us: the gift of life, the gift of this world, the gift of each other.

And the gift of the present. It is this present, this time that now we must seize. I leave you with a reflection from Mahatma Gandhi, spoken with those in mind who said that the disputes and conflicts of the modern world are too great to overcome; it was spoken shortly after Gandhi's quest for independence had taken him to Britain.

"I am not conscious of a single experience throughout my three months' stay in England and Europe," he said, "that made me feel that after all East is East and West is West. On the contrary, I have been convinced more than ever that human nature is much the same, no matter under what clime it flourishes, and that if you approached people with trust and affection, you would have ten-fold trust and thousand-fold affection returned to you."

For the sake of a peaceful world, a world where human dignity and freedom is respected and enshrined, let us approach each other with ten-fold trust and thousand-fold affection. A new future awaits us. The time is here, the moment is now.

One of the Founding Fathers of our nation, Thomas Paine, spoke words that apply to all of us gathered here today — they apply directly to all sitting here in this room. He said, "We have it in our power to begin the world over again."

Thank you. God bless you.

GROMYKO ADDRESS

Mr. Lusaka, I congratulate you on your election to the office of President of the thirty-ninth session of the General Assembly.

Our congratulations also go to the representatives of Brunei Darussalam, a State which has become the 159th Member of the United Nations.

For almost 40 years now, the words "the United Nations" have been firmly established in the world's political vocabulary. There is virtually no major international problem in connection with which those words would not be spoken in different languages, both in this Hall and outside it.

The extensive involvement of the United Nations in world affairs and developments is determined by the very mission of this forum, which was brought into being in order to unite the political will and potential of States for the purpose of maintaining international peace and security.

The conclusion reached by the founding Members of the United Nations was very simple indeed. It was born of the experience of the most bloody and destructive war that has ever befallen mankind. Indeed, it was precisely through united efforts that the aggressor was crushed. High was the cost of the great victory whose fortieth anniversary will be observed next year. All the peoples who fought against fascism contributed to that victory, but the Soviet Union's decisive role in it is indisputable.

United efforts were and are still needed today in order to build the post-war world. For it is the main lesson of the Second World War that States must stand together in the fight against war.

It is common knowledge, however, that as the war-ravaged earth was still smoldering and thousands of towns and villages were in ruins, the international atmosphere once again began to deteriorate and ultimately to become critical. This happened through the fault of those who, in their quest for world hegemony, began to behave contrary to their obligations as allies in the anti-Hitlerite coalition, oblivious to the lessons of the past.

In disregard of the lofty purposes and principles of the United Nations Charter, which they too had just signed, a group of States set out to escalate their military preparations by putting together a system of aggressive military blocs with the North Atlantic Alliance as its pivot. Those States pledged themselves to a policy based on a position of strength, a policy of brinkmanship. They are responsible for the advent of the cold war, which for a long time froze the normal flow of international life for which the peoples of the world yearned.

As a result, in the post-war years the world has been in a state of fever. And whenever international relations were marked — as was the case during the period of détente — by budding cooperation between States with different social systems, no effort was spared to undermine those positive processes, which is exactly what happened at the whim of the North Atlantic Treaty Organization (NATO) military bloc. It is precisely this trend in world politics that is the source of the situation that characterizes the international climate today. The threat of war has grown and the foundations of world peace have become more shaky.

This course, which is manifest as never before in the current policies of the United States and of those who choose to be its accomplices, is opposed by a broad front of peace-loving forces....

[Threat of Nuclear War]

The Soviet Union and the States of the socialist community are concentrating their efforts on attaining the key objective of preventing a nuclear disaster. For if the destructive potential currently amassed in the world were unleashed the human race would probably cease to exist. To prevent that from happening is a goal of overriding importance. All States represented in the United Nations should contribute to this achievement. No one and nothing can relieve them of the responsibility they have assumed under the United Nations Charter for the destiny of present and succeeding generations....

It took Washington a long time to send its team to the negotiating table in Geneva. However, at the talks the United States side followed a scenario that was not designed to lead to agreement. How else can one describe the fact that while negotiating the limitation of nuclear arms in Europe our partners did exactly the opposite? Beforehand — I repeat, beforehand — they set the date for deploying new United States medium-range missiles on the territories of several Western European States. We were told to accept the United States position or else there would be no agreement. So there is no agreement.

As to the Soviet proposals paving the way to agreements, they were rejected out of hand. Anything aimed at reaching agreement on the basis of equality was opposed with hostility.

It was Washington's deliberate intention to wreck the negotiations on nuclear arms — both medium-range and strategic. And it succeed [sic] in this. Juggling with words ostensibly in favour of negotiations is a false propaganda ploy. Its purpose is obvious.

Now they rejoice that they were able to begin the deployment of their missiles in Europe, as planned. Even here in the course of the General Assembly one can meet representatives of Western European States who are rubbing their hands with pleasure over the fact that the plan for deployment is being implemented....

The Soviet Union is in favour of serious talks. Not only are we prepared for such talks, but we are insisting on them. Our proposals on the limitation and reduction of strategic arms and on the limitation of nuclear arms in Europe remain valid. They neither offer advantages nor do any harm to either side. The United States must remove the obstacles it has put up in the way of the talks. Unless these obstacles are removed, of course, these talks will not take place and this is what the United States has in mind.

It is often asked: since it is difficult for the time being to arrive at a radical solution to the problem of nuclear arms, would it not be possible to take steps that would create a favourable atmosphere for that, raise the level of trust among States and ease international tension?

We are convinced that such steps are both possible and necessary. An effective measure of this kind would be the implementation of our proposal, endorsed by the United Nations, for a quantitative and qualitative freeze of nuclear weapon arsenals by all States which possess them. This could be done in the first place by the USSR and the United States on a bilateral basis — I repeat, the USSR and the United States on a bilateral basis — to set an example for other nuclear Powers to follow. Why should we do this? We propose to Washington: let us set such an example.

For the time being it is necessary at least to suspend the nuclear arms race. The world has crossed the line beyond which any further buildup and improvement of these arms is not only dangerous but senseless.

In the present circumstances it is futile and hopeless for anyone to expect to get ahead and gain military superiority. It is absolutely illusory to hope to win a nuclear war: whether global or limited, blitzkrieg or protracted — whatever the nuclear war doctrines.... What kind of people can fail to see that peace today is fragile? In spite of the obvious, they once again proclaim a policy of "peace through strength"....

[Weapons In Outer Space]

In view of its special urgency it is necessary to single out the question of preventing the race in nuclear and other weapons in outer space, which some want to turn into a staging area for war. We all know who is seeking this.

The extension of the arms race to outer space, unless checked in time, could become an irreversible process. Effective measures are needed to keep outer space peaceful.

Our country put forward a proposal, which was approved at the last session of the United Nations General Assembly, to conclude a treaty on the prohibition of the use of force in outer space and from space against the Earth. The Soviet Union unilaterally declared a moratorium on the placing of anti-satellite weapons in outer space as long as the United States of America and other States did likewise.

Another major step has been our initiative in calling for Soviet-United States talks on preventing the militarization of outer space. We believe that the Soviet Union and the United States of America, as the leading Powers in the field of outer space exploration, should do all they can to keep outer space peaceful and in particular, with a view to accomplishing this task, to lay the foundations for multilateral agreement. Full responsibility for the failure to hold the talks rests with the United States side. Washington is unwilling to engage in the talks. . . .

We urge the United States Government to recognize that the militarization of outer space threatens the whole of mankind, including the American people themselves. We express the hope that the United States of America will refrain from actions which would make irreversible the process of turning outer space into an arena of military rivalry and that it will be willing to engage in talks with a view to reaching an agreement. For its part, the Soviet Union continues to be in favour of starting such talks as soon as possible. . . .

In seeking to promote this goal in every possible way, the Soviet Union proposes the inclusion in the agenda of the current session of the General Assembly of an important and urgent item entitled "Use of outer space exclusively for peaceful purposes, for the benefit of mankind." What we are talking about is, in the first place, the banning, without delay and for all time, of the use of force in and from outer space against the Earth, as well as from the Earth against objects in outer space. In other words, agreement must be reached on the prohibition and elimination of space attack weapons of all systems, whatever their mode of basing, designed to destroy objects in space. This applies above all to States with major space capabilities. . . .

Surely the implementation of the proposal of the socialist countries to conclude a treaty on the mutual non-use of military force in relations between the States of the Warsaw Treaty and the North Atlantic Treaty Alliance would help to dissipate mutual apprehensions. It would be a welcome decision if an obligation not to be the first to use either nuclear or conventional weapons against one another — in other words, not to use force — were undertaken by States whether or not they belong to military alliances or have a neutral or non-aligned status. . . .

Some two years ago in Geneva the Soviet Union introduced at the Conference on Disarmament in Geneva draft basic provisions for a convention on the prohibition of chemical weapons. That draft constitutes a well-balanced basis for agreement. Some of those provisions were subsequently revised and amended to accommodate the positions of the other participants in the talks. Not everyone wants to see a successful completion of those talks. Some would rather see them fail. It would seem that the ostensible interest of certain States serves to conceal their plans for a build-up of chemical weapons. Such tactics should be strongly condemned. Where is the policy in certain War Departments that are doing this, when a true sobriety or far-sightedness would favour peace and the fate of the world? The drafting of an international convention on the prohibition and elimination of chemical weapons should be speeded up and the United Nations could contribute to this in no small measure. With time this problem will become even more intractable.

Our country expresses its readiness to take part in multilateral negotiations on the limitation of naval activities and naval armaments and on the extension of confidence-building measures to seas and oceans, especially to regions with the busiest sea lanes or with the highest likelihood of conflict situations. We have already put forward a proposal — and this is worth recalling — for an agreement on appropriate measures, including those applicable to particular regions, such as the Indian, Atlantic or Pacific Oceans, the Mediterranean Sea or the Persian Gulf. . . .

The arms race is seriously damaging to people even when the guns are silent, for it is increasingly consuming intellectual and material wealth and impedes the solution of global problems such as hunger, diseases, the search for new sources of energy, and the preservation of the environment.

These tasks will not be accomplished either by declaratory statements or by attempts to make assistance to other countries contingent on their acceptance of a particular model of socio-economic development. Something else is required, namely, the renunciation of all forms of exploitation and of the use of trade and economic ties as tools of political pressure; and a restructuring of international economic relations on a just and democratic basis.

By pressing for the implementation of tangible measures for curbing the arms race and achieving disarmament in close connection with the solution of world economic and social development problems, we consider that reduction of military budgets in either percentage or absolute terms is a promising way to achieve such a goal. And yes, I am talking about military budgets.

Together with the other State signatories of the Warsaw Treaty the USSR has submitted a proposal to the countries of NATO to begin talks on the question of the mutual non-increase of military expenditures and their subsequent reduction. In our view, there should be no obstacles to the participation of States that do not belong to these military and political groupings in implementing the proposed measures.

However, so far there has been no response from NATO, and that is no accident. If a picture were taken today using the most sophisticated modern technology to show on a planetary scale the magnitude of the world-wide military preparations by the United States and its allies, it would reveal a view that would stun any thinking person: a palisade of missiles; strategic bombers; naval armadas plying the waters of the seas and oceans; hundreds of military bases scattered all over the globe; and colossal stockpiles of weapons of every type.

Some may say that the Soviet Union too has weapons on land, in the air and on and under water. Our answer is: Yes, we do have them, but not by our choice. The objective facts of post-war history irrefutably show that it was not the Soviet Union, not socialism, but rather the other side that initiated the arms race and each of its new spirals. That is where the truth lies.

Forced to take countermeasures, our country did so only in response to, and to the extent commensurate with, the protection of its own security and that of its friends and allies. We have never sought, nor are we seeking, superiority. We stand for maintaining military equilibrium, and at the lowest possible level at that....

[Proposals]

The world community welcomed the Soviet initiatives that brought forth major international treaties and agreements — on the non-proliferation of nuclear weapons, on banning nuclear-weapons tests in the three environments, on the prohibition of the emplacement of weapons of mass destruction on the sea-bed and the ocean floor, on the prohibition of bacteriological weapons, etc. They continue to serve their purpose to this day and serve it well.

We have voluntarily and unilaterally assumed a number of obligations ranging from no-first-use of nuclear weapons to practical steps limiting our armed forces and armaments in Central Europe.

While making its own constructive contributions, the Soviet Union reacts favourably to proposals made by other countries. We support the idea of establishing nuclear-free zones and zones of peace in various parts of the globe. We have responded positively to the recent initiative by Argentina, Greece, India, Mexico, Tanzania and Sweden which urged all nuclear Powers to stop the build-up of nuclear weapons and begin to reduce their stockpiles.

The proposals that we have made constitute an impressive list of initiatives aimed at easing international tensions and developing peaceful cooperation among States.

Yet no matter what proposals or arguments we advance, our counterparts say "no" — they are not acceptable.

They swear that they favour a halt in the arms race, but only through modernization of arms and through improvement and stockpiling of weapons. Is it not absurd? It is absurd, indeed, and it underlies the entire policy. They would have people believe that they favour a reduction in world tensions, but only by establishing more and more military bases, by intensifying military preparations, by militarizing outer space and by deploying new kinds of United States nuclear weapons in Europe....

The Soviet delegation is authorized to state before this high forum that the USSR will follow the same policy course it has pursued up to now, namely, the course aimed at peace, disarmament, limitation and subsequent elimination of nuclear armaments, and the solution of other acute problems of today....

[International Conflicts]

It is understandable that prevention of war is a difficult task. The flywheel of military production is revolving continuously and influential forces — which place the interests of dominating the world above everything else — will not stop it.

Examples are readily available; they are at hand — all you have to do is reach for them. In defiance of the elementary norms of international law and morality an act of banditry was committed against tiny Grenada, which dared to assert its sovereignty. It was occupied and robbed of its independence.

We are witnessing gross interference in the internal affairs of El Salvador. No effort is being spared to prop up the regime of the stooges who are committing brutal crimes against the Salvadoran people.

A real siege — military, political and economic — has been mounted against Nicaragua, whose people, defending their national freedom, independence and democratic achievements, are heroically resisting in the face of the undeclared war organized against it by Washington. But the Nicaraguan people want just one thing; they want their independence and they want to resolve their internal affairs as they themselves see fit.

They still cannot reconcile themselves to the existence of socialist Cuba. Threats are being made against Cuba to force that country off the course to which it has been committed in both words and deeds....

Turning now to the Middle East, here again we can see what the imperialist policies mean for peoples and countries. Still fresh in our memories are the barbaric acts in Lebanon undertaken in an attempt to force upon it a capitulation agreement with Israel, and these acts are still going on today.

Yet the facts show that the United States, which relies upon "strategic cooperation" with Israel, has no intention of establishing lasting peace in that region. The Soviet Union has recently put forward a proposal on the

827

principles of a Middle East settlement. That proposal is well known and has evoked a broad response. We call upon all parties to the conflict to act with sober-minded regard for each other's legitimate rights and interests and all other States to facilitate the search for a just settlement in the Middle East.

Provocative intrigues continue against sovereign and non-aligned Afghanistan. The foes of the Afghan people will stop at nothing and will not abandon their hope of plunging it back into medieval darkness. To this end military incursions from outside are being organized. Is it possible to solve the foreign policy aspect of this problem? Yes, it is. The way to do that is to stop forming, arming and infiltrating into the country from outside gangs of anti-Government bandits and saboteurs and not to interfere in the international affairs of Afghanistan. There can be no doubt that Afghanistan has followed, and will continue to follow, the path it has chosen — the path of independence, freedom, social progress, peace and non-alignment.

In South-East Asia the situation is being exacerbated by the policy pursued by outside forces. Acts of provocation against Viet Nam, Laos and Kampuchea are going on unabated. Attempts are being made to pit their neighbours, the members of the Association of South-East Asian Nations, against those countries. We regard the initiative of the three countries of Indo-China on turning South-East Asia into a zone of peace, good-neighbourliness and cooperation, as also their efforts to start a political dialogue among the States of the region, as constructive.

The Soviet leadership has repeatedly stated its positions on the question of its relations with the People's Republic of China. Those positions are well known. The Soviet Union favours normal good-neighbourly relations between these two great States. . . .

We are convinced that the time is ripe to take the most serious notice of the fact that certain States, having set out to achieve military superiority and to pursue the policy of terrorism in international affairs, have resorted to actions designed to undermine the socio-political systems of other countries. . . .

This destroys the very possibility of ensuring peaceful relations and mutual trust among States and increases the threat of war. Such policies and actions flout the international rules of conduct. They cannot be tolerated and must be terminated. The United Nations, in our view, should speak out emphatically in support of the rule of law in international relations.

In the light of what I have said, the USSR is submitting to the General Assembly of the United Nations for its consideration an important and urgent item entitled, "Inadmissibility of the policy of State terrorism and any actions by States aimed at undermining the socio-political system of other sovereign States."

We propose that the United Nations resolutely condemn the policy and practice of State terrorism as a method of dealing with other countries and peoples. It is necessary to renounce any action aimed at changing or undermining by force the social systems of sovereign States, destabilizing and overthrowing their legitimate Governments, or initiating military action to that end on any pretext whatsoever, and to halt any such action already in progress.

All States are duty-bound to respect the inalienable right of the peoples of the world to decide for themselves their own destinies and to pursue independently their own political or any other kind of development....

There is much truth in the statement that the international situation is directly dependent on the state of Soviet-United States relations. Today, as always, our country believes in the maintenance of normal relations with the United States — and there has been much talk about this. Until the recent past, that is precisely how these relations were developing, although not without certain vicissitudes, whereas in the years of the Second World War they were relations of allies....

History does not begin on the day when a particular United States Administration comes into office. The periods when the two Powers combined their efforts to defeat fascism will stand out as the best pages in the history of Soviet-United States relations; and those who determine United States policy today have a great deal to do if they wish their words and the obligations they assume to be trusted. No attempts to substitute modifications in form for the substance of a policy and for the need to move away from militarism towards a policy of peace can be meaningful. That is nothing but an empty vessel. What is required is the determination to make such a move if one is truly guided by good intentions in United States-Soviet relations and is really working towards peace. That alone can carry some weight on the political scales.

The Soviet Union believes that it is precisely concrete deeds, not verbal assurances, that can lead to normalizing the situation in our relations with the United States. The USSR will not be found wanting. Every American, every American family, should know that the Soviet Union wants peace — and only peace — with the United States....

It is our firm conviction that it is possible to correct the current alarming tilt in international developments, to halt the arms race and to set it on a downward spiral, to reduce and then totally eliminate the threat of war. This requires the combined efforts of States, nuclear and non-nuclear, big and small, regardless of their social systems....

The future of mankind is the common responsibility of all countries, and the peoples of the world are entitled to expect that the whole of the activities of the United Nations will be imbued with a sense of that responsibility.

October

MENTAL HEALTH REPORT

October 2, 1984

One adult American in five, 19 percent of the adult population, suffers from a mental disorder, according to studies announced October 2 and published in the October issue of The Archives of General Psychiatry. *The National Institute of Mental Health (NIMH), which conducted the research, released the first results of a continuing study that was to eventually survey 20,000 people in five cities. Because the study permitted follow-up and evaluation of change, the results could provide useful information on risk factors for mental illness, alterations in mental conditions, and the relation of disorders to the use of mental health services.*

Types and Incidence of Mental Disorders

Interviews of approximately 10,000 people in Baltimore, Md., St. Louis, Mo., and New Haven, Conn., disclosed that more that 8 percent were afflicted with anxiety disorders (including phobias, compulsive behavior, and panic attacks). More than 6 percent had substance abuse disorders, and an additional 6 percent suffered from affective disorders (major depression, manic-depression, and morbid anxiety). Schizophrenia and antisocial personality disorders each afflicted 1 percent of the population surveyed.

Prior to this study women were thought to have a higher incidence of mental illness than men, perhaps because previous research emphasized anxieties, depression, and phobias — the types of disorders that proved to be more common among women. Ratios of mental disorders, however, were shown in the NIMH study to occur at the same rate for men as for women. According to the results, men tended to have problems of drug and alcohol abuse, as well as anti-social personality disorders, and having one disorder was shown to increase the likelihood of having a second. The research indicated that certain disorders may be related and some people may be predisposed to mental illness.

No significant racial differences were found in the rates or types of mental illness, but lower socioeconomic groups appeared to have more problems. The college-educated population had fewer psychiatric disorders. Age also played a key role as adults under 45 suffered from twice the mental disorders of older individuals, especially from substance abuse, anti-social personality, and anxiety disorders.

Differences between rural and urban environments were cited, with city dwellers having a higher rate of disorders. A differing prevalence of certain disorders was noted in each research site, showing greater incidence of phobia in Baltimore, of alcohol abuse and dependence in St. Louis, and of major depression in New Haven.

One goal of the study was to determine how mental health services were used. According to statistics in one of the reports included in the study, fewer than 20 percent of adult Americans with mental illnesses seek treatment for their problems, and most consult general practitioners rather than mental health specialists. Women tend to seek treatment more often than men, visiting generalists and specialists equally. Men are more likely to see specialists. The elderly visit general medical providers more often; visits by this group to mental health specialists are rare. Schizophrenics received treatment at the highest rate (50 percent).

Methods of Study

The groundwork for the NIMH study was laid by the development of strict and detailed diagnostic criteria by the American Psychiatric Association. This Diagnostic and Statistical Manual of Mental Disorders (the DSM-III), applied for the first time by this study to a randomly selected population (rather than to a population of those already receiving treatment), made possible a more careful accounting of the severe and significant forms of mental disorder. Very mild, non-disabling disorders were not counted, and serious problems were identified according to more precise definitions than ever had been used before on such a comprehensive scale. Symptoms experienced both over a lifetime and in the six-month period before the interview were part of the study.

The categories in the DSM-III were translated into questionnaires containing hundreds of questions administered by lay interviewers in two face-to-face sessions a year apart, with a contact at six months. Data for the second interviews were still to be completed, as were studies of populations in Durham, N.C., and Los Angeles, Calif. "Oversamples" of the elderly and of minority groups also were to be examined in future studies, as was a sampling of residents of mental institutions.

Following are excerpts of three articles from The Archives of General Psychiatry, *Vol. 41, October 1984:*

LIFETIME PREVALENCE OF SPECIFIC PSYCHIATRIC DISORDERS IN THREE SITES

Lee N. Robins, PhD; John E. Helzer, MD; Myrna M. Weissman, PhD; Helen Orvaschel, PhD; Ernest Gruenberg, MD, DPH; Jack D. Burke, Jr, MD, MPH; Darrel A. Regier, MD, MPH

This study reports on the lifetime prevalence of specific psychiatric disorders in the community as found in the first three of the five sites of the Epidemiologic Catchment Area (ECA) program. . . . Briefly, the ECA program is a collaborative effort to apply common diagnostic and health utilization instruments at six-month intervals to large general population samples, including both persons in households and those who are institutionalized.

The ECA program is still in progress. However, results available from the initial interviews in three of the five sites can provide prevalence rates of specific psychiatric disorders in three metropolitan areas, New Haven, Conn, Baltimore, and St. Louis, and can show their relation to demographic characteristics. The goal of this report is to answer the following questions: (1) What is the lifetime prevalence of 15 *DSM-III* [Diagnostic and Statistical Manual of Mental Disorders, Third Edition, which includes cognitive impairment, drug or alcohol abuse or dependence, antisocial personality, schizophrenia, panic, dysthymia, agoraphobia, somatization, manic or depressive episodes, anorexia, simple phobia, and obsessive-compulsive disorder] diagnoses in three metropolitan areas; (2) What are the major demographic correlates of these disorders; (3) What notable intersite variation exists, and how can it be explained?

The lifetime prevalence of a particular disorder is stated as the proportion of persons in a representative sample of the population who have *ever* experienced that disorder up to the date of assessment. This measure has also been called the "proportion of survivors affected" (PSA).

The National Institute of Mental Health (NIMH) ECA program estimates the lifetime prevalence of specific mental disorders in the general population by means of the Diagnostic Interview Schedule (DIS). . . . Its administration by lay interviewers has been found approximately equivalent in diagnostic results to its administration by psychiatrists. In the current report, it will be used to make only *DSM-III* diagnoses.

Respondents are asked whether they have ever had each symptom that serves as a criterion for the diagnoses covered. With respect to each symptom that the respondent has experienced, a set of standard probes are then asked that assess, where appropriate, whether criteria were met for possible psychiatric importance (ie, was the symptom severe enough to be of clinical interest, and did it occur at least once when it had no definitive physical cause). The number and variety of symptoms of possible psychiatric importance experienced are compared with *DSM-III* criteria. For diagnoses that are characteristically episodic (eg, major depression, mania, panic disorder), a further requirement is the concurrence of symptoms within a period of specified length, so that an episode can be said to have occurred. . . .

RESULTS
Prevalence of Specific Disorders

. . . In each site, from 29% to 38% of the sample had experienced at least one of these disorders in their lifetime. Rates differed by only 2.1% between St. Louis and New Haven and were not significantly different, while Baltimore's rate was significantly higher ($P<.001$). The higher rate for Baltimore was explained by the higher rates of phobia assessed there. If phobias are excluded, prevalence rates of at least one of the remaining diagnoses vary across sites by a nonsignificant 2.3%.

Alcohol abuse or dependence was the most common disorder in New Haven and St. Louis; phobia was the most common disorder in Baltimore. In all three sites, alcohol abuse or dependence affected between 11% and 16%. Drug abuse and dependence was less common, affecting between 5% and 6% at some time in their lives prior to interview in every site. Without the substance abuse disorders, rates of persons having had at least one of the covered diagnoses at some time in their lives would drop by about one third in New Haven and St. Louis, and about one fifth in Baltimore.

When the three sites' rates are averaged, about one in 20 adults are found to have suffered a major depressive episode. Dysthymia [excessive morbidity] affected about one in 30 persons, while antisocial personality and obsessive-compulsive disorder each affected about one in 40. Less than one (noninstitutionalized) adult in 50 suffered from panic disorder, cognitive impairment, or schizophrenia. Schizophreniform disorder, somatization disorder, and anorexia nervosa were all rare, occurring in less than one of 500 persons in every site.

We noted that these diagnoses were made using, insofar as was possible, only those questions available in all three sites. How much would the picture have changed if the full DIS had been available in all sites? We can estimate these effects by examining the frequency with which questions and diagnoses unavailable in some sites were positive in St. Louis, where the complete DIS was used. First, the most common diagnoses would have been tobacco use disorder, found in St. Louis in 36%, and psychosexual dysfunction, found in 24%. The Yale criteria applied to the New Haven data for schizophrenia were slightly different from those applied to data from the other two sites, because the early version of the DIS lacked two questions and had slightly different instructions for the interviewers. When St. Louis data were analyzed using the Yale program, the St. Louis schizophrenia prevalence rose from 1.0% to 2.5%. This suggests that the rate of schizophrenia (1.9%) in New Haven is probably an overestimate. Seven questions for the diagnosis of antisocial personality had been deleted by sites other than St. Louis. When answers to these seven questions were added to the St. Louis data for use in making a computer diagnosis of antisocial personality, the rate positive rose from 3.3% o 5.1%. In New Haven and Baltimore, therefore, the estimate for antisocial personality is slightly low.

These results show that prevalence estimates for these disorders can be considerably affected by what may seem only minor variations in the questions used and interviewer instructions. They underscore the danger of attributing differences between results of studies conducted in different places or in different eras to regional differences or a change in times unless precisely identical instruments have been applied in precisely the same way.

Furthermore, it must be recalled that estimates presented herein will be modified by the addition of the institutionalized sample. However, the institutionalized population is not large enough to alter the finding that the leading lifetime diagnoses among the 15 studied are alcohol abuse or dependence, phobia major depressive episode, antisocial personality, and drug abuse and dependence. . . .

Demographic Correlates of Disorder

Race.—. . . The New Haven site is only 10% black according to the 1980 census, while the St. Louis site has twice as many blacks, and the Baltimore site has three times as many. Therefore, a look at the relationship between race and diagnosis is potentially helpful in explaining intersite differences.

However, . . . differences between blacks and others in rates of psychiatric disorders are generally modest and rarely statistically significant. . . . In addition, only for simple phobia is there any replication across sites, with significantly higher rates for blacks in Baltimore and St. Louis, but not New Haven. When blacks were compared with nonblacks, they were found to have the higher rate in about half (24) of the 45 comparisons (given 15 disorders in three sites), approximately what we would expect by chance. Where differences exist, they tend to be small compared with age and sex differences, and much less consistent across sites.

Since Baltimore had the largest proportion of blacks of the three sites, its high rate of simple phobia and agoraphobia might be explained in part by its higher proportion of blacks. However, . . . Baltimore's rates of simple phobia and agoraphobia were higher for both blacks and nonblacks than rates in the same ethnic groups elsewhere. Thus, intersite differences in the proportion of blacks did not explain away intersite differences in prevalence rates.

Education.—Differences between sites with respect to the proportions holding a college degree are the inverse of differences with respect to race. New Haven had the highest proportion of college graduates (27%), and Baltimore had the lowest (9%). . . . Therefore, a relationship between education and psychiatric disorder might help to explain intersite differences.

[O]verall, college graduates had fewer psychiatric disorders than others. They showed a significantly lower rate in every site with respect to cognitive impairment, and significantly lower rates in at least one site for simple phobia, agoraphobia, schizophrenia, schizophreniform disorder, alcohol abuse and dependence, and somatization disorder. The low rate of cognitive impairment in college-educated persons probably reflects the fact that because of the increase in educational level in recent years, most living college graduates tend to be young. It may also show that Mini-Mental State Examination scores are affected by IQ and educational level as well as by dementia. . . . More persons in Baltimore than in New Haven or St. Louis were found to have agoraphobia and simple phobia among both graduates and nongraduates, and more alcohol abuse and dependence was found in St. Louis than in New Haven or Baltimore among both groups.

Urbanization.—A final demographic variable of interest is urbanization. As we noted earlier, of the three sites, only St. Louis includes a rural and small-town catchment area. Therefore, it is the only site so far in which the relationship between urbanization and disorder can be assessed.

[O]verall, the inner-city environment was associated with a higher rate of disorder. Drug abuse and dependence, alcohol abuse and dependence, and antisocial behavior were significantly more common in the inner city than in rural areas. Schizophrenia was more common in the inner city than in the suburbs. Cognitive impairment was higher in the central city than in either suburbs or rural areas. For only one disorder, panic, was the rate significantly high in the rural small-town area compared with the suburbs.

The inclusion of a small-town and rural area in the St. Louis site does not explain any of the intersite differences. Indeed, the rate of alcohol abuse and dependence in St. Louis would have differed even more from that of other sites if the rural area had been excluded. . . .

The finding that is most challenging to our expectations is that the distribution of disorders by age does not seem to reflect the fact that older groups, having always passed through as much or more of the age-of-risk than younger groups, should have lifetime rates as high or higher than those of the young. Instead, lifetime prevalence was generally lowest in those older than 65 years, and highest in those 25 to 44 years old. It is not yet clear why the rates in the elderly are so low. Hypotheses discussed include a possible historical increase in risk among the younger generation, less willingness to report symptoms, disorder-associated mortality, and difficulty in recall. . . .

SIX-MONTH PREVALENCE OF PSYCHIATRIC DISORDERS IN THREE COMMUNITIES
1980 to 1982

Jerome K. Meyers, PhD; Myrna M. Weissman, PhD; Gary L. Tischler, MD; Charles E. Holzer III, PhD; Philip J. Leaf, PhD; Helen Orvaschel, PhD; James C. Anthony, PhD; Jeffrey H. Boyd, MD, MPH; Jack D. Burke, Jr, MD, MPH; Morton Kramer, ScD; Roger Stoltzman, MD

Prevalence and incidence rates of specific psychiatric disorders derived from community-based surveys have important scientific and health policy implications. Variations in such rates can provide clues to etiology and can be used as base rates for family genetic studies. In health care policy, such rates are useful in planning health programs and in evaluating the impact of community treatment programs. . . .

The original specifications for the ECA project called for each site to contact a random sample of approximately 4,000 household residents 18 years and older to obtain at least 3,000 interviews. The specific procedures for developing a sample frame varied from site to site along two important dimensions. First, the differences in the geographic areas to be surveyed and differences in available information about housing units influenced the sampling procedures at each site. Second, each site contained an oversampling of individuals to produce better estimates for specific subsets of the population.

The New Haven survey developed a list of all housing units and produced a systematic sample of household clusters using a random starting point. One adult from each household was selected at random. Elderly residents were oversampled. In Baltimore, blocks were selected with probability proportionate to size, and households were sampled systematically from blocks. One person between the ages of 18 and 64 years was selected from each household, with all persons 65 years and older also being selected to provide an oversample. In St. Louis, census enumeration districts were selected from each of three catchment areas, with enumeration districts with a preponderence of blacks being oversampled. Two blocks were selected from each enumeration district (or clusters of enumeration districts) with probability proportionate to size followed by a systematic sampling of households. As in New Haven, only one adult (18 years or older) was selected at random from each household.

Lay interviewers were recruited, trained, and supervised at each site. These interviewers gathered and recorded data on sociodemographic characteristics and mental status by following the highly standardized NIMH DIS. More than 3,000 interviews were conducted at each site with completion rates of between 76% and 80%. Common computer programs were used to analyze the data, ascertain cases of particular categories of mental disorder, and estimate prevalence rates and their variances. . . .

The DIS determines *DIS-III* disorders with reference to several discrete time periods, including two weeks prior to interview, one month, six months, and one year prior to interview, and the entire lifetime prior to interview. In this report, current mental status has generally been defined in terms of disturbance that the DIS indicates as active in the six months prior to interview. . . .

In summary, while age distribution of disorders by sex is generally similar, there are some important differences. The basis for ranking within age groups was the mean six-month prevalence rates for New Haven, Baltimore, and St. Louis combined. Alcohol abuse and/or dependence predominates among men 18 to 24 years, followed closely by drug abuse and/or dependence, whereas for women in this age group, phobias are the most common, followed by drug abuse and/or dependence and major depression. In the age group 25 to 44 years, alcohol abuse and/or dependence continues to be the most common disorder for men. However, phobias now are the second highest disorder covered, followed closely by drug abuse and/or dependence. For women, the most common disorders are phobias and major depression. In the age group 45 to 64 years, phobias remain the most frequent diagnosis for women, and nearly equals the rate of alcohol abuse and/or dependence for men. Dysthymia is the second most common diagnosis found among women. In the age group 65 years and older, severe cognitive impairment is the most common disorder for men, followed by phobia and alcohol abuse and/or dependence. For women in this age group, the most common disorder is phobia, followed by severe cognitive impairment. . . .

The comparison of DIS/*DSM-III* rates across the three ECA sites indicates considerable similarity of results at all sites. The only major discrepancy is the much higher rate of the phobic disorders found in Baltimore, which may be explained by methodological factors in the collection of data.

Summarizing our substantive findings, the most common disorders in the three communities studied are phobias, alcohol abuse and/or dependence, dysthymia, and major depression. In all three communities, there were similar sex and age differences in rates of disorder. The most common diagnoses for women were phobias and major depression, whereas for men, the predominant disorder was alcohol abuse and/or dependence. The total rates of disorder drop sharply after age 45 years. Most individual disorders follow the same pattern except cognitive impairment. The most striking

but expected differences by age are that substance abuse and/or dependence and antisocial personality disorder are predominantly a younger
person's disorder, whereas cognitive impairment is most prevalent in
persons aged 65 years and older.

UTILIZATION OF HEALTH
AND MENTAL HEALTH SERVICES
Three Epidemiologic Catchment Area Sites

*Sam Shapiro; Elizabeth A. Skinner, MSW; Larry G. Kessler, ScD;
Michael Von Korff, ScD; Pearl S. German, ScD; Gary L. Tischler, MD;
Philip J. Leaf, PhD; Lee Benham, PhD; Linda Cottler, MPH; Darrel A.
Regier, MD*

...A substantial body of knowledge has accumulated during the past
ten to 15 years regarding the utilization of health and mental health
services by persons who are given diagnoses of mental or emotional
disorders by mental health specialists and other practitioners. The information has been used to derive estimates of the national requirements
for mental health personnel and facilities and the costs for meeting the
demand for mental health care. An issue of special interest in many of the
studies has been the existing and potential role of primary care providers
in meeting the need for treatment of mental or emotional problems
presented by patients.

The picture that has emerged is that patients with such problems are
relatively high users of ambulatory health services generally and that more
than half of them present these problems only to primary care providers.
Women more often than men use mental health services, and there are
large differences in utilization related to age, with the aged having
particularly low rates. On a more limited basis, other relationships have
been examined, such as the extent to which primary care providers
recognize the existence of mental and emotional problems among their
patients, differences between types of mental disorders seen by primary
care providers and mental health specialists, and patterns of utilization of
general medical services prior to and following a diagnosis of mental
disorder or episode of psychiatric care.

Useful as this information has been, great uncertainty has existed about
the ability to generalize from such observations to the situation in the
community at large. The data come primarily from structured care settings
(health maintenance organizations, other multispecialty group practices,
community mental health centers), and the utilization levels and patterns
derived may differ from what occurs in the majority of the US population
whose source for medical care is physicians outside of such settings.

Moreover, while the relationship of mental and emotional status to use of ambulatory health services has been studied, there is little information describing the relationship of mental and emotional status to use of inpatient health services. The ECA surveys are yielding new findings concerning this relationship.

An important restriction of many of the previous studies of utilization is inherent in the source of information, ie, the provider-patient encounter....

Most studies in this country are limited to persons whose mental or emotional disorders become known only in the course of their seeking care; excluded are nonutilizers and patients receiving general medical care whose psychological problems are undetected or not recorded in the medical record. A consequence is that we are limited in any attempt to measure need for services by the absence of information about the magnitude and characteristics of these groups. Furthermore, studies of experiences in specific practices, including group practices, will miss services received elsewhere unless supplemented by additional inquiry. Movement from one provider or group of providers to another, when not on referral, will more often than not be unknown, and help-seeking in special treatment programs and admissions to long-stay institutions will remain largely undetermined. An additional issue that arises in assessing the information is that reliability and validity of mental disorder diagnoses may vary greatly among providers of general medical care and criteria used by mental health specialists in making a diagnosis may differ sufficiently to affect interpretation of the data. The ECA program is structured to overcome these restrictions by deriving data on help-seeking through surveys of probability samples of noninstitutional adult populations in defined geographic areas, complemented by interviews with samples of institutionalized persons from these areas, and administration of the DIS....

This exploration of mental health care received by noninstitutionalized adult populations is based on the experience in three ECAs, New Haven, Baltimore, and St. Louis, areas that are predominantly urban or suburban with major health care resources inside the areas or in close proximity to them. Attention is focused on ambulatory care in the six-month period prior to interviews among persons with cognitive impairment or a DIS/*DSM-III* disorder in this interval (characterized as "recent"). Several conclusions can be drawn from the data.

1. Broad patterns of utilization are similar among the ECAs; more detailed examination of relationships shows differences of some consequence. In all areas, total ambulatory care is substantially greater in the presence of a recent DIS disorder, a finding consistent with results from studies based on clinic patients with a psychiatric diagnosis. The study also shows that the increased utilization extends to hospital admissions for physical conditions during the previous year, a new observation.

2. One of the clearest differences concerns which sector of health services

is used when people seek care for mental or emotional problems. In New Haven, where the ratio of psychiatrists to population is relatively high, the population more often turns to the specialty mental health sector than only to general medical providers; in the other two areas, there is little difference in which sector is used. Between 9% and 22% of all ambulatory visits are to mental health specialists, with New Haven at the high end of the ECA experience. Among persons with a recent DIS disorder, 24% to 38% of all visits are made to this type of specialist.

3. Women with a recent DIS disorder more frequently than men seek care for their mental or emotional problems, and persons 18 to 24 years are less likely than those 25 to 64 years to do so; again, these are situations expected from other studies. The new observations concern which sector of care they turn to. In all areas, men are more dependent on the specialty sector than women, and in two of the sites, the aged infrequently receive their mental health care from the specialty sector. This will need to be examined further to see how these relationships are affected by differences in rates of specific DIS disorders.

4. The question of need for services has not been addressed in this presentation. However, the data indicate that it is a large issue. A majority of persons in virtually all recent DIS disorder categories do not see any provider for mental health reasons during a six-month period; the proportions are especially low among persons with cognitive disorders and substance abuse and/or dependence. Whether functional status, family or economic circumstances, or usual source of care are any different among nonutilizers compared with utilizers will provide considerable insight to the meaning of nonutilization. The opportunity to probe into the issue exists through the data available in the ECA program.

5. Persons classified as having no DIS disorder constitute a heterogeneous group. Although their utilization is low compared with that of the subgroups with a DIS disorder, they account for about one third of all the people who see a provider for a mental or emotional problem. This indicates that any effort to estimate the burden of mental or emotional problems on the health care system will need to go beyond those with a DIS disorder and use available information on conditions not covered by the DIS and symptoms that do not meet the DIS disorder criteria.

This overview is not designed to detail the full range of issues to be dealt with later. With the inclusion of data on the institutionalized population, a more complete picture will be obtained about utilization by a community's total population. Also, the data from the surveys that cover a year's experience following the baseline interviews will provide a more substantial basis for understanding utilization of general health and mental health services by persons with mental or emotional conditions. . . .

PRESIDENTIAL DEBATES

October 7, 21, 1984

The final weeks of the 1984 presidential campaign were highlighted by two televised debates between Republican president Ronald Reagan and Democratic challenger Walter F. Mondale. Reagan had been the front-runner throughout the campaign, but Mondale was widely acknowledged as the winner in the first debate, held October 7 in Louisville, Ky., temporarily boosting his long-shot presidential campaign. The results of the October 21 debate, held in Kansas City, Mo., were less clear-cut with most observers calling the confrontation a draw, or giving a narrow edge to Mondale.

Age Issue

Mondale's strong showing in Louisville helped to lessen his negative image in the mind of many voters. An October 10 Washington Post-ABC News *poll found that the share of voters expressing a favorable opinion of Mondale increased from 41 percent before the debate to 54 percent after it.*

But perhaps the more significant outcome of the debate was the perception that Reagan turned in a relatively poor performance. The 73-year-old incumbent seemed tired and disorganized by the end of the 100-minute debate, leading journalists and Democrats to suggest that age was finally catching up with him. He drew criticism from several quarters for giving stumbling, unfocused responses to some questions.

But Reagan's second debate performance seemed to deflect questions about his age and competence. Many observers gave him credit for a more polished performance. In the debate's most memorable moment, Reagan tried to deflate much of the age issue. Asked if he would be able to function during a crisis, Reagan quipped, "I will not make age an issue of this campaign. I am not going to exploit, for political purposes, my opponent's youth and inexperience."

First Debate

The first encounter, devoted to domestic issues, was largely a repetition of the candidates' views on economics and religion, two issues that dominated much of the campaign. Mondale lashed out at the size of the federal budget deficit under Reagan; the incumbent in turn attacked his challenger for proposing to raise taxes. Reagan angrily denounced Mondale's claim that he would cut Social Security benefits in a second term. Reagan criticized abortion, while Mondale warned that Christian fundamentalists, led by the Rev. Jerry Falwell, would control future Supreme Court appointments.

But two incidents during the debate provided the most dramatic illustrations of the candidates' differing performances. The first came when Reagan repeated his most famous line from his 1980 debate with President Jimmy Carter. (Historic Documents of 1980, p. 919) "There you go again," Reagan said, responding to Mondale's claim that Reagan would move to raise taxes during a second term. But Mondale pounced on the comment, reminding his opponent that the 1980 remark was in response to Carter's warning that Reagan would cut the Medicare program. Yet, Mondale continued, "you went right out and tried to cut $20 billion out of Medicare."

The candidates' concluding remarks provided an even more telling contrast. After the debate, Reagan's aides conceded that his performance at the end was unimpressive for a master of televised communication. His final remarks were rambling and disjointed, jumping within a few sentences from the poverty rate in 1979 to the rate of business investment since 1949, and from the number of Navy ships to the cost of military pensions.

Mondale, on the other hand, presented a more focused concluding statement. Latching on to Reagan's repetition of his famous question from the 1980 debate, "Are you better off than you were four years ago?" Mondale said that the real issue was the future. "Will we be better off?" he asked, with a continued arms race, a swelling deficit and a spoiled environment.

Second Debate

Squaring off in their much-anticipated rematch October 21, Reagan and Mondale produced sharp rhetoric over foreign policy and defense. On the issues of arms control and relations with the Soviet Union, each candidate appeared intent on countering the negative image raised by his opponent during the campaign.

Mondale charged that Reagan's inability to reach an arms control agreement with the Soviets was due in part to his lack of understanding of the issues. The two also clashed over Reagan's proposed futuristic anti-missile defense system, which critics lampooned as "Star Wars." (Historic Documents of 1983, p. 305) Reagan argued that the plan would free the world from the dangers of "mutually assured destruction" as a deterrent to war. He suggested that the technology could be offered to the Soviets as an incentive to negotiate a ban on all nuclear arms.

Mondale, who made his call to "draw a line and keep the heavens free from war" a centerpiece of the final weeks of his campaign, warned that the program would lead to a new arms race in space and sharply criticized the idea of sharing the technology.

On the topic of foreign policy, Mondale focused on the administration's effort to undermine Nicaragua's leftist government. Noting that a recently disclosed Central Intelligence Agency manual had urged "contra" rebels in Nicaragua to use violence against government officials, he charged that this policy had "hurt us, strengthened our opposition and undermined the moral authority of our country in that region." (CIA manual, p. 903) In rebuttal, Reagan attributed the manual to "a gentleman down in Nicaragua who is on contract to the CIA, advising supposedly on military tactics of the contras." But he quickly retracted the statement, which was an admission of a greater U.S. role in the country than the administration previously had acknowledged.

Although Reagan's second performance was deemed an improvement over the first debate, he appeared to falter at the end. His concluding statement, an anecdote about a letter to be put in a time capsule, was seen by many observers as lacking coherence, and time ran out before he could finish.

Most commentators credited Mondale with effectively presenting one of his key themes: that Reagan was a detached president whose leadership was marred by an inadequate grasp of the facts. "A president must know what is essential to command and to leadership and to strength," he stressed. Mondale's positive performance in the debates, especially during the first match, however, had little effect on the outcome of the campaign. Reagan won the election by a landslide, carrying every state except Minnesota, Mondale's home state, and the District of Columbia. (Victory and concession speeches, p. 953)

> *Following are the texts of the presidential debate on domestic issues held in Louisville, Ky., October 7, and the debate on foreign policy October 21 in Kansas City, Mo., between*

847

President Ronald Reagan and former vice president Walter F. Mondale. (Boldface headings in brackets have been added by Congressional Quarterly to highlight the organization of the text.):

FIRST PRESIDENTIAL DEBATE

MRS. DOROTHY S. RIDINGS, Chair, The League of Women Voters Education Fund: Good evening from the Kentucky Center for the Arts in Louisville, Kentucky. I am Dorothy Ridings, President of The League of Women Voters, the sponsor of tonight's first Presidential debate between Republican Ronald Reagan and Democrat Walter Mondale.

Tonight's debate marks the third consecutive Presidential election in which the League is presenting the candidates for the nation's highest office in face-to-face debate. Our panelists are James Wieghart [James G. Wieghart], National Political Correspondent for Scripps-Howard News Service; Diane Sawyer, Correspondent for the CBS program *60 Minutes*; and Fred Barnes, National Political Correspondent for *The Baltimore Sun*. Barbara Walters of ABC News, who is appearing in her fourth Presidential debate, is our moderator. Barbara.

MS. BARBARA WALTERS, Moderator; Correspondent, ABC News: Thank you, Dorothy. A few words as we begin tonight's debate about the format. The position of the candidates — that is, who answers questions first and who gives the last statement — was determined by a toss of the coin between the two candidates. Mr. Mondale won. And that means that he chose to give the final closing statement. It means, too, that the President will answer the first question first. I hope that's clear. If it isn't, it will become clear as the debate goes on.

Further, the candidates will be addressed as they each wanted, and will therefore be called "Mr. President" and "Mr. Mondale." Since there will also be a second debate between the two Presidential candidates, tonight will focus primarily on the economy and other domestic issues. The debate itself is built around questions from the panel. In each of its segments, a reporter will ask the candidate the same general question. Then — and this is important — each candidate will have the chance to rebut what the other has said. In the final segment of the debate will be the closing segment, and the candidates will each have four minutes for their closing statements. And, as I have said, Mr. Mondale will be the last person on the program to speak.

And now I would like to add a personal note, if I may. As Dorothy Ridings pointed out, I have been involved now in four Presidential debates, either as a moderator or as a panelist. In the past, there was no problem in selecting panelists. Tonight, however, there were to have been four panelists participating in this debate. The candidates were given a list of almost 100 qualified journalists from all the media and could agree on only these three fine journalists. As moderator, and on behalf of my fellow journalists, I very much regret, as does The League of Women Voters, that this situation has occurred.

And now let us begin the debate with the first question from James Wieghart. Mr. Wieghart?

[Balanced Budget]

MR. JAMES G. WIEGHART, National Political Correspondent, Scripps-Howard News Service: Mr. President, in 1980, you promised the American people, in your campaign, a balanced budget by 1983. We've now had more and bigger deficits in the four years you have been in office. Mr. President, do you have a secret plan to balance the budget sometime in the second turn ... term? And if so, would you lay out that plan for us tonight?

THE HONORABLE RONALD REAGAN, President of the United States of America: I have a plan, not a secret plan. As a matter of fact, it is the economic recovery program that we presented when I took office in 1981. It is true that earlier, working with some very prominent economists, I had come up, during the campaign, with an economic program that I thought could rectify the great problems confronting us: the double-digit inflation, the high tax rates that I think were hurting the economy, the stagflation that we were undergoing.

Before even the election day, something that none of those economists had even predicted had happened: that the economy was so worsened that I was openly saying that what we had thought, on the basis of our plan, could have brought a balanced budget — no, that was no longer possible. So the plan that we have had and that we are following is a plan that is based on growth in the economy, recovery without inflation, and reducing the share of the ... of ... that the Government is taking from the Gross National Product, which has become a drag on the economy.

Already we have a recovery that has been going on for about 21 months, to the point that we can now call it an expansion. Under that, this year we have seen a $21 billion reduction in the deficit from last year, based mainly on the increased revenues the Government is getting without raising tax rates. Our tax cut, we think, was very instrumental in bringing about this economic recovery. We have reduced inflation to about a third of what it was. The interest rates have come down about nine or ten points and, we think, must come down further. In the last 21 months, more than six million people have gotten jobs. We've found.... There have been created new jobs for those people, to where there are now 105 million civilians working, where there were only 99 million before, 107 [million] if you count the military.

So we believe that, as we continue to reduce the level of Government spending — the increase, rate of increase in Government spending, which has come down from 17 to 6 percent — and at the same time as the growth in the economy increases the revenues the Government gets without raising taxes, those two lines will meet. And when they meet, that is a balanced budget.

MR. WIEGHART: Mr. President, the Congressional Budget Office has some bad news. The lines aren't about to meet, according to their projections. They project that the budget deficit will continue to climb. In the year 1989, they project a budget deficit of $273 billion. In view of that, and in view of the economic recovery we are now enjoying, would it make sense to propose a tax increase, or take some other fiscal measures to reduce that deficit now, when times are relatively good?

MR. REAGAN: The deficit is a result . . . it is the result of excessive government spending. I do not, very frankly, take seriously the Congressional Budget Office projections, because they have been wrong on virtually all of them, including the fact that our recovery wasn't going to take place to begin with. But it has taken place. But as I said, we have the rate of increase in Government spending down to 6 percent. If the rate of increase in Government spending can be held at 5 percent — we're not far from there — by 1989 that would have reduced budget deficits down to a $30 or $40 billion level. At the same time, if we can have a 4 percent recovery continue through that same period of time, that will mean, without an increase in tax rates, that will mean $400 billion more in Government revenues. And so I think that the lines can meet.

Actually, in constant dollars, in the domestic side of the budget, there has been no spending increase in the four years that we have been here.

MR. WIEGHART: Mr. Mondale, the Carter-Mondale Administration didn't come close to balancing the budget in its four years in office either, despite the fact that President Carter [President Jimmy Carter] did promise a balanced budget during his term. You have proposed a plan, combining tax increases and budgetary cuts and other changes in the administration of the Government, that would reduce the projected budget deficit by two-thirds, to approximately $87 billion in 1989. That still is an enormous deficit that we'll be running for these four years. What other steps do you think should be taken to reduce this deficit and for . . . position the country for economic growth?

THE HONORABLE WALTER MONDALE, former Vice President of the United States of America: One of the key tests of leadership is whether one sees clearly the nature of the problems confronted by our nation. And perhaps *the* dominant domestic issue of our times is: What do we do about these enormous deficits? I respect the President. I respect the Presidency, and I think he knows that. But the fact of it is, every estimate by this Administration about the size of the deficit has been off by billions and billions of dollars. As a matter of fact, over four years, they have missed the mark by nearly $600 billion. We were told we would have a balanced budget in 1983. It was a $200 billion deficit instead. And now, we have a major question facing the American people as to whether we'll deal with this deficit and get it down for the sake of a healthy recovery. Virtually every economic analysis that I've heard of, including that of the distinguished Congressional Budget Office — which is respected by, I think, almost everyone — says that even with historically high levels of economic growth, we will suffer a $263 billion deficit. In other words, it doesn't converge, as the President suggests — it gets larger even with growth.

What that means is that we will continue to have devastating problems with foreign trade: this is the worst trade year in American history, by far. Our rural and farm friends will have continued devastation. Real interest rates, the real cost of interest, will remain very, very high. And many economists are predicting that we're moving into a period of very slow growth because the economy is tapering off, and maybe a recession.

I get it down to a level below 2 percent of Gross National Product with a policy that's fair. I've stood up and told the American people that I think it's a real problem, that it can destroy long-term economic growth, and I've told you what I think should be done. I think this is a test of leadership, and I think the American people know the difference.

MR. WIEGHART: Mr. Mondale, one other way to attack the deficit is further reductions in spending. The President has submitted a number of proposals to Congress to do just that and, in many instances, the House — controlled by the Democrats — has opposed them. Isn't it one aspect of leadership for a prominent Democrat such as yourself to encourage responsible reductions in spending and thereby reduce the deficit?

MR. MONDALE: Absolutely, and I have proposed over $100 billion in cuts in Federal spending over four years. But I am not going to cut it out of Social Security and Medicare and student assistance and things that people need. These people depend upon all of us for the little security that they have, and I'm not going to do it that way. The rate of defense spending increase can be slowed. Certainly we can find a coffee pot that costs something less than $7,000. And there are other ways of squeezing this budget without constantly picking on our senior citizens and the most vulnerable in American life. And that's why the Congress, including the Republicans, have not gone along with the President's recommendations.

MS. WALTERS: I would like to ask the audience please to refrain from applauding either side.

It just takes away from the time for your candidates.

And now it is time for the rebuttal. Mr. President, one minute for rebuttal.

MR. REAGAN: Yes. I don't believe that Mr. Mondale has a plan for balancing the budget; he has a plan for raising taxes. As a matter of fact, the biggest single tax increase in our nation's history took place in 1977. And, for the five years previous to our taking office, taxes doubled in the United States and the budgets increased $318 billion. So, there is no ratio between taxing and balancing a budget. Whether you borrow the money or whether you simply tax it away from the people, you're taking the same amount of money out of the private sector unless and until you bring down government's share of what it is taking.

With regard to Social Security, I hope there will be more time than just this minute to mention that, but I will say this: a President should never say, "Never," but I'm going to violate that rule and say, "Never." I will never stand for a reduction of the Social Security benefits for the people that are now getting them.

MS. WALTERS: Mr. Mondale?

MR. MONDALE: Well, that's exactly the commitment that was made to the American people in 1980 — he would never reduce benefits. And of course, what happened right after the election is, they proposed to cut Social Security benefits by 25 percent, reducing the adjustment for inflation, cutting out minimum benefits for the poorest on Social Security, removing educational benefits for dependents whose widows were trying ... with widows trying to get them through college. Everybody remembers that. People know what happened. There is a difference. I have fought for Social Security and Medicare, and for things to help people who are vulnerable, all my life. And I will do it as President of the United States.

MS. WALTERS: Thank you very much.

We will now begin with segment number two with my colleague, Diane Sawyer. Ms. Sawyer.

[Leadership]

MS. DIANE SAWYER, CBS News: Mr. President, Mr. Mondale, the public opinion polls do suggest that the American people are most concerned about the personal leadership characteristics of the two candidates, and each of you has questioned the other's leadership ability. Mr. President, you have said that Mr. Mondale's leadership would take the country down the path of defeatism and despair, and Vice President Bush has called him "whining" and "hoping for bad news." And Mr. Mondale, you have said that President Reagan offers showmanship, not leadership, that he has not mastered what he must know to command his government.

I'd like to ask each of you to substantiate your claims — Mr. Mondale first. Give us specifics to support your claim that President Reagan is a showman, not a leader, has not mastered what he must know to be President after four years. And then second, tell us what personal leadership characteristics you have that he does not.

MR. MONDALE: Well, first of all, I think the first answer this evening suggests exactly what I'm saying. There is no question that we face this massive deficit, and almost everybody agrees unless we get it down the chances for long-term healthy growth are nil. And it's also unfair to dump these tremendous bills on our children. The President says it will disappear overnight because of some reason. No one else believes that's the case. I do, and I'm standing up to the issue with an answer that's fair. I think that's what leadership is all about. There's a difference between being a quarterback and a cheerleader, and when there's a real problem, a President must confront it.

What I was referring to, of course, in the comment that you referred to, was the situation in Lebanon. Now, for three occasions, one after another, our embassies were assaulted in the same way by a truck with demolitions. The first time . . . and I did not criticize the President because these things can happen once and sometimes twice. The second time the barracks in Lebanon were assaulted, as we all remember, there were two or three commission reports, recommendations by the CIA, the State Department and the others. And the third time, there was even a warning from the terrorists themselves.

Now, I believe that a President must command that White House and those who work for him. It's the toughest job on earth, and you must master the facts and insist that things that must be done are done. I believe that the way in which I will approach the Presidency is what's needed, because all my life, that has been the way in which I have sought to lead. And that's why, in this campaign, I'm telling you exactly what I want to do. I am answering your questions. I am trying to provide leadership now, before the election, so that the American people can participate in that decision.

MS. SAWYER: You have said, Mr. Mondale, that the polls have given you lower ratings on leadership than President Reagan because your message has failed to get through. Given that you have been in public office for so many years, what accounts for the failure of your message to get through?

MR. MONDALE: Well, I think we're getting better all the time, and I think tonight, as we contrast for the first time our differing approach to government, to values, to the leadership in this country — I think as this debate goes forward, the American people will have, for the first time, a chance to weigh the two of us against each other. And I think, as a process ... as a part of that process, what I am trying to say will come across, and that is that we must lead, we must command, we must direct. And a President must see it like it is. He must stand for the values of decency that the American people stand for, and he must use the power of the White House to try to control these nuclear weapons and lead this world toward a safer world.

MS. SAWYER: Mr. President, the issue is leadership in personal terms. First, do you think, as Vice President Bush said, that Mr. Mondale's campaign is one of whining and hoping for bad news? And, second, what leadership characteristics do you possess that Mr. Mondale does not?

MR. REAGAN: Well, whether he does or not, let me suggest my own idea about the leadership factor — and since you've asked it. And, incidentally, I might say that, with regard to the 25 percent cut to Social Security — before I get to the answer to your question — the only 25 percent cut that I know of was accompanying that huge 1977 tax increase, was a cut of 25 percent in the benefits for every American who was born after 1916.

Now, leadership — first of all, I think you must have some principles you believe in. In mine, I happen to believe in the people, and believe that the people are supposed to be dominant in our society. That they, not government, are to have control of their own affairs to the greatest extent possible with an orderly society. Now, having that, I think also that in leadership. . . . Well, I believe that you find people, in positions such as I'm in, who have the talent and ability to do the things that are needed in the various departments of government. I don't believe that a leader should be spending his time in the Oval Office deciding who is going to play tennis on the White House court. And you let those people go with the guidelines of overall policy, and not looking over their shoulder and nit-picking the manner in which they go at the job. You are ultimately responsible, however, for that job.

But I also believe something else about that. I believe that. . . . And when I became Governor of California I started this, and I continue it in this Office — that any issue that comes before me, I have instructed Cabinet members and Staff: they are not to bring up any of the political ramifications that might surround the issue. I don't want to hear them. I want to hear only arguments as to whether it is good or bad for the people. Is it morally right? And on that basis, and that basis alone, we make a decision on every issue.

Now, with regard to my feeling about why I thought that his record bespoke his possible taking us back to the same things that we knew under the previous Administration — his record is that he spoke in praise of deficits several times, said they weren't to be abhorred, that, as a matter of fact, he at one time said he wished the deficit could be doubled because they stimulate the economy and help reduce unemployment.

MS. SAWYER: As a follow-up, let me draw in another specific, if I could, a specific that the Democrats have claimed about your campaign — that it is, essentially, based on imagery. And one specific that they allege is that, for instance, recently you showed up at the opening ceremony of a Buffalo old-age housing project when, in fact, your policy was to cut Federal housing subsidies for the elderly. Yet you were there to have your picture taken with them.

MR. REAGAN: Our policy was not to cut subsidies. We have believed in partnership, and that was an example of a partnership between not only local government and the Federal Government, but also between the private sector that built that particular structure. And this is what we have been trying to do, is involve the Federal Government in such partnerships. We are today subsidizing housing for more than 10 million people. And we're going to continue along that line. We have no thought of throwing people out into the snow, whether because of age or need. We have preserved the safety net for the people with true need in this country. And it has been pure demagoguery that we have in some way shut off all the charitable programs, or many of them, for the people who have real need. The safety net is there, and we are taking care of more people than has ever been taken care of before by any Administration in this country.

MS. WALTERS: Mr. Mondale, the opportunity for you to rebut.

MR. MONDALE: Well, I guess I'm reminded a little bit of what Will Rogers once said about Hoover. He said, "It's not what he doesn't know that bothers me, it's what he knows for sure that just ain't so." The fact of it is . . . [Laughter] the fact of it is . . . the fact of it is, the President's budget sought to cut Social Security by 25 percent. It's not an opinion — it's a fact. And when the President was asked the other day, "What do you want to cut in the budget?" he said, "Cut those things I asked for but didn't get." That's Social Security and Medicare.

The second fact is that the housing unit for senior citizens that the President dedicated in Buffalo was only made possible through a Federal assistance program for senior citizens that the President's budget sought to terminate. So if he'd had his way, there wouldn't have been any housing project there at all. This Administration has taken a meat cleaver out, in terms of Federal-assisted housing, and the record is there. We have to see the facts before we can draw conclusions.

MS. WALTERS: Mr. President?

MR. REAGAN: Well, let me just respond with regard to Social Security. When we took office, we discovered that the program that the Carter-Mondale Administration had said would solve the fiscal problems of Social Security for the next 50 years, wouldn't solve them for five. Social Security was due to go bankrupt before 1983. Any proposals that I made at that time were at the request of the Chairman — a Democrat — of one of the leading committees, who said we have to do something before the program goes broke and the checks bounce.

And so we made a proposal. And then in 1982 they used that proposal in a demagogic fashion for the 1982 campaign. And three days after the election in 1982 they came to us and said, "Social Security, we know, is broke." Indeed, we had to borrow $17 billion to pay the checks. And then I asked for a bipartisan commission, which I'd asked for from the beginning, to sit down and work out a solution. And so the whole matter of what to do with Social Security has been resolved by bipartisan legislation. And it is on a sound basis now for as far as you can see into the next century.

MS. WALTERS: Mr. President, we begin segment number three with Fred Barnes.

[Religion and Politics]

MR. FRED BARNES, National Political Correspondent, *The Baltimore Sun*: Mr. President, would you describe your religious beliefs, noting particularly whether you consider yourself a born-again Christian, and explain how these beliefs affect your presidential decisions?

MR. REAGAN: Well, I was raised to have a faith and a belief, and have been a member of a church since I was a small boy. In our particular church we did not use that term, "born again," so I don't know whether I would fit that, that particular term. But I have, thanks to my mother — God rest her soul — the firmest possible belief and faith in God. And I don't believe. . . . I believe, I should say, as Lincoln once said, that I could not — I would be the most stupid man in the world if I thought I could confront the duties of the office I hold if I could not turn to someone who was stronger and greater than all others. And I do resort to prayer.

At the same time, however, I have not believed that prayer should be introduced into an election, or be a part of a political campaign, or religion a part of that campaign. As a matter of fact, I think religion became a part of this campaign when Mr. Mondale's running mate said I wasn't a good Christian. So it does play a part in my life. I have no hesitancy in saying so. And, as I say, I don't believe that I could carry on unless I had a belief in a higher authority and a belief that prayers are answered.

MR. BARNES: Given those beliefs, Mr. President, why don't you attend services regularly, either by going to church or by inviting a minister to the White House as President Nixon used to do, or someone to Camp David, as President Carter used to do?

MR. REAGAN: The answer to your question is very simple about why I don't go to church. I have gone to church regularly all my life. And I started to here in Washington. And now, in the position I hold, and in the world in which we live, where embassies do get blown up in Beirut.... We're supposed to talk about that on the debate the twenty-first, I understand. But I pose a threat to several hundred people if I go to church. I know the threats that are made against me. We all know the possibilities of terrorism. We have seen the barricades that have had to be built around the White House. And, therefore, I don't feel — and my minister knows this and supports me in this position — I don't feel that I have a right to go to church knowing that my being there could cause something of the kind that we have seen in other places — in Beirut, for example. I think the Lord understands.

MS. WALTERS: May I ask the audience, please to refrain from applause. Fred, your second question.

MR. BARNES: Mr. Mondale, would you describe your religious beliefs and mental whether you consider yourself a born-again Christian, and explain how those beliefs would affect your decisions as President?

MR. MONDALE: First of all, I accept President Reagan's affirmation of faith. I am sure that we all accept and admire his commitment to his faith, and we are strengthened, all of us, by that fact. I am a son of a Methodist minister. My wife is the daughter of a Presbyterian minister. I don't know if I've been born again, but I know I was born into a Christian family, and I believe I have sung at more weddings and more funerals than anybody ever to seek the Presidency. Whether that helps or not I don't know. I have a deep religious faith, our family does, it is fundamental, it's probably the reason that I'm in politics. I think our faith tells us ... instructs us about the moral life that we should lead, and I think we are all together on that.

What bothers me is this growing tendency to try to use one's own personal interpretation of faith politically to question others' faith, and to try to use the instrumentalities of government to impose those views on others. All history tells us that that's a mistake. When the Republican platform says that from here on out we're going to have a religious test for judges before they're selected for the Federal Court, and then Jerry Falwell [Dr. Jerry Falwell, President, Moral Majority, Incorporated] announces that that means they get at least two Justices of the Supreme Court, I think that's an abuse of faith in our country.

This nation is the most religious nation on earth. More people go to church and synagogues than any other nation on earth, and it's because we kept the politicians and the state out of the personal exercise of our faith. That's why faith in the United States is pure and unpolluted by the intervention of politicians. And I think if we want to continue, as I do, to have a religious nation let's keep that line and never cross it.

MS. WALTERS: Thank you. Mr. Barnes, next question.

We have time for rebuttal now.

MR. BARNES: I think I have a follow-up.

MS. WALTERS: Yes, I asked you if you did. I'm sorry. I thought you waived it.

MR BARNES: Yes, I do. Yes. Mr. Mondale. The . . . you've complained, just now, about Jerry Falwell, and you've complained other times about other fundamentalists in politics. Correct me if I'm wrong, but I don't recall you ever complaining about ministers who were involved in the civil rights movement, or in the anti-Vietnam War demonstrations, or about black preachers, who've been so involved in American politics. Is it only conservative ministers that you object to?

MR. MONDALE: No, what I object to . . . what I object to is someone seeking to use his faith to question the faith of another, or to use that faith and seek to use the power of government to impose it on others. A minister who is in civil rights, or in the conservative movement, because he believes his faith instructs him to do that, I admire. The fact that the faith speaks to us, and that we are moral people, hopefully, I accept and rejoice in. It's when you try to use that to undermine the integrity of private political — uh, private religious — faith, and the use of the state is where — for the most personal decisions in American life — that's where I draw the line.

MS. WALTERS: Thank you. Now, Mr. President, rebuttal.

PRESIDENT REAGAN: Yes, it's very difficult to rebut, because I find myself in so much agreement with Mr. Mondale. I, too, want that wall that is in the Constitution of separation of church and state to remain there. The only attacks I have made are on people who have not . . . apparently would break away at that wall from the Government side, using the Government, using the power of the courts and so forth, to hinder that part of the Constitution that says the Government shall not only not establish a religion, it shall not inhibit the practice of religion. And they have been using these things to have government, through court orders, inhibit the practice of religion. A child wants to say grace in its school cafeteria and a court rules that they can't do it, because it's school property. These are the types of things that I think have been happening in a kind of a secular way that have been eroding that separation, and I am opposed to that.

With regard to a platform on the Supreme Court I can only say one thing about that. I don't . . . I have appointed one member of the Supreme Court, Sandra Day O'Connor. I'll stand on my record on that, and if I have the opportunity to appoint any more, I'll do it in the same manner that I did in selecting her.

MS. WALTERS: Mr. Mondale, your rebuttal please.

MR. MONDALE: The platform to which the President refers, in fact, calls for a religious test in the selection of judges. And Jerry Falwell says, "That means we get two or three judges," and it would involve a religious test for the first time in American life. Let's take the example that the President cites; I believe in prayer. My family prays. We've never had any difficulty finding time to pray, but do we want a Constitutional amendment adopted of the kind proposed by the President that gets the local politicians into the business of selecting prayers that our children must either recite in school, or be embarrassed and asked to excuse themselves? Who would write the prayer? What would it say? How would it be resolved when those disputes occurred?

It seems to me that a moment's reflection tells you why the United States Senate turned that amendment down — because it will undermine the practice of honest faith in our country by politicizing it. We don't want that.

MS. WALTERS: Thank you, Mr. Mondale. Our time is up for this round. We go into the second round of our questioning, begin again with Jim Wieghart. Jim?

[Democratic Party]

MR. WIEGHART: After that discussion this may be like going from the sublime to the ridiculous, but here it goes: I have a political question for you, Mr. Mondale.

Polls indicate a massive change in the electorate away from the coalition that has long made the Democratic Party a majority. Blue-collar workers, young professionals, their children, and much of the middle class now regard themselvs as independents or Republican, instead of Democrats, and the gap ... the edge that the Democrats had in party registration seems to be narrowing. I'd like to ask you, Mr. Mondale, what is causing this? Is the Democratic Party out of synch with the majority of Americans, and will it soon be replaced as a majority party by the Republicans? What do you think needs to be done about it as a Democrat?

MR. MONDALE: My answer is that this campaign isn't over yet, and when people vote I think you're going to see a very strong verdict by the American people that they favor the approach that I'm talking about.

The American people want arms control. They don't want this arms race, and they don't want this deadly new effort to bring weapons into the heavens, and they want an American foreign policy that leads toward a safer world. The American people see this debt, and they know it's got to come down, and if it won't come down the economy is gonna slow down, maybe go into a recession. They see this tremendous influx and swamping of cheap foreign imports in this country, that has cost over 3 million jobs, given farmers the worst year in American history, and they know this debt must come down as well, because it's unfair to our children.

The American people want this environment protected. They know that these toxic-waste dumps should have been cleaned up a long time ago, and they know that people's lives and health are being risked because we've had an Administration that has been totally insensitive to the law and the demand for the protection of the environment.

The American people want their children educated, they want to get our edge back in science, and they want a policy headed by the President that helps close this gap that's widening between the United States and Europe and Japan. The American people want to keep opening doors. They want those civil rights laws enforced, they want the Equal Rights Amendment ratified, they want equal pay for comparable effort for women, and they want it because they've understood from the beginning that when we open doors, we're all stronger, just as we were at the Olympics.

I think as you make the case, the American people will increasingly come to our cause.

MR. WIEGHART: Mr. Mondale, isn't it possible that the American people have heard your message and they are listening, but they are rejecting it?

MR. MONDALE: Well, tonight we had the first debate over the deficit. The President says it will disappear automatically. I have said it is going to take some work. I think the American people will draw their own conclusions. Secondly, I have said that I will not support the cuts in Social Security and Medicare and the rest that the President has proposed. The President answers that it didn't happen, or if it did, it was resolved later in a commission. As the record develops, I think it's going to become increasingly clear that what I am saying and where I want to take this country is exactly where the country wants to go, and the comparison of approaches is such that I think will lead to further strength.

MR. WIEGHART: Mr. President, you and your party are benefiting from what appears to be an erosion of the old Democratic coalition. But you have not laid out a specific agenda to take this shift beyond November 6. What is your program for America for the next decade — with, with some specificity?

MR. REAGAN: Well, again, I am running on the record. I think sometimes Mr. Mondale is running away from his. But I am running on the record of what we have asked for. We will continue to try and get things that we didn't get in the program that has already brought the rate of spending of Government down from 17 percent to 6.1 percent, a program of returning authority and autonomy to the local and state governments that has been unjustly seized by the Federal Government. And you might find those words in a Democratic platform of some years ago. I know because I was a Democrat at that time. And I left the Party eventually because I could no longer follow the turn in the Democratic leadership that they took us down an entirely different path — a path of centralizing authority in the Federal Government, lacking trust in the American people.

I promised when we took office that we would reduce inflation. We have, to one-third of what it was. I promised that we would reduce taxes. We did — 25 percent across the board. That barely held even with, if it did that much, with the gigantic tax increase imposed in 1977. But at least it took that burden away from them. I said that we would create jobs for our people. And we did — six million in the last 20 or 21 months. I said that we would become respected in the world once again, and that we would refurbish our national defense to the place that we could deal on the world scene, and then seek disarmament, reduction of arms, and, hopefully, an elimination of nuclear weapons. We have done that.

All of the things that I said we would do — from inflation being down, interest rates being down, unemployment falling — all of those things we have done. And I think this is something the American people see.

I think they also know that we have . . . we had a commission that came in a year ago with a recommendation on education, on excellence in education. And today, without the Federal Government being involved other than passing on to them, the school districts, the words from that commission, we find 35 states with task forces now dealing with their educational problems. We find that schools are now extending the curriculum to now have forced teaching of mathematics and science and so forth. All of these things have brought an improvement in the college entrance exams for the first time in some 20 years.

So I think that many Democrats are seeing the same thing this Democrat saw. The leadership isn't taking us where we want to go.

MR. WIEGHART: Mr. President, there is a. . . . Much of what you said affects the quality of life of many Americans — their income, the way they live, and so forth. But there's an aspect to quality of life that lies beyond the private sector, which has to do with our neighborhoods, with our cities, our streets, our parks, our environment. In those areas, I have a difficulty seeing what your program is and what you feel the Federal responsibility is in these areas of the quality of life in the public sector that affects everybody. And even enormous wealth by one individual can't create the kind of environment that he might like.

MR. REAGAN: There are tasks that government legitimately should enforce and tasks that government performs well. And you've named some of them. Crime has come down the last two years for the first time in many, many decades that it has come down — or since we've kept records — two consecutive years. And last year it came down, the biggest drop in crime that we've had. I think that we've had something to do with that, just as we have with the drug problem nationwide.

The environment? Yes, I feel as strongly as anyone about the preservation of the environment. When we took office we found that the national parks were so dirty, and contained so many hazards, lack of safety features, that we stopped buying additional park land until we had rectified this with what was to be a five-year program, but is just about finished already — $1 billion — and now we're going back to budgeting for additional lands for our parks. We have added millions of acres to the wilderness lands, to the game refuges. I think that we are out in front of most. And I see the red light is blinking, so I can't continue, but I've got more.

MS. WALTERS: Well, you'll have a chance when your rebuttal time comes up, perhaps, Mr. President.

MR. REAGAN: All right.

MS. WALTERS: Mr. Mondale, now it's your turn for rebuttal.

MR. MONDALE: The President says that when the Democratic Party made its turn, he left it. The year that he decided we had lost our way was the year that John F. Kennedy was running against Richard Nixon. I was Chairman of Minnesotans for Kennedy. President Reagan was Chairman of a thing called Democrats for Nixon.

Now, maybe we've made a wrong turn with Kennedy, but I'll be proud of supporting him all of our life ... all of my life, and I'm very happy that John Kennedy was elected. Because John Kennedy looked at the future with courage, saw what needed to be done, and understood his own government. The President just said that his government is shrinking. It's not; it's now the largest peacetime government ever, in terms of the take from the total economy. And instead of retreating where we ... instead of being strong where we should be strong, he wants to make it strong and intervene in the most private and personal questions in American life. That's where government should not be.

MS. WALTERS: Mr. President?

MR. REAGAN: Before I campaigned as a Democrat for a Republican candidate for President, I had already voted for Dwight Eisenhower to be President of the United States. So my change had come earlier than that. I hadn't gotten around to re-registering as yet. I found that was rather difficult to do. But I finally did it.

There are some other things that have been said here, Barb, you said that I might be able to dredge them up. Mr. Mondale referred to the farmers' worst year. The farmers are not the victims of anything this Administration has done. The farmers were the victims of the double-digit inflation and the 21.5 percent interest rates of the Carter-Mondale Administration, and the grain embargo ... which destroyed our reliability nationwide as a supplier. All of these things are presently being rectified, and I think that we are going to salvage the farmers. As a matter of fact, the ... there has been less than one-quarter of one percent of foreclosures of the 270,000 loans from Government that the farmers have.

MS. WALTERS: Thank you, Mr. President. We will now turn to Diane Sawyer for her round of questions. Diane?

[Abortion]

MS. SAWYER: I'd like to turn to an area that I think few people enjoy discussing, but that we probably should tonight, because the positions of the two candidates are so clearly different and lead to very different policy consequences — and that is abortion and right to life. I'm exploring for your personal views of abortion, and specifically how you would want them applied as public policy.

First, Mr. President, do you consider abortion murder or a sin? And second, how hard would you work, what kind of priority would you give in your second term legislation to make abortion illegal? And specifically, would you make certain, as your party platform urges, that Federal Justices that you appoint be pro-life?

MR. REAGAN: I believe that in the appointment of judges that all that was specified in the party platform was that they observe ... have a ... they respect the sanctity of human life. Now that I would want to see in any judge, and with regard to any issue having to do with human life.

But with regard to abortion — and I have a feeling that this is ... there's been some reference without naming it here, in remarks of Mr. Mondale, tied to injecting religion into government. With me, abortion is not a problem of religion; it's a problem of the Constitution. I believe that until and unless someone can establish that the unborn child is not a living human being, then that child is already protected by the Constitution which guarantees life, liberty, and the pursuit of happiness to all of us. And I think that this is what we should concentrate on, is trying. . . .

I know there was weeks and weeks of testimony before a Senate committee. There were medical authorities, there were religious ... there were clerics there, everyone talking about this matter of pro-life. And at the end of all of that, not one shred of evidence was introduced that the unborn child was not alive. We have seen premature births that are now grown-up, happy people going around.

Also, there is a strange dichotomy in this whole position about our courts ruling that abortion is not the taking of a human life. In California some time ago, a man beat a woman so savagely that her unborn child was born dead with a fractured skull. And the California state legislature unanimously passed a law that was signed by the then Democratic governor — signed a law that said that any man who so abuses a pregnant woman that he causes the death of her unborn child shall be charged with murder. Now, isn't it strange that that same woman could have taken the life of her unborn child and it was abortion, not murder, but if somebody else does it, that's murder? And it recognizes — it used the term "death of the unborn child."

So this has been my feeling about abortion, that we have a problem now to determine. And all evidence so far comes down on the side of the unborn child being a living human being.

MS. SAWYER: A two-part follow-up — do I take it from what you said about the platform, then, that you don't regard the language, and don't regard in your own appointments, abortion position a test of any kind for justices that it should be? And also, if abortion is made illegal, how would you want it enforced? Who would be the policing units that would investigate, and would you want the women who have abortions to be prosecuted?

MR. REAGAN: The laws regarding that always were state laws. It was only when the Supreme Court handed down a decision that the Federal Government intervened in what had always been a state policy. Our laws against murder are state laws. So, I would think that this would be the — the point of enforcement on this.

I . . . as I say, I feel that we have a problem here to resolve, and no one has approached it from that matter. It is . . . it does not happen that the church that I belong to had that as part of its dogma. I know that some churches do. Now, it is a sin if you're taking a human life. At the same time, in our Judeo-Christian tradition, we recognize the right of taking human life in self-defense, and therefore I've always believed that a mother — if medically, it is determined that her life is at risk if she goes through with the pregnancy — she has a right then to take the life of even her own unborn child in defense of her own.

MS. SAWYER: Mr. Mondale, to turn to you, do you consider abortion a murder or a sin? And, bridging from what President Reagan said, he has written that if society doesn't know whether life — does human life, in fact, does begin at conception — as long as there is a doubt, that the unborn child should at least be given the benefit of the doubt, and that there should be protection for that unborn child?

MR. MONDALE: This is one of the most emotional and difficult issues that could possibly be debated. I think your questions, however, underscore the fact: there is probably no way that government should or could answer this question in every individual case and in the private lives of the American people.

The Constitutional amendment proposed by President Reagan would make it a crime for a woman to have an abortion if she had been raped or suffered from incest. Is it really the view of the American people, however you feel on the question of abortion, that government ought to be reaching into your living rooms and making choices like this? I think it cannot work, won't work, and will lead to all kinds of cynical evasions of the law. Those who can afford to have them will continue to have them. The disadvantaged will go out in the back alley, as they used to do. I think these questions are inherently personal and moral, and every individual instance is different. Every American should beware . . . be aware of the seriousness of the step. But there are some things that government can do, and some things they cannot do.

Now, the example that the President cites has nothing to do with abortion. Somebody went to a woman and nearly killed her. That's always been a serious crime, and always should be a serious crime. But how does that compare with the problem of a woman who's raped? Do we really want those decisions made by judges who've been picked because they will agree to find the person guilty? I don't think so, and I think it's going in exactly the wrong direction. In America, on basic moral questions, we have always let the people decide in their own personal lives. We haven't felt so insecure that we've reached for the club of state to have our point of view. It's been a good instinct, and we're the most religious people on earth.

One final point. President Reagan, as Governor of California, signed a bill which is perhaps the most liberal pro-abortion bill of any state in the union.

MS. SAWYER: But if I can get you back for a moment on my point, which was the question of when human life begins, a two-part follow-up. First of all, at what point do *you* believe that human life begins in the growth of a fetus, and second of all, you said that government shouldn't be involved in the decisions, yet there are those who would say that government is involved, and the consequence of the involvement was 1.5 million abortions in 1980. And how do you feel about that?

MR. MONDALE: The basic decision of the Supreme Court is that each person has to make this judgment in her own life, and that's the way it's been done. And it's a personal and private moral judgment. I don't know the answer to when life begins, and it's not that simple, either. You've got another life involved. And if it's rape, how do you draw moral judgments on that? If it's incest, how do you draw moral judgments on that? Does every woman in America have to present himself ... herself before some judge picked by Jerry Falwell to clear her personal judgment? It won't work.

MS. WALTERS: I'm sorry to do this, but I really must talk to the audience. You're all invited guests. I know I'm wasting time in talking to you, but it really is very unfair of you to applaud, sometimes louder or less loud. And I ask you, as people who were invited here, and polite people, to refrain.

We have our time now, for rebuttal. Mr. President.

MR. REAGAN: Yes. But with regard to this being a personal choice, isn't that what a murderer is insisting on, his or her right to kill someone because of whatever fault they think justifies that?

Now, I'm not capable — and I don't think you are, any of us — to make this determination that must be made with regard to human life. I am simply saying that I believe that that's where the effort should be directed to make that determination. I don't think that any of us should be called upon here to stand and make a decision as to what other things might come under the self-defense tradition. That, too, would have to be worked out then, when you once recognize that we're talking about a life.

But in this great society of ours, wouldn't it make a lot more sense — in this gentle and kind society — if we had a program that made it possible for when incidents come along in which someone feels they must do away with that unborn child, that instead we make it available for the adoption? There are a million and a half people out there standing in line waiting to adopt children who can't have them any other way.

MS. WALTERS: Mr. Mondale?

MR. MONDALE: I agree with that, and that's why I was the principal sponsor of a liberal adoption law so that more of these children could come to term, so that the young mothers were educated, so we found an option — an alternative. I'm all for that. But the question is whether this other option, proposed by the President, should be pursued. And I don't agree with it.

Since I've got about 20 seconds, let me just say one thing. The question of agriculture came up a minute ago. Net farm income is off 50 percent in the last three years and every farmer knows it. And the effect of these economic policies is like a massive grain embargo which has caused farm exports to drop 20 percent. It's been a big failure. I opposed the grain embargo in my Administration. I'm opposed to these policies as well.

MS. WALTERS: I'm sitting here like the great schoolteacher letting you both get away with things, because one did it, the other one did it. May I ask in the future that the rebuttals stick to what the rebuttal is. And, also, foreign policy will be the next debate. Stop dragging it in by its ear into this one.

Now, having admonished you, I would like to say to the panel, you are allowed one question and one follow-up. Would you try, as best you could, not to ask two and three. I know it's something we all want to do. Two or three questions is part I, and two and three is part II. Having said that, Fred, it's yours.

[Taxes]

MR. BARNES: Thank you. Mr. Mondale, let me ask you about middle class Americans and the taxes they pay. I'm talking about, not about the rich or the poor — I know your views on their taxes — but about families earning $25,000 to $45,000 a year. Do you think that those families are overtaxed or undertaxed by the Federal Government?

MR. MONDALE: In my opinion, as we deal with this deficit, people from about $70,000 a year on down have to be dealt with very, very carefully because they are the ones who didn't get any relief the first time around. Under the 1981 tax bill, people making $200,000 a year got $60,000 in tax relief over three years, while people making $30,000 a year, all taxes considered, got no relief at all or their taxes actually went up. That's why my proposal protects everybody from $25,000 a year or less against any tax increases, and treats those $70,000 and under in a way that is more beneficial than the way the President proposes with a sales tax or a flat tax.

What does this mean in real life? Well, the other day Vice President Bush disclosed his tax returns to the American people. He's one of the wealthiest Americans, and he's our Vice President. In 1981, I think he paid about 40 percent in taxes. In 1983, as a result of these tax preferences, he paid a little over 12 percent — 12.8 percent in taxes. That meant that he paid a lower percent in taxes than the janitor who cleaned up his office or the chauffeur who drives him to work.

I believe we need some fairness. And that's why I proposed what I think is a fair and responsible proposal that helps protect these people who have already got no relief or actually got a tax increase.

MR. BARNES: It sounds as if you were saying you think this group of taxpayers making $25,000 to $45,000 a year is already overtaxed. Yet your tax proposal would increase their taxes. I think your aides have said those earning about $25,000 to $35,000, their tax rate . . . their tax bill would go up $100, and from $35,000 to $45,000 — more than that, several hundred dollars. Wouldn't that stifle their incentive to work and invest and so on, and also hurt the recovery?

MR. MONDALE: The first thing is, everybody $25,000 and under would have no tax increase. Mr. Reagan, after the election, is going to have to propose a tax increase. And you will have to compare what he proposes. And his Secretary of the Treasury said he is studying a sales tax, or value-added tax. They're the same thing. They hit middle- and moderate-income Americans and leave wealthy Americans largely untouched.

Up until about $70,000, as you go up the ladder, my proposals will be far more beneficial. As soon as we get the economy on a sound ground, as well, I'd like to see the total repeal of indexing. I don't think we can do that for a few years. But at some point we want to do that as well.

MR. BARNES: Mr. President, let me try this on you. Do you think middle-income Americans are overtaxed or undertaxed?

MR. REAGAN: You know, I wasn't going to say this at all, but I can't help it. There you go again. [Laughter.] I don't have a plan to tax or increase taxes. I'm not going to increase taxes. I can understand why you are, Mr. Mondale, because as a Senator you voted 16 times to increase taxes. Now, I believe that our problem has not been that anybody in our country is undertaxed: it's that Government is overfed. And I think that most of our people, this is why we had a 25 percent tax cut across the board, which maintained the same progressivity of our tax structure in the brackets on up. And, as a matter of fact, it just so happens that in the quirks of administering these taxes, those above $50,000 actually did not get quite as big a tax cut, percentage-wise, as did those from $50,000 down. From $50,000 down, those people paid two-thirds of the taxes. And those people got two-thirds of the tax cut.

Now, the Social Security tax of '77 — this, indeed, was a tax that hit people in the lower brackets the hardest. It had two features. It had several tax increases phased in over a period of time. There are two more yet to come between now and 1989. At the same time every year, it increased the amount of money — virtually every year, there may have been one or two that were skipped in there — that was subject to that tax. Today it is up to about $38,000 of earnings that is subject to the payroll tax for Social Security. And that tax, there are not deductions. So a person making anywhere from ten, fifteen, twenty . . . they're paying that tax on the full gross earnings that they have after they have already paid an income tax on that same amount of money.

Now, I don't think that to try and say that we were taxing the rich and not the other way around: it just doesn't work out that way. The system is still where it was with regard to the progressivity, as I've said. And that has not been changed. But if you take it in numbers of dollars instead of percentage, yes, you can say, "Well, that person got ten times as much as this other person." Yes — but he paid ten times as much also. But if you take it in percentages, then you find out that it is fair and equitable across the board.

MR. BARNES: I thought I caught, Mr. President, a glimmer of a stronger statement, there in your answer, than you've made before. I think the operative position you had before was that you would only raise taxes in a second term as a last resort. And I thought you said flatly that, "I'm not going to raise taxes." Is that what you meant to say — that you will flatly not raise taxes in your second term as President?

MR. REAGAN: Yes, I had used. . . . "Last resort" would always be with me. If you got the Government down to the lowest level that you yourself could say it could not go any lower and still perform the services for the people; and if the recovery was so complete that you knew you were getting the ultimate amount of revenues that you could get through that growth and there was still some slight difference there between those two lines, then I had said once that, "Yes, you would have to then look to see if taxes should not be adjusted." I don't foresee those things happening. So I say with great confidence I'm not going to — I'm not going to go for a tax.

With regard to assailing Mr. Bush about his tax problems, and the difference from the tax he once paid, and then the later tax he paid, I think, if you looked at the deductions, there were great legal expenses in there. It had to do, possibly, with the sale of his home. And they had to do with his setting up of a blind trust. All of those are legally deductions — deductible in computing your tax. And it was a one-year thing with him.

MS. WALTERS: Mr. Mondale, here we go again, this time for rebuttal.

MR. MONDALE: Well, first of all, I gave him the benefit of the doubt on the house deal. I'm just talking about the 12.8 percent that he paid. And that's what's happening all over this country with wealthy Americans. They've got so many loopholes; they don't have to pay much in taxes. Now, Mr. President, you said, "There you go again." Right? Remember the last time you said that?

MR. REAGAN: Um-hummm.

MR. MONDALE: You said it when President Carter said that you were going to cut Medicare. And you said, "Oh no, there you go again, Mr. President." And what did you do right after the election? You went out and tried to cut $20 billion out of Medicare. And so, when you say, "There you go again," people remember this, you know. And people will remember that you signed the biggest tax increase in the history of California, and the biggest tax increase in the history of the United States. And what are you going to do? You've got a $260 billion deficit. You can't wish it away. You won't slow defense spending. You refuse to do that.

MS. WALTERS: Mr. Mondale? I'm afraid your time is up.

MR. MONDALE: Sorry.

MS. WALTERS: Mr. President.

MR. REAGAN: Yes. With regard to Medicare, no. But it's time for us to say that Medicare is in pretty much the same condition that Social Security was. And something is going to have to be done in the next several years to make it fiscally sound. And, no, I never proposed any $20 billion should come out of Medicare. I have proposed that the program we must treat with that particular problem. And maybe part of that problem is because during the four-year period medical costs in this country went up 87 percent.

MS. WALTERS: All right ... fine ... we can't. ...

MR. REAGAN: I gave you back some of that time.

MS. WALTERS: We can't keep going back for other rebuttals. There will be time later. We now go to our final round. The way things stand now, we have time for only two sets of questions, and by lot it will be Jim and Diane. And we'll start with Jim Wieghart.

[Economic Recovery]

MR. WIEGHART: Mr. President, the economic recovery is real but uneven. The Census Bureau, just a month ago, reported that there are more people living under poverty now — a million more people living under it — than when you took office. There have been a number of studies, including studies by the Urban Institute and other nonpolitical organizations, that say that the impact of the tax and budget cuts in your economic policies have impacted severely on certain classes of Americans: working mothers head of households, minority groups, elderly poor. In fact, they're saying the rich are getting richer and the poor are getting poorer under your policies. What relief can you offer to the working poor, to the minorities and the women head of households who have borne the brunt of these economic programs? What can you offer them in the future in your next term?

MR. REAGAN: Well, some of those facts and figures just don't stand up. Yes, there has been an increase in poverty, but it is a lower rate of increase than it was in the preceding years, before we got here. It has begun to decline, but it is still going up. On the other hand, women heads of household — single women heads of household — have for the first time ... there has been a turn down in the rate of poverty for them. We have found also in our studies that in this increase in poverty it all had to do with their private earnings. It had nothing to do with the transfer payments from Government the ... by way of many programs. We are spending now 37 percent more on food for the hungry in all the various types of programs that was spent in 1980. We're spending a third more on all of the ... well, all of the programs of human service. We have more people receiving food stamps than were ever receiving them before — 2,300,000 more are receiving them — even though we took 850,000 off the food-stamp rolls, because they were making an income that was above anything that warranted their fellow citizens having to support them.

We found people making 185 percent of the poverty level were getting Government benefits. We have set a line at 130 percent so that we can direct that aid down to the truly needy. Sometime ago Mr. Mondale said something about education, and college students, and help of that kind. Half — one out of two — of the full-time college students in the United States are receiving some form of federal aid. But there again we've found people that there were ... under the previous Administration, families that had no limit to income were still eligible for low-interest college loans. We didn't think that was right, and so we have set a standard, but those loans and those grants are directed to the people who otherwise could not go to college, their family incomes were so low. So, there are a host of other figures that reveal that the grant programs are greater than they have ever been, taking care of more people than they ever have. 7.7 million elderly citizens who were living in the lowest 20 percent of earnings . . . 7.7 million have moved up into another bracket since our administration took over, leaving only 5 million of the elderly in that bracket, when there had been more than 13 million.

MR. WIEGHART: Mr. President, in a visit to Texas — in Brownsville, I believe it was in the Rio Grande Valley — you did observe that the economic recovery was uneven in that —

MR. REAGAN: Oh, yes.

MR. WIEGHART: — particular area of Texas, unemployment was over 14 percent, whereas state-wide it was the lowest in the country, I believe 5.6 percent. And you made the comment that, however, that man does not live by bread alone. What did you mean by that comment, and, is it . . . if I interpret it correctly, it would be a comment more addressed to the affluent who, obviously, can look beyond just the bread that they need to sustain them with their wherewithal.

MR. REAGAN: That had nothing to do with the other thing of talking about their needs, or anything. I remember distinctly, I was segueing into another subject. I was talking about the things that have been accomplished, and that was referring to the revival of patriotism and optimism, the new spirit that we're finding all over America, and it is a wonderful thing to see when you get out there among the people. So, that was the only place that that was used. I did avoid, I'm afraid, in my previous answer also, the idea of uneven . . . yes, there is no way that the recovery is even across the country, just as in the depths of the recession there was some parts of the country that were worse off, but some that didn't even feel the pain of the recession. We're not going to rest, are not going to be happy until every person in this country who wants a job can have one, until the recovery is complete across the country.

MR. WIEGHART: Mr. Mondale, the . . . as you can gather from the question of the President the celebrated war on poverty obviously didn't end the problem of poverty, although it may have dented it. The poor and the homeless, and the disadvantaged are still with us. What should the Federal Government's role be to turn back the growth in the number of people living below the poverty level, which is now 35 million in the United States, and to help deal with the structural unemployment problems that the President was referring to in an uneven recovery?

MR. MONDALE: Number one, we've got to get the debt down to get the interest rates down so the economy will grow, and people will be employed. Number two, we have to work with cities and others to help generate economic growth in those communities. To the Urban Development Action Grant Program . . . I don't mind those enterprise zones, let's try them, but not as a substitute for the others. Certainly, education and training is crucial. If these young Americans don't have the skills that make them

869

attractive to employees, they're not going to get jobs.

The next thing is to try to get more entrepreneurship in business within the reach of minorities, so that these businesses are located in the communities in which they're found.

The other thing is we need the business community, as well as government, heavily involved in these communities to try to get economic growth. There is no question that the poor are worse off. I think the President genuinely believes that they're better off, but the figures show that about 8 million more people are below the poverty line than 4 years ago. How you can cut school lunches, how you can cut student assistance, how you can cut housing, how you can cut disability benefits, how you can do all of these things, and then the people receiving them — for example, the disabled, who have no alternative. How they're going to do better I don't know. Now, we need a tight budget, but there's no question that this Administration has singled out things that affect the most vulnerable in American life, and they're hurting.

One final point if I might. There's another part of the lopsided economy that we're in today, and that is that these heavy deficits have killed exports, and are swamping the nation with cheap imports. We are now $120 billion of imports, 3 million jobs lost and farmers are having their worst year. That's another reason to get the deficit down.

MR. WIEGHART: Mr. Mondale, is it possible that the vast majority of Americans who appear to be prosperous have lost interest in the kinds of programs you're discussing to help those less privileged than they are?

MR. MONDALE: I think the American people want to make certain that that dollar is wisely spent. I think they stand for civil rights. I know they're all for education and science and training, which I strongly support. They want these young people to have a chance to get jobs, and the rest. I think the business community wants to get involved. I think they're asking for new and creative ways to try to reach it with everyone involved. I think that's part of it.

I think also that the American people want a balanced program that gives us long-term growth, so that they're not having to take money that's desperate to themselves and their families and give it to someone else. I'm opposed to that too.

MS. WALTERS: And now it's time for our rebuttal for this period. Mr. President?

MR. REAGAN: Yes. The connection has been made again between the deficit and the interest rates. There is no connection between them. There is a connection between interest rates and inflation, but I would call to your attention that in 1981, while we were operating still on the Carter-Mondale budget that we inherited, that the interest rates came down from 21.5 [percent] toward the 12 or 13 [percent] figure. And while they were coming down, the deficits had started their great increase. They were going up. Now, if there was a connection, I think that there would be a different parallel between the deficit getting larger and interest rates going down.

The interest rates are based on inflation. And right now, I have to tell you, I don't think there is any excuse for the interest rates being as high as they are because we have brought inflation down so low. I think it can only be that they are anticipating, or hope — or expecting, not hoping, that maybe we don't have a control of inflation, and it's going to go back up again. Well, it isn't going to go back up. We are going to see that it doesn't.

MS. WALTERS: Mr. President —

MR. REAGAN: I haven't got time to answer with regard to the disabled.

MS. WALTERS: Thank you, Mr. President. Mr. Mondale?

MR. MONDALE: Mr. President, if I heard you correctly, you said that these deficits don't have anything to do with interest rates. I will grant you that interest rates were too high in 1980, and we can have another debate as to why energy prices and so on. There is no way of glossing around that. But when these huge deficits went in place until 1981, what's called the real interest rates — the spread between inflation and what a loan costs you — doubled. And that's still the case today. And the result is interest costs that have never been seen before in terms of real charges. And it's attributable to the deficit.

Everybody — every economist, every businessman — believes that. Your own Council of Economic Advisers — Mr. Feldstein [Martin S. Feldstein, former Chairman, Council of Economic Advisers], in his report, told you that. Every chairman of the [Senate] Finance and [House] Ways and Means Committee[s], Republican leaders in the Senate and House, are telling you that: that deficit is ruining the long-term hopes for this economy. It is causing high interest rates. It is ruining us in trade. It has given us the highest small-business failure in 50 years. The economy is starting downhill, with housing failures —

MS. WALTERS: Thank you, Mr. Mondale.

MR. MONDALE: Go ahead.

MS. WALTERS: They are both very obedient. I have to give you credit for that. We now start our final round of questions. We do want to have time for your rebuttal. And we start with Diane ... Diane Sawyer.

[Campaign Rhetoric]

MS. SAWYER: Since we are reaching the end of the question period, and since in every Presidential campaign, the candidates tend to complain that the opposition candidate is not held accountable for what he or she says, let me give you the chance to do that. Mr. Mondale, beginning with you. What do you think the most outrageous thing is your opponent said in this debate tonight?

MR. MONDALE: You want to give me some suggestions? I'm going to use my time a little differently. I'm going to give the President some credit. I think the President has done some things to raise the sense of spirit, morale, good feeling in this country. He is entitled to credit for that. What I think we need, however, is not just that, but to move forward, not just congratulating ourselves, but challenging ourselves to get on with the business of dealing with America's problems.

I think in education, when he lectured the country about the importance of discipline, I didn't like it at first, but I think it helped a little bit. But now we need both that kind of discipline, and the resources, and the consistent leadership that allows this country to catch up in education and science and training. I like President Reagan. This is not personal. These are deep differences about our future, and that's the basis of my campaign.

MS. SAWYER: To follow up in a similar vein then, what remaining question would you most like to see your opponent forced to answer?

MR. MONDALE: Without any doubt, I have stood up and told the American people that that $263 billion deficit must come down. And I have done what no candidate for President has ever done: I told you before the election what I would do. Mr. Reagan, as you saw tonight ... President Reagan takes the position that it will disappear by magic. It was once called "voodoo economics." I wish the President would say, "Yes, the CBO is right. Yes, we have a $263 billion deficit. This is how I'm going to get it done." Don't talk about growth, because even though we need growth, that's not helping. It's going to go in the other direction, as they've estimated.

And give us a plan. What will you cut? Whose taxes will you raise? Will you finally touch that defense budget? Are you going to go after Social Security, and Medicare, and student assistance, and the handicapped again, as you did last time? If you'll just tell us what you're going to do, then the American people could compare my plan for the future with your plan. And that's the way it should be. The American people would be in charge.

MS. SAWYER: Mr. President, the most outrageous thing your opponent has said in the debate tonight?

MR. REAGAN: Well now, I have to start with a smile, since his kind words to me. I'll tell you what I think has been the most outrageous thing in political dialogue, both in this campaign and the one in '82. And that is the continued discussion and claim that somehow I am the villain who is going to pull the Social Security checks out from those people who are dependent on them. And why I think it is outrageous — first of all, it isn't true — but why it is outrageous is because, for political advantage, every time they do that, they scare millions of senior citizens who are totally dependent on Social Security, have no place else to turn. And they have to live and go to bed at night thinking, "Is this true? Is someone going to take our check away from us and leave us destitute?" And I don't think that that should be a part of political dialogue.

Now ... now to ... and I still, I just have a minute here?

MS. WALTERS: You have more time.

MR. REAGAN: Oh, I —

MS. WALTERS: You can keep going.

MR. REAGAN: O.K. All right. Now, Social Security, let's lay it to rest once and for all. I told you, never would I do such a thing. But I tell you also now: Social Security has nothing to do with the deficit. Social Security is totally funded by the payroll tax levied on employer and employee. If you reduce the outgo of Social Security, that money would not go into the General Fund to reduce a deficit. It would go into the Social Security Trust Fund. So Social Security has nothing to do with balancing a budget or erasing or lowering the deficit.

Now, as, again, to get to whether I have ... I am depending on magic, I think I have talked in straight economic terms about a program of recovery that was ... I was told wouldn't work. And then after it worked, I was told that lowering taxes would increase inflation. And none of these things happened. It is working, and we are going to continue on that same line.

As to what we might do and find in further savings cuts, no, we're not going to starve the hungry. But we have 2,478 specific recommendations from a commission of more than 2,000 business people in this country, through the Grace Commission, that we're studying right now — and we've already implemented 17 percent of them — that are recommendations as to how to make government more efficient and more economic.

MS. SAWYER: And, to keep it even, what remaining question would you most like to see your opponent forced to answer?

MR. REAGAN: Why the deficits are so much of a problem for him now, but that in 1976, when the deficit was $52 billion and everyone was panicking about that, he said no, that he thought it ought to be bigger, because a bigger deficit would stimulate the economy and would help do away with unemployment. In 1979, he made similar statements ... the same effect. But ... but the ... deficits ... there was nothing wrong with having deficits. Remember, there was a trillion dollars in debt before we got here. That's got to be paid by our children and grandchildren too, if we don't do it. And I'm hoping we can start some payments on it before we get through here. That's why I want another four years.

MS. WALTERS: Well, we have time now, if you'd like to answer the President's question, or whatever rebuttal.

MR. MONDALE: Well, we just finished almost the whole debate, and the American people don't have the slightest clue about what President Reagan will do about these deficits. And yet that's the most important single issue of our time.

I did support the '76 measure that he told about, because we were in a deep recession and we needed some stimulation. But I will say, as a Democrat, I was a real piker, Mr. President. In 1979, we ran a $29 billion deficit all year. This Administration seems to run that every morning. And the result is exactly what we see. This economy is starting to run downhill. Housing is off. Last report on new purchases, it's the lowest since 1982. Growth is a little over three percent now. Many people are predicting a recession. And the flow of imports into this country is swamping the American people.

We've got to deal with this problem. And those of us who want to be your President should tell you now what we're going to do, so you can make a judgment.

MS. WALTERS: Thank you very much. We must stop now. I want to give you time for your closing statements. It's indeed time for that. From each of you, we will begin with President Reagan.

I'm sorry. Mr. Reagan, you had your rebuttal, and I just cut you off, because our time is going. You have a chance now for rebuttal before your closing statement. Is that correct?

MR. REAGAN: No. I might as well just go with what I —

MS. WALTERS: Do you want to go with your. . . ?

MR. REAGAN: I don't think so.

MS. WALTERS: Do you want to wait?

MR. REAGAN: I'm all confused now.

MS. WALTERS: Technically, you did. I have little voices that come in my ear. You don't get those same voices. I'm not hearing it from here. I'm hearing it from here.

MR. REAGAN: All right.

MS. WALTERS: You have waived your rebuttal. You can go with your closing statement.

MR. REAGAN: We'll include it in that.

MS. WALTERS: O.K.

[Closing Statements]

MR. REAGAN: Four years ago, in similar circumstances to this I asked you, the American people, a question. I asked, are you better off than you were four years before. The answer to that, obviously, was no. And as a result I was elected to this office, and promised a new beginning. Now, maybe I'm expected to ask that same question again. I'm not going to because I think that all of you, or almost everyone; those people that have . . . are in the pockets of poverty and haven't caught up. They couldn't answer the way I would want them to. But I think that the most of the people in this country would say yes, they are better off than they were four years ago.

The question, I think, should be enlarged. Is America better off than it was four years ago? And I believe the answer to that has to also be yes.

I'd promised a new beginning. So far it is only a beginning. If the job were finished, I might have thought twice about seeking reelection for this job. But we now have an economy that, for the first time. . . .

Well, let's put it this way. In the first half of 1980, Gross National Product was down, a minus 3.7 percent. First half of '84, it's up eight and a half percent. Productivity in the first half of 1980 was down a minus 2 percent. Today, it is up a plus 4 percent. Personal earnings after taxes, per capita, have gone up almost $3,000 in these four years. In 1980 or 1979, a person with a fixed income of $8,000 would . . . was $500 above the poverty line. And this may explain why there are the numbers still in poverty. By 1980, that same person was $500 below the poverty line.

We have restored much of our economy. With regard to business investment, it is higher than it has been since 1949. So there seems to be no shortage of investment capital. We have, as I said, cut the taxes, but we have reduced inflation, and for two years now it has stayed down there —

not at double-digit, but in the range of 4 [percent] or below.

We believe that. . . . We had also promised that we would make our country more secure. Yes, we have an increase in the defense budget. But back then, we had planes that couldn't fly for lack of spare parts or pilots. We had Navy vessels that couldn't leave harbor because of lack of crew, or again, lack of spare parts. Today, we're well on our way to a 600-ship Navy. We have 543 at present. We have. . . . Our military, the morale is high. The . . . I think the people should understand that two-thirds of the defense budget pays for pay and salary, or pay and pension. And then you add to that food and wardrobe and all the other things, and you only have a small portion going for weapons. But I am determined that if ever our men are called on, they should have the best that we can provide in the . . . in the manner of tools and weapons.

There has been reference to expensive spare parts: hammers costing $500. Well, we are the ones who found those.

I think we've given the American people back their spirit. I think there's an optimism in the land and a patriotism. And I think that we're in a position once again to heed the words of Thomas Paine, who said, "We have it in our power to begin the world over again."

MS. WALTERS: Thank you, Mr. Reagan. Mr. Mondale, the closing words are now yours.

MR. MONDALE: I want to thank The League of Women Voters and the City of Louisville for hosting this evening's debate. I want to thank President Reagan for agreeing to debate. He didn't have to, and he did. And we all appreciate it.

The President's favorite question is, "Are you better off?" Well, if you're wealthy, you're better off. If you're middle-income, you're about where you were. And if you're of modest income, you're worse off. That's what the economists tell us. But is that really the question that should be asked? Isn't the real question "Will we be better off? Will our children be better off? Are we building the future that this nation needs?"

I believe that if we ask those questions that bear on our future — not just congratulate ourselves, but challenge us to solve those problems — you'll see that we need new leadership. Are we better off with this arms race? Would we be better off if we start this "Star Wars" escalation into the heavens? Are we better off when we deemphasize our values of human rights? Are we better off when we load our children with this fantastic debt? Would fathers and mothers feel proud of themselves if they loaded their children with debts like this nation is now — over a trillion dollars on the shoulders of our children? Can we be . . . say, really say that we will be better off when we pull away from sort of that basic American instinct of decency and fairness?

I would rather lose a campaign about decency than win a campaign about self-interest. I don't think this nation is composed of people who care only for themselves. And when we sought to assault Social Security and Medicare, as the record shows we did, I think that was mean-spirited. When we terminated 400,000 desperate, hopeless, defenseless Americans who were on disability — confused and unable to defend themselves — and just laid them out on the street, as we did for four years, I don't think that's what America is all about.

America is a fair society, and it is not right that Vice President Bush pays less in taxes than the janitor who helps him. I believe there is fundamental fairness crying out that needs to be achieved in our tax system. I believe that we will be better off if we protect this environment. And contrary to what the President says, I think their record on the environment is inexcusable and often shameful. These laws are not being enforced, have not been enforced, and the public health and the air and the water are paying the price. That's not fair for our future.

I think our future requires a President to lead us in an all-out search to advance our education, our learning, and our science and training, because this world is more complex, and we are being pressed harder all the time.

I believe in opening doors. We won the Olympics in part because we've had civil rights laws and the laws to prohibit discrimination against women. I have been for those efforts all my life. The President's record is quite different.

The question is our future. President Kennedy once said, in response to similar arguments, "We are great, but we can be greater." We can be better if we face our future, rejoice in our strengths, face our problems, and by solving them, build a better society for our children.

Thank you.

MS. WALTERS: Thank you, Mr. Mondale. Please, we have not finished quite yet. Thank you, Mr. Mondale, and thank you, Mr. President, and our thanks to our panel members as well. And so we bring to a close this first of The League of Women Voters Presidential Debates of 1984. You two can go at each other again in the final League debate on October 21 in Kansas City, Missouri.

And this Thursday night, October 11, at 9 p.m. Eastern Daylight Time, the Vice President, George Bush, will debate Congresswoman Geraldine Ferraro in Philadelphia. And I hope that you will all watch once again.

No matter what the format is, these debates are very important. We all have an extremely vital decision to make. Once more, gentlemen, our thanks. Once more to you our thanks. And now, this is Barbara Walters wishing you a good evening.

SECOND PRESIDENTIAL DEBATE

MRS. DOROTHY S. RIDINGS, Chair, The League of Women Voters Education Fund: Good evening. Good evening from the Municipal Auditorium in Kansas City. I'm Dorothy Ridings, the President of the League of Women Voters, the sponsor of this final Presidential debate of the 1984 campaign between Republican Ronald Reagan and Democrat Walter Mondale. Our panelists for tonight's debate on defense and foreign policy issues are Georgie Anne Geyer, syndicated columnist for Universal Press

Syndicate, Marvin Kalb, chief diplomatic correspondent for NBC News, Morton Kondracke, executive editor of *The New Republic* magazine, and Henry Trewhitt, diplomatic correspondent for *The Baltimore Sun.* Edwin Newman, formerly of NBC News and now a syndicated columnist for King Features, is our moderator. Ed.

MR. EDWIN NEWMAN, King Features Syndicate: Dorothy Ridings, thank you. A brief word about our procedure tonight. The first question will go to Mr. Mondale. He will have two and a half minutes to reply. Then the panel member who put the question will ask a follow-up. The answer to that will be limited to one minute. After that, the same question will be put to President Reagan. Again, there will be a follow-up, and then each man will have one minute for rebuttal. The second question will go to President Reagan first. After that, the alternating will continue. At the end there will be four-minute summations, with President Reagan going last. We have asked the questioners to be brief. Let's begin. Ms. Geyer, your question to Mr. Mondale.

[Central America]

MS. GEORGIE ANNE GEYER, Universal Press Syndicate: Mr. Mondale, two related questions on the crucial issue of Central America. You and the Democratic Party have said that the only policy toward the horrendous civil wars in Central America should be on the economic development and negotiations, with perhaps a quarantine of Marxist Nicaragua. Do you believe that these answers would in any way solve the bitter conflicts there? Do you really believe that there is no need to resort to force at all? Are not these solutions to Central America's gnawing problems simply, again, too weak and too late?

FORMER VICE PRESIDENT MONDALE: I believe that the question oversimplifies the difficulties of what we must do in Central America. Our objectives ought to be to strengthen the democracies, to stop Communist and other extremist influences, and stabilize the community in that area.

To do that, we need a three-pronged attack. One is military assistance to our friends who are being pressured. Secondly, a strong and sophisticated economic aid program and human rights program that offers a better life and a sharper alternative to the alternative offered by the totalitarians who oppose us. And finally, a strong diplomatic effort that pursues the possibilities of peace in the area. That's one of the big disagreements that we have with the President — that they have not pursued the diplomatic opportunities, either within El Salvador or between the countries, and have lost time during which we might have been able to achieve a peace.

This brings up the whole question of what Presidential leadership is all about. I think the lesson in Central America — this recent embarrassment in Nicaragua, where we are giving instructions for hired assassins, hiring criminals, and the rest — all of this has strengthened our opponents. A President must not only assure that we're tough, but we must also be wise and smart in the exercise of that power.

We saw the same thing in Lebanon, where we spent a good deal of America's assets. But because the leadership of this Government did not pursue wise policies, we have been humiliated and our opponents are stronger. The bottom line of national strength is that the President must be in command. He must lead. And when a President doesn't know that submarine missiles are recallable, says that 70 percent of our strategic forces are conventional, discovers three years into his Administration that our arms control efforts have failed because he didn't know that most Soviet missiles were on land — these are things a President must know to command. A President is called the Commander in Chief. He is called that because he is supposed to be in charge of the facts and run our Government and strengthen our nation.

MS. GEYER: Mr. Mondale, if I could broaden the question just a little bit. Since World War II, every conflict that we as Americans have been involved with has been in nonconventional or traditional terms — military terms. The Central American wars are very much in the same pattern as China, as Lebanon, as Iran, as Cuba in the early days. Do you see any possibility that we are going to realize the change in warfare in our time or react to it in those terms?

MR. MONDALE: We absolutely must, which is why I responded to your first question the way I did. It's more — it's much more complex. You must understand the region, you must understand the politics of the area, you must provide a strong alternative, and you must show strength — and all at the same time. That's why I object to the covert action in Nicaragua. That's a classic example of a strategy that's embarrassed us, strengthened our opposition, and it undermined the moral authority of our people and our country in the region. Strength requires knowledge, command. We've seen, in the Nicaraguan example, a policy that has actually hurt us, strengthened our opposition, and undermined the moral authority of our country in that region.

MS. GEYER: Mr. President, in the last few months it has seemed more and more that your policies in Central America were beginning to work. Yet, just at this moment, we are confronted with the extraordinary story of a C.I.A. guerrilla manual for the anti-Sandinista Contras whom we are backing which advocates not only assassinations of Sandinistas, but the hiring of criminals to assassinate the guerrillas we are supporting in order to create martyrs. Is this not, in effect, our own state-supported terrorism?

PRESIDENT REAGAN: No, and I'm glad you asked that question, because I know it's on many people's minds. I have ordered an investigation. I know that the C.I.A. is already going forward with one. We have a gentleman down in Nicaragua who is on contract to the C.I.A., advising supposedly on military tactics of the Contras. And he drew up this manual. It was turned over to the Agency head in — of the C.I.A. in Nicaragua to be printed. And a number of pages were excised by that Agency head there — the man in charge — and he sent it on up here to C.I.A., where more pages were excised before it was printed. But some way or other, there were 12 of the original copies that got out down there and were not submitted for this printing process of the C.I.A. Now, those are the details as we have them. And as soon as we have an investigation and find out where any blame lies for the few that did not get excised or changed, we certainly are going to do something about that. We will take the proper action at the proper time.

I was very interested to hear about Central America and our process down there, and I thought for a moment that instead of a debate I was going to find Mr. Mondale in complete agreement with what we're doing. Because the plan that he has outlined is the one that we have been following for quite some time, including diplomatic processes throughout Central America and working closely with the Contadora Group. So I can only tell you, about the manual, that we're not in the habit of assigning guilt before there has been proper evidence produced and proof of that guilt. But if guilt is established — whoever is guilty — we will treat with that situation then, and they will be removed.

MS. GEYER: Well, Mr. President, you are implying, then, that the C.I.A. in Nicaragua is directing the Contras there? I would also like to ask whether having the C.I.A. investigate its own manual in such a sensitive area is not sort of like sending the fox into the chicken coop a second time?

MR. REAGAN: I'm afraid I misspoke when I said "a C.I.A. head in Nicaragua." There is not someone there directing all of this activity. There are, as you know, C.I.A. men stationed in other countries in the world, and certainly in Central America. And so it was a man down there in that area that this was delivered to, and he recognized that what was in that manual was in direct contravention of my own executive order in December of 1981 that we would have nothing to do with regard to political assassinations.

MR. NEWMAN: Mr. Mondale, your rebuttal.

MR. MONDALE: What is a President charged with doing when he takes his oath of office? He raises his right hand and takes an oath of office to take care to faithfully execute the laws of the land. The President can't know everything, but a President has to know those things that are essential to his leadership and the enforcement of our laws.

This manual, several thousands of which were produced, was distributed, ordering political assassinations, hiring of criminals, and other forms of terrorism. Some of it was excised, but the part dealing with political terrorism was continued. How can this happen? How can something this serious occur in an Administration and have a President of the United States, in a situation like this, say he didn't know? A President must know these things. I don't know which is worse — not knowing or knowing and not stopping it. And what about the mining of the harbors in Nicaragua, which violated international law? This has hurt this country, and a President is supposed to command.

MR. NEWMAN: Mr. President, your rebuttal.

MR. REAGAN: Yes. I have so many things there to respond to, I'm going to pick out something you said earlier. You've been all over the country repeating something that I will admit the press has also been repeating — that I believe that nuclear missiles could be fired and then called back. I never, ever conceived of such a thing. I never said any such thing. In a discussion of our strategic arms negotiations, I said the submarines carrying missiles and airplanes carrying missiles were more conventional type weapons, not as destabilizing as the land-based missiles, and that they were also weapons that ... or carriers, that if they were sent out and there was a change, you could call them back before they had launched their missiles. But I hope that from here on you will no longer be saying that particular thing, which is absolutely false. How anyone could think that any sane person would believe you could call back a nuclear missile, I think, is as ridiculous as the whole concept has been. So, thank you for giving me a chance to straighten the record. I'm sure that you appreciate that.

MR. NEWMAN: Mr. Kalb ... Mr. Kalb, your question to President Reagan.

[Soviet Union]

MR. MARVIN KALB, NBC News: Mr. President, you have often described the Soviet Union as a powerful, evil empire intent on world domination. But this year you have said, and I quote, "If they want to keep their Mickey Mouse system, that's O.K. with me." Which is it, Mr. President? Do you want to contain them within their present borders, and perhaps try to reestablish détente or what goes for détente, or do you really want to roll back their empire?

MR. REAGAN: I have said on a number of occasions exactly what I believe about the Soviet Union. I retract nothing that I have said. I believe that many of the things they have done are evil in any concept of morality that we have. But I also recognize that as the two great superpowers in the world, we have to live with each other. And I told Mr. Gromyko [Andrei Gromyko, Foreign Minister, U.S.S.R.] we don't like their system. They don't like ours. We're not going to change their system, and they sure better not try to change ours. But, between us, we can either destroy the world or we can save it. And I suggested that certainly it was to their common interest, along with ours, to avoid a conflict and to attempt to save the world and remove the nuclear weapons. And I think that, perhaps, we established a little better understanding.

I think that in dealing with the Soviet Union one has to be realistic. I know that Mr. Mondale in the past has made statements as if they were just people like ourselves, and if we were kind and good and did something nice, they would respond accordingly. And the result was unilateral disarmament. We canceled the B-1 under the previous Administration. What did we get for it? Nothing. The Soviet Union has been engaged in the biggest military buildup in the history of man at the same time that we tried the policy of unilateral disarmament — of weakness, if you will. And now we are putting up a defense of our own. And I've made it very plain to them: we seek no superiority. We simply are going to provide a deterrent so that it will be too costly for them if they are nursing any ideas of aggression against us.

Now, they claim they are not. And I made it plain to them, we're not. But this ... there's been no change in my attitude at all. I just thought, when I came into office, it was time that there was some realistic talk to and about the Soviet Union. And we did get their attention.

MR. KALB: Mr. President, perhaps the other side of the coin — a related question, sir. Since World War II, the vital interests of the United States have always been defined by treaty commitments and by Presidential proclamations. Aside from what is obvious — such as NATO, for example — which countries, which regions in the world do you regard as vital national interests of this country — meaning that you would send American troops to fight there if they were in danger?

MR. REAGAN: Ah, well, now you've added a hypothetical there at the end, Mr. Kalb, about that — where we would send troops in to fight. I am not going to make the decision as to what the tactics could be. But obviously, there are a number of areas in the world that are of importance to us. One is the Middle East. And that is of interest to the whole Western world and the industrialized nations, because of the great supply of energy on which so many depend there. The ... our neighbors here in America are vital to us. We're working right now and trying to be of help in southern Africa with regard to the independence of Namibia and the removal of the Cuban surrogates — the thousands of them — from Angola. So, I can say there are a great many interests. I believe that we have a great interest in the Pacific Basin. That is where I think the future of the world lies. But I am not going to pick out one and in advance hypothetically say, "Oh yes. We would send troops there." I don't want to send troops any place —

MR. NEWMAN: I'm sorry, Mr. President. Your time was up.

MR. KALB: Mr. Mondale, you have described the Soviet leaders as, and I'm quoting, "cynical, ruthless, and dangerous," suggesting an almost total lack of trust in them. In that case, what makes you think that the annual summit meetings with them that you've proposed will result in agreements that would satisfy the interests of this country?

MR. MONDALE: Because the only type of agreements to reach with the Soviet Union are the types that are specifically defined, so we know exactly what they must do, subject to full verification — which means we know every day whether they're living up to it, and follow-ups wherever we find suggestions that they're violating it, and the strongest possible terms. I have no illusions about the Soviet Union leadership or the nature of that state. They are a tough and a ruthless adversary, and we must be prepared to meet that challenge. And I would.

Where I part with the President is that, despite all of those differences, we must — as past Presidents before this one have done — meet on the common ground of survival. And that's where the president has opposed practically every arms control agreement by every President of both political parties since the bomb went off. And he now completes this term with no progress toward arms control at all, but with a very dangerous arms race under way instead. There are now over 2,000 more warheads pointed at us today than there were when he was sworn in. And that does not strengthen us. We must be very, very realistic in the nature of that leadership, but we must grind away and talk to find ways to reducing these differences, particularly where arms races are concerned and other danger-ous exercises of Soviet power.

There will be no unilateral disarmament under my Administration. I will keep this nation strong. I understand exactly what the Soviets are up to. But that, too, is a part of national strength. To do that, a President must know what is essential to command and to leadership and to strength. And that's where the President's failure to master, in my opinion, the essential elements of arms control has cost us dearly. These four years.... Three years into this Administration, he said he just discovered that most Soviet missiles are on land, and that's why his proposal didn't work. I invite the American people tomorrow ... because I will issue the statement quoting President Reagan. He said exactly what I said he said. He said that these missiles were less dangerous than ballistic missiles because you could fire them and you could recall them if you decide there had been a miscalculation.

MR. NEWMAN: I'm sorry, Mr. —

MR. MONDALE: A President must know those things.

[Eastern Europe]

MR. KALB: A related question, Mr. Mondale, on Eastern Europe: Do you accept the conventional diplomatic wisdom that Eastern Europe is a Soviet sphere of influence? And, if you do, what could a Mondale Administration realistically do to help the people of Eastern Europe achieve the human rights that were guaranteed to them as a result of the Helsinki Accords?

MR. MONDALE: I think the essential strategy of the United States ought not accept any Soviet control over Eastern Europe. We ought to deal with each of these countries separately. We ought to pursue strategies with each of them, economic and the rest, that help them pull away from their dependence upon the Soviet Union. Where the Soviet Union has acted irresponsibly, as they have in many of those countries — especially, recently, in Poland — I believe we ought to insist that Western credits extended to the Soviet Union bear the market rate. Make the Soviets pay for their irresponsibility. That is a very important objective — to make certain that we continue to look forward to progress toward greater independence by these nations, and work with each of them separately.

MR. NEWMAN: Mr. President, your rebuttal.

MR. REAGAN: Yes. I'm not going to continue trying to respond to these repetitions of the falsehoods that have already been stated here. But with regard to whether Mr. Mondale would be strong, as he said he would be, I know that he has a commercial out where he is appearing on the deck of the [U.S.S.] *Nimitz* and watching the F-14s take off, and that's an image of strength. Except that if he had had his way when the *Nimitz* was being planned, he would have been deep in the water out there, because there wouldn't have been any *Nimitz* to stand on. He was against it. He was against the F-14 fighter; he was against the M-1 tank; he was against the B-1 bomber; he wanted to cut the salary of all of the military; he wanted to bring home half of the American forces in Europe. And he has a record of weakness with regard to our national defense that is second to none. Indeed, he was on that side virtually throughout all his years in the Senate, and he opposed even President Carter when, toward the end of his term, President Carter wanted to increase the defense budget.

MR. NEWMAN: Mr. Mondale, your rebuttal.

MR. MONDALE: Mr. President, I accept your commitment to peace, but I want you to accept my commitment to a strong national defense. I have proposed a budget which would increase our nation's strength by . . . in real terms, by double that of the Soviet Union. I'll tell you where we disagree. It is true, over ten years ago, I voted to delay production of the F-14, and I'll tell you why. The plane wasn't flying supposed to . . . the way it was supposed to be. It was a waste of money. Your definition of national strength is to throw money at the Defense Department. My definition of national strength is to make certain that a dollar spent buys us a dollar's worth of defense. There is a big difference between the two of us. A President must manage that budget. I will keep us strong, but you'll not do that unless you command that budget and make certain we get the strength that we need. When you pay out $500 for a $5 hammer, you're not buying strength.

MR. NEWMAN: I would ask the audience not to applaud. All it does is take up time that we would like to devote to the debate. Mr. Kondracke, your question to Mr. Mondale.

[Use of Military Force]

MR. MORTON M. KONDRACKE, *The New Republic:* Mr. Mondale, in an address earlier this year, you said that before this country resorts to military force, and I'm quoting, "American interests should be sharply defined, publicly supported, Congressionally sanctioned, militarily feasible, internationally defensible, open to independent scrutiny, and alert to regional history." Now, aren't you setting up such a gauntlet of tests here that adversaries could easily suspect that as President you would never use force to protect American interests?

MR. MONDALE: No. As a matter of fact, I believe every one of those standards is essential to the exercise of power by this country. And we can see that in both Lebanon and in Central America. In Lebanon, this President exercised American power all right, but the management of it was such that our Marines were killed; we had to leave in humiliation; the Soviet Union became stronger; terrorists became emboldened. And it was because they did not think through how power should be exercised, did not have the American public with them on a plan that worked, that we ended up the way we did.

Similarly, in Central America, what we're doing in Nicaragua with this covert war — which the Congress, including many Republicans, have tried to stop — is finally end up with the public definition of American power that hurts us, where we get associated with political assassins and the rest. We have to decline, for the first time in modern history, jurisdiction of the World Court, because they will find us guilty of illegal actions.

And our enemies are strengthened from all of this. We need to be strong. We need to be prepared to use that strength. But we must understand that we are a democracy. We are a Government by the people, and when we move, it should be for very severe and extreme reasons that serve our national interest and end up with a stronger country behind us. It is only in that way that we can persevere.

MR. KONDRACKE: You've been quoted as saying that you might quarantine Nicaragua. I'd like to know what that means. Would you stop Soviet ships, as President Kennedy did in 1962, and wouldn't that be more dangerous than President Reagan's covert war?

MR. MONDALE: What I'm referring to there is the mutual self-defense provisions that exist in the Inter-American treaty, the so-called Rio pact, that permits the nations that are friends in that region to combine to take steps, diplomatic and otherwise, to prevent Nicaragua when she acts irresponsibly in asserting power in other parts outside of her border . . . to take those steps, whatever they might be, to stop it.

The Nicaraguans must know that it is the policy of our government that those . . . that that leadership must stay behind the boundaries of their nation, not interfere in other nations. And by working with all of the nations in the region, unlike the policies of this Administration — and unlike the President said, they have *not* supported negotiations in that region — we will be much stronger, because we will have the moral authority that goes with those efforts.

MR. KONDRACKE: President Reagan, you introduced U.S. forces into Lebanon as neutral peacekeepers, but then you made them combatants on the side of the Lebanese Government. Eventually, you were forced to withdraw them under fire, and now Syria, a Soviet ally, is dominant in the country. Doesn't Lebanon represent a major failure on the part of your Administration and raise serious questions about your capacity as a foreign policy strategist and as Commander in Chief?

MR. REAGAN: No, Morton, I don't agree to all of those things. First of all, when we and our allies — the Italians, the French, and the United Kingdom — went into Lebanon, we went in there at the request of what was left of the Lebanese Government, to be a stabilizing force while they tried to establish a government. But the first — pardon me — the first time we went in, we went in at their request, because the war was going on right in Beirut between Israel and the P.L.O. terrorists. Israel could not be blamed for that. Those terrorists had been violating their northern border consistently, and Israel chased them all the way to there. Then, we went in with a multinational force to help remove — and did remove — more than 13,000 of those terrorists from Lebanon. We departed, and then the Government of Lebanon asked us back in as a stabilizing force while they established a government and sought to get the foreign forces all the way out of Lebanon, and that they could then take care of their own borders.

And we were succeeding. We were there for the better part of a year. Our position happened to be at the airport. Oh, there were occasional snipings and sometimes some artillery fire. But we did not engage in conflict that was out of line with our mission. I will never send troops anywhere on a mission of that kind without telling them that if somebody shoots at them, they can darn well shoot back. And this is what we did. We never initiated any kind of action. We defended ourselves there. But we were succeeding to the point that the Lebanese Government had been organized. If you will remember, there were the meetings in Geneva in which they began to meet with the hostile factional forces and try to put together some kind of a peace plan.

We were succeeding, and that was why the terrorist acts began. There are forces there — and that includes Syria, in my mind — who don't want us to succeed, who don't want that kind of a peace with a dominant Lebanon, dominant over its own territory. And so the terrorist acts began, and led to the one great tragedy when they were killed in that suicide bombing of the building. Then the multilateral force withdrew for only one reason: we withdrew because we were no longer able to carry out the mission for which we had been sent in. But we went in in the interest of peace, and to keep Israel and Syria from getting into the sixth war between them. And I have no apologies for our going on a peace mission.

[Lebanon and Terrorism]

MR. KONDRACKE: Mr. President, four years ago you criticized President Carter for ignoring ample warnings that our diplomats in Iran might be taken hostage. Haven't you done exactly the same thing in Lebanon, not once, but three times, with 300 Americans not hostages but dead. And you vowed swift retaliation against terrorists, but doesn't our lack of response suggest that you're just bluffing?

MR. REAGAN: Morton, no. I think there's a great difference between the Government of Iran threatening our diplomatic personnel — and there is a Government that you can see and can put your hand on. In the terrorist situation, there are terrorist factions all over.... In a recent 30-day period, 37 terrorist acts in 20 countries have been committed. The most recent has been the one in Brighton [England]. In dealing with terrorists, yes, we want to retaliate, but only if we can put our finger on the people responsible and not endanger the lives of innocent civilians there in the various communities and in the city of Beirut where these terrorists are operating. I have just signed legislation to add to our ability to deal, along with our allies, with this terrorist problem. And it's going to take all the nations together, just as when we banded together we pretty much resolved the whole problem of skyjackings some time ago. Well, the red light went on. I could have gone on forever.

MR. NEWMAN: Mr. Mondale, your rebuttal.

MR. MONDALE: Groucho Marx said, "Who do you believe — me or your own eyes?" And what we have in Lebanon is something that the American people have seen. The Joint Chiefs urged the President not to put our troops in that barracks because they were undefensible. They urged ... they went to him five days before they were killed and said, "Please take them out of there." The Secretary of State admitted that this morning. He did not do so. The report following the explosion of the barracks disclosed that we had not taken any of the steps that we should have taken. That was the second time. Then the Embassy was blown up a few weeks ago, and once again, none of the steps that should have been taken were taken. And we were warned five days before that explosives were on their way, and they weren't taken.

The terrorists have won each time. The President told the terrorists he was going to retaliate. He didn't. They called their bluff. And the bottom line is, the United States left in humiliation and our enemies are stronger.

MR. NEWMAN: Mr. President, your rebuttal.

MR. REAGAN: Yes. First of all, Mr. Mondale should know that the President of the United States did not order the Marines into that barracks. That was a command decision made by the commanders on the spot and based with what they thought was best for the men there. That is one.

On the other things that you've just said about the terrorists, I'm tempted to ask you what you would do. These are unidentified people, and, after the bomb goes off, they're blown to bits because they are suicidal individuals who think that they're going to go to paradise if they perpetrate such an act and lose their life in doing it. We are going to ... as I say, we're busy trying to find the centers where these operations stem from, and retaliation will be taken. But we are not going to simply kill some people to say, "Oh, look — we got even." We want to know, when we retaliate, that we're retaliating with those who are responsible for the terrorist acts. And terrorist acts are such that our own United States Capitol in Washington has been bombed twice.

MR. NEWMAN: Mr. Trewhitt, your question to President Reagan.

[Age and Missiles]

MR. HENRY L. TREWHITT, *The Baltimore Sun:* Mr. President, I want to raise an issue that I think has been lurking out there for two or three weeks, and cast it specifically in national security terms. You already are the oldest President in history, and some of your staff say you were tired after your most recent encounter with Mister ... Mr. Mondale. I recall, yet, that President Kennedy, who had to go for days on end with very little sleep during the Cuba missile crisis. . . . Is there any doubt in your mind that you would be able to function in such circumstances?

MR. REAGAN: Not at all, Mr. Trewhitt. And I want you to know that also, I will not make age an issue of this campaign. I am not going to exploit, for political purposes, my opponent's youth and inexperience.

If I still have time, I might add, Mr. Trewhitt, I might add that it was Seneca or it was Cicero — I don't know which — that said, "If it was not for the elders correcting the mistakes of the young, there would be no state."

MR. TREWHITT: Mr. President, I'd like to head for the fence and try to catch that one before it goes over, but ... but I'll go on to another question.

The ... you and Mr. Mondale have already disagreed about what you had to say about recalling submarine-launched missiles. There's another ... a similar issue out there that relates to your ... it is said, at least, that you were unaware that the Soviet retaliatory power was based on land-based missiles. First, is that correct? Secondly, if it is correct, have you informed yourself in the meantime? And third, is it even necessary for the President to be so intimately involved in strategic details?

MR. REAGAN: Yes. This had to do with our disarmament talks. And the whole controversy about land missiles came up because we thought that the strategic nuclear weapons, the most destabilizing, are the land-based. You put your thumb on a button and somebody blows up twenty minutes later. So, we thought that it would be simpler to negotiate first with those, and then we made it plain, a second phase — take up the submarine-launched ... the air ... the airborne missiles. The Soviet Union — to our surprise, and not just mine — made it plain when we brought this up that they placed, they thought, a greater reliance on the land-based missiles, and therefore they wanted to take up all three. And we agreed; we said, "All right, if that's what you want to do." But it was a surprise to us because they outnumbered us 64 to 36 in submarines and 20 percent more bombers capable of carrying nuclear missiles than we had.

So, why should we believe that they had placed that much more reliance on land-based? But even after we gave in and said, "All right, let's discuss it all," they walked away from the table. We didn't.

MR. TREWHITT: Mr. Mondale, I'm going to hang in there. Should the President's age and stamina be an issue in the political campaign?

MR. MONDALE: No, and I have not made it an issue, nor should it be. What's at issue here is the President's application of his authority to understand what a President must know to lead this nation, secure our defense, and make the decisions and the judgments that are necessary.

A minute ago, the President quoted Cicero, I believe. I want to quote somebody a little closer to home, Harry Truman. He said, "The buck stops here." We just heard the President's answer for the problems at the barracks in Lebanon, where 241 Marines were killed. What happened? First, the Joint Chiefs of Staff went to the President, said, "Don't put those troops there." They did it. And then, five days before the troops were killed, they went back to the President through the Secretary of Defense and said, "Please, Mr. President, take those troops out of there because we can't defend them." They didn't do it. And we know what's ... what happened. After that, once again our Embassy was exploded. This is the fourth time this has happened — an identical attack in the same region, despite warnings, even public warnings from the terrorists. Who's in charge? Who's handling this matter? That's my main point.

Now, on arms control, we're completing four years. This is the first Administration since the bomb went off that made no progress. We have an arms race under way instead. A President has to lead his Government or it won't be done. Different people with different views fight with each other. For three and a half years, this Administration avoided arms control, resisted tabling arms control proposals that had any ... hope of agreeing, rebuked their negotiator in 1981 when he came close to an agreement, at least in principle, on medium-range weapons. And we have this arms race under way.

And a recent book that just came out by the ... perhaps the nation's most respected author in this field, Strobe Talbott, called "The Deadly Gambits," concludes that this President has failed to master the essential details needed to command and lead us, both in terms of security and terms of arms control. That's why they call the President the Commander in Chief. Good intentions, I grant, but it takes more than that. You must be tough and smart.

MR. TREWHITT: This question of leadership keeps arising in different forms in this discussion already. And the President, Mr. Mondale, has called you "whining and vacillating" — among the more charitable phrases, "weak," I believe. It is ... it is a question of leadership, and he has made the point that you have not repudiated some of the semidiplomatic activity of the Reverend Jackson, particularly in Central America. Do you ... did you approve of his diplomatic activity, and are you prepared to repudiate him now?

MR. MONDALE: I ... I read his statement the other day. I don't admire Fidel Castro at all, and I've said that. Che Guevara was a contemptible figure in civilization's history. I know the Cuban state as a police state, and all my life I've worked in a way that demonstrates that. But Jesse Jackson is an independent person. I don't control him. And let's talk about people we do control. In the last debate, the Vice President of the United States said that I said the Marines had died shamefully and died in shame in Lebanon. I demanded an apology from Vice President Bush because I had instead honored these young men, grieved for their families, and think they were wonderful Americans that honored us all. What does the President have to say about taking responsibility for a Vice President who won't apologize for something like that?

MR. NEWMAN: Mr. President, your rebuttal.

MR. REAGAN: Yes. I know it'll come as a surprise to Mr. Mondale, but I am in charge. And, as a matter of fact, we haven't avoided arms control talks with the Soviet Union. Very early in my Administration I proposed — and I think something that had never been proposed by any previous Administration — I proposed a total elimination of intermediate-range missiles, where the Soviets had better than a ten ... and still have better than a ten-to-one advantage over the Allies in Europe. When they protested that and suggested a smaller number, perhaps, I went along with that. The so-called negotiation that you said I walked out on was the so-called "walk in the wood" between one of our representatives and one of the Soviet Union, and it wasn't me that turned it down; the Soviet Union disavowed it.

MR. NEWMAN: Mr. Mondale, your rebuttal.

MR. MONDALE: Now, there are two distinguished authors in arms control in this country. There are many others, but two that I want to cite tonight. One is Strobe Talbott in his classic book, "The Deadly Gambits." The other is John Newhouse, who's one of the most distinguished arms control specialists in our country. Both said that this Administration turned down the "walk in the woods" agreement first, and that would have been a perfect agreement from the standpoint of the United States and Europe and our security. When Mr. Nitze [Paul Nitze, Chairman, Intermediate Range Nuclear Forces Negotiations], a good negotiator, returned, he was rebuked and his boss was fired.

This is the kind of leadership that we've had in this Administration in the most deadly issue of our times. Now we have a runaway arms race. All they've got to show for four years in U.S.-Soviet relations is one meeting in the last weeks of an Administration and nothing before. They're tough negotiators, but all previous Presidents have made progress. This one has not.

[Illegal Immigration]

MR. NEWMAN: Miss Geyer, your question to Mr. Mondale.

MS. GEYER: Mr. Mondale, many analysts are now saying that actually our number one foreign policy problem today is one that remains almost totally unrecognized: massive illegal immigration from economically collapsing countries. They are saying that it is the only real territorial threat to the American nation-state. You yourself said in the 1970s that we had a, quote, "hemorrhage on our borders," unquote. Yet today you have backed off any immigration reform, such as the balanced and highly-crafted Simpson-Mazzoli bill. Why? What would you do instead today, if anything?

MR. MONDALE: This is a very serious problem in our country, and it has to be dealt with. I object to that part of the Simpson-Mazzoli bill which I think is very unfair and would prove to be so. That is the part that requires employers to determine the citizenship of an employee before they're hired. I am convinced that the result of this would be that people who are Hispanic, people who have different languages or speak with an accent, would find it difficult to be employed. I think that's wrong. We've never had citizenship tests in our country before, and I don't think we should have a citizenship card today. That is counterproductive.

I do support the other aspects of the Simpson-Mazzoli bill that strengthen enforcement at the border, strengthen other ways of dealing with undocumented workers in this . . . in this difficult area, and dealing with the problem of settling people who have lived here for many, many years and do not have an established status. I have further strongly recommended that this Administration do something it has not done, and that is to strengthen enforcement at the border, strengthen the officials in this Government that deal with undocumented workers, and to do so in a way that's responsible and within the Constitution of the United States. We need an answer to this problem, but it must be an American answer that is consistent with justice and due process. Everyone in this room, practically, here tonight, is an immigrant. We came here loving this nation, serving it, and it has served all of our most bountiful dreams. And one of those dreams is justice. And if we need a measure, and I will support a measure that brings about those objectives but voids that one aspect that I think is very serious.

The second part is to maintain and improve our relations with our friends to the south. We cannot solve this problem all on our own. And that's why the failure of this Administration to deal in effective and good-faith way with Mexico, with Costa Rica, with the other nations, in trying to find a peaceful settlement to the dispute in Central America has undermined our capacity to effectively to deal diplomatic in this . . . diplomatically in this area, as well.

MS. GEYER: Sir, people as well-balanced and just as Father Theodore Hesburgh at Notre Dame [University of Notre Dame], who headed the Select Commission on Immigration, have pointed out repeatedly that there will be no immigration reform without employer sanctions, because it would be an unbalanced bill and there would be simply no way to reinforce it.

However, putting that aside for the moment, your critics have also said repeatedly that you have not gone along with the bill, or with any immigration reform, because of the Hispanic groups or Hispanic leadership groups, who actually do not represent what the Hispanic Americans want — because polls show that they overwhelmingly want some kind of immigration reform. Can you say, or . . . how can you justify your position on this? And how do you respond to the criticism that this is another, or that this is an example of your flip-flopping and giving in to special interest groups at the expense of the American nation?

MR. MONDALE: I think you're right that the polls show that the majority of Hispanics want that bill. So, I'm not doing it for political reasons. I'm doing it because all my life I've fought for a system of justice in this country, a system in which every American has a chance to achieve the fullness in life without discrimination. This bill imposes upon employers the responsibility of determining whether somebody who applies for a job is an American or not. And, just inevitably, they're going to be reluctant to hire Hispanics or people with a different accent.

If I were dealing with politics here, the polls show the American people want this. I am for reform in this area, for tough enforcement at the border, and for many other aspects of the Simpson-Mazzoli bill. But all my life, I've fought for a fair nation, and despite the politics of it, I stand where I stand and I think I'm right. And before this fight is over, we're going to come up with a better bill, a more effective bill that does not undermine the liberties of our people.

MS. GEYER: Mr. President, you, too, have said that our borders are out of control. Yet, this fall, you allowed the Simpson-Mazzoli bill — which would at least have minimally protected our borders and the rights of citizenship — because of a relatively unimportant issue of reimbursement to the states for legalized aliens. Given that, may I ask what priority can we expect you to give this forgotten national security element? How sincere are you in your efforts to control, in effect, the nation-state that is the United States?

MR. REAGAN: Georgie Anne, we, believe me, supported the Simpson-Mazzoli bill strongly, and the bill that came out of the Senate. However, there were things added in the House side that we felt made it less of a good bill — as a matter of fact, made it a bad bill. And in conference, we stayed with them in conference all the way to where even Senator Simpson [Alan Kooi Simpson, Republican, Wyoming] did not want the bill in the manner in which it would come out of the conference committee. There were a number of things in there that weakened that bill. I can't go into detail about them here. But it is true, our borders are out of control. It is also true that this has been a situation on our borders back through a number of Administrations. And I supported this bill. I believe in the idea of amnesty for those who have put down roots and who have lived here, even though some time back they . . . they may have entered illegally.

With regard to the employer sanctions, this . . . we must have that, not only to ensure that we can identify the illegal aliens, but also, while some keep protesting about what it would do to employers, there is another employer that we shouldn't be so concerned about. And these are employers, down through the years, who have encouraged the illegal entry into this country because they then hire these individuals, and hire them at starvation wages, and with none of the benefits that we think are normal and natural for workers in our country. And the individuals can't complain because of their illegal status. We don't think that those people should be allowed to continue operating free. And this was why the provisions that we had in with regard to sanctions and so forth. And I'm going to do everything I can — and all of us in the Administration are — to join in again, when Congress is back at it, to get an immigration bill that will give us, once again, control of our borders.

And with regard to friendship below the border and with the countries down there — yes, no Administration that I know has established the relationship that we have with our Latin friends. But as long as they have an economy that leaves so many people in dire poverty and unemployment, they are going to seek that employment across our borders. And we work with those other countries.

[Population Explosion]

MS. GEYER: Mr. President, the experts also say that the situation today is terribly different, quantitatively, qualitatively different from what it has been in the past because of the gigantic population growth. For instance, Mexico's population will go from about 60 million today to 120 million at the turn of the century. Many of these people will be coming into the United States not as citizens, but as illegal workers.

You have repeatedly said, recently, that you believe that Armageddon, the destruction of the world, may be imminent in our times. Do you ever feel that we are in for an Armageddon, or a . . . a situation, a time of anarchy regarding the population explosion in the world?

MR. REAGAN: No, as a matter of fact, the population explosion . . . and if you will look at the actual figures, has been vastly exaggerated . . . overexaggerated. As a matter of fact, there are some pretty scientific and solid figures about how much space there still is in the world and how many more people we can have. It's almost like going back to the Malthusian theory, when even then they were saying that everyone would starve, with the limited population they had then. But the problem of population growth is one here with regard to our immigration, and we have been the safety valve, whether we wanted to or not, with the illegal entry here, in Mexico, where their population is increasing and they don't have an economy that can absorb them and provide the jobs. And this is what we're trying to work out, not only to protect our own borders, but have some kind of fairness and recognition of that problem.

MR. NEWMAN: Mr. Mondale, your rebuttal.

MR. MONDALE: One of the biggest problems today is that the countries to our south are so desperately poor that these people, who will almost lose their lives if they don't come north, come north despite all the risks. And if we're going to find a permanent, fundamental answer to this, it goes to American economic and trade policies to permit these nations to have a chance to get on their own two feet and to get prosperity so that they can have jobs for themselves and their people.

And that's why this enormous national debt, engineered by this Administration, is harming these countries and fueling this immigration. These high interest rates, real rates that have doubled under this Administration, have had the same effect on Mexico and so on. And the cost of repaying those debts is so enormous that it results in massive unemployment, hardship, and heartache. And that drives our friends to the north . . . to the south up into our region. And we need to end those deficits, as well.

MR. NEWMAN: Mr. President, your rebuttal.

MR. REAGAN: Well, my rebuttal is, I've heard the national debt blamed for a lot of things, but not for illegal immigration across our border, and it has nothing to do with it. But with regard to these high interest rates too, at least give us the recognition of the fact that when you left office, Mr. Mondale, they were 21.5 [percent], the prime rate. It's now 12.25 [percent], and I predict it will be coming down a little more shortly. So, we're trying to undo some of the things that your Administration did.

MR. NEWMAN: Mister . . . no applause, please. Mr. Kalb, your question to President Reagan.

[A Nuclear Armageddon?]

MR. KALB: Mr. President, I'd like to pick up this Armageddon theme. You've been quoted as saying that you do believe, deep down, that we are heading for some kind of biblical Armageddon. Your Pentagon and your Secretary of Defense have plans for the United States to fight and prevail in a nuclear war. Do you feel that we are now heading, perhaps, for some kind of nuclear Armageddon, and do you feel that this country and the world could survive that kind of calamity?

MR. REAGAN: Mr. Kalb, I think what has been hailed as something I'm supposedly, as President, discussing as principle is the result of just some philosophical discussions with people who are interested in the same things, and that is the prophecies down through the years, the biblical prophecies of what would portend the coming of Armageddon and so forth, and the fact that a number of theologians, for the last decade or more, have believed that this was true, that the prophecies are coming together to portend that. But no one knows whether Armageddon . . . those prophecies mean that Armageddon is a thousand years away or day after tomorrow. So, I have never seriously warned and said, "We must plan according to Armageddon."

Now, with regard to having to say whether we would try to survive in the event of a nuclear war, of course we would. But let me also point out that to several parliaments around the world, in Europe and in Asia, I have made a statement in . . . to each one of them, and I'll repeat it here: A nuclear war cannot be won and must never be fought. And that is why we are maintaining a deterrent and trying to achieve a deterrent capacity to where no one would believe that they could start such a war and escape with limited damage. But the deterrent — and that's what it is for — is also what led me to propose what is now being called the "Star Wars" concept: to propose that we research to see if there isn't a defensive weapon that could defend against incoming missiles. And if such a defense could be found, wouldn't it be far more humanitarian to say that now we can defend against a nuclear war by destroying missiles instead of slaughtering millions of people?

['Star Wars' Technology]

MR. KALB: Mr. President, when you made that proposal, the so-called "Star Wars" proposal, you said, if I am not mistaken, that you would share this very supersophisticated technology with the Soviet Union. After all of the distrust over the years, sir, that you have expressed towards the Soviet Union, do you really expect anyone to take seriously that offer — that you would share the best of America's technology in this weapons area with our principal adversary?

MR. REAGAN: Why not? What if we did? And I hope we can. We're still researching. What if we come up with a weapon that renders those

893

missiles obsolete? There has never been a weapon invented in the history of man that has not led to a defensive, a counterweapon. But suppose we came up with that? Now, some people have said, "Ah, that would make a war imminent, because they would think that we could now launch a first strike, because we could defend against the enemy." But why not do what I have offered to do and ask the Soviet Union to do? Say, "Look, here's what we can do. We'll even give it to you. Now, will you sit down with us and once and for all get rid, all of us, of these nuclear weapons, and free mankind from that threat?" I think that would be the greatest use of a defensive weapon.

MR. KALB: Mr. Mondale, you have been very sharply critical of the President's strategic defense initiative. And yet, what is wrong with a major effort by this country to try to use its best technology to knock out as many incoming nuclear warheads as possible?

MR. MONDALE: First of all, let me sharply disagree with the President on sharing the most advanced, the most dangerous, the most important technology in America with the Soviet Union. We have had for many years, understandably, a system of restraints on high technology, because the Soviets are behind us. And any research or development along the "Star Wars" schemes would inevitably involve our most advanced computers, most advanced engineering, and the thought that we would share this with the Soviet Union is, in my opinion, a total nonstarter. I would not let the Soviet Union get their hands on it at all.

Now what's wrong with "Star Wars?" There's nothing wrong with the theory of it. If we could develop a principle that would say both sides could fire all their missiles and no one would get hurt. I suppose it's a good idea. But the fact of it is, we're so far away from research that even comes close to that, that the director of engineering research in the Defense Department said to get there, we would have to solve eight problems, each of which are more difficult than the atomic bomb and the Manhattan Project. It would cost something like a trillion dollars to test and deploy weapons.

The second thing is, this all assumes that the Soviets wouldn't respond in kind. And they always do. We don't get behind, they won't get behind, and that's been the tragic story of the arms race. We have more at stake in space satellites than they do. If we could stop right now the testing and the deployment of these space weapons — and the President's proposals go clear beyond research — if it was just research, we wouldn't have any argument, because maybe someday somebody will think of something. But to commit this nation to a build-up of antisatellite and space weapons at this time, and their crude state, would bring about an arms race that's very dangerous indeed.

One final point — the most dangerous aspect of this proposal is, for the first time, we would delegate to computers the decision as to whether to start a war. That's dead wrong. There wouldn't be time for a President to decide. It would be decided by these remote computers; it might be an oil fire, it might be a jet exhaust, the computer might decide it's a missile, and off we go. Why don't we stop this madness now and draw a line and keep the heavens free from war?

[Nuclear Freeze]

MR. KALB: Mr. Mondale, in this general area, sir, of arms control, President Carter's National Security Advisor, Zbig Brzezinski [Zbigniew Brzezinski] said, "A nuclear freeze is a hoax." Yet, the basis of your arms proposals, as I understand them, is a mutual and verifiable freeze on existing weapons systems. In your view, which specific weapons systems could be subject to a mutual and verifiable freeze, and which could not?

MR. MONDALE: Every system that is verifiable should be placed on the table for negotiations for an agreement. I would not agree to any negotiations or any agreement that involved conduct on the part of the Soviet Union that we couldn't verify every day. I would not agree to any agreement in which the United States' security interest was not fully recognized and supported. That's ... that's why we say "mutual and verifiable" freezes.

Now, why do I support the freeze? Because this ever-rising arms race madness makes both nations less secure. It's more difficult to defend this nation. It is putting a hair trigger on nuclear war. This Administration, by going into the "Star Wars" system, is going to add a dangerous new escalations. We have to be tough on the Soviet Union. But I think the American people —

MR. NEWMAN: Time is up, Mr. Mondale.

MR. MONDALE: — and the people of the Soviet Union want it to stop.

MR. NEWMAN: President Reagan, your rebuttal.

MR. REAGAN: Yes. My rebuttal, once again, is that this invention that has just been created here of how I would go about the rolling over for the Soviet Union ... no, Mr. Mondale. My idea would be, with that defensive weapon, that we would sit down with them and then say, "Now, are you willing to join us? Here's what we can...." Give them, give them a demonstration. And then say, "Here's what we can do." Now, if you're willing to join us in getting rid of all the nuclear weapons in the world, then we'll give you this one so that we would both know that no one can cheat; that we've both got something that if anyone tries to cheat.... But when you keep "Star-Warring" it — I never suggested where the weapons should be or what kind. I'm not a scientist. I said, and the Joint Chiefs of Staff agreed with me, that it was time for us to turn our research ability to seeing if we could not find this kind of a defensive weapon. And suddenly somebody says, "Oh, it's got to be up there, and it's 'Star Wars,'" and so forth. I don't know what it would be. But if we can come up with one, I think the world will be better off.

MR. NEWMAN: Mr. Mondale, your rebuttal.

MR. MONDALE: Well, that's what a President's supposed to know — where those weapons are going to be. If they're space weapons, I assume they'll be in space. If they're antisatellite weapons, I assume they're going to be an aid ... armed against antisatellites.

Now, this is the most dangerous technology that we possess. The Soviets try to spy on us, steal this stuff. And to give them technology of this kind, I disagree with. You haven't just accepted research, Mr. President. You've set up a strategic defense initiative, an agency. You're beginning to test. You're talking about deploying. You're asking for a budget of some $30 billion for this purpose. This is an arms escalation, and we will be better off — far better off — if we stop right now, because we have more to lose in space than they do. If someday somebody comes along with an answer, that's something else. But that there would be an answer in our lifetime is unimaginable. Why do we start things that we know the Soviets will match and make us all less secure? That's what the President is for.

MR. NEWMAN: Mr. Kondracke, your question to Mr. Mondale.

MR. KONDRACKE: Mr. Mondale, you say that with respect to the Soviet Union, you want to negotiate a mutual nuclear freeze. Yet you would unilaterally give up the MX missile and the B-1 bomber before the talks have even begun. And you have announced, in advance, that reaching an agreement with the Soviets is the most important thing in the world to you. Aren't you giving away half the store before you even sit down to talk?

MR. MONDALE: No. As a matter of fact, we have a vast range of technology and weaponry right now that provides all the bargaining chips that we need. And I support the air-launched cruise missile, ground-launched cruise missile, the Pershing missile, the Trident submarine, the D-5 submarine, the Stealth technology, the Midgetman — we have a whole range of technology. Why I disagree with the MX is that it's a sitting duck. It'll draw an attack. It puts a hair trigger ... and it is a dangerous, destabilizing weapon. And the B-1 is similarly to be opposed, because for 15 years the Soviet Union has been preparing to meet the B-1. The Secretary of Defense himself said it would be a suicide mission if it were built.

Instead, I want to build the Midgetman, which is mobile and thus less vulnerable, contributing to stability, and a weapon that will give us security and contribute to an incentive for arms control. That's why I'm for Stealth technology: to build the Stealth bomber, which I've supported for years, that can penetrate the Soviet air defense system without any hope that they can perceive where it is because their radar system is frustrated. In other words, a President has to make choices. This makes us stronger.

The final point is, that we can use this money that we save on these weapons to spend on things that we really need. Our conventional strength in Europe is under strength. We need to strengthen that in order to assure our Western allies of our presence there — a strong defense — but also to diminish and reduce the likelihood of a commencement of a war and the use of nuclear weapons. It's in this way, by making wise choices, that we are stronger; we enhance the chances of arms control. Every President till this one has been able to do it. And this nation — the world — is more dangerous as a result.

MR. KONDRACKE: I want to follow up on Mr. Kalb's question. It seems to me on the question of verifiability that you do have some problems with the extent of the freeze. It seems to me, for example, that testing would be very difficult to verify because the Soviets encode their telemetry; research would be impossible to verify; numbers of warheads would be impossible to verify by satellite, except with on-site inspection; and production of any weapon would be impossible to verify. Now, in view of that, what is going to be frozen?

MR. MONDALE: I will not agree to any arms control agreement, including a freeze, that's not verifiable. Let's take your warhead principle. The warhead principle — there've been counting rules for years. Whenever a weapon is tested we count the number of warheads on it, and whenever that warhead is used, we count that number warheads, whether they have that number or less on it or not. These are standard rules. I will not agree to any production restrictions or agreements unless we have the ability to verify those agreements. I don't trust the Russians. I believe that every agreement we reach must be verifiable, and I will not agree to anything that we cannot tell every day. In other words, we've got to be tough. But in order to stop this arms madness we've got to push ahead with tough negotiations that are verifiable, so that we know the Soviets are agreeing and living up to their agreement.

[Negotiating with Friends]

MR. KONDRACKE: Mr. President, I want to ask you a question about negotiating with friends. You severely criticized President Carter for helping to undermine two friendly dictators who got into trouble with their own people: the Shah of Iran and President Somoza of Nicaragua. Now there are other such leaders heading for trouble, including President Pinochet [Augusto Pinochet Ugarte] of Chile and President Marcos [Ferdinand E. Marcos] of the Philippines. What should you do, and what can you do, to prevent the Philippines from becoming another Nicaragua?

MR. REAGAN: Morton, I did criticize the President because of our undercutting of what was a stalwart ally: the Shah of Iran. But I am not at all convinced that he was that far out of line with his people, or that they wanted that to happen. The Shah had done our bidding and carried our load in the Middle East for quite some time, and I did think that it was a blot on our record that we let him down. Have things gotten better? The Shah, whatever he might have done, was building low-cost housing, had taken land away from the mullahs, and was distributing it to the peasants so they could be landowners — things of that kind. But we turned it over to a maniacal fanatic who has slaughtered thousands and thousands of people, calling it executions.

The matter of Somoza — no. I never defended Somoza. As a matter of fact, the previous Administration stood by him. So did I. Not that I could have done anything in my position at that time. But for this revolution to take place ... and the promise of the revolution was democracy, human rights, free labor unions, free press. And then, just as Castro had done in Cuba, the Sandinistas ousted the other parties to the revolution. Many of them are now the Contras. They exiled some, they jailed some, they murdered some, and they installed a Marxist-Leninist totalitarian government. And what I have to say about this is: many times — and this has to do with the Philippines also.... I know there are things there in the Philippines that do not look good to us from the standpoint, right now, of democratic rights. But what is the alternative? It is a large Communist movement to take over the Philippines. They have been our friend for ... since their inception as a nation. And I think that we've had enough of a record of letting, under the guise of revolution, someone that we thought was a little more right than we would be, letting that person go and then winding up with totalitarianism, pure and simple, as the alternative. And I think that we're better off, for example, with the Philippines, of trying to retain our friendship and help them right the wrongs we see, rather than throwing them to the wolves and then facing a Communist power in the Pacific.

[Philippines]

MR. KONDRACKE: Mr. President, since the United States has two strategically important bases in the Philippines, would the overthrow of President Marcos constitute a threat to vital American interests? And, if so, what would you do about it?

MR. REAGAN: Well, as I say, we have to look at what an overthrow there would mean and what the government would be that would follow. And there is every evidence, every indication, that that government would be hostile to the United States. And that would be a severe blow to the ... to our abilities there in the Pacific.

MR. KONDRACKE: And what would you do about it?

MR. NEWMAN: Sorry. Sorry, you've asked the follow-up question. Mr. Mondale, your rebuttal.

MR. MONDALE: Perhaps in no area do we disagree more than this Administration's policies on human rights. I went to the Philippines as Vice President, pressed for human rights, called for the release of Aquino, *and* made progress that had been stalled on both the Subic [Bay] and Clark Airfield bases.

What explains this Administration cozying up to the Argentine dictators after they took over? Fortunately, a democracy took over. But this nation was embarrassed by this current Administration's adoption of their policies. What happens in South Africa where, for example, the Nobel Prize winner two days ago said this Administration is seen as working with the oppressive government of that reg ... of South Africa. That hurts this nation. We need to stand for human rights. We need to make it clear we're for human liberty. National security and human rights must go together. But this Administration, time and time again, has lost its way in this field.

MR. NEWMAN: President Reagan, your rebuttal.

MR. REAGAN: Well, the invasion of Afghanistan didn't take place on our watch. I have described what has happened in Iran. And we weren't here then, either. I don't think that our record of human rights can be assailed. I think that we have observed ourselves and have done our best to see that human rights are extended throughout the world. Mr. Mondale has recently announced a plan of his to get the democracies together and to work with the whole world to turn to democracy. And I was glad to hear him say that, because that's what we've been doing ever since I announced to the British Parliament that I thought we should do this.

And human rights are not advanced when, at the same time, you then stand back and say, "Whoops, we didn't know the gun was loaded." And you have another totalitarian power on your hands.

MR. NEWMAN: In this segment, because of the pressure of time, there will be no rebuttals and there will be no follow-up questions. Mr. Trewhitt, your question to President Reagan.

MR. TREWHITT: One question to each candidate?

MR. NEWMAN: One question to each candidate.

[Nuclear Strategy]

MR. TREWHITT: Mr. President, can I take you back to something you said earlier? And if I am misquoting you, please correct me. But I understood you to say that if the development of space military technology was successful you might give the Soviets a demonstration and say, "Here it is," which sounds to me as if you might be trying to gain the sort of advantage that would enable you to dictate terms, and which, I would then suggest to you, might mean scrapping a generation of nuclear strategy called mutual deterrence, in which we, in effect, hold each other hostage. Is that your intention?

MR. REAGAN: Well, I can't say that I have round-tabled that and sat down with the Chiefs of Staff. But I have said that it seems to me that this could be a logical step in what is my ultimate goal, my ultimate dream: and that is the elimination of nuclear weapons in the world. And it seems to me that this could be an adjunct, or certainly a great assisting agent, in getting that done. I am not going to roll over, as Mr. Mondale suggests, and give them something that could turn around and be used against us. But I think it's a very interesting proposal — to see if we can find, first of all, something that renders those weapons obsolete, incapable of their mission. But Mr. Mondale seems to approve MAD. MAD is mutual assured destruction, meaning if you use nuclear weapons on us, the only thing we have to keep you from doing it is that we'll kill as many people of yours as you'll kill of ours. I think that to do everything we can to find, as I say, something that would destroy weapons and not humans, is a great step forward in human rights.

MR. TREWHITT: Mr. Mondale, could I ask you to address the question of nuclear strategy? Then let's. . . . The formal document is very arcane, but I'm going to ask you to deal with it anyway. Do you believe in MAD —

mutual assured destruction, mutual deterrence — as it has been practiced for the last generation?

MR. MONDALE: I believe in a sensible arms control approach that brings down these weapons to manageable levels. I would like to see their elimination. And in the meantime, we have to be strong enough to make certain that the Soviet Union never tempts us. Now, here we have to decide between generalized objectives and reality. The President says he wants to eliminate or reduce the number of nuclear weapons. But, in fact, these last four years have seen more weapons built, a wider and more vigorous arms race than in human history. He says he wants a system that will make nuclear arms — wars — safe, so nobody's going to get hurt. Well, maybe someday somebody can dream of that. Why threaten our space satellites upon which we depend? Why pursue a strategy that would delegate to computers the question of starting a war? A President, to defend this country and to get arms control, must master what's going on. We all ... I accept his objective of ... and his dreams. We all do. But the hard reality is that we must know what we are doing and pursue those objectives that are possible in our time. He's opposed every effort of every President to do so. And the four years of his Administration he's failed to do so. And if you want a tough President who uses that strength to get arms control and draws the line in the heavens, vote for Walter Mondale.

MR. NEWMAN: Please — I must, I must again ask the audience not to applaud, not to cheer, not to demonstrate its feelings in any way.

We've arrived at the point in the debate now where we call for closing statements. You have the full four minutes, each of you. Mr. Mondale, will you go first?

[Mondale's Closing Statement]

MR. MONDALE: I want to thank The League of Women Voters, the good citizens of Kansas City, and President Reagan for agreeing to debate this evening. This evening we talked about national strength. I believe we need to be strong. And I will keep us strong. By strength ... I think strength must also require wisdom and smarts in its exercise. That's key to the strength of our nation. A President must know the essential facts — essential to command. But a President must also have a vision of where this nation should go. Tonight, as Americans, you have a choice. And you're entitled to know where we would take this country if you decide to elect us.

As President, I would press for long-term, vigorous economic growth. That's why I want to get these debts down and these interest rates down, restore America's exports, help rural America, which is suffering so much, and bring the jobs back here for our children. I want this next generation to be the best educated in American history, to invest in the human mind and science again so we're out front. I want this nation to protect its air, its water, its land, and its public health. America is not temporary. We're forever. And, as Americans, our generation should protect this wonderful land for our children. I want a nation of fairness, where no one is denied the fullness of life or discriminated against, and we deal compassionately with those in our midst who are in trouble. And, above all, I want a nation that's strong. Since we debated two weeks ago, the United States and the Soviet Union have built 100 more warheads, enough to kill millions of Americans and millions of Soviet citizens. This doesn't strengthen us. This weakens the chances of civilization to survive.

I remember the night before I became Vice President. I was given a briefing and told that any time, night or day, I might be called upon to make the most fateful decision on earth: whether to fire these atomic weapons that could destroy the human species. That lesson tells us two things. One, pick a President that you know will know — if that tragic moment ever comes — what he must know. Because there'd be no time for staffing, committees, or advisors. A President must know right then. But, above all, pick a President who will fight to avoid the day when that god-awful decision ever needs to be made. And that's why this election is so terribly important. America and Americans decide not just what's happening in this country.

We are the strongest and most powerful free society on earth. When you make that judgment, you are deciding not only the future of our nation. In a very profound respect, you're providing the future . . . deciding the future of the world. We need to move on. It's time for America to find new leadership. Please join me in this cause to move confidently and with a sense of assurance and command, to build the blessed future of our nation.

MR. NEWMAN: President Reagan, your summation please.

[Reagan's Closing Statement]

MR. REAGAN: Yes. My thanks to The League of Women Voters, to the panelists, the moderator, and to the people of Kansas City for their warm hospitality and greeting.

I think the American people tonight have much to be grateful for: an economic recovery that has become expansion, freedom, and most of all, that we are at peace. I am grateful for the chance to reaffirm my commitment to reduce nuclear weapons and, one day, to eliminate them entirely. The question before you comes down to this: Do you want to see America return to the policies of weakness of the last four years, or do we want to go forward, marching together, as a nation of strength, and that's going to continue to be strong?

The. . . . We shouldn't be dwelling on the past, or even the present. The meaning of this election is the future, and whether we're going to grow and provide the jobs and the opportunities for all Americans, and that they need.

Several years ago, I was given an assignment to write a letter. It was to go into a time capsule and would be read in a hundred years, when that time capsule was opened. I remember driving down the California coast one day. My mind was full of what I was going to put in that letter about the problems and the issues that confront us in our time and what we did about them.

But I couldn't completely neglect the beauty around me: the Pacific out there on one side of the highway, shining in the sunlight, the mountains of the coast range rising on the other side. And I found myself wondering what it would be like for someone ... wondering if someone, a hundred years from now, would be driving down that highway, and if they would see the same thing.

With that thought, I realized what a job I had with that letter. I would be writing a letter to people who know everything there is to know about us. We know nothing about them. They would know all about our problems. They would know how we solved them and whether our solution was beneficial to them down through the years or whether it hurt them. They would also know that we lived in a world with terrible weapons, nuclear weapons of terrible destructive power aimed at each other, capable of crossing the ocean in a matter of minutes and destroying civilization as we knew it. And then, I thought to myself, "What ... what are they going to say about us? What are those people a hundred years from now going to think?" They will know whether we used those weapons or not.

Well, what they will say about us a hundred years from now depends on how we keep our rendezvous with destiny. Will we do the things that we know must be done, and know that one day, down in history a hundred years, or perhaps before, someone will say, "Thank God for those people back in the 1980s — for preserving our freedom, for saving for us this blessed planet called Earth with all its grandeur and its beauty."

You know, I am grateful to all of you for giving me the opportunity to serve you for these four years, and I seek reelection because I want more than anything else to try to complete the new beginning that we charted four years ago. George Bush — who I think is one of the finest Vice Presidents this country has ever had — George Bush and I have criss-crossed the country, and we've had, in these last few months, a wonderful experience. We have met young America. We have met your sons and daughters.

MR. NEWMAN: Mr. President, I am obliged to cut you off there under the rules of the debate. I'm sorry.

MR. REAGAN: All right. I was just going to.... All right.

MR. NEWMAN: Perhaps I ... perhaps I should point out that the rules under which I did that were agreed upon by the two campaigns, with The League, as you know, sir.

MR. REAGAN: I know. I know. Yes.

MR. NEWMAN: Thank you, Mr. President. Thank you, Mr. Mondale. Our thanks also to the panel. Finally, to our audience, we thank you, and The League of Women Voters asks me to say to you: Don't forget to vote on November 6.

C I A MANUAL

October 14, 1984

The Associated Press disclosed October 14 that the Central Intelligence Agency (CIA) had approved in 1983 a manual giving instructions on the military and political means of overthrowing the Sandinista government of Nicaragua. Entitled "Psychological Operations in Guerrilla Warfare," the 90-page document explains how to kidnap officials, blow up public buildings, and blackmail citizens. Much of the manual describes how to meet the practical needs of a guerrilla army, such as maintaining remote mountain camps, but its major focus was on the use of violence as a propaganda tool.

As translated by the Congressional Research Service, the manual states that "It is possible to neutralize carefully selected and planned targets, such as court judges, ... police and state Security officials, CDS [Sandinista Defense Committee] chiefs, etc. For psychological purposes, it is necessary to take extreme precautions, and it is absolutely necessary to gather together the population affected, so that they will be present, take part in the act, and formulate accusations against the oppressor." Among the things that should be considered in choosing a target to "neutralize," the manual said, were "the degree of violence necessary to carry out the change," the "degree of violence acceptable to the population affected," and the "degree of violence possible without causing damage or danger to other individuals in the area of the target."

The disclosure that the CIA had approved a manual that appeared to advocate the killing of Nicaraguan officials by U.S.-backed guerrillas prompted a political furor just weeks before the 1984 presidential

election and renewed controversy over whether the intelligence organiza-
tion was following the rules prohibiting assassinations. The rules were
promulgated in 1976 after a lengthy and controversial congressional
investigation into CIA abuses of power, in which it was disclosed that the
agency had plotted the deaths of two leaders, Premier Fidel Castro of
Cuba and Patrice Lumumba of the Congo (Zaire). The rules were
updated by President Ronald Reagan in 1981 by an order that read, "No
person employed by or acting on behalf of the United States government
shall engage in, or conspire to engage in assassination."

The controversy also brought into question the aims of the Reagan
administration in Nicaragua. Believing that the left-wing Sandinista
government was aiding leftist guerrillas in El Salvador, Reagan insisted
early in his first term that the arms flow be halted. Covert U.S. assistance
to the Nicaraguan anti-Sandinista rebels, known as the contras, began in
1981. Congress approved the covert aid but put restrictions on the funds,
prohibiting the use of "military equipment, training or advice or other
support for military activities, to any group or individual, not part of a
country's armed forces, for the purpose of overthrowing the government
of Nicaragua or provoking a military exchange between Nicaragua and
Honduras."

On October 10, 1984, Congress voted to slash Reagan's requested covert
aid to the contras by half and said that none of the $14 million could be
given before February 28, 1985, when the Nicaraguan situation would be
reviewed.

Controversy Over Instructions

In the wake of the Associated Press disclosure, controversy swirled
around the use of the word, "neutralize," which some said was a
euphemism for assassinate. After an October 21 briefing by the CIA,
Senate Intelligence Committee member Sam Nunn, D-Ga., said the use of
the word "could lead one to the conclusion that the president's policy [of
prohibiting assassinations] was being or could possibly be breached."
However, Wyoming Republican Malcolm Wallop, another member of the
committee, said the statement on neutralizing, when read within the
context of the entire manual, advocated "restraint" and not necessarily
assassinations. "As a whole, the manual is a code of conduct for which the
United States ought not to be ashamed," he said.

CIA director William J. Casey endorsed Wallop's statement in a letter
delivered October 31 to the Senate Intelligence Committee. He quoted at
length from the manual to demonstrate that its "thrust and purpose" was
to show the guerrillas how to deal humanely with civilians and Sandinis-
tas. President Reagan called Casey's explanation "very forthcoming." He
told reporters there was "nothing in that manual that talked assassina-

tion at all" and said the reference to "neutralizing" officials meant removing them from office.

Questions also arose over how much the manual had been edited. Reagan said that it had been written by "a gentleman down in Nicaragua who is on contract to the CIA advising supposedly on the military tactics of the contras." It was later reviewed by a CIA official in Central America "who recognized that what was in that manual was in direct contravention of my own executive order," and several pages were deleted from the document. The manual was then forwarded to CIA headquarters in Virginia, where more pages were excised. "But some way or another," said Reagan , "there were 12 of the original copies that got out down there and were not submitted for this printing process of the CIA."

However, Nunn, after being briefed by CIA officials, said that the controversial section on neutralization was included in the several thousand copies of the manual that were printed. The administration's explanation also was contradicted by Edgar Chamorro, a senior official in the largest Nicaraguan rebel group, the Nicaraguan Democratic Force. Chamorro, who said he was in charge of the manual's publication, told The New York Times that "there was only one draft" and that the manual used in Nicaragua included all the material that was eventually made public.

A Political Issue

The manual became an intense political issue in the closing weeks of the campaign as Democratic presidential candidate Walter F. Mondale and other Democrats cited it as evidence of Reagan's intention to overthrow the Sandinista government. They said the manual demonstrated the lengths to which the administration was willing to go to battle the Nicaraguan regime. Mondale raised the issue in his second televised debate with Reagan, saying that "giving instructions for hired assassins, hiring criminals and the rest — all of this has strengthened our opponents." (Debates, p. 845) Michael D. Barnes, D-Md., chairman of the House Western Hemisphere Affairs Subcommittee, called the manual "an outrage and most certainly a violation of the rules governing the CIA."

Edward P. Boland, D-Mass., chairman of the House Intelligence Committee, said the manual "should never have been produced by any element of the United States government. It espouses the doctrine of Lenin, not Jefferson. . . . I am appalled by the image of the United States that this manual portrays. . . . Something such as this manual points to the wisdom of congressional action to cut off funding for the secret war. Unfortunately, the cutoff comes too late to repair the damage in this instance."

Investigations

On November 10, the White House announced that two government investigations had found that there had been no violation of law in the preparation of the manual but that there may have been "lapses in judgment" by some lower-level CIA officials. The statement said both investigations had showed that "despite portions which could be misinterpreted, the manual had worthy purposes — instilling in Nicaraguan freedom fighters the knowledge of how to promote understanding of their goals among the people and counseling them on appropriate behavior in dealing with civilians." According to the Associated Press, three CIA officials received letters of reprimand, two officials were suspended from duty temporarily and a contract employee known by the pseudonym John Kirkpatrick was "allowed" to resign. Several of the disciplined officials objected, contending they were "scapegoats" to protect senior officials.

Conducting its own investigation, the House Intelligence Committee concluded December 5 that the manual reflected "negligence" but no legal intent to violate the law. In a press release prepared with bipartisan support, the committee added that "the incident of the manual illustrates once again to a majority of the committee that the CIA did not have adequate command and control of the entire Nicaraguan covert action." The release followed a two-hour closed hearing with Director Casey, who acknowledged to the committee that the agency had been negligent in the affair.

Following are excerpts from "Psychological Operations in Guerrilla Warfare," *disclosed by the Associated Press October 14, 1984, and translated by the Congressional Research Service:*

Preface

Guerrilla warfare is essentially a political war. Therefore, its area of operations exceeds the territorial limits of conventional warfare, to penetrate the political entity itself: the "political animal" that Aristotle defined.

In effect, the human being should be considered the priority objective in a political war. And conceived as the military target of guerrilla war, the human being has his most critical point in his mind. Once his mind has been reached, the "political animal" has been defeated, without necessarily receiving bullets.

Guerrilla warfare is born and grows in the political environment; in the constant combat to dominate that area of political mentality that is inherent to all human beings and which collectively constitutes the "environment" in which guerrilla warfare moves, and which is where precisely its victory or failure is defined.

This conception of guerrilla warfare as political war turns Psychological Operations into the decisive factor of the results. The target, then, is the minds of the population, all the population: our troops, the enemy troops and the civilian population.

This book is a manual for the training of guerrillas in psychological operations, and its application to the concerte case of the Christian and democratic crusade being waged in Nicaragua by the Freedom Commandos.

Welcome!

Introduction

1 — GENERALITIES

The purpose of this book is to introduce the guerrilla student to the psychological operations techniques that will be of immediate and practical value to him in guerrilla warfare. This section is introductory and general; subsequent sections will cover each point set forth here in more detail.

The nature of the environment of guerrilla warfare does not permit sophisticated psychological operations, and it becomes necessary for the chiefs of groups, chiefs of detachments and squadron leaders to have the ability to carry out, with minimal instructions from the higher levels, psychological action operations with the contacts that are thoroughly aware of the situation, i.e. the foundations.

2 — COMBATANT, PROPAGANDIST GUERRILLAS

In order to obtain the maximum results from the psychological operations in guerrilla warfare, every combatant should be as highly motivated to carry out propaganda face to face as he is as a combatant. This means that the individual political awareness of the guerrilla of the reason for his struggle will be as acute as his ability to fight.

Such a political awareness and motivation is obtained through the dynamic of groups and self-criticism, as a standard method of instruction for the guerrilla training and operations. Group discussions raise the spirit and improve the unity of thought of the guerrilla squads and exercise social pressure on the weak members to carry out a better role in future training or in combative action. Self-criticism is in terms of one's contribution or defects in his contribution to the cause, to the movement, the struggle, etc.; and gives a positive individual commitment to the mission of the group.

The desired result is a guerrilla who can persuasively justify his actions when he comes into contact with any member of the People of Nicaragua, and especially with himself and his fellow guerrillas in dealing with the vicissitudes of guerrilla warfare. This means that every guerrilla will be persuasive in his face-to-face communication — propagandist-combatant — in his contact with the people; he should be able to give 5 to 10 logical reasons why, for example, a peasant should give him cloth, needle and thread to mend his clothes. When the guerrilla behaves in this manner, enemy propaganda will never succeed in making him an enemy in the eyes of the people. It also means that hunger, cold, fatigue and insecurity will have a meaning, psychologically, in the cause of the struggle due to his constant orientation.

3 — ARMED PROPAGANDA

Armed propaganda includes every act carried out, and the good impression that this armed force causes will result in positive attitudes in the population toward that force; and it does not include forced indoctrination. Armed propaganda improves the behavior of the population toward them, and it is not achieved by force.

This means that a guerrilla armed unit in a rural town will not give the impression that arms are their strength over the peasants, but rather that they are the strength of the peasants against the Sandinista government of repression. This is achieved through a close identification with the people, as follows: hanging up weapons and working together with them on their crops, in construction, in the harvesting of grains, in fishing, etc. explanations to young men about basic weapons, e.g. giving them an unloaded weapon and letting them touch it, see it, etc., describing in a rudimentary manner its operation; describing with simple slogans how weapons will serve the people to win their freedom; demanding the requests by the people for hospitals and education, reducing taxes, etc.

All these acts have as their goal the creation of an identification of the people with the weapons and the guerrillas who carry them, so that the population feels that the weapons are, indirectly, their weapon to protect them and help them in the struggle against a regime of oppression. Implicit terror always accompanies weapons, since the people are internally "aware" that they can be used against them, but as long as explicit coersion [sic] is avoided, positive attitudes can be achieved with respect to the presence of armed guerrillas within the population.

4 — ARMED PROPAGANDA TEAMS

Armed Propaganda Teams (EPA) are formed through a careful selection of persuasive and highly motivated guerrillas who move about within the population, encouraging the people to support the guerrillas and put up resistance against the enemy. It combines a high degree of political awareness and the 'armed' propaganda ability of the guerrillas toward a planned, programmed, and controlled effort.

The careful selection of the staff, based on their persuasiveness in informal discussions and their ability in combat, is more important than their degree of education or the training program. The tactics of the Armed Propaganda Teams are carried out covertly, and should be parallel to the tactical effort in guerrilla warfare. The knowledge of the psychology of the population is primary for the Armed Propaganda Teams, but much more intelligence data will be obtained from an EPA program in the area of operations.

5 — DEVELOPMENT AND CONTROL OF THE "FRONT" ORGANIZATIONS

The development and control of "front" (or facade) organizations is carried out through subjective internal control at group meetings of "inside cadres," and the calculations of the time for the fusion of these combined efforts to be applied to the masses.

Established citizens — doctors, lawyers, businessmen, teachers, etc. — will be recruited initially as "Social Crusaders" in typically "innocuous" movements in the area of operations. When their "involvement" with the clandestine organization is revealed to them, this supplies the psychological pressure to use them as "inside cadres" in groups to which they already belong or of which they can be members.

Then they will receive instruction in techniques of persuasion over control of target groups to support our democratic revolution, through a gradual and skillful process. A cell control system isolates individuals from one another, and at the appropriate moment, their influence is used for the fusion of groups in a united national front.

6 — CONTROL OF MEETINGS AND MASS ASSEMBLIES

The control of mass meetings in support of guerrilla warfare is carried out internally through a covert commando element, bodyguards, messengers, shock forces (initiators of incidents), placard carriers (also used for making signals), shouters of slogans, everything under the control of the outside commando element.

When the cadres are placed or recruited in organizations such as labor unions, youth groups, agrarian organizations or professional associations, they will begin to manipulate the objectives of the groups. The psychological apparatus of our movement through inside cadres prepares a mental attitude which at the crucial moment, can be turned into a fury of justified violence.

Through a small group of guerrillas infiltrated within the masses this can be carried out; they will have the mission of agitating by giving the impression that there are many of them and that they have a large popular backing. Using the tactics of a force of 200-300 agitators, a demonstration can be created in which 10,000-20,000 persons take part.

7 — SUPPORT OF CONTACTS WITH
THEIR ROOTS IN REALITY

The support of local contacts who are familiar with the deep reality is achieved through the exploitation of the social and political weaknesses of the target society, with propagandist-combatant guerrillas, armed propaganda, armed propaganda teams, cover organizations and mass meetings.

The combatant-propagandist guerrilla is the result of a continuous program of indoctrination and motivation. They will have the mission of showing the people how great and fair our movement is in the eyes of all Nicaraguans and the world. Identifying themselves with our people, they will increase the sympathy towards our movement, which will result in greater support of the population for the freedom commandos, taking away support for the regime in power.

Armed propaganda will extend this identification process of the people with the Christian guerrillas, providing converging points against the Sandinista regime.

The Armed Propaganda Teams provide a several-stage program of persuasive planning in guerrilla warfare in all areas of the country. Also, these teams are the "eyes and ears" of our movement.

The development and control of the cover organizations in guerrilla warfare will give our movement the ability to create a "whiplash" effect within the population, when the order for fusion is given. When the infiltration and internal subjective control have been developed in a manner parallel to other guerrilla activities, a *commandante* of ours will literally be able to shape up the Sandinista structure, and replace it.

The mass assemblies and meetings are the culmination of a wide base support among the population and it comes about in the later phrases [*sic*] of the operation. This is the moment in which the overthrow can be achieved and our revolution can become an open one, requiring the close collaboration of the entire population of the country, and of contacts with their roots in reality.

The tactical effort in guerrilla warfare is directed at the weaknesses of the enemy and at destroying their military resistance capacity and should be parallel to a psychological effort to weaken and destroy their socio-political capacity at the same time. In guerrilla warfare, more than in any other type of military effort, the psychological activities should be simultaneous with the military ones, in order to achieve the objectives desired.

II Combatant-Propagandist Guerrilla

1 — GENERALITIES

The objective of this section is to familiarize the guerrilla with the techniques of psychological operations, which maximizes [*sic*] the social psychological effect of a guerrilla movement, converting the guerrilla into a propagandist, in addition to being a combatant. The nature of the environment in guerrilla warfare does not permit sophisticated facilities for psychological operations, so that use should be made of the effective face-to-face persuasion of each guerrilla.

2 — POLITICAL AWARENESS

The individual political awareness of the guerrilla, the reason for his struggle, will be as important as his ability in combat. This political awareness and motivation will be achieved:

— By improving the combat potential of the guerrilla by improving his motivation for fighting.

— By the guerrilla recognizing himself as a vital tie between the democratic guerrillas and the people, whose support is essential for the subsistence of both.

— By fostering the support of the population for the national insurgence through the support for the guerrillas of the locale, which provides a psychological basis in the population for politics after the victory has been achieved.

— By developing trust in the guerrillas and in the population, for the reconstruction of a local and national government.

— By promoting the value of participation by the guerrillas and the people in the civic affairs of the insurrection and in the national programs.

— By developing in each guerrilla the ability of persuasion face-to-face, at the local level, to win the support of the population, which is essential for success in guerrilla warfare. . . .

III Armed Propaganda

1 — GENERALITIES

Frequently a misunderstanding exists on "armed propaganda," that this tactic is a compulsion of the people with arms. In reality, it does not include compulsion, but the guerrilla should know well the principles and methods of this tactic. The objective of this section is to give the guerrilla student an understanding of the armed propaganda that should be used, and that will be able to be applied in guerrilla warfare.

2 — CLOSE IDENTIFICATION WITH THE PEOPLE

Armed propaganda includes all acts carried out by an armed force, whose results improve the attitude of the people toward this force, and it does not include forced indoctrination. This is carried out by a close identification with the people at any occasion. For example:

—Putting aside weapons and working side by side with the peasants in the countryside: building, fishing, repairing roofs, transporting water, etc.

— When working with the people, the guerrillas can use slogans such as "many hands doing small things, but doing them together."

—Participating in the tasks of the people, they can establish a strong tie between them and the guerrillas and at the same time a popular support for our movement is generated.

During the patrols and other operations around or in the midst of villages, each guerrilla should be respectful and courteous with the people. In addition he should move with care and always be well prepared to fight, if necessary. But he should not always see all the people as enemies, with suspicions or hostility. Even in war, it is possible to smile, laugh or greet people. Truly, the cause of our revolutionary base, the reason why we are struggling, is our people. We must be respectful to them on all occasions that present themselves.

In places and situations wherever possible, e.g. when they are resting during the march, the guerrillas can explain the operation of weapons to the youths and young men. They can show them an unloaded rifle so that they will learn to load and unload it; their use, and aiming at imaginary targets since they are potential recruits for our forces.

The guerrillas should always be prepared with simple slogans in order to explain to the people, whether in an intentional form or by chance, the reason for the weapons.

"The weapons will be for winning freedom; they are for you."

"With weapons we can impose demands such as hospitals, schools, better roads, and social services for the people, for you."

"Our weapons are, in truth, the weapons of the people, yours."

"With weapons we can change the Sandino-Communist regime and return to the people a true democracy so that we will all have economic opportunities."

All of this should be designed to create an identification of the people with the weapons and the guerrillas who carry them. Finally, we should make the people feel that we are thinking of them and that the weapons are the people's, in order to help them and protect them from a Communist, totalitarian, imperialist regime, indifferent to the needs of the population.

3 — IMPLICIT AND EXPLICIT TERROR

A guerrilla armed force always involves implicit terror because the population, without saying it aloud, feels terror that the weapons may be used against them. However, if the terror does not become explicit, positive results can be expected.

In a revolution, the individual lives under a constant threat of physical damage. If the government police cannot put an end to the guerrilla activities, the population will lose confidence in the government, which has the inherent mission of guaranteeing the safety of citizens. However, the guerrillas should be careful not to become an explicit terror, because this would result in a loss of popular support.

In the words of a leader of the HUK guerrilla movement of the Philippine Islands:

> "The population is always impressed by weapons, not by the terror that they cause, but rather by a sensation of strength/force. We must appear before the people, giving them support with our weapons; that will give them the message of the struggle."

This is then, in few words, the essence of armed propaganda.

An armed guerrilla force can occupy an entire town or small city which is neutral or relatively passive in the conflict. In order to conduct the armed propaganda in an effective manner, the following should be carried out simultaneously:

— Destroy the military or police installations and remove the survivors to a "public place."

— Cut all outside lines of communication: cables, radio, messengers.

— Set up ambushes, in order to delay the reinforcements in all the possible entry routes.

— Kidnap all officials or agents of the Sandinista government and replace them in "public places" with military or civilian persons of trust to our movement; in addition, carry out the following:

— Establish a public tribunal that depends on the guerrillas and cover the town or city in order to gather the population for this event.

— Shame, ridicule and humiliate the "personal symbols" of the government of repression in the presence of the people and foster popular participation through guerrillas within the multitude, shouting slogans and jeers.

— Reduce the influence of individuals in tune with the regime, pointing out their weaknesses and taking them out of the town, without damaging them publicly.

— Mix the guerrillas within the population and show very good conduct by all members of the column, practicing the following:

— Any article taken will be paid for with cash;

— The hospitality offered by the people will be accepted and this opportunity will be exploited in order to carry out face-to-face persuasion about the struggle.

— Courtesy visits should be made to the prominent persons and those with prestige in the place, such as doctors, priests, teachers, etc.

— The guerrillas should instruct the population that with the end of the operative, and when the Sandinista repressive forces interrogate them, they may reveal EVERYTHING about the military operation carried out. For example, the type of weapons they use, how many men arrived, from what direction they came and in what direction they left, in short, EVERYTHING.

— In addition, indicate to the population that at meetings or in private discussions they can give the names of the Sandinista informants, who will be removed together with the other officials of the government of repression.

— When a meeting is held, conclude it with a speech by one of the leaders of guerrilla political cadres (the most dynamic), which includes explicit references to:

— The fact that the "enemies of the people" — the officials or Sandinista agents, must not be mistreated in spite of their criminal acts, although the guerrilla force may have suffered casualties, and that this is done due to the generosity of the Christian guerrillas.

— Give a declaration of gratitude for the "hospitality" of the population, as well as let them know that the risks that they will run when the Sandinistas return are greatly appreciated.

— The fact that the Sandinista regime, although it exploits the people with taxes, control of money, grains and all aspects of public life through associations, which they are forced to become part of, will not be able to resist the attacks of our guerrilla forces.

— Make the promise to the people that you will return to ensure that the "leeches" of the Sandinista regime of repression will not be able to hinder our guerrillas from integrating in the population.

— A statement repeated to the population to the effect that they can reveal everything about this visit of our commandos, because we are not afraid of anything or anyone, neither the Soviets nor the Cubans. Emphasize that we are Nicaraguans, that we are fighting for the freedom of Nicaragua and to establish a very Nicaraguan government.

4 — GUERRILLA WEAPONS ARE THE STRENGTH OF THE PEOPLE OVER AN ILLEGAL GOVERNMENT

The armed propaganda in populated areas does not give the impression that weapons are the power of the guerrillas over the people, but rather that the weapons are the strength of the people against a regime of repression. Whenever it is necessary to use armed force in an occupation or visit to a town or village, guerrillas should emphasize making sure that they:

— Explain to the population that in the first place this is being done to protect them, the people, and not themselves.

— Admit frankly and publicly that this is an "act of the democratic guerrilla movement," with appropriate explanations.

— That this action, although it is not desirable, is necessary because the final objective of the insurrection is a free and democratic society, where acts of force are not necessary.

— The force of weapons is a necessity caused by the oppressive system, and will cease to exist when the "forces of justice" of our movement assume control.

If, for example, it should be necessary for one of the advanced posts to have to fire on a citizen who was trying to leave the town or city in which the guerrillas are carrying out armed propaganda or political proselitism, the following is recommended:

— Explain that if that citizen had managed to escape, he would have alerted the enemy that is near the town or city, and they would carry out acts of reprisal such as rapes, pillage, destruction, captures, etc., in this way terrorizing the inhabitants of the place for having given attention and hospitalities to the guerrillas of the town.

— If a guerrilla fires at an individual, make the town see that he was an enemy of the people, and that they shot him because the guerrillas recognized as their first duty the protection of citizens.

— The commando tried to detain the informant without firing because he, like all Christian guerrillas, espouses nonviolence. Having fired at the Sandinista informant, although it is against his own will, was necessary to prevent the repression of the Sandinista government against innocent people.

— Make the population see that it was the repressive system of the regime that was the cause of this situation, what really killed the informer, and that the weapon fired was one recovered in combat against the Sandinista regime.

— Make the population see that if the Sandinista regime ends the repression, the corruption backed by foreign powers, etc., the freedom commandos would not have had [sic] to brandish arms against brother Nicaraguans, which goes against our Christian sentiments. If the informant hadn't tried to escape he would be enjoying life together with the rest of the population, because he would not have tried to inform the enemy. This death would have been avoided, if justice and freedom existed in Nicaragua, which is exactly the objective of the democratic guerrilla.

5 — SELECTIVE USE OF VIOLENCE FOR PROPAGANDISTIC EFFECTS

It is possible to neutralize carefully selected and planned targets, such as court judges, *mesta* judges, police and State Security officials, CDS chiefs, etc. For psychological purposes it is necessary to take extreme precautions, and it is absolutely necessary to gather together the population affected, so that they will be present, take part in the act, and formulate accusations against the oppressor.

The target or person should be chosen on the basis of:

— The spontaneous hostility that the majority of the population feels toward the target.

— Use rejection or potential hatred by the majority of the population affected toward the target, stirring up the population and making them see all the negative and hostile actions of the individual against the people.

— If the majority of the people give their support or backing to the target or subject, do not try to change these sentiments through provocation.

— Relative difficulty of controlling the person who will replace the target.

The person who will replace the target should be chosen carefully, based on:

— Degree of violence necessary to carry out the change.

— Degree of violence acceptable to the population affected.

— Degree of violence possible without causing damage or danger to other individuals in the area of the target.

— Degree of reprisal predictable by the enemy on the population affected or other individuals in the area of the target.

The mission to replace the individual should be followed by:

— Extensive explanation within the population affected of the reason why it was necessary for the good of the people.

— Explain that Sandinista retaliation is unjust, indiscriminate, and above all, a justification for the execution of this mission.

— Carefully test the reaction of the people toward the mission, as well as control this reaction, making sure that the population's reaction is beneficial towards the Freedom Commandos.

6 — CONCLUSIONS

Armed propaganda includes all acts executed and the impact achieved by an armed force, which as a result produces positive attitudes in the population toward this force, and it does not include forced indoctrination. However, armed propaganda is the most effective available instrument of a guerrilla force....

CHERNENKO INTERVIEW

October 16, 1984

Konstantin Chernenko, president of the Soviet Union, granted an interview with a Western reporter October 16, eight months after he assumed leadership following the death of Yuri Andropov. (Andropov death, p. 145) Agreeing to the interview, the Soviet leader demonstrated his interest in renewing a dialogue with the United States. In contrast to the hard-line approach taken by Foreign Minister Andrei Gromyko in his address to the United Nations General Assembly on September 27, Chernenko's manner was characterized by the Washington Post *reporter, Dusko Doder, as warm and his tone as conciliatory. (U.N. address, p. 811)*

Chernenko reiterated the four issues raised by Gromyko before the United Nations that the Soviets considered vital in the resumption of arms-control talks between the two nations: a freeze on nuclear weapons buildup and an eventual reduction and elimination of weapons already deployed; a pledge not to strike first with nuclear force; a ban on the militarization of outer space; and ratification of the test-ban treaties of 1974 and 1976. Chernenko claimed that the Soviet Union had taken steps in all four areas, and that a U.S. commitment in any one of them could be an opportunity for dialogue between the two countries. As did Gromyko, Chernenko emphasized the Soviet desire for "practical deeds," not rhetoric, from the American side.

Discussions with the Soviet Union broke down in Geneva in 1983 when the United States deployed nuclear missiles in Western Europe. Chernenko did not mention the removal of these missiles as a condition for a resumption of arms-control negotiations, but he returned to the same four points raised by Gromyko.

Circumstances of Interview

Chernenko agreed to respond in writing to questions submitted six days in advance by the Washington Post *reporter. Contrary to the Soviet disinclination to meet with the Western press, Chernenko sent for the reporter, offered written responses, and allowed a 20-minute interview as well. Doder described the encounter as "genial" and said the Soviet leader looked fit and relaxed.*

Soviet-American relations during the administration of Ronald Reagan had been characterized by extremely harsh words and deeds from both sides. Gromyko, in his U.N. address, had blamed the United States in strong terms for world tensions. Reagan, in turn, had often denounced the Soviet Union's "evil" intentions, although his U.N. speech in September had taken a conciliatory tone. Throughout his first term, Reagan had made the rearming of America a top priority and had gone ahead with deployment of nuclear missiles in Western Europe, over the objection of some European groups. Reagan also had proposed the development of anti-satellite weapons. The Soviets had added to their arsenal of missiles in Eastern Europe and, a few days before the Chernenko interview, had begun deploying long-range cruise missiles on strategic bombers and submarines.

Chernenko's Washington Post *interview was seen as a gesture toward détente. Following this initial contact with the Western press, Chernenko answered written questions by Marvin Kalb, an NBC correspondent. In Washington, the Soviet Embassy held a reception honoring the English publication of a collection of Chernenko's speeches, and cultural exchanges between the U.S. and the Soviet Union were being arranged.*

Shultz-Gromyko Meeting

Perhaps the most significant event in Soviet-American relations in 1984 was the announcement on November 23 in both Washington and Moscow that Secretary of State George Shultz and Gromyko would meet in Geneva in January 1985 to begin negotiations toward an arms control agreement. The possibility of a high-level meeting had been discussed since early fall, following a summer of disagreement about an agenda.

The Soviets' top priority had been the banning of militarization of outer space, while the United States had wanted to hold "umbrella talks" covering the full range of strategic weapons. The initiative for the January meeting was a November 17 message by Chernenko to Reagan, to which the administration quickly responded.

Reaction

Much of the American reaction to the interview centered on the timing ot the Chernenko comments. Coming only a few days before the presidential election debate on foreign policy, the sudden interest in communicating with Americans was seen by some as an attempt to influence the election or to inject the four main Soviet concerns into the debate. Three of the four topics appeared in the Democratic Party platform, and Democratic candidate Walter F. Mondale had been attacking President Reagan for his failure to meet with a high Soviet official in his four years in office. (Democratic Party platform, p. 549) Chernenko might also, considering his lengthy illness and the prominence of Foreign Minister Gromyko on the world scene, have wanted to demonstrate publicly his leadership in foreign policy and his physical health. With additional U.S. missiles due to be deployed in Belgium in March 1985, the Soviet Union was undoubtedly anxious to renew negotiations.

Following are written questions and answers and the abridged version of the oral interview given to Dusko Doder of the Washington Post, *October 16, 1984:*

Soviet Attitude

[Q] President Reagan has said that the United States is prepared to resume a dialogue with the Soviet Union on a broad range of questions including arms control. What is the attitude of the Soviet Union toward President Reagan's expression of readiness for talks?

[A] In the past, we have already heard words about the U.S. administration's readiness for talks. But they have never been supported by real deeds that would attest to a genuine desire to reach agreement on a just and mutually acceptable basis at least on one of the essential questions of our relations, particularly in the field of arms limitation and a reduction of the war danger.

Every time we put forward concrete proposals, they would run into a blind wall. Let me give some examples.

Such was the case last March when we identified a whole set of problems. Reaching agreement on them — or at least on some of them — would mean a real shift both in Soviet-U.S. relations and in the international situation as a whole. But what they did was simply to shirk responding to our proposals.

Such was the case in June when we proposed reaching agreement on preventing the militarization of outer space. This time we were answered, but with what? An attempt was made to substitute the very subject of negotiations. It was proposed to discuss issues related to nuclear weapons, i.e., issues which had previously been discussed at the talks in Geneva that were wrecked by the United States itself.

At the same time, the United States not only refused to remove the obstacles created by the deployment of new U.S. missiles in Western Europe but is going ahead with their deployment.

And what about outer space? Instead of preventing an arms race in space, we were invited to proceed to working out some rules for such a race, and in fact to legalize it. Obviously, we cannot agree to that. Our objective is genuinely peaceful outer space and we shall persistently strive for this objective.

These are the facts.

Turning now to President Reagan's statement which you have referred to. If what the president has said about readiness to negotiate is not merely a tactical move, I wish to state that the Soviet Union will not be found wanting. We have always been prepared for serious and businesslike negotiations and have repeatedly said so.

We are ready to proceed to negotiations with a view to working out and concluding an agreement to prevent the militarization of outer space, including complete renunciation of antisatellite systems, with a mutual moratorium — to be established from the date of the beginning of the talks—on testing and deployment of space weapons. This is precisely the way we formulated our proposal from the outset. Now it is for Washington to respond.

The Soviet proposal that the nuclear powers freeze quantitatively and qualitatively all nuclear weapons at their disposal also remains valid.

Agreement on that matter would mean mutual cessation of the buildup of all components of the existing nuclear arsenals, including delivery vehicles and nuclear warheads. The nuclear arms race would thus be stopped. That would radically facilitate further agreements on reductions in and eventual complete elimination of such weapons.

The White House still has before it our official proposal that the Soviet Union and the United States initially agree to freeze their nuclear weapons, thus setting an example for other nuclear powers.

There is a real opportunity to finalize the agreement on the complete and general prohibition of nuclear weapon tests. Should there be no such tests, these weapons will not be improved, which will put the brakes on the nuclear arms race.

Here, too, the United States could prove in deeds the sincerity of its declarations in favor of nuclear arms limitation. The United States can also prove it by ratifying the Soviet-American treaties on underground nuclear explosions. These treaties were signed as far back as 1974 and 1976. Prove it precisely by ratifying them and not by inviting observers, as suggested by the American side, who would merely dispassionately ascertain the fact of explosion.

The Soviet Union has repeatedly called upon Washington to follow our example in assuming an obligation not to be the first to use nuclear weapons. Every time the answer was "no."

Imagine the reverse situation: the United States assumes an obligation not to be the first to use nuclear weapons and calls upon us to reciprocate while we say "no," this does not suit us and we reserve the right to a first nuclear strike. What would people in the United States think of our intentions in that case? There can be no two views on that score.

I have mentioned several most pressing problems related to the cessation of the arms race and the strengthening of security. There are other important questions which, I believe, the president is well aware of. All of them call for solutions and for making concrete efforts. Unsupported by practical deeds, words about readiness to negotiate remain mere words. I believe the above answers your question.

No Shift Seen

[Q] A view is widely spread that recently a shift has become discernible which could lead to better Soviet-U.S. relations. What do you think about this and what is your view of the prospects for these relations in the time to come?

[A] Indeed, sentiments in favor of a shift for the better in Soviet-U.S. relations are widely spread in the world. This, in our view, reflects the growing understanding of the importance of these relations, particularly in the current international situation.

Unfortunately, so far there has been no ground to speak of such a shift in Soviet-U.S. relations as a fact of life. It is possible? The resolution of the problems to which I referred earlier would help to bring it about.

I am convinced there is no sound alternative at all to a constructive development of Soviet-U.S. relations. At the same time, we do not overlook the fact that we have different social systems and world outlooks.

But if the responsibility which rests with our two countries is constantly kept in mind, if policy is oriented toward peace and not war, these differences not only do not exclude the search for mutual understanding, but call for it.

I have already said in the past and I wish to stress it once again: we stand for good relations with the U.S.A. and experience shows that they can be such. This requires a mutual desire to build relations as equals, to mutual benefit and for the good of the cause of peace.

Oral Exchange

[Q] I want to use this opportunity to hear your opinion as to what specific steps the Soviet leadership would like to see after the American elections to get out of the current impasse in Soviet-American relations.

[A] First of all, of course, the elections should take place in order to answer what will happen after the elections. The elections are in the future and therefore to determine now, in advance, what, when and where we are going to discuss is obviously too early. But you know our general official point of view.

Whoever is the president in America, our policy—a policy of peace which we are carrying out persistently [*sic*] and systematically—is going, I think, to remain the same. The same. That is why peace is the main question for us, and I think that any president who comes to the White House after the election will, I think, will be thinking about the same question.

As a matter of fact, two great countries can, as we became convinced in the past and are being convinced each day, can do a great deal, if fact they can do everything, in order that flames of another world war do not flare up. This is our objective, this is our direction, our general direction, and we think that any sober-minded person can understand us correctly.

We are doing this not because we . . . like it, but because we experienced in reality what such a war means, war without a hydrogen bomb, without such bombs. And what about a war with atomic bombs? We are now convinced that this is a very terrible weapon and naturally we would like to see in the face of American president a partner in this sacred human task — for peace.

Limited Optimism

[Q] What about specific measures?

[A] There [in the written answers] is our program on this score.

[Q] Are you optimistic about the present development of Soviet-American relations?

[A] Well, there are considerable possibilities in Soviet-American relations, very considerable possibilities. We have been making attempts, and you know if we enumerate the numbers of our proposals, which we have advanced and which I mentioned in my answers, you can easily see that . . . .

Chernenko's foreign policy adviser Andrei Alexandrov-Agentov: So far, there is no. . . .

Chernenko: No, so far there is no serious shift, businesslike shifts, such moves which could convince people and which could be convincing in themselves. In principle, I am an optimist, an optimist, but that does not mean an endless optimism, since there are limits to everything. I think nevertheless that things are going to get normalized if the American side indeed takes some practical steps in the direction of the struggle for peace. Practical steps.

[Q] And should not both sides take some small steps?

[A] You see, you will find the answers there. And not small steps but big steps that we have made in the direction of peace. But the White House is silent on this question. They are silent and they do not answer . . . or they do not even simply notice them. Or they consciously do not respond. One thing is clear: there has been no practical shift in the direction of peace by the White House. You can see that yourself.

It is necessary of course to translate those talks, all our agreements, questions and answers onto practical tracks. Here is the essence of the issue. It is not that we lack peace proposals, there are very many of them, but there are no practical solutions, no practical approaches for their resolution.

This is the most important point. And small steps, yes, yes, they only cloud people's eyes. That's it. But I believe that my answers to your questions are also one of our steps, our practical steps, on this important road.

REPORTS ON ASSASSINATION OF BENIGNO S. AQUINO JR.
October 23, 24, 1984

A commission investigating the 1983 murder of Philippine opposition leader Benigno S. Aquino Jr. made public its findings in two reports released October 23 and 24. Both reports stated that Aquino's death was the result of a military conspiracy. Corazon J. Agrava, chairwoman of the commission, implicated seven military members in her report issued October 23. The majority report, however, made public by the four other panel members October 24, pointed to a much broader military plot. According to this report, 25 military men and one civilian were involved in the conspiracy.

Background

Aquino, a former mayor, governor, and senator, was the opposition party leader and political archrival of Philippine president Ferdinand Marcos. After several years of detainment by the Marcos government, Aquino had been permitted to leave the Philippines in 1980 for heart surgery in the United States. He remained in self-imposed exile in the United States for three years. In June of 1983, however, he announced his decision to return to the Philippines to participate in preparations for the 1984 national assembly elections. The Marcos government urged Aquino not to return, citing concern for his safety.

Nonetheless, on August 21 Aquino arrived at the Manila International Airport aboard a China Airlines' flight. An escort of military guards surrounded him as he descended the service stairs of the plane. Seconds later Aquino was shot in the head and killed.

*Circumstances surrounding the assassination were unclear. An un-
known gunman, later identified as Rolando Galman, had been on the
ground near the plane. Military officials claimed that Galman had been
hired by communists to kill Aquino and that he had fired the fatal shot.
The military guards surrounding Aquino shot and killed Galman as soon
as Aquino had been hit. Opposition leaders, however, maintained that
the Marcos government was responsible for Aquino's death and demanded an investigation.*

*The Philippine government, a presidential-parliamentary system giv-
ing a strong degree of control to the chief executive, had been plagued by
stories of corruption, nepotism, and human rights violations since Marcos
assumed power in 1965. (1983 human rights reports, p. 155) In the
aftermath of Aquino's murder, street rioting and anti-government demonstrations deteriorated Marcos' control of the government. The increasingly uncertain political climate led to an economic crisis as worried
investors pulled their money out of the country. However, with Aquino's
death as a rallying point, the opposition party was strengthened and
fared well in the May 1984 elections.*

*Although the United States, with two military installations in the
Philippines, had been a supporter of the Marcos government, the growing
economic and political instability of the nation led to speculation of how
long the government would survive.*

Panels Appointed

*On August 24, three days after Aquino's death, Marcos appointed a
five-member commission, headed by Supreme Court Chief Justice
Enrique Fernando, to investigate the shooting. All five members of the
panel were government supporters, and public confidence in the group's
impartiality was low. Lawsuits challenging the commission's biases and
legality forced Fernando's resignation. When the second designated
chairman, Arturo Tolentino, refused the job, the other commission
members resigned.*

*Marcos appointed a new commission October 22, 1983, this time
drawing on names submitted by community leaders. Agrava, a retired
justice of the Court of Appeals, chaired the board. Other members were
Dante Santos, a prominent businessman; Amado C. Dizon, a college
administrator; Ernesto F. Herrera, leader of a pro-government labor
union; and Luciano E. Salazar, a corporate leader.*

*For eleven months the group investigated the Aquino killing. Commis-
sion members questioned almost 200 witnesses, including Imelda Marcos,
the president's wife, and Gen. Fabian C. Ver, chief of staff of the armed
forces and a close friend and adviser to Marcos. Commission members
traveled to Japan and to the United States to interview witnesses; they*

gathered approximately 1,400 documents, exhibits, and audio and video tape recordings. After an initial period of public doubt about its impartiality, the panel began to win the faith of many Philippine citizens.

Commission Reports

Agrava made public her 121-page report on October 23. In it, she accused Gen. Luther Custodio, head of the Aviation Security Command, and six soldiers who had been in the airport escort of plotting Aquino's death. Galman, Agrava stated, did not shoot Aquino but had been set up to take the blame. Rather, one of the military group on the stairs with Aquino fired the fatal shot; to pinpoint the actual assassin could be impossible, she said. Agrava specifically noted in her report that Ver "was not a plotter."

The other four commission members, however, claimed in their 457-page report that Ver was involved in the conspiracy. The majority report found Ver and 25 others, including Custodio and another general, "indictable for the premeditated killing" of Aquino and Galman.

Because of Ver's longstanding and close relationship with Marcos, the accusations against the general were embarrassing and potentially damaging to the president. Ver took a leave of absence from his post, protesting his innocence and demanding a speedy trial. Marcos publicly defended the general.

While many Filipinos praised the commission's findings, some Marcos opponents charged that the panel had not gone far enough. "The moment you implicate Ver, you implicate the president," one opposition leader said. A government ombudsman evaluated the commission reports and referred the matter to a prosecution panel. On November 5, prosecutors announced that Ver and the 25 others named in the majority report were accused of the double murder of Aquino and Galman. A three-man prosecution panel was scheduled to review the evidence and replies of the accused to decide whether there was "probable cause" to refer the case for trial.

Following are excerpts of Chairwoman Corazon J. Agrava's report on the assassination of Benigno S. Aquino, released October 23, and excerpts of the commission's majority report, released October 24, 1984:

AGRAVA REPORT

(A) With the finding that Senator [Benigno S.] Aquino [Jr.] was shot on the service stairs, all testimony that [Rolando] Galman had shot him has to be rejected. No evidence had placed Galman on the stairs before the shooting.

(B) Having found that Galman could not have shot Senator Aquino, it has to be further concluded that one of the military group on the service stairs with Senator Aquino was the triggerman.

There is no evidence pinpointing who he is. He could not have been [Sgt. Claro] Lat, who was close to the right of Senator Aquino, nor could have been [Sgt. Arnulf] de Mesa, who was slightly to the left of Senator Aquino and whose right hand was holding the left wrist of Senator Aquino. He could have been either [Sgt. Filomeno] Miranda or [Constable 1st Class Pogelio] Moreno, who were immediately to the rear of the trio of Lat, Senator Aquino and de Mesa, or Constable 1st Class [Mario] Lazaga farther back. Or it could have been one of the other escort party who was on the stairway. To pinpoint the actual assassin might not be provable beyond reasonable doubt with the available evidence. . . .

It has been found that Senator Aquino was shot while he was on the last steps of the service stairs. Of the six persons with him on the stairs, two had testified that Senator Aquino was shot after he had left the service stairs, while the other four claimed they did not see who fired the fatal shot. These statements of the six definitely show that they were in a criminal plot.

Under the proven circumstances, the board has concluded that there was a criminal plot to assassinate Senator Aquino on his way from the airplane to the SWAT van.

The indications are that the plotters had agreed that only one would be the assassin, that the others can either point to Galman as the killer or they can state that they did not see the shooting and that they will give false testimony to mislead and confuse. Thus, Sergeant [Armando] dela Cruz initially testified he was inside the tube when Senator Aquino was felled by the fatal shot. However, after he was confronted with photographs, he had to admit that he was on the platform of the service stairs at the moment of killing.

As previously stated, two of the six who had descended the service stairs with Senator Aquino testified that it was Galman who had fired the fatal shot, that is, to mislead. The other four, consonant with the plot, said they did not see the shooting.

The assassin could not have done it on his own. The personal circumstances of the six who were on the service stairs when Senator Aguino made his descent indicate that none of them could have a personal motive to assassinate him. Moreover, in the absence of a plot, the other five would not have hesitated to name the assassin so that they could free themselves from criminal responsibility.

It stands to reason that another had induced the assassin to fire the fatal shot and had arranged for the other five to take the positions they actually afterward took. The finding of the existence of a criminal plot is inevitable. . . .

Within the realm of possibility, howsoever improbable, there could have been only three intentional plotters, the one who actually shot Senator Aquino, the one who ordered him to shoot and the one behind the latter. If the one who ordered the assassin to shoot had authority to require other persons to do anything in regard to the planned assassination, those others may not be included among the plotters, except when their actions are such as to indicate that they knew of the plot and had opted to participate. It should be very difficult, if not impossible, to determine who the prime mover was.

From the evidence gathered, those who can be definitely identified as plotters are:

(A) The six persons who were on the service stairs while Senator Aquino was descending, to wit: Sergeant Lat, Sergeant de Mesa, Sergeant Miranda, Constable 1st Class Moreno, Constable 1st Class Lazaga and Sergeant dela Cruz.

(B) Gen. Luther Custodio is included as a plotter because the criminal plot could not have been planned and implemented without his intervention.

General [Fabian C.] Ver was not a plotter.... Even if General Ver should assume command responsibility for the assassination of Senator Aquino, it will not make him an actual plotter....

It bears repeating that the task of the board, if at all possible, was to determine the assassin of Senator Aquino and to ascertain if there were others who had induced the assassin to commit the murder. To the full extent that the evidence gathered had established them, I have arrived at the conclusions incorporated in this report. With this, and the reports of the other members, the board had accomplished its work.

The transcripts of the testimonial evidence heard during the hearings of the board, together with all submitted exhibits, will be turned over to the Ministry of Justice, as well as sundry records. The epilogue to our work lies in what will transpire in accordance with the action that the office of the President any thereafter direct to be taken....

MAJORITY'S REPORT

The SWAT troopers who gunned down [Rolando] Galman, and the soldiers who escorted Senator Aquino down the service stairs, deliberately and in conspiracy with one another, gave a perjured story to us regarding the alleged shooting by Galman of Senator Aquino and the mowing down, in turn, of Galman himself, these persons being Sergeant Lat, Sergeant de Mesa, Constable 1st Class Moreno, Constable 1st Class Lazaga, Sergeant Miranda, Sergeant de Guzman, Sergeant Mateo, Sergeant Desolong, Airman 1st Class Estelo.

The conspiracy to lie to and mislead us extended to the other officers and men who regaled us with the same concocted tale, these persons being Captain Kavinta, Sergeant Martinez, Sergeant Fernandez, Sergeant Mojica, Sergeant Torio, Airman 1st Class Acupido.

It was not a .357 Magnum revolver that was used in the assassination of

Senator Aquino but a .38 or .45-caliber pistol.

Gen. Prospero A. Olivas sought to mislead us upon this matter of the .357 Magnum revolver by citing, in substantiation of his theory that this was the murder weapon, a chemical report that he knew or ought to have known involved a lead fragment that was not one of those retrieved from the head of Senator Aquino, and completely disregarding and deliberately omitting to cite a second chemical report, which admittedly involved two of the three lead fragments recovered from Senator Aquino's head, just as he also sought to mislead us by his theory of the "deformed copper jacket" claimed by him to have exited from Senator Aquino's chin, and his theory of the "corrupted" or spurious ABC videotape adopted by NHK-TV for its special program on the Aquino assassination — these with the evident purpose of concealing the body or effects of the crime and bring about exoneration of the military. . . .

Contrary to the claims of the military investigators, there is no evidence to link the N.P.A.-C.P.P. to the killing of Senator Aquino; if at all, the evidence shows that Rolando Galman had no subversive affiliations.

Senator Aquino was shot behind the head as he reached the bottom of the service stairs attached to the airbridge of Bay 8. He was not shot by Rolando Galman, who was never at the stairway. It was in fact only the soldiers in the staircase with Senator Aquino who could have shot him, and considering the relative positions of the persons in that fatal stairway, it was either Constable 1st Class Rogelio Moreno or Sergeant Filomeno Miranda who had the best opportunity to do so.

The military officers in charge of the security preparations for Senator Aquino were fully cognizant of the fact that it was on C.A.L. [China Airlines] CI-811 that Senator Aquino would arrive at the M.I.A. [Manila International Airport] on Aug. 21, 1983, and, therefore, the ostensible acts of having to meet and search every arriving flight in order to identify Senator Aquino were fictitious and sham, and the various other acts of ostensible protection to Senator Aquino, considered conjointly with the facts above-mentioned, the concerted lies of the SWAT troopers and escorts, the misleading evidence submitted to us relative to the murder weapon and the subversive connections, all relate to and interact with one another so closely as to disclose a definite common design and common objective — in a word, criminal conspiracy.

We now address ourselves to the final question: Who are the other persons who are involved in this conspiracy, either as principals, upon the theory that the act of one is the act of all, or as accessories, for attempting to hide the corpus of the offense? . . .

General Custodio's involvement in the conspiracy is indubitable.

Custodio presided over the whole clockwork-like proceeding at the M.I.A. on August 21, 1983, giving such orders and doing such acts as were necessary, in line with either the real plan, or the apparent one.

We also satisfied that the evidence proves the complicity of General Fabian C. Ver in this tragic affair, in attempting, like General Olivas, to cover up the crime, or hide the corpus of effects of the crime.

Ver at first denied any "monitoring" of Aquino's activities in the U.S.A. It was only after intensive questioning that he finally admitted to "following up" Aquino's movements in America. He had to admit he was being regularly informed of the messages from the Philippine Embassy at Singapore. Those messages leave no doubt about the close surveillance of Senator Aquino's activities.

The evidence shows the military authorities knew that Aquino was coming via C.A.L. CI-811. Yet Ver denied awareness of this fact.

Col. Vincente Tigas also took part in the conspiracy. He limited the number of media representatives who would supposedly be allowed to meet Senator Aquino at the airbridge at Gate 8, effectively precluded their view and photographing of the service stairs of the airbridge, prevented their interviewing of potential eyewitnesses, ordered the collection of negatives of these journalists which he retained in his custody or control and did not offer to surrender the same to the board until required to do so by subpoena duces tecum. . . .

With respect to Col. Arturo Custodio, Galman could not have moved around and remained on the tarmac or the airport building except with the knowledge and consent of the Avsecom officers and men engaged in the operations at the time.

He and Hermilo Gosuico were the ones who picked up Rolando Galman from his house.

We close our report with a candid and honest exhortation to our people to demonstrate sobriety and to remain calm while pursuing with vigor and tenacity our firm resolve to see that justice is done to former Sen. Benigno S. Aquino, Jr., and the Filipino people.

To be sure, there are forces around us that will use this report to discredit our traditionally revered institutions as they have unscrupulously done with the valid grievances that we have always articulated. We hope and pray that the Filipino people are able to recognize and resist the subtle entrapment that these forces have so carefully designed in order that, in their naïveté, the people will find themselves unwittingly supporting these forces, objectives to destabilize our country and to fall prey to an intolerable political ideology. This ideology is antithetical to the Filipino people's traditional love of freedom, justice and adherence to democratic ideals. . . .

More than any other event in contemporary Philippine history, the killing of the late former Senator Aquino has brought into sharper focus the ills pervading Philippine society. It was the concretization of the horror that has been haunting this country for decades, routinely manifested by the breakdown of peace and order, economic instability, subversion, graft and corruption, and an increasing number of abusive elements in what are otherwise noble institutions in our country — the military and law enforcement agencies. We are, however, convinced that, by and large, the great majority of the officers and men of these institutions have remained decent and honorable, dedicated to their noble mission in the service of our country and people. . . .

A tragedy like that which happened on August 21, 1983, and the crisis that followed, would have normally caused the resignation of the chief of the armed forces in a country where public office is viewed with highest esteem and respect and where the moral responsibilities of public officials transcend all other considerations.

We anticipate that there will be those who, because of their prejudices, will express dissatisfaction over our conclusions. To them, we can only say that we did what the law mandated, using as basis nothing but the evidence, and, invoking as guide in our search for truth in the Aquino assassination, nothing but our conscience.

GEORGE SHULTZ ON TERRORISM

October 25, 1984

Strongly speaking out against terrorism, Secretary of State George P. Shultz said the United States should take swift retaliatory measures against terrorists, sometimes before they strike, even if these actions may mean the loss of innocent lives. The October 25 speech before the Jewish Community Relations Council at Park Avenue Synagogue in Manhattan came after three terrorist attacks on U.S. facilities in Lebanon within a period of 18 months.

"We must reach a consensus in this country that our responses should go beyond passive defense to consider means of active prevention, pre-emption and retaliation," Shultz said. "Our goal must be to prevent and deter future terrorist acts and experience has taught us over the years that one of the best deterrents to terrorism is the certainty that swift and sure measures will be taken against those who engage in it."

The secretary asked for broad public support for the use of military force in fighting terrorism. There will be no time for a national debate after every terrorist attack and "we cannot allow ourselves to become the Hamlet of nations, worrying endlessly over whether and how to respond," he said. Shultz pointed out that the public must understand that the lives of U.S. military men and even innocent civilians might be lost in retaliatiory attacks against terrorists. He added that the government may often have to act before "each and every fact is known."

A few days later, shortly before he left the country to attend the funeral of slain Indian prime minister Indira Gandhi, Shultz expanded upon his theme of the threat of international terrorism. (Gandhi assas-

sination, p. 945) *"I feel very strongly about it,"* he said. *"We in the United States have to wake up that it is an international form of warfare and it is directed largely against us and our way of life and our way of thinking, and we have to recognize it and be prepared to defend ourselves and our values against it."*

Administration Reaction

The immediate response from within the administration to the secretary of state's forceful statement suggested a government at odds on dealing with terrorists. State Department spokesman John Hughes told reporters that Shultz was voicing the administration's position. However, Vice President George Bush came out in disagreement with the secretary's contention that the public should be ready to accept some loss of innocent life.

"I think you have got to pinpoint the source of the attack," said Bush. *"We are not going to go out and bomb innocent civilians or something of that nature. I don't think we ever get to the point where you kill 100 innocent women and children just to kill one terrorist."* The United States *"has a great difficulty in fine tuning retaliation,"* he said. *"It has been our policy not to needlessly risk the lives of innocent civilians. This makes it difficult to retaliate."*

Bush claimed administration policy was expressed by President Ronald Reagan in his October 21 foreign policy debate with former vice president Walter F. Mondale. "We want to retaliate," Reagan said in the debate, *"but only if we can put our finger on the people responsible and not endanger the lives of innocent civilians."* (Presidential debates, p. 845) *When later questioned about the strident nature of the secretary of state's speech, President Reagan replied, "I don't think it was a statement of policy. He was saying all these things must be considered. I think what Secretary Shultz was saying was that you couldn't rule out the possibility of innocent people being killed. . . . He was not saying that we would do that."*

Thirty minutes after Reagan's comments, White House spokesman Larry Speakes issued a clarification. "Shultz's speech was administration policy from top to bottom," Speakes said. *"Shultz was saying that, in isolated cases, innocent civilians may be killed in a retaliatory strike. I emphasize may be, not will be."*

Terrorist Activities

The administration's defense of Shultz's statement reflected a discrepancy between what officials said publicly about terrorism and what they had been able to do to counter terrorist activities. In the 1980 presidential campaign, Reagan repeatedly castigated President Jimmy Carter for allowing Americans to be held hostage for 444 days by Iranian militants and for the failure of the U.S. government's attempted rescue mission of the hostages. At the beginning of his first term, he promised retaliation against similar acts of terrorism.

On April 18, 1983, 17 Americans were among 51 people killed when a van filled with explosives raced into the driveway of the U.S. Embassy in Beirut and blew up. Six months later, a truck drove into the parking lot at Beirut International Airport where approximately 1,600 U.S. Marines had been headquartered for more than a year. The truck broke through metal fences and sandbag barriers and came to a stop in the lobby of a four-story concrete building housing hundreds of servicemen. The driver detonated an estimated 2,000 pounds of explosives, killing himself and most of the sleeping Americans inside and demolishing the building. The attack left 241 Americans dead. A similar attack the same day at the French barracks killed 58 members of the French peace-keeping force.

Following the bombing at the Marine barracks, Reagan said that "We have strong circumstantial evidence linking the perpetrators of this latest atrocity to others that have occurred against us in the recent past, including the bombing of our embassy in Beirut last April. Every effort will be made to find the criminals responsible for this act of terrorism so that this despicable act will not go unpunished."

The American military presence abroad was attacked again September 20, 1984, when a truck carrying explosives crashed at the newly opened U.S. Embassy Annex near Beirut killing 14 people, two of them Americans. A shadowy group calling itself the "Islamic Jihad" claimed responsibility for the bombing. Speaking of the assaults in the Middle East, Reagan pointed out that there is "a great difference" between terrorism perpetrated by the Iranian government, "a government you can see and put your hand on," and of finding and punishing the terrorists responsible for the killings in Lebanon.

Following are excerpts of Secretary of State George P. Shultz's address on terrorism delivered to the Jewish Community Relations Council October 25, 1984:

Someday terrorism will no longer be a timely subject for a speech, but that day has not arrived. Less than two weeks ago, one of the oldest and greatest nations of the Western world almost lost its Prime Minister, Margaret Thatcher, to the modern barbarism that we call terrorism. A month ago the American Embassy Annex in East Beirut was nearly destroyed by a terrorist truck bomb, the third major attack on Americans in Lebanon within the past two years. To list all the other acts of brutality that terrorists have visited upon civilized society in recent years would be impossible here because that list is too long. It is too long to name and too long to tolerate.

But I am here to talk about terrorism as a phenomenon in our modern world — about what terrorism is and what it is not. We have learned a great deal about terrorism in recent years. We have learned much about the terrorists themselves, their supporters, their diverse methods, their underlying motives, and their eventual goals. What once may have seemed the random, senseless, violent acts of a few crazed individuals has come into clearer focus. A pattern of terrorist violence has emerged. It is an alarming pattern, but it is something that we can identify and, therefore, a threat that we can devise concrete measures to combat.

The knowledge we have accumulated about terrorism over the years can provide the basis for a coherent strategy to deal with the phenomenon, if we have the will to turn our understanding into action.

The Meaning of Terrorism

We have learned that terrorism is, above all, a form of political violence. It is neither random nor without purpose. Today we are confronted with a wide assortment of terrorist groups which, alone or in concert, orchestrate acts of violence to achieve distinctly political ends. Their stated objectives may range from separatist causes to revenge for ethnic grievances to social and political revolution. Their methods may be just as diverse: from planting homemade explosives in public places to suicide car-bombings to kidnappings and political assassinations. But the overarching goal of all terrorists is the same: they are trying to impose their will by force — a special kind of force designed to create an atmosphere of fear. . . .

They succeed when governments change their policies out of intimidation. But the terrorist can even be satisfied if a government responds to terror by clamping down on individual rights and freedoms. Governments that overreact, even in self defense, may only undermine their own legitimacy, and they unwittingly serve the terrorists' goals. The terrorist succeeds if a government responds to violence with repressive, polarizing behavior that alienates the government from the people.

The Threat to Democracy

We must understand, however, that terrorism, wherever it takes place, is directed in an important sense against *us*, the democracies — against our most basic values and often our fundamental strategic interests. Because terrorism relies on brutal violence as its only tool, it will always be the enemy of democracy. For democracy rejects the indiscriminate or improper use of force and relies instead on the peaceful settlement of disputes through legitimate political processes.

The moral bases of democracy — the principles of individual rights, freedom of thought and expression, freedom of religion — are powerful barriers against those who seek to impose their will, their ideologies, or their religious beliefs by force. Whether in Israel or Lebanon or Turkey or

Italy or West Germany or Northern Ireland, a terrorist has no patience for the orderly processes of democratic society, and, therefore, he seeks to destroy it. Indeed, terrorism seeks to destroy what all of us here are seeking to build.

The United States and the other democracies are morally committed to certain ideals and to a humane vision of the future. Nor is our vision limited to within our borders. In our foreign policies, as well, we try to foster the kind of world that promotes peaceful settlement of disputes, one that welcomes beneficial change. We do not practice terrorism and we seek a world which holds no place for terrorist violence, a world in which human rights are respected by all governments, a world based on the rule of law.

And there is yet another reason why we are attacked. If freedom and democracy are the targets of terrorism, it is clear that totalitarianism is its ally. The number of terrorist incidents in totalitarian states is minimal and those against their personnel abroad are markedly fewer than against the West. And this is not only because police states offer less room for terrorists to carry out acts of violence. States that support and sponsor terrorist actions have managed in recent years to co-opt and manipulate the terrorist phenomenon in pursuit of their own strategic goals.

It is not a coincidence that most acts of terrorism occur in areas of importance to the West. More than 80 percent of the world's terrorist attacks in 1983 occurred in Western Europe, Latin America, and the Middle East. Terrorism in this context is not just criminal activity, but an unbridled form of warfare.

Today, international links among terrorist groups are more clearly understood. And Soviet and Soviet-bloc support is also more clearly understood. We face a diverse family of dangers. Iran and the Soviet Union are hardly allies, but they both share a fundamental hostility to the West. When Libya and the PLO provide arms and training to the Communists in Central America, they are aiding Soviet-supported Cuban efforts to undermine our security in that vital region. When the Red Brigades in Italy and the Red Army Faction in Germany assault free countries in the name of Communist ideology, they hope to shake the West's self-confidence, unity, and will to resist intimidation. The terrorists who assault Israel — and indeed the Marxist Provisional IRA in Northern Ireland — are ideological enemies of the United States. We cannot and we will not succumb to the likes of Khomeini and Qaddafi....

We should understand the Soviet role in international terrorism without exaggeration or distortion. One does not have to believe that the Soviets are puppeteers and the terrorists marionettes; violent or fanatic individuals and groups can exist in almost any society.

But in many countries, terrorism would long since have withered away had it not been for significant support from outside. When Israel went into Lebanon in 1982, Israeli forces uncovered irrefutable evidence that the Soviet Union had been arming and training the PLO and other groups. Today, there is no reason to think that Soviet support for terrorist groups around the world has diminished. Here as elsewhere, there is a wide gap

937

between Soviets *[sic]* words and Soviet deeds, a gap that is very clear, for instance, when you put Soviet support for terrorist groups up against the empty rhetoric of the resolution against so-called "state terrorism" which the USSR has submitted to this year's UN General Assembly. The Soviets condemn terrorism, but in practice they connive with terrorist groups when they think it serves their own purposes, and their goal is always the same: to weaken liberal democracy and undermine world stability.

The Moral and Strategic Stakes

The stakes in our war against terrorism, therefore, are high. We have already seen the horrible cost in innocent lives that terrorist violence has incurred. But perhaps even more horrible is the damage that terrorism threatens to wreak on our modern civilization. For centuries mankind has strived to build a world in which the highest human aspirations can be fulfilled.

We have pulled ourselves out of a state of barbarism and removed the affronts to human freedom and dignity that are inherent to that condition. We have sought to free ourselves from that primitive existence described by Hobbes where life is lived in "continual fear and danger of violent death ... nasty, brutish, and short." We have sought to create instead a world where universal respect for human rights and democratic values makes a better life possible. . . .

Terrorism is a step backward; it is a step toward anarchy and decay. In the broadest sense, terrorism represents a return to barbarism in the modern age. If the modern world cannot face up to the challenge, then terrorism, and the lawlessness and inhumanity that come with it, will gradually undermine all that the modern world has achieved and make further progress impossible. . . .

Combatting Moral Confusion

. . . We cannot begin to address this monumental challenge to decent, civilized society until we clear our heads of the confusion about terrorism, in many ways the *moral* confusion, that still seems to plague us. Confusion can lead to paralysis, and it is a luxury that we simply cannot afford.

The confusion about terrorism has taken many forms. In recent years, we have heard some ridiculous distortions, even about what the word "terrorism" means. The idea, for instance, that denying food stamps to some is a form of terrorism cannot be entertained by serious people. And those who would argue, as recently some in Great Britain have, that physical violence by strikers can be equated with "the violence of unemployment," are, in the words of *The Economist*, "a menace to democracy everywhere." In a real democracy, violence is unequivocally bad. Such distortions are dangerous, because words are important. When we distort our language we may distort our thinking, and we hamper our efforts to find solutions to the grave problems we face.

There has been, however, a more serious kind of confusion surrounding the issue of terrorism: the confusion between the terrorist act itself and the political goals that the terrorists claim to seek.

The grievances that terrorists supposedly seek to redress through acts of violence may or may not be legitimate. The terrorist acts themselves, however, can never be legitimate. And legitimate causes can never justify or excuse terrorism. Terrorist means discredit their ends.

We have all heard the insidious claim that "one man's terrorist is another man's freedom fighter." When I spoke on the subject of terrorism this past June, I quoted the powerful rebuttal to this kind of moral relativism made by the late Senator Henry Jackson. His statement bears repeating today:

> "The idea that one person's 'terrorist' is another's 'freedom fighter' cannot be sanctioned. Freedom fighters or revolutionaries don't blow up buses containing non-combatants; terrorist murderers do. Freedom fighters don't set out to capture and slaughter school children; terrorist murderers do. Freedom fighters don't assassinate innocent businessmen, or hijack and hold hostage innocent men, women, and children; terrorist murderers do. It is a disgrace that democracies would allow the treasured word 'freedom' to be associated with acts of terrorists."

We cannot afford to let an Orwellian corruption of language obscure our understanding of terrorism. We know the difference between terrorists and freedom fighters, and as we look around the world, we have no trouble telling one from the other.

How tragic it would be if democratic societies so lost confidence in their own moral legitimacy that they lost sight of the obvious: that violence directed against democracy or the hopes for democracy lacks fundamental justification. Democracy offers the opportunity for peaceful change, legitimate political competition, and redress of grievances. We must oppose terrorists no matter what banner they may fly. For terrorism in *any* cause is the enemy of freedom.

And we must not fall into the deadly trap of giving justification to the unacceptable acts of terrorists by acknowledging the worthy-sounding motives they may claim. Organizations such as the Provisional IRA, for instance, play on popular grievances, and political and religious emotions, to disguise their deadly purpose. They find ways to work through local political and religious leaders to enlist support for their brutal actions. As a result, we even find Americans contributing, we hope unwittingly, to an organization which has killed — in cold blood and without the slightest remorse — hundreds of innocent men, women, and children in Great Britain and Ireland; an organization which has assassinated senior officials and tried to assassinate the British Prime Minister and her entire cabinet; a professed Marxist organization which also gets support from Libya's Qadhafi [*sic*] and has close links with other international terrorists. The Government of the United States stands firmly with the Government of the United Kingdom and the Government of Ireland in opposing any action that lends aid or support to the Provisional IRA.

Moral confusion about terrorism may take many forms. When two Americans and twelve Lebanese were killed at our Embassy Annex in East Beirut last month, for instance, we were told by some that this mass murder was an expression, albeit an extreme expression, of Arab hostility to American policy in the Middle East. We were told that this bombing happened because of our policies in Lebanon, or because of the overall state of our relations with the Arab nations, or because of our support for Israel. And we were advised by some that if we want to stop terrorism — if we want to put an end to these vicious murders — then what we need to do is change our policies. In effect, we have been told that terrorism is in some measure our own fault, and we deserved to be bombed. I tell you here and now that the United States will not be driven off or stayed from our course or change our policy by terrorist brutality. . . .

The terrorists' principal goal in the Middle East is to destroy any progress toward a negotiated peace. And the more our policies succeed, the closer we come toward achieving our goals in the Middle East, the harder terrorists will try to stop us. The simple fact is, the terrorists are more up-set about *progress* in the Middle East than they are about any alleged failures to achieve progress. Let us not forget that President Sadat was murdered because he made peace, and that threats continue to be issued daily in that region because of the fear — yes, fear — that others might favor a negotiated path toward peace.

Whom would we serve by changing our policies in the Middle East in the face of the terrorist threat? Not Israel, not the moderate Arabs, not the Palestinian people, and certainly not the cause of peace. Indeed, the worst thing we could do is change our principled policies under the threat of violence. What we *must* do is support our friends and remain firm in our goals. . . .

The Response to Terrorism

While terrorism threatens many countries, the United States has a special responsibility. It is time for this country to make a broad national commitment to treat the challenge of terrorism with the sense or urgency and priority it deserves.

The essence of our response is simple to state: Violence and aggression must be met by firm resistance. This principle holds true whether we are responding to full-scale military attacks or to the kinds of low-level conflicts that are more common in the modern world.

We are on the way to being well prepared to deter an all-out war or a Soviet attack on our principal allies; that is why these are the least likely contingencies. It is not self-evident that we are as well prepared and organized to deter and counter the "gray area" of intermediate challenges that we are more likely to face — the low intensity conflict of which terrorism is a part.

We have worked hard to deter large-scale aggression by strengthening our strategic and conventional defenses, by restoring the pride and confidence of the men and women in our military, and by displaying the kind of national resolve to confront aggression that can deter potential adversaries. We have been more successful than in the past in dealing with many forms of low-level aggression. We have checked Communist aggression and subversion in Central America and the Caribbean and opened the way for peaceful, democratic processes in that region. And we successfully liberated Grenada from Marxist control and returned that tiny island to freedom and self-determination.

But terrorism, which is also a form of low-level aggression, has so far posed an even more difficult challenge, for the technology of security has been outstripped by the technology of murder. And, of course, the United States is not the only nation that faces difficulties in responding to terrorism. To update President Reagan's report in the debate last Sunday, since September first, 41 acts of terrorism have been perpetrated by no less than 14 terrorist groups against the people and property of 21 countries. Even Israel has not rid itself of the terrorist threat, despite its brave and prodigious efforts.

But no nation has had more experience with terrorism than Israel, and no nation has made a greater contribution to our understanding of the problem and the best ways to confront it. By supporting organizations like the Jonathan Institute, named after the brave Israeli soldier who led and died at Entebbe, the Israeli people have helped raise international awareness of the global scope of the terrorist threat. . . .

Much of Israel's success in fighting terrorism has been due to broad public support for Israel's anti-terrorist policies. Israel's people have shown the will, and they have provided their government the resources, to fight terrorism. They entertain no illusions about the meaning or the danger of terrorism. Perhaps because they confront the threat everyday, they recognize that they are at war with terrorism. The rest of us would do well to follow Israel's example.

But part of our problem here in the United States has been our seeming inability to understand terrorism clearly. Each successive terrorist incident has brought too much self-condemnation and dismay, accompanied by calls for a change in our policies and our principles, or calls for withdrawal and retreat. We *should* be alarmed. We *should* be outraged. We *should* investigate and strive to improve. But widespread public anguish and self-condemnation only convince the terrorists that they are on the right track. It only encourages them to commit more acts of barbarism in the hope that American resolve will weaken. . . .

The Requirements for an Active Strategy

We must reach a consensus in this country that our responses should go beyond passive defense to consider means of active prevention, preemption, and retaliation. Our goal must be to prevent and deter future terrorist acts, and experience has taught us over the years that one of the best deterrents to terrorism is the certainty that swift and sure measures will be taken against those who engage in it. We should take steps toward carrying out such measures. There should be no moral confusion on this issue. Our aim is not to seek revenge, but to put an end to violent attacks against innocent people, to make the world a safer place to live for all of us. Clearly, the democracies have a moral right, indeed a duty, to defend themselves.

A successful strategy for combatting terrorism will require us to face up to some hard questions and to come up with some clear-cut answers. The questions involve our intelligence capability, the doctrine under which we would employ force, and, most important of all, our public's attitude toward this challenge. Our nation cannot assume the will to act without firm public understanding and support.

First, our intelligence capabilities, particularly our human intelligence, are being strengthened. Determination and capacity to act are of little value unless we can come close to answering the questions: who? where? and when? We have to do a better job of finding out who the terrorists are, where they are, and the nature, composition, and patterns of behavior of terrorist organizations. Our intelligence services are organizing themselves to do the job, and they must be given the mandate and the flexibility to develop techniques of detection and contribute to deterrence and response.

Second, there is no question about our ability to use force where and when it is needed to counter terrorism. Our nation has forces prepared for action — from small teams able to operate virtually undetected, to the full weight of our conventional military might. But serious issues are involved — questions that need to be debated, understood, and agreed if we are to be able to utilize our forces wisely and effectively.

If terrorists strike here at home, it is a matter for police action and domestic law enforcement. In most cases overseas, acts of terrorism against our people and installations can be dealt with best by the host government and its forces. It is worth remembering that just as it is the responsibility of the United States Government to provide security for foreign embassies in Washington, so the internationally agreed doctrine is that the security of our embassies abroad in the first instance is the duty of the host government, and we work with those governments cooperatively and with considerable success. The ultimate responsibility of course is ours, and we will carry it out with total determination and all the resources available to us. Congress, in a bipartisan effort, is giving us the legislative tools and the resources to strengthen the protection of our facilities and our people overseas — and they must continue to do so. But while we strengthen our defenses, defense alone is not enough.

The heart of the challenge lies in those cases where international rules and traditional practices do not apply. Terrorists will strike from areas where no governmental authority exists or they will base themselves behind what they expect will be the sanctuary of an international border. And they will design their attacks to take place in precisely those "gray areas" where the full facts cannot be known, where the challenge will not bring with it an obvious or clear-cut choice of response.

In such cases we must use our intelligence resources carefully and completely. We will have to examine the full range of measures available to us to take. The outcome may be that we will face a choice between doing nothing or employing military force. We now recognize that terrorism is being used by our adversaries as a modern tool of warfare. It is no aberration. We can expect more terrorism directed at our strategic interests around the world in the years ahead. To combat it we must be willing to use military force.

What will be required, however, is public understanding *before the fact* of the risks involved in combatting terrorism with overt power.

The public must understand *before the fact* that there is potential for loss of life of some of our fighting men and the loss of life of some innocent people.

The public must understand *before the fact* that some will seek to cast any preemptive or retaliatory action by us in the worst light and will attempt to make our military and our policy-makers — rather than the terrorists — appear to be the culprits.

The public must understand *before the fact* that occasions will come when their government must act before each and every fact is known — and that decisions cannot be tied to the opinion polls.

Public support for U.S. military actions to stop terrorists before they commit some hideous act or in retaliation for an attack on our people is crucial if we are to deal with this challenge.

Our military has the capability and the techniques to use power to fight the war against terrorism. This capability will be used judiciously. To be successful over the long term, it will require solid support from the American people.

I can assure you that in this Administration our actions will be governed by the rule of law; and the rule of law is congenial to action against terrorists. We will need the flexibility to repond to terrorist attacks in a variety of ways, at times and places of our own choosing. Clearly, we will not respond in the same manner to every terrorist act. Indeed, we will want to avoid engaging in a policy of automatic retaliation which might create a cycle of escalating violence beyond our control.

If we are going to respond or pre-empt effectively, our policies will have to have an element of unpredictability and surprise. And the prerequisite for such a policy must be a broad public consensus on the moral and strategic necessity of action. We will need the capability to act on a moment's notice. There will not be time for a renewed national debate after every terrorist attack. We may never have the kind of evidence that can stand up in an American court of law. But we cannot allow ourselves to become the Hamlet of nations, worrying endlessly over whether and how to respond. A great nation with global responsibilities cannot afford to be hamstrung by confusion and indecisiveness. Fighting terrorism will not be a clean or pleasant contest, but we have no choice but to play it.

We will also need a broader international effort. If terrorism is truly a threat to Western moral values, our morality must not paralyze us; it must give us the courage to face up to the threat. And if the enemies of these values are united, so too must the democratic countries be united in defending them. . . .

Sanctions, when exercised in concert with other nations, can help to isolate, weaken, or punish states that sponsor terrorism against us. Too often, countries are inhibited by fear of losing commercial opportunities or fear of provoking a bully. Economic sanctions and other forms of countervailing pressure impose costs and risks on the nations that apply them, but some sacrifices will be necessary if we are not to suffer even greater costs down the road. Some countries are clearly more vulnerable to extortion than others; surely this is an argument for banding together in mutual support, not an argument for appeasement.

If we truly believe in the values of our civilization, we have a duty to defend them. The democracies must have the self-confidence to tackle this menacing problem or else they will not be in much of a position to tackle other kinds of problems. If we are not willing to set limits to what kinds of behavior are tolerable, then our adversaries will conclude that there are no limits. As Thomas Jefferson once said, when we were confronted with the problem of piracy, "an insult unpunished is the parent of others." In a basic way, the democracies must show whether they believe in themselves.

We must confront the terrorist threat with the same resolve and determination that this nation has shown time and again throughout our history. There is no room for guilt or self-doubt about our right to defend a way of life that offers *all* nations hope for peace, progress, and human dignity. The sage Hillel expressed it well: "If I am not for myself, who will be? If I am for myself alone, who am I?"

As we fight this battle against terrorism, we must always keep in mind the values and way of life we are trying to protect. Clearly, we will not allow ourselves to descend to the level of barbarism that terrorism represents. We will not abandon our democratic traditions, our respect for individual rights, and freedom, for these are precisely what we are struggling to preserve and promote. Our values and our principles will give us the strength and the confidence to meet the great challenge posed by terrorism. If we show the courage and the will to protect our freedom and our way of life, we will prove ourselves again worthy of these blessings.

ASSASSINATION
OF INDIRA GANDHI
October 31, 1984

In an act of religious retribution, Sikh bodyguards on October 31 shot and killed Indian prime minister Indira Gandhi as she walked from her home to her office at her official residence in New Delhi. The two bodyguards, trusted members of the prime minister's security force, fired at close range with a submachine gun and pistol at Gandhi, who was later pronounced dead at a nearby hospital of injuries resulting from as many as 11 bullet wounds. One assassin was killed by loyal guards and the other wounded.

The assassination touched off a major political crisis; outraged Hindus attacked Sikhs across India, and more than 1,200 people were reported killed during the bloody two-week aftermath of the assassination. The army was put on alert to counteract the hostilities, and many Sikhs fled their homes to go into hiding. Hours after Gandhi's death, her son, Rajiv Gandhi, was sworn in as the new prime minister. Joined by several opposition party leaders, he immediately issued an appeal for an end to the violence, urging "sanity and harmony." When reports of beatings and murders of Sikhs continued, he addressed the nation by radio, saying, "Nothing would hurt the soul of our beloved Indira Gandhi more than the occurrence of violence in any part of the country."

In the midst of mob outbreaks and rioting, Gandhi's body was taken to the Teen Murti House, a former British imperial palace and residence of her father's, where thousands of mourners filed by to pay homage. Three days later, on November 3, her body was transported in a funeral cortege through the streets of New Delhi. Gandhi, who had served as India's prime minister for 16 years, was cremated in a traditional Hindu funeral ceremony witnessed by tens of thousands, including nearly 100 foreign leaders and dignitaries. Outrage at the assassination was expressed by leaders from around the world. President Ronald Reagan said Gandhi had been "a source of global leadership" and expressed "shock, revulsion, and grief at the brutal assassination."

Assassination Motive

Gandhi's assassins apparently were motivated by the military's June 1984 invasion of the Golden Temple of Armistar, Sikhism's holiest shrine, situated in the state of Punjab. Sikh extremists had been using the temple as a base for terrorist operations in the Punjab, hoping to force the government to create a separate Sikh state in that region. In the early morning hours of June 6, Gandhi tried to break the separatist drive by storming the temple where the Sikhs' militant leader, Jarnail Singh Bhindranwale, accompanied by hundreds of his followers, had taken refuge to avoid arrest for his terrorist activities. After 36 hours of fierce fighting, the 72-acre temple complex was strewn with bodies. According to government figures, nearly 600 people were killed in the raid, including Bhindranwale. Gandhi's assassins reportedly had vowed at that time to kill her in retribution for the raid.

One of the assassins, Bengt Singh, who had been on Gandhi's security staff for 12 years, reportedly shouted defiantly after emptying his rifle into her, "I have done what I had to do. Now you do what you have to do." He was then led to a guardhouse where a skirmish erupted and he was shot and killed by security guards. The second assassin, Satwant Singh, a 21-year police constable who had been assigned to guard Gandhi five months earlier, was wounded. He told police that he was a member of a Sikh conspiracy that included Rajiv Gandhi among its targets.

Hindu-Sikh conflicts have been rare in the long history of religious conflict in India, but a recent movement to create a separate Sikh state in the Punjab region of northern India, where Sikhs have a numerical majority, had aroused government concern. Sikh extremists had been carrying on a two-year terrorist campaign in the region that had resulted in the death of nearly 600 people. Sikhism, a 15th-century offshoot of Hinduism, does not adhere to the Hindu caste system and stresses monotheism. Although Sikhs compose only 2 percent of India's 750 million population, they are among its most prosperous minorities. They have become successful farmers in the Punjab region, and many have set up thriving businesses outside their home state in New Delhi, Bombay, Calcutta, Madras, and other important trade centers. They are easily identifiable by their traditional long hair, beards, and turbans.

In the outbreak of violence following the assassination, reports indicated that authorities showed indifference or reluctance to stop Hindu attacks against Sikhs, as vigilante groups moved through the city streets attacking Sikhs and destroying their shops and homes.

Indira Gandhi's Rule

Indira Gandhi, granddaughter of Motilal Nehru, an early leader of the Indian independence movement, and daughter of Jawaharlal Nehru, who was India's first prime minister, was born into a life of politics and power. Educated in England and Switzerland, she was a constant companion to and official hostess for her father. Despite her apparent shyness and retiring manner as a young woman, she proved after her father's death to be a tough and powerful leader. First elected to political office in 1955, she was named president of the Congress Party four years later. Upon her father's death in 1964, she was elected to the lower house of parliament and two years later began the first of her four terms as prime minister.

She served as India's prime minister for a total of 16 years, her first stay in office lasting from 1966 to 1977, when she was defeated in a general election. Throughout her tenure, she had worked for a strong central government, independence from foreign influence, and the build-up of a strong military force. Under her leadership, India became the sixth country to explode a nuclear device and one of the first to launch its own satellite. But by the end of her first stay in office she had gained a reputation as an authoritarian leader, willing to sacrifice democratic freedoms to maintain her power and the strength of the national government. Her political stature and strong identification with the Indian people won her re-election as prime minister in 1980 when her newly formed Congress (I) Party — the "I" for Indira — won a sweeping victory. In recent years, the United States frequently criticized her friendliness toward the Soviet Union, which demonstrated itself in her refusal to openly condemn the invasion of Afghanistan in 1980. She was seen as a tough and sometimes inflexible leader who was unafraid to use military force to ensure a strong and unified India.

In 1980 she met with personal tragedy when her younger son, Sanjay, was killed in a flying accident. Gandhi allegedly had been grooming Sanjay to succeed her as prime minister. After his death she called upon the elder son, Rajiv, to enter the political arena. Rajiv had been a pilot for Indian Airways and had shown little inclination for political life. However, after his brother's death he ran for Sanjay's seat in parliament and in January 1983 was named secretary general of the Congress (I) Party.

Doubts in the Wake of Gandhi's Death

The major question confronting India upon Gandhi's assassination was whether Rajiv Gandhi, with only three years of political experience, would be able to fulfill adequately his role as prime minister and bring stability to the country. Hours after Gandhi's death, the country erupted into violence. Curfews were imposed on several Indian cities and Sikhs were shipped to army and paramilitary camps to protect them from mob attacks. The night of the assassination, Sikhs were attacked on trains making their way into New Delhi. In one of the worst incidents of violence, dozens of people were slain in a Sikh neighborhood in Trilokpuri, a colony of slum dwellers on the outskirts of New Delhi. The police said 95 bodies had been found, but residents and witnesses put the toll much higher.

A day after Gandhi's funeral, Rajiv Gandhi made his first move toward asserting his authority by reinstating all but one of his mother's cabinet ministers and firing the country's chief civil servant for his failure to move more quickly to control the violence. He also quelled speculation that a flare-up with Pakistan might be imminent by meeting with Pakistani president Mohammed Zia ul-Haq. A full inquiry into Gandhi's death was initiated and mob violence was finally put under control. In a radio address November 12, Gandhi pledged continuity with the foreign and domestic policies of his grandfather and mother. In a further effort to ensure democratic stability, he called for general elections to be held before the end of 1984.

> *Following is the address of Rajiv Gandhi as the newly sworn in prime minister of India following the assassination of Indira Gandhi, and the address of President Giani Zail Singh to the nation October 31, 1984:*

PRIME MINISTER RAJIV GANDHI'S ADDRESS

Indira Gandi, India's Prime Minister, has been assassinated. She was mother not ony to me but to the whole nation. She served the Indian people to the last drop of her blood. The country knows with what tireless dedication she toiled for the development of India.

You all know how dear to her heart was the dream of a united, peaceful and prosperous India. An India in which all Indians, irrespective of their religion, language or political persuasion live together as one big family in an atmosphere free from mutual rivalries and prejudices.

By her untimely death her work remains unfinished. It is for us to complete this task.

This is a moment of profound grief. The foremost need now is to maintain our balance. We can and must face this tragic ordeal with fortitude, courage and wisdom. We should remain calm and exercise the maximum restraint. We should not let our emotions get the better of us, because passions would cloud judgement.

Nothing would hurt the soul of our beloved Indira Gandhi more than the ocurrence of violence in any part of the country. It is of prime importance at this moment that every step we take is in the correct direction.

Indira Gandhi is no more but her soul lives. India lives. India is immortal. The spirit of India is immortal. I know that the nation will recognise its responsibilities and that we shall shoulder the burden heroically and with determination.

The nation has placed a great responsibility on me by asking me to head the Government. I shall be able to fulfill it only with your support and co-operation. I shall value your guidance in upholding the unity, integrity and honour of the country.

PRESIDENT GIANI ZAIL SINGH'S ADDRESS

My Dear Countrymen,

On this the saddest day of my life I speak to you when I am totally over-taken by the dark cloud of cruel fate. Our beloved Mrs. Indira Gandhi is no longer with us. I have lost my dearest friend; we have all lost one of the greatest leaders our country has ever produced; and the world has lost a harbinger of peace who was undoubtedly the greatest woman leader mankind has ever produced.

My association with her family spans over four decades. Panditji's passing away was my first personal bereavement. The loss of Mrs. Gandhi is for me unbearable. In spite of her preoccupation with her official duties we met often. For me each such meeting was a memorable experience. She was gentle, soft spoken, brilliant and above all an epitome of culture. She was a daughter Panditji would have been proud of.

Now all that has ended. The dastardly act of assassins which is not only heinous but a crime against humanity itself, has put the nation to test at an extremely critical juncture of our history. The unity and integrity of the nation is being challenged. Let our grief not cloud our good sense and maturity both as individuals and a nation. God shall grant us the strength to meet the new challenges. Let us rally behnd the ideals we have inherited from our forefathers. Let us demonstrate to the world that India's stability cannot be jeopardised by a handful of subhuman assassins.

November

1984 ELECTION RESULTS

November 6, 1984

The presidential campaign of 1984 ended November 6 with the sweeping victory of Republican president Ronald Reagan, who took a near record-breaking 59 percent of the vote in his race against Democratic challenger Walter F. Mondale. He captured the electoral votes of all but one state, Mondale's home state of Minnesota, and the District of Columbia. The magnitude of the Reagan victory was topped only by that of Lyndon Johnson, who carried 61 percent of the vote in 1964.

Reagan's success was no surprise to most observers. Pollsters had been predicting a win by the president since August and election-eve polls showed him far ahead of Mondale. His smashing victory dashed Democratic hopes of building a class-oriented anti-Reagan majority. Democrats had tried to galvanize the millions of voters who were hurt by the president's cuts in spending for social programs or objected to his redirection of the federal government. There was evidence of a massive anti-Reagan vote in 1982 when Democrats made impressive gains in congressional elections, but it had evaporated with the economic recovery in 1984. Democrats did register millions of new voters, many of them black, but those gains were blunted by a well-financed Republican registration drive and the common perception that developed in late summer that the race was not even close.

In Reagan's victory speech and in Mondale's concession of defeat, both men touched on the themes that dominated their campaigns. Reagan, who essentially ran on the record of his first four years in the White House, reiterated what he saw as his first-term successes.

"We said we would get inflation under control and we did," Reagan told supporters gathered in the Century Plaza Hotel in Los Angeles for an election-night celebration. "We said we would get America working again and we've created more than six and a half million new jobs. We said that we would work to restore traditional values in our society and we have begun. We said that we would slow down government and the rate of its spending increases, and we did. We said we would rebuild our defenses and make America prepared for peace and we have."

During the campaign, Mondale had charged that Reagan's economic policies favored the rich at the expense of the poor. He had also attacked the president's foreign policy for what he said was its emphasis on military aid instead of negotiations and an arms race that was out of control. (Presidential debates, p. 845)

Speaking to supporters and campaign workers at the St. Paul Civic Center, Mondale urged them to continue to fight for "the poor, the unemployed, the elderly, the handicapped." He also pleaded for the control of nuclear weapons "before they destroy us all."

Following are excerpts from Ronald Reagan's presidential victory address and excerpts from Walter F. Mondale's concession speech of November 6, 1984:

REAGAN VICTORY SPEECH

...And now, I have a special thanks to you for something that began here in this state almost 20 years ago....

We set out, I remember, back there almost 20 years ago and said that we could start a prairie fire here in California, one that would capture the intensity of our devotion to freedom and the strength of our commitment to American ideals.

Well, we began to carry a message to every corner of the nation, a simple message. The message is here in America, the people are in charge. And that's really why we're here tonight. This electoral victory belongs to you and the principles that you cling to, principles struck by the brilliance and bravery of patriots more than 200 years ago. They set forth the course of liberty and hope that makes our country special in the world.

To the extent that what has happened today reaffirms those principles, we are part of that prairie fire that we still think defines America — a fire of hope that will keep alive the promise of opportunity as we head into the next century.

Four years ago, when we celebrated victory in this same room, our country was faced by some deep and serious problems. But instead of complaining together, we rolled up our sleeves and began working together. We said we would get inflation under control, and we did.

We said we would get America working again — and we've created more than six and a half million new jobs. We said that we would work to restore traditional values in our society, and we have begun. And we said that we would slow down government and the rate of its spending increases, and we did.

We said we'd get interest rates down, and we did. We said we would rebuild our defenses and make America prepared for peace, and we have.

Now — now, I wish I could take credit for this . . . but the credit — no, the credit belongs to the American people — to each of you. Our work isn't finished; there's much more to be done. We want to make every family more secure; to help those in our inner cities, on our farms, and in some of our older industries which are not yet back on their feet. And the recovery will not be complete until it's complete for everyone.

By rebuilding our strength, we can bring ourselves closer to the day when all nations can begin to reduce nuclear weapons and ultimately banish them from the earth entirely.

You know, so many people act as if this election means the end of something —

The vision that we outlined in 1980, indeed, the passion of the fire that we kept burning for two decades doesn't die just because four years have passed. To each one of you I say: tonight is the end of nothing. It is the beginning of everything.

. . . What we've done only prepares us for what we're going to do. We must continue, not only into those next four years, but into the next decade and the next century, to meet our goal of sustained economic growth without inflation, and to keep America strong.

Our society is a society of unlimited opportunity which will reach out to every American and includes lifting the weak and nurturing the less fortunate.

We fought many years for our principles. Now we'll work to keep those principles in practice. That's what we have to leave to our children, and to their children, and they are what this campaign was all about.

We come together again. We're united again. And now, let's start building together and keep the prairie fire alive and let's never stop shaping that society which lets each person's dreams unfold into a life of unending hope. America's best days lie ahead. And, you know, you'll forgive me. I've got — I'm going to do it just one more time — You ain't seen nothing yet.

God bless you. Thank you all very much. Thank you.

MONDALE CONCESSION SPEECH

A few minutes ago, I called the president of the United States and congratulated him on his victory for re-election as president of the United States.

He has won. We are all Americans. He is our president, and we honor him tonight.

Again tonight, the American people in town halls, in homes, in firehouses, in libraries, chose the occupant of the most powerful office on earth. Their choice was made peacefully, with dignity and with majesty.

Although I would rather have won, tonight we rejoice in our democracy, we rejoice in the freedom of a wonderful people, and we accept their verdict.

I thank the people of America for hearing my case. I have travelled this nation, I believe, more than any living American. Wherever I've gone, the American people have heard me out.

They've listened to me. They've treated me fairly. They've lifted my spirits, and they've added to my strength. If there's one thing I'm certain of, it is that this is a magnificent nation with the finest people on earth. . . .

I thank Geraldine Ferraro. We're very proud of Gerry. We didn't win, but we made history, and that fight has just begun. . . .

I've been around for a while, and I have noticed in the seeds of almost every victory are to be found the seeds of defeat, and in every defeat are to be found the seeds of victory. Let us fight on. Let us fight on.

My loss tonight does not in any way diminish the worth of importance of our struggle. The America we want to build is just as important tomorrow as it was yesterday. Let us continue to seek an America that is just and fair.

Tonight, especially, I think of the poor, the unemployed, the elderly, the handicapped, the helpless, and the sad, and they need us more than ever tonight.

Let us fight for jobs and fairness. Let us fight for these kids and make certain that they have the best education that any generation ever had.

Let us fight for our environment and protect our air, our water and our land.

While we keep America strong, let us use that strength to keep the peace, to reflect our values and to control these weapons before they destroy us all.

That has been my fight. That has been our fight in this campaign. We must fight for those goals with all of our heart in the future.

I am honored by Minnesota, by all of the people of this country who have permitted me to wage this fight. What an honor it is. I'm at peace with the knowledge that I gave everything I've got.

I am confident that history will judge us honorably so tonight let us be determined to fight on.

Good night and God bless you and God bless America.

Thank you very much.

BISHOPS' PASTORAL LETTER ON U.S. ECONOMIC POLICIES
November 11, 1984

A panel of Roman Catholic bishops made public the first draft of a pastoral letter on American economic conditions and social responsibility November 11 at the National Conference of Catholic Bishops. The 120-page document, entitled "Catholic Social Teaching and the U.S. Economy," criticized the country's economic practices and called for changes in attitudes and policies to help the poor. "The fact that so many people are poor in a nation as wealthy as ours is a social and moral scandal that must not be ignored," the draft stated. Many of the bishops' proposals, including greater government responsibility for helping the poor and the jobless, clashed with President Ronald Reagan's positions.

The draft was the work of a five-man committee chaired by Archbishop Rembert Weakland of Milwaukee. The panel worked on the draft for three years and purposely delayed its publication until after the November 1984 elections to preclude any partisan use of the document.

Nonetheless, anticipation of the letter stirred controversy even before its release. On November 7 a group of prominent business and professional lay Catholics issued their own, more conservative, view of the role of the U.S. economy in solving problems of poverty. The group organized in May 1984 out of concern that the bishops' letter "would not be consistent with our deep beliefs in the market system and its capacity for self-correction" said its chairman, former Treasury secretary William E. Simon. The self-selected lay committee denied that its report was an attempt to undercut the forthcoming pastoral draft.

Human Dignity

The bishops cited a two-fold purpose behind the pastoral draft: to provide guidance for members of the church and to add to the public debate about U.S. economic policies. "The theme of human dignity is central to Catholic social thought and forms the basis for our perspectives and recommendations in this letter," the draft began. The first section of the document discussed the biblical and theological foundations upon which economic life should be based. The second part focused on application of moral principles to American economic practices.

Much of the bishops' draft was in keeping with stands voiced by Pope John Paul II in various addresses. The draft quoted, for example, several statements the pontiff made during his September visit to Canada, including his condemnation of countries that amass "for themselves the imperialistic monopoly of economic and political supremacy at the expense of others." (Pope's Canadian trip, p. 777)

However, the bishops did not go so far as some "liberation theologists" who condemn American capitalism generally and view economic inequality as a struggle between rich and poor. (The Vatican on liberation theology, p. 759) Rather, the bishops suggested that American capitalism be evaluated from an ethical viewpoint and that the economy be reshaped to guarantee "the minimum conditions of human dignity."

Major recommendations set forth in the draft include:
● reduction of the unemployment rate to 3 or 4 percent, with increased government support for job creation programs;
● total overhaul of the welfare system;
● reduction in arms race spending and redirection of that money to social programs;
● government, business, and labor participation in economic reforms to aid the chronically unemployed and others living on the margin of poverty;
● reform of labor laws to aid in formation of unions, to prevent intimidation of workers and to provide more timely remedies of unfair labor practices;
● redirection of U.S. foreign policy to concentrate on human, rather than military, needs.

Reactions

The draft received a favorable response from the almost 300 bishops attending the national conference in Washington at which the document was presented. The bishops had three months in which to submit comments on the draft; in the spring of 1985 a second draft, based on these comments, was to be issued. After discussion of the second draft at a general meeting of bishops in June, a third version was to be prepared.

Final revisions and voting on the pastoral letter were planned for November 1985.

Several Democrats on Capitol Hill praised the bishops' call for increased government aid for the poor. Some, however, criticized the delayed publication of the document until after the elections. Sen. William Proxmire, D-Wis., for example, said "It's coming out when the game is over and the fans have left the field and a few beer cans are still lying around." Others countered that the bishops, by issuing the draft after the election, kept alive debate about economic policies toward the nation's poor. The White House reported that President Reagan welcomed the draft and shared "the bishops' concern for the poor."

Regardless of the draft's controversial proposals, some questioned whether the bishops should speak out on public policy issues. The bishops said they must. On "dignity of life" issues such as abortion, nuclear war, human rights, and economic justice, "silence on our part would approximate dereliction of pastoral duty and civic irresponsibility," Bishop James W. Malone of Youngstown, Ohio, told the conference. He added that "Our impact on the public will be directly proportionate to the persuasiveness of our positions."

Following are excerpts from "The Pastoral Letter on Catholic Social Teaching and the U.S. Economy," *prepared by a committee of Roman Catholic bishops and released November 11, 1984.* (Boldface-headings in brackets have been added by Congressional Quarterly to highlight the organization of the text.):

[Introduction]

1. Every perspective on economic life that is human, moral and Christian must be shaped by two questions: What does the economy do *for* people? What does it do *to* people? It is concern for the effects of the U.S. economy on the lives of millions of human beings that leads us to issue this pastoral letter....

3. The poor have a special claim on our concern because they are vulnerable and needy. We believe that all — Christians, Jews, those of other faiths or no faith at all — must measure their actions and choices by what they do *for* and *to* the poor. As pastors and as citizens we are convinced of one fundamental criterion for economic decisions, policies and institutions: They must all be at the service of human beings. The economy was made for people, *all* people, and not the other way around.

4. ... Everyone knows the significance of economic policy, economic organizations and economic relationships, a significance that goes beyond purely secular or technical questions to profoundly human, and therefore moral, matters. It touches our very faith in God and what we hope and be-

lieve about the destiny of humanity. The signs of our time direct the pastoral concern of the church to these moral aspects of economic activity. Interpreting this activity in the light of the Gospel — at the local, national and international levels — is the task we have set for outselves in this pastoral letter. . . .

7. In this effort to discern the signs of the times in U.S. economic life we have listened to many ways of analyzing the problems and many proposed solutions. In our discussion, study and reflection one thing has become evident. There is no clear consensus about the nature of the problems facing the country or about the best ways to address these problems effectively. The nation wonders whether it faces fundamentally new economic challenges that call for major changes in its way of doing business or whether adjustments within the framework of existing institutions will suffice. Public opinion polls and daily press reports fluctuate between optimism and pessimism over the future, whether national or global.

8. This uncertainty and alteration between hope and apprehension has many causes. The U.S. economy has been immensely successful in providing for the material needs and in raising the living standard of its citizens. Our nation is one of the richest on earth. Despite this great wealth the country has recently gone through a severe recession with the highest unemployment rates since the Great Depression of the 1930s. In the recovery from this painful period the situation has improved, but very serious doubts remain about the future. The rate of poverty has risen sharply in recent years and is now at the highest level since 1965. Unemployment is exceptionally high even in the midst of the recovery, especially for minorities and youth. Some regions have been especially hard hit and their economic futures are in doubt. Farmers with moderate-sized holdings, workers in aging heavy industries, owners of vulnerable small businesses, and the poor and minority population in many central cities are often tempted to despair.

9. Some analysts argue that these problems result from a fundamental structural transition in the U.S. economy, caused by new international competition, the movement of labor-intensive industries out of the country, the displacement of jobs by advanced technology and a shift from a manufacturing and industrial economy to a service economy with lower-paying jobs. Add to this a major threat to the stability of the international financial system posed by the huge debts of several developing countries. A deepening crisis would leave no one untouched.

10. Others see the situation in less dramatic terms. They recognize that very serious problems exist, such as the aging of the industrial base in cities of the northern and central regions of the country, the displacement of many farmers from the land, the large trade deficits which eliminate jobs in the United States and the fraying of the social "safety net" which protects those at the bottom of society. But they consider these grave problems to be the result of particular policies that can be changed incrementally rather than as the sign of a deep shift in the nature of the

economy. They believe, for example, that by reducing deficits, increasing productivity, taking remedial action to assist declining cities, farms and industries, and by carefully managing and rescheduling the Third-World debt, a crisis can be avoided within the framework of existing institutions.

11. The investment of human creativity and material resources in the production of the weapons of war only makes these economic problems more intractable. The rivalry and mutual fear between the superpowers channel resources away from the task of creating a more just and productive economy into a seemingly endless effort to create more powerful and technologically sophisticated weaponry. . . .

12. Even more damaging from the viewpoint of economic justice are the arms races between developing countries and their neighbors. Poor countries can ill afford to use their scarce resources to buy weapons when they lack food, education and health care for large parts of their population. The willingness of the superpowers and other developed countries to fan the flames of arms competition among many developing countries poses another serious threat to global economic justice. . . .

14. One thing is certain in all this discussion: the stakes are enormously high. U.S. economic institutions and policies directly affect the dignity and well-being of millions of U.S. citizens. Choices made here have worldwide effects. Decisions made abroad have immediate consequences in the lives of U.S. citizens. How our country responds to the economic problems it faces will help or harm people all around the globe.

15. We are well aware of the difficulties involved in relating moral and religious values to economic life. Modern society has become so complex and fragmented that people have difficulty sensing the relationship among the different dimensions of their lives, such as the economic, the moral and the religious. During the preparation of this letter we have often been asked what possible connection there could be between Christian morality and the technical questions of economic policy. We acknowledge the problem of discovering these links, and we also fully accept the fact that social and economic affairs "enjoy their own laws and values which must be gradually deciphered, put to use and regulated by human beings." Religious and moral conviction cannot, simply by itself, produce solutions to economic dilemmas. We are confident, however, that the Christian moral tradition can make an important contribution to finding the right path.

16. In this letter we seek to support human dignity, strengthen the bonds of life in society and uncover the deeper meaning of the many activities that form economic life. These themes are the basis of the perspectives and recommendations proposed in this letter.

17. We write with two purposes. The first is to provide guidance for members of our own church as they seek to form their consciences and reach moral decisions about economic matters. The second is to add our voice to the public debate about U.S. economic policies. In pursuing the first of these purposes we argue from a distinctively Christian perspective

that has been shaped by the Bible and by the content of Christian tradition, and from a standpoint that reflects our faith in God: Father, Son and Holy Spirit. The second purpose demands that our arguments be developed in a reasoned manner that will be persuasive to those who do not share our faith or our tradition. . . .

21. In addition, our perspective and our conclusions are shaped by an overriding concern for the impact of decisions and policies on the lives of people, especially the poor. *Our fundamental norm is this: Will this decision or policy help the poor and deprived members of the human community and enable them to become more active participants in economic life?...*

[Theological Foundations]

23. The basis for all that the church believes about the moral dimensions of economic life is its vision of the transcendent worth — the sacredness — of human beings. *The dignity of the human person, realized in community with others, is the criterion against which all aspects of economic life must be measured....*

39. The biblical motifs of creation, covenant and community provide fundamental perspectives and obligatory ideals which should inform our thoughts and our hopes. To stand before God as creator is to respect God's creation, both the world of nature and that of human history. Misuse of the resources of the world or appropriation of them by a minority of the world's population betrays the gift of creation meant for all people who are created in God's image with a mandate to make the earth fruitful. Creation by God and recreation in Christ make us realize that the communality we share with people of other nations is more basic than the barriers national borders create. A true biblical vision of the human condition relativizes the claims of any state or government to total allegiance. It also makes us realize that people of other nations and with other ways of living share equally in God's image and should be equal recipients of God's bounty.

40. As we reflect that we are people of the new covenant, we recognize also that the gifts of God involve corresponding responsibilities. God made a covenant with the people delivered from Egypt and granted them the land of promise with the mandate that they remain a faithful people. As a people in a land which has been greatly gifted by God in natural and human resources we are also a people with great responsibility. As John Paul II said on his visit to the United States, "Riches and freedom create a special obligation," and the Holy Father went on to exhort us not to be blind to the needs of the poor who, like Lazarus, sit at our gates. . . .

61. John Paul II has summoned the church to be a community of disciples, a community in which "we must see first and foremost Christ saying to each member of the community: Follow me." When the first followers of Jesus heard and answered this call they left all things to

become one with Jesus in the mystery of the cross. In many areas of church life, to be a follower of Christ demands suffering and renunciation. Questions of family life, sexual morality, and war and peace face Catholics of the United States with challenges that summon them to the deepest commitment of faith. This is no less true in the area of economics and social justice. We live in one of the most affluent cultures in history, where many of the values of an increasingly materialistic society stand in direct conflict with the gospel vision. We have been exhorted by John Paul II to break with "the frenzy of consumerism" and to adopt a "simple way of living." Our contemporary prosperity exists alongside the poverty of many both at home and abroad, and the image of disciples who "left all" to follow Jesus is difficult to reconcile with a contemporary ethos that encourages amassing as much as possible. . . .

[HUMAN DIGNITY]

77. . . . [I]f the economy is to function in a way that respects the dignity of persons, these qualities should be present: *It should enable persons to find a significant measure of self-realization in their labor; it should permit persons to fulfill their material needs through adequate remuneration; and it should make possible the enhancement of unity and solidarity within the family, the nation and the world community. . . .*

81. When we consider the performance of the American economy and its success in respecting these basic economic rights, we see an encouraging record. In its comparatively short history the United States has made impressive strides in the effort to provide material necessities, employment, health care, education and social services for its people. It has done this within a political system based on the precious value of freedom. While the United States can be rightfully proud of its achievements as a society, we know full well that there have been failures, some of them massive and ugly. Hunger persists in our country, as our church-sponsored soup kitchens testify. Far too many people are homeless and must seek refuge from the cold in our church basements. As pastors we know the despair that can devastate individuals, families and whole communities when the plague of unemployment strikes. Inadequate funding for education puts a high mortgage on our economic future. Racial discrimination has devastating effects on the economic well-being of minorities. Inequality in employment opportunity, low wages for women and lack of sufficient child-care services can undermine family life. The blighted and decaying environment of some disadvantaged communities stands in stark contrast with the natural and architectural beauty of others. Real space for leisure, contemplation and prayer seems increasingly scarce in our driven society. . . .

88. Finally, the citizenry of the United States needs a new and stronger will to pursue this task in a sustained way in the years ahead. It will be an

undertaking which involves struggle: a struggle for greater understanding, a struggle with our own selfishness and a struggle to develop institutions that support active participation in economic life for all. The effort to guarantee the economic rights of all will face resistance until the fullness of the kingdom of God has been established by God's gracious initiative. Until that day arrives, Christ calls us to the conversion of heart which will enable us to engage in this struggle with courage and hope. . . .

89. . . .We believe the time has come for a similar experiment in economic democracy: the creation of an order that guarantees the minimum conditions of human dignity in the economic sphere for every person. By drawing on the resources of the Catholic moral-religious tradition, we hope to make a contribution to such a new "American experiment" in this letter. . . .

103. *The fulfillment of the basic needs of the poor is of the highest priority.* Personal decisions, social policies and power relationships must all be evaluated by their effects on those who lack the minimum necessities of nutrition, housing, education and health care. Our society has to consider other goals that these, such as productivity and economic efficiency, but not to the further detriment of the disadvantaged of our world. This evaluation of decisions, policies and institutions primarily in light of their impact on the poor constitutes the "preferential option for the poor" which flows from biblical faith. It is also a priority fully supported by human experience and reason. In particular, this principle grants priority to meeting fundamental human needs over the fulfillment of desires for luxury consumer goods or for profits that do not ultimately benefit the common good of the community.

104. *Increased economic participation for the marginalized takes priority over the preservation of privileged concentrations of power, wealth and income.* This principle follows from the fact that economic rights and responsibilities must find expression in the institutional order of society. It grants priority to policies and programs that enhance participation through work. It also points out the need for policies to improve the situation of groups unjustly discriminated against in the past. And it has very important implications for the institutions that shape the international economic order.

105. *Meeting human needs and increasing participation should be priority targets in the investment of wealth, talent and human energy.* Increasing productivity both in the United States and in less-developed parts of the world is a clear need. But different sorts of investment of human and financial resources can have very different outcomes for people even when they have similar rates of productivity. This principle presents a strong moral challenge to policies that put large amounts of talent and capital into the production of luxury consumer goods and military technology while failing to invest sufficiently in education, in the basic infrastructure of our society or in economic sectors that produce the jobs, goods and services that we urgently need. . . .

[RESPONSIBILITIES AND RIGHTS]

111. ...[T]he church fully supports the right of workers to form unions or other associations to secure their rights to fair wages and working conditions. This is a specific application of the more general right to associate. Trade unions express the essentially social nature of human persons and manifest the human need for solidarity. In the words of Pope John Paul II, "The experience of history teaches that organizations of this type are an indispensable element of social life, especially in modern industrialized societies." Unions may also legitimately resort to strikes in situations where they are the only available means for pursuing the justice owed to workers. No one may deny the right to organize for purposes of collective bargaining or coercively suppress unions without attacking human dignity itself. Therefore we firmly oppose organized efforts, such as those regrettably now seen in this country, to break existing unions or to prevent workers from organizing through intimidation and threats. U.S. labor-law reform is needed to give greater substance to the right to organize, to prevent intimidation of workers and to provide remedies in a more timely manner for unfair labor practices....

117. The responsibilities of the business and financial sectors are expressions of the duty to exercise faithful stewardship over the resources with which God has blessed our society. We have great wealth, both in fertile land and natural resources. In addition, the ingenuity and inventiveness of our forebears have left us a legacy of vast industrial and technological capacity. Those in our society who own and manage this wealth hold it in trust, both for all who depend on it today as well as for generations yet to come. As St. Paul observed, "What is expected of stewards is that each one be found worthy of his trust" (1 Cor. 4:2)....

120. Within the framework of this basic vision of stewardship and concern for the common good, the Catholic tradition has long defended the right to private ownership of property. Private ownership has value for many reasons. It provides incentives for diligence at work. It allows parents to contribute to the welfare of their children. Directly and indirectly it protects political liberty....

121. This support of private ownership does not mean that any individual, group, organization or nation has the right to unlimited accumulation of wealth. Especially when there are so many needy people in our world, the right to own must bow to the higher principles of stewardship and the common use of the goods of creation. There is a "social mortgage" on private property which implies that "private property does not constitute for anyone an absolute or unconditioned right. No one is justified in keeping for his exclusive use what he does not need, when others lack necessities." In our increasingly complex economy, true stewardship may also sometimes demand that the right to own cede to public involvement in the planning or ownership of certain sectors of the economy. The church's teaching opposes collectivist and statist economic approaches. But it also

resists the notion that an unimpeded market automatically produces justice. . . .

138. We measure the justice of our economic institutions in part by their ability to deliver those goods and services which fulfill basic human needs and provide a living worthy of human dignity. In our economy consumption is a stimulus to production, and increased production generates employment. As consumers, therefore, all of us play an important role in the pursuit of economic justice.

139. Nevertheless, both our Christian faith and the norms of human justice impose distinct limits on what we consume and how we view material goods. The Gospel calls us to renounce disordered attachment to earthly possessions. Jesus blessed the poor, though he did not teach that degrading poverty is somehow a blessed condition. He called us to seek first the kingdom of God rather than an ever-increasing store of goods and wealth. Similarly, the earliest Christians sought to alleviate poverty and called upon the wealthy in their community to relinquish their goods in the service of their brothers and sisters. Such limits on consumption and the accumulation of wealth are essential if we are to avoid what Pope Paul VI called "the most evident form of moral underdevelopment," namely avarice. They are also essential to the realization of the justice that protects human dignity. . . .

141. All U.S. citizens, especially parents, must nurture the inner freedom to resist these pressures constantly to seek more. Also, men and women in the advertising and marketing field must examine the methods they use to see if they can really stand scrutiny in this light. During his visit to our country, Pope John Paul II challenged us to recognize the urgency of our responsibility "even if it involves a notable change in the attitudes and lifestyles of those blessed with a larger share of the world's goods."

142. . . . A consumerist mentality which encourages immediate gratification mortgages our future and ultimately risks undermining the foundations of a just order. Both our cultural values and our tax structures need to be revised to discourage excessively high levels of consumption and to encourage saving and consequent investment in both private and public endeavors that promote the economic rights of all persons. . . .

143. . . . All the moral principles that govern the just operation of any economic endeavor apply to the church and its many agencies and institutions. . . .

[Policy Applications]

151. The principles of Catholic social teaching provide a rich tradition from which to approach a discussion of economic justice. They form the basis for the reflections on specific public-policy issues that will be addressed in this section. We shall attempt here to focus the light of moral principles on certain of the economic realities and choices that are central

to American life. In doing so, we are aware that the movement from principle to practice is a complex and sometimes difficult task. We undertake this task with the firm conviction that moral values have an important role to play in determining public policies, but with the understanding that ethical principles in themselves do not dictate specific kinds of programs or provide blueprints for action. . . .

[RECOMMENDATIONS]

179. *1. We recommend that the nation make a major new policy commitment to achieve full employment.* We believe that an unemployment rate in the range of 3 percent or 4 percent is a reasonable definition of full employment in the United States today. We have noted above that considerably higher rates have received growing public and professional acceptance in recent years for a number of reasons: demographic changes, institutional rigidities and employment/inflation tradeoffs. In light of the possibilities for reducing unemployment and the criteria for doing so successfully, we believe that 6 percent to 7 percent unemployment is unacceptable and is not the best the United States can do. . . .

180. *2. We recommend increased support by the government for direct job-creation programs targeted on the structurally unemployed.* Such programs can take the form of direct public-service employment and also of public subsidies for employment in the private sector. . . .

The United States has no shortage of major needs which are not likely to be met unless we take concerted public action. Our roads and bridges need to be repaired, farmland needs to be conserved and restored, parks and recreation facilities need to be improved, low-cost housing needs to be built and our public transportation system needs to be expanded. Private industry must play a major role in meeting these needs through ordinary contractual relations with government. Direct public-service employment programs also have a role to play in the effort. . . .

181. *3. We recommend expansion of apprenticeship and job-training programs in the private sector which are administered and supported jointly by business, labor unions and government.* . . .

184. *4. We recommend the formation of local, state and national coalitions to press for the design and implementation of job-creation strategies.* . . .

185. *5. In order to bring frictional unemployment to a truly minimal level we recommend improvement and expansion of job-placement services on both the local and national level.* . . .

[POVERTY LEVELS]

187. The extent of poverty in the United States must be a matter of grave concern to all citizens. At the end of 1983 there were about 35 million Americans, who, by the government's official definition, were poor. An-

other 20 million or 30 million had so little that by any reasonable standard they were also needy. After a decline in the annual rate of proverty from 14.7 percent in 1966 to 11.7 percent in 1979, the figure climbed to 15.2 percent by the end of 1983 — the sharpest increase since poverty statistics began to be collected. In the four years between 1979 and 1983 the number of those living in poverty increased by over 9 million people. During this same period the number of poor children under the age of 6 jumped by 51 percent. The fact that so many people are poor in a nation as wealthy as ours is a social and moral scandal that must not be ignored. . . .

193. One much-discussed condition that does not appear to be either a cause or a cure of poverty is personal motivation. Some claim that the poor are poor because they do not try hard enough to find a job, do not work hard enough when they have one and generally do not try to get ahead. In fact, one of the most detailed studies ever done on poverty in this country showed that initial attitudes were not an important predictor of later income. Indeed, some of those who worked the longest hours remained poor because of low wages. Until there is real evidence that motivation significantly contributes to poverty, this kind of argument should be abandoned. It is not only unsupported but is insulting to the poor. . . .

194. Here we cannot enter into a full discussion of the nature of poverty, but we want to raise a few central points. Poverty is not merely the lack of adequate financial resources. To be poor entails a more profound kind of deprivation, for it means being denied full participation in the economic, social and political life of society. It means being without sufficient control over and access to the decisions that affect your life. It means being marginalized and powerless in a way that assaults not only your pocketbook but also your fundamental human dignity.

195. Our nation's response to poverty, therefore, must not only include improvements in welfare programs for the poor, as we shall discuss below. It must also address broader social and institutional factors that are an integral part of this problem. We call attention here to three such factors: 1) racial discrimination; 2) the feminization of poverty; and 3) the distribution of income and wealth. . . .

202. If the United States were a country in which poverty existed amid relatively equitable income distribution, one might argue that we do not have the resources to provide everyone with an adequate living. But, in fact, this is a country marked by glaring disparities of wealth and income. As noted earlier Catholic social teaching does not suggest that absolute equality in the distribution of income and wealth is required. Some degree of inequality is not only acceptable, but may be desirable for economic and social reasons. However, gross inequalities are morally unjustifiable, particularly when millions lack even the basic necessities of life. In our judgment, the distribution of income and wealth in the United States is so inequitable that it violates this minimum standard of distributive justice. In 1982 the richest 20 percent of Americans received more income than the bottom 70 percent combined and nearly as much as all other Americans

combined. The poorest 20 percent of the people received only about 4 percent of the nation's income while the poorest 40 percent received only 13 percent. . . .

[SOCIAL WELFARE PROGRAMS]

218. We have emphasized that social welfare programs are no substitute for the fundamental reforms in social and economic policy that are necessary to empower the poor, to provide jobs at decent wages and to reduce the growing inequities in America's economic life. Nevertheless, for millions of poor Americans the only economic safety net is the public welfare system. We believe that programs in this area are essential and should be designed to serve the needs of the poor in a manner that respects their human dignity. In our judgment the present welfare system does not meet that criterion and is in need of major reform.

219. The United States has numerous separate programs to assist the needy, including four with broad coverage: Aid to Families with Dependent Children, Supplemental Security Income, food stamps and Medicaid, which provides certain health services to some of the poor. In general our welfare system is woefully inadequate. It is a patchwork arrangement marked by benefit levels that leave recipients poor; gaps in coverage; inconsistent treatment of poor people in similar situations; wide variations in benefits across states; humiliating treatment of clients; and frequent complaints about "red tape". . . .

222. One reason why we do not have a humane welfare system is our punitive attitude toward the poor. Americans have a tendency to blame poverty on laziness, to stigmatize welfare recipients, to exaggerate the benefits actually received by the poor and to overstate the extent of fraud in welfare payments. The belief persists in this country that the poor are poor by choice, that anyone can escape poverty by hard work and that welfare programs make it easier for people to avoid work. Hence we devise programs that single out the poor for special treatment, provide meager benefits and are often demeaning in the way they are administered. In violation of the spirit of solidarity, the needy are kept at the edge of society and told in dozens of ways that they are a burden. In this climate, politicians often find that they can score points by producing cuts in welfare programs, even when the cost is a sharp increase in human misery. . . .

226. We strongly recommend that the United States undertake a thorough reform of its welfare and income-support programs. Building on our earlier discussion of moral principles, we propose six guidelines for that effort.

227. *1. Public-assistance programs should be adequately funded and provide recipients with decent support.* . . .

229. *2. The United States should establish national eligibility standards and a national minimum-benefit level for public-assistance programs.* . . .

231. *3. Public-assistance programs should strengthen rather than weaken marriage and the family....*

234. *4. Within the limits just stated, public-assistance programs should encourage rather than penalize gainful employment.* Individuals ought not be worse off because they work outside the home than if they relied solely on public assistance....

236. *5. The design of public-assistance programs should involve the participation of the recipient population and avoid or minimize stigma to clients....*

238. *6. The administration of public-assistance programs should show respect for clients.* With the punitive spirit behind our present welfare programs, a premium is often put on deterring applications, using regulations to create difficulties for clients and otherwise showing the poor that they are not to be trusted. Such practices seldom occur in most social-benefit programs for the non-poor....

[U.S. AND WORLD ECONOMY]

268. The U.S. economy is linked with the rest of the world economy in multiple ways. Many of these links are of positive benefit both to the people of the United States and to those of other nations. It is also clear, however, that the present pattern does harm as well as good to large numbers of persons....

271. In that interdependent world the United States is still the economic giant — despite its own recent recession and the rise of other economic powers. The American economy has an enormous influence on the rest of the world, especially the developing countries; and those countries are increasingly important participants in international economic activity, with a growing impact on the United States. Such interdependence, as we emphasized earlier in this letter and in our pastoral letter on war and peace, is central to any assessment of the role of the United States in the world....

285. We do not intend to evaluate the various proposals for international economic reform or to provide a blueprint for a new international system. Rather we want to urge a basic and overriding consideration; that both empirical and moral evidence, especially the precarious situation of the developing countries, calls for the renewal of the dialogue urged by Pope John Paul II between North and South. *We strongly recommend that such a dialogue aim at restructuring the existing patterns of economic relations so as to establish greater equity and meet the basic human needs of the poor people of the South....*

290. In recent years U.S. policy toward the developing world has shifted from its earlier emphasis on basic human needs and social and economic development to a selective assistance based on an East-West assessment of a North-South set of problems. Such a view makes the principal policy issue one of "national security," which in turn is described in political-

military terms. Developing countries thus become largely test cases in the East-West struggle; they have meaning or value only in terms of the larger geopolitical calculus. The result is that issues of political and economic development take second place to the political-strategic argument. We deplore this change. . . .

292. In our view, however, the most damaging single retrenchment is the decline in the U.S. support for the International Development Association, the "soft-line window" of the World Bank. Its clients are countries whose per capita income is $410 per year or less. Through a series of recent policy decisions the United States has shifted its role in IDA from being a leading supporter of the poorest countries to becoming an obstacle to multilateral efforts to help poor people in these countries. . . .

314. . . . In 1982 the military expenditures of the developed countries were 17 times larger than their foreign assistance; in 1984 the United States alone budgeted more than 20 times as much for defense as for foreign assistance and nearly two-thirds of the latter took the form of military assistance or went to countries because of their perceived security value to the United States. *Rather than promoting U.S. arms sales to countries that cannot afford them, we should be campaigning for an international agreement to reduce this lethal trade.*

315. The international economic order is in crisis; the gap between rich and poor countries and between rich and poor people within countries is widening. The United States represents the most powerful single factor in the international economic equation. With that kind of power comes a commensurate responsibility. But even as we speak of crisis, we see an opportunity for the United States to launch, on both a national and a global scale, a campaign for economic democracy and justice to match the still incomplete, but encouraging political democracy we have achieved here with so much pain and sacrifice.

316. To restructure the international order along lines of greater equality and participation will require a far more stringent application of the principles of affirmative action than we have seen in the United States itself. Like the struggle for political democracy at home, it will entail sacrifices. But that is what the recognition and acceptance of responsibility means. As a nation founded on Judeo-Christian religious principles, we are called to make those sacrifices in order to bring justice and peace to the world, as well as for our own long-term self-interest. The times call for the kinds of leadership and vision that have characterized our nation in the past when the choices were clear. Now we need to call upon these qualities again. As Pope John Paul II said to President Carter during his visit to the United States, "America, which in the past decades has demonstrated goodness and generosity in providing food for the hungry of the world, will, I am sure, be able to match this generosity with an equally convincing contribution to the establishing of a world order that will create the necessary economic and trade conditions for a more just relationship between all the nations of the world."

317. We hope that this letter has begun to clarify how Catholic social teaching applies to the situations we are describing, so that our country can move in the direction the pope indicated. We share his conviction that many of these issues generally called economic are, at root, moral and therefore require the appplication of moral principles derived from the Gospels and from the evolving social teaching of the church. . . .

325. On another level, overcoming the split between the Christian vision and economic life calls for a deeper awareness in the church of the integral connection between worship and the world of work. Worship and prayer are the center of Christian existence and the pre-eminent purpose of the church. They are also the wellspring that gives life to our reflection on economic problems. . . .

330. There are indeed different paths to holiness in the church and vocations to different forms of sharing in the effort to achieve the goals presented in this letter. These reflections on worship and liturgy, however, make vividly clear that none of us can afford to live a spiritually schizophrenic existence in which our private lives are oriented toward Christian discipleship while our economic activities are devoid of these same values. All Christians are called to put into practice the eucharistic promise in our daily lives and work. This vision of human dignity realized in solidarity with others should be at the foundation of our economic life. The value and dignity of each person is no mere philosophical or theological assertion, but a living conviction that leads to concrete decisions affecting our society and our environment. . . .

REPORT ON 'NATURAL' DISASTERS

November 13, 1984

A famine of staggering proportions spread across huge areas of sub-Saharan Africa in 1984. Although the news media were slow to bring the disaster to light in the United States, the outpouring of contributions to international relief organizations was immense after newspapers and television networks showed images of starvation in October and November.

Many specialists believed that the human role in the "natural" disasters was large, and some of them said that traditional food relief might be useless or even counterproductive. A report, "Natural Disasters: Acts of God or Acts of Man?" released November 13 by Earthscan, a United Nations-supported news and information service, reflected some of these views. The report was written by the head of the Swedish Red Cross and by the editorial director of Earthscan.

The Earthscan report said that its discussion of the value of international relief was "not meant to be an attack on relief." In many disasters, it said, "nothing but relief" was possible.

African Famine

The famine, said to be the worst in African history, followed two broad belts of drought across the continent. In November 1984 the United Nations Food and Agriculture Organization (FAO) said the 24 African nations and 150 million people confronted, at the least, hardship and malnutrition. In Ethiopia alone, the famine was believed to have been a factor in the deaths of 300,000 people. Another 200,000 were said to have died in Mozambique.

Beginning in 1981, drought had spread from Mozambique in the southeast to a belt running from Mauritania in the northwest through Mali and Niger and Burkina Faso to Somalia and Kenya. Newsweek magazine quoted Peter Onu, acting secretary-general of the Organization of African Unity, as saying, "What we know is that millions of people are starving and hundreds of thousands are dying because we are no longer able to provide our own staple food."

Relief Efforts

Contributions from Americans for famine relief reached a crescendo in late November when news coverage in the United States suddenly peaked. Established relief organizations such as the American Red Cross and Oxfam American earlier had been unsuccessful in trying to interest the U.S. media in the disaster. The New York Times *November 11, 1984, quoted Trevor Page, an executive of the Rome-based World Food Pro gram, as saying, "The blame seems to have tipped in the last few weeks in favor of not letting a million people die of starvation."*

The famine in Ethiopia was the focus of much of the print and television coverage. In that country, the government of Colonel Mengistu Haile Mariam, an ally of the Soviet Union, was widely blamed for not giving priority to the disaster. Critics pointed out that in September 1984 the government spent more than $150 million on celebrations marking the 10th anniversary of the revolution that established the regime.

Writing for Newsweek, *Jean Mayer, the president of Tufts University and one of the world's leading experts on nutrition, said that in most cases famines could be coped with much more effectively "than we now do." Pointing to "abundant" U.S. grain surpluses, he said that "all that has to be done" was to get the food to where it was needed as quickly as possible.*

Mayer recommended that military commanders be used in relief efforts "since they are trained to move men and materials." And he urged that when a famine did strike, local populations be kept in place. "The social breakdown that develops [when people move about in search of food] makes that famine harder to cope with," he wrote.

Earthscan Report

The report on disasters, "Natural Disasters: Acts of God or Acts of Man?" was supported financially by the Swedish Red Cross and the Swedish International Development Authority (SIDA). It was written by Anders Wijkman, secretary-general of the Swedish Red Cross, and Lloyd

Timberlake, Earthscan editorial director. The London-based Earthscan, which covers global environmental developments, is financed by the United Nations and by several industrialized nations.

The study on which the report was based found that the average number of disasters each year worldwide increased from 54 in the 1960s to 81 in the 1970s. It was impossible, the report said, to explain the increases by changes in climate or geological processes. Instead, the report pointed to "human vulnerability resulting from poverty and inequality; environmental degradation owing to poor land use; and rapid population growth, especially among the poor."

People did not starve in a drought-related famine just because there was no food, the Earthscan report pointed out. Citing a study by the International Labor Organization (ILO), it said that a famine "chose" its victims by class and occupation. Traditional food relief usually arrived too late, did not meet the most serious problems, and frequently worked against needed change by propping up existing regimes.

> *Following are excerpts from "Natural Disasters: Acts of God or Acts of Man?" released in London November 13, 1984, by Earthscan, a United Nations-supported news and information service:*

A Question of Balance

Events called "natural disasters" are killing more and more people every year. Yet there is no evidence that the climatological mechanisms associated with droughts, floods and cyclones are changing. And no geologist is claiming that the earth movements associated with earthquakes, volcanoes and tsunami (earthquake waves) are becoming more violent.

If nature is not changing, why are "natural disasters" becoming more frequent, more deadly and more destructive?

This ... [report] sets out to show that it is because people are changing their environment to make it more *prone* to some disasters, and are behaving so as to make themselves more *vulnerable* to these hazards. Growing Third World populations are forced to overcultivate, deforest and generally overuse their land, making it more prone to both floods and droughts. Growing numbers of Third World poor are forced to live on dangerous ground: in shantytowns in flood-prone river basins or foreshores, or in huts of heavy mud-brick on steep hills in earthquake-prone cities.

The common view of "natural disasters" is due for a radical change. A new term may even be needed, such as "nature disaster", to distinguish calamities associated with the forces of nature from such tribulations as war and factory explosions. Today humans are playing too large a role in natural disasters for us to go on calling them "natural".

975

So a distinction must be made between the "trigger events" — too little rain, too much rain, earthshocks, hurricanes — which may be natural, and the associated disasters, which may be largely man-made. For instance, a strong earthquake in an unoccupied desert area, which affects no one, is hardly a disaster. A mild earthquake in a shantytown of heavy mud-brick houses on the side of a steep ravine may well prove a disaster in terms of human deaths and suffering. But is the disaster more the result of the earthshocks or of the fact that people are living in such dangerous houses on such dangerous ground? Viewed another way, is it easier to prevent the earthshock or improve the housing conditions? ...

This ... [report] stresses a few basic thoughts about disasters and how to cope with them.

- Natural disasters are an integral part of human life, especially in the Third World. Their impact is affected by people's relations to their environment, to their government and to the other institutions of their society.
- Everyday acts by humans — farming, cutting fuelwood, building homes, choosing sites for housing — can make their land more or less prone to calamity and the people more or less vulnerable.
- Current disaster relief may not be the most charitable, efficient or more cost-effective means of alleviating the human suffering caused by disasters. It can even, in some circumstances, do more harm than good.
- As people develop economically and politically they become less vulnerable to natural disasters. Organisations concerned with disasters must be concerned with development.

If these ideas contain any great amount of truth, then most of those agencies working with natural disasters should rethink their methods of operation.

However, in stressing the ways in which humans make their land more prone to drought and flood, and thus increase their own suffering, we do not mean to imply that unpredictable Nature does not have a key role to play in triggering these disasters....

Droughts: Too Little Water

... Lack of vegetation and topsoil means that the land cannot retain the water. The old irrigation channels actually take water away from the crops. So normal rains become "floods", and these are followed quickly by "droughts". And all of this can happen in years of normal average rainfall. After several years work, the IRRI [International Rice Research Institute] has been unable to produce a rice strain that can flourish when drought follows quickly on the heels of total submersion.

These "droughts" during plentiful rainfall — with the damage to crops associated with seasons of little rain — make nonsense of the three types of drought defined by geographers:

- "precipitation drought" due to lack of rainfall;
- "runoff drought" due to low levels of river flow; and
- "aquifer drought" due to a lack of groundwater.

In fact, US disaster expert I. Burton defines drought in Tanzania not in terms of rainfall, but in terms of crop production. A "major" drought is one that diminishes crop yields by as much as 30% and a "severe" drought would "cause a loss of crop and animal production of about 8%". This definition not only removes drought from a measurement of rain but emphasises how narrow the margins are in Third World agriculture.

RAIN, SOIL, DROUGHT AND CLIMATE

When US climatologist C.W. Thornthwaite measured average monthly rainfall for Lagos, Sokoto (in northern Nigeria on the southern border of the Sahel region) and London, he found that Sokoto receives 100 mm (4 inches) more rain a year than London. But most of Sokoto's rain comes in July, August and September. There are five months during which Sokoto receives no rain at all. London's rain is evenly spread throughout the year.

The Sahel's rains come during a few months — when they come at all — and during those months it often comes in downpours. Most of the tropics, whether rainy or arid, gets its rain in seasons of intense rainfall between dry seasons. For these rains to do crops any good, the soil must retain water.

Yet most of Africa's soil is infertile sand and laterite soils (with a high content of iron and aluminium compounds, which become hard on exposure to sun and air). Sand and laterite not only erode easily, but hold little water compared to the clayey and humus-rich soils of the temperate zones. Laterite soils, when devegetated and exposed to sun and rain, can bake into a hard, concrete-like texture which is almost impossible to cultivate and absorbs virtually no rainfall. Soils throughout the tropics generally tend to be poorer than temperate soils. There are, however, many exceptions, such as the volcanic soils of Indonesia and Burundi, the deep clays of the northeast coast of Brazil, the Gezira area of Sudan and south of Lake Chad.

In the tropics, soils naturally prone of erosion receive a harder buffeting by rainstorms. At a rainfall rate of 35 mm (1.4 ins) per hour, there is a sharp rise in rain's ability to cause "splash erosion": to knock crumbs of soil loose, beginning the process of wash erosion that cuts deep into the soil.

Vegetation helps fragile tropical soils to retain water. When this vegetation is removed, topsoil rapidly erodes, according to Dr. W.E. Ormerod of the London School of Hygiene and Tropical Medicine (who assembled most of the above data on Sahel rainfall and soil).

Areas with widespread erosion are more prone to drought — because the soils can retain less and less water — and more prone to floods for the same reason.

THE BIG DROUGHTS

But surely the major droughts of several years affecting several nations are due plainly and simply to lack of rain?

In early 1984, more than 150 million people in 24 western, eastern and southern African nations were "on the brink of starvation" because of droughts, and "famine has already caused deaths in some countries", according to a UN Food and Agriculture Organization (FAO) report. In October 1983, FAO had launched a general alert concerning the food situation in Africa.

Rains in 1983-84 either did not come, or came too little, too early or too late. Countries outside the Sahel were also affected:

- Ethiopia: in four northern regions five million people were suffering after several consecutive years of drought. Eritrea had little rain except on the coast. Civil war also disrupted agriculture and food distribution schemes.
- Sudan: Eastern Sudan had a poor harvest, but refugees from Ethiopia continued to pour in. The British relief organisation OXFAM reported that in one camp the new arrivals were not fleeing war, but were drought refugees — farmers from Tigre and Wollo regions who were malnourished upon arrival.
- Mozambique: Central and southern areas had had little or no rain since 1979, and with drought affecting the entire region many of the rivers normally flowing into the country had dried up. The government reported in late 1983 that "for the rural population in many areas the only food supply during the last months were some fruits and leaves growing in the savannah forest". A UN report in early 1984 said 10,000 people had already died in three of the worst hit provinces and at least 750,000 people were in need of urgent aid.
- Zimbabwe: All eight districts got some rain in late 1983, but the water supply remained critical, with cattle dying in some areas. Living cattle were weak, so in some areas there was no draught power, causing people to use hoes to plough, reducing the area they could plant and so affecting future harvests.

The weather was clearly to blame. But in each nation human activity made the disaster worse:

- Ethiopia: Robert Lamb of UNEP [United Nations Environment Program] reported that "the highlands, especially the regions of Wollo, Tigre, and Gondor have been so overfarmed, overgrazed and deforested that efforts to scrape a bare living from this land threaten to destroy it permanently. The erosion resulting from overuse causes the Ethiopian highlands to lose one billion tonnes of topsoil each year, according to UN estimates." The situation is so desperate that the government has begun a major resettlement scheme to transfer farmers from the highlands to underpopulated lowlands. Government officials have referred to the people to be moved as "environment refugees".

- Sudan: For some time the Sahara has been encroaching upon the Sudan across a broad front at a rate of about five kilometres (3 miles) a year, claimed Sudanese President Jaafar Mohamed Al Nimeri in late 1983 at the FAO annual conference. In fact, scientists say the process of desertification is less like the advance of a wall of sand than the outbreak of a blotchy skin disease, here and there over an area of 100-200 sq km (60-125 sq miles). Yet the Sudanese government continues to allow, even to encourage, overcultivation and overgrazing in the afflicted areas. President Nimeri told the FAO meeting that the nation's motto was "agriculture and more agriculture".

- Mozambique: Some 8,000-10,000 Mozambique National Resistance Movement fighters, widely reported to be backed by South Africa, destroyed homes, state-run shops, health centres and crops in late 1983 and early 1984, according to OXFAM. They prevented government delivery of relief supplies, frightened people out of planting their crops and caused many to flee to safer areas, especially in the two southernmost provinces, Gaza and Inhambane. Mozambique has suffered both drought and destabilisation.

- Zimbabwe: As Zimbabwe approached independence in 1980, the whites — 5% of the population — controlled 50% of the land. Economic and security problems have meant that land redistribution since then has been slow. African families crowded onto poor quality "tribal lands" have been forced to overcultivate and deforest these fragile areas. Poor rainfall has been the final blow. The cattle-herding Ndebele people do not feel they are getting their fair share of the redistributed land under the Shona-dominated government of Premier Mugabe. Their own land has been overgrazed by their herds, and the Ndebele appeared to be suffering the worst from the drought.

An FAO report released in July 1984 listed six African countries which would face severe food shortages right through 1985, due to the failures of three successive harvests. Zimbabwe and Mozambique were joined on the list by Angola, Botswana, Lesotho and Zambia.

THE SAHEL: 1968-73

The 1968-73 Sahel drought, which most directly affected Chad, Mali, Mauritania, Niger, Senegal and Upper Volta (now called Burkina-Faso), was made worse by human action and inaction. According to a report to the 1977 UN Conference on Desertification (UNCOD), between 100,000 and 150,000 died in the region. And in a report by the Club du Sahel (an informal collection of countries giving aid to the region) and the Permanent Interstate Committee for Drought Control in the Region (CILSS — an organisation of Sahelian governments) the toll was 50,000-100,000.

But the death toll tells little of the story. Jean Copans of the Centre for African Studies in Paris, claims that by 1974 there were 200,000 people in Niger (5% of the population) completely dependent on food distribution; 250,000 people in Mauritania (20% of the population) had moved to towns and were completely destitute; and in Mali another 250,000 people (5%) were totally dependent on aid in towns.

The drought focused scientific and public attention on the Sahel in particular, and on the climate in general. Scientists checked to see if climatic change was to blame.

"No serious analysis of the available data is known to show a falling trend of rainfall in the zone over the period for which records are available", concluded E. G. Davy in a report for the UN World Meteorological Organization; his findings also covered arid zones in India and the Middle East. Other climatologists agreed. Rainfall has been lower in the past 15-20 years than during the 1950s and early 1960s, but there is no evidence that this represents a major climate change. Scientists also looked at the historical record and found that rains have often failed in the Sahel. The nomadic Tuareg tribespeople have given earlier droughts names like "Forget your wife" and "The sale of children".

Alan Grainger of Oxford University, UK wrote in a 1982 Earthscan report:

> "Drought triggers a crisis, but does not cause it. Overcultivation and overgrazing weaken the land, allowing no margin when drought arrives. The high human pressure will continue during the drought, leading ultimately to even greater and more visible damage to the land and the deaths of large numbers of animals."

After the drought, both the Club du Sahel and CILSS agreed that food self-sufficiency was the main goal of national and regional development. Over 1975-80, donor countries committed $7.5 billion in aid. Yet only 24% of this was actually directed toward agriculture, and less than 40% of all agriculture and forestry projects were rural. The rest went to urban-based support projects. Of the $7.5 billion, only 8% went for cropping which depends on rain rather than irrigation. (Some 28% of all agricultural aid went to cash crops, most of which were exported. In 1960-70, almost all aid to "rainfed" cropping went to cotton and peanut projects.) Only 5% of the $7.5 billion went to livestock raising, a major activity in the region. Only 1.4% of aid went to forestry/ecology in 1980, up from 0.35% in 1975. Writing in 1983 of the ways in which both aid-giving and aid-receiving nations had been spending money to combat desertification, Dr. Harold Dregne of Texas Tech University (US), noted:

> "Governments do not see desertification as a high-priority item. Rangeland deterioration, accelerated soil erosion and salinisation and waterlogging do not

command attention until they become crisis items. Lip service is paid to combating desertification, but the political will is directed elsewhere. There seems to be little appreciation that a major goal of many developing nations, that of food self-sufficiency, cannot be attained if soil and plant resources are allowed to deteriorate."

Each year the region falls further and further behind its goal of food self-sufficiency. Population is increasing at the rate of 2.5% a year and cereal production rises at 1% a year. Between 1955 and 1979, the land area under millet and sorghum increased at an average rate of 3.4% per year, but production rose only 2.5% per year. Thus yields per hectare are falling. Food aid to the region never falls below 100,000 tonnes a year.

Why, when everyone seems agreed that food self-sufficiency is of utmost importance for the Sahel, does so little money go to agriculture?

First, the peasants who live in arid lands have little political power. The governments — civil servants, police, army — are in the capitals. So leaders like to keep aid in the capitals — whether it be food aid or the construction of buildings and other projects which generate employment.

Second, for the same political reasons, Sahelian governments have a policy of providing cheap food to urban centres. So subsistence farmers rarely produce extra food to sell in the market — because the selling price does not pay for the fertiliser or better seed they need to increase production.

Third, the donor nations have few experts who can increase yields of sorghum and millet in arid lands, but do have experts at constructing roads and buildings, and they have companies manufacturing equipment for such purposes.

Yield per hectare of foods is falling because increasing populations tend to push farmers and herders onto marginal lands, and because plantations of cash crops get the best land along southern rivers, pushing subsistence farmers and nomads north toward the desert.

Fourth, livestock numbers are climbing toward their pre-drought (1968) levels. The contribution of domestic animals to desertification is a controversial issue, but overgrazing is certainly playing a role in degrading land in the Sahel. In 1980, the numbers of cows and sheep in the Sahel were at 70% of their pre-drought levels; the numbers of goats, horses and donkeys, were equal to 1968 levels, according to a UNDP [United Nations Development Program] report.

"The situation has become extremely precarious in the Sudan, as in all countries in the region, and is today much more delicate than in the late 1960s. The next serious drought might well entail more severe consequences than the last one", predicted French rangeland expert Michel Baumer in 1982.

"Whether you see the desert as advancing or the Sahel as losing ground, a real catastrophe is on the way", predicted Mamadou Mahamane, director of a Niger forestry aid project the same year.

THE SAHEL TODAY

In 1983, rains were either too late or too little across much of the Sahel, except in the south.

In Mauritania, the rains failed in 1982 and 1983. The Mauritanian government distributed food in late 1983, but this went to centres up to 100 km (60 miles) away from some villages. There was a mass migration to the capital Nouakchott, which already contained half the country's population.

In Burkina-Faso (formerly called Upper Volta), there was almost no 1983 harvest in the north. Waterholes were only a quarter full. An aid worker in Oudalan reported that peasants there were as badly off as in 1972.

All the Sahelian countries except Niger were on the FAO's list of threatened African countries. Niger also suffered from late 1983 rains, but its government has perhaps done more than any other Sahelian government to promote food self-sufficiency, emphasising food rather than cash crops after the 1968-73 drought. Niger seems to be the lead country in the region in terms of extending advice and services to the countryside. Its leaders took quick action in 1983, selling off 5,000 head of cattle from government farms as a warning to pastoralists that grazing lands would not be sufficient for several months. It advised herders to move to better pastures and began to provide animal fodder to help get the herds through the 1983-84 dry season ....

DROUGHT AND FAMINE

Just as poor rainfall is not the single and direct cause of drought, drought is not the single and direct cause of famine.

People do not starve in a drought-related famine simply because there is no food. No relief worker has starved to death during a drought; no journalist has died of hunger while covering a drought. Because of a complex set of economic, cultural and political factors, these people are "entitled" to food, to borrow a concept from economist Amartya Sen. Due to economic, cultural and political reasons, the "victims" of the famine are not entitled to food.

Critics of this analysis point out that just because there is enough food available for journalists and relief workers to buy does not necessarily mean there would be enough for all the hungry to buy if they had money.

The International Labour Organisation (ILO) studied the famines in Bengal in 1943, in Ethiopia in 1973 and in Bangladesh in 1974. It found that famine "chose" its victims by class and occupation, and there were many other factors at work besides food scarcity. In Bengal, food stocks were below the level of 1942 but were within the normal range of fluctuation. But wartime inflation had destroyed the Bengal currency. In Ethiopia, the lack of food was a highly localised phenomenon. But richer farmers had dismissed labourers and household staff because of low yields, so there were no wages to buy food. Dr. John Rivers of the International Disaster Institute maintains that throughout the famine Ethiopia was a net exporter of food. In Bangladesh, there was actually more food available on a per person basis than in some recent non-famine years. But floods had disrupted industry and thus cut other employment opportunities.

In each case people's options were diminished. Those who suffered most were the landless labourers and the pastoralists who had to sell their livelihood — their cattle — to survive, at a time when there was no market for cattle.

B. M. Bhatia, in his 1967 study of Indian famines, also concluded that famine is not an imbalance between populations and natural resources, but that "instead of absolute want, famine under modern conditions had come to signify a sharp and abrupt rise in food prices which renders food beyond the reach of the poor who suffer starvation".

FLEXIBILITY AND DROUGHT

Up to fairly recent times, people have relied on flexible responses to avoid the effects of droughts and other disasters.

The most basic form of flexibility is mobility, notes Canadian geographer Eric Waddell, who quotes an old Chinese proverb, "Of thirty ways to escape danger, running away is best".

Many of the coping mechanisms of the nomadic herdsmen of the Sahel depend on movement to another area, but there are also other ways of increasing flexibility. The Wodaabe Fulani people of Niger not only move seasonally (transhumance) from the southern cropped fields during the dry season to the northern Sahelian pastures as the rains begin in June, but move out of camps in different directions daily to seek water and grass. They carefully diversify their herds, mixing camels, sheep and goats with cows. Different animals have different needs for water and pasture and breed at different times, spreading risk. They trade their sheep, goats, hides, milk, butter and cheese with Hausa farmers for such staples as millet and sorghum. They rely on certain "fallback activities" such as short-term, spontaneous sedentarisation and wage labour. (The government has discouraged one traditional fallback activity: raiding other tribes.) They share animals in a very complex system of kinship duties and traditional exchanges. Animals may be given, loaned or rented out. A cow may be loaned until she has three calves; the borrower keeps the calves and returns the cow.

Flexibility can aid farmers as well as herders. New Guinea cultivators once moved into other areas during drought. But before doing so, they exhausted other possibilities. They typically planted gardens far apart and at different elevations, sowing crops resistant to various climate extremes — rain, drought, frost — in different gardens....

Recently, a number of factors have virtually eliminated the flexibility of response of many marginal people in drought-prone areas. Most governments discourage "mobility" as a response to an emergency, and have also tried to settle nomads. Yet through custom, the herders still keep large numbers of animals. Population pressure — especially the growing numbers of cultivators — and government regulations such as grazing fees and range block systems also hinder mobility. Cultivators' flexibility is limited by their need to earn money by concentrating on perhaps only one cash crop. Also, their poverty and the lack of government agricultural extension means that they have little or no choice in the varieties of subsistence crops which they plant. Investing all one's efforts in one variety of one staple is dangerous, expecially in drought-prone areas.

US geographer Ben Wisner, studying ways used by traditional societies to diminish the effects of drought in Kenya in the past, found 157 different mechanisms at work, most of them complex sharing systems among extended families. Looking at the same society recently, he found only two of these mechanisms still at work: leaving the countryside for urban jobs, and prayer.

Flexibility today can cover a number of possibilities: the ability to move; a choice of types and varieties of cash and subsistence crops; a choice of markets for crops and livestock (in a drought, herders cannot sell their livestock locally because the bottom has dropped out of the market); alternative ways of making money, such as light industry; and government insurance schemes.

Flexibility is not only a defensive approach. Under the right conditions, it can even bring prosperity in drought-prone areas.

In the late 1920s a group of Mennonite Christians of German-Russian origin left Canada seeking cultural and religious freedom and settled in the remote "Chaco" region of Paraguay, some 750 km (465 miles) by small riverboat, rail and road from Asunción. Severe floods alternate with drought in this region of fine clayey and sandy soils.

Canadian geographers A. Hecht and J. W. Fretz, who studied three Mennonite settlements of almost 10,000 people, found that "in about one out of four years, major drought conditions exist in the Chaco". Yet after 50 years of hard struggle, these settlers, admittedly the offspring of immigrants with industrial and professional backgrounds, are flourishing.

They appear to succeed by spreading their options as widely as possible, planting cotton and castor beans as cash crops and peanuts, beans and sorghum as food crops. Harvests vary wildly from year to year; wheat proved so vulnerable to drought that the Mennonites ceased planting it in 1970. They have imported "buffalo grass" from Texas, which is an excellent cattle feed, does well on the Chaco soils and recuperates quickly after a drought. Milk from their cattle is turned into cheese and butter at their own dairy, thus providing a market for their milk, which they would not be able to sell as milk. A local tree provides a resin which is sold for use in perfumes and various industrial purposes.

Other local industries include a tannery, a shoe factory, a metal foundry, tile and brick yards, a furniture factory, a blacksmith and tinsmiths. The Paraguayan Mennonites have even set up an agriculture experiment station.

Such industries help the settlements survive drought years such as 1975, when harvests were only 48% of 1974 yields, in that the people can continue to produce things to sell. And today they also have supplies of saved capital upon which to draw.

Hecht and Fretz attribute the Mennonites' prosperity to "the ability to specialise in agricultural endeavours suitable to the environment" and the abandonment of unsuccessful crops attempted in the early years of the settlements. The authors draw from this the lesson that "environmentally sensitive regions are vulnerable when crop production strives to meet all needs", as in subsistence farming.

The Mennonites have moved beyond subsistence by overcoming great transport problems in getting products to markets, but more importantly by relying on a wide range of food and cash-producing options.

The cultivators of the Sahelian countryside lack agricultural options, markets which pay reasonable prices for any surpluses, and any manufacturing or industrial opportunities. The Mennonite experience offers the hope that well-considered tactics and economic development can offer at least the possibility of doing well amidst droughts. . . .

Relief

. . . [I]t may appear churlish to question the value of international relief after a natural disaster. We have become familiar with problems connected with military aid, long-term food aid and even much development aid. By comparison, disaster relief — getting food, medicine and shelter to populations suddenly bereft of these things — seems like benign and selfless charity.

But it is becoming more and more doubtful, say growing numbers of relief experts and field workers, whether relief is a cost-effective operation in terms of the best way to spend a given amount of money to help the afflicted people. Some disaster relief is being planned and managed on the basis of incorrect assumptions and mixed political and economic motives. These doubts about relief are only slowly percolating into the consciousness of the general public. They are in fact felt most strongly in the collective minds of the relief agencies themselves. For it is these agencies which must cope with the growing flood of disaster appeals from the poorer developing nations. The relief agencies are coming to realise that emergency relief by itself is no longer an adequate response.

The following chapter is not meant to be an attack on relief. Yet documenting as it does many of the ways well-intended relief schemes can go wrong, it may sound like such. In many disasters, nothing but relief is possible, due perhaps to warfare or to regimes which will not accept long-term development assistance and instead insist on short-term, emergency aid.

Relief work is steadily more difficult, not only from the point of view of deciding whether or to what extent intervention in a disaster which has both "natural" and "political" causes, but also from the point of view of basic logistics — getting material effectively to the field. Third World disasters have reached such overwhelming proportions that foreign disaster assistance, even if efficiently planned and organised, can play only a marginal role in mitigating them. Relief work today is like bandaging a wound that is constantly growing.

Third World disasters — particularly droughts and floods, the two which are increasing most rapidly — will demand increasing amounts of international attention in the future. Traditional relief will continue to be a major part of the international response. But to at least slow the rate of increase in disasters, governments and aid donors will have to recognize the human hand in causing these catastrophes, and stop treating each disaster only as a logistical exercise in moving men and equipment. Whenever possible, short-term assistance should be linked to longer-term improvements aimed at disaster prevention.

Thus in critically analysing some aspects of relief assistance in its more traditional forms, the following chapter does not mean to question the value of relief itself in all cases, but to point out the need for improvements in execution and for a redefinition of the basic objectives of relief operations.

THE HELPLESSNESS MYTH

Despite constant debunking the prevailing image of disaster victims is of a huddled mass of dazed humanity, deep in shock after the initial panic has worn off.

However, one of the key findings of the US National Opinion Research Council's 1950-54 research into human behaviour in disasters was that panic and other forms of uncontrolled behaviour were relatively rare. In 1953, the US National Academy of Sciences (NAS) became interested in disasters and formed a Disaster Research Group which worked in the field until 1963. During its 10 years of study, it divided disasters into various "phases" and examined how people acted in each.

It found that during the *impact phase* there was virtually no panic. Ad hoc leaders tended to emerge who had no tested leadership ability but who had skills to offer which were needed in the situation. In the *inventory phase* immediately following impact, people engaged in search and rescue activities and sought family and friends. Social coordination gave way to loose, informal organisational structures among and within groups.

In the *rescue phase* some people became docile or passive, a condition which rendered them more receptive to suggestions and authority, but this phase tended to be restricted to really large disasters in which there had been great disruption and destruction. During the *remedy phase* there was a heightening of interaction between individuals and groups, with class barriers breaking down and outside relief groups being ostracised by the stricken community.

These NAS findings have remained disputed, and in the early 1960s some researchers were attacking the entire disaster research field as being politically controversial, empirically weak and experimentally difficult. Nevertheless, the early work did a lot to dispel myths — myths which have needed repeated dispelling ever since. The League of Red Cross Societies' *Disaster Relief Handbook,* published in 1976 and still in use in early 1984, carried the following definition of "disaster":

> "A disaster is a catastrophic situation in which the day-to-day patterns of life are — in many instances — suddenly disrupted and people are plunged into helplessness and suffering and, as a result, need protection, food, clothing, shelter, medical and social care, and other necessities of life."

... Experience shows that it is always the victims who bear the brunt of work and expense in providing their own post-disaster relief. According to US disaster consultant Frederick Cuny, foreign disaster aid has never covered more than 40% of the costs of relief in a Third World disaster. In many cases it covers a much smaller proportion.

The office of the UN Disaster Relief Co-ordinator (UNDRO) noted in its 1982 report *Shelter After Disaster* that "often, far from being dazed and distraught by the loss of their homes, the survivors are amazingly resilient — the best resource for reconstruction". It advised relief workers to harness this resource . . . .

RELIEF AS INTERVENTION

On a normal day-to-day basis, a Third World community — whether a nation, city or shantytown — is an extremely complex network of deals, debts, kinships and relationships. During a disaster these relationships do not vanish; they aid the recovery and rebuilding processes. Thus it is not an easy task for relief agencies from other lands to bring into such complicated systems goods and advice which are appropriate and helpful.

"Agencies repeatedly attempt to simplify what is a complex process; and by doing so, they create innumerable problems, not only for themselves, but also for the society which they are trying to assist", writes US disaster consultant Frederick Cuny. "It is naive to believe that an agency can go into a society and provide a structure which meets their definition of shelter or of a house, without participating in the process through which houses are normally provided", Cuny adds.

What goes for houses also goes for food and other goods. Stories abound in the relief field of completely inappropriate aid: the British charity that sent packs of tea, tissues and Tampax; the European Community sending powdered milk into an earthquake area where few cows had perished, but there was no water; and the West German charity which constructed 1,000 polystyrene igloos which proved too hot to live in. But the igloos could not be dismantled or moved. They had to be burned down, and when burning they gave off toxic fumes. Tins of chicken cooked in pork-fat have been sent to Moslem countries which do not eat pork. Blankets donated to India were donated by India to Nepal, which donated them back to India; the blankets were never needed or used. Turkey after a 1983 earthquake asked donors not to send any medicine or second-hand clothes, but a Northern donor flew in a few days later with a planeload of precisely these items — and a TV crew to cover the distribution.

Tony Jackson of OXFAM has found potato crisps, slimming foods, children's sweet fruit drinks and spaghetti sauce sent as food aid to Chad, Guatemala, Kampuchea and the Dominican Republic.

The Red Cross delivered 3,000 tents to the town of San Martin after the 1976 Guatemalan earthquake. Some $850,000 had been donated for this relief effort, and photos appearing in a later Red Cross brochure showed neat rows of tents. But despite efforts by the Guatemalan Army to virtually march the "victims" into the tents at gunpoint, the townsfolk declined; they wanted to be near their possessions and livestock. After two weeks, seven tents were occupied.

A major problem with relief is that the "relief period" following a sudden, violent disaster — as opposed to the reconstruction and rehabilitation periods, which may last some years — is very short; some experts put it at only 48 hours. Depending on climate, if victims have not found shelter, warmth, water and at least the hope of food within a day or two, it is too late. Few international relief agencies can deliver in such a short time. Such necessities are almost always more quickly available near the disaster area. So when tents and blankets arrive from Europe, the victims are either sheltered and warm, or past help.

Yet human nature dictates that when a plane lands with free goods, people will stop what they are doing and queue for hours to get whatever is available, whether they need it or not. Thus relief can actually slow down reconstruction and interfere with self-help.

Examples of inappropriate aid raise the question of to whom the agencies and other "intervenors" are accountable. Who forms their constituency? Ian Davis, from Oxford Polytechnic, UK, looked at the accountability of various outsiders: UN agencies, overseas governments, overseas charities, foreign experts and local elite. He found that none is accountable to the victims of the quake, except in the cases of overseas charities and local elite when they work through grassroots groups, as when the Red Cross works through the local Red Cross chapters or other international volunteer agencies work through local organisations. UN agencies and foreign government agencies are officially accountable to the recipient government and — in the case of national agencies — to their home governments. But in practice, on the disaster scene, they are accountable to no one except a possible journalistic exposé . . . .

It would be unfair to put all the blame for inappropriate help on foreign agencies. Very often the national governments of the afflicted countries are insensitive, to say the least, to the needs of the victims. Given that human activity causes or exacerbates many natural disasters, then the governments of the victim nations have a large responsibility in doing so little to prevent these disasters. Once a calamity has occurred, government policies often complicate relief work and rehabilitation. In some situations, the needs of afflicted populations are neglected. In others, security problems, real or alleged for political reasons, prevent relief agencies from operating efficiently.

In most disasters, the military plays a key role in restoring order. This follows European and US practices in the 1950s and 1960s, and makes a certain amount of sense because the military can get self-sufficient units to the field quickly, has good communications and access to transport and heavy machinery. It is a disciplined organization. But the military does things in a military manner. Army units have been known to move into a disaster area like an invading army and to treat the survivors like prisoners of war, ordering them here and there. In some cases troops have organised victims in orderly, compact tent camps — far from their domestic animals and the homes they want to rebuild. The density of such camps can encourage the spread of disease. Such a military approach can create feelings of helplessness and passivity among the victims which would not be there if they were allowed to get on with the job . . . .

THE RELIEF "CONSTITUENCY"

An examination of the "constituencies" of the foreign intervenors in disasters — whether UN agency, foreign government or relief agency — helps explain the mixed motives.

Rarely, except when intervenors work through local organisations, does this constituency include the actual victims of the disaster. For the big Western governments, the constituency is the voters at home — especially around election time — and the other branches of government, especially those concerned with foreign policy.

Over the period 1965-73, the total of US government disaster aid exceeded that of the rest of the international community in five of the nine years. In the case of some disasters, US aid exceeded that provided by total country self-help, according to British geographer Phil O'Keefe. However, by themselves these figures give the wrong impression. Over that nine-year period, in-country self-help more than doubled the amount of external assistance received. The domestic self-help is also probably underestimated. So despite international relief efforts, the local people still do most of their own "relieving" and reconstructing.

It is possible to make three broad generalisations about disaster aid from the North. First, it is highly variable and follows no logic of need and cost-effectiveness. Second, it tends to follow the pattern of the donor country's development and military aid; i.e., relief aid tends to go to allies and those already getting aid. Third, a lot of "relief" is merely the export of surplus commodities.

As for lack of logic, the most telling statistic is that the dead seem to attract more "relief" than those still struggling. A ranking of disaster types in terms of numbers killed during the 1970s beginning with the deadliest, would read as follows: earthquake, cyclone, civil strife, drought and flood. In terms of numbers affected, the ranking is almost reversed: drought (almost 25 million), flood, civil strife, cyclone and earthquake (about two million). But a ranking of donor response to League of Red Cross and Red Crescent Societies appeals during the 1970s reads: civil strife, earthquake, cyclone, flood, drought. So except for the civil strife category, disasters that kill a few quickly get much more "relief" than disasters that grind people down slowly.

Accidents of newsworthiness and politics can affect response. In Europe, the attempt by the Ethiopian government under Haile Selassie to virtually ignore the drought in the early 1970s became an international scandal with enormous media coverage. Contributions through volunteer agencies exceeded $21 million. In the United States, the media was focused on Watergate, and US aid was only about $1.5 million. In early 1984, US congressmen trying to vote through more grain for drought-afflicted African nations were frustrated because the appropriation had been tacked onto a controversial vote for military aid for Central America.

Some disasters are simply more fashionable than others. In 1983, the Red Cross launched separate appeals for Polish food needs and for the Brazilian drought victims. Poland got four times more than was appealed for. By the end of 1983, the northeastern Brazilian drought appeal had brought in only 2.4% of the expressed needs, though this figure rose slowly to above 50% by March 1984. A November 1983 Red Cross appeal for Turkish earthquake victims almost immediately brought in $233 per person assisted; the Brazil drought appeal, also launched in November, had gathered no more than 56 cents per person to be assisted by the end of the year. The League launched a total of 48 international appeals in 1983, the biggest for drought victims in India and Mauritania. But Poland and Turkey got 26.7% of the total gift value of $57 million raised that year; India got one-third of the amount appealed for, and Mauritania got about half.

In Europe, appeals from former colonies in Africa and Asia tend to raise more money than disasters in Latin America. But the United States, which regards Latin America as its sphere of influence, is more disposed to help those governments which it regards as favourably disposed to its policies. During the 1973-74 crop year, the US contributed $130 million dollars to the Sahel region. At the same time the US also airlifted $2.2 billion to Israel, during the October 1973 Yom Kippur War. And in fiscal 1974-75, the US Congress approved $700 million for South Vietnam. Africa, which tends to suffer most from drought and famine today, is low in US aid priorities; less than 10% of USAID foreign appropriation goes to Africa, and the majority of that to only 10 African states.

US "PL 480" food aid, which covers both concessional sales and donations, does go to feed people in need. But it is unreliable; when US farmers can get higher prices abroad for their grain, the PL 480 programme is drastically cut. During the Sahel famine, low domestic cereal prices encouraged the US government to pay $3 billion to US farmers not to produce food. The downturn in production and large Soviet purchases meant there was little US grain available for aid. The United States gave 6.1 million tonnes of wheat in food aid in 1970, but it provided only 2.5 million tonnes in 1973. In the 1974 fiscal year, more than 59% of the Food for Peace shipments went to countries reflecting US security concerns such as Vietnam, Cambodia, Laos, Malta, Jordan and Israel.

Politics — along with a growing sense of pride and a growing realisation of the limitations of foreign relief efforts — also has a role to play in limiting what disaster-stricken nations will accept today. After the Guatemala City earthquake of 1976, Guatemala refused to accept aid from Britain because the two countries were in dispute over Belize. China, India, Mexico and the Philippines are all countries which have recently declined disaster aid in certain cases, apparently through a mixture of pride and seeing no real gain in accepting it.

CHARITY AND ITS MOTIVES

Governments are not the only relief organisations which overlook the needs of disaster victims in planning their activities. The non-governmental relief agencies may also be prone to similar "political" motivation.

Voluntary agencies find relief efforts helpful in book-keeping in two ways. First, delivering a planeload of food to earthquake victims generates great amounts of publicity, and publicity brings in more contributions to the agency. Such efforts catch more press attention than, say, helping villagers build cyclone-resistant houses. This may be one reason relief agencies expend so much effort to be first in getting goods to disaster areas, even if there is no way to distribute the goods to victims once they arrive. Such publicity is a two-edged sword, as it can mean that agencies let the media set priorities for them. OXFAM disaster co-ordinator Marcus Thompson describes how difficult it is to explain to an OXFAM donor why the agency is not involved in a flood which has just been shown on television: " . . . 'Of course it's a disaster; I saw it on the news. Send food in', the donor is likely to tell me. It is hard pressure to ignore."

Second, volunteer agencies and charities like to be able to demonstrate that a high percentage of the funds collected go to "the field", and that only a small percentage stays home for such things as salaries and office rent. Disaster relief efforts are a great help in making this ratio appear impressive to would-be donors, because a disaster relief operation — whether effective or ineffective — may consume a great deal of money and material with relatively little manpower overheads. Other activities which may keep experts in the field for long periods can make this ratio of expenditure look less favorable.

There have also been charges that disaster relief appeals are planned not as a response to disasters but as a response to fund-raising strategies. One or two big campaigns a year (especially around Christmas time) for dramatic events like earthquakes tend to pull in many more donations than a long-term appeal for those affected by drought.

The debate over the motives and efficiency of relief has not been ignored by the charities. The UK charities — the British Red Cross Society, Save the Children Fund, Christian Aid, CAFOD (the Catholic charity) and OXFAM — have all banded together to form the Disasters Emergency Committee (DEC). It pools information and launches joint appeals for funds; each organisation disposes of its share according to its interests. DEC has helped to avoid competition between appeals and has raised the amounts the appeals can raise. After the Vietnam war, Save the Children, a UK relief-focused organisation, wanted to launch a DEC appeal for relief. War on Want argued that the disaster was continuing and required a longer term effort. War on Want has since left DEC, dissatisfied with its concentration on relief rather than on continuing development aid. OXFAM is also moving away from "relief" toward development.

Frederick Cuny has been involved directly in relief operations in the Biafra war, the Bangladesh civil war and the Lebanese fighting; he has also participated in relief work in Israel, Burundi, Nicaragua, Honduras, Guatemala and Peru. He believes that:

> "A lot of these (large relief) agencies have known for a long time that their programmes do not work. However, they respond to pressure not only from their own donors but from the countries they are working in. Local governments sometimes don't have any better idea than the agencies of what's going on in the field."

Cuny described a large US voluntary agency as being simply "too big" and "locked into providing free assistance. Their entire advertising campaign is based around giving money for welfare for poor people in developing countries. Because of this policy, they can't sell the food or other materials when it is appropriate. I have heard the director talk about why he has to keep doing this. I guess it is more important to have the money coming in than to worry about where it is going or what it is doing."

FOOD AS RELIEF

There has been such a backlash against food aid recently that organisations such as the World Food Programme (WFP) believe that it soon may become difficult to mount any successful appeals for such aid in emergencies.

In early 1984, FAO Director-General Edouard Saouma asked for 1.6 million tonnes of food aid for the 24 African countries most affected by drought. Though much of this aid, if raised, will go astray and be used inefficiently, it would be a tragedy if people starved because of changing aid fashions in the North. Any criticism of food aid for disaster relief must be balanced by the knowledge that food aid can and does save lives.

This ... [report] is not addressing the complex debate on food aid in general; our discussion centres on the effectiveness of using food as part of post-disaster relief. About 70% of all food aid is given or sold on concessional terms to Third World governments, and most of this is resold to help these governments' budgets. The remaining 30% — "project food aid" — is designated for free distribution to the poor. Only 10% of all food aid is used for disaster relief and feeding refugees.

OXFAM's Tony Jackson, whose book *Against the Grain* (Oxford, 1982) best describes the problems connected with various types of food aid, says firmly in his conclusions: "Food aid is often needed for emergency relief and this will often entail imports, especially for refugees". He asserts elsewhere: "A well-organised and equitable relief programme is possible". He gives as an example of such a programme the efforts following the destruction in southwest Dominican Republic by Hurricanes David and Frederick in 1979. The Netherlands office of the international relief agency Caritas organised the import of food, paid for by the Dutch, first from nearby Caribbean islands and then from the Netherlands itself. WFP brought in food from Haiti. Some 300,000 people received food over a five-month period. The distribution programme was designed and run locally, and recipients were told they would get food for five months only, so reliance on food aid was not institutionalised ....

Once begun, food aid may never stop. Since the 1976 earthquake, Guatemala has continued to receive much larger amounts of non-disaster food aid than it received before. Haiti first received food aid after Hurricane Hazel in 1954; according to one priest, "it never stopped coming".

Post-disaster food aid is often of the wrong type. Some examples of this are listed above. During the Biafran war of 1968, Switzerland sent large amounts of Emmenthaler cheese to people who normally drank little milk and had never eaten cheese. Relief workers had to bury the cheese ....

There is a large body of opinion which holds that relief food aid has actually been responsible for much of the turmoil Bangladesh has suffered since the 1971 civil war. So much food aid poured in after the fighting that market prices for rice fell. Farmers planted less; production fell, and as production fell, agencies sent in more food. In 1975, World Food Programme director Trevor Page asked donor countries to stop sending food. He told a meeting that the more food which came in, the more starvation there appeared to be. By the mid-1970s, the ports were becoming jammed by food shipments, and Bengali farmers began to sell their food to marketeers who smuggled it into India, where they could make a bigger profit. By the start of the 1980s, the aid and relief agencies had accomplished little more than to build up "a dependency relationship on foreign resources", according to US disaster consultant Frederick Cuny. "Now the idea of having a foreign adviser had permeated the entire Bengali society, all the way down to the village level, to the point where nobody makes decisions unless it's been OK'd by a foreigner, and the foreigners are much less equipped than the Bengalis to run Bangladesh."

The controversy over food aid generally and disaster relief food aid in particular has not been ignored by the WFP, which noted in a 1982 issue of *World Food Programme News* that wherever possible WFP purchases its emergency and relief assistance food regionally, as for instance when purchasing for such countries as Burma, Thailand and Zimbabwe. It is able to bring food aid to disaster areas in sufficient quantities and in time to prevent starvation by diverting food from development projects in a given country or even from ships at sea. While asserting that a substantial part of its relief resources was used to feed starving people too weak to work after disaster had struck, WFP advocated the phasing out of free relief distribution as soon as local governments could organise constructive rehabilitation.

HELPING THE "PRE-DISASTER VICTIMS"

Theories on ways to minimise the effects of disasters have been buffeted by fashion. The Cold War of the 1950s led to stress on "preparedness". During the highly technological 1960s, the emphasis switched to "prevention", and then during the 1970s, "mitigation" came into fashion. Now it appears that a more sophisticated form of preparedness may be the strategy of the 1980s.

Preparedness has to do with having everything and everybody in place before a disaster so that order can more quickly be established during the chaos that the event will bring. Examples include stockpiles and action plans. Prevention involves such things as building levees to prevent flooding, and seeding to dissipate cyclones. It is very expensive and, in the case of rivers which are rapidly silting, must be done repeatedly. Mitigation has to do with pre-disaster measures to minimise effects: zoning and building laws to cope with earthquakes and cyclones; drought-resistant crops; public education and insurance.

Few non-government agencies concerned with disasters can afford to get involved in expensive, traditional prevention activities such as building levees. Nor can agencies, except perhaps the large UN bodies, expect to get involved in the "top-down" national preparedness and mitigation strategies. But there are numerous opportunities for working with the potential victims to make their environment less prone and themselves less vulnerable. Such programmes would have several things in common, all being:

- directed toward those on the margins;
- family-based and village-based;
- environmentally sustainable;
- concerned with protection and rehabilitation of soil, water and forests;
- aimed at reducing poverty among the vulnerable;

- concerned with nutrition, as it is the malnourished who are the most vulnerable to the hardships accompanying disaster, especially those interrupting food supplies;
- concerned with fostering self-reliance, as this is the only way the programmes themselves will be sustainable;
- focused on subsistence agriculture, as it is the peasant farmers whose lives and livelihoods are most vulnerable to most disasters.

Agencies which could work these goals into their programmes would be making people less vulnerable to disaster and less in need of "relief and rehabilitation" after disasters. They would also be improving the overall quality of people's lives, not just the quality of their lives during a cyclone or earthquake. A subsistence farmer able to cope with a drought is better able to cope in non-drought years.

There is a danger in the realisation that disaster vulnerability and poverty are inseparable. It can lead one up the classic cul-de-sac: the Catch 22 of all development, and the rationalisation of many Northern opponents of development assistance. Their argument is: "The poor are vulnerable. Poverty cannot be eliminated. Therefore, nothing can be done".

In fact, there are many low-cost projects which can both mitigate the effects of disaster and help to "develop" a Third World community. Some disaster experts are fond of saying that almost any good development project will alleviate the effects of a disaster. Cuny points out that the introduction of high-yielding wheat varieties into India in the 1960s-70s not only improved that nation's nutritional balance but helped reduce the possibility of a major famine due to the failure of the rice crop. Also, savings and loan programmes introduced into Guatemala by the cooperative movement mitigated the economic effects of disasters and gave people money reserves with which to rebuild after the 1976 earthquake.

Natural disasters are failures in interactions between vulnerable people and a vulnerable environment. Disaster mitigation, therefore, should aim at changes to improve both human and environmental conditions and the interactions between them. One cannot be isolated from the other. The major disaster problems are essentially unsolved development problems . . . .

REPORT ON HUMANITIES EDUCATION IN THE UNITED STATES

November 25, 1984

A National Endowment for the Humanities (NEH) panel report issued November 25 decried the state of the humanities in higher education and called for changes in teaching and curriculum at the undergraduate level.

William J. Bennett, chairman of the NEH and author of the 42-page report, wrote that college students today lack "even the most rudimentary knowledge about the history, literature, art, and philosophical foundations of their nation and civilization." Uninspired teaching and a "steady erosion" in structured curricula over two decades were largely responsible for the decline in humanities programs, Bennett wrote. He placed much of the blame on educators themselves. "The fault lies principally with those of us whose business it is to educate these students," he said. At the beginning of his second term, President Ronald Reagan nominated Bennett to succeed T. H. Bell as secretary of education.

The report recommended that college students be required to take a "core of common studies" on Western civilization and that these courses be taught by top-flight faculty members. Areas of knowledge in the humanities that the panel believed essential to a college education included:

● Study of the development of Western civilization.
● "Careful" reading of several masterworks of English, American and European literature.
● Study of the significant ideas and debates in the history of philosophy.

● Proficiency in a foreign language.

*Bennett convened a 31-member panel, composed of teachers, adminis-
trators and authorities on higher education, in March to assess the state
of humanities learning at the undergraduate level. The group held three
public meetings during the spring and summer, studied a variety of
material and information from colleges, universities, and national surveys. After eight months of study, Bennett wrote a report, "To Reclaim A
Legacy," based on the group's findings. The report stirred controversy in
the humanities field, with some scholars publicly disagreeing with the
group's recommendations.*

*An Education Department report, issued in October, offered more
general criticisms of undergraduate education. "Student learning, curricular coherence, the quality of facilities, faculty morale and academic
standards no longer measure up to our expectations," the Education
Department report stated. In line with the NEH report's proposal, the
Education Department document recommended that students pursue a
liberal arts education for two years.*

*The Association of American Colleges and the Carnegie Foundation for
the Advancement of Teaching were also preparing studies on the quality
of higher education. All of these efforts, said a* Washington Post *editorial
on the Bennett report, "mark a new stage in building back the structure
of intellectual values that was severely damaged in the upheavals of the
late 1960s and early 1970s."*

*Following are excerpts from "To Reclaim A Legacy: A
Report on the Humanities in Higher Education" by William
J. Bennett, released by the National Endowment for the
Humanities November 25, 1984:*

Although more than 50 percent of America's high school graduates
continue their education at American colleges and universities, few of
them can be said to receive there an adequate education in the culture and
civilization of which they are members. Most of our college graduates
remain shortchanged in the humanities — history, literature, philosophy,
and the ideals and practices of the past that have shaped the society they
enter. The fault lies principally with those of us whose business it is to educate these students. We have blamed others, but the responsibility is ours.
Not by our words but by our actions, by our indifference, and by our
intellectual diffidence we have brought about this condition. It is we the
educators — not scientists, business people, or the general public — who
too often have given up the great task of transmitting a culture to its
rightful heirs. Thus, what we have on many of our campuses is an
unclaimed legacy, a course of studies in which the humanities have been si-
phoned off, diluted, or so adulterated that students graduate knowing
little of their heritage. . . .

I. Why Study the Humanities?

The federal legislation that established the National Endowment for the Humanities in 1965 defined the humanities as specific disciplines: "language, both modern and classical; linguistics; literature; history; jurisprudence; philosophy; archaeology; comparative religion; ethics; the history, criticism, and theory of the arts"; and "those aspects of the social sciences which have humanistic content and employ humanistic methods." But to define the humanities by itemizing the academic fields they embrace is to overlook the qualities that make them uniquely important and worth studying. Expanding on a phrase from Matthew Arnold, I would describe the humanities as the best that has been said, thought, written, and otherwise expressed about the human experience. The humanities tell us how men and women of our own and other civilizations have grappled with life's enduring, fundamental questions: What is justice? What should be loved? What deserves to be defended? What is courage? What is noble? What is base? Why do civilizations flourish? Why do they decline? . . .

The members of the study group discussed at length the most effective ways to teach the humanities to undergraduates. Our discussion returned continually to two basic prerequisites for learning in the humanities: good teaching and a good curriculum. . . .

. . . The humanities are not an educational luxury, and they are not just for majors. They are a body of knowledge and a means of inquiry that convey serious truths, defensible judgments, and significant ideas. Properly taught, the humanities bring together the perennial questions of human life with the greatest works of history, literature, philosophy, and art. Unless the humanities are taught and studied in this way, there is little reason to offer them.

Based on our discussion, we recommend the following knowledge in the humanities as essential to a college education:

- Because our society is the product and we the inheritors of Western civilization, American students need an understanding of its origins and development, from its roots in antiquity to the present. This understanding should include a grasp of the major trends in society, religion, art, literature, and politics, as well as a knowledge of basic chronology.
- A careful reading of several masterworks of English, American, and European literature.
- An understanding of the most significant ideas and debates in the history of philosophy.
- Demonstrable proficiency in a foreign language (either modern or classical) and the ability to view that language as an avenue into another culture.

In addition to these areas of fundamental knowledge, study group members recommended that undergraduates have some familiarity with the history, literature, religion, and philosophy of at least one non-Western culture or civilization. We think it better to have a deeper understanding of a single non-Western culture than a superficial taste of many. Finally, the study group thought that all students should study the history of science and technology....

... Preliminary findings from a 1984-85 survey by the American Council on Education indicate that a student can obtain a bachelor's degree from 75 percent of all American colleges and universities without having studied European history; from 72 percent without having studied American literature or history; and from 86 percent without having studied the civilizations of classical Greece and Rome. The Modern Language Association reports that both entrance and graduation requirements in foreign languages have been weakened significantly since 1966. In that year, 33 percent of all colleges and universities required some foreign language study for admission. By 1975, only 18 percent required a foreign language, and by 1983 only 14 percent. The picture is similar for graduation requirements. In 1966, 89 percent of all institutions required foreign language study for the bachelor's degree, dropping to 53 percent in 1975 and 47 percent in 1983.

Conventional wisdom attributes the steep drop in the number of students who major in the humanities to a concern for finding good-paying jobs after college. Although there is some truth in this, we believe that there is another, equally important reason — namely, that we in the academy have failed to bring the humanities to life and to insist on their value....

The past twenty years have seen a steady erosion in the place of the humanities in the undergraduate curriculum and in the coherence of the curriculum generally. So serious has this erosion become that Mark Curtis, president of the Association of American Colleges, wrote: "The chaotic state of the baccalaureate curriculum may be the most urgent and troubling problem of higher education in the final years of the twentieth century." Clark Kerr has called the undergraduate curriculum "a disaster area," and Professor Frederick Rudolph of Williams College has written:

> ... when the professors abandoned a curriculum that they thought students needed they substituted for it one that, instead, catered either to what the professors needed or what the students wanted. The results confirmed the authority of professors and students but they robbed the curriculum of any authority at all. The reaction of students to all this activity in the curriculum was brilliant. They concluded that the curriculum really didn't matter.

A collective loss of nerve and faith on the part of both faculty and academic administrators during the late 1960s and early 1970s was undeniably destructive of the curriculum. When students demanded a greater role in setting their own education agendas, we eagerly responded by abandoning course requirements of any kind and with them the intellectual authority to say to students what the outcome of a college education ought to be. With intellectual authority relinquished, we found that we did not need to worry about what was worth knowing, worth defending, worth believing. The curriculum was no longer a statement about what knowledge mattered; instead, it became the product of a political compromise among competing schools and departments overlaid by marketing considerations. In a recent article Frederick Rudolph likened the curriculum to "a bazaar and the students [to] tourists looking for cheap bargains."

Once the curriculum was dissolved, colleges and universities found it difficult to reconstruct because of the pressures of the marketplace. All but the most selective institutions must now compete for scarce financial resources — students' tuition and enrollment-driven state subsidies. As a consequence, many are reluctant to reinstate meaningful course requirements for fear of frightening away prospective applicants. (I believe such a fear is misplaced, but more on this later.)

Intellectual authority came to be replaced by intellectual relativism as a guiding principle of the curriculum. Because colleges and universities believed they no longer could or should assert the primacy of one fact or one book over another, all knowledge came to be seen as relative in importance, relative to consumer or faculty interest. This loss was accompanied by a shift in language. The desired ends of education changed from knowledge to "inquiry," from content to "skills." We began to see colleges listing their objectives as teaching such skills as reading, critical thinking, and awareness of other points of view. These are undeniably essential ends to a college education, but they are not sufficient. One study group member said, "What good is knowing how to write if you are ignorant of the finest examples of the language? Failure to address content allows colleges and universities to beg the question of what an educated man or woman in the 1980s needs to know. The willingness of too many colleges to act as if all learning were relative is a self-inflicted wound that has impaired our ability to defend our subjects as necessary for learning or important for life. . . .

It is not surprising that once colleges and universities decided the curriculum did not have to represent a vision of an educated person, the secondary schools (and their students) took the cue and reached the same conclusion. Vanderbilt University Professor Chester Finn pointed out that college entrance requirements constitute *de facto* high school exit requirements for high school graduates — now nearly six of every ten — who seek postsecondary education. With exit requirements relaxed, college-bound students no longer perceive a need to take electives in English and history, let alone foreign languages. Instead, they choose courses thought to offer immediate vocational payoff. . . .

Curricular reform must begin with the president. In their research on presidential leadership, Clark Kerr and David Riesman found that only 2 percent of the more than seven hundred college and university presidents interviewed described themselves as playing a major role in academic affairs. This is an alarming finding. A president should be the chief academic officer of the institution, not just the chief administrative, recruitment, or fund raising officer. The president and other principal academic officers (provosts, deans, vice presidents for academic affairs) are solely accountable for all its parts and the needs of all its students. They are ultimately responsible for the quality of the education these students receive. . . .

But . . . the curriculum cannot be reformed without the enthusiastic support of the faculty. . . . Philip Phibbs [president, University of Puget Sound] called upon humanities faculty to recognize their common interests:

> Leadership . . . must also come from the humanities faculty itself. This group must assert itself aggressively within the larger faculty and make its case with confidence and clarity. In too many cases, I think, faculty members in the humanities assume that any intelligent human being, and certainly any intelligent faculty colleague, understands the value of the humanities. It should not, therefore, be necessary to articulate the case. This is a dangerous and misguided assumption.

V. Concluding Thoughts

The humanities are important, not to just a few scholars, gifted students, or armchair dilettantes, but to any person who would be educated. They are important precisely because they embody mankind's age-old effort to ask the questions that are central to human existence. As Robertson Davies told a college graduating class, "a university education is meant to enlarge and illuminate your life." A college education worthy of the name must be constructed upon a foundation of the humanities. Unfortunately, our colleges and universities do not always give the humanities their due. All too often teaching is lifeless, arid, and without commitment. On too many campuses the curriculum has become a self-service cafeteria through which students pass without being nourished. Many academic leaders lack the confidence to assert that the curriculum should stand for something more than salesmanship, compromise, or special interest politics. Too many colleges and universities have no clear sense of their educational mission and no conception of what a graduate of their institution ought to know or be.

The solution is not a return to an earlier time when the classical curriculum was the only curriculum and college was available to only a privileged few. American higher education today serves far more people and many more purposes than it did a century ago. Its increased accessibility to women, racial and ethnic minorities, recent immigrants, and students of limited means is a positive accomplishment of which our nation is rightly proud. As higher education broadened, the curriculum became more sensitive to the long-overlooked cultural achievements of many groups, with what Janice Harris of the University of Wyoming referred to as "a respect for diversity." This too is a good thing. But our eagerness to assert the virtues of pluralism should not allow us to sacrifice the principle that formerly lent substance and continuity to the curriculum, namely that each college and university should recognize and accept its vital role as conveyor of the accumulated wisdom of our civilization.

We are a part and a product of Western civilization. That our society was founded upon such principles as justice, liberty, government with the consent of the governed, and equality under the law is the result of ideas descended directly from great epochs of Western civilization — Enlightenment England and France, Renaissance Florence, and Periclean Athens. These ideas, so revolutionary in their times yet so taken for granted now, are the glue that binds together our pluralistic nation. The fact that we as Americans — whether black or white, Asian or Hispanic, rich or poor — share these beliefs aligns us with other cultures of the Western tradition. It is not enthnocentric or chauvinistic to acknowledge this. No student citizen of our civilization should be denied access to the best that tradition has to offer.

Ours is not, of course, the only great cultural tradition the world has seen. There are others, and we should expect an educated person to be familiar with them because they have produced art, literature, and thought that are compelling monuments to the human spirit and because they have made significant contributions to our history. Those who know nothing of these other traditions can neither appreciate the uniqueness of their own nor understand how their own fits with the larger world. They are less able to understand the world in which they live. The college curriculum must take the non-Western world into account, not out of political expediency or to appease interest groups, but out of respect for its importance in human history. But the core of the American college curriculum — its heart and soul — should be the civilization of the West, source of the most powerful and pervasive influences on America and all of its people. It is simply not possible for students to understand their society without studying its intellectual legacy. If their past is hidden from them, they will become aliens in their own culture, strangers in their own land. . . .

WEINBERGER ON THE USES OF U.S. MILITARY FORCE

November 28, 1984

In a speech delivered at the National Press Club on November 28, Secretary of Defense Caspar W. Weinberger outlined six major conditions to be met before U.S. combat troops were sent into battle abroad. The speech, regarded by some as the clearest statement of the administration's military policy since Reagan took office in 1981, reportedly was prompted by congressional concern that U.S. troops would be sent into Central America. Weinberger said the United States should follow a restrained, cautious approach to the use of military force. Drawing from the lesson of Vietnam, he said there must be reasonable assurance that any military intervention would have the support of the American public.

Weinberger stressed in his speech, "The Uses of Military Power," that "commitment of U.S. forces to combat must be a last resort" used only when other means have failed or have no prospect of succeeding. If troops are committed, he said they should enter combat "with the clear intention of winning." If applied carefully, he argued, the six tests he had outlined would help the United States avoid a gradual approach that almost always meant an insufficient use of force. "These tests," he said, "can help us to avoid being drawn inexorably into an endless morass, where it is not vital to our national interest to fight."

Weinberger offered assurances that U.S. responses to Soviet intervention in Central America would be in economic and military assistance and training rather than in the deployment of troops. "The president," Weinberger said, "will not allow our military forces to creep, or be drawn gradually, into a combat role in Central America or any other place in the world."

Genesis of Tests

Defense Department officials said Weinberger had drawn up his list of tests after reading the history of Vietnam and other conflicts and after discussions with the Joint Chiefs of Staff and other military officials. His conditions echoed those of Pentagon officers who since the end of the Vietnam War had advocated that a well-defined goal, with the freedom to employ the means to achieve it, must be assured before military intervention begins. In stressing that force would not be used indiscriminately, Weinberger also hinted that congressional restraints on presidential use of military force — as imposed by the War Powers Act — should perhaps be modified.

Weinberger said the relationship between U.S. forces and military objectives should be continually reassessed, and that allies must be willing to share part of the burden for their defense. "We have learned that there are limits to how much of our spirit and blood and treasure we can afford to forfeit in meeting our responsibility to keep peace and freedom," he said. "... We cannot assume for other sovereign nations the responsibility to defend their territory, without their strong invitation, when our freedom is not threatened."

Weinberger-Shultz Conflict

Weinberger's speech, which he wrote himself but cleared with the White House and National Security Council, contained an implied statement concerning the use of military strikes against terrorists. In direct contrast to Secretary of State George P. Shultz, who on October 25 had urged retaliation against terrorist attacks, even if it cost innocent lives, Weinberger suggested a cautious approach. He said that "... the United States should not commit forces to combat overseas unless the particular engagement or occasion is deemed vital to our national interest." (Shultz on terrorism, p. 933)

Differences between President Reagan's two top foreign policy advisers had been apparent since 1982 when U.S. troops were deployed in Lebanon. Shultz had led administration policy makers advocating the use of American military units both there and in Grenada and as a weapon against international terrorists. Weinberger had been reluctant to send troops in those cases, and reports had surfaced that the two advisers had differed in other policy areas, including arms control, the treatment of North Atlantic Treaty Organization allies, and the extent of U.S. intervention in Central America. (Lebanon bombing, Grenada invasion, Historic Documents of 1983, pp. 874-853 and 933-966)

Although Weinberger had been in Reagan's Cabinet when he was governor of California in the 1960s and reportedly had a close personal relationship with the president, Shultz, who joined the Cabinet in 1982, had gradually gained influence among the president's advisers. Press reports said that conflicts between the two had begun to filter down to lower levels of the bureaucracy, giving rise to concern that stalemates over policy decisions might result.

Shultz responded to Weinberger's speech on December 10 at a convocation address for Yeshiva University at the Waldorf-Astoria Hotel in New York City, saying that "there is no such thing as guaranteed public support in advance" of a military operation and that "diplomacy backed by strength will always be ineffectual at best, dangerous at worst." The two speeches had been almost in direct contrast to one another, the diplomatic chief calling for more military action and the defense chief calling for diplomatic intervention.

> *Following is the Defense Department news release text of a speech, "The Uses of Military Power," delivered by Defense Secretary Caspar W. Weinberger at the National Press Club November 28, 1984. (Boldface headings in brackets have bee₁ added by Congressional Quarterly to highlight the organization of the text.):*

Thank you for inviting me to be here today with the members of the National Press Club, a group most important to our national security. I say that because a major point I intend to make in my remarks today is that the single most critical element of a successful democracy is a strong consensus of support and agreement for our basic purposes. Policies formed without a clear understanding of what we hope to achieve will never work. And you help to build that understanding among our citizens.

Of all the many policies our citizens deserve — and need — to understand, none is so important as those related to our topic today — the uses of military power. Deterrence will work only if the Soviets understand our firm commitment to keeping the peace, ... and only from a well-informed public can we expect to have that national will and commitment.

So today, I want to discuss with you perhaps the most important question concerning keeping the peace. Under what circumstances, and by what means, does a great democracy such as ours reach the painful decision that the use of military force is necessary to protect our interests or to carry out our national policy?

National power has many components, some tangible, — like economic wealth, technical pre-eminence. Other components are intangible — such as moral force, or strong national will. Military forces, when they are strong and ready and modern, are a credible — and tangible — addition to a nation's power. When both the intangible national will and those forces are forged into one instrument, national power becomes effective.

In today's world, the line between peace and war is less clearly drawn than at any time in our history. When George Washington, in his farewell address, warned us, as a new democracy, to aviod foreign entanglements, Europe then lay 2-3 months by sea over the horizon. The United States was protected by the width of the oceans. Now in this nuclear age we measure time in minutes rather than months.

Aware of the consequences of any misstep, yet convinced of the precious worth of the freedom we enjoy, we seek to avoid conflict, while maintaining strong defenses. Our policy has always been to work hard for peace, but to be prepared if war comes. Yet, so blurred have the lines become between open conflict and half-hidden hostile acts that we cannot confidently predict where, or when, or how, or from what direction aggression may arrive. We must be prepared, at any moment, to meet threats ranging in intensity from isolated terrorist acts, to guerilla *[sic]* action, to full-scale military confrontation.

Alexander Hamilton, writing in the *Federalist Papers*, said that "It is impossible to foresee or define the extent and variety of national exigencies, or the correspondent extent and variety of the means which may be necessary to satisfy them." If it was true then, how much more true it is today, when we must remain ready to consider the means to meet such serious indirect challenges to the peace as proxy wars and individual terrorist action. And how much more important is it now, considering the consequences of failing to deter conflict at the lowest level possible. While the use of military force to defend territory has never been questioned when a democracy has been attacked and its very survival threatened, most democracies have rejected the unilateral aggressive use of force to invade, conquer or subjugate other nations. The extent to which the use of force *is* acceptable remains unresolved for the host of other situations which fall between these extremes of defensive and aggressive use of force.

We find ourselves, then, face to face with a modern paradox: the most likely challenge to the peace — the gray area conflicts — are precisely the most difficult challenges to which a democracy must respond. Yet, while the source and nature of today's challenges are uncertain, our response must be clear and understandable. Unless we are certain that force is essential, we run the risk of inadequate national will to apply the resources needed.

Because we face a spectrum of threats — from covert aggression, terrorism, and subversion, to overt intimidation, to use of brute force — choosing the appropriate level of our response is difficult. Flexible response does not mean just any response is appropriate. But once a decision to employ some degree of force has been made, and the purpose clarified, our government must have the clear mandate to carry out, and continue to carry out, that decision until the purpose has been achieved. That, too, has been difficult to accomplish.

The issue of which branch of government has authority to define that mandate and make decisions on using force is now being strongly contended. Beginning in the 1970s Congress demanded, and assumed, a far more active role in the making of foreign policy and in the decisionmaking process for the employment of military forces abroad than had been thought appropriate and practical before. As a result, the centrality of decision-making authority in the executive branch has been compromised by the legislative branch to an extent that actively interferes with that process. At the same time, there has not been a corresponding acceptance of responsibility by Congress for the outcome of decisions concerning the employment of military forces.

Yet the outcome of decisions on whether — and when — and to what degree — to use combat forces abroad has never been more *important* than it is today. While we do not seek to deter or settle all the world's conflicts, we must recognize that, as a major power, our responsibilities and interests are now of such scope that there are few troubled areas we can afford to ignore. So we must be prepared to deal with a range of possibilities, a spectrum of crises, from local insurgency to global conflict. We prefer, of course, to *limit* any conflict in its early stages, to contain and control it — but to do that our military forces must be deployed in a *timely* manner, and be fully supported and prepared *before* they are engaged, because many of those difficult decisions must be made extremely quickly.

[Inaction vs. Force]

Some on the national scene think they can always avoid making tough decisions. Some reject entirely the question of whether any force can ever be used abroad. They want to avoid grappling with a complex issue because, despite clever rhetoric disguising their purpose, these people are in fact advocating a return to post-World War I isolationism. While they may maintain in principle that military force has a role in foreign policy, they are never willing to name the circumstance or the place where it would apply.

On the other side, some theorists argue that military force can be brought to bear in any crisis. Some of these proponents of force are eager to advocate its use even in limited amounts simply because they believe that if there are American forces of *any* size present they will somehow solve the problem.

Neither of these two extremes offers us any lasting or satisfactory solutions. The first — undue reserve — would lead us ultimately to withdraw from international events that require free nations to defend their interests from the aggressive use of force. We would be abdicating our responsibilities as the leader of the free world — responsibilities more or less thrust upon us in the aftermath of World War II — a war incidentally that isolationism did nothing to deter. These are responsibilities we must fulfill unless we desire the Soviet Union to keep expanding its influence unchecked throughout the world. In an international system based on mutual interdependence among nations, and alliances between friends, stark isolationism quickly would lead to a far more dangerous situation for the United States: we would be without allies and faced by many hostile or indifferent nations.

The second alternative — employing our forces almost indiscriminately and as a regular and customary part of our diplomatic efforts — would surely plunge us headlong into the sort of domestic turmoil we experienced during the Vietnam War, without accomplishing the goal for which we committed our forces. Such policies might very well tear at the fabric of our society, endangering the *single* most critical element of a successful democracy: *a strong consensus of support and agreement for our basic purposes.*

Policies formed without a clear understanding of what we hope to achieve would also earn us the scorn of our troops, who would have an understandable opposition to being *used* — in every sense of the word — casually and without intent to support them fully. Ultimately this course would reduce their morale and their effectiveness for engagements we *must* win. And if the military were to distrust its civilian leadership, recruitment would fall off and I fear an end to the all-volunteer system would be upon us, requiring a return to a draft, sowing the seeds of riot and discontent that so wracked the country in the '60s.

We have now restored high morale and pride in the uniform throughout the services. The all-volunteer system is working spectacularly well. Are we willing to forfeit what we have fought so hard to regain?

In maintaining our progress in strengthening America's military deterrent, we face difficult challenges. For we have entered an era where the dividing lines between peace and war are less clearly drawn, the identity of the foe is much less clear. In World Wars I and II, we not only knew who our enemies were, but we shared a clear sense of *why* the principles espoused by our enemies were unworthy.

Since these two wars threatened our very survival as a free nation and the survival of our allies, they were total wars, involving every aspect of our society. All the means of production, all our resources were devoted to winning. Our policies had the unqualified support of the great majority of our people. Indeed, World Wars I and II ended with the unconditional surrender of our enemies. . . the only acceptable ending when the alternative was the loss of our freedom.

But in the aftermath of the Second World War, we encountered a more subtle form of warfare — warfare in which, more often than not, the face of the enemy was masked. Territorial expansionism could be carried out indirectly by proxy powers, using surrogate forces aided and advised from afar. Some conflicts occurred under the name of "national liberation," but far more frequently ideology or religion provided the spark to the tinder.

Our adversaries can also take advantage of our open society, and our freedom of speech and opinion to use alarming rhetoric and disinformation to divide and disrupt our unity of purpose. While they would never dare to allow such freedoms to their own people, they are quick to exploit ours by conducting simultaneous military and propaganda campaigns to achieve their ends.

They realize that if they can divide our national will at home, it will not be necessary to defeat our forces abroad. So by presenting issues in bellicose terms, they aim to intimidate Western leaders and citizens, encouraging us to adopt conciliatory positions to their advantage. Meanwhile *they* remain sheltered from the force of public opinion in their countries, because public opinion there is simply prohibited and does not exist.

Our freedom presents both a challenge and an opportunity. It is true that until democratic nations have the support of the people, they are inevitably at a disadvantage in a conflict. But when they *do* have that support they cannot be defeated. For democracies have the power to send a compelling message to friend and foe alike by the vote of their citizens. And the American people have sent such a signal by re-electing a strong chief executive. They know that President Reagan is willing to accept the responsibility for his actions and is able to lead us through these complex times by insisting that we regain *both* our military and our economic strength.

[Limits to U.S. Power]

In today's world where minutes count, such decisive leadership is more important than ever before. Regardless of whether conflicts are limited, or threats are ill-defined, we *must* be capable of quickly determining that the threats and conflicts either *do* or *do not* affect the vital interests of the United States and our allies ... and then responding appropriately.

Those threats may not entail an immediate, direct attack on our territory, and our response may not necessarily require the immediate or direct defense of our homeland. But when our vital national interests and those of our allies *are* at stake, we cannot ignore our safety, or forsake our allies.

At the same time, recent history has proven that we cannot assume unilaterally the role of the world's defender. We have learned that there are limits to how much of our spirit and blood and treasure we can afford to forfeit in meeting our responsibility to keep peace and freedom. So while we may and should offer substantial amounts of economic and military assistance to our allies in their time of need, and help them maintain forces to deter attacks against them — usually we cannot substitute our troops or our will for theirs.

We should only engage *our* troops if we must do so as a matter of our *own* vital national interest. We cannot assume for other sovereign nations the responsibility to defend *their* territory — without their strong invitation — when our freedom is not threatened.

On the other hand, there have been recent cases where the United States has seen the need to join forces with other nations to try to preserve the peace by helping with negotiations, and by separating warring parties, and thus enabling those warring nations to withdraw from hostilities safely. In the Middle East, which has been torn by conflict for millennia, we have sent our troops in recent years both to the Sinai and to Lebanon, for just such a peacekeeping mission. But we did not configure or equip those forces for combat — they were armed only for their self-defense. Their mission required them to be — and to be recognized as — peacekeepers. We knew that if conditions deteriorated so they were in danger, or if because of the actions of the warring nations, their peace keeping mission could not be realized, then it would be necessary either to add sufficiently to the number and arms of our troops — in short to equip them for combat. . . or to withdraw them. And so in Lebanon, when we faced just such a choice, because the warring nations did not enter into withdrawal or peace agreements, the President properly withdrew forces equipped only for peacekeeping.

In those cases where our national interests require us to commit combat forces, we must never let there be doubt of our resolution. When it is necessary for our troops to be committed to combat, we *must* commit them, in sufficient numbers and we *must* support them, as effectively and resolutely as our strength permits. When we commit our troops to combat we must do so with the sole object of winning.

[Six Tests to Apply]

Once it is clear our troops are required, because our vital interests are at stake, then we must have the firm national resolve to commit every ounce of strength necessary to win the fight to achieve our objectives. In Grenada we did just that.

Just as clearly, there are other situations where United States combat forces should *not* be used. I believe the postwar period has taught us several lessons, and from them I have developed *six* major tests to be applied when we are weighing the use of U.S. combat forces abroad. Let me now share them with you.

(1) *First*, the United States should not commit forces to *combat* overseas unless the particular engagement or occasion is deemed vital to our national interest or that of our allies. That emphatically does not mean that we should *declare* beforehand, as we did with Korea in 1950, that a particular area is outside our strategic perimeter.

(2) *Second*, if we decide it *is* necessary to put *combat* troops into a given situation, we should do so wholeheartedly, and with the clear intention of winning. If we are *un*willing to commit the forces or resources necessary to achieve our objectives, we should not commit them at all. Of course if the particular situation requires only limited force to win our objectives, then we should not hesitate to commit forces sized accordingly. When Hitler broke treaties and remilitarized the Rhineland, small combat forces then could perhaps have prevented the holocaust of World War II.

(3) *Third*, if we *do* decide to commit forces to combat overseas, we should have clearly defined political and military objectives. And we should know precisely how our forces can accomplish those clearly defined objectives. And we should have and send the forces needed to do just that. As Clausewitz wrote, "No one starts a war — or rather, no one in his senses ought to do so — without first being clear in his mind what he intends to achieve by that war, and how he intends to conduct it."

War may be different today than in Clausewitz's time, but the need for well-defined objectives and a consistent strategy is still essential. If we determine that a combat mission has become necessary for our vital national interests, then we must send forces capable to do the job — and not assign a combat mission to a force configured for peacekeeping.

(4) *Fourth*, the relationship between our objectives and the forces we have committed — their size, composition and disposition — must be continually reassessed and adjusted if necessary. Conditions and objectives invariably change during the course of a conflict. When they do change, then so must our combat requirements. We must continuously keep as a beacon light before us the basic questions: *"Is this conflict in our national interest?"* "Does our national interest require us to fight, to use force of arms?" If the answers are "yes", then we *must* win. If the answers are "no", then we should not be in combat.

(5) *Fifth*, before the U.S. commits combat forces abroad, there must be some reasonable assurance we will have the support of the American people and their elected representatives in Congress. This support cannot be achieved unless we are candid in making clear the threats we face; the support cannot be sustained without continuing and close consultation. We cannot fight a battle with the Congress at home while asking our troops to win a war overseas or, as in the case of Vietnam, in effect asking our troops *not* to win, but just to be there.

(6) *Finally*, the commitment of U.S. forces to combat should be a last resort.

I believe that these tests can be helpful in deciding whether or not we should commit our troops to combat in the months and years ahead. The point we must all keep uppermost in our minds is that if we ever decide to commit forces to combat, we must support those forces to the *fullest* extent of our national will for as long as it takes to win. So we must have in mind objectives that are clearly defined and understood and supported by the widest possible number of our citizens. And those objectives must be vital to our survival as a free nation and to the fulfillment of our responsibilities as a world power. We must also be farsighted enough to sense when immediate and strong reactions to apparently small events can prevent lion-like responses that may be required later. We must never forget those isolationists in Europe who shrugged that "Danzig is not worth a war", and "Why should we fight to keep the Rhineland demilitarized?"

These tests I have just mentioned have been phrased negatively for a purpose — they are intended to sound a note of caution — caution that we must observe prior to commiting forces to combat overseas. When we ask our military forces to risk their very lives in such situations, a note of caution is not only prudent, it is morally required.

In many situations we may apply these tests and conclude that a combatant role is not appropriate. Yet no one should interpret what I am saying here today as an abdication of America's responsibilities — either to its own citizens or to its allies. Nor should these remarks be misread as a signal that this country, or this administration, is unwilling to commit forces to combat overseas.

We have demonstrated in the past that, when our vital interests or those of our allies are threatened, we are ready to use force, and use it decisively, to protect those interests. Let no one entertain any illusions — if our vital interests are involved, we are prepared to fight. And we are resolved that if we *must* fight, we *must* win.

So, while these tests are drawn from lessons we have learned from the past, they also can — and should — be applied to the future. For example, the problems confronting us in Central America today are difficult. The possibility of more extensive Soviet and Soviet-proxy penetration into this hemisphere in months ahead is something we should recognize. If this happens we will clearly need more economic and military assistance and training to help those who want democracy.

The President will not allow our military forces to creep — or be drawn gradually — into a combat role in Central America or any other place in the world. And indeed our policy is designed to prevent the need for direct American involvement. This means we will need sustained Congressional support to back and give confidence to our friends in the region.

I believe that the tests I have enunciated here today can, if applied carefully, avoid the danger of this gradualist incremental approach which almost always means the use of insufficient force. These tests can help us to avoid being drawn inexorably into an endless morass, where it is not vital to our national interest to fight.

But policies and principles such as these require decisive leadership in both the executive and legislative branches of government — and they also require strong and sustained public support. Most of all, these policies require national unity of purpose. I believe the United States now possesses the policies and leadership to gain that public support and unity. And I believe that the future will show we have the strength of character to protect peace with freedom.

In summary, we should all remember these are the policies —indeed the *only* policies — that can preserve for ourselves, our friends, and our posterity, peace with freedom.

I believe we *can* continue to deter the Soviet Union and other potential adversaries from pursuing their designs around the world. We *can* enable our friends in Central America to defeat aggression and gain the breathing room to nurture democratic reforms. We *can* meet the challenge posed by the unfolding complexity of the 1980's.

We will then be poised to begin the last decade of this century amid a peace tempered by realism, and secured by firmness and strength. And it will be a peace that will enable all of us — ourselves at home, and our friends abroad — to achieve a quality of life, both spiritually and materially, far higher than man has even dared to dream.

December

AMA CALL FOR
BAN ON BOXING
December 5, 1984

After years of recommending various reforms to lessen the danger of prize fighting for its participants, the American Medical Association's House of Delegates adopted a resolution on December 5, 1984, calling for a complete ban on professional and amateur boxing in the United States.

Dr. Joseph R. Boyle, AMA president, told The New York Times *that physicians need to persuade legislators and the public that boxing "is indeed a very dangerous sport and that it ought to be outlawed.... It seems to us an extraordinarily incongruous thing that we have a sport in which two people are literally paid to get into a ring and try to beat one another to death, or at least beat them into a state of senselessness that will leave them permanently brain-damaged."*

Boyle noted that the United States has laws banning dog fighting and cock fighting, while "putting two human beings in the ring . . . is perfectly legal."

The AMA resolution sparked a number of editorials and commentaries, both for and against banning the sport. One prominent defender of boxing, Washington Post *columnist Carl Rowan, wrote that the physicians were trying to deny poor young men the right to a lucrative sports career. Rowan argued that injuries are common in other sports such as football and professions such as coal mining, yet the AMA was not proposing to abolish football or coal mining. Other writers such as veteran sports broadcaster Red Barber sided with the AMA, pointing out that boxing differs from football and other contact sports because its primary objective is to harm the opponent.*

Angelo Dundee, the boxing coach who trained Muhammad Ali and Sugar Ray Leonard, labeled as "baloney" one doctor's characterization of the sport as a "sacrifice of minority youth." "You go out and whip each other," he said. "And see who's the best man, that's all. Nobody's out to maim nobody."

Dundee and others had recommended reforms to eliminate most of the deaths and injuries resulting from boxing. Some of the suggestions included the use of thumbless boxing globes, to eliminate the possibility of thumbing out an opponent's eye; the wearing of protective head gear, as boxers did in the 1984 Olympics; and limiting the number of rounds a bout may run.

In previous years, the AMA had stopped short of calling for an outright ban on the sport. In 1983 the physicians' organization advised giving ringside doctors the right to stop bouts that they thought might result in serious injury to the fighters.

Young boxers interviewed after the AMA's resolution was made public condemned the idea of a ban. Most of them said that boxing was not intrinsically brutal but rather a sport requiring skill. They added that fighting gives them an opportunity to make money that they would not have otherwise. Kenny Baysmore, a Washington, D.C., fighter, told The Washington Post on December 23, 1984, that "You always recover, or you think you do."

"When I see what's happened to Muhammad Ali, it affects me from a sympathetic point of view," Baysmore added. "But he just hung around too long. You have to know when to get out. I see myself fighting for six more years. Hopefully no more. I won't let myself go out punch drunk." (Ali, world heavyweight champion for many years, was diagnosed in 1984 as suffering from a form of Parkinson's disease.)

"Punch drunk" is the term used to describe a boxer who, in the words of Dr. Russell H. Patterson Jr., a member of the AMA's advisory panel on brain injury in boxing, "is unable to coordinate voluntary muscular movements..., has a broad-based gait, slurred speech and dementia."

The punch-drunk syndrome is sometimes found in older boxers who have sustained a number of knockouts. But the AMA cited results of a study published in the May 25, 1984, issue of The Journal of the American Medical Association, showing that younger boxers with no history of alcohol and drug abuse also showed signs of brain damage. The physicians examined 15 former and active professional boxers and found varying degrees of brain damage in 13.

The men demonstrated symptoms such as disorientation, loss of memory and confusion. They underwent tests for short-term memory and received computed tomographic (CT) scans of the brain, clinical neurological exams and electro-encephalograms.

Researchers found that boxers sustain brain damage because blows to the head cause the brain to respond at a speed different from that of the skull that contains it. This causes blood vessels to stretch and snap. If the blow is hard enough to tear the vessels, blood builds up between the brain and the skull lining, putting pressure on the brain. In the most severe instances, this pressure can kill a fighter. Duk Doo Kim, a South Korean boxer who died in 1982 as a result of blows he received during a boxing match, was killed by such an accumulation of blood on the brain.

Autopsies on older boxers suffering from the punch-drunk syndrome often reveal brain changes similar to those of Alzheimer's disease patients. In some cases, researchers have found the nerve cells almost completely missing from some areas of a boxer's brain, leaving only neurofibrillary tangles also found in Alzheimer's patients.

The possibility of death in the ring caused by blows to the head is a very real one for boxers. In an editorial in the May 25, 1984, issue, the editor of The Journal of the American Medical Association, *Dr. George D. Lundberg, quoted* Ring *magazine statistics showing that 11 fighters had died from ring injuries since January 1983.*

"Some have argued that boxing has a redeeming social value in that it allows a few disadvantaged or minority individuals an opportunity to rise to spectacular wealth or fame," wrote Lundberg in the January 14, 1983, issue of the Journal. *"This does occur, but at what price? The price in this country includes chronic brain damage for them and the thousands of others who do not achieve wealth, fame or even a decent living from the ring. Others argue that man must fight and that surreptitious fights will occur if boxing is outlawed, producing an even worse situation. I suggest that such is equivalent to arguing that gunfighter duels should be instituted, tickets sold, and betting promoted since, after all, homicide by gunshot is also common in our society."*

> *Following is the resolution on boxing adopted December 5, 1984, in Honolulu by the American Medical Association House of Delegates:*

RESOLVED, That the American Medical Association:

1) Encourage the elimination of both amateur and professional boxing, a sport in which the primary objective is to inflict injury;

2) Communicate its opposition to boxing to appropriate regulatory bodies;

3) Assist state medical societies to work with their state legislators to enact a law to eliminate boxing in their jurisdictions;

4) Educate the American public, especially children and young adults, about the dangerous effects of boxing on the health of participants.

MASS GAS POISONING
AT BHOPAL, INDIA
December 9, 1984

One of the worst industrial accidents in history occurred December 3, 1984, in Bhopal, India, when a deadly cloud of methyl isocyanate escaped from a Union Carbide India chemical processing plant, killing more than 2,000 people and injuring as many as 50,000.

The accident happened when the chemical, normally kept in a liquid state through refrigeration, became heated, changing it into a gas. As pressure built up in the main tank, the gas was diverted into a holding tank where scrubbers and a caustic wash normally neutralize the chemical before it is released. Although the exact cause of the accident was unclear, it appeared that the gas gushed into the holding tank too fast for the neutralizing process to work, allowing the unaltered methyl isocyanate to escape into the open air. V. P. Gokhale, managing director of Union Carbide India, denied in an interview that the valves had malfunctioned. He said the failures were those of workers inside the plant.

The deadly gas leaked at approximately midnight and was borne by the wind to the Jai Prakash Nagar, a government-sponsored resettlement area south of the plant where thousands of poor, many of them part of the plant's support staff, lived. Most of the victims were asleep as the gas, kept low to the ground by the cool night air, washed over the shantytown. When a warning alarm finally was sounded, many people ran to the plant fearing a fire. A large number of the victims were children, the elderly, and those too infirm to escape from the gas. People not killed in their sleep were felled in the streets, blinded and unable to breathe.

Liability Issue

Methyl isocyanate is an intermediary chemical used in the production of Sevin and other agricultural pesticides, major products for Union Carbide. As the cleanup process and the cremation of the dead got under way, the company's safety procedures and liability were hotly debated. Union Carbide issued a statement December 9 announcing its intention to contribute 10 million rupees, approximately $1 million, to establish a relief fund and to provide medical supplies and treatment for the victims. The company also promised to conduct a full investigation of the tragedy. Union Carbide's other plant producing methyl isocyanate, located in Institute, West Virginia, temporarily halted production of the chemical following the accident.

Warren M. Anderson, chairman of Union Carbide, flew to India to assess the incident and was arrested by local officials upon his arrival in Bhopal December 7. Charged with criminal conspiracy and detained for a day, he was released on $2,000 bond. Because the parent company owned 50.9 percent of the plant against India's 49.1 percent, Indian officials insisted that it had been Union Carbide's responsibility to notify the local plant of the potential dangers. A computerized safety system used in the American plant had not been installed in Bhopal. But as events leading to the accident began to unravel, it became apparent that the Indian nationals operating the plant had neglected to prevent the tank from overheating. The Indian staff on duty reportedly ran from the scene instead of taking the prescribed measures to halt the escaping gas.

Transfer of Technology

Aside from the legal and moral liabilities in the Bhopal tragedy, the case illustrated vividly many of the complex problems involved in attempts to transfer sophisticated industrial capabilities to less-developed countries, even to one of the so-called middle-tier countries such as India. Construction and operation of modern industrial plants require a working knowledge of the technology on which they are based and of the managerial and administrative skills required to translate technological capabilities into viable commercial processes and products. The less-developed countries lack people with both types of skills. India is better off in that regard than most, ranking, at least on paper, either third or fourth in the world in the number of scientists and engineers.

In an effort to increase the knowledge and skills central for a modern industrial state, many developing countries, with India foremost among them, have insisted that foreign corporations employ the host countries' own nationals to operate their plants, and to provide training for those nationals when necessary. Similarly, they often have required that the plants be located away from large urban centers where a ready supply of adequately trained personnel might be available.

From this perspective, the government of India must have considered Bhopal, capital of the relatively backward state of Madhya Pradesh and located almost in the dead center of India, as an ideal location for the Union Carbide plant. Not only did the plant provide jobs in an area of relatively high unemployment, it also promised to increase the pool of technically skilled people that the country needed in its drive toward modernization.

The accident in Bhopal, reminiscent of the 1976 tragedy in Seveso, Italy, when a dioxin cloud poisoned the entire city, and more recently in Mexico City, when a gas explosion killed 400 people in November 1984, underscored this threat of advanced technology in developing nations. Tragedies on a lesser scale are common in these countries. Oftentimes, materials banned for production or sale in the United States are made and sold in other parts of the world.

Much of the responsibility lies with the host countries as well. Many Third World nations, besides welcoming industries that will aid their economies, are willing consumers of potentially dangerous chemicals to help produc₂ desperately needed food supplies and to combat disease.

Examining the potential for technological disasters three weeks before the Bhopal gas leak, the Organization for Economic Cooperation and Development, meeting outside Paris, considered revising its industrial code of ethics to require a disclosure to host nations of possible catastrophes, emergency procedures, and environmental impact studies before a facility is constructed.

> *Following is a statement Union Carbide India Ltd. released December 9 in New Delhi, setting forth the company's intention to aid the victims of the gas leak that took place in Bhopal, India, December 3, 1984:*

The Bhopal tragedy has shocked the entire management and the employees of the company. It is regrettable that, owing to certain unexpected developments which took place in the last few days, there has been some delay in giving information to the press and the public.

Questions are being raised regarding compensation. It is to be recognized that the matter of compensation for those who have suffered in this tragedy is a very complex issue, but it is hoped that it can be decided upon as soon as possible.

Meanwhile, the company has decided to make a contribution of 10 million rupees to the Madhya Pradesh Chief Minister's relief fund to assist in the treatment and rehabilitation of those who have suffered injury due to exposure to M.I.C. [methyl isocyanate] vapour.

Arrangements have also been made to shortly open an orphanage at

Bhopal in consultation with the state government. . . .

The company made arrangements to rush in medical supplies including hydrocortisone, respirators, oxygen regulators, etc., to Bhopal. A U.S. physician has also been brought in and the company has arranged to bring in eminent experts from overseas for chest and eye physiology, with the active support and cooperation of Union Carbide Corporation, U.S.A.

The management is extending full cooperation to the technical teams deputed by the authorities to investigate the causes which led to this tragedy. Simultaneously, investigations are also under way by a technical team from the U.S.A.

The company offers sincere condolences to the families of the deceased and sympathies to those who have suffered. The management sincerely hopes that the efforts the company is making and shall continue to make, together with the mutual cooperation and understanding of everyone concerned, the suffering caused by this tragedy shall be mitigated as early as is humanly possible.

TUTU'S NOBEL PEACE PRIZE

December 10, 1984

Calling him a "unifying leader figure in the campaign to resolve the problems of apartheid in South Africa," the Norwegian Nobel Committee announced Bishop Desmond Tutu, general secretary of the South African Council of Churches, as the winner of the 1984 Nobel Peace Prize on October 16. Tutu's award, accepted December 10, followed in the tradition of honors for another South African opponent of apartheid, Albert Lutuli, president of the outlawed African National Congress. Lutuli won the coveted award in 1960.

The committee said that the 1984 award "should be seen as a renewed recognition of the courage and heroism shown by black South Africans in their use of peaceful methods in the struggle against apartheid." Egil Aarvik, committee chairman, agreed that the choice of Tutu was a gesture to promote change in his country.

Renewed Unrest in South Africa

Bishop Tutu's honor came in a time of the most violent unrest in South Africa in eight years. Protests and riots began in September over rent increases and what blacks claimed were inferior schools. The violence spread when President P. W. Botha implemented his new constitution that gave limited parliamentary representation to the country's 850,000 Indians and 2.8 million coloreds (mixed-race), but no political voice to more than 23 million blacks. In a two-week period, 163 residents were killed and hundreds more were injured, most by government security forces.

In 1976 bloody riots erupted in Soweto and other black townships where more than 500 persons were killed. One month before the outbreak, Tutu, as the first black dean of Johannesburg, wrote to former prime minister John Vorster warning him of the troubles. Vorster ignored the letter but Tutu became widely known among white South Africans as a determined opponent of apartheid.

In 1978 Tutu was appointed general secretary of the South African Council of Churches (SACC), the first black to hold this position of leadership that represents more than 12 million Christians. According to Richard Bissell, author of a study of U.S.-African politics, the SACC "became a rallying point for open radical dissent from the government inside South Africa," with Tutu orchestrating the vocal opposition. In 1979 at a World Council of Churches meeting in Copenhagen, Tutu expressed the "angry response" of blacks to the post-Soweto period in South Africa and called for other nations to boycott South African coal, even if it meant the loss of black miners' jobs. The South African Broadcasting Corp. then characterized the World Council as "pro-communist, pro-revolutionary, and pro-Soviet." As a result of Tutu's controversial posture, government authorities conducted three investigations into the activities of the South African Council, causing most of the white churches to withdraw their membership.

Not surprisingly, many white Anglican clergymen adamantly opposed the November 13 election of Tutu as the first black bishop of Johannesburg because of his protests against military conscription in South Africa and his support for the withdrawal of foreign investment in South African companies.

Similarly, the South African government reacted with distaste when Tutu was named Nobel Prize winner. Botha's office refused to comment and conservative newspapers expressed disgust at the choice. Said one Johannesburg paper, "To South Africans who have so often read about his vicious verbal attacks, Bishop Desmond Tutu ... must be one of the strangest recipients yet to receive a Peace Prize." However, when Tutu returned to Johannesburg from the United States, where he had been visiting professor at the General Theological Seminary in New York, hundreds of joyful supporters met him, singing, dancing, and parading with posters proclaiming freedom from apartheid.

Tutu's Meeting with Reagan

The bishop's December 7 visit to Washington, D.C., spurred on anti-apartheid protesters, who began marching in front of the South African Embassy on November 21. Thirteen members of Congress and Dr. George Wald, 1967 Nobel Prize winner for medicine, were among the more than 200 persons arrested as the demonstrations gained momentum and spread to more than 13 American cities.

President Ronald Reagan and Tutu met on December 7 to discuss U.S. policies on South Africa. The bishop said that he asked Reagan to call for an end to the current violence in South Africa, a halt to forced population removals to impoverished "homelands," amnesty for all political prisoners, the release of all detainees, and a national convention to create a model for a new society. After the meeting, Tutu said that Reagan had expressed interest in some of his ideas but that neither one had changed his views about how the United States should regard the South African system.

Tutu charged that the administration's "constructive engagement" policy that opts for gentle behind-the-scenes nudging instead of political confrontation was "immoral, evil and unchristian" and that it had only made the South African government "more intransigent." The bishop accused the administration of "aligning itself with the perpetrators of the most vicious system since Nazism" when the U.S. abstained from voting on a United Nations Security Council proposition condemning South Africa's apartheid system October 23.

Letter from Republican Members of Congress

In an unusual move, 35 conservative Republican members of Congress, whose views normally coincide with those of Reagan, wrote to South African ambassador Bernardus G. Fourie, warning of diplomatic and economic sanctions against South Africa unless it took immediate measures to abolish apartheid. During the week before, the incoming chairman of the Senate Foreign Relations Committee, Richard G. Lugar, R-Ind., and Nancy Kassebaum, R-Kan., chairman of the panel's African Affairs Subcommittee, wrote to Reagan asking for more "public criticism" of South Africa.

Whether responding to political pressure at home or his conscience, as he claimed, Reagan spoke out against apartheid in an international Human Rights Day speech December 10. Calling for an end to the forced removal of several million blacks to predominantly impoverished "homelands" and the detention without trial of black leaders, Reagan asked the South African government "to reach out to its black majority [and] move toward a more just society." Responding to Reagan's unexpected gesture, Tutu said, "Reagan must have disliked my calling his policy ... 'evil, immoral, and unchristian.'"

Meanwhile, Tutu collected his Nobel Peace Prize in Oslo on the same day, December 10, as Reagan's address. But before the bishop could accept the $180,000 cash award and a 7.2-ounce gold medal, he and all of the other prize winners were evacuated from the hall by police who had received a bomb threat. Commented Tutu after the scare had passed, "This just shows how desperate our enemies have become." At the Nobel laureate's lecture the following day, Tutu delivered an impassioned speech attacking the South African government for depriving blacks of *their South African citizenship and turning them into "aliens in the land of their birth."*

> *Following is the lecture delivered by Bishop Desmond Mpilo Tutu of South Africa upon receipt of the 1984 Nobel Peace Prize in Oslo December 10, 1984. (Boldface headings in brackets have been added by Congressional Quarterly to highlight the organization of the text.):*

Your Majesty, members of the Royal Family, Mr. Chairman, Ladies and Gentlemen:

Before I left South Africa, a land I love passionately, we had an emergency meeting of the Executive Committee of the South African Council of Churches with the leaders of our member churches. We called the meeting because of the deepening crisis in our land, which has claimed nearly 200 lives this year alone. We visited some of the troublespots on the Witwatersrand. I went with others to the East Rand. We visited the home of an old lady. She told us that she looked after her grandson and the children of neighbors while their parents were at work. One day the police chased some pupils who had been boycotting classes, but they disappeared between the township houses. The police drove down the old lady's street. She was sitting at the back of the house in her kitchen, whilst her charges were playing in the front of the house in the yard. Her daughter rushed into the house, calling out to her to come quickly. The old lady dashed out of the kitchen into the living room. Her grandson had fallen just inside the door, dead. He had been shot in the back by the police. He was 6 years old. A few weeks later, a white mother, trying to register her black servant for work, drove through a black township. Black rioters stoned her car and killed her baby of a few months old, the first white casualty of the current unrest in South Africa. Such deaths are two too many. These are part of the high cost of apartheid.

[Black Family Life Undermined]

Every day in a squatter camp near Cape Town, called K.T.O., the authorities have been demolishing flimsy plastic shelters which black mothers have erected because they were taking their marriage vows seriously. They have been reduced to sitting on soaking mattresses, with their household effects strewn round their feet, and whimpering babies on their laps, in the cold Cape winter rain. Every day the authorities have carried out these callous demolitions. What heinous crime have these women committed, to be hounded like criminals in this manner? All they wanted is to be with their husbands, the fathers of their children. Everywhere else in the world they would be highly commended, but in South Africa, a land which claims to be Christian, and which boasts a public holiday called Family Day, these gallant women are treated so inhumanely, and yet all they want is to have a decent and stable family life. Unfortunately, in the land of their birth, it is a criminal offence for them to live happily with their husbands and the fathers of their children. Black family life is thus being undermined, not accidentally, but by deliberate Government policy. It is part of the price human beings, God's children, are called to pay for apartheid. An unacceptable price.

I come from a beautiful land, richly endowed by God with wonderful natural resources, wide expanses, rolling mountains, singing birds, bright shining stars out of blue skies, with radiant sunshine, golden sunshine. There is enough of the good things that come from God's bounty, there is enough for everyone, but apartheid has confirmed some in their selfishness, causing them to grasp greedily a disproportionate share, the lion's share, because of their power. They have taken 87% of the land, though being only about 20% of our population. The rest have had to make do with the remaining 13%. Apartheid has decreed the politics of exclusion. 73% of the population is excluded from any meaningful participation in the political decision-making processes of the land of their birth. The new constitution, making provision for three chambers, for whites, coloureds, and Indians, mentions blacks only once, and thereafter ignores them completely. Thus this new constitution, lauded in parts of the West as a step in the right direction, entrenches racism and ethnicity. The constitutional committees are composed in the ratio of 4 whites to 2 coloreds and 1 Indian. 0 black. 2 + 1 can never equal, let alone be more than, 4. Hence this constitution perpetuates by law and entrenches white minority rule. Blacks are expected to exercise their political ambitions in unviable, poverty-striken, arid, bantustan homelands, ghettoes of misery, inexhaustible reservoirs of cheap black labour, bantustans into which South Africa is being balkanised. Blacks are systematically being stripped of their South African citizenship and being turned into aliens in the land of their birth. This is apartheid's final solution, just as Nazism had its final solution for the Jews in Hitler's Aryan madness. The South African Government is smart. Aliens can claim but very few rights, least of all political rights.

[Removal to 'Homelands']

In pursuance of apartheid's ideological racist dream, over 3,000,000 of God's children have been uprooted from their homes, which have been demolished, whilst they have then been dumped in the bantustan homeland resettlement camps. I say dumped advisedly; only things or rubbish is dumped, not human beings. Apartheid has, however, ensured that God's children, just because they are black, should be treated as if they were things, and not as of infinite value as being created in the image of God. These dumping grounds are far from where work and food can be procured easily. Children starve, suffer from the often irreversible consequences of malnutrition—this happens to them not accidentally, but by deliberate Government policy. They starve in a land that could be the bread basket of Africa, a land that normally is a net exporter of food.

The father leaves his family in the bantustan homeland, there eking out a miserable existence, whilst he, if he is lucky, goes to the so-called white man's town as a migrant, to live an unnatural life in a single sex hostel for 11 months of the year, being prey there to prostitution, drunkenness, and worse. This migratory labour policy is declared Government policy, and has been condemned, even by the white D.R.C. [Dutch Reformed Church], not noted for being quick to criticise the Government, as a cancer in our society. This cancer, eating away at the vitals of black family life, is deliberate Government policy. It is part of the cost of apartheid, exorbitant in terms of human suffering.

[Discriminatory Education]

Apartheid has spawned discriminatory education, such as Bantu Education, education for serfdom, ensuring that the Government spends only about one tenth on one black child per annum for education what it spends on a white child. It is education that is decidedly separate and unequal. It is to be wantonly wasteful of human resources, because so many of God's children are prevented, by deliberate Government policy, from attaining to their fullest potential. South Africa is paying a heavy price already for this iniquitous policy because there is a desperate shortage of skilled manpower, a direct result of the short-sighted schemes of the racist regime. It is a moral universe that we inhabit, and good and right and equity matter in the universe of the God we worship. And so, in this matter, the South African Government and its supporters are being properly hoisted with their own petard.

[Laws of Apartheid]

Apartheid is upheld by a phalanx of iniquitous laws, such as the Population Registration Act, which decrees that all South Africans must be classified ethnically, and duly registered according to these race categories. Many times, in the same family one child has been classified white whilst another, with a slightly darker hue, has been classified coloured, with all the horrible consequences for the latter of being shut out from membership of a greatly privileged caste. There have, as a result, been several child suicides. This is too high a price to pay for racial purity, for it is doubtful whether any end, however desirable, can justify such a means. There are laws, such as the Prohibition of Mixed Marriages Act, which regard marriages between a white and a person of another race as illegal. Race becomes an impediment to a valid marriage. Two persons who have fallen in love are prevented by race from consummating their love in the marriage bond. Something beautiful is made to be sordid and ugly. The Immorality Act decrees that fornication and adultery are illegal if they happen between a white and one of another race. The police are reduced to the level of peeping Toms to catch couples red-handed. Many whites have committed suicide rather than face the disastrous consequences that follow in the train of even just being charged under this law. The cost is too great and intolerable.

Such an evil system, totally indefensible by normally acceptable methods, relies on a whole phalanx of draconian laws such as the security legislation which is almost peculiar to South Africa. There are the laws which permit the indefinite detention of persons whom the Minister of Law and Order has decided are a threat to the security of the State. They are detained at his pleasure, in solitary confinement, without access to their family, their own doctor, or a lawyer. That is severe punishment when the evidence apparently available to the Minister has not been tested in an open court — perhaps it could stand up to such rigorous scrutiny, perhaps not; we are never to know. It is a far too convenient device for a repressive regime, and the minister would have to be extra special not to succumb to the temptation to curcumvent the awkward process of testing his evidence in an open court, and thus he lets his power under the law to be open to the abuse where he is both judge and prosecutor. Many, too many, have died mysteriously in detention. All this is too costly in terms of human lives. The minister is able, too, to place people under banning orders without being subjected to the annoyance of the checks and balances of due process. A banned person for 3 or 5 years becomes a non-person, who cannot be quoted during the period of her banning order. She cannot attend a gathering, which means more than one other person. Two persons together talking to a banned person are a gathering! She cannot attend the wedding or funeral of even her own child without special permission. She must be at home from 6:00 PM of one day to 6:00 AM of the next and on all public holidays, and from 6:00 PM on Fridays until 6:00 AM on Mondays for 3 years. She cannot go on holiday outside the magisterial area to which she has been confined. She cannot go to the cinema, nor to a picnic. That is severe punishment, inflicted without the evidence allegedly justifying it being made available to the banned person, nor having it scrutinized in a court of law. It is a serious erosion and violation of basic human rights, of which blacks have precious few in the land of their birth. They do not enjoy the rights of freedom of movement and association. They do not enjoy freedom of security of tenure, the right to participate in the making of decisions that affect their lives. In short, this land, richly endowed in so many ways, is sadly lacking in justice.

Once a Zambian and a South African, it is said, were talking. The Zambian then boasted about their Minister of Naval Affairs. The South African asked, "But you have no navy, no access to the sea. How then can you have a Minister of Naval Affairs?" The Zambian retorted, "Well, in South Africa you have a Minister of Justice, don't you?"

[Peaceful Protest Against Apartheid]

It is against this system that our people have sought to protest peacefully since 1912 at least, with the founding of the African National Congress. They have used the conventional methods of peaceful protest — petitions, demonstrations, deputations, and even a passive resistance campaign. A tribute to our people's commitment to peaceful change is the fact that the only South Africans to win the Nobel Peace Prize are both black. Our people are peace-loving to a fault. The response of the authorities has been an escalating intransigence and violence, the violence of police dogs, tear gas, detention without trial, exile, and even death. Our poeple protested peacefully against the Pass Laws in 1960, and 69 of them were killed on March 21, 1960, at Sharpeville, many shot in the back runnning away. Our children protested against inferior education, singing songs and displaying placards and marching peacefully. Many in 1976, on June 16th and subsequent times, were killed or imprisoned. Over 500 people died in that uprising. Many children went into exile. The where-abouts of many are unknown to their parents. At present, to protest that self-same discriminatory education, and the exclusion of blacks from the new constitutional dispensation, the sham local black government, rising unemployment, increased rents and General Sales Tax, our people have boycotted and demonstrated. They have staged a successful 2-day stay away. Over 150 people have been killed. It is far too high a price to pay. There has been little revulsion or outrage at this wanton destruction of human life in the West. In parenthesis, can somebody please explain to me something that has puzzled me. When a priest goes missing and is subsequently found dead, the media in the West carry his story in very ex-tensive coverage. I am glad that the death of one person can cause so much concern. But in the self-same week when this priest is found dead, the South African Police kill 24 blacks who had been participating in the protest, and 6,000 blacks are sacked for being similarly involved, and you are lucky to get that much coverage. Are we being told something I do not want to believe, that we blacks are expendable and that blood is thicker than water, that when it comes to the crunch, you cannot trust whites, that they will club together against us? I don't want to believe that is the message being conveyed to us.

[Civil War Being Waged]

Be that as it may, we see before us a land bereft of much justice, and therefore without peace and security. Unrest is endemic, and will remain an unchanging feature of the South African scene until apartheid, the root cause of it all, is finally dismantled. At this time, the Army is being quartered on the civilian population. There is a civil war being waged. South Africans are on either side. When the ANC [African National Congress] and the PAC [Pan-Africanist Congress] were banned in 1960, they declared that they had no option but to carry out the armed struggle. We in the SACC [South African Council of Churches] have said we are opposed to all forms of violence — that of a repressive and unjust system, and that of those who seek to overthrow that system. However, we have added that we understand those who say they have had to adopt what is a last resort for them. Violence is not being introduced into the South African situation de novo from outside by those who are called terrorists or freedom fighters, depending on whether you are an oppressed or an oppressor. The South African situation is violent already, and the primary violence is that of apartheid, the violence of forced population removals, of inferior education, of detention without trial, of the migratory labour systems, etc.

There is war on the border of our country. South African faces follow South African. South African soldiers are fighting against Namibians who oppose the illegal occupation of their country by South Africa, which has sought to extend its repressive systems of apartheid, unjust and exploitative.

There is no peace in Southern Africa. There is no peace because there is no justice. There can be no real peace and security until there be first justice enjoyed by all the inhabitants of that beautiful land. The Bible knows nothing about peace without justice, for that would be crying "peace, peace, where there is no peace." God's Shalom, peace, involves inevitably righteousness, justice, wholeness, fullness of life, participation in decision making, goodness, laughter, joy, compassion, sharing and reconciliation.

[South Africa as a Microcosm of the World]

I have spoken extensively about South Africa, first because it is the land I know best, but because it is also a microcosm of the world and an example of what is to be found in other lands in differing degree — when there is injustice, invariably peace becomes a casualty. In El Salvador, in Nicaragua, and elsewhere in Latin America, there have been repressive regimes which have aroused opposition in those countries. Fellow citizens are pitted against one another, sometimes attracting the unhelpful attention and interest of outside powers, who want to extend their spheres of influence. We see this in the Middle East, in Korea, in the Philippines, in Kampuchea, in Vietnam, in Ulster, in Afghanistan, in Mozambique, in Angola, in Zimbabwe, behind the Iron Curtain.

[Cost of Arms Race]

Because there is global insecurity, nations are engaged in a mad arms race, spending billions of dollars wastefully on instruments of destruction, when millions are starving. And yet, just a fraction of what is expended so obscenely on defence budgets would make the difference in enabling God's children to fill their stomachs, be educated, and given the chance to lead fulfilled and happy lives. We have the capacity to feed ourselves several times over, but we are daily haunted by the spectacle of the gaunt dregs of humanity shuffling along in endless queues, with bowls to collect what the charity of the world has provided, too little too late. When will we learn, when will the people of the world get up and say, Enough is enough. God created us for fellowship. God created us so that we should form the human family, existing together because we were made for one another. We are not made for an exclusive self-sufficiency but for interdependence, and we break the law of our being at our peril. When will we learn that an escalated arms race merely escalates global insecurity? We are now much closer to a nuclear holocaust than when our technology and our spending were less.

Unless we work assiduously so that all of God's children, our brothers and sisters, members of our one human family, all will enjoy basic human rights, the right to a fulfilled life, the right of movement, of work, the freedom to be fully human, within a humanity measured by nothing less than the humanity of Jesus Christ Himself, then we are on the road inexorably to self-destruction, we are not far from global suicide; and yet it could be so different.

When will we learn that human beings are of infinite value because they have been created in the image of God, and that it is a blasphemy to treat them as if they were less than this and to do so ultimately recoils on those who do this? In dehumanising others, they are themselves dehumanised. Perhaps oppression dehumanises the oppressor as much as, if not more than, the oppressed. They need each other to become truly free to become human. We can be human only in fellowship, in community, in koinonia, in peace.

Let us work to be peacemakers, those given a wonderful share in Our Lord's ministry of reconciliation. If we want peace, so we have been told, let us work for justice. Let us beat our swords into ploughshares.

[God's Plea to All Human Beings]

God calls us to be follow workers with Him, so that we can extend His Kingdom of shalom, of justice, of goodness, of compassion, of caring, of sharing, of laughter, joy and reconciliation, so that the kingdoms of this world will become the Kindgom of our God and of His Christ, and He shall reign forever and ever. Amen. Then there will be a fulfillment of the wonderful vision in the Revelation of St. John the Divine (Rev 7:9ff):

> 9. After this I beheld, and lo, a great multitude, which no man could number, of all nations and kindreds and people and tongues, stood before the throne and before the Lamb, clothed with white robes, and palms in their hands,
>
> 10. And cried with a loud voice, saying, "Salvation to our God, who sitteth upon the throne, and unto the Lamb."

11. And all the angels stood round about the throne, and about the elders and the four beasts, and fell before the throne on their faces, and worshipped God

12. saying, "Amen; Blessing and glory and wisdom and thanksgiving and honour and power and might, be unto our God forever and ever. Amen."

NIH PANEL REPORT LINKING CHOLESTEROL AND HEART DISEASE
December 13, 1984

Seeking to end the 25-year debate about cholesterol, a National Institutes of Health (NIH) panel decisively concluded December 13 after a two-day conference that high blood cholesterol is a direct cause of heart disease and not just an associated "risk factor." The 14-member advisory panel of doctors, researchers, and non-scientists urged Americans, more than half of whom have undesirably high levels of cholesterol exceeding 200 milligrams, to "lower total [dietary] fat, saturated fat and cholesterol" to help combat heart disease. The panel established by the National Heart, Lung, and Blood Institute and the NIH Office of Medical Applications of Research stressed that cholesterol-lowering drugs should be used only as a last resort.

The panel based its recommendations on the results of numerous laboratory experiments, the most recent being a 10-year study that used diet and an anti-cholesterol drug to pinpoint cholesterol's role in heart disease. The study, released by NIH in January 1984, showed that every 1 percent drop in cholesterol was accompanied by a 2 percent reduction in the rate of heart attack.

The experiments cost $150 million and involved 3,806 men aged 35 to 59 with abnormally high blood cholesterol levels. The participants had no previous symptoms of coronary disease and had been found to be inadequately responding to the diet slated for the experiment.

For seven to 10 years, all the men were given the same low-cholesterol diet, with half of the men receiving daily doses of the cholesterol-reducing drug cholestyramine and the other half a placebo. At the end of the study, coronary heart disease risk had been lowered by 19 percent among the group receiving the drug as compared with the group on the diet only. The study was believed to be the first to demonstrate that reducing cholesterol levels for a number of years actually decreases the risk of heart attacks.

In its latest findings, the NIH noted that the Japanese have a much lower cholesterol rate than their American counterparts and suffer from much less heart disease. But when these same people immigrate to Hawaii and San Francisco, the study said, they develop a higher cholesterol level and a greater risk of heart disease as the result of their acquired American diet. On the other end of the scale, the panel said, the Finns have a much higher cholesterol rate than Americans and a much increased risk of coronary heart disease.

Citing heart disease as the number-one killer in the United States, with more than 550,000 deaths yearly and more than 5.4 million persons showing symptoms of the disease, the NIH panel advised Americans to make substantial changes in their diets. The panel specified as a "reasonable goal" 180 milligrams per deciliter (180 mg/dl) of blood cholesterol for persons under 30 and about 220 mg/dl for those who were older, thus calling for lower levels than those that many doctors traditionally considered "normal."

In a related action, Health and Human Services Secretary Margaret M. Heckler urged Americans to reduce fat in their diets and to add fiber, fresh fruits, and vegetables in an effort to fight cancer. Heckler, stating that the biggest cancer-causing factors "are ones we can control," estimated that diet is responsible for one-third of all cancers. Her statements were part of a new anti-cancer campaign introduced in March 1984.

The NIH panel's recommendations for a diet lower in fat and cholesterol were hardly revolutionary. The American Heart Association, later accompanied by at least 12 other health organizations, had advocated such a diet for more than 10 years. However, the panel's recommendations represented a new turn in federal health policy. The group urged the food industry, including fast-food chains, to develop products that would provide healthier diets; to state on food labels the amount and source of fat content; and to create nutrition education programs for medical professionals and the public alike.

> *Following is the introduction to* Lowering Blood Cholesterol,
> *a National Institutes of Health (NIH) panel report released*
> *December 13.*

Coronary heart disease is responsible for more than 550,000 deaths in the United States each year. It is responsible for more deaths than all forms of cancer combined. There are over 5.4 million Americans with symptomatic coronary heart disease and a large number of others with undiagnosed coronary disease. It has been estimated that coronary heart disease costs the United States over $60 billion a year in direct and indirect costs.

Coronary heart disease is due to atherosclerosis, a slowly progressive disease of the large arteries that begins early in life but rarely produces symptoms until middle age. Often the disease goes undetected until the time of the first heart attack, and this first heart attack is often fatal. Modern methods of treatment have improved greatly the outlook for patients having heart attacks, but major progress in our battle against this number 1 killer must rest on finding preventive measures.

A number of risk factors have been identified as strongly associated with coronary heart disease. Cigarette smoking, high blood pressure, and high blood cholesterol are the most clearly established of these factors. Risk is greater in men, increases with age, and has a strong genetic factor. Obesity, diabetes mellitus, physical inactivity, and behavior pattern are also risk factors.

A large body of evidence of many kinds links elevated blood cholesterol levels to coronary heart disease. However, some doubt remains about the strength of the evidence for a cause-and-effect relationship. Questions remain regarding the exact relationship between blood cholesterol and heart attacks and the steps that should be taken to diagnose and treat elevated blood cholesterol levels.

To resolve some of these questions, the National Heart, Lung, and Blood Institute convened a Consensus Development Conference on Lowering Blood Cholesterol to Prevent Heart Disease on December 10-12, 1984. After hearing a series of expert presentations and reviewing all of the available data, a consensus panel of lipoprotein experts, cardiologists, primary care physicians, epidemiologists, biomedical scientists, bio-statisticians, experts in preventive medicine, and lay representatives considered the evidence and agreed on answers to the following questions:

- Is the relationship between blood cholesterol levels and coronary heart disease causal?
- To what extent will reduction of cholesterol levels reduce the prevalence and severity of coronary heart disease?
- Under what circumstances and at what level of blood cholesterol should dietary or drug treatment be started?
- Should an attempt be made to reduce the blood cholesterol levels of the general population?
- What research directions should be pursued on the relationship between blood cholesterol and heart disease?

PANEL'S CONCLUSIONS

Elevated blood cholesterol level is a major cause of coronary artery disease. It has been established beyond a reasonable doubt that lowering definitely elevated blood cholesterol levels (specifically blood levels of low-density lipoprotein cholesterol) will reduce the risk of heart attacks due to coronary heart disease. This has been demonstrated most conclusively in men with elevated blood cholesterol levels, but much evidence justifies the conclusion that similar protection will be afforded in women with elevated levels. After careful review of genetic, experimental, epidemiologic, and clinical trial evidence, we recommend treatment of individuals with blood cholesterol levels above the 75th percentile (upper 25 percent of values). Further, we are persuaded that the blood cholesterol level of most Americans is undesirably high, in large part because of our high dietary intake of calories, saturated fat, and cholesterol. In countries with diets lower in these constituents, blood cholesterol levels are lower, and coronary heart disease is less common. There is no doubt that appropriate changes in our diet will reduce blood cholesterol levels. Epidemiologic data and over a dozen clinical trials allow us to predict with reasonable assurance that such a measure will afford significant protection against coronary heart disease.

For these reasons we recommend that:

1. Individuals with *high-risk blood cholesterol levels* (values above the 90th percentile) be treated intensively by dietary means and, if response to diet is inadequate, with appropriate drugs. Guidelines for children are somewhat different, as discussed below.

2. Individuals with *moderate-risk blood cholesterol levels* (values between the 75th and 90th percentiles) be treated intensively by dietary means. Only a small proportion should require drug treatment.

3. All Americans (except children under 2 years of age) be advised to adopt a diet that reduces total dietary fat intake from the current level of about 40 percent of total calories to 30 percent of total calories, reduces saturated fat intake to less than 10 percent of total calories, limits polyunsaturated fat intake to 10 percent of total calories, and reduces daily cholesterol intake to 250 to 300 mg.

4. Intake of total calories be reduced, if necessary, to correct obesity and adjusted to maintain ideal body weight.

5. In individuals with elevated blood cholesterol, special attention be given to the management of other risk factors (hypertension, cigarette smoking, diabetes, and physical inactivity).

These dietary recommendations are similar to those of the American Heart Association and the Inter-Society Commission for Heart Disease Resources.

We further recommend that:

6. Programs be planned and initiated soon to educate physicians, other health professionals, and the public to the significance of elevated blood cholesterol and the importance of treating it. We

recommend that the National Heart, Lung, and Blood Institute develop plans for a National Cholesterol Education Program to this purpose.

7. The food industry be encouraged to continue and intensify efforts to develop and market foods that will make it easier for individuals to adhere to the recommended diets and that restaurants serve meals consistent with these dietary recommendations.

8. Food labeling should include the source of fat, total fat, saturated and polyunsaturated fat, and cholesterol content as well as other nutritional information.

9. All physicians be encouraged to include whenever possible a blood cholesterol measurement on every patient seen; to ensure reliability of data, we recommend steps to improve and standardize methods for cholesterol measurement in clinical laboratories.

10. Further research be encouraged to compare the effectiveness of currently recommended diets with that of alternative diets; to study human behavior as it relates to food choices and adherence to diets; to develop more effective, safe, and economical drugs for lowering blood cholesterol levels; to assess the effectiveness of treatment of high blood cholesterol levels in patients with established clinical coronary artery disease; to develop more precise and sensitive noninvasive artery imaging methods; to apply basic cell and molecular biology to increase our understanding of lipoprotein metabolism (particularly the role of HDL as a protective factor) and artery wall metabolism as they relate to coronary heart disease.

11. Plans be developed that will permit assessment of the impact of the changes recommended here as implementation proceeds and to provide the basis for changes when and where appropriate. . . .

AGREEMENT ON RETURN OF HONG KONG TO CHINA

December 19, 1984

A final agreement on the return of Hong Kong from British sovereignty to Chinese jurisdiction was signed in the Great Hall of the People in Peking December 19 by British prime minister Margaret Thatcher and Chinese premier Zhao Ziyang. The transfer will take place in 1997 when a 99-year lease expires. A draft agreement had been initialed by government representatives September 26 and approved by the British Parliament in early December. The accord included assurances that Hong Kong would become a special administrative zone with a great deal of local autonomy.

Hong Kong, originally a province of China, was taken over by the British in 1841. The Qing Dynasty was forced to cede the island of Hong Kong, or Victoria Island, and a portion of the Kowloon Peninsula, to Great Britain under the provisions of the Treaty of Nanjing in 1842 after China's loss of the Opium War. The Kowloon Peninsula, on the mainland, and Stonecutters Island were acquired by the British by the Convention of Peking in 1860. The New Territories, also on mainland China, were leased by a treaty for 99 years in 1898.

Although the leased land was due to return to Chinese sovereignty in 1997, the government long had contended that the treaties governing the annexed territories were invalid because they were signed under duress, and the return of these lands had become a major foreign policy goal of the Chinese for years.

As a crown colony, and given its ideal port location in the Far East, Hong Kong became a major commercial and economic center bolstered by international investment. The colony's capitalistic system has reaped benefits for the Chinese. Abutting the communist mainland, Hong Kong has served as Peking's outlet to Western markets, generating a third of China's foreign exchange. The territory of Hong Kong is 410 square miles with more than five million people, making it one of the most densely populated areas in the world.

Treaty Provisions

The future of Hong Kong weighed heavily on foreign policy analysts, its residents, and investors as the termination of leased period drew nearer. After more than two years and 22 rounds of intense negotiations, a treaty finally was reached, with the Chinese government agreeing to retain the territory's basic democratic freedoms for at least 50 years after the lease expired. Those important provisions included Hong Kong's judicial and educational systems. The agreement will allow Britons and other foreigners to work in the Hong Kong government but will deny them positions of authority. Although the territory will retain its status as a free port and commercial center, China will represent Hong Kong in foreign and military affairs. Warships may enter the port only under the permission of the government in Peking.

Residents of Hong Kong will enjoy far greater personal freedoms than those allowed in China, maintaining the right to travel freely, to continue religious ties with the Church of England and the Roman Catholic Church, and to strike. Although China has agreed that Hong Kong's laws will remain valid after 1997, the agreement states that any existing law that is contrary to those China's National Peoples Congress enact in Hong Kong will be nullified.

Transition Period

To allow for a smooth transition of power, the Chinese and British announced the formation of a joint liaison group to monitor Hong Kong's progress beginning in 1988 and terminating in 2000. In addition, the British government initiated an assessment office for the colony's residents to voice opinions and field questions. The treaty did not allow for a public referendum in Hong Kong, a provision strongly opposed by China. In the months that followed the treaty's initialing, the assessment office was flooded by responses indicating the serious reservations that Hong Kong's residents had over the long-term future of the territory. A member of a British team monitoring the activities of the assessment office was quoted in the Washington Post *as saying that "nobody in Hong Kong can escape the uncertainties of the future.... The minority who reject the draft agreement do so either because they can never accept reunification with Communist China or because they are bitter about the consequences*

*for themselves as British Dependent Territories citizens. The majority
who accept it do so chiefly because they regard reunification as inevitable
and are relieved that the terms of the draft agreement are as good as they
are." China had indicated that negotiations could be resumed in the
future if both parties agreed.*

Taiwan Issue

*Upon reaching an agreement with Great Britain over Hong Kong, the
Chinese began to make overtures to the Nationalist government on
Taiwan for reunification with mainland China. Historically a haven for
ousted regimes, Taiwan had been occupied by several countries since the
17th century. The Spaniards were expelled from the island in 1662 by the
Ming Dynasty, who were fleeing after takeover of the mainland by the
Qing Dynasty. Japan took control of Taiwan after China's loss in the
Sino-Japanese war in 1895. The island was finally returned to China
after World War II, but following the communists' victory in 1949, Chiang
Kai-shek fled to the island with the Nationalists.*

*From the onset of the Korean War in 1950, the United States had given
military and economic support to the Nationalist government, maintaining a highly visible presence in the Far East. As the United States and
China began renewing political and cultural ties, U.S. support for the
small nation weakened, with the communist Chinese strongly encouraging the United States to stay out of the reunification debate.*

*Striving for reunification with Taiwan, Chinese Prime Minister Zhao
Ziyang offered the Nationalist government terms similar to those agreed
to by Great Britain. Zhao proposed to retain the Taiwanese economic and
capitalist system but stressed the cultural and social significance of
reuniting the island with the mainland.*

> *Following is the introduction of the agreement between the
> United Kingdom of Great Britain and Northern Ireland and
> the People's Republic of China on the future of Hong Kong,
> as signed December 19, 1984:*

The Government of the United Kingdom of Great Britain and Northern
Ireland and the Government of the People's Republic of China have
reviewed with satisfaction the friendly relations existing between the two
Governments and peoples in recent years and agreed that a proper
negotiated settlement of the question of Hong Kong, which is left over
from the past, is conducive to the maintenance of the prosperity and
stability of Hong Kong and to the further strengthening and development
of the relations between the two countries on a new basis. To this end, they
have, after talks between the delegations of the two Governments, agreed
to declare as follows:

1. The Government of the People's Republic of China declares that to
recover the Hong Kong area (including Hong Kong Island, Kowloon and

the New Territories, hereinafter referred to as Hong Kong) is the common aspiration of the entire Chinese people, and that it has decided to resume the exercise of sovereignty over Hong Kong with effect from 1 July 1997.

2. The Government of the United Kingdom declares that it will restore Hong Kong to the People's Republic of China with effect from 1 July 1997.

3. The Government of the People's Republic of China declares that the basic policies of the People's Republic of China regarding Hong Kong are as follows:

(1) Upholding national unity and territorial integrity and taking account of the history of Hong Kong and its realities, the People's Republic of China has decided to establish, in accordance with the provisions of Article 31 of the Constitution of the People's Republic of China, a Hong Kong Special Administrative Region upon resuming the exercise of sovereignty over Hong Kong.

(2) The Hong Kong Special Administrative Region will be directly under the authority of the Central People's Government of the People's Republic of China. The Hong Kong Special Administrative Region will enjoy a high degree of autonomy, except in foreign and defence affairs which are the responsibilities of the Central People's Government.

(3) The Hong Kong Special Administrative Region will be vested with executive, legislative, and independent judicial power, including that of final adjudication. The laws currently in force in Hong Kong will remain basically unchanged.

(4) The Government of the Hong Kong Special Administrative Region will be composed of local inhabitants. The chief executive will be appointed by the Central People's Government on the basis of the results of elections or consultations to be held locally. Principal officials will be nominated by the chief executive of the Hong Kong Special Administrative Region for appointment by the Central People's Government. Chinese and foreign nationals previously working in the public and police services in the government departments of Hong Kong may remain in employment. British and other foreign nationals may also be employed to serve as advisers or hold certain public posts in government departments of the Hong Kong Special Administrative Region.

(5) The current social and economic systems in Hong Kong will remain unchanged, and so will the life-style. Rights and freedoms, including those of the person, of speech, of the press, of assembly, of association, of travel, of movement, of correspondence, of strike, of choice of occupation, of academic research and of religious belief will be ensured by law in the Hong Kong Special Administrative Region. Private property, ownership of enterprises, legitimate right of inheritance and foreign investment will be protected by law.

(6) The Hong Kong Special Administrative Region will retain the status of a free port and a separate customs territory.

(7) The Hong Kong Special Administrative Region will retain the status of an international financial centre, and its markets for foreign exchange, gold, securities and futures will continue. There will be free flow of capital. The Hong Kong dollar will continue to circulate and remain freely convertible.

(8) The Hong Kong Special Administrative Region will have independent finances. The Central People's Government will not levy taxes on the Hong Kong Special Administrative Region.

(9) The Hong Kong Special Administrative Region may establish mutually beneficial economic relations with the United Kingdom and other countries, whose economic interests in Hong Kong will be given due regard.

(10) Using the name of "Hong Kong, China", the Hong Kong Special Administrative Region may on its own maintain and develop economic and cultural relations and conclude relevant agreements with states, regions and relevant international organisations.

The Government of the Hong Kong Special Administrative Region may on its own issue travel documents for entry into and exit from Hong Kong.

(11) The maintenance of public order in the Hong Kong Special Administrative Region will be the responsibility of the Government of the Hong Kong Special Administrative Region.

(12) The above-stated basic policies of the People's Republic of China regarding Hong Kong and the elaboration of them in Annex I to this Joint Declaration will be stipulated, in a Basic Law of the Hong Kong Special Administrative Region of the People's Republic of China, by the National People's Congress of the People's Republic of China, and they will remain unchanged for 50 years.

4. The Government of the United Kingdom and the Government of the People's Republic of China declare that, during the transitional period between the date of the entry into force of this Joint Declaration and 30 June 1997, the Government of the United Kingdom will be responsible for the administration of Hong Kong with the object of maintaining and preserving its economic prosperity and social stability; and that the Government of the People's Republic of China will give its cooperation in this connection.

5. The Government of the United Kingdom and the Government of the People's Republic of China declare that, in order to ensure a smooth transfer of government in 1997, and with a view to the effective implementation of this Joint Declaration, a Sino-British Joint Liaison Group will be set up when this Joint Declaration enters into force; and that it will be established and will function in accordance with the provisions of Annex II to this Joint Declaration.

6. The Government of the United Kingdom and the Government of the People's Republic of China declare that land leases in Hong Kong and other related matters will be dealt with in accordance with the provisions

of Annex III to this Joint Declaration.

7. The Government of the United Kingdom and the Government of the People's Republic of China agree to implement the preceding declarations and the Annexes to this Joint Declaration.

8. This Joint Declaration is subject to ratification and shall enter into force on the date of the exchange of instruments of ratification, which shall take place in Beijing before 30 June 1985. This Joint Declaration and its Annexes shall be equally binding.

CUMULATIVE INDEX, 1980-84

A

Tutu Nobel Prize Speech, 1027-1037 *(1984)*

U.S. Withdrawal from UNESCO, 967-971 *(1983)*

United Nations Effectiveness, 769-779 *(1982)*

Vance Speech at Harvard, 475-483 *(1980)*

Vatican-U.S. Relations, 19-22 *(1984)*

World Court on Mining Nicaragua, 339-345 *(1984)*

Zhao Visit, 23-30 *(1984)*

Foreign Aid

Caribbean Basin Initiative, 179-190 *(1982)*

Economic Summit (Mexico), 777 *(1981)*

Economic Summit (Ottawa), 598 *(1981)*

Economic Summit (Williamsburg), 512 *(1983)*

El Salvador, 242 *(1981)*

IMF-World Bank Conference, 883-896 *(1980)*; 801-814 *(1983)*

Kissinger Commission Report, 31-52 *(1984)*

Natural Disasters Report, 973-995 *(1984)*

Reagan, Congressional Democrats on Central America, 449-454 *(1983)*

Foreign Trade

Caribbean Basin Initiative, 179-190 *(1982)*; 88, 449, 450 *(1983)*

China/U.S. Accords, 293-294 *(1984)*

Democratic Party Platform, 586-589 *(1984)*

Economic Advisers' Report, 133-137 *(1983)*; 140-141 *(1984)*

Economic Summit (London), 356, 361 *(1984)*

Economic Summit (Mexico), 777 *(1981)*

Economic Summit (Ottawa), 598 *(1981)*

Economic Summit (Venice), 512 *(1980)*

Economic Summit (Versailles) 469-476 *(1982)*

Economic Summit (Williamsburg), 511 *(1983)*

IMF-World Bank Conference, 807-808, 810-822 *(1983)*; 796 *(1984)*

Inter-American Dialogue Report, 378-381 *(1983)*

Kissinger Commission Report, 40-42 *(1984)*

OPEC Oil Price Changes, 979-981 *(1982)*

President's Economic Report, 126-127 *(1983)*; 119-120, 124 *(1984)*

Reagan Speeches in Japan, 903, 907-908 *(1983)*

Republican Party Platform, 679-680 *(1984)*

Soviet Agricultural Trade and Foreign Policy, 823-835 *(1982)*

Soviet Pipeline Sanctions, 879-884 *(1982)*

State of the Union, 98 *(1980)*; 63-64, 74-75 *(1981)*; 81, 84-85, 88 *(1983)*

Supreme Court on Unitary Taxation of Multinational Corporations, 645-658 *(1983)*

U.S.-China, 829-846 *(1980)*; 23-30 *(1984)*

Forests. *See Environment.*

Fourteenth Amendment

Busing, 619-652 *(1982)*

Constitutional Rights of Mentally Retarded, 521-530 *(1982)*

Death Penalty, 53, 60 *(1982)*

Education of Illegal Aliens, 489-506 *(1982)*

Parental Rights, 259-280 *(1982)*

Sex Discrimination, 758 *(1983)*

Unitary Taxation of Multinational Corporations, 645-658 *(1983)*

Fourth Amendment

Automobile Search and Seizure, 425-446 *(1982)*

Exclusionary Rule, 505-519 *(1984)*

Home Arrests, 281-297 *(1980)*

Prisoners' Rights, 479-491 *(1984)*

France

Klaus Barbie Report, 737-747 *(1983)*

Versailles Economic Summit, 469-476 *(1982)*

Free Speech. *See First Amendment.*

Freedom of Information Act. *See also Press.*

Census Data Confidentiality, 171-178 *(1982)*

Crime Report, 655-658 *(1981)*

Reagan Policy, 393-400 *(1981)*

Fuel. *See Energy Policy.*

G

Galiber, Joseph L., 803-809 *(1984)*

Galman, Rolando, 925-932 *(1984)*

Gandhi, Indira

Assassination, 945-949 *(1984)*

Non-aligned Nations Summit Address, 263-268 *(1983)*

Gandhi, Rajiv, 945-949 *(1984)*

Garwood, Robert T., 197-201 *(1981)*

Gas. *See Natural Gas.*

General Accounting Office

Grace Commission Report, 169-179 *(1984)*

General Agreement on Tariffs and Trade (GATT), 468-476 *(1982)*

Genetic Engineering

Court on Patenting of Living Organisms, 493-502 *(1980)*

Human Genetic Engineering Resolution, 525-532 *(1983)*

Georgia

Death Penalty, 455 *(1980)*

Germany, Federal Republic of

Common Market Summit, 443 *(1984)*

Geyer, Georgie Anne, 876-902 *(1984)*

Gierek, Edward, 794 *(1980)*; 881 *(1981)*

Giscard d'Estaing, Valery

Economic Summit (Venice), 503 *(1980)*

Global Future Report, 13-30 *(1981)*

Global 2000 Report, 665-697 *(1980)*

Godfrey v. Georgia, 455-472 *(1980)*

I